Current Events — Summaries and analyses of current events written by finance instructors. See how finance theory gets applied in practice every day.

Current Events
- Tobacco Stoc
- The Greenspan Effect: Fed Chairman Speaks And The Market Reacts
- 1995 Was One for the Books
- Stocks Rise On Rate Cut From Fed

Internet Resources — Annotated links to topic-specific sites on the Web.

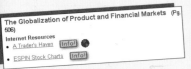

The Globalization of Product and Financial Markets (Pg. 506)

Internet Resources
- A Trader's Haven Info!
- ESPIN Stock Charts Info!

Study Hall — Includes ***Ask the Tutor*** for finance-specific help, a ***Writing Center***, computer help, and more. One of the most popular spots on the PHLIP site!

PHLIP '98

STUDY HALL RESOURCES

ASK THE TUTOR

Ask the Tutor allows students to post questions or comments to the threaded conference message board for their course. There is also a general conference where students can ask questions that don't fall within a particular course.

WRITING CENTER

The Writing Center has tools, tips and techniques for authoring powerful business communications.

CAREER CENTER

The Career Center is designed for business students in general, but we have resources for everyone. There are also great resources for each of our supported business disciplines.

STUDY SKILLS CENTER

The overall key to college success is being able to manage ourselves in an academic environment. To do that

THE CAREERS CENTER

The **big picture** of finance includes the career possibilities that a finance degree opens to you! ***Careers in Finance*** explores the working life of finance professionals who tell you how they got there, what you can expect when you get there, and what it takes to be successful.

The Career Center contains:

- Video interviews with finance professionals explaining what they do every day.
- Industry surveys of current salaries at all levels among the finance professions.

Interviewing and resume writing tips and other advice that will help you land your first job in finance.

For Installation Instructions see the README file on this CD-ROM

-3
all

Windows® 3.1, Windows® 95

AND THE BIG PICTURE OF FINANCIAL MANAGEMENT

WORKSHOPS

LEARN MORE ABOUT:
RESUME WRITING

TARGET YOUR APPROACH

Different Resumé Formats:
Chronological
Functional
Technical Skills

Cover Letter Templates:
Formal Introduction
Campus Visit
Office Visit
Negotiations

CAREERS

LEARN MORE ABOUT:
INVESTMENT BANKING

KEY JOBS
RESOURCES
FACTS & TRENDS
SKILL REQUIREMENTS
SALARY SURVEYS
TOP TIER FIRMS

the INSIDE SCOOP

Runner
Outrade Clerk
Deck Holder
Phone Clerk

TEXAS INSTRUMENTS

BAII PLUS Rebate Terms and Conditions

This offer is valid only for BAII PLUS purchases between July 1, 1998 and December 31, 1999. All claims must be postmarked by January 31, 2000. Allow 8 to 10 weeks for processing. All purchases must be made in the U.S. or Canada. Rebates will be sent only to addresses in the U.S. and Canada and paid in U.S. dollars. Not redeemable at any store. Send this completed form along with the cash register receipt (original or copy) and the UPC bar code to the address indicated. This original mail-in certificate must accompany your request and may not be duplicated or reproduced. Offer valid only as stated on this form. Offer void where prohibited, taxed, licensed, or restricted. Limit one rebate per household or address. Texas Instruments reserves the right to discontinue this program at any time and without notice.

Yes! I Want $5 Back On My Purchase of the BAII PLUS.

BASIC FINANCIAL MANAGEMENT

Basic Financial Management

Eighth Edition

David F. Scott, Jr.

University of Central Florida
Holder, Phillips-Schenck Chair in American Private Enterprise
Executive Director, Dr. Phillips Institute for the Study of
American Business Activity
Professor of Finance

John D. Martin

Baylor University
Carr P. Collins Chair in Finance

J. William Petty

Baylor University
Professor of Finance
W. W. Caruth Chair in Entrepreneurship

Arthur J. Keown

Virginia Polytechnic Institute and State University
R. B. Pamplin Professor of Finance

Prentice Hall, Upper Saddle River, New Jersey 07458

Senior Acquisitions Editor: Paul Donnelly
Developmental Editor: Bruce Kaplan
Assistant Editor: Gladys Soto
Editorial Assistant: Jodi Hirsh
Editorial Director: James C. Boyd
Marketing Manager: Patrick Lynch
Production Editor: Susan Rifkin
Managing Editor: Dee Josephson
Manufacturing Supervisor: Paul Smolenski
Manufacturing Manager: Vincent Scelta
Design Manager: Patricia Smythe
Interior and Cover Design: Jill Little
Cover Illustration: Joseph Page Kovach
Composition: TSI Graphics

 © 1999, 1996 by Prentice Hall, Inc.
A Simon & Schuster Company
Upper Saddle River, New Jersey 07458

Library of Congress Cataloging-in-Publication Data
Basic financial management/ David F. Scott, Jr.…[et al.].—8th ed.
    p. cm
    Includes index.
    ISBN 0-13-794074-2 (hard: alk. paper)
    1. Business enterprises—Finance.   2. Corporations—Finance.
Scott, David F., Jr.
HG4026.B318   1999
658.15—dc21   98-30595
                                           CIP
                                           AC

Printed in the United States of America

10 9 8 7 6 5 4 3 2 1

ISBN 0-13-794074-2

Prentice-Hall International (UK) Limited, *London*
Prentice-Hall of Australia Pty. Limited, *Sydney*
Prentice-Hall Canada Inc., *Toronto*
Prentice-Hall Hispanoamericana, S.A., *Mexico*
Prentice-Hall of India Private Limited, *New Delhi*
Prentice-Hall of Japan, Inc., *Tokyo*
Simon & Schuster Asia Pte. Ltd., *Singapore*
Editora Prentice-Hall do Brasil, Ltda., *Rio de Janeiro*

The eighth edition of *Basic Financial Management* is dedicated to our families—the ones who love us the most.

Peggy

—David F. Scott, Jr.

Sally, David, and Melanie, and Jess

—John D. Martin

To my brother James, who has given much to his little brother, and been the finest of role models and one of my greatest encouragers.

—J. William Petty

Barb, Emily, and Artie

—Arthur J. Keown

Brief Contents

Preface   xix

AN INTRODUCTION TO FINANCIAL MANAGEMENT   1   CHAPTER 1

THE ROLE OF FINANCIAL MARKETS AND INTEREST RATES IN FINANCIAL MANAGEMENT   37   CHAPTER 2

EVALUATING A FIRM'S FINANCIAL PERFORMANCE AND MEASURING CASH FLOW   79   CHAPTER 3

FINANCIAL FORECASTING, PLANNING, AND BUDGETING   142   CHAPTER 4

THE TIME VALUE OF MONEY   172   CHAPTER 5

RISK AND RATES OF RETURN   211   CHAPTER 6

BOND VALUATION   259   CHAPTER 7

STOCK VALUATION   290   CHAPTER 8

CAPITAL-BUDGETING DECISION CRITERIA   322   CHAPTER 9

CHAPTER 10   CASH FLOWS AND OTHER TOPICS
IN CAPITAL BUDGETING   357

CHAPTER 11   CAPITAL BUDGETING AND RISK ANALYSIS   398

CHAPTER 12   COST OF CAPITAL   431

CHAPTER 13   ANALYSIS AND IMPACT OF LEVERAGE   464

CHAPTER 14   PLANNING THE FIRM'S FINANCING MIX   513

CHAPTER 15   DIVIDEND POLICY AND INTERNAL FINANCING   573

CHAPTER 16   WORKING-CAPITAL MANAGEMENT
AND SHORT-TERM FINANCING   611

CHAPTER 17   CASH AND MARKETABLE SECURITIES
MANAGEMENT   638

CHAPTER 18   ACCOUNTS RECEIVABLE, INVENTORY,
AND TOTAL QUALITY MANAGEMENT   685

CHAPTER 19   TERM LOANS AND LEASES   718

CHAPTER 20   THE USE OF FUTURES, OPTIONS, AND CURRENCY
SWAPS TO REDUCE RISK   744

CHAPTER 21   CORPORATE RESTRUCTURING:
COMBINATIONS AND DIVESTITURES   782

Appendixes   835

Glossary   858

Indexes   865

CONTENTS

Preface   xix

AN INTRODUCTION TO FINANCIAL MANAGEMENT   1
CHAPTER 1

Introduction   1

What Is Finance?   2

Goal of the Firm   2

Legal Forms of Business Organization   4

The Tax Environment   7

Ten Axioms That Form the Basics of Financial Management   12

Axiom 1: The Risk-Return Trade-Off—We Won't Take on Additional Risk Unless We Expect to Be Compensated with Additional Return   13

Axiom 2: The Time Value of Money—A Dollar Received Today Is Worth More Than a Dollar Received in the Future   14

Axiom 3: Cash—Not Profits—Is King   15

Axiom 4: Incremental Cash Flows—It's Only What Changes That Counts   15

Axiom 5: The Curse of Competitive Markets—Why It's Hard to Find Exceptionally Profitable Projects   16

Axiom 6: Efficient Capital Markets—The Markets Are Quick and the Prices Are Right   17

Axiom 7: The Agency Problem—Managers Won't Work for Owners Unless It's in Their Best Interest   18

Axiom 8: Taxes Bias Business Decisions   19

Axiom 9: All Risk Is Not Equal—Some Risk Can Be Diversified Away, and Some Cannot   19

Axiom 10: Ethical Behavior Is Doing the Right Thing, and Ethical Dilemmas Are Everywhere in Finance   21

Overview of the Text   22

How Financial Managers Use This Material   24

Summary   24

METHODS OF DEPRECIATION   33
APPENDIX 1A

CHAPTER 2

THE ROLE OF FINANCIAL MARKETS AND INTEREST RATES IN FINANCIAL MANAGEMENT   37

Introduction   37

The Financial Manager, Internal and External Funds, and Flexibility   39

The Mix of Corporate Securities Sold in the Capital Market   41

Why Financial Markets Exist   42

Financing of Business: The Movement of Funds Through the Economy   45

Components of the U.S. Financial Market System   48

The Investment Banker   51

Private Placements   54

Flotation Costs   56

Regulation   56

More Recent Regulatory Developments   58

Rates of Return in the Financial Markets   59

Interest Rate Determinants in a Nutshell   63

Inflation and Real Rates of Return: The Financial Analyst's Approach   72

How Financial Managers Use This Material   73

Summary   73

CHAPTER 3

EVALUATING A FIRM'S FINANCIAL PERFORMANCE AND MEASURING CASH FLOW   79

Introduction   79

Basic Financial Statements   81

Financial Ratio Analysis   95

The DuPont Analysis: An Integrative Approach to Ratio Analysis   108

Measuring Firm Performance the EVA Way   112

How Financial Managers Use This Material   113

Summary   114

CHAPTER 4

FINANCIAL FORECASTING, PLANNING, AND BUDGETING   142

Introduction   142

Financial Forecasting   143

The Sustainable Rate of Growth   151

Financial Planning and Budgeting   152

How Financial Managers Use This Material   156

Summary   157

THE TIME VALUE OF MONEY   172

CHAPTER 5

Introduction   172

Compound Interest and Future Value   173

Present Value   181

Annuities—A Level Stream   184

Making Interest Rates Comparable   196

How Financial Managers Use This Material   197

Summary   197

RISK AND RATES OF RETURN   211

CHAPTER 6

Introduction   211

Expected Return   213

Risk   214

The Investor's Required Rate of Return   228

The Fama and French Attack on the CAPM   232

The Investor's Experience in the Capital Markets   235

How Financial Managers Use This Material   240

Summary   241

MEASURING THE REQUIRED RATE OF RETURN: THE ARBITRAGE PRICING MODEL   256

APPENDIX 6A

BOND VALUATION   259

CHAPTER 7

Introduction   259

Definitions of Value   260

Valuation: Understanding the Process   262

Characteristics of Bonds   264

The Different Kinds of Bonds   266

Bond Valuation   271

Bondholders' Expected Rates of Return (Yield to Maturity)   274

Bond Valuation: Five Important Relationships   277

How Financial Managers Use This Material   283

Summary   283

CHAPTER 8

STOCK VALUATION 290

Introduction   290

Features and Types of Preferred Stock   291

Valuing Preferred Stock   294

Characteristics of Common Stock   296

Valuing Common Stock   301

Stockholder's Expected Rate of Return   307

How Financial Managers Use This Material   311

Summary   311

APPENDIX 8A

THE RELATIONSHIP BETWEEN VALUE AND EARNINGS   318

CHAPTER 9

CAPITAL-BUDGETING DECISION CRITERIA   322

Introduction   322

Finding Profitable Projects   323

Payback Period   324

Net Present Value   328

Profitability Index (Benefit/Cost Ratio)   330

Internal Rate of Return   332

Ethics in Capital Budgeting   343

A Glance at Actual Capital-Budgeting Practices   343

How Financial Managers Use This Material   345

Summary   345

CHAPTER 10

CASH FLOWS AND OTHER TOPICS IN CAPITAL BUDGETING   357

Introduction   357

Guidelines for Capital Budgeting   358

Measuring a Project's Benefits and Costs   361

Complications in Capital Budgeting: Capital Rationing and Mutually Exclusive Projects   371

How Financial Managers Use This Material   377

Summary   378

CAPITAL BUDGETING AND RISK ANALYSIS   398

CHAPTER 11

Introduction   398

Risk and the Investment Decision   399

Methods for Incorporating Risk Into Capital Budgeting   403

Other Approaches to Evaluating Risk in Capital Budgeting   411

How Financial Managers Use This Material   417

Summary   417

COST OF CAPITAL   431

CHAPTER 12

Introduction   431

The Cost of Capital: Key Definitions and Concepts   432

Determining Individual Costs of Capital   433

The Weighted Average Cost of Capital   441

Cost of Capital in Practice: Briggs & Stratton   444

Calculating Divisional Costs of Capital: PepsiCo, Inc.   446

Using a Firm's Cost of Capital to Evaluate New Capital Investments   448

Market Value Added and Economic Profit   449

How Financial Managers Use This Material   454

Summary   455

ANALYSIS AND IMPACT OF LEVERAGE   464

CHAPTER 13

Introduction   464

Business and Financial Risk   465

Breakeven Analysis   468

Operating Leverage   478

Financial Leverage   483

Combination of Operating and Financial Leverage   487

How Financial Managers Use This Material   490

Summary   492

PLANNING THE FIRM'S FINANCING MIX   513

CHAPTER 14

Introduction   513

Key Terms and Getting Started   514

A Glance at Capital Structure Theory   516

Basic Tools of Capital Structure Management   534

How Financial Managers Use This Material   543

Summary   552

CHAPTER 15   **DIVIDEND POLICY AND INTERNAL FINANCING   573**

Introduction   573

Dividend Payment versus Profit Retention   575

Does Dividend Policy Affect Stock Price?   576

The Dividend Decision in Practice   590

Dividend Payment Procedures   594

Stock Dividends and Stock Splits   594

Stock Repurchases   597

How Financial Managers Use This Material   600

Summary   601

CHAPTER 16   **WORKING-CAPITAL MANAGEMENT
AND SHORT-TERM FINANCING   611**

Introduction   611

Managing Current Assets and Liabilities   612

Appropriate Level of Working Capital   614

Hedging Principle   615

Estimation of the Cost of Short-Term Credit   619

Sources of Short-Term Credit   620

How Financial Managers Use This Material   628

Summary   628

CHAPTER 17   **CASH AND MARKETABLE SECURITIES
MANAGEMENT   638**

Introduction   638

What Are Liquid Assets?   639

Why a Company Holds Cash   640

Cash-Management Objectives and Decisions   642

Collection and Disbursement Procedures   644

Composition of Marketable Securities Portfolio   653

How Financial Managers Use This Material   660

Summary   660

APPENDIX 17A   **CASH-MANAGEMENT MODELS:
SPLIT BETWEEN CASH AND NEAR CASH   676**

ACCOUNTS RECEIVABLE, INVENTORY, AND TOTAL QUALITY MANAGEMENT 685

CHAPTER 18

Introduction 685

Accounts Receivable Management 686

Inventory Management 695

TQM and Inventory-Purchasing Management: The New Supplier
Relationships 703

How Financial Managers Use This Material 706

Summary 708

TERM LOANS AND LEASES 718

CHAPTER 19

Introduction 718

Term Loans 719

Leases 722

How Financial Managers Use This Material 735

Summary 736

THE USE OF FUTURES, OPTIONS, AND CURRENCY SWAPS TO REDUCE RISK 744

CHAPTER 20

Introduction 744

Futures 745

Options 753

Currency Swaps 766

How Financial Managers Use This Material 766

Summary 768

CONVERTIBLE SECURITIES AND WARRANTS 771

APPENDIX 20A

CORPORATE RESTRUCTURING: COMBINATIONS AND DIVESTITURES 782

CHAPTER 21

Introduction 782

Why Mergers Might Create Wealth 784

Determination of a Firm's Value 787

Divestitures 797

How Financial Managers Use This Material 797

Summary 799

INTERNATIONAL BUSINESS FINANCE 805

Introduction   805

The Globalization of Product and Financial Markets   807

Exchange Rates   808

Interest-Rate Parity Theory   818

Purchasing Power Parity   818

Exposure to Exchange Rate Risk   820

Multinational Working-Capital Management   824

International Financing and Capital Structure Decisions   825

Direct Foreign Investment   828

How Financial Managers Use This Material   829

Summary   829

Appendix A   835

Appendix B   847

Appendix C   849

Appendix D   851

Appendix E   853

Appendix F   855

Glossary   858

Organization Index   865

Subject Index   867

PREFACE

Over the past 30 years, the teaching of finance has evolved from a descriptive presentation of ill-defined decision rules, taught through the use of case examples, to a science where the logic and decision rules spring from basic economic principles. Today, finance continues to change and develop at an ever-increasing pace. Sparked by the changing business environment and developments in the academic world, new financing and risk management techniques seem to appear on almost a daily basis.

To prepare for a field as dynamic as finance you must go beyond the answers and understand the logic that drives them. For this reason the presentation in this text has been crafted around 10 basic axioms. Using these axioms, we provide an introduction to financial decision making that is rooted both in current financial theory and in the current state of world economic conditions. Our objective is to provide the student with a theory-based and relevant understanding of financial decision making.

OUR APPROACH TO *BASIC FINANCIAL MANAGEMENT*

The first-time student of finance will find that corporate finance builds upon both accounting and economics. Economics provides much of the theory that underlies our techniques, whereas accounting provides the input or data on which decision making is based. Unfortunately, it is all too easy for students to lose sight of the logic that drives finance and to focus instead on memorizing formulas and procedures. As a result, students have a difficult time understanding the interrelationships between the topics covered. Moreover, later in life when the problems encountered do not fit neatly into the textbook presentation, the student may have problems abstracting from what was learned. To overcome this problem, the opening chapter presents 10 basic principles or axioms of finance that are woven throughout the book. What results is a text tightly bound around these guiding principles. In essence, the student is presented with a cohesive, interrelated subject from which future, as yet unknown, problems can be approached.

Teaching an introductory finance class while faced with an ever-expanding discipline puts additional pressures on the instructor. What to cover, what to omit, and how to do this while maintaining a cohesive presentation are inescapable questions. In dealing with these questions, we have attempted to present the chapters in a stand-alone fashion so that they could be easily rearranged to fit almost any desired course structure and course length. Because the axioms are woven into every chapter, the presentation of the text remains tight regardless of whether or not the chapters are rearranged. Again, our goal is to provide an enduring understanding of the basic tools and fundamental principles upon which finance is based. This foundation will give a student beginning his or her studies in finance a strong base on which to build future studies and give the student who will take only one finance class a lasting understanding of the basics of finance.

Although historical circumstances continue to serve as the driving force behind the development and practice of finance, the underlying principles that guide our discipline remain the same. These principles are presented in an intuitively appealing manner in chapter 1 and thereafter are tied to all that follows. With a focus upon the big picture, we provide an introduction to financial decision making rooted in current financial theory and in the current state of world economic conditions. This focus can be seen in a number of ways, perhaps most obvious being the attention paid both to valuation and to the capital markets and their influence on corporate financial decisions. What results is an introductory treatment of a discipline rather than the treatment of a series of isolated finance problems. The goal of this text is to go beyond teaching the tools of a discipline or a trade, and help students gain a complete understanding of the subject. This will give them the ability to apply what he or she has learned to new and yet unforeseen problems—in short, to educate students in finance.

A TOTAL LEARNING PACKAGE

Basic Financial Management is not simply another introductory finance text. It is a total learning package and reflects the vitality and ever-expanding nature of the discipline. Finance has grown too complex not to teach with an eye on the big picture, focusing on the interrelationships between the materials that are covered. Listed below are some of the distinctive pedagogical features that assist the student in understanding how concepts in finance link to the big picture of finance.

LEARNING AIDS IN THE TEXT

Ten Axioms of Finance

The fundamental principles that drive the practice of corporate finance are presented in the form of 10 axioms. These axioms first appear in chapter 1 and thereafter appear in in-text inserts called "Relate to the Big Picture." These inserts serve to refocus the student's attention on the underlying principles behind what is being done. In effect, they serve to keep the student from becoming so wrapped up in specific calculations that the interrelationships and overall scheme is lost.

Integrative End-of-Chapter Problems

An Integrative Problem is provided at the end of each chapter and covers all the major topics included in that chapter. This comprehensive problem can be used as a lecture or review tool by the professor. To aid the instructor in presenting this material, the solution is provided to the instructor in Microsoft PowerPoint format. For students, the integrative end-of-chapter problems provide an opportunity to apply all the concepts presented within the chapter in a realistic setting, thereby strengthening their understanding of the material.

Stop and Think

In-text inserts titled "Stop and Think" appear throughout the text to allow the student to take time out and reflect upon the meaning of what has just been presented. The use of these "Stop and Think" inserts, coupled with the use of the 10 axioms, keeps the student from losing sight of the interrelationships and motivating factors behind what is being done.

Basic Financial Management in Practice

Strong emphasis is also placed upon practice, where practice is used to demonstrate both the relevance of the topics discussed and the implementation of theory. Moreover, to add life to the discussion, "Basic Financial Management in Practice" boxed inserts are provided throughout the text. These boxes are largely taken from the popular press with analysis and implications provided following each box. In this way, the subject matter comes to life with added relevance to the student.

Introductory Examples

Each chapter opens with an introductory example of the related experiences of an actual company and sets the stage for what is to follow. In this way, the relevance, use, and importance of the material to be presented can be easily understood by the student.

Unique Treatment of Value-Based Management

An important addition to the eighth edition of *Basic Financial Management* is the discussion of value-based management (VBM). Value-based management is the generic term used to refer to the set of management tools designed to help firms manage their operations in such a way as to enhance shareholder value. In principle, VBM applies the methods of discounted cash flow analysis that have long been advocated as the basis for analyzing new investments to the analysis of the performance of the firm's existing assets or assets already in place. Traditionally, the finance profession has had relatively little to say about performance appraisal of the firm as an entity. As a result, firms have typically used a variety of accounting-based performance metrics such as earnings per share, growth in earnings, and various financial ratios like return on net assets to monitor firm performance. These methods have a number of widely recognized deficiencies related to the fact that they focus on the results of a single year's operations and ignore the opportunity cost of capital employed by the firm. Currently available materials that discuss VBM have been prepared by the various consulting firms, each of whom is promoting its particular method. Furthermore, no book has yet undertaken the task of synthesizing these seemingly unrelated tools within a common valuation framework.

International Financial Management

In view of the continued globalization of world markets, we have integrated examples of international finance throughout the text. In addition, recognizing the fact that many of us approach the teaching of international finance in different ways, a separate chapter on international financial management is also provided.

Chapter Learning Objectives and Key Terms

Each chapter begins by setting out the learning objectives for that chapter, and setting in mind what that chapter will enable the student to do. In addition, at the end of each chapter, key terms and their locations in the text are identified, making for an easy review for the student.

Financial Calculators

The use of financial calculators has been integrated through this text, especially with respect to the presentation of the time value of money. Where appropriate, calculator solutions appear in the margin.

Extensive Use of Real-World Examples

In this edition we have greatly expanded the illustrative use of examples of problems facing real firms. This adds to student interest both by showing the relevance of the subjects covered and by providing an exciting framework within which to discuss financial concepts.

How Financial Managers Use This Material

A new section entitled "How Financial Managers Use This Material" has been added to close each chapter. This section ties the material presented in the chapter both to the student's future job setting and to real-world companies, thereby enhancing the student's interest and displaying the relevance of the material covered.

NEW TO THIS EDITION

The following list includes the major additions that are new to *Basic Financial Management*, eighth edition:

- New, relatively simple problems have been added to almost every chapter to give the professor more choice in homework assignments. Changes in the tax environment, for example, the changes in the net operating loss carryback and carryforward resulting from the 1997 Taxpayer Relief Act, are reflected in the presentation.
- We have substantially revised and streamlined chapter 2 with regard to both organization and content in order to provide a more useful and teachable introduction to the financial markets. Several new sections are included in the chapter dealing with (1) the financial manager and financing flexibility, (2) analyzing interest rates by use of risk premiums, and (3) analyzing real and nominal interest rates from a financial analyst's viewpoint. In addition, interest rate determinants are given special attention and explanation.
- The movement of "Evaluating Financial Performance" from chapter 12 in the previous edition to chapter 3 in this edition reflects the fundamental importance of basic accounting concepts to all facets of the study of corporate finance. In addition to changing this chapter's location in the text, we have completely re-written it in an effort to simplify and open up the presentation. We recognize that the purpose of much of this material is to refresh the concepts in the minds of the student and set forth basic concepts that will be used throughout the text.
- Chapters 3 and 4 were revised to smooth and simplify the flow while increasing the use of real-world examples and thereby highlighting the relevance and importance of the material being presented. For example, we used McDonald's in chapter 3 to illustrate the financial analysis of a real-world firm. Real-world companies were also used in some of the end-of-chapter problems.
- In discussing the use of accounting information to evaluate a firm's financial performance in chapter 3, we note that such an approach fails to connect performance directly to the goal of enhancing shareholder value. For this reason, we now include a section entitled "Measuring Firm Performance the EVA Way," which explains the use of EVA as a way to evaluate management's performance in terms of their contribution to increased shareholder value.
- Our revision of chapter 5 involved both a title change to "The Time Value of Money" and a dramatic increase in the use of examples to intuitively demonstrate the power of compounding.
- We have updated the risk-return and valuation chapters using new examples of actual companies to illustrate the concepts presented.

- The capital budgeting chapters, chapters 9, 10, and 11, now contain a plethora of examples using companies like McDonald's and GM to illustrate the concepts presented. In addition, chapter 9 now contains a section on net present value profiles.
- With respect to chapter 12, "Cost of Capital," we simplified the presentation by eliminating the discussion of breaks in the cost-of-capital schedule. In addition, we added a discussion of Briggs and Stratton's computation of the cost of capital and include a section on market value added and economic profit. We also include a discussion of why a firm might choose to go public and an international box discussing differences in capital costs across national boundaries.
- In chapter 13, we expanded the real-world discussions to include: The Coca-Cola Company, Chevron Corporation, IBM, and Archer Daniels Midland Corporation. The distinction between operating leverage and financial leverage is sharpened by using examples from these actual firms.
- Chapter 14, "Planning the Firm's Financing Mix," was revised with a totally new introduction that draws upon policies at the Georgia-Pacific Corporation. Actual examples of how firms design their capital structures and what influences their debt capacities are now included. Further, we stress the relationship between financial strategy and operating (commercial) strategy.
- In chapter 15, we provide a new introduction that relates dividend policy to the risk-return trade-off (Axiom 1). The changes in corporate dividend policies induced by extraordinarily high equity market returns over the 1995–1997 period are discussed. Dividend policies from firms like the Coca-Cola Company and the Walt Disney Company are examined.
- The focus of chapter 16, "Working-Capital Management and Short-Term Finance," was sharpened and more tightly focused on the issues that arise in the management of working capital and the choice of a source of short-term credit.
- Chapter 17, "Cash and Marketable Securities Management," has been shortened and includes updated data on interest rate levels on popular liquid asset investments. We stress the concept of cash management as a system.
- Coverage of the concept of supply chain management which is a company-wide systems approach to quality, is now provided in chapter 18. Supply chain management is actually the greater umbrella under which inventory management and TQM fall. Supply chain management deals with any activity aimed at providing customers with prompt and reliable service or products at the lowest cost, and, as such, includes not only inventory management, but also management of plants, warehouses, distribution centers, and retail operations.
- Chapter 19, "Term Loans and Leases" has been updated and has additional problems. New problems emphasize the basic calculations underlying the analysis of financial leases and term loans.
- A basic introduction to LEAPS is now provided in chapter 20.
- Chapter 21, "Corporate Restructuring: Combinations and Divestitures," has been streamlined by eliminating the discussion of '80s LBO restructuring. A section was also added to discuss the agency problem arising out of the separation of ownership and management and the various approaches that can be taken to deal with it. This discussion includes incentive-based compensation, external oversight or monitoring, and the use of financial policies designed to minimize managerial choice.
- In chapter 22, we emphasize the influence of the global economy on firm-level activity. Financial management no longer ends at the borders. The financial-economic crisis that affected the so-called "Asian tigers" is discussed and put in the context of efficient capital markets (Axiom 6). Examples from actual firms on the management of foreign exchange rate risk are provided and discussed.

As a final, but important, comment to the teacher, we know how frustrating errors in a textbook or instructor's manual can be. Thus we have worked diligently to provide you with as error-free a book as possible. Not only did we check and recheck the answers ourselves, but Prentice Hall hired faculty members at other universities to check the accuracy of the problem solutions. We therefore make the following offer to users of *Basic Financial Management*.

Any professor or student identifying an error of substance (e.g., an incorrect number in an example or problem) in *Basic Financial Management*, in the text, that has not been previously reported to the authors, will receive a $10 reward. If a series of related errors occurs resulting from an original error, the reward will be limited to a maximum of $20 for the group of errors. Please report any errors to Dave Scott at the following address:

Dave Scott

College of Business Administration, 427
University of Central Florida
Orlando, FL 32816-1400

LEARNING AIDS SUPPLEMENTAL TO THE TEXT

Basic Financial Management integrates the most advanced technology available to assist the student and the instructor. Not only does it make their financial management come alive with the most current information, but also enhances a total understanding of all tools and concepts necessary in mastering the course.

FOR THE STUDENT

THE PRENTICE HALL FINANCE CENTER CD

Contained in the inside back cover of this text is the ***Prentice Hall Finance Center CD,*** referred to in the text as the ***Finance Learning and Development CD***.
This robust learning tool contains the following features all designed to increase student awareness of what finance professionals do, ensure comprehension and mastery of the financial mathematics contained in the text, and supply a direct link to PHLIP—the Prentice Hall Learning on the Internet Partnership.

Careers Center

This Web site introduces the student to a vast array of professional opportunities in finance through video interviews with professionals and insights into what they do on the job in an average day. Here the student will meet an options trader, a mutual fund manager, investment analysts, a CFO, and others. Also accessible are features for personal development, resume writing, interviewing techniques, and career planning information.

FINCOACH—The Financial Math Practice Center

The Financial Math Practice Center contains more than 5 million problems and self-tests in virtually all math areas

covered in this text and financial management. Save problems, review them, print them. This is a step-by-step guide to solving any corporate finance mathematics problem and allows the student to rapidly gain mastery in all mathematical challenges.

PHLIP—The *Basic Financial Management* Web Center

PHLIP (Prentice Hall Learning on the Internet Partnership) can be accessed either directly from the CD or remotely at *www.prenhall.com/bfm*. Here's what the student can do on PHLIP:

- Read current news items from the popular business press that are directly related to chapters and use chapter terminology and providing links to more related information, discussion questions, and projects for assignment by the instructor.
- Download Excel spreadsheet templates related to specific chapter problems.
- Access additional careers information.
- Learn study skills, writing skills, and engage in conferences with other students who are studying financial management.

Case Connect

Also linked through the PHLIP Web site and applicable to specific chapters in the text are cases using interactive and linked features to provide the student and the instructor with a means of understanding concepts through real-world applications. Generally, these cases focus on a broad area of corporate finance and are appropriate for the level of this text.

On-Line Study Guide Companion Web Site

The Prentice Hall Companion Web site is another feature accessible by the student on the PHLIP site and designed specifically for this text. This Companion Web site allows the student to test their understanding of concepts within each chapter and relay via e-mail their answers to their instructor. Instructors will find this custom site useful for allocating student assignments and on-line quizzes; and its built-in grading feature can grade exams and provide students with immediate feedback.

Student Lecture Notes

Accessible through PHLIP, the PowerPoint Lecture Notes can be downloaded and printed as a handy lecture aid for the student with per chapter PowerPoints and space on the page for lecture note taking of material covered by the instructor.

OTHER SUPPLEMENTS AVAILABLE FOR THE STUDENT

Student Workbook—Available for purchase at the bookstore, this workbook is written by the authors of the text and contains innovative features to help the student using *Basic Financial Management*, eighth edition.

Each chapter begins with an overview of the key points in its respective text chapter and serves as a useful review. Additional problems with detailed solutions and self-tests can be used as an aid in preparing for examinations or for preparation of outside assignments.

FOR THE INSTRUCTOR

Instructor's Manual with Solutions

Prepared by the authors of the text, this manual contains concise chapter orientations, detailed chapter outlines, complete answers to end-of-chapter questions, and worked out solutions to all problems in the text. An Instructor's Guide to using PHLIP and a Guide to Using the Prentice Hall Finance Center are also contained in this manual.

Test Item File

Completely revised and updated by Professor Philip Thames of California State University, Fullerton, the eighth edition test bank contains over 5,000 true/false, multiple choice, and short answer questions.

PH Custom Tests

Available for both Windows and Macintosh, PH Custom is the computerized version of the test item file. It permits the instructor to edit, add, or delete questions from the test item file and generate his or her own custom exams.

FINCOACH Test Manager and FINCOACH Instructor's Manual

Test Manager software has been developed to allow instructors to generate tests based on **FINCOACH—*The Financial Management Math Practice Program*** contained within the Prentice Hall Finance Center CD, referred to in the text as the Finance Learning and Development CD, available to all students using ***Basic Financial Management***, eighth edition. In addition, an Instructor's Manual for using FINCOACH Test Manager and FINCOACH in the course has been developed and is available to all instructors.

PowerPoint Presentation

Over 50 slides per chapter of new lecture notes have been prepared by Professor Anthony Byrd of the University of Central Florida. These electronic transparencies allow the instructor to make full-color presentations coordinated with the *Basic Financial Management,* eighth edition *Student Lecture Notes.* To encourage more active learning, the slides include sample problems for students to solve in class. The Power-Points are available from the Prentice Hall PHLIP Web site (www.prenhall.com/bfm) by clicking "faculty site" for *Basic Financial Management*, eighth edition. ID and Password designations are available from the local Prentice Hall representative.

PHLIP Faculty Web Site
(Go to: *http://www.prenhall.com/bfm*)

Instructors will need to acquire a password and ID code from their local Prentice Hall representative in order to open the faculty site and gain access to the following materials:

- Downloadable PowerPoint Presentations with an average of 50 per chapter.
- Downloadable per chapter Instructor's Manual.

- Downloadable Excel spreadsheet Solutions to selected end-of-chapter problems, including solutions to Integrated Problems.
- "Talk To Team" faculty chat room.
- "Teaching Archive" resources for enhancing lecture materials and doing research on the Web.
- "Help With Computers" provides tips and access to getting answers to tricky computer problems.
- Solutions and Answers to all Cases on the **Case Connect Web site**.
- *Basic Financial Management,* eighth edition **On-Line Companion Web Site** for creating syllabuses and assignments and assessing student progress via e-mail relay of answers given on the On-Line Study Guide available to all students using the text.

Color Transparencies

All figures and tables from the text are available as full-color images on $8\frac{1}{2} \times 11$ acetate transparencies.

ACKNOWLEDGMENTS

We gratefully acknowledge the assistance, support, and encouragement of those individuals who have contributed to *Basic Financial Management*. Specifically, we wish to recognize the very helpful insights provided by many of our colleagues. For their careful comments and helpful reviews of this edition of the text, we are indebted to:

Theodore F. Byrley	SUNY Buffalo
Michael W. Carter	University of Arkansas—Fayetteville
James Forjan	York College of Pennsylvania
Stephen M. Horan	Saint Bonaventure University
Rajiv Karla	Moorhead State University
Michael G. McMillan	Northern Virginia Community College
John Primus	California State University—Hayward
Jane B. Romal	State University of New York at Fredonia
Edward J. Stendardi	St. John Fisher College
Bob G. Wood Jr.	Tennessee Technological University
Iqbal A. Memon	Fort Lewis College

We would also like to thank those who have provided helpful insights in past editions. For their comments and reviews, we would like to thank:

Kamal Abouzeid, V. T. Alaganan, Michael T. Alderson, Dwight C. Anderson, Nasser Arshadi, Sung C. Bea, Gary Benesh, Laura Berk, Sam G. Berry, Randy Billingsley, Eric Blazer, Laurence E. Blouse, Russell P. Boisjoly, Robert Boldin, Michael Bond, Waldo L. Born, Virgil L. Brewer, Jozelle Brister, Paul Burzik, John Byrd, Don M. Chance, Perikolam Raman Chandy, K. C. Chen, Santosh Choudhury, Jeffrey S. Christensen, M. C. Chung, Albert H. Clark, David W. Cole, Steven M. Dawson, Yashwant S. Dhatt, Bernard C. Dill, Mark Dorfman, John W. Ellis, Suzanne Erickson, Marjorie Evert, Slim Feriani, Greg Filbeck, Sidney R. Finkel, Fredrick G. Floss, Lyn Fraser, John Glister, Sharon S. Graham, Jack Griggs, Nancy Lee Halford, Ken Halsey, James D. Harris, William R. Henry, Dr. Linda C. Hittle, Keith Howe, Charles R. Idol, Vahan Janjigian, Nancy Jay, Jeff Jenkins, William Jens, Steve A. Johnson, Ravi Kamath, Djavad Kashefinejad, Terry Keele, James D. Keys, David R. Klock, Reinhold P. Lamb, Larry Lang, George B. F. Lanigan, William R. Lasher, Howard C. Launstein, David E. Letourneau, Leonard T. Long, Richard MacMinn, Judy E. Maese, Abbas Mamoozadeh, Terry S. Maness, Surendra K. Mansinghka, James A. Miller, Naval Modani, Eric J. Moon, Scott Moore, M. P. Narayan, Willliam E. O'Connell Jr., Shalini Perumpral, Jeffrey H. Peterson, Mario Picconi, John M. Pinkerton, Stuart Rosenstein, Ivan C. Roten, Marjorie A. Rubash, Jack H. Rubens, Todd Schank, Peter A. Sharp, Jackie Shu, Michael Solt, Raymond F. Spudeck, Suresh Srivastava, Joseph Stanford, Donald L. Stevens, David Suk, Elizabeth Sun, L. E. Sweeney, Philip R. Swensen, R. Bruce Swensen, Amir Tavakkol, Lee Tenpao, John G. Thatcher, Gary L. Trennepohl, Ronald Tsang, Paul A. Vanderheiden, K. G. Viswananthan, Al Webster, Patricia Webster, Herbert Weintraub, Kenneth L. Westby, Sandra Williams, Lawrence C. Wolken, Kevin Woods, Steve B. Wyatt, Wold Zemedkun, Marc Zenner.

We also thank our friends at Prentice Hall. They are a great group of folks. We offer our personal expression of appreciation to Paul Donnelly, our current editor who added real value to this project through his vision and insightfulness and whose energy and devotion to the project have been inspirational. He is simply the best. Our thanks to Patrick Lynch, for his marketing genius; to Janet Ferrugia, the marketing communications director, for her great job in alerting the market to the eighth edition; to Jodi Hirsh, for her attention to detail, she was the glue that kept this project together; to Gladys Soto, our assistant editor, who serves as both a sounding board and source for new ideas.

We benefited greatly from what has to be Prentice Hall's very best production team: to Susan Rifkin and Dee Josephson we are enormously grateful for making this edition one of our best experiences ever with a production group. Paul Smolenski has redefined our idea of the word "miracle" with the challenging schedule he faced to get this book to market on time and in near perfect form. We tip our hats once more to the splendid design group of Pat Smythe, Jill Little, and John Romer. We thank Glenn Furney at Texas Instruments for all his help in integrating calculator solutions into the text; and the Prentice Hall field representatives for their input based on their interaction with teachers from across the nation.

As a final word, we express our sincere thanks to those using *Basic Financial Management* in the classroom. We thank you for making us a part of your team. Always feel free to give any of us a call or contact us through the Internet when you have questions or needs.

D. F. S.
J. D. M.
J. W. P.
A. J. K.

Learning Objectives

Active Applications

World Finance

Practice

THE *BIG PICTURE* OF FINANCIAL MANAGEMENT

A Note to the Students about Using This Book

Corporate finance texts, out of necessity, contain vast amounts of information, computations, theory, and explanation. Competent students will read and remember the material, at least enough of it to pass the class. The best students, however, will go beyond the pages, to the "answers behind the answers" to truly understand what those equations mean, and how the theory works in the real world. The only way to do this is to see the logical foundation that these details, financial tools, and economic theory are built upon—the **big picture** of financial management. *Basic Financial Management* and the Prentice Hall Finance Center CD-ROM are designed to help your studies by presenting the material in an understandable, memorable framework, containing all the details but focusing on the logic behind them. Simply put, we present the forest and not just the trees. Whether this is your last course in finance or you are going on to additional courses in the increasingly important, exciting, and lucrative finance industry, this book will help you take away an understanding that you can refer to and rely upon the rest of your life.

KEEPING IT ORGANIZED

The Ten Axioms of Finance — the golden thread that ties everything together

Axiom 1:

THE RISK-RETURN TRADE-OFF—WE WON'T TAKE ON ADDITIONAL RISK UNLESS WE EXPECT TO BE COMPENSATED WITH ADDITIONAL RETURN

At some point, we have all saved some money. Why have we done this? The answer is simple: to expand our future consumption opportunities—for example, save for a house, a car, or retirement. We are able to invest those savings and earn a return on our dollars because some people would rather forgo future consumption opportunities to consume more now—maybe they're borrowing money to open a new business or a company is borrowing money to build a new plant. Assuming there are a lot of different people that would like to use our savings, how do we decide where to put our money?

First, investors demand a minimum return for delaying consumption that must be greater than the anticipated rate of inflation. If they didn't receive enough to compensate for anticipated inflation, investors would purchase whatever goods they desired ahead of time or invest in assets that were subject to inflation and earn the rate of inflation on those assets. There isn't much incentive to postpone consumption if your savings are going to decline in terms of purchasing power.

The previous explanations rely on the capital asset pricing model (CAPM)—and beta—as our standard bearer for estimating a stock's market risk and the rate of return that we should expect for a given beta. However, not everyone is happy with this approach, as discussed in the next section.

STOP AND THINK

*The conclusion of the matter is that **Axiom 1** is alive and well. It tells us, **We Won't Take on Additional Risk Unless We Expect to Be Compensated with Additional Return**. That is, there is a risk-return trade-off in the market.*

RELATE TO THE BIG PICTURE

Valuing preferred stock relies on three of our axioms presented in chapter 1, namely:

- *Axiom 1: The Risk-Return Trade-Off—We Won't Take on Additional Risk Unless We Expect to Be Compensated with Additional Return.*
- *Axiom 2: The Time Value of Money—A Dollar Received Today Is Worth More Than a Dollar Received in the Future.*
- *Axiom 3: Cash—Not Profits—Is King.*

As we have already observed with bonds, determining the economic worth or value of an asset always relies on these three axioms. Without them, we would have no basis for explaining value. With them, we can know that the amount and timing of cash, not earnings, drives value. Also, we must be rewarded for taking risk; otherwise, we will not invest.

The ***Ten Axioms*** are introduced and explained intuitively in chapter 1 . . .

. . . reappear throughout the textbook to tie the details of the material back to the Axioms . . .

. . . and are revisited at strategic points to ensure students can take complex material and ***Relate to the Big Picture***.

Learning Objectives — tying together the **_big picture_** of the chapter

CHAPTER PREVIEW

In chapter 7, we developed a general concept about valuation, where economic value was defined as the present value of the expected future cash flows generated by the asset. We then applied that concept to valuing bonds.

We now give our attention to valuing stocks, both preferred stock and common stock. As already noted at the outset of our study of finance and on several occasions since, the financial manager's objective should be to maximize the value of the firm's common stock. Thus we need to understand what determines stock value.

As we have done in all other chapters, it is important to begin by identifying the axioms that are important in understanding the topic to be studied—in this case, the basic considerations in issuing and valuing stock. These axioms are as follows: **Axiom 1: The Risk-Return Trade-Off—We Won't Take on Additional Risk Unless We Expect to Be Compensated with Additional Return; Axiom 2: The Time Value of Money—A Dollar Received Today Is Worth More Than a Dollar Received in the Future; Axiom 3: Cash—Not Profits—Is King; Axiom 7: The Agency Problem—Managers Won't Work for the Owners Unless It's in Their Best Interest.**

The first three axioms listed above relate to our definition of value—present value of cash flows. The last axiom, **Axiom 7,** indicates that the value of a firm's stock is in part dictated by the willingness of management to work in the best interest of the owners, which for most large companies are not the same group.

Numbered **_Learning Objectives_** outline the key points the chapter will cover and set expectations for what should be learned. The Chapter Preview ties this current chapter to what came before, to the Axioms that apply, and to what may come later.

OBJECTIVE 4

...ALUING COMMON STOCK

e both bonds and preferred stock, a common stock's value is equal to the present ue of all future cash flows expected to be received by the stockholder. However, in trast to bonds, common stock does not promise its owners interest income or a matu- y payment at some specified time in the future. Nor does common stock entitle the lder to a predetermined constant dividend, as does preferred stock. For common stock, e dividend is based on (1) the profitability of the firm, and (2) on management's deci- on to pay dividends or to retain the profits to grow the firm.

Thus dividends will vary with a firm's profitability and its stage of growth. The funds are any's early years, little if any dividends are typically paid. The funds are nance the firm's growth—to capture the opportunity that was identified by the As a company's growth slows—additional investment opportunities become sive—and the business becomes more profitable, the financial manager will paying dividends to the common stockholders. As the firm eventually reach and growth is no longer a priority, the financial manager should increase th even more. In short, a firm's stage of growth has direct implications on the be paid and on the value of the stock.

The Learning Objectives then appear at appropriate places in the chapter and in the chapter's **_Summary_** to tie the details to the chapter's outline and expectations. This feature also functions as a great tool for quick reference and your pre-exam reviews!

SUMMARY

Valuation is an important process in financial management. An understanding of valuation, both the concepts and procedures, supports the financial officer's objective of maximizing the value of the firm.

Preferred stock has no fixed maturity date and the dividends are fixed in amount. Following are some of the more frequent characteristics of preferred stock.

OBJECTIVE 1

- There are multiple classes of preferred stock.
- Preferred stock has a priority of claim on assets and income over common stock.
- Any dividends, if not paid as promised, must be paid before any common stock dividends may be paid. That is, they are cumulative.
- Protective provisions are included in the contract for the preferred shareholder in order to reduce the investor's risk.
- Many preferred stocks are convertible into common stock shares.

For a few preferred stocks:

- The dividend rate may be adjustable as interest rates change.
- The preferred stockholder may be allowed to participate in the firm's earnings in certain situations.
- The preferred stockholder may receive dividends in the form of more shares—payment in kind (PIK).

In addition, there are provisions frequently used to retire an issue of preferred stock, such as the ability for the firm to call its preferred stock or to use a sinking fund provision.

Value is the present value of future cash flows discounted at the investor's required rate of return. Although the valuation of any security entails the same basic principles, the procedures used in each situation vary. For example, we learned in chapter 7 that valuing a bond involves calculating the present value of future interest to be received plus the present value of the principal returned to the investor at the maturity of the bond.

For securities with cash flows that are constant in each year but where there is no specified maturity, such as preferred stock, the present value equals the dollar amount of the annual dividend divided by the investor's required rate of return; that is,

OBJECTIVE 2

$$\text{preferred stock value} = \frac{\text{dividend}}{\text{required rate of return}}$$

Bondholders and preferred stockholders can be viewed as creditors, whereas the common stockholders are the owners of the firm. Common stock does not have a maturity date, but exists as long as the firm does. Nor does common stock have an upper limit

OBJECTIVE 3

HANDLING THE MATH

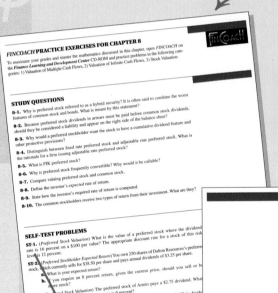

EXAMPLE

If we place $100 in a savings account that yields 12 percent compounded quarterly, what will our investment grow to at the end of 5 years? Substituting $n = 5$, $m = 4$, $i = 12$ percent, and $PV = \$100$ into equation (5-7), we find

$$FV_5 = \$100\left(1 + \frac{.12}{4}\right)^{4 \cdot 5}$$
$$= \$100(1 + .03)^{20}$$
$$= \$100(1.806)$$
$$= \$180.60$$

Thus we will have $180.60 at the end of 5 years. Notice that the calculator solution is slightly different because of rounding errors in the tables, as explained in the previous section, and that it also takes on a negative value.

Calculator Solution

DATA INPUT	FUNCTION KEY
20	N
3	I/Y
100	PV
0	PMT

FUNCTION KEY	ANSWER
CPT	
FV	−180.61

The text contains *hundreds of detailed examples, many with in-text Calculator Solutions,* keyed to the TI BAII+ (an HP conversion sheet is also included with every book), which remove uncertainty by showing the exact key-strokes needed to solve problems. The authors explain any differences between calculator solutions and problem solutions. Check the front of this text for your $5 discount offer from Texas Instruments on the TI BAII+, the best-selling, least expensive financial calculator for students!

The chapter refers students to the appropriate module in *FinCoach™*, the Windows-based math finance practice program, for an unlimited number of computer-generated, instantaneously corrected, heavily supported practice and self-test problems. **FinCoach™ comes FREE with the Prentice Hall Finance Center CD-ROM included in the back of this textbook. Using it will improve your grade!** (See the following description of the Prentice Hall Finance Center for more details.)

FINCOACH PRACTICE EXERCISES FOR CHAPTER 8

To maximize your grades and master the mathematics discussed in this chapter, open *FINCOACH* on the *Finance Learning and Development Center* CD-ROM and practice problems in the following categories: 1) Valuation of Multiple Cash Flows, 2) Valuation of Infinite Cash Flows, 3) Stock Valuation

STUDY QUESTIONS

8-1. Why is preferred stock referred to as a hybrid security? It is often said to combine the worst features of common stock and bonds. What is meant by this statement?

8-2. Because preferred stock dividends in arrears must be paid before common stock dividends, should they be considered a liability and appear on the right side of the balance sheet?

8-3. Why would a preferred stockholder want the stock to have a cumulative dividend feature and other protective provisions?

8-4. Distinguish between fixed rate preferred stock and adjustable rate preferred stock. What is the rationale for a firm issuing adjustable rate preferred stock?

8-5. What is PIK preferred stock?

8-6. Why is preferred stock frequently convertible? Why would it be callable?

8-7. Compare valuing preferred stock and common stock.

8-8. Define the investor's *expected* rate of return.

8-9. State how the investor's required rate of return is computed. What are they?

8-10. The common stockholders receive two types of return from their investment. What are they?

SELF-TEST PROBLEMS

ST-1. (*Preferred Stock Valuation*) What is the value of a preferred stock where the dividend rate is 16 percent on a $100 par value? The appropriate discount rate for a stock of this risk level is 12 percent.

ST-2. (*Preferred Stockholder Expected Return*) You own 250 shares of Dalton Resources's preferred stock, which currently sells for $38.50 per share and pays annual dividends of $3.25 per share.
   a. What is your expected return?
   b. If you require an 8 percent return, given the current price, should you sell or buy more stock?

ST-3. (*Preferred Stock Valuation*) The preferred stock of Armlo pays a $2.75 dividend. What is the value of the stock if your required return is 9 percent?

ST-4. (*Common Stock Valuation*) Crosby Corporation's common stock paid $1.32 in dividends last year and is expected to grow indefinitely at an annual 7 percent rate. What is the value of the stock if you require an 11 percent return?

ST-5. (*Common Stockholder Expected Return*) Blackburn & Smith's common stock currently sells for $23 per share. The company's executives anticipate a constant growth rate of 10.5 percent and an end-of-year dividend of $2.50.
   a. What is your expected rate of return?
   b. If you require a 17 percent return, should you purchase the stock?

STUDY PROBLEMS (SET A)

8-1A. (*Preferred Stock Valuation*) Calculate the value of a preferred stock that pays a dividend of $6 per share and your required rate of return is 12 percent.

8-2A. (*Measuring Growth*) If Pepperdine, Inc.'s return on equity is 16 percent and the management plans to retain 60 percent of earnings for investment purposes, what will be the firm's growth rate?

8-3A. (*Preferred Stock Valuation*) What is the value of a preferred stock where the dividend rate is 14 percent on a $100 par value? The appropriate discount rate for a stock of this risk level is 12 percent.

8-4A. (*Preferred Stockholder Expected Return*) Solitron's preferred stock is selling for $42.16 and pays $1.95 in dividends. What is your expected rate of return if you purchase the security at the market price?

8-5A. (*Preferred Stockholder Expected Return*) You own 200 shares of Somner Resources's preferred stock, which currently sells for $40 per share and pays annual dividends of $3.40 per share.
   a. What is your expected return?
   b. If you require an 8 percent return, given the current price should you sell or buy more stock?

Two sets of Study Problems (A&B), each problem is identified by topic, provide dozens more practice problems per chapter. Solutions to odd-numbered study problems are contained in the Student Solutions Manual. (Available through your bookstore.)

Self-Test Problems with detailed solutions further reinforce your understanding of the math.

Integrative Problems tie together multiple chapters in a real-world scenario to illustrate how the concepts work together to help form the big picture.

INTEGRATIVE PROBLEM

You are considering three investments. The first is a bond that is selling in the market at $1,200. The bond has a $1,000 par value, pays interest at 14 percent, and is scheduled to mature in 12 years. For bonds of this risk class, you believe that a 12 percent rate of return should be required. The second investment that you are analyzing is a preferred stock ($100 par value) that sells for $90 and pays an annual dividend of $12. Your required rate of return for this stock is 14 percent. The last investment is a common stock ($25 par value) that recently paid a $3 dividend. The firm's earnings per share have increased from $4 to $8 in 10 years, which also reflects the expected growth in dividends per share for the indefinite future. The stock is selling for $25, and you think a reasonable required rate of return for the stock is 20 percent.

1. Calculate the value of each security based on your required rate of return.
2. Which investment(s) should you accept? Why?
3. If your required rates of return changed to 14 percent for the bond, 16 percent for the preferred stock, and 18 percent for the common stock, how would your answers change to parts 1 and 2?
4. Assuming again that your required rate of return for the common stock is 20 percent, but the anticipated constant growth rate changes to 12 percent, how would your answers to parts 1 and 2 change?

GO TO:
http://www.prenhall.com/bfm
For downloads and current events associated with this chapter

MAKING THE MATERIAL RELEVANT

Basic Financial Management in Practice boxes bring articles from the top newspapers, magazines, and financial journals right into the text.

The ***Analysis and Implications*** section then shows you how to analyze the article using the financial tools the student has just accumulated, showing how the big picture of finance extends beyond the covers of this book!

Basic Financial Management in Practice articles help students analyze:

- **Current events** (chapter 8: "Promoting Stock on the Internet")
- **Ethical dilemmas** (chapter 1: "Right vs. Wrong: Just Take Your Time")
- Cutting-edge **financial innovations** (chapter 6: "Morgan Stanley Develops Way to Measure Mutual Fund Risk")
- **Personal finance** (chapter 5: "Make a Child a Millionaire")
- **Global applications** (chapter 12: "Why Do Interest Rates Differ Between Countries?")
- The **cross-functionality of finance** in the workplace (chapter 11: "Scientific Management at Merck: An Interview with CFO Judy Lewent")

www.prenhall.com/bfm

This icon means that students can use the power of the Internet to help grasp the big picture! ***The Basic Financial Management*** Web site contains Current Events, Internet Resources, and additional cases customized to the text! The Prentice Hall Finance Center CD-ROM contains a hot-link to the site. (See the Prentice Hall Finance Center description for more details.)

HOW FINANCIAL MANAGERS USE THIS MATERIAL

Not only is the financial manager responsible for finding and then properly evaluating new projects, but the financial manager must be certain that the numbers going into the analysis are correct. Let's look at what the financial managers at Burger King faced when they decided to introduce the Big King, a new burger that looks an awful lot like the Big Mac. The first task they face is to estimate what the sales from this new product will be—a task that is easier said than done. Not only will sales be dependent upon how good the product is, or in this case, how good the product tastes, but they will also be dependent upon how good a job the marketing department does in selling the public on this new product. But just looking at sales is not enough. To properly perform the analysis on this product, Burger King needs to know what portion of sales will simply be sales diverted from Whoppers, and what portion of sales will be new to Burger King as a whole. In other words, when they introduce the Big King, how much of the sales are from new customers—those "Big Mac attack" eaters.

This is truly an area where finance and marketing meet. Much of the job of the financial manager is to make sure that the numbers are correct. That is, have the marketing people considered any synergistic effects? If new customers are drawn into Burger King, are they likely to buy a drink and some fries?—two very high markup sales. Will they bring in their families or friends when they make their Big King purchase? How about the increased inventory associated with carrying the Big King line? If it all sounds pretty

Case Problems ask students to think critically about the material and apply it to a large-scale problem or project.

CASE PROBLEMS

DANFORTH & DONNALLEY LAUNDRY PRODUCTS COMPANY

Capital Budgeting: Relevant Cash Flows

On April 14, 1998, at 3:00 P.M., James Danforth, president of Danforth & Donnalley (D&D) Laundry Products Company, called to order a meeting of the financial directors. The purpose of the meeting was to make a capital-budgeting decision with respect to the introduction and production of a new product, a liquid detergent called Blast. Chemical Company, formed in 1973 with the merger of Danforth D&D was headquartered in Seattle, Washington, producers of Lift-Off detergent, the leading laundry detergent on the West Coast, and Donnalley Home Products Company, headquartered in Detroit, Michigan, makers of Wave detergent, a major Midwestern laundry product. As a result of the merger, D&D was producing and marketing two major product lines. Although these products were in direct competition, they were not without product differentiation: Lift-Off was a low-suds, concentrated powder, and Wave was a more traditional powder detergent. Each line brought with it considerable brand

---

Every chapter concludes with a discussion of ***How Financial Managers Use This Material.*** This section helps students see the applicability and implications of this material in a new way, through the eyes of a financial manager.

Make a Child a Millionaire
Just Take Your Time

THE WALL STREET JOURNAL, APRIL 22, 1994

BASIC FINANCIAL MANAGEMENT IN PRACTICE

Thanks a million.

Even if you haven't got a lot of money, you can easily give $1 million or more to your children, grandchildren, or favorite charity. All it takes is a small initial investment and a lot of time.

Suppose your 16-year-old daughter plans to take a summer job, which will pay her at least $2,000. Because she has earned income, she can open an individual retirement account. If you would like to help fund her retirement, Kenneth Klegon, a financial planner in Lansing, Michigan, suggests giving her $2,000 to set up the IRA. He then advises doing the same in each of the next 5 years, so that your daughter stashes away a total of $12,000.

Result? If the money is invested in stocks, and stocks deliver their historical average annual return of 10%, your daughter will have more than $1 million by the time she turns 65.

Because of the corrosive effect of inflation, that $1 million will only buy a quarter of what $1

million buys today, presuming the cost of living rises at 3% a year. Nonetheless, your $12,000 gift will go a long way toward paying for your daughter's retirement. The huge gain is possible because of the way stock-market compounding works, with money earned each year not only on your initial investment, but also on the gains accumulated from earlier years.

"The beauty of this strategy is that it will grow tax-deferred," Klegon says. "There's no cost. You can set up an IRA with a no-load mutual fund for nothing." Similarly, Mr. Klegon says, once your children enter the work force full time, you can encourage them to participate in their company's 401(k) plan by reimbursing them for their contributions.

SOURCE: Jonathan Clements, "Make a Child a Millionaire," *The Wall Street Journal* (April 22, 1994): C1. Reprinted by permission of *The Wall Street Journal*, ©1994 by Dow Jones & Co., Inc. All Rights Reserved Worldwide.

Analysis and Implications:

A. Using the principles and techniques set out in this chapter, we can easily see how much this IRA investment will accumulate to. We can first take the $2,000 6-year annuity and determine its future value—that is, its value when your daughter is 21 and receives the last payment. This would be done as follows:

$$FV = PMT(FVIFA_{10\%, 6yrs})$$
$$= \$2,000(FVIFA_{10\%, 6yrs})$$
$$= \$15,431.22$$

We could then take this amount that your daughter has when she is 21 and compound it out 44 years to when she is 65, as follows:

$$FV = PV(FVIF_{10\%, 44yrs})$$
$$= \$15,431.22(FVIF_{10\%, 44yrs})$$
$$= \$1,022,535.54$$

Thus your daughter's IRA would have accumulated to $1,022,535.54 by age 65 if she grew at 10 percent compounded annually.

B. To determine how much this is worth in today's dollars, if inflation increases at an annual rate of 3 percent compounded annually this period, we need only calculate the present value of $1,022,535.54 to be received 49 years from now given a discount rate of 3 percent. This would determine the future value of this IRA measured in dollars with the same spending power as those around when your daughter was 16. This is done as follows:

$$PV = FV(PVIF_{3\%, 49yrs})$$
$$= \$1,022,535.54(PVIF_{3\%, 49yrs})$$
$$= \$240,245.02$$

You can change the growth and inflation rates and come up with all kinds of numbers, but one thing holds: There is incredible power in compounding!

187

USING TECHNOLOGY TO REVEAL THE *BIG PICTURE* BEYOND

The Prentice Hall Finance Center CD-ROM in the back of this book is designed to both support your coursework and extend your finance education into the real world to show you the "Big Picture" of financial management!

THE MATH PRACTICE CENTER

One of the most challenging parts of a corporate finance/financial management course is often the math— but you don't have to let it stand in your way of a good grade. Using the FinCoach finance math practice software, you'll get all the practice you need, on your own time, at your own speed, with immediate feedback, and supported at every step with:

 FinAide Help on which equation to use.

 FinDoc Help on what the variables mean.

 FinHelp Background help on the financial concept at work.

 FinCalc An on-line financial calculator.

And more, all designed to get you comfortable with the math of finance so you can focus on the **big picture** — the logic behind the math and what the numbers tell you!

THE WEB CENTER

Take finance from theory in a textbook to real world practice! The Web site supporting your *Basic Financial Management* eighth edition textbook — part of the PHLIP (Prentice Hall Learning on the Internet Partnership) project — is created and maintained by finance instructors and designed to incorporate the power of the Internet into your textbook and your course with:

Excel templates for the spread-sheet problems contained in the textbook.

An on-line study guide with multiple choice, essay, and Web destination questions. Answers and results can be e-mailed to your instructor.

This Book and the Classroom

Current Events — Summaries and analyses of current events written by finance instructors. See how finance theory gets applied in practice every day.

Current Events
- Tobacco Stocks Recoup After Bill is Extinguished
- The Greenspan Effect: Fed Chairman Speaks And The Market Reacts
- 1995 Was One for the Books
- Stocks Rise On Rate Cut From Fed

Internet Resources — Annotated links to topic-specific sites on the Web.

The Globalization of Product and Financial Markets (Pg. 506)
Internet Resources
- A Trader's Haven [info]
- ESPIN Stock Charts [info]

Study Hall — Includes ***Ask the Tutor*** for finance-specific help, a ***Writing Center***, computer help, and more. One of the most popular spots on the PHLIP site!

STUDY HALL RESOURCES

ASK THE TUTOR

Ask the Tutor allows students to post questions or comments to the threaded conference message board for their course. There is also a general conference where students can ask questions that don't fall within a particular course.

CAREER CENTER

The Career Center is designed for business students in general, but we have resources for everyone. There are also great resources for each of our supported business disciplines.

WRITING CENTER

The Writing Center has tools, tips and techniques for authoring powerful business communications.

STUDY SKILLS CENTER

The overall key to college success is being able to manage ourselves in an academic environment. To do that

The Careers Center

The **big picture** of finance includes the career possibilities that a finance degree opens to you! ***Careers in Finance*** explores the working life of finance professionals who tell you how they got there, what you can expect when you get there, and what it takes to be successful.
The Career Center contains:

- Video interviews with finance professionals explaining what they do every day.
- Industry surveys of current salaries at all levels among the finance professions.

Interviewing and resume writing tips and other advice that will help you land your first job in finance.

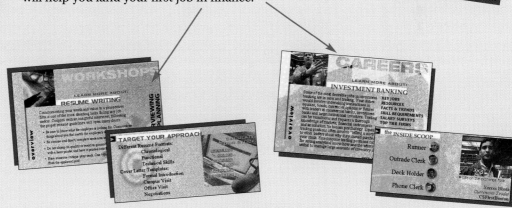

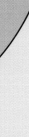

For Installation Instructions see the README file on this CD-ROM

6-3
Hall

Windows® 3.1, Windows®95

And the Big Picture of Financial Management

Also available

Basic Financial Management eighth edition   Study Guide
0-13-083375-4

Written by the authors of *Basic Financial Management*, this study guide offers study hints, extra help on the topics, and dozens of extra practice questions per chapter to help you prepare for exams. If your bookstore does not carry the Study Guide already, simply ask the manager to order a copy for you using the ISBN number above!

BASIC FINANCIAL MANAGEMENT

Learning Objectives

Active Applications

World Finance

Practice

CHAPTER 1

AN INTRODUCTION TO FINANCIAL MANAGEMENT

LEARNING OBJECTIVES

After reading this chapter, you should be able to

1. Describe what the subject of financial management is about.

2. Explain the goal of the firm.

3. Compare the various legal forms of business and explain why the corporate form of business is the most logical choice for a firm that is large or growing.

4. Identify the corporate tax features that affect business decisions.

5. Explain the 10 axioms that form the basics of financial management.

INTRODUCTION

In 1996, stockholders at Walt Disney Co. approved a compensation package for Michael Eisner, the chairman at Disney, that included $196 million of stock options. This is in addition to the $203 million he received in 1993. Needless to say, Disney has made Eisner a rich man. However, Eisner has also made the Disney shareholders rich. At the time the new compensation package was approved, Disney's stock had risen about 2,400 percent since 1984 when Eisner took over a then struggling Disney. That's an average annual return of over 30 percent per year!

In this chapter, we aren't so concerned with how much a firm's CEO earns, but whether the compensation package helps align the interests of the managers with those of the shareholders. We will see that this alignment between managers and shareholders is necessary to realize the goal of the firm that we develop. We will also see that aligning the interests of the shareholders and managers serves as one of the basic axioms of finance developed in this chapter. Moreover, the tax laws were recently changed to encourage corporations to incorporate pay for performance into management contracts, thereby aligning the interests of shareholders and managers.

CHAPTER PREVIEW

In this chapter, we will lay a foundation for the entire book. We will explain what finance is, and then we will explain the key goal that guides financial decision making: maximization of shareholder wealth. We will show the legal and tax environment of financial decisions. Finally, we will describe the golden thread that ties everything together: the 10 basic axioms of finance.

WHAT IS FINANCE?

Financial management is concerned with the maintenance and creation of economic value or wealth. Consequently, this course focuses on decision making with an eye toward creating wealth. As such, we will deal with financial decisions such as when to introduce a new product, when to invest in new assets, when to replace existing assets, when to borrow from banks, when to issue stocks or bonds, when to extend credit to a customer, and how much cash to maintain.

To illustrate, consider two firms, Merck and IBM. At the end of 1995, the total market value of Merck, a large pharmaceutical company, was $83 billion. Over the life of the business, Merck's investors had invested about $20 billion in the business. In other words, management created $63 billion in additional wealth for the shareholders. IBM, on the other hand, was valued at $63 billion at the end of 1995. But over the years, IBM's investors had actually invested $69 billion—a loss in value of $6 billion. Therefore, Merck created wealth for its shareholders, while IBM lost shareholder wealth.

In introducing decision-making techniques, we will emphasize the logic behind those techniques, thereby insuring that we do not lose sight of the concepts when dealing with the calculations. To the first-time student of finance, this may sound a bit overwhelming. However, as we will see, the techniques and tools introduced in this text are all motivated by 10 underlying principles or axioms that will guide us through the decision-making process.

GOAL OF THE FIRM

We believe that the preferable goal of the firm should be *maximization of shareholder wealth*, by which we mean maximization of the price of the existing common stock. Not only will this goal be in the best interest of the shareholders, but it will also provide the most benefits to society. This will come about as scarce resources are directed to their most productive use by businesses competing to create wealth.

To better understand this goal, we will first discuss profit maximization as a possible goal for the firm. Then we will compare it to maximization of shareholder wealth to see why, in financial management, the latter is the more appropriate goal for the firm.

Profit Maximization

In microeconomics courses, profit maximization is frequently given as the goal of the firm. Profit maximization stresses the efficient use of capital resources, but it is not specific with respect to the time frame over which profits are to be measured. Do we maximize profits over the current year, or do we maximize profits over some longer period? A financial manager could easily increase current profits by eliminating research and development expenditures and cutting down on routine maintenance. In the short run, this might result in increased profits, but this clearly is not in the best long-run interests of the firm. If we are to base financial decisions on a goal, that goal must be precise, not allow for misinterpretation, and deal with all the complexities of the real world.

In microeconomics, profit maximization functions largely as a theoretical goal, with economists using it to prove how firms behave rationally to increase profit. Unfortunately, it ignores many real-world complexities that financial managers must address in their decisions. In the more applied discipline of financial management, firms must deal every day with two major factors not considered by the goal of profit maximization: uncertainty and timing.

Microeconomics courses ignore uncertainty and risk to present theory more easily. Projects and investment alternatives are compared by examining their expected values or weighted average profits. Whether one project is riskier than another does not enter into these calculations; economists do discuss risk, but only tangentially.[1] In reality, projects differ a great deal with respect to risk characteristics, and to disregard these differences in the practice of financial management can result in incorrect decisions. As we will discover later in this chapter, there is a very definite relationship between risk and expected return—that is, investors demand a higher expected return for taking on added risk—and to ignore this relationship would lead to improper decisions.

Another problem with the goal of profit maximization is that it ignores the timing of the project's returns. If this goal is only concerned with this year's profits, we know it inappropriately ignores profit in future years. If we interpret it to maximize the average of future profits, it is also incorrect. Inasmuch as investment opportunities are available for money in hand, we are not indifferent to the timing of the returns. Given equivalent cash flows from profits, we want those cash flows sooner rather than later. Thus the real-world factors of uncertainty and timing force us to look beyond a simple goal of profit maximization as a decision criterion.

Finally, and possibly most important, accounting profits fail to recognize one of the most important costs of doing business. When we calculate accounting profits, we consider interest expense as a cost of borrowing money, but we ignore the cost of the funds provided by the firm's shareholders (owners). If a company could earn 8 percent on a new investment, that would surely increase the firm's profits. However, what if the firm's shareholders could earn 12 percent with that same money in another investment of similar risk? Should the company's managers accept the investment because it will increase the firm's profits? Not if they want to act in the best interest of the firm's owners (shareholders). Now look at what happened with Burlington Northern.

Burlington Northern is a perfect example of erroneous thinking. In 1980, Richard Bressler was appointed as CEO of the company. Bressler, unlike his predecessor, was not a "railroad man." He was an "outsider" who was hired for the express purpose of improving the value of the shareholders' stock. The reason for the change was that Burlington Northern had been earning about 4 percent on the shareholders' equity, when CDs with no risk were paying 6 percent. Management was certainly increasing the firm's profits, but they were destroying shareholder wealth by investing in railroad lines that were not even earning a rate of return equal to that paid on government securities. We will turn now to an examination of a more robust goal for the firm: maximization of shareholder wealth.

Maximization of Shareholder Wealth

In formulating the goal of maximization of shareholder wealth, we are doing nothing more than modifying the goal of profit maximization to deal with the complexities of the operating environment. We have chosen maximization of shareholder wealth—that is, maximization of the market value of the existing shareholders' common stock—because the effects of all financial decisions are thereby included. Investors react to poor investment or dividend decisions by causing the total value of the firm's stock to fall, and they react to good decisions by pushing up the price of the stock. In effect, under this goal, good decisions are those that create wealth for the shareholder.

Obviously, there are some serious practical problems in implementing this goal and in using changes in the firm's stock to evaluate financial decisions. We know the price of

---

[1]See, for example, Robert S. Pindyck and Daniel Rubenfield. *Microeconomics*, 2d ed. (New York: Macmillan, 1992), 244–46.

a firm's stock fluctuates, often for no apparent reason. However, over the long run, price equals value. We will keep this long-run balancing in mind and focus on the effect that our decision *should* have on the stock price if everything else were held constant. The market price of the firm's stock reflects the value of the firm as seen by its owners and takes into account the complexities and complications of the real-world risk. As we follow this goal throughout our discussions, we must keep in mind that the shareholders are the legal owners of the firm.

O B J E C T I V E 3

LEGAL FORMS OF BUSINESS ORGANIZATION

In the chapters ahead, we will focus on financial decisions for corporations. Although the corporation is not the only legal form of business available, it is the most logical choice for a firm that is large or growing. It is also the dominant business form in terms of sales in this country. In this section, we will explain why this is so. This will in turn allow us to simplify the remainder of the text, as we will assume that the proper tax code to follow is the corporate tax code, rather than examine different tax codes for different legal forms of businesses. Keep in mind that our primary purpose is to develop an understanding of the logic of financial decision making. Taxes will become important only when they affect our decisions, and our discussion of the choice of the legal form of the business is directed at understanding why we will limit our discussion of taxes to the corporate form.

Legal forms of business organization are diverse and numerous. However, there are three categories: the sole proprietorship, the partnership, and the corporation. To understand the basic differences between each form, we need to define each form and understand its advantages and disadvantages. As we will see, as the firm grows, the advantages of the corporation begin to dominate. As a result, most large firms take on the corporate form.

Sole Proprietorship

Sole proprietorship

A business owned by a single individual.

The **sole proprietorship** is a business owned by a single individual. The owner maintains title to the assets and is personally responsible, generally without limitation, for the liabilities incurred. The proprietor is entitled to the profits from the business but must also absorb any losses. This form of business is initiated by the mere act of beginning the business operations. Typically, no legal requirement must be met in starting the operation, particularly if the proprietor is conducting the business in his or her own name. If a special name is used, an assumed-name certificate should be filed, requiring a small registration fee. Termination occurs on the owner's death or by the owner's choice. Briefly stated, the sole proprietorship is, for all practical purposes, the absence of any formal *legal* business structure.

Partnership

Partnership

An association of two or more individuals joining together as co-owners to operate a business for profit.

The primary difference between a **partnership** and a sole proprietorship is that the partnership has more than one owner. A partnership is an association of two or more persons coming together as co-owners for the purpose of operating a business for profit. Partnerships fall into two types: (1) general partnerships and (2) limited partnerships.

General partnership. In a general partnership, each partner is fully responsible for the liabilities incurred by the partnership. Thus, any partner's faulty conduct even having the appearance of relating to the firm's business renders the remaining partners liable as well. The relationship among partners is dictated entirely by the partnership agreement, which may be an oral commitment or a formal document.

THE WALL STREET JOURNAL, APRIL 29, 1994

Promotion Cost More Than a Contribution

Does Corporate Charity Increase Shareholder Wealth?

(A) Harper's magazine reported without comment that Miller Brewing gives $150,000 a year to its black scholarship program, but spends double that to promote it. Miller won't comment on the figures but it notes that the Thurgood Marshall Scholarship Fund keeps 87 deserving black students in college.

Noel Hankin, director of corporate relations for the Philip Morris unit, says part of the promotional budget goes to expensive television plugs linking Miller and the fund. It also bought advertising in black publications saluting black education. The ads carried modest logos for Miller as well as for the fund, and an 800 number.

(B) The fund spends about $348,000 a year on the students, Mr. Hankin says, and Miller is by far the largest contributor. He says Miller spends more on promoting the fund to attract donations than it receives in contributions to it.

Mr. Hankin says the tiny fund wants to get out from behind the shadow of the well-known United

Negro College Fund, a prodigious fund raiser. The UNCF aids black private colleges. The Thurgood Marshall fund serves a larger number of black public universities, which enroll more than 70% of all students at historical black schools. "Yes, we do mention Miller, but for good reason; we're the ones promoting the awareness of the fund," Mr. Hankin says.

It isn't unusual for firms to donate far less than they spend on promoting charities. "A ratio of 2-to-1 or 3-to-1 is common," says Craig Smith, president of Corporate Citizen, a Seattle think tank that studies corporate giving.

SOURCE: Excerpted from Leon E. Wynter, Business and Race, "Promotion Cost More Than a Contribution," *The Wall Street Journal* (April 29, 1994): B1. Reprinted by permission of *The Wall Street Journal*, © 1994 by Dow Jones & Co., Inc. All Rights Reserved Worldwide.

Analysis and Implications ...

A. Most firms do provide donations to worthy causes. Milton Friedman, the Nobel-Prize-winning economist, has argued, however, that because financial managers are employees of the corporation, and the corporation is owned by the shareholders, the financial managers should run the corporation in such a way that shareholder wealth is maximized and then allow the shareholders to decide if they would like to pass on any of the profits to deserving causes. Friedman argues that the executive making the decision to donate should be serving as an agent of the stockholders. In effect, by donating earnings to a charity that would have gone to the shareholders, the executive is both imposing taxes and deciding how the tax proceeds shall be spent.

B. In this case, it does not appear that Miller made this donation without any consideration of the benefits they might reap. For Miller, the decision to donate may have had more to do with marketing than with social responsibility. This would explain the fact that Miller spent twice what it donated to the fund on promotion. In this way, corporate donations can be attempts to maximize shareholder wealth by casting the firm in a more positive light.

Limited partnership. In addition to the general partnership, in which all partners are jointly liable without limitation, many states provide for a limited partnership. The state statutes permit one or more of the partners to have limited liability, restricted to the amount of capital invested in the partnership. Several conditions must be met to qualify as a limited partner. First, at least one general partner must remain in the association for whom the privilege of limited liability does not apply. Second, the names of the limited partners may not appear in the name of the firm. Third, the limited partners may not participate in the management of the business. If one of these restrictions is violated, all partners forfeit their right to limited liability. In essence, the intent of the statutes creating the limited partnership is to provide limited liability for a person whose interest in the partnership is purely as an investor. That individual may not assume a management function within the organization.

Corporation

The **corporation** has been a significant factor in the economic development of the United States. As early as 1819, Chief Justice John Marshall set forth the legal definition of a corporation as "an artificial being, invisible, intangible, and existing only in the contemplation of law."[2] This entity *legally* functions separate and apart from its owners. As such, the corporation can individually sue and be sued, and purchase, sell, or own property; and its personnel are subject to criminal punishment for crimes. However, despite this legal separation, the corporation is composed of owners who dictate its direction and policies. The owners elect a board of directors, whose members in turn select individuals to serve as corporate officers, including president, vice-president, secretary, and treasurer. Ownership is reflected in common stock certificates, designating the number of shares owned by its holder. The number of shares owned relative to the total number of shares outstanding determines the stockholder's proportionate ownership in the business. Because the shares are transferable, ownership in a corporation may be changed by a shareholder simply remitting the shares to a new shareholder. The investor's liability is confined to the amount of the investment in the company, thereby preventing creditors from confiscating stockholders' personal assets in settlement of unresolved claims. This is an extremely important advantage of a corporation. After all, would you be willing to invest in General Electric if you would be liable in the event that one of their airplane engines malfunctions and people die in a crash? Finally, the life of a corporation is not dependent on the status of the investors. The death or withdrawal of an investor does not affect the continuity of the corporation. The management continues to run the corporation when stock is sold or when it is passed on through inheritance.

Comparison of Organizational Forms

Owners of new businesses have some important decisions to make in choosing an organizational form. Whereas each business form seems to have some advantages over the others, we will see that, as the firm grows and needs access to the capital markets to raise funds, the advantages of the corporation begin to dominate.

Large and growing firms choose the corporate form for one reason: ease in raising capital. Because of the limited liability, the ease of transferring ownership through the sale of common shares, and the flexibility in dividing the shares, the corporation is the ideal business entity in terms of attracting new capital. In contrast, the unlimited liabilities of the sole proprietorship and the general partnership are deterrents to raising equity capital. Between the extremes, the limited partnership does provide limited liability for limited partners, which has a tendency to attract wealthy investors. However, the impracticality of

---

[2]*The Trustees of Dartmouth College* v. *Woodard*, 4 Wheaton 636 (1819).

having a large number of partners and the restricted marketability of an interest in a partnership prevent this form of organization from competing effectively with the corporation. Therefore, when developing our decision models, we will assume that we are dealing with the corporate form. The taxes incorporated in these models will deal only with the corporate tax codes. Because our goal is to develop an understanding of the management, measurement, and creation of wealth, and not to become tax experts, we will only focus on those characteristics of the corporate tax code that will affect our financial decisions.

THE TAX ENVIRONMENT

OBJECTIVE 4

The tax environment sets up the ground rules under which financial decisions are made. As the nation's politics change, so does the tax system. The purpose of looking at the current tax structure is not to become tax experts, but rather to gain an understanding of taxes and how they affect business decisions. There is a good chance that corporate tax rates may change significantly before you enter the workforce. However, although rates may change, taxes will continue to remain a cash outflow and therefore something to avoid. Thus, we will pay close attention to which expenses are and are not deductible for tax purposes, and in doing so focus on how taxes affect business decisions.

Objectives of Income Taxation

Originally, the sole objective of the federal government in taxing income was to generate financing for government expenditures. Although this purpose continues to be important, social and economic objectives have been added. For instance, a company may receive possible reductions in taxes if: (1) it undertakes certain technological research, (2) it pays wages to certain economically disadvantaged groups, or (3) it locates in certain economically depressed areas. Other socially oriented stipulations in the tax laws include exemptions for dependents, old age, and blindness, and a reduction in taxes on retirement income. In addition, the government uses tax legislation to stabilize the economy. In recessionary periods, corporate taxes may be lowered to generate job growth.

In short, three objectives may be given for the taxation of revenues: (1) the provision of revenues for government expenditures, (2) the achievement of socially desirable goals, and (3) economic stabilization.

Types of Taxpayers

To understand the tax system, we must first ask, "Who is the taxpayer?" For the most part, there are three basic types of taxable entities: individuals, corporations, and fiduciaries. Individuals include company employees, self-employed persons owning their own businesses, and members of a partnership. Income is reported by these individuals in their personal tax returns.[3] The corporation, as a separate legal entity, reports its income and pays any taxes related to these profits. The owners (stockholders) of the corporation need not report these earnings in their personal tax returns, except when all or a part of the profits are distributed in the form of dividends. Finally, fiduciaries, such as estates and trusts, file a tax return and pay taxes on the income generated by the estate or trust which isn't distributed to (and included in the taxable income of) a beneficiary.

Although taxation of individual and fiduciary income is an important source of income to the government, neither is especially relevant to the financial manager. Because most

---

[3]Partnerships report income from the partnership but do not pay taxes. The income is then reported again by each partner, who each pay any taxes owed.

firms of any size are corporations, we will restrict our discussion to the corporation. A caveat is necessary however. Tax legislation can be quite complex, with numerous exceptions to most general rules. The laws can also change quickly, and certain details discussed here may no longer apply in the near future. However, the general approach should remain the same, regardless of changes.

Computing Taxable Income

The taxable income for a corporation is based on the gross income from all sources, except for allowable exclusions, less any tax-deductible expenses. *Gross income* equals the firm's dollar sales from its product less the cost of producing or acquiring the product. Tax-deductible expenses include any operating expenses, such as marketing expenses and administrative expenses. Also, *interest expense* paid on the firm's outstanding debt is a tax-deductible expense. However, dividends paid to the firm's stockholders are *not* deductible expenses, but rather distributions of income. Other taxable income includes interest income and dividend income that the corporation receives.

To demonstrate how to compute a corporation's taxable income, consider the J and S Corporation, a manufacturer of home accessories. The firm, originally established by Kelly Stites, had sales of $50 million for the year. The cost of producing the accessories totaled $23 million. Operating expenses were $10 million. The corporation has $12,500,000 in debt outstanding with an 8 percent interest rate, which has resulted in $1 million in interest expense ($12,500,000 × .08 = $1,000,000). Management paid $1 million in dividends to the firm's common stockholders. No other income, such as interest or dividend income, was received. The taxable income for the J and S Corporation would be $16 million, as shown in Table 1.1.

Once we know the J and S Corporation's taxable income, we can next determine the amount of taxes the firm will owe.

Computing the Taxes Owed

The taxes to be paid by the corporation on its taxable income are based on the corporate tax rate structure. The specific rates effective for the corporation, as of 1997, are given in Table 1.2. Under the Revenue Reconciliation Act of 1993, a new top marginal corporate tax rate of 35 percent was added for taxable income in excess of $10 million. Also, a surtax of 3 percent was imposed on taxable income between $15 million and $18,333,333.

Table 1.1 J and S Corporation Taxable Income

Sales		$50,000,000
Cost of goods sold		(23,000,000)
Gross profit		$27,000,000
Operating expenses		
Administrative expenses	$4,000,000	
Depreciation expenses	1,500,000	
Marketing expenses	4,500,000	
Total operating expenses		(10,000,000)
Operating income (earnings before interest and taxes)		$17,000,000
Other income		0
Interest expense		(1,000,000)
Taxable income		$16,000,000

NOTE: Dividends paid to common stockholders ($1,000,000) are not tax-deductible.

Table 1.2 Corporate Tax Rates

Rates	Income Levels
15%	$0–$50,000
25%	$50,001–$75,000
34%	$75,001–$10,000,000
35%	over $10,000,000

NOTE: Additional surtaxes:
- 5% on income between $100,000 and $335,000
- 3% on income between $15,000,000 and $18,333,333

This, in combination with the previously existing 5 percent surtax on taxable income between $100,000 and $335,000, recaptures the benefits of the lower marginal rates and, as a result, both the average and marginal tax rates on taxable income above $18,333,333 become 35 percent.

Tax liability for the J and S Corporation, which had $16 million in taxable earnings, would be $5,530,000, as shown in Table 1.3:

Table 1.3 Tax Calculations for J and S Corporation

Earnings	×	Marginal Tax Rate	=	Taxes
$ 50,000	×	15%	=	$ 7,500
25,000	×	25%	=	6,250
9,925,000	×	34%	=	3,374,500
6,000,000	×	35%	=	2,100,000
				$5,488,250

Additional surtaxes:
- Add 5% surtax on income between
  $100,000 and $335,000
  (5% × [$335,000 − $100,000])   11,750
- Add 3% surtax on income between
  $15,000,000 and $18,333,333
  (3% × [$16,000,000 − $15,000,000])   30,000

Total tax liability $5,530,000

The tax rates shown in Table 1.2 are defined as the **marginal tax rates**, or rates applicable to the next dollar of income. For instance, if a firm has earnings of $60,000 and is contemplating an investment that would yield $10,000 in additional profits, the tax rate to be used in calculating the taxes on this added income is 25 percent; that is, the marginal tax rate is 25 percent. However, if the corporation already expects $20 million without the new investment, the extra $10,000 in earnings would be taxed at 35 percent, the marginal tax rate at the $20 million level of income. In the example, where the J and S Corporation has taxable income of $16 million, its marginal tax rate is 38 percent (this is because $16 million falls into the 35 percent tax bracket *with* a 3 percent surtax); that is, any additional income from new investments will be taxed at a rate of 38 percent. However, after taxable income exceeds $18,333,333, the marginal tax rate declines to 35 percent, when the 3 percent surtax no longer applies.

Marginal tax rate

The tax rate that would be applied to the next dollar of income.

For financial decision making it's the *marginal tax rate* rather than the average tax rate that we will be concerned with. As will become increasingly clear throughout the text, we always want to consider the tax consequences of any financial decision. The appropriate rate to be used in the analysis is the marginal tax rate, because it is this rate that will be applicable for any changes in earnings as a result of the decision being made. Thus, when making financial decisions involving taxes, always use the marginal tax rate in your calculations.[4]

The tax rate structure used in computing the J and S Corporation's taxes assumes that the income occurs in the United States. Given the globalization of the economy, it may well be that some of the income originates in a foreign country. If so, the tax rates, and the method of taxing the firm, frequently vary. International tax rates can vary substantially and the job of the financial manager is to minimize the firm's taxes by reporting as much income as possible in the low-tax-rate countries and as little as possible in the high-tax-rate countries. Of course, other factors, such as political risk, may discourage your efforts to minimize taxes across national borders.

Other Tax Considerations

Several major aspects of existing tax legislation have relevance for the financial manager: (1) the dividend income exclusion on dividends received by corporations, (2) the effects of depreciation on the firm's taxes, (3) the tax treatment of operating losses, and (4) the recognition of capital gains and losses. We also need to consider any additional taxes that may be imposed on a firm for the "excessive accumulation" of profits within the business in an effort to avoid double taxation. Finally, we should be familiar with the tax provision that allows a corporation to be taxed as a partnership, which became increasingly important with the Tax Reform Act of 1986. Let's look at each of these tax provisions in turn.

Dividend exclusion. A corporation may normally exclude 70 percent of any dividends received from another corporation. For instance, if corporation A owns common stock in corporation B and receives dividends of $1,000 in a given year, only $300 will be subject to tax, and the remaining $700 (70 percent of $1,000) will be tax exempt. If the corporation receiving the dividend income is in a 34 percent tax bracket, only $102 in taxes (34 percent of $300) will result.[5]

Depreciation. The methods for computing depreciation expense are explained in Appendix 1C. Essentially, there are three methods for computing **depreciation** expenses: (1) the straight-line depreciation method, (2) the double-declining balance method, and (3) the modified accelerated cost recovery system. Any one of the three methods results in the same depreciation expense over the life of the asset; however, the last two approaches allow the firm to take the depreciation earlier as opposed to later, which in turn defers taxes until later. Assuming a time value of money, there is an advantage to using the accelerated techniques. (Chapter 5 fully explains the time value of money.)

Depreciation

The means by which an asset's value is expensed over its useful life for federal income tax purposes.

---

[4]On taxable income between $335,000 and $10 million, both the marginal and average tax rates equal 34 percent, owing to the imposition of the 5 percent surtax that applies to taxable income between $100,000 and $335,000. After the company's taxable income exceeds $18,333,333, both the marginal and average tax rate equal 35 percent, because the 3 percent surtax on income between $15 million and $18,333,333 eliminates the benefits of having the first $10 million of income taxed at 34 rather than 35 percent.

[5]If corporation A owns at least 20 percent of corporation B, but less than 80 percent, 80 percent of any dividends received may be excluded from taxable income. If 80 percent or more is owned, all the dividends received may be excluded.

Also, management may use straight-line depreciation for reporting income to the shareholders but use an accelerated method for calculating taxable income.

Net operating loss deduction. If a corporation has an operating loss (which is simply a loss from operating a business), that loss may be applied against income in other years. The tax laws provide for a **net operating loss carryback** and **carryforward**. A carryback permits the taxpayer to apply the loss against the profits for the previous 2 years. If the loss has not been completely absorbed by the profits in these 2 years, the loss may be carried forward to each of the next 20 years (carryforward).[6] At the end of that 20-year period, any loss still remaining may no longer be used as a tax deduction. To illustrate, a 1998 operating loss may be used to recover, in whole or in part, the taxes paid during 1997 and 1996. If any part of the loss still remains, this amount may be used to reduce taxable income, if any, during the 20-year period for 1999 through 2018.

Capital gains and losses. An important tax consideration prior to 1987 was the preferential tax treatment for **capital gains**; that is, gains from the sale of assets not bought or sold in the ordinary course of business. The Tax Reform Act of 1986 repealed any special treatment of capital gains and, although the Revenue Reconciliation Act of 1993 reinstituted preferential treatment in certain unique circumstances, in general, capital gains are taxed at the same rates as ordinary income. However, if a corporation has capital losses that exceed capital gains in any year, these net **capital losses** may not be deducted from ordinary income. The net losses may, however, be carried back and applied against net capital gains in each of the 3 years before the current year. If the loss is not completely used in the 3 prior years, any remaining loss may be carried forward and applied against any net gains in each of the next 5 years. For example, if a corporation has an $80,000 net capital loss in 1998, it may apply this loss against any net gains in 1995, 1996, and 1997. If any loss remains, it may be carried forward and applied against any gains through 2003.

Accumulated earnings tax. The earnings generated by a corporation are subject to "double taxation," first at the corporate level and then at the stockholder level as the firm's profits are distributed in the form of dividends. If the shareholders have no immediate need for dividend income, the corporation could retain its profits and perhaps even employ the funds for the personal benefit of the company's owners. For example, management could retain the corporate profits but make a personal loan to the stockholders. Also, if the profits were accumulated within the firm, the price of the common stock, assuming the profits are reinvested at a rate above the shareholders' required rate of return, should rise. Until the stock is sold, the investor would not be required to pay any tax.

To prevent such stratagems of tax avoidance, a 28 percent surtax in addition to the regular income tax is assessed at the corporate level on any accumulation of earnings by a corporation for the purpose of avoiding taxes on its shareholders. The tax does not apply to the retention of profits for *reasonable business* needs. Nor must the money be reinvested immediately as long as there is evidence that future needs require the current accumulation of earnings. Although it is difficult to state exactly when the accumulation of profits is thought to be reasonable, examples would include: (1) providing for the replacement of plant and equipment, (2) retiring debt created in connection with the corporation's business, (3) extending more credit to customers, and (4) financing the

Net operating loss carryback and carryforward

A tax provision that permits the taxpayer first to apply a loss against the profits in the 2 prior years (carryback). If the loss has not been completely absorbed by the profits in these 2 years, it may be applied to taxable profits in each of the 20 following years (carryforward).

Capital gain or loss

As defined by the revenue code, a gain or loss resulting from the sale or exchange of a capital asset.

---

[6]The carryback period was reduced by the Taxpayer Relief Act of 1997. For years prior to August 5, 1997, the carryback was 3 years and the carryforward was 15 years. The purpose of reducing the carryback to 2 years (from 3 years) was to increase revenue to the government, which was then passed on to taxpayers in the form of reduced taxes.

acquisition of a new business. The bottom line here is that you can use earnings for business purposes, but you can't hold on to them just as a tax dodge.

Subchapter S Corporation. In deciding between the sole proprietorship or partnership form and the corporation, tax considerations are important. Owners attempt to select the form of business organization that maximizes their after-tax returns. To minimize the tax influence on the decision, Congress established the **Subchapter S Corporation**, which enables a corporation to be taxed as a partnership. This provision eliminates the "double taxation" effect on the corporation. The Subchapter S Corporation files a tax return for information purposes only and pays no taxes. The taxes from the business are paid by the stockholders, whether or not the earnings are distributed. However, to qualify as a Subchapter S Corporation, the following requirements must be met:

1. The firm must be a domestic corporation.
2. There may be no more than 35 shareholders at the beginning of the corporation's life. These shareholders must be individuals, estates, or certain trusts.
3. The corporation cannot be a member of an affiliated group eligible to file a consolidated tax return with another corporation.
4. There may be only one class of stock.
5. A nonresident alien cannot be a stockholder.

Only small to moderate-sized firms typically can satisfy the Subchapter S Corporation requirements. However, if the qualifications can be met, the company may potentially receive the benefits of a corporation but be taxed as a partnership.

Putting It All Together: An Example

To illustrate certain portions of the tax laws for a corporation, assume that the Griggs Corporation had sales during the past year of $5 million; its cost of goods sold was $3 million; and it incurred operating expenses of $1 million. In addition, it received $185,000 in interest income and $100,000 in dividend income from another corporation. In turn, it paid $40,000 in interest and $75,000 in dividends. Finally, the company sold a piece of land for $100,000 that had cost $50,000 six years ago. Given this information, the firm's taxable income is $1,225,000, as computed in the top part of Table 1.4.

Based on the tax rates from Table 1.2, Griggs's tax liability is $416,500, as shown at the bottom of Table 1.4. Note that the $75,000 Griggs paid in dividends is not tax deductible. Also, since the firm's taxable income exceeds $335,000, and the 5 percent surtax no longer applies, the marginal tax rate and the average tax rate both equal 34 percent; that is, we could have computed Griggs's tax liability as 34 percent of $1,225,000, or $416,500. As we will see, as the tax code changes, different investments become more and less profitable, which demonstrates the role taxes play in the financial manager's decisions.

OBJECTIVE 5

TEN AXIOMS THAT FORM THE BASICS OF FINANCIAL MANAGEMENT

We have just discussed the legal and tax foundations of financial decisions. We will now look at the *finance* foundations that lie behind the decisions made by financial managers. To the first-time student of finance, the subject matter may seem like a collection of unrelated decision rules. This could not be further from the truth. In fact, our decision rules, and the logic that underlies them, spring from 10 simple axioms that do not require knowledge of finance to understand. *However, while it is not necessary to understand finance in order to understand these axioms, it is necessary to understand these axioms in order to understand finance.* Keep in mind that although these axioms may at first appear

Subchapter S Corporation

A corporation that, because of specific qualifications, is taxed as though it were a partnership.

Table 1.4 Griggs Corporation Tax Computations

Sales			$5,000,000
Cost of goods sold			(3,000,000)
Gross profit			2,000,000
Operating expenses			(1,000,000)
Operating income			$1,000,000
Other taxable income and expenses:			
Interest income		$185,000	
Dividend income	$100,000		
Less 70% exclusion	(70,000)	30,000	
Interest expense		(40,000)	175,000
Gain on land sale:			
Selling price		$100,000	
Cost		(50,000)	$ 50,000
Total taxable income			$1,225,000
Tax computation:			
15% × $ 50,000 =	$ 7,500		
25% × 25,000 =	6,250		
34% × 1,150,000 =	391,000		
$1,225,000			
Add 5% surtax for income between			
$100,000 and $335,000	$ 11,750		
Tax liability	$416,500		

simple or even trivial, they will provide the driving force behind all that follows. These axioms will weave together concepts and techniques presented in this text, thereby allowing us to focus on the logic underlying the practice of financial management. In order to make the learning process easier for you as a student, we will keep returning to these axioms throughout the book in the form of "Relate to the Big Picture" boxes—tying the material together and letting you sort the "forest from the trees."

Axiom 1:

THE RISK-RETURN TRADE-OFF—WE WON'T TAKE ON ADDITIONAL RISK UNLESS WE EXPECT TO BE COMPENSATED WITH ADDITIONAL RETURN

At some point, we have all saved some money. Why have we done this? The answer is simple: to expand our future consumption opportunities—for example, save for a house, a car, or retirement. We are able to invest those savings and earn a return on our dollars because some people would rather forgo future consumption opportunities to consume more now—maybe they're borrowing money to open a new business or a company is borrowing money to build a new plant. Assuming there are a lot of different people that would like to use our savings, how do we decide where to put our money?

First, investors demand a minimum return for delaying consumption that must be greater than the anticipated rate of inflation. If they didn't receive enough to compensate for anticipated inflation, investors would purchase whatever goods they desired ahead of time or invest in assets that were subject to inflation and earn the rate of inflation on those assets. There isn't much incentive to postpone consumption if your savings are going to decline in terms of purchasing power.

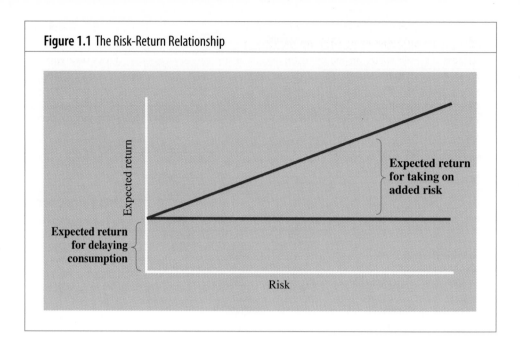

Figure 1.1 The Risk-Return Relationship

Investment alternatives have different amounts of risk and expected returns. Investors sometimes choose to put their money in risky investments because these investments offer higher expected returns. The more risk an investment has, the higher will be its expected return. This relationship between risk and expected return is shown in Figure 1.1.

Notice that we keep referring to *expected* return rather than *actual* return. We may have expectations of what the returns from investing will be, but we can't peer into the future and see what those returns are actually going to be. If investors could see into the future, no one would have invested money in the drug maker Liposme, whose stock dropped 61.5 percent on July 24, 1997. This is when the results of a late stage clinical study of Liposme's Ventus respiratory drug were announced, showing no difference between patients who received the drug and those who received a placebo. Until after the fact, you are never sure what the return on an investment will be. That is why General Motors bonds pay more interest than U.S. Treasury bonds of the same maturity. The additional interest convinces some investors to take on the added risk of purchasing a General Motors bond.

This risk-return relationship will be a key concept as we value stocks, bonds, and proposed new projects throughout this text. We will also spend some time determining how to measure risk. Interestingly, much of the work for which the 1990 Nobel Prize for Economics was awarded centered on the graph in Figure 1.1 and how to measure risk. Both the graph and the risk-return relationship it depicts will reappear often in this text.

Axiom 2:

THE TIME VALUE OF MONEY—A DOLLAR RECEIVED TODAY IS WORTH MORE THAN A DOLLAR RECEIVED IN THE FUTURE

A fundamental concept in finance is that money has a time value associated with it: A dollar received today is worth more than a dollar received a year from now. Because we can earn interest on money received today, it is better to receive money earlier rather than later. In your economics courses, this concept of the time value of money is referred to as the opportunity cost of passing up the earning potential of a dollar today.

In this text, we focus on the creation and measurement of wealth. To measure wealth or value, we will use the concept of the time value of money to bring the future benefits and costs of a project back to the present. Then, if the benefits outweigh the costs, the project creates wealth and should be accepted; if the costs outweigh the benefits, the project does not create wealth and should be rejected. Without recognizing the existence of the time value of money, it is impossible to evaluate projects with future benefits and costs in a meaningful way.

To bring future benefits and costs of a project back to the present, we must assume a specific opportunity cost of money, or interest rate. Exactly what interest rate to use is determined by **Axiom 1: The Risk-Return Trade-Off**, which states investors demand higher returns for taking on more risky projects. Thus, when we determine the present value of future benefits and costs, we take into account that investors demand a higher return for taking on added risk.

Axiom 3:

CASH—NOT PROFITS—IS KING

In measuring wealth or value, we will use cash flows, not accounting profits, as our measurement tool. That is, we will be concerned with when the money hits our hand, when we can invest it and start earning interest on it, and when we can give it back to the shareholders in the form of dividends. Remember, it is the cash flows, not profits, that are actually received by the firm and can be reinvested. Accounting profits, on the other hand, appear when they are earned rather than when the money is actually in hand. As a result, a firm's cash flows and accounting profits may not be the same. For example, a capital expense, such as the purchase of new equipment or a building, is depreciated over several years, with the annual depreciation subtracted from profits. However, the cash flow, or actual dollars, associated with this expense generally occurs immediately. Therefore cash inflows and outflows involve the actual receiving and payout of money—when the money hits or leaves your hands. As a result, cash flows correctly reflect the timing of the benefits and costs.

Axiom 4:

INCREMENTAL CASH FLOWS—IT'S ONLY WHAT CHANGES THAT COUNTS

In 1997, General Mills, the maker of Cheerios, Frosted Cheerios, Apple Cinnamon Cheerios, and Multi Grain Cheerios, introduced Team Cheerios—"3 delicious O's Teamed Up for One Sweet Crunch." There is no doubt that Team Cheerios competed directly with General Mill's other cereals and, in particular, its Cheerios products. In fact, Team Cheerios, with its brown sugar and frosting, tastes very much like Frosted Cheerios. Certainly some of the sales dollars that ended up with Team Cheerios would have been spent on other Cheerios and General Mills products if Team Cheerios had not been available. Although General Mills was targeting younger consumers with this sweetened cereal, there is no question that Team sales bit into—actually cannibalized—sales from Cheerios and other General Mills's lines. Realistically, there's only so much cereal anyone can eat. The *difference* between revenues General

Mills generated after introducing Team Cheerios versus simply maintaining its existing line of cereals is the incremental cash flows. This difference reflects the true impact of the decision.

In making business decisions, we are concerned with the results of those decisions: What happens if we say yes versus what happens if we say no? **Axiom 3** states that we should use cash flows to measure the benefits that accrue from taking on a new project. We are now fine tuning our evaluation process so that we only consider **incremental** cash flows. The incremental cash flow is the difference between the cash flows if the project is taken on versus what they will be if the project is not taken on.

What is important is that we *think* incrementally. Our guiding rule in deciding whether a cash flow is incremental is to look at the company with and without the new product. In fact, we will take this incremental concept beyond cash flows and look at all consequences from all decisions on an incremental basis.

Axiom 5:

THE CURSE OF COMPETITIVE MARKETS— WHY IT'S HARD TO FIND EXCEPTIONALLY PROFITABLE PROJECTS

Our job as financial managers is to create wealth. Therefore, we will look closely at the mechanics of valuation and decision making. We will focus on estimating cash flows, determining what the investment earns, and valuing assets and new projects. But it will be easy to get caught up in the mechanics of valuation and lose sight of the process of creating wealth. Why is it so hard to find projects and investments that are exceptionally profitable? Where do profitable projects come from? The answers to these questions tell us a lot about how competitive markets operate and where to look for profitable projects.

In reality, it is much easier evaluating profitable projects than finding them. If an industry is generating large profits, new entrants are usually attracted. The additional competition and added capacity can result in profits being driven down to the required rate of return. Conversely, if an industry is returning profits below the required rate of return, then some participants in the market drop out, reducing capacity and competition. In turn, prices are driven back up. This is precisely what happened in the VCR video rental market in the mid-1980s. This market developed suddenly with the opportunity for extremely large profits. Because there were no barriers to entry, the market quickly was flooded with new entries. By 1987, the competition and price cutting produced losses for many firms in the industry, forcing them to flee the market. As the competition lessened with firms moving out of the video rental industry, profits again rose to the point where the required rate of return could be earned on invested capital.

In competitive markets, extremely large profits simply cannot exist for very long. Given that somewhat bleak scenario, how can we find good projects—that is, projects that return more than their expected rate of return given their risk level (remember Axiom 1). Although competition makes them difficult to find, we have to invest in markets that are not perfectly competitive. The two most common ways of making markets less competitive are to differentiate the product in some key way or to achieve a cost advantage over competitors.

Product differentiation insulates a product from competition, thereby allowing a company to charge a premium price. If products are differentiated, consumer choice is no longer made by price alone. For example, many people are willing to pay a premium for Starbucks coffee. They simply want Starbucks and price is not important. In the pharmaceutical industry, patents create competitive barriers. Schering-Plough's Claritin, an allergy relief medicine, and Hoffman-La Roche's Valium, a tranquilizer, are protected from direct competition by patents.

Service and quality are also used to differentiate products. For example, Levi's has long prided itself on the quality of its jeans. As a result, it has been able to maintain its market share. Similarly, much of Toyota and Honda's brand loyalty is based on quality. Service can also create product differentiation, as shown by McDonald's fast service, cleanliness, and consistency of product that brings customers back.

Whether product differentiation occurs because of advertising, patents, service, or quality, the more the product is differentiated from competing products, the less competition it will face and the greater the possibility of large profits.

Economies of scale and the ability to produce at a cost below competition can effectively deter new entrants to the market and thereby reduce competition. Wal-Mart is one such case. For Wal-Mart, the fixed costs are largely independent of the store's size. For example, inventory costs, advertising expenses, and managerial salaries are essentially the same regardless of annual sales. Therefore, the more sales that can be built up, the lower the per-sale dollar cost of inventory, advertising, and management. Restocking from warehouses also becomes more efficient as delivery trucks can be used to full potential.

Regardless of how the cost advantage is created—by economies of scale, proprietary technology, or monopolistic control of raw materials—the cost advantage deters new market entrants while allowing production at below industry cost. This cost advantage has the potential of creating large profits.

The key to locating profitable investment projects is to first understand how and where they exist in competitive markets. Then the corporate philosophy must be aimed at creating or taking advantage of some imperfection in these markets, either through product differentiation or creation of a cost advantage, rather than looking to new markets or industries that appear to provide large profits. Any perfectly competitive industry that looks too good to be true won't be for long. It is necessary to understand this to know where to look for good projects and to accurately measure the project's cash flows. We can do this better if we recognize how wealth is created and how difficult it is to create it.

Axiom 6:

EFFICIENT CAPITAL MARKETS—THE MARKETS ARE QUICK AND THE PRICES ARE RIGHT

Our goal as financial managers is the maximization of shareholder wealth. How do we measure shareholder wealth? It is the value of the shares that the shareholders hold. To understand what causes stocks to change in price, as well as how securities such as bonds and stocks are valued or priced in the financial markets, it is necessary to have an understanding of the concept of **efficient markets**.

Efficient market

A market in which the values of all assets and securities at any instant in time fully reflect all available public information.

Whether a market is efficient or not has to do with the speed with which information is impounded into security prices. An efficient market is characterized by a large number of profit-driven individuals who act independently. In addition, new information regarding securities arrives in the market in a random manner. Given this setting, investors adjust to new information immediately and buy and sell the security until they feel the market price correctly reflects the new information. Under the efficient market hypothesis, information is reflected in security prices with such speed that there are no opportunities for investors to profit from publicly available information. Investors competing for profits ensure that security prices appropriately reflect the expected earnings and risks involved and thus the true value of the firm.

What are the implications of efficient markets for us? First, the price is right. Stock prices reflect all publicly available information regarding the value of the company. This means we can implement our goal of maximization of shareholder wealth by focusing on the effect each decision *should* have on the stock price if everything else were held constant. That is, over time good decisions will result in higher stock prices and bad ones, lower stock prices. Second, earnings manipulations through accounting changes will not result in price changes. Stock splits and other changes in accounting methods that do not affect cash flows are not reflected in prices. Market prices reflect expected cash flows available to shareholders. Thus, our preoccupation with cash flows to measure the timing of the benefits is justified.

As we will see, it is indeed reassuring that prices reflect value. It allows us to look at prices and see value reflected in them. While it may make investing a bit less exciting, it makes corporate finance much less uncertain.

Axiom 7:

THE AGENCY PROBLEM—MANAGERS WON'T WORK FOR OWNERS UNLESS IT'S IN THEIR BEST INTEREST

Agency problem

Problem resulting from conflicts of interest between the manager (the stockholder's agent) and the stockholders.

Although the goal of the firm is the maximization of shareholder wealth, in reality, the agency problem may interfere with the implementation of this goal. The **agency problem** results from the separation of management and the ownership of the firm. For example, a large firm may be run by professional managers who have little or no ownership in the firm. Because of this separation of the decision makers and owners, managers may make decisions that are not in line with the goal of maximization of shareholder wealth. They may approach work less energetically and attempt to benefit themselves in terms of salary and perquisites at the expense of shareholders.

To begin with, an agent is someone who is given the authority to act on behalf of another, referred to as the principal. In the corporate setting, the shareholders are the principals, because they are the actual owners of the firm. The Board of Directors, the CEO, the corporate executives, and all others with decision-making power are agents of the shareholders. Unfortunately, the Board of Directors, the CEO, and the other corporate executives don't always do what's in the best interest of the shareholders. Instead, they act many times in their own best interest. Not only might they benefit themselves in terms of salary and perquisites, but they might also avoid any projects that have risk associated with them—even if they're great projects with huge potential returns and a small chance of failure. Why is this so? Because if the project doesn't turn out, these agents of the shareholders may lose their jobs.

The costs associated with the agency problem are difficult to measure, but occasionally we see the problem's effect in the marketplace. For example, if the market feels management of a firm is damaging shareholder wealth, we might see a positive reaction in stock price to the removal of that management. In 1989, on the day following the death of John Dorrance, Jr., chairman of Campbell Soup, Campbell's stock price rose about 15 percent. Some investors felt that Campbell's relatively small growth in earnings might be improved with the departure of Dorrance. There was also speculation that Dorrance was the major obstacle to a possible positive reorganization.

If the management of the firm works for the owners, who are the shareholders, why doesn't the management get fired if they don't act in the shareholder's best interest? *In theory*, the shareholders pick the corporate board of directors and the board of directors in turn picks the management. Unfortunately, *in reality* the system frequently works the other way around. Management selects the board of director nominees and then distributes the ballots. In effect, shareholders are offered a slate of nominees selected by the management. The end result is management effectively selects the directors, who then may have more allegiance to managers than to shareholders. This in turn sets up the potential for agency problems with the board of directors not monitoring managers on behalf of the shareholders as they should.

We will spend considerable time monitoring managers and trying to align their interests with shareholders. Managers can be monitored by auditing financial statements and managers' compensation packages. The interests of managers and shareholders can be aligned by establishing management stock options, bonuses, and perquisites that are directly tied to how closely their decisions coincide with the interest of shareholders. The agency problem will persist unless an incentive structure is set up that aligns the interests of managers and shareholders. In other words, what's good for shareholders must also be good for managers. If that is not the case, managers will make decisions in their best interests rather than maximizing shareholder wealth.

Axiom 8:

TAXES BIAS BUSINESS DECISIONS

Earlier in this chapter, we saw how taxes influence financial decisions. Hardly any decision is made by the financial manager without considering the impact of taxes. When we introduced **Axiom 4**, we said that only incremental cash flows should be considered in the evaluation process. More specifically, the cash flows we will consider will be *after-tax incremental cash flows to the firm as a whole*.

When we evaluate new projects, we will see income taxes playing a significant role. When the company is analyzing the possible acquisition of a plant or equipment, the returns from the investment should be measured on an after-tax basis. Otherwise, the company will not truly be evaluating the true incremental cash flows generated by the project.

The government also realizes taxes can bias business decisions and uses taxes to encourage spending in certain ways. If the government wanted to encourage spending on research and development projects it might offer an *investment tax credit* for such investments. This would have the effect of reducing taxes on research and development projects, which would in turn increase the after-tax cash flows from those projects. The increased cash flow would turn some otherwise unprofitable research and development projects into profitable projects. In effect, the government can use taxes as a tool to direct business investment to research and development projects, to the inner cities, and to projects that create jobs.

Axiom 9:

ALL RISK IS NOT EQUAL—SOME RISK CAN BE DIVERSIFIED AWAY, AND SOME CANNOT

Much of finance centers around **Axiom 1: The Risk-Return Trade-Off**. But before we can fully use **Axiom 1**, we must decide how to measure risk. As we will see, risk is difficult to measure. **Axiom 9** introduces you to the process of diversification and demonstrates how it can reduce risk. We will also provide you with an understanding of how diversification makes it difficult to measure a project or an asset's risk.

You are probably already familiar with the concept of diversification. There is an old saying, "don't put all of your eggs in one basket." Diversification allows good and bad events or observations to cancel each other out, thereby reducing total variability without affecting expected return.

To see how diversification complicates the measurement of risk, let us look at the difficulty Louisiana Gas has in determining the level of risk associated with a new natural gas well drilling project. Each year, Louisiana Gas might drill several hundred wells, with each well having only a 1 in 10 chance of success. If the well produces, the profits are quite large, but if it comes up dry, the investment is lost. Thus with a 90 percent chance of losing everything, we would view the project as being extremely risky. However, if Louisiana Gas each year drills 2,000 wells, all with a 10 percent, independent chance of success, then they would typically have 200 successful wells. Moreover, a bad year may result in only 190 successful wells, and a good year may result in 210 successful wells. If we look at all the wells together, the extreme good and bad results tend to cancel each other out and the well drilling projects taken together do not appear to have much risk or variability of possible outcome.

The amount of risk in a gas well project depends upon our perspective. Looking at the well standing alone, it looks like a lot; however, if we consider the risk that each well contributes to the overall firm risk, it is quite small. This is because much of the risk associated with each individual well is diversified away within the firm. The point is: We can't look at a project in isolation. Later, we will see that some of this risk can be further diversified away within the shareholder's portfolio.

Perhaps the easiest way to understand the concept of diversification is to look at it graphically. Consider what happens when we combine two projects, as depicted in Figure 1.2. In this case, the cash flows from these projects move in opposite directions, and when they are combined, the variability of their combination is totally eliminated. Notice that the return has not changed—each individual project's and their combination's return averages 10 percent. In this case, the extreme good and bad observations cancel each other out. The degree to which the total risk is reduced is a function of how the two sets of cash flows or returns move together.

As we will see for most projects and assets, some risk can be eliminated through diversification, whereas some risk cannot. This will become an important distinction later in our studies. *For now, we should realize that the process of diversification can reduce risk, and as a result, measuring a project's or an asset's risk is very difficult.* A project's risk changes depending on whether you measure it standing alone or together with other projects the company may take on.

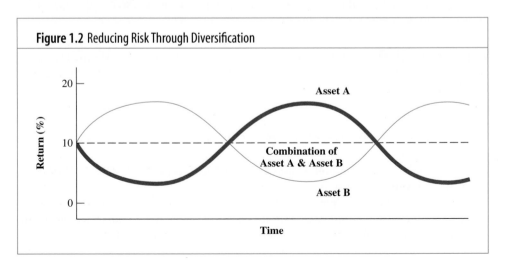

Figure 1.2 Reducing Risk Through Diversification

Axiom 10:

ETHICAL BEHAVIOR IS DOING THE RIGHT THING, AND ETHICAL DILEMMAS ARE EVERYWHERE IN FINANCE

Ethics, or rather a lack of ethics, in finance is a recurring theme in the news. During the late 1980s and early 1990s, the fall of Ivan Boesky and Drexel, Burnham, Lambert, and the near collapse of Salomon Brothers seemed to make continuous headlines. Meanwhile, the movie *Wall Street* was a hit at the box office and the book *Liar's Poker*, by Michael Lewis, chronicling unethical behavior in the bond markets, became a best seller. As the lessons of Salomon Brothers and Drexel, Burnham, Lambert illustrate, ethical errors are not forgiven in the business world. Not only is acting in an ethical manner morally correct, it is congruent with our goal of maximization of shareholder wealth.

Ethical behavior means "doing the right thing." A difficulty arises, however, in attempting to define "doing the right thing." The problem is that each of us has his or her own set of values, which forms the basis for our personal judgments about what is the right thing to do. However, every society adopts a set of rules or laws that prescribe what it believes to be "doing the right thing." In a sense, we can think of laws as a set of rules that reflect the values of the society as a whole, as they have evolved. For purposes of this text, we recognize that individuals have a right to disagree about what constitutes "doing the right thing," and we will seldom venture beyond the basic notion that ethical conduct involves abiding by society's rules. However, we will point out some of the ethical dilemmas that have arisen in recent years with regard to the practice of financial management. So as we embark on our study of finance and encounter ethical dilemmas, we encourage you to consider the issues and form your own opinions.

Many students ask, "Is ethics really relevant?" This is a good question and deserves an answer. First, although business errors can be forgiven, ethical errors tend to end careers and terminate future opportunities. Why? Because *unethical behavior eliminates trust, and without trust, businesses cannot interact*. Second, *the most damaging event a business can experience is a loss of the public's confidence in its ethical standards*. In finance, we have seen several recent examples of such events. It was the ethical scandals involving insider trading at Drexel, Burnham, Lambert that brought down that firm. In 1991, the ethical scandals involving attempts by Salomon Brothers to corner the Treasury bill market led to the removal of its top executives and nearly put the company out of business.

Beyond the question of ethics is the question of social responsibility. In general, corporate social responsibility means that a corporation has responsibilities to society beyond the maximization of shareholder wealth. It asserts that a corporation answers to a broader constituency than shareholders alone. As with most debates that center on ethical and moral questions, there is no definitive answer. One opinion is that because financial managers are employees of the corporation, and the corporation is owned by the shareholders, the financial managers should run the corporation in such a way that shareholder wealth is maximized and then allow the shareholders to decide if they would like to fulfill a sense of social responsibility by passing on any of the profits to deserving causes. Very few corporations consistently act in this way. For example, in 1992 Bristol-Myers Squibb Co. announced it would start an ambitious program to give away heart medication to those who cannot pay for it. This announcement came in the wake of an American Heart Association report showing that many of the nation's working poor face severe health risks because they cannot afford heart drugs.

Clearly, Bristol-Myers Squibb felt it had a social responsibility to provide this medicine to the poor at no cost.

How do you feel about this decision?

A Final Note on the Axioms

Hopefully, these axioms are as much statements of common sense as they are theoretical statements. These axioms provide the logic behind what is to follow. We will build on them and attempt to draw out their implications for decision making. As we continue, try to keep in mind that although the topics being treated may change from chapter to chapter, the logic driving our treatment of them is constant and is rooted in these 10 axioms.

OVERVIEW OF THE TEXT

In this text, we will focus on the maintenance and creation of wealth. Although this will involve attention to decision-making techniques, we will emphasize the logic behind those techniques to ensure that you do not lose sight of the concepts driving finance and the creation of wealth. The text begins by discussing the goal of maximization of shareholder wealth, a goal that is to be used in financial decision making, and presents the legal and tax environment in which these decisions are to be made. Since this environment sets the ground rules, it is necessary to understand it before decision rules can be formulated. The 10 guiding axioms that provide the underpinnings for what is to follow are then presented. Chapter 2 examines the financial markets and interest rates, looking at both the determinants of interest rates and their effect on business decisions. Chapters 3 and 4 introduce the basic financial tools the financial manager uses to maintain control over the firm and its operations. These tools enable the financial manager to locate potential problem areas and plan for the future.

Chapter 5 explores how the firm and its assets are valued. It begins with an examination of the mathematics of finance and the concept of the time value of money. An understanding of this topic allows us to compare benefits and costs that occur in different time periods. We move on in chapter 6 to develop an understanding of the meaning and measurement of risk. Valuation of fixed income securities is examined in chapter 7, and chapter 8 looks at valuation models that attempt to explain how different financial decisions affect the firm's stock price.

Using the valuation principles just developed, chapter 9 discusses the capital-budgeting decision, which involves the financial evaluation of investment proposals in fixed assets. We then examine the measurement of cash flows in chapter 10, and introduce methods to incorporate risk in the analysis in chapter 11. Finally, in chapter 12, we will examine the financing of a firm's chosen projects, looking at what costs are associated with alternative ways of raising new funds.

Chapter 13 examines the firm's capital structure along with the impact of leverage on returns to the enterprise. Once these relationships between leverage and valuation are developed, we move on to the process of planning the firm's financing mix in chapter 14. This is followed in chapter 15 with a discussion of the determination of the dividend-retained earnings decision.

Chapters 16 through 19 deal with working-capital management, the management of current assets. We will discuss methods for determining the appropriate investment in cash, marketable securities, inventory, and accounts receivable, as well as the risks associated with these investments and the control of these risks.

NATIONAL BUSINESS EMPLOYMENT WEEKLY

Right vs. Wrong
Just Take Your Time

Dilemma #1: Degree in hand, you've just landed a dream job in finance and accounting with a Fortune 500 company. But because of several quarters of poor financial results, your boss asks you to make improper changes in the accounting records "to help the company look a little better." Nobody will get hurt, he assures you.

"You're just keeping the stockholders happy—and protecting employees' jobs."

What should you do?

Dilemma #2: Your friends are envious of your new job as an assistant buyer for a major retail chain. While the salary isn't quite what you'd hoped for, the company gives employees significant discounts on purchases. Suddenly, friends and family members are inundating you with requests to buy things for them using your employee discount. Company policy states, however, that discounts are for employees only. You think, "everybody else in the store does this. Besides, who really gets hurt?" But what should you do?

Many new graduates will confront ethics issues at work according to a forthcoming study by the Ethics Resource Center Inc., a nonprofit organization in Washington, D.C. Of 4,000 employees surveyed, 30% admit to feeling pressured to compromise their company's ethical standards because of deadlines, overly aggressive objectives, concerns about the company's survival and other factors.

Additionally, 30% say they personally observed conduct that violated the law or their company's standards in the past year. Frequently mentioned types of misconduct include lying to superiors, falsifying reports or records, theft and sexual harassment. However, less than half the respondents say they attempted to report their observations to others in the company. Lack of confidentiality in the reporting process and fears of retribution were the main reasons for not reporting.

Ethical issues are particularly difficult for new grads to deal with. Young employees often feel too insecure to risk questioning current practices or reporting their concerns. Thus, they're likely to follow a superior's instructions—regardless of the ethical implications. Lack of experience also can make new hires susceptible to such rationalizations as, "That's the way things are done in the real world," or "Everybody does it."

SOURCE: Excerpted from Lori A. Tansey, "Right vs. Wrong," *The College Edition of the National Business Employment Weekly,* (Spring/Summer 1994, *Managing Your Career*): 11. Reprinted by permission from the *National Business Employment Weekly,* © by Dow Jones & Co., Inc. All rights reserved.

A (marker)

B (marker)

Analysis and Implications ...

A. Going into the workplace, students tend to have strong textbook training, but are not adequately prepared to face ethical dilemmas. Still, the answer to these dilemmas should be clear: It is wrong to manipulate financial statements and it is wrong to violate company policy.

B. According to Lori Tansey, the director of advisory services and a consultant with the Ethics Resource Center, Inc., to determine whether an action or decision involves an ethics problem, you can ask yourself the following:

1. Are my actions fair? If I was affected by this decision, would I feel it is reasonable?
2. Would I be comfortable reading about my actions in the newspaper?
3. Is it legal?

She then moves on to say that if you have any questions about your answers to these questions, you should talk to your supervisor or to your supervisor's manager, if your supervisor is involved.

Chapter 20 presents discussion of the use of futures, options, and swaps by financial managers to reduce risk. This is followed in chapter 21 by an introduction to corporate restructuring including mergers, spinoffs, and leveraged buyouts. The final chapter in the text, chapter 22, deals with international financial management, focusing on how financial decisions are affected by the international environment.

HOW FINANCIAL MANAGERS USE THIS MATERIAL

As the chapter title states, this chapter provides you with an introduction to financial management. The axioms presented in this chapter provide you with some clues as to the types of questions that will be dealt with by financial managers. As you will find out over the course of your studies, financial questions abound. In late 1997, headlines in *The Wall Street Journal* were full of financial decisions including WorldCom's decision to offer $37 billion for MCI, Apple Computer's decision to sell built-to-order computers directly to customers, and Friendly Ice Cream selling its stock to the public for the first time at $18 per share. But financial questions and decisions also appeared in the headlines in the sports section when the Florida Marlins, the World Series champs, decided to clear the deck of highly paid players, selling and trading off some of baseball's best players, and when the Big Ten and Pac 12 decided between sending their top teams to the Rose Bowl or to the Alliance bowls. In the future, the news will likely be that financial decisions driven by television contracts will dictate a further realignment of major college football conferences.

What do all of these financial decisions have in common? They are all based on the principles laid out in the 10 axioms presented in this chapter, and they all deal with decision making. They are all financial decisions, because the focus of finance is how to raise and spend or invest money. Your goal as a financial manager is to manage the firm in such a way that shareholder wealth is maximized. As you will see, there are few, if any, major decisions that a manager makes that don't have financial implications.

SUMMARY

OBJECTIVE 1

This chapter outlines a framework for the maintenance and creation of wealth. In introducing decision-making techniques aimed at creating wealth, we will emphasize the logic behind those techniques. This chapter begins with an examination of the goal of the firm. The commonly accepted goal of profit maximization is contrasted with the more complete goal of maximization of shareholder wealth. Because it deals well with uncertainty and time in a real-world environment, the goal of maximization of shareholder wealth is found to be the proper goal for the firm.

OBJECTIVE 2

OBJECTIVE 3

The sole proprietorship is a business operation owned and managed by a single individual. Initiating this form of business is simple and generally does not involve any substantial organizational costs. The proprietor has complete control of the firm, but must be willing to assume full responsibility for its outcomes.

The general partnership, which is simply a coming together of two or more individuals, is similar to the sole proprietorship. The limited partnership is another form of partnership sanctioned by states to permit all but one of the partners to have limited liability if this is agreeable to all partners.

The corporation increases the flow of capital from public investors to the business community. Although larger organizational costs and regulations are imposed on this legal entity, the corporation is more conducive to raising large amounts of capital. Limited liability, continuity of life, and ease of transfer in ownership, which increase the marketability of the investment, have contributed greatly in attracting large numbers of investors to the corporate environment. The formal control of the corporation is vested in the parties who own the greatest number of shares. However, day-to-day operations are managed by the corporate officers, who theoretically serve on behalf of the common stockholders.

In introducing taxes, we focus on taxes that affect our business decisions. Three taxable entities exist: the individual, including partnerships; the corporation; and the fiduciary. Only information on the corporate tax environment is given here.

For the most part, taxable income for the corporation is equal to the firm's operating income plus capital gains less any interest expense. The corporation is allowed an income exclusion of 70 percent of the dividends received from another corporation. Also, if the Internal Revenue Service considers the corporation to be retaining unreasonable amounts of earnings within the business, an accumulated earnings tax may be imposed.

To minimize the tax influence in selecting the form of legal organization, a corporation may choose to be a Subchapter S Corporation and be taxed as a partnership, provided certain qualifications can be satisfied.

This chapter closes with an examination of the 10 axioms on which finance is built and which motivate the techniques and tools introduced in this text:

Axiom 1:	The Risk-Return Trade-Off—We Won't Take on Additional Risk Unless We Expect to Be Compensated with Additional Return
Axiom 2:	The Time Value of Money—A Dollar Received Today Is Worth More Than a Dollar Received in the Future
Axiom 3:	Cash—Not Profits—Is King
Axiom 4:	Incremental Cash Flows—It's Only What Changes That Counts
Axiom 5:	The Curse of Competitive Markets—Why It's Hard to Find Exceptionally Profitable Projects
Axiom 6:	Efficient Capital Markets—The Markets Are Quick and the Prices Are Right
Axiom 7:	The Agency Problem—Managers Won't Work for Owners Unless It's in Their Best Interest
Axiom 8:	Taxes Bias Business Decisions
Axiom 9:	All Risk Is Not Equal—Some Risk Can Be Diversified Away, and Some Cannot
Axiom 10:	Ethical Behavior Is Doing the Right Thing, and Ethical Dilemmas Are Everywhere in Finance

KEY TERMS

Agency problem, 18	**Efficient market**, 17	**Partnership**, 4
Capital gain or loss, 11	**Marginal tax rate**, 9	**Sole proprietorship**, 4
Corporation, 6	**Net operating loss carryback and carryforward**, 11	**Subchapter S Corporation**, 12
Depreciation, 10		

GO TO:
http://www.prenhall.com/bfm
For downloads and current events
associated with this chapter

STUDY QUESTIONS

1-1. What are some of the problems involved in the use of profit maximization as the goal of the firm? How does the goal of maximization of shareholder wealth deal with those problems?

1-2. Compare and contrast the goals of profit maximization and maximization of shareholder wealth.

1-3. Firms often involve themselves in projects that do not result directly in profits; for example, IBM and Mobil Oil frequently support public television broadcasts. Do these projects contradict the goal of maximization of shareholder wealth? Why or why not?

1-4. What is the relationship between financial decision making and risk and return? Would all financial managers view risk-return trade-offs similarly?

1-5. Define (a) sole proprietorship, (b) partnership, and (c) corporation.

1-6. Identify the primary characteristics of each form of legal organization.

1-7. Using the following criteria, specify the legal form of business that is favored: (a) organizational requirements and costs, (b) liability of the owners, (c) continuity of business, (d) transferability of ownership, (e) management control and regulations, (f) ability to raise capital, and (g) income taxes.

1-8. Does a partnership pay taxes on its income? Explain.

1-9. When a corporation receives a dividend from another corporation, how is it taxed?

1-10. What is the purpose of the net operating loss deduction?

1-11. What is the rationale for an accumulated earnings tax?

1-12. What is the purpose of the Subchapter S Corporation? In general, what type of firm would qualify as a Subchapter S Corporation?

SELF-TEST PROBLEMS

ST-1. (*Corporate Income Tax*) The Dana Flatt Corporation had sales of $2 million this past year. Its cost of goods sold was $1.2 million, and its operating expenses were $400,000. Interest expenses on outstanding debts were $100,000, and the company paid $40,000 in preferred stock dividends. The corporation received $10,000 in preferred stock dividends and interest income of $12,000. The firm sold stock that had been owned for 2 years for $40,000; the original cost of the stock was $30,000. Determine the corporation's taxable income and its tax liability.

STUDY PROBLEMS (SET A)

1-1A. (*Corporate Income Tax*) The William B. Waugh Corporation is a regional Toyota dealer. The firm sells new and used trucks and is actively involved in the parts business. During the most recent year, the company generated sales of $3 million. The combined cost of goods sold and the operating expenses were $2.1 million. Also, $400,000 in interest expense was paid during the year. The firm received $6,000 during the year in dividend income from 1,000 shares of common stock that had been purchased 3 years previously. However, the stock was sold toward the end of the year for $100 per share; its initial cost was $80 per share. The company also sold land that had been recently purchased and had been held for only 4 months. The selling price was $50,000; the cost was $45,000. Calculate the corporation's tax liability.

1-2A. (*Corporate Income Tax*) Sales for L. B. Menielle, Inc., during the past year amounted to $5 million. The firm provides parts and supplies for oil field service companies. Gross profits for the year were $3 million. Operating expenses totaled $1 million. The interest and dividend income from securities owned were $20,000 and $25,000, respectively. The firm's interest expense was $100,000. The firm sold securities on two occasions during the year, receiving a gain of $40,000 on the first sale but losing $50,000 on the second. Compute the corporation's tax liability.

1-3A. (*Corporate Income Tax*) Sandersen, Inc., sells minicomputers. During the past year, the company's sales were $3 million. The cost of its merchandise sold came to $2 million, and cash operating expenses were $400,000; depreciation expense was $100,000, and the firm paid $150,000 in interest on bank loans. Also, the corporation received $50,000 in dividend income but paid $25,000 in the form of dividends to its own common stockholders. Calculate the corporation's tax liability.

1-4A. (*Corporate Income Tax*) A. Don Drennan, Inc., had sales of $6 million during the past year. The company's cost of goods sold was 70 percent of sales; operating expenses, including depreciation, amounted to $800,000. The firm sold a capital asset (stock) for $75,000, which had been purchased 5 months earlier at a cost of $80,000. Determine the company's tax liability.

1-5A. (*Corporate Income Tax*) The Robbins Corporation is an oil wholesaler. The company's sales last year were $1 million, with the cost of goods sold equal to $600,000. The firm paid interest of $200,000, and its cash operating expenses were $100,000. Also, the firm received $40,000 in dividend income and paid only $10,000 in dividends to its preferred stockholders. Depreciation expense was $150,000. Compute the firm's tax liability. Based on your answer, does management need to take any additional action?

1-6A. (*Corporate Income Tax*) The Fair Corporation had sales of $5 million this past year. The cost of goods sold was $4.3 million, and operating expenses were $100,000. Dividend income totaled $5,000. The firm sold land for $150,000 that had cost $100,000 five months ago. The firm received $150 per share from the sale of 1,000 shares of stock. The stock was purchased for $100 per share 3 years ago. Determine the firm's tax liability.

1-7A. (*Corporate Income Tax*) Sales for J. P. Hulett, Inc., during the past year amounted to $4 million. The firm supplies statistical information to engineering companies. Gross profits totaled $1 million, and operating and depreciation expenses were $500,000 and $350,000, respectively. Dividend income for the year was $12,000. Compute the corporation's tax liability.

1-8A. (*Corporate Income Tax*) Anderson & Dennis, Inc., sells computer software. The company's past year's sales were $5 million. The cost of its merchandise sold came to $3 million. Operating expenses were $175,000, plus depreciation expenses totaling $125,000. The firm paid $200,000 interest on loans. The firm sold stock during the year, receiving a $40,000 gain on a stock owned 6 years but losing $60,000 on stock held 4 months. Calculate the company's tax liability.

1-9A. (*Corporate Income Tax*) G. R. Edwin, Inc., had sales of $6 million during the past year. The cost of goods sold amounted to $3 million. Operating expenses totaled $2.6 million and interest expense was $30,000. Determine the firm's tax liability.

1-10A. (*Corporate Income Tax*) The Analtoly Corporation is an electronics dealer and distributor. Sales for the last year were $4.5 million, and cost of goods sold and operating expenses totaled $3.2 million. Analtoly also paid $150,000 in interest expense, and depreciation expense totaled $50,000. In addition, the company sold securities for $120,000 that it had purchased 4 years earlier at a price of $40,000. Compute the tax liability for Analtoly.

1-11A. (*Corporate Income Tax*) Utsumi, Inc., supplies wholesale industrial chemicals. Last year, the company had sales of $6.5 million. Cost of goods sold and operating expenses amounted to 70 percent of sales, and depreciation and interest expenses were $75,000 and $160,000, respectively. Furthermore, the corporation sold 40,000 shares of Sumitono Industries for $10 a share. These shares were purchased a year ago for $8 each. In addition, Utsumi received $60,000 in dividend income. Compute the corporation's tax liability.

The final stage in the interview process for an Assistant Financial Analyst at Caledonia Products involves a test of your understanding of basic financial concepts and of the corporate tax code. You are given the following memorandum and asked to respond to the questions. Whether or not you are offered a position at Caledonia will depend on the accuracy of your response.

To: Applicants for the position of Financial Analyst

From: Mr. V. Morrison, CEO, Caledonia Products

Re: A test of your understanding of basic financial concepts and of the Corporate Tax Code

Please respond to the following questions:

1. What are the differences between the goals of profit maximization and maximization of shareholder wealth? Which goal do you think is more appropriate?

2. What does the risk-return trade-off mean?

3. Why are we interested in cash flows rather than accounting profits in determining the value of an asset?

4. What is an efficient market and what are the implications of efficient markets for us?

5. What is the cause of the agency problem and how do we try to solve it?

6. What do ethics and ethical behavior have to do with finance?

7. Define (a) sole proprietorship, (b) partnership, and (c) corporation.

8. The Carrickfergus Corporation had sales of $4 million this past year. Its cost of goods sold was $2.4 million, and its operating expenses were $600,000. Interest expenses on outstanding debts were $300,000, and the company paid $60,000 in preferred stock dividends. The corporation received $30,000 in preferred stock dividends and interest income of $22,000. The firm sold stock that had been owned for 2 years for $100,000; the original cost of the stock was $60,000. Determine the corporation's taxable income and its tax liability.

STUDY PROBLEMS (SET B)

1-1B. (*Corporate Income Tax*) The M. M. Roscoe Corporation is a regional truck dealer. The firm sells new and used trucks and is actively involved in the parts business. During the most recent year, the company generated sales of $4 million. The combined cost of goods sold and the operating expenses were $3.2 million. Also, $300,000 in interest expense was paid during the year. The firm received $5,000 during the year in dividend income from 1,000 shares of common stock that had been purchased 3 years previously. However, the stock was sold toward the end of the year for $100 per share; its initial cost was $80 per share. The company also sold land that had been recently purchased and had been held for only 4 months. The selling price was $55,000; the cost was $45,000. Calculate the corporation's tax liability.

1-2B. (*Corporate Income Tax*) Sales for J. P. Enterprises during the past year amounted to $5 million. The firm provides parts and supplies for oil field service companies. Gross profits for the year were $2.5 million. Operating expenses totaled $900,000. The interest and dividend income from securities owned were $15,000 and $25,000, respectively. The firm's interest expense was $100,000. The firm sold securities on two occasions during the year, receiving a gain of $45,000 on the first sale but losing $60,000 on the second. Compute the corporation's tax liability.

1-3B. (*Corporate Income Tax*) Carter B. Daltan, Inc., sells minicomputers. During the past year, the company's sales were $3.5 million. The cost of its merchandise sold came to $2 million, and cash operating expenses were $500,000; depreciation expense was $100,000, and the firm paid $165,000 in interest on bank loans. Also, the corporation received $55,000 in dividend income but paid $25,000 in the form of dividends to its own common stockholders. Calculate the corporation's tax liability.

1-4B. (*Corporate Income Tax*) Kate Menielle, Inc., had sales of $8 million during the past year. The company's cost of goods sold was 60 percent of sales; operating expenses, including depreciation, amounted to $900,000. The firm sold a capital asset (stock) for $75,000, which had been purchased 5 months earlier at a cost of $80,000. Determine the company's tax liability.

1-5B. (*Corporate Income Tax*) The Burgess Corporation is an oil wholesaler. The company's sales last year were $2.5 million, with the cost of goods sold equal to $700,000. The firm paid interest of $200,000, and its cash operating expenses were $150,000. Also, the firm received $50,000 in dividend income and paid only $15,000 in dividends to its preferred stockholders. Depreciation expense was $150,000. Compute the firm's tax liability.

1-6B. (*Corporate Income Tax*) The A.K.U. Corporation had sales of $5.5 million this past year. The cost of goods sold was $4.6 million and operating expenses were $125,000. Dividend income totaled $5,000. The firm sold land for $150,000 that had cost $100,000 five months ago. The firm received $140 per share from the sale of 1,000 shares of stock. The stock was purchased for $100 per share 3 years ago. Determine the firm's tax liability.

1-7B. (*Corporate Income Tax*) Sales for Phil Schubert, Inc., during the past year amounted to $5 million. The firm supplies statistical information to engineering companies. Gross profits totaled $1.2 million, and operating and depreciation expenses were $500,000 and $400,000, respectively. Dividend income for the year was $15,000. Compute the corporation's tax liability.

1-8B. (*Corporate Income Tax*) Williams & Crisp, Inc., sells computer software. The company's past year's sales were $4.5 million. The cost of its merchandise sold came to $2.2 million. Operating expenses were $175,000, plus depreciation expenses totaling $130,000. The firm paid $150,000 interest on loans. The firm sold stock during the year, receiving a $50,000 gain on a stock owned 6 years but losing $70,000 on stock held 4 months. Calculate the company's tax liability.

1-9B. (*Corporate Income Tax*) J. Johnson, Inc., had sales of $7 million during the past year. The cost of goods sold amounted to $4 million. Operating expenses totaled $2.6 million and interest expense was $40,000. Determine the firm's tax liability.

1-10B. (*Corporate Income Tax*) The Kusomoto Corporation is an electronics dealer and distributor. Sales for the last year were $6.9 million, and cost of goods sold and operating expenses totaled $4.3 million. Kusomoto also paid $180,000 in interest expense, and depreciation expense totaled $40,000. In addition, the company sold securities for $117,000 that it had purchased 4 years earlier at a price of $37,000. Compute the tax liability for Kusomoto.

1-11B. (*Corporate Income Tax*) Martinez, Inc., supplies wholesale industrial chemicals. Last year the company had sales of $8.3 million. Cost of goods sold and operating expenses amounted to 77 percent of sales, and depreciation and interest expense were $79,000 and $150,000, respectively. Furthermore, the company sold 50,000 shares of Rose Corporation for $7.50 a share. These shares were purchased a year ago for $5 each. In addition, Martinez received $72,000 in dividend income. Compute the corporation's tax liability.

LIVING AND DYING WITH ASBESTOS

What happens when you find your most profitable product is dangerous—an ethical dilemma for the financial manager.

Much of what we deal with in financial management centers around the evaluation of projects—when they should be accepted and when they should be terminated. As new information surfaces regarding the future profitability of a project, the firm always has the choice of terminating that project. When this new information raises the question of whether or not it is ethical to produce a profitable project, the decision becomes more difficult. Many times, ethical dilemmas pit profits versus ethics. These decisions become even more difficult when continuing to produce the product is within the law.

Asbestos is a fibrous mineral used for fireproofing, electrical insulation, building materials, brake linings, and chemical filters. If you are exposed long enough to asbestos particles—usually 10 or more years—you can develop a chronic lung inflammation called asbestosis, which makes breathing difficult and infection easy. Also linked to asbestos exposure is mesethelioma, a cancer of the chest lining. This disease sometimes doesn't develop until 40 years after the first exposure. Although the first major scientific conference on the dangers of asbestos was not held until 1964, the asbestos industry knew of the dangers of asbestos 60 years ago.

As early as 1932, the British documented the occupational hazards of asbestos dust inhalation.[a] Indeed, on September 25, 1935, the editors of the trade journal *Asbestos* wrote to Sumner Simpson, president of Raybestos-Manhattan, a leading asbestos company, asking permission to publish an article on the dangers of asbestos. Simpson refused and later praised the magazine for not printing the article. In a letter to Vandivar Brown, secretary of Johns-Manville, another asbestos manufacturer, Simpson observed: "The less said about asbestos the better off we are." Brown agreed, adding that any article on asbestosis should reflect American, not English, data.

In fact, American data were available, and Brown, as one of the editors of the journal, knew it. Working on behalf of Raybestos-Manhattan and Johns-Manville and their insurance carrier, Metropolitan Life Insurance Company, Anthony Lanza had conducted research between 1929 and 1931 on 126 workers with 3 or more years of asbestos exposure. But Brown and others were not pleased with the paper Lanza submitted to them for editorial review. Lanza, said Brown, had failed to portray asbestosis as milder than silicosis, a lung disease caused by long-term inhalation of silica dust and resulting in chronic shortness of breath. Under the then-pending Workmen's Compensation law, silicosis was categorized as a compensable disease. If asbestosis was worse than silicosis or indistinguishable from it, then it too would have to be covered. Apparently Brown didn't want this and thus requested that Lanza depict asbestosis as less serious than silicosis. Lanza complied and also omitted from his published report the fact that more than half the workers examined—67 of 126—were suffering from asbestosis.

Meanwhile, Sumner Simpson was writing F. H. Schulter, president of Thermoid Rubber Company, to suggest that several manufacturers sponsor further asbestos experiments. The sponsors, said Simpson, could exercise oversight prerogatives; they "could determine from time to time after the findings are made whether they wish any publication or not." Added Simpson: "It would be a good idea to distribute the information to the medical fraternity, providing it is of the right type and would not injure our companies." Lest there should be any question about the arbiter of publication, Brown wrote to officials at the laboratory conducting the tests:

> It is our further understanding that the results obtained will be considered the property of those who are advancing the required funds, who will determine whether, to what extent and in what manner they shall be made public. In the event it is deemed desirable that the results be made public, the manuscript of your study will be submitted to us for approval prior to publication.

Industry officials were concerned with more than controlling information flow. They also sought to deny workers early evidence of their asbestosis. Dr. Kenneth Smith, medical director of a Johns-Manville plant in Canada, explained why seven workers he found to have asbestosis should not be informed of their disease:

> It must be remembered that although these men have the X-ray evidence of asbestosis, they are working today and definitely are not disabled from asbestosis. They have not been told of this diagnosis, for it is felt that as long as the man feels well, is happy at home and at work, and his physical condition remains good, nothing should be said. When he becomes disabled and sick, then the diagnosis should be made and the claim submitted *by the Company*. The fibrosis of this disease is irreversible and permanent so that eventually compensation will be paid to each of these men. But as long as the man is not disabled, it is felt that he should not be told of his condition so that he can live and work in peace and the Company can benefit by his many years of experience. Should the man be told of his condition today there is a very definite possibility that he would become mentally and physically ill, simply through the knowledge that he has asbestosis.

When lawsuits filed by asbestos workers who had developed cancer reached the industry in the 1950s, Dr. Smith suggested

---

[a]See Samuel S. Epstein, "The Asbestos 'Pentagon Papers,'" in Mark Green and Robert Massie, Jr., eds., *The Big Business Reader: Essays on Corporate America* (New York: Pilgrim Press, 1980) 154–65. This article is the primary source of the facts and quotations reported here.

that the industry retain the Industrial Health Foundation to conduct a cancer study that would, in effect, squelch the asbestos-cancer connection. The asbestos companies refused, claiming that such a study would only bring further unfavorable publicity to the industry, and that there wasn't enough evidence linking asbestos and cancer industry-wide to warrant it.

Shortly before his death in 1977, Dr. Smith was asked whether he had ever recommended to Johns-Manville officials that warning labels be placed on insulation products containing asbestos. He provided the following testimony:

> The reasons why the caution labels were not implemented immediately, it was a business decision as far as I could understand. Here was a recommendation, the corporation is in business to make, to provide jobs for people and make money for stockholders and they had to take into consideration the effects of everything they did, and if the application of a caution label identifying a product as hazardous would cut out sales, there would be serious financial implications. And the powers that be had to make some effort to judge the necessity of the label vs. the consequences of placing the label on the product.

Dr. Smith's testimony and related documents have figured prominently in hundreds of asbestos-related lawsuits, totaling more than $1 billion. In March 1981, a settlement was reached in nine separate lawsuits brought by 680 New Jersey asbestos workers at a Raybestos-Manhattan plant. Several asbestos manufacturers, as well as Metropolitan Life Insurance, were named as defendants. Under the terms of the settlement, the workers affected will share in a $9.4 million court-administered compensation fund. Each worker will be paid compensation according to the length of exposure to asbestos and the severity of the disease contracted.

By 1982, an average of 500 new asbestos cases were being filed each month against Manville (as Johns-Manville was now called), and the company was losing more than half the cases that went to trial. In 10 separate cases, juries had also awarded punitive damages, averaging $616,000 a case. By August, 20,000 claims had been filed against the company, and Manville filed for bankruptcy in federal court. This action froze the lawsuits in their place and forced asbestos victims to stand in line with other Manville creditors. After more than 3 years of legal haggling, Manville's reorganization plan was finally approved by the bankruptcy court. The agreement set up a trust fund valued at approximately $2.5 billion to pay Manville's asbestos claimants. To fund the trust, shareholders were required to surrender half the value of their stock, and the company had to give up much of its projected earnings over the next 25 years.[b]

Claims, however, soon overwhelmed the trust, which ran out of money in 1990. With many victims still waiting for payment, federal Judge Jack B. Weinstein ordered the trust to restructure its payments and renegotiate Manville's contributions to the fund. As a result, the most seriously ill victims will now be paid first, but average payments to victims have been lowered significantly, from $145,000 to $43,000. Meanwhile, the trust's stake in Manville has been increased to 80 percent, and Manville has been required to pay $300 million to it in additional dividends.[c]

Questions

1. Should the asbestos companies be held morally responsible in the sense of being capable of making a moral decision about the ill effects of asbestos exposure? Or does it make sense to consider only the principal people involved as morally responsible— for example, Simpson and Brown?

2. Simpson and Brown presumably acted in what they thought were the best profit interests of their companies. Nothing they did was illegal. On what grounds, if any, are their actions open to criticism?

3. Suppose that Simpson and Brown reasoned this way: "While it may be in our firms' short-term interests to suppress data about the ill effects of asbestos exposure, in the long run it may ruin our companies. We could be sued for millions, and the reputation of the entire industry could be destroyed. So we should reveal the true results of the asbestos-exposure research and let the chips fall where they may." Would that be appropriate?

4. If you were a stockholder in Raybestos-Manhattan or Johns-Manville, would you approve of Simpson and Brown's conduct? If not, why not?

5. "Hands of government" proponents would say that it is the responsibility of government, not the asbestos industry, to ensure health and safety with respect to asbestos. In the absence of appropriate government regulations, asbestos manufacturers have no responsibility other than to operate efficiently. Do you agree?

6. Does Dr. Smith's explanation for concealing from workers the nature of their health problems illustrate how adherence to industry and corporate goals can militate against individual moral behavior? Or do you think Dr. Smith did all he was morally obliged to do as an employee of an asbestos firm? What about Lanza's suppression of data in his report?

7. It has been shown that spouses of asbestos workers can develop lung damage and cancer simply by breathing the fibers carried home on work clothes and that people living near asbestos plants experience higher rates of cancer than the general population does. Would it be possible to assign responsibility for these effects to individual members of asbestos companies? Should the companies themselves be held responsible?

Note: Adapted by permission: William Shaw and Vincent Barry, "Living and Dying with Asbestos," *Moral Issues in Business*, 6th ed., 224–27. © 1995 by Wadsworth, Inc.

[b]See Robert Mokhiber, *Corporate Crime and Violence* (San Francisco: Sierra Club Books, 1988), 285–86; and Arthur Sharplin, "Manville Lives on as Victims Continue to Die," *Business and Society Review 65* (Spring 1988): 27–28.

---

[c]"Asbestos Claims to Be Reduced Under New Plan," *The Wall Street Journal* (November 20, 1990): A4; and "MacNeil-Lehrer Newshour," December 18, 1990.

SELF-TEST SOLUTIONS

ST-1.

Sales		$2,000,000
Cost of goods sold		(1,200,000)
Gross profit		800,000
Tax-deductible expenses:		
Less: Operating expenses	$400,000	
Less: Interest expenses	100,000	(500,000)
		$ 300,000
Other income:		
Interest income		$ 12,000
Preferred dividend income	$ 10,000	
Less 70% exclusion	(7,000)	3,000
Taxable ordinary income		$ 315,000
Gain on sale:		
Selling price	$ 40,000	
Less: Cost	(30,000)	10,000
Taxable Income		$ 325,000
Tax liability		
.15 × $ 50,000 =	$ 7,500	
.25 × 25,000 =	6,250	
.34 × 250,000 =	85,000	
5% surtax =	11,250	
	$110,000	

METHODS OF DEPRECIATION

If an asset purchased has a limited life beyond 1 year but its usefulness gradually declines over time, the taxpayer is not permitted to show the cost of the asset as a tax deduction in the year it is acquired. However, if the property is used in a business or profession or in the production of income, a part of the original cost may be written off as a tax deduction in each year of the asset's anticipated economic life. Examples of assets that may be depreciated include machinery and buildings.

STRAIGHT AND DOUBLE-DECLINING BALANCE METHODS

Historically, there have been 2 commonly used methods for computing depreciation: straight-line (SL) and double-declining balance (DDB). Of the 2, straight-line is the simplest to understand and to use. Consider the following example: A firm purchases a fixed asset for $12,000 that has a 5-year expected life and a $2,000 anticipated salvage value at the end of that period. Straight-line depreciation on the asset would be $2,400 per year ($12,000 ÷ 5 years = $2,400). Although there is a $2,000 salvage value, this value is disregarded in computing annual depreciation expense for tax purposes.

The double-declining balance method (DDB) is referred to as an accelerated depreciation method, because it provides for a more rapid rate of expensing the asset cost than the straight-line method does. This method involves depreciating the *undepreciated* value of the asset at twice the rate of the straight-line method. This method is demonstrated in Table 1A.1. In terms of the preceding example, the straight-line rate was $2,400 ÷ $12,000, or .2. Thus the double-declining rate is $2 \times .2$, or .4.

Under the DDB method, the asset would never be fully depreciated. The Internal Revenue Code allows the firm to switch over from DDB to straight-line any time before the end of the asset's useful life. The optimal time to make the switch is in that year when straight-line depreciation exceeds that of the double-declining balance method: Note in Table 1A-1 that the switch occurs in year 4.

With regard to the two methods for computing depreciation, note that the double-declining balance method offers the very real advantage of deferring the payment of taxes.

Table 1A.1 Computation of Double-Declining Balance Depreciation Expense

Year	Book Value of Asset (First of Year)	Depreciation Rate	Depreciation Expense	Accumulated Depreciation	Book Value (End of Year)
1	$12,000.00	.40	$4,800.00	$ 4,800.00	$7,200.00
2	7,200.00	.40	2,880.00	7,680.00	4,320.00
3	4,320.00	.40	1,728.00	9,408.00	2,592.00
4	2,592.00	—	1,296.00[a]	10,704.00	1,296.00
5	1,296.00	—	1,296.00	12,000.00	.00

[a]Switching to straight-line depreciation in year 4 produced a depreciation expense of $1,296 ($2,592/2) for each of the two remaining years in the useful life of the asset, which exceeds the depreciation expense in these years if the double-declining balance method had been used.

Table 1A.2 Depreciation Methods and Lives

Type of Asset	Method	Lives (Class)
Property with ADR of 4 years or less, excluding automobiles and light trucks.	Double-declining balance	3-year
Property with ADR of more than 4 years and less than 10 years. Automobiles, light trucks, and R&D are property to be included.	Double-declining balance	5-year
Property with ADR of 10 years or more and less than 16 years, and property without ADR that is not classified elsewhere are to be included.	Double-declining balance	7-year
Property with ADR of 16 years or more and less than 20 years.	Double-declining balance	10-year
Property with ADR of 20 years or more and less than 25 years.	150% declining balance	15-year
Property with ADR of 25 years or more, other than real property, such as buildings.	Straight-line	27.5-year
Real property (buildings) with ADR greater than 25 years.	Straight-line	39-year

The larger amounts of depreciation in the earlier years decrease taxable income in these years; however, smaller amounts of depreciation in later years subsequently increase taxable income. Consequently, taxes are deferred until these later years.

THE MODIFIED ACCELERATED COST RECOVERY SYSTEM

For assets acquired in 1987 or later, the **modified accelerated cost recovery system (ACRS)** is to be used in computing annual depreciation. Initially established in 1981, the ACRS was modified by tax law, effective January 1, 1987, to include three key variables in computing depreciation: (1) the asset depreciation range, (2) the method of depreciation, and (3) the averaging convention.

Prior to 1981, a depreciable asset was depreciated over its economic useful life. Now the depreciation period is based on the **asset depreciation range (ADR)** system, which groups assets into classes by asset type and industry. Given the type of asset, both the method of depreciation and the actual number of years to be used in depreciating the asset may then be determined. These methods and lives (classes) are presented in Table 1A.2. The first column classifies depreciable property into eight groups. The second column designates whether the asset is to be depreciated using double-declining balance (200 percent), 150 percent declining balance, or straight-line. The last column indicates the depreciation life (class), which designates the number of years to be used in calculating depreciation.

The last consideration in computing depreciation is that tax legislation restricts the amount of depreciation that may be taken in the year an asset is acquired or sold. These limitations have been called **averaging conventions**. The two primary conventions, or limitations, may be stated as follows:

1. *Half-Year Convention:* Personal property, such as machinery, is treated as having been placed in service or disposed of at the midpoint of the taxable year. Thus, a half-year of depreciation generally is allowed for the taxable year in which property is placed in service or is disposed of.
2. *Mid-Month Convention:* Real property, such as buildings, is treated as being placed in service or disposed of in the middle of the month. Accordingly, a half-month of depreciation is allowed for the month disposed of or placed in service.

Table 1A.3 Percentages for Personal Property[a]

Recovery Year	3-Year (200% DDB)	5-Year (200% DDB)	7-Year (200% DDB)	10-Year (200% DDB)	15-Year (150% DB)	20-Year (150% DB)
1	33.0%	20.0%	14.3%	10.0%	5.0%	3.8%
2	45.0	32.0	24.5	18.0	9.5	7.2
3	15.0	19.2	17.5	14.4	8.6	6.7
4	7.0	11.5[b]	12.5	11.5	7.7	6.2
5		11.5	8.9[b]	9.2	6.9	5.7
6		5.8	8.9	7.4	6.2	5.3
7			8.9	6.6[b]	5.9[b]	4.9
8			4.5	6.6	5.9	4.5[b]
9				6.5	5.9	4.5
10				6.5	5.9	4.5
11				3.3	5.9	4.5
12					5.9	4.5
13					5.9	4.5
14					5.9	4.5
15					5.9	4.5
16					3.0	4.5
17						4.5
18						4.5
19						4.5
20						4.5
21						1.7
Total	100.0	100.0	100.0	100.0	100.0	100.0

[a]Assumes half-year convention applies.
[b]Switch over to straight-line depreciation over remaining useful life.

Using the modified ACRS to compute the depreciation for assets other than buildings results in a different percentage of the asset being depreciated each year. These percentages are shown in Table 1A.3. For buildings, the straight-line depreciation method is used. In lieu of the double-declining balance method, a firm may use straight-line depreciation for any asset, regardless of asset class. However, the number of years designated for the particular asset class must still be used.

To demonstrate the use of the modified ACRS, assume that a piece of equipment costs $12,000 and has been assigned to a 5-year class. Using the percentages in Table 1A.3 for a 5-year class asset, the depreciation deductions would be calculated as shown in Table 1A.4.

Table 1A.4 Modified ACRS Demonstrated

Year	Depreciation Percentage	Annual Depreciation
1	20.0%	2,400
2	32.0	3,840
3	19.2	2,304
4	11.5	1,380
5	11.5	1,380
6	5.8	696
	100.0%	$12,000

Note that the averaging convention that allows for the half-year of depreciation in the first year results in a half-year of depreciation beyond the fifth year, or in year 6.

STUDY PROBLEMS

1C-1. (*Depreciation*) Compute the annual depreciation for an asset that costs $250,000 and that has an ADR of 6 years. Use the modified ACRS in your calculations.

1C-2. (*Depreciation*) You acquired a depreciable asset this year, costing $500,000. Your accountant tells you it has a 12-year ADR.

    a. Using the modified ACRS, compute the annual depreciation.

    b. What assumption is being made about when within the year you bought the asset?

Learning Objectives

Active Applications

World Finance

Practice

CHAPTER 2

THE ROLE OF FINANCIAL MARKETS AND INTEREST RATES IN FINANCIAL MANAGEMENT

INTRODUCTION

From February 4, 1994, through March 25, 1997, the Federal Reserve System (Fed), the nation's central bank, voted to change the "target" federal funds rate on 11 different occasions. Eight of these interest rate changes were in the upward direction. The federal funds rate is a short-term market rate of interest, influenced by the Fed, that serves as a sensitive indicator of the direction of future changes in interest rates. In early 1994, the central bank feared that inflationary pressures were building up in the U.S. economy and decided to take action, via raising nominal short-term interest rates, to stem those pressures by slowing down aggregate economic growth. The Fed remained committed to a course of higher interest rates throughout 1994 and the first half of 1995; then on July 6, 1995, these monetary policy makers reversed course and began a series of three interest rate decreases. For over a year, from January 31, 1996, to March 25, 1997, the Fed stayed on the sidelines and let the nation's financial markets direct the course of interest rates. However, during the first quarter of 1997, the Fed again became concerned that increased inflationary pressures were building up within the U.S. economic system. For example, the national economy was growing at a faster inflation-adjusted rate in the 1997 first quarter than had been experienced since the

LEARNING OBJECTIVES

After reading this chapter, you should be able to

1. Understand the historical relationship between internally generated corporate sources of funds and externally generated sources of funds.

2. Understand the financing mix that tends to be used by firms raising long-term financial capital.

3. Explain why financial markets exist in a developed economy.

4. Explain the financing process by which savings are supplied and raised by major sectors in the economy.

5. Describe the key components of the U.S. financial market system.

6. Understand the role of the investment banking business in the context of raising corporate capital.

7. Distinguish between privately placed securities and publicly offered securities.

8. Be acquainted with the concepts of securities flotation costs and securities markets regulations.

9. Understand the rate of return relationships among various classes of financing vehicles that persist in the financial markets.

10. Be acquainted with recent interest rate levels.

11. Explain the fundamentals of interest rate determination.

first quarter of 1987—the year of the major equity market crash that occurred during October. As a result, the Fed chose to raise the target federal funds rate on March 25, 1997. These policy actions and the resultant changes are shown in the accompanying table.

Changes in the Target Federal Funds Rate and Commercial Bank Prime Lending Rate			
Date	Old Target Rate (%)	New Target Rate (%)	Prime Lending Rate (%)
1994			
February 4	3.00	3.25	6.00 (no change)
March 22	3.25	3.50	6.25
April 18	3.50	3.75	6.75
May 17	3.75	4.25	7.25
August 16	4.25	4.75	7.75
November 19	4.75	5.50	8.50
1995			
February 1	5.50	6.00	9.00
July 6	6.00	5.75	8.75
December 19	5.75	5.50	8.50
1996			
January 31	5.50	5.25	8.25
1997			
March 25	5.25	5.50	8.50

From a financial management viewpoint, the eight overt actions by the Fed to raise rates caused the opportunity cost of funds *to rise. This means the firm's cost of capital funds rose, which in turn made it more difficult for real capital projects to be financed and be included in the firm's capital budget. The three decisions to lower the target federal funds rate had the exact opposite effect (i.e., the firm's cost of capital funds decreased.) In this latter case, the firm can take on more capital projects.*

Also note in the far right column of the table that the commercial bank prime lending rate typically changes in the same direction and at about the same time that a shift in the federal funds rate occurs. The prime lending rate is the interest rate that banks charge their most creditworthy customers. Thus the transmission of the central bank's policy move to the explicit cost of funds that the firm faces in the financial markets happens quickly. The commercial banking industry helps it along.

As you read this chapter, you will learn about (1) the importance of financial markets to a developed economy, (2) how funds are raised in the financial markets, and (3) the fundamentals of interest rate determination. This will help you, as a financial executive, understand the likely effects of federal monetary policy actions on your firm's ability to do business.

CHAPTER PREVIEW

This chapter focuses on the market environment in which long-term financial capital is raised. Long-term funds are raised in the capital market. By the term *capital-market*, we mean all institutions and procedures that facilitate transactions in long-term financial instruments (such as common stocks and bonds).

The sums involved in tapping the capital markets can be vast. For example, new corporate securities offered to the investing marketplace for cash during 1996 totaled $503 billion. To be able to distribute and absorb security offerings of such enormous size, an economy must have a well-developed financial market system. To use that system effectively, the financial manager must possess a basic understanding of its structure. This chapter will help you gain that understanding.

Moreover, we will introduce the logic behind the determination of interest rates and required rates of return in the capital markets. We will also explore interest rate levels and risk differentials (premia) over recent time periods. This knowledge of financial market history will permit you as both a financial manager and investor to realize that earning, say, a 40 percent annual return on a common stock investment does not occur very often.

As you work through this chapter, be on the lookout for direct applications of several of our axioms that form the basics of business financial management. Specifically, your attention will be directed to: Axiom 1: The Risk-Return Trade-Off—We Won't Take on Additional Risk Unless We Expect to Be Compensated with Additional Return; Axiom 6: Efficient Capital Markets—The Markets Are Quick and the Prices Are Right; and Axiom 10: Ethical Behavior Is Doing the Right Thing, and Ethical Dilemmas Are Everywhere in Finance.

THE FINANCIAL MANAGER, INTERNAL AND EXTERNAL FUNDS, AND FLEXIBILITY

At times, internally generated funds will not be sufficient to finance all of the firm's proposed expenditures. In these situations, the corporation may find it necessary to attract large amounts of financial capital externally or otherwise forgo projects that are forecast to be profitable.[1] Year in and year out, business firms in the nonfinancial corporate sector of the U.S. economy rely heavily on the nation's financial market system to raise cash.

Table 2.1 displays the relative internal and external sources of funds for such corporations over the 1981 to 1996 period. Notice that the percentage of external funds raised in any given year can vary substantially from that of other years. In 1982, for example, the nonfinancial business sector raised 25.4 percent of its funds in the financial markets. This was substantially less than the 39.4 percent raised externally only 1 year earlier, during 1981. After that, the same type of significant adjustment made by financial managers is evident. During 1988, we see that nonfinancial firms raised 36.3 percent of new funds in the external markets. By the end of 1991, this proportion dropped drastically to 9.7 percent.

Such adjustments illustrate an important point: Financial executives are perpetually on their toes regarding market conditions and the state of the overall economy. Both are reflected in interest rate levels and changes, which are discussed later in this chapter. Changes in market conditions influence the precise way corporate funds will be raised. High relative interest rates, for instance, will deter use of debt instruments by the financial manager.

OBJECTIVE 1

---

[1]By *externally generated*, we mean that the funds are obtained by means other than through retentions or depreciation. Funds from these latter two sources are commonly called *internally generated* funds.

Table 2.1 Nonfinancial Corporate Business Sources of Funds

Year	Total Sources ($ Billions)	Percent Internal Funds	Percent External Funds
1996	711.0	83.5	16.5
1995	741.8	73.4	26.6
1994	677.6	77.8	22.2
1993	587.5	82.1	17.9
1992	560.5	78.2	21.8
1991	471.7	90.3	9.7
1990	535.5	76.9	23.1
1989	567.9	70.4	29.6
1988	634.2	63.7	36.3
1987	564.7	66.6	33.4
1986	538.8	62.5	37.5
1985	493.8	71.3	28.7
1984	511.4	65.8	34.2
1983	444.6	65.7	34.3
1982	331.7	74.6	25.4
1981	394.4	60.6	39.4

NOTE: Data from *Economic Report of the President*, February 1995, p. 384; *Federal Reserve Bulletin*, June 1997, Table 1.57; and *Flow of Funds Accounts of the United States*, First Quarter 1997, Table F. 102.

The financial market system must be both organized and resilient. Periods of economic recession test the financial markets and those firms that continually use the markets. Economic contractions are especially challenging to financial decision makers because all recessions are unique. This forces financing policies to become unique.

During the 1981 to 1982 recession, which lasted 16 months, interest rates remained high by historic standards during the worst phases of the downturn. This occurred because policy makers at the Fed decided to wring a high rate of inflation out of the economy by means of a tight monetary policy. Simultaneously, stock prices were depressed. These business conditions induced firms to forgo raising funds via external means. During 1982, 74.6 percent of corporate funds were generated internally (see Table 2.1). The same general pattern followed after the 1990 to 1991 recession ended in the first quarter of 1991. During 1991, businesses paid down their short-term borrowing and relied on internally generated sources for 90.3 percent of their net financing needs.

Corporate profitability also plays a role in the determination of the internal–external financing choice. In 1997, the U.S. economy began the seventh year of economic expansion, making it, at that time, the third longest expansion on record. The good economy translated into good corporate profits. Other things held equal, greater profits reduce the need for external financing. Thus, over the 1993 to 1996 period, the reliance on external finance averaged 21 percent. Whereas, when profits were more strained over the 1981 to 1984 period, financial managers relied more heavily on the market system for an average of 33 percent of their total funds needed

The point here is an important one for the executive: As economic activity and policy shape the environment of the financial markets, financial managers must understand the meaning of the economic ups and downs and remain flexible in their decision-making processes. Remaining excessively rigid leads to financing mistakes. Those mistakes will generate costs that are ultimately borne by the firm's stockholders.

In chapter 13, we will learn how to assess leverage use—both operating and financial leverage. In addition, we also will examine the corporate financing decision. Portions of those discussions will identify financial managers' confirmed preferences for raising funds through new debt contracts. The next section presents some near-term history of that financing behavior.

THE MIX OF CORPORATE SECURITIES SOLD IN THE CAPITAL MARKET

OBJECTIVE 2

When corporations decide to raise cash in the capital market, what type of financing vehicle is most favored? Many individual investors think that common stock is the answer to this question. This is understandable, given the coverage of the level of common stock prices by the popular news media. All the major television networks, for instance, quote the closing price of the Dow Jones Industrial Average on their nightly news broadcasts. Common stock, though, is not the financing method relied on most heavily by corporations. The answer to this question is *corporate bonds. The corporate debt markets clearly dominate the corporate equity markets when new funds are being raised.* This is a long-term relationship—it occurs year after year. Table 2.2 bears this out.

In Table 2.2, we see the total volume (in millions of dollars) of domestic corporate securities sold for cash over the 1981 to 1996 period. The percentage breakdown among common stock, preferred stock, and bonds is also displayed. We will learn from our discussions of the cost of capital and planning the firm's financing mix that the U.S. tax

Table 2.2 Corporate Securities Offered for Cash (Domestic Offerings), 1981–1996

Year	Total Volume ($ Millions)	Percent Common Stock	Percent Preferred Stock	Percent Bonds and Notes
1996	502,540	16.5	6.6	76.9
1995	477,579	12.1	2.3	85.6
1994	425,620	11.2	2.9	85.9
1993	588,583	14.0	3.3	82.7
1992	456,515	12.5	4.7	82.8
1991	352,245	13.7	4.9	81.4
1990	212,712	9.1	1.9	89.0
1989	213,617	12.2	2.9	84.9
1988	244,670	14.7	2.7	82.6
1987	262,725	16.4	3.9	79.7
1986	248,722	23.7	4.9	71.4
1985	133,460	27.5	5.3	67.2
1984	95,287	23.3	4.5	72.2
1983	103,355	43.9	7.7	48.4
1982	73,397	32.3	6.7	61.0
1981	64,500	39.5	2.6	57.9
Mean	—	20.2	4.2	75.6 = 100.0%

NOTE: Data from *Economic Report of the President*, January 1989, 415, and *Federal Reserve Bulletin*, Table 1.46, various issues.

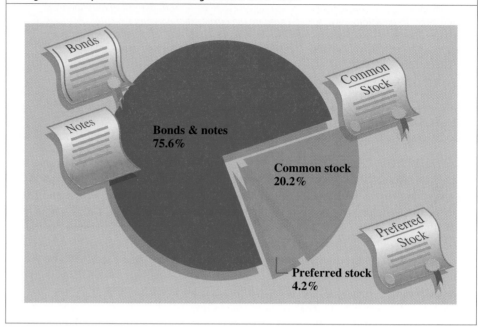

Figure 2.1 Corporate External Financing Patterns 1981–1996

Bonds & notes
75.6%

Common stock
20.2%

Preferred stock
4.2%

Bonds

Notes

Common Stock

Preferred Stock

system inherently favors debt as a means of raising capital. Quite simply, interest expense is deductible from other income when computing the firm's federal tax liability, whereas the dividends paid on both preferred and common stock are not.

Financial executives responsible for raising corporate cash know this. When they have a choice between marketing new bonds and marketing new preferred stock, the outcome is usually in favor of bonds. The after-tax cost of capital on the debt is less than that incurred on the preferred stock. Likewise, if the firm has unused debt capacity and the general level of equity prices is depressed, financial executives favor the issuance of debt securities over the issuance of new common stock. It is always good to keep some benchmark figures in your head. The average (unweighted) mix of corporate securities sold for cash over the 1981 to 1996 period is displayed in Figure 2.1. This *excludes* private debt placements or the bonds and notes categories would be a bit higher.

OBJECTIVE 3

WHY FINANCIAL MARKETS EXIST

Financial markets

Those institutions and procedures that facilitate transactions in all types of financial claims (securities).

Financial markets are institutions and procedures that facilitate transactions in all types of financial claims. The purchase of your home, the common stock you may own, and your life insurance policy all took place in some type of financial market. Why do financial markets exist? What would the economy lose if our complex system of financial markets were not developed? We will address these questions here.

Some *economic units*, such as households, firms, or governments, spend more during a given period than they earn. Other economic units spend less on current consumption than they earn. For example, business firms in the aggregate usually spend more during a specific period than they earn. Households in the aggregate spend less on current consumption than they earn. As a result, some mechanism is needed to facilitate the transfer of savings from those economic units with a surplus to those with a deficit. That is precisely the function of financial markets. Financial markets exist in order to allocate the supply of savings in the economy to the demanders of those savings. The central characteristic of a financial market is that it acts as the vehicle through which the forces of demand and supply for a specific type of financial claim (such as a corporate bond) are brought together.

Now, why would the economy suffer without a developed financial market system? The answer is that the wealth of the economy would be less without the financial markets. The rate of capital formation would not be as high if financial markets did not exist. This means that the net additions during a specific period to the stocks of (1) dwellings, (2) productive plant and equipment, (3) inventory, and (4) consumer durables would occur at lower rates. Figure 2.2 helps clarify the rationale behind this assertion. The abbreviated balance sheets in the figure refer to firms or any other type of economic units that operate in the private as opposed to governmental sectors of the economy. This means that such units cannot issue money to finance their own activities.

At stage 1 in Figure 2.2, only real assets exist in the hypothetical economy. **Real assets** are tangible assets, such as houses, equipment, and inventories. They are distinguished from **financial assets**, which represent claims for future payment on other economic units. Common and preferred stocks, bonds, bills, and notes all are types of financial assets. If only real assets exist, then savings for a given economic unit, such as a firm, must be accumulated in the form of real assets. If the firm has a great idea for a new product, that new product can be developed, produced, and distributed only out of company savings (retained earnings). Furthermore, all investment in the new product must occur simultaneously as the savings are generated. If you have the idea, and we have the savings, there is no mechanism to transfer our savings to you. This is not a good situation.

At stage 2, paper money (cash) comes into existence in the economy. Here, at least, you can *store* your own savings in the form of money.

Thus you can finance your great idea by drawing down your cash balances. This is an improvement over stage 1, but there is still no effective mechanism to transfer our savings to you. You see, we will not just hand you our dollar bills. We will want a receipt.

The concept of a receipt that represents the transfer of savings from one economic unit to another is a monumental advancement. The economic unit with excess savings can lend

Real assets

Tangible assets such as houses, equipment, and inventories.

Financial assets

Claims for future payment by one economic unit on another.

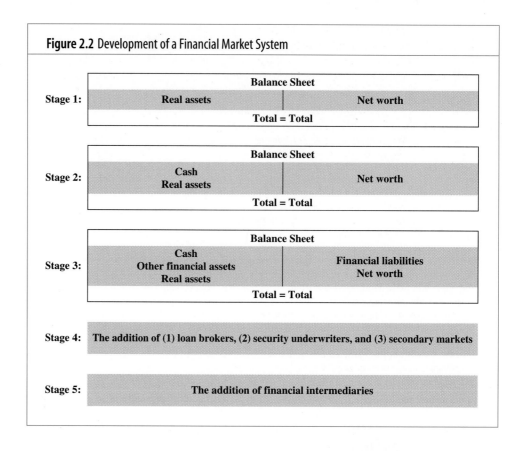

Figure 2.2 Development of a Financial Market System

Stage 1:

Balance Sheet	
Real assets	Net worth
Total = Total	

Stage 2:

Balance Sheet	
Cash Real assets	Net worth
Total = Total	

Stage 3:

Balance Sheet	
Cash Other financial assets Real assets	Financial liabilities Net worth
Total = Total	

Stage 4: The addition of (1) loan brokers, (2) security underwriters, and (3) secondary markets

Stage 5: The addition of financial intermediaries

---

the savings to an economic unit that needs them. To the lending unit, these receipts are identified as "other financial assets" in stage 3 of Figure 2.2. To the borrowing unit, the issuance of financial claims (receipts) shows up as "financial liabilities" on the stage 3 balance sheet. The economic unit with surplus savings will earn a rate of return on those funds. The borrowing unit will pay that rate of return, but it has been able to finance its great idea.

In stage 4, the financial market system moves further toward full development. Loan brokers come into existence. These brokers help locate pockets of excess savings and channel such savings to economic units needing the funds. Some economic units will actually purchase the financial claims of borrowing units and sell them at a higher price to other investors; this process is called **underwriting**. Underwriting is discussed in more detail later in this chapter. In addition, **secondary markets** develop. Secondary markets simply represent trading existing financial claims. If you buy your brother's General Motors common stock, you have made a secondary market transaction. Secondary markets reduce the risk of investing in financial claims. Should you need cash, you can liquidate your claims in the secondary market. This induces savers to invest in securities.

The progression toward a developed and complex system of financial markets ends with stage 5. Here, financial intermediaries come into existence. You can think of financial intermediaries as the major financial institutions with which you are used to dealing. These include commercial banks, savings and loan associations, credit unions, life insurance companies, and mutual funds. Financial intermediaries share a common characteristic: They offer their own financial claims, called **indirect securities**, to economic units with excess savings. The proceeds from selling their indirect securities are

Underwriting

The purchase and subsequent resale of a new security issue. The risk of selling the new issue at a profitable price is assumed (underwritten) by an investment banker.

Secondary market

Transactions in currently outstanding securities.

Indirect securities

The unique financial claims issued by financial intermediaries. Mutual fund shares are an example.

then used to purchase the financial claims of other economic units. These latter claims can be called **direct securities**. Thus a mutual fund might sell mutual fund shares (their indirect security) and purchase the common stocks (direct securities) of some major corporations. A life insurance company sells life insurance policies and purchases huge quantities of corporate bonds. Financial intermediaries thereby involve many small savers in the process of capital formation. This means there are more "good things" for everybody to buy.

Direct securities

The pure financial claims issued by economic units to savers. These can later be transformed into indirect securities.

A developed financial market system provides for a greater level of wealth in the economy. In the absence of financial markets, savings are not transferred to the economic units most in need of those funds. It is difficult, after all, for a household to build its own automobile. The financial market system makes it *easier* for the economy to build automobiles and all the other goods that economic units like to accumulate.

STOP AND THINK

The movement of financial capital (funds) throughout the economy just means the movement of savings to the ultimate user of those savings. Some sectors of the economy save more than other sectors. As a result, these savings are moved to a productive use—say to manufacture that Corvette you want to buy.

The price of using someone else's savings is expressed in terms of interest rates. The financial market system helps to move funds to the most-productive end use. Those economic units with the most promising projects should be willing to bid the highest (in terms of rates) to obtain the savings. The concepts of financing and moving savings from one economic unit to another are now explored.

FINANCING OF BUSINESS: THE MOVEMENT OF FUNDS THROUGH THE ECONOMY

OBJECTIVE 4

We now understand the crucial role that financial markets play in a capitalist economy. At this point, we will take a brief look at how funds flow across some selected sectors of the U.S. economy. In addition, we will focus a little more closely on the process of financial intermediation that was introduced in the preceding section. Some actual data are used to sharpen our knowledge of the financing process. We will see that financial institutions play a major role in bridging the gap between savers and borrowers in the economy. Nonfinancial corporations, we already know, are significant borrowers of financial capital.

The Financing Process

Table 2.3 shows how funds were supplied and raised by the major sectors of our economy in 1996. Households were a large net supplier of funds to the financial markets. This is the case, by the way, year in and year out. In 1996, households made available $145.3 billion in funds to other sectors. That was the excess of their funds supplied over the funds raised in the markets. In the jargon of economics, the household sector is a *savings-surplus* sector.

Notice that during 1996, the nonfinancial business sector was also a *savings-surplus sector* to the net extent of $41.9 billion. This means nonfinancial firms supplied $41.9 billion more to the financial markets than they took out in the form of borrowings or new equity issues. In fact, during 1996, these companies were actually net buyers of their own stocks. Quite often the nonfinancial business sector is a *savings-deficit sector*. Such was the case for each year during the 1982 to 1990 period. A buoyant period for corporate

Table 2.3 Sector View of Flow of Funds in U.S. Financial Markets for 1996 (Billions of Dollars)

Sector	[1] Funds Raised	[2] Funds Supplied	[2] – [1] Net Funds Supplied
Households[a]	$429.7	$575.0	$145.3
Nonfinancial corporate business	355.1	397.0	41.9
U.S. government	189.6	−9.4	−199.0
State and local governments	15.0	−48.4	−63.4
Foreign	276.6	509.8	233.2

[a]Includes personal trusts and nonprofit organizations.
NOTE: Data from *Flow of Funds Accounts, First Quarter 1997*, Flow of Funds Section (Washington, DC; Board of Governors of the Federal Reserve System, June 12, 1997).

profitability following the 1990 to 1991 recession is largely responsible for this sector returning to a savings-surplus status. This sector often "switches" from deficit to surplus to deficit depending on aggregate economic conditions.

Next, it can also be seen that the U.S. government sector was a savings-deficit sector for 1996. In 1996, the federal government raised $199.0 billion in excess of the funds it supplied to the financial markets.

This highlights a serious problem for the entire economy and a challenge for the financial manager. Persistent federal deficits have increased the role of the federal government in the market for borrowed funds. Prior to 1998, the last time the federal government posted a budget surplus was 1969; the last time prior to that was 1960. The federal government has thus become a "quasi-permanent" savings-deficit sector. Most financial economists agree that this tendency puts upward pressure on interest rates in the financial marketplace and thereby raises the general (overall) cost of capital to corporations. This phenomenon has become known as *crowding-out:* The private borrower is pushed out of the financial markets in favor of the government borrower.

Table 2.3 further highlights how important *foreign* financial investment is to the activity of the U.S. economy. As the federal government has become more of a "confirmed" savings-deficit sector, the need for funds has been increasingly supplied by foreign interests. Thus, in 1996 the foreign sector *supplied* a net $233.2 billion to the domestic capital markets. Back in 1982, the foreign sector *raised*—rather than supplied—$29.9 billion in the U.S. financial markets! This illustrates the dynamic nature of financial management.

Table 2.3 demonstrates that the financial market system must exist to facilitate the orderly and efficient flow of savings from the surplus sectors to the deficit sectors of the economy. The result during *long* periods is that the nonfinancial business sector is typically dependent on the household sector to finance its investment needs. The governmental sectors—especially the federal government—are quite reliant on foreign financing.

Movement of Savings

Figure 2.3 provides a useful way to summarize our discussion of (1) why financial markets exist and (2) the movement of funds through the economy. It also serves as an introduction to the role of the investment banker—a subject discussed in detail later in this chapter.

Figure 2.3 Three Ways to Transfer Financial Capital in the Economy

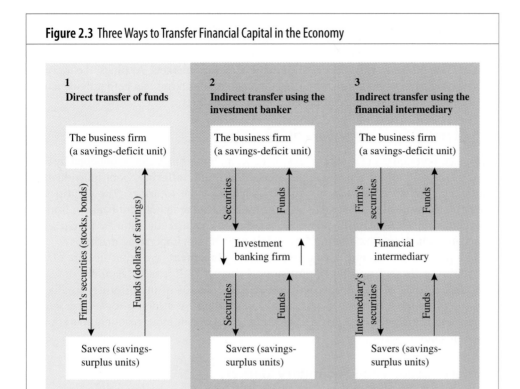

We see that savings are ultimately transferred to the business firm in need of cash in three ways:

1. **The direct transfer of funds.** Here the firm seeking cash sells its securities directly to savers (investors) who are willing to purchase them in hopes of earning a reasonable rate of return. New business formation is a good example of this process at work. The new business may go directly to a saver or group of savers called venture capitalists. The venture capitalists will lend funds to the firm or take an equity position in the firm if they feel the product or service the new firm hopes to market will be successful.

2. **Indirect transfer using the investment banker.** In a common arrangement under this system, the managing investment banking house will form a syndicate of several investment bankers. The syndicate will buy the entire issue of securities from the firm that is in need of financial capital. The syndicate will then sell the securities at a higher price than it paid for them to the investing public (the savers). Merrill Lynch Capital Markets and Goldman Sachs are examples of investment banking firms. They tend to be called "houses" by those who work in the financial community. Notice that under this second method of transferring savings, the securities being issued just pass through the investment banking firm. They are not transformed into a different type of security.

3. **Indirect transfer using the financial intermediary.** This is the type of system life insurance companies and pension funds operate within. The financial intermediary collects the savings of individuals and issues its own (indirect) securities in exchange for these savings. The intermediary then uses the funds collected from the individual savers to acquire the business firm's (direct) securities, such as stocks and bonds.

We all benefit from the three transfer mechanisms displayed in Figure 2.3. Capital formation and economic wealth are greater than they would be in the absence of this financial market system.

Numerous approaches exist for classifying the securities markets. At times, the array can be confusing. An examination of four sets of dichotomous terms can help provide a basic understanding of the structure of the U.S. financial markets.

Public Offerings and Private Placements

When a corporation decides to raise external capital, those funds can be obtained by making a public offering or a private placement. In a **public offering**, both individual and institutional investors have the opportunity to purchase the securities. The securities are usually made available to the public at large by a managing investment banking firm and its underwriting (risk-taking) syndicate. The firm does not meet the ultimate purchasers of the securities in the public offering. The public market is an impersonal market.

In a **private placement**, also called a **direct placement**, the securities are offered and sold to a limited number of investors. The firm will usually hammer out, on a face-to-face basis with the prospective buyers, the details of the offering. In this setting, the investment banking firm may act as a finder by bringing together potential lenders and borrowers. The private placement market is a more personal market than its public counterpart.

Primary Markets and Secondary Markets

Primary markets are those in which securities are offered for the *first* time to potential investors. A new issue of common stock by AT&T is a primary market transaction. This type of transaction increases the total stock of financial assets outstanding in the economy.

As mentioned in our discussion of the development of the financial market system, *secondary markets* represent transactions in currently outstanding securities. If the first buyer of the AT&T stock subsequently sells it, he or she does so in the secondary market. All transactions after the initial purchase take place in the secondary market. The sales do *not* affect the total stock of financial assets that exist in the economy. Both the money market and the capital market, described next, have primary and secondary sides.

Money Market and Capital Market

The key distinguishing feature between the money and capital markets is the maturity period of the securities traded in them. The **money market** refers to all institutions and procedures that provide for transactions in short-term debt instruments generally issued by borrowers with very high credit ratings. By financial convention, *short-term* means maturity periods of 1 year or less. Notice that equity instruments, either common or preferred, are not traded in the money market. The major instruments issued and traded are U.S. Treasury bills, various federal agency securities, bankers' acceptances, negotiable certificates of deposit, and commercial paper. Keep in mind that the money market is an intangible market. You do not walk into a building on Wall Street that has the words "Money Market" etched in stone over its arches. Rather, the money market is primarily a telephone and computer market.

Capital Market

The **capital market** refers to all institutions and procedures that provide for transactions in long-term financial instruments. *Long-term* here means having maturity periods that extend beyond 1 year. In the broad sense, this encompasses term loans and financial

---

Public offering

A security offering where all investors have the opportunity to acquire a portion of the financial claims being sold.

Private placement

A security offering limited to a small number of potential investors.

Primary market

Transactions in securities offered for the first time to potential investors.

Money market

All institutions and procedures that facilitate transactions in short-term credit instruments.

Capital market

All institutions and procedures that facilitate transactions in long-term financial instruments.

leases, corporate equities, and bonds. The funds that comprise the firm's capital structure are raised in the capital market. Important elements of the capital market are the organized security exchanges and the over-the-counter markets.

Organized Security Exchanges and Over-the-Counter Markets

Organized security exchanges are tangible entities; they physically occupy space (such as a building or part of a building), and financial instruments are traded on their premises. The **over-the-counter markets** include all security markets *except* the organized exchanges. The money market, then, is an over-the-counter market. Because both markets are important to financial officers concerned with raising *long-term capital*, some additional discussion is warranted.

Organized security exchanges

Formal organizations involved in the trading of securities. They are tangible entities that conduct auction markets in listing securities.

Over-the-counter markets

All security markets except the organized exchanges.

Organized Security Exchanges

For practical purposes there are seven major security exchanges in the United States.[2] These are the (1) New York Stock Exchange, (2) American Stock Exchange, (3) Chicago Stock Exchange, (4) Pacific Stock Exchange, (5) Philadelphia Stock Exchange, (6) Boston Stock Exchange, and (7) Cincinnati Stock Exchange. The New York Stock Exchange (NYSE) and the American Stock Exchange (AMEX) are called *national* exchanges, whereas the others are loosely described as *regionals*. All of these seven active exchanges are registered with the Securities and Exchange Commission (SEC). Firms whose securities are traded on the registered exchanges must comply with reporting requirements of both the specific exchange and the SEC.

An indication of the importance of the NYSE to our financial market system is reflected in something known as "consolidated tape volume." The Consolidated Tape prints all of the transactions on stocks that are listed on the NYSE and are traded on other organized markets. These markets include the exchanges mentioned earlier plus over-the-counter markets. In 1995, the NYSE accounted for 82.9 percent of consolidated volume.[3]

The business of an exchange, including securities transactions, is conducted by its *members*. Members are said to occupy "seats." There are 1,366 seats on the NYSE, a number that has remained constant since 1953. Major brokerage firms own seats on the exchanges. An officer of the firm is designated to be the member of the exchange, and this membership permits the brokerage house to use the facilities of the exchange to effect trades. During 1995, the prices of seats that were exchanged for cash ranged from a low of $785,000 to a high of $1,050,000.[4]

Stock exchange benefits. Both corporations and investors enjoy several benefits provided by the existence of organized security exchanges. These include

1. **Providing a continuous market.** This may be the most important function of an organized security exchange. A continuous market provides a series of continuous security prices. Price changes from trade to trade tend to be smaller than they would be in the absence of organized markets. The reasons are that there is a relatively large sales volume in each security, trading orders are executed quickly, and the range between the price asked for a security and the offered price tends to be narrow. The result is that price volatility is reduced.

---

[2]Others include (1) the Honolulu Stock Exchange, which is unregistered; (2) the Board of Trade of the City of Chicago, which does not now trade stocks; and (3) the Chicago Board Options Exchange, Inc., which deals in options rather than stocks. The cities of Colorado Springs, Salt Lake City, and Spokane also have small exchanges.

[3]New York Stock Exchange, *1995 Fact Book* (New York, 1996), 27.

[4]New York Stock Exchange, *1995 Fact Book* (New York, 1996), 73.

2. **Establishing and publicizing fair security prices.** An organized exchange permits security prices to be set by competitive forces. They are not set by negotiations off the floor of the exchange, where one party might have a bargaining advantage. The bidding process flows from the supply and demand underlying each security. This means the specific price of a security is determined in the manner of an auction. In addition, the security prices determined at each exchange are widely publicized.

3. **Helping business raise new capital.** Because a continuous secondary market exists where prices are competitively determined, it is easier for firms to float new security offerings successfully. This continuous pricing mechanism also facilitates the determination of the offering price of a new issue. This means that comparative values are easily observed.

Listing requirements. To receive the benefits provided by an organized exchange, the firm must seek to have its securities listed on the exchange. An application for listing must be filed and a fee paid. The requirements for listing vary from exchange to exchange; those of the NYSE are the most stringent. The general criteria for listing fall into these categories: (1) profitability, (2) size, (3) market value, and (4) public ownership. To give you the flavor of an actual set of listing requirements, those set forth by the NYSE are displayed in Table 2.4.[5]

Over-the-Counter Markets

Many publicly held firms do not meet the listing requirements of major stock exchanges. Others may want to avoid the reporting requirements and fees required to maintain listing. As an alternative, their securities may trade in the over-the-counter markets. On the basis of sheer numbers (not dollar volume), more stocks are traded over-the-counter than on organized exchanges. As far as secondary trading in corporate bonds is concerned, the over-the-counter markets are where the action is. In a typical year, more than 90 percent of corporate bond business takes place over-the-counter.

Most over-the-counter transactions are done through a loose network of security traders who are known as broker-dealers and brokers. Brokers do not purchase securities for their own account, whereas dealers do. Broker-dealers stand ready to buy and sell specific securities at selected prices. They are said to "make a market" in those securities.

Table 2.4 NYSE Listing Requirements

Profitability
Earnings before taxes (EBT) for the most recent year must be at least $2.5 million.
For the 2 years preceding that, EBT must be at least $2.0 million.
Size
Net tangible assets must be at least $40.0 million.
Market Value[a]
The market value of publicly held stock must be at least $40.0 million.
Public Ownership
There must be at least 1.1 million publicly held common shares.
There must be at least 2,000 holders of 100 shares or more.

---

[a]The market value is tied to the level of common stock prices prevailing in the marketplace at the time of the listing application. From time to time, the $40.0 million requirement noted above may be lessened. Under current regulations of the NYSE, the requirement can never be less than $9.0 million.

---

[5]New York Stock Exchange, *1995 Fact Book* (New York, 1996), 39.

Their profit is the spread or difference between the price they will pay for a security (bid price) and the price at which they will sell the security (asked price).

Price quotes. The availability of prices is not as continuous in the over-the-counter market as it is on an organized exchange. Since February 8, 1971, however, when a computerized network called NASDAQ came into existence, the availability of prices in this market has improved substantially. NASDAQ stands for National Association of Security Dealers Automated Quotation System. It is a telecommunications system that provides a national information link among the brokers and dealers operating in the over-the-counter markets. Subscribing traders have a terminal that allows them to obtain representative bids and ask prices for thousands of securities traded over-the-counter. NASDAQ is a quotation system, not a transactions system. The final trade is still consummated by direct negotiation between traders.

NASDAQ price quotes for many stocks are published daily in *The Wall Street Journal*. This same financial newspaper also publishes prices on hundreds of other stocks traded over-the-counter. Local papers supply prices on stocks of regional interest.

STOP AND THINK

We touched briefly on the investment banking industry and the investment banker earlier in this chapter when we described various methods for transferring financial capital (see Figure 2.3). The investment banker is to be distinguished from the commercial banker in that the former's organization is not a permanent depository for funds. For the moment, it is important for you to learn about the role of the investment banker in the funding of commercial activity due to the importance of this institution within the financial market system.

THE INVESTMENT BANKER

OBJECTIVE 6

Most corporations do not raise long-term capital frequently. The activities of working-capital management go on daily, but attracting long-term capital is, by comparison, episodic. The sums involved can be huge, so these situations are considered of great importance to financial managers. Because most managers are unfamiliar with the subtleties of raising long-term funds, they enlist the help of an expert. That expert is an investment banker.

Definition

The **investment banker** is a financial specialist involved as an intermediary in the merchandising of securities. He or she acts as a "middle person" by facilitating the flow of savings from those economic units that want to invest to those units that want to raise funds. We use the term *investment banker* to refer both to a given individual and to the organization for which such a person works, variously known as an **investment banking firm** or an **investment banking house**. Although these firms are called investment bankers, they perform no depository or lending functions. The activities of commercial banking and investment banking as we know them today were separated by the Banking Act of 1933 (also known as the Glass-Steagall Act of 1933). Just what does this middle-man role involve? That is most easily understood in terms of the basic functions of investment banking.

Investment banker

A financial specialist who underwrites and distributes new securities and advises corporate clients about raising external financial capital.

Functions

The investment banker performs three basic functions: (1) underwriting, (2) distributing, and (3) advising.

Underwriting. The term **underwriting** is borrowed from the field of insurance. It means "assuming a risk." The investment banker assumes the risk of selling a security issue at a satisfactory price. A satisfactory price is one that will generate a profit for the investment banking house.

The procedure goes like this. The managing investment banker and its syndicate will buy the security issue from the corporation in need of funds. The **syndicate** is a group of other investment bankers who are invited to help buy and resell the issue. The managing house is the investment banking firm that originated the business because its corporate client decided to raise external funds. On a specific day, the firm that is raising capital is presented with a check (cash) in exchange for the securities being issued. At this point, the investment banking syndicate owns the securities. The corporation has its cash and can proceed to use it. The firm is now immune from the possibility that the security markets might turn sour. If the price of the newly issued security falls below that paid to the firm by the syndicate, the syndicate will suffer a loss. The syndicate, of course, hopes that the opposite situation will result. Its objective is to sell the new issue to the investing public at a price per security greater than its cost.

Distributing. Once the syndicate owns the new securities, it must get them into the hands of the ultimate investors. This is the distribution or selling function of investment banking. The investment banker may have branch offices across the United States, or it may have an informal arrangement with several security dealers who regularly buy a portion of each new offering for final sale. It is not unusual to have 300 to 400 dealers involved in the selling effort. The syndicate can properly be viewed as the security wholesaler, and the dealer organization can be viewed as the security retailer.

Advising. The investment banker is an expert in the issuance and marketing of securities. A sound investment banking house will be aware of prevailing market conditions and can relate those conditions to the particular type of security that should be sold at a given time. Business conditions may be pointing to a future increase in interest rates. The investment banker might advise the firm to issue its bonds in a timely fashion to avoid the higher yields that are forthcoming. The banker can analyze the firm's capital structure and make recommendations as to what general source of capital should be issued. In many instances, the firm will invite its investment banker to sit on the board of directors. This permits the banker to observe corporate activity and make recommendations on a regular basis.

Distribution Methods

Several methods are available to the corporation for placing new security offerings in the hands of final investors. The investment banker's role is different in each of these. Sometimes, in fact, it is possible to bypass the investment banker. These methods are described in this section. Private placements, because of their importance, are treated separately later in the chapter.

Negotiated purchase. In a negotiated underwriting, the firm that needs funds makes contact with an investment banker, and deliberations concerning the new issue begin. If all goes well, a *method* is negotiated for determining the price the investment banker and the syndicate will pay for the securities. For example, the agreement might state that the

---

Syndicate

A group of investment bankers who contractually assist in the buying of a new security issue.

syndicate will pay $2 less than the closing price of the firm's common stock on the day before the offering date of a new stock issue. The negotiated purchase is the most prevalent method of securities distribution in the private sector. It is generally thought to be the most profitable technique as far as investment bankers are concerned.

Competitive bid purchase. The method by which the underwriting group is determined distinguishes the competitive bid purchase from the negotiated purchase. In a competitive underwriting, several underwriting groups bid for the right to purchase the new issue from the corporation that is raising funds. The firm does not directly select the investment banker. The investment banker that underwrites and distributes the issue is chosen by an auction process. The syndicate willing to pay the greatest dollar amount per new security will win the competitive bid.

Most competitive bid purchases are confined to three situations, compelled by legal regulations: (1) railroad issues, (2) public utility issues, and (3) state and municipal bond issues. The argument in favor of competitive bids is that any undue influence of the investment banker over the firm is mitigated and the price received by the firm for each security should be higher. Thus, we would intuitively suspect that the cost of capital in a competitive bid situation would be less than in a negotiated purchase situation. Evidence on this question, however, is mixed. One problem with the competitive bid purchase as far as the fundraising firm is concerned is that the benefits gained from the advisory function of the investment banker are lost. It may be necessary to use an investment banker for advisory purposes and then by law exclude that same banker from the competitive bid process.

Commission or best-efforts basis. Here, the investment banker acts as an agent rather than as a principal in the distribution process. The securities are *not* underwritten. The investment banker attempts to sell the issue in return for a fixed commission on each security actually sold. Unsold securities are returned to the corporation. This arrangement is typically used for more speculative issues. The issuing firm may be smaller or less established than the investment banker would like. Because the underwriting risk is not passed on to the investment banker, this distribution method is less costly to the issuer than a negotiated or competitive bid purchase. On the other hand, the investment banker only has to give it his or her "best effort." A successful sale is not guaranteed.

Privileged subscription. Occasionally, the firm may feel that a distinct market already exists for its new securities. When a new issue is marketed to a definite and select group of investors, it is called a **privileged subscription**. Three target markets are typically involved: (1) current stockholders, (2) employees, or (3) customers. Of these, distributions directed at current stockholders are the most prevalent. Such offerings are called *rights offerings*. In a privileged subscription, the investment banker may act only as a selling agent. It is also possible that the issuing firm and the investment banker might sign a *standby agreement*, which would obligate the investment banker to underwrite the securities that are not accepted by the privileged investors.

Privileged subscription

The process of marketing a new security issue to a select group of investors.

Direct sale. In a **direct sale**, the issuing firm sells the securities directly to the investing public without involving an investment banker. Even among established corporate giants, this procedure is relatively rare. A variation of the direct sale, though, was used more frequently in the 1970s than in previous decades. This involves the private placement of a new issue by the fund-raising corporation *without* use of an investment banker as an intermediary. Texaco, Mobil Oil, and International Harvester (now Navistar) are examples of large firms that have followed this procedure.

Direct sale

The sale of securities by the corporation to the investing public without the services of an investment banking firm.

Table 2.5 Leading U.S. Investment Bankers, 1996

Firm	Underwriting Volume (Billions of Dollars)	Percent of Market
1. Merrill Lynch	$155.9	16.4%
2. Lehman Brothers	$100.7	10.6
3. Goldman, Sachs	$ 98.5	10.3
4. Salomon Brothers	$ 96.2	10.1
5. Morgan Stanley	$ 83.7	8.8
6. J.P. Morgan	$ 68.7	7.2
7. CS First Boston	$ 60.0	6.3
8. Bear, Stearns	$ 41.7	4.4
9. Donaldson, Lufkin & Jenrette	$ 34.8	3.6
10. Smith Barney	$ 29.9	3.1

SOURCE: Securities Data Co. as reported in *The Wall Street Journal* (January 2, 1997): R 38.

Industry leaders. All industries have their leaders, and investment banking is no exception. We have discussed investment bankers at some length in this chapter. Table 2.5 gives us some idea who the major players are within the investment banking industry. It lists the top 10 houses in 1996 based on the dollar volume of security issues that were managed. Notice in the table that the U.S. investment banking industry is a highly concentrated one. The top four bankers with regard to underwriting volume during 1996 accounted for a full 47.4 percent of the total market. This degree of concentration is pervasive over time.

OBJECTIVE 7

PRIVATE PLACEMENTS

Private placements are an alternative to the sale of securities to the public or to a restricted group of investors through a privileged subscription. Any type of security can be privately placed (directly placed). This market, however, is clearly dominated by debt issues. Thus we restrict this discussion to debt securities. From year to year the volume of private placements will vary greatly. Table 2.6 shows, though, that the private placement market is always a significant portion of the U.S. capital market.

The major investors in private placements are large financial institutions. Based on the volume of securities purchased, the three most important investor groups are (1) life insurance companies, (2) state and local retirement funds, and (3) private pension funds.

In arranging a private placement, the firm may (1) avoid the use of an investment banker and work directly with the investing institutions or (2) engage the services of an investment banker. If the firm does not use an investment banker, of course, it does not have to pay a fee. Conversely, investment bankers can provide valuable advice in the private placement process. They are usually in contact with several major institutional investors; thus, they will know if a firm is in a position to invest in its proposed offering, and they can help the firm evaluate the terms of the new issue.

Private placements have advantages and disadvantages compared with public offerings. The financial manager must carefully evaluate both sides of the question. The advantages associated with private placements are these:

1. **Speed.** The firm usually obtains funds more quickly through a private placement than a public offering. The major reason is that registration of the issue with the SEC is not required.

Table 2.6 Publicly and Privately Placed Corporate Debt Placed Domestically — 1981–1995
(gross proceeds of all new U.S. corporate debt issues)

Year	Total Volume ($ million)	Percent Publicly Placed	Percent Privately Placed
1995	$496,296	82.4%	17.6%
1994	441,287	82.8	17.2
1993	608,255	80.1	19.9
1992	443,911	85.2	14.8
1991	361,860	79.3	20.7
1990	276,259	68.5	31.5
1989	298,813	60.7	39.3
1988	329,919	61.3	38.7
1987	301,447	69.5	30.5
1986	313,502	74.2	25.8
1985	165,754	72.1	27.9
1984	109,903	66.9	33.1
1983	68,370	69.1	30.9
1982	53,636	81.7	18.3
1981	45,092	84.5	15.5

NOTE: Data from *Federal Reserve Bulletin*, various issues including June 1997, p. A31.

2. **Reduced flotation costs.** These savings result because the lengthy registration statement for the SEC does not have to be prepared, and the investment banking underwriting and distribution costs do not have to be absorbed.
3. **Financing flexibility.** In a private placement, the firm deals on a face-to-face basis with a small number of investors. This means that the terms of the issue can be tailored to meet the specific needs of the company. For example, all of the funds need not be taken by the firm at once. In exchange for a commitment fee, the firm can "draw down" against the established amount of credit with the investors. This provides some insurance against capital market uncertainties, and the firm does not have to borrow the funds if the need does not arise. There is also the possibility of renegotiation. The terms of the debt issue can be altered. The term to maturity, the interest rate, or any restrictive covenants can be discussed among the affected parties.

The following disadvantages of private placements must be evaluated:

1. **Interest costs.** It is generally conceded that interest costs on private placements exceed those of public issues. Whether this disadvantage is enough to offset the reduced flotation costs associated with a private placement is a determination the financial manager must make. There is some evidence that on smaller issues, say $500,000 as opposed to $30 million, the private placement alternative would be preferable.
2. **Restrictive covenants.** Dividend policy, working-capital levels, and the raising of additional debt capital may all be affected by provisions in the private-placement debt contract. That is not to say that such restrictions are always absent in public debt contracts. Rather, the financial officer must be alert to the tendency for these covenants to be especially burdensome in private contracts.
3. **The possibility of future SEC registration.** If the lender (investor) should decide to sell the issue to a public buyer before maturity, the issue must be registered with the SEC. Some lenders, then, require that the issuing firm agree to a future registration at their option.

FLOTATION COSTS

Flotation costs

The underwriter's spread and issuing costs associated with the issuance and marketing of new securities.

The firm raising long-term capital incurs two types of **flotation costs**: (1) the underwriter's spread and (2) issuing costs. Of these two costs, the underwriter's spread is the larger. The *underwriter's spread* is simply the difference between the gross and net proceeds from a given security issue expressed as a percent of the gross proceeds. The *issue costs* include (1) printing and engraving, (2) legal fees, (3) accounting fees, (4) trustee fees, and (5) several other miscellaneous components. The two most significant issue costs are printing and engraving and legal fees.

Data published by the SEC have consistently revealed two relationships about flotation costs. First, the costs associated with issuing common stock are notably greater than the costs associated with preferred stock offerings. In turn, preferred stock costs exceed those of bonds. Second, flotation costs (expressed as a percent of gross proceeds) decrease as the size of the security issue increases.

In the first instance, the stated relationship reflects the fact that issue costs are sensitive to the risks involved in successfully distributing a security issue. Common stock is riskier to own than corporate bonds. Underwriting risk is, therefore, greater with common stock than with bonds. Thus, flotation costs just mirror these risk relationships. In the second case, a portion of the issue costs is fixed. Legal fees and accounting costs are good examples. So, as the size of the security issue rises, the fixed component is spread over a larger gross proceeds base. As a consequence, average flotation costs vary inversely with the size of the issue.

STOP AND THINK

*Since late 1986, there has been a renewal of public interest in the regulation of the country's financial markets. The key event was a massive insider trading scandal that made the name Ivan F. Boesky one of almost universal recognition—but unfortunately, in a negative sense. This should remind you of **Axiom 10** that you recall deals with ethical behavior. This was followed by the October 19, 1987, crash of the equity markets. In early 1990, the investing community (both institutional and individual) became increasingly concerned over a weakening in the so-called "junk bond market." The upshot of all of this enhanced awareness is a new appreciation of the crucial role that regulation plays in the financial system. The basics of regulation follow.*

REGULATION

Following the severe economic downturn of 1929 to 1932, Congressional action was taken to provide for federal regulation of the securities markets. State statutes (blue sky laws) also govern the securities markets where applicable, but the federal regulations are clearly more pressing and important. The major federal regulations are reviewed here.

Primary Market Regulations

The new issues market is governed by the Securities Act of 1933. The intent of the act is important. It aims to provide potential investors with accurate, truthful disclosure about the firm and the new securities being offered to the public. This does *not* prevent firms from issuing highly speculative securities. The SEC says nothing whatsoever about the possible investment worth of a given offering. It is up to the investor to separate the junk from the jewels. The SEC does have the legal power and responsibility to enforce the 1933 act.

Full public disclosure is achieved by the requirement that the issuing firm file a registration statement with the SEC containing requisite information. The statement details particulars about the firm and the new security being issued. During a minimum 20-day waiting period, the SEC examines the submitted document. In numerous instances, the 20-day wait has been extended by several weeks. The SEC can ask for additional information that was omitted in order to clarify the original document. The SEC can also order that the offering be stopped.

During the registration process, a preliminary prospectus (the "red herring") may be distributed to potential investors. When the registration is approved, the final prospectus must be made available to the prospective investors. The prospectus is actually a condensed version of the full registration statement. If, at a later date, the information in the registration statement and the prospectus is found to be lacking, purchasers of the new issue who incurred a loss can sue for damages. Officers of the issuing firm and others who took part in the registration and marketing of the issue may suffer both civil and criminal penalties.

Generally, the SEC defines public issues as those that are sold to more than 25 investors. Some public issues need not be registered. These include

1. Relatively small issues, where the firm sells less than $1.5 million of new securities per year.
2. Issues that are sold entirely intrastate.
3. Issues that are basically short-term instruments. This translates into maturity periods of 270 days or less.
4. Issues that are already regulated or controlled by some other federal agency. Examples here are the Federal Power Commission (public utilities) and the Interstate Commerce Commission (railroads).

Secondary Market Regulations

Secondary trading is regulated by the Securities Exchange Act of 1934. This act created the SEC to enforce securities laws. The Federal Trade Commission enforced the 1933 act for 1 year. The major aspects of the 1934 act can be best presented in outline form:

1. Major security exchanges must register with the SEC. This regulates the exchanges and places reporting requirements on the firms whose securities are listed on them.
2. Insider trading is regulated. Insiders can be officers, directors, employees, relatives, major investors, or anyone having information about the operation of the firm that is not public knowledge. If an investor purchases the security of the firm in which the investor is an insider, he or she must hold it for at least 6 months before disposing of it. Otherwise, profits made from trading the stock within a period of less than 6 months must be returned to the firm. Furthermore, insiders must file with the SEC a monthly statement of holdings and transactions in the stock of their corporation.[6]
3. Manipulative trading of securities by investors to affect stock prices is prohibited.
4. The SEC is given control over proxy procedures.
5. The Board of Governors of the Federal Reserve System is given responsibility for setting margin requirements. This affects the flow of credit into the securities markets. Buying securities on margin simply means using credit to acquire a portion of the subject financial instruments.

---

[6]On November 14, 1986, the SEC announced that Ivan F. Boesky had admitted to illegal insider trading after an intensive investigation. Boesky at the time was a very well-known Wall Street investor, speculator, and arbitrageur. Boesky was an owner or part owner in several companies, including an arbitrage fund named Ivan F. Boesky & Co. L. P. Boesky agreed to pay the U.S. government $50 million, which represented a return of illegal profits, another $50 million in civil penalties; to withdraw permanently from the securities industry; and to plead guilty to criminal charges. The far-reaching investigation continued into 1987 and implicated several other prominent investment figures.

MORE RECENT REGULATORY DEVELOPMENTS

Securities Acts Amendments of 1975

The Securities Acts Amendments of 1975 touched on three important issues. First, Congress mandated the creation of a national market system (NMS). Only broad goals for this national exchange were identified by Congress. Implementation details were left to the SEC and, to a much lesser extent, the securities industry in general. Congress was really expressing its desire for (1) widespread application of auction market trading principles, (2) a high degree of competition across markets, and (3) the use of modern electronic communication systems to link the fragmented markets in the country into a true NMS. The NMS is still a goal toward which the SEC and the securities industry are moving. Agreement as to its final form and an implementation date have not occurred.

A second major alteration in the habits of the securities industry also took place in 1975. This was the elimination of fixed commissions (fixed brokerage rates) on public transactions in securities. This was closely tied to the desire for an NMS in that fixed brokerage fees provided no incentive for competition among brokers. A third consideration of the 1975 amendments focused on such financial institutions as commercial banks and insurance firms. These financial institutions were prohibited from acquiring membership on stock exchanges in order to reduce or save commissions on their own trades.

Shelf Registration

Shelf registration

A procedure for issuing new securities where the firm obtains a master registration statement approved by the SEC.

On March 16, 1982, the SEC began a new procedure for registering new issues of securities. Formally it is called SEC Rule 415; informally the process is known as a **shelf registration**, or a **shelf offering**. The essence of the process is rather simple. Rather than go through the lengthy, full registration process each time the firm plans an offering of securities, it can get a blanket order approved by the SEC. A master registration statement that covers the financing plans of the firm over the coming 2 years is filed with the SEC. On approval, the firm can market some or all of the securities over this 2-year period. The securities are sold in a piecemeal fashion, or "off the shelf." Prior to each specific offering, a short statement about the issue is filed with the SEC.

Corporations raising funds approve of this new procedure. The tedious, full registration process is avoided with each offering pulled off the shelf. This should result in a saving of fees paid to investment bankers. Moreover, an issue can more quickly be brought to the market. Also, if market conditions change, an issue can easily be redesigned to fit the specific conditions of the moment.

As is always the case, there is another side to the story. Recall that the reason for the registration process in the first place is to give investors useful information about the firm and the securities being offered. Under the shelf registration procedure, some of the information about the issuing firm becomes old as the 2-year horizon unfolds. Some investment bankers feel they do not have the proper amount of time to study the firm when a shelf offering takes place. This is one of those areas of finance where more observations are needed before any final conclusions can be made.

Earlier in the chapter, in discussing "the financing process," we noted that net users of funds (saving-deficit economic units) must compete with one another for the funds supplied by net savers (savings-surplus economic units). Consequently, to obtain financing for projects that will benefit the firm's stockholders, that firm must offer the supplier (savings-surplus unit) a rate of return *competitive* with the next best investment alternative available to that saver (investor). This rate of return on the next best investment alternative to the saver is known as the supplier's **opportunity cost of funds**. The opportunity cost concept is crucial in financial management and will be referred to often.

Opportunity cost of funds

The next best rate of return available to the investor for a given level of risk.

Next we will review the levels and variability in rates of return that have occurred over the lengthy period of 1926 to 1996. This review focuses on returns from a wide array of financial instruments. In chapter 12, we will discuss at length the concept of an *overall* cost of capital. Part of that overall cost of capital is attributed to interest rate levels at given points in time. So we will follow this initial broad look at interest rate levels with a discussion of the more recent period of 1981 to 1996.

Rates of Return over Long Periods

History can tell us a great deal about the returns that investors earn in the financial markets. A primary source for a historical perspective comes from Ibbotson and Sinquefield's *Stocks, Bonds, Bills, and Inflation*, which examines the realized rates of return for a wide variety of securities spanning the period from 1926 through 1996.[7] As part of their study, Ibbotson and Sinquefield calculated the average annual rates of return investors earned over the preceding 70 years, along with the average inflation rate for the same period. They also calculated the standard deviations of the returns for each type of security. The concept of standard deviation comes from our statistical colleagues, who use this measurement to indicate quantitatively how much dispersion or variability there is around the mean, or average, value of the item being measured—in this case, the rates of return in the financial markets.

Ibbotson and Sinquefield's results are summarized in Figure 2.4. These returns represent the average inflation rate and the average observed rates of return for different types of securities. The average inflation rate was 3.2 percent for the period covered by the study. We will refer to this rate as the "inflation-risk premium." The investor who earns only the rate of inflation has earned no "real return." That is, the *real return* is the return earned above the rate of increase in the general price level for goods and services in the economy, which is the inflation rate. In addition to the danger of not earning above the inflation rate, investors are concerned about the risk of the borrower defaulting or failing to repay the loan when due. Thus we would expect a default-risk premium for long-term corporate bonds over long-term government bonds. The premium for 1926 to 1996 as shown in Figure 2.4, was 0.6 percent, or what is called 60 basis points (6.0 percent on long-term corporate bonds minus 5.4 percent on long-term government bonds). We would also expect an even greater risk premium for common stocks vis-a-vis long-term corporate bonds, because the variability in average returns is greater for common stocks. The Ibbotson and Sinquefield study verifies such a risk premium, with common stocks (all firms) earning 6.7 percent more than the rate earned on long-term corporate bonds (12.7 percent for common stocks minus 6.0 percent for long-term corporate bonds).

Remember that these returns are "averages" across many securities and over an extended period of time. However, these averages reflect the conventional wisdom

---

[7]Roger G. Ibbotson and Rex A. Sinquefield, *Stocks, Bonds, Bills, and Inflation: Historical Returns* (Chicago: Ibbotson Associates, 1997): 33. © Ibbotson Associates.

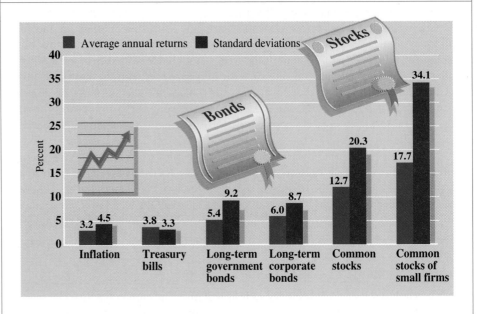

Figure 2.4 Average Annual Returns and Standard Deviations of Returns, 1926–1996

SOURCE: Roger G. Ibbotson, Rex A. Sinquefield, *Stocks, Bonds, Bills, and Inflation: Historical Returns* (Chicago: Ibbotson Associates, 1997): 33. © Ibbotson Associates.

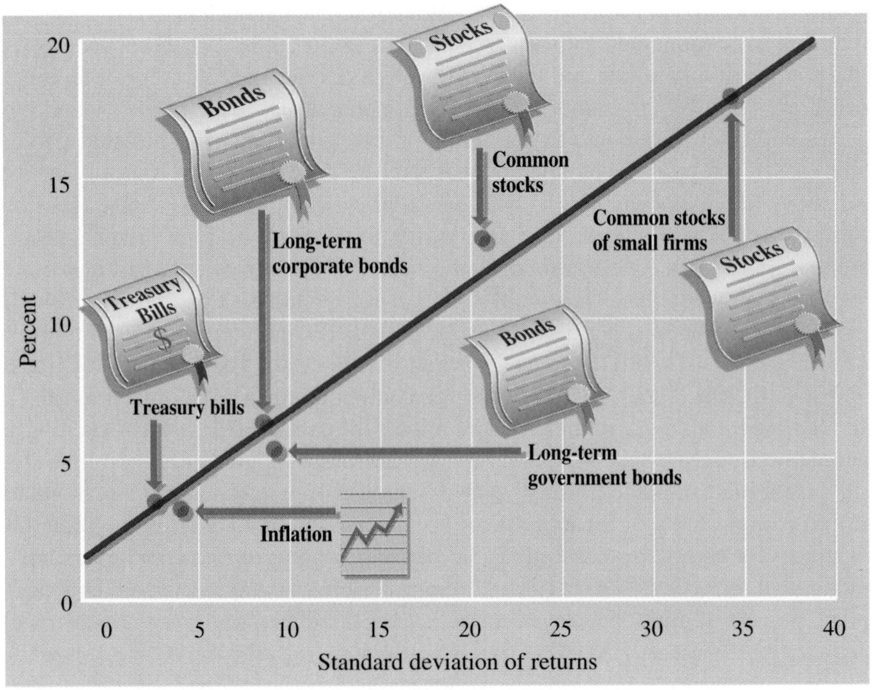

Figure 2.5 Rates of Return and Standard Deviations, 1926–1996

regarding risk premiums: The greater the risk, the greater will be the expected returns. Such a relationship is shown in Figure 2.5, where the average returns are plotted against their respective deviations; note that higher average returns have historically been associated with higher dispersion in these returns.

Interest Rate Levels over Recent Periods

OBJECTIVE 10

The *nominal* interest rates on some key fixed-income securities are displayed within both Table 2.7 and Figure 2.6 for the most recent 1981 to 1996 time frame. The rate of inflation at the consumer level is also presented in those two exhibits. This allows us to observe quite easily several concepts that were mentioned in the section above. Specifically, we can observe (1) the inflation-risk premium, (2) the default-risk premium across the several instruments, and (3) the approximate real return for each instrument. Looking at the mean (average) values for each security and the inflation rate at the bottom of Table 2.7 will facilitate the discussion.

Notice that the average inflation rate over this more recent period is higher than reported in the longer period covered by the Ibbotson and Sinquefield analysis. Over the period from 1981 to 1996, the consumer price index (December to December change) increased by an average of 3.89 percent each year. According to the logic of the financial markets, investors will *require* a nominal rate of interest that exceeds the inflation rate or else their realized *real* return will be negative. Earning a negative return over long periods of time is not very smart.

Table 2.7 indicates that investor rationality prevailed. For example, the average inflation-risk premium demanded on U.S. Treasury bills with a 3-month maturity was 3.06 percent (or 306 basis points). That is, an average 6.95 percent yield on Treasury bills over the

Table 2.7 Interest Rate Levels and Inflation Rates 1981–1996			
Year	**3-Month Treasury Bills** %	**30-Year Treasury Bonds** %	**Aaa-Rated Corporate Bonds** %	**Inflation Rate** %
1981	14.08	13.44	14.17	8.9
1982	10.69	12.76	13.79	3.9
1983	8.63	11.18	12.04	3.8
1984	9.52	12.39	12.71	4.0
1985	7.49	10.79	11.37	3.8
1986	5.98	7.80	9.02	1.1
1987	5.82	8.58	9.38	4.4
1988	6.68	8.96	9.71	4.4
1989	8.12	8.45	9.26	4.6
1990	7.51	8.61	9.32	6.1
1991	5.42	8.14	8.77	3.1
1992	3.45	7.67	8.14	2.9
1993	3.02	6.59	7.22	2.7
1994	4.29	7.37	7.97	2.7
1995	5.51	6.88	7.59	2.5
1996	5.02	6.71	7.37	3.3
Mean	6.95	9.15	9.86	3.89

NOTE: Data from *Federal Reserve Bulletin*, various issues, and *Federal Reserve Statistical Releases* H.15 (519), G.13 (415), various issues.

Figure 2.6 Interest Rate Levels and Inflation Rates 1981–1996

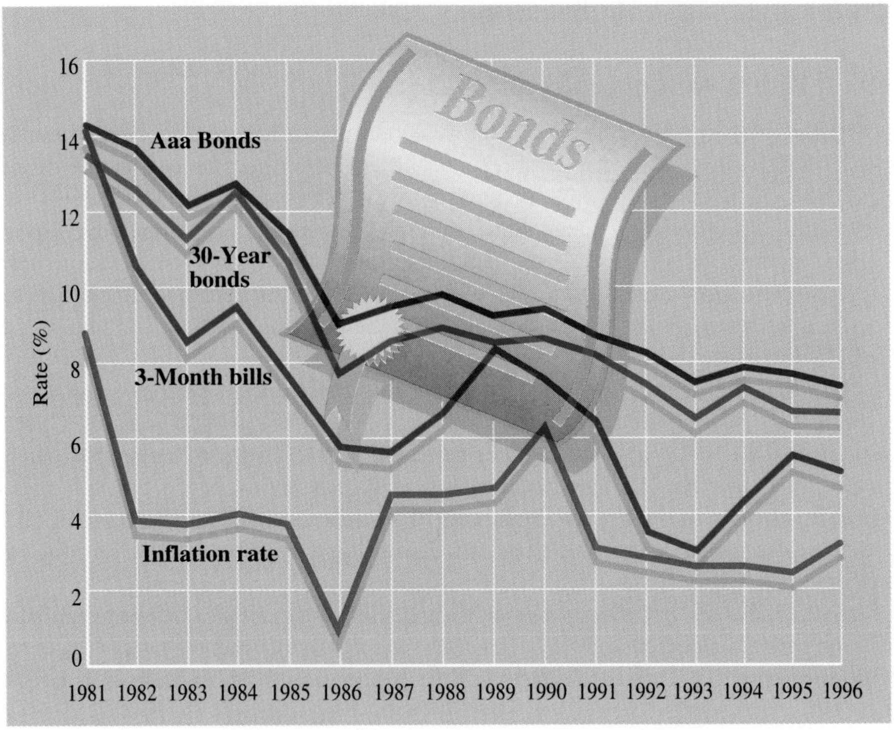

period *minus* the average inflation rate of 3.89 percent over the same period produces a premium of 3.06 percent.

The default-risk premium is also evident in Table 2.7 and Figure 2.6. If we array the securities in these two exhibits from low risk to high risk, the following tabulation results:

Security	Yield
3-month Treasury bills	6.95%
30-year Treasury bonds	9.15
Aaa Corporate bonds	9.86

Again, the basic rationale of the financial markets prevailed. The default-risk premium on high-rated (Aaa) corporate bonds relative to long-term Treasury bonds of 30-year maturity was 0.71 percent.

The array above can also be used to identify another factor that affects interest rate levels. It is referred to as the "maturity premium." This maturity premium arises even if securities possess equal (or approximately equal) odds of default. This is the case with Treasury bills and Treasury bonds, for instance, because the full faith and credit of the U.S. government stands behind these financial contracts. They are considered risk free (that is, possessing no chance of default).

Notice that Treasury bonds with a 30-year maturity commanded a 2.20 percent yield differential over the shorter, 3-month-to-maturity Treasury bonds. This provides an estimate of the maturity premium demanded by investors over this specific 1981 to 1996 period. More precisely, the *maturity premium* can be defined as: **the additional return required by investors in longer-term securities (bonds, in this case) to compensate them for the greater risk of price fluctuations on those securities caused by interest rate changes.**

When you study the basic mathematics of financial decisions in chapter 5 and the characteristics of fixed-income securities in chapter 7, you will learn how to quantify this maturity premium that is imbedded in nominal interest rates.

One other type of risk premium that helps determine interest rate levels needs to be identified and defined. It is known as the "liquidity premium." The *liquidity premium* is defined as: **the additional return required by investors in securities that cannot be quickly converted into cash at a reasonably predictable price.**

The secondary markets for small-bank stocks, especially community banks, provide a good example of the liquidity premium. A bank holding company that trades on the New York Stock Exchange, such as SunTrust Bank, will be more liquid to investors than, say, the common stock of Citizens National Bank of Leesburg, Florida. Such a liquidity premium will be reflected across the spectrum of financial assets, from bonds to stocks.

RELATE TO THE BIG PICTURE

Our first axiom, ***Axiom 1: The Risk-Return Trade-Off—We Won't Take on Additional Risk Unless We Expect to Be Compensated with Additional Return,*** *established the fundamental risk-return trade-offs that govern the financial markets. We are now trying to provide you with an understanding of the kinds of risks that are rewarded in the risk-return trade-off.*

INTEREST RATE DETERMINANTS IN A NUTSHELL

OBJECTIVE 11

Our review of rates of return and interest rate levels in the financial markets permits us to synthesize our introduction to the different types of risks that impact interest rates. We can, thereby, generate a simple equation with the **nominal** (that is, observed) **rate of interest** being the output variable from the equation. The nominal interest rate is sometimes called the "quoted" rate. It is the rate that you would read about in *The Wall Street Journal* for a specific fixed-income security. That equation follows:

Nominal rate of interest

The observed rate of interest on a specific fixed-income security; no adjustment is made for expected inflation.

$$k = k^* + IRP + DRP + MP + LP \tag{2-1}$$

where: k = the nominal or observed rate of interest on a specific fixed-income security.

k^* = the real risk-free rate of interest; it is the required rate of interest on a fixed-income security that has no risk and in an economic environment of zero inflation. This can be reasonably thought of as the rate of interest demanded by investors in U.S. Treasury securities during periods of no inflation.

IRP = the inflation-risk premium.

DRP = the default-risk premium.

MP = the maturity premium.

LP = the liquidity premium.

Sometimes in analyzing interest rate relationships over time, it is of use to focus on what is called the "nominal risk-free rate of interest." Again, by nominal we mean "observed." So let us designate the nominal risk-free interest rate as k_{rf}. Drawing, then, on our discussions and notation from above, we can write this expression for k_{rf}:

$$k_{rf} = k^* + IRP \qquad (2\text{-}2)$$

This equation just says that the nominal risk-free rate of interest is equal to the real risk-free interest rate plus the inflation-risk premium. It also provides a quick and *approximate* way of estimating the risk-free rate of interest, k^*, by solving directly for this rate. This basic relationship in equation (2-2) contains important information for the financial decision maker. It has also been for years the subject of fascinating and lengthy discussions among financial economists. We will look more at the substance of the real rate of interest in the second section that follows here. In that discussion, we will improve on equation (2-2) by making it more precise. But first, we want to put our knowledge of interest rate determinants into action.

Estimating Specific Interest Rates Using Risk Premiums: An Example

By making use of our knowledge of various risk premiums as contained in equation (2-1), the financial manager can generate useful information for the firm's financial planning process. For instance, if the firm is about to offer a new issue of corporate bonds to the investing marketplace, it is possible for the financial manager or analyst to estimate what interest rate (yield) will satisfy the markets and help ensure that the bonds are actually bought by investors. Offering too high of a yield by the firm is unwise in that unnecessary interest expense will be incurred by the firm and will, thereby, negatively impact earnings. On the other hand, offering too low of a yield will hinder the bonds from being attractive to investors (savers) in a competitive marketplace. This situation can be clarified and illustrated by use of a specific example.

Problem situation. You have been asked to provide a reasonable estimate of the nominal interest rate for a new issue of Aaa-rated bonds to be offered by Big Truck Producers, Inc. The final format that the chief financial officer of Big Truck has requested is that of equation (2-1) in the text. Your assignment also requires that you consult the data in Table 2.7.

Some agreed-upon procedures related to generating estimates for key variables in equation (2-1) follow:

1. The financial market environment over the 1993 to 1995 period is considered representative of the prospective tone of the market near the time of offering the new bonds to the investing public. This means that 3-year averages will be used as benchmarks for some of the variable estimates. All estimates will be rounded off to hundredths of a percent; thus, 6.288 becomes 6.29 percent.
2. The real risk-free rate of interest is the difference between the calculated average yield on 3-month Treasury bills and the inflation rate.
3. The default-risk premium is estimated by the difference between the average yield on Aaa-rated bonds and 30-year Treasury bonds.
4. The maturity premium is estimated by the difference between the average yield on 30-year Treasury bonds and 3-month Treasury bills.
5. Big Truck's bonds will be traded on the New York Exchange for Bonds so the liquidity premium will be slight. It will be greater than zero, however, because the secondary market for the firm's bonds is more uncertain than that of some other truck producers. It is estimated at 3 basis points. A basis point is one-hundredth of 1 percent.

THE NEW YORK TIMES, JUNE 5, 1994

Pick a Number, Any Number

The economy is growing a lot faster than expected. Or maybe it is growing much more slowly than thought.

Or maybe the numbers are just messed up.

There is something for everyone in the economic statistics from Washington. And never was that clearer, or perhaps we mean less clear, than it was Friday.

First, the good news. The unemployment rate dropped from 6.4 percent in April to 6 percent in May, far below any forecast. The report, President Clinton was quick to say, "clearly supports the wisdom of the economic strategy we have been following."

Unfortunately, there was more. The government also said that just 191,000 new jobs were created last month, a lot fewer than anyone had expected. If that's right, the economy is weaker than thought.

How can such clearly incompatible figures coexist? The answer is that they are based on different surveys, each with its own inaccuracies. The unemployment figure comes from a household survey, which asks people whether they worked in the previous week and whether they were looking for work. The number of jobs comes from a survey of employers. Add in seasonal adjustments that probably are flawed, and the numbers could mean anything.

If nothing else, the numbers produced wild times for bond traders. If the economy is as strong as the 6 percent figure indicates, then inflation fears are likely to be rekindled and the Federal Reserve is likely to try to push up interest rates even more than it already has. So when the 6 percent headline flashed on news tickers, everybody wanted to sell bonds. Prices plunged, and the yield on 30-year Treasury bonds rose from around 7.3 percent to over 7.4 percent. **(A) (B)**

But within a few minutes, sentiment began to turn as the report on job totals came in. Bond prices rose, and by the end of the day the yield, which falls as prices rise, was back down to 7.26 percent.

All of which proved only that those who rely on quick readings of complicated and flawed economic reports can lose a lot of money very quickly.

And where is the economy really going?

Wait a bit. The government will have more numbers this week, including figures on inflation and on how much money Americans are borrowing. **(C)**

Maybe the new set of numbers will make some sense. But don't bet on it.

Analysis and Implications …

A. Note the linkage here between a seemingly strong aggregate economy and rising inflationary expectations. A larger than expected drop in the national unemployment rate *could* cause bond traders to implicitly forecast a rising rate of inflation. This is because when more people work, they have the money from wages to demand more goods and services. Such a situation typically translates into a greater level of inflation.

B. So we see that bond traders in general are a pessimistic lot compared to most other economic units. To them, good overall economic news means higher inflation. Higher inflation means that an inflation-risk premium must be built into long-term bond yields. The upshot is that bond prices will fall, so that bond yields (interest rates) can rise.

C. Also, observe that it is unwise to pin all of your business hopes on a single set of economic numbers. Why? Because those numbers will both be revised and there will be new numbers out tomorrow. The new numbers may paint or imply a different picture. The moral is: If the numbers are not to your liking, refrain from jumping off the top floor of the nearest tall building—by the time you hit the ground, the numbers will have changed. You can see how very difficult it is to accurately forecast interest rate changes.

Now place your output into the format of equation (2-1) so that the nominal interest rate can be estimated and the size of each variable can also be inspected for reasonableness and discussion with the chief financial officer.

Solution. Let's now look at the building blocks that will comprise our forecast of the nominal interest rate on Big Truck's new issue of bonds. The nominal rate (k) that is forecast to satisfy the market turns out to be 7.62 percent. The tabular presentations, below, aid us in obtaining this estimate. The top portion generates the 3-year averages thought to be representative of the basic financial market environment. The bottom portion is a worksheet that "builds up" the nominal interest rate. It is just equation (2-1) in worksheet form.

Year	(1) 3-Month Treasury Bills %	(2) 30-Year Treasury Bonds %	(3) Aaa-Rated Corporate Bonds %	(4) Inflation Rate %
1993	3.02	6.59	7.22	2.70
1994	4.29	7.37	7.97	2.70
1995	5.51	6.88	7.59	2.50
Mean	4.27	6.95	7.59	2.63

Table Columns as Shown Above	Equation (2-1)	
(1) − (4)	$k*$	1.64
	+	+
(4)	IRP	2.63
	+	+
(3) − (2)	DRP	0.64
	+	+
(2) − (1)	MP	2.68
	+	+
Given	LP	0.03
	=	=
	k	7.62

Thus the real risk-free rate of interest is estimated to be 1.64 percent. It is the difference between the 3-year average yield on 3-month Treasury bills and the inflation rate (column 1 minus column 4). In similar fashion, the inflation-risk premium of 2.63 percent (IRP) is the 3-year average of the change in the inflation rate (column 4). The default-risk premium (DRP) is the difference in the 3-year average rates that were available to investors in Aaa-rated bonds and Treasury bonds with a 30-year maturity (column 3 minus column 2). The maturity premium (MP) of 2.68 percent is the difference in the 3-year average rates that were earned by investors in 30-year Treasury bonds and 3-month Treasury bills (column 2 minus column 1). The liquidity premium (LP) was estimated for us by a sharp financial analyst—such as yourself.

When we put this altogether as an estimate of the nominal interest rate needed to satisfy the financial markets on Big Truck's new bond issue, we have:

$k = k^* + IRP + DRP + MP + LP$ = nominal rate on Big Truck's bonds,

$k = 1.64 + 2.63 + 0.64 + 2.68 + 0.03 = 7.62\%$

Understanding the analysis, above, will help you deal with the Integrative Problem at the end of this chapter. We move now to an examination of the relationship between real and nominal interest rates.

The Effects of Inflation on Rates of Return and the Fisher Effect

When a rate of interest is quoted, it is generally the nominal, or observed rate. The **real rate of interest**, on the other hand, represents the rate of increase in actual purchasing power, after adjusting for inflation. For example, if you have $100 today and loan it to someone for a year at a nominal rate of interest of 11.3 percent, you will get back $111.30 in 1 year. But if during the year, prices of goods and services rise by 5 percent, it will take $105 at year end to purchase the same goods and services that $100 purchased at the beginning of the year. What was your increase in purchasing power over the year? The quick and dirty answer is found by subtracting the inflation rate from the nominal rate, $11.3\% - 5\% = 6.3\%$, but this is not exactly correct. To be more precise, let the nominal rate of interest be represented by k_{rf}, the anticipated rate of inflation by IRP, and the real rate of interest by k^*. Using these notations, we can express the relationship among the nominal interest rate, the rate of inflation, and the real rate of interest as follows:

Real rate of interest

The nominal rate of interest less the expected rate of inflation over the maturity of the fixed-income security. This represents the expected increase in actual purchasing power to the investor.

$$1 + k_{rf} = (1 + k^*)(1 + IRP) \tag{2-3}$$

or

$$k_{rf} = k^* + IRP + (k^* \cdot IRP)$$

Consequently, the nominal rate of interest (k_{rf}) is equal to the sum of the real rate of interest (k^*), the inflation rate (IRP), and the product of the real rate and the inflation rate. This relationship among nominal rates, real rates, and the rate of inflation has come to be called the *Fisher effect*.[8] It means that the observed nominal rate of interest includes both the real rate and an *inflation premium* as noted in the previous section.

Substituting into equation (2-3) using a nominal rate of 11.3 percent and an inflation rate of 5 percent, we can calculate the real rate of interest, k^*, as follows:

$$k_{rf} = k^* + IRP + (k^* \cdot IRP)$$

$$.113 = k^* + .05 + .05k^*$$

$$k^* = .06 = 6\%$$

Thus, at the new higher prices, your purchasing power will have increased by only 6 percent, although you have $11.30 more than you had at the start of the year. To see why, let's assume that at the outset of the year, one unit of the market basket of goods and services costs $1, so you could purchase 100 units with your $100. At the end of the year, you have $11.30 more, but each unit now costs $1.05 (remember the 5 percent rate of inflation). How many units can you buy at the end of the year? The answer is $111.30 ÷ $1.05 = 106$, which represents a 6 percent increase in real purchasing power.[9]

---

[8]This relationship was analyzed many years ago by Irving Fisher. For those who want to explore Fisher's theory of interest in more detail, a fine overview is contained in Peter N. Ireland, "Long-Term Interest Rates and Inflation: A Fisherian Approach," *Federal Reserve Bank of Richmond, Economic Quarterly*, 82 (Winter 1996), pp. 22–26.

[9]In chapter 5, we will study more about the time value of money.

The Federal Reserve and Interest Rates

Organization

Many people are not aware that the Federal Reserve System is not part of the executive branch of the federal government, like the U.S. Treasury or Commerce Departments. Rather it is a blend of public and private enterprise. The nation's central bank is an agency created by Congress, but the Fed's decentralized structure of 12 district banks and 25 branches gives each unit some aspects of privately owned businesses. The Fed's operational arms at the various banks and branches, for example, compete with one another—and with private sector organizations—to provide quality financial services.

The Federal Reserve System is also similar to private businesses in that each bank and branch elects a board of directors. Contributing expertise gained from their own professions, the Fed directors play an integral role in the system's ability to formulate monetary policy and provide high-quality financial services to depository institutions and the U.S. Treasury.[a]

Ⓐ

The Fed and Interest Rates

It is often suggested that the Federal Reserve tightly controls all interest rates. Actually, the Federal Reserve sets only one interest rate, its discount rate. In addition, the Federal Reserve's open market operations in recent years have been aimed at holding another rate, the federal funds rate, close to levels indicated by the Federal Open Market Committee (FOMC), the Federal Reserve's primary monetary policy-making body.

This article explains how changes in the federal funds rate and the discount rate work through financial markets to affect other short-term interest rates such as those on Treasury bills and certificates of deposit. It also explains why the influence of changes in the funds rate and the discount rate on long-term rates, such as mortgage rates and corporate bond yields, is relatively weak.[b]

Monetary Policy in Brief

The Federal Reserve's monetary policy can be defined as the Fed's use of its influence on reserves in the banking system to influence money and credit and, through them, the economy. The federal funds rate and the discount rate figure importantly in the conduct of monetary policy, and many observers regard these two rates as the principal indicators of the direction of policy. Declines in these rates are taken as signs that the Federal Reserve wants to encourage money and credit growth, or "ease" money and credit conditions, whereas increases in money and credit conditions are interpreted as Fed efforts to restrain money and credit growth, or "tighten" money and credit conditions.

Federal funds are reserves lent overnight by depository institutions with excess reserves to depository institutions with insufficient reserves. The **federal funds** rate is a market rate of interest determined by the supply and demand for reserves. The Fed directly affects the funds rate by buying and selling government securities in the "open market" to influence the supply of reserves, and, therefore, federal funds in the banking system. When the Federal Reserve wants to ease money and credit conditions through open market operations, for example, it supplies additional reserves to the banking system by purchasing additional short-term government securities.

Ⓑ

When a depository institution is short on the reserves it needs to meet regulatory requirements, it may also borrow reserves from its regional Federal Reserve Bank at the discount rate. The **discount rate** is an "administered" rate, set at a certain level and held there by administrative decision. Changes in the discount rate are initiated by the boards of directors of the individual Reserve Banks, but the Federal Reserve's Board of Governors in Washington must approve all changes. This coordination generally results in roughly simultaneous changes to all Reserve Banks.

Effect of Changes in the Funds Rate on Short-Term Rates

The Federal Reserve exercises a strong influence on other short-term rates through its influence on the federal funds rate, because the funds rate is the base rate to which other money market rates are anchored. To see this, consider the rate on bank certificates of deposit (CDs), which are generally arranged for a few months. Banks can raise funds either through CDs or federal funds and therefore choose whichever option is expected to be cheaper. CD rates are roughly aligned with an average of expected future funds rates over the term of the CD. Hence if bankers see a rise in the federal funds rate and expect it to persist, they will bid up the rate on CDs. Likewise, corporations considering a Treasury bill purchase have the option of lending their funds daily over the term of the bill at the overnight rate on repurchase agreements, which is closely tied to the federal funds rate. Hence they will require a higher Treasury bill rate following an increase in the funds rate that they believe to be persistent.

As these examples illustrate, the arbitrage activities of money market participants will generally keep other short-term rates in line with the federal funds rate, abstracting from differences in default risk. Hence persistent increases in the federal funds rate engineered by the Federal Reserve will generally lead to comparable increases in other short-term interest rates.

Changes in the Discount Rate

As indicated above, banks can borrow reserves at the discount window or they can acquire reserves in the federal funds market. (Of course, individual banks can also acquire reserves by selling off securities.) Under the operating procedures used by the Federal Reserve in the 1980s, increases in the discount rate that raise the cost of acquiring borrowed reserves also can lead quickly to an increase in the cost of acquiring reserves in the federal funds market. Hence under these procedures the discount rate can have a strong direct effect on the funds rate and other market rates.

More generally, if changes in the discount rate are viewed by market participants as signaling a "tighter" monetary policy in the future, then they can influence the current level of market interest rates regardless of the Fed's operating procedures. The reason is that anticipation of a tighter policy will raise the expected future level of the funds rate. A higher expected funds rate will then raise current rates on CDs and Treasury bills as in the examples above. Such effects are usually labeled "announcement effects" by market participants.

Long-Term Rates

The ability of the Federal Reserve to directly influence the level of interest rates diminishes greatly at longer maturities. The reason is that longer-term interest rates, such as mortgage rates and corporate bond yields, are largely determined by the expected rate of inflation. To appreciate the influence of inflation

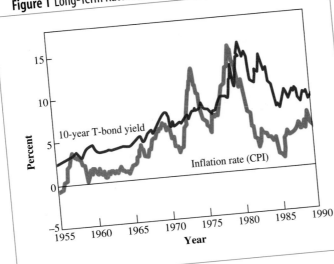

Figure 1 Long-Term Rates Fall After Inflation Falls

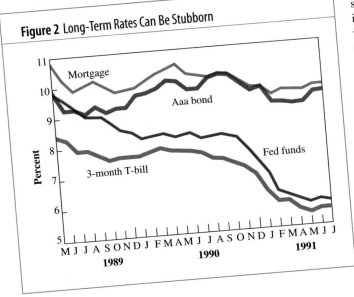

Figure 2 Long-Term Rates Can Be Stubborn

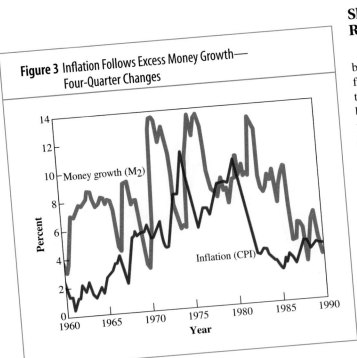

Figure 3 Inflation Follows Excess Money Growth—Four-Quarter Changes

expectations on longer-term rates, suppose that the long-term expected inflation rate were 5 percent. Lenders would be unwilling to lend at 5 percent because the interest income would be completely offset by the inflation loss. Lenders want to cover the expected inflation loss and earn some real rate of return, considered usually to be about 4 percent. Borrowers, for their part, are willing to pay the inflation premium because they expect to repay their debts with cheaper dollars. Therefore, one can reasonably expect long-term interest rates to be about 4 percentage points above the expected inflation rate. It follows that an important way to reduce long-term rates is to lower the expected rate of inflation. The historical data in Figure 1 show that long-term rates have come down only after inflation has declined.

Short- and Long-Term Rates: A Case Study

The relatively weak link between movements in the federal funds rate and movements in long-term rates can be illustrated by the behavior of rates over 2 recent years. From June 1989 through June 1991, the federal funds rate fell 4 percentage points, from about 9.75 percent to about 5.75 percent, and other short-term rates also declined about 4 percentage points. Long-term rates, however, fell only about 1 percentage point over this period, as illustrated in Figure 2.

How should these declines be interpreted in light of the previous discussion? Apparently, the public's inflation outlook did not change much from June 1989 through June 1991 because long-term rates did not move much over this period. Evidently, the public believed that the Fed's downward pressure on short-term rates were anti-recession moves that would not significantly alter the inflation outlook. In July and August of 1991, however, declines in long-term rates suggested perceived progress in reducing expected inflation.

The Fed's Role

The historical data show that long-term interest rates decline when the expected rate of inflation declines. Furthermore, empirical evidence strongly suggests that, over time, inflation results from excessive increases in the money supply (Figure 3). To prevent inflation and to concurrently bring down long-term rates, policy makers must ensure that, over time, the money supply grows only as fast as the economy's potential growth in output.

SOURCES: [a]"Board Member Finds Parallels between the Fed and His Own Business," *Financial Update*, Federal Reserve Bank of Atlanta, 3 (Fall 1990): 3; [b]Craig Carlock, "How the Federal Reserve Influences Interest Rates," *Cross Sections*, Federal Reserve Bank of Richmond, 8 (Fall 1991), 12–14.

Analysis and Implications ...

A. Many analysts suggest that the Federal Reserve System (our nation's central bank) is the most powerful institution in the United States. At the very least, it is an agency necessary for the financial manager to understand as it has tremendous power to influence the level of short-term interest rates and, thereby, the nominal cost of credit to firms.

"Fed-watching" is a pervasive exercise among not only financial economists, but also wise business practitioners. Analysts try to gain some insight into the direction of interest rate changes by studying public statements by Fed officials. Keep in mind that the Federal Reserve is both a quasi-public and quasi-private organization. Interestingly enough, not a single member of this powerful group is elected by the public. Some in Congress would like to change that. What do you think about such a proposal?

B. As was mentioned in the lead in to this chapter, the federal funds rate is a visible indicator of the tone of monetary policy in the United States. The Fed does not directly "set" this rate but tries to keep it close to a targeted level by influencing the supply of reserves in the banking system. The Federal Open Market Committee (FOMC) determines the target level. Thus when the FOMC meets roughly every 6 weeks, all serious financial executives look for clues as to what occurred at those meetings. Sometimes an immediate announcement is made by Fed officials; sometimes it is not. In this latter case, you as an analyst have to "read the tea leaves."

C. The discount rate is one interest rate that the Fed can directly set. Changes in the federal funds rate are more subtle, but tend to be used more often by the Fed in setting the tone of monetary policy. Rarely is the discount rate changed without the federal funds target rate being changed in the same direction. But the federal funds target rate is often altered without the discount rate being altered.

D. The Federal Reserve's main influence on interest rates occurs at the short-end of the yield curve. Inflationary expectations become the dominant factor affecting the level of and changes in *long-term* interest rates. Thus changes in the producer price index for finished goods and the consumer price index become important indicators for those analysts who like to anticipate interest rate movements in long-term securities.

Although the algebraic methodology presented in the preceding section is strictly correct, few practicing analysts or executives use it. Rather, they will employ some version of the following relationship, an approximation method, to estimate the real rate of interest over a selected past time frame.

(Nominal interest rate) − (inflation rate) = real interest rate

The concept is straightforward, but implementation requires that several judgments be made. For example, which interest rate series and maturity period should be used? Suppose we settle for using some U.S. Treasury security as a surrogate for a nominal risk-free interest rate. Then should we use the yield on 3-month U.S. Treasury bills or, perhaps, that on 30-year Treasury bonds? Guess what? There is no absolute answer to the question.

So, we can have a real risk-free short-term interest rate, as well as a real risk-free long-term interest rate, and several variations in between. In essence, it just depends on what the analyst wants to accomplish. We could also calculate the real rate of interest on some rating class of corporate bonds (such as Aaa-rated bonds) and have a risky real rate of interest as opposed to a real risk-free interest rate.

Further, the choice of a proper inflation index is equally challenging. Again, we have several choices. We could use the consumer price index, the producer price index for finished goods, or some price index out of the national income accounts, such as the gross domestic product chain price index. Again, there is no precise scientific answer as to which specific price index to use. Logic and consistency do narrow the boundaries of the ultimate choice.

Let's tackle a very basic example. Suppose that an analyst wants to estimate the approximate real interest rate on (1) 3-month Treasury bills, (2) 30-year Treasury bonds, and (3) Aaa-rated corporate bonds over the 1981 to 1995 time frame. Further, the annual rate of change in the consumer price index (measured from December to December) is considered a logical measure of past inflation experience. Most of our work is already done for us in Table 2.7. Some of the data from Table 2.7 are as follows:

Security	Mean Nominal Yield %	Mean Inflation Rate %	Inferred Real Rate %
Treasury bills	7.08	3.93	3.15
Treasury bonds	9.31	3.93	5.38
Corporate bonds	10.03	3.93	6.10

Notice that the mean yield over the 15 years from 1981 to 1995 on all three classes of securities has been used as a reasonable proxy for the ex-post return. Likewise, the mean inflation rate over the same time period has been used as an estimate of the inflation-risk premium (*IRP* from our earlier notation). The last column, above, provides the approximation for the real interest rate on each class of securities.

Thus over the 15-year examination period, the real rate of interest on 3-month Treasury bills was 3.15 percent, 5.38 percent on 30-year Treasury bonds, and 6.10 percent on

Aaa-rated corporate bonds. These three estimates (approximations) of the real interest rate provide a rough guide as to the increase in real purchasing power associated with an investment position in each security. Remember that the real rate on the corporate bonds is expected to be greater than that on long-term government bonds because of the default-risk premium (*DRP*) placed on the corporate securities.

HOW FINANCIAL MANAGERS USE THIS MATERIAL

Corporate financial executives are constantly balancing the internal demand for funds against the costs of raising external financial capital. In order to finance favorable projects, the financial executive at times will have to choose between issuing new debt, preferred stock, or common stock. Further, the executive will decide whether to raise the external capital via a public offering or private placement of the new securities to a limited number of potential investors. Most of these activities will involve the counsel of an investment banking firm and an awareness of securities markets regulations.

We know that when financial executives decide to raise cash in the capital market, the issuance of corporate debt clearly dominates other forms of financing instruments. This preference rests on economic logic: Interest expense is deductible from other taxable income when computing the firm's tax liability; dividends paid on either preferred stock or common stock are not. This puts **Axiom 8: Taxes Bias Business Decisions** into action. Stated alternatively, firms would rather suffer a lower tax bill as opposed to a higher tax bill. Wouldn't you? As a result of this knowledge, U.S. corporate executives raised 76.9 percent of their external cash from bonds and notes (debt capital) during 1996.

Financial executives are fully aware of **Axiom 8**, but also the need to create wealth for their common stock investors. The use of fixed-income financing (leverage) has to be wisely done—not overdone, or it will ultimately raise overall capital costs and the risk of bankruptcy. The Walt Disney Company displays this perspective in the following statement: "Disney shareholders benefit from the prudent leverage in the company's capital structure represented by total borrowings of $11.1 billion at year end. Attractive borrowing rates help to reduce the company's overall cost of capital, thereby creating value for shareholders. Disney still has substantial financial flexibility to borrow, should sound business opportunities present themselves."[10]

SUMMARY

This chapter centers on the market environment in which corporations raise long-term funds, including the structure of the U.S. financial markets, the institution of investment banking, and the various methods for distributing securities. It also discusses the role of interest rates in allocating savings to ultimate investment.

When corporations go to the capital market for cash, the most favored financing method is debt. The corporate debt markets clearly dominate the equity markets when new funds are raised. The U.S. tax system inherently favors debt capital as a fundraising

OBJECTIVES
1 AND 2

---

[10]The Walt Disney Company, *Annual Report* (1997), 17.

method. In an average year over the 1981 to 1996 period, bonds and notes made up 75.6 percent of external cash that was raised.

OBJECTIVE 3

The function of financial markets is to allocate savings efficiently in the economy to the ultimate demander (user) of the savings. In a financial market, the forces of supply and demand for a specific financial instrument are brought together. The wealth of an economy would not be as great as it is without a fully developed financial market system.

OBJECTIVE 4

Every year, households are a net supplier of funds to the financial markets. The nonfinancial business sector is most always a net borrower of funds. Both life insurance companies and private pension funds are important buyers of corporate securities. Savings are ultimately transferred to the business firm seeking cash by means of (1) the direct transfer, (2) the indirect transfer using the investment banker, or (3) the indirect transfer using the financial intermediary.

OBJECTIVE 5

Corporations can raise funds through public offerings or private placements. The public market is impersonal in that the security issuer does not meet the ultimate investors in the financial instruments. In a private placement, the securities are sold directly to a limited number of institutional investors.

The primary market is the market for new issues. The secondary market represents transactions in currently outstanding securities. Both the money and capital markets have primary and secondary sides. The money market refers to transactions in short-term debt instruments. The capital market, on the other hand, refers to transactions in long-term financial instruments. Trading in the money and capital markets can occur in either the organized security exchanges or the over-the-counter market. The money market is exclusively an over-the-counter market.

OBJECTIVE 6

The investment banker is a financial specialist involved as an intermediary in the merchandising of securities. He or she performs the functions of (1) underwriting, (2) distributing, and (3) advising. Major methods for the public distribution of securities include (1) the negotiated purchase, (2) the competitive bid purchase, (3) the commission or best-efforts basis, (4) privileged subscriptions, and (5) direct sales. The direct sale bypasses the use of an investment banker. The negotiated purchase is the most profitable distribution method to the investment banker. It also provides the greatest amount of investment banking services to the corporate client.

OBJECTIVE 7

Privately placed debt provides an important market outlet for corporate bonds. Major investors in this market are (1) life insurance firms, (2) state and local retirement funds, and (3) private pension funds. Several advantages and disadvantages are associated with private placements. The financial officer must weigh these attributes and decide if a private placement is preferable to a public offering.

OBJECTIVE 8

Flotation costs consist of the underwriter's spread and issuing costs. The flotation costs of common stock exceed those of preferred stock, which, in turn, exceed those of debt. Moreover, flotation costs as a percent of gross proceeds are inversely related to the size of the security issue.

OBJECTIVE 8

The new issues market is regulated at the federal level by the Securities Act of 1933. It provides for the registration of new issues with the SEC. Secondary market trading is regulated by the Securities Exchange Act of 1934. The Securities Acts Amendments of

1975 placed on the SEC the responsibility for devising a national market system. This concept is still being studied. The shelf registration procedure (SEC Rule 415) was initiated in March 1982. Under this regulation and with the proper filing of documents, firms that are selling new issues do not have to go through the old, lengthy registration process each time the firm plans an offering of securities.

The financial markets give managers an informed indication of investors' opportunity costs. The more efficient the market, the more informed the indication. This information is a useful input about the rates of return that investors require on financial claims. In turn, this will become useful to financial managers as they estimate the overall cost of capital used as a screening rate in the capital budgeting process.

Rates of return on various securities are based on the underlying supply of loanable funds (savings) and demand for those loanable funds. In addition to a risk-free return, investors will want to be compensated for the potential loss of purchasing power resulting from inflation. Moreover, investors require a greater return the greater the default-risk, maturity premium, and liquidity premium are on the securities being analyzed.

OBJECTIVES
9, 10, 11

KEY TERMS

Capital market, 48

Direct sale, 53

Direct securities, 45

Financial assets, 43

Financial markets, 42

Flotation costs, 56

Indirect securities, 44

Investment banker, 51

Money market, 48

Nominal rate of interest, 63

Opportunity cost of funds, 59

Organized security
exchanges, 49

Over-the-counter markets, 49

Primary markets, 48

Private placement, 48

Privileged subscription, 53

Public offering, 48

Real assets, 43

Real rate of interest, 67

Secondary markets, 44

Shelf registration, 58

Syndicate, 52

Underwriting, 44

PHLIP

GO TO:
http://www.prenhall.com/bfm
For downloads and current events associated with this chapter

STUDY QUESTIONS

2-1. What are financial markets? What function do they perform? How would an economy be worse off without them?

2-2. Define in a technical sense what we mean by *financial intermediary*. Give an example of your definition.

2-3. Distinguish between the money and capital markets.

2-4. What major benefits do corporations and investors enjoy because of the existence of organized security exchanges?

2-5. What are the general categories examined by an organized exchange in determining whether an applicant firm's securities can be listed on it?

(Specific numbers are not needed here, but rather areas of investigation.)

2-6. Why do you think most secondary market trading in bonds takes place over-the-counter?

2-7. What is an investment banker, and what major functions does he or she perform?

2-8. What is the major difference between a negotiated purchase and a competitive bid purchase?

2-9. Why is an investment banking syndicate formed?

2-10. Why might a large corporation want to raise long-term capital through a private placement rather than a public offering?

2-11. As a recent business school graduate, you work directly for the corporate treasurer. Your corporation is going to issue a new security plan and is concerned with the probable flotation costs. What tendencies about flotation costs can you relate to the treasurer?

2-12. When corporations raise funds, what type of financing vehicle (instrument or instruments) is most favored?

2-13. What is the major (most significant) savings-surplus sector in the U.S. economy?

2-14. Identify three distinct ways that savings are ultimately transferred to business firms in need of cash.

2-15. Explain the term *opportunity cost* with respect to cost of funds to the firm.

2-16. Compare and explain the historical rates of return for different types of securities.

2-17. Explain the impact of inflation on rates of return.

STUDY PROBLEMS (SET A)

2-1A. (*Real Interest Rates: Financial Analyst's Method*) The chief financial officer of your firm has asked you for an approximate answer to this question: What was the increase in real purchasing power associated with both 3-month Treasury bills and 30-year Treasury bonds over the 1991 to 1995 period? (Hints: (a) consult Table 2.7 in the text, and (2) simple averages on the key variables will provide a defensible response to your boss.) Also, the chief financial officer wants a short explanation should the 3-month real rate turn out to be *less* than the 30-year real rate.

2-2A. (*Inflation and Interest Rates*) What would you expect the nominal rate of interest to be if the real rate is 4.5 percent and the expected inflation rate is 7.3 percent?

2-3A. (*Inflation and Interest Rates*) Assume the expected inflation rate is 3.8 percent. If the current real rate of interest is 6.4 percent, what ought the nominal rate of interest be?

2-4A. (*Inflation and Interest Rates*) What would you expect the nominal rate of interest to be if the real rate is 4 percent and the expected inflation rate is 7 percent?

2-5A. (*Inflation and Interest Rates*) Assume the expected inflation rate is 4 percent. If the current real rate of interest is 6 percent, what ought the nominal rate of interest be?

2-6A. (*Inflation and Interest Rates*) Assume the expected inflation rate is 5 percent. If the current real rate of interest is 7 percent, what would you expect the nominal rate of interest to be?

INTEGRATIVE PROBLEM

You have been asked to provide a reasonable estimate of the nominal interest rate for a new issue of Aaa-rated bonds to be offered by Large Truck Producers, Inc. The final format that the chief financial officer of Large Truck has requested is that of equation (2-1) in the text. You'll also need to consult the data in the table that follows this discussion.

Some agreed-upon procedures related to generating estimates for key variables in equation (2-1) follow:

> **1.** The financial market environment over the 1993 to 1996 period is considered representative of the prospective tone of the market near the time of offering the new bonds to the investing public. This means that 4-year averages will be used as benchmarks for some

of the variable estimates. All estimates will be rounded off to hundredths of a percent; thus, 6.288 becomes 6.29 percent.

2. The real risk-free rate of interest is the difference between the calculated average yield on 3-month Treasury bills and the inflation rate.

3. The default-risk premium is estimated by the difference between the average yield on Aaa-rated bonds and 30-year Treasury bonds.

4. The maturity premium is estimated by the difference between the average yield on 30-year Treasury bonds and 3-month Treasury bills.

5. Large Truck's bonds will be traded on the New York Exchange for bonds, so the liquidity premium will be slight. It will be greater than zero, however, because the secondary market for the firm's bonds is more uncertain than that of some other truck producers. It is estimated at 3 basis points. A basis point is one-hundredth of 1 percent.

Now place your output into the format equation (2-1) so that the nominal interest rate can be estimated and the size of each variable can also be inspected for reasonableness and discussion with the chief financial officer. Make sure that you can identify the size of: the inflation-risk premium, the default-risk premium, the maturity premium, and the liquidity premium.

The data necessary to solve this problem are contained in the following table.

Interest Rate Levels and Inflation Rates 1981–1996			
Year	3-Month Treasury Bills %	30-Year Treasury Bonds %	Aaa-Rated Corporate Bonds %	Inflation Rate %
1981	14.08	13.44	14.17	8.9
1982	10.69	12.76	13.79	3.9
1983	8.63	11.18	12.04	3.8
1984	9.52	12.39	12.71	4.0
1985	7.49	10.79	11.37	3.8
1986	5.98	7.80	9.02	1.1
1987	5.82	8.58	9.38	4.4
1988	6.68	8.96	9.71	4.4
1989	8.12	8.45	9.26	4.6
1990	7.51	8.61	9.32	6.1
1991	5.42	8.14	8.77	3.1
1992	3.45	7.67	8.14	2.9
1993	3.02	6.59	7.22	2.7
1994	4.29	7.37	7.97	2.7
1995	5.51	6.88	7.59	2.5
1996	5.02	6.71	7.37	3.3
Mean	6.95	9.15	9.86	3.89

SOURCE: *Federal Reserve Bulletin,* various issues, and *Federal Reserve Statistical Releases* H.15 (519), G.13 (415), various issues.

STUDY PROBLEMS (SET B)

2-1B. (*Inflation and Interest Rates*) What would you expect the nominal rate of interest to be if the real rate is 6 percent and the expected inflation rate is 4 percent?

2-2B. (*Inflation and Interest Rates*) Assume the expected inflation rate is 5 percent. If the current real rate of interest is 7 percent, what ought the nominal rate of interest be?

2-3B. (*Inflation and Interest Rates*) What would you expect the nominal rate of interest to be if the real rate is 5 percent and the expected inflation rate is 3 percent?

2-4B. (*Inflation and Interest Rates*) Assume the expected inflation rate is 4 percent. If the current real rate of interest is 6 percent, what ought the nominal rate of interest be?

2-5B. (*Inflation and Interest Rates*) Assume the expected inflation rate is 9 percent. If the current real rate of interest is 5 percent, what would you expect the nominal rate of interest to be?

Learning Objectives

Active Applications

World Finance

Practice

CHAPTER 3

EVALUATING A FIRM'S FINANCIAL PERFORMANCE AND MEASURING CASH FLOW

INTRODUCTION

E valuating the performance of a firm using its financial statements can be a tricky business. The difficulty is generally not due to deliberate attempts by corporate managers and their accountants to mislead you. The problem relates to the substantial flexibility inherent in the set of rules and principles that accountants follow in preparing a firm's financial statements (generally accepted accounting principles, or GAAP). For example, consider the words of wisdom offered by Warren Buffet in the 1990 annual report of Berkshire Hathaway, Inc.

> The term "earnings" has a precise ring to it. And when an earnings figure is accompanied by an unqualified auditor's certificate, a naive reader might think it comparable in certitude to pi, calculated to dozens of decimal places. In reality, however, earnings can be as pliable as putty when a charlatan heads the company reporting them. Eventually truth will surface, but in the meantime a lot of money can change hands. Indeed, some important American fortunes have been created by the monetization of accounting mirages....
>
> So where does this leave the analyst who attempts to evaluate the financial performance of a firm using its financial statements? The answer is that one must seek to understand the subtle differences in accounting practice and the effect that they can have on reported earnings. Analyzing financial performance using accounting statements is not simply a mechanical process. It requires the analyst not only to "crunch the numbers" but to understand where the numbers came from.

With this caveat from one of the most successful investors ever, we begin our study of how to interpret and use a firm's financial statements.

CHAPTER PREVIEW

In chapter 2, we looked at the workings of the financial markets. We found that these markets provide the means for bringing together investors (savers) with the users of capital (businesses that provide products and services to the consumer). There we looked at the world as the economist sees it, with an eye for understanding the marketplace where managers go to acquire capital. It is these financial markets that determine the value of a firm, and, given our goal of maximizing shareholder value, no issue is more fundamental to our study. However, we now want to alter our perspective. In this chapter, we will see the world of finance more as the accountant sees it.

Although some might argue that the accountant has less to say to us than the economist, it is an undeniable fact that a significant part of the data used in financial management is provided by the accountant. Accounting is the language of finance. Thus chapter 3 reviews the firm's basic financial statements and discusses the use of financial ratios to analyze them. The basic financial statements include the income statement, balance sheet, and cash flow statement. We first review the basic format of the firm's financial statements with particular attention given to the cash flow statement. This statement is important in financial analysis because it focuses on cash rather than income or profits. Our discussion of financial ratios incorporates four categories of ratios: firm liquidity, operating profitability, financing decisions, and return on equity. We conclude our discussion of financial statements analysis with an overview of an integrative approach to ratio analysis known as Du Pont analysis.

Two axioms are especially important in this chapter: Axiom 3 tells us that Cash—Not Profits—Is King. At times, cash is more important than profits. Thus in this chapter, considerable time will be devoted to learning how to measure cash flows. Axiom 7 warns us there may be a conflict between management and owners, especially in large firms where managers and owners have different incentives. That is, **Managers Won't Work for the Owners Unless It's in Their Best Interest to do so.**

Although the management is an agent of the owners, experience suggests that managers do not always act in the best interest of the owners.[1] The incentives for the managers are at times different from those of the owners. Thus the firm's common stockholders, as well as other providers of capital (such as bankers), have a need for information that can be used to monitor the managers' actions. Because the owners of large companies do not have access to internal information about the firm's operations, they must rely on public information from any and all sources. One of the main sources of such information comes from the company's financial statements provided by the firm's accountants. Although this information is by no means perfect, it is an important source used by outsiders to assess a company's activities.

In addition to the investors, the managers themselves have a need for financial information to evaluate their decisions. If they are to have any hope of evaluating their own decisions and the decisions of others within their organization, they need to understand the financial consequences of their decisions. Only with this information can a financial decision maker plan and control activities within the firm effectively.[2]

---

[1]For a general discussion of this issue, including a comparison of perspectives from different countries, see Steven Kaplan, "Corporate Governance and Corporate Performance," *Journal of Applied Corporate Finance*, Winter 1997, pp. 86–93.

[2]Chapter 4 develops the use of financial planning and control techniques based on the firm's pro forma or projected financial statements.

BASIC FINANCIAL STATEMENTS

As we set the stage for gaining a better understanding of financial management, it is imperative to know the "coin of the realm" used to describe a company's financial position. To a large extent, this "coin" is the firm's financial or accounting statements.

We can think of financial statements as consisting of certain pieces of important information about the firm's operations that are reported in the form of (1) an income statement, (2) a balance sheet, and (3) statement of cash flows. We will look at each of these statements of cash flows in turn.

The Income Statement

An **income statement** measures the financial results of a firm's operations for a specific period, such as a year. The statement measures the income the firm provides to its owners, which can either be (1) paid out to them in dividends, or (2) retained and reinvested by the firm. It is helpful to think of the income statement as comprising four types of activities:

1. Selling the product or service.
2. The cost of producing or acquiring the goods or services sold.
3. The expenses incurred in marketing and distributing the product or service to the customer, along with administrative operating expenses.
4. The financing costs of doing business; for example, interest paid to creditors and dividend payments to the preferred stockholders (but not to the common stockholders).

These "income-statement activities" are represented graphically in Figure 3.1. In this figure, we observe that the top part of the income statement, beginning with sales and continuing down through the **operating income** or **earnings before interest and taxes**, is affected solely by the first three activities, or what is considered the firm's operating activities. No financing costs are included to this point.

Below the line reporting operating income, we see the results of the firm's financing decisions, along with the taxes that are due on the company's income. Here the company's **financing costs** are shown, first in the form of interest expenses and then preferred

Income statement

The statement of profit or loss for the period is comprised of net revenues less expenses for the period.

Operating income (earnings before interest and taxes)

Profit from sales minus total operating expenses.

Financing costs

Costs incurred by a company that often include interest expenses and preferred dividends.

Figure 3.1 The Income Statement: An Overview

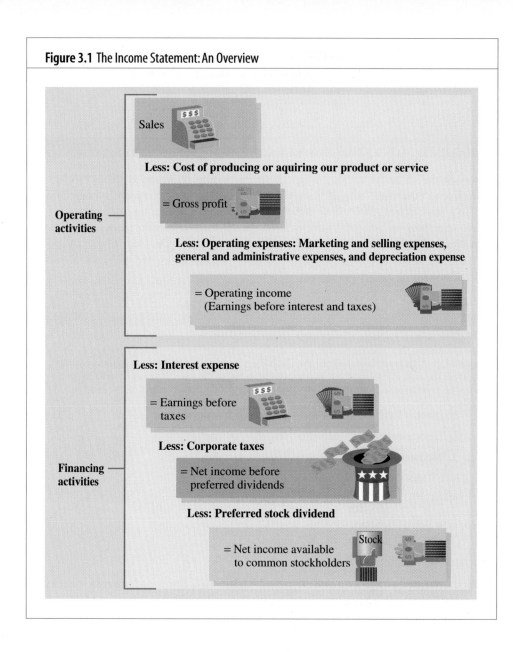

Earnings before taxes

Operating income minus interest expense.

Tax expenses

Tax liability determined by earnings before taxes.

Net income available to common stockholders (net income)

A figure representing the firm's profit or loss for the period. It also represents the earnings available to the firm's common and preferred stockholders.

dividends. The tax rates imposed on the company's **earnings before taxes** determine the amount of the tax liability, or the **tax expenses**. (It is important to note here that interest expense is a tax-deductible expense—it is subtracted to compute earnings before taxes, which is also the firm's taxable income, whereas preferred dividends are not tax deductible.)[3] The final number, **net income available to common stockholders** (frequently just called **net income**), is the income that may be distributed to the company's owners (usually in the form of dividends) or reinvested in the company, provided of course there is cash available to do so. As we shall see later, however, the fact that a firm has a positive net income does not necessarily mean it has any cash—possibly a surprising result to us, but one we shall come to understand.

---

[3]Notice that interest is a tax-deductible expense, whereas preferred dividends are paid after taxes have been calculated.

Table 3.1

	McDonald's Corporation Consolidated Income Statement For year ended December 31, 1996 (in millions)
Sales	$10,648
Cost of goods sold	6,163
Gross profit	$ 4,485
Operating expenses:	
Marketing expenses and general and administrative expenses	$ 1,435
Depreciation	456
Total operating expenses	$ 1,891
Operating income	$ 2,594
Interest expense	343
Earnings before taxes	$ 2,251
Income taxes	678
Net income available to common stockholders	$ 1,573
Net income available to common stockholders	$ 1,573
Dividends	820
Change in retained earnings	$ 753

An example of an income statement is provided in Table 3.1 for the McDonald's Corporation. As shown in the table, McDonald's had sales of $10,648 million for the 12-month period ending December 31, 1996, and the cost of goods sold was $6,163 million. (The numbers for McDonald's are expressed in millions, so McDonald's sales were actually about $10.6 billion, with cost of goods sold of almost $6.2 billion.) The result is a gross profit of $4,485 million ($4.5 billion). The firm then had $1,891 million in operating expenses, which included selling or marketing expenses, general and administrative expenses, and depreciation expenses. After deducting operating expenses, the firm's operating profits (earnings before interest and taxes) amounted to $2,594 million ($2.6 billion). This amount represents the before-tax profits generated as if the McDonald's Corporation were an all-equity company. To this point, we have calculated the profits resulting only from operating activities, as opposed to financing decisions such as how much debt or equity is used to finance the company's operations.[4]

We next deduct McDonald's interest expense (the amount paid for using debt financing) of $343 million to arrive at the company's earnings before tax of $2,251 million ($2.25 billion). Finally, we deduct the income taxes of $678 million to leave the net income available to common stockholders of $1,573 ($1.57 billion). At the bottom of the income statement, we also see the amount of common dividends paid by the firm to its owners in the amount of $820 million, leaving $753 million, which increases retained earnings in the firm's 1996 balance sheet. (When we look at McDonald's balance sheet in the next section, notice that the firm's retained earnings increased by $753 million.)

---

[4]The McDonald's Corporation financial statements presented in this chapter have been simplified considerably with some loss of accuracy in details, but doing so avoids unnecessary complexity.

The Balance Sheet

Whereas the income statement reports the results from operating the business for a period of time, such as a year, the **balance sheet** provides a snapshot of the firm's financial position at a specific point in time, presenting its asset holdings, liabilities, and owner-supplied capital. Assets represent the resources owned by the firm, whereas the liabilities and owners' equity indicate how those resources are financed.

The difference between the timing of an income statement and a balance sheet may be represented graphically as follows.

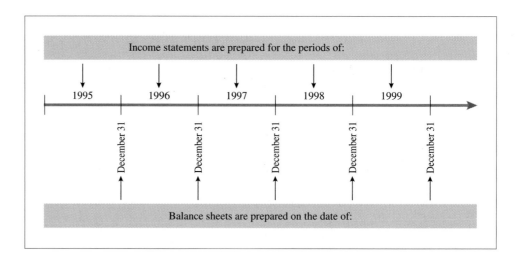

Here we see five periods of operations, 1995 through 1999. There would be an income statement for the period of January 1 through December 31 for each of the five years' operations and a balance sheet reporting the company's financial position as of December 31 of each year. Thus, the balance sheet on December 31, 1998, is a statement of the company's financial position at that particular date, which is the result of all financial transactions since the company began its operations.

Figure 3.2 gives us the basic ingredients of a balance sheet. In the figure, the assets fall into three categories:

1. **Current assets**—consisting primarily of cash, marketable securities, accounts receivable, inventories, and prepaid expenses.
2. **Fixed or long-term assets**—comprising equipment, buildings, and land.
3. **Other assets**—all assets not otherwise included in the firm's current assets or fixed assets, such as patents, long-term investments in securities, and goodwill.

In reporting the dollar amounts of these various assets, the conventional practice is to report the value of the assets and liabilities on a historical cost basis. Thus the balance sheet is not intended to represent the current market value of the company, but rather reports the historical transactions recorded at their cost. Determining a fair value of the business is a different matter.

The remaining part of the balance sheet (the right side of Figure 3.2), headed "Liabilities and Equity," indicates how the firm has financed its investments in assets. The principal sources of financing are debt (liabilities) and equity. The **debt** consists of such sources as credit extended from suppliers (accounts payable) or a loan from a bank (including notes payable and mortgages). The **equity** includes the stockholders' investment in the firm (par value plus paid in capital) and the cumulative profits retained in the business up to the date of the balance sheet, or **retained earnings**.

Balance sheet

A statement of financial position at a particular date. The form of the statement follows the balance sheet equation: total assets = total liabilities + owner's equity.

Current assets

Current assets consist primarily of cash, marketable securities, accounts receivable, inventories, and prepaid expenses.

Fixed or long-term assets

Assets comprising equipment, buildings, and land.

Other assets

Assets not included in current assets or fixed assets.

Debt

Consists of such sources as credit extended by suppliers or a loan from a bank.

Equity

Stockholder's investment in the firm and the cumulative profits retained in the business up to the date of the balance sheet.

Retained earnings

The cumulative earnings that have been retained and reinvested in the firm over its life.

Figure 3.2 The Balance Sheet: An Overview

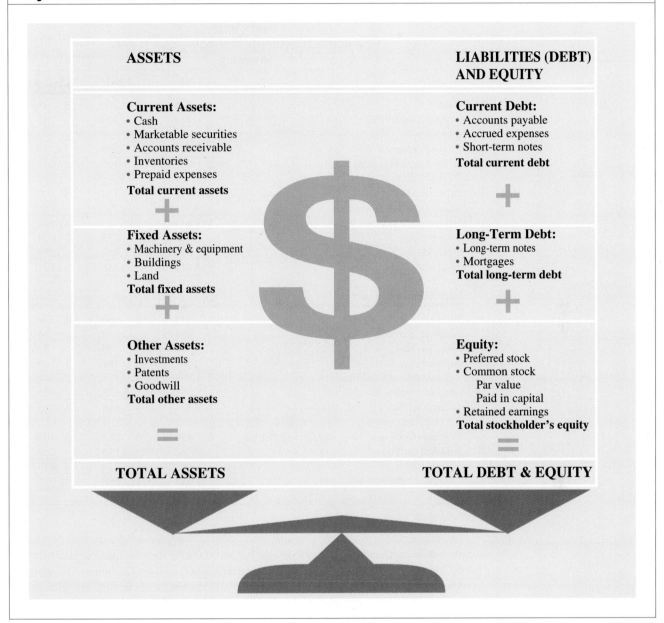

It is important to remember that the change in retained earnings each year is equal to the firm's net income for the year less the dividends paid to the shareholders during the year—thus the name *retained earnings*.

Balance sheets for the McDonald's Corporation are presented in Table 3.2 for both December 31, 1995, and December 31, 1996, along with the changes in each amount between years. By referring to the two balance sheets, we can see the financial position of the firm both at the beginning and end of 1996. Furthermore, by examining the two balance sheets, along with the income statement for 1996, we will have a more complete picture of the firm's operations. We are then able to see what McDonald's looked like at the beginning of 1996

Table 3.2

McDonald's Corporation
Balance Sheet
For years ended December 31, 1995 and December 31, 1996
(in millions)

Assets	1995	1996	Change
Cash	$ 335	$ 330	$ (5)
Accounts receivable	414	495	81
Inventory	58	70	12
Prepaid expenses	149	208	59
Total current assets	$ 956	$ 1,103	$ 147
Gross fixed assets	$17,137	$19,134	$1,997
Accumulated depreciation	(4,326)	(4,782)	(456)
Net fixed assets	$12,811	$14,352	$1,541
Investments	755	779	24
Other assets	893	1,152	259
Total assets	$15,415	$17,386	$1,971

Liabilities and Equity	1995	1996	Change
Short-term notes payable	$ 611	$ 660	$ 49
Accounts payable	564	638	74
Taxes payable	23	55	32
Accrued expenses	597	782	185
Total current liabilities	$ 1,795	$ 2,135	$ 340
Long-term notes payable	5,758	6,533	775
Total liabilities	$ 7,553	$ 8,668	$1,115
Common stock (par value and paid-in capital)	$ 480	$ 583	$ 103
Retained earnings	7,382	8,135	753
Total equity	$ 7,862	$ 8,718	$ 856
Total liabilities and equity	$15,415	$17,386	$1,971

(balance sheet on December 31, 1995), what happened during the year (income statement for 1996), and the final outcome at the end of the year (balance sheet on December 31, 1996).

The balance sheet data for the McDonald's Corporation show that the firm ended the prior year (1995) with about $15.4 billion ($15,415 million) in assets, compared to $17.4 billion ($17,386 million) a year later at the end of 1996, an increase of $1.97 billion. Most of this growth was in long-term assets, namely, an increase of $2 billion ($1,997 million) in gross plant and equipment, also called fixed assets. In the bottom half of the balance sheet, we should notice the growth in debt and equity primarily occurred in the long-term notes payable (an increase of $775 million), along with an increase in retained earnings of $753 million. This growth in long-term debt (liabilities) and retained earnings (equity) accounts for a majority of the increase in total assets.

Thus far, we have examined two important financial statements used by managers and investors alike: (1) to know how profitable the firm has been for a given time period (income statement), and (2) to see a firm's financial position at a given point in time (balance sheet). While these two statements are indispensable for measuring firm performance, we still have not examined how the firm's cash flows were generated and

How Much Were Daimler-Benz's Profits?

Foreign companies are not subject to the same financial reporting standards as U.S. firms. How much difference is there? Consider two examples.

The first German firm to list its stock on the New York Stock Exchange, Daimler-Benz, reported a $100-million profit in 1994 under German accounting rules, but that translated into a $1-billion loss after applying U.S. GAAP. Second, the 1995 earnings for the Italian firm, Gucci, would have been 66 percent higher under international accounting standards than under U.S. standards.

Owing to the large differences in earnings that can result depending on the country where the earnings are reported, an International Accounting Standards Committee (IASC) is developing international accounting guidelines for firms to follow. If accepted by the Securities and Exchange Commission, these standards could allow more foreign businesses to list their stocks on U.S. exchanges—an aspiration that many have as a way to raise more capital. Thus, in anticipation, some European companies have already converted to international rules in the hopes of being able to list their stocks on the New York Stock Exchange or on NASDAQ within the next few years.

This change, if made, will require U.S. investors interested in foreign companies to understand the differences in accounting between the international rules and the U.S. GAAP, which will not be an easy task. Otherwise, who is to say how much a company made in profits?

used in its operations—a very important consideration. After all, **Axiom 3** tells us that cash is king. That leads us to our last financial statement critical to managing and evaluating a firm—the statement of cash flow.

Statement of Cash Flows

> **STOP AND THINK**
>
> *In this section, we will learn how to construct a firm's statement of cash flows. We could limit our study to interpreting the statement and not get into the computations. However, experience suggests that our understanding of cash flows is limited if we do not know what drives the numbers. Also, without the computations, we will not be able to grasp the relationship between a firm's profits and its cash flows—an item of considerable importance.*

The final statement for consideration is the **statement of cash flows**, which shows the actual cash flows generated by the firm for the year. The primary categories for this statement are presented in Figure 3.3. Here we see that the cash flows generated are divided into three main areas: (1) cash flows from operations, (2) cash flows from investments made by the firm, and (3) cash flows from financing transactions, such as issuing stock and borrowing or repaying debt.

Table 3.3 shows a statement of cash flow for the McDonald's Corporation. The data needed to construct a statement of cash flow come from two sources: (1) balance sheets for

Statement of cash flows

The statement of cash flow enumerates the cash receipts and cash disbursements for a specified interval of time (usually 1 year).

the beginning of 1996 (actually December 31, 1995) and the end of 1996, and (2) the income statement for 1996. Let's look at the computations required in determining the cash flow for McDonald's. To do so, we will need to make frequent use of the company's income statement (Table 3.1) and the balance sheets (Table 3.2).

Figure 3.3 The Cash Flow Statement: An Overview

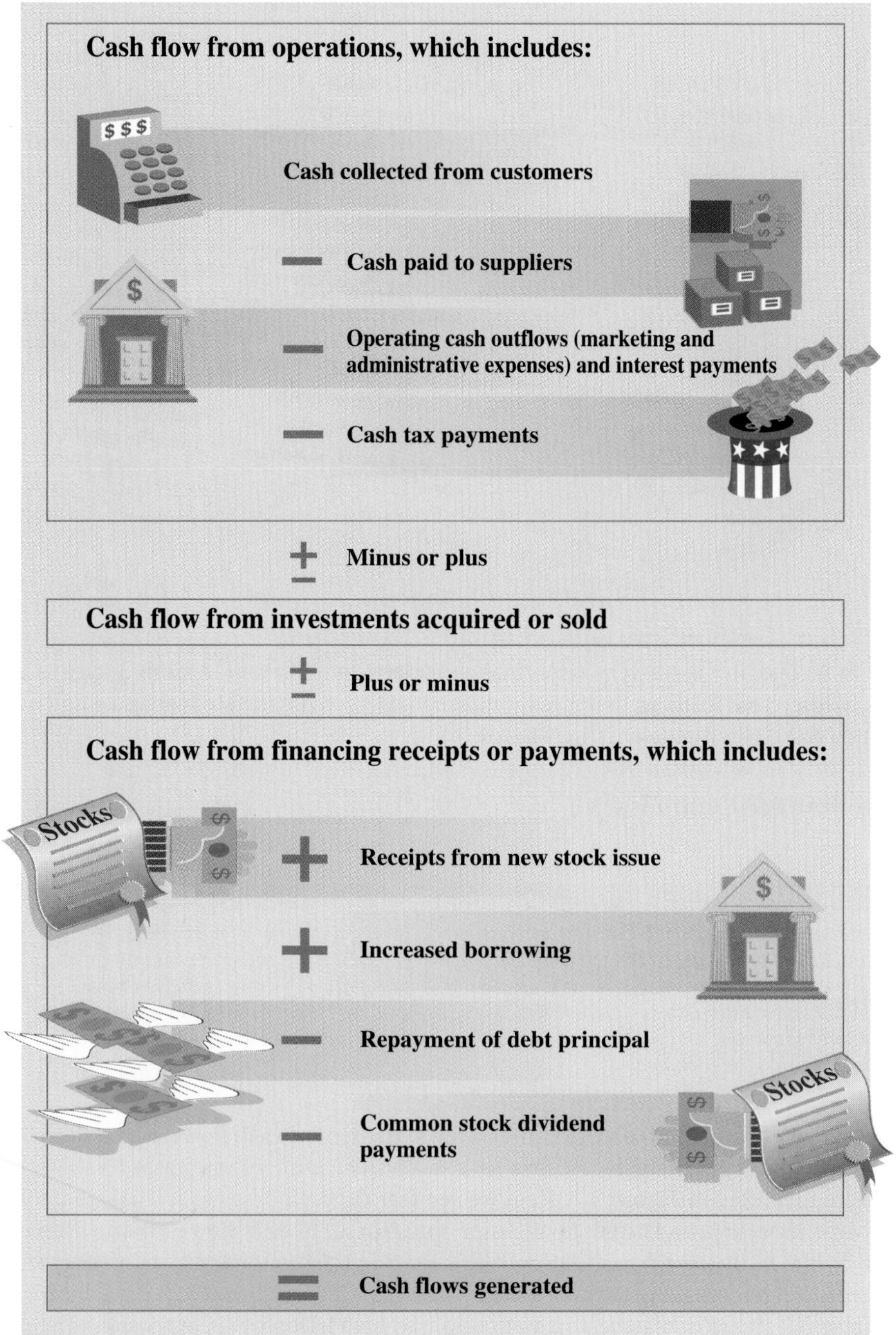

Cash flow from operations, which includes:

Cash collected from customers

— Cash paid to suppliers

— Operating cash outflows (marketing and administrative expenses) and interest payments

— Cash tax payments

± Minus or plus

Cash flow from investments acquired or sold

± Plus or minus

Cash flow from financing receipts or payments, which includes:

+ Receipts from new stock issue

+ Increased borrowing

— Repayment of debt principal

— Common stock dividend payments

= Cash flows generated

Table 3.3

McDonald's Corporation
Statement of Cash Flows
For Year ended December 31, 1996
(in millions)

Cash Flow From Operating Activities

Cash inflows received from customers

Net sales	$10,648	
Less increase in accounts receivable	(81)	
Cash inflows from customers		$10,567
Cash paid to suppliers		
Cost of goods sold	$ (6,163)	
Plus increase in inventory	(12)	
Less increase in accounts payable	74	
Cash paid to suppliers		$ (6,101)
Other operating cash outflows		
Marketing expenses and general and		
administrative expenses	$ (1,435)	
Interest expense	(343)	
Plus increase in prepaid expenses	(59)	
Less increase in accrued expenses	185	
Other operating cash outflows		$ (1,652)
Cash tax payments		
Provision for income taxes	$ (678)	
Less increase in taxes payable	22	
Cash tax payments		$ (656)
Cash flow from operating activities		$ 2,168

Cash Flow From Investing Activities

Increase in gross plant and equipment	$ (1,997)	
Increase in investments	(24)	
Increase in other assets	(259)	
Cash flow from investing activities		$ (2,280)

Cash Flow From Financing Activities

Increase in short-term notes	$ 49	
Increase in long-term notes	775	
Net change in common stock	103	
Common stock dividends	(820)	
Cash flow from financing activities		$ 107
Net Change in Cash		$ (5)

Cash Flows from Operations

As already noted, a firm's **cash flows from operations** consist of (1) collections from customers, (2) payments to suppliers for the purchase of materials, (3) other operating cash outflows, such as marketing and administrative expenses and interest payments, and (4) cash tax payments.

Cash flows from operations

Cash flow that consists of (1) collections from customers; (2) payments to suppliers for the purchase of materials; (3) other operating cash flows such as marketing and administrative expenses and interest payments; and (4) cash tax payments.

1. **Collections from customers.** Our beginning point is to determine how much the firm has collected from its customers. We know how much they sold (sales revenue), but we want to know what was actually collected in cash. To find this number, we simply take the firm's sales and subtract the change in accounts receivable. For example, if a firm had $200,000 in sales during a year, but its accounts receivable increased from $50,000 to $70,000, or by $20,000, that means that $20,000 of the sales were not collected. Thus the firm's collections were only $180,000 ($200,000 − $20,000). For the McDonald's Corporation, sales were $10,648 million (about $10.6 billion), but accounts receivable increased $81 million from $414 million to $495 million. (See the change in accounts receivable in Table 3.2). Thus actual collections were $10,567 million ($10.6 billion), calculated as $10,648 million less $81 million. This small difference means that the firm's sales and its cash collections from customers are essentially the same.

2. **Payments to suppliers.** When a firm purchases products from suppliers, the firm's inventories are increased. When the product is sold, the inventory decreases, and cost of goods sold in the income statement increases. Thus total purchases of products from suppliers are reflected in the cost of goods sold plus any increase in inventories. Then the firm will either pay for the products or rely on additional credit from the supplier, which is shown in accounts payable in the balance sheet. The actual payment to suppliers may therefore be calculated as follows:

$$\begin{pmatrix} \text{payment} \\ \text{to suppliers} \end{pmatrix} = \begin{pmatrix} \text{cost of} \\ \text{goods sold} \end{pmatrix} + \begin{pmatrix} \text{change in} \\ \text{inventories} \end{pmatrix} - \begin{pmatrix} \text{change in} \\ \text{accounts} \\ \text{payable} \end{pmatrix} \qquad (3\text{-}1)$$

For McDonald's, the cost of goods sold for 1996 was $6,163 million ($6.16 billion); inventories increased from $58 million to $70 million, or by $12 million, and accounts payable increased $74 million, from $564 million to $638 million. Thus payments to suppliers were $6,101 million, computed as follows:

$$\begin{pmatrix} \text{payment} \\ \text{to suppliers} \end{pmatrix} = \begin{pmatrix} \text{cost of} \\ \text{goods sold} \end{pmatrix} + \begin{pmatrix} \text{change in} \\ \text{inventories} \end{pmatrix} - \begin{pmatrix} \text{change in} \\ \text{accounts} \\ \text{payable} \end{pmatrix} \cdot$$

$$= \$6,163 + 12 - \$74 \text{ million}$$

$$= \$6,101$$

3. **Other operating cash outflows and interest payments.** We next calculate the actual cash outflows listed as operating expenses and interest expense in the income statement. We only include those operating expenses that are cash outflows and not such items as depreciation expense or other noncash items. In addition, we adjust for any other changes in the balance sheets that relate to operating expenses. Typically these adjustments involve the changes in prepaid expenses and accrued expenses:

   a. We add any changes in prepaid expenses; even though they have not been expensed on an accrual basis, they have been paid.

   b. We deduct the changes in accrued expenses and interest payable; although these items have been expensed, they have not yet been paid.

   We see in Table 3.3 that the other operating cash outflows for McDonald's came to $1,435 million, the combination of marketing expenses, general and administrative expenses (without any depreciation expense), interest expense, plus the $59 million increase in prepaid expenses, and less the $185 million increase in accrued expenses.[5]

4. **Cash tax payments.** The tax expense shown in a firm's income statement is often not the actual amount paid at that time. The provision for taxes in the income statement is the

---

[5]In the income statement, we made a point to compute operating income before deducting interest expenses; that is, operating income or earnings before interest and taxes represents the profits from operations without regard to financing costs, such as interest. Now when calculating cash flows from operations, we deduct interest payments. Why the inconsistency? The answer is that our cash flow statement follows the conventional format used by accountants.

amount attributable to the income reported, but the company may be permitted to defer part of the payment. Thus the cash payment would equal the provision for taxes reported in the income statement less (plus) any increase (decrease) in accrued or deferred taxes in the balance sheet. For the McDonald's Corporation, the cash tax payment is $656 million—the $678 in the provision for taxes in the income statement less the $22 million increase in taxes payable as reflected from a comparison of the two balance sheets in Table 3.2.

The final cash flows from operations are shown to be $2,375 million, the net change from the above cash flows ($10,567 − $6,101 − $1,435 − $656 million).

Cash Flows—Investment Activities

Now that we have calculated the cash flows that were generated from the day-to-day operations at McDonald's, we next want to determine the amount of cash used for investments by the firm—the **cash flows from investment activities**. As shown in Table 3.3, $2,280 million ($2.28 billion) was expended for investments during 1996, including $1,997 million ($2 billion) for gross fixed assets (an increase from $17,137 million to $19,134 million); plus the $24 million increase in investments ($779 − $755 million) and the $259 million increase in other assets ($1,152 − $893 million). We should note that we view the change in *gross* fixed assets, not *net* fixed assets. Nor do we consider the change in accumulated depreciation. Since depreciation is a noncost expense, it is to be ignored when measuring cash flows.

Cash flows from investment activities

Cash flows that include the purchase of fixed assets and other assets.

Cash Flows—Financing Activities

The last area is **cash flows from financing activities**, including any cash inflows or outflows to or from the firm's investors, both lenders of debt and owners. For 1996, McDonald's Corporation, had a small positive cash flow from financing activities in the amount of $107 million. The company increased both short-term debt ($49 million) and long-term debt ($775 million), and had an increase in common stock ($130 million), and paid $820 million in common stock dividends.

Cash flows from financing activities

Cash flow that includes proceeds from long-term debt or issuing common stock, and payments made for stock dividends.

We may now summarize the cash flows shown in Table 3.3 for the McDonald's Corporation as follows:

Cash flows from operations	$2,168
Cash flows—investment activities	(2,280)
Cash flows—financing activities	107
Total cash flows	$ (5)

Thus the total cash flows generated by the McDonald's Corporation from all its activities come to a negative $5 million in 1996. (We should also note that the firm's change in cash balances between two balance sheets will always equal the cash flow shown in the statement of cash flows for McDonald's cash balance in 1995 ($335 million) decreased $5 million ($330 million)—the exact amount of the firm's 1996 cash flows.

Measuring Cash Flows From Operations: An Alternative Approach

The format used in Table 3.3 to measure cash flow from operations is called the **direct method**. It begins with the cash flow collected from the firm's customers and then subtracts the different cash outflows occurring in regular operations of the business, such as the money paid to suppliers and for employee wages, just to mention two examples. We could also measure cash flow from operations by the **indirect method**. This approach,

Direct method

A statement of cash flow that begins with sales and converts the income statement from an accrual basis to a cash basis.

Indirect method

A statement of cash flow that beings with net income and then adds back the non-cash expenses, and other items that affect a company's cash flows.

which gives us the same answer as the direct method, is shown for the McDonald's Corporation in Table 3.4. In this table, we see that the indirect method begins with net income and then adds back all expenses related to the firm's operations that did not result in a cash outflow for the period. The actual steps for calculating cash flows from operations using the indirect method follow.

To the firm's net income:

1. Add back any noncash expenses that have been deducted, such as depreciation.
2. Subtract (add) any increases (decreases) in current assets, excluding cash.
3. Add (subtract) any increases (decreases) in non-interest bearing, short-term liabilities, such as payables and accruals.

(Note that the last two adjustments—changes in current assets and non-interest bearing current liabilities are the same ones made when we computed cash flows from operations using the direct method.)

So, in a sense, the two methods for arriving at cash flow from operations differ only in terms of whether we start at the top (direct method) or the bottom (indirect method) of the income statement. Both methods simply convert the firm's statement of net income to its cash flow equivalent.

The McDonald's Corporation: What Have We Learned?

Based on our review of the McDonald's financial statements, we can now draw some conclusions. To this point, we have learned that:

- The firm has used its cash flows from operations and from new financing to expand the asset base of the company.
- The main sources of new financing for the firm came from borrowing long-term.
- McDonald's has little in the way of current assets, especially accounts receivable and inventory. Most of the firm's investments are in fixed assets.
- The primary use of the firm's cash flows during 1996 went to investing in fixed assets.

To better understand the small investment in accounts receivable and inventories and the large amounts in fixed assets, we have to think about the nature of McDonald's business. For a restaurant business, inventories will be small—you don't want to keep a lot of lettuce on hand. Also, many of the restaurants are owned by franchisees and not the McDonald's Corporation itself. Thus McDonald's has no inventory whatsoever related to

Table 3.4 The Indirect Method for Measuring Cash Flows From Operations The McDonald's Corporation for Year Ending December 31, 1996 ($ Millions)		
Net income available to common stockholders (from the income statement)		$1,573
Add (deduct) to reconcile net income to net cash flow		
Depreciation expense		456
Less		
Increase in accounts receivable	$ (81)	
Increase in inventories	(12)	
Increase in prepaid expenses	(59)	(152)
Plus		
Increase in accounts payable	74	
Increase in accrued expenses	185	
Increase in taxes payable	32	291
Cash flows from operations		$2,168

Phar-Mor Officers Embezzle $500 million

In April 1992, five executives at the drugstore chain, Phar-Mor, Inc., gathered for a Saturday meeting at the company's Youngstown, Ohio, headquarters. Phar-Mor President Michael "Mickey" Monus, Chief Financial Officer Patrick Finn, and several members of the company's accounting staff were present. On the agenda was Phar-Mor's upcoming audit by its outside accountant, Coopers & Lybrand.

There was a problem: Phar-Mor had to keep the auditors from discovering that over the past 4 years, Monus, Finn, and other top executives had been cooking the company's books—which by now were done to a turn. For fiscal year 1991 alone, reported income was overstated by $145 million. "We're getting real close to audit time again," accountant John Anderson said nervously. "And we got some major problems down here. . . . You know I'm on the front line with these auditors, and if something comes out to light, I'm there first and I have to sit there and try and cover this stuff."

The participants ran through ways to "cover this stuff." They could hide the $145 million income overstatement with payments from vendors, couldn't they? "We gotta put some things in, in place that automatically take it down so we don't gotta look at it," said Monus. He began pacing back and forth. "Gotta get through the audit. . . . We're not in a good spot here. Keep our fingers crossed and get through it and get the number down."

Monus would have understood that he was in far too deep for a lucky break if he had known that one of his subordinates was secretly taping the meeting. Almost 4 years later, the recording of that Saturday afternoon discussion would help convict the Phar-Mor president on 109 felony counts of fraud, embezzlement, and tax charges. It would also become one of the defense weapons wielded most vigorously by Phar-Mor's auditors, Coopers & Lybrand, which faced a trial of its own stemming from Phar-Mor's collapse.

Phar-Mor's success was based on a simple idea that initially showed tremendous promise. In the early 1980s, Monus visited a deep-discount store in Cleveland and came away with his own plan for a drugstore chain, one that he managed to convince Giant Eagle to bankroll. All non-pharmaceutical items would be bought in special, high-volume deals with suppliers and marked up a flat 20 percent. Phar-Mor stores might not carry every brand, size, or flavor of toothpaste all the time, but the toothpaste it did carry would be extraordinarily cheap for consumers. The concept proved to be an immediate hit.

It was, however, a dangerous strategy. The 20 percent markup translated into a gross profit margin—markup as a percentage of sale price—that was razor thin: 16.5 percent, as compared to about 25 percent gross profit margin for discount stores such as Kmart or 40 percent for nondiscount drugstores. A small drop in gross profit margin, as little as one percentage point, could have a dramatic effect on the company's net income.

That's exactly what happened in the late 1980s, as Phar-Mor opened stores in states beyond its base in Ohio and Pennsylvania and began running into serious competition from national chains, such as Wal-Mart. In response, the company cut prices and began selling loss leaders—cans of Coke for 35 cents each, for example. In 1988 Phar-Mor's Vice-President of Finance Jeffrey Walley spot-checked more than 500 items in Phar-Mor stores and discovered to his alarm that the gross profit margin had dropped by a full percentage point. "It will be extremely difficult to remain profitable at 15.5 percent gross [profit margin]," he warned in a memo to Phar-Mor management. To raise prices, though, would have meant admitting to the world—including potential investors—that the beguilingly simple Phar-Mor strategy just didn't work.

The Phar-Mor story suggests that even professional accountants can be deceived by a firm's managers if that is the intent. Also, many of the investors in Phar-Mor were sophisticated businesses, including such firms as Sears, Roebuck & Company, Westinghouse Electric, Debartolo Realty and the Equitable. The moral of the story: If someone is determined to cheat you, they can most likely find a way.

SOURCE: Adapted from "Knocked Off Balance," *The American Lawyer* (July/August 1996). Used by permission from *The American Lawyer* © 1996 American Lawyer Media, L.P.

these units. Regarding accounts receivable, the business is largely a cash operation, with the receivables being primarily money owed the firm by the franchises. On the other hand, the McDonald's Corporation owns the real estate for all the stores, whether company-owned or a franchise, which explains the large amount of fixed assets. So by looking at the financial statements for the McDonald's Corporation, we have gained a better understanding of the business.

Profits and Cash Flows

As a final thought about measuring cash flows, there is a popular belief that income plus depreciation is a reasonable measure of a company's cash flows. For instance, taking net income available to common stockholders for McDonald's of $1,573 million and adding back depreciation of $456 million, gives us $2,029 million. Given conventional thought, someone might be tempted to use this amount as an estimate of the firm's cash flows. However, from the cash flow statement, we can see that the cash flows actually decreased $5 million. Thus we can conclude that calculating a firm's cash flow is more complicated than merely adding depreciation expense back to net income. The changes in asset balances resulting from growth are just as important in determining the firm's cash flows as is profits, maybe even more important sometimes. Hence management, particularly of a growth company, is well advised not to limit its attention to profits, but to also focus on cash flows, because they are not the same thing.

Interpreting the Cash Flow Statement

OBJECTIVE 2

As already noted, there are three basic categories of activities related to a firm's cash flows, these being

- Cash flows from operations.
- Cash flows related to the investment or sale of assets (investment activities).
- Cash flows related to financing the firm (financing activities).

To help us understand the basic nature of a firm's cash flows, consider the following cash flow patterns with respect to the three categories:

| | Cash Flow Related To | | |
Cash Flow Pattern	Operations	Investments	Financing
1	+	−	+
2	+	+	−
3	+	−	−
4	−	+	+

For example, a firm with cash flow pattern 1 has positive cash flows from operations, negative investment cash flows, and positive cash flows from financing. How would we describe this company? It is a firm (as is the case of McDonald's) that is using its cash flows from operations and new financing to expand the firm's operations. On the other hand, a company with cash flow pattern 2 is one that is using its positive cash flows from operations and selling off assets to pay down debt and pay owners. Cash flow pattern 3 depicts a firm that is using cash flows from operations to expand the business and to pay down debt and pay owners. Finally, cash flow pattern 4 describes a company that is encountering cash flow problems from operations, which are being covered by selling assets and by borrowing more and/or acquiring more equity financing. There are obviously other possible cash flow patterns—four to be exact—but the above cash flow patterns are sufficient to see the process to be used in interpreting the cash flow statement.[6]

FINANCIAL RATIO ANALYSIS

OBJECTIVE 3

To this point, we have examined financial statements in absolute dollar terms for the purpose of coming to understand a firm's financial position. We chose to use the financial statements for the McDonald's Corporation to illustrate the format and content of the statements. We next want to restate the accounting data in relative terms, or what we call **financial ratios**. Financial ratios help us identify some of the financial strengths and weaknesses of a company. The ratios give us two ways of making meaningful comparisons of a firm's financial data: (1) we can examine the ratios across time (say for the last 5 years) to identify any trends; and (2) we can compare the firm's ratios with those of other firms.

In making a comparison of our firm with other companies, we could select a peer group of companies, or we could use industry norms published by firms such as Dun and Bradstreet, Robert Morris Associates, Standard and Poor's, and Prentice Hall. Dun and Bradstreet, for instance, annually publishes a set of 14 key ratios for each of 125 lines of business. Robert Morris Associates, the association of bank loan and credit officers, publishes a set of 16 key ratios for more than 350 lines of business. In both cases, the ratios are classified by industry and by firm size to provide the basis for more meaningful comparisons.

Financial ratios

Restating the accounting data in relative terms to identify some of the financial strengths and weaknesses of a company.

STOP AND THINK

Mathematically, a financial ratio is nothing more than a ratio whose numerator and denominator are comprised of financial data. Sound simple? Well, in concept it is. The objective in using a ratio when analyzing financial information is simply to standardize the information being analyzed so that comparisons can be made between ratios of different firms or possibly the same firm at different points in time. So try to keep this in mind as you read through the discussion of financial ratios. All we are doing is trying to standardize financial data so that we can make comparisons with industry norms or recognize trends.

We use financial ratios to answer questions about a firm's operations and to evaluate the company's financial performance. Specifically, we can address four important questions:

1. How liquid is the firm?
2. Is management generating adequate *operating* profits on the firm's assets?
3. How is the firm financing its assets?
4. Are the owners (stockholders) receiving an adequate return on *their* investment?

Let's look at each of these questions in turn. In doing so, we will use the balance sheet (Table 3.2) and the income statement (Table 3.3) for the McDonald's Corporation to demonstrate how these questions can be answered.

Question 1: How Liquid Is the Firm?

The **liquidity** of a business is defined as its ability to meet maturing debt obligations. That is, does or will the firm have the resources to pay the creditors when the debt comes due?

Liquidity

The ability of a firm to pay its bills on time, and how quickly a firm converts its liquid assets (accounts receivables and inventories) into cash.

---

[6]For a more complete discussion of these cash flow patterns, see Benton E. Gup, William D. Samson, Michael T. Dugan, Myung J. Kim, and Thawatfchai Jittrapanun, "An Analysis of the Statement of Cash Flow Patterns," *Financial Practice and Education*, Fall 1993, pp. 72–79.

There are two ways to approach the liquidity question. First, we can look at the firm's assets that are relatively liquid in nature and compare them to the amount of the debt coming due in the near term.[7] Second, we can look at how quickly the firm's liquid assets—namely, accounts receivable and inventories—are being converted into cash.

Measuring liquidity: approach 1. The first approach compares (a) cash and the assets that should be converted into cash within the year with (b) the debt (liabilities) that is coming due and payable within the year. The assets here are the *current assets*, and the debt is the *current liabilities* in the balance sheet. Thus we could use the following measure, called the **current ratio**, to estimate a company's relative liquidity:

$$\text{current ratio} = \frac{\text{current assets}}{\text{current liabilities}} \tag{3-2}$$

Furthermore, remembering that the three primary current assets include (1) cash, (2) accounts receivable, and (3) inventories, we could make our measure of liquidity more restrictive by *excluding inventories*, the least liquid of the current assets, in the numerator. This revised ratio is called the **acid-test** (or **quick**) **ratio**, and is calculated as follows:

$$\text{acid-test ratio} = \frac{\text{current assets} - \text{inventories}}{\text{current liabilities}} \tag{3-3}$$

To demonstrate how to compute the current ratio and acid-test ratio, we will use the 1996 balance sheet for the McDonald's Corporation (refer to Table 3.2). To have a standard for comparison, we could use industry norms published by Dun and Bradstreet or any of the other sources mentioned above. However, we had difficulty at finding industry norms that we thought represented comparable companies—not an unusual problem in practice. Thus we chose instead to calculate the average ratios for a group of similar firms or what could be called a *peer group*. The 1996 results for these first two ratios are as follows:

McDonald's Corporation	**Peer-Group Average**

$$\text{current ratio} = \frac{\text{current assets}}{\text{current liabilities}}$$

$$= \frac{\$1,103\text{M}}{\$2,135\text{M}} = 0.52 \qquad\qquad 0.90$$

$$\text{acid-test ratio} = \frac{\text{current assets} - \text{inventories}}{\text{current liabilities}}$$

$$= \frac{\$1,103\text{M} - 70\text{M}}{\$2,135\text{M}} = 0.48 \qquad\qquad 0.62$$

So, in terms of the current ratio and acid-test ratio, McDonald's is significantly less liquid than the average peer-group firm. McDonald's only has $0.52 in current assets for every $1 in current liabilities (debt), compared to $0.90 for comparable firms, and only $0.48 in current assets less inventories per $1 of current debt, compared to $0.62 for the peer group. Given the conventional wisdom that firms should maintain about $2 in current assets for every $1 in current debt—an idea that fails to recognize the unique needs of various companies—McDonald's, and even the industry itself, is less liquid than most other companies.

---

[7]This approach has long been used in the finance community; however, it really measures solvency, not liquidity. A firm is solvent when its assets exceed its liabilities, which is in essence what we will be measuring by this approach. For an in-depth discussion of this issue, see chapter 2 of Terry S. Maness and John T. Zietlow, *Short-Term Financial Management* (New York: Dryden Press, 1997).

Measuring liquidity: approach 2. The second view of liquidity examines the firm's ability to convert accounts receivable and inventory into cash on a timely basis. The conversion of accounts receivable into cash may be measured by computing how long it takes to collect the firm's receivables; that is, how many days of sales are outstanding in the form of accounts receivable? We can answer this question by computing the **average collection period**:

$$\text{average collection period} = \frac{\text{accounts receivable}}{\text{daily credit sales}} \qquad (3\text{-}4)$$

If we assume all the McDonald's Corporation's 1996 sales ($10,648 million in Table 3.1) to be credit sales, as opposed to some cash sales, then the firm's average collection period is 17 days, compared to a peer-group norm of 6 days:

McDonald's Corporation	**Peer-Group Average**

$$\text{average collection period} = \frac{\text{accounts receivable}}{\text{daily credit sales}}$$

$$= \frac{\$495\text{M}}{\$10,648\text{M} \div 365} = 17.0 \text{ days} \qquad\qquad 6 \text{ days}$$

Thus McDonald's does not collect its receivables as quickly as the average firm in the comparison group—17 days compared to only 6 days for the industry. The short collection period for the industry is undoubtedly the result of being in the restaurant industry, which has more cash sales than most industries. By our using total sales, as opposed to credit sales, in our calculation, we have understated the actual collection period, both for McDonald's and for the industry. Nevertheless, the fact remains that McDonald's does extend longer credit terms than do its competitors.

We could have reached the same conclusion by measuring how many times accounts receivable are "rolled over" during a year, or the **accounts receivable turnover ratio**. For instance, the McDonald's Corporation turns its receivables over 21.5 times a year.[8]

McDonald's Corporation	**Peer-Group Average**

$$\text{accounts receivable turnover} = \frac{\text{credit sales}}{\text{accounts receivable}} \qquad (3\text{-}5)$$

$$= \frac{\$10,648\text{M}}{\$495\text{M}} = 21.5 \text{ times/year} \qquad\qquad 60.81 \text{ times/year}$$

Whether we use the average collection period or the accounts receivable turnover ratio, the conclusion is the same. The McDonald's Corporation is slower at collecting its receivables than competing firms.[9] Whether the longer credit terms are good or bad depends on the reason for the slower collections. As a general rule, management would want to collect receivables sooner rather than later—that is, lower collection period and higher turnover ratios. However, it may be that McDonald's management intentionally extends longer terms as a policy for reasons they deem

---

Average collection period

Average collection period indicates how rapidly a firm is collecting its credit, as measured by the average number of days it takes to collect its accounts receivable.

Accounts receivable turnover ratio

Accounts receivable turnover ratio indicates how rapidly the firm is collecting its credit, as measured by the number of times its accounts receivable are collected or "rolled over" during the year.

---

[8]We could also measure the accounts receivable turnover by dividing 365 days by the average collection period: 365/17 = 21.5.

[9]Although it will not be discussed here, we could also evaluate how effectively management is managing accounts receivable by aging the firm's receivables. For example, we could calculate how many of the accounts are 0 to 30 days old, 30 to 60 days old, and over 60 days.

justifiable. Alternatively, slower collection could mean that management is simply not being as careful at enforcing their collection policies. In other words, they are not effectively managing receivables.

We now want to know the same thing for inventories that we just determined for accounts receivable: How many times are we turning over inventories during the year? In this manner, we gain some insight into the liquidity of inventories. The **inventory turnover ratio** is calculated as follows:

$$\text{inventory turnover} = \frac{\text{cost of goods sold}}{\text{inventory}} \qquad (3\text{-}6)$$

Note that sales in this ratio is replaced by cost of goods sold. Since the inventory (the denominator) is measured at cost, we want to use a cost-based measure of sales in the numerator. Otherwise, our answer would vary from one firm to the next solely due to differences in how each firm marks up its sales over costs.[10]

Given that the McDonald's Corporation's cost of goods sold was $6,163 million (Table 3.1) and its inventory was $70 million (Table 3.2), the firm's 1996 inventory turnover, along with the peer-group average, is as follows:

McDonald's Corporation	**Peer-Group Average**

$$\frac{\text{inventory}}{\text{turnover}} = \frac{\text{cost of goods sold}}{\text{inventory}}$$

$$= \frac{\$6,163M}{\$70M} = 88.0 \text{ times/year} \qquad 56.3 \text{ times/year}$$

Given the above results, we can conclude that McDonald's is clearly excellent in its management of inventory, turning its inventory over 88 times per year compared to 56 times for the peer group. In other words, McDonald's sells its inventory in 4.1 days on average (365 days ÷ 88.0 times), whereas the average firm takes 6.5 days (365 days ÷ 56.3 times).

Thus when it comes to McDonald's liquidity, we see that the firm has low current and acid-test ratios, but that the firm collects its receivables in about 17 days and turns its inventory over 88 times per year (about every 4 days), indicating that these individual assets are relatively liquid, even though collections are slower than the peer group.

In summary, a firm's liquidity—its ability to meet maturing debt obligations (short-term debt) and the ability to convert accounts receivables and inventories into cash on a timely basis—represents an important dimension to managers, lenders, and investors. The less liquid the firm, the greater the chance that the firm will be unable to pay creditors when payments are due.

Question 2: Is Management Generating Adequate Operating Profits on the Firm's Assets?

We now begin a different line of thinking that will carry us through all the remaining questions. At this point, we want to know if the profits are sufficient relative to the assets being invested. The question is similar to a question one might ask about the interest being earned on a savings account at the bank. When you invest $1,000 in a savings account and receive $40 in interest during the year, you are earning a 4 percent return on your investment ($40 ÷ $1,000 = .04 = 4%). With respect to the McDonald's

---

[10]Whereas our logic may be correct to use cost of goods sold in the numerator, practicality may dictate that we use sales instead. Some suppliers of peer-group norm data use sales in the numerator. Thus for consistency in our comparisons, we too may need to use sales.

Corporation, we want to know something similar: the rate of return management is earning on the firm's assets.

In answering this question, we have several choices as to how we measure profits: gross profits, operating profits, or net income. Gross profits would not be an acceptable choice because it does not include some important information, such as the cost of marketing and distributing the firm's product. Thus we should choose between operating profits and net income. For our purposes, we prefer to use operating profits, because this measure of firm profits is calculated before the costs of the company's financing policies have been deducted. Because financing is explicitly considered in our next question, we want to isolate only the operating aspects of the company's profits at this point. In this way, we are able to compare the profitability of firms with different debt-to-equity mixes. Therefore, to examine the level of operating profits relative to the assets, we would use the **operating income return on investment** (OIROI):

$$\frac{\text{operating income}}{\text{return on investment}} = \frac{\text{operating income}}{\text{total assets}} \qquad (3\text{-}7)$$

The operating income return on investment for the McDonald's Corporation 1996 (based on the financial data in Table 3.1 and Table 3.2), and the corresponding peer-group norm, are shown below:

McDonald's Corporation	**Peer-Group Average**

$$\frac{\text{operating income}}{\text{return on investment}} = \frac{\text{operating income}}{\text{total assets}}$$

$$= \frac{\$2,594\text{M}}{\$17,386\text{M}} = .149 = 14.9\% \qquad\qquad 13.2\%$$

Hence we see that the McDonald's Corporation is earning an above-average return on investment relative to the average firm in the peer group. Management is generating more income on $1 of assets than similar firms.[11]

If we were the managers of the McDonald's Corporation, we should not be satisfied with merely knowing that we are earning more than a competitive return on the firm's assets. We should also want to know why we are above average. To understand this issue, we may separate the operating income return on investment, OIROI, into two important pieces: the operating profit margin and the total asset turnover. The firm's OIROI is a multiple of these two ratios and may be shown algebraically as follows:

$$\text{OIROI} = \left(\begin{array}{c}\text{operating}\\ \text{profit margin}\end{array}\right) \times \left(\begin{array}{c}\text{total asset}\\ \text{turnover}\end{array}\right) \qquad (3\text{-}8a)$$

or more completely,

$$\text{OIROI} = \frac{\text{operating income}}{\text{sales}} \times \frac{\text{sales}}{\text{total assets}} \qquad (3\text{-}8b)$$

OIROI: component 1. The first component of the OIROI, the **operating profit margin**, is an extremely important variable in understanding a company's operating profitability.

---

[11]The **return on assets** (ROA) is often used as an indicator of a firm's profitability and is measured as follows: return on assets = net income ÷ total assets.

We choose not to use this ratio because *net income* is influenced both by operating decisions and how the firm is financed. We want to restrict our attention only to operating activities; financing is considered later in questions 3 and 4. Nevertheless, sometimes the peer-group norm for operating income return on investment is not available. Instead, return on assets is provided. If so, we have no option but to use the return on assets for measuring the firm's profitability.

It is important that we know exactly what drives this ratio. In coming to understand the ratio, think about the makeup of the ratio, which may be expressed as follows:

$$\frac{\text{operating}}{\text{profit margin}} = \frac{\text{operating income}}{\text{sales}}$$

$$= \frac{\text{total} - \text{cost of} - \text{general and} - \text{marketing}}{\text{sales} \quad \text{goods sold} \quad \text{administrative} \quad \text{expenses}}{\text{sales}}$$

Because total sales equals the number of units sold times the sales price per unit, and the cost of goods sold equals the number of units sold times the cost of goods sold per unit, we may conclude that the driving forces of the operating profit margin are the following:

1. The number of units of product sold.[12]
2. The average selling price for each product unit.
3. The cost of manufacturing or acquiring the firm's product.
4. The ability to control general and administrative expenses.
5. The ability to control expenses in marketing and distributing the firm's product.

These influences are also apparent simply by looking at the income statement and thinking about what is involved in determining the firm's operating profits or income.[13] For the McDonald's Corporation and its peer group, the operating profit margins are 24.4 percent and 8 percent, respectively, determined as follows:

McDonald's Corporation	**Peer-Group Average**

$$\frac{\text{operating}}{\text{profit margin}} = \frac{\text{operating income}}{\text{sales}}$$

$$= \frac{\$2,594M}{\$10,648M} = .244 = 24.4\% \qquad\qquad 8\%$$

Based on these findings, we may conclude that the McDonald's Corporation is more than competitive when it comes to keeping costs and expenses in line relative to sales, as is reflected by the operating profit margin. In other words, management is extremely effective in managing the five driving forces of the operating profit margin listed above. In terms of its high operating profit margin, McDonald's has no equal.

Total asset turnover

Total asset turnover indicates management's effectiveness at managing a firm balance sheet—its assets—as indicated by the amount of sales generated per 1 dollar of assets.

OIROI: component 2. As shown in Equation (3.8b), the **total asset turnover** is the second component of the operating income return on investment. The total asset turnover measures the dollar sales per one dollar of assets. The ratio is calculated as follows:

$$\frac{\text{Total asset}}{\text{turnover}} = \frac{\text{sales}}{\text{total assets}} \tag{3-9}$$

----

[12]The number of units affects the operating profit margin only if some of the firm's costs and expenses are fixed. If a company's expenses are all variable in nature, then the ratio would not change as the number of units sold increases or decreases, because the numerator and the denominator would change at the same rate.

[13]We could have used the **net profit margin**, rather than the operating profit margin, which is measured as follows: net profit margin = net income ÷ sales.

Net profit margin

Net profit margin measures the net income of a firm as a percent of sales.

The net profit margin measures the amount of net income per one dollar of sales. However, because net income includes both operating expenses and interest expense, this ratio is influenced both by operating activities and financing activities. We prefer to defer the effect of financing decisions until questions 3 and 4, which follow shortly.

Intel Announces Lower Than Expected Profits

The following excerpts were taken from an article appearing in *The Wall Street Journal* regarding Intel's announcement that the firm's profits would not be as good as expected. The reason: lower profit margins as a result of carrying too much inventory. Don Clark, the author of the article, suggests that the firm's stock will be negatively affected.

Intel, based in Santa Clara, California, said profits were hurt because it bought too many memory chips for use in motherboards, the circuit boards that contain most electronic components in PCs. Andrew Grove, Intel's chief executive officer, said the company took unusually large write downs that totaled about $70 million.

Intel said the write downs helped push down its gross profit margin (gross profit ÷ sales) to 48 percent from 52 percent in the preceding quarter. Looking ahead, the company projected that margins will stay in the "high 40s" in the first quarter [1996].

Those comments are expected to be another blow to investors, who have hammered high-tech stocks in general recently and have been particularly tough on Intel. Intel's stock is down more than 40% since July [1995], and investors were especially nervous about the fourth-quarter report.

This ratio indicates how efficiently a firm is using its assets in generating sales. For instance, if Company A can generate $3 in sales with $1 in assets, compared to $2 in sales per asset dollar for Company B, we may say that Company A is using its assets more efficiently in generating sales, which is a major determinant in the firm's operating income return on investment.

Returning to the McDonald's Corporation, the firm's total asset turnover is calculated as follows:

McDonald's Corporation **Peer-Group Average**

$$\text{total asset turnover} = \frac{\text{sales}}{\text{total assets}}$$

$$= \frac{\$10,648M}{\$17,386M} = 0.61 \qquad 1.65$$

Based on the forgoing results, we see that the McDonald's Corporation generates only about $0.61 in sales per dollar of assets, whereas the competition on average produces $1.65 from every dollar in assets. That is, the McDonald's Corporation is not using its assets as efficiently as the average firm in its peer group.

We should not stop here with our analysis of McDonald's asset utilization; we should dig deeper. We have concluded that the assets are not being used efficiently, but now we should try to determine which assets are the problem. Are we overinvested in all assets or more so in accounts receivable or inventory or fixed assets? To answer this question, we merely examine the turnover ratios for the primary assets held by the firm—accounts receivables, inventories, and fixed assets. We have already calculated these ratios for accounts receivables and inventories, which are repeated as follows:

McDonald's Corporation		**Peer-Group Average**

Accounts receivable turnover:

$$\frac{\text{credit sales}}{\text{accounts receivable}} = \frac{\$10,648M}{\$495M} = 21.51 \qquad\qquad 60.8$$

Inventory turnover:

$$\frac{\text{cost of goods sold}}{\text{inventory}} = \frac{\$6,163M}{\$70M} = 88.04 \qquad\qquad 56.3$$

We next calculate a firm's fixed assets turnover ratio as follows:

$$\frac{\text{fixed assets}}{\text{turnover}} = \frac{\text{sales}}{\text{fixed assets}} \qquad\qquad\qquad (3\text{-}10)$$

For the McDonald's Corporation:

Peer-Group Average

$$\frac{\text{sales}}{\text{net fixed assets}} = \frac{\$10,648M}{\$14,352M} = 0.74 \qquad\qquad 2.0$$

To summarize, we should remember that a firm's operating income return on investment (OIROI) is a function of two elements, the operating profit margin and the firm's total asset turnover. For the McDonald's Corporation, the OIROI was determined as follows:

$$\text{OIROI}_{\text{McD}} = 24.4\% \times 0.61 = .149 = 14.9\%$$

and for the peer group, this same ratio is

$$\text{OIROI}_{\text{pg}} = 8\% \times 1.65 = .132 = 13.2\%$$

Based on these results, we can know that the McDonald's Corporation is extremely effective at keeping its cost of goods sold and operating expenses low relative to its sales (high operating profit margin), but that the company is not particularly efficient in managing the firm's assets.

In particular, the company has excessive accounts receivable, which we had known from our earlier discussions, and also there is too large an investment in fixed assets (for example, buildings and lands) for the sales being produced. It would appear that these two asset categories are not being managed well, and the consequence is a lower overall or total asset turnover ratio. Moreover, given the far greater amount invested in fixed assets ($14.4 billion) than accounts receivable ($495 million)—see the balance sheet in Table 3.2—the heart of the problem is with the firm's large amount of fixed assets relative to the firm's sales.

Question 3: How Is the Firm Financing Its Assets?

We now turn for the moment to the matter of how the firm is financed. We shall return to the firm's profitability shortly. The basic issue is the use of debt versus equity: Do we finance the assets more by debt or equity? In answering this question, we will use two ratios. Many more could be used. First, we simply ask what percentage of

The Lack of Accounting Controls Results in Unethical Behavior

The following excerpts from an article from *The Wall Street Journal* describe what can go wrong when ethical behavior is absent in our business dealings.

"Always another loan, always another deal." That was how Charn Uswachoke, better known in Thailand as "Mr. Chips," fended off jittery bankers, when a group of them asked why Alphatec Electronics PCL had just violated some terms of its international debt.

An independent audit by Price Waterhouse in July revealed that Alphatec, once a star on the Stock Exchange of Thailand, overstated profits by at least $164 million between 1994 and 1997, at a time when the report says the company should have been reporting "significant losses." Revenue was said to be six to 10 times as high as it actually was, say current and former employees familiar with Alphatec's true numbers.

Once featured as Thailand's best hope for joining the upper ranks of the world's technology producers, Alphatec instead became an object lesson in the dangers of doing business in a country where management accountability is lacking. The stark absence of corporate controls at Alphatec—the mingling of funds, listed and closely held companies run by the same family, the use of multiple sets of accounting books and misleading accounting methods, the highly paid, rubber-stamp board—mirrors the problems at other Thai companies that have brought this country's economy to the brink of collapse.

Accounting irregularities surfaced in May. After several months of trying to restructure Alphatec for an initial public offering, Lehman Brothers changed strategies and initiated a $300 million high-yield-bond proposal. On May 11, [1997], a team of New York lawyers and investment bankers, led by Lehman technology chief Jack Skydel, visited Bangkok to run through the numbers with Alphatec's people.

Fifteen minutes before the meeting, Mr. Charn dropped a bombshell on Mr. Merszei [Alphatec's chief financial officer]: Alphatec's debt had expanded not by $35 million, as Mr. Charn had recently indicated, but by $100 million. Most of the increase had resulted from financial transfers to Mr. Charn's other companies, Mr. Merszei says Mr. Charn told him.

In another office, Mr. Merszei and a colleague, Robert Book, took Lehman's Mr. Skydel aside. "I said, 'This company is not a candidate in any debt to equity market in the world.'" Mr. Book, a long-time financial consultant to Mr. Charn, recalls. "'The financial practices here are not in keeping with the Western value system, or any value system. I'm sorry you came.'" The New Yorkers flew home that night.

SOURCE: "A Company's Travails Show Why Economy in Thailand Is Shot," *The Wall Street Journal* (September 8, 1997): Section A; p. 1. © by Dow Jones & Co., Inc. All rights reserved. Reprinted with permission.

---

the firm's assets are financed by debt, including *both* short-term and long-term debt, realizing the remaining percentage must be financed by equity. We would compute the **debt ratio** as follows:[14]

$$\text{debt ratio} = \frac{\text{total debt}}{\text{total assets}}$$

(3-11)

Debt ratio

Debt ratio indicates how much debt is used to finance a firm's assets.

---

[14]We will often see the relationship stated in terms of debt to equity, or the debt-equity ratio, rather than debt to total assets. We come to the same conclusion with either ratio.

For the McDonald's Corporation, debt as a percentage of total assets is 49.9 percent (taken from McDonald's balance sheet in Table 3.2) compared to a peer-group norm of 66 percent. The computation is as follows:

McDonald's Corporation   **Peer-Group Average**

$$\text{debt ratio} = \frac{\text{total debt}}{\text{total assets}}$$

$$= \frac{\$8,668M}{\$17,386M} = .499 = 49.9\% \qquad\qquad 66\%$$

Thus the McDonald's Corporation uses significantly less debt than the average firm in the peer group.

We should note that companies in general finance about 40 percent of their assets with debt and 60 percent in equity. Firms with more real assets, such as land and buildings (as with the McDonald's Corporation), are able to finance more of their assets with debt. High-technology firms where the assets are "soft," such as research and development, are less able to acquire debt financing. Thus the amount of debt a firm uses depends on its proven income record and the availability of assets that can be used as collateral for the loan—and how much risk management is willing to assume.

Our second perspective regarding the firm's financing decisions comes by looking at the income statement. When we borrow money, there is a minimum requirement that the firm pay the interest on the debt. Thus it is informative to compare the amount of operating income that is available to service the interest with the amount of interest that is to be paid. Stated as a ratio, we compute the number of times we are earning our interest. Thus a **times interest earned** *ratio* is commonly used when examining the firm's debt position and is computed in the following manner:

$$\text{times interest earned} = \frac{\text{operating income}}{\text{interest expense}} \qquad\qquad (3\text{-}12)$$

Based on the income statement for the McDonald's Corporation (Table 3.1), the firm's times interest earned is 7.56, computed as follows:

McDonald's Corporation   **Peer-Group Average**

$$\genfrac{}{}{0pt}{}{\text{times}}{\genfrac{}{}{0pt}{}{\text{interest}}{\text{earned}}} = \frac{\text{operating income}}{\text{interest expense}}$$

$$= \frac{\$2,594M}{\$343M} = 7.56 \qquad\qquad 4.0$$

Thus the McDonald's Corporation is able to service its interest expense without any great difficulty. In fact, the firm's operating income could fall to as little as one-eighth (1/7.56) its current level and still have the income to pay the required interest. We should remember, however, that interest is not paid with income but with cash, and that the firm may be required to repay some of the debt principal as well as the interest. Thus the times interest earned is only a crude measure of the firm's capacity to service its debt. Nevertheless, it does give us a general indication of a company's debt capacity.

Question 4: Are the Owners (stockholders) Receiving an Adequate Return on Their Investment?

Our one remaining question looks at the accounting return on the common stockholders' investment or **return on common equity**; that is, we want to know if the earnings available to the firm's owners or common equity investors are attractive when compared to the returns of owners of companies in the peer group.

We measure the return to the owners as follows:

$$\text{return on common equity} = \frac{\text{net income}}{\begin{array}{c}\text{common equity (including par, paid}\\\text{in capital and retained earnings)}\end{array}} \quad (3\text{-}13)$$

The return on common equity for the McDonald's Corporation and the peer group are 18 percent and 20 percent, respectively:

McDonald's Corporation   **Peer-Group Average**

$$\frac{\text{return on}}{\text{common equity}} = \frac{\text{net income}}{\text{common equity}}$$

$$\frac{\$1,573M}{\$8,718M} = .18 = 18\% \qquad\qquad 20\%$$

It would appear that the owners of the McDonald's Corporation are not receiving a return on their investment equivalent to what owners involved with competing businesses receive. However, we should also ask, "Why not?" To answer, we need to draw on what we have already learned, namely that:

1. The McDonald's Corporation is more profitable in its operations than its competitors. (Remember, the operating income return on investment, OIROI, was 14.9 percent for McDonald's compared to 13.2 percent for the competition.) Thus this fact would suggest that McDonald's should have a higher, not a lower, return on common equity.
2. McDonald's uses considerably less debt (more equity) financing than does the average firm in the peer group. As we will see shortly, the more debt a firm uses, the higher its return on equity will be, provided that the firm is earning a return on investment greater than its cost of debt. Thus the competition, on average, provides a higher return for its shareholders by using more debt, not by being better at generating profits on the firm's assets. That's the good news. The bad news for the competitors' shareholders is the more debt a firm uses, the greater the company's financial risk, which translates to more risk for the shareholders as well.

To help us understand the forgoing conclusion about the reason for McDonald's lower return on common equity and its implications, consider the following example.

Firms A and B are identical in size, both having $1,000 in total assets and both having an operating income return on investment of 14 percent. However, they are different in one respect: Firm A uses no debt, but Firm B finances 60 percent of its investments with debt at an interest cost of 10 percent. For the sake of simplicity, we will assume there are no income taxes. The financial statements for the two companies would be as follows:

	Firm A	Firm B
Total assets	$1,000	$1,000
Debt (10% interest rate)	$ 0	$ 600
Equity	1,000	400
Total	$1,000	$1,000
Operating income (OIROI = 14%)	$ 140	$ 140
Interest expense (10%)	0	60
Net profit	$ 140	$ 80

Computing the return on common equity for both companies, we see that Firm B has a much more attractive return to its owners, 20 percent compared to Firm A's 14 percent:

$$\text{return on equity} = \frac{\text{net income}}{\text{common equity}}$$

$$\text{Firm A: } = \frac{\$140}{\$1,000} = .14 = 14\% \quad \text{Firm B: } \frac{\$80}{\$400} = .20 = 20\%$$

Why the difference? Firm B is earning 14 percent on its investments, but is only having to pay 10 percent for its borrowed money. The difference between the return on the firm's investments and the interest rate, 14 percent less the 10 percent, goes to the owners, thus boosting Firm B's return on equity above that of Firm A. We are seeing the favorable results of debt at work, where we borrow at 10 percent and invest at 14 percent. The result is an increase in the return on equity.

If debt enhances the owners' returns, why would we not use lots of it all the time? We may continue our example to find the answer. Assume now that the economy falls into a deep recession, business declines sharply, and Firms A and B only earn a 6 percent operating income return on investment. Let's recompute the return on common equity now.

	Firm A	Firm B
Operating income (OIROI = 6%)	$60	$60
Interest expense	0	60
Net profit	$60	$ 0
Return on equity:	Firm A: $\dfrac{\$60}{\$1,000} = .06 = 6\%$	Firm B: $\dfrac{\$0}{\$400} = .00 = 0\%$

Now the use of debt has a negative influence on the return on equity, with Firm B earning less than Firm A for its owners. This results from the fact that now Firm B earns less than the interest rate of 10 percent; consequently, the equity investors have to make up the difference. Thus using debt is a two-edged sword; when times are good, debt financing can make them very, very good, but when times are bad, debt financing makes them very, very bad. Thus financing with debt can potentially enhance the returns of the equity investors, but it also increases the uncertainty or risk for the owners.

Let's review what we have learned about the use of financial ratios in evaluating a company's financial position. We have presented the financial ratios calculated for the McDonald's Corporation in Table 3.5. The ratios are grouped by the issue being addressed: liquidity, operating profitability, financing, and profits for the owners. As before, we use some ratios for more than one purpose, namely the turnover ratios for accounts receivable and inventories. These ratios have implications both for the firm's liquidity and its profitability; thus they are listed in both areas. Also, we have included both average collection period and accounts receivable turnover; typically, we would only use one in our analysis, because they are just different ways of expressing the same thing.

Conducting Financial Analysis Over Time

To this point, we have been comparing the McDonald's Corporation with a peer group as of 1996. As mentioned earlier, we should also be interested in a firm's performance over time. To illustrate this process, Table 3.6, shows the financial ratios for the

Table 3.5 McDonald's Corporation Financial Ratio Analysis

Financial Ratios	McDonald's Corporation	Industry Average
1. Firm Liquidity		
Current ratio $= \dfrac{\text{current assets}}{\text{current liabilities}}$	$\dfrac{1{,}103M}{2{,}135M} = 0.52$	0.90
Acid test ratio $= \dfrac{\text{current assets} - \text{inventories}}{\text{current liabilities}}$	$\dfrac{1{,}103M - 70M}{2{,}135M} = 0.48$	0.62
Average collection period $= \dfrac{\text{accounts receivable}}{\text{daily credit sales}}$	$\dfrac{495M}{10{,}648M \div 365M} = 17.0$	6.0
Accounts receivable turnover $= \dfrac{\text{credit sales}}{\text{accounts receivable}}$	$\dfrac{\$10{,}648M}{\$495M} = 21.5$	60.8
Inventory turnover $= \dfrac{\text{cost of goods sold}}{\text{inventory}}$	$\dfrac{6{,}163M}{70M} = 88.0$	56.3
2. Operating Profitability		
Operating income return on investment $= \dfrac{\text{operating income}}{\text{total assets}}$	$\dfrac{2{,}594M}{17{,}386M} = 14.9\%$	13.2
Operating profit margin $= \dfrac{\text{operating income}}{\text{sales}}$	$\dfrac{2{,}594M}{10{,}648M} = 24.4\%$	8.0
Total asset turnover $= \dfrac{\text{sales}}{\text{total assets}}$	$\dfrac{10{,}648M}{17{,}386M} = 0.61$	1.65
Accounts receivable turnover $= \dfrac{\text{sales}}{\text{accounts receivable}}$	$\dfrac{10{,}648M}{495M} = 21.5$	60.8
Inventory turnover $= \dfrac{\text{cost of goods sold}}{\text{inventory}}$	$\dfrac{6{,}163M}{70M} = 88.0$	56.3
Fixed assets turnover $= \dfrac{\text{sales}}{\text{net fixed assets}}$	$\dfrac{10{,}648M}{14{,}352M} = 0.74$	2.0
3. Financing Decisions		
Debt ratio $= \dfrac{\text{total debt}}{\text{total assets}}$	$\dfrac{8{,}668M}{17{,}386M} = 49.9\%$	66.0%
Times interest earned $= \dfrac{\text{operating income}}{\text{interest expense}}$	$\dfrac{2{,}594M}{343M} = 7.56\%$	4.0%
4. Return on Equity		
Return on equity $= \dfrac{\text{net income}}{\text{common equity}}$	$\dfrac{1{,}573M}{8{,}718M} = 18.0\%$	20.0%

Table 3.6 Gillette Company Ratio Analysis 1992–1996

	1992	1993	1994	1995	1996
Current ratio	1.50	1.44	1.54	1.46	1.62
Quick Ratio	0.95	0.94	1.01	0.97	1.16
Accounts receivable turnover	4.35	4.41	4.40	4.09	3.56
Inventory turnover	2.16	2.12	2.13	2.21	2.43
Operating income return on investment	23.1%	21.3%	22.3%	21.6%	19.6%
Operating profit margin	18.7%	20.1%	20.2%	20.2%	21.1%
Gross profit margin	64.4%	65.7%	66.9%	66.3%	66.0%
Total asset turnover	1.23	1.06	1.10	1.07	0.93
Fixed asset turnover	4.80	4.45	4.30	4.15	3.78
Debt ratio	0.64	0.71	0.63	0.60	0.57
Times interest earned	11.65	18.13	20.08	23.24	26.68
Return on equity	34.8%	19.7%	35.3%	33.4%	21.4%

Gillette Company for the years 1992 through 1996. Based on the trends, we can draw the following conclusions:

1. Gillette's liquidity has been relatively stable over time. The quick ratio has declined somewhat, but probably in part due to an increase in the accounts receivable turnover, which is good. The current ratio has increased slightly, but possibly as a result of a slower inventory turnover, which is not ideal. Nevertheless, all in all, the firm's liquidity has been constant for the most part.

2. The firm's operating profitability on its assets (OIROI) has declined significantly from 23.1 percent to 19.6 percent. The decrease occurred in spite of increasing profit margins (operating and gross profits). Thus the reason for the decrease has been management's failure to use the firm's assets as efficiently in the later years (total asset turnover went from 1.23 in 1992 to 0.93 in 1996). The decline comes from less efficient use of fixed assets and inventories.

3. Gillette's use of debt financing has declined over the 5 years. Also, the firm has significantly increased its ability to cover interest, as a result of increasing operating profits along with significantly lower interest payments.

4. The return on equity for Gillette's stockholders has fallen sharply from almost 35 percent to slightly over 23 percent. This trend comes from lower operating income return on investment and less debt financing.

From the forgoing trend analysis we are able to see clearly how the firm is performing financially over time, which gives us additional insights not possible from only looking at industry norms.

OBJECTIVE 4

THE DUPONT ANALYSIS: AN INTEGRATIVE APPROACH TO RATIO ANALYSIS

In the previous section, we used ratio analysis to answer four questions thought to be important in understanding a company's financial position. The last three of the four questions dealt with a company's earnings capabilities and the common stockholders' return on the equity capital. In our analysis, we measured the return on equity as follows:

$$\text{return on equity} = \frac{\text{net income}}{\text{common equity}} \tag{3-14}$$

Another approach can be used to evaluate a firm's return on equity. The **duPont analysis** is a method used to analyze a firm's profitability and return on equity. Figure 3.4 shows graphically the duPont technique, along with the numbers for the McDonald's Corporation. Beginning at the top of the figure, we see that the return on equity is calculated as follows:

$$\text{return on equity} = \left(\frac{\text{return}}{\text{on assets}}\right) \div \left(1 - \frac{\text{total debt}}{\text{total assets}}\right) \tag{3-15}$$

where the return on assets, or ROA, equals:

$$\text{return on assets} = \frac{\text{net income}}{\text{total assets}} \tag{3-16}$$

Thus we see that the return on equity is a function of (1) the firm's overall profitability (net income relative to the amount invested in assets), and (2) the amount of debt used to finance the assets. We also know that the return on assets may be represented as follows:

$$\text{return on assets} = \left(\frac{\text{net profit}}{\text{margin}}\right) \times \left(\frac{\text{total asset}}{\text{turnover}}\right) \tag{3-17}$$

$$= \left(\frac{\text{net income}}{\text{sales}}\right) \times \left(\frac{\text{sales}}{\text{total assets}}\right)$$

Combining equations (3-15) and (3-17) gives us the basic duPont equation that shows the firm's return on equity as follows:

$$\text{return on equity} = \left(\frac{\text{net profit}}{\text{margin}}\right) \times \left(\frac{\text{total asset}}{\text{turnover}}\right) \div \left(1 - \frac{\text{total debt}}{\text{total assets}}\right) \tag{3-18}$$

$$= \left(\frac{\text{net income}}{\text{sales}}\right) \times \left(\frac{\text{sales}}{\text{total assets}}\right) \div \left(1 - \frac{\text{total debt}}{\text{total assets}}\right)$$

Using the duPont equation and the diagram in Figure 3.4 allows management to see more clearly what drives the return on equity and the interrelationships among the net profit margin, the asset turnover, and the debt ratio. Management is provided with a road map to follow in determining their effectiveness in managing the firm's resources to maximize the return earned on the owners' investment. In addition, the manager or owner can determine why that particular return was earned.

Let's return to the McDonald's Corporation to demonstrate the use of the duPont analysis. Taking the information from the McDonald's Corporation's income statement (Table 3.1) and balance sheet as of December 31, 1996 (Table 3.2), we can calculate the company's return on equity as follows:

$$\text{return on equity} = \left(\frac{\text{net income}}{\text{sales}}\right) \times \left(\frac{\text{sales}}{\text{total assets}}\right) \div \left(1 - \frac{\text{total debt}}{\text{total assets}}\right)$$

$$= \left(\frac{\$1,573}{\$10,648}\right) \times \left(\frac{\$10,648}{\$17,386}\right) \div \left(1 - \frac{\$8,668}{\$17,386}\right)$$

$$= \frac{14.77\% \times .612}{(1 - .499)}$$

$$= 18.04\%$$

We can also visualize the relationships graphically for the McDonald's Corporation, as shown in Figure 3.4.

duPont analysis

The duPont analysis is an approach to evaluate a firm's profitability and return on equity.

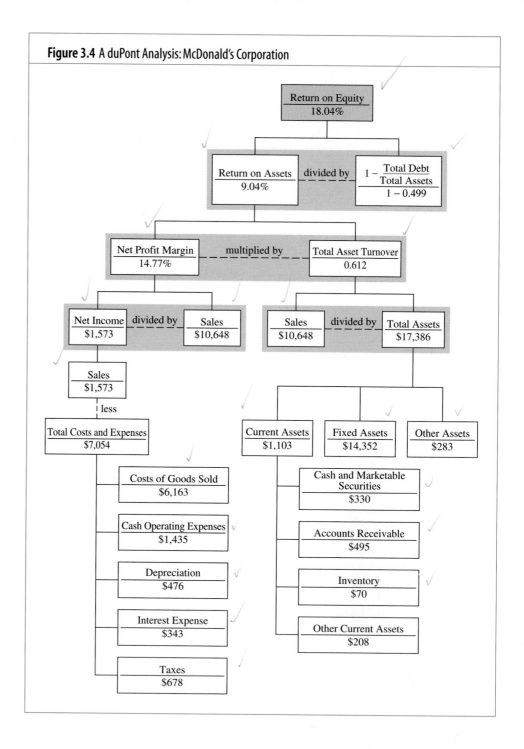

Figure 3.4 A duPont Analysis: McDonald's Corporation

If the McDonald's Corporation's management wants to improve the company's return on equity, they should carefully examine Figure 3.4 for possible avenues. As we study the figure, we quickly see that improvement in the return on equity can come in one or more of four ways:

1. Increase sales without a disproportionate increase in costs and expenses.
2. Reduce the firm's cost of goods sold or operating expenses shown in the left side of Figure 3.4.

3. Increase the sales relative to the asset base, either by increasing sales or by reducing the amounts invested in company assets. From our earlier examination of the McDonald's Corporation, we learned that the firm had excessive accounts receivables and fixed assets. Thus management needs to reduce these assets to the point possible, which would in turn result in an increase in the return on assets and then the return on equity.
4. Increase the use of debt relative to equity, but only to the extent that it does not unduly jeopardize the firm's financial position.

The choice between using the four-question approach as described earlier or the duPont analysis is largely a matter of personal preference. Both approaches are intended to let us see the variables that determine a firm's profitability. There are, however, limitations to either technique because of the inherent limitations in using financial ratios—a topic addressed in the next section.

Limitations of Ratio Analysis

OBJECTIVE 5

We have shown how financial ratios may be used to understand a company's financial position, but anyone who works with these ratios ought to be aware of the limitations involved in their use. The following list includes some of the more important pitfalls that may be encountered in computing and interpreting financial ratios:

1. It is sometimes difficult to identify the industry category to which a firm belongs when the firm engages in multiple lines of business. Thus we frequently must select our own set of peer firms and construct tailor-made norms. Such was the case with our analysis of the McDonald's Corporation.
2. Published industry averages are only approximations and provide the user with general guidelines rather than scientifically determined averages of the ratios of all or even a representative sample of the firms within an industry.
3. Accounting practices differ widely among firms and can lead to differences in computed ratios. In addition, firms may choose different methods of depreciating their fixed assets.
4. An industry average may not provide a desirable target ratio or norm. At best, an industry average provides a guide to the financial position of the average firm in the industry, which includes all the dogs and the stars. It does not mean it is the ideal or best value for the ratio. Thus we may choose to compare our firm's ratios with a self-determined peer group or even a single competitor.[15]
5. Many firms experience seasonality in their operations. Thus balance sheet entries and their corresponding ratios will vary with the time of year when the statements are prepared. For example, a firm may have a fiscal year that ends on June 30, whereas another company in the same industry may have a December 31 fiscal-year end. To avoid this problem, an average account balance should be used (for several months or quarters during the year) rather than the year-end total. For example, an average of month-end inventory balances might be used to compute a firm's inventory turnover ratio when the firm is subject to a significant seasonality in its sales (and correspondingly in its investment in inventories).

In spite of their limitations, financial ratios provide us with a very useful tool for assessing a firm's financial conditions. We should, however, be aware of these potential weaknesses when performing a ratio analysis. In many cases, the real value derived from analyzing financial ratios is that they tell us what questions to ask and what avenues to pursue.

---

[15]See Donald F. Cunningham and John T. Rose, "Industry Norms in Financial Statement Analysis: A Comparison of RMA and D&B Benchmark Data," *The Credit and Financial Management Review*, 1995, pp. 42–48, for a comparison of the industry financial ratios provided by Robert Morris and Associates with those of Dun and Bradstreet. They find significant differences within the same industry classifications. This finding points out the need to carefully consider the choice of an industry norm. In fact, your analysis may require that you construct your own norm from, say, a list of the four or five firms in a particular industry that might provide the most appropriate standard of comparison for the firm being analyzed.

MEASURING FIRM PERFORMANCE THE EVA WAY

To this point, we have considered firm performance only from an accounting perspective. Questions 2 and 4 of our *four-question approach* have specifically measured the rate of return on the firm's total assets (operating income return on investment) and the return earned on the shareholder's investment (return on equity). We suggested that these returns should be compared with returns earned by other firms in comparable businesses or against industry norms to see how management is doing with the firm's assets. However, in none of our discussions have we connected these return measurements to the financial goal of the firm, that of creating shareholder value. For instance, we observed that McDonald's is earning almost a 15 percent operating income return on investment, compared to about 13 percent by a peer group of companies. We concluded that management is performing better than its competition, but we never said whether McDonald's is creating or destroying shareholder value from its investments.

How is shareholder value created or destroyed? Quite simply, shareholder value is created when a firm earns a rate of return on the capital invested in excess of the investors' required rate of return. If we invest in a firm and have a 12 percent required rate of return and the firm earns 15 percent on our capital, then management is creating value for the investor. If instead, the firm only earns 10 percent, then investor value is being destroyed. This concept, although followed faithfully by many firms when making accept/reject decisions on large capital investments in plant and equipment, has traditionally not been part of management's thought process in evaluating firm—and management—performance. Instead, most managers are more focused on the accounting results—earnings growth, profit margins, and the return on equity.

More recently, attention has been given to determining whether a firm's management is in fact creating shareholder value on all the capital invested and linking their compensation, mostly through bonuses, to the amount of shareholder value created. Although several techniques have been developed for assessing whether management is creating shareholder value, the one seeming to capture the most attention presently is economic value added (EVA®). This approach, developed by the consulting firm Stern Stewart & Co., is an attempt to measure a firm's *economic* profit rather than *accounting* profit in a given year. Economic profits assign a cost to the equity capital (the opportunity cost of the funds provided by the shareholders) in addition to the interest cost on the firm's debt; many accountants only recognize the interest expense as a financing cost. For example, assume a firm has total assets of $1,000 and is financed 40 percent with debt ($400) and 60 percent with equity ($600). If the interest rate on the debt is 10 percent, the interest cost is $40 ($400 × 10%) and would be reported in the income statement. However, there would be no cost shown for the equity financing. On the other hand, to compute economic profits, we recognize not only the interest cost, but also the opportunity cost of the $600 equity. That is, if the shareholders could earn 15 percent on another investment of similar risk (their opportunity cost is therefore 15 percent), then we should count this cost just as surely as we do the interest payment.[16] Thus in computing economic profits, we would subtract not only the $40 in interest, but also $90 ($600 equity × 15%) as the cost of equity. Thus economic profits exist only if our operating profits exceed $130 ($40 + $90).[17] Stated as a percentage, the firm must earn at least a 13 percent operating income return on its investment ($130 ÷ $1,000) in order to meet the investors' required rates of return.

---

[16]In chapter 13, we will explain much more about the investor's opportunity cost of funds and how that is used to compute a cost of capital for the firm.

[17]We are ignoring the effect of taxes in these computations for simplicity sake. The basic idea is the same.

In this context, EVA® (the value created for the shareholders) is computed as follows:

$$EVA = (r - k) \times C \tag{3-19}$$

where r = the firm's operating income return on invested capital

k = the total cost of all capital, both debt and equity

C = amount of capital (total assets) invested in the firm

That is, the value created by management is determined by the amount the firm earns on its invested capital relative to the cost of these funds—both debt and equity—and the amount of capital invested in the firm. Continuing with our previous example, assume that our company is earning a 16 percent operating return on its assets (capital). Then we could say that the firm's economic value added is $30, determined as follows:

$$EVA = (16\% - 13\%) \times \$1,000$$

$$= \$30$$

The forgoing explains the EVA concept in its simplest form. However, computing EVA requires our converting a firm's financial statements from an accountant's perspective (GAAP) to an economist's view of the world (i.e., converting from accounting book values to economic book values). This process is much more involved than is being presented here, but we have at least an understanding of the basic premises involved in its computation. For now, we simply want to remember that management should be working to create shareholder value, and ideally, the evaluation of management's performance should be tied to that objective. Taken alone, financial ratios fail to capture this important dimension of financial management, and should therefore be used with a measure of caution. Much more will be said about the goal of creating shareholder value as we continue our study of finance.

HOW FINANCIAL MANAGERS USE THIS MATERIAL

In this chapter, we have explained the contents of key financial statements. But more importantly, we provided a framework for using the information in evaluating a firm's performance. Accounting data is the basis for so much that is done in finance. It is used in almost every aspect of financial management, either directly or indirectly. In any firm of any significance, the data is used both to evaluate historical performance and to project future expectations.

Not only do the financial managers use the data, but financial analysts and lenders rely on the firm's financial information to advise investors and to make loans. Increasingly, managers are being evaluated and compensated based on the firm's performance, where performance is measured in terms of the company's profitability, and more recently, management's ability to earn rates of return that exceed the investors' required rates of return. For instance, Michael Eisner, the CEO for Disney, received large bonuses based on the company earning a superior return on the common stockholders' investment. The same is true for Al Dunlap when he went to Scott Paper to turn the company around and make it more profitable.

So, if a manager or a common stockholder wants to know the effectiveness of a firm's strategies, the ultimate test is the rate of return being earned on the company's assets, which is measured to a large extent by the accounting data. Without such information, managers cannot make any definite conclusions as to the success of their strategies.

SUMMARY

 OBJECTIVE 1

Three basic financial statements are commonly used to describe the financial condition and performance of the firm: the balance sheet, the income statement, and the statement of cash flows. The balance sheet provides a picture of the firm's assets, liabilities, and owners' equity on a particular date, whereas the income statement reflects the net revenues from the firm's operations over a given period. The statement of cash flows combines information from both the balance sheet and income statement to describe sources and uses of cash for a given period in the firm's history.

 OBJECTIVE 2

There are three basic categories of activities related to a firm's cash flows:

- Cash flows from operations
- Cash flows related to the investment or sale of assets (investment activities)
- Cash flows related to financing the firm (financing activities)

The first category, cash flows from operations, converts the income statement from an accrual basis to a cash basis. Also, by identifying the positive or negative signs of these three areas of cash flows, we gain an understanding of where cash is coming from and how it is being used. After all, it is cash that pays the bills, not an accounting entry called "profits."

 OBJECTIVE 3

Financial ratios are the principal tools of financial analysis. Sometimes referred to simply as benchmarks, ratios standardize financial information so that comparisons can be made between firms of varying sizes.

Two groups find financial ratios useful. The first is comprised of managers who use them to measure and track company performance over time. The focus of their analysis is frequently related to various measures of profitability used to evaluate the performance of the firm from the perspective of the owners. The second group of users of financial ratios includes analysts external to the firm who, for one reason or another, have an interest in the firm's economic well-being. An example of this group would be a loan officer of a commercial bank who wishes to determine the credit worthiness of a loan applicant. Here the focus of the analysis is on the firm's previous use of financial leverage and its ability to pay the interest and principal associated with the loan request.

Financial ratios may be used to answer at least four questions: (1) How liquid is the company? (2) Is management effective at generating operating profits on the firm's assets? (3) How is the firm financed? (4) Are the returns earned by the common stockholders adequate?

Two methods may be used in analyzing financial ratios. The first involves trend analysis for the firm over time; the second involves making ratio comparisons with a selected peer group of similar firms. In our example, a peer group was chosen for analyzing the financial position of the McDonald's Corporation.

 OBJECTIVE 4

Another approach frequently used to evaluate a firm's profitability and the return on equity is the duPont analysis. The basic format of the duPont analysis dissects the return on equity into three drivers, represented as follows:

$$\text{return on equity} = \left(\frac{\text{net income}}{\text{sales}}\right) \times \left(\frac{\text{sales}}{\text{total assets}}\right) \div \left(1 - \frac{\text{total debt}}{\text{total assets}}\right)$$

OBJECTIVE 5

The following limitations may be encountered in computing and interpreting financial ratios:

1. It is sometimes difficult to identify an appropriate industry category.
2. Published industry averages are only approximations rather than scientifically determined averages.
3. Accounting practices differ widely among firms and can lead to differences in computed ratios.

4. An industry average may not provide a desirable target ratio or norm.
5. Many firms experience seasonality in their operations. Thus ratios will vary with the time of year when the statements are prepared.

In spite of their limitations, financial ratios provide us with very useful tools for assessing a firm's financial condition.

Financial ratios provide a popular way to evaluate a firm's financial performance. However, when evaluating a company's use of assets (capital) to create firm value, financial ratio analysis may not be enough. Economic value added is one approach (there are others) being used by managements to evaluate their firm's performance in terms of shareholder value creation. Economic value added, or EVA, is equal to the return on invested capital less the investors' opportunity cost of the funds times the total amount of capital invested.

OBJECTIVE 6

KEY TERMS

Accounts receivable turnover ratio, 97

Acid-test (quick) ratio, 96

Average collection period, 97

Balance sheet, 84

Cash flows from financing activities, 91

Cash flows from investment activities, 91

Cash flows from operations, 89

Current assets, 84

Current ratio, 96

Debt, 84

Debt ratio, 103

Direct method, 91

duPont analysis, 109

Earnings before taxes, 82

Equity, 84

Financial ratios, 95

Financing costs, 81

Fixed or long-term assets, 84

Income statement, 81

Indirect method, 91

Inventory turnover ratio, 98

Liquidity, 95

Net income available to common stockholders (net income), 82

Net profit margin, 100

Operating income (earnings before interest and taxes), 81

Operating income return on investment, 99

Operating profit margin, 99

Other assets, 84

Retained earnings, 84

Return on assets, 99

Return on common equity, 104

Statement of cash flows, 87

Tax expenses, 82

Times interest earned, 104

Total asset turnover, 100

GO TO:
http://www.prenhall.com/bfm
For downloads and current events associated with this chapter

STUDY QUESTIONS

3-1. The basic financial statements of an organization consist of the balance sheet, income statement, and statement of cash flow. Describe the nature of each and explain how their functions differ.

3-2. Describe the eight cash flow patterns that can exist in a statement of cash flow (the direct method).

3-3. Why is it that the preferred stockholders' section of the balance sheet would change only when new shares are sold or repurchased, whereas the common equity section would change from year to year regardless of whether new shares are bought or sold?

3-4. Discuss the reasons why net income for a particular period does not necessarily reflect a firm's cash flow during that period.

3-5. Describe the "four-question approach" to using financial ratios.

3-6. Discuss briefly the two perspectives that can be taken in performing ratio analyses.

3-7. Where can we obtain industry norms? What are the limitations of industry average ratios? Discuss briefly.

SELF-TEST PROBLEMS

ST-1. (*Ratio Analysis and Short-Term Liquidity*) Ray's Tool and Supply Company of Austin, Texas, has been expanding its level of operation for the past 2 years. The firm's sales have grown rapidly as a result of the expansion of the Austin economy. However, Ray's is a privately held company, and the only source of available funds it has is a line of credit with the firm's bank. The company needs to expand its inventories to meet the needs of its growing customer base but also wishes to maintain a current ratio of at least 3. If Ray's current assets are $6 million, and its current ratio is now 4, how much can it expand its inventories (financing the expansion with its line of credit) before the target current ratio is violated?

ST-2. (*Ratio Analysis*) The statements for M & G Industries are as follows:

M & G Industries Balance Sheet for December 31, 1997 and 1998

	1997	1998
Cash	$ 9,000	$ 500
Accounts receivable	12,500	16,000
Inventories	29,000	45,500
Total current assets	$ 50,500	$ 62,000
Land	20,000	26,000
Buildings and equipment	70,000	100,000
Less: allowance for depreciation	(28,000)	(38,000)
Total fixed assets	$ 62,000	$ 88,000
Total assets	$112,500	$150,000
Accounts payable	$ 10,500	$ 22,000
Short-term bank notes	17,000	47,000
Total current liabilities	$ 27,500	$ 69,000
Long-term debt	28,750	22,950
Common stock	31,500	31,500
Retained earnings	24,750	26,550
Total debt and equity	$112,500	$150,000

M & G Industries Income Statement for the Years Ended December 31, 1997 and 1998

	1997	1998
Sales (all credit)	$125,000	$160,000
Cost of goods sold	75,000	96,000
Gross profit	$ 50,000	$ 64,000
Operating expenses		
Fixed cash operating expenses	$ 21,000	$ 21,000
Variable operating expenses	12,500	16,000
Depreciation	4,500	10,000
Total operating expenses	$ 38,000	$ 47,000
Earnings before interest and taxes	$ 12,000	$ 17,000
Interest expense	3,000	6,100
Earnings before taxes	$ 9,000	$ 10,900
Taxes	4,500	5,450
Net income	$ 4,500	$ 5,450

a. Based on the preceding statements, complete the following table:

M & G Industries Ratio Analysis			
	Industry Averages	**Actual 1997**	**Actual 1998**
Current ratio	1.80		
Acid-test ratio	.70		
Average collection period	37.00		
Inventory turnover	2.50		
Debt ratio	58%		
Times interest earned	3.80		
Gross profit margin	38%		
Operating profit margin	10%		
Total asset turnover	1.14		
Fixed asset turnover	1.40		
Operating income return on investment	11.4%		
Return on total assets	4.0%		
Return on common equity	9.5%		

b. Evaluate the firm's financial position using the "four-question approach" described in the chapter.

ST-3. (*Cash Flow Statement*)

a. Using the indirect method, prepare a cash flow statement for M & G Industries for 1998 using information given in Self-Test Problem ST-2.

b. How does this statement supplement your ratio analysis from Self-Test Problem ST-2? Explain.

STUDY PROBLEMS (SET A)

3-1A. (*Ratio Calculation*) Given the following information for the McNabb Construction Company, calculate the firm's total asset turnover and return on equity ratios:

Net profit margin (net income ÷ sales)	8%
Return on total assets (net income ÷ total assets)	15%
Debt ratio (total liabilities ÷ total assets)	30%

3-2A. (*Balance Sheet Analysis*) Complete the following balance sheet using the following information:

Cash		Accounts payable	100,000
Accounts receivable		Long-term debt	
Inventory		Total liabilities	
Current assets		Common equity	
Net fixed assets	1,500,000	Total	$2,100,000
Total	$2,100,000		

Current ratio = 6.0   Total asset turnover = 1.0
Inventory turnover = 8.0   Average collection period = 30 days
Debt ratio = 20%   Gross profit margin = 15%

3-3A. (*Ratio Analysis*) The Mitchem Marble Company has a target current ratio of 2.0 but has experienced some difficulties financing its expanding sales in the past few months. The firm has a current ratio of 2.5 with current assets of $2.5 million. If Mitchem expands its receivables and inventories using its short-term line of credit, how much additional short-term funding can it borrow before its current ratio standard is reached?

3-4A. (*Ratio Analysis*) The balance sheet and income statement for the J. P. Robard Mfg. Company are as follows:

Balance Sheet ($000)	
Cash	$ 500
Accounts receivable	2,000
Inventories	1,000
Current assets	3,500
Net fixed assets	4,500
Total assets	$8,000
Accounts payable	$1,100
Accrued expenses	600
Short-term notes payable	300
Current liabilities	$2,000
Long-term debt	2,000
Owners' equity	4,000
Total liabilities and owners' equity	$8,000

Income Statement ($000)	
Net sales (all credit)	$8,000
Cost of goods sold	(3,300)
Gross profit	4,700
Operating expenses (includes $500 depreciation)	(3,000)
Operating income	1,700
Interest expense	(367)
Earnings before taxes	$1,333
Income taxes (40%)	(533)
Net income	$ 800

Calculate the following ratios:

Current ratio	Debt ratio
Times interest earned	Average collection period
Inventory turnover	Fixed asset turnover
Total asset turnover	Gross profit margin
Operating profit margin	Return on equity
Operating income return on investment	

3-5A. (*Analyzing Operating Income Return on Investment*) The R. M. Smithers Corporation earned an operating profit margin of 10 percent based on sales of $10 million and total assets of $5 million last year.

    a. What was Smithers's total asset turnover ratio?

b. During the coming year, the company president has set a goal of attaining a total asset turnover of 3.5. How much must firm sales rise, other things being the same, for the goal to be achieved? (State your answer in both dollars and percentage increase in sales.)

c. What was Smithers's operating income return on investment last year? Assuming the firm's operating profit margin remains the same, what will the operating income return on investment be next year if the total asset turnover goal is achieved?

3-6A. (*Using Financial Ratios*) The Brenmar Sales Company had a gross profit margin (gross profits/sales) of 30 percent and sales of $9 million last year. Seventy-five percent of the firm's sales are on credit and the remainder are cash sales. Brenmar's current assets equal $1.5 million, its current liabilities equal $300,000, and it has $100,000 in cash plus marketable securities.

a. If Brenmar's accounts receivable are $562,500, what is its average collection period?

b. If Brenmar reduces its average collection period to 20 days, what will be its new level of accounts receivable?

c. Brenmar's inventory turnover ratio is 9 times. What is the level of Brenmar's inventories?

3-7A. (*Ratio Analysis*) Using Pamplin Inc.'s financial statements shown on the following pages:

a. Compute the following ratios for both 1997 and 1998.

	Industry Norm
Current ratio	5.00
Acid-test (quick) ratio	3.00
Inventory turnover	2.20
Average collection period	90.00
Debt ratio	0.33
Times interest earned	7.00
Total asset turnover	0.75
Fixed asset turnover	1.00
Operating profit margin	20%
Return on common equity	9%

b. How liquid is the firm?

c. Is management generating adequate operating profit on the firm's assets?

d. How is the firm financing its assets?

e. Are the common stockholders receiving a good return on their investment?

Pamplin, Inc., Balance Sheet at 12/31/97 and 12/31/98

Assets	1997	1998
Cash	$ 200	$ 150
Accounts receivable	450	425
Inventory	550	625
Current assets	$1,200	$1,200
Plant and equipment	$2,200	$2,600
Less: accumulated depreciation	(1,000)	(1,200)
Net plant and equipment	$1,200	$1,400
Total assets	$2,400	$2,600

(continued)

Liabilities and Owner's Equity	1997	1998
Accounts payable	$ 200	$ 150
Notes payable—current (9%)	0	150
Current liabilities	$ 200	$ 300
Bonds (8 1/3% interest)	$ 600	$ 600
Owners' equity		
Common stock	$ 300	$ 300
Paid-in capital	600	600
Retained earnings	700	800
Total owners' equity	$1,600	$1,700
Total liabilities and owners' equity	$2,400	$2,600

Pamplin, Inc., Income Statement for years ending 12/31/97 and 12/31/98

	1997		1998	
Sales (all credit)		$1,200		$1,450
Cost of goods sold		700		850
Gross profit		$ 500		$ 600
Operating expenses	30		40	
Depreciation	220	250	200	240
Operating income		$ 250		$ 360
Interest expense		50		64
Net income before taxes		$ 200		$ 296
Taxes (40%)		80		118
Net income		$ 120		$ 178

3-8A. (*Statement of Cash Flow*) Prepare a statement of cash flow for Pamplin, Inc., for the year ended December 31, 1998 (problem 3-7A). Use both the direct method and the indirect method in calculating cash flow from operations.

3-9A. (*Statement of Cash Flow*) (a) Prepare a cash flow statement for the Waterhouse Co. for the year 1998. Use both the direct method and the indirect method in calculating cash flow from operations. (b) What were the firm's primary sources and uses of cash?

	1997	1998
Cash	$ 75,000	$ 82,500
Receivables	102,000	90,000
Inventory	168,000	165,000
Prepaid expenses	12,000	13,500
Total current assets	$357,000	$351,000
Gross fixed assets	325,500	468,000
Accumulated depreciation	(94,500)	(129,000)
Patents	61,500	52,500
Total assets	$649,500	$742,500

(*continued*)

	1997	1998
Accounts payable	$124,500	$112,500
Taxes payable	97,500	105,000
Total current liabilities	$222,000	$217,500
Mortgage payable	150,000	0
Preferred stock	0	225,000
Additional paid-in capital—preferred	0	6,000
Common stock	225,000	225,000
Retained earnings	52,500	69,000
Total liabilities and equity	$649,500	$742,500

Additional Information:

1. The only entry in the accumulated depreciation account is the depreciation expense for the period.

2. The only entries in the retained earning account are for dividends paid in the amount of $18,000 and for the net income for the year.

3. Expenses include a $9,000 amortization of patents.

4. The income statement for 1998 is as follows:

Sales (all credit)	$ 187,500
Cost of goods sold	(111,000)
Gross profit	76,500
Operating expenses	(32,000)
Provision for taxes	(10,000)
Net income	$ 34,500

(Cost of goods sold includes depreciation expense of $34,500)

3-10A. (*Review of Financial Statements*) Prepare a balance sheet and income statement on December 31, 1998, for the Sharpe Mfg. Co. from the following scrambled list of items.

Accounts receivable	$120,000
Machinery and equipment	700,000
Accumulated depreciation	236,000
Notes payable	100,000
Net sales	800,000
Inventory	110,000
Accounts payable	90,000
Long-term debt	160,000
Cost of goods sold	500,000
Operating expenses	280,000
Common stock	320,000
Cash	96,000
Retained earnings—prior year	?
Retained earnings—current year	?

3-11A. (*Financial Ratios—Investment Analysis*) The annual sales for Salco, Inc., were $4.5 million last year. The firm's end-of-year balance sheet appeared as follows:

Current assets	$ 500,000	Liabilities	$1,000,000
Net fixed assets	1,500,000	Owners' equity	1,000,000
	$2,000,000		$2,000,000

The firm's income statement for the year was as follows:

Sales	$4,500,000
Less: cost of goods sold	(3,500,000)
Gross profit	$1,000,000
Less: operating expenses	(500,000)
Operating income	$500,000
Less: interest expense	(100,000)
Earnings before taxes	$ 400,000
Less: taxes (50%)	(200,000)
Net income	$ 200,000

a. Calculate Salco's total asset turnover, operating profit margin, and operating income return on investment.

b. Salco plans to renovate one of its plants, which will require an added investment in plant and equipment of $1 million. The firm will maintain its present debt ratio of .5 when financing the new investment and expects sales to remain constant, while the operating profit margin will rise to 13 percent. What will be the new operating income return on investment for Salco after the plant renovation?

c. Given that the plant renovation in part (b) occurs and Salco's interest expense rises by $50,000 per year, what will be the return earned on the common stockholders' investment? Compare this rate of return with that earned before the renovation.

3-12A. (*Statement of Cash Flow*) The consolidated balance sheets of the TMU Processing Company are presented below for May 31, 1998 and May 31, 1999 (millions of dollars). TMU earned $14 million after taxes during the year ended May 31, 1999, and paid common dividends of $10 million.

	May 31 1998	May 31 1999
Cash	$ 10	$ 8
Accounts receivable	12	22
Inventories	8	14
Current assets	$ 30	$ 44
Gross fixed assets	$100	$110
Less: accumulated depreciation	(40)	(50)
Net fixed assets	$ 60	$ 60
Total assets	$ 90	$104
Accounts payable	$ 12	$ 9
Notes payable	7	7
Long-term debt	11	24
Common stock	20	20
Retained earnings	40	44
Total liabilities	$ 90	$104

a. Prepare a statement of cash flow for 1999 for TMU Processing Company. (Hint: You will only be able to use the indirect method.)

b. Summarize your findings.

3-13A. (*Preparing the Statement of Cash Flow*) Comparative balance sheets for December 31, 1997, and December 31, 1998, for the Abrams Mfg. Company are as follows:

	1997	1998
Cash	$ 89,000	$100,000
Accounts receivable	64,000	70,000
Inventory	112,000	100,000
Prepaid expenses	10,000	10,000
Total current assets	275,000	280,000
Plant and equipment	238,000	311,000
Accumulated depreciation	(40,000)	(66,000)
Total assets	$473,000	$525,000
Accounts payable	$ 85,000	$ 90,000
Accrued liabilities	68,000	63,000
Total current debt	153,000	153,000
Mortgage payable	70,000	0
Preferred stock	0	120,000
Common stock	205,000	205,000
Retained earnings	45,000	47,000
Total debt and equity	$473,000	$525,000

Abrams's 1996 income statement is as follows:

Sales (all credit)	$184,000
Cost of sales	150,000
Gross profit	$ 34,000
Operating, interest, and tax expenses	10,000
Net income	$ 24,000

Additional Information:

a. The only entry in the accumulated depreciation account is for 1998 depreciation.

b. The firm paid $22,000 in dividends during 1998.

Prepare a 1998 statement of cash flow for Abrams using the indirect method.

3-14A. (*Analyzing the Statement of Cash Flow*) Identify any financial weaknesses revealed in the statement of cash flow for the Westlake Manufacturing Co.

Westlake Manufacturing Co. Statement of Cash Flow for Current Year	
Cash flow from operating activities	
Net income	$ 540,000
Add (deduct) to reconcile net income to cash flow	
Decrease in accounts receivable	40,000
Increase in inventories	(240,000)
	(continued)

Westlake Manufacturing Co. Statement of Cash Flow for Current Year *(continued)*		
Increase in prepaid expenses	(10,000)	
Depreciation expense	60,000	
Decrease in accrued wages	(50,000)	
Net cash flow from operations		$ 340,000
Cash flow from investing activities		
Sale (purchase) of plant and equipment		$2,400,000
Cash flow from financing activities		
Issuance of bonds	$1,000,000	
Repayment of short-term debt	(3,000,000)	
Payment of long-term debt	(500,000)	
Payment of dividends	(1,000,000)	
Net cash from financing activities		(3,500,000)
Net increase (decrease) in cash for the period		($760,000)

3-15A. The T. P. Jarmon Company manufactures and sells a line of exclusive sportswear. The firm's sales were $600,000 for the year just ended, and its total assets exceeded $400,000. The company was started by Mr. Jarmon just 10 years ago and has been profitable every year since its inception. The chief financial officer for the firm, Brent Vehlim, has decided to seek a line of credit from the firm's bank totaling $80,000. In the past, the company has relied on its suppliers to finance a large part of its needs for inventory. However, in recent months, tight money conditions have led the firm's suppliers to offer sizable cash discounts to speed up payments for purchases. Mr. Vehlim wants to use the line of credit to supplant a large portion of the firm's payables during the summer months, which are the firm's peak seasonal sales period.

The firm's two most recent balance sheets were presented to the bank in support of its loan request. In addition, the firm's income statement for the year just ended was provided to support the loan request. These statements are as follows:

T. P. Jarmon Company, Balance Sheet for 12/31/97 and 12/31/98		
Assets	**1997**	**1998**
Cash	$ 15,000	$ 14,000
Marketable securities	6,000	6,200
Accounts receivable	42,000	33,000
Inventory	51,000	84,000
Prepaid rent	1,200	1,100
Total current assets	$115,200	$138,300
Net plant and equipment	286,000	270,000
Total assets	$401,200	$408,300
Liabilities and Equity	**1997**	**1998**
Accounts payable	$ 48,000	$ 57,000
Notes payable	15,000	13,000
Accruals	6,000	5,000
Total current liabilities	$ 69,000	$ 75,000
Long-term debt	$160,000	$150,000
Common stockholders' equity	$172,200	$183,300
Total liabilities and equity	$401,200	$408,300

T. P. Jarmon Company, Income Statement for the Year Ended 12/31/98		
Sales (all credit)		$600,000
Less: cost of goods sold		460,000
Gross profits		$140,000
Less: operating and interest expenses		
General and administrative	$30,000	
Interest	10,000	
Depreciation	30,000	
Total		70,000
Earnings before taxes		$ 70,000
Less: taxes		27,100
Net income available to common stockholders		$ 42,900
Less: cash dividends		31,800
Change in retained earnings		$ 11,100

Jan Fama, associate credit analyst for the Merchants National Bank of Midland, Michigan, was assigned the task of analyzing Jarmon's loan request.

a. Calculate the financial ratios for 1998 corresponding to the industry norms provided as follows:

	Ratio Norm
Current ratio	1.8
Acid-test ratio	0.9
Debt ratio	0.5
Times interest earned	10.0
Average collection period	20.0
Inventory turnover (based on cost of goods sold)	7.0
Return on common equity	12.0%
Gross profit margin	25.0%
Operating income return on investment	16.8%
Operating profit margin	14.0%
Total asset turnover	1.20
Fixed asset turnover	1.80

b. Which of the ratios reported above in the industry norms do you feel should be most crucial in determining whether the bank should extend the line of credit?

c. Prepare a statement of cash flow for Jarmon covering the year ended December 31, 1998.

d. Use the information provided by the financial ratios and the statement of cash flow to decide if you would support making the loan.

e. Use the duPont analysis to evaluate the firm's financial position.

3-16A. PepsiCo's income statement for 1996 and the balance sheets for December 31, 1995, and December 31, 1996, follow.

a. Go to your library and find industry norms for the beverages industry. (PepsiCo is considered to be in the beverages industry [Standard Industrial Code 2086].)

b. Are there any ratios that are not provided for the industry that prevent you from using the "four-question approach" as described in this chapter? How would you adapt your approach to compensate for any missing industry norms?

c. Compute the financial ratios for PepsiCo for 1996, and using your industry norms, evaluate the firm in the following areas:

(1) liquidity

(2) operating profitability

(3) financing policies

(4) return of the shareholders' investment

d. Prepare a statement of cash flow for PepsiCo. Interpret your findings.

PepsiCo, Inc., Income Statement for Year Ending 1996

Net sales		$31,645
Costs and expenses, net		
Costs of sales	$15,383	
Selling, general, and administrative expenses[a]	12,593	
Amortization of intangible assets[b]	301	
Impairment of long-lived assets[c]	822	$29,099
Operating profit		$ 2,546
Interest expense		(600)
Interest income		101
Income before income taxes		$ 2,047
Provision for income taxes		898
Net income		$ 1,149

[a]Selling expenses and general and administrative expenses include $1,740 in depreciation and amortization (noncash expenses).
[b]Amortization of intangible assets is a noncash expense for the purposes of writing off the intangible assets over time—much like depreciation of fixed assets.
[c]Impairment of long-lived assets (plant and equipment or fixed assets) is a noncash expense, also similar to depreciation.

PepsiCo, Inc., Balance Sheet December 31, 1995 and 1996

	1995	1996
Assets		
Current assets		
Cash and cash equivalents	$ 382	$ 447
Short-term investments, at cost	1,116	339
Accounts and notes receivable	2,407	2,516
Inventories	1,051	1,038
Prepaid expenses	590	799
Total current assets	$ 5,546	$ 5,139
Investments in unconsolidated affiliates	1,635	1,375
Property, plant, and equipment, net	9,870	10,191
Intangible assets, net	7,584	7,136
Other assets	797	671
Total assets	$25,432	$24,512

(continued)

Liabilities and Shareholders Equity		
Current liabilities		
Accounts payable	$ 1,556	$ 1,565
Accrued compensation and benefits	815	847
Short-term borrowings	706	26
Accrued marketing	469	573
Income taxes payable	387	487
Other current liabilities	1,297	1,641
Total current liabilities	$ 5,230	$ 5,139
Long-term debt	8,509	8,439
Other liabilities	2,495	2,533
Deferred income taxes	1,885	1,778
Shareholders' equity		
Capital stock, par value 1 2/3 cents per share:		
authorized 3,600 shares, issued 1,726 shares	$ 14	$ 29
Capital in excess of par value	1,060	1,201
Retained earnings	8,730	9,184
Currency translation adjustment and other	(808)	(768)
	$ 8,996	$ 9,646
Less: treasury stock, at cost	(1,683)	(3,023)
Total shareholders' equity	$ 7,313	$ 6,623
Total liabilities and shareholders' equity	$25,432	$24,512

3-17A. (*Economic Value Added*) Stegemoller Inc.'s management wants to evaluate its firm's prior-year performance in terms of its contribution to shareholder value. This past year, the firm earned an operating income return on investment of 12 percent, compared to an industry norm of 11 percent. It has been estimated that the firm's investors have an opportunity cost on their funds of 14 percent. The firm's total assets for the year were $100 million. Compute the amount of economic value created or destroyed by the firm. How does your finding support or fail to support what you would conclude using ratio analysis to evaluate the firm's performance?

INTEGRATIVE PROBLEM

F̲ollowing are the 1992 to 1996 financial statements both for Reebok International LTD and Nike, two head-to-head competitors in the athletic footwear industry.

1. Evaluate the two respective firms in terms of their financial performance over time (1992 to 1996) as it relates to (1) liquidity, (2) operating profitability, (3) financing the assets, and (4) the shareholders' (common equity) return on investment. (A computer spreadsheet is extremely helpful here. In fact, the financial statements for these two companies are available at http://nikebiz.com/invest/invest_nj.html and http://www.reebok.com/annual/19.html, which would save you some time in doing the assignment.)

2. Compare the two firms' financial performances against each other. How are they different and how are they similar?

3. Compute the firms' cash flows only for 1996 and compare the results. (Again, the computer spreadsheet would be a real time saver here.)

GO TO:
http://www.prenhall.com/bfm
For downloads and current events associated with this chapter

Reebok International LTD, Financial Statements 1992–1996

Income Statements
($Millions)

	1992	1993	1994	1995	1996
Sales	$3,023	$2,894	$3,280	$3,481	$3,479
Cost of goods sold	1,799	1,695	1,938	2,084	2,108
Gross profit	$1,224	$1,199	$1,342	$1,397	$1,371
Selling, general & admin.	807	770	890	1,000	1,078
Depreciation	27	35	32	35	28
Operating profit	$ 390	$ 394	$ 420	$ 362	$ 265
Interest expense	20	25	17	26	42
Non-operating income/expense	14	11	14	10	15
Special items	(125)	(8)	—	(72)	—
Earnings before taxes	$ 258	$ 372	$ 417	$ 274	$ 238
Income taxes	143	140	154	100	84
Minority interest	—	8	9	11	15
Net income	$ 115	$· 223	$ 254	$ 163	$ 139

Balance Sheets
($Millions)

	1992	1993	1994	1995	1996
ASSETS					
Cash & equivalents	$ 105	$ 79	$ 84	$ 80	$ 232
Accounts receivable	418	457	532	507	591
Inventories	434	514	625	635	545
Prepaid expenses	24	22	30	—	—
Other current assets	79	55	66	121	96
Total current assets	$1,060	$1,127	$1,337	$1,343	$1,464
Gross plant & equipment	$ 196	$ 220	$ 283	$ 336	$ 357
Accumulated depreciation	69	89	118	144	172
Net plant, property & equipment	$ 128	$ 131	$ 165	$ 192	$ 185
Other assets	158	134	147	121	138
Total assets	$1,345	$1,392	$1,649	$1,656	$1,787
LIABILITIES					
Long-term debt due in 1 year	$ 4	$ 3	$ 5	$ 1	$ 53
Notes payable	4	24	64	67	33
Accounts payable	281	138	171	166	196
Taxes payable	89	81	102	48	66
Accrued expenses	—	144	157	145	169
Other current liabilities	7	6	6	6	—
Total current liabilities	$ 386	$ 396	$ 506	$ 432	$ 517
Long-term debt	116	134	132	254	854
Deferred taxes	5	—	—	5	—
Minority interest	—	15	22	31	34
Total liabilities	$ 507	$ 545	$ 659	$ 723	$1,405

(continued)

	1992	1993	1994	1995	1996
EQUITY					
Preferred stock	$ —	$ —	$ —	$ 39	$ —
Common stock	$ 1	$ 1	$ 1	$ 1	$ 1
Capital surplus	447	264	165	—	—
Retained earnings	993	1,185	1,427	1,497	998
Less: treasury stock	603	603	603	604	617
Common equity	$ 839	$ 847	$ 991	$ 894	$ 382
Total equity	$ 839	$ 847	$ 991	$ 933	$ 382
Total liabilities & equity	$1,345	$1,392	$1,649	$1,656	$1,787

Nike, Financial Statements 1992–1996

Income Statement
($Millions)

	1992	1993	1994	1995	1996
Sales	$3,405	$3,931	$3,790	$4,761	$6,471
Cost of goods sold	2,050	2,337	2,245	2,805	3,825
Gross profit	$1,355	$1,594	$1,544	$1,956	$2,646
Selling, general & admin.	761	922	974	1,210	1,640
Depreciation	48	60	72	84	68
Operating profit	$ 546	$ 611	$ 499	$ 662	$ 938
Interest expense	31	27	16	24	39
Non-operating income/expense	7	10	15	24	1
Special items	—	—	(7)	(11)	—
Earnings before taxes	$ 522	$ 595	$ 491	$ 651	$ 900
Income taxes	193	230	192	250	346
Net income	$ 329	$ 365	$ 299	$ 401	$ 554

Balance Sheet
($Millions)

	1992	1993	1994	1995	1996
ASSETS					
Cash & equivalents	$ 260	$ 291	$ 519	$ 216	$ 262
Accounts receivable	596	668	704	1,053	1,346
Inventories	471	593	470	630	931
Prepaid expenses	33	42	40	74	94
Other current assets	28	26	38	73	93
Total current assets	$1,388	$1,621	$1,770	$2,046	$2,726
Gross plant & equipment	$ 498	$ 571	$ 639	$ 891	$1,048
Accumulated depreciation	152	193	233	336	404
Net plant, property & equipment	$ 346	$ 378	$ 406	$ 555	$ 644
Intangibles	110	158	157	496	475
Other assets	29	31	40	46	106
Total assets	$1,873	$2,187	$2,374	$3,143	$3,951

(continued)

	1992	1993	1994	1995	1996
LIABILITIES					
Long-term debt due in 1 year	$ 4	$ 53	$ 4	$ 32	$ 7
Notes payable	106	108	127	397	445
Accounts payable	135	136	211	298	455
Taxes payable	42	17	38	36	79
Accrued expenses	134	139	182	345	480
Total current liabilities	$ 421	$ 453	$ 562	$1,108	$1,466
Long-term debt	69	15	12	11	10
Deferred taxes	27	30	18	18	2
Other liabilities	24	44	40	42	41
Total liabilities	$ 541	$ 541	$ 633	$1,179	$1,519
EQUITY					
Common stock	$ 3	$ 3	$ 3	$ 3	$ 3
Capital surplus	94	108	108	122	155
Retained earnings	1,235	1,535	1,630	1,839	2,274
Common equity	1,332	1,646	1,741	1,964	2,432
Total equity	$1,332	$1,646	$1,741	$1,964	$2,432
Total liabilities & equity	$1,873	$2,187	$2,374	$3,143	$3,951

Industry Averages: Athletic Footwear

Current ratio	2.04
Quick ratio	1.30
Average collection period	69.96
Accounts receivable turnover	5.22
Inventory turnover	3.90
Operating income return on investment	18.6%
Operating profit margin	10.8%
Gross profit margin	39.6%
Total asset turnover	1.72
Debt ratio	52.9%
Times interest earned	10.72
Return on equity	21.2%

STUDY PROBLEMS (SET B)

3-1B. (*Ratio Calculation*) Given the following information for the Marcus Food Distributing Company, calculate the firm's total asset turnover and return on equity ratios:

Net profit margin (net income ÷ sales)	12%
Return on total assets (net income ÷ total assets)	15%
Debt ratio (total liabilities ÷ total assets)	45%

3-2B. (*Balance Sheet Analysis*) Complete the following balance sheet using this information:

Cash		Accounts payable	100,000
Accounts receivable		Long-term debt	
Inventory		Total liabilities	
Current assets		Common equity	
Net fixed assets	1,000,000	Total	$1,300,000
Total	$1,300,000		

Current ratio = 3.0   Total asset turnover = .5
Inventory turnover = 10.0   Average collection period = 45 days
Debt ratio = 30%   Gross profit margin = 30%

3-3B. (*Ratio Analysis*) The Allandale Office Supply Company has a target current ratio of 2.0 but has experienced some difficulties financing its expanding sales in the past few months. At present, the firm has a current ratio of 2.75 with current assets of $3 million. If Allandale expands its receivables and inventories using its short-term bank loan (a current liability), how much additional short-term funding can it borrow before its current ratio standard is reached?

3-4B. (*Ratio Analysis*) The balance sheet and income statement for the Simsboro Paper Company are as follows:

Balance Sheet ($000)		Income Statement ($000)	
Cash	$1,000	Net sales (all credit)	$7,500
Accounts receivable	1,500	Cost of goods sold	(3,000)
Inventories	1,000	Gross profit	$4,500
Current assets	$3,500	Operating expenses[a]	(3,000)
Net fixed assets	$4,500	Operating income (EBIT)	$1,500
Total assets	$8,000	Interest expense	(367)
Accounts payable	$1,000	Earnings before taxes	$1,133
Accrued expenses	600	Income taxes (40%)	(453)
Short-term notes payable	200	Net income	$ 680
Current liabilities	$1,800		
Long-term debt	2,100		
Owners' equity	$4,100		
Total liabilities and owners' equity	$8,000		

[a]Including depreciation expense of $500 for the year.

Calculate the following ratios:

Current ratio	Debt ratio
Times interest earned	Average collection period
Inventory turnover	Fixed asset turnover
Total asset turnover	Gross profit margin
Operatingt profit margin	Return on equity
Operating income return on investment	

3-5B. (*Analyzing Operating Income Return on Investment*) The R. M. Senchack Corporation earned an operating profit margin of 6 percent based on sales of $11 million and total assets of $6 million last year.

   a. What was Senchack's total asset turnover ratio?

b. During the coming year, the company president has set a goal of attaining a total asset turnover of 2.5. How much must firm sales rise, other things being the same, for the total asset goal to be achieved? (State your answer in both dollars and as a percent increase in sales.)

c. What was Senchack's operating income return on investment last year? Assuming the firm's operaating profit margin remains the same, what will the operataing income return on investment be next year if the total asset turnover goal is achieved?

3-6B. (*Using Financial Ratios*) Brenda Smith, Inc., had a gross profit margin (gross profits ÷ sales) of 25 percent and sales of $9.75 million last year. Seventy-five percent of the firm's sales are on credit and the remainder are cash sales. Smith's current assets equal $1,550,000, its current liabilities equal $300,000, and it has $150,000 in cash plus marketable securities.

a. If Smith's accounts receivable are $562,500, what is its average collection period?

b. If Smith reduces its average collection period to 20 days, what will be its new level of accounts receivable?

c. Smith's inventory turnover ratio is 8 times. What is the level of Smith's inventories?

3-7B. (*Ratio Analysis of Loan Request*) Using Chavez Corporation's financial statements following:

a. Compute the following ratios for both 1997 and 1998.

	Industry Norm
Current ratio	5.00
Acid-test (quick) ratio	3.00
Inventory turnover	2.20
Average collection period	90.00
Debt ratio	0.33
Times interest earned	7.00
Total asset turnover	0.75
Fixed asset turnover	1.00
Operating profit margin	20%
Operating income return on investment	15%
Return on common equity	13.43%

b. How liquid is the firm?

c. Is management generating adequate operating profit on the firm's assets?

d. How is the firm financing its assets?

e. Are the common stockholders receiving a good return on their investment?

J. B. Chavez Corporation, Balance Sheet at 12/31/97 and 12/31/98 ($000)

Assets	12/31/97	12/31/98	Liabilities and Owners' Equity	12/31/97	12/31/98
Cash	$ 225	$ 175	Account payable	$ 250	$ 115
Accounts receivable	450	430	Notes payable—current (9%)	0	115
Inventory	575	625	Current liabilities	$ 250	$ 230
Current assets	$1,250	$1,230	Bonds	$ 600	$ 600
Plant and equipment	$2,200	$2,500	Owners' equity		
Less: Accumulated depreciation	(1,000)	(1,200)	Common stock	$ 300	$ 300
Net plant and equipment	$1,200	$1,300	Paid-in capital	600	600
Total assets	$2,450	$2,530	Retained earnings	700	800
			Total owners' equity	$1,600	$1,700
			Total liabilities and owners' equity	$2,450	$2,530

J. B. Chavez Corporation, Income Statement for the Years Ending 12/31/97 and 12/31/98				
		1997		1998
Sales		$1,250		$1,450
Cost of goods sold		(700)		(875)
Gross profit		$ 550		$ 575
Operating expenses	(30)		(45)	
Depreciation	(220)	(250)	(200)	(245)
Net operating income		$ 300		$ 330
Interest expense		(50)		(60)
Net income before taxes		$ 250		$ 270
Taxes (40%)		(100)		(108)
Net income		$ 150		$ 162

3-8B. (*Statement of Cash Flow*) Prepare a statement of cash flow for J. B. Chavez Corporation for the year ended December 31, 1998 (problem 3-7B). Use both the direct method and the indirect method in calculating cash flow from operations.

3-9B. (*Statement of Cash Flows*) (a) Prepare a statement of cash flow for Cramer, Inc., for the year 1998. Use both the direct method and the indirect method in calculating cash flow from operations. (b) What were the firm's primary sources and uses of cash?

	1997	1998
Cash	$ 76,000	$ 82,500
Receivables	100,000	91,000
Inventory	168,000	163,000
Prepaid expenses	11,500	13,500
Total current assets	$355,500	$350,000
Gross fixed assets	325,500	450,000
Accumulated depreciation	(94,500)	(129,000)
Patents	61,500	52,500
Total assets	$648,000	$723,500

	1997	1998
Accounts payable	$123,000	$ 93,500
Taxes payable	97,500	105,000
Current liabilities	$220,500	$198,500
Mortgage payable	150,000	—
Preferred stock	—	231,000
Common stock	225,000	225,000
Retained earnings	52,500	69,000
Total liabilities and equity	$648,000	$723,500

Additional Information:

1. The only entry in the accumulated depreciation account is the depreciation expense for the period.

2. The only entries in the retained earnings account are for dividends paid in the amount of $20,000 and for the net income for the year.

3. Expenses include a $9,000 amortization of patents.

4. The income statemeant for 1998 is as follows:

Sales (all credit)	$190,000
Cost of goods sold	(86,000)
Gross profit	$104,000
Operating expenses (incl. interest expense)	(43,500)
Provisions for taxes	(24,000)
Net income	$ 36,500

(Cost of goods sold included depreciation expense of $34,500)

3-10B. (*Review of Basic Financial Statements*) Prepare a balance sheet and income statement on December 31, 1998 for the Sabine Mfg. Co. from the scrambled list of items below. Ignore income taxes and interest expense.

Accounts receivable	$150,000
Machinery and equipment	700,000
Accumulated depreciation	236,000
Notes payable—current	90,000
Net sales	900,000
Inventory	110,000
Accounts payable	90,000
Long-term debt	160,000
Cost of goods sold	550,000
Operating expenses	280,000
Common stock	320,000
Cash	90,000
Retained earnings—prior year	?
Retained earnings—current year	?

3-11B. (*Financial Ratios—Investment Analysis*) The annual sales for Mel's, Inc, were $5 million last year. The firm's end-of-year balance sheet appeared as follows:

Current assets	$ 500,000	Liabilities	$1,000,000
Net fixed assets	$1,500,000	Owners' equity	$1,000,000
	$2,000,000		$2,000,000

The firm's income statement for the year was as follows:

Sales	$5,000,000
Less: Cost of goods sold	(3,000,000)
Gross profit	$2,000,000
Less: Operating expenses	(1,500,000)
Operating income	$ 500,000
Less: Interest expense	(100,000)
Earnings before taxes	$ 400,000
Less: Taxes (40%)	(160,000)
Net income	$ 240,000

a. Calculate Mel's total asset turnover, operating profit margin, and operating income return on investment.

b. Mel plans to renovate one of its plants, which will require an added investment in plant and equipment of $1 million. The firm will maintain its present debt ratio of .5 when financing the new investment and expects sales to remain constant, whereas the operating profit margin will rise to 13 percent. What will be the new operating income return on investment for Mel after the plant renovation?

c. Given that the plant renovation in part (b) occurs and Mel's interest expense rises by $40,000 per year, what will be the return earned on the common stockholders' investment? Compare this rate of return with that earned before the renovation.

3-12B. (*Statement of Cash Flow*) The consolidated balance sheets of the SMU Processing Company are presented below for May 31, 1997, and May 31, 1998 (millions of dollars). SMU earned $14 million after taxes during the year ended May 31, 1998, and paid common dividends of $10 million.

	1997	1998
Cash	$ 10	$ 8
Accounts receivable	12	22
Inventories	8	14
Current assets	$ 30	$ 44
Gross fixed assets	$100	$110
Less: Accumulated depreciation	(40)	(50)
Net fixed assets	$ 60	$ 60
Total assets	$ 90	$104
Accounts payable	$ 12	$ 9
Notes payable	7	7
Long-term debt	11	24
Common stock	20	20
Retained earnings	40	44
Total liabilities and owners' equity	$ 90	$104

a. Prepare a statement of cash flow for 1998 for SMU Processing Company. (Hint: You will only be able to use the indirect method.)

b. Summarize your findings.

3-13B. (*Preparing the Statement of Cash Flow*) Comparative balance sheets for December 31, 1997, and December 31, 1998, for the J. Ng Company follow:

	1998	1997
Cash	$ 70,000	$ 89,000
Accounts receivable	70,000	64,000
Inventory	80,000	102,000
Prepaid expenses	10,000	10,000
Total current assets	230,000	265,000
Plant and equipment	301,000	238,000
Accumulated depreciation	−66,000	−40,000
Total assets	$465,000	$463,000
Accounts payable	$ 80,000	85,000
Accrued liabilities	63,000	68,000
Total current liabilities	143,000	153,000

(continued)

	1998	1997
Mortgage payable	0	60,000
Preferred stock	$ 60,000	0
Additional paid-in capital—preferred stock	10,000	0
Common stock	205,000	205,000
Retained earnings	47,000	45,000
Total debt and equity	$465,000	$463,000

Ng's 1996 Income Statement is as follows:

	1998
Sales	$204,000.00
Cost of sales	160,000.00
Gross profit	44,000.00
Operating, interest, and tax expenses	10,000.00
Net income	$ 34,000.00

Additional Information:

    a. The only entry in the accumulated depreciation account is for 1996 depreciation.

    b. The firm paid $32,000 in dividends during 1998.

Prepare a statement of cash flows for J. Ng Inc. for 1998 using the indirect method.

3-14B. (*Analyzing the Statement of Cash Flow*) Identify by financial weaknesses revealed in the statement of cash flow for the Simsboro Pulpwood Mill, Inc.

Simsboro Pulpwood Mill, Inc., Statement of Cash Flow		
Cash flow from operating activities		
Net income	$ 500,000	
Add (deduct) to reconcile		
net income to net cash flow		
Decrease in accounts receivable	$ 200,000	
Increase in inventories	(400,000)	
Increase in prepaid expenses	(100,000)	
Depreciation expense	600,000	
Decrease in accrued wages	(50,000)	
Net cash flow from operating activities		$ 750,000
Cash flow from investing activities		
Purchase (sale) of plant and equipment		(2,250,000)
Cash flow from financing activities		
Issuance of bonds payable	$5,000,000	
Repayment of short-term debt	(3,000,000)	
Repayment of long-term debt	(500,000)	
Payment of dividends	(1,000,000)	
Net cash from financing activities		500,000
Net increase (decrease) in cash for the period		$(1,000,000)

3-15B. RPI Inc. is a manufacturer and retailer of high-quality sports clothing and gear. The firm was started several years ago by a group of serious outdoors enthusiasts who felt there was a need for a firm that could provide quality products at reasonable prices. The result was RPI Inc. Since its inception, the firm has been profitable with sales that last year totaled $700,000 and assets in excess of $400,000. The firm now finds its growing sales outstrip its ability to finance its inventory needs and estimates that it will need to borrow $100,000 in a short-term loan from its bank during the coming year.

The firm's most recent financial statements were provided to its bank as support for the firm's loan request. Joanne Peebie, a loan analyst trainee for the Morristown Bank and Trust, has been assigned the task of analyzing the firm's loan request.

RPI Inc., Balance Sheets for 12/31/97 and 12/31/98

Assets	1997	1998	Liabilities and Stockholders' Equity	1997	1998
Cash	$ 16,000	$ 17,000	Accounts payable	$ 48,000	$ 55,000
Marketable securities	7,000	7,200	Notes payable	16,000	13,000
Accounts receivable	42,000	38,000	Accruals	6,000	5,000
Inventory	50,000	93,000	Total current liabilities	$ 70,000	$ 73,000
Prepaid rent	1,200	1,100	Long-term debt	$160,000	$150,000
Total current assets	$116,200	$156,300	Common stockholders' equity	$172,200	$223,300
Net plant and equipment	286,000	290,000	Total liabilities and equity	$402,200	$446,300
Total assets	$402,200	$446,300			

RPI Inc., Income Statement for the Year Ended 12/31/98

Sales (all credit)		$700,000
Less: Cost of goods sold		500,000
Gross profits		$200,000
Less: Operating and interest expenses		
General and administrative	$ 50,000	
Interest	10,000	
Depreciation	30,000	
Total		90,000
Profit before taxes		$110,000
Less: Taxes		27,100
Net income available to common stockholders		$ 82,900
Less: Cash dividends		31,800
Change in retained earnings		$ 51,100

a. Calculate RPI's financial ratios corresponding to these industry norms provided for 1998:

	Ratio Norm		Ratio Norm
Current ratio	1.80	Return on total assets	8.40%
Acid-test ratio	0.90	Gross profit margin	25.0%
Debt ratio	0.50	Operating income return on investment	16.8%
Long-term debt to total assets	0.70	Operating profit margin	14.0%
Times interest earned	10.00	Total asset turnover	1.20
Average collection period	20.00	Fixed asset turnover	1.80
Inventory turnover (based on cost of goods sold)	7.00		

b. Which of the ratios reported in these industry norms do you feel should be most crucial in determining whether the bank should extend the loan?

c. Prepare a statement of cash flow for RPI covering the year ended December 31, 1996.

d. Use the information provided by the financial ratios and the statement of cash flow to decide if you would support making the loan.

e. Use the Du Pont analysis to evaluate the firm's financial position as of December 31, 1996.

3-16B. The Gillette Company's income statement for 1996 and the balance sheets for December 31, 1995, and December 31, 1996 follow.

a. Go to your library and find industry norms for the cutlery industry. (Gillette is considered to be in the cutlery industry [Standard Industrial Code 3420].)

b. Are there any ratios that are not provided for the industry that prevent you from using the "four-question approach" as described in this chapter? How would you adapt your approach to compensate for any missing industry norms?

c. Compute the financial ratios for Gillette for 1996, and using your industry norms, evaluate the firm in the following areas:

(1) liquidity

(2) operating profitability

(3) financing policies

(4) return on the shareholders' investment

d. Prepare a statement of cash flow for the Gillette Company. Interpret your findings.

Gillette Co., Financial Statements

Income Statements
($Millions)

	1996
Sales	$ 9,698
Cost of goods sold	3,301
Gross profit	$ 6,397
Selling, general, & administrative expense	3,978
Depreciation	370
Operating profit	$ 2,049
Interest expense	77
Non-operating income/expense	(35)
Special items	(413)
Earnings before taxes	$ 1,524
Income taxes	576
Earnings after taxes	$ 948
Preferred dividends	5
Extraordinary items	—
Net income	$ 943

	1995	1996
ASSETS		
Cash & equivalents	$ 50	$ 84
Accounts receivable	1,660	2,725
Inventories	1,035	1,358
Prepaid expenses	140	227
Other current assets	220	359

(continued)

	1995	1996
Total current assets	$3,105	$ 4,753
Gross plant, property & equipment	$3,262	$ 4,561
Accumulated depreciation	1,625	1,995
Net plant, property & equipment	$1,637	$ 2,566
Intangibles	1,221	2,626
Other assets	378	490
Total assets	$6,341	$10,435
LIABILITIES		
Long-term debt due in one year	$ 27	$ 15
Notes payable	576	656
Accounts payable	400	547
Taxes payable	248	299
Accrued expenses	806	1,318
Other current liabilities	67	100
Total current liabilities	$2,124	$ 2,935
Long-term debt	691	1,490
Deferred taxes	73	299
Minority interest	20	30
Other liabilities	919	1,190
Total liabilities	$3,827	$ 5,944
EQUITY		
Preferred stock	$ 63	$ 70
Common stock	$ 560	$ 671
Capital surplus	31	1,159
Retained earnings	2,906	3,647
Less: treasury stock	1,046	1,056
Common equity	$2,451	$ 4,421
Total equity	2,514	4,491
Total liabilities & equity	$6,341	$10,435

3-17B. (*Economic Value Added*) MacKenzie Inc.'s management wants to evaluate its firm's prior-year performance in terms of its contribution to shareholder value. This past year, the firm earned an operating income return on investment of 15 percent, compared to an industry norm of 13 percent. It has been estimated that the firm's investors have an opportunity cost on their funds of 12 percent. The firm's total assets for the year were $200 million. Compute the amount of economic value created or destroyed by the firm. How does your finding support or fail to support what you would conclude using ratio analysis to evaluate the firm's performance?

SELF-TEST SOLUTIONS

SS-1. Note that Ray's current inventory expansion is as follows:

current ratio = $6,000,000/current liabilities = 4

Thus the firm's level of current liabilities is $1,500,000. If the expansion in inventories is financed entirely with borrowed funds, then the change in inventories is equal to the change in current liabilities, and the firm's current ratio after the expansion can be defined as follows:

$$\text{current ratio} = \frac{\$6,000,000 + \text{change in inventory}}{\$1,500,000 + \text{change in inventory}} = 3$$

Note that we set the new current ratio equal to the firm's target of 3. Solving for the change in inventory in the above equation, we determine that the firm can expand its inventories by $750,000 and finance the expansion with current liabilities and still maintain its target current ratio.

SS-2. a.

M & G Industries, Ratio Analysis			
	Industry Averages	Actual 1997	Actual 1998
Current ratio	1.80	1.84	0.90
Acid-test ratio	0.70	0.78	0.24
Average collection periods (based on a 365-day year and end-of-year figures.)	37.00	36.50	36.50
Inventory turnover	2.50	2.59	2.11
Debt ratio	58%	50%	61.3%
Times interest earned	3.80	4.00	2.79
Gross profit margin	38%	40%	40%
Operating profit margin	10%	9.6%	10.6
Total asset turnover	1.14	1.11	1.07
Fixed asset turnover	1.40	2.02	1.82
Operating income return on investment	11.4%	10.67%	11.3%
Return on common equity	9.5%	8.0%	9.4%

b. M & G's liquidity in 1998 is poor, as suggested by the low current ratio and acid-test ratio: also, inventories are turning slowly. In 1998, management is doing a satisfactory job at generating profits on the firm's operating assets, as indicated by the operating income return on investment. Note that the operating income return on investment in 1998 is average, owing to a slightly above-average operating profit margin combined with a slightly below-average asset turnover. The problem with the asset turnover ratio comes from a slow inventory turnover.

M & G has increased its use of debt to the point of using slightly more debt than the average company in the industry. As a result, the firm's coverage of interest has decreased to a point well below the industry norm.

As of 1998, M & G's return on equity is average because the operating income return on investment and the debt ratio are average.

SS-3. a.

M & G Industries, Statement of Cash Flow for the Year Ended December 31, 1998		
Cash flow from *operating* activities		
Net income (from the income statement)	$ 5,450	
Add (deduct) to reconcile		
Net income to net cash flow		
Increase in accounts payable	11,500	
Increase in inventories	(16,500)	
Depreciation expense	10,000	
Increase in accounts receivable	(3,500)	
Net cash inflow from operating activities		$ 6,950
Cash flow from *investing* activities		
Purchase of land	($6,000)	
Purchase of plant and equipment	(30,000)	
Net cash outflow from *investing* activities		(36,000)
Cash flows from *financing* activities		
Cash inflows		
Increase in bank notes	$30,000	
Cash outflows		
Decrease in long-term debt	(5,800)	
Common stock dividend	(3,650)	
Net cash inflow from financing activities		20,550
Net increase (decrease) in cash for the period		($ 8,500)
Cash balance at the beginning of the period		$ 9,000
Cash balance at the end of the period		$ 500

b. The statement of cash flow is an important supplement to ratio analysis. The statement directs analysts' attention to where M & G Industries obtained financing during the period and how those funds were spent. For example, a very large portion of M & G's funds came from an increase in bank notes and from an increase in accounts payable. In addition, the largest uses of funds were additions to buildings and equipment and increases in inventories. Thus M & G did little in the most recent operating period to alleviate the financial problems we noted earlier in our ratio analysis. In fact, M & G aggravated matters by purchasing fixed assets using short-term sources of financing. It would appear that another short-term loan at this time is *not* warranted.

Learning Objectives

Active Applications

World Finance

Practice

CHAPTER 4

LEARNING OBJECTIVES

After reading this chapter, you should be able to

1. Use the percent of sales method to forecast the financing requirements of a firm.

2. Describe the limitations of the percent of sales forecast method.

3. Calculate a firm's sustainable rate of growth.

4. Prepare a cash budget and use it to evaluate the amount and timing of a firm's financing needs.

FINANCIAL FORECASTING, PLANNING, AND BUDGETING

INTRODUCTION

Forecasting is an integral part of the planning process, yet there are countless examples where our ability to predict the future has been simply awful. During the mid-eighties oil prices were roughly $30 a barrel, and many firms were developing new reserves that would cost well over this amount to produce. Why? Oil prices were projected to continue to rise and many thought the price might eventually reach $50 a barrel by the end of the decade. Then in January 1986, the collapse of the oil producer's cartel in combination with the benefits of energy conservation efforts produced a dramatic drop in oil prices to below $10 a barrel.

If forecasting the future is so difficult, and plans are built on forecasts, why do firms engage in planning efforts? The answer, oddly enough, does not lie in the accuracy of the firm's projections, for planning offers its greatest value when the future is the most uncertain. The reason is that planning is the process of thinking about what the future might bring and devising strategies for dealing with the likely outcomes. Planning is thinking in advance and thinking in advance provides an opportunity to devise contingency plans that can be quickly and easily initiated should the need arise. This increased speed of response to uncertain events means that the firm can reduce the costs of responding to adverse circumstances and quickly respond to take advantage of unexpected opportunities.

Financial managers spend a significant portion of their time planning for their firm's uncertain future. Financial planning entails collecting sales forecasts from marketing personnel and production plans from operations, and then combining them to make projections of the firm's future financing requirements. In this chapter, we will see that the financial plan takes the form of a set of pro forma or planned *financial statements and a cash budget. These statements provide a benchmark to which day-to-day actual results can be compared. If actual performance results begin to deviate from the plan, then this provides the financial manager with an early warning signal that her financing plans may be inadequate and appropriate actions can be taken: for example, contacting the firm's banker to request an increase in the firm's prearranged credit line.*

CHAPTER PREVIEW

Chapter 4 has two primary objectives: First, we develop an appreciation for the financial manager's role in financial forecasting. Firms go through an annual planning and budgeting exercise in which the financial manager is asked to bring together revenue forecasts from marketing and production plans from operations to develop a forecast of the firm's cash flow. This cash flow forecast then becomes the basis for estimating the firm's financing requirements. Second, we review the cash budget, pro forma (planned) income statement and pro forma balance sheet. These statements constitute the principal elements of the firm's financial forecast and serve as a benchmark against which future performance can be compared.

This chapter emphasizes Axiom 3: Cash—Not Profits—Is King, and Axiom 7: The Agency Problem—Managers Won't Work for Owners Unless It's in Their Best Interest. Firm's pay bills and dividends with cash and investors make mortgage payments using cash not profits. In addition, financial planning entails the construction of detailed budgets which can be used as an oversight tool for monitoring the activities of the firm's employees.

RELATE TO THE BIG PICTURE

Financial decisions are made today in light of our expectations of an uncertain future. Financial forecasting involves making estimates of the future financing requirements of the firm. Axiom 3: Cash—Not Profits—Is King speaks directly to this problem. Remember that effective financial management requires that consideration be given to cash flow and when it is received or dispersed.

FINANCIAL FORECASTING

OBJECTIVE 1

Forecasting in financial management is used to estimate a firm's future financial needs. If the financial manager has not attempted to anticipate his firm's future financing requirements, then a crisis occurs every time the firm's cash inflows fall below its cash outflows. Proper planning means anticipating and preparing for those times in every firm's future when it will need to obtain additional financing and also when the firm will have excess cash. For example, the financing requirements of growth firms frequently outstrip the firm's ability to generate cash. Planning for growth means that the financial manager can anticipate the firm's financing requirements and plan for them well in advance of the need. Advance planning means the financial manager can explore more alternatives and obtain the most favorable set of financing terms available.

The basic steps involved in predicting those financing needs are the following: **Step 1:** Project the firm's sales revenues and expenses over the planning period. **Step 2:** Estimate the levels of investment in current and fixed assets that are necessary to support the projected sales. **Step 3:** Determine the firm's financing needs throughout the planning period.

Sales Forecast

The key ingredient in the firm's planning process is the *sales forecast*. This projection is generally derived using information from a number of sources. At a minimum, the sales forecast for the coming year would reflect (1) any past trends in sales that are expected to carry through into the new year, and (2) the influence of any events that might materially affect those trends.[1] An example of the latter would be the initiation of a major advertising campaign or a change in the firm's pricing policy.

Forecasting Financial Variables

Traditional financial forecasting takes the sales forecast as a given and makes projections of its impact on the firm's various expenses, assets, and liabilities. The amount of financing—as we will see—can vary greatly if sales grow by 1 percent versus 5 percent or 10 percent. The amount of the variation depends on the interplay of the key variables that determine the firm's financing requirements.

Percent of Sales Method of Financial Forecasting

The most commonly used method for making these projections is the percent of sales method. The **percent of sales method** involves estimating the level of an expense, asset, or liability for a future period as a percent of the sales forecast. The percentage used can come from the most recent financial statement as a percent of current sales, from an average computed over several years, from the judgment of the analyst, or from some combination of these sources.

Table 4.1 presents a complete example of the use of the percent of sales method of financial forecasting. In this example, each item in the firm's balance sheet that varies with sales is converted to a percentage of 1998 sales of $10 million. The forecast of the new balance for each item is then calculated by multiplying this percentage times the $12 million in projected sales for the 1999 planning period. This method of forecasting future financing is not as precise or detailed as the method using a cash budget, which is presented later; however, it offers a relatively low-cost and easy-to-use first approximation of the firm's financing needs for a future period.

Note that in the example in Table 4.1, both current and fixed assets are assumed to vary with the level of firm sales. This means that the firm does not have sufficient productive capacity to absorb a projected increase in sales. Thus if sales were to rise by $1, fixed assets would rise by $.40, or 40 percent of the projected increase in sales. Note that if the fixed assets the firm currently owns were sufficient to support the projected level of new sales (such as when the firm has excess capacity), these assets should not be allowed to vary with sales. If this were the case, then fixed assets would not be converted to a percent of sales and would be projected to remain unchanged for the period being forecast.

Also, we note that accounts payable and accrued expenses are the only liabilities allowed to vary with sales. Both these accounts might reasonably be expected to rise and fall with the level of firm sales; hence the use of the percent of sales forecast. Because these two categories of current liabilities normally vary directly with the level of sales, they are often referred to as **spontaneous sources of financing**. Chapter 16, which discusses working-capital management, has more to say about these forms of financing. Notes payable, long-term debt, common stock, and paid-in capital are not assumed to vary

---

[1]A complete discussion of forecast methodologies is outside the scope of this book. The interested reader will find the following references helpful: F. Gerard Adams, *The Business Forecasting Revolution* (Oxford: Oxford University Press, 1986); C. W. J. Granger, *Forecasting in Business and Economics*, 2d ed. (Boston: Academic Press, 1989); and Paul Newbold and Theodore Bos, *Introductory Business Forecasting* (Cincinnati: Southwestern, 1990).

Table 4.1 Using the Percent of Sales Method to Forecast Future Financing Requirements

Assets	Present (1998)	Percent of Sales (1998 Sales = $10M)	Projected (Based on 1999 Sales = $12M)
Current assets	$2.0M	$\dfrac{\$2M}{\$10M} = 20\%$	$.2 \times \$12M = \$2.4M$
Net fixed assets	$4.0M	$\dfrac{\$4M}{\$10M} = 40\%$	$.4 \times \$12M = \$4.8M$
Total	$6.0M		$7.2M

Liabilities and Owners' Equity	Present (1998)	Percent of Sales (1998 Sales = $10M)	Projected (Based on 1999 Sales = $12M)
Accounts payable	$1.0M	$\dfrac{\$1M}{\$10M} = 10\%$	$.10 \times \$12M = \$1.2M$
Accrued expenses	1.0M	$\dfrac{\$1M}{\$10M} = 10\%$	$.10 \times \$12M = \$1.2M$
Notes payable	.5M	NA[a] no change	.5M
Long-term debt	$2.0M	NA[a] no change	2.0M
Total liabilities	$4.5M		$4.9M
Common stock	$ .1M	NA[a] no change	$ .1M
Paid-in capital	.2M	NA[a] no change	.2M
Retained earnings	1.2M	$\$1.2M + [.05 \times \$12M \times (1 - .5)] =$	1.5M[b]
Common equity	$1.5M		$1.8M
Total	$6.0M	Total financing provided	$6.7M
		Discretionary financing needed	.5M[c]
		Total	$7.2M

[a] Not applicable. These account balances are assumed not to vary with sales.
[b] Projected retained earnings equals the beginning level ($1.2M) plus projected net income less any dividends paid. In this case, net income is projected to equal 5 percent of sales, and dividends are projected to equal half of net income: $.05 \times \$12M \times (1 - .5) = \$300,000$.
[c] Discretionary financing needed equals projected total assets ($7.2M) less projected total liabilities ($4.9M) less projected common equity ($1.8), or $\$7.2M - 4.9M - 1.8M = \$500,000$.

directly with the level of firm sales. These sources of financing are termed **discretionary**, in that the firm's management must make a conscious decision to seek additional financing using any one of them. An example of discretionary financing is a bank note which requires that negotiations be undertaken and an agreement signed setting forth the terms and conditions for the financing. Finally, we note that the level of retained earnings does vary with estimated sales. The predicted change in the level of retained earnings equals the estimated after-tax profits (projected net income) equal to 5 percent of sales or $600,000 less the common stock dividends of $300,000.

Thus using the example from Table 4.1, we estimate that firm sales will increase from $10 million to $12 million, which will cause the firm's needs for total assets to rise to $7.2 million. These assets will then be financed by $4.9 million in existing liabilities plus spontaneous liabilities; $1.8 million in owner funds, including $300,000 in retained earnings from next year's sales; and finally, $500,000 in discretionary financing, which can be raised by issuing notes payable, selling bonds, offering an issue of stock, or some combination of these sources. By far the most frequently used source of discretionary financing is a bank loan. As we learn later when we study financial policy, if the need for financing persists, then the firm may later issue bonds or stock to retire the bank loan.

In summary, we can estimate the firm's needs for discretionary financing, using the percent of sales method of financial forecasting, by following a four-step procedure:

Discretionary financing

Sources of financing that require an explicit decision on the part of the firm's management every time funds are raised.

FORBES, FEBRUARY 9, 1987

Now You See It . . .

Cash flow is at least as important a measure of corporate health as reported earnings. But put a dozen investors in a room and you'll get almost as many different definitions.

After grappling with the problem for more than six years, the Financial Accounting Standards Board has come up with the beginnings of a more precise definition. It would require all companies to use the same format to explain how cash and cash equivalents change from one reporting period to the next. The proposal still leaves companies with room for flexibility but will make investors' lives much easier. Why? Companies will have to show sources and uses of cash in three areas: operations, investing, and financing.

Let's take a specific case: Lowe's Cos., the North Carolina-based retailer of building materials. The company said in its annual report that cash flow amounted to $2.31 per share in 1985 as compared with $2.20 the year before. An investor looking at these numbers might have assumed Lowe's had plenty of cash left over for dividends and other purposes.

Not necessarily so. Although Lowe's used a generally accepted definition of cash flow, it was not a strict definition. It failed to subtract the cash absorbed by higher inventories and receivables. Lowe's ended the year with hardly more cash than it started the year,

(A)

and its long-term debt almost doubled from 1984 to 1985—despite the positive cash flow.

Does it really matter how you measure cash flow? Very much. While Lowe's is healthy—the increased inventory and receivables simply reflect growth in revenues—there are situations where a company can go broke while reporting positive cash flow. How can this be? Simple.

Suppose inventories and receivables rise faster than sales, reflecting slow pay by customers and unsold goods. Under the simpler method of reporting cash flow (which would not include working-capital components), such a company could report a positive cash flow even while it was fast running out of cash.

(B)

When the smoke clears, investors will still need to do lots of homework. It's never enough to know just what the numbers are. You still have to figure out what the numbers mean. Again, Lowe's is an example. Even if it were forced to report a negative cash flow, it would still be a very healthy business; it would cease being one only if inventories and receivables increased faster than sales and the company's credit were deteriorating.

When it comes to some things, the more you try simplifying them, the more complicated they become.

SOURCE: Excerpted from T. Pouschine, "Now You See It . . . ," *Forbes* (February 9, 1987): 70. Reprinted by Permission of FORBES Magazine © Forbes Inc., 1987.

Step 1: Convert each asset and liability account that varies directly with firm sales to a percent of current year's sales, for example:

$$\frac{\text{current assets}}{\text{sales}} = \frac{\$2M}{\$10M} = .2 \text{ or } 20\%$$

Step 2: Project the level of each asset and liability account in the balance sheet using its percent of sales multiplied by projected sales or by leaving the account balance unchanged where the account does not vary with the level of sales, for example:

projected current assets =

$$\text{projected sales} \times \frac{\text{current assets}}{\text{sales}} = \$12M \times .2 = \$2.4M$$

Analysis and Implications . . .

A. A crude way to estimate a firm's cash flow is to add depreciation and other noncash expenses to a firm's reported net income. This does not measure the cash flow that actually passes through the firm during the period, however. The reason is that firm's account for their income using the accrual method of accounting. The accrual method recognizes as income for the period all revenues "earned" during the period and recognizes as expenses all those expenses incurred in generating those revenues. This means, for example, that a firm might sell $4,000,000 worth of merchandise in February that cost it $3,000,000. This generates $1,000,000 in gross profit. Now, let's assume that the items sold during February were actually purchased and paid for in January such that the firm does not pay out any cash during February. Furthermore, let's assume that the items sold in February are all sold on terms of net 60 meaning that no cash will be received for 60 days. What is the firm's cash flow for the period? Zero. The cash flow statement (discussed in chapter 3) provides a uniform method of accounting for differences in the way that we account for income and the actual flow of cash.

B. Even highly profitable firms that are growing rapidly can experience cash shortages. This problem arises out of the mismatching of cash receipts (collections from credit sales are delayed by the firm's credit terms) and cash disbursements for items being sold as well as plant and equipment expenditures. We will discuss this problem in more depth later when we discuss the Sustainable Rate of Growth concept.

Step 3: Project the addition to retained earnings available to help finance the firm's operations. This equals projected net income for the period less planned common stock dividends, for example:

projected addition to retained earnings =

$$\text{projected sales} \times \frac{\text{net income}}{\text{sales}} \times \left(1 - \frac{\text{cash dividends}}{\text{net income}} \right)$$

$$= \$12M \times .05 \times [1 - .5] = \$300,000$$

Step 4: Project the firm's need for discretionary financing as the projected level of total assets less projected liabilities and owners' equity, for example:

discretionary financing needed =

projected total assets − projected total liabilities − projected owner's equity

$$= \$7.2M - \$4.9M - \$1.8M = \$500,000$$

STOP AND THINK

The key to financial forecasting is the identification of the firm's anticipated future financing requirements. These requirements can be identified as the "plug" figure, or simply the number that balances the financial manager's pro forma balance sheet.

The Discretionary Financing Needed (DFN) Model

In the preceding discussion, we estimated DFN (discretionary financing needed) as the difference in projected total assets and the sum of projected liabilities and owner's equity. We can estimate DFN directly using the predicted change in sales (ΔS) and corresponding changes in assets, liabilities, and owner's equity as follows:

$$
\text{DFN}_{t+1} = \begin{array}{c} \text{projected} \\ \text{change in} \\ \text{assets} \end{array} - \begin{array}{c} \text{projected} \\ \text{change in} \\ \text{liabilities} \end{array} - \begin{array}{c} \text{projected} \\ \text{change in} \\ \text{owners' equity} \end{array} \tag{4-1}
$$

or

$$
\text{DFN}_{t+1} = \left[\frac{\text{assets}_t^*}{\text{sales}_t} \Delta \text{sales}_{t+1} \right] - \left[\frac{\text{liabilities}_t^*}{\text{sales}_t} \Delta \text{sales}_{t+1} \right] - [\text{NPM}_{t+1}(1-b)\text{sales}_{t+1}]
$$

where

DFN_{t+1} = predicted discretionary financing needed for period $t+1$.

assets_t^* = those assets in period t that are expected to change in proportion to the level of sales. In our example, we have assumed that all the firm's assets vary in proportion to sales. We will have more to say about this assumption in the next section, where we consider economies of scale and lumpy fixed asset investments.

sales_t = the level of sales for the period t.

$\Delta \text{sales}_{t+1}$ = the change in sales projected for period $t+1$, i.e., $\text{sales}_{t+1} - \text{sales}_t$. Note that "$\Delta$" is the Greek symbol delta which is used here to represent "change."

liabilities_t^* = those liabilities in period t that are expected to change in proportion to the level of sales. In our preceding example, we assumed that accounts payable and accrued expenses varied with sales but notes payable and long-term debt did not.

NPM_{t+1} = the net profit margin (Net Income ÷ sales) projected for period $t+1$.

b = dividends as a percent of net income or the dividend payout ratio such that $(1-b)$ is the proportion of the firm's projected net income that will be retained and reinvested in the firm (that is, $(1-b)$ is the retention ratio).

Using the numbers from the preceding example, we estimate DFN_{1999} as follows:

$$
\text{DFN}_{1999} = \left(\frac{\$2M + 4M}{10M} \right) \$2M - \left(\frac{\$1M + 1M}{\$10M} \right) \$2M - [.05(1 - .5)\$12M]
$$

$$
= \$.5 \text{ million or } \$500{,}000
$$

Analyzing the Effects of Profitability and Dividend Policy on DFN

Using the DFN model, we can quickly and easily evaluate the sensitivity of our projected financing requirements to changes in key variables. For example, using the information from the preceding example, we evaluate the effect of net profit margins (NPM) equal to 1 percent, 5 percent, and 10 percent in combination with dividend payout ratios of 30 percent, 50 percent, and 70 percent as follows:

Discretionary Financing Needed for Various Net Profit Margins and Dividend Payout Ratios			
Net Profit Margin	Dividend Payout Ratios (Dividends ÷ Net Income)		
	30%	50%	70%
1%	$716,000	$740,000	$764,000
5%	380,000	500,000	620,000
10%	(40,000)	200,000	440,000

Let's first consider the dividend payout ratio. The higher the payout percentage is, other things being equal, the lower the firm's internal source of financing will be. Consider the row corresponding to a 5 percent net profit margin. If the firm pays out 30 percent of its earnings in dividends (retains 70 percent), then its need for discretionary financing is estimated to be $380,000, whereas a 70 percent dividend payout ratio requires $620,000 in discretionary financing. Later in chapter 14, we will learn that firms tend to have dividend policies that are similar to other firms in their industry. For example, firms in high growth industries such as Intel pay out a very small fraction of their earnings in dividends. In fact, until 1992 Intel paid no dividends to its common stockholders and the firm currently pays less than 5 percent of its earnings in dividends. Thus a firm's discretionary financing needs are in part a function of its growth prospects and industry practice with respect to the payment of dividends.

Discretionary financing needs are also a function of the firm's profitability. The higher the net profit margin is, all things being the same, the lower the firm's need for discretionary financing will be. For example, with a 1 percent net profit margin and 30 percent dividend payout ratio, the firm will require $716,000 in discretionary financing. If the net profit margin were 10 percent with the same payout ratio, the firm would have surplus funds of $40,000. Thus a firm's discretionary financing needs swing from year to year with the firm's profitability that is, to a large degree, due to economy-wide and industry influences, and are outside the control of the firm's management. Financial planning is particularly crucial for firms subject to wide variability in their year to year profitability.

Limitations of the Percent of Sales Forecast Method

OBJECTIVE 2

The percent of sales method of financial forecasting provides reasonable estimates of a firm's financing requirements only where asset requirements and financing sources can be accurately forecast as a constant percent of sales. For example, predicting inventories using the percent of sales method involves the following predictive equation:

$$\text{inventories}_t = \frac{\text{inventories}_t}{\text{sales}_t} \times \text{sales}_t$$

Figure 4.1a depicts this predictive relationship. Note that the percent-of-sales predictive model is simply a straight line that passes through the origin (that is, has a zero intercept). Thus the percent-of-sales model is appropriate where there is no level of inventories which remains constant regardless of the level of firm sales, and inventories rise and fall in direct proportion to changes in the level of sales.

There are some fairly common instances in which this type of relationship fails to describe the relationship between an asset category and sales. Two such examples involve

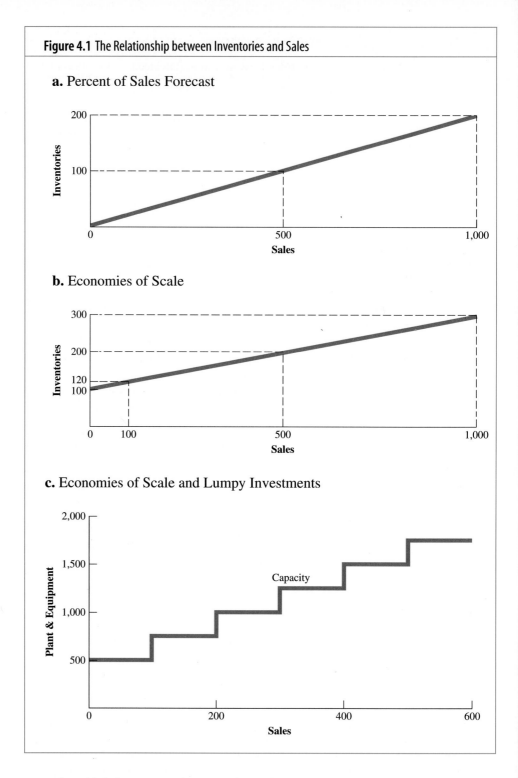

Figure 4.1 The Relationship between Inventories and Sales

a. Percent of Sales Forecast

b. Economies of Scale

c. Economies of Scale and Lumpy Investments

assets for which there are scale economics and assets that must be purchased in discrete quantities ("lumpy assets").

Economies of scale are sometimes realized from investing in certain types of assets such as finished goods inventories. For example, a retail drugstore requires a full range of drug products in order to operate. This inventory can be replenished on a daily basis in response to firm sales. However, a constant level of investment is necessary to open the doors of the enterprise. This means that these assets do not increase in direct proportion to sales. Figure 4.1b reflects one instance in which the firm realizes economies of scale from its investment in inventory. Note that inventories as a percent of sales decline from 120 percent where sales are $100, to 30 percent where sales equal $1,000. This reflects the fact that there is a fixed component of inventories (in this case $100) that the firm must have on hand regardless of the level of sales, plus a variable component (20 percent of sales). In this instance, the predictive equation for inventories is as follows:

$$\text{inventories}_t = a + b \text{ sales}_t$$

In this example, a is equal to 100 and b equals .20.

Figure 4.1c is an example of *lumpy assets*, that is, assets that must be purchased in large, nondivisible components such as plant and equipment. For example, firms in the semiconductor industry now invest approximately $2 billion in each new wafer fab (factory) they build. They then spend the next 2 to 3 years filling the fab's productive capacity with production. Consequently, when a block of assets is purchased, it creates excess capacity until sales grow to the point where the capacity is fully used. The result is a step function such as the one depicted in Figure 4.1c. Thus if the firm does not expect sales to exceed the current capacity of its plant and equipment, there would be no projected need for added plant and equipment capacity.

THE SUSTAINABLE RATE OF GROWTH

OBJECTIVE 3

Growing firms require expenditures for new assets which outstrip the firm's ability to finance those purchases using internally generated profits. This means that the firm must go out and borrow the additional funds or issue new equity. Because selling new shares of stock is a very involved and expensive endeavor, the question arises as to how fast a firm can grow without having to borrow more than the firm's desired debt ratio and without having to sell more stock. This growth rate is referred to as the sustainable rate of growth. Specifically, the **sustainable rate of growth** (g^*) represents the rate at which a firm's sales can grow if it wants to maintain its present financial ratios and does not want to resort to the sale of new equity shares.[2] A simple formula can be derived for g^* where we assume that a firm's assets and liabilities all grow at the same rate as its sales, that is,

Sustainable rate of growth

The maximum rate of growth in sales that the firm can sustain while maintaining its present capital structure (debt and equity mix) and without having to sell new common stock.

$$\text{sustainable rate of growth } (g^*) = \text{ROE} \, (1 - b) \tag{4-3}$$

ROE is the firm's return on equity, which was defined in chapter 3 as follows:

$$\text{ROE} = \frac{\text{net income}}{\text{common equity}}$$

and b is the firm's dividend payout ratio, that is, $\frac{\text{dividends}}{\text{net income}}$. The term $(1 - b)$ is sometimes referred to as the **plowback ratio** because it indicates the fraction of earnings that are reinvested or plowed back into the firm. Thus $g^* = \text{ROE} \times \text{Plowback Ratio}$.

Equation (4-3) is deceptively simple. Recall that ROE can also be written as follows:

Plowback ratio

The percent of a firm's earnings that are reinvested in the firm.

$$\text{ROE} = \left(\frac{\text{net income}}{\text{sales}} \right) \times \left(\frac{\text{sales}}{\text{assets}} \right) \times \left(\frac{\text{assets}}{\text{common equity}} \right)$$

[2]For an extensive discussion of this concept, see Robert C. Higgins, "Sustainable Growth with Inflation," *Financial Management* (Autumn 1981): 36–40.

Consequently, a firm's sustainable rate of growth is determined by its ROE (i.e., its anticipated net profit margin, asset turnover, and capital structure), as well as its dividend policy.

EXAMPLE: CALCULATING THE SUSTAINABLE RATE OF GROWTH

Consider the three firms found below:

Firm	Net Profit Margin	Asset Turnover	Leverage (assets/equity)	Plowback Ratio	g^*
A	15%	1	1.2	50%	9.0%
B	15%	1	1.2	100%	18.0%
C	15%	1	1.5	100%	22.5%

Comparing Firms A and B, we see that the only difference is that Firm A pays out half its earnings in common dividends (i.e., plows back half its earnings) whereas Firm B retains or plows back all of its earnings. The net result is that Firm B with its added source of internal equity financing can grow at twice the rate of Firm A (18 percent compared to only 9 percent). Similarly, comparing Firms B and C, we note that they differ only in that Firm B finances only 83 percent of its assets with equity whereas Firm C finances 67 percent of its assets with equity. The result is that Firm C's sustainable rate of growth is 22.5 percent compared to only 18 percent for Firm B.

Before leaving our discussion of the sustainable rate of growth concept, it is important that we stress the underlying assumptions behind equation (4-2). For this equation to accurately depict a firm's sustainable rate of growth, the following assumptions must hold: First, the firm's assets must vary as a constant percent of sales (i.e., even fixed assets expand and contract directly with the level of firm sales). Second, the firm's liabilities must all vary directly with firm sales. This means that the firm's management will expand its borrowing (both spontaneous and discretionary) in direct proportion with sales to maintain its present ratio of debt to assets. Finally, the firm pays out a constant proportion of its earnings in common stock dividends regardless of the level of firm sales. Since all three of these assumptions are only rough approximations to the way that firms actually behave, equation (4-3) provides a crude approximation of the firm's actual sustainable rate of growth. However, an estimate of g^* using equation (4-3) can be a very useful first step in the firm's financial planning process.

FINANCIAL PLANNING AND BUDGETING

As we noted earlier, the primary virtue of the percent-of-sales method of financial forecasting is its simplicity. To obtain a more precise estimate of the amount and timing of a firm's future financing requirements requires that a cash budget be prepared. The percent-of-sales method of financial forecasting provides a very useful, low-cost forerunner to the development of the more detailed cash budget, which the firm will ultimately use to estimate its financing needs.

Budget Functions

A *budget* is simply a forecast of future events. For example, students preparing for final exams make use of time budgets, which help them allocate their limited preparation time among their courses. Students also must budget their financial resources among competing uses, such as books, tuition, food, rent, clothes, and extracurricular activities.

Budgets perform three basic functions for a firm. First, they indicate the amount and timing of the firm's needs for future financing. Second, they provide the basis for taking corrective action in the event budgeted figures do not match actual or realized figures. Third, budgets provide the basis for performance evaluation. Plans are carried out by people, and budgets provide benchmarks that management can use to evaluate the performance of those responsible for carrying out those plans and, in turn, to control their actions. Thus budgets are valuable aids in both the planning and controlling aspects of the firm's financial management.

The Cash Budget

OBJECTIVE 4

The **cash budget** represents a detailed plan of future cash flows and is composed of four elements: cash receipts, cash disbursements, net change in cash for the period, and new financing needed.

Cash budget

A detailed plan of future cash receipts and disbursements.

To demonstrate the construction and use of the cash budget, consider Salco Furniture Company, Inc., a regional distributor of household furniture. Management is in the process of preparing a monthly cash budget for the upcoming 6 months (January through June 1999). Salco's sales are highly seasonal, peaking in the months of March through May. Roughly 30 percent of Salco's sales are collected 1 month after the sale, 50 percent 2 months after the sale, and the remainder during the third month following the sale.

Salco attempts to pace its purchases with its forecast of future sales. Purchases generally equal 75 percent of sales and are made 2 months in advance of anticipated sales. Payments are made in the month following purchases. For example, June sales are estimated at $100,000, thus April purchases are .75 × $100,000 = $75,000 and are paid in May. Wages, salaries, rent, and other cash expenses are recorded in Table 4.2, which gives Salco's cash budget for the 6-month period ended in June 1999. Additional expenditures are recorded in the cash budget related to the purchase of equipment in the amount of $14,000 during February and the repayment of a $12,000 loan in May. In June, Salco will pay $7,500 interest on its $150,000 in long-term debt for the period of January through June 1999. Interest on the $12,000 short-term note repaid in May for the period January through May equals $600 and is paid in May. In addition, tax payments of $4,460 and $5,200 are made in March and June.

Salco currently has a cash balance of $20,000 and maintains a minimum balance of $10,000 to meet any unanticipated shortfall in net cash flow. Additional borrowing necessary to maintain that minimum balance is estimated in the final section of Table 4.2.

Table 4.2 Salco Furniture Co., Inc., Cash Budget for the 6 Months Ended June 30, 1999

Worksheet	Oct.	Nov.	Dec.	Jan.	Feb.	Mar.	Apr.	May	June	July	Aug.
Sales	$55,000	$62,000	$50,000	$60,000	$75,000	$88,000	$100,000	$110,000	$100,000	$80,000	$75,000
Collections:											
First month (30%)				15,000	18,000	22,500	26,400	30,000	33,000		
Second month (50%)				31,000	25,000	30,000	37,500	44,000	50,000		
Third month (20%)				11,000	12,400	10,000	12,000	15,000	17,600		
Total				$57,000	55,400	62,500	75,900	89,000	100,600		
Purchases (75% of sales in 2 months)			$56,250	66,000	75,000	82,500	75,000	60,000	56,250		
Payments (1-month lag)				$56,250	66,000	75,000	82,500	75,000	60,000		
Cash budget											
Cash receipts											
Collections (see worksheet)				$57,000	55,400	62,500	75,900	89,000	100,600		
Cash disbursements:											
Payments (see worksheet)				$56,250	66,000	75,000	82,500	75,000	60,000		
Wages and salaries				3,000	10,000	7,000	8,000	6,000	4,000		
Rent				4,000	4,000	4,000	4,000	4,000	4,000		
Other expenses				1,000	500	1,200	1,500	1,500	1,200		
Interest expense on existing debt ($12,000 note and $150,000 in long-term debt)								600	7,500		
Taxes						4,460			5,200		
Purchase of equipment					14,000						
Loan repayment ($12,000 note due in May)								12,000			
Total disbursements:				$64,250	94,500	91,660	96,000	99,100	81,900		
Net monthly change				$(7,250)	(39,100)	(29,160)	(20,100)	(10,100)	18,700		
Plus: Beginning cash balance				20,000	12,750	10,000	10,000	10,000	10,000		
Less: Interest on short-term borrowing				—	—	(364)	(659)	(866)	(976)		
Equals: Ending cash balance before short-term borrowing				$12,750	(26,350)	(19,524)	(10,759)	(966)	27,724		
Financing needed[a]				—	36,350	29,524	20,759	10,966	(17,724)[b]		
Ending cash balance				$12,750	10,000	10,000	10,000	10,000	10,000		
Cumulative borrowing				—	36,350	65,874	86,633	97,599	79,875		

[a]The amount of financing that is required to raise the firm's ending cash balance up to its $10,000 desired cash balance.

[b]Negative financing needed simply means the firm has excess cash that can be used to retire a part of its short-term borrowing from prior months.

Borrowing takes place at the beginning of the month in which the funds are needed. Interest on borrowed funds equals 12 percent per annum, or 1 percent per month, and is paid in the month following the one in which funds are borrowed. Thus interest on funds borrowed in January will be paid in February equal to 1 percent of the loan amount outstanding during January.

The financing-needed line in Salco's cash budget indicates that the firm's cumulative short-term borrowing will be $36,350 in February, $65,874 in March, $86,633 in April, and $97,599 in May. In June, the firm will be able to reduce its borrowing to $79,875. Note that the cash budget indicates not only the amount of financing needed during the period but also when the funds will be needed.

Fixed versus Flexible Budgets

The cash budget given in Table 4.2 for Salco, Inc., is an example of a fixed budget. Cash flow estimates are made for a single set of monthly sales estimates. Thus the estimates of expenses and new financing needed are meaningful only for the level of sales for which they were computed. To avoid this limitation, several budgets corresponding to different sets of sales estimates can be prepared. Flexible budgeting fulfills two basic needs: First, it gives information regarding the firm's possible financing needs, and second, it provides a standard against which to measure the performance of subordinates who are responsible for the various cost and revenue items contained in the budget.

This second function deserves some additional comment. The obvious problem that arises relates to the fact that costs vary with the actual level of sales experienced by the firm. Thus if the budget is to be used as a standard for performance evaluation or control, it must be constructed to match realized sales and production figures. This can involve much more than simply adjusting cost figures up or down in proportion to the deviation of actual from planned sales; that is, costs may not vary in strict proportion to sales, just as inventory levels may not vary as a constant percent of sales. Thus preparation of a flexible budget involves reestimating all the cash expenses that would be incurred at each of several possible sales levels. This process might utilize a variation of the percent of sales method discussed earlier.

Budget Period

There are no strict rules for determining the length of the budget period. However, as a general rule, it should be long enough to show the effect of management policies, yet short enough so that estimates can be made with reasonable accuracy. Applying this rule of thumb to the Salco example in Table 4.2, it appears that the 6-month budget period is too short. The reason is that we cannot tell whether the planned operations of the firm will be successful over the coming fiscal year. That is, for most of the first 6-month period, the firm is operating with a cash flow deficit. If this does not reverse in the latter 6 months of the year, then a reevaluation of the firm's plans and policies is clearly in order.

Longer-range budgets are also prepared in the form of the capital-expenditure budget. These budget details the firm's plans for acquiring plant and equipment over a 5-year, 10-year, or even longer period. Furthermore, firms often develop comprehensive long-range plans extending up to 10 years into the future. These plans are generally not as detailed as the annual cash budget, but they do consider such major components as sales, capital expenditures, new-product development, capital funds acquisition, and employment needs.

To Bribe or Not to Bribe

In many parts of the world, bribes and payoffs to public officials are considered the norm in business transactions. This raises a perplexing ethical question. If paying bribes is not considered unethical in a foreign country, should you consider it unethical to make these payments?

This situation provides an example of an ethical issue that gave rise to legislation. The Foreign Corrupt Practices Act of 1977 (as amended in the Omnibus Trade and Competitiveness Act of 1988) established criminal penalties for making payments to foreign officials, political parties, or candidates in order to obtain or retain business. Ethical problems are frequently found in the gray areas just outside the boundaries of current legislation and often lead to the passage of new legislation. **(A)**

Consider the following question: If you were involved in negotiating an important business deal in a foreign country, and the success or failure of the deal hinged on whether you paid a local government official to help you consummate the deal, would you authorize the payment? Assume that the form of the payment is such that you do not expect to be caught and punished; for example, your company agrees to purchase supplies from a family member of the government official at a price slightly above the competitive price. **(B)**

Analysis and Implications ...

A. Ethical dilemmas arise in those situations that are not clearly prescribed by law or social custom. It is the gray areas that give us trouble. Ethical behavior is simple to define and difficult to implement. Very simply, ethical behavior is "doing the right thing." The hard part comes when defining what is right, for this requires that each of us search our own personal values for guidance. In these situations, it is ultimately your own conscience, dictated by your personal beliefs and system of values, that will serve as your guide to action.

B. What would you do?

HOW FINANCIAL MANAGERS USE THIS MATERIAL

In the introduction, we pointed out examples that illustrate the difficulties involved in making financial forecasts. The difficulty of making a forecast, we learned, often varied directly with the value of the effort. That is, it is precisely where forecasts are most difficult that our attempts and the plans we formulate based upon the forecast are the most valuable.

Every business of any size makes and uses financial forecasts as an integral part of its planning process. The typical firm makes revenue and expense projections for at least 1 and usually 5 years. These forecasts are then used to develop pro forma financial statements that can be used to evaluate the financial condition of the firm if the forecast proves to be accurate. In addition, it is common practice to develop one or more contingency plans based on alternative sales and cost outcomes. The alternative scenarios frequently reflect optimistic and pessimistic scenarios.

The forecast methods used in practice can be varied. The firm may actually contract with a consulting firm for long-run forecasts that they feel demand skills not possessed by the finance staff. In the majority of the cases, however, the firm's finance personnel gather information concerning historical revenue and cost relationships and use this as the basis for developing the firm's financial forecast in conjunction with the firm's sales forecast. The sales forecast is frequently constructed by polling the heads of the firm's various operating divisions and then combining the results. In this way, the finance staff relies on the individuals who are directly responsible for the revenues being forecast.

SUMMARY

This chapter develops the role of forecasting within the context of the firm's financial planning activities. Forecasts of the firm's sales revenues and related expenses provide the basis for projecting future financing needs. The most popular method for forecasting financial variables is the percent of sales method.

OBJECTIVE 1

The percent of sales method presumes that the asset or liability being forecast is a constant percent of sales for all future levels of sales. There are instances where this assumption is not reasonable, and consequently, the percent of sales method does not provide reasonable predictions. One such instance arises where there are economies of scale in the use of the asset being forecast. For example, the firm may need at least $10 million in inventories to open its doors and operate even for sales as low as $100 million per year. If sales double to $200 million, inventories may only increase to $15 million. Thus inventories do not increase with sales in a constant proportion. A second situation where the percent of sales method fails to work properly is where asset purchases are lumpy. That is, if plant capacity must be purchased in $50 million increments, then plant and equipment will not remain a constant percent of sales.

OBJECTIVE 2

How serious are these possible problems and should we use the percent of sales method at all? Even in the face of these problems, the percent of sales method predicts reasonably well where predicted sales levels do not differ drastically from the level used to calculate the percent of sales. For example, if the current sales level used in calculating percent of sales for inventories is $40 million, then we can feel more comfortable forecasting the level of inventories corresponding to a new sales level of $42 million than if sales were predicted to rise to $60 million.

A firm's sustainable rate of growth is the maximum rate at which its sales can grow if it is to maintain its present financial ratios and not have to resort to issuing new equity. We calculate the sustainable rate of growth as follows:

OBJECTIVE 3

$$\text{sustainable rate of growth } (g^*) = \text{ROE} (1 - b)$$

where ROE is the return earned on common equity and b is the dividend payout ratio (that is, the ratio of dividends to earnings). Consequently, a firm's sustainable rate of growth increases with ROE and decreases with a higher fraction of its earnings paid out in dividends.

The cash budget is the primary tool of financial forecasting and planning. It contains a detailed plan of future cash flow estimates and is comprised of four elements or segments: cash receipts, cash disbursements, net change in cash for the period, and new financing needed. Once prepared, the cash budget also serves as a tool for monitoring and controlling the firm's operations. By comparing actual cash receipts and disbursements to those in the cash budget, the financial manager can gain an appreciation for how well the firm is performing. In addition, deviations from the plan serve as an early warning system to signal the need for external financing in response to either the presence of future investment opportunities or poor business performance.

OBJECTIVE 4

KEY TERMS

Cash budget, 153	**Percent of sales method**, 144	**Spontaneous financing**, 144
Discretionary financing, 145	**Plowback ratio**, 151	**Sustainable rate of growth**, 151

STUDY QUESTIONS

4-1. Discuss the shortcomings of the percent of sales method of financial forecasting.

4-2. Explain how a fixed cash budget differs from a variable or flexible cash budget.

4-3. What two basic needs does a flexible (variable) cash budget serve?

4-4. What would be the probable effect on a firm's cash position of the following events?
  a. Rapidly rising sales
  b. A delay in the payment of accounts payable
  c. A more liberal credit policy on sales (to the firm's customers)
  d. Holding larger inventories

4-5. How long should the budget period be? Why would a firm not set a rule that all budgets be for a 12-month period?

4-6. A cash budget is usually thought of as a means of planning for future financing needs. Why would a cash budget also be important for a firm that had excess cash on hand?

4-7. Explain why a cash budget would be of particular importance to a firm that experiences seasonal fluctuations in its sales.

SELF-TEST PROBLEMS

ST-1. (*Financial Forecasting*) Use the percent of sales method to prepare a pro forma income statement for Calico Sales Co., Inc. Projected sales for next year equal $4 million. Cost of goods sold is expected to be 70 percent of sales, administrative expense equals $500,000, and depreciation expense is $300,000. Interest expense equals $50,000 and income is taxed at a rate of 40 percent. The firm plans to spend $200,000 during the period to renovate its office facility and will retire $150,000 in notes payable. Finally, selling expense equals 5 percent of sales.

ST-2. (*Cash Budget*) Stauffer, Inc., has estimated sales and purchase requirements for the last half of the coming year. Past experience indicates that it will collect 20 percent of its sales in the month of the sale, 50 percent of the remainder 1 month after the sale, and the balance in the second month following the sale. Stauffer prefers to pay for half its purchases in the month of the purchase and the other half the following month. Labor expense for each month is expected to equal 5 percent of that month's sales, with cash payment being made in the month in which the expense is incurred. Depreciation expense is $5,000 per month; miscellaneous cash expenses are $4,000 per month and are paid in the month incurred. General and administrative expenses of $50,000 are recognized and paid monthly. A $60,000 truck is to be purchased in August and is to be depreciated on a straight-line basis over 10 years with no expected salvage value. The company also plans to pay a $9,000 cash dividend to stockholders in July. The company feels that a minimum cash balance of $30,000 should be maintained. Any borrowing will cost 12 percent annually, with interest paid in the month following the month in which the funds are borrowed. Borrowing takes place at the beginning of the month in which the need for funds arises. For example, if during the month of July, the firm should need to borrow $24,000 to maintain its $30,000 desired minimum balance, then $24,000 will be taken out on July 1 with interest owed for the entire month of July. Interest for the month of July would then be paid on August 1. Sales and purchase estimates are shown below. Prepare a cash budget for the months of July and August (cash on hand June 30 was $30,000, whereas sales for May and June were $100,000 and purchases were $60,000 for each of these months).

Month	Sales	Purchases
July	$120,000	$50,000
August	150,000	40,000
September	110,000	30,000

STUDY PROBLEMS (SET A)

4-1A. (*Financial Forecasting*) Zapatera Enterprises is evaluating its financing requirements for the coming year. The firm has only been in business for 1 year, but its chief financial officer predicts that the firm's operating expenses, current assets, net fixed assets, and current liabilities will remain at their current proportion of sales.

Last year Zapatera had $12 million in sales with net income of $1.2 million. The firm anticipates that next year's sales will reach $15 million with net income rising to $2 million. Given its present high rate of growth, the firm retains all its earnings to help defray the cost of new investments.

The firm's balance sheet for the year just ended is as follows:

Zapatera Enterprises, Inc.

Balance Sheet

	12/31/98	% of Sales
Current assets	$3,000,000	25%
Net fixed assets	6,000,000	50%
Total	$9,000,000	
Liabilities and Owners' Equity		
Accounts payable	$3,000,000	25%
Long-term debt	2,000,000	NA*
Total liabilities	$5,000,000	
Common stock	1,000,000	NA
Paid-in capital	1,800,000	NA
Retained earnings	1,200,000	
Common equity	4,000,000	
Total	$9,000,000	

*Not applicable. This figure does not vary directly with sales and is assumed to remain constant for purposes of making next year's forecast of financing requirements.

GO TO:
http://www.prenhall.com/bfm
For downloads and current events associated with this chapter

Estimate Zapatera's total financing requirements (i.e., total assets) for 1999 and its net funding requirements (discretionary financing needed).

4-2A. (*Pro forma accounts receivable balance calculation*) On March 31, 1998, the Sylvia Gift Shop had outstanding accounts receivable of $20,000. Sylvia's sales are roughly evenly split between credit and cash sales, with the credit sales collected half in the month after the sale and the remainder 2 months after the sale. Historical and projected sales for the gift shop are given:

Month	Sales	Month	Sales
January	$15,000	March	30,000
February	20,000	April (projected)	40,000

a. Under these circumstances, what should the balance in accounts receivable be at the end of April?

b. How much cash did Sylvia realize during April from sales and collections?

4-3A. (*Financial Forecasting*) Sambonoza Enterprises projects its sales next year to be $4 million and expects to earn 5 percent of that amount after taxes. The firm is currently in the process of projecting its financing needs and has made the following assumptions (projections):

1. Current assets will equal 20 percent of sales, and fixed assets will remain at their current level of $1 million.

2. Common equity is currently $0.8 million, and the firm pays out half its after-tax earnings in dividends.

3. The firm has short-term payables and trade credit that normally equal 10 percent of sales, and has no long-term debt outstanding.

What are Sambonoza's financing needs for the coming year?

4-4A. (*Financial Forecasting—Percent of Sales*) Tulley Appliances, Inc., projects next year's sales to be $20 million. Current sales are at $15 million based on current assets of $5 million and fixed assets of $5 million. The firm's net profit margin is 5 percent after taxes. Tulley forecasts that current assets will rise in direct proportion to the increase in sales, but fixed assets will increase by only $100,000. Currently, Tulley has $1.5 million in accounts payable (which vary directly with sales), $2 million in long-term debt (due in 10 years) and common equity (including $4 million in retained earnings) totaling $6.5 million. Tulley plans to pay $500,000 in common stock dividends next year.

a. What are Tulley's total financing needs (that is, total assets) for the coming year?

b. Given the firm's projections and dividend payment plans, what are its discretionary financing needs?

c. Based on your projections, and assuming that the $100,000 expansion in fixed assets will occur, what is the largest increase in sales the firm can support without having to resort to the use of discretionary sources of financing?

4-5A. (*Pro Forma Balance Sheet Construction*) Use the following industry average ratios to construct a pro forma balance sheet for Carlos Menza, Inc.

Total asset turnover	2 times
Average collection period (assume a 365-day year)	9 days
Fixed asset turnover	5 times
Inventory turnover (based on cost of goods sold)	3 times
Current ratio	2 times
Sales (all on credit)	$4.0 million
Cost of goods sold	75% of sales
Debt ratio	50%

Cash	_____	Current liabilities	_____
Inventory	_____	Long-term debt	_____
Accounts receivable	_____	Common stock plus	_____
Net fixed assets	_____	Retained earnings	_____
Total	$_____	Total	$_____

4-6A. (*Cash Budget*) The Sharpe Corporation's projected sales for the first 8 months of 1999 are as follows:

January	$ 90,000	May	$300,000
February	120,000	June	270,000
March	135,000	July	225,000
April	240,000	August	150,000

Of Sharpe's sales, 10 percent is for cash, another 60 percent is collected in the month following sale, and 30 percent is collected in the second month following sale. November and December sales for 1998 were $220,000 and $175,000, respectively.

Sharpe purchases its raw materials 2 months in advance of its sales equal to 60 percent of their final sales price. The supplier is paid 1 month after it makes delivery. For example, purchases for April sales are made in February and payment is made in March.

In addition, Sharpe pays $10,000 per month for rent and $20,000 each month for other expenditures. Tax prepayments of $22,500 are made each quarter, beginning in March.

The company's cash balance at December 31, 1998, was $22,000; a minimum balance of $15,000 must be maintained at all times. Assume that any short-term financing needed to maintain the cash balance would be paid off in the month following the month of financing if sufficient funds are available. Interest on short-term loans (12 percent) is paid monthly. Borrowing to meet estimated monthly cash needs takes place at the beginning of the month. Thus if in the month of April the firm expects to have a need for an additional $60,500, these funds would be borrowed at the beginning of April with interest of $605 (.12 × 1/12 × $60,500) owed for April and paid at the beginning of May.

a. Prepare a cash budget for Sharpe covering the first 7 months of 1999.

b. Sharpe has $200,000 in notes payable due in July that must be repaid or renegotiated for an extension. Will the firm have ample cash to repay the notes?

4-7A. (*Percent of Sales Forecasting*) Which of the following accounts would most likely vary directly with the level of firm sales? Discuss each briefly.

	Yes	No		Yes	No
Cash	____	____	Notes payable	____	____
Marketable securities	____	____	Plant and equipment	____	____
Accounts payable	____	____	Inventories	____	____

4-8A. (*Financial Forecasting—Percent of Sales*) The balance sheet of the Thompson Trucking Company (TTC) follows:

Thompson Trucking Company Balance Sheet, December 31, 1998 ($ millions)			
Current assets	$10	Accounts payable	$ 5
Net fixed assets	15	Notes payable	0
Total	$25	Bonds payable	10
		Common equity	10
		Total	$25

TTC had sales for the year ended 12/31/98 of $50 million. The firm follows a policy of paying all net earnings out to its common stockholders in cash dividends. Thus TTC generates no funds from its earnings that can be used to expand its operations. (Assume that depreciation expense is just equal to the cost of replacing worn-out assets.)

a. If TTC anticipates sales of $80 million during the coming year, develop a pro forma balance sheet for the firm for 12/31/99. Assume that current assets vary as a percent of sales, net fixed assets remain unchanged, accounts payable vary as a percent of sales, and use notes payable as a balancing entry.

b. How much "new" financing will TTC need next year?

c. What limitations does the percent of sales forecast method suffer from? Discuss briefly.

4-9A. (*Financial Forecasting—Discretionary Financing Needed*) The most recent balance sheet for the Armadillo Dog Biscuit Co. is shown in the table following. The company is about to embark on an advertising campaign, which is expected to raise sales from the current level of $5 million to $7 million by the end of next year. The firm is currently operating at full capacity and will have to increase its investment in both current and fixed assets to support the projected level of new sales. In fact, the firm estimates that both categories of assets will rise in direct proportion to the projected increase in sales.

Armadillo Dog Biscuit Co., Inc. ($ millions)			
	Present Level	**Percent of Sales**	**Projected Level**
Current assets	$2.0		
Net fixed assets	3.0		
Total	$5.0		
Accounts payable	$0.5		
Accrued expenses	0.5		
Notes payable	—		
Current liabilities	$1.0		
Long-term debt	$2.0		
Common stock	0.5		
Retained earnings	1.5		
Common equity	$2.0		
Total	$5.0		

The firm's net profits were 6 percent of current year's sales but are expected to rise to 7 percent of next year's sales. To help support its anticipated growth in asset needs next year, the firm has suspended plans to pay cash dividends to its stockholders. In past years, a $1.50 per share dividend has been paid annually.

Armadillo's payables and accrued expenses are expected to vary directly with sales. In addition, notes payable will be used to supply the funds that are needed to finance next year's operations and that are not forthcoming from other sources.

a. Fill in the table and project the firm's needs for discretionary financing. Use notes payable as the balancing entry for future discretionary financing needed.

b. Compare Armadillo's current ratio and debt ratio (total liabilities/total assets) before the growth in sales and after. What was the effect of the expanded sales on these two dimensions of Armadillo's financial condition?

c. What difference, if any, would have resulted if Armadillo's sales had risen to $6 million in one year and $7 million only after 2 years? Discuss only; no calculations required.

4-10A. (*Forecasting Discretionary Financing Needs*) Fishing Charter, Inc., estimates that it invests 30 cents in assets for each dollar of new sales. However, 5 cents in profits are produced by each dollar of additional sales, of which 1 cent can be reinvested in the firm. If sales rise from their current level of $5 million by $500,000 next year, and the ratio of spontaneous liabilities to sales is .15, what will be the firm's need for discretionary financing? (*Hint:* In this situation you do not know what the firm's existing level of assets is, nor do you know how those assets have been financed. Thus you must estimate the change in financing needs and match this change with the expected changes in spontaneous liabilities, retained earnings, and other sources of discretionary financing.)

4-11A. (*Preparation of a Cash Budget*) Harrison Printing has projected its sales for the first eight months of 1999 as follows:

GO TO:
http://www.prenhall.com/bfm
For downloads and current events
associated with this chapter

January	$100,000	April	$300,000	July	$200,000
February	120,000	May	275,000	August	180,000
March	150,000	June	200,000		

Harrison collects 20 percent of its sales in the month of the sale, 50 percent in the month following the sale, and the remaining 30 percent 2 months following the sale. During November and December of 1998 Harrison's sales were $220,000 and $175,000, respectively.

Harrison purchases raw materials 2 months in advance of its sales equal to 65 percent of its final sales. The supplier is paid 1 month after delivery. Thus purchases for April sales are made in February and payment is made in March.

In addition, Harrison pays $10,000 per month for rent and $20,000 each month for other expenditures. Tax prepayments of $22,500 are made each quarter beginning in March. The company's cash balance as of December 31, 1998, was $22,000; a minimum balance of $20,000 must be maintained at all times to satisfy the firm's bank line of credit agreement. Harrison has arranged with its bank for short-term credit at an interest rate of 12 percent per annum (1 percent per month) to be paid monthly. Borrowing to meet estimated monthly cash needs takes place at the end of the month, and interest is not paid until the end of the following month. Consequently, if the firm were to need to borrow $50,000 during the month of April, then it would pay $500 (= .01 × $50,000) in interest during May. Finally, Harrison follows a policy of repaying its outstanding short-term debt in any month in which its cash balance exceeds the minimum desired balance of $20,000.

a. Harrison needs to know what its cash requirements will be for the next 6 months so that it can renegotiate the terms of its short-term credit agreement with its bank, if necessary. To evaluate this problem, the firm plans to evaluate the impact of a ± 20 percent variation in its monthly sales efforts. Prepare a 6-month cash budget for Harrison and use it to evaluate the firm's cash needs.

b. Harrison has a $200,000 note due in June. Will the firm have sufficient cash to repay the loan?

4-12A. (*Sustainable Rate of Growth*) ADP, Inc., is a manufacturer of specialty circuit boards in the personal computer industry. The firm has experienced phenomenal sales growth over its short 5-year life. Selected financial statement data are found in the following table:

	1995	1994	1993	1992	1991
Sales	$3,000	$2,200	$1,800	$1,400	$1,200
Net income	150	110	90	70	60
Assets	2,700	1,980	1,620	1,260	1,080
Dividends	60	44	36	28	24
Common equity	812	722	656	602	560
Liabilities	1,888	1,258	964	658	520
Liabilities and equity	2,700	1,980	1,620	1,260	1,080

a. Calculate ADP's sustainable rate of growth for each of the 5 years of its existence.

b. Compare the actual rates of growth in sales to the firm's sustainable rates calculated in part a. How has ADP been financing its growing asset needs?

4-13A. (*Sustainable Rate of Growth*) The Carrera Game Company has experienced a 100 percent increase in sales over the last 5 years. The company president, Jack Carrera, has become increasingly alarmed by the firm's rising debt level even in the face of continued profitability.

	1997	1996	1995	1994	1993
Sales	$60,000	$56,000	$48,000	$36,000	$30,000
Net income	3,000	2,800	2,400	1,800	1,500
Assets	54,000	50,400	43,200	32,400	27,000
Dividends	1,200	1,120	960	720	600
Common equity	21,000	19,200	17,520	16,080	15,000
Liabilities	33,000	31,200	25,680	16,320	12,000
Liabilities and equity	54,000	50,400	43,200	32,400	27,000

a. Calculate the debt to assets ratio, return on common equity, actual rate of growth in firm sales and retention ratio for each of the 5 years of data provided.

b. Calculate the sustainable rates of growth for Carrera for each of the last 5 years. Why has the firm's borrowing increased so dramatically?

4-14A. (*Forecasting Inventories*) Findlay Instruments produces a complete line of medical instruments used by plastic surgeons and has experienced rapid growth over the last 5 years. In an effort to make more accurate predictions of its financing requirements, Findlay is currently attempting to construct a financial planning model based on the percent of sales forecasting method. However, the firm's chief financial analyst (Sarah Macias) is concerned that the projections for inventories will be seriously in error. She recognizes that the firm has begun to accrue substantial economies of scale in its inventory investment and has documented this fact in the following data and calculations:

Year	Sales (000)	Inventory (000)	% of Sales
1991	$15,000	1,150	7.67%
1992	18,000	1,180	6.56%
1993	17,500	1,175	6.71%
1994	20,000	1,200	6.00%
1995	25,000	1,250	5.00%
		Average	6.39%

a. Plot Findlay's sales and inventories for the last 5 years. What is the relationship between these two variables?

b. Estimate firm inventories for 1996 where firm sales are projected to reach $30,000,000. Use the average percent of sales for the last 5 years, the most recent percent of sales, and your evaluation of the true relationship between the sales and inventories from part a to make three predications.

Phillips Petroleum is an integrated oil and gas company with headquarters in Bartlesville, Oklahoma, where it was founded in 1917. The company engages in petroleum exploration and production worldwide. In addition, it engages in natural gas gathering and processing, as well as petroleum refining and marketing primarily in the United States. The company has three operating groups—Exploration and Production, Gas and Gas Liquids, and Downstream Operations, which encompasses Petroleum Products and Chemicals.

INTEGRATIVE PROBLEM

GO TO:
http://www.prenhall.com/bfm
For downloads and current events
associated with this chapter

In the mid-1980s, Phillips engaged in a major restructuring following two failed takeover attempts, one led by T. Boone Pickens and the other by Carl Icahn.* The restructuring resulted in a $4.5 billion plan to exchange a package of cash and debt securities for roughly half the company's shares and to sell $2 billion worth of assets. Phillips's long-term debt increased from $3.4 billion in late 1984 to a peak of $8.6 billion in April 1985.

During 1992, Phillips was able to strengthen its financial structure dramatically. Its subsidiary Phillips Gas Company completed an offering of $345 million of Series A 9.32% Cumulative Preferred Stock. As a result of these actions and prior year's debt reductions, the company lowered its long-term debt to capital ratio over the last 5 years from 75 to 55 percent. In addition, the firm refinanced over a billion dollars of its debt at reduced rates. A company spokesman said that "Our debt-to-capital ratio is still on the high side, and we'll keep working to bring it down. But the cost of debt is manageable, and we're beyond the point where debt overshadows everything else we do."[†]

Summary Financial Information for Phillips Petroleum Corporation: 1986–1992 (in millions of dollars except for per share figures)							
	1986	**1987**	**1988**	**1989**	**1990**	**1991**	**1992**
Sales	10,018.00	10,917.00	11,490.00	12,492.00	13,975.00	13,259.00	12,140.00
Net income	228.00	35.00	650.00	219.00	541.00	98.00	270.00
EPS	0.89	0.06	2.72	0.90	2.18	0.38	1.04
Current assets	2,802.00	2,855.00	3,062.00	2,876.00	3,322.00	2,459.00	2,349.00
Total assets	12,403.00	12,111.00	11,968.00	11,256.00	12,130.00	11,473.00	11,468.00
Current liabilities	2,234.00	2,402.00	2,468.00	2,706.00	2,910.00	2,603.00	2,517.00
Long-term liabilities	8,175.00	7,887.00	7,387.00	6,418.00	6,501.00	6,113.00	5,894.00
Total liabilities	10,409.00	10,289.00	9,855.00	9,124.00	9,411.00	8,716.00	8,411.00
Preferred stock	270.00	205.00	0.00	0.00	0.00	0.00	359.00
Common equity	1,724.00	1,617.00	2,113.00	2,132.00	2,719.00	2,757.00	2,698.00
Dividends per share	2.02	1.73	1.34	0.00	1.03	1.12	1.12

SOURCE: Phillips Annual Reports for the years 1987–1992.

Highlights of Phillips's financial condition spanning the years 1986–1992 are found in the preceding table.[‡] These data reflect the modern history of the company as a result of its financial restructuring following the downsizing and reorganization of Phillips's operations begun in the mid-1980s.

Phillips's management is currently developing its financial plans for the next 5 years and wants to develop a forecast of its financing requirements. As a first approximation, they have asked you to develop a model that can be used to make "ballpark" estimates of the firm's financing needs under the proviso that existing relationships found in the firm's financial statements remain the same over the period. Of particular interest is whether or not Phillips will be able to further reduce its reliance on debt financing. You may assume that Phillips's projected sales (in millions) for 1993 through 1997 are as follows: $13,000, $13,500, $14,000, $14,500, and $15,500.

---

*This discussion is based on a story in *The New York Times*, January 7, 1986.

†From *SEC Online*, 1992.

‡Extracted from Phillips's Annual Reports for the years represented.

1. Project net income for 1993 to 1997 using the percent of sales method based on an average of this ratio for 1986 to 1992.

2. Project total assets and current liabilities for the period 1993 to 1997 using the percent of sales method and your sales projections from part 1.

3. Assuming that common equity increases only as a result of the retention of earnings and holding long-term liabilities and preferred stock equal to their 1992 balances, project Phillips's discretionary financing needs for 1993 to 1997. (*Hint:* Assume that total assets and current liabilities vary as a percent of sales as per your answer. In addition, assume that Phillips plans to continue to pay its dividend of $1.12 per share in each of the next 5 years.)

STUDY PROBLEMS (SET B)

4-1B. (*Financial Forecasting*) Hernandez Trucking Company is evaluating its financing requirements for the coming year. The firm has only been in business for 3 years and the firm's chief financial officer (Eric Stevens) predicts that the firm's operating expenses, current assets, and current liabilities will remain at their current proportion of sales.

Last year, Hernandez had $20 million in sales with net income of $1 million. The firm anticipates that next year's sales will reach $25 million with net income rising to $2 million. Given its present high rate of growth, the firm retains all its earnings to help defray the cost of new investments.

The firm's balance sheet for the year just ended is found below:

Hernandez Trucking Company, Inc. Balance Sheet		
	12/31/98	**% of Sales**
Current assets	$ 4,000,000	20%
Net fixed assets	8,000,000	40%
Total	$12,000,000	
Liabilities and Owner's Equity		
Accounts payable	$ 3,000,000	15%
Long-term debt	2,000,000	NA*
Total liabilities	$ 5,000,000	
Common stock	1,000,000	NA
Paid-in capital	1,800,000	NA
Retained earnings	4,200,000	
Common equity	7,000,000	
Total	$12,000,000	

*Not applicable. This figure does not vary directly with sales and is assumed to remain constant for purposes of making next year's forecast of financing requirements.

Estimate Hernandez's total financing requirements for 1999 and its net funding requirements (discretionary financing needed).

4-2B. (*Pro Forma Accounts Receivable Balance Calculation*) On March 31, 1998, the Floydata Food Distribution Company had outstanding accounts receivable of $52,000. Sales are roughly

40 percent credit and 60 percent cash, with the credit sales collected half in the month after the sale and the remainder 2 months after the sale. Historical and projected sales for Floydata Food are given below:

Month	Sales
January	$100,000
February	100,000
March	80,000
April (projected)	60,000

    a. Under these circumstances, what should the balance in accounts receivable be at the end of April?

    b. How much cash did Floydata realize during April from sales and collections?

4-3B. (*Financial Forecasting*) Simpson, Inc., projects its sales next year to be $5 million and expects to earn 6 percent of that amount after taxes. The firm is currently in the process of projecting its financing needs and has made the following assumptions (projections):

    a. Current assets will equal 15 percent of sales and fixed assets will remain at their current level of $1 million.

    b. Common equity is presently $0.7 million, and the firm pays out half its after-tax earnings in dividends.

    c. The firm has short-term payables and trade credit that normally equal 11 percent of sales and has no long-term debt outstanding.

What are Simpson's financing needs for the coming year?

4-4B. (*Financial Forecasting—Percent of Sales*) Carson Enterprises is in the midst of its annual planning exercise. Bud Carson, the owner, is a mechanical engineer by education and has only modest skills in financial planning. In fact, the firm has operated in the past on a "crisis" basis with little attention paid to the firm's financial affairs until a problem arose. This worked reasonably well for several years, until the firm's growth in sales created a serious cash flow shortage last year. Bud was able to convince the firm's bank to come up with the needed funds, but an outgrowth of the agreement was that the firm would begin to make forecasts of its financing requirements annually. To support its first such effort, Bud has made the following estimates for next year: Sales are currently $18 million with projected sales of $25 million for next year. The firm's current assets equal $7 million, and its fixed assets are $6 million. The best estimate Bud can make is that current assets will equal the current proportion of sales and fixed assets will rise by $100,000. At the present time, the firm has accounts payable of $1.5 million, $2 million in long-term debt, and common equity totaling $9.5 million (including $4 million in retained earnings). Finally, Carson Enterprises plans to continue paying its dividend of $600,000 next year and has a 5 percent profit margin.

    a. What are Carson's total financing needs (that is, total assets) for the coming year?

    b. Given the firm's projections and dividend payment plans, what are its discretionary financing needs?

    c. Based on the projections given and assuming that the $100,000 expansion in fixed assets will occur, what is the largest increase in sales the firm can support without having to resort to the use of discretionary sources of financing?

4-5B. (*Pro Forma Balance Sheet Construction*) Use the following industry average ratios to construct a pro forma balance sheet for the V. M. Willet Co.

Total asset turnover	2.5 times
Average collection period (assume a 360-day year)	10 days
Fixed asset turnover	6 times
Inventory turnover (based on cost of goods sold)	4 times
Current ratio	3 times
Sales (all on credit)	$5 million
Cost of goods sold	80% of sales
Debt ratio	60%

Cash		Current liabilities	
Accounts receivables		Long-term debt	
Inventories		Common stock plus	
Net fixed assets	$_____	retained earnings	$_____
	$‗‗‗‗		$‗‗‗‗

4-6B. (*Cash Budget*) The Carmel Corporation's projected sales for the first 8 months of 1999 are as follows:

January	$100,000	May	$275,000
February	110,000	June	250,000
March	130,000	July	235,000
April	250,000	August	160,000

Of Carmel's sales, 20 percent is for cash, another 60 percent is collected in the month following sale, and 20 percent is collected in the second month following sale. November and December sales for 1998 were $220,000 and $175,000, respectively.

Carmel purchases its raw materials 2 months in advance of its sales equal to 70 percent of their final sales price. The supplier is paid 1 month after it makes delivery. For example, purchases for April sales are made in February and payment is made in March.

In addition, Carmel pays $10,000 per month for rent and $20,000 each month for other expenditures. Tax prepayments for $23,000 are made each quarter beginning in March.

The company's cash balance at December 31, 1998, was $22,000; a minimum balance of $20,000 must be maintained at all times. Assume that any short-term financing needed to maintain cash balance would be paid off in the month following the month of financing if sufficient funds are available. Interest on short-term loans (12 percent) is paid monthly. Borrowing to meet estimated monthly cash needs takes place at the beginning of the month. Thus if in the month of April the firm expects to have a need for an additional $60,500, these funds would be borrowed at the beginning of April with interest of $605 ($.12 \times 1/12 \times $60,500$) owed for April and paid at the beginning of May.

    a. Prepare a cash budget for Carmel covering the first 7 months of 1999.

    b. Carmel has $250,000 in notes payable due in July that must be repaid or renegotiated for an extension. Will the firm have ample cash to repay the notes?

4-7B. (*Percent of Sales Forecasting*) Which of the following accounts would most likely vary directly with the level of firm sales? Discuss each briefly.

	Yes	No		Yes	No
Cash	___	___	Notes payable	___	___
Marketable securities	___	___	Plant and equipment	___	___
Accounts payable	___	___	Inventories	___	___

4-8B. (*Financial Forecasting—Percent of Sales*) The balance sheet of the Chavez Drilling Company (CDC) follows:

Chavez Drilling Company Balance Sheet for January 31, 1998 ($ millions)			
Current assets	$15	Accounts payable	$10
Net fixed assets	15	Notes payable	0
Total	$30	Bonds payable	10
		Common equity	10
		Total	$30

CDC had sales for the year ended 1/31/98 of $60 million. The firm follows a policy of paying all net earnings out to its common stockholders in cash dividends. Thus CDC generates no funds from its earnings that can be used to expand its operations (assume that depreciation expense is just equal to the cost of replacing worn-out assets).

   a. If CDC anticipates sales of $80 million during the coming year, develop a pro forma balance sheet for the firm for 1/31/99. Assume that current assets vary as a percent of sales, net fixed assets remain unchanged, accounts payable vary as a percent of sales, and use notes payable as a balancing entry.

   b. How much "new" financing will CDC need next year?

   c. What limitations does the percent of sales forecast method suffer from? Discuss briefly.

4-9B. (*Financial Forecasting—Discretionary Financing Needed*) Symbolic Logic Corporation (SLC) is a technological leader in the application of surface mount technology in the manufacture of printed circuit boards used in the personal computer industry. The firm has recently patented an advanced version of its original path-breaking technology and expects sales to grow from their present level of $5 million to $8 million in the coming year. Since the firm is at present operating at full capacity, it expects to have to increase its investment in both current and fixed assets in proportion to the predicted increase in sales.

The firm's net profits were 7 percent of current year's sales and are expected to be the same next year. To help support its anticipated growth in asset needs next year, the firm has suspended plans to pay cash dividends to its stockholders. In years past, a $1.25 per share dividend has been paid annually.

Symbolic Logic Corporation ($ millions)			
	Present Level	**Percent of Sales**	**Projected Level**
Current assets	$2.5		
Net fixed assets	3.0		
Total	5.5		
Accounts payable	$1.0		
Accrued expenses	0.5		
Notes payable	—		
Current liabilities	$1.5		
Long-term debt	$2.0		
Common stock	0.5		
Retained earnings	1.5		
Common equity	$2.0		
Total	$5.5		

SLC's payables and accrued expenses are expected to vary directly with sales. In addition, notes payable will be used to supply the funds needed to finance next year's operations and that are not forthcoming from other sources.

    a. Fill in the table and project the firm's needs for discretionary financing. Use notes payable as the balancing entry for future discretionary financing needed.

    b. Compare SLC's current ratio and debt ratio (total liabilities/total assets) before the growth in sales and after. What was the effect of the expanded sales on these two dimensions of SLC's financial condition?

    c. What difference, if any, would have resulted if SLC's sales had risen to $6 million in one year and $8 million only after 2 years? Discuss only; no calculations required.

4-10B. (*Forecasting Discretionary Financing Needs*) Royal Charter, Inc., estimates that it invests 40 cents in assets for each dollar of new sales. However, 5 cents in profits are produced by each dollar of additional sales, of which 1 cent can be reinvested in the firm. If sales rise from their present level of $5 million by $500,000 next year, and the ratio of spontaneous liabilities to sales is .15, what will be the firm's need for discretionary financing? (*Hint:* In this situation you do not know what the firm's existing level of assets is, nor do you know how those assets have been financed. Thus you must estimate the change in financing needs and match this change with the expected changes in spontaneous liabilities, retained earnings, and other sources of discretionary financing. Note that spontaneous liabilities are those liabilities that vary with sales.)

4-11B. (*Preparation of a Cash Budget*) Halsey Enterprises has projected its sales for the first eight months of 1999 as follows:

January	$120,000	May	$225,000
February	160,000	June	250,000
March	140,000	July	210,000
April	190,000	August	220,000

Halsey collects 30 percent of its sales in the month of the sale, 30 percent in the month following the sale, and the remaining 40 percent 2 months following the sale. During November and December of 1998, Halsey's sales were $230,000 and $225,000, respectively.

Halsey purchases raw materials 2 months in advance of its sales equal to 75 percent of its final sales. The supplier is paid in the month after delivery. Thus purchases for April sales are made in February and payment is made in March.

In addition, Halsey pays $12,000 per month for rent and $20,000 each month for other expenditures. Tax prepayments of $26,500 are made each quarter beginning in March. The company's cash balance as of December 31, 1998, was $28,000; a minimum balance of $25,000 must be maintained at all times to satisfy the firm's bank line of credit agreement. Halsey has arranged with its bank for short-term credit at an interest rate of 12 percent per annum (1 percent per month) to be paid monthly. Borrowing to meet estimated monthly cash needs takes place at the beginning of the month, but interest is not paid until the end of the following month. Consequently, if the firm were to need to borrow $50,000 during the month of April, then it would pay $500 (= .01 × $50,000) in interest during May. Finally, Halsey follows a policy of repaying any outstanding short-term debt in any month in which its cash balance exceeds the minimum desired balance of $25,000.

    a. Halsey needs to know what its cash requirements will be for the next 6 months so that it can renegotiate the terms of its short-term credit agreement with its bank, if necessary. To evaluate this problem the firm plans to evaluate the impact of a ± 20 percent variation in its monthly sales efforts. Prepare a 6-month cash budget for Halsey and use it to evaluate the firm's cash needs.

    b. Halsey has a $200,000 note due in July. Will the firm have sufficient cash to repay the loan?

SELF-TEST SOLUTIONS

SS-1.

Calico Sales Co., Inc., Pro Forma Income Statement		
Sales		$4,000,000
Cost of goods sold (70%)		(2,800,000)
Gross profit		1,200,000
Operating expense		
Selling expense (5%)	$200,000	
Administrative expense	500,000	
Depreciation expense	300,000	(1,000,000)
Net operating income		200,000
Interest		(50,000)
Earnings before taxes		150,000
Taxes (40%)		(60,000)
Net income		$ 90,000

Although the office renovation expenditure and debt retirement are surely cash outflows, they do not enter the income statement directly. These expenditures affect expenses for the period's income statement only through their effect on depreciation and interest expense. A cash budget would indicate the full cash impact of the renovation and debt retirement expenditures.

SS-2.

	May	June	July	Aug.
Sales	$100,000	$100,000	$ 120,000	$150,000
Purchases	60,000	60,000	50,000	40,000
Cash Receipts:				
Collections from month of sale (20%)	20,000	20,000	24,000	30,000
1 month later (50% of uncollected amount)		40,000	40,000	48,000
2 months later (balance)			40,000	40,000
Total receipts			$ 104,000	$ 118,000
Cash Disbursements:				
Payments for purchases—				
From 1 month earlier			$ 30,000	$ 25,000
From current month			$ 25,000	20,000
Total			$ 55,000	$ 45,000
Miscellaneous cash expenses			4,000	4,000
Labor expense (5% of sales)			6,000	7,500
General and administrative expense				
($50,000 per month)			50,000	50,000
Truck purchase			0	60,000
Cash dividends			9,000	—
Total disbursements			$(124,000)	$(166,500)
Net change in cash			(20,000)	(48,500)
Plus: Beginning cash balance			30,000	30,000
Less: Interest on short-term borrowing				
(1% of prior month's borrowing)				(200)
Equals: Ending cash balance—without borrowing			10,000	(18,700)
Financing needed to reach target cash balance			20,000	48,700
Cumulative borrowing			$ 20,000	$ 68,700

Learning Objectives

Active Applications

World Finance

Practice

CHAPTER 5

LEARNING OBJECTIVES

After reading this chapter, you should be able to

1. Explain the mechanics of compounding: how money grows over time when it is invested.

2. Determine the future or present value of a sum when there are nonannual compounding periods.

3. Discuss the relationship between compounding (future value) and bringing money back to the present (present value).

4. Define an ordinary annuity and calculate its compound or future value.

5. Differentiate between an ordinary annuity and an annuity due, and determine the future and present value of an annuity due.

6. Calculate the annual percentage yield or effective annual rate of interest and then explain how it differs from the nominal or stated interest rate.

THE TIME VALUE OF MONEY

INTRODUCTION

In business, there is probably no other single concept with more power or applications than that of the time value of money. Homer (Sidney Homer, that is) in his landmark book, *A History of Interest Rates*, noted that if $1,000 was invested for 400 years at 8 percent interest it would grow to $23 quadrillion—that would work out to approximately $5 million per person on earth. He was not giving a plan to make the world rich, but effectively pointing out the power of the time value of money.

The time value of money is certainly not a new concept. Benjamin Franklin had a good understanding of how it worked when he left £1,000 each to Boston and Philadelphia. With the gift he left instructions that the cities were to lend the money, charging the going interest rate, to worthy apprentices. Then after the money had been invested in this way for 100 years, they were to use a portion of the investment to build something of benefit to the city, holding some back for the future. Two hundred years later, Franklin's Boston gift resulted in the construction of the Franklin Union, has helped countless medical students with loans, and still has over $3 million left in the account. Philadelphia, likewise, has reaped a significant reward from his gift. Bear in mind that all this has come from a gift of £2,000, with some serious help from the time value of money.

The power of the time value of money can also be illustrated through a story Andrew Tobias tells in his book *Money Angles*. There he tells of a peasant who wins a chess tournament put on by the king. The king then asks the peasant what he would like as the prize. The peasant answers that he would like for his village one piece of grain to be placed on the first square of his chessboard, two pieces of grain on the second square, four pieces of grain on the third, eight on the fourth, and so forth. The king, thinking he was getting off easy, pledged on his word of honor that it would be done. Unfortunately for the king, by the time all 64 squares on the chess board were filled, there were 18.5 million trillion grains of wheat on the board—the kernels were compounding at a rate of 100 percent over the 64 squares of the chessboard. Needless to *say, no one in the village ever went hungry. In fact, that is so much wheat that if the kernels were one-quarter inch long (quite frankly, I have no idea how long a kernel of wheat is, but Andrew Tobias's guess is one-quarter inch), if laid end to end they could stretch to the sun and back 391,320 times.*

Not only is there incredible power in compounding, but it also allows us to compare projects that provide benefits in different time periods. For example, a manager may have to choose between three projects, one that promises $1,000 next year, one that promises $1,500 in 5 years, and one that promises $2,500 in 10 years. How does the manager evaluate these projects with cash flows in different periods? The time value of money holds the key to doing this. Not only will an understanding of the time value of money help you to evalute projects, but it will also allow you to understand how stocks and bonds are valued, how much you should save for your children's education, and how much your mortgage payments will be.

CHAPTER PREVIEW

In the next six chapters, we will focus on determining the value of the firm and the value of investment proposals. A key concept that underlies this material is the *time value of money*; that is, a dollar today is worth more than a dollar received a year from now because a dollar today can be invested and earn interest. Intuitively this idea is easy to understand. We are all familiar with the concept of interest. This concept illustrates what economists call an *opportunity cost* of passing up the earning potential of a dollar today. This opportunity cost is the time value of money.

Different investment proposals produce different sets of cash flows over different time periods. How does the manager compare these? We will see that the concept of the time value of money will let us do this. Thus an understanding of the time value of money is essential to an understanding of financial management, whether basic or advanced. In this chapter, we develop the tools to incorporate Axiom 2: The Time Value of Money—A Dollar Received Today Is Worth More Than a Dollar Received in the Future into our calculations. In coming chapters, we will use this concept to measure value by bringing the benefits and costs from a project back to the present.

COMPOUND INTEREST AND FUTURE VALUE

Most of us encounter the concept of compound interest at an early age. Anyone who has ever had a savings account or purchased a government savings bond has received compound interest. **Compound interest** occurs when interest paid on the investment during the first period is added to the principal; then, during the second period, interest is earned on this new sum.

For example, suppose we place $100 in a savings account that pays 6 percent interest, compounded annually. How will our savings grow? At the end of the first year we have earned 6 percent, or $6 on our initial deposit of $100, giving us a total of $106 in our savings account. The mathematical formula illustrating this phenomenon is

Compound interest

Interest that occurs when interest paid on the investment during the first period is added to the principal; then, during the second period, interest is earned on this new sum.

$$FV_1 = PV(1 + i) \tag{5-1}$$

where FV_1 = the future value of the investment at the end of 1 year

i = the annual interest (or discount) rate

PV = the present value, or original amount invested at the beginning of the first year

In our example

$$FV_1 = PV(1 + i)$$
$$= \$100(1 + .06)$$
$$= \$100(1.06)$$
$$= \$106$$

Carrying these calculations one period further, we find that we now earn the 6 percent interest on a principal of $106, which means we earn $6.36 in interest during the second year. Why do we earn more interest during the second year than we did during the first? Simply because we now earn interest on the sum of the original principal, or present value, and the interest we earned in the first year. In effect, we are now earning interest on interest—this is the concept of compound interest. Examining the mathematical formula illustrating the earning of interest in the second year, we find

$$FV_2 = FV_1(1 + i) \tag{5-2}$$

which for our example, gives

$$FV_2 = \$106(1.06)$$
$$= \$112.36$$

Looking back at equation (5-1) we can see that FV_1, or $106, is actually equal to $PV(1 + i)$, or $100 (1 + .06). If we substitute these values into equation (5-2), we get

$$FV_2 = PV(1 + i)(1 + i) \tag{5-3}$$
$$= PV(1 + i)^2$$

Carrying this forward into the third year, we find that we enter the year with $112.36 and we earn 6 percent, or $6.74, in interest, giving us a total of $119.10 in our savings account. Expressing this mathematically

$$FV_3 = FV_2(1 + i) \tag{5-4}$$
$$= \$112.36(1.06)$$
$$= \$119.10$$

If we substitute the value in equation (5-3) for FV_2 into equation (5-4), we find

$$FV_3 = PV(1 + i)(1 + i)(1 + i) \tag{5-5}$$
$$= PV(1 + i)^3$$

Table 5.1 Illustration of Compound Interest Calculations

Year	Beginning Value	Interest Earned	Ending Value
1	$100.00	$ 6.00	$106.00
2	106.00	6.36	112.36
3	112.36	6.74	119.10
4	119.10	7.15	126.25
5	126.25	7.57	133.82
6	133.82	8.03	141.85
7	141.85	8.51	150.36
8	150.36	9.02	159.38
9	159.38	9.57	168.95
10	168.95	10.13	179.08

By now a pattern is beginning to be evident. We can generalize this formula to illustrate the value of our investment if it is compounded annually at a rate of i for n years to be

$$FV_n = PV(1 + i)^n \tag{5-6}$$

where FV_n = the future value of the investment at the end of n years
n = the number of years during which the compounding occurs
i = the annual interest (or discount) rate
PV = the present value or original amount invested at the beginning of the first year

Table 5.1 illustrates how this investment of $100 would continue to grow for the first 10 years at a compound interest rate of 6 percent. Notice how the amount of interest earned annually increases each year. Again, the reason is that each year interest is received on the sum of the original investment plus any interest earned in the past.

When we examine the relationship between the number of years an initial investment is compounded for and its future value as shown graphically, in Figure 5.1, we see that we can increase the future value of an investment by increasing the number of years we let it compound or by compounding it at a higher interest rate. We can also see this from equation (5-6), because an increase in either i or n while PV is held constant will result in an increase in FV_n.

STOP AND THINK

Keep in mind that future cash flows are assumed to occur at the end of the time period during which they accrue. For example, if a cash flow of $100 occurs in time period 5, it is assumed to occur at the end of time period 5, which is also the beginning of time period 6. In addition, cash flows that occur in time $t = 0$ occur right now; that is, they are already in present dollars.

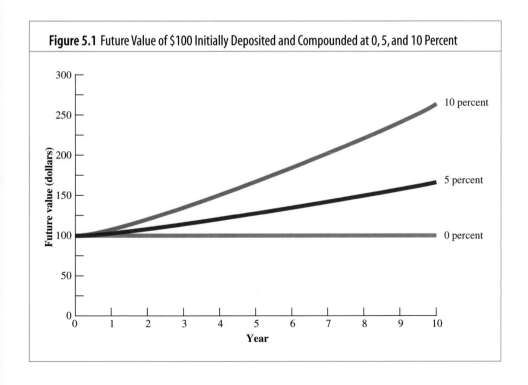

Figure 5.1 Future Value of $100 Initially Deposited and Compounded at 0, 5, and 10 Percent

EXAMPLE

If we place \$1,000 in a savings account paying 5 percent interest compounded annually, how much will our account accrue to in 10 years? Substituting $PV = \$1,000$, $i = 5$ percent, and $n = 10$ years into equation (5-6), we get

$$
\begin{aligned}
FV_n &= PV(1 + i)^n \\
&= \$1,000(1 + .05)^{10} \\
&= \$1,000(1.62889) \\
&= \$1,628.89
\end{aligned}
$$

Thus at the end of 10 years, we will have \$1,628.89 in our savings account.

Future-value interest factor ($FVIF_{i,n}$)

The value $(1 + i)^n$ used as a multiplier to calculate an amount's future value.

As the determination of future value can be quite time consuming when an investment is held for a number of years, the **future-value interest factor** for i and n (**$FVIF_{i,n}$**), defined as $(1 + i)^n$, has been compiled in the back of the book for various values of i and n. An abbreviated compound interest or future-value interest factor table appears in Table 5.2, with a more comprehensive version of this table appearing in appendix B at the back of this book. Alternatively, the $FVIF_{i,n}$ values could easily be determined using a calculator. Note that the compounding factors given in these tables represent the value of \$1 compounded at rate i at the *end* of the nth period. Thus to calculate the future value of an initial investment, we need only determine the $FVIF_{i,n}$ using a calculator or the tables in appendix B and multiply this times the initial investment. In effect, we can rewrite equation (5-6) as follows:

$$FV_n = PV(FVIF_{i,n}) \tag{5-6a}$$

EXAMPLE

If we invest \$500 in a bank where it will earn 8 percent compounded annually, how much will it be worth at the end of 7 years? Looking at Table 5.2 in row $n = 7$ and column $i = 8\%$, we find that $FVIF_{8\%,7\text{yrs}}$ has a value of 1.714. Substituting this in equation (5-6a), we find

$$
\begin{aligned}
FV_n &= PV(FVIF_{8\%,7\text{yrs}}) \\
&= \$500(1.714) \\
&= \$857
\end{aligned}
$$

Thus we will have \$857 at the end of 7 years.

We will find several uses for equation (5-6): not only will we find the future value of an investment, but we can also solve for PV, i, or n. When we will be given three of the four variables, we can solve for the fourth.

STOP AND THINK

As you read through the chapter, it is a good idea to solve the problems as they are presented. If you just read the problems, the principles behind them often do not sink in. The material presented in this chapter forms the basis for the rest of the course; therefore, a good command of the concepts underlying the time value of money is crucial.

Table 5.2 $FVIF_{i,n}$ or the Compound Sum of $1

n	1%	2%	3%	4%	5%	6%	7%	8%	9%	10%
1	1.010	1.020	1.030	1.040	1.050	1.060	1.070	1.080	1.090	1.100
2	1.020	1.040	1.061	1.082	1.102	1.124	1.145	1.166	1.188	1.210
3	1.030	1.061	1.093	1.125	1.158	1.191	1.225	1.260	1.295	1.331
4	1.041	1.082	1.126	1.170	1.216	1.262	1.311	1.360	1.412	1.464
5	1.051	1.104	1.159	1.217	1.276	1.338	1.403	1.469	1.539	1.611
6	1.062	1.126	1.194	1.265	1.340	1.419	1.501	1.587	1.677	1.772
7	1.072	1.149	1.230	1.316	1.407	1.504	1.606	1.714	1.828	1.949
8	1.083	1.172	1.267	1.369	1.477	1.594	1.718	1.851	1.993	2.144
9	1.094	1.195	1.305	1.423	1.551	1.689	1.838	1.999	2.172	2.358
10	1.105	1.219	1.344	1.480	1.629	1.791	1.967	2.159	2.367	2.594
11	1.116	1.243	1.384	1.539	1.710	1.898	2.105	2.332	2.580	2.853
12	1.127	1.268	1.426	1.601	1.796	2.012	2.252	2.518	2.813	3.138
13	1.138	1.294	1.469	1.665	1.886	2.133	2.410	2.720	3.066	3.452
14	1.149	1.319	1.513	1.732	1.980	2.261	2.579	2.937	3.342	3.797
15	1.161	1.346	1.558	1.801	2.079	2.397	2.759	3.172	3.642	4.177

EXAMPLE

Let's assume that the Chrysler Corporation has guaranteed that the price of a new Jeep will always be $20,000, and you'd like to buy one but currently have only $7,752. How many years will it take for your initial investment of $7,752 to grow to $20,000 if it is invested at 9 percent compounded annually? We can use equation (5-6a) to solve for this problem as well. Substituting the known values in equation (5-6a), you find

$$FV_n = PV(FVIF_{i,n})$$
$$\$20,000 = \$7,752(FVIF_{9\%,\ nyrs})$$
$$\frac{\$20,000}{\$7,752} = \frac{\$7,752(FVIF_{9\%,\ nyrs})}{\$7,752}$$
$$2.58 = FVIF_{9\%,\ nyrs}$$

Thus you are looking for a value of 2.58 in the $FVIF_{i,n}$ tables, and you know it must be in the 9% column. To finish solving the problem, look down the 9% column for the value closest to 2.58. You find that it occurs in the $n = 11$ row. Thus it will take 11 years for an initial investment of $7,752 to grow to $20,000 if it is invested at 9 percent compounded annually.

EXAMPLE

Now let's solve for the compound annual growth rate, and let's go back to that Jeep that always costs $20,000. In 10 years, you'd really like to have $20,000 to buy a new Jeep, but you only have $11,167. At what rate must your $11,167 be compounded annually for it to grow to $20,000 in 10 years? Substituting the known variables into equation (3-6a), you get

$$FV_n = PV(FVIF_{i,n})$$
$$\$20,000 = \$11,167(FVIF_{i,\ 10yrs})$$
$$\frac{\$20,000}{\$11,167} = \frac{\$11,167\ (FVIF_{i,\ 10yrs})}{\$11,167}$$
$$1.791 = FVIF_{i,\ 10yrs}$$

You know you are looking in the $n = 10$ row of the $FVIF_{i,n}$ tables for a value of 1.791, and you find this in the $i = 6\%$ column. Thus if you want your initial investment of $11,167 to grow to $20,000 in 10 years, you must invest it at 6 percent.

Just how powerful is the time value of money? Manhattan Island was purchased by Peter Miniut from the Indians in 1624 for $24 in "knickknacks" and jewelry. If at the end of 1624 the Indians had invested their $24 at 8 percent compounded annually, it would be worth over $70.3 trillion today (by the end of 1997, 373 years later). That's certainly enough to buy back all of Manhattan. In fact, with $70 trillion in the bank, the $50 to $60 billion you'd have to pay to buy back all of Manhattan would only seem like pocket change. This story illustrates the incredible power of time in compounding. There simply is no substitute for it.

Moving Money Through Time with the Aid of a Financial Calculator

Time value of money calculations can be made simple with the aid of a *financial calculator*. In solving time value of money problems with a financial calculator, you will be given three of four variables and will have to solve for the fourth. Before presenting any solutions using a financial calculator, we will introduce the calculator's five most common keys. (In most time value of money problems, only four of these keys are relevant.) These keys are:

Menu Key	Description
N	Stores (or calculates) the total number of payments or compounding periods.
I/Y	Stores (or calculates) the interest or discount rate.
PV	Stores (or calculates) the present value of a cash flow or series of cash flows.
FV	Stores (or calculates) the future value, that is, the dollar amount of a final cash flow or the compound value of a single flow or series of cash flows.
PMT	Stores (or calculates) the dollar amount of each annuity payment deposited or received at the end of each year.

When you use a financial calculator, remember that outflows generally have to be entered as negative numbers. In general, each problem will have two cash flows: one an outflow with a negative value, and one an inflow with a positive value. The idea is that you deposit money in the bank at some point in time (an outflow), and at some other point in time you take money out of the bank (an inflow). Also, every calculator operates a bit differently with respect to entering variables. Needless to say, it is a good idea to familiarize yourself with exactly how your calculator functions.

In any problem, you will be given three of four variables. These four variables will always include *N* and *I/Y*; in addition, two out of the final three variables *PV*, *FV*, and *PMT* will also be included. To solve a time value of money problem using a financial calculator, all you need to do is enter the appropriate numbers for three of the four variables, and press the key of the final variable to calculate its value. It is also a good idea to enter zero for any of the five variables not included in the problem in order to clear that variable.

Now let's solve the previous example using a financial calculator. We were trying to find at what rate must $100 be compounded annually for it to grow to $179.10 in 10 years. The solution using a financial calculator would be as follows:

Step 1: Input values of known variables

Data Input	Function Key	Description
10	N	Stores $N = 10$ years
−100	PV	Stores $PV = -\$100$
179.10	FV	Stores $FV = \$179.10$
0	PMT	Clears PMT to $= 0$

Step 2: Calculate the value of the unknown variable

Function Key	Answer	Description
CPT		
I/Y	6.00%	Calculates $I/Y = 6.00\%$

Any of the problems in this chapter can easily be solved using a financial calculator; and the solutions to many examples using a Texas Instrument BAII Plus financial calculator are provided in the margins. If you are using the TI BAII Plus, make sure that you have selected both the "END MODE" and "one payment per year" ($P/Y = 1$). This sets the payment conditions to a maximum of one payment per period occurring at the end of the period. One final point: You will notice that solutions using the present-value tables versus solutions using a calculator may vary slightly—a result of rounding errors in the tables.

For further explanation of the TI BAII Plus, see appendix A at the end of the book.

STOP AND THINK

The concepts of compound interest and present value will follow us through the remainder of this book. Not only will they allow us to determine the future value of any investment, but they will allow us to bring the benefits and costs from new investment proposals back to the present and thereby determine the value of the investment in today's dollars.

Compound Interest with Nonannual Periods

OBJECTIVE 2

Until now, we have assumed that the compounding period is always annual; however, it need not be, as evidenced by savings and loan associations and commercial banks that compound on a quarterly, and in some cases daily, basis. Fortunately, this adjustment of the compounding period follows the same format as that used for annual compounding. If we invest our money for 5 years at 8 percent interest compounded semiannually, we are really investing our money for 10 six-month periods during which we receive 4 percent interest each period. If it is compounded quarterly, we receive 2 percent interest per period for 20 three-month periods. Table 5.3 illustrates the importance of nonannual compounding. For example, if you invested $100 at 15 percent you'd end up with about 5 percent more if it was compounded semiannually instead of annually, and about 10 percent more if the compounding occurred daily. This process can easily be generalized, giving us the following

Table 5.3 The Value of $100 Compounded at Various Nonannual Periods

For 1 Year at i Percent	$i =$	2%	5%	10%	15%
Compounded annually		$102.00	$105.00	$110.00	$115.00
Compounded semiannually		102.01	105.06	110.25	115.56
Compounded quarterly		102.02	105.09	110.38	115.87
Compounded monthly		102.02	105.12	110.47	116.08
Compounded weekly (52)		102.02	105.12	110.51	116.16
Compounded daily (365)		102.02	105.13	110.52	116.18

For 10 Years at i Percent	$i =$	2%	5%	10%	15%
Compounded annually		$121.90	$162.89	$259.37	$404.56
Compounded semiannually		122.02	163.86	265.33	424.79
Compounded quarterly		122.08	164.36	268.51	436.04
Compounded monthly		122.12	164.70	270.70	444.02
Compounded weekly (52)		122.14	164.83	271.57	447.20
Compounded daily (365)		122.14	164.87	271.79	448.03

formula for finding the future value of an investment for which interest is compounded in nonannual periods:

$$FV_n = PV\left(1 + \frac{i}{m}\right)^{mn} \tag{5-7}$$

where FV_n = the future value of the investment at the end of n years
n = the number of years during which the compounding occurs
i = annual interest (or discount) rate
PV = the present value or original amount invested at the beginning of the first year
m = the number of times compounding occurs during the year

EXAMPLE

If we place $100 in a savings account that yields 12 percent compounded quarterly, what will our investment grow to at the end of 5 years? Substituting $n = 5$, $m = 4$, $i = 12$ percent, and $PV = \$100$ into equation (5-7), we find

$$FV_5 = \$100\left(1 + \frac{.12}{4}\right)^{4 \cdot 5}$$
$$= \$100(1 + .03)^{20}$$
$$= \$100(1.806)$$
$$= \$180.60$$

Thus we will have $180.60 at the end of 5 years. Notice that the calculator solution is slightly different because of rounding errors in the tables, as explained in the previous section, and that it also takes on a negative value.

Calculator Solution

DATA INPUT	FUNCTION KEY
20	N
3	I/Y
100	PV
0	PMT

FUNCTION KEY	ANSWER
CPT	
FV	−180.61

Obviously, the choice of the interest rate plays a critical role in how much an investment grows, but do small changes in the interest rate have much of an impact on future values? To answer this question, let's look back to Peter Minuit's purchase of Manhattan.

If the Indians had invested their $24 at 10 percent rather than 8 percent compounded annually at the end of 1624, they would have over $66 quadrillion by the end of 1997 (373 years). That is 66 followed by 15 zeros or $66,000,000,000,000,000. Actually, that is enough to buy back not only Manhattan Island, but the entire world and still have plenty left over! Now let's assume a lower interest rate—say 6 percent. In that case, the $24 would have only grown to a mere $65.0 billion—less than 1/100th of what it grew to at 8 percent, and only one-millionth of what it would have grown to at 10 percent. With today's real estate prices, you could probably buy Manhattan, but you probably couldn't pay your taxes! To say the least, the interest rate is extremely important in investing.

PRESENT VALUE

OBJECTIVE 3

Up until this point, we have been moving money forward in time; that is, we know how much we have to begin with and are trying to determine how much that sum will grow in a certain number of years when compounded at a specific rate. We are now going to look at the reverse question: What is the value in today's dollars of a sum of money to be received in the future? The answer to this question will help us determine the desirability of investment projects in chapters 9 through 11. In this case, we are moving future money back to the present. We will be determining the **present value** of a lump sum, which in simple terms is the current value of a future payment. What we will be doing is, in fact, nothing other than inverse compounding. The differences in these techniques come about merely from the investor's point of view. In compounding, we talked about the compound interest rate and the initial investment; in determining the present value, we will talk about the discount rate, and the present value of future cash flows. Determination of the discount rate is the subject of chapter 6, and can be defined as the rate of return available on an investment of equal risk to what is being discounted. Other than that, the technique and the terminology remain the same, and the mathematics are simply reversed. In equation (5-6), we attempt to determine the future value of an initial investment. We now want to determine the initial investment or present value. By dividing both sides of equation (5-6) by $(1 + i)^n$, we get

Present value

The current value of a future sum.

$$PV = FV_n \left[\frac{1}{(1 + i)^n} \right] \tag{5-8}$$

where PV = the present value of the future sum of money
FV_n = the future value of the investment at the end of n years
n = the number of years until the payment will be received
i = the annual discount (or interest) rate

Because the mathematical procedure for determining the present value is exactly the inverse of determining the future value, we also find that the relationships among n, i, and PV are just the opposite of those we observed in future value. The present value of a future sum of money is inversely related to both the number of years until the payment will be received and the discount rate. Graphically, this relationship can be seen in Figure 5.2.

STOP AND THINK

Although the present value equation [equation (5-8)] will be used extensively in evaluating new investment proposals, it should be stressed that the present value equation is actually the same as the future value or compounding equation [equation (5-6)] where it is solved for PV.

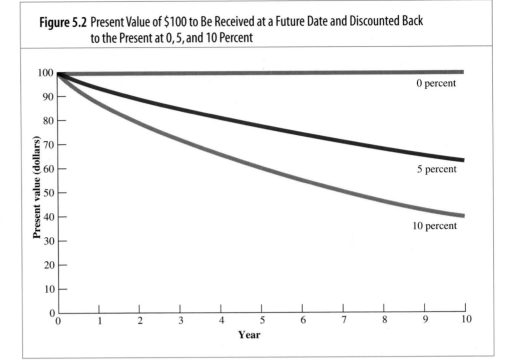

Figure 5.2 Present Value of $100 to Be Received at a Future Date and Discounted Back to the Present at 0, 5, and 10 Percent

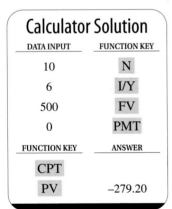

Calculator Solution

DATA INPUT	FUNCTION KEY
10	N
6	I/Y
500	FV
0	PMT
FUNCTION KEY	**ANSWER**
CPT	
PV	–279.20

EXAMPLE

What is the present value of $500 to be received 10 years from today if our discount rate is 6 percent? Substituting $FV_{10} = \$500$, $n = 10$, and $i = 6$ percent into equation (5-8), we find

$$PV = \$500 \left[\frac{1}{(1 + .06)^{10}} \right]$$

$$= \$500 \left(\frac{1}{1.791} \right)$$

$$= \$500(.558)$$

$$= \$279$$

Thus the present value of the $500 to be received in 10 years is $279.

Present-value interest factor ($PVIF_{i,n}$)

The value $[1/(1 + i)^n]$ used as a multiplier to calculate an amount's present value.

To aid in the computation of present values, the **present-value interest factor** for i and n or $\boldsymbol{PVIF_{i,n}}$, which is equal to $[1/(1 + i)^n]$, has been compiled for various combinations of i and n and appears in appendix C at the back of this book. An abbreviated version of appendix C appears in Table 5.4. A close examination shows that the values in Table 5.4 are merely the inverse of those found in appendix B. This, of course, is as it should be, as the values in appendix B are $(1 + i)^n$ and those in appendix C are $[1/(1 + i)^n]$. Now to determine the present value of a sum of money to be received at some future date, we need only determine the value of the appropriate $PVIF_{i,n}$, either by using a calculator or consulting the tables, and multiply it by the future value. In effect, we can use our new notation and rewrite equation (5-8) as follows:

$$PV = FV_n(PVIF_{i,n}) \tag{5-8a}$$

Table 5.4 $PVIF_{i,n}$ or the Present Value of $1

n	1%	2%	3%	4%	5%	6%	7%	8%	9%	10%
1	.990	.980	.971	.962	.952	.943	.935	.926	.917	.909
2	.980	.961	.943	.925	.907	.890	.873	.857	.842	.826
3	.971	.942	.915	.889	.864	.840	.816	.794	.772	.751
4	.961	.924	.888	.855	.823	.792	.763	.735	.708	.683
5	.951	.906	.863	.822	.784	.747	.713	.681	.650	.621
6	.942	.888	.837	.790	.746	.705	.666	.630	.596	.564
7	.933	.871	.813	.760	.711	.655	.623	.583	.547	.513
8	.923	.853	.789	.731	.677	.627	.582	.540	.502	.467
9	.914	.837	.766	.703	.645	.592	.544	.500	.460	.424
10	.905	.820	.744	.676	.614	.558	.508	.463	.422	.386
11	.896	.804	.722	.650	.585	.527	.475	.429	.388	.350
12	.887	.789	.701	.625	.557	.497	.444	.397	.356	.319
13	.879	.773	.681	.601	.530	.469	.415	.368	.326	.290
14	.870	.758	.661	.577	.505	.442	.388	.340	.299	.263
15	.861	.743	.642	.555	.481	.417	.362	.315	.275	.239

EXAMPLE

You're on vacation in a rather remote part of Florida and see an advertisement stating that if you take a sales tour of some condominiums that "you will be given $100 just for taking the tour." However, the $100 that you get is in the form of a savings bond that will not pay you the $100 for 10 years. What is the present value of $100 to be received 10 years from today if your discount rate is 6 percent? By looking at the $n = 10$ row and $i = 6\%$ column of Table 5.4, you find the $PVIF_{6\%,10yrs}$ is .558. Substituting $FV_{10} = \$100$ and $PVIF_{6\%,10yrs} = .558$ into equation (5-8a), you find

$$PV = \$100 \, (PVIF_{6\%,10yrs})$$
$$= \$100(.558)$$
$$= \$55.80$$

Thus the value in today's dollars of that $100 savings bond is only $55.80.

Calculator Solution

DATA INPUT	FUNCTION KEY
10	N
6	I/Y
100	FV
0	PMT

FUNCTION KEY	ANSWER
CPT	
PV	−55.84

Dealing with Multiple, Uneven Cash Flows

Again, we only have one present-value–future-value equation; that is, equations (5-6) and (5-8) are identical. We have introduced them as separate equations to simplify our calculations; in one case, we are determining the value in future dollars and in the other case, the value in today's dollars. In either case, the reason is the same: To compare values on alternative investments and to recognize that the value of a dollar received today is not the same as that of a dollar received at some future date, we must measure the dollar values in dollars of the same time period.

Remember those three projects we spoke of in the chapter opening, the one that promised $1,000 in 1 year, one that promised $1,500 in 5 years, and one that promised $2,500 in 10 years? The concept of present value allows us to bring their flows back to the present and make those projects comparable. Moreover, because all present values are comparable (they are all measured in dollars of the same time period), we can add and subtract the present value of inflows and outflows to determine the present value of an investment. Let's now look at an example of an investment that has two cash flows in different time periods and determine the present value of this investment.

EXAMPLE

What is the present value of an investment that yields $500 to be received in 5 years and $1,000 to be received in 10 years if the discount rate is 4 percent? Substituting the values of $n = 5$, $i = 4$ percent, and $FV_5 = \$500$; and $n = 10$, $i = 4$ percent, and $FV_{10} = \$1,000$ into equation (5-8) and adding these values together, we find

$$PV = \$500\left[\frac{1}{(1 + .04)^5}\right] + \$1,000\left[\frac{1}{(1 + .04)^{10}}\right]$$
$$= \$500(PVIF_{4\%,5yrs}) + \$1,000(PVIF_{4\%,10yrs})$$
$$= \$500(.822) + \$1,000(.676)$$
$$= \$411 + \$676$$
$$= \$1,087$$

Again, present values are comparable because they are measured in the same time period's dollars.

OBJECTIVE 4

ANNUITIES—A LEVEL STREAM

An **annuity** is a series of equal dollar payments for a specified number of years. Because annuities occur frequently in finance—for example, interest payments on bonds are in effect annuities—we will treat them specially. Although compounding and determining the present value of an annuity can be dealt with using the methods we have just described, these processes can be time consuming, especially for larger annuities. Thus we have modified the formulas to deal directly with annuities.

Although all annuities involve a series of equal dollar payments for a specified number of years, there are two basic types of annuities: an **ordinary annuity** and an **annuity due**. With an ordinary annuity, we assume that the payments occur at the end of each period; with an annuity due, the payments occur at the beginning of each period. Because an annuity due provides the payments earlier (at the beginning of each period instead of the end as with an ordinary annuity), it has a greater present value. After we master ordinary annuities, we will examine annuities due. However, in finance, ordinary annuities are used much more frequently than are annuities due. Thus, in this text, whenever the term "annuity" is used, you should assume that we are referring to an ordinary annuity unless otherwise specified.

Compound Annuities

A **compound annuity** involves depositing or investing an equal sum of money at the end of each year for a certain number of years and allowing it to grow. Perhaps we are saving money for education, a new car, or a vacation home. In any case, we want to know how much our savings will have grown by some point in the future.

Actually, we can find the answer by using equation (5-6), our compounding equation, and compounding each of the individual deposits to its future value. For example, if to provide for a college education we are going to deposit $500 at the end of each year for

Annuity

A series of equal dollar payments for a specified number of years.

Ordinary annuity

An annuity in which the payments occur at the end of each period.

Annuity due

An annuity in which the payments occur at the beginning of each period.

Compound annuity

Depositing an equal sum of money at the end of each year for a certain number of years and allowing it to grow.

the next 5 years in a bank where it will earn 6 percent interest, how much will we have at the end of 5 years? Compounding each of these values using equation (5-6), we find that we will have $2,818.50 at the end of 5 years.

$$FV_5 = \$500(1 + .06)^4 + \$500(1 + .06)^3 + \$500(1 + .06)^2 + \$500(1 + .06) + \$500$$
$$= \$500(1.262) + \$500(1.191) + \$500(1.124) + \$500(1.060) + \$500$$
$$= \$631.00 + \$595.50 + \$562.00 + \$530.00 + \$500.00$$
$$= \$2,818.50$$

To better understand what's happening, lets look at this problem using a time line. A time line is simply a horizontal line on which the present—time period zero—is at the left most end. Future time periods are then shown along the line moving from left to right. The dollar amount of the cash flow is shown below the line, with positive values representing cash inflows, and negative values representing cash outflows. We will frequently use time lines to illustrate the timing of an investment's cash flows. In the present example, cash flows of $500 are received at the end of years 1 through 5, and is presented graphically in Table 5.5. From examining the mathematics involved and the graph of the movement of money through time in Table 5.5, we can see that this procedure can be generalized to

$$FV_n = PMT\left[\sum_{t=0}^{n-1}(1 + i)^t\right] \tag{5-9}$$

where FV_n = the future value of the annuity at the end of the nth year
PMT = the annuity payment deposited or received at the end of each year
i = the annual interest (or discount) rate
n = the number of years for which the annuity will last

To aid in compounding annuities, the **future-value interest factor for an annuity** for i and n ($FVIFA_{i,n}$), defined as $\left[\sum_{t=0}^{n-1}(1 + i)^t\right]$ is provided in appendix D for various combinations of n and i. An abbreviated version is shown in Table 5.6.

Using this new notation, we can rewrite equation (5-9) as follows:

$$FV_n = PMT(FVIFA_{i,n}) \tag{5-9a}$$

The $FVIFA_{i,n}$ can also be calculated as follows:

$$FVIFA_{i,n} = \frac{(1 + i)^n - 1}{i} \tag{5-9b}$$

This formula is useful if you don't have a financial calculator or tables.

Future-value interest factor of an annuity ($FVIFA_{i,n}$)

The value $\left[\sum_{t=0}^{n-1}(1 + i)^t\right]$ used as a multiplier to calculate the future value of an annuity.

Calculator Solution

DATA INPUT	FUNCTION KEY
5	N
6	I/Y
0	PV
500	PMT

FUNCTION KEY	ANSWER
CPT	
FV	–2,818.55

Table 5.5 Illustration of a 5-Year $500 Annuity Compounded at 6 Percent

Year	0	1	2	3	4	5
Dollar deposits at end of year		500	500	500	500	500
						$ 500.00
						530.00
						562.00
						595.50
						631.00
Future value of the annuity						$2,818.50

Table 5.6 $FVIFA_{i,n}$ or the Sum of an Annuity of $1 for n Years

n	1%	2%	3%	4%	5%	6%	7%	8%	9%	10%
1	1.000	1.000	1.000	1.000	1.000	1.000	0.000	1.000	1.000	1.000
2	2.010	2.020	2.030	2.040	2.050	2.060	2.070	2.080	2.090	2.100
3	3.030	3.060	3.091	3.122	3.152	3.184	3.215	3.246	3.278	3.310
4	4.060	4.122	4.184	4.246	4.310	4.375	4.440	4.506	4.573	4.641
5	5.101	5.204	5.309	5.416	5.526	5.637	5.751	5.867	5.985	6.105
6	6.152	6.308	6.468	6.633	6.802	6.975	7.153	7.336	7.523	7.716
7	7.214	7.434	7.662	7.898	8.142	8.394	8.654	8.923	9.200	9.487
8	8.286	8.583	8.892	9.214	9.549	9.897	10.260	10.637	11.028	11.436
9	9.368	9.755	10.159	10.583	11.027	11.491	11.978	12.488	13.021	13.579
10	10.462	10.950	11.464	12.006	12.578	13.181	13.816	14.487	15.193	15.937
11	11.567	12.169	12.808	13.486	14.207	14.972	15.784	16.645	17.560	18.531
12	12.682	13.412	14.192	15.026	15.917	16.870	17.888	18.977	20.141	21.384
13	13.809	14.680	15.618	16.627	17.713	18.882	20.141	21.495	22.953	24.523
14	14.947	15.974	17.086	18.292	19.598	21.015	22.550	24.215	26.019	27.975
15	16.097	17.293	18.599	20.023	21.578	23.276	25.129	27.152	29.361	31.772

Reexamining the previous example, in which we determined the value after 5 years of $500 deposited at the end of each of the next 5 years in the bank at 6 percent, we would look in the $i = 6\%$ column and $n = 5$ year row and find the value of the $FVIFA_{6\%,5yrs}$ to be 5.637. Substituting this value into equation (5-9a), we get

$$FV_5 = \$500(5.637)$$
$$= \$2,818.50$$

This is the same answer we obtained earlier.

Rather than asking how much we will accumulate if we deposit an equal sum in a savings account each year, a more common question is how much we must deposit each year to accumulate a certain amount of savings. This problem frequently occurs with respect to saving for large expenditures and pension funding obligations.

For example, we may know that we need $10,000 for education in 8 years; how much must we deposit at the end of each year in the bank at 6 percent interest to have the college money ready? In this case, we know the values of n, i, and FV_n in equation (5-9); what we do not know is the value of PMT. Substituting these example values in equation (5-9), we find

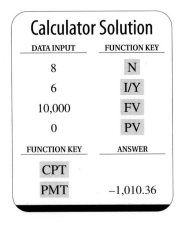

Calculator Solution

DATA INPUT	FUNCTION KEY
8	N
6	I/Y
10,000	FV
0	PV

FUNCTION KEY	ANSWER
CPT	
PMT	−1,010.36

$$\$10,000 = PMT\left[\sum_{t=0}^{8-1}(1+.06)^t\right]$$

$$\$10,000 = PMT(FVIFA_{6\%,8yrs})$$

$$\$10,000 = PMT(9.897)$$

$$\frac{\$10,000}{9.897} = PMT$$

$$PMT = \$1,010.41$$

Thus we must deposit $1,010.41 in the bank at the end of each year for 8 years at 6 percent interest to accumulate $10,000 at the end of 8 years.

THE WALL STREET JOURNAL, APRIL 22, 1994

Make a Child a Millionaire
Just Take Your Time

Thanks a million.

Even if you haven't got a lot of money, you can easily give $1 million or more to your children, grandchildren, or favorite charity. All it takes is a small initial investment and a lot of time.

Suppose your 16-year-old daughter plans to take a summer job, which will pay her at least $2,000. Because she has earned income, she can open an individual retirement account. If you would like to help fund her retirement, Kenneth Klegon, a financial planner in Lansing, Michigan, suggests giving her $2,000 to set up the IRA. He then advises doing the same in each of the next 5 years, so that your daughter stashes away a total of $12,000.

(A) Result? If the money is invested in stocks, and stocks deliver their historical average annual return of 10%, your daughter will have more than $1 million by the time she turns 65.

(B) Because of the corrosive effect of inflation, that $1 million will only buy a quarter of what $1 million buys today, presuming the cost of living rises at 3% a year. Nonetheless, your $12,000 gift will go a long way toward paying for your daughter's retirement. The huge gain is possible because of the way stock-market compounding works, with money earned each year not only on your initial investment, but also on the gains accumulated from earlier years.

"The beauty of this strategy is that it will grow tax-deferred," Klegon says. "There's no cost. You can set up an IRA with a no-load mutual fund for nothing." Similarly, Mr. Klegon says, once your children enter the work force full time, you can encourage them to participate in their company's 401(k) plan by reimbursing them for their contributions.

SOURCE: Jonathan Clements, "Make a Child a Millionaire," *The Wall Street Journal* (April 22, 1994): C1. Reprinted by permission of *The Wall Street Journal*, © 1994 by Dow Jones & Co., Inc. All Rights Reserved Worldwide.

Analysis and Implications …

A. Using the principles and techniques set out in this chapter, we can easily see how much this IRA investment will accumulate to. We can first take the $2,000 6-year annuity and determine its future value—that is, its value when your daughter is 21 and receives the last payment. This would be done as follows:

$$FV = PMT(FVIFA_{10\%, 6yrs})$$
$$= \$2,000(FVIFA_{10\%, 6yrs})$$
$$= \$15,431.22$$

We could then take this amount that your daughter has when she is 21 and compound it out 44 years to when she is 65, as follows:

$$FV = PV(FVIF_{10\%, 44yrs})$$
$$= \$15,431.22(FVIF_{10\%, 44yrs})$$
$$= \$1,022,535.54$$

Thus your daughter's IRA would have accumulated to $1,022,535.54 by age 65 if it grew at 10 percent compounded annually.

B. To determine how much this is worth in today's dollars, if inflation increases at an annual rate of 3 percent over this period, we need only calculate the present value of $1,022,535.54 to be received 49 years from now given a discount rate of 3 percent. This would determine the future value of this IRA measured in dollars with the same spending power as those around when your daughter was 16. This is done as follows:

$$PV = FV(PVIF_{3\%, 49yrs})$$
$$= \$1,022,535.54(PVIF_{3\%, 49yrs})$$
$$= \$240,245.02$$

You can change the growth and inflation rates and come up with all kinds of numbers, but one thing holds: There is incredible power in compounding!

EXAMPLE

How much must we deposit in an 8 percent savings account at the end of each year to accumulate \$5,000 at the end of 10 years? Substituting the values $FV_{10} = \$5,000$, $n = 10$, and $i = 8$ percent into equation (5-9), we find

$$\$5,000 = PMT\left[\sum_{t=0}^{10-1}(1 + .08)^t\right] = PMT(FVIFA_{8\%,10\text{yrs}})$$

$$\$5,000 = PMT(14.487)$$

$$\frac{\$5,000}{14.487} = PMT$$

$$PMT = \$345.14$$

Thus we must deposit \$345.14 per year for 10 years at 8 percent to accumulate \$5,000.

STOP AND THINK

A time line often makes it easier to understand time value of money problems. By visually plotting the flow of money, you can better determine which formula to use. Arrows placed above the line are inflows, whereas arrows below the line represent outflows. One thing is certain: Time lines reduce errors.

Present Value of an Annuity

Pension funds, insurance obligations, and interest received from bonds all involve annuities. To value them, we need to know the present value of each. Although we can find this by using the present-value table in appendix C, this can be time consuming, particularly when the annuity lasts for several years. For example, if we wish to know what \$500 received at the end of the next 5 years is worth to us today given the appropriate discount rate of 6 percent, we can simply substitute the appropriate values into equation (5-8), such that

$$PV = \$500\left[\frac{1}{(1 + .06)^1}\right] + \$500\left[\frac{1}{(1 + .06)^2}\right] + \$500\left[\frac{1}{(1 + .06)^3}\right]$$

$$+ \$500\left[\frac{1}{(1 + .06)^4}\right] + \$500\left[\frac{1}{(1 + .06)^5}\right]$$

$$= \$500(.943) + \$500(.890) + \$500(.840) + \$500(.792) + \$500(.747)$$

$$= \$2,106$$

Thus the present value of this annuity is \$2,106.00. From examining the mathematics involved and the graph of the movement of these funds through time in Table 5.7, we see that we are simply summing up the present values of each cash flow. Thus this procedure can be generalized to

$$PV = PMT\left[\sum_{t=1}^{n}\frac{1}{(1 + i)^t}\right] \tag{5-10}$$

where PMT = the annuity payment deposited or received at the end of each year
i = the annual discount (or interest) rate
PV = the present value of the future annuity
n = the number of years for which the annuity will last

Table 5.7 Illustration of a 5-Year $500 Annuity Discounted Back to the Present at 6 Percent

Year	0	1	2	3	4	5
Dollars received at the end of year		500	500	500	500	500
	$ 471.50 ◄┘					
	445.00 ◄					
	420.00 ◄					
	396.00 ◄					
	373.50 ◄					
Present value of the annuity	$2,106.00					

To simplify the process of determining the present value for an annuity, the **present-value interest factor for an annuity** for i and n (**PVIFA$_{i,n}$**), defined as $\left[\sum_{t=1}^{n} \frac{1}{(1+i)^t}\right]$, has been compiled for various combinations of i and n in appendix E with an abbreviated version provided in Table 5.8.

Present-value interest factor for an annuity (*PVIFA$_{i,n}$*)

The value $\left[\sum_{t=1}^{n} \frac{1}{(1+i)^t}\right]$ used as a multiplier to calculate the present value of an annuity.

Using this new notation, we can rewrite equation (5-10) as follows:

$$PV = PMT(PVIFA_{i,n}) \tag{5-10a}$$

The $PVIFA_{i,n}$ can also be calculated as follows:

$$PVIFA_{i,n} = \frac{1 - \dfrac{1}{(1+i)^n}}{i} \tag{5-10b}$$

This formula is useful if you don't have a financial calculator or tables.

Solving the previous example to find the present value of $500 received at the end of each of the next 5 years discounted back to the present at 6 percent, we look in the $i = 6\%$

Table 5.8 *PVIFA$_{i,n}$* or the Present Value of an Annuity of $1

n	1%	2%	3%	4%	5%	6%	7%	8%	9%	10%
1	0.990	0.980	0.971	0.962	0.952	0.943	0.935	0.926	0.917	0.909
2	1.970	1.942	1.913	1.886	1.859	1.833	1.808	1.783	1.759	1.736
3	2.941	2.884	2.829	2.775	2.723	2.673	2.624	2.577	2.531	2.487
4	3.902	3.808	3.717	3.630	3.546	3.465	3.387	3.312	3.240	3.170
5	4.853	4.713	4.580	4.452	4.329	4.212	4.100	3.993	3.890	3.791
6	5.795	5.601	5.417	5.242	5.076	4.917	4.767	4.623	4.486	4.355
7	6.728	6.472	6.230	6.002	5.786	5.582	5.389	5.206	5.033	4.868
8	7.652	7.326	7.020	6.733	6.463	6.210	5.971	5.747	5.535	5.335
9	8.566	8.162	7.786	7.435	7.108	6.802	6.515	6.247	5.995	5.759
10	9.471	8.983	8.530	8.111	7.722	7.360	7.024	6.710	6.418	6.145
11	10.368	9.787	9.253	8.760	8.306	7.887	7.499	7.139	6.805	6.495
12	11.255	10.575	9.954	9.385	8.863	8.384	7.943	7.536	7.161	6.814
13	12.134	11.348	10.635	9.986	9.394	8.853	8.358	7.904	7.487	7.103
14	13.004	12.106	11.296	10.563	9.899	9.295	8.746	8.244	7.786	7.367
15	13.865	12.849	11.938	11.118	10.380	9.712	9.108	8.560	8.061	7.606

column and $n = 5$ year row and find the $PVIFA_{6\%,5yr}$ to be 4.212. Substituting the appropriate values into equation (5-10a), we find

$$PV = \$500(4.212)$$
$$= \$2,106$$

This, of course, is the same answer we calculated when we individually discounted each cash flow to the present. The reason is that we really only have one table: all of the tables are derived from Table 5.2; the Table 5.8 value for an n-year annuity for any discount rate i is merely the sum of the first n values in Table 5.4. We can see this by comparing the value in the present-value-of-an-annuity table (Table 5.8) for $i = 8$ percent and $n = 6$ years, which is 4.623, with the sum of the values in the $i = 8\%$ column and $n = 1, \ldots,$ six rows of the present-value table (Table 5.4), which is equal to 4.623, as shown in Table 5.9.

EXAMPLE

What is the present value of a 10-year $1,000 annuity discounted back to the present at 5 percent? Substituting $n = 10$ years, $i = 5$ percent, and $PMT = \$1,000$ into equation (5-10), we find

$$PV = \$1,000\left[\sum_{t=1}^{10}\frac{1}{(1 + .05)^t}\right] = \$1,000(PVIFA_{5\%,10yrs})$$

Determining the value for the $PVIFA_{5\%,10yrs}$ from Table 5.8, row $n = 10$, column $i = 5\%$, and substituting it in, we get

$$PV = \$1,000(7.722)$$
$$= \$7,722$$

Thus the present value of this annuity is $7,722.

As with our other compounding and present-value tables, given any three of the four unknowns in equation (5-10), we can solve for the fourth. In the case of the present-value-of-an-annuity table, we may be interested in solving for PMT if we know i, n, and PV. The financial interpretation of this action would be: How much can be withdrawn, perhaps as a pension or to make loan payments, from an account that earns i percent compounded annually for each of the next n years if we wish to have nothing left at the end of n years?

Table 5.9 Present Value of a 6-Year Annuity Discounted at 8 Percent

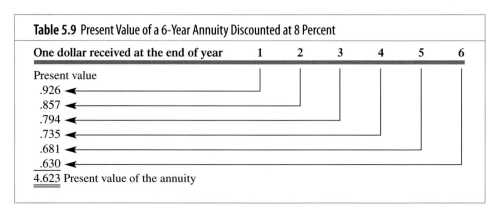

One dollar received at the end of year	1	2	3	4	5	6

Present value
.926
.857
.794
.735
.681
.630
4.623 Present value of the annuity

For an example, if we have $5,000 in an account earning 8 percent interest, how large an annuity can we draw out each year if we want nothing left at the end of 5 years? In this case, the present value, PV, of the annuity is $5,000, $n = 5$ years, $i = 8$ percent, and PMT is unknown. Substituting this into equation (5-10), we find

$5,000 = PMT(3.993)$
$1,252.19 = PMT$

Thus this account will fall to zero at the end of 5 years if we withdraw $1,252.19 at the end of each year.

Annuities Due

Because **annuities due** are really just **ordinary annuities** where all the annuity payments have been shifted forward by 1 year, compounding them and determining their present value is actually quite simple. Remember, with an annuity due, each annuity payment occurs at the beginning of each period rather than at the end of the period. Let's first look at how this affects our compounding calculations.

Because an annuity due merely shifts the payments from the end of the year to the beginning of the year, we now compound the cash flows for 1 additional year. Therefore, the compound sum of an annuity due is simply

$$FV_n(\text{annuity due}) = PMT(FVIFA_{i,n})(1 + i)$$

For example, earlier we calculated the value of a 5-year ordinary annuity of $500, invested in the bank at 6 percent to be $2,818.50. If we now assume this to be a 5-year annuity due, its future value increases from $2,818.50 to $2,987.61.

$$\begin{aligned}
FV_5 &= \$500(FVIFA_{6\%,5\text{yrs}})(1 + .06) \\
&= \$500(5.637)(1.06) \\
&= \$2,987.61
\end{aligned}$$

Likewise, with the present value of an annuity due, we simply receive each cash flow 1 year earlier—that is, we receive it at the beginning of each year rather than at the end of each year. Thus since each cash flow is received 1 year earlier, it is discounted back for one less period. To determine the present value of an annuity due, we merely need to find the present value of an ordinary annuity and multiply that by $(1 + i)$, which in effect cancels out 1 year's discounting.

$$PV(\text{annuity due}) = PMT(PVIFA_{i,n})(1 + i)$$

Reexamining the earlier example where we calculated the present value of a 5-year ordinary annuity of $500 given an appropriate discount rate of 6 percent, we now find that if it is an annuity due rather than an ordinary annuity, the present value increases from $2,106 to $2,232.36.

$$\begin{aligned}
PV &= \$500(PVIFA_{6\%,5\text{yrs}})(1 + .06) \\
&= \$500(4.212)(1.06) \\
&= \$2,232.36
\end{aligned}$$

The result of all this is that both the future and present values of an annuity due are larger than that of an ordinary annuity because in each case all payments are received earlier. Thus when *compounding* an annuity due, it compounds for 1 additional year; whereas when *discounting* an annuity due, the cash flows are discounted for 1 less year. Although annuities due are used with some frequency in accounting, their usage is quite limited in finance. Therefore, in the remainder of this text, whenever the term annuity is used, you should assume that we are referring to an ordinary annuity.

Calculator Solution

DATA INPUT	FUNCTION KEY
5	N
8	I/Y
5,000	PV
0	FV

FUNCTION KEY	ANSWER
CPT	
PMT	−1,252.28

EXAMPLE

The Virginia State Lottery runs like most other state lotteries: You must select six out of 44 numbers correctly in order to win the jackpot. If you come close, there are some significantly lesser prizes—we will ignore them for now. For each million dollars in the lottery jackpot, you receive $50,000 per year for 20 years, and your chance of winning is 1 in 7.1 million. One of the recent advertisements for the Virginia State Lottery went as follows: "Okay, you got two kinds of people. You've got the kind who play Lotto all the time and the kind who play Lotto some of the time. You know, like only on a Saturday when they stop in at the store on the corner for some peanut butter cups and diet soda and the jackpot happens to be really big. I mean, my friend Ned? He's like, 'Hey, it's only 2 million dollars this week.' Well, hellloooo, anybody home? I mean, I don't know about you, but I wouldn't mind having a measly 2 mill coming *my* way. . . ."

What is the present value of these payments? The answer to this question depends upon what assumption you make as to the time value of money—in this case, let's assume that your required rate of return on an investment with this level of risk is 10 percent. Keeping in mind that the Lotto is an annuity due—that is, on a $2 million lottery you would get $100,000 immediately and $100,000 at the end of each of the next 19 years. Thus the present value of this 20-year annuity due discounted back to present at 10 percent becomes:

$$
\begin{aligned}
PV_{\text{annuity due}} &= PMT(PVIFA_{i\%,\,n\text{yrs}})(1 + i) \\
&= \$100,000(PVIFA_{10\%,\,20\text{yrs}})(1 + .10) \\
&= \$100,000(8.514)(1.10) \\
&= \$851,400(1.10) \\
&= \$936,540
\end{aligned}
$$

Thus the present value of the $2 million Lotto jackpot is less than $1 million if 10 percent is the appropriate discount rate. Moreover, because the chance of winning is only 1 in 7.1 million, the expected value of each dollar "invested" in the lottery is only (1/7.1 million) × ($936,540) = 13.19 cents. That is, for every dollar you spend on the lottery, you should expect to get (*on average*) about 13 cents back—not a particularly good deal. Although this ignores the minor payments for coming close, it also ignores taxes. In this case, it looks like "my friend Ned" is doing the right thing by staying clear of the lottery. Obviously, the main value of the lottery is entertainment. Unfortunately, without an understanding of the time value of money, it can sound like a good investment.

Amortized Loans

Amortized loan

A loan paid off in equal installments.

The procedure of solving for *PMT* is also used to determine what payments are associated with paying off a loan in equal installments over time. Loans that are paid off this way, in equal periodic payments, are called **amortized loans**. For example, suppose you want to buy a used car. To do this, you borrow $6,000 to be repaid in four equal payments at the end of each of the next 4 years, and the interest rate that is paid to the lender is 15 percent on the outstanding portion of the loan. To determine what the annual payment associated with the repayment of this debt will be, we simply use equation (5-10) and solve for the value of *PMT*, the annual annuity. Again, we know three of the four values in that equation, *PV*, *i*, and *n*. *PV*, the present value of the future annuity, is $6,000; *i*, the annual interest rate, is 15 percent; and *n*, the number of years for which the annuity will last, is 4 years. *PMT*, the annuity payment received (by the

Table 5.10 Loan Amortization Schedule Involving a $6,000 Loan at 15 Percent to Be Repaid in 4 Years

Year	Annuity	Interest Portion of the Annuity[a]	Repayment of the Principal Portion of the Annuity[b]	Outstanding Loan Balance after the Annuity Payment
1	$2,101.58	$900.00	$1,201.58	$4,798.42
2	2,101.58	719.76	1,381.82	3,416.60
3	2,101.58	512.49	1,589.09	1,827.51
4	2,101.58	274.07	1,827.51	

[a]The interest portion of the annuity is calculated by multiplying the outstanding loan balance at the beginning of the year by the interest rate of 15 percent. Thus for year 1 it was $6,000.00 × .15 = $900.00, for year 2 it was $4,798.42 × .15 = $719.76, and so on.
[b]Repayment of the principal portion of the annuity was calculated by subtracting the interest portion of the annuity (column 2) from the annuity (column 1).

lender and paid by you) at the end of each year, is unknown. Substituting these values into equation (5-10), we find

$$\$6,000 = PMT\left[\sum_{t=1}^{4}\frac{1}{(1+.15)^t}\right]$$

$$\$6,000 = PMT(PVIFA_{15\%,4\text{yrs}})$$

$$\$6,000 = PMT(2.855)$$

$$\$2,101.58 = PMT$$

To repay the principal and interest on the outstanding loan in 4 years, the annual payments would be $2,101.58. The breakdown of interest and principal payments is given in the **loan amortization schedule** in Table 5.10, with very minor rounding error. As you can see, the interest payment declines each year as the loan outstanding declines, and more of the principal is repaid each year.

Present Value of Complex Stream

Although some projects will involve a single cash flow and some annuities, many projects will involve uneven cash flows over several years. Chapter 9, which examines investments in fixed assets, presents this situation repeatedly. There we will be comparing not only the present value of cash flows between projects, but also the cash inflows and outflows within a particular project, trying to determine that project's present value. However, this will not be difficult because the present value of any cash flow is measured in today's dollars and thus can be compared, through addition for inflows and subtraction for outflows, to the present value of any other cash flow also measured in today's dollars.

Year	Cash Flow	Year	Cash Flow
1	$500	6	$500
2	200	7	500
3	−400	8	500
4	500	9	500
5	500	10	500

Calculator Solution

DATA INPUT	FUNCTION KEY
4	N
15	I/Y
6,000	PV
0	FV

FUNCTION KEY	ANSWER
CPT	
PMT	−2,101.59

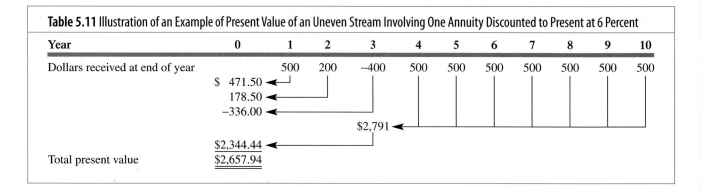

Table 5.11 Illustration of an Example of Present Value of an Uneven Stream Involving One Annuity Discounted to Present at 6 Percent

Year	0	1	2	3	4	5	6	7	8	9	10
Dollars received at end of year		500	200	−400	500	500	500	500	500	500	500
	$ 471.50 ◂┘										
	178.50 ◂────										
	−336.00 ◂────										
				$2,791 ◂────							
	$2,344.44 ◂────										
Total present value	$2,657.94										

Table 5.12 Determination of the Present Value of an Uneven Stream Involving One Annuity Discounted to Present at 6 Percent

1. Present value of $500 received at the end of 1 year = $500(.943) = $ 471.50
2. Present value of $200 received at the end of 2 years = $200(.890) =   178.00
3. Present value of a $400 outflow at the end of 3 years = −$400(.840) =   −336.00
4. (a) Value at the end of year 3 of a $500 annuity, years 4 through 10 = $500(5.582) = $2,791
     (b) Present value of $2,791 received at the end of year 3 = $2,791(.840) = $2,344.44
5. Total present value = $2,657.94

For example, if we wished to find the present value of the following cash flows given a 6 percent discount rate, we would merely discount the flows back to the present and total them by adding in the positive flows and subtracting the negative ones. However, this problem also contains the annuity of $500 that runs from years 4 through 10. To accommodate this, we can first discount the annuity back to the beginning of period 4 (or end of period 3) by multiplying it by the value of $PVIFA_{6\%,7\text{yrs}}$ and get its present value at that point in time. We then multiply this value times the $PVIF_{6\%,3\text{yrs}}$ in order to bring this single cash flow (which is the present value of the 7-year annuity) back to the present. In effect, we discount twice—first back to the end of period 3, then back to the present. This is shown graphically in Table 5.11 and numerically in Table 5.12. Thus the present value of this uneven stream of cash flows is $2,657.94.

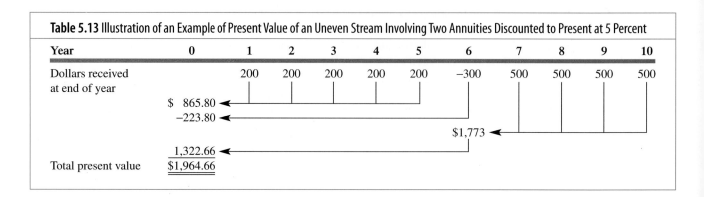

Table 5.13 Illustration of an Example of Present Value of an Uneven Stream Involving Two Annuities Discounted to Present at 5 Percent

Year	0	1	2	3	4	5	6	7	8	9	10
Dollars received at end of year		200	200	200	200	200	−300	500	500	500	500
	$ 865.80 ◂────										
	−223.80 ◂────										
							$1,773 ◂────				
	1,322.66 ◂────										
Total present value	$1,964.66										

EXAMPLE

What is the present value of an investment involving $200 received at the end of years 1 through 5, a $300 cash outflow at the end of year 6, and $500 received at the end of years 7 through 10, given a 5 percent discount rate? Here we have two annuities, one that can be discounted directly back to the present by multiplying it by the value of the $PVIFA_{5\%,5yrs}$ and one that must be discounted twice to bring it back to the present. This second annuity, which is a 4-year annuity, must first be discounted back to the beginning of period 7 (or end of period 6) by multiplying it by the value of the $PVIFA_{5\%,4yrs}$. Then the present value of this annuity at the end of period 6 (which can be viewed as a single cash flow) must be discounted back to the present by multiplying it by the value of the $PVIF_{5\%,6yrs}$. To arrive at the total present value of this investment, we subtract the present value of the $300 cash outflow at the end of year 6 from the sum of the present value of the two annuities. Table 5.13 shows this graphically; Table 5.14 gives the calculations. Thus the present value of this series of cash flows is $1,964.66.

Remember, once the cash flows from an investment have been brought back to present they can be combined by adding and subtracting to determine the project's total present value.

Perpetuities and Infinite Annuities

A **perpetuity** is an annuity that continues forever; that is, every year from its establishment, this investment pays the same dollar amount. An example of a perpetuity is preferred stock that yields a constant dollar dividend infinitely. Determining the present value of a perpetuity is delightfully simple; we merely need to divide the constant flow by the discount rate.[1] For example, the present value of a $100 perpetuity discounted back to the present at 5 percent is $100/.05 = $2,000. Thus the equation representing the present value of a perpetuity is

$$PV = \frac{PP}{i} \tag{5-11}$$

where PV = the present value of the perpetuity

PP = the constant dollar amount provided by the perpetuity

i = the annual interest (or discount) rate

Table 5.14 Determination of Present Value of an Example with Uneven Stream Involving Two Annuities Discounted to Present at 5 Percent

1. Present value of first annuity, years 1 through 5 = $200(4.329) =	$ 865.80
2. Present value of $300 cash outflow = –$300(.746) =	–223.80
3. (a) Value at end of year 6 of second annuity, years 7 through 10 = $500(3.546) = $1,773	
(b) Present value of $1,773 received at the end of year 6 = $1,773(.746) =	1,322.66
4. Total present value =	$1,964.66

---

[1]See chapter 8 for a mathematical derivation.

What is the present value of a $500 perpetuity discounted back to the present at 8 percent? Substituting $PP = \$500$ and $i = .08$ into equation (5-11), we find

$$PV = \frac{\$500}{.08} = \$6{,}250$$

Thus the present value of this perpetuity is $6,250.

OBJECTIVE 6

MAKING INTEREST RATES COMPARABLE

Nominal or quoted interest rate

The stated rate of interest on the contract.

Annual percentage yield (APY) or effective annual rate

The annual compound rate that produces the same return as the nominal or quoted rate.

In order to make intelligent decisions on where to invest or borrow money, it is important that we make the stated interest rates comparable. Unfortunately, some rates are quoted as compounded annually, whereas others are quoted as compounded quarterly or compounded daily. But we already know that it is not fair to compare interest rates with different compounding periods to each other. Thus the only way interest rates can logically be compared is to convert them to some common compounding period and then compare them. That is what is done with the **annual percentage yield**. In order to understand the process of making different interest rates comparable, it is first necessary to define the **nominal** or **quoted interest rate**.

The nominal or quoted rate is the rate of interest stated on the contract. For example, if you shop around for loans and are quoted 8 percent compounded annually and 7.85 percent compounded quarterly, then 8 percent and 7.85 percent would both be nominal rates. Unfortunately, because on one, the interest is compounded annually, but on the other, interest is compounded quarterly, they are not comparable. In fact, it is never appropriate to compare nominal rates *unless* they include the same number of compounding periods per year. To make them comparable, we must calculate their equivalent rate at some common compounding period. We do this by calculating the **annual percentage yield** (**APY**) or **effective annual rate**. This is the annual compound rate that produces the same return as the nominal or quoted rate.

Let's assume that you are considering borrowing money from a bank at 12 percent compounded monthly. To convert this to an APY, we must determine the annual rate that would produce the same return as the nominal rate. In the case of a 12 percent loan compounded monthly, by looking in the *FVIF* Table in the back of the book, we see that the future value of $1 in 1 year at 12 percent compounded monthly (that is, compounded at 1 percent per month for 12 one-month periods) is $1.1268 ($FVIF_{1\%,12\text{periods}} = 1.1268$). This tells us that 12.68 percent is the APY, because if we compound $1 at the nominal rate of 12 percent compounded monthly, we would have $1.1268 after 1 year.

Generalizing on this process, we can calculate the APY using the following equation:

$$\text{APY} = (1 + i/m)^m - 1 \tag{5-12}$$

where APY is the annual percentage yield, i is the nominal rate of interest per year, and m is the number of compounding periods within a year. Given the wide variety of compounding periods used by businesses and banks, it is important to know how to make these rates comparable so that logical decisions can be made.

HOW FINANCIAL MANAGERS USE THIS MATERIAL

Almost all business decisions involve cash flow occurring in different time periods. It is the techniques and tools introduced in this chapter that allow you to compare these cash flows and, therefore, make the appropriate decision. Perhaps you'll work for Marriott and you'll be deciding whether to build a hotel resort or some new time share units on the beachfront land Marriott owns on Hilton Head Island. That's a decision that involves spending the money right now to build the complex and then, sometime in the future, either selling the time share units or receiving rent from tourists at the new hotel resort. It's an understanding of the time value of money that allows you to compare these cash flows that occur in different time periods. In fact, any time you're evaluating a new product, the time value of money comes into play. In short, there isn't another tool in business that is more essential to making good decisions.

As you will see later, the time value of money also plays a central role in determining the price a share of common stock sells for. That is to say, it was an understanding of the time value of money that allowed the folks at Friendly Ice Cream to determine that Friendly's common stock should be offered to the public at $18 per share when it was first sold. Those same people use the time value of money to determine how much they should save for their children's college education and for retirement, and whether they should refinance their home mortgage. Truly, the concept of the time value of money is one that not only affects all corporate finance decisions, but also affects all personal finance decisions as well.

SUMMARY

To make decisions, financial managers must compare the costs and benefits of alternatives that do not occur during the same time period. Whether to make profitable investments or to take advantage of favorable interest rates, financial decision making requires an understanding of the time value of money. Managers who use the time value of money in all of their financial calculations assure themselves of more logical decisions. The time value process first makes all dollar values comparable; because money has a time value, it moves all dollar flows either back to the present or out to a common future date. All time value formulas presented in this chapter actually stem from the single compounding formula $FV_n = PV(1 + i)^n$. The formulas are used to deal simply with common financial situations, for example, discounting single flows, compounding annuities, and discounting annuities. Table 5.15 provides a summary of these calculations.

KEY TERMS

Amortized loan, 192

Annual percentage yield (APY) or effective annual rate, 196

Annuity, 184

Annuity due, 184

Compound annuity, 184

Compund interest, 173

Future-value interest factor ($FVIF_{i,n}$), 176

Future-value interest factor of an annuity ($FVIFA_{i,n}$), 185

Nominal or quoted interest rate, 196

Ordinary annuity, 184

Present value, 181

Present-value interest factor ($PVIF_{i,n}$), 182

Present-value interest factor of an annuity ($PVIFA_{i,n}$), 189

GO TO:
http://www.prenhall.com/bfm
For downloads and current events associated with this chapter

Table 5.15 Summary of Time Value of Money Equations*

Calculation	Equation
Future value of a single payment	$FV_n = PV(1 + i)^n$ or $PV(FVIF_{i,n})$
Future value of a single payment with nonannual compounding	$FV_n = PV\left(1 + \dfrac{i}{m}\right)^{mn}$
Present value of a single payment	$PV = FV_n\left[\dfrac{1}{(1 + i)^n}\right]$ or $FV_n(PVIF_{i,n})$
Future value of an annuity	$FV_n = PMT\left[\displaystyle\sum_{t=0}^{n-1}(1 + i)^t\right]$ or $PMT(FVIFA_{i,n})$
Present value of an annuity	$PV = PMT\left[\displaystyle\sum_{t=1}^{n}\dfrac{1}{(1 + i)^t}\right]$ or $PMT(PVIFA_{i,n})$
Present value of a perpetuity	$PV = \dfrac{PP}{i}$
Annual Percentage Yield (APY)	$APY = \left(1 + \dfrac{1}{m}\right)^{m} - 1$

Notation: FV_n = the future value of the investment at the end of n years

n = the number of years until payment will be received or during which compounding occurs

i = the annual interest or discount rate

PV = the present value of the future sum of money

m = the number of times compounding occurs during the year

PMT = the annuity payment deposited or received at the end of each year

PP = the constant dollar amount provided by the perpetuity

*Related tables appear in appendices B through E at the end of the book.

OBJECTIVE 1

OBJECTIVE 2

OBJECTIVE 3

OBJECTIVE 4

OBJECTIVE 5

OBJECTIVE 6

STUDY QUESTIONS

5-1. What is the time value of money? Why is it so important?

5-2. The processes of discounting and compounding are related. Explain this relationship.

5-3. How would an increase in the interest rate (i) or a decrease in the holding period (n) affect the future value (FV_n) of a sum of money? Explain why.

5-4. Suppose you were considering depositing your savings in one of three banks, all of which pay 5 percent interest; bank A compounds annually, bank B compounds semiannually, and bank C compounds daily. Which bank would you choose? Why?

5-5. What is the relationship between the $PVIF_{i,n}$ (Table 5.4) and the $PVIFA_{i,n}$ (Table 5.8)? What is the $PVIFA_{10\%,10yr}$? Add up the values of the $PVIF_{10\%,n}$ for $n = 1, \ldots, 10$. What is this value? Why do these values have the relationship they do?

5-6. What is an annuity? Give some examples of annuities. Distinguish between an annuity and a perpetuity.

SELF-TEST PROBLEMS

ST-1. You place $25,000 in a savings account paying annual compound interest of 8 percent for 3 years and then move it into a savings account that pays 10 percent interest compounded annually. How much will your money have grown at the end of 6 years?

ST-2. You purchase a boat for $35,000 and pay $5,000 down and agree to pay the rest over the next 10 years in 10 equal annual payments that include principal payments plus 13 percent of compound interest on the unpaid balance. What will be the amount of each payment?

ST-3. For an investment to grow eightfold in 9 years, at what rate would it have to grow?

STUDY PROBLEMS (SET A)

5-1A. (*Compound Interest*) To what amount will the following investments accumulate?
- **a.** $5,000 invested for 10 years at 10 percent compounded annually
- **b.** $8,000 invested for 7 years at 8 percent compounded annually
- **c.** $775 invested for 12 years at 12 percent compounded annually
- **d.** $21,000 invested for 5 years at 5 percent compounded annually

5-2A. (*Compound Value Solving for* n) How many years will the following take?
- **a.** $500 to grow to $1,039.50 if invested at 5 percent compounded annually
- **b.** $35 to grow to $53.87 if invested at 9 percent compounded annually
- **c.** $100 to grow to $298.60 if invested at 20 percent compounded annually
- **d.** $53 to grow to $78.76 if invested at 2 percent compounded annually

5-3A. (*Compound Value Solving for* i) At what annual rate would the following have to be invested?
- **a.** $500 to grow to $1,948.00 in 12 years
- **b.** $300 to grow to $422.10 in 7 years
- **c.** $50 to grow to $280.20 in 20 years
- **d.** $200 to grow to $497.60 in 5 years

5-4A. (*Present Value*) What is the present value of the following future amounts?
- **a.** $800 to be received 10 years from now discounted back to present at 10 percent
- **b.** $300 to be received 5 years from now discounted back to present at 5 percent
- **c.** $1,000 to be received 8 years from now discounted back to present at 3 percent
- **d.** $1,000 to be received 8 years from now discounted back to present at 20 percent

5-5A. (*Compound Annuity*) What is the accumulated sum of each of the following streams of payments?
- **a.** $500 a year for 10 years compounded annually at 5 percent
- **b.** $100 a year for 5 years compounded annually at 10 percent
- **c.** $35 a year for 7 years compounded annually at 7 percent
- **d.** $25 a year for 3 years compounded annually at 2 percent

5-6A. (*Present Value of an Annuity*) What is the present value of the following annuities?
- **a.** $2,500 a year for 10 years discounted back to the present at 7 percent
- **b.** $70 a year for 3 years discounted back to the present at 3 percent
- **c.** $280 a year for 7 years discounted back to the present at 6 percent
- **d.** $500 a year for 10 years discounted back to the present at 10 percent

5-7A. (*Compound Value*) Brian Mosallam, who recently sold his Porsche, placed $10,000 in a savings account paying annual compound interest of 6 percent.

    a. Calculate the amount of money that will have accrued if he leaves the money in the bank for 1, 5, and 15 years.

    b. If he moves his money into an account that pays 8 percent or one that pays 10 percent, rework part (a) using these new interest rates.

    c. What conclusions can you draw about the relationship between interest rates, time, and future sums from the calculations you have done above?

5-8A. (*Compound Interest with Nonannual Periods*) Calculate the amount of money that will be in each of the following accounts at the end of the given deposit period:

Account	Amount Deposited	Annual Interest Rate	Compounding Period (Compounded Every __Months)	Deposit Period (Years)
Theodore Logan III	$ 1,000	10%	12	10
Vernell Coles	95,000	12	1	1
Thomas Elliott	8,000	12	2	2
Wayne Robinson	120,000	8	3	2
Eugene Chung	30,000	10	6	4
Kelly Cravens	15,000	12	4	3

5-9A. (*Compound Interest with Nonannual Periods*)

    a. Calculate the future sum of $5,000, given that it will be held in the bank 5 years at an annual interest rate of 6 percent.

    b. Recalculate part (a) using a compounding period that is (1) semiannual and (2) bimonthly.

    c. Recalculate parts (a) and (b) for a 12 percent annual interest rate.

    d. Recalculate part (a) using a time horizon of 12 years (annual interest rate is still 6 percent).

    e. With respect to the effect of changes in the stated interest rate and holding periods on future sums in parts (c) and (d), what conclusions do you draw when you compare these figures with the answers found in parts (a) and (b)?

5-10A. (*Solving for* i *in Annuities*) Nicki Johnson, a sophomore mechanical engineering student, receives a call from an insurance agent who believes that Nicki is an older woman ready to retire from teaching. He talks to her about several annuities that she could buy that would guarantee her an annual fixed income. The annuities are as follows:

Annuity	Initial Payment into Annuity (at $t = 0$)	Amount of Money Received per Year	Duration of Annuity (Years)
A	$50,000	$8,500	12
B	$60,000	$7,000	25
C	$70,000	$8,000	20

If Nicki could earn 11 percent on her money by placing it in a savings account, should she place it instead in any of the annuities? Which ones, if any? Why?

5-11A. (*Future Value*) Sales of a new finance book were 15,000 copies this year and were expected to increase by 20 percent per year. What are expected sales during each of the next 3 years? Graph this sales trend and explain.

5-12A. (*Future Value*) Reggie Jackson, formerly of the New York Yankees, hit 41 home runs in 1980. If his home-run output grew at a rate of 10 percent per year, what would it have been over the following 5 years?

5-13A. (*Loan Amortization*) Mr. Bill S. Preston, Esq., purchased a new house for $80,000. He paid $20,000 down and agreed to pay the rest over the next 25 years in 25 equal annual payments that include principal payments plus 9 percent compound interest on the unpaid balance. What will these equal payments be?

5-14A. (*Solving for* PMT *in an Annuity*) To pay for your child's education, you wish to have accumulated $15,000 at the end of 15 years. To do this, you plan to deposit an equal amount into the bank at the end of each year. If the bank is willing to pay 6 percent compounded annually, how much must you deposit each year to obtain your goal?

5-15A. (*Solving for* i *in Compound Interest*) If you were offered $1,079.50 10 years from now in return for an investment of $500 currently, what annual rate of interest would you earn if you took the offer?

5-16A. (*Future Value of an Annuity*) In 10 years, you plan to retire and buy a house in Oviedo, Florida. The house you are looking at currently costs $100,000 and is expected to increase in value each year at a rate of 5 percent. Assuming you can earn 10 percent annually on your investments, how much must you invest at the end of each of the next 10 years to be able to buy your dream home when you retire?

5-17A. (*Compound Value*) The Aggarwal Corporation needs to save $10 million to retire a $10 million mortgage that matures in 10 years. To retire this mortgage, the company plans to put a fixed amount into an account at the end of each year for 10 years. The Aggarwal Corporation expects to earn 9 percent annually on the money in this account. What equal annual contribution must it make to this account to accumulate the $10 million by the end of 10 years?

5-18A. (*Compound Interest with Nonannual Periods*) After examining the various personal loan rates available to you, you find that you can borrow funds from a finance company at 12 percent compounded monthly or from a bank at 13 percent compounded annually. Which alternative is the most attractive?

5-19A. (*Present Value of an Uneven Stream of Payments*) You are given three investment alternatives to analyze. The cash flows from these three investments are as follows:

Investment			
End of Year	A	B	C
1	$10,000		$10,000
2	10,000		
3	10,000		
4	10,000		
5	10,000	$10,000	
6		10,000	50,000
7		10,000	
8		10,000	
9		10,000	
10		10,000	10,000

Assuming a 20 percent discount rate, find the present value of each investment.

5-20A. (*Present Value*) The Kumar Corporation plans to issue bonds that pay no interest but can be converted into $1,000 at maturity, 7 years from their purchase. To price these bonds competitively with other bonds of equal risk, it is determined that they should yield 10 percent, compounded annually. At what price should the Kumar Corporation sell these bonds?

5-21A. (*Perpetuities*) What is the present value of the following?

    a. A $300 perpetuity discounted back to the present at 8 percent

    b. A $1,000 perpetuity discounted back to the present at 12 percent

    c. A $100 perpetuity discounted back to the present at 9 percent

    d. A $95 perpetuity discounted back to the present at 5 percent

5-22A. (*Present Value of an Annuity Due*) What is the present value of a 10-year annuity due of $1,000 annually given a 10 percent discount rate?

5-23A. (*Solving for* n *with Nonannual Periods*) About how many years would it take for your investment to grow fourfold if it were invested at 16 percent compounded semiannually?

5-24A. (*Present Value of an Uneven Stream of Payments*) You are given three investment alternatives to analyze. The cash flows from these three investments are as follows:

Investment			
End of Year	A	B	C
1	$2,000	$2,000	$5,000
2	$3,000	$2,000	$5,000
3	$4,000	$2,000	−$5,000
4	−$5,000	$2,000	−$5,000
5	$5,000	$5,000	$15,000

What is the present value of each of these three investments if 10% is the appropriate discount rate?

5-25A. (*Complex Present Value*) How much do you have to deposit today so that beginning 11 years from now you can withdraw $10,000 a year for the next 5 years (periods 11 through 15) plus an *additional* amount of $20,000 in the last year (period 15)? Assume an interest rate of 6 percent.

5-26A. (*Loan Amortization*) On December 31, Beth Klemkosky bought a yacht for $50,000, paying $10,000 down and agreeing to pay the balance in 10 equal annual installments that include both the principal and 10 percent interest on the declining balance. How big would the annual payments be?

5-27A. (*Solving for i in an Annuity*) You lend a friend $30,000, which your friend will repay in 5 equal annual payments of $10,000, with the first payment to be received 1 year from now. What rate of return does your loan receive?

5-28A. (*Solving for i in Compound Interest*) You lend a friend $10,000, for which your friend will repay you $27,027 at the end of 5 years. What interest rate are you charging your "friend"?

5-29A. (*Loan Amortization*) A firm borrows $25,000 from the bank at 12 percent compounded annually to purchase some new machinery. This loan is to be repaid in equal annual installments at the end of each year over the next 5 years. How much will each annual payment be?

5.30A. (*Present Value Comparison*) You are offered $1,000 today, $10,000 in 12 years, or $25,000 in 25 years. Assuming that you can earn 11 percent on your money, which should you choose?

5-31A. (*Compound Annuity*) You plan to buy some property in Florida 5 years from today. To do this, you estimate that you will need $20,000 at that time for the purchase. You would like to accumulate these funds by making equal annual deposits in your savings account, which pays 12 percent annually. If you make your first deposit at the end of this year, and you would like your account to reach $20,000 when the final deposit is made, what will be the amount of your deposits?

5-32A. (*Complex Present Value*) You would like to have $50,000 in 15 years. To accumulate this amount, you plan to deposit each year an equal sum in the bank, which will earn 7 percent interest compounded annually. Your first payment will be made at the end of the year.

    a. How much must you deposit annually to accumulate this amount?

    b. If you decide to make a large lump-sum deposit today instead of the annual deposits, how large should this lump-sum deposit be? (Assume you can earn 7 percent on this deposit.)

c. At the end of 5 years, you will receive $10,000 and deposit this in the bank toward your goal of $50,000 at the end of 15 years. In addition to this deposit, how much must you deposit in equal annual deposits to reach your goal? (Again assume you can earn 7 percent on this deposit.)

5-33A. (*Comprehensive Present Value*) You are trying to plan for retirement in 10 years and currently you have $100,000 in a savings account and $300,000 in stocks. In addition, you plan to add to your savings by depositing $10,000 per year in your *savings account* at the end of each of the next 5 years and then $20,000 per year at the end of each year for the final 5 years until retirement.

a. Assuming your savings account returns 7 percent compounded annually and your investment in stocks will return 12 percent compounded annually, how much will you have at the end of 10 years? (Ignore taxes.)

b. If you expect to live for 20 years after you retire, and at retirement you deposit all of your savings in a bank account paying 10 percent, how much can you withdraw each year after retirement (20 equal withdrawals beginning 1 year after you retire) to end up with a zero balance at death?

5-34A. (*Loan Amortization*) On December 31, Son-Nan Chen borrowed $100,000, agreeing to repay this sum in 20 equal annual installments that include both the principal and 15 percent interest on the declining balance. How large will the annual payments be?

5-35A. (*Loan Amortization*) To buy a new house you must borrow $150,000. To do this, you take out a $150,000, 30-year, 10 percent mortgage. Your mortgage payments, which are made at the end of each year (one payment each year), include both principal and 10 percent interest on the declining balance. How large will your annual payments be?

5-36A. (*Present Value*) The state lottery's million-dollar payout provides for $1 million to be paid over 19 years in $50,000 amounts. The first $50,000 payment is made immediately and the 19 remaining $50,000 payments occur at the end of each of the next 19 years. If 10 percent is the appropriate discount rate, what is the present value of this stream of cash flows? If 20 percent is the appropriate discount rate, what is the present value of the cash flows?

5-37A. (*Compounding an Annuity Due*) Find the future value at the end of year 10 of an annuity due of $1,000 per year for 10 years compounded annually at 10 percent. What would be the future value of this annuity if it were compounded annually at 15 percent?

5-38A. (*Present Value of an Annuity Due*) Determine the present value of an annuity due of $1,000 per year for 10 years discounted back to present at an annual rate of 10 percent. What would be the present value of this annuity due if it were discounted at an annual rate of 15 percent?

5-39A. (*Present Value of a Future Annuity*) Determine the present value of an ordinary annuity of $1,000 per year for 10 years with the first cash flow from the annuity coming at the end of year 8 (that is, no payments at the end of years 1 through 7 and annual payments at the end of years 8 through 17) given a 10 percent discount rate.

5-40A. (*Solving for i in Compound Interest—Financial Calculator Needed*) In September 1963, the first issue of the comic book *X-MEN* was issued. The original price for the issue was 12 cents. By September 1998, 35 years later, the value of this comic book had risen to $5,000. What annual rate of interest would you have earned if you had bought the comic in 1963 and sold it in 1998?

5-41A. (*Comprehensive Present Value*) You have just inherited a large sum of money and you are trying to determine how much you should save for retirement and how much you can spend now. For retirement, you will deposit today (January 1, 1999) a lump sum in a bank account paying 10 percent compounded annually. You don't plan on touching this deposit until you retire in 5 years (January 1, 2004) and you plan on living for 20 additional years and then drop dead on December 31, 2023. During your retirement, you would like to receive income of $50,000 per year to be received the first day of each year, with the first payment on January 1, 2004, the last payment on January 1, 2023. Complicating this objective is your desire to have one final 3-year fling during which time you'd like to track down all the original members of *Leave It to Beaver* and *The Brady Bunch* and get their autographs. To finance this, you want to receive $250,000 on January 1, 2019, and *nothing* on January 1, 2020 and January 1, 2021, because you will be on the road. In addition, after you pass on (January 1, 2024), you would like to have a total of $100,000 to leave to your children.

    a. How much must you deposit in the bank at 10 percent on January 1, 1999 to achieve your goal? (Use a time line to answer this question.)

    b. What kinds of problems are associated with this analysis and its assumptions?

INTEGRATIVE PROBLEM

For your job as the business reporter for a local newspaper, you are given the task of putting together a series of articles that explains the power of the time value of money to your readers. Your editor would like you to address several specific questions in addition to demonstrating for the readership the use of the time value of money techniques by applying them to several problems. What would be your response to the following memorandum from your editor?

TO: Business Reporter

FROM: Perry White, Editor, *Daily Planet*

RE: Upcoming Series on the Importance and Power of the Time Value of Money

In your upcoming series on the time value of money, I would like to make sure you cover several specific points. In addition, before you begin this assignment, I want to make sure we are all reading from the same script, because accuracy has always been the cornerstone of the *Daily Planet*. In this regard, I'd like a response to the following questions before we proceed:

1. What is the relationship between discounting and compounding?

2. What is the relationship between the $PVIF_{i,n}$ and $PVIFA_{i,n}$?

3. (1) What will $5,000 invested for 10 years at 8 percent compounded annually grow to?

    (2) How many years will it take $400 to grow to $1,671, if it is invested at 10 percent compounded annually?

    (3) At what rate would $1,000 have to be invested to grow to $4,046 in 10 years?

4. Calculate the future sum of $1,000, given that it will be held in the bank for 5 years and earn 10 percent compounded semiannually?

5. What is an annuity due? How does this differ from an ordinary annuity?

6. What is the present value of an ordinary annuity of $1,000 per year for 7 years discounted back to present at 10 percent? What would be the present value if it were an annuity due?

7. What is the future value of an ordinary annuity of $1,000 per year for 7 years compounded at 10 percent? What would be the future value if it were an annuity due?

8. You have just borrowed $100,000, and you agree to pay it back over the next 25 years in 25 equal end-of-year annual payments that include the principal payments plus 10 percent compound interest on the unpaid balance. What will be the size of these payments?

9. What is the present value of a $1,000 perpetuity discounted back to present at 8 percent?

10. What is the present value of a $1,000 annuity for 10 years with the first payment occurring at the end of year 10 (that is, ten $1,000 payments occurring at the end of year 10 through year 19) given an appropriate discount rate of 10 percent?

11. Given a 10 percent discount rate, what is the present value of a perpetuity of $1,000 per year if the first payment does not begin until the end of year 10?

12. What is the annual percentage yield (APY) on an 8 percent bank loan compounded quarterly?

STUDY PROBLEMS (SET B)

5-1B. (*Compound Interest*) To what amount will the following investments accumulate?

    a. $4,000 invested for 11 years at 9 percent compounded annually

    b. $8,000 invested for 10 years at 8 percent compounded annually

c. $800 invested for 12 years at 12 percent compounded annually

d. $21,000 invested for 6 years at 5 percent compounded annually

5-2B. (*Compound Value Solving for* n) How many years will the following take?

a. $550 to grow to $1,043.90 if invested at 6 percent compounded annually

b. $40 to grow to $88.44 if invested at 12 percent compounded annually

c. $110 to grow to $614.79 if invested at 24 percent compounded annually

d. $60 to grow to $78.30 if invested at 3 percent compounded annually

5-3B. (*Compound Value Solving for* i) At what annual rate would the following have to be invested?

a. $550 to grow to $1,898.60 in 13 years

b. $275 to grow to $406.18 in 8 years

c. $60 to grow to $279.66 in 20 years

d. $180 to grow to $486.00 in 6 years

5-4B. (*Present Value*) What is the present value of the following future amounts?

a. $800 to be received 10 years from now discounted back to present at 10 percent

b. $400 to be received 6 years from now discounted back to present at 6 percent

c. $1,000 to be received 8 years from now discounted back to present at 5 percent

d. $900 to be received 9 years from now discounted back to present at 20 percent

5-5B. (*Compound Annuity*) What is the accumulated sum of each of the following streams of payments?

a. $500 a year for 10 years compounded annually at 6 percent

b. $150 a year for 5 years compounded annually at 11 percent

c. $35 a year for 8 years compounded annually at 7 percent

d. $25 a year for 3 years compounded annually at 2 percent

5-6B. (*Present Value of an Annuity*) What is the present value of the following annuities?

a. $3,000 a year for 10 years discounted back to the present at 8 percent

b. $50 a year for 3 years discounted back to the present at 3 percent

c. $280 a year for 8 years discounted back to the present at 7 percent

d. $600 a year for 10 years discounted back to the present at 10 percent

5-7B. (*Compound Value*) Trish Nealon, who recently sold her Porsche, placed $20,000 in a savings account paying annual compound interest of 7 percent.

a. Calculate the amount of money that will have accrued if she leaves the money in the bank for 1, 5, and 15 years.

b. If she moves her money into an account that pays 9 percent or one that pays 11 percent, rework part (a) using these new interest rates.

c. What conclusions can you draw about the relationship between interest rates, time, and future sums from the calculations you have done above?

5-8B. (*Compound Interest with Nonannual Periods*) Calculate the amount of money that will be in each of the following accounts at the end of the given deposit period:

Account	Amount Deposited	Annual Interest Rate	Compounding Period (Compounded Every __Months)	Deposit Period (Years)
Korey Stringer	$ 2,000	12%	2	2
Erica Moss	50,000	12	1	1
Ty Howard	7,000	18	2	2
Rob Kelly	130,000	12	3	2
Mary Christopher	20,000	14	6	4
Juan Diaz	15,000	15	4	3

5-9B. (*Compound Interest with Nonannual Periods*)

   a. Calculate the future sum of $6,000, given that it will be held in the bank 5 years at an annual interest rate of 6 percent.

   b. Recalculate part (a) using a compounding period that is (1) semiannual and (2) bimonthly.

   c. Recalculate parts (a) and (b) for a 12 percent annual interest rate.

   d. Recalculate part (a) using a time horizon of 12 years (annual interest rate is still 6 percent).

   e. With respect to the effect of changes in the stated interest rate and holding periods on future sums in parts (c) and (d), what conclusions do you draw when you compare these figures with the answers found in parts (a) and (b)?

5-10B. (*Solving for* i *in Annuities*) Ellen Denis, a sophomore mechanical engineering student, receives a call from an insurance agent, who believes that Ellen is an older woman ready to retire from teaching. He talks to her about several annuities that she could buy that would guarantee her an annual fixed income. The annuities are as follows:

Annuity	Initial Payment into Annuity (at $t = 0$)	Amount of Money Received per year	Duration of Annuity (Years)
A	$50,000	$8,500	12
B	$60,000	$7,000	25
C	$70,000	$8,000	20

If Ellen could earn 12 percent on her money by placing it in a savings account, should she place it instead in any of the annuities? Which ones, if any? Why?

5-11B. (*Future Value*) Sales of a new marketing book were 10,000 copies this year and were expected to increase by 15 percent per year. What are expected sales during each of the next 3 years? Graph this sales trend and explain.

5-12B. (*Future Value*) Reggie Jackson, formerly of the New York Yankees, hit 41 home runs in 1980. If his home-run output grew at a rate of 12 percent per year, what would it have been over the following 5 years?

5-13B. (*Loan Amortization*) Stefani Moore purchased a new house for $150,000. She paid $30,000 down and agreed to pay the rest over the next 25 years in 25 equal annual payments that include principal payments plus 10 percent compound interest on the unpaid balance. What will these equal payments be?

5-14B. (*Solving for* PMT *in an Annuity*) To pay for your child's education, you wish to have accumulated $25,000 at the end of 15 years. To do this, you plan to deposit an equal amount into the bank at the end of each year. If the bank is willing to pay 7 percent compounded annually, how much must you deposit each year to obtain your goal?

5-15B. (*Solving for* i *in Compound Interest*) If you were offered $2,376.50 ten years from now in return for an investment of $700 currently, what annual rate of interest would you earn if you took the offer?

5-16B. (*Future Value of an Annuity*) In 10 years, you plan to retire and buy a house in Marco Island, Florida. The house you are looking at currently costs $125,000 and is expected to increase in value each year at a rate of 5 percent. Assuming you can earn 10 percent annually on your investments, how much must you invest at the end of each of the next 10 years to be able to buy your dream home when you retire?

5-17B. (*Compound Value*) The Knutson Corporation needs to save $15 million to retire a $15 million mortgage that matures in 10 years. To retire this mortgage, the company plans to put a fixed amount into an account at the end of each year for 10 years. The Knutson Corporation expects to earn 10 percent annually on the money in this account. What equal annual contribution must it make to this account to accumulate the $15 million by the end of 10 years?

5-18B. (*Compound Interest with Nonannual Periods*) After examining the various personal loan rates available to you, you find that you can borrow funds from a finance company at 24 percent compounded monthly or from a bank at 26 percent compounded annually. Which alternative is the most attractive?

5-19B. (*Present Value of an Uneven Stream of Payments*) You are given three investment alternatives to analyze. The cash flows from these three investments are as follows:

Investment			
End of Year	A	B	C
1	$15,000		$20,000
2	15,000		
3	15,000		
4	15,000		
5	15,000	$15,000	
6		15,000	60,000
7		15,000	
8		15,000	
9		15,000	
10		15,000	20,000

Assuming a 20 percent discount rate, find the present value of each investment.

5-20B. (*Present Value*) The Shin Corporation is planning on issuing bonds that pay no interest but can be converted into $1,000 at maturity, 8 years from their purchase. To price these bonds competitively with other bonds of equal risk, it is determined that they should yield 9 percent, compounded annually. At what price should the Shin Corporation sell these bonds?

5-21B. (*Perpetuities*) What is the present value of the following?
   a. A $400 perpetuity discounted back to the present at 9 percent
   b. A $1,500 perpetuity discounted back to the present at 13 percent
   c. A $150 perpetuity discounted back to the present at 10 percent
   d. A $100 perpetuity discounted back to the present at 6 percent

5-22B. (*Present Value of an Annuity Due*) What is the present value of a 5-year annuity due of $1,000 annually given a 10 percent discount rate?

5-23B. (*Solving for n with Nonannual Periods*) About how many years would it take for your investment to grow sevenfold if it were invested at 10 percent compounded semiannually?

5-24B. (*Present Value of an Uneven Stream of Payments*) You are given three investment alternatives to analyze. The cash flows from these three investments are as follows:

Investment			
End of Year	A	B	C
1	$ 5,000	$ 1,000	$10,000
2	$ 5,000	$ 3,000	$10,000
3	$ 5,000	$ 5,000	$10,000
4	−$15,000	$10,000	$10,000
5	$15,000	−$10,000	−$40,000

What is the present value of each of these three investments if 10 percent is the appropriate discount rate?

5-25B. (*Complex Present Value*) How much do you have to deposit today so that beginning 11 years from now you can withdraw $10,000 a year for the next 5 years (periods 11 through 15) plus an *additional* amount of $15,000 in the last year (period 15)? Assume an interest rate of 7 percent.

5-26B. (*Loan Amortization*) On December 31, Loren Billingsley bought a yacht for $60,000, paying $15,000 down and agreeing to pay the balance in 10 equal annual installments that include both the principal and 9 percent interest on the declining balance. How big would the annual payments be?

5-27B. (*Solving for* i *in an Annuity*) You lend a friend $45,000, which your friend will repay in five equal annual payments of $9,000 with the first payment to be received 1 year from now. What rate of return does your loan receive?

5-28B. (*Solving for* i *in Compound Interest*) You lend a friend $15,000, for which your friend will repay you $37,313 at the end of 5 years. What interest rate are you charging your "friend"?

5-29B. (*Loan Amortization*) A firm borrows $30,000 from the bank at 13 percent compounded annually to purchase some new machinery. This loan is to be repaid in equal annual installments at the end of each year over the next 4 years. How much will each annual payment be?

5-30B. (*Present Value Comparison*) You are offered $1,000 today, $10,000 in 12 years, or $25,000 in 25 years. Assuming that you can earn 11 percent on your money, which should you choose?

5-31B. (*Compound Annuity*) You plan to buy some property in Florida 5 years from today. To do this, you estimate that you will need $30,000 at that time for the purchase. You would like to accumulate these funds by making equal annual deposits in your savings account, which pays 10 percent annually. If you make your first deposit at the end of this year and you would like your account to reach $30,000 when the final deposit is made, what will be the amount of your deposits?

5-32B. (*Complex Present Value*) You would like to have $75,000 in 15 years. To accumulate this amount, you plan to deposit each year an equal sum in the bank, which will earn 8 percent interest compounded annually. Your first payment will be made at the end of the year.

  a. How much must you deposit annually to accumulate this amount?
  b. If you decide to make a large lump-sum deposit today instead of the annual deposits, how large should this lump-sum deposit be? (Assume you can earn 8 percent on this deposit.)
  c. At the end of 5 years, you will receive $20,000 and deposit this in the bank toward your goal of $75,000 at the end of 15 years. In addition to this deposit, how much must you deposit in equal annual deposits to reach your goal? (Again assume you can earn 8 percent on this deposit.)

5-33B. (*Comprehensive Present Value*) You are trying to plan for retirement in 10 years and currently you have $150,000 in a savings account and $250,000 in stocks. In addition, you plan to add to your savings by depositing $8,000 per year in your *savings account* at the end of each of the next 5 years and then $10,000 per year at the end of each year for the final 5 years until retirement.

  a. Assuming your savings account returns 8 percent compounded annually and your investment in stocks will return 12 percent compounded annually, how much will you have at the end of 10 years? (Ignore taxes.)
  b. If you expect to live 20 years after you retire, and at retirement you deposit all of your savings in a bank account paying 11 percent, how much can you withdraw each year after retirement (20 equal withdrawals beginning 1 year after you retire) to end up with a zero-balance at death?

5-34B. (*Loan Amortization*) On December 31, Eugene Chung borrowed $200,000, agreeing to repay this sum in 20 equal annual installments that include both the principal and 10 percent interest on the declining balance. How large will the annual payments be?

5-35B. (*Loan Amortization*) To buy a new house, you must borrow $250,000. To do this, you take out a $250,000, 30-year, 9 percent mortgage. Your mortgage payments, which are made at the end of each year (one payment each year), include both principal and 9 percent interest on the declining balance. How large will your annual payments be?

5-36B. (*Present Value*) The state lottery's million-dollar payout provides for $1 million to be paid over 24 years in $40,000 amounts. The first $40,000 payment is made immediately with the 24 remaining $40,000 payments occurring at the end of each of the next 24 years. If 10 percent is the appropriate discount rate, what is the present value of this stream of cash flows? If 20 percent is the appropriate discount rate, what is the present value of the cash flows?

5-37B. (*Compounding an Annuity Due*) Find the future value at the end of year 5 of an annuity due of $1,000 per year for 5 years compounded annually at 5 percent. What would be the future value of this annuity if it were compounded annually at 8 percent?

5-38B. (*Present Value of an Annuity*) Determine the present value of an annuity due of $1,000 per year for 15 years discounted back to present at an annual rate of 12 percent. What would be the present value of this annuity due if it were discounted at an annual rate of 15 percent?

5-39B. (*Present Value of a Future Annuity*) Determine the present value of an ordinary annuity of $1,000 per year for 10 years with the first cash flow from the annuity coming at the end of year 8 (that is, no payments at the end of years 1 through 7 and annual payments at the end of years 8 through 17) given a 15 percent discount rate.

5-40B. (*Solving for i in Compound Interest—Financial Calculator Needed*) In March 1963, issue number 39 of *Tales of Suspense* was issued. The original price for that issue was 12 cents. By March of 1998, 35 years later, the value of this comic book had risen to $3,000. What annual rate of interest would you have earned if you had bought the comic in 1963 and sold it in 1998?

5-41B. (*Comprehensive Present Value*) You have just inherited a large sum of money and you are trying to determine how much you should save for retirement and how much you can spend now. For retirement you will deposit today (January 1, 1999) a lump sum in a bank account paying 10 percent compounded annually. You don't plan on touching this deposit until you retire in 5 years (January 1, 2004), and you plan on living for 20 additional years and then drop dead on December 31, 2023. During your retirement, you would like to receive income of $60,000 per year to be received the first day of each year, with the first payment on January 1, 2004 and the last payment on January 1, 2023. Complicating this objective is your desire to have one final 3-year fling, during which time you'd like to track down all the original members of *The Mr. Ed Show* and *The Monkees* and get their autographs. To finance this, you want to receive $300,000 on January 1, 2019, and *nothing* on January 1, 2020, and January 1, 2021, as you will be on the road. In addition, after you pass on (January 1, 2024), you would like to have a total of $100,000 to leave to your children.

    a. How much must you deposit in the bank at 10 percent on January 1, 1999 in order to achieve your goal? (Use a time line in order to answer this question.)

    b. What kinds of problems are associated with this analysis and its assumptions?

SELF-TEST SOLUTIONS

SS-1. This is a compound interest problem in which you must first find the future value of $25,000 growing at 8 percent compounded annually for 3 years and then allow that future value to grow for an additional 3 years at 10 percent. First, the value of the $25,000 after 3 years growing at 8 percent is

$$FV_3 = PV(1 + i)^n$$
$$FV_3 = \$25,000(1 + .08)^3$$
$$FV_3 = \$25,000(1.260)$$
$$FV_3 = \$31,500$$

Thus after 3 years, you have $31,500. Now this amount is allowed to grow for 3 years at 10 percent. Plugging this into equation (5-6), with $PV = \$31,500$, $i = 10$ percent, $n = 3$ years, we solve for FV_3:

$$FV_3 = \$31,500(1 + .10)^3$$
$$FV_3 = \$31,500(1.331)$$
$$FV_3 = \$41,926.50$$

Thus after 6 years, the $25,000 will have grown to $41,926.50.

SS-2. This loan amortization problem is actually just a present-value-of-an-annuity problem in which we know the values of i, n, and PV, and are solving for PMT. In this case, the value of i is 13 percent, n is 10 years, and PV is $30,000. Substituting these values into equation (5-10), we find

$$\$30,000 = PMT\left[\sum_{t=1}^{10}\frac{1}{(1+.13)^t}\right]$$

$$\$30,000 = PMT(5.426)$$

$$\$5,528.93 = PMT$$

SS-3. This is a simple compound interest problem in which FV_9 is eight times larger than PV. Here again, three of the four variables are known: $n = 9$ years, $FV_9 = 8$, and $PV = 1$, and we are solving for i. Substituting these values into equation (5-6), we find

$$FV_9 = PV(1+i)^n$$

$$FV_9 = PV(FVIF_{i,n})$$

$$8 = 1(FVIF_{i,9\text{yr}})$$

$$8.00 = FVIF_{i,9\text{yr}}$$

Thus we are looking for an $FVIF_{i,9\text{yr}}$ with a value of 8 in appendix B, which occurs in the 9-year row. If we look in the 9-year row for a value of 8.00, we find it in the 26% column (8.004). Thus the answer is 26 percent.

1993 BERKSHIRE HATHAWAY ANNUAL REPORT

Negotiating a Deal— the Old-Fashioned Way

Warren Buffett is world renowned as an investor. The stock of his firm, Berkshire Hathaway, traded at a price of about $43,000 per share in 1994. His philosophy is to invest in only a small number of companies and then be actively involved with the management. He also believes it is better to invest in a superior company at a fair price rather than a mediocre firm at a cheap price. The following is an excerpt from the 1993 Berkshire Hathaway annual report, and gives us a great (and unique) example of a business transaction based not on the technicalities of a long and involved contract, but on trust. Mr. Buffett writes:

Mrs. B—Rose Blumkin—had her 100th birthday on December 3, 1993. (The candles cost more than the cake.) That was a day on which the store was scheduled to be open in the evening. Mrs. B, who works seven days a week, for however many hours the store operates, found the proper decision quite obvious: She simply postponed her party until an evening when the store was closed.

Mrs. B's story is well known but worth telling again. She came to the United States 77 years ago, unable to speak English and devoid of formal schooling. In 1937, she founded the Nebraska Furniture Mart with $500. Last year the store had sales of $200 million, a larger amount by far than that recorded by any other home furnishings store in the United States. Our part in all of this began ten years ago when Mrs. B sold control of the business to Berkshire Hathaway, a deal we completed without obtaining audited financial statements, checking real estate records, or getting any warranties. In short, her word was good enough for us.

Naturally, I was delighted to attend Mrs. B's birthday party. After all, she's promised to attend *my* 100th birthday party.

SOURCE: Berkshire Hathaway 1993 Annual Report, Omaha Nebraska, pp. 19–20.

To gain a basic understanding of investment risk, we might ask: What is risk and how is it measured? To begin, we will answer this question when we are only making a single investment, and then for a portfolio, or group of investments.

STOP AND THINK

The first Chinese symbol represents danger, the second stands for opportunity. The Chinese define risk as the combination of danger and opportunity. Greater risk, according to the Chinese, means we have greater opportunity to do well, but also greater danger to do badly.

Risk and a Single Investment

To help us grasp the fundamental meaning of risk, consider two possible investments:

1. The first investment is a U.S. Treasury bill, which is a government security that matures in 90 days and promises to pay an annual return of 6 percent. If we purchase and hold this security for 90 days, we are virtually assured of receiving no more and no less than 6 percent. For all practical purposes, the risk of loss is nonexistent.
2. The second investment involves the purchase of the stock of a local publishing company. Looking at the past returns of the firm's stock, we have made the following estimate of the annual returns from the investment:

Chance (Probability) of Occurrence	Rate of Return on Investment
1 chance in 10 (10%)	−10%
2 chances in 10 (20%)	5%
4 chances in 10 (40%)	15%
2 chances in 10 (20%)	25%
1 chance in 10 (10%)	40%

Investing in the publishing company could conceivably provide a return as high as 40 percent if all goes well or we could lose 10 percent if everything goes against the firm. However, in future years, both good and bad, we could expect a 15 percent return on average computed as follows:[3]

$$\overline{k} = (.10)(-10\%) + (.20)(5\%) + (.40)(15\%) + (.20)(25\%) + (.10)(40\%)$$

$$= 15\%$$

Comparing the Treasury bill investment with the publishing company investment, we see that the Treasury bills offer an expected 6 percent rate of return, whereas the publishing company has an expected rate of return of 15 percent. However, our investment in the publishing firm is clearly more "risky"—that is, there is greater uncertainty about the final outcome. Stated somewhat differently, there is a greater variation or dispersion of possible returns, which in turn implies greater **risk**.[4] Figure 6.1 shows these differences graphically in the form of discrete probability distributions.

Although the return from investing in the publishing firm is clearly less certain than for Treasury bills, quantitative measures of risk are useful when the difference between two investments is not so evident. Just as we used the time value of money in chapter 5 to compare cash flow streams of different investments, we need a way to compare the riskiness of different projects. Furthermore, the problem is similar for a financial manager who must consider different investments. At times the choice is obvious, but at others it is not—so the manager needs a way to be more precise in analyzing a project's level of risk. The standard deviation (σ) is such a measure. The **standard deviation** is

Risk

The prospect of an unfavorable outcome. This concept has been measured operationally as the standard deviation or beta, which will be explained later.

Standard deviation

A measure of the spread or dispersion about the mean of a probability distribution. We calculate it by squaring the difference between each outcome and its expected value, weighting each squared difference by its associated probability, summing over all possible outcomes, and taking the square root of this sum.

---

[3]We assume that the particular outcome or return earned in 1 year does *not* affect the return earned in the subsequent year. Technically speaking, the distribution of returns in any year is assumed to be independent of the outcome in any prior year.

[4]How can we possibly view variations above the expected return as risk? Should we not be concerned only with the negative deviations? Some would agree and view risk as only the negative variability in returns from a predetermined minimum acceptable rate of return. However, as long as the distribution of returns is symmetrical, the same conclusions will be reached.

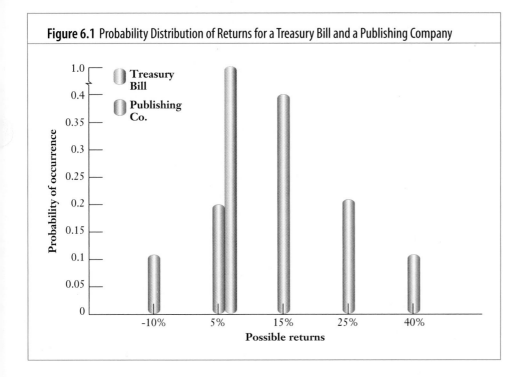

Figure 6.1 Probability Distribution of Returns for a Treasury Bill and a Publishing Company

simply the square root of the *average squared deviation of each possible return from the expected return*; that is

$$\sigma = \sqrt{\sum_{i=1}^{n}(k_i - \overline{k})^2\, P(k_i)} \qquad (6\text{-}3)$$

where n = the number of possible outcomes or different rates of return on the investment
$\quad k_i$ = the value of the ith possible rate of return
$\quad \overline{k}$ = the expected rate of return
$\quad P(k_i)$ = the chance or probability that the ith outcome or return will occur.

For the publishing company, the standard deviation would be 12.85 percent, determined as follows:

$$\sigma = \left[\begin{array}{l} (-10\% - 15\%)^2(.10) + (5\% - 15\%)^2(.20) \\ + (15\% - 15\%)^2(.40) + (25\% - 15\%)^2(.20) \\ + (40\% - 15\%)^2(.10) \end{array}\right]^{\frac{1}{2}}$$

$$= \sqrt{165\%} = 12.85\%$$

Although the standard deviation of returns provides us with a quantitative measure of an asset's riskiness, how should we interpret the result? What does it mean? Is the 12.85 percent standard deviation for the publishing company investment good or bad? First, we should remember that statisticians tell us that two-thirds of the time, an event will fall within plus or minus one standard deviation of the expected value (assuming the distribution is normally distributed; that is, it is shaped like a bell). Thus given a 15 percent expected return and a standard deviation of 12.85 percent for the publishing company investment, we may reasonably anticipate that the actual returns will fall between 2.15 percent and 27.85 percent (15% ± 12.85%) two-thirds of the time—not much certainty with this investment.

A second way to interpret the standard deviation as a measure of risk is to compare the investment in the publishing firm against other investments. The attractiveness of a security with respect to its return and risk cannot be determined in isolation. Only by examining other available alternatives can we reach a conclusion about a particular investment's risk. For example, if another investment, say an investment in a firm that owns a local radio station, has the same expected return as the publishing company, 15 percent, but with a standard deviation of 7 percent, we would consider the risk associated with the publishing firm, 12.85 percent, to be excessive. In the technical jargon of modern portfolio theory, the radio company investment is said to "dominate" the publishing firm investment. In common sense terms, this means that the radio company investment has the same expected return as the publishing company investment but is less risky.

What if we compare the investment in the publishing company with one in a quick oil-change franchise, an investment in which the expected rate of return is an attractive 24 percent, but in which the standard deviation is estimated at 18 percent? Now what should we do? Clearly, the oil-change franchise has a higher expected rate of return, but it also has a larger standard deviation. In this example, we see that the real challenge in selecting the better investment comes when one investment has a higher expected rate of return but also exhibits greater risk. *Here the final choice is determined by our attitude toward risk, and there is no single right answer.* You might select the publishing company, whereas I might choose the oil-change investment, and neither of us would be wrong. We would simply be expressing our tastes and preferences about risk and return.

STOP AND THINK

As we shall see, risk is the potential variability in future cash flows. The wider the range of possible events that can occur, the greater the risk. If we think about it, this is a relatively intuitive concept.

OBJECTIVE 3

Risk and Diversification

In the preceding discussion, we defined risk as the variability of anticipated returns as measured by the standard deviation. However, more can be said about risk, especially as to its nature, when either an individual or a firm holds more than one asset. Let's consider for the moment how risk is affected if we diversify our investment by holding a variety of securities.

To begin, assume that the date is July 20, 1996. When you awake this morning, you follow your daily routine, which includes reading *The Wall Street Journal*. You always begin by scanning "What's News—Business and Finance," with an eye for anything related to the stocks you own—and there they are. Two of your stocks made the front page, the first being Motorola. The firm announced that profits had declined 32 percent, owing to a cellular-phone price war and the declining demand for computer chips, both products Motorola sells. The result: Motorola's stock fell 15 percent on the announcement. That hurts! The only consolation is the article on Nike, another one of your investments. For Nike, profits were up 38 percent as the result of an unexpected surge in sales. In response, the company's stock increased 4.3 percent—not as much as your loss in Motorola, but it helps. You also notice that these events

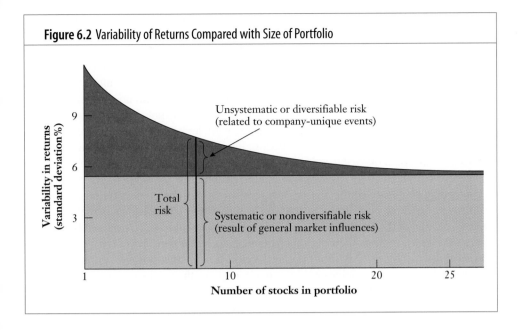

Figure 6.2 Variability of Returns Compared with Size of Portfolio

occurred on a day that the overall market on the New York Stock Exchange increased only one-half of 1 percent.

Clearly, what we have described about Motorola and Nike were events unique to these two companies, and as we would expect, the investors reacted accordingly; that is, the value of the stock changed in light of the new information. Although we might have wished we had owned only Nike stock at the time, most of us would prefer to avoid such uncertainties; that is, we are risk averse. Instead, we would like to reduce the risk associated with our investment portfolio without having to accept a lower expected return. Good news: It is possible by diversifying our portfolio!

If we diversify our investments across different securities rather than invest in only one stock, the variability in the returns of our portfolio should decline. The reduction in risk will occur if the stock returns within our portfolio do not move precisely together over time—that is, if they are not perfectly correlated. Figure 6.2 shows graphically what we can expect to happen to the variability of returns as we add additional stocks to the portfolio. The reduction occurs because some of the volatility in returns of a stock are unique to that security. The unique return variability of a single stock tends to be countered by the unique variability of another security. However, we should not expect to eliminate all risk from our portfolio. In practice, it would be rather difficult to cancel all the variations in returns of a portfolio, because stock prices have some tendency to move together; that is, a rising stock market tends to boost *most* (not all) stocks. Furthermore, investing in Intel, Microsoft, and Dell Computers would provide little reduction in the variabiality of returns. These firms are concentrated in the same industry, and as a result, their stocks tend to move together. On the other hand, investing in Coca-Cola, Exxon, and Citibank would have a greater effect on the variability of returns. To be even more effective at reducing the variability of returns, we could invest in various large and small firms in different industries, as well as foreign companies. But even then, you will not be able to remove all the risk (variation in returns). Thus we can divide the total risk (total variability) of our portfolio into two types of risk: (1) **firm-specific** or **company-unique risk** and (2) **market-related risk**. Company-unique risk might also be called **diversifiable risk**, because it can be diversified away. Market risk is **nondiversifiable risk**; it

Firm-specific risk or company-unique risk (diversifiable risk or unsystematic risk)

The portion of the variation in investment returns that can be eliminated through investor diversification. This diversifiable risk is the result of factors that are unique to the particular firm.

Market-related risk (nondiversifiable risk or systematic risk)

The portion of variations in investment returns that cannot be eliminated through investor diversification. This variation results from factors that affect all stocks.

cannot be eliminated, no matter how much we diversify. These two types of risk are shown graphically in Figure 6.2.

Total risk declines until we have approximately 20 securities, and then the decline becomes very slight.[5] The remaining risk, which would typically be about 40 percent of the total risk, is the portfolio's market risk. At this point, our portfolio is highly correlated with all securities in the marketplace. Events that affect our portfolio now are not so much unique events but changes in the general economy or major political events. Examples include changes in general interest rates, changes in tax legislation that affects companies, or increasing public concern about the effect of business practices on the environment.

Because we can remove the company-unique, or unsystematic risk, there is no reason to believe that the market will reward us with additional returns for assuming risk that could be avoided by simply diversifying. Our new measure of risk should therefore measure how responsive a stock or portfolio is to changes in a *market portfolio*, such as the New York Stock Exchange or the S&P 500 Index.[6] This relationship could be determined by plotting past returns, say on a monthly basis, of a particular stock or a portfolio of stocks against the returns of the *market portfolio* for the same period. The market portfolio is one that only has systematic (nondiversifiable) risk. We frequently use the stocks making up the S & P 500 Index (500 large U.S. companies) as a surrogate for the overall market portfolio.

STOP AND THINK

We have just explained **Axiom 9: All Risk Is Not Equal—Some Risk Can Be Diversified Away, and Some Cannot.** *As we diversify our portfolio, we reduce the effects of company-unique risk, but some risk—nondiversifiable or market risk—still remains, no matter how much we diversify.*

OBJECTIVE 4

Measuring Market Risk

To help clarify the idea of systematic risk, let's examine the relationship between the common stock returns of PepsiCo and the returns of the S&P 500 Index. The monthly returns for PepsiCo. and for the S&P 500 Index for the 24 months ending December 1996 are presented in Table 6.2, and in Figure 6.3. These monthly returns, or **holding-period returns**, as they are often called, are calculated as follows:[7]

$$k_t = \frac{P_t}{P_{t-1}} - 1 \qquad (6\text{-}4)$$

where k_t = the holding period return in month t for a particular firm such as PepsiCo or for a market portfolio such as the S&P Index.

P_t = a firm's stock price such as PepsiCo (or the S&P Index) at the end of month t.

Holding-period return

The return an investor would receive from holding a security for a designated period of time. For example, a monthly holding-period return would be the return for holding a security for a month.

---

[5]A number of studies have noted that portfolios consisting of approximately 20 randomly selected common stocks have virtually no company-unique or diversifiable risk. See Robert C. Klemkosky and John D. Martin, "The Effect of Market Risk on Portfolio Diversification," *Journal of Finance* (March 1975):147–54.

[6]The New York Stock Exchange Index is an index that reflects the performance of all stocks listed on the New York Stock Exchange. The Standard and Poor (S&P) 500 Index is similarly an index that measures the combined performance of the companies that constitute the largest 500 companies in the United States, as designated by Standard and Poor.

[7]For simplicity's sake, we are ignoring the dividend that the investor receives from the stock as part of the total return. In other words, letting D_t equal the dividend received by the investor in month t, the holding period return would more accurately be measured as:

$$k_1 = \frac{P_t + D_t}{P_{t-1}} - 1$$

Table 6.2 Monthly Holding Period Returns, PepsiCo and the S&P 500 Index
          January 1995–December 1996

Month and Year	PepsiCo		S&P 500 Index	
	Price	Return	Price	Return
1994				
December	$18.13		$459.27	
1995				
January	$18.44	1.72%	$470.42	2.43%
February	19.56	6.10%	487.39	3.61%
March	19.56	0.00%	500.71	2.73%
April	20.81	6.39%	514.71	2.80%
May	24.50	17.72%	533.40	3.63%
June	22.75	−7.14%	544.75	2.13%
July	23.44	3.02%	562.06	3.18%
August	22.63	−3.47%	561.66	−0.07%
September	25.50	12.71%	584.41	4.05%
October	26.31	3.18%	581.50	−0.50%
November	27.69	5.23%	605.37	4.10%
December	27.94	0.90%	615.96	1.75%
1996				
January	$29.81	6.71%	$636.02	3.26%
February	31.63	6.08%	640.43	0.69%
March	31.63	0.00%	645.50	0.79%
April	31.75	0.40%	654.17	1.34%
May	33.25	4.72%	669.12	2.29%
June	35.50	6.77%	670.63	0.23%
July	31.75	−10.56%	639.95	−4.57%
August	28.75	−9.45%	651.99	1.88%
September	28.25	−1.74%	687.31	5.42%
October	29.63	4.87%	705.27	2.61%
November	30.25	2.11%	757.02	7.34%
December	29.25	−3.31%	740.74	−2.15%
Average monthly return		2.21%		2.04%
Standard deviation		6.40%		3.21%

For instance, the holding-period return for PepsiCo and the S&P Index for December 1995 is computed as follows:

$$\text{PepsiCo return} = \frac{\text{stock price end of December 95}}{\text{stock price end of November 95}} - 1$$

$$= \frac{\$27.94}{\$27.69} - 1 = .00903 = 0.9\%$$

$$\text{S\&P 500 Index return} = \frac{\text{index value end of December 95}}{\text{index value end of November 95}} - 1$$

$$= \frac{\$615.96}{\$605.37} - 1 = .01749 = 1.75\%$$

At the bottom of Table 6.2, we have also computed the averages of the returns for the 24 months, both for PepsiCo and for the S&P 500, and the standard deviation for these returns. Because we are using historical return data, we assume each observation has an

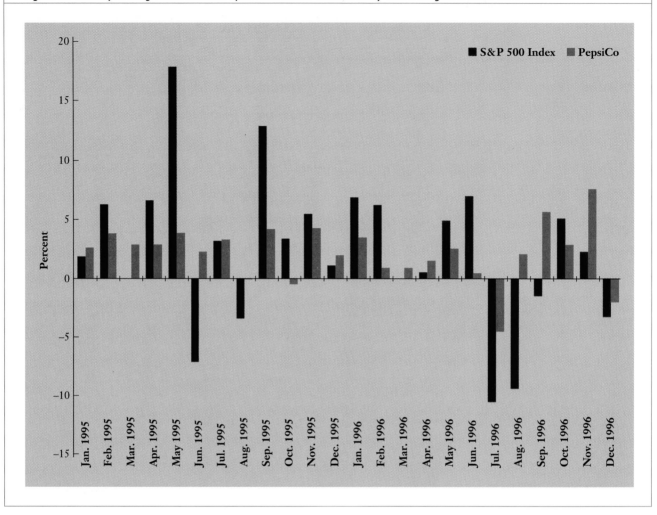

Figure 6.3 Monthly Holding-Period Returns: PepsiCo and the S&P Index, January 1995 through December 1996

equal probability of occurrence. Thus the average return, $\bar{k}$, is found by summing the returns and dividing by the number of months; that is,

$$\text{average return} = \frac{\sum_{t=1}^{n} \text{return in month } t}{\text{number of months}} = \frac{\sum_{t=1}^{n}(k_t)}{n} \qquad (6\text{-}5)$$

and the standard deviation is computed as:

$$\begin{aligned} \text{standard} \\ \text{deviation} \end{aligned} = \sqrt{\frac{\sum_{t=1}^{n} (\text{return in month } t - \text{average return})^2}{\text{number of months} - 1}} \qquad (6\text{-}6)$$

$$= \sqrt{\frac{\sum_{t=1}^{n} (k_t - \bar{k})^2}{n - 1}}$$

Morgan Stanley Develops Way to Measure Mutual-Fund Risk

By 1997, the stock market had been on a seven-year roll of increasing prices. Many investors had not been in the market long enough to have experienced a real downturn. Believing that investors had become so focused on the continuing high rates of return and had forgotten about risk, Morgan Stanley & Co. developed a way to help investors better understand how much risk they were incurring in their search for return.

Experience suggests that helping investors link risk to returns has two problems. First, it is hard to devise a risk-adjusted return that will be widely accepted. Second, it is hard to get investors to pay attention to risk.

As noted by one investment advisor, "For the past two years, nobody's enhanced the value of their portfolio by focusing on risk, even though at this stage in the market it might be prudent to do that."

Leah Modigliani, a stock strategist at Morgan Stanley, who helped design the approach, says that her firm's new risk-adjusted return will help investors decide whether they are being paid enough for the risk they are taking. To measure that risk-adjusted return, Morgan Stanley adjusts a fund's portfolio until the volatility exactly equals that of a benchmark like the Standard & Poor's 500 Index. To illustrate, consider that Fidelity's giant Magellan Fund posted an average annual total return of 16.2 percent over a 10-year period, beating the S&P 500 return of 15.2 percent. But its risk-adjusted return, as calculated by Morgan Stanley, was 14.9 percent, meaning Magellan's holders earned less for the risk they took than did an investor who had invested in the stocks comprising the Standard & Poor's 500 Index.

Morgan Stanley's efforts to develop a rate of return that is risk adjusted—that is, it allows us to compare investments with different amounts of risk—suggests that an investor cannot speak about a return without also talking about the accompanying riskiness of the investment. *They go together like a horse and carriage.* The same thing could be said for financial managers who have to compare the expected rates of returns of projects that have different levels of risk. In later chapters, we will see how this might be done in business.

In looking at Table 6.2 and Figure 6.3, we notice the following things about PepsiCo's holding-period returns over the 2 years ending in December 1996, these being:

1. PepsiCo's stockholders have had slightly higher average monthly returns than the average stock in the S&P 500 Index, 2.21 percent compared to 2.04 percent. That's the good news.
2. The bad news is PepsiCo's greater volatility of returns—in other words, greater risk—as evidenced by PepsiCo's higher standard deviation. As shown at the bottom of Table 6.2, the standard deviation of the returns is 6.40 percent for PepsiCo's versus 3.21 percent for the S&P 500 Index. PepsiCo's more volatile returns are also evident in Figure 6.3, where we see the PepsiCo's returns frequently being higher and lower than the corresponding S&P 500 returns.
3. We should also notice the tendency of PepsiCo's stock price to increase (decrease) when the value of the S&P 500 Index increases (decreases). In 20 of the 24 months, PepsiCo's returns were positive (negative) when the S&P 500 Index returns were positive (negative). That is, there is a positive, although not perfect, relationship between PepsiCo's stock returns and the S&P 500 Index returns.

Figure 6.4 Monthly Holding-Period Returns: PepsiCo and the S&P Index
January 1995–December 1996

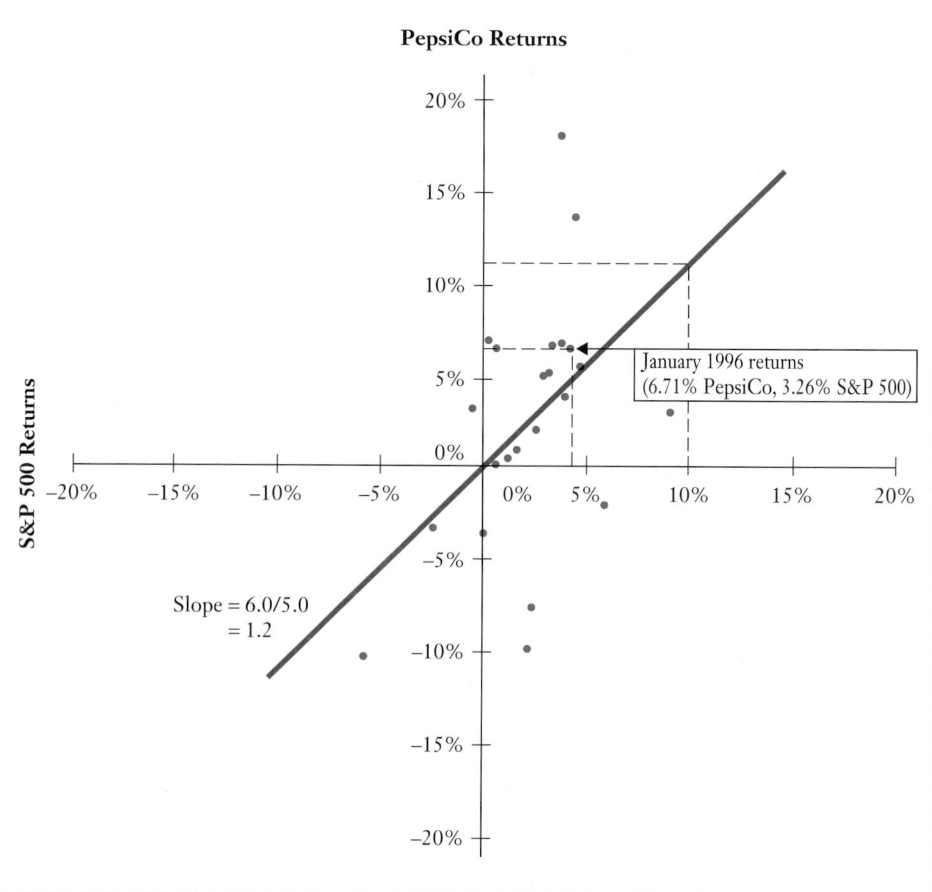

With respect to our third observation, that there is a relationship between the stock returns for PepsiCo's and the S&P 500 Index, it is helpful to see this relationship by graphing PepsiCo's returns against the S&P 500 Index returns. We provide such a graph in Figure 6.4. In the figure, we have plotted PepsiCo's returns on the vertical axis and the returns for the S&P 500 Index on the horizontal axis. Each of the 24 dots in the figure represent the returns for PepsiCo's and the S&P 500 Index for a particular month. For instance, the returns for January 1996 for PepsiCo's and the S&P 500 Index were 6.71 percent and 3.26 percent, respectively, which are noted in the figure.

In addition to the dots in the graph, we have drawn a line of "best fit," which we call the **characteristic line**. The slope of the characteristic line measures the average relationship between a stock's returns and those of the S&P 500 Index; or stated differently, the slope of the line indicates the average movement in a stock's price to a movement in the S&P 500 Index price. For PepsiCo's, the slope of the line is 1.2, which simply equals the rise of the line relative to the run of the line.[8] A slope of 1.2, as

Characteristic line

The line of "best fit" through a series of returns for a firm's stock relative to the market returns. The slope of the line, frequently called beta, represents the average movement of the firm's stock returns in response to a movement in the market's returns.

---

[8]Linear regression analysis is the statistical technique used to determine the slope of the line of best fit.

for PepsiCo., means that as the market return (S&P 500 Index returns) increases or decreases 1 percentage point, the return for McDonald's on average increases or decreases 1.2 percentage points.

We can also think of the 1.2 slope of the characteristic line as indicating that PepsiCo's returns are 1.2 times as volatile on average as those of the overall market (S&P 500 Index). This slope has come to be called **beta** in investor jargon, and measures the average relationship between a stock's returns and the market's returns. It is a term you will see almost anytime you read an article written by a financial analyst about the riskiness of a stock.

Looking once again at Figure 6.4, we see that the dots (returns) are scattered all about the characteristic line—most of the returns do not fit neatly on the characteristic line. That is, the average relationship may be 1.2, but the variation in PepsiCo's returns is only partly explained by the stock's average relationship with the S&P 500 Index. There are other driving forces unique to PepsiCo that also affect the firm's stock returns. (Earlier, we called this company-unique risk.) If we were, however, to diversify our holdings and own, say, 20 stocks with betas of 1.2, we could essentially eliminate the variation about the characteristic line. That is, we would remove almost all the volatility in returns, except for what is caused by the general market, which is represented by the slope of the line in Figure 6.4. If we plotted the returns of our 20-stock portfolio against the S&P 500 Index, the points in our new graph would fit nicely along a straight line with a slope of 1.2, which means that the beta of the portfolio is also 1.2. The new graph would look something like the one shown in

Beta

A measure of the relationship between an investment's returns and the market returns. This is a measure of the investment's nondiversifiable risk.

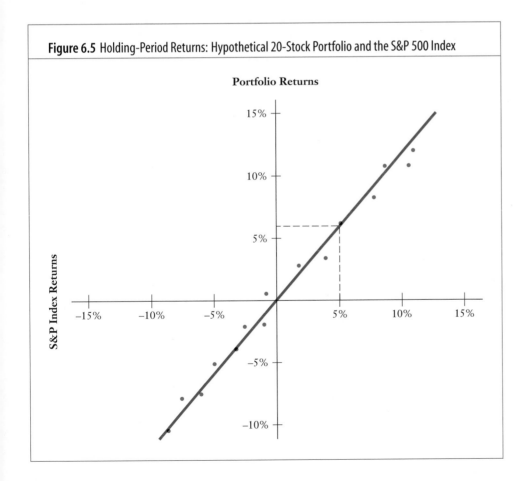

Figure 6.5 Holding-Period Returns: Hypothetical 20-Stock Portfolio and the S&P 500 Index

Figure 6.5. In other words, by diversifying our portfolio, we can essentially eliminate the variations about the characteristic line, leaving only the variation in returns for a company that comes from variations in the general market returns.

So beta—the slope of the characteristic line—is a measure of a firm's market risk or systematic risk, which is the risk that remains for a company even after we have diversified our portfolio. It is this risk—and only this risk—that matters for any investors who have broadly diversified portfolios.

We have said that beta is a measure of a stock's systematic risk, but how should we interpret a specific beta? For instance, when is a beta considered low and when is it considered high? In general, a stock with a beta of 0 has no systematic risk; a stock with a beta of 1 has systematic or market risk equal to the "typical" stock in the marketplace; and a stock with a beta exceeding 1 has more market risk than the typical stock. Most stocks, however, have betas between 0.60 and 1.60.

We should also realize that calculating beta is no exact science. The final estimate of a firm's beta is heavily dependent on one's methodology. For instance, it matters whether you use 24 months in your measurement or 60 months, as most professional investment companies do. Take our computation of PepsiCo's beta. We said PepsiCo's beta was 1.2 but Standard and Poor's and Value Line, two well-known investment services, have estimated PepsiCo's beta to be 1.24 and 1.00, respectively. The difference in results can be observed by comparing Standard and Poor's and Value Line's beta estimates for a number of firms as follows:

	S&P	Value Line
Ford Motor	0.65	1.10
McDonald's	0.84	0.95
IBM	1.25	1.10
Exxon	0.62	0.70
Nevada Power	0.14	0.70
Hershey Foods	0.58	0.90

Thus although close in many instances, even the professionals may not agree in their measurement of a given firm's beta.

To this point, we have talked about measuring an individual stock's beta. We will now consider how to measure the beta for a portfolio of stocks.

> **STOP AND THINK**
>
> *Remember that the slope of the characteristic line is called beta and it is a measure of a stock's systematic or market risk. The slope of the characteristic line indicates the average response of a stock's returns to the change in the market as a whole. How an investor and a financial manager uses beta will be explained in the section that follows. We will see it again in chapter 12 when we explain how a firm computes its cost of capital.*

OBJECTIVE 5 ## Measuring a Portfolio's Beta

From Figure 6.4, we see that the stock price of PepsiCo moves 1.2 percent on average for a 1 percent change in the market. However, we also see a lot of fluctuation around this characteristic line. If we were to diversify our holdings and own 20 stocks with betas of about 1.2, like that of PepsiCo, we could essentially eliminate the variation around the line; that is, we would remove almost all the volatility in returns, except for what is caused by the general market, represented by the slope of the line. If we plotted the returns of our 20-stock portfolio against the S&P 500 Index, the points in our new graph would fit nicely along a straight line with a slope of 1.2. The new graph would look something like the one that was shown in Figure 6.5.

What if we were to diversify our portfolio, as we have just suggested, but instead of acquiring stocks with the same beta as PepsiCo (1.2), we buy eight stocks with betas of 1 and 12 stocks with betas of 1.5. What is the beta of our portfolio? As it works out, the **portfolio beta** is merely the average of the individual stock betas. Actually, the portfolio beta is a weighted average of the individual security's betas, the weights being equal to the proportion of the portfolio invested in each security. Thus the beta (β) of a portfolio consisting of n stocks is equal to:

Portfolio beta

The relationship between a portfolio's returns and the market returns. It is a measure of the portfolio's nondiversifiable risk.

$$\beta_{\text{portfolio}} = \sum_{j=1}^{n} (\text{percentage invested in stock } j) \times (\beta \text{ of stock } j) \qquad (6\text{-}7)$$

So, assuming we bought equal amounts of each stock in our new 20-stock portfolio, the beta would simply be 1.3, calculated as follows:

$$\beta_{\text{portfolio}} = \left(\frac{8}{20} \times 1.0\right) + \left(\frac{12}{20} \times 1.50\right)$$
$$= 1.3$$

Thus whenever the general market increases or decreases 1 percent, our new portfolio's returns would on average change 1.3 percent, which says that our new portfolio has more systematic or market risk than has the market as a whole.

We can conclude that the beta of a portfolio is determined by the betas of the individual stocks. If we have a portfolio consisting of stocks with low betas, then our portfolio will have a low beta. The reverse is true as well. Figure 6.6 presents these situations graphically.

Although portfolio betas tend to be stable, individual betas are not necessarily stable and not always particularly meaningful. A classic example of how individual stock betas can be misleading comes from Burton G. Malkiel's book *A Random Walk Down Wall Street*.[9] Malkiel describes how Meade Johnson (following its takeover by Bristol-Myers) had a negative beta in the 1960s. Apparently, Meade Johnson introduced a product called "Metrecal," a dietary supplement that Meade Johnson sold to consumers, who drank this instead of eating their normal lunches. In any case, the public loved it, and Meade Johnson's stock shot up in price just as the market sank into a deep slump. As the market rebounded in 1963 and 1964, the Metrecal fad died and Meade Johnson dropped in price, again moving in an opposite direction from the market. Later in the 1960s, just as the market began to drop, Meade Johnson reintroduced the exact same product, this time called "Nutrament," telling consumers to buy it and drink it in addition to their normal lunch to put on weight. Once again, Meade Johnson's stock price went up as the market went down. The result of all this was that Meade Johnson had a negative beta. Needless to say, it would be unfortunate if capital-budgeting decisions were made using Meade Johnson's beta as the yardstick by which they were measured. The point here is that betas for individual stocks are not always reliable. In fact, typically only about 30 percent of the variation in returns

---

[9]Burton Malkiel, *A Random Walk Down Wall Street*, 4th ed. (New York: W.W. Norton, 1996)

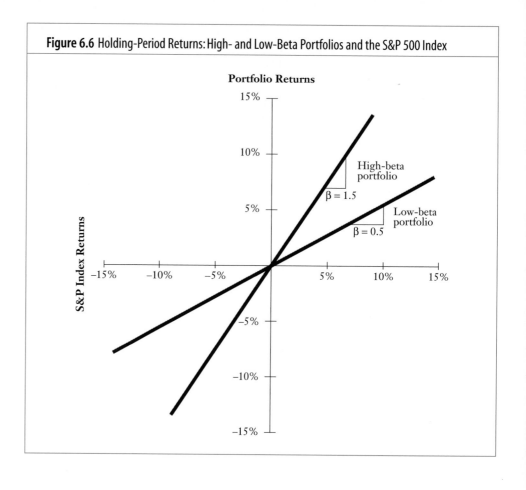

Figure 6.6 Holding-Period Returns: High- and Low-Beta Portfolios and the S&P 500 Index

of a stock can be statistically related (correlated) to the market portfolio, and sometimes as low as 5 percent.

In summary, beta is the underlying basis often used for measuring a security's or a portfolio's risk. It also proves useful to a financial manager when attempting to specify what the relationship should be between an investor's required rate of return and the stock's or portfolio's risk—market risk, that is. In other words, a financial manager can use beta to estimate an *appropriate* required rate of return for the firm's stockholders. The use of beta in this regard is the topic of the following section and will be seen again in later chapters.

OBJECTIVE 6 **THE INVESTOR'S REQUIRED RATE OF RETURN**

In this section, we examine the concept of the investor's required rate of return, especially as it relates to the riskiness of the asset, and then we see how the required rate of return is measured.

THE WALL STREET JOURNAL, JUNE 24, 1994

A Calmer Portfolio
Just Add a Little Risk

It is possible to reduce the riskiness of a portfolio of investments by adding other, riskier assets to our portfolio. The objective is to find other securities that, although risky when viewed alone, actually reduce the risk of our portfolio of investments because they move counter to the assets already contained in the portfolio. The following excerpts from *The Wall Street Journal* article address this possibility.

If you want to make your mutual fund portfolio more tranquil, try buying some risky funds.[a] Sound absurd? It's not at all, says Gerald Perritt, editor of the *Mutual Fund Letter*, a Chicago newsletter: "People look at a fund and say, 'how risky is it?' But it's not the risk of the individual fund that counts, but what the addition of that fund does to your overall portfolio."

Venturing into high-risk funds—such as those specializing in small-company, foreign, or natural-resource stock—is a way to spread your market bets. And that, in turn, lowers the risk that all your investments will sink at once. In the long run, such diversification tends not only to smooth returns, but also to boost them.

If you only buy low-risk funds, "you'll end up with a lot of large-company stocks," says John Rekenthaler, editor of *Morningstar Mutual Funds*, a newsletter published by Chicago's Morningstar Inc. "You're not going to get a very diversified portfolio."

To protect themselves against a protracted decline in large-company stocks, many investors salt away some of their money in bond or money-market funds. But that may cost them dearly over time by dragging down their long-term investment returns. A better strategy, say financial advisers, is to select the types of stock funds that tend to blaze a different path than the large-stock bellwethers.

Funds that hold shares of small companies, foreign firms or natural-resource producers fit that bill. But these funds also are prone to wild swings in price. Paradoxically, when you combine these risky funds with large-company stock funds, they can have a marvelously soothing effect. How come? Such funds often provide offsetting gains when large-company stocks are tumbling, so including them in your mix will tend to damp the gyrations of your overall portfolio.

[a] A mutual fund invests in stocks and bonds on behalf of its investors. This approach allows smaller investors to own a part of a portfolio that is more diversified than if they invested directly in a given company, such as in Coca-Cola or Walmart.

SOURCE: Jonathan Clements, "For a Calmer Portfolio: Just Add a Little Risk," *The Wall Street Journal* (June 24, 1994): C1. Reprinted by permission of *The Wall Street Journal*, © 1994 by Dow Jones & Co., Inc. All Rights Reserved Worldwide.

The Required Rate of Return Concept

The **investor's required rate of return** can be defined as the minimum rate of return necessary to attract an investor to purchase or hold a security. This definition considers the investor's opportunity cost of making an investment; that is, if an investment is made, the investor must forgo the return available from the next best investment. This forgone return is the **opportunity cost of funds** and consequently is the investor's required rate of return. In other words, we invest with the intention of achieving a rate sufficient to warrant making the investment. The investment will be made only if the purchase price is low enough relative to expected future cash flows to provide a rate of return greater than or equal to our required rate of return. To help us better understand the nature of an investor's required rate of return, we can separate the return into its basic components: the *risk-free rate of return* plus a *risk premium*. Expressed as an equation:

$$k = k_{rf} + k_{rp} \tag{6-8}$$

where k = the investor's required rate of return
$\quad k_{rf}$ = the risk-free return
$\quad k_{rp}$ = the risk premium

As noted in chapter 2, the **risk-free rate of return**, k_{rf}, rewards us for deferring consumption, and not for assuming risk; that is, the risk-free return reflects the basic fact that we invest today so that we can consume more later. By itself, the risk-free rate should be used only as the required rate of return, or discount rate, for *riskless* investments. Typically, our measure for the risk-free rate is the rate of return on a U.S. government security.

The **risk premium**, k_{rp}, is the additional return we expect to receive for assuming risk.[10] As the level of risk increases, we will demand additional expected returns. Even though we may or may not actually receive this incremental return, we must have reason to expect it; otherwise, why expose ourselves to the chance of losing all or part of our money?

EXAMPLE

To demonstrate the required rate of return concept, let us take Southwestern Bell, which has bonds that mature in 2007. Based on the market price of these bonds at year end 1996, we can determine that investors were expecting a 7 percent return. The 90-day Treasury bill rate at that time was about 5 percent, which means that Southwestern Bell bondholders were requiring a risk premium of 2 percent. Stated as an equation, we have

$$\text{required rate } (k) = \text{risk-free rate } (k_{rf}) + \text{risk premium } (k_{rp})$$
$$= 5\% \qquad\qquad + 2\%$$
$$= 7\%$$

Measuring the Required Rate of Return

We have seen that (1) systematic risk is the only relevant risk—the rest can be diversified away, and (2) the required rate of return, k, equals the risk-free rate, k_{rf}, plus a risk premium, k_{rp}. We can now put these elements together to estimate required

---

[10]The risk premium here can be thought of as a composite of a "default risk premium" (reflected in the difference in the bond's rate of return and the rate on a similar maturity government bond) and "term structure" premium (reflected in the difference in the 90-day Treasury bill rate and the long-term government bond rate).

rates of return. Looking at equation (6-8), the really tough task is how to estimate the risk premium.

The finance profession has had difficulty in developing a practical approach to measure the investor's required rates of return; however, financial managers often use a method called the **capital asset pricing model (CAPM)**. The capital asset pricing model is an equation that equates the expected rate of return on a stock to the risk-free rate plus a risk premium for the stock's systematic risk. Although not without its critics, the CAPM provides an intuitive approach for thinking about the return that an investor should require on an investment, given the asset's systematic or market risk.

Equation (6-8), as shown on the opposite page, provides the natural starting point for measuring the investor's required rate of return and sets us up to use the CAPM. Rearranging this equation to solve for the risk premium (k_{rp}), we have

$$k_{rp} = k - k_{rf} \qquad (6\text{-}9)$$

which simply says that the risk premium for a security, k_{rp}, equals the security's expected return, k, less the risk-free rate existing in the market, k_{rf}. For example, if the expected return for a security is 15 percent and the risk-free rate is 5 percent, the risk premium is 10 percent. Also, if the expected return for the market, k_m, is 13 percent, and the risk-free rate, k_{rf}, is 5 percent, the risk premium, k_{rp}, for the general market would be 8 percent. This 8 percent risk premium would apply to any security having systematic (nondiversifiable) risk equivalent to the general market, or a beta of 1.

In the same market, a security with a beta of 2 should provide a risk premium of 16 percent, or twice the 8 percent risk premium existing for the market as a whole. Hence in general, the appropriate required rate of return for the jth security, k_j, should be determined by

$$k_j = k_{rf} + \beta_j(k_m - k_{rf}) \qquad (6\text{-}10)$$

Equation (6-10) is the CAPM. This equation designates the risk-return trade-off existing in the market, where risk is defined in terms of beta. Figure 6.7 graphs the

Capital asset pricing model (CAPM)

An equation stating that the expected rate of return on a project is a function of (1) the risk-free rate, (2) the investment's systematic risk, and (3) the expected risk premium for the market portfolio of all risky securities.

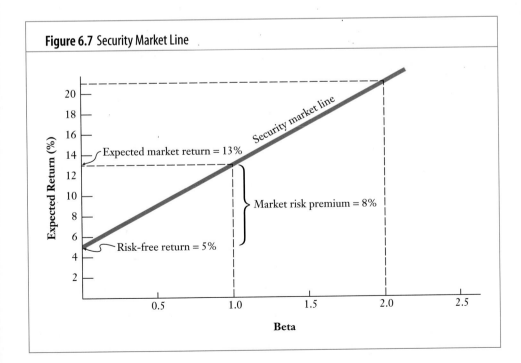

Figure 6.7 Security Market Line

Security market line

The return line that reflects the attitudes of investors regarding the minimal acceptable return for a given level of systematic risk.

CAPM as the **security market line**.[11] As presented in this figure, securities with betas equal to 0, 1, and 2 should have required rates of return as follows:

$$If\ \beta_j = 0:\ k_j = 5\% + 0(13\% - 5\%) = 5\%$$
$$If\ \beta_j = 1:\ k_j = 5\% + 1(13\% - 5\%) = 13\%$$
$$If\ \beta_j = 2:\ k_j = 5\% + 2(13\% - 5\%) = 21\%$$

where the risk-free rate, k_{rf}, is 5 percent and the expected market return, k_m, is 13 percent.[12]

EXAMPLE

To illustrate the use of beta in estimating a fair rate of return for a given stock, consider IBM. Standard and Poor's estimates IBM's beta to be 1.25. We will see later in the chapter that the risk premium for large company stocks (return on large company stocks less a risk-free rate) has been about 9 percent over the last seven decades. The risk-free rate of return (U.S. Treasury bill) in early 1997 was about 5 percent. Thus an investor should expect a 16.25 percent rate of return from investing in IBM, computed as follows:

$$k_{ibm} = k_{rf} + \beta_{ibm} (k_m - k_{rf})$$
$$= 5\% + 1.25\ (9\%)$$
$$= 5\% + 11.25\% = 16.25\%$$

The previous explanations rely on the capital asset pricing model (CAPM)—and beta—as our standard bearer for estimating a stock's market risk and the rate of return that we should expect for a given beta. However, not everyone is happy with this approach, as discussed in the next section.

STOP AND THINK

*The conclusion of the matter is that **Axiom 1** is alive and well. It tells us, **We Won't Take on Additional Risk Unless We Expect to Be Compensated with Additional Return**. That is, there is a risk-return trade-off in the market.*

OBJECTIVE 7

THE FAMA AND FRENCH ATTACK ON THE CAPM

The primary implication of the capital asset pricing model (CAPM) is that higher returns accrue to securities which have higher levels of nondiversifiable or systematic risk (measured by the security's beta coefficient). However, recent evidence by Fama and French

---

[11]Two key assumptions are made in using the security market line. First, we assume that the marketplace where securities are bought and sold is highly efficient. Market efficiency indicates that the price of an asset responds quickly to new information, thereby suggesting that the price of a security reflects all available information. As a result, the current price of a security is considered to represent the best estimate of its future price. Second, the model assumes that a perfect market exists. A perfect market is one in which information is readily available to all investors at a nominal cost. Also, securities are assumed to be infinitely divisible, with any transaction costs incurred in purchasing or selling a security being negligible. Furthermore, investors are assumed to be single-period wealth maximizers who agree on the meaning and the significance of the available information. Finally, within the perfect market, all investors are *price takers*, which simply means that a single investor's actions cannot affect the price of a security. These assumptions are obviously not descriptive of reality. However, from the perspective of positive economics, the mark of a good theory is the accuracy of its predictions, not the validity of the simplifying assumptions that underlie its development.

[12]For a more in-depth explanation of the CAPM, see B. Rosenberg, "The Capital Asset Pricing Model and the Market Model," *Journal of Portfolio Management* (Winter 1981):5–16.

Value-at-Risk Management: A New Approach to Measuring Risk

In 1994, many financial institutions discovered that they had inadvertently "put all of their eggs in one basket." Although diversified among such assets as debt, commodities, and cash, they discovered that every asset class contained a built-in assumption that interest rates would decline. The results were devastating; billions of dollars were lost.

As a result of the lessons learned by their mistakes, a new risk-management technique called *value at risk* (VAR) was developed. The approach assesses the amount of risk inherent in a financial portfolio at any given time. For instance, it might be designed to estimate the amount of money (with a level of confidence of 95 percent) that could be lost in a given portfolio in the next 24 hours. The technique also assesses how risk exposures in different parts of a portfolio can either magnify each other or offset each other. Value-at-risk management determines for certain that the portfolio is truly diversified. It can also indicate when an investor is being unnecessarily cautious.

In 1994, VAR was used primarily by a small group of international banks and stock brokerage firms to manage risks incurred in buying and selling securities. However by 1997, VAR was being used for risks other than those arising from market movements; for instance, the model would evaluate the risk of default by another trader. Also, mutual-fund managers and even CFOs at nonfinancial companies, including Xerox, General Motors, and GTE, are finding VAR to be helpful. Enron, the largest wholesale marketer of natural gas and electricity in the United States, calculates its VAR every day.

The value-at-risk model is not perfect by any means. Similar to most mathematical models, it is typically based on historical patterns that may or may not be applicable in the future—especially in time of turmoil. So most firms complement the analysis by "stress-testing" a portfolio to evaluate how it would perform in various worst-case scenarios. But for all its imperfections, value-at-risk management is an approach to uncovering sources of risk that financial managers might otherwise not notice.

---

indicates that over the period 1963 to 1990, differences in beta do not explain differences in the performance (rates of returns) of stocks.[13]

To illustrate their finding, let's return to the previous example. There we used IBM's beta of 1.25 to suggest that the investor should earn a 16.25 percent rate of return on their investment. But in fact, IBM shareholders received a return of 22 percent for the year. So in this instance, CAPM was not accurate in estimating a shareholder's return. Fama and French found that, as a whole, CAPM is not particularly effective at forecasting a stock's rate of return. What they did find was that stock returns are much more related to firm size (the smaller the company, the higher the return) and to the ratio of a firm's accounting book value to its market value (book value ÷ market value), where the lower the ratio the lower the stock's return. From this evidence, they conclude that "beta is dead."

---

[13]Eugene Fama and Kenneth French, "The Cross-Section of Expected Stock Returns," *Journal of Finance* XLVII, No. 2 (June 1992), pp. 427–65.

The Defense of the CAPM

Two counter arguments have been offered in response to the Fama and French criticisms of CAPM and beta. First, some argue that Fama and French's research methodology was flawed; others contend that Fama and French's contentions are theoretically incomplete. The bottom line is that CAPM is not dead, but our faith in its ability to explain the world of risk and return has been shaken.

Two research studies have addressed the "empirical refinement" line of defense of the CAPM. Chan and Lakonishok look at a much longer series of returns than do Fama and French.[14] They evaluate the entire period 1926 to 1991 and found that for the period ended in 1982, higher betas were indeed associated with higher returns. However, for the period after 1982 they found again that beta and stock returns were unrelated. Furthermore, when they looked at the returns of the 10 worst and 10 best months in terms of the stock market's performance, they found that stocks with higher betas did worse in the worst months and better in the best months than their lower beta counterparts. Thus we have some limited evidence supporting the basic CAPM prediction that higher betas are associated with higher stock returns.

The second empirical study is by Kothari, Shankin, and Sloan. These authors reexamined the issue as to whether beta explains variation in average returns over the post-1940 period as well as the longer post-1926 period.[15] They, like Fama and French before them, tested the notion that book-to-market value of the firm's equity captures the variation in average returns over a longer period, 1947 to 1987, using a somewhat different data set than that used by Fama and French. Two of their conclusions are as follows:

- They found a 6 percent risk premium in the sample of stocks used, compared to Fama and French's results indicating there was no risk premium relative to increasing systematic risk.
- Using a different sample of firms in their study, they found that book-to-market value was only weakly related to average stock returns, which sharply disagrees with Fama and French. Based upon this observation, they argue that the Fama-French results are limited to their sample of companies, and do not necessarily apply to a broader sample of companies.

The theoretical argument against the Fama and French allegations was offered by Roll and Ross.[16] They argue that using an index, such as the S&P 500 Index or the New York Stock Exchange Index, to calculate the market returns may not accurately reflect the returns of the true market portfolio. Because the market portfolio proxy used by Fama and French may not be the correct one, there is no reason to believe that the betas and rates of return should be positively related.[17] Thus the Fama and French results may either be the result of using an incorrect market portfolio proxy or due to a failure of the model to explain any relationship between risk and return. We cannot tell which.

Weighing the Evidence

So what are we to conclude? Is beta dead? At the very least, this latest salvo of criticism has forced the academic community to again come to grips with the fundamental shortcomings of the CAPM. The model, like all models which attempt to explain complex real

---

[14]Louis Chan and Josef Lakonishok, "Are the Reports of Beta's Death Premature?" University of Illinois working paper (December 1992).

[15]S. P. Kothari, J. Shankin, and R. Sloan, "Another Look at the Cross-Section of Expected Stock Returns," *Journal of Finance* L, No.1 (March 1995).

[16]Richard Roll and Stephen A. Ross, "On the Cross-Sectional Relation Between Expected Returns and Betas," UCLA working paper (July 8, 1992).

[17]Technically, Roll and Ross noted that where the correct market portfolio is used, beta and expected returns are exactly linear and positively related. Where the market portfolio is even slightly inefficient, this positive relation no longer holds.

world phenomena using simplifying assumptions, is an abstraction and does not completely and perfectly "fit the facts" as to the way the world works. Does this mean that the model lacks usefulness? We think not. The model points toward the need to diversify and identifies the source of the market risk premium as being tied to the risk of the security which cannot be diversified away. Is the model a complete guide to the underlying determinants of risk premiums? Probably not—we know that insolvency risk is ignored by the CAPM and this risk is a significant fact of life in the way investors evaluate and value securities. So just how useful is the model? We are reminded by the Fama and French results that the CAPM is, at best, only a rough approximation to the relationship between risk and return. Thus we are reminded to treat beta estimates and corresponding market risk premium estimates with great care.

The attacks and counterattacks on the effectiveness of the CAPM will, we believe, continue until a more appealing theory comes along that better explains the relationship between risk and returns. In fact, to this point, only one alternative theory has been offered as a substitute, or as a possible complement, for the CAPM. This newer theory, the **arbitrage pricing model** (**APM**) considers multiple economic factors when explaining required rates of return, rather than looking at systematic risk or general market returns as a single determinant of an investor's required rate of return.[18] Despite having some desirable features and potential, the arbitrage pricing model has yet to be put to widespread use. We have, nevertheless, provided a brief treatment of the model in appendix 6A.

Whatever method is used to assess an appropriate required rate of return for an investment, one key point remains. To formulate a complete concept or understanding of security valuation, a financial manager must understand the nature of the investor's required rate of return. The required rate of return, which serves as the discount rate in the valuation process, is the investor's minimum acceptable return that would induce him or her to purchase or hold a security. It is also used by the financial manager to value investment projects, as discussed in chapters 9 and 10. Thus despite the problems with establishing a link between risk and return, the financial manager is given no choice but to make a good faith effort to recognize and adapt to the risk-return relationship.

Arbitrage-pricing model (APM)

An alternative theory to the capital asset pricing model for relating stock returns and risk. The theory maintains that security returns vary from their expected amounts when there are unanticipated changes in basic economic forces.

THE INVESTOR'S EXPERIENCE IN THE CAPITAL MARKETS

OBJECTIVE 8

In explaining risk and rates of return, we have generally used hypothetical examples; however, we can add a great deal to our understanding by looking at the rates of returns that have been earned by investors and the riskiness of these returns. In other words, it is one thing to talk about the theory but another to see if the theory is consistent with the real world. Let's have a reality check by answering the following three questions based on available evidence about risk and rates of return:

1. What has been the historical relationship between risk and rates of return for different types of investments?
2. What have investors been able to accomplish through diversification?
3. How much risk could have been avoided if we had invested for a longer time period? That is, was risk, as measured by the volatility of returns, the same if we held our investment for 5 years versus 1 year?

These questions are important from a managerial perspective, but also for anyone thinking about making investments in the capital markets—the market where bonds and stocks are

---

[18]A description of the APM is found in Dorothy H. Bower, Richard S. Bower, and Dennis E. Logue, "A Primer on Arbitrage Pricing Theory," in Joel M. Stern and Donald H. Chew, Jr., eds., *The Revolution in Corporate Finance* (New York: Basil Blackwell, 1986): 69–77.

bought and sold. As managers, we need to understand the investor's opportunity cost of investing; that is, what could an investor earn by investing in another company of similar risk? Only by answering this question can a financial manager begin to understand whether the shareholders are receiving a fair return on their investments. Also, from an investor's perspective, there is a need to know the historical experience of other investors in the capital markets; otherwise, there is no basis for knowing what can be reasonably expected in terms of rates of returns.

The Relationship Between Risk and Rates of Return

The information used to answer the above questions comes primarily from Ibbotson Associates, a research company that has compiled data about rates of return all the way back to 1926. Their data are comprehensive and extremely useful both to investors and financial managers in their respective needs for understanding rates of returns in the capital markets. In their results, they summarize, among other things, the annual returns for different portfolios of securities, five of them being:[19]

1. Common stocks of small firms
2. Common stocks of large companies
3. Long-term corporate bonds
4. Long-term U.S. government bonds
5. U.S. Treasury bills

Before comparing the actual rates of returns and their variability (risk), we should first think about what to expect. First, we would intuitively expect a Treasury bill to be the least risky of the five portfolios. Because a Treasury bill has a short-term maturity date, the price is less volatile (less risky) than the price of a long-term government security.[20] In turn, because there is a chance of default on a corporate bond, which is essentially nonexistent for government securities, a long-term government bond is less risky than a long-term corporate bond. Finally, common stock of large companies is more risky than a corporate bond, with small-company stocks being more risky than the portfolio of large-firm stocks.

By smaller firm, we do not mean the "mom-and-pop" store down on the corner, but rather the smallest companies listed on the New York Stock Exchange (the bottom 20 percent, to be exact). It is believed that these smaller companies are more risky than the really large firms. Why might that be? First, smaller businesses experience greater risk in their operations—they are more sensitive to business downturns and some operate in niche markets which can quickly appear and then quickly disappear. Second, they rely more heavily on debt financing than larger firms. These differences create more variability in their profits and cash flows, which translates into greater risk.

With the forgoing in mind, we should expect different rates of return to the holders of these varied securities. If the market rewards an investor for assuming risk, the average annual rates of return should increase as risk increases.

A comparison of the annual rates of return for the five portfolios listed above for the years 1926 to 1996 is provided in Figure 6.8. Four attributes of these returns are included: (1) the *nominal* average annual rate of return; (2) the standard deviation of the returns, which measures the volatility or riskiness of the portfolios; (3) the *real* average annual rate of return, which is the nominal return less the inflation rate; and (4) the risk premium, which represents the additional return received beyond the risk-free rate (Treasury bill rate) for assuming risk. Also, a frequency distribution of returns is provided to give us a visual sense of the variability of the returns.

---

[19]Roger G. Ibbotson and Rex A. Sinquefield, *Stocks, Bonds, Bills, and Inflation: Historical Return* (1926–1996) (Chicago, IL: Dow Jones-Irwin, 1997).

[20]For an explanation of the greater volatility for long-term bonds relative to short-term bonds, see chapter 7.

Figure 6.8 Annual Rates of Return 1926–1996

Securities	Nominal Average Annual Returns	Standard Deviation of Returns	Real Average Annual Returns[a]	Risk Premium[b]	Frequency Distributions of Returns
Small Company Stocks	17.7%	34.1%	14.5%	13.9%	
Large Company Stocks	12.7	20.3	9.5	8.9	
Long-Term Corporate Bonds	6.0	8.7	2.8	2.2	
Long-Term Government Bonds	5.4	9.2	2.2	1.6	
U.S. Treasury Bills	3.8	3.3	0.6	0	

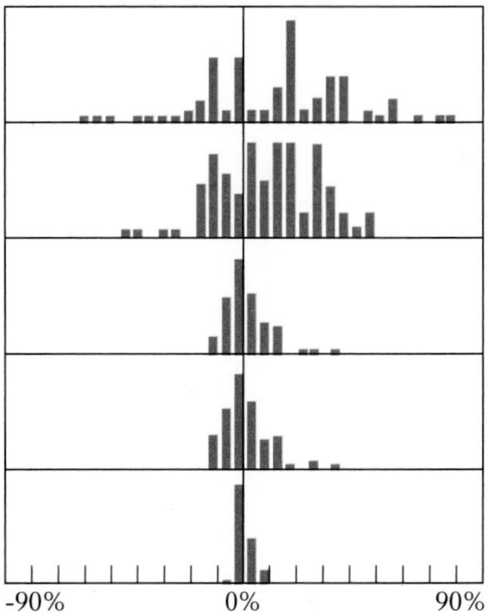

-90%   0%   90%

[a]Real return equals the nominal return less the average inflation rate from 1926 through 1996 of 3.2 percent.
[b]Risk premium equals the nominal security return less the average risk-free rate (Treasury bills) of 3.7 percent.

SOURCE: R. G. Ibbotson and R. A. Sinquefield, *Stocks, Bonds, Bills, and Inflation: Historical Returns* (Chicago: Ibbotson Associates, 1997): 33.
© Ibbotson Associates.

Looking first at the two columns of average annual returns and standard deviations, we gain an overview of the risk-return relationships that have existed over the 70 years ending in 1996. For the most part, there has been a positive relationship between risk and return, with Treasury bills being the least risky and common stocks of small companies being the most risky.

The return information in Figure 6.8 demonstrates that common stock has been the investor's primary inflation hedge in the long run—the average inflation rate has been 3.2 percent—and offered the highest risk premium. However, it is equally apparent that the common stockholder is exposed to sizable risk, as demonstrated by a 20.3 percent standard deviation for large-company stocks and a 34.1 percent standard deviation for small-company stocks. In fact, in the 1926 to 1996 time frame, large-common share-holders received negative returns in 20 of the 70 years, compared with only one in 70 for Treasury bills.

Risk and Diversification[21]

We now want to know what we could have accomplished from diversifying across different portfolios. Here again, we can draw on Ibbotson Associates for our answer. To demonstrate the effect of diversification on risk and rates of return, compare three portfolios (A, B, and C) consisting of the following investments:

---

[21]This presentation is based on material developed by Ibbotson Associates. Copyright 1994.

Types of securities	Investment Mix in Portfolio:		
	A	B	C
Short-term government securities (Treasury bills)	0%	63%	34%
Long-term government bonds	100%	12%	14%
Large-company stocks	0%	25%	52%
	100%	100%	100%

Figure 6.9 shows the average returns and standard deviations of the three portfolios. The results show that an investor can use diversification to improve the risk-return characteristics of a portfolio. Specifically, we see that:

1. Portfolio A, which consists entirely of long-term government bonds, had an average annual return of 5.5 percent with a standard deviation of 11.3 percent.[22]
2. In Portfolio B, we have diversified across all three security types, with the majority of the funds (63 percent) now invested in Treasury bills and a lesser amount (25 percent) in stocks. The effects are readily apparent. The average returns of the two portfolios, A and B, are identical, but the risk associated with Portfolio B is almost half that of Portfolio A—standard deviation of 6.1 percent for Portfolio B compared to 11.3 percent for Portfolio A. Notice that risk has been reduced in Portfolio B even though stocks, a far more risky security, have been included in the portfolio. How could this be? Simple: Stocks behave differently than both government bonds and Treasury bills, with the effect being a less risky (lower standard deviation) portfolio.

Figure 6.9 The Effect of Diversification on Average Returns and Risk

Portfolio		Average Annual Return	Risk (Standard Deviation)
A	100% Long-term government bonds	5.5%	11.3%
B	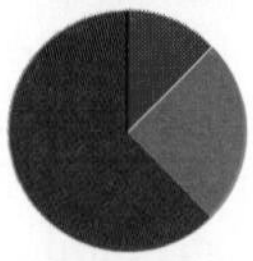 25% Large company stocks 12% Long-term government bonds 63% Treasury bills	5.5%	6.1%
C	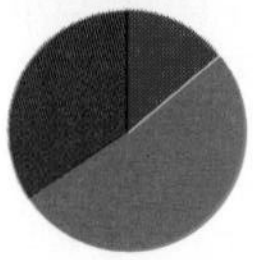 52% Large company stocks 14% Long-term government bonds 34% Treasury bills	8.0%	11.3%

■ Large company stocks ■ Long-term government bonds ■ Treasury bills

NOTE: Adapted from Ibbotson Associates, Copyright 1994, Chicago, Illinois.

---

[22]In this example, Ibbotson Associates use 1970–1993 data to compute the standard deviation for the long-term government bonds; all other computations use the total 1926–1993 time frame.

The Investor and Asset Allocation

As suggested in this chapter, how an investor allocates his or her assets is important in terms of the resulting returns and the variability of these returns over time. As we have also noted, stocks are more volatile in their returns than bonds or Treasury bills. The importance of this issue for investors was captured in an article appearing in *The Wall Street Journal*. Some of the author's ideas follow.

Amid the recent market turmoil, maybe you are wondering whether you really have the right mix of investments. Here are a few thoughts to keep in mind:

Taking Stock

If you are a bond investor who is petrified of stocks, the wild price swings of the past few weeks have probably confirmed all your worst suspicions. But the truth is, adding stocks to your bond portfolio could bolster your returns, without boosting your portfolio's overall gyrations.

How can that be? While stocks and bonds often move up and down in tandem, this isn't always the case, and sometimes stocks rise when bonds are tumbling. That happened in this year's [1996] first six months, when U.S. stock-mutual funds soared 10.8% while taxable bonds slipped 0.3%, according to Lipper Analytical Services.

Indeed, Chicago researchers Ibbotson Associates figures a portfolio that's 100% in longer-term government bonds has the same risk profile as a mix that includes 83% in longer-term government bonds and 17% in the blue chip stocks that constitute Standard & Poor's 500 stock index.

But while the risk level is similar, the bond-stock mix had better returns over the past 25 years, gaining 10.2% a year, compared with 9.6% for longer-term government bonds alone. The bottom line? Everybody should own some stocks. Even cowards.

Same Great Taste, Even More Filling

All right, you will buy a few stocks. But you are sticking strictly to the blue chips. A good move?

Here's another fun fact from Ibbotson Associates.

The Chicago firm calculates that a portfolio that's 100% in the S&P 500 is about as risky as a mix that includes 73% S&P 500, 6% smaller company stocks and 21% foreign stocks. But the globally diverse portfolio was more rewarding over the past 25 years, climbing 12.9% a year, compared with 12.2% for the S&P 500. If you're going to own stocks, it clearly pays to diversify.

SOURCE: Jonathan Clements, "The Right Mix: Fine-Tuning a Portfolio to Make Money and Sleep Soundly," *The Wall Street Journal*, (July 23, 1996): Cl. Reprinted by permission of *The Wall Street Journal*, © 1996 by Dow Jones & Co., Inc. All Rights Reserved Worldwide.

3. Portfolio B demonstrated how an investor can reduce risk while keeping returns constant, and Portfolio C, with its increased investment in stocks (52 percent), shows how an investor can increase average returns while keeping risk constant. This portfolio has a risk level identical to that of long-term government bonds alone (Portfolio A), but achieves a higher average return of 8 percent, compared to 5.5 percent for the government bond portfolio.

The conclusion to be drawn from this example is clear: The market rewards diversification. By diversifying our investments, we can indeed lower risk without sacrificing expected return, or we can increase expected return without having to assume more risk.

The preceding example gives us real-world evidence as to the merits of diversification; however, a clarification is in order. Note that the diversification in the above example is across different asset types—Treasury bills versus long-term government bonds versus

Asset allocation

Identifying and selecting the asset classes appropriate for a specific investment portfolio and determining the proportions of these assets within the given portfolio.

common stocks. Diversifying among different kinds of assets—such as stocks, bonds, and real estate—is called **asset allocation**, as compared to diversification within the different asset classes—such as investing only in PepsiCo, National Semiconductor, and American Airlines. The benefit we receive from diversifying is far greater through effective asset allocation than through merely selecting individual securities (e.g., stocks) to include within an asset category. For instance, Brinson, Singer, and Beebower studied quarterly data from 82 large U.S. pension funds over the period 1977 to 1987.[23] They found that the asset allocation decision accounted for over 91 percent of the differences among the returns of pension funds. Deciding what specific securities to hold accounted for only 4.6 percent of the variation in the different pension returns.[24]

Risk and Being Patient

As clearly shown by Ibbotson Associates, investors are rewarded for assuming risk. Then why would we not always invest in common stocks, especially of smaller companies, rather than in bonds? The answer relates to the length of time the investor is willing and able to wait for the returns. An investor in common stocks must often wait longer to earn the higher returns than those provided by bonds—maybe as long as 20 years.

To demonstrate this phenomenon, the Vanguard Group, a mutual fund company, compared the rates of return you would have earned on the S&P 500 stocks for different holding periods, such as 1 year or 5 years. The time frame of their study included the years from 1950 through 1980. The results of their study, summarized in Figure 6.10, are quite interesting.

Looking at individual years, the *annual* returns for the S&P 500 stocks from 1950 through 1980 averaged 11.4 percent, but were as high as 52.3 percent in 1 year and as low as −26.3 percent in another year. If, however, we invested for 5 years, say for 1951 through 1956, 1952 through 1957, and so on, our annual return would have varied between −2.4 percent and 20.1 percent, a nice reduction in variability. But if we really want to reduce the variability, we should invest for 15, 20, or 25 years—a long time, but not much of a problem for people in their twenties or thirties.

In conclusion, the capital markets reward us not just for diversifying our investments, but also for being patient investors. That is, the returns tend to converge toward the average as we lengthen our holding period, a principle our statistics professor told us about and called it the central tendency theorem. Now we see it in real life in the capital markets.

HOW FINANCIAL MANAGERS USE THIS MATERIAL

We have now completed our study of risk, and most importantly, how rates of return for investments are explicitly tied to risk. The greater the risk, the greater the required rate of return needed to attract investors. This concept, although presented at this point mostly from an investor's perspective, holds equally well for a financial manager considering an investment to develop a new product line. Thus this chapter will serve as the basis for much that we do in later chapters when it comes to evaluating investment decisions. However, because any investment decision made by a firm should be linked to the goal of enhancing shareholder value, we will next study the concepts and procedures for valuing bonds and stocks.

[23]Gary P. Brinson, Brian D. Singer, and Gilbert L. Beebower, "Determinants of Portfolio Performance," *Financial Analysts Journal* (May–June 1991).

[24]It is also interesting to know that Brinson, Singer, and Beebower found that timing investments explained a meager 1.8 percent of the variation in pension fund returns. That is, none of the investors of these pension funds were any better than their peers at timing market movements when making investments.

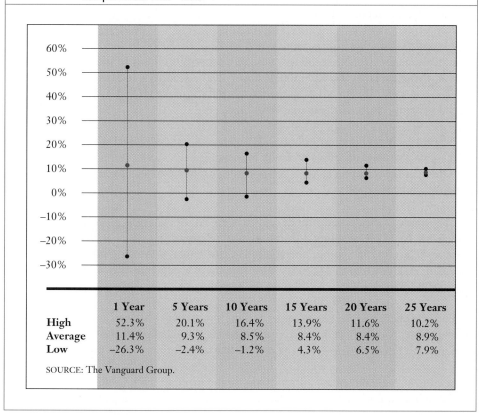

Figure 6.10 Average and Range of Returns by Length of Holding Period
Sample Period 1950–1980

	1 Year	5 Years	10 Years	15 Years	20 Years	25 Years
High	52.3%	20.1%	16.4%	13.9%	11.6%	10.2%
Average	11.4%	9.3%	8.5%	8.4%	8.4%	8.9%
Low	−26.3%	−2.4%	−1.2%	4.3%	6.5%	7.9%

SOURCE: The Vanguard Group.

SUMMARY

In chapter 2, we referred to the discount rate as the interest rate or the opportunity cost of funds. At that point, we considered a number of important factors that influence interest rates, including the price of time, expected or anticipated inflation, the risk premium related to maturity (liquidity) and variability of future returns.

In this chapter, we returned to our study of rates of return, and looked carefully at the relationship between risk and rates of returns.

In a world of uncertainty, we cannot make forecasts with certainty. Thus we must speak in terms of *expected* events. The expected return on an investment may therefore be stated as the arithmetic mean or average of all possible outcomes where those outcomes are weighted by the probability that each will occur.

Risk, for our purposes, is the prospect of an unfavorable outcome and may be measured by the standard deviation.

OBJECTIVE 1

OBJECTIVE 2

 **OBJECTIVE 3**

We have made an important distinction between nondiversifiable risk and diversifiable risk. We concluded that the only relevant risk given the opportunity to diversify our portfolio is a security's nondiversifiable risk, which we called by two other names: systematic risk and market risk.

 **OBJECTIVE 4**

A security's market risk is represented by beta, the slope of the characteristic line. Beta measures the average responsiveness of a security's returns to the movement of the general market, such as the S&P 500. If beta is 1, the security's returns move 1-to-1 with the market returns; if beta is 1.5, the security's returns move up and down 1.5 percent for every 1 percent change in the market's returns.

 **OBJECTIVE 5**

A portfolio's beta is simply a weighted average of the individual stock's betas, where the weights are the percentage of funds invested in each stock. The portfolio beta measures the average responsiveness of the portfolio's returns to the movement of the general market, such as the S&P 500.

 **OBJECTIVE 6**

The capital asset pricing model, even with its weaknesses, provides an intuitive framework for understanding the risk-return relationship. The CAPM suggests that investors determine an appropriate required rate of return, depending upon the amount of systematic risk inherent in a security. This minimum acceptable rate of return is equal to the risk-free rate plus a return premium for assuming risk.

 **OBJECTIVE 7**

For several years, the capital asset pricing model (CAPM) was touted as the "new investment technology" and received the blessings of the vast majority of professional investors and finance professors. The model, like any abstract theory, creates some unresolved issues. For example, we might question whether the risk of an asset can be totally captured in a single dimension of sensitivity to the market, as the CAPM proposes. Fama and French, two financial economists, argue that they have developed evidence that the CAPM does not explain why stock returns differ. Thus beta, at least according to Fama and French, does not adequately explain the risk-return relationship in the markets.

 **OBJECTIVE 8**

Ibbotson Associates has provided us with annual rates of return earned on different types of security investments as far back as 1926. They summarize, among other things, the annual returns for five portfolios of securities made up of (1) common stocks of small firms, (2) common stocks of large companies, (3) long-term corporate bonds, (4) long-term U.S. government bonds, and (5) U.S. Treasury bills. A comparison of the annual rates of return for these respective portfolios for the years 1926 to 1993 shows there to be a positive relationship between risk and return, with Treasury bills being least risky and common stocks of small firms being most risky. From the data, we are able to see the benefit of diversification in terms of improving the return-risk relationship. Also, the data clearly demonstrates that common stock has in the long run served as the best inflation hedge, and that risk associated with common stocks can be reduced if investors will be patient in receiving their returns.

GO TO:
http://www.prenhall.com/bfm
For downloads and current events
associated with this chapter

KEY TERMS

Arbitrage-pricing model
  (APM), 235

Asset allocation, 240

Beta, 225

Capital asset pricing model
  (CAPM), 231

Characteristic line, 224

Expected rate of return, 214

Firm-specific risk or
  company-unique risk
  (diversifiable risk or
  unsystematic risk), 219

Holding-period return, 220

Investor's required rate
  of return, 230

Market-related risk
  (nondiversifiable risk or
  systematic risk), 219

Opportunity cost of funds, 230
Portfolio beta, 227
Risk, 216

Risk-free or riskless rate of return, 230
Risk premium, 230

Security market line, 232
Standard deviation, 216

FINCOACH PRACTICE EXERCISES FOR CHAPTER 6

To maximize your grades and master the mathematics discussed in this chapter, open *FINCOACH* on the *Finance Learning and Development Center* CD-ROM and practice problems in the following categories: 1) Portfolio Diversification 2) CAPM

STUDY QUESTIONS

6-1. a. What is meant by the investor's required rate of return?

   b. How do we measure the riskiness of an asset?

   c. How should the proposed measurement of risk be interpreted?

6-2. What is (a) unsystematic risk (company-unique or diversifiable risk) and (b) systematic risk (market or nondiversifiable risk)?

6-3. What is the meaning of beta? How is it used to calculate k, the investor's required rate of return?

6-4. Define the security market line. What does it represent?

6-5. How do we measure the beta for a portfolio?

6-6. If we were to graph the returns of a stock against the returns of the S&P 500 Index, and the points did not follow a very ordered pattern, what could we say about that stock? If the stock's returns tracked the S&P 500 returns very closely, then what could we say?

6-7. Over the past 6 decades, we have had the opportunity to observe the rates of return and variability of these returns for different types of securities. Summarize these observations.

SELF-TEST PROBLEMS

ST-1. (*Expected Return and Risk*) Universal Corporation is planning to invest in a security that has several possible rates of return. Given the following probability distribution returns, what is the expected rate of return on the investment? Also, compute the standard deviation of the returns. What do the resulting numbers represent?

Probability	Return
.10	−10%
.20	5%
.30	10%
.40	25%

ST-2. (*Capital Asset Pricing Model*) Using the CAPM, estimate the appropriate required rate of return for the following three stocks, given that the risk-free rate is 5 percent, and the expected return for the market is 17 percent.

Stock	Beta
A	.75
B	.90
C	1.40

ST-3. (*Expected Return and Risk*) Given the following holding-period returns, calculate the average returns and the standard deviations for the Kaifu Corporation and for the market.

Month	Kaifu Corp.	Market
1	4%	2%
2	6	3
3	0	1
4	2	−1

ST-4. (*Holding-Period Returns*) From the following price data, compute the holding-period returns.

Time	Stock Price
1	$10
2	13
3	11
4	15

ST-5. a. (*Security Market Line*) Determine the expected return and beta for the following portfolio:

Stock	Percentage of Portfolio	Beta	Expected Return
1	40%	1.00	12%
2	25	0.75	11
3	35	1.30	15

b. Given the preceding information, draw the security market line and show where the securities fit on the graph. Assume that the risk-free rate is 8 percent and that the expected return on the market portfolio is 12 percent. How would you interpret these findings?

STUDY PROBLEMS (SET A)

6-1A. (*Expected Rate of Return and Risk*) Pritchard Press, Inc., is evaluating a security. One-year Treasury bills are currently paying 9.1 percent. Calculate the following investment's expected return and its standard deviation. Should Pritchard invest in this security?

Probability	Return
.15	5%
.30	7%
.40	10%
.15	15%

6-2A. (*Expected Rate of Return and Risk*) Syntex, Inc., is considering an investment in one of two common stocks. Given the information that follows, which investment is better, based on risk (as measured by the standard deviation) and return?

Common Stock A		Common Stock B	
Probability	Return	Probability	Return
		.20	−5%
.30	11%	.30	6%
.40	15%	.30	14%
.30	19%	.20	22%

6-3A. (*Expected Rate of Return and Risk*) Friedman Manufacturing, Inc., has prepared the following information regarding two investments under consideration. Which investment should be accepted?

Common Stock A		Common Stock B	
Probability	Return	Probability	Return
.20	−2%	.10	4%
.50	18%	.30	6%
.30	27%	.40	10%
		.20	15%

6-4A. a. (*Required Rate of Return Using CAPM*) Compute a fair rate of return for Intel common stock, which has a 1.2 beta. The risk-free rate is 6 percent and the market portfolio (New York Stock Exchange stocks) has an expected return of 16 percent.

b. Why is the rate you computed a fair rate?

6-5A. (*Estimating Beta*) From the following graph relating the holding-period returns for Aram, Inc., to the S&P 500 Index, estimate the firm's beta.

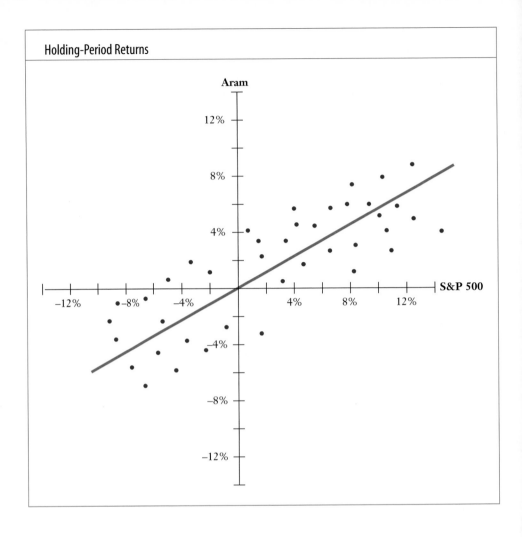

Holding-Period Returns

6-6A. (*Capital Asset Pricing Model*) Johnson Manufacturing, Inc., is considering several investments. The rate on Treasury bills is currently 6.75 percent, and the expected return for the market is 12 percent. What should be the required rates of return for each investment (using the CAPM)?

Security	Beta
A	1.50
B	.82
C	.60
D	1.15

6-7A. (*Capital Asset Pricing Model*) CSB, Inc., has a beta of .765. If the expected market return is 11.5 percent and the risk-free rate is 7.5 percent, what is the appropriate required rate of return of CSB (using the CAPM)?

6-8A. (*Capital Asset Pricing Model*) The expected return for the general market is 12.8 percent, and the risk premium in the market is 4.3 percent. Tasaco, LBM, and Exxos have betas of .864, .693, and .575, respectively. What are the appropriate required rates of return for the three securities?

6-9A. (*Computing Holding-Period Returns*) From the following price data, compute the holding-period returns for Asman and Salinas.

Time	Asman	Salinas
1	$10	$30
2	12	28
3	11	32
4	13	35

How would you interpret the meaning of a holding-period return?

6-10A. (*Measuring Risk and Rates of Return*)
 a. Given the following holding-period returns, compute the average returns and the standard deviations for the Zemin Corporation and for the market.

Month	Zemin Corp.	Market
1	6%	4%
2	3	2
3	1	−1
4	−3	−2
5	5	2
6	0	2

 b. If Zemin's beta is 1.54 and the risk-free rate is 8 percent, what would be an appropriate required return for an investor owning Zemin? (*Note:* Because the preceding returns are based on monthly data, you will need to annualize the returns to make them comparable with the risk-free rate. For simplicity, you can convert from monthly to yearly returns by multiplying the average monthly returns by 12.)

 c. How does Zemin's historical average return compare with the return you believe to be a fair return, given the firm's systematic risk?

6-11A. (*Portfolio Beta and Security Market Line*) You own a portfolio consisting of the following stocks:

Stock	Percentage of Portfolio	Beta	Expected Return
1	20%	1.00	16%
2	30%	0.85	14%
3	15%	1.20	20%
4	25%	0.60	12%
5	10%	1.60	24%

The risk-free rate is 7 percent. Also, the expected return on the market portfolio is 15.5 percent.

   a. Calculate the expected return of your portfolio. (*Hint:* The expected return of a portfolio equals the weighted average of the individual stock's expected return, where the weights are the percentage invested in each stock.)

   b. Calculate the portfolio beta.

   c. Given the information preceding, plot the security market line on paper. Plot the stocks from your portfolio on your graph.

   d. From your plot in part (c), which stocks *appear* to be your winners and which ones appear to be losers?

   e. Why should you consider your conclusion in part (d) to be less than certain?

6-12A. (*Expected Return, Standard Deviation, and Capital Asset Pricing Model*) Following you will find the end-of-month prices, both for the S&P 500 Index and for John Deere common stock.

   a. Using the following data, calculate the holding-period returns for each month from April 1996 to March 1997.

	Prices	
Month and year	S&P 500	John Deere
1996		
March	$645.50	$41.63
April	$654.17	$38.88
May	$669.12	$41.63
June	$670.63	$40.00
July	$639.95	$35.75
August	$651.99	$39.75
September	$687.31	$42.00
October	$705.27	$41.88
November	$757.02	$44.63
December	$740.74	$40.50
1997		
January	$786.16	$42.75
February	$790.82	$42.63
March	$757.12	$43.50

   b. Calculate the average monthly return and the standard deviation of these returns both for the S&P 500 and John Deere.

   c. Develop a graph that shows the relationship between the John Deere stock returns and the S&P 500 Index (Show the John Deere returns on the vertical axis and the S&P 500 Index returns on the horizontal, as done in Figure 6.4).

   d. From your graph, describe the nature of the relationship between John Deere stock returns and the returns for the S&P 500 Index.

INTEGRATIVE PROBLEM

Note: Although not absolutely necessary, you are advised to use a computer spreadsheet to work the following problem.

   1. Use the following price data for the S&P 500 Index, Bristol-Myer-Squibb and General Electric to calculate the holding-period returns for the 24 months during 1995 and 1996.

		S&P 500	Bristol-Myers-Squibb	GE
1994	December	$459.27	$28.94	$25.50
1995	January	470.42	30.75	25.75
	February	487.39	30.94	27.38
	March	500.71	31.44	27.00
	April	514.71	32.56	28.00
	May	533.40	33.19	29.00
	June	544.75	34.06	28.19
	July	562.06	34.63	29.50
	August	561.88	34.38	29.44
	September	584.41	36.44	31.88
	October	581.50	38.13	31.63
	November	605.37	40.13	33.56
	December	615.93	42.94	36.00
1996	January	636.02	44.25	38.38
	February	640.43	42.56	37.75
	March	645.50	42.81	38.94
	April	654.17	41.13	38.63
	May	669.12	42.69	41.38
	June	670.63	45.00	43.38
	July	639.95	43.31	41.13
	August	651.99	43.88	41.56
	September	687.31	48.19	45.50
	October	705.27	52.88	48.38
	November	757.02	56.88	52.00
	December	740.74	54.50	49.44

GO TO:
http://www.prenhall.com/bfm
For downloads and current events
associated with this chapter

2. Calculate the average monthly holding-period return and the standard deviation of these returns for the S&P 500 Index, Bristol-Myers-Squibb, and General Electric.

3. Plot (1) the holding-period returns for Bristol-Myers-Squibb against the S&P 500 Index, and (2) plot the General Electric holding-period returns against the S&P 500 Index. (Use Figure 6.4 as the format for your graph.)

4. From your graphs in part 3, describe the nature of the relationship between the Bristol-Myers-Squibb stock returns and the returns for the S&P 500 Index. Make the same comparison for General Electric.

5. Assume that you have decided to invest one-half of your money in Bristol-Myers-Squibb and the remaining in General Electric. Calculate the monthly holding-period returns for your two-stock portfolio. (*Hint:* The monthly return for the portfolio is the average of the two stock's monthly returns.)

6. Plot the returns of your two-stock portfolio against the S&P 500 Index as you did for the individual stocks in part 3. How does this graph compare to the graphs for the individual stocks? Explain the difference.

7. Following are the returns on an *annualized* basis that were realized from holding long-term government bonds during 1995 and 1996. Calculate the average *monthly* holding-period return and the standard deviations of these returns. (*Hint:* You will need to convert the annual returns to monthly returns by dividing each return by 12 months.)

Month and Year	Annualized Rate of Return	Month and Year	Annualized Rate of Return
1995 January	7.84%	1996 January	5.58%
February	7.60	February	5.60
March	7.22	March	6.13
April	7.20	April	6.34
May	7.07	May	6.66
June	6.30	June	6.85
July	6.21	July	6.73
August	6.45	August	6.80
September	6.28	September	6.96
October	6.17	October	6.72
November	6.03	November	6.37
December	5.76	December	6.12

8. Now assume that you have decided to invest equal amounts of money in Bristol-Myers-Squibb, General Electric, and the long-term government securities. Calculate the monthly returns for your three-asset portfolio. What are the average return and the standard deviation?

9. Make a comparison of the average returns and the standard deviations for all the individual assets and the two portfolios that we designed. What conclusions can be reached by your comparison?

10. The betas for Bristol-Myers-Squibb and General Electric are 1.11 and 1.23, respectively. Compare the meaning of these betas relative to the preceding standard deviations calculated.

11. The Treasury bill rate at the end of 1996 was approximately 5 percent. Given the betas for Bristol-Myers-Squibb and General Electric and using the preceding data for the S&P 500 Index as a measure for the market portfolio expected return, estimate an appropriate required rate of return given the level of systematic risk for each stock.

STUDY PROBLEMS (SET B)

6-1B. (*Expected Rate of Return and Risk*) B. J. Gautney Enterprises is evaluating a security. One-year Treasury bills are currently paying 8.9 percent. Calculate the following investment's expected return and its standard deviation. Should Gautney invest in this security?

Probability	Return
.15	6%
.30	5%
.40	11%
.15	14%

6-2B. (*Expected Rate of Return and Risk*) Kelly B. Stites, Inc., is considering an investment in one of two common stocks. Given the information that follows, which investment is better, based on risk (as measured by the standard deviation) and return?

Security A		Security B	
Probability	Return	Probability	Return
.20	−2%	.10	5%
.50	19%	.30	7%
.30	25%	.40	12%
		.20	14%

6-3B. (*Expected Rate of Return and Risk*) Clevenger Manufacturing, Inc., has prepared the following information regarding two investments under consideration. Which investment should be accepted?

Common Stock A		Common Stock B	
Probability	Return	Probability	Return
		.15	6%
.20	10%	.30	8%
.60	13%	.40	15%
.20	20%	.15	19%

6-4B. a. (*Required Rate of Return Using CAPM*) Compute a *fair* rate of return for Compaq common stock, which has a 1.5 beta. The risk-free rate is 8 percent and the market portfolio (New York Stock Exchange stocks) has an expected return of 16 percent.

b. Why is the rate you computed a fair rate?

6-5B. (*Estimating Beta*) From the following graph relating the holding-period returns for Bram, Inc., to the S&P 500 Index, estimate the firm's beta.

Holding-Period Returns

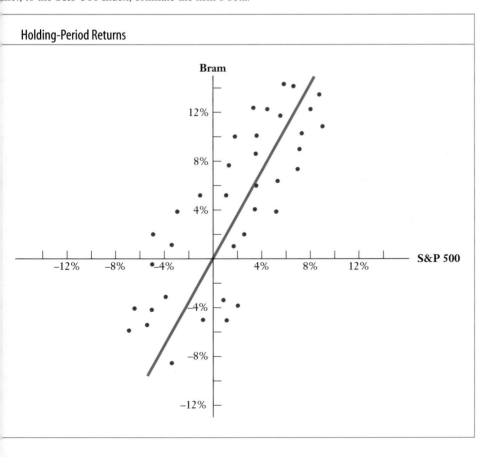

6-6B. (*Capital Asset Pricing Model*) Bobbi Manufacturing, Inc., is considering several invest-ments. The rate on Treasury bills is currently 6.75 percent, and the expected return for the market is 12 percent. What should be the required rates of return for each investment (using the CAPM)?

Security	Beta
A	1.40
B	.75
C	.80
D	1.20

6-7B. (*Capital Asset Pricing Model*) Breckenridge, Inc., has a beta of .85. If the expected market return is 10.5 percent and the risk-free rate is 7.5 percent, what is the appropriate required return of Breckenridge (using the CAPM)?

6-8B. (*Capital Asset Pricing Model*) The expected return for the general market is 12.8 percent, and the risk premium in the market is 4.3 percent. Dupree, Yofota, and MacGrill have betas of .82, .570, and .680, respectively. What are the appropriate required rates of return for the three securities?

6-9B. (*Computing Holding-Period Returns*) From the following price data, compute the holding-period returns for O'Toole and Baltimore.

Time	O'Toole	Baltimore
1	$22	$45
2	24	50
3	20	48
4	25	52

How would you interpret the meaning of a holding-period return?

6-10B. (*Measuring Risk and Rates of Return*)

a. Given the following holding-period returns, compute the average returns and the stan-dard deviations for the Sugita Corporation and for the market.

Month	Sugita Corp.	Market
1	1.8%	1.5%
2	−0.5	1.0
3	2.0	0.0
4	−2.0	−2.0
5	5.0	4.0
6	5.0	3.0

b. If Sugita's beta is 1.18 and the risk-free rate is 8 percent, what would be an appropriate required return for an investor owning Sugita? (*Note:* Because the preceding returns are based on monthly data, you will need to annualize the returns to make them comparable with the risk-free rate. For simplicity, you can convert from monthly to yearly returns by multiplying the average monthly returns by 12.)

c. How does Sugita's historical average return compare with the return you believe to be a fair return, given the firm's systematic risk?

6-11B. (*Portfolio Beta and Security Market Line*) You own a portfolio consisting of the following stocks:

Stock	Percentage of Portfolio	Beta	Expected Return
1	10%	1.00	12%
2	25	0.75	11
3	15	1.30	15
4	30	0.60	9
5	20	1.20	14

The risk-free rate is 8 percent. Also, the expected return on the market portfolio is 11.6 percent.

a. Calculate the expected return of your portfolio. (*Hint:* The expected return of a portfolio equals the weighted average of the individual stock's expected return, where the weights are the percentage invested in each stock.)

b. Calculate the portfolio beta.

c. Given the preceding information, plot the security market line on paper. Plot the stocks from your portfolio on your graph.

d. From your plot in part (c), which stocks *appear* to be your winners and which ones *appear* to be losers?

e. Why should you consider your conclusion in part (d) to be less than certain?

6-12B. (*Expected Return, Standard Deviation, and Capital Asset Pricing Model*) Below you will find the end-of-month prices, both for the S&P 500 Index and for Colgate-Palmolive common stock.

a. Using the following data, calculate the holding-period returns for each month from April 1996 to March 1997.

	Prices	
Month and Year	S&P 500	Colgate-Palmolive
1996		
March	$645.50	$38.94
April	$654.17	$38.31
May	$669.12	$39.38
June	$670.63	$42.38
July	$639.95	$39.25
August	$651.99	$40.63
September	$687.31	$43.44
October	$705.27	$46.06
November	$757.02	$46.31
December	$740.74	$46.13
1997		
January	$786.16	$48.38
February	$790.82	$51.75
March	$757.12	$49.81

b. Calculate the average monthly return and the standard deviation of these returns both for the S&P 500 and Colgate-Palmolive.

c. Develop a graph that shows the relationship between the Colgate-Palmolive stock returns and the S&P 500 Index. (Show the Colgate-Palmolive returns on the vertical axis and the S&P 500 Index returns on the horizontal as done in Figure 6.4.)

d. From your graph, describe the nature of the relationship between Colgate-Palmolive stock returns and the returns for the S&P 500 Index.

SELF-TEST SOLUTIONS

SS-1.

(A) Probability $P(k_i)$	(B) Return(k_i)	Expected Return ($\bar{k}$) $(A) \times (B)$	Weighted Deviation $(k_i - \bar{k})^2 P(k_i)$
.10	−10%	−1%	52.9%
.20	5%	1%	12.8%
.30	10%	3%	2.7%
.40	25%	10%	57.6%
		$\bar{k} = 13\%$	$\sigma^2 = 126.0\%$
			$\sigma = 11.22\%$

From our studies in statistics, we know that if the distribution of returns were normal, then Universal could expect a return of 13 percent with a 67 percent possibility that this return would vary up or down by 11.22 percent between 1.78 percent (13% − 11.22%) and 24.22 percent (13% + 11.22%). However, it is apparent from the probabilities that the distribution is not normal.

SS-2.

Stock A	5% + .75(17% − 5%) = 14%
Stock B	5% + .90(17% − 5%) = 15.8%
Stock C	5% + 1.40(17% − 5%) = 21.8%

SS-3.

Kaifu

Average return:

$$\frac{4\% + 6\% + 0\% + 2\%}{4} = 3\%$$

Standard deviation:

$$\sqrt{\frac{\begin{array}{l}(4\% - 3\%)^2 \\ + (6\% - 3\%)^2 \\ + (0\% - 3\%)^2 \\ + (2\% - 3\%)^2\end{array}}{4-1}} = 2.58\%$$

Market

Average return:

$$\frac{2\% + 3\% + 1\% - 1\%}{4} = 1.25$$

Standard deviation:

$$\sqrt{\dfrac{\begin{array}{l}(2\% - 1.25\%)^2 \\ + (3\% - 1.25\%)^2 \\ + (1\% - 1.25\%)^2 \\ + (-1\% - 1.25\%)^2\end{array}}{4 - 1}} = 1.71\%$$

SS-4.

Time	Stock Price	Holding-Period Return
1	$10	
2	13	($13 ÷ $10) − 1 = 30.0%
3	11	($11 ÷ $13) − 1 = −15.4%
4	15	($15 ÷ $11) − 1 = 36.4%

SS-5. a. Portfolio expected return:

$(.4 \times 12\%) + (.25 \times 11\%) + (.35 \times 15\%) = 12.8\%$

Portfolio beta:

$(.4 \times 1) + (.25 \times .75) + (.35 \times 1.3) = 1.04$

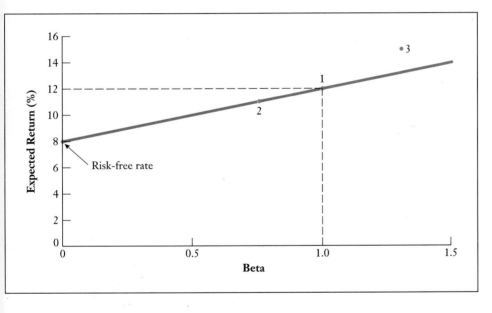

b. Stocks 1 and 2 seem to be right in line with the security market line, which suggests that they are earning a fair return, given their systematic risk. Stock 3, on the other hand, is earning more than a fair return (above the security market line). We might be tempted to conclude that security 3 is undervalued. However, we may be seeing an illusion; it is possible to misspecify the security market line by using bad estimates in our data.

APPENDIX 6A

MEASURING THE REQUIRED RATE OF RETURN: THE ARBITRAGE PRICING MODEL

The basic theme of the arbitrage pricing model (APM) may be summarized as follows:[25]

1. Actual security returns vary from their expected amounts because *of unanticipated* changes—anticipated changes are already reflected in the stock price—in a number of basic economic forces, such as industrial production, inflation rates, the term structure of interest rates, and the difference in interest rates between high- and low-risk bonds.[26]
2. Just as the CAPM defined a portfolio's systematic risk to be its sensitivity to the general-market returns (that is, its beta coefficient), APM suggests that the risk of a security is reflected in its sensitivity to the unexpected changes in important economic forces.
3. Any two stocks or portfolios that have the same sensitivity to meaningful economic forces (that is, the same relevant or systematic risk) must have the same expected return. Otherwise, we could replace some of the stocks in our portfolio with other stocks having the same sensitivities but higher expected returns and earn riskless profits.
4. We would expect portfolios that are highly sensitive to unexpected changes in macroeconomic forces to offer investors high expected returns. This relationship may be represented quantitatively as follows:

$$E(k_i) = k_{rf} + (S_{i1})(RP_1) + (S_{i2})(RP_2) + \ldots + (S_{ij})(RP_j) + \ldots + (S_{in})(RP_n) \tag{6A-1}$$

where $E(k_i)$ = the expected return for stock or portfolio i
k_{rf} = the risk-free rate
S_{ij} = the sensitivity of stock i returns to unexpected changes in economic force j
RP_j = the market risk premium associated with an unexpected change in the jth economic force
n = the number of relevant economic forces

To help understand the APM model, we will draw from the actual research of Bower, Bower, and Logue, (BBL).[27] After computing returns for 815 stocks from 1970 through 1979, BBL used a technique called factor analysis to study the general movement of monthly returns for the 815 stocks. The technique identified four factors that help explain the movement of the returns, and also used equation (6A-1) to represent the risk-return relationship in an APM format. The actual model appears as follows:

$$\text{expected return for stock } i = 6.2\% - 185.5\% \, (S_{i1}) + 144.5\% \, (S_{i2})$$
$$+ \ 12.4\% \, (S_{i3}) - 274.4\% \, (S_{i4})$$

The value 6.2% in the equation is an estimate of the risk-free rate, as determined by the model; the remaining values, −185.5%, . . . , −274.4%, signify the market risk premiums for each of the four factors; and the $S_{i1}, \ldots, S_{i4}$ represent the sensitivities of stock i to the four factor.

The BBL factors are determined statistically from past return data and were not intuitively or economically identified; that is, the technique provides *factors* that tell us more

---

[25]The following description of the APM is taken in part from Dorothy H. Bower, Richard S. Bower, and Dennis E. Logue, "A Primer on Arbitrage Pricing Theory," in Joel M. Stern and Donald H. Chew, Jr., eds., *The Revolution in Corporate Finance* (New York: Basil Blackwell, 1986), 69–77.

[26]See R. Roll and S. Ross, "The Arbitrage Pricing Theory Approach to Strategic Portfolio Planning," *Financial Analysts Journal* (May–June 1984):14–26.

[27]Dorothy A. Bower, Richard S. Bower, and Dennis E. Logue, "Equity Screening Rates Using Arbitrage Pricing Theory," in C. F. Lee, ed., *Advances in Financial Planning* (Greenwich, CT: JAI Press, 1984).

about the movement in the returns than would any other factors. Each factor could conceivably relate to a single economic variable; however, it is more likely that each factor represents the influence of several economic variables.

Having specified the APM risk-return relationship, BBL then used the model to estimate the expected (required) rates of return for 17 stocks. This estimation required BBL to use regression analysis to study the relationships of the returns of the 17 stocks to the four factors. From this regression analysis, they were able to measure the sensitivity of each security's return to a particular factor. These *sensitivity coefficients* for a particular stock may then be combined with the APM model in equation (6A-1) to estimate the investors' required rate of return.

Using 3 of the 17 stocks to demonstrate the calculation, the regression coefficients (sensitivity coefficients) for American Hospital Supply, CBS, and Western Union are shown here:

Stock Sensitivity Coefficients (S)				
	Factor 1	Factor 2	Factor 3	Factor 4
American Hospital Supply	−0.050	0.010	0.040	0.020
CBS	−0.050	0.002	0.005	0.010
Western Union	−0.050	−0.020	−0.010	0.009

Using these stock sensitivity coefficients and the APM model, as developed by BBL, we can estimate the investors' expected (required) rate of return for each stock as follows:

$$\text{American Hospital Supply} = 6.2\% - 185.5\%(-0.050) + 144.5\%(0.010)$$
$$+ 12.4\%(0.040) - 74.4\%(.020)$$
$$= 11.93\%$$

$$\text{CBS} = 6.2\% - 185.5\%(-0.050) + 144.5\%(0.002)$$
$$+ 12.4\%(0.005) - 274.4\%(0.010)$$
$$= 13.08\%$$

$$\text{Western Union} = 6.2\% - 185.5\%(-0.050) + 144.5\%(-0.020)$$
$$+ 12.4\%(-0.010) - 274.4\%(0.009)$$
$$= 9.99\%$$

STUDY PROBLEMS

6A–1. (*Arbitrage Pricing Model*) Using the APM along with the results of the Bower, Bower, and Logue research just discussed, estimate the appropriate required rates of return for the following three stocks:

Sensitivity Factor				
Stock	Factor 1	Factor 2	Factor 3	Factor 4
A	−0.070	−0.020	0.010	0.003
B	−0.070	0.030	0.005	0.010
C	−0.070	−0.010	0.006	0.009

6A–2. a. (*Required Rate of Return Using APM*) If we use the arbitrage pricing model to measure investors' required rate of return, what is our concept of risk?

b. Using the results of the Bower, Bower, and Logue study of return variability, as captured in equation (6A-1), calculate the investors' required rate of return for the following stocks:

Sensitivity Factor				
Stock	**Factor 1**	**Factor 2**	**Factor 3**	**Factor 4**
A	−0.070	0.030	0.005	0.010
B	−0.070	−0.010	0.006	0.009
C	−0.050	−0.004	−0.010	−0.007
D	−0.060	−0.007	−0.006	0.006

c. Assuming (1) a risk-free rate of 6.1 percent and (2) an expected market return of 17.25 percent, estimate the investors' required rate of return for the four stocks in part (b), using the CAPM.

Stock	Beta
A	1.40
B	1.70
C	1.20
D	1.10

d. What might explain the differences in your answers to parts (b) and (c)?

Learning Objectives

Active Applications

World Finance

Practice

CHAPTER 7

BOND VALUATION

INTRODUCTION

During 1995, the chief financial officers for IBM and Pacific Bell watched the price of their firms' bonds (a form of debt issued by public corporations) increase by over 20 percent. IBM's bonds were valued at $970 at the beginning of 1995, but sold for $1,180 by year end. Pacific Bell's bonds were selling for $842 in January 1995, but by the end of the year, they were worth $1,060. If you had purchased these bonds at the outset of 1995 and sold them at the end of the year, you would have earned a 30 percent and 33 percent rate of return on the two bonds, respectively (including the interest income you received from the bonds). These investments would have certainly beat a savings account at a bank. However, 1995 was no typical year for bond investors. The rate of returns earned on bonds were unusually attractive in 1995—a 27 percent average return for bonds of large companies. In 1994, however, investors in long-term corporate bonds received a negative 6 percent return. How could the returns be so volatile from year to year, when these aren't even stocks that we usually think of as being risky investments? Read on, and you will find the answer to this puzzle.

CHAPTER PREVIEW

Knowing the fair value of an asset is not always an easy matter to know. The *Maxims* of the French writer La Rouchefoucauld, written over three centuries ago, still speak to us: "The greatest of all gifts is the power to estimate things at their true worth."

How is the value of an asset, such as a bond or stock or real estate, determined? Why does the value of an asset change so radically at times? To illustrate the point, the market price of Chrysler's bonds—the value as perceived by the investors buying and selling the bonds—was as low as $1,000 and as high as $1,200 within a matter of months during 1994. These questions are important for managers committed to maximizing the value of the firm. It is absolutely essential for them to know what drives the value of an asset.

LEARNING OBJECTIVES

After reading this chapter, you should be able to

1. Define the term *value* as used for several different purposes.

2. Describe the basic process for valuing assets.

3. Explain the key features of bonds.

4. Distinguish between different kinds of bonds.

5. Estimate the value of a bond.

6. Compute a bondholder's expected rate of return.

7. Explain five important relationships that exist in bond valuation.

Specifically, they need to understand how bonds and stocks are valued in the marketplace; otherwise, they cannot act in the best interest of the firm's investors. In this chapter, we will show how to value a bond.

A bond is one form of a company's long-term debt. We will look at the features or characteristics of most bonds and then identify the different kinds of bonds. We will then shift our attention to valuing a bond, bringing in the concept of the bondholder's expected rate of return. Finally, we will discuss five important relationships on bond valuation.

Throughout the chapter, we will rely on the first three axioms given in chapter 1, which are as follows:

> Axiom 1: The Risk-Return Trade-Off—We Won't Take on Additional Risk Unless We Expect to Be Compensated with Additional Return; Axiom 2: The Time Value of Money—A Dollar Received Today Is Worth More Than a Dollar Received in the Future; Axiom 3: Cash—Not Profit—Is King.

We cannot overstate the significance of these axioms in understanding the valuation of a bond, the topic of this chapter.

OBJECTIVE 1

DEFINITIONS OF VALUE

The term *value* is often used in different contexts, depending on its application. Examples of different uses of this term include the following:

Book value

The value of an asset as shown on a firm's balance sheet. It represents the historical cost of the asset rather than its current market value or replacement cost.

Book value is the value of an asset as shown on a firm's balance sheet. It represents the historical cost of the asset rather than its current worth. For instance, the book value of land is the amount the firm originally paid for the land.

Liquidation value

The amount that could be realized if an asset were sold individually and not as a part of a going concern.

Liquidation value is the dollar sum that could be realized if an asset were sold individually and not as part of a going concern. For example, if a firm's operations were discontinued and its assets were divided up and sold, the sales price would represent the asset's liquidation value.

Market value

The observed value for the asset in the marketplace.

Market value of an asset is the observed value for the asset in the marketplace. This value is determined by supply and demand forces working together in the marketplace, where buyers and sellers negotiate a mutually acceptable price for the asset. For instance, the market price for Ford common stock on September 23, 1997, was $27. This price is a result of a large number of buyers and sellers interacting through the New York Stock Exchange. In theory, a market price exists for all assets. However, many assets have no readily observable market price because trading seldom occurs. For instance, the market price for the common stock of the Rosewood Corporation, a large but privately held firm in Dallas, would be more difficult to establish than the market value of J. C. Penney's common stock, which is traded daily on the New York Stock Exchange.

Intrinsic or economic value

The present value of the asset's expected future cash flows. This value is the amount the investor considers to be a fair value, given the amount, timing, and riskiness of future cash flows.

The **intrinsic** or **economic value** of an asset can be defined as the present value of the asset's expected future cash flows discounted at the appropriate required rate of return. This value is the amount the investor considers to be a **fair value**, given the amount, timing, and riskiness of future cash flows. Once the investor has estimated the intrinsic value of a security, this value could be compared with its market value when available. If the intrinsic value is greater than the market value, then the security is undervalued in the eyes of the investor. Should the market value exceed the investor's intrinsic value, then the security is overvalued.

Efficient market

A market in which the values of securities at any instant in time fully reflect all available information, which results in the market value and the intrinsic value being the same.

We hasten to add that if the securities market is working efficiently, the market value and the intrinsic value of a security will be equal. Whenever a security's intrinsic value differs from its current market price, the competition among investors seeking opportunities to make a profit will quickly drive the market price back to its intrinsic value. Thus we may define an **efficient market** as one in which the values of all securities at any instant fully reflect all available public information. In such a market, the market value and the intrinsic

Bondholders Beware

We have learned that the bond rating attached to a bond when it is issued does not necessarily continue with it until maturity. In fact, with all the debt that corporations piled on in the late 1980s, it seemed that the only direction debt ratings went was down. The ethical question here: Does management have a duty to bondholders to watch out for their interests? Is just living by the letter of the bond covenants—while working hard to evade them—all right?

Let's look at a couple of examples that have infuriated bondholders. In early 1988, Shearson Lehman Hutton helped sell $1 billion of RJR Nabisco bonds. About 6 months later, Shearson helped Kohlberg Kravis Roberts (KKR), an investment banker, buy RJR. The way the purchase was arranged, RJR issued large amounts of new debt, driving the market value of the previously issued bonds down by $100 million. Needless to say, a lot of bondholders were angry.

Texaco is another company that has worked around bond covenants. Several years ago, Pennzoil sued Texaco for $10 billion and won the case. To minimize damage to shareholders as a result of their court battle with Pennzoil, Texaco filed for Chapter 11 bankruptcy protection. The company entered bankruptcy, bond interest payments were passed, and later it emerged from bankruptcy with its credit standing unchanged.

Was what Shearson did unethical—to issue, then destroy? Should Texaco have used bankruptcy to protect its shareholders at the expense of its bondholders? What do you think? How would you have viewed each situation if you had been a bondholder? What if you had been a stockholder? Is it ethical for one group of investors to benefit at the expense of another group? What do you think?

value are the same. If the markets are efficient, it is extremely difficult for an investor to make extra profits from an ability to predict prices, because prices respond very quickly to the arrival of new information.

RELATE TO THE BIG PICTURE

*The fact that investors have difficulty in truly identifying stocks that are undervalued relates to **Axiom 6: Efficient Capital Market—The Markets Are Quick and the Prices Are Right.** In an efficient market, prices reflect all available public information about the security, and therefore it is priced fairly.*

The idea of market efficiency has been the backdrop for an intense battle between professional investors and university professors. The academic community has contended that someone throwing darts at the list of securities in *The Wall Street Journal* could do as well as a professional money manager. Market professionals retort that academicians are grossly mistaken in this view. The war has been intense but also one that the student of finance should find intriguing. It can be followed each month in *The Wall Street Journal* where the investment performance of dart throwers and different professional investors are compared. Through August 1997, there had been 61 contests between these rivals. The score: 34 for the professional managers and 27 for the dart throwers.

While the debate rages on between the academic community and many investment professionals, the financial manager should use the intrinsic value to guide decisions. It is this value that provides the manager the connection between operating decisions and shareholder value. By maximizing intrinsic value, the manager can reasonably assume that shareholder value is being enhanced. Thus for the financial manager's purpose, understanding intrinsic value is a foundation to many topics that we will cover in future chapters. So our attention is directed to this important topic.

OBJECTIVE 2

VALUATION: UNDERSTANDING THE PROCESS

As already noted, *intrinsic value of an asset is equal to the present value of its expected future cash flows*, where these cash flows are discounted back to the present using the investor's required rate of return. This statement is true for valuing all assets and serves as the basis of almost all that we do in finance. Thus value is affected by three elements:

1. The amount and timing of the asset's expected cash flows
2. The riskiness of these cash flows
3. The investor's required rate of return for undertaking the investment

The first two factors are characteristics of the asset; the third, the required rate of return, is the minimum rate of return necessary to attract an investor to purchase or hold a security. This rate must be high enough to compensate the investor for the risk perceived in the asset's future cash flows.

RELATE TO THE BIG PICTURE

Our discussions thus far remind us of three of our axioms:

- *Axiom 1: The Risk-Return Trade-Off—We Won't Take on Additional Risk Unless We Expect to Be Compensated with Additional Return.*
- *Axiom 2: The Time Value of Money—A Dollar Received Today Is Worth More Than a Dollar Received in the Future.*
- *Axiom 3: Cash—Not Profit—Is King*

Determining the economic worth or value of an asset always relies on these three axioms. Without them, we would have no basis for explaining value. With them, we can know that the amount and timing of cash, not earnings, drive value. Also, we must be rewarded for taking risk; otherwise, we will not invest.

Figure 7.1 depicts the basic factors involved in valuation. As the figure shows, finding the value of an asset involves:

1. Assessing the asset's characteristics, which include the amount and timing of the expected cash flow and the riskiness of these cash flows;
2. Determining the investor's required rate of return, which embodies the investor's attitude about assuming risk and perception of the riskiness of the asset; and
3. Discounting the expected cash flows back to the present, using the investor's required rate of return as the discount rate.

STOP AND THINK

Intrinsic value is the present value of expected future cash flows. Intrinsic value is a function of the cash flows yet to be received, the riskiness of these cash flows, and the investor's required rate of return. This statement is true regardless of what type of asset we are valuing. If you remember only one thing from this chapter, remember that intrinsic value is the present value of expected future cash flows.

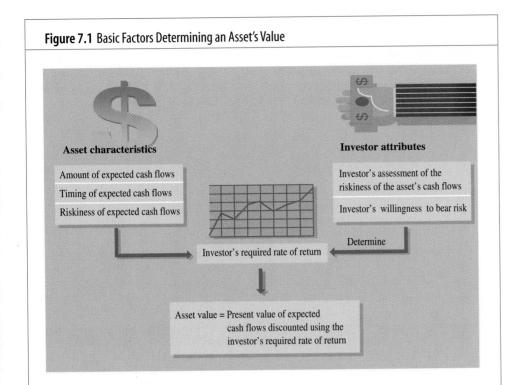

Figure 7.1 Basic Factors Determining an Asset's Value

Asset characteristics

Amount of expected cash flows

Timing of expected cash flows

Riskiness of expected cash flows

Investor attributes

Investor's assessment of the riskiness of the asset's cash flows

Investor's willingness to bear risk

Determine

Investor's required rate of return

Asset value = Present value of expected cash flows discounted using the investor's required rate of return

The valuation process can be described as follows: It is assigning value to an asset by calculating the present value of its expected future cash flows using the investor's required rate of return as the discount rate. The investor's required rate of return, k, is determined by the level of the risk-free rate of interest and the risk premium that the investor feels is necessary to compensate for the risks assumed in owning the asset. Therefore, a basic security valuation model can be defined mathematically as follows:

$$V = \frac{C_1}{(1+k)^1} + \frac{C_2}{(1+k)^2} + \ldots + \frac{C_n}{(1+k)^n} \tag{7-1}$$

or

$$V = \sum_{t=1}^{n} \frac{C_t}{(1+k)^1}$$

where C_t = cash flow to be received at time t

V = the intrinsic value or present value of an asset producing expected future cash flows, C_t in years 1 through n

k = the investor's required rate of return

n = the number of years cash flows are to be received

Using equation (7-1), there are three basic steps in the valuation process:

Step 1: Estimate the C_t in equation (7-1), which is the amount and timing of the future cash flows the security is expected to provide.

Step 2: Determine k, the investor's required rate of return.

Step 3: Calculate the intrinsic value, V, as the present value of expected cash flows discounted at the investor's required rate of return.

Equation (7-1), which measures the present value of future cash flows, is the basis of the valuation process. It is the most important equation in this chapter, because all the remaining equations in this chapter and in chapter 8 are merely reformulations of this one equation. If we understand equation (7-1), all the valuation work we do, and a host of other topics as well, will be much clearer in our minds. With the forgoing brief but important principles of valuation as our foundation, let's now look at the nature and kinds of bonds and then how they are valued.

STOP AND THINK

There are three easy rules about cash flows and valuation:

1. *We prefer more cash over less cash.*
2. *We prefer cash sooner rather than later.*
3. *We prefer less risky cash flow over more risky cash flows.*

These three rules capture the essence of what we do in determining an asset's value.

OBJECTIVE 3

CHARACTERISTICS OF BONDS

As to its nature, a bond represents a fixed claim on a firm, which must be met legally or the company can be forced into bankruptcy—the claim must be paid as promised. In contrast, common stock, which we will study in the next chapter, has a residual claim: A dividend can be canceled and it does not have to be made up, and the common stock can have negative earnings without bankruptcy necessarily following.

It should also be understood that not all bonds are equal in terms of the nature and priority of claim against the company issuing them. As we will see later, some bonds are secured, which means specific assets have been designated as collateral for the loan; others have not. Unsecured bonds do not have first claim to any individual assets—that is, their claim is unsecured and more general in nature. Also, some bonds are not to be paid until other debt claims have been completely satisfied if the firm is liquidated. That is, their claim is junior or *subordinated* to senior debt. Thus if the firm fails, these bondholders are paid after the senior debt payment has been satisfied, but before any claims are paid to the stockholders.

Let us now turn to a discussion of the different features or characteristics associated with bonds. Some of the more important characteristics are as follows:

- claim on assets and income
- par value
- coupon interest rate
- maturity
- indenture
- current yield
- bond ratings

Let's consider each in turn.

Claim on Assets and Income

In the case of insolvency, claims of debt in general, including bonds, are honored before those of both common stock and preferred stock. However, different types of debt may also have a hierarchy among themselves as to the order of their claim on assets.

Bonds also have a claim on income that comes ahead of common and preferred stock. In general, if interest on bonds is not paid, the bond trustees can classify the firm insolvent and force it into bankruptcy. Thus the bondholder's claim on income is more likely to be honored than that of common and preferred stockholders, whose dividends are paid at the discretion of the firm's management.

Par Value

The **par value** of a bond is its face value that is returned to the bondholder at maturity. In general, corporate bonds are issued in denominations of $1,000, although there are some exceptions to this rule. Also, when bond prices are quoted in the financial press, prices are generally expressed as a percentage of the bond's par value. For example, a Detroit Edison bond that pays $90 per year interest and matures in 2002 was recently quoted in *The Wall Street Journal* as selling for 95 1/8. That does not mean you can buy the bond for $95.125. It means that this bond is selling for 95 1/8 percent of its par value of $1,000. Hence the market price of this bond is actually $951.25. At maturity in 2002, the bondholder will receive the $1,000.

Par value of a bond

The bond's face value that is returned to the bondholder at maturity, usually $1,000.

Coupon Interest Rate

The **coupon interest rate** on a bond indicates the percentage of the par value of the bond that will be paid out annually in the form of interest. Thus regardless of what happens to the price of a bond with an 8 percent coupon interest rate and a $1,000 par value, it will pay out $80 annually in interest until maturity (.08 × $1,000 = $80).

Coupon interest rate

A bond's coupon interest rate indicates what percentage of the par value of the bond will be paid out annually in the form of interest.

Maturity

The **maturity** of a bond indicates the length of time until the bond issuer returns the par value to the bondholder and terminates or redeems the bond.

Maturity

The length of time until the bond issuer returns the par value to the bondholder and terminates the bond.

Indenture

An **indenture** is the legal agreement between the firm issuing the bond and the bond trustee who represents the bondholders. The indenture provides the specific terms of the loan agreement, including a description of the bonds, the rights of the bondholders, the rights of the issuing firm, and the responsibilities of the trustee. This legal document may run 100 pages or more in length, with the majority of it devoted to defining protective provisions for the bondholder.

Typically, the restrictive provisions included in the indenture attempt to protect the bondholder's financial position relative to that of other outstanding securities. Common provisions involve (1) limitations on issuing common stock dividends, (2) restrictions on the purchase or sale of fixed assets, and (3) constraints on additional borrowing.

Indenture

The legal agreement or contract between the firm issuing the bonds and the bond trustee who represents the bondholders.

Current Yield

The **current yield** on a bond refers to the ratio of the annual interest payment to the bond's current market price. If, for example, we have a bond with an 8 percent coupon interest rate, a par value of $1,000, and a market price of $700, it would have a current yield of

Current yield

The ratio of the annual interest payment to the bond's market price.

$$\text{current yield} = \frac{\text{annual interest payments}}{\text{market price of the bond}} \tag{7-2}$$

$$= \frac{.08 \times \$1,000}{\$700} = \frac{\$80}{\$700} = 0.114 = 11.4 \text{ percent}$$

Interest Tax Shield

One of the primary differences between debt and equity is the way each is taxed. The interest paid on debt is tax deductible, but dividends are not. For instance, assume that a $1,000 bond pays 8 percent, or $80 (8% × $1,000), and that the firm paying the interest is in a 34 percent tax bracket. Because the company can take the interest as a tax deduction, the after-tax cost of the debt is 5.28 percent [8% × (1 − .34)]. In other words, although the firm actually pays $80 in interest to the bondholder, the firm's dollar interest cost after taxes is only $52.80 ($1,000 × 5.28%) or a savings in taxes of $27.20 ($80.00 − $52.80). This savings in taxes resulting from the tax deductibility of the interest expense is called the **interest tax shield**. On the other hand, an $80 dividend payment is not tax deductible; thus a company paying the dividend incurs the full $80 cost.

Interest tax shield

The savings in taxes resulting from the tax deductibility of the interest expense.

Bond Ratings

John Moody first began to rate bonds in 1909; since that time, three rating agencies— Moody's, Standard & Poor's, and Fitch Investor Services—have provided ratings on corporate bonds. These ratings involve a judgment about the future risk potential of the bond. Although they deal with expectations, several historical factors seem to play a significant role in their determination.[1] Bond ratings are favorably affected by (1) a greater reliance on equity than debt in financing the firm, (2) profitable operations, (3) a low variability in past earnings, (4) large firm size, and (5) little use of subordinated debt. In turn, the rating a bond receives affects the rate of return demanded on the bond by the investors. The poorer the bond rating, the higher the rate of return demanded in the capital markets. Table 7.1 provides an example and description of these ratings. Thus, for the financial manager, bond ratings are extremely important. They provide an indicator of default risk that in turn affects the rate of return that must be paid on borrowed funds.

> **STOP AND THINK**
>
> *When we say that a lower bond rating means a higher interest rate charged by the investors (bondholders), we are observing an application of **Axiom 1: The Risk-Return Trade-Off—We Won't Take on Additional Risk Unless We Expect to be Compensated with Additional Return.***

Now that we have finished our study of the key features of most bonds, we will now classify the main types of bonds.

OBJECTIVE 3

THE DIFFERENT KINDS OF BONDS

A **bond** is simply a long-term promissory note, issued by the borrower, promising to pay its holder a predetermined and fixed amount of interest each year. Whereas the term *bond* may be defined simply as long-term debt, there are many types of bonds. In the following section, we will briefly explain several different kinds of bonds that you frequently hear about in financial circles.

Bond

A type of debt or a long-term promissory note, issued by the borrower, promising to pay its holder a predetermined and fixed amount of interest each year.

---

[1]See Willard T. Carlton, Brian Dragun and Victor Lazear, "The WPPSS Mess, or 'What's in a Bond Rating?' A Case Study," *International Review of Financial Analysis*, 1993, Vol. 2, No.1, 1–16 and John M. Cheny, "Rating Classification and Bond Yield Volatility," *Journal of Portfolio Management*, 1983, Vol. 9, No. 3, 51–57.

Table 7.1 Standard & Poor's Corporate Bond Ratings

AAA	This is the highest rating assigned by Standard & Poor's for debt obligation and indicates an extremely strong capacity to pay principal and interest.
AA	Bonds rated AA also qualify as high-quality debt obligations. Their capacity to pay principal and interest is very strong, and in the majority of instances they differ from AAA issues only in small degree.
A	Bonds rated A have a strong capacity to pay principal and interest, although they are somewhat more susceptible to the adverse effects of changes in circumstances and economic conditions.
BBB	Bonds rated BBB are regarded as having an adequate capacity to pay principal and interest. Whereas they normally exhibit adequate protection parameters, adverse economic conditions or changing circumstances are more likely to lead to a weakened capacity to pay principal and interest for bonds in this category than for bonds in the A category.
BB B CCC CC	Bonds rated BB, B, CCC, and CC are regarded, on balance, as predominantly speculative with respect to the issuers' capacity to pay interest and repay principal in accordance with the terms of the obligation. BB indicates the lowest degree of speculation and CC the highest. Although such bonds will likely have some quality and protective characteristics, these are outweighed by large uncertainties or major risk exposures to adverse conditions.
C	The rating C is reserved for income bonds on which no interest is being paid.
D	Bonds rated D are in default, and payment of principal and/or interest is in arrears.

Plus (+) or Minus (−): To provide more detailed indications of credit quality, the ratings from "AA" to "BB" may be modified by the addition of a plus or minus sign to show relative standing within the major rating categories.

SOURCE: *Standard & Poor's Fixed Income Investor*, Vol. 8 (1994). Reprinted by permission.

Mortgage Bonds

A **mortgage bond** is a bond secured by a lien on real property. Typically, the value of the real property is greater than that of the mortgage bonds issued. This provides the mortgage bondholders with a margin of safety in the event the market value of the secured property declines. In the case of foreclosure, the trustees have the power to sell the secured property and use the proceeds to pay the bondholders. In the event that the proceeds from this sale do not cover the bonds, the bondholders become general creditors, similar to debenture bondholders, for the unpaid portion of the debt.

Mortgage bond

A bond secured by a lien on real property.

Debentures

The term **debenture** applies to any unsecured long-term debt; by *unsecured*, we mean that no specific asset has been designated to be used as collateral for the loan. Because these bonds are unsecured, the earning ability of the issuing corporation is of great concern to the bondholder. They are also viewed as being more risky than secured bonds and, as a result, must provide investors with a higher yield than secured bonds provide. Often the issuing firm attempts to provide some protection to the holder through the prohibition of any additional encumbrance of assets. This prohibits the future issuance of secured long-term debt that would further tie up the firm's assets and leave the bondholders less protected. To the issuing firm, the major advantage of debentures is that no property has to be secured by them. This allows the firm to issue debt and still preserve some future borrowing power.

Debenture

Any unsecured long-term debt.

Subordinated Debentures

Subordinated debenture

A debenture that is subordinated to other debentures in being paid in the case of insolvency.

Many firms have more than one issue of debentures outstanding. In this case, a hierarchy may be specified, in which some debentures are given subordinated standing in case of insolvency. This means that the claims of the **subordinated debentures** are honored only after the claims of secured debt and unsubordinated debentures have been satisfied.

Zero and Very Low Coupon Bonds

Zero and very low coupon bonds

Bonds issued at a substantial discount from their $1,000 face value that pay no or little interest.

Zero and very low coupon bonds allow the issuing firm to issue bonds at a substantial discount from their $1,000 face value with a zero or very low coupon rate. The investor receives a large part (or all on the zero coupon bond) of the return from the appreciation of the bond. For example, in 1983, IntelComm, a telecommunications firm, issued $300 million of debt maturing in 2001 with a zero coupon rate. These bonds were sold at a 71 percent discount from their par value; that is, investors only paid $288 for a bond with a $1,000 par value. Investors who purchased these bonds for $288 and hold them until they mature in 2001 will receive a 13.25 percent yield to maturity, with all of this yield coming from appreciation of the bond. IntelComm, on the other hand, will have no cash outflows until these bonds mature; however, at that time it will have to pay back $300 million even though it only received $86 million when the bonds were first issued.

As with any form of financing, there are both advantages and disadvantages of issuing zero or very low coupon bonds. Let's look at them from the issuing firm's perspective. As a disadvantage, IntelComm faced an extremely large cash outflow when the bonds matured, much greater than the cash inflow it experienced when the bonds were first issued. Second, discount bonds can only be retired at maturity. That is, the company issuing the bond can not require the bondholder to sell the bond back to the company before the maturity date. Thus if interest rates fall, a firm cannot benefit by requiring its investors to sell their bonds back to the company. The advantages of zero and low coupon bonds are, first, that annual cash outflows associated with interest payments do not occur with zero coupon bonds and are at a relatively low level with low coupon bonds. Second, because there is relatively strong investor demand for this type of debt, prices tend to be bid up and the investor's rate of return tends to be bid down. That is to say, IntelComm was able to issue zero coupon bonds at about half a percent less than it would have been if they had been traditional coupon bonds. Finally, IntelComm was able to deduct the annual amortization of the discount from taxable income, which provided a positive annual cash flow to IntelComm.

Junk Bonds (High-Yield Bonds)

Junk or high-yield bonds

Bonds rated BB or below.

Junk bonds are high-risk debt with *ratings of BB or below* by Moody's and Standard & Poor's. The lower the rating, the higher the chance of default; the lowest class is CC for Standard & Poor's and Ca for Moody's. Originally, the term was used to describe bonds issued by "fallen angels"; that is, firms with sound financial histories that were facing severe financial problems and suffering from poor credit ratings.

Junk bonds are also called **high-yield bonds** for the high interest rates they pay the investor, typically having an interest rate of between 3 and 5 percent more than AAA-grade long-term debt.

Before the mid-1970s, smaller firms simply did not have access to the capital markets because of the reluctance of investors to accept speculative grade bonds. However,

Reading a Bond Quote in *The Wall Street Journal*

Below is shown a section of *The Wall Street Journal* that gives the quotes on July 1, 1996, for some of the corporate bonds traded on the New York Stock Exchange on that date.

Bonds	Cur Yld	Vol	Close	Net Chg
Caterpinc 6s07	6.8	49	$88\frac{3}{8}$	$+\frac{3}{8}$
ChsCp 8s04	7.9	1	101	$-\frac{5}{8}$
ChsCp $6\frac{1}{8}$08	6.8	8	$89\frac{1}{2}$	$-\frac{1}{2}$
CPWV $7\frac{1}{4}$13	7.8	30	$93\frac{1}{2}$	$-\frac{5}{8}$
Chiquta $10\frac{1}{2}$04	10.5	3	100	-1
ChckFul 7s12	cv	65	84	-1
Chryslr 10.4s99	10.0	61	$104\frac{1}{8}$	$\dots$
Chryslr 10.95s17	10.0	8	109	$\dots$
ChryF $6\frac{1}{2}$98	6.4	6	101	$\dots$
Clardge $11\frac{3}{4}$02	13.6	341	$86\frac{3}{8}$	$+\frac{1}{8}$
ClrkOil $9\frac{1}{2}$04	9.3	51	$102\frac{1}{8}$	$+\frac{1}{4}$
ClevEl $8\frac{3}{4}$05	9.0	25	$97\frac{1}{4}$	

The bonds shown in the list above as "CaterpInc 6s07" were issued by Caterpillar, Inc.; they pay a 6 percent coupon interest rate (indicated by the "6s"), or $60 interest paid semiannually (actually $30 paid semiannually) on a par value of $1,000; and they mature in 2007 (07 is the last two digits of the year the bonds mature). The closing price of the bonds on July 1, 1996, was $88\frac{3}{8}$, which is stated as a percent of the bond's $1,000 par value; thus the bond's closing price on July 1 was $883.75 = .88375 \times $1,000. The current yield on the bonds is 6.8 percent, calculated as the annual interest divided by the closing price, or $60 \div $883.75 = 6.8%. During the trading day, 49 bonds were traded on the exchange, as reflected by the "Vol" heading.[a] Finally, the net change "Net Chg" in the price of the bond from the previous day's close was an increase of $\frac{3}{8}$ of 1 percent.

[a]There may have been a lot more than 49 bonds changing hands on July 1, 1996. Many bond trades are negotiated directly between institutional investors or through bankers and are not listed in *The Wall Street Journal*.

by the late 1980s, junk bonds became the way to finance hostile takeovers—buying a firm without the management's approval. For example, the purchase of RJR Nabisco for some $20 billion by the investment group KKR was largely accomplished by junk bond financing. However, the eventual bankruptcy of Drexel Burnham Lambert, the investment banker most responsible for developing a large junk bond market, the jailing of the "king of junk bonds" Michael Milken, and increasing interest rates brought an end to the extensive use of junk bonds for financing corporate takeovers (Michael Milken, a partner at Drexel Burnham Lambert, used to have an annual conference in Beverly Hills, California, nicknamed "The Predator's Ball" for attracting takeover investors and corporate raiders who needed junk bond financing to accomplish their takeovers.)

When corporate takeovers subsided from their highs, most people thought the junk bond was forever dead. By 1990, the junk bond market was virtually nonexistent. Then, in 1992, with investors looking for higher interest rates and a rebounding economy, the junk bond market was revitalized. The following year, new junk bond issues reached a record $62 billion. Also, less than 20 percent of the proceeds from junk bonds in 1995 were used to finance mergers and acquisitions, compared to 60 percent in the 1980s. Also, in 1995, more than 800 companies had issued junk bonds, up from several hundred in the 1980s. The borrowers in the 1990s come from a variety of industries, including manufacturing, media, retailing, consumer products, financial services, and housing. Also, credit quality improved. Only 17 percent of new issues in 1995 fell into the lower ratings of creditworthiness, compared with 66 percent in 1988.

As we look forward to the late 1990s and the next millennium, junk bonds will continue to play an important role in the financing of many middle-sized firms. Mutual funds and pension funds, which owned 40 percent of all junk bonds in 1995, should continue to provide an active market for such securities. So, contrary to the conventional wisdom of the early 1990s, the junk bond market is alive and well.

STOP AND THINK

*Some have thought junk bonds were fundamentally different from other securities, but they are not. They are bonds with a great amount of risk, and therefore promise high expected returns. Thus **Axiom 1: The Risk-Return Trade-Off—We Won't Take on Additional Risk Unless We Expect to Be Compensated with Additional Return.***

Eurobonds

Eurobonds

Bonds issued in a country different from the one in whose currency the bond is denominated—for instance, a bond issued in Europe or in Asia by an American company that pays interest and principal to the lender in U.S. dollars.

Eurobonds are not so much a different type of security as they are securities, in this case bonds, issued in a country different from the one in whose currency the bond is denominated. For example, a bond that is issued in Europe or in Asia by an American company and that pays interest and principal to the lender in U.S. dollars would be considered a Eurobond. Thus even if the bond is not issued in Europe, it merely needs to be sold in a country different from the one in whose currency it is denominated to be considered a Eurobond. The Eurobond market actually had its roots in the 1950s and 1960s as the U.S. dollar became increasingly popular because of its role as the primary international reserve currency. The primary attractions to borrowers in the Eurobonds market, aside from favorable rates, are the relative lack of regulation (Eurobonds are not registered with the Securities and Exchange Commission, or SEC), less rigorous disclosure requirements than those of the SEC, and the speed with which they can be issued. Interestingly, not only are Eurobonds not registered with the SEC, but they legally cannot be offered to U.S. citizens and residents during their initial distribution.

We have to this point defined value and explained the basic valuation process; we have also described the common features and kinds of bonds that are commonly used by corporations. Now we can turn our attention to actually valuing a bond.

Issuing Junk Bonds: A Case Example

(A) On the matter of junk bonds, Lea Carty, an economist at the bond rating agency Moody's Investors Service in New York says, "The junk bond market is here to stay. It's become a very important form of financing for younger, riskier firms." One such young, risky company is CommNet.

CommNet, which went public in 1986 and had yet to make a profit by 1995, is an example of a hot, young company that issued junk bonds. A 10-year-old firm with $90 million in sales, CommNet was one of the first companies in the cellular telephone industry to use junk bond financing in 1993. The company's first issue raised $100 million to expand its eight-state rural telephone systems. CommNet sold more junk bonds in 1995, raising $80 million by selling 10-year notes with an 11.25 percent coupon.

(B) Proceeds from CommNet's second junk sale were used to pay investors of convertible stock. A conventional bank loan wasn't a viable alternative because banks don't allow companies to buy back stock with bank proceeds, he said.

The firm's chief financial officer, Dan Dwyer, **(C)** remembers the experience this way: "I think it was a combination of the quality of our company and market timing. The company's philosophy chose to sell bonds instead of stock in hopes of increasing value to shareholders."

Dwyer doesn't rule out a third junk bond issue in the future. "If we see an acquisition opportunity out there, we may well be back in the high-yield market," he said.

SOURCE: John Accola, "Junk Is Looking Good: Denver Companies Find Raising Cash with Risky Securities Easy as ATM," *Rocky Mountain News* (January 14, 1996): 80A, Denver, CO: Denver Publishing Company.

Analysis and Implications ...

A. After the collapse of the junk bond market and Drexel B (the primary supporter of such issues) filed bankruptcy, most people thought that junk bonds would no longer be an active financing source. Experience now suggests that they were wrong. The junk bond market revived and is alive and well. Many non-rated companies, such as CommNet, rely on junk bonds as an important source of financing.

B. Investors in junk bonds can be more creative and flexible in designing a bond issue than banks can be, owing to bank regulations.

C. There is some strong evidence that a firm's stock price can be expected to increase when debt is issued, but decrease when stock is issued.

BOND VALUATION

OBJECTIVE 4

The value of an asset is equal to the present value of the expected future cash flows. When applying this concept to valuing a bond, there are three essential elements that we must know. These are: (1) the amount and timing of the cash flows to be received by the investor, (2) the maturity date of the bond, and (3) the investor's required rate of return.

Figure 7.2 Data Requirements for Bond Valuation

(A) Cash Flow Information	Periodic interest payments For example, $65 per year Principal amount or par value For example, $1,000
(B) Term to Maturity	For example, 12 years
(C) Investor's Required Rate of Return	For example, 8 percent

These three elements are shown in Figure 7.2, along with an illustration of the data needed. The first item, the amount of cash flows is dictated by the periodic interest to be received and by the par value to be paid at maturity. Given these elements, we can compute the value of the bond, or the present value of the bond's future cash flows.

STOP AND THINK

The value of a bond is the present value both of future interest to be received and the par or maturity value of the bond. Simply list these cash flows, use your required rate of return as the discount rate, and find the value.

EXAMPLE

Consider a bond issued by Alaska Airlines in 1984, with a maturity date of 2014 and a stated coupon rate of 6.875 percent.[2] In 1997, with 17 years left to maturity, investors owning the bonds were requiring an 8 percent rate of return. We can calculate the value of the bonds to these investors using the following three-step valuation procedure:

Step 1:   Estimate the amount and timing of the expected future cash flows. Two types of cash flows are received by the bondholder:

a. Annual interest payments equal to the coupon rate of interest times the face value of the bond. In this example, the interest payments equal $68.75 = .06875 × $1,000. Assuming that 1997 interest payments have already been made, these cash flows will be received by the bondholder in each of the 17 years before the bond matures (1998 through 2014 = 17 years).

b. The face value of the bond of $1,000 to be received in 2014.

To summarize, the cash flows received by the bondholder are as follows:

Years	1	2	3	4 . . .	16	17
	$68.75	$68.75	$68.75	$68.75 . . .	$68.75	$ 68.75 + $1,000.00 $1,068.75

---

[2]Alaska Airlines remits the interest to its bondholders on a semiannual basis on January 15 and July 15. However, for simplicity, assume the interest is to be received annually. The effect of semiannual payments will be examined later.

Step 2: Determine the investor's required rate of return by evaluating the riskiness of the bond's future cash flows. An 8 percent required rate of return for the bondholders is given.

Step 3: Calculate the intrinsic value of the bond as the present value of the expected future interest and principal payments discounted at the investor's required rate of return.

The present value of Alaska Airline's bonds is found as follows:

$$\text{bond value} = V_b = \frac{\$ \text{ interest in year 1}}{(1 + \text{required rate of return})^1}$$

$$+ \frac{\$ \text{ interest in year 2}}{(1 + \text{required rate of return})^2}$$

$$+ \ldots + \frac{\$ \text{ interest in year 17}}{(1 + \text{required rate of return})^{17}}$$

$$+ \frac{\$ \text{ par value of bond}}{(1 + \text{required rate of return})^{17}}$$

or, summing over the interest and principal payments,

$$V_b = \underbrace{\sum_{t=1}^{17} \frac{\$ \text{ interest in year } t}{(1 + \text{required rate of return})^t}}_{\text{present value of interest}} + \underbrace{\frac{\$ \text{ par value of bond}}{(1 + \text{required rate of return})^{17}}}_{\text{present value of par value}}$$

STOP AND THINK

The forgoing equation is a restatement in a slightly different form of equation (7-1). Recall that equation (7-1) states that the value of an asset is the present value of future cash flows to be received by the investor.

Using I_t to represent the interest payment in year t, M to represent the bond's maturity (or par) value, and k_b to equal the bondholder's required rate of return, we may express the value of a bond maturing in year n as follows:

$$V_b = \sum_{t=1}^{n} \frac{\$I_t}{(1 + k_b)^t} + \frac{\$M}{(1 + k_b)^n} \qquad (7\text{-}3a)$$

Equivalently, we can use the notation from chapter 5 and the present value tables to compute the bond value as follows:

$$V_b = \$I_t (PVIFAk_{b,n}) + \$M(PVIFk_{b,n})$$

$$= \$68.75 (9.1216) + \$1,000 (0.2703)$$

$$\doteq \$897.41$$

The same answer, subject to a three cent rounding difference, can be found using a financial calculator, such as a TI BAII Plus. The computation is shown in the margin.[3]

Thus if investors consider 8 percent to be an appropriate required rate of return in view of the risk level associated with Alaska Airline's bonds, paying a price of $897.41 would satisfy their return requirement.

Calculator Solution

DATA INPUT	FUNCTION KEY
17	N
8	I/Y
68.75	PMT
1,000	FV

FUNCTION KEY	ANSWER
CPT PV	−897.38

---

[3]As noted in chapter 5, we are using the TI BAII Plus. You may want to return to the chapter 5 section, *Moving Through Time with the Aid of a Financial Calculator* or appendix A, to see a more complete explanation of using the TI BAII Plus. For an explanation of other calculators, see the study guide that accompanies this text.

Semiannual Interest Payments

In the preceding illustration, the interest payments were assumed to be paid annually. However, companies typically pay interest to bondholders semiannually. For example, rather than disbursing $68.75 in interest at the conclusion of each year, Alaska Airlines pays $34.375 (half of $68.75) on January 15 and July 15.

Several steps are involved in adapting equation (7-3a), as shown on the previous page, for semiannual interest payments.[4] First, thinking in terms of *periods* instead of years, a bond with a life of n years paying interest semiannually has a life of $2n$ periods. In other words, a 5-year bond ($n = 5$) that remits its interest on a semiannual basis actually makes 10 payments. Yet although the number of periods has doubled, the *dollar* amount of interest being sent to the investors for each period and the bondholders' required rate of return are half of the equivalent annual figures. I_t becomes $I_t/2$ and k_b is changed to $k_b/2$; thus, for semiannual compounding, equation (7-3a) becomes

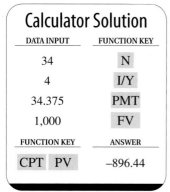

Calculator Solution

DATA INPUT	FUNCTION KEY
34	N
4	I/Y
34.375	PMT
1,000	FV

FUNCTION KEY	ANSWER
CPT PV	−896.44

$$V_b = \sum_{t=1}^{2n} \frac{\$I_t/2}{\left(1 + \dfrac{k_b}{2}\right)^t} + \frac{\$M}{\left(1 + \dfrac{k_b}{2}\right)^{2n}} \qquad (7\text{-}3b)$$

Again, using the present-value-interest-factor notations for discounting cash flows:

$$V_b = (\$I_t \div 2)(PVIFA_{k_b/2,\ 2n}) + \$M(PVIF_{k_b/2,\ 2n})$$

$$V_b = (\$68.75 \div 2)(18.4112) + \$1,000(0.2636)$$

$$= \$896.49$$

Thus in this instance, the value of the Alaskan Airline bonds is slightly less if interest is paid semiannually.

OBJECTIVE 5

BONDHOLDERS' EXPECTED RATES OF RETURN (YIELD TO MATURITY)

Theoretically, each investor could have a different required rate of return for a particular security. However, the financial manager is only interested in the required rate of return that is implied by the market prices of the firm's securities. That is, when a financial manager issues a bond in the capital markets, only one price is set—not one for each individual investor. In other words, the consensus of a firm's investors about the expected rate of return is reflected in the current market price of the bond.

Bondholder's expected rate of return

The discount rate that equates the present value of the future cash flows (interest and maturity value) with the current market price of the bond. It is the rate of return an investor will earn if a bond is held to maturity.

Yield to maturity

The same as the expected rate of return (see above).

To measure the **bondholder's expected rate of return**, $\bar{k}_b$, we would find the discount rate that equates the present value of the future cash flows (interest and maturity value) with the current market price of the bond.[5] The expected rate of return for a bond is also the rate of return the investor will earn if the bond is held to maturity, or the **yield to maturity**. Thus when referring to bonds, the terms *expected rate of return* and *yield to maturity* are often used interchangeably.

To illustrate this concept, consider the Brister Corporation's bonds, which are selling for $1,100. The bonds carry a coupon interest rate of 9 percent and mature in 10 years.

---

[4]The logic for calculating the value of a bond that pays interest semiannually is similar to the material presented in chapter 5, where compound interest with nonannual periods was discussed.

[5]When we speak of computing an expected rate of return, we are not describing the situation very accurately. Expected rates of return are *ex ante* (before the fact). They are based on "expected and unobservable future cash flows," and therefore can only be estimated.

Sure, Markets Are Rational, Just Like Life

To mainstream economists, markets are the great citadel of rational man. When buying a car, you and I may indulge a fantasy, or a neurosis. But as participants in impersonal markets, we are cool, calculating and predictable. And be there, somewhere in the land, an investor who succumbs to fantasy and pays an irrational price, then the army of rational soldiers will step into the breach and profit from the error, thereby correcting it (by selling). In this sense, financial markets are different. Even if you think the Land Rover I purchase is overpriced, there is no way you can sell it short. But the presence of other investors will keep me from paying too much for a stock.

This is true, usually. According to economics texts, it is true all the time—a significant leap. (A) According to the state religion of economics departments and business schools, prices are so uniformly rational that no one can constantly profit from exploiting stocks. Harvard's Michael Jenson long ago deemed this view "accepted as a fact of life."

Indeed it permeates every breath of modern finance. Since beating the stock market is a presumed impossibility, consistently successful investors are dismissed as lucky coin-flippers. (B) Moreover, the assumption of market rationality has perverted the notion of "risk." Since each stock price is assumed to be "right," each bounce of every stock is also assumed to be right,

and the amount that any one stock has bounced around has been widely accepted as a proxy for its "riskiness." (C) There is another interpretation—the stock prices are occasionally silly and many short-term bounces are meaningless, the product of the herd listing to one direction and then another. A small but growing band of economists are coming around. In their view, the human traits that influence behavior—among them fear of ridicule—also affect markets. "One of the biggest errors in human judgment is to pay attention to the crowd," says Robert Shiller, a Yale economist. This explains the crash of 1987, when stocks fell 23% on no news.

Welcome to the school of behavioral economics. It is loosely knit and boasts no grand theory—only that the old theory of pervasive rationality doesn't fit the human actors who actually buy and sell . . . Such work once was considered heretical . . . But behavior is now a hot topic, even among statistically oriented economists. No less a sage than Prof. Jensen is studying neurology. "I have been driven by the idea that rationality doesn't describe a whole lot of behavior," the former apostle of rationalism says.

SOURCE: Excerpts from Roger Lowenstein, "Sure, Markets Are Rational, Just Like Life," *The Wall Street Journal* (June 13, 1996): C1. Reprinted by permission of *The Wall Street Journal*, © 1996 by Dow Jones & Co., Inc. All Rights Reserved Worldwide.

Analysis and Implications . . .

A. When we say *uniformly rational*, at least according to the Capital Asset Pricing Model, we mean that prices are determined by expected return and risk.

B. Remember that our notion of "risk" is variability of returns—and nothing else.

C. The idea that the markets are efficient has long been the belief of the academicians who study market efficiency. However, some people have argued that the markets are inefficient. But they have had difficulty arguing their case in a convincing way. Intuitively, they have felt that the psychological aspects of investing—such as greed and fear—could make investors behave differently than might be expected by our finance models. This argument of irrationality may have some merit in support of their beliefs.

(Remember the coupon rate determines the interest payment, where the interest payment equals coupon rate $\times$ par value.)

In determining the expected rate of return $(\bar{k}_b)$ implicit in the current market price, we need to find the rate that discounts the anticipated cash flows back to a present value of $1,100, which is the existing market price (P_0) for the bond.

Finding the expected rate of return for a bond using the present value tables is done by trial and error. We have to keep trying new rates until we find the discount rate that results in the present value of the future interest and maturity value of the bond just equaling the current market value of the bond. If the expected rate is somewhere between rates in the present value tables, we then must interpolate between the rates.

For our example, if we try 7 percent, the bond's present value is $1,140.16. Because the present value of $1,140.16 is greater than the market price of $1,100, then the current interest rate (expected rate of return) is higher than 7 percent. Thus we should try a higher rate. Increasing the discount rate, say, to 8 percent gives a present value of $1,066. Now the present value is less than the market price; thus we know that the investor's expected rate of return is between 7 percent and 8 percent. The calculations are shown as follows:

| Years | Cash flow | 7 percent | | 8 percent | |
		Present value factors	Present value	Present value factors	Present value
1–10	$ 90 per year	7.024	$ 632.16	6.710	$ 603.90
10	$1,000 in year 10	0.508	508.00	0.463	463.00
		Present value at 7 percent:	$1,140.16	Present value at 8 percent:	$1,066.90

Because we now know the rate is between 7 percent and 8 percent, we may interpolate to find the expected return. Because a 7 percent discount rate yields a value of $1,140.16, we want to increase the discount rate just enough to lower the value to $1,100 (the current market price), or by $40.16. But when we increase the rate to 8 percent, the value of the bond is lowered by $73.26 to $1,066.90. Thus we should only increase the interest rate by 0.55 of 1 percent ($40.16 ÷ $73.26) and not a full 1 percent. This process may be shown as follows:

Rate	Value	Differences in Value	
7%	$1,140.16		
$\bar{k}_b$	1,100.00	$40.16	$73.26
8%	1,066.90		

Solving for $\bar{k}_b$ by interpolation, we have:

$$\bar{k}_b = 7\% + \left(\frac{\$40.16}{\$73.26}\right)(8\% - 7\%) = 7.55\%$$

Thus the expected rate of return on the Brister Corporation's bonds for an investor who purchases the bonds for $1,100 is approximately 7.55 percent.

Rather than using the present value tables to compute the expected return for the Brister Corporation's bonds, which is cumbersome, it is much easier to use a calculator. The solution (using a TI BAII Plus) is shown in the left margin.

Calculator Solution

DATA INPUT	FUNCTION KEY
10	N
1,100	PV
90	+/– PMT
1,000	+/– PV

FUNCTION KEY	ANSWER
CPT I/Y	7.54

Given our understanding of bond valuation and a bondholder's expected rate of return, let's discover what else a financial manager needs to know to understand why bond prices and interest rates perform as they do.

BOND VALUATION: FIVE IMPORTANT RELATIONSHIPS

We have now learned to find the value of a bond (V_b), given (1) the amount of interest payments, (2) the maturity or par value, (3) the length of time to maturity, and (4) the investor's required rate of return. We also know how to compute the expected rate of return, $\bar{k}_b$, which also happens to be the *current interest rate* on the bond, given (1) the current market value, (2) the amount of interest payments, (3) the maturity value, and (4) the length of time to maturity. We now have the basics. However, a financial manager needs to know more in order to understand how the firm's bonds will react to changing conditions. So let's go further in our understanding of bond valuation by studying several important relationships.

First Relationship

The value of a bond is inversely related to changes in the investor's present required rate of return (the current interest rate). In other words, as interest rates increase (decrease), the value of the bond decreases (increases).

To illustrate, assume that an investor's required rate of return for a given bond is 12 percent. The bond has a par value of $1,000 and annual interest payments of $120, indicating a 12 percent coupon interest rate ($120 ÷ $1,000 = 12%). Assuming a 5-year maturity date, the bond would be worth $1,000, computed as follows by using equation (7-3a):

$$V_b = \frac{I_1}{(1+k_b)^1} + \ldots + \frac{I_n}{(1+k_b)^n} + \frac{M}{(1+k_b)^n}$$

$$= \sum_{t=1}^{n} \frac{I_t}{(1+k_b)^t} + \frac{M}{(1+k_b)^n}$$

$$= \sum_{t=1}^{5} \frac{\$120}{(1+.12)^t} + \frac{\$1,000}{(1+.12)^5} = \$1,000$$

Using present value tables, we have:

$$V_b = \$120\,(PVIFA_{12\%,5yr}) + \$1,000(PVIF_{12\%,5yr})$$

$$V_b = \$120(3.605) + \$1,000(.567)$$

$$= \$432.60 + \$567.00$$

$$= \$999.60 \cong \$1,000.00$$

If, however, the investor's required rate of return increases from 12 percent to 15 percent, the value of the bond would decrease to $899.24, computed as follows:

$$V_b = \$120\,(PVIFA_{15\%,5yr}) + \$1,000(PVIF_{15\%,5yr})$$

$$V_b = \$120(3.352) + \$1,000(.497)$$

$$= \$402.24 + \$497.00$$

$$= \$899.24$$

Figure 7.3 Value and Required Rates for a 5-Year Bond at 12 Percent Coupon Rate

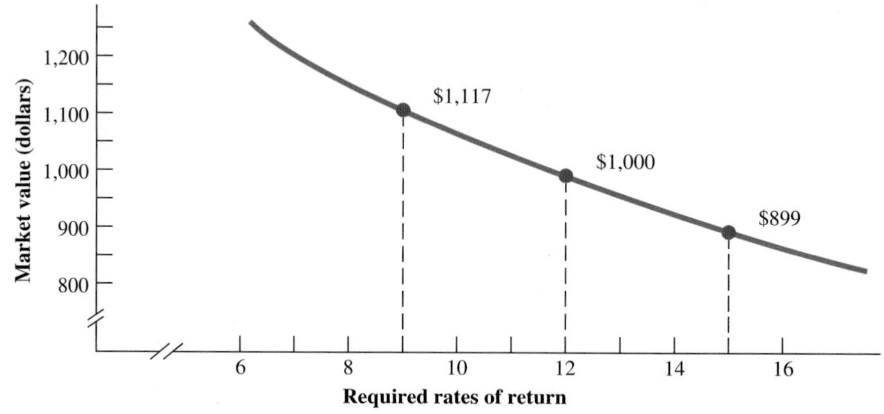

On the other hand, if the investor's required rate of return decreases to 9 percent, the bond would increase in value to $1,116.80:

$$V_b = \$120 \ (PVIFA_{9\%,5\text{yr}}) + \$1,000(PVIF_{9\%,5\text{yr}})$$

$$V_b = \$120(3.890) + \$1,000(.650)$$

$$= \$466.80 + \$650.00$$

$$= \$1,116.80$$

This inverse relationship between the investor's required rate of return and the value of a bond is presented in Figure 7.3. Clearly, as an investor demands a higher rate of return, the value of the bond decreases. Because the interest payments and par value are fixed, the higher rate of return the investor desires can be achieved only by paying less for the bond. Conversely, a lower required rate of return yields a higher market value for the bond.

Changes in bond prices represent an element of uncertainty for the bond investor as well as the financial manager. If the current interest rate (required rate of return) changes, the price of the bond also fluctuates. An increase in interest rates causes the bondholder to incur a loss in market value. Because future interest rates and the resulting bond value cannot be predicted with certainty, a bond investor is exposed to the risk of changing values as interest rates vary. This risk has come to be known as **interest-rate risk**.

Interest-rate risk

The variability in a bond's value (risk) caused by changing interest rates.

Second Relationship

The market value of a bond will be less than the par value if the investor's required rate is above the coupon interest rate; but it will be valued above par value if the investor's required rate of return is below the coupon interest rate.

Using the previous example, we observed that:

1. The bond has a *market* value of $1,000, equal to the par or maturity value, when the investor's required rate of return equals the 12 percent coupon interest rate. In other words, if

   required rate = coupon rate, then *market value = par value*

        12%   =   12%,   then $1,000   = $1,000

2. When the required rate is 15 percent, which exceeds the 12 percent coupon rate, the market value falls below par value to $899.24; that is, if

> *required rate > coupon rate*, then *market value < par value*

> 15%   >   12%,   then $899.24   < $1,000

In this case, the bond sells at a discount below par value; thus it is called a **discount bond**.

3. When the required rate is 9 percent, or less than the 12 percent coupon rate, the market value, $1,116.80, exceeds the bond's par value. In this instance, if

> *required rate < coupon rate*, then *market value > par value*

> 9%   <   12%,   then $1,116.80   > $1,000

The bond is now selling at a premium above par value; thus it is a **premium bond**.

Discount bond

A bond that is selling below its par value.

Premium bond

A bond that is selling above its par value.

Third Relationship

As the maturity date approaches, the market value of a bond approaches its par value.

Continuing to draw from our example, the bond has 5 years remaining until the maturity date. The bond sells at a discount below par value ($899.24), when the required rate is 15 percent; and it sells at a premium above par value ($1,116.80), when the required rate is only 9 percent.

In addition to knowing value today, an investor would also be interested in knowing how these values would change over time, assuming no change in the current interest rates. For example, how will these values change when only 2 years remain until maturity rather than 5 years? Table 7.2 shows (1) the values with 5 years remaining to maturity, (2) the values as recomputed with only 2 years left until the bonds mature, and (3) the changes in values between the 5-year bonds and the 2-year bonds. The following conclusions can be drawn from these results:

1. The premium bond sells for less as maturity approaches. The price decreases from $1,116.80 to $1,053.08 over the 3 years.
2. The discount bond sells for more as maturity approaches. The price increases from $899.24 to $951.12 over the 3 years.

The change in prices over the entire life of the bond is shown in Figure 7.4. The graph clearly demonstrates that the value of a bond, either a premium or a discount bond, approaches par value as the maturity date becomes closer in time.

Fourth Relationship

Long-term bonds have greater interest rate risk than do short-term bonds.

As already noted, a change in current interest rates (required rate of return) causes a change in the market value of a bond. However, the impact on value is greater for long-term bonds than it is for short-term bonds.

Table 7.2 Values Relative to Maturity Dates

Required Rate	Market Value If Maturity Is:		Change in Value
	5 Years	2 Years	
9%	$1,116.80	$1,053.08	–$63.72
12	1,000.00	1,000.00	.00
15	899.24	951.12	51.88

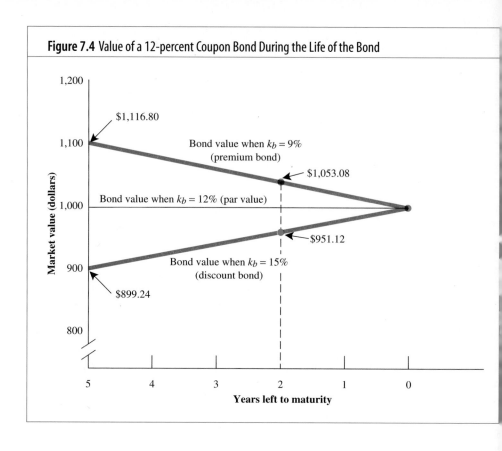

Figure 7.4 Value of a 12-percent Coupon Bond During the Life of the Bond

In Figure 7.3, we observed the effect of interest rate changes on a 5-year bond paying a 12 percent coupon interest rate. What if the bond did not mature until 10 years from today instead of 5 years? Would the changes in market value be the same? Absolutely not. The changes in value would be more significant for the 10-year bond. For example, if we vary the current interest rates (the bondholder's required rate of return) from 9 percent to 12 percent and then to 15 percent, as we did earlier with the 5-year bond, the values for both the 5-year and the 10-year bonds would be as follows:

| | Market Value for a 12% Coupon Rate Bond Maturing in | |
Required Rate	5 Years	10 Years
9%	$1,116.80	$1,192.16
12	1,000.00	1,000.00
15	899.24	849.28

Using these values and the required rates, we can graph the changes in values for the two bonds relative to different interest rates. These comparisons are provided in Figure 7.5. The figure clearly illustrates that the long-term bond (say 10 years) is more responsive or sensitive to interest rate changes than the price of a short-term bond (say 5 years).

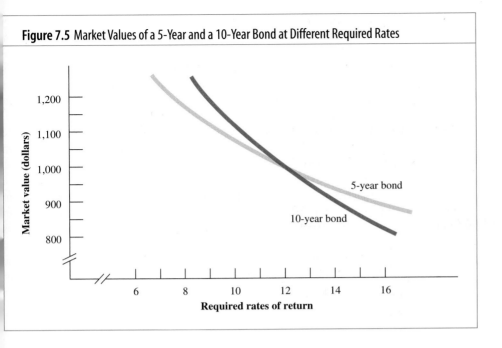

Figure 7.5 Market Values of a 5-Year and a 10-Year Bond at Different Required Rates

The reason long-term bond prices fluctuate more than short-term bond prices in response to interest rate changes is simple. Assume an investor bought a 10-year bond yielding a 12 percent interest rate. If the current interest rate for bonds of similar risk increased to 15 percent, the investor would be locked into the lower rate for 10 years. If, on the other hand, a shorter-term bond had been purchased, say one maturing in 2 years, the investor would have to accept the lower return for only 2 years and not the full 10 years. At the end of year 2, the investor would receive the maturity value of $1,000 and could buy a bond offering the higher 15 percent rate for the remaining 8 years. Thus interest rate risk is determined, at least in part, by the length of time an investor is required to commit to an investment. However, the holder of a long-term bond may take some comfort from the fact that long-term interest rates are usually not as volatile as short-term rates. If the short-term rate changed 1 percentage point, for example, it would not be unusual for the long-term rate to change only 0.3 percentage points.

Fifth Relationship

The sensitivity of a bond's value to changing interest rates depends not only on the length of time to maturity, but also on the pattern of cash flows provided by the bond.

It is not at all unusual for two bonds with the same maturity to react differently to a change in interest rates. Consider two bonds, A and B, both with 10-year maturities and the same 10 percent coupon interest rate. Although the bonds are similar in terms of maturity date and the contractual interest rate, the structure of the interest payments is different for each bond. Bond A pays $100 interest annually, with the $1,000 principal being repaid at the end of the tenth year. Bond B is a zero-coupon bond; it pays no interest until the bond matures. At that time, the bondholder receives $1,593.70 in interest plus $1,000 in principal. The value of both bonds, assuming a market interest rate (required rate of return) of 10 percent, is $1,000. However, if interest rates fell to 6 percent, bond A's market value would be $1,294, compared with $1,447 for bond B. Why the difference? Both bonds have the same maturity, and each promises the same 10 percent rate of return. The answer lies in the differences in their cash flow patterns. Bond B's cash flows are received in the more distant future on average than are the cash flows for bond A. Because a change in interest rates always has a greater impact on the present value of later cash flows than on earlier cash flows (due to the effects of compounding), bonds with cash flows coming later, on average, will be more sensitive to interest rate changes than will bonds with earlier cash flows. This phenomenon was recognized in 1938 by Macaulay, who devised the concept of duration.

The **duration** of a bond is simply a measure of the responsiveness of its price to a change in interest rates. The greater the relative percentage change in a bond price in response to a given percentage change in the interest rate, the longer the duration. In computing duration, we consider not only the maturity or term over which cash flows are received but also the time pattern of interim cash flows. Specifically, duration is a weighted average time to maturity in which the weight attached to each year is the present value of the cash flow for that year. A measurement of duration may be represented as follows:

$$\text{duration} = \frac{\sum_{t=1}^{n} \dfrac{tC_t}{(1+k_b)^t}}{P_0}$$

(7-4)

where t = the year the cash flow is to be received

n = the number of years to maturity

C_t = the cash flow to be received in year t

k_b = the bondholder's required rate of return

P_0 = the bond's present value

For our two bonds, A and B, duration would be calculated as follows:

$$\text{duration bond A} = \frac{\left((1)\dfrac{\$100}{(1.1)^1} + (2)\dfrac{\$100}{(1.1)^2} + (3)\dfrac{\$100}{(1.1)^3} + \ldots + (9)\dfrac{\$100}{(1.1)^9} + (10)\dfrac{\$1,100}{(1.1)^{10}} \right)}{\$1,000}$$

$$= 6.759$$

$$\text{duration bond B} = \frac{\left((1)\dfrac{0}{(1.1)^1} + (2)\dfrac{0}{(1.1)^2} + (3)\dfrac{0}{(1.1)^3} + \ldots + (9)\dfrac{0}{(1.1)^9} + (10)\dfrac{\$2,593.70}{(1.1)^{10}} \right)}{\$1,000}$$

$$= 10$$

Thus although both bonds have the same maturity, 10 years, the zero-coupon bond (bond B) is more sensitive to interest rate changes, as suggested by its higher duration, which in this instance equals its maturity. The lesson learned: in assessing a bond's sensitivity to changing interest rates, the bond's duration is the more appropriate measure, not the term to maturity.

HOW FINANCIAL MANAGERS USE THIS MATERIAL

To be effective as a financial manager, we must have a good understanding of the capital markets, where a company's bonds and stocks are issued and are bought and sold. The forgoing presentation has provided us the foundation to that understanding. Much of what has been said has been from an investor's perspective, but it is crucial that the financial manager see the "territory" from that perspective as well. Otherwise, the manager is likely to be blindsided by the markets. Also, many firms not only issue bonds, but also buy and sell bonds of other companies as well as the federal and state governments. The financial manager then becomes an investor in his or her own right.

SUMMARY

Valuation is an important issue if we are to manage a company effectively. An understanding of the concepts and how to compute the value of a security underlie much that we do in finance and in making correct decisions for the firm as a whole. Only if we know what matters to our investors can we maximize the firm's value.

Value is defined differently depending on the context. But for us, value is the present value of future cash flows expected to be received from an investment discounted at the investor's required rate of return.

OBJECTIVE 1

The valuation process can be described as follows: It is assigning value to an asset by calculating the present value of its expected future cash flows using the investor's required rate of return as the discount rate. The investor's required rate of return, k, equals the risk-free rate of interest plus a risk premium to compensate the investor for assuming risk.

OBJECTIVE 2

A bond, as a form of debt, is a promisory note issued by a firm, committing to pay a fixed amount of interest and to repay the amount borrowed. Some of the more important terms and characteristics about bonds include the following:

OBJECTIVE 3

- claims on assets and income
- par value
- coupon interest rate
- maturity
- indenture
- current yield
- interest tax shield
- bond ratings

There are a variety of types of bonds, including: Eurobonds, subordinated debentures, mortgage bonds, debentures, zero and very low coupon bonds, and junk bonds.

OBJECTIVE 3

The value of a bond is the present value both of future interest to be received and the par or maturity value of the bond.

OBJECTIVE 4

To measure the bondholders' expected rate of return, we find the discount rate that equates the present value of the future cash flows (interest and maturity value) with the current market price of the bond. The expected rate of return for a bond is also the rate of return the investor will earn if the bond is held to maturity, or the *yield to maturity*.

OBJECTIVE 5

OBJECTIVE 6

Five key relationships exist in bond valuation:

1. A decrease in interest rates (required rates of return) will cause the value of a bond to increase; an interest rate increase will cause a decrease in value. The change in value caused by changing interest rates is called interest rate risk.
2. If the bondholder's required rate of return (current interest rate):
   a. Equals the coupon interest rate, the bond will sell at par, or maturity value.
   b. Exceeds the bond's coupon rate, the bond will sell below par value, or at a *discount*.
   c. Is less than the bond's coupon rate, the bond will sell above par value, or at a *premium*.
3. As a bond approaches maturity, the market price of the bond approaches the par value.
4. A bondholder owning a long-term bond is exposed to greater interest rate risk than one owning a short-term bond.
5. The sensitivity of a bond's value to interest rate changes is not only affected by the time to maturity, but also by the time pattern of interim cash flows, or its *duration*.

GO TO:
http://www.prenhall.com/bfm
For downloads and current events associated with this chapter

KEY TERMS

Bond, 266	**Efficient market**, 260	**Market value**, 260
Bondholder's expected rate of return, 274	**Eurobonds**, 270	**Maturity**, 265
	Indenture, 265	**Mortgage bond**, 267
Book value, 260	**Interest-rate risk**, 278	**Par value of a bond**, 265
Coupon interest rate, 265	**Interest tax shield**, 266	**Premium bond**, 279
Current yield, 265	**Intrinsic or economic value**, 260	**Subordinated debenture**, 268
Debenture, 267		**Yield to maturity**, 274
Discount bond, 279	**Junk or low-rated bonds**, 268	**Zero and very low coupon bonds**, 268
Duration, 282	**Liquidation value**, 260	

FINCOACH PRACTICE EXERCISES FOR CHAPTER 7

To maximize your grades and master the mathematics discussed in this chapter, open *FINCOACH* on the *Finance Learning and Development Center* CD-ROM and practice problems in the following categories: 1) Valuation of Multiple Cash Flows, 2) Bond Valuation

STUDY QUESTIONS

7-1. What are the basic differences between book value, liquidation value, market value, and intrinsic value?

7-2. What is a general definition of the intrinsic value of a security?

7-3. Explain the three factors that determine the intrinsic or economic value of an asset.

7-4. Explain the relationship between an investor's required rate of return and the value of a security.

7-5. **a.** How does a bond's par value differ from its market value?
   b. Explain the difference between a bond's coupon interest rate, the current yield, and a bondholder's required rate of return.

7-6. Describe the bondholder's claim on the firm's assets and income.

7-7. What factors determine a bond's rating? Why is the rating important to the firm's manager?

7-8. Distinguish between debentures and mortgage bonds.

7-9. Define (a) Eurobonds, (b) zero coupon bonds, and (c) junk bonds.

7-10. Define the bondholder's expected rate of return.

7-11. How does the market value of a bond differ from its par value when the coupon interest rate does not equal the bondholder's required rate of return?

7-12. Differentiate between a premium bond and discount bond. What happens to the premium or discount for a given bond over time?

7-13. Why is the value of a long-term bond more sensitive to a change in interest rates than a short-term bond?

7-14. Explain duration.

SELF-TEST PROBLEMS

ST-1. (*Bond Valuation*) Trico bonds have a coupon rate of 8 percent, a par value of $1,000, and will mature in 20 years. If you require a return of 7 percent, what price would you be willing to pay for the bond? What happens if you pay *more* for the bond? What happens if you pay *less* for the bond?

ST-2. (*Bond Valuation*) Sunn Co.'s bonds, maturing in 7 years, pay 8 percent on a $1,000 face value. However, interest is paid semiannually. If your required rate of return is 10 percent, what is the value of the bond? How would your answer change if the interest were paid annually?

ST-3. (*Bondholder's Expected Rate of Return*) Sharp Co. bonds are selling in the market for $1,045. These 15-year bonds pay 7 percent interest annually on a $1,000 par value. If they are purchased at the market price, what is the expected rate of return?

ST-4. (*Duration*) Calculate the value and the duration for the following bonds:

Bond	Years to Maturity	Annual Interest	Maturity Value
Argile	10	$80	$1,000
Terathon	15	65	1,000

The required rate of return is 8 percent.

STUDY PROBLEMS (SET A)

7-1A. (*Bond Valuation*) Calculate the value of a bond that expects to mature in 12 years and has a $1,000 face value. The coupon interest rate is 8 percent and the investors' required rate of return is 12 percent.

7-2A. (*Bond Valuation*) Enterprise, Inc., bonds have a 9 percent coupon rate. The interest is paid semiannually and the bonds mature in 8 years. Their par value is $1,000. If your required rate of return is 8 percent, what is the value of the bond? What is its value if the interest is paid annually?

7-3A. (*Bondholder's Expected Rate of Return*) The market price is $900 for a 10-year bond ($1,000 par value) that pays 8 percent interest (4 percent semiannually). What is the bond's expected rate of return?

7-4A. (*Bond Expected Rate of Return*) Exxon 20-year bonds pay 9 percent interest annually on a $1,000 par value. If bonds sell at $945, what is the bond's expected rate of return?

7-5A. (*Bondholder's Expected Rate of Return*) Zenith Co.'s bonds mature in 12 years and pay 7 percent interest annually. If you purchase the bonds for $1,150, what is your expected rate of return?

7-6A. (*Bond Valuation*) National Steel 15-year, $1,000 par value bonds pay 8 percent interest annually. The market price of the bonds is $1,085, and your required rate of return is 10 percent.

    a. Compute the bond's expected rate of return.

    b. Determine the value of the bond to you, given your required rate of return.

    c. Should you purchase the bond?

7-7A. (*Bond Valuation*) You own a bond that pays $100 in annual interest, with a $1,000 par value. It matures in 15 years. Your required rate of return is 12 percent.

    a. Calculate the value of the bond.

    b. How does the value change if your required rate of return (*i*) increases to 15 percent or (*ii*) decreases to 8 percent?

    c. Explain the implications of your answers in part (b) as they relate to interest rate risk, premium bonds, and discount bonds.

    d. Assume that the bond matures in 5 years instead of 15 years. Recompute your answers in part (b).

    e. Explain the implications of your answers in part (d) as they relate to interest rate risk, premium bonds, and discount bonds.

7-8A. (*Bondholder Expected Return*) Abner Corporation's bonds mature in 15 years and pay 9 percent interest annually. If you purchase the bonds for $1,250, what is your expected rate of return?

7-9A. (*Bond Valuation*) Telink Corporation bonds pay $110 in annual interest, with a $1,000 par value. The bonds mature in 20 years. Your required rate of return is 9 percent.

    a. Calculate the value of the bond.

    b. How does the value change if (*i*) your required rate of return (*k*) increases to 12 percent or (*ii*) decreases to 6 percent?

    c. Interpret your finding in parts (a) and (b).

7-10A. (*Duration*) Calculate the value and the duration for the following bonds:

Bond	Years to Maturity	Annual Interest	Maturity Value
P	5	$100	$1,000
Q	5	70	1,000
R	10	120	1,000
S	10	80	1,000
T	15	65	1,000

Your required rate of return is 8 percent.

INTEGRATIVE PROBLEM

Following you will find data on $1,000 par value bonds issued by Atari, Sun Company, and Time Warner at the end of 1997. Assume you are thinking about buying these bonds as of January 1998. Answer the following questions for each of these bonds:

    1. Calculate the values of the bonds if your required rates of return are as follows: Atari 11 percent, Sun Company 7 percent, and Time Warner 9 percent where:

	Atari	Sun	Time Warner
Coupon interest rates	5.25%	9.375%	7.45%
Years to maturity	8	22	5

2. At the end of 1997, the bonds were selling for the following amounts:

Atari	$ 630
Sun Company	$1,050
Time Warner	$ 976

What were the expected rates of return for each bond?

3. How would the values of the bonds change if (*i*) your required rate of return (*k*) increases 3 percentage points or (*ii*) decreases 3 percentage points?

4. Explain the implications of your answers in part 2 as they relate to interest rate risk, premium bonds, and discount bonds.

5. Compute the duration for each of the bonds. Interpret your results.

6. What are some of the things you can conclude from the above computations?

7. Should you buy the bonds? Explain.

STUDY PROBLEMS (SET B)

7-1B. (*Bond Valuation*) Calculate the value of a bond that expects to mature in 10 years and has a $1,000 face value. The coupon interest rate is 9 percent and the investors' required rate of return is 15 percent.

7-2B. (*Bond Valuation*) Pybus, Inc., bonds have a 10 percent coupon rate. The interest is paid semiannually and the bonds mature in 11 years. Their par value is $1,000. If your required rate of return is 9 percent, what is the value of the bond? What is it if the interest is paid annually?

7-3B. (*Bondholder Expected Return*) A bond's market price is $950. It has a $1,000 par value, will mature in 8 years, and pays 9 percent interest (4.5 percent semiannually). What is your expected rate of return?

7-4B. (*Bond Expected Rate of Return*) Doisneau 20-year bonds pay 10 percent interest annually on a $1,000 par value. If you buy the bonds at $975, what is your expected rate of return?

7-5B. (*Bondholder Expected Return*) Hoyden Co.'s bonds mature in 15 years and pay 8 percent interest annually. If you purchase the bonds for $1,175, what is your expected rate of return?

7-6B. (*Bond Valuation*) Fingen 14-year, $1,000 par value bonds pay 9 percent interest annually. The market price of the bonds is $1,100 and your required rate of return is 10 percent.

   a. Compute the bond's expected rate of return.

   b. Determine the value of the bond to you, given your required rate of return.

   c. Should you purchase the bond?

7-7B. (*Bond Valuation*) Arizona Public Utilities issued a bond that pays $80 in interest, with a $1,000 par value. It matures in 20 years. Your required rate of return is 7 percent.

   a. Calculate the value of the bond.

   b. How does the value change if your required rate of return (*i*) increases to 10 percent or (*ii*) decreases to 6 percent?

   c. Explain the implications of your answers in part (b) as they relate to interest rate risk, premium bonds, and discount bonds.

   d. Assume that the bond matures in 10 years instead of 20 years. Recompute your answers in part (b).

   e. Explain the implications of your answers in part (d) as they relate to interest rate risk, premium bonds, and discount bonds.

7-8B. (*Bondholder Expected Return*) Zebner Corporation's bonds mature in 14 years and pay 7 percent interest annually. If you purchase the bonds for $1,110, what is your expected rate of return?

7-9B. (*Bond Valuation*) Visador Corporation bonds pay $70 in annual interest, with a $1,000 par value. The bonds mature in 17 years. Your required rate of return is 8.5 percent.

    a. Calculate the value of the bond.

    b. How does the value change if (*i*) you required rate of return (*k*) increases to 11 percent or (*ii*) decreases to 6 percent?

    c. Interpret your finding in parts (a) and (b).

7-10B. (*Duration*) Calculate the value and the duration for the following bonds:

Bond	Years to Maturity	Annual Interest	Maturity Value
A	5	$ 90	$1,000
B	5	60	1,000
C	10	120	1,000
D	15	90	1,000
E	15	75	1,000

Your required rate of return is 7 percent.

SELF-TEST SOLUTIONS

SS-1.

$$\text{Value } (V_b) = \sum_{t=1}^{20} \frac{\$80}{(1.07)^t} + \frac{\$1,000}{(1.07)^{20}}$$

Thus

Present value of interest: $80(10.594) = \$\ \ 847.52$

Present value of par value: $1,000(0.258) = \underline{\ \ \ 258.00}$

                            Value $(V_b) = \underline{\underline{\$1,105.52}}$

If you pay more for the bond, your required rate of return will not be satisfied. In other words, by paying an amount for the bond that exceeds $1,105.52, the expected rate of return for the bond is less than the required rate of return. If you have the opportunity to pay less for the bond, the expected rate of return exceeds the 7 percent required rate of return.

SS-2. If interest is paid semiannually:

$$\text{Value } (V_b) = \sum_{t=1}^{14} \frac{\$40}{(1+0.05)^t} + \frac{\$1,000}{(1+0.05)^{14}}$$

Thus

    $40(9.899) = \$395.96$

$1,000(0.505) = \underline{\ \ 505.00}$

    Value $(V_b) = \underline{\underline{\$900.96}}$

If interest is paid annually:

$$\text{Value } (V_b) = \sum_{t=1}^{7} \frac{\$80}{(1.10)^t} + \frac{\$1,000}{(1.10)^7}$$

$$V_b = \$80 \ (4.868) + \$1,000 \ (0.513)$$

$$V_b = \$902.44$$

SS-3.

$$\$1,045 = \sum_{t=1}^{15} \frac{\$70}{(1+\bar{k}_b)^t} + \frac{\$1,000}{(1+\bar{k}_b)^{15}}$$

At 6%: $\$70(9.712) + \$1,000(0.417) = \$1,096.84$

At 7%: Value must equal $1,000.

Interpolation:

Expected rate of return: $\bar{k}_b = 6\% + \dfrac{\$51.84}{\$96.84}(1\%) = 6.54\%$

SS-4.

Calculator Solution	
DATA INPUT	FUNCTION KEY
15	N
70	+/− PMT
1,000	+/− FV
1,045	PV
FUNCTION KEY	ANSWER
CPT I/Y	6.52

	Bond			
	Argile $1,000 (value)		Terathon $872 (value)	
Years	C_t	$(t)(PV(C_t))$	C_t	$(t)(PV(C_t))$
1	$ 80	$ 74	$ 65	$ 60
2	80	137	65	111
3	80	191	65	155
4	80	235	65	191
5	80	272	65	221
6	80	302	65	246
7	80	327	65	265
8	80	346	65	281
9	80	360	65	293
10	1,080	5,002	65	301
11			65	307
12			65	310
13			65	311
14			65	310
15			1,065	5,036
Sum of $(t)(PV(C_t))$		$7,247		$8,398
Duration		7.25		9.63

Learning Objectives

Active Applications

World Finance

Practice

CHAPTER 8

LEARNING OBJECTIVES

After reading this chapter, you should be able to

1. Identify the basic characteristics and features of preferred stock.

2. Value preferred stock.

3. Identify the basic characteristics and features of common stock.

4. Value common stock.

5. Calculate a stock's expected rate of return.

STOCK VALUATION

INTRODUCTION

Throughout the 1990s, a record number of privately owned companies issued stock for the first time to the public—often called initial public offerings, or IPOs. For instance, on May 31, 1997, online bookseller Amazon.com raised $54 million from issuing 3 million shares of common stock at $18 per share. Before the end of the day, the shares had increased to $30, before declining to $23.50. Given that only about one-tenth of the total shares were issued to the public, the firm's market value for all its stock was about $550 million. Although Amazon.com shares rose as much as 67 percent in first-day trading, that was mild compared with earlier, high-profile Internet stock offerings. Yahoo shares soared 154 percent; Netscape Communications increased 108 percent in its first day of trading.

Even though these are the glamour stories, they could be told by many other young firms from cosmetic makers to oil companies, all having one thing in common—a need for additional equity capital to finance the firm's growth. FPA Medical Management is one such firm that was able to grow by issuing common stock to investors:

> Dr. Sol Lizerbram heads up FPA Medical Management, a small San Diego company that assembles networks of doctors. A tiny startup just five years ago, FPA did its IPO in October of 1994. Armed with $11.5 million raised at the initial offering and $26 million raised in another offering last fall, Lizerbram hired staff, acquired medical and management services groups, and seeded new startups. From zero earnings, 40 employees, and just $18 million in revenue 18 months ago, FPA now employs nearly 700, reaches throughout California and beyond to six other states, and will pull in an estimated $170 million in revenue this year. "We owe that growth to public capital," says Lizerbram.[1]

---

[1]John Wyatt, "America's Amazing IPO Bonanza," *Fortune* (May 27, 1996): 77.

Thus the financial managers of firms wanting to issue stock, whether for the first time or not, need to have a clear understanding of the different features of stock and how stock is valued. In this chapter, we will address these important issues.

CHAPTER PREVIEW

In chapter 7, we developed a general concept about valuation, where economic value was defined as the present value of the expected future cash flows generated by the asset. We then applied that concept to valuing bonds.

We now give our attention to valuing stocks, both preferred stock and common stock. As already noted at the outset of our study of finance and on several occasions since, the financial manager's objective should be to maximize the value of the firm's common stock. Thus we need to understand what determines stock value.

As we have done in all other chapters, it is important to begin by identifying the axioms that are important in understanding the topic to be studied—in this case, the basic considerations in issuing and valuing stock. These axioms are as follows: Axiom 1: The Risk-Return Trade-Off—We Won't Take on Additional Risk Unless We Expect to Be Compensated with Additional Return; Axiom 2: The Time Value of Money—A Dollar Received Today Is Worth More Than a Dollar Received in the Future; Axiom 3: Cash—Not Profits—Is King; Axiom 7: The Agency Problem—Managers Won't Work for the Owners Unless It's in Their Best Interest.

The first three axioms listed above relate to our definition of value—present value of cash flows. The last axiom, Axiom 7, indicates that the value of a firm's stock is in part dictated by the willingness of management to work in the best interest of the owners, which for most large companies are not the same group.

FEATURES AND TYPES OF PREFERRED STOCK

OBJECTIVE 1

Preferred stock is often referred to as a hybrid security because it has many characteristics of both common stock and bonds. Preferred stock is similar to common stock in that it has no fixed maturity date, the nonpayment of dividends does not bring on bankruptcy, and dividends are not deductible for tax purposes. On the other hand, preferred stock is similar to bonds in that dividends are fixed in amount.

The size of the preferred stock dividend is generally fixed either as a dollar amount or as a percentage of the par value. For example, Texas Power and Light has issued $4 preferred stock, whereas Toledo Edison has some 4.25 percent preferred stock outstanding. The par value on the Toledo Edison preferred stock is $100; hence each share pays 4.25% × $100, or $4.25 in dividends annually. Because these dividends are fixed, preferred stockholders do not share in the residual earnings of the firm but are limited to their stated annual dividend.

In examining preferred stock, we will first discuss several features common to almost all preferred stock. Next we will investigate features less frequently included and take a brief look at methods of retiring preferred stock. We will then learn how to value preferred stock.

Although each issue of preferred stock is unique, a number of characteristics are common to almost all issues. Some of these more frequent traits include:

- multiple classes of preferred stock
- preferred stock's claim on assets and income
- cumulative dividends
- protective provisions
- convertibility

Preferred stock

A hybrid security with characteristics of both common stock and bonds. It is similar to common stock because it has no fixed maturity date, the nonpayment of dividends does not bring on bankruptcy, and dividends are not deductible for tax purposes. Preferred stock is similar to bonds in that dividends are limited in amount.

Other features that are less common include:

- adjustable rates
- participation
- payment in kind (PIK)

In addition, there are provisions frequently used to retire an issue of preferred stock, including the ability of the firm to call its preferred stock or to use a sinking-fund provision to repurchase preferred shares. All these features are presented in the discussion that follows.

Multiple Classes

If a company desires, it can issue more than one series or class of preferred stock, and each class can have different characteristics. In fact, it is quite common for firms that issue preferred stock to issue more than one series. For example, Philadelphia Electric has 13 different issues of preferred stock outstanding. These issues can be further differentiated in that some are convertible into common stock and others are not, and they have varying priority status regarding assets in the event of bankruptcy.

Claim on Assets and Income

Preferred stock has priority over common stock with regard to claims on assets in the case of bankruptcy. If a firm is liquidated, the preferred stock claim is honored after that of bonds and before that of common stock. Multiple issues of preferred stock may be given an order of priority. Preferred stock also has a claim on income prior to common stock. That is, the firm must pay its preferred stock dividends before it pays common stock dividends. Thus in terms of risk, preferred stock is safer than common stock because it has a prior claim on assets and income. However, it is riskier than long-term debt because its claims on assets and income come after those of bonds.

Cumulative Feature

Most preferred stocks carry a cumulative feature. **Cumulative preferred stock** requires all past unpaid preferred stock dividends be paid before any common stock dividends are declared. This feature provides some degree of protection for the preferred shareholder. Without a cumulative feature, management might be tempted not to pay preferred dividends when common stock dividends were passed. Because preferred stock does not have the dividend enforcement power of interest from bonds, the cumulative feature is necessary to protect the rights of preferred stockholders.

Protective Provisions

In addition to the cumulative feature, protective provisions are common to preferred stock. These **protective provisions** generally allow for voting rights in the event of nonpayment of dividends, or they restrict the payment of common stock dividends if sinking-fund payments are not met or if the firm is in financial difficulty. In effect, the protective features included with preferred stock are similar to the restrictive provisions included with long-term debt.

To examine typical protective provisions, consider Tenneco Corporation and Reynolds Metals preferred stocks. The Tenneco preferred stock has a protective provision that provides preferred stockholders with voting rights whenever six quarterly dividends are in arrears. At that point, the preferred shareholders are given the power to elect a majority of the board of directors. The Reynolds Metals preferred stock includes a protective provision that precludes the payment of common stock dividends during any period in which the preferred stock sinking fund is in default. Both provisions, which yield protection beyond that provided by the cumulative provision and thereby reduce shareholder risk, are desirable. Given these protective provisions for the investor, they reduce the cost of preferred stock to the issuing firm.

Convertibility

Much of the preferred stock that is issued today is **convertible** at the discretion of the holder into a predetermined number of shares of common stock. In fact, today about one-third of all preferred stock issued has a convertibility feature. The convertibility feature is, of course, desirable to the investor and thus reduces the cost of the preferred stock to the issuer.

Convertible preferred stock

Convertible preferred stock allows the preferred stockholder to convert the preferred stock into a predetermined number of shares of common stock, if he or she so chooses.

Adjustable Rate Preferred Stock

Adjustable preferred stock was developed to provide investors with some protection against wide swings in principal that occur when interest rates move up and down. With this kind of preferred stock, quarterly dividends fluctuate with interest rates under a formula that ties the dividend payment at either a premium or discount to the highest of (1) the 3-month Treasury bill rate, (2) the 10-year Treasury bond rate, or (3) the 20-year Treasury bond rate. For instance, BankAmerica has adjustable rate preferred stock, where the dividend rate is adjusted every 3 months to 2 percentage points below the highest of the interest rates on three U.S. Treasury securities, but no lower than 6.5 percent and no greater than 14.5 percent.

Although adjustable rate preferred stock allows dividend rates to be tied to the rates on Treasury securities, it also provides a maximum and a minimum level to which they can climb or fall, called the *dividend rate band*. The purpose of allowing the dividend rate on this preferred stock to fluctuate is, of course, to minimize the fluctuation in the value of the preferred stock. In times of high and fluctuating interest rates, this is a very appealing feature indeed.

Adjustable rate preferred stock

Preferred stock intended to provide investors with some protection against wide swings in the stock value that occur when interest rates move up and down. The dividend rate changes along with prevailing interest rates.

Another type of adjustable rate preferred stock is **auction rate preferred stock**. With this stock, the dividend rate is set every 49 days by an auction process. At each auction, buyers and sellers place bids for shares, specifying the yield they are willing to accept for the next 7-week period. The yield is then set at the lowest level necessary to match buyers and sellers. As a result, the yield offered on auction rate preferred stock accurately reflects current interest rates, while keeping the market price of these securities at par.

Auction rate preferred stock

Variable rate preferred stock in which the dividend rate is set by an auction process.

Participation

Although *participating* features are infrequent in preferred stock, their inclusion can greatly affect its desirability to investors and cost to the issuing firm. The **participation feature** allows the preferred stockholder to participate in earnings beyond the payment of the stated dividend. This is usually done in accordance with some set formula. For example, Borden Series A preferred stock currently provides for a dividend of *no less than* 60 cents per share, to be determined by the board of directors.[2] Preferred stock of this sort actually resembles common stock as much as it does normal preferred stock. Although a participating feature is certainly desirable from the point of view of the investor, it is infrequently included in preferred stock.

Participating preferred stock

Allows the preferred stockholder to participate in earnings beyond the payment of the stated dividend.

---

[2]During the early 1990s, Borden ran into financial problems. By fall of 1994, the firm was being restructured financially and later acquired, which altered some of the agreements with investors. As a result, the Borden Series A preferred shareholders did not participate in earnings in the ensuing years.

PIK Preferred

One byproduct of the acquisition boom of the late 1980s was the creation of payment-in-kind (PIK) preferred stock. With **PIK preferred**, investors receive no dividends initially; they merely get more preferred stock, which in turn pays dividends in even more preferred stock. Eventually (usually after 5 or 6 years if all goes well for the issuing company), cash dividends should replace the preferred stock dividends. Needless to say, the issuing firm has to offer hefty dividends, generally ranging from 12 percent to 18 percent, to entice investors to purchase PIK preferred.

Retirement Features

Although preferred stock does not have a set maturity associated with it, issuing firms generally provide for some method of retirement. If preferred stock could not be retired, issuing firms could not take advantage of falling interest rates. In other words, if interest rates decline, a financial manager would want to retire (pay off) the preferred stock that is currently outstanding and issue new debt or preferred stock at the lower rate. Without the retirement feature, the manager would be unable to do so.

Most preferred stock has some type of **call provision** associated with it. A call provision allows a company to repurchase its preferred stock (or bonds) from their holders at stated prices over a given time period. In fact, the Securities and Exchange Commission discourages the issuance of preferred stock without some call provision. The SEC has taken this stance on the grounds that if a method of retirement is not provided, the issuing firm will not be able to retire its preferred stock if interest rates fall.

The call feature on preferred stock usually involves an initial premium above the par value or issuing price of the preferred of approximately 10 percent. Then over time, the call premium generally falls. By setting the initial call price above the initial issue price and allowing it to decline slowly over time, the firm protects the investor from an early call that carries no premium. A call provision also allows the financial manager to plan the retirement of its preferred stock at predetermined prices.

A **sinking fund** provision requires the firm periodically to set aside an amount of money for the retirement of its preferred stock. This money is then used to purchase the preferred stock in the open market or through the use of the call provision, whichever method is cheaper. Although preferred stock does not have a maturity date associated with it, the use of a call provision in addition to a sinking fund can effectively create a maturity date. For example, a Quaker Oats issue of preferred stock has an annual sinking fund, operating between the years 1981 and 2005, which requires the annual elimination of a minimum of 20,000 shares and a maximum of 40,000 shares. The minimum payments are designed so that the entire issue will be retired by the year 2005. If any sinking fund payments are made above the minimum amount, the issue will be retired prior to 2005. Thus the size of the outstanding issue decreases each year after 1981.

OBJECTIVE 2 ◦ **VALUING PREFERRED STOCK**

As already explained, the owner of preferred stock generally receives a *constant income* from the investment in each period. However, the return from preferred stock comes in the form of *dividends* rather than *interest*. In addition, whereas bonds generally have a specific maturity date, most preferred stocks are perpetuities (nonmaturing). In this instance, finding the value (present value) of preferred stock, V_{ps}, with a level cash flow stream continuing indefinitely, may best be explained by an example.

EXAMPLE

Consider AT&T's preferred stock issue. In the same way that we valued bonds in chapter 7, we will use a three-step valuation procedure.

Step 1: Estimate the amount and timing of the receipt of the future cash flows the preferred stock is expected to provide. AT&T's preferred stock pays an annual dividend of $3.64. The shares do not have a maturity date; that is, they go to perpetuity.

Step 2: Evaluate the riskiness of the preferred stock's future dividends and determine the investor's required rate of return. For AT&T, assume that the investor's required rate of return is 7 percent.[3]

Step 3: Calculate the economic or intrinsic value of the share of preferred stock, which is the present value of the expected dividends discounted at the investor's required rate of return. The valuation model for a share of preferred stock (V_{ps}) is therefore defined as follows:

$$V_{ps} = \frac{\text{dividend in year 1}}{(1 + \text{required rate of return})^1}$$
$$+ \frac{\text{dividend in year 2}}{(1 + \text{required rate of return})^2}$$
$$+ \ldots + \frac{\text{dividend in infinity}}{(1 + \text{required rate of return})^\infty}$$
$$= \frac{D_1}{(1 + k_{ps})^1} + \frac{D_2}{(1 + k_{ps})^2} + \ldots + \frac{D_\infty}{(1 + k_{ps})^\infty}$$
$$V_{ps} = \sum_{t=1}^{\infty} \frac{D_t}{(1 + k_{ps})^t} \tag{8-1}$$

Because the dividends for preferred stock represent a perpetuity—they continue indefinitely—equation (8-1) can be reduced to the following relationship:[4]

$$V_{ps} = \frac{\text{annual dividend}}{\text{required rate of return}} = \frac{D}{k_{ps}} \tag{8-2}$$

---

[3]How do we know the investor's required rate of return is 7 percent? Return to chapter 6 for an explanation of how we ascertain an investor's required rate of return.

[4]To verify this result, consider the following equation:

(i) $\qquad V_{ps} = \frac{D_1}{(1 + k_{ps})^1} + \frac{D_2}{(1 + k_{ps})^2} + \ldots + \frac{D_n}{(1 + k_{ps})^n}$

If we multiply both sides of this equation by $(1 + k_{ps})$, we have

(ii) $\qquad V_{ps}(1 + k_{ps}) = D_1 + \frac{D_2}{(1 + k_{ps})} + \ldots + \frac{D_n}{(1 + k_{ps})^{n-1}}$

Subtracting (i) from (ii) yields

$$V_{ps}(1 + k_{ps} - 1) = D_1 + \frac{D_n}{(1 + k_{ps})^n}$$

As n approaches infinity, $D_n/(1 + k_{ps})^n$ approaches zero. Consequently,

$$V_{ps}k_{ps} = D_1 \text{ and } V_{ps} = \frac{D_1}{k_{ps}}$$

Because $D_1 = D_2 = \ldots = D_n$, we need not designate the year. Therefore,

(iii) $\qquad V_{ps} = \frac{D}{k_{ps}}$

Equation (8-2) represents the present value of an infinite stream of constant cash flows. We can determine the value of the AT&T preferred stock, using equation (8-2), as follows:

$$V_{ps} = \frac{D}{k_{ps}} = \frac{\$3.64}{.07} = \$52$$

In summary, the value of a preferred stock is the present value of all future dividends. But because most preferred stocks are nonmaturing—the dividends continue to infinity—we therefore have to come up with another way for finding value as represented by equation (8-2).

RELATE TO THE BIG PICTURE

Valuing preferred stock relies on three of our axioms presented in chapter 1, namely:

- **Axiom 1: The Risk-Return Trade-Off—We Won't Take on Additional Risk Unless We Expect to Be Compensated with Additional Return.**
- **Axiom 2: The Time Value of Money—A Dollar Received Today Is Worth More Than a Dollar Received in the Future.**
- **Axiom 3: Cash—Not Profits—Is King.**

As we have already observed with bonds, determining the economic worth or value of an asset always relies on these three axioms. Without them, we would have no basis for explaining value. With them, we can know that the amount and timing of cash, not earnings, drives value. Also, we must be rewarded for taking risk; otherwise, we will not invest.

OBJECTIVE 3

Common stock

Common stock shares represent the ownership in a corporation.

CHARACTERISTICS OF COMMON STOCK

Common stock represents ownership in the corporation. Bondholders can be viewed as creditors, whereas the common stockholders are the true owners of the firm. Common stock does not have a maturity date, but exists as long as the firm does. Nor does common stock have an upper limit on its dividend payments. Dividend payments must be declared by the firm's board of directors before they are issued. In the event of bankruptcy, the common stockholders—as owners of the corporation—cannot exercise claims on assets until the firm's creditors, including the bondholders and preferred shareholders, have been satisfied.

In examining common stock, we will look first at several of its features or characteristics. Then we will focus on valuing common stock.

Claim on Income

As the owners of the corporation, the common shareholders have the right to the residual income after bondholders and preferred stockholders have been paid. This income may be paid directly to the shareholders in the form of dividends or retained and reinvested by the firm. Although it is obvious the shareholder benefits immediately from the distribution of income in the form of dividends, the reinvestment of earnings also benefits the shareholder. Plowing back earnings into the firm should result in an increase in the value of the firm, in its earning power, and in its future dividends. This action in turn results in an increase in the value of the stock. In effect, residual income is distributed directly to shareholders in the form of dividends or indirectly in the form of capital gains (a rising stock price) on their common stock.

What Does a Stock Look Like?

The right to residual income has both advantages and disadvantages for the common stockholder. The advantage is that the potential return is limitless. Once the claims of the more senior securities (bonds and preferred stock) have been satisfied, the remaining income flows to the common stockholders in the form of dividends or capital gains. The disadvantage: If the bond and preferred stock claims on income totally absorb earnings, common shareholders receive nothing. In years when earnings fall, it is the common shareholder who suffers first.

Claim on Assets

Just as common stock has a residual claim on income, it also has a residual claim on assets in the case of liquidation. Only after the claims of debt holders and preferred stockholders have been satisfied do the claims of common shareholders receive attention. Unfortunately, when bankruptcy does occur, the claims of the common shareholders generally go unsatisfied. This residual claim on assets adds to the risk of common stock. Thus although common stock has historically provided a higher return than

Warren Buffett: Responding to the Capital Markets

If you look in *The Wall Street Journal* at the shares traded on the New York Stock Exchange, you might be surprised to see that one firm, Berkshire Hathaway, has shares that traded at $47,000 per share (as of November 1997). The firm, founded and operated by Warren Buffett, began as an insurance company in Omaha, Nebraska, and has since grown into a multibillion-dollar enterprise that now owns a portfolio of companies. But few of us could afford to buy very many (if even one) of the shares.

Thus when a need arises in the financial markets, there is always someone who responds to that need. Why not create an investment fund in which small investors could buy shares and these amounts would be accumulated to buy Berkshire Hathaway shares? In this way, small investors could own small slices of the "big shares."

When this possibility arose, Buffett did not like the idea. He feared these general investors would be led astray or engage in frequent trading of the stock, rather than be long-term investors. So Buffett made a decision to issue class B shares that would be priced at a small fraction of the original shares' price. The following is a Dow Jones News Service release announcing the new shares.

Berkshire Hathaway Class B Shares Priced at $1,110

OMAHA, Neb. (Dow Jones)—Berkshire Hathaway, Inc.'s (BRK) offer of 450,000 new class B shares was priced at $1,100 each.

In a press release the company said class A common shares closed today at $33,400. The company has said the class B shares would come to market at about one-thirtieth of the price of the class A shares.

The offering may be increased to 517,000 shares of the lower-priced stock if the underwriter, Salomon Brothers, Inc., exercises the over allotment option in full.

Berkshire Hathaway, which is about 40% owned by Warren Buffett, is an insurance holding company.

other securities, averaging 12 percent annually since the late 1920s, it also has more risks associated with it.

Voting Rights

The common shareholders elect the board of directors and are in general the only security holders given a vote. Early in this century, it was not uncommon for a firm to issue two classes of common stock that were identical, except that only one carried voting rights. For example, both the Parker Pen Co. and the Great Atlantic and Pacific Tea Co. (A&P) had two such classes of common stock. This practice was virtually eliminated by (1) the Public Utility Holding Company Act of 1935, which gave the Securities and Exchange Commission the power to require that newly issued common stock carry voting rights; (2) the New York Stock Exchange's refusal to list common stock without voting privileges; and (3) investor demand for the inclusion of voting rights. However, with the merger boom of the 1980s, dual classes of common stock with different voting rights again emerged, this time as a defensive tactic used to prevent takeovers.

Reading a Stock Quote in *The Wall Street Journal*

Following is a section of *The Wall Street Journal* that gives the quotes for some of the stocks traded on the New York Stock Exchange on February 12, 1997.

| 52 Weeks | | Stock | Sym | Div | Yld % | PE | Vol. 100s | Hi | Lo | Close | Net Chg |
Hi	Lo										
$107\frac{7}{8}$	$73\frac{5}{8}$	GenElec	GE	2.08	2.0	24	28140	$106\frac{1}{8}$	$104\frac{1}{4}$	$105\frac{7}{8}$	$+1\frac{3}{4}$
$32\frac{7}{8}$	$27\frac{1}{8}$	GenGrowProp	GGP	1.72	5.5	14	1498	$31\frac{1}{2}$	$31\frac{1}{4}$	$31\frac{1}{4}$	$-\frac{1}{4}$
$4\frac{1}{4}$	$2\frac{3}{8}$	GenHost	GH		...	dd	439	$3\frac{1}{2}$	$3\frac{3}{8}$	$3\frac{3}{8}$	$-\frac{3}{4}$
$14\frac{1}{8}$	8	GenHouse	GHW	.32	3.1	dd	65	$10\frac{5}{8}$	$10\frac{3}{8}$	$10\frac{3}{8}$	$-\frac{1}{8}$
$34\frac{3}{8}$	$18\frac{1}{8}$	GeninstrCp	GIC		...	dd	7091	$23\frac{5}{8}$	$23\frac{1}{4}$	$23\frac{1}{2}$	$+\frac{3}{8}$
$68\frac{3}{4}$	52	GenMills	GIS	2.00	2.9	24	5591	$68\frac{1}{4}$	$67\frac{3}{8}$	$67\frac{7}{8}$	$-\frac{3}{4}$
$63\frac{3}{4}$	$45\frac{3}{4}$	GenMotor	GM	2.00f	3.5	10	29880	$57\frac{7}{8}$	$56\frac{3}{4}$	$57\frac{5}{8}$	$+\frac{7}{8}$

These stocks include some familiar companies, such as General Electric (GE), General Mills, and General Motors, that are listed in *The Wall Street Journal* on a daily basis. To help us understand how to read the quotes, consider General Electric:

- The 52-week *Hi* column shows that General Electric stock reached a high of $107\frac{7}{8}$ ($107.88) during the past year.
- The 52-week *Lo* column shows that General Electric sold for a low of $73\frac{5}{8}$ ($73.63) during the past year.
- The *Stock* (GenElec) and *Sym* (GE) columns give an abbreviated version of the corporation's name and the ticker symbol, respectively.
- *Div*, the dividend column, gives the amount of dividend that General Electric paid its common stockholder's in the last year; $2.08 per share.

- *Yld %* (2.0) is the stock's dividend yield—the amount of the dividend divided by the day's closing price ($2.08 ÷ $105.88).
- *PE* (24) gives the current market price ($105\frac{7}{8}$) divided by the firm's earnings per share.
- The amount of General Electric stock traded on February 12, 1997 is represented in the *Vol 100s* column, or 2,814,000 shares.
- General Electric stock traded at a high price (*Hi* – $106\frac{1}{8}$) and a low price (*Lo* – $104\frac{1}{4}$) during the day.
- The previous day's closing price is subtracted from the closing price (*Close*) of $105\frac{7}{8}$ for February 12, 1997 for a net change (Net Chg) of $+1\frac{1}{4}$.

Common shareholders not only have the right to elect the board of directors, they also must approve any change in the corporate charter. A typical charter change might involve the authorization to issue new stock or perhaps a merger proposal.

Voting for directors and charter changes occur at the corporation's annual meeting. Whereas shareholders may vote in person, the majority generally vote by proxy.

Proxy

A proxy gives a designated party the temporary power of attorney to vote for the signee at the corporation's annual meeting.

Proxy fight

When rival groups compete for proxy votes in order to control the decisions made in a stockholder meeting.

Majority voting

Each share of stock allows the shareholder one vote, and each position on the board of directors is voted on separately. As a result, a majority of shares has the power to elect the entire board of directors.

A **proxy** gives a designated party the temporary power of attorney to vote for the signee at the corporation's annual meeting. The firm's management generally solicits proxy votes and, if the shareholders are satisfied with its performance, has little problem securing them. However, in times of financial distress or when management takeovers are being attempted, **proxy fights**—battles between rival groups for proxy votes—occur.

Although each share of stock carries the same number of votes, the voting procedure is not always the same from company to company. The two procedures commonly used are majority and cumulative voting. Under **majority voting**, each share of stock allows the shareholder one vote, and each position on the board of directors is voted on separately. Because each member of the board of directors is elected by a simple majority, a majority of shares has the power to elect the entire board of directors.

With **cumulative voting**, each share of stock allows the shareholder a number of votes equal to the number of directors being elected. The shareholder can then cast all of his or her votes for a single candidate or split them among the various candidates. The advantage of a cumulative voting procedure is that it gives minority shareholders the power to elect a director.

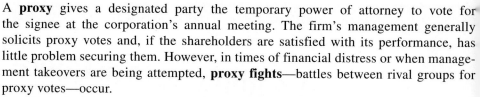

RELATE TO THE BIG PICTURE

*In theory, the shareholders pick the corporate board of directors, generally through proxy voting, and the board of directors in turn picks the management. Unfortunately, in reality the system frequently works the other way around. Shareholders are offered a slate of nominees selected by management from which to choose. The end result is that management effectively selects the directors, who then may have more allegiance to the managers than to the shareholders. This in turn sets up the potential for agency problems in which a divergence of interests between managers and shareholders is allowed to exist, with the board of directors not monitoring the managers on behalf of the shareholders as they should. The result: **Axiom 7: The Agency Problem—Managers Won't Work for the Owners Unless It's in Their Best Interest**. A former president for Archer-Daniels-Midland, is one example among many of the agency problem. At one time, he would place his own family members and personal friends on the firm's board, paying them at rates twice the norm.*

Cumulative voting

Each share of stock allows the shareholder a number of votes equal to the number of directors being elected. The shareholder can then cast all of his or her votes for a single candidate or split them among the various candidates.

Preemptive rights

The right of a common shareholder to maintain a proportionate share of ownership in the firm. When new shares are issued, common shareholders have the first right of refusal.

Rights

Certificates issued to shareholders giving them an option to purchase a stated number of new shares of stock at a specified price during a 2- to 10-week period.

Preemptive Rights

The **preemptive right** entitles the common shareholder to maintain a proportionate share of ownership in the firm. When new shares are issued, common shareholders have the first right of refusal. If a shareholder owns 25 percent of the corporation's stock, then he or she is entitled to purchase 25 percent of the new shares. Certificates issued to the shareholders giving them an option to purchase a stated number of new shares of stock at a specified price typically during a 2- to 10-week period are called **rights**. These rights can be exercised (generally at a price set by management below the common stock's current market price), can be allowed to expire, or can be sold in the open market.

Limited Liability

Although the common shareholders are the actual owners of the corporation, their liability in the case of bankruptcy is limited to the amount of their investment. The advantage is that investors who might not otherwise invest their funds in the firm become willing to do so.

ETHICS IN AMERICAN BUSINESS: A SPECIAL REPORT, 1988

Ethics: Keeping Perspective

Ethical and moral lapses in the business and financial community, academia, politics, and religion fill the daily press. But the rash of insider-trading cases on Wall Street against recent graduates of top business and law schools seems particularly disturbing because the cream of the crop, with six-figure incomes and brilliant careers ahead, is being convicted.

Most appear to have been very bright, highly motivated overachievers, driven by peer rivalries to win a game in which the score had a dollar sign in front of it. Although there have been a few big fish, most sold their futures for $20,000 to $50,000 of illicit profits. They missed the point—that life is a marathon, not a sprint.

In fact, most business school graduates become competent executives, managing people and resources for the benefit of society. The rewards—the titles and money—are merely byproducts of doing a good job.

To illustrate the point, consider the owner of a small company who had the opportunity to acquire a contract with a large Fortune 500 company to produce a product for the large firm. Verbal agreement was reached on the deal, but when the owner met with the president of the large company to sign the contract, the price of the product to be produced by the small firm was $0.25 per unit higher than originally agreed upon—in the small owner's favor. When questioned, the president of the large firm informed the small firm owner she was to deposit the difference in a personal account and then periodically send the money to the president's personal bank account. Because the small firm owner was not directly profiting from the president's clearly unethical behavior, should she have accepted the terms? It would have increased her firm's profits—but only by a legitimate amount. How about the president of the large company? Why would he be willing to act unethically for what would have meant $40,000 or $50,000 to him?

NOTE: Adapted from John S. R. Shad, "Business's Bottom Line: Ethics," *Ethics in American Business: A Special Report*, Touche Ross & Co., 1988, 56.

VALUING COMMON STOCK

OBJECTIVE 4

Like both bonds and preferred stock, a common stock's value is equal to the present value of all future cash flows expected to be received by the stockholder. However, in contrast to bonds, common stock does not promise its owners interest income or a maturity payment at some specified time in the future. Nor does common stock entitle the holder to a predetermined constant dividend, as does preferred stock. For common stock, the dividend is based on (1) the profitability of the firm, and (2) on management's decision to pay dividends or to retain the profits to grow the firm.

Thus dividends will vary with a firm's profitability and its stage of growth. In a company's early years, little if any dividends are typically paid. The funds are needed to finance the firm's growth—to capture the opportunity that was identified by the founders. As a company's growth slows—additional investment opportunities become less attractive—and the business becomes more profitable, the financial manager will then begin paying dividends to the common stockholders. As the firm eventually reaches maturity and growth is no longer a priority, the financial manager should increase the dividends even more. In short, a firm's stage of growth has direct implications on the dividends to be paid and on the value of the stock.

The Growth Factor in Valuing Common Stock

What is meant by the term *growth* when used in the context of valuing common stock? A company can grow in a variety of ways. It can become larger by borrowing money to invest in new projects. Likewise, it can issue new stock for expansion. Management could also acquire another company to merge with the existing firm, which would increase the firm's assets. In all these cases, the firm is growing through the use of new financing, by issuing debt or common stock. Although management could accurately say that the firm has grown, the original stockholders may or may not participate in this growth. Growth is realized through the infusion of new capital. The firm's assets have clearly increased, but unless the original investors increase their investment in the firm, they will own a smaller portion of the expanded business.

Another means of growing is internal growth, which comes from management retaining some or all of the firm's profits for reinvestment in the firm, in turn resulting in the growth of future earnings and hopefully the value of the existing common stock. Although not a direct investment in the company—the shareholders did not send the firm any additional money—the retention of profits is a form of investment by the current common stockholders. The money made from existing product lines could be distributed to the shareholders, but instead is retained as a source of financing future growth. In this way, the current stockholders participate in the growth of the company. It is this internal growth (no financing was acquired from new external sources) that matters in valuing the shares of the present common stockholders.[5]

EXAMPLE

To illustrate the nature of internal growth, assume that the return on equity for PepsiCo is 16 percent.[6] If PepsiCo's management decides to pay all the profits out in dividends to its stockholders, the firm will experience no growth internally. It might become larger by borrowing more money or issuing new stock, but internal growth will come only through the retention of profits. If, on the other hand, PepsiCo retained all the profits, the stockholders' investment in the firm would grow by the amount of profits retained, or by 16 percent. If, however, management kept only 50 percent of the profits for reinvestment, the common shareholders' investment would increase only by half of the 16 percent return on equity, or by 8 percent. Generalizing this relationship, we have

$$g = ROE \times r, \tag{8-3}$$

where g = the growth rate of future earnings and the growth in the common stockholders' investment in the firm

ROE = the return on equity (net income/common book value)

r = the company's percentage of profits retained, called the profit-retention rate.[7]

---

[5]We are not arguing that the existing common stockholders never benefit from the use of external financing; however, such benefit is more evasive when dealing with competitive capital markets.

[6]The return on equity is the percentage return on the common shareholders investment in the company and is computed as follows:

$$\text{return on equity} = \frac{\text{net income}}{(\text{par value} + \text{paid in capital} + \text{retained earnings})}$$

[7]The retention rate is also equal to (1 – the percentage of profits paid out in dividends). The percentage of profits paid out in dividends is often called the dividend-payout ratio.

Promoting Stock on the Internet

The following story reported in *The Wall Street Journal* shows both the potential for communicating with investors and the ethical issues that can arise.

When Todd Bakar, a securities analyst with Hambrecht & Quist, began following Iomega Corp., he considered himself prudent. On the plus side, Iomega has a hot product: an affordable and removable storage disk with far more capacity than conventional floppies. On the other hand, Mr. Bakar observed, the stock price was rich. At $9.50 a share, price had risen a remarkable 17 times in 15 months.

That was in March [1996]. Two months later in May, Iomega had quintupled to $54. All based on one positive earnings report and literally thousands of messages over the Motley Fool, an on-line bulletin board on America Online. Some of the messages were informative; some were "financial trash."

According to Iomega and Hambrecht & Quist, some of these cyberscribes, both bulls and bears, have taken liberties with the truth. As a result, the Securities and Exchange Commission has opened a probe into trading in the stock, as part of which the Fool has turned over thousands of postings. Kenneth Israel Jr., the SEC's district administrator in Salt Lake City says, "Obviously there is some concern with what is going on over the Internet generally—not to say there is anything illegal going on—is a new world for everybody." What should the SEC look at? For starters, is aggressive and possibly manipulative promotion—an activity rightly regulated in traditional "public" forums—getting a free ride on the info highway?

David and Tom Gardner, the brothers who run the Fool, and who recommend Iomega in their model portfolio, say the Fool provides the best research going—and provides it to the little guy. A bulletin board open to thousands can dig up more than any Wall Street firm—or journalist. "The exciting thing now, we have an open environment," Tom Gardner says, "It's a meritocracy." The brothers concede that their service is open to manipulators, but add that they are open to swift refutation.

Therefore, if only 25 percent of the profits were retained by PepsiCo, we would expect the common stockholders' investment in the firm and the value of the stock price to increase or grow by only 4 percent; that is,

$$g = 16\% \times 0.25 = 4\%$$

In summary, common stockholders frequently rely on an increase in the stock price as a source of return. If the company is retaining a portion of its earnings for reinvestment, future profits and dividends should grow. This growth should be reflected in an increased market price of the common stock in future periods, provided that the return on the funds reinvested exceeds the investor's required rate of return. Therefore, both types of return (dividends and price appreciation) are necessary in the development of a valuation model for common stock.

To explain this process, let us begin by examining how an investor—and financial manager—might value a common stock that is to be held for only 1 year.

Common Stock Valuation—Single Holding Period

For an investor holding a common stock for only 1 year, the value of the stock should equal the present value of both the expected dividend to be received in 1 year, D_1, and the anticipated market price of the share at year end, P_1. If k_{cs} represents a common stockholder's required rate of return, the value of the security, V_{cs}, would be

$$V_{cs} = \begin{bmatrix} \text{present value of dividend} \\ \text{received in 1 year } (D_1) \end{bmatrix} + \begin{bmatrix} \text{present value of market price} \\ \text{received in 1 year } (P_1) \end{bmatrix}$$

$$= \frac{D_1}{(1 + k_{cs})} + \frac{P_1}{(1 + k_{cs})}$$

EXAMPLE

Suppose an investor is contemplating the purchase of RMI common stock at the beginning of this year. The dividend at year end is expected to be $1.64, and the market price by the end of the year is projected to be $22. If the investor's required rate of return is 18 percent, the value of the security would be

$$V_{cs} = \frac{\$1.64}{(1 + .18)} + \frac{\$22}{1 + .18}$$

$$= \$1.39 + \$18.64$$

$$= \$20.03$$

Once again we see that valuation is a three-step process. First, we estimate the expected future cash flows from common stock ownership (a $1.64 dividend and a $22 end-of-year expected share price). Second, we estimate the investor's required rate of return by assessing the riskiness of the expected cash flows (assumed to be 18 percent). Finally, we discount the expected dividend and end-of-year share price back to the present at the investor's required rate of return.

Common Stock Valuation—Multiple Holding Periods

Because common stock has no maturity date and is frequently held for many years, a multiple-holding-period valuation model is needed. This model is an equation used to value stock that has no maturity date, but continues in perpetuity (or as long as the firm exists). The general common stock valuation model can be defined as follows:

$$V_{cs} = \frac{D_1}{(1 + k_{cs})^1} + \frac{D_2}{(1 + k_{cs})^2} + \ldots + \frac{D_n}{(1 + k_{cs})^n} + \ldots + \frac{D_\infty}{(1 + k_{cs})^\infty} \tag{8-4}$$

STOP AND THINK

Turn back to chapter 7, and compare equation (7-1) with equation (8-4). Equation (8-4) is merely a restatement in a slightly different form of equation (7-1). Recall that equation (7-1), which is the basis for our work in valuing securities, states that the value of an asset is the present value of future cash flows to be received by the investor. Equation (8-4) simply applies equation (7-1) to valuing common stock.

Equation (8-4) indicates that we are discounting the dividend at the end of the first year, D_1, back 1 year; the dividend in the second year, D_2, back 2 years; the dividend in the nth year back n years; and the dividend in infinity back an infinite number of years.

Netscape Issues Stock to the Public

(A) Below is *The New York Times* account of Netscape Communications Corporation issuing stock to the public on August 10, 1995—an event that set a new record for a first-day stock offering.

(B) A 15-month-old company that has never made a dime of profit had one of the most stunning debuts in Wall Street history yesterday as investors rushed to pour their money into cyberspace.

Netscape Communications Corporation, founded in April 1994, produces a popular software program (C) that allows users of personal computers and modems to pilot their way through the Internet's World Wide Web.

Netscape became the latest—and hottest—company in the Internet business to list shares on the nation's stock exchanges. Shares of Netscape, which had been priced at $28 before trading began at 11 A.M., (D) opened far higher—at $71. The shares soon surged to as high as $74.75. By noon, money managers at big mutual funds and other institutional investors fortunate enough to be in on the ground floor could have cashed in profit of more than 150 percent and gone to lunch.

But that left plenty of action for other investors, some of whom racked up losses, during an afternoon of frantic buying and selling. Indeed, many of the 5.75 million available shares—13 percent of the total number of outstanding shares—traded hands more than once yesterday. The volume of trading of the stock reached 13.88 million shares by the time the

closing bell rang. The price of Netscape shares ended at $58.25 apiece, up $30.25 from the offering price.

It was the best opening day for a stock in Wall Street history for an issue of its size. The overall dollar value of the one-day gain in the stock was $173.9 million. And the total market value of Netscape, including the shares held previously by management and venture capital firms, grew to $2.2 billion.

(E) As a result of the phenomenal demand, some people are riding the Internet wave to phenomenal wealth—on paper at least. At the company's current valuation, James H. Clark, the company's 50-year-old chairman and largest shareholder, holds a stake worth $566 million. Marc L. Andreessen, Netscape's 24-year-old vice president of technology and an inventor of its prize software, based on yesterday's closing price, is worth more than $58 million.

(F) Still, Netscape's future is by no means assured. Many hot new issues have soared only to come crashing down to earth. The Internet is still considered to be in its infancy and there are many wealthy and powerful competitors. Microsoft, for example, has licensed a rival browser from Spyglass and plans to distribute it along with the Microsoft Windows 95 software later this year.

SOURCE: Laurence Zuckerman, "With Internet Cachet, Not Profit, a New Stock Is Wall Street's Darling," *The New York Times* (August 10, 1995): A1. Copyright © 1995 by The New York Times Co. Reprinted by permission.

Analysis and Implications …

A. Issuing stock to the public for the first time is called an initial public offering (IPO).

B. You might think that before a stock would be attractive to the public as a prospective investment that the firm would have reported profits. That is not necessarily the case for high-tech firms. The value of such companies is more a function of their anticipated future potential, so that the company's current financial position has little significance.

C. For many years, only the "glamour" stocks could go public. The firm had to be in certain industries that had a "story" that investors could get excited about. More recently, even car dealerships in the larger cities are combining and taking the company public.

D. It is not unusual for the price of the stock to increase sharply when it is first issued, although not as much as Netscape.

E. Entrepreneurs who found companies eventually need a way to cash out of their investment in the company. Going public is one way they can gain liquidity in their investment; that is, there is a ready market for their stock if they want to sell. However, they usually cannot sell their stock immediately after the new offering. By law, they have to wait a couple of years.

F. By the end of 1997, Netscape was trading for less than $20 per share—easy come, easy go.

The required rate of return is k_{cs}. In using equation (8-4), note that the value of the stock is established at the beginning of the year, say January 1, 1999. The most recent past dividend D_0 would have been paid the previous day, December 31, 1998. Thus if we purchased the stock on January 1, the first dividend would be received in 12 months, on December 31, 1999 which is represented by D_1.

Fortunately, equation (8-4) can be reduced to a much more manageable form if dividends grow each year at a constant rate, g. The constant-growth common stock valuation equation may be represented as follows:[8]

$$\text{common stock value} = \frac{\text{dividend in year 1}}{\text{required rate of return} - \text{growth rate}} \tag{8-5}$$

$$V_{cs} = \frac{D_1}{k_{cs} - g}$$

Consequently, the intrinsic value (present value) of a share of common stock whose dividends grow at a constant annual rate in perpetuity can be calculated using equation (8-5). Although the interpretation of this equation may not be intuitively obvious, simply remember that it solves for the present value of the future dividend stream growing at a rate, g, to infinity, assuming that k_{cs} is greater than g.

STOP AND THINK

The intrinsic value of a common stock, like preferred stock, is the present value of all future dividends. And we have the same problem we had with preferred stock: It is hard to value cash flows that continue in perpetuity. So we must make some assumptions about the expected growth of future dividends. If, for example, we assume that dividends grow at a constant rate forever, we can then calculate the present value of the stock.

---

[8]Where common stock dividends grow at a constant rate of g every year, we can express the dividend in any year in terms of the dividend paid at the end of the previous year, D_0. For example, the expected dividend 1 year hence is simply $D_0(1 + g)$. Likewise, the dividend at the end of t years is $D_0(1 + g)^t$. Using this notation, the common stock valuation equation in (8-4) can be written as follows:

$$V_{cs} = \frac{D_0(1 + g)^1}{(1 + k_{cs})^1} + \frac{D_0(1 + g)^2}{(1 + k_{cs})^2} + \ldots + \frac{D_0(1 + g)^n}{(1 + k_{cs})^n} + \ldots + \frac{D_0(1 + g)^{\infty}}{(1 + k_{cs})^{\infty}}$$

If both sides of equation (8-5) are multiplied by $(1 + k_{cs})/(1 + g)$ and then equation (8-4) is subtracted from the product, the result is

$$\frac{V_{cs}(1 + k_{cs})}{1 + g} - V_{cs} = D_0 - \frac{D_0(1 + g)^{\infty}}{(1 + k_{cs})^{\infty}}$$

If $k_{cs} > g$, which normally should hold, $\left[D_0(1 + g)^{\infty}/(1 + k_{cs})^{\infty} \right]$ approaches zero. As a result,

$$\frac{V_{cs}(1 + k_{cs})}{1 + g} - V_{cs} = D_0$$

$$V_{cs}\left(\frac{1 + k_{cs}}{1 + g}\right) - V_{cs}\left(\frac{1 + g}{1 + g}\right) = D_0$$

$$V_{cs}\left[\frac{(1 + k_{cs}) - (1 + g)}{1 + g}\right] = D_0$$

$$V_{cs}(k_{cs} - g) = D_0(1 + g)$$

$$V_{cs} = \frac{D_1}{k_{cs} - g} \tag{8-7}$$

Consider the valuation of a share of common stock that paid a $2 dividend at the end of the last year and is expected to pay a cash dividend every year from now to infinity. Each year the dividends are expected to grow at a rate of 10 percent. Based on an assessment of the riskiness of the common stock, the investor's required rate of return is 15 percent. Using this information, we would compute the value of the common stock as follows:

1. Because the $2 dividend was paid last year (actually yesterday), we must compute the next dividend to be received, that is, D_1, where

$$D_1 = D_0(1 + g)$$
$$= \$2(1 + .10)$$
$$= \$2.20$$

2. Now, using equation (8-5)

$$V_{cs} = \frac{D_1}{k_{cs} - g}$$
$$= \frac{\$2.20}{.15 - .10}$$
$$= \$44$$

We have argued that the value of a common stock is equal to the present value of all future dividends, which is without question a fundamental premise of finance. In practice, however, managers, along with many security analysts, often talk about the relationship between stock value and earnings, rather than dividends. We would encourage you to be very cautious in using earnings to value a stock. Even though it may be a popular practice, the evidence available suggests that investors look to the cash flows generated by the firm, not the earnings, for value. A firm's value truly is the present value of the cash flows it produces. (We look at this issue in appendix 8A.)

We now turn to our last issue in stock valuation, that of the stockholder's expected returns, a matter of key importance to the financial manager.

RELATE TO THE BIG PICTURE

Valuing common stock is no different from valuing preferred stock; the pattern of the cash flows changes, but nothing else. Thus the valuation of common stock relies on the same three axioms that were used in valuing preferred stock:

- *Axiom 1: The Risk-Return Trade-Off—We Won't Take on Additional Risk Unless We Expect to Be Compensated with Additional Return.*
- *Axiom 2: The Time Value of Money—A Dollar Received Today Is Worth More Than a Dollar Received in the Future.*
- *Axiom 3: Cash—Not Profits—Is King.*

STOCKHOLDER'S EXPECTED RATE OF RETURN

OBJECTIVE 5

As stated in chapter 7, the expected rate of return on a bond is the return the bondholder expects to receive on the investment by paying the existing market price for the security. This rate of return is of interest to the financial manager because it tells the manager about the investor's expectations, which in turn affects the firm's cost of financing new projects. The same can be said for the financial manager needing to know the expected rate of return of the firm's stockholders, which is the topic of this next section.

The Preferred Stockholder's Expected Rate of Return

In computing the preferred stockholder's expected rate of return, we use the valuation equation for preferred stock. Earlier, equation (8-2) specified the value of a preferred stock (V_{ps}) as

$$V_{ps} = \frac{\text{annual dividend}}{\text{required rate of return}} = \frac{D}{k_{ps}}$$

Solving equation (8-2) for the preferred stockholder's required rate of return (k_{ps}), we have:

$$k_{ps} = \frac{\text{annual dividend}}{\text{intrinsic value}} = \frac{D}{V_{ps}} \qquad (8\text{-}6)$$

That is, preferred stockholder's *required* rate of return simply equals the stock's annual dividend divided by the intrinsic value. We may also restate equation (8-6) to solve for a preferred stock's *expected* rate of return, $\bar{k}_{ps}$, as follows:[9]

$$\bar{k}_{ps} = \frac{\text{annual dividend}}{\text{market price}} = \frac{D}{P_0} \qquad (8\text{-}7)$$

Note that we have merely substituted the current market price P_0, for the intrinsic value, V_{ps}. The expected rate of return $\bar{k}_{ps}$, therefore, equals the annual dividend relative to the price the stock is presently selling for, P_0. Thus the expected rate of return $\bar{k}_{ps}$, is the rate of return the investor can expect to earn from the investment if bought at the current market price. For example, if the present market price of preferred stock is $50 and it pays a $3.64 annual dividend, the expected rate of return implicit in the present market price is

$$\bar{k}_{ps} = \frac{D}{P_0} = \frac{\$3.64}{\$50} = 7.28\%$$

Therefore, investors at the margin (who pay $50 per share for a preferred security that is paying $3.64 in annual dividends) are expecting a 7.28 percent rate of return.

The Common Stockholder's Expected Rate of Return

The valuation equation for common stock was defined earlier in equation (8-4) as

$$\text{value} = \frac{\text{dividend in year 1}}{(1 + \text{required rate of return})^1} + \frac{\text{dividend in year 2}}{(1 + \text{required rate of return})^2}$$

$$+ \ldots + \frac{\text{dividend in year infinity}}{(1 + \text{required rate of return})^\infty}$$

$$V_{cs} = \frac{D_1}{(1 + k_{cs})^1} + \frac{D_2}{(1 + k_{cs})^2} + \ldots + \frac{D_\infty}{(1 + k_{cs})^\infty}$$

$$V_{cs} = \sum_{t=1}^{\infty} \frac{D_t}{(1 + k_{cs})^t}$$

---

[9]We will use $\bar{k}$ to represent a security's expected rate of return versus k for the investor's required rate of return.

MANAGEMENT COST ACCOUNTING, SEPTEMBER 21, 1992

Falsifying of Corporate Information Becoming Financial Fraud of the '90s

The names are toppling like financial dominoes: Phar-Mor, the Ohio drugstore chain; College Bound, a school test-coaching service in Florida, and Gottschalks, a retailer in California. In the last year, each has been found to have provided regulators and investors with seriously inaccurate information about its activities.

They are part of a growing parade of companies sent to the regulatory woodshed in the 1990s in what some securities lawyers and regulators say is a sharp change in the type of corporate frauds being committed—from those involving stock trading to those involving the way public companies are run.

Solid numbers are hard to come by, since the cases fall across several legal and regional jurisdictions. But in the last year alone, at least twenty public companies traded on national stock exchanges have come forward to disclose serious lapses in their past financial statements ranging from inflated sales and hidden ownership to the possibility of outright embezzlement.

"There's no doubt about it," said Charles Harper, the chief of the Miami office of the S.E.C. and one of the agency's most experienced fraud fighters. "We're seeing the serious problems migrating upstream, from the brokers to the issuers."

Cases tracked by Securities Class Action Alert, a research service in Cresskill, N.J., show the same trend.

"In the 1980s, most of the lawsuits were takeover related," said James Newman, publisher of the service. "In the '90s, we've seen a very significant rise in suits charging significant fraud and failures to disclose losses or poor earnings."

What is driving this apparent upswing in "issuer fraud" cases? Experts point to the combined effects of a strong stock market, which has enabled often-shaky companies to sell stock to big institutions, and a weak economy, which has made it harder for those companies to deliver on their promises.

"That's when you see fraud cases increase," said Richard C. Breeden, chairman of the S.E.C. "People have made projections—some mixture of hype and dream—and along comes a weak economy and the results don't measure up. So they 'cook' the books."

SOURCE: Diane B. Henrique, "Falsifying of Corporate Information Becoming Financial Fraud of the '90s," *Management Cost Accounting* (September 21, 1992): 12.

Owing to the difficulty of discounting to infinity, we made the key assumption that the dividends, D_t, increase at a constant annual compound growth rate of g. If this assumption is valid, equation (8-4) was shown to be equivalent to

$$\text{value} = \frac{\text{dividend in year 1}}{\text{required rate of return} - \text{growth rate}}$$

$$V_{cs} = \frac{D_1}{k_{cs} - g}$$

Thus V_{cs} represents the maximum value that an investor having a required rate of return of k_{cs} would pay for a security having an anticipated dividend in year 1 of D_1, that is expected to grow in future years at rate g. Solving for k_{cs}, we can compute the common stockholder's required rate of return as follows:[10]

$$k_{cs} = \left(\frac{D_1}{V_{cs}}\right) + g \qquad (8\text{-}8)$$

$$\uparrow \qquad\qquad \uparrow$$

dividend   annual
yield   growth rate

From this equation, the common stockholder's required rate of return is equal to the dividend yield plus a growth factor. Although the growth rate, g, applies to the growth in the company's dividends, given our assumptions the stock's value may also be expected to increase at the same rate. For this reason, g represents the annual percentage growth in the stock value. In other words, the investors' required rate of return is satisfied by receiving dividends and capital gains, as reflected by the expected percentage growth rate in the stock price.

As was done for preferred stock earlier, we may revise equation (8-8) to measure a common stock's *expected* rate of return, $\bar{k}_{cs}$. Replacing the intrinsic value, V_{cs}, in equation (8-8) with the stock's current market price, P_0, we may express the stock's expected rate of return as follows:

$$\bar{k}_{cs} = \frac{\text{dividend in year 1}}{\text{market price}} + \text{growth rate} = \frac{D_1}{P_0} + g$$

EXAMPLE

As an example of computing the expected rate of return for a common stock where dividends are anticipated to grow at a constant rate to infinity, assume that a firm's common stock has a current market price of $44. If the expected dividend at the conclusion of this year is $2.20 and dividends and earnings are growing at a 10 percent annual rate (last year's dividend was $2), the expected rate of return implicit in the $44 stock price is as follows:

$$\bar{k}_{cs} = \frac{\$2.20}{\$44} + 10\% = 15\%$$

As a final note, we should understand that the *expected* rate of return implied by a given market price equals the *required* rate of return for investors at the margin. For these investors, the expected rate of return is just equal to their required rate of return, and therefore they are willing to pay the current market price for the security. These investors' required rate of return is of particular significance to the financial manager because it represents the cost of new financing to the firm.

---

[10]At times, the expected dividend at year end (D_1) is not given. Instead, we might only know the most recent dividend (paid yesterday), that is, D_0. If so, we must restate the equation as follows:

$$V_{cs} = \frac{D_1}{(k_{cs} - g)} = \frac{D_0(1 + g)}{(k_{cs} - g)}$$

In this chapter, we have looked at the nature and process for valuing both preferred stock and common stock—sources of equity capital for a business. Although we have taken an investor perspective in much of what we have said, we are ultimately interested in the implications of valuation for a financial manager. But a financial manager must first and foremost view valuation from the investor's vantage point. What matters to the investor should matter to the financial manager. Otherwise, a financial manager cannot be effective in enhancing firm value—the criterion for evaluating much that the financial manager does. This relationship will become increasingly clear as we move into future chapters dealing with making capital investments and financing these expenditures.

SUMMARY

Valuation is an important process in financial management. An understanding of valuation, both the concepts and procedures, supports the financial officer's objective of maximizing the value of the firm.

Preferred stock has no fixed maturity date and the dividends are fixed in amount. Following are some of the more frequent characteristics of preferred stock.

OBJECTIVE 1

- There are multiple classes of preferred stock.
- Preferred stock has a priority of claim on assets and income over common stock.
- Any dividends, if not paid as promised, must be paid before any common stock dividends may be paid. That is, they are cumulative.
- Protective provisions are included in the contract for the preferred shareholder in order to reduce the investor's risk.
- Many preferred stocks are convertible into common stock shares.

For a few preferred stocks:

- The dividend rate may be adjustable as interest rates change.
- The preferred stockholder may be allowed to participate in the firm's earnings in certain situations.
- The preferred stockholder may receive dividends in the form of more shares—payment in kind (PIK).

In addition, there are provisions frequently used to retire an issue of preferred stock, such as the ability for the firm to call its preferred stock or to use a sinking fund provision.

Value is the present value of future cash flows discounted at the investor's required rate of return. Although the valuation of any security entails the same basic principles, the procedures used in each situation vary. For example, we learned in chapter 7 that valuing a bond involves calculating the present value of future interest to be received plus the present value of the principal returned to the investor at the maturity of the bond.

OBJECTIVE 2

For securities with cash flows that are constant in each year but where there is no specified maturity, such as preferred stock, the present value equals the dollar amount of the annual dividend divided by the investor's required rate of return; that is,

$$\text{preferred stock value} = \frac{\text{dividend}}{\text{required rate of return}}$$

Bondholders and preferred stockholders can be viewed as creditors, whereas the common stockholders are the owners of the firm. Common stock does not have a maturity date, but exists as long as the firm does. Nor does common stock have an upper limit

OBJECTIVE 3

on its dividend payments. Dividend payments must be declared by the firm's board of directors before they are issued. In the event of bankruptcy, the common stockholders, as owners of the corporation, cannot exercise claims on assets until the firm's creditors, including the bondholders and preferred shareholders, have been satisfied. However, common stockholders' liability is limited to the amount of their investment.

The common shareholders are in general the only security holders given a vote. Common shareholders have the right to elect the board of directors and to approve any change in the corporate charter. Although each share of stock carries the same number of votes, the voting procedure is not always the same from company to company.

The preemptive right entitles the common shareholder to maintain a proportionate share of ownership in the firm.

 OBJECTIVE 4

For common stock where the future dividends are expected to increase at a constant growth rate, value may be given by the following equation:

$$\text{common stock value} = \frac{\text{dividend in year 1}}{\text{required rate of return} - \text{growth rate}}$$

Growth here relates to *internal* growth only, where management retains part of the firm's profits to be reinvested and thereby grow the firm—as opposed to growth through issuing new stock or acquiring another firm.

Growth in and of itself does not mean that we are creating value for the stockholders. Only if we are reinvesting at a rate of return that is greater than the investors' required rate of return will growth result in increased value to the firm. In fact, if we are investing at rates less than the required rate of return for our investors, the value of the firm will actually decline.

 OBJECTIVE 5

The expected rate of return on a security is the required rate of return of investors who are willing to pay the present market price for the security, but no more. This rate of return is important to the financial manager because it equals the required rate of return of the firm's investors.

The expected rate of return for preferred stock is computed as follows:

$$\text{expected return preferred stock} = \frac{\text{annual dividend}}{\text{stock market price}}$$

The expected rate of return for common stock is calculated as follows:

$$\text{expected return common stock} = \frac{\text{dividend in year 1}}{\text{stock market price}} + \text{dividend growth rate}$$

GO TO:
http://www.prenhall.com/bfm
For downloads and current events associated with this chapter

KEY TERMS

Adjustable rate preferred stock, 293

Auction rate preferred stock, 293

Call provision, 294

Common stock, 298

Convertible preferred stock, 293

Cumulative preferred stock, 292

Cumulative voting, 300

Majority voting, 300

Participating preferred stock, 293

PIK preferred stock, 294

Preemptive rights, 300

Preferred stock, 291

Protective provisions, 292

Proxy, 300

Proxy fight, 300

Rights, 300

Sinking fund, 294

FINCOACH PRACTICE EXERCISES FOR CHAPTER 8

To maximize your grades and master the mathematics discussed in this chapter, open *FINCOACH* on the *Finance Learning and Development Center* CD-ROM and practice problems in the following categories: 1) Valuation of Multiple Cash Flows, 2) Valuation of Infinite Cash Flows, 3) Stock Valuation

STUDY QUESTIONS

8-1. Why is preferred stock referred to as a hybrid security? It is often said to combine the worst features of common stock and bonds. What is meant by this statement?

8-2. Because preferred stock dividends in arrears must be paid before common stock dividends, should they be considered a liability and appear on the right side of the balance sheet?

8-3. Why would a preferred stockholder want the stock to have a cumulative dividend feature and other protective provisions?

8-4. Distinguish between fixed rate preferred stock and adjustable rate preferred stock. What is the rationale for a firm issuing adjustable rate preferred stock?

8-5. What is PIK preferred stock?

8-6. Why is preferred stock frequently convertible? Why would it be callable?

8-7. Compare valuing preferred stock and common stock.

8-8. Define the investor's *expected* rate of return.

8-9. State how the investor's required rate of return is computed.

8-10. The common stockholders receive two types of return from their investment. What are they?

SELF-TEST PROBLEMS

ST-1. (*Preferred Stock Valuation*) What is the value of a preferred stock where the dividend rate is 16 percent on a $100 par value? The appropriate discount rate for a stock of this risk level is 12 percent.

ST-2. (*Preferred Stockholder Expected Return*) You own 250 shares of Dalton Resources's preferred stock, which currently sells for $38.50 per share and pays annual dividends of $3.25 per share.
  a. What is your expected return?
  b. If you require an 8 percent return, given the current price, should you sell or buy more stock?

ST-3. (*Preferred Stock Valuation*) The preferred stock of Armlo pays a $2.75 dividend. What is the value of the stock if your required return is 9 percent?

ST-4. (*Common Stock Valuation*) Crosby Corporation's common stock paid $1.32 in dividends last year and is expected to grow indefinitely at an annual 7 percent rate. What is the value of the stock if you require an 11 percent return?

ST-5. (*Common Stockholder Expected Return*) Blackburn & Smith's common stock currently sells for $23 per share. The company's executives anticipate a constant growth rate of 10.5 percent and an end-of-year dividend of $2.50.
  a. What is your expected rate of return?
  b. If you require a 17 percent return, should you purchase the stock?

STUDY PROBLEMS (SET A)

8-1A. (*Preferred Stock Valuation*) Calculate the value of a preferred stock that pays a dividend of $6 per share and your required rate of return is 12 percent.

8-2A. (*Measuring Growth*) If Pepperdine, Inc.'s return on equity is 16 percent and the management plans to retain 60 percent of earnings for investment purposes, what will be the firm's growth rate?

8-3A. (*Preferred Stock Valuation*) What is the value of a preferred stock where the dividend rate is 14 percent on a $100 par value? The appropriate discount rate for a stock of this risk level is 12 percent.

8-4A. (*Preferred Stockholder Expected Return*) Solitron's preferred stock is selling for $42.16 and pays $1.95 in dividends. What is your expected rate of return if you purchase the security at the market price?

8-5A. (*Preferred Stockholder Expected Return*) You own 200 shares of Somner Resources's preferred stock, which currently sells for $40 per share and pays annual dividends of $3.40 per share.
   a. What is your expected return?
   b. If you require an 8 percent return, given the current price should you sell or buy more stock?

8-6A. (*Common Stock Valuation*) You intend to purchase Marigo common stock at $50 per share, hold it 1 year, and sell after a dividend of $6 is paid. How much will the stock price have to appreciate for you to satisfy your required rate of return of 15 percent?

8-7A. (*Common Stockholder Expected Return*) Made-It's common stock currently sells for $22.50 per share. The company's executives anticipate a constant growth rate of 10 percent and an end-of-year dividend of $2.
   a. What is your expected rate of return if you buy the stock for $22.50?
   b. If you require a 17 percent return, should you purchase the stock?

8-8A. (*Common Stock Valuation*) Header Motor, Inc., paid a $3.50 dividend last year. At a constant growth rate of 5 percent, what is the value of the common stock if the investors require a 20 percent rate of return?

8-9A. (*Measuring Growth*) Given that a firm's return on equity is 18 percent and management plans to retain 40 percent of earnings for investment purposes, what will be the firm's growth rate?

8-10A. (*Common Stockholder Expected Return*) The common stock of Zaldi Co. is selling for $32.84. The stock recently paid dividends of $2.94 per share and has a projected constant growth rate of 9.5 percent. If you purchase the stock at the market price, what is your expected rate of return?

8-11A. (*Common Stock Valuation*) Honeywag common stock is expected to pay $1.85 in dividends next year, and the market price is projected to be $42.50 by year end. If the investor's required rate of return is 11 percent, what is the current value of the stock?

8-12A. (*Common Stockholder Expected Return*) The market price for Hobart common stock is $43. The price at the end of 1 year is expected to be $48, and dividends for next year should be $2.84. What is the expected rate of return?

8-13A. (*Preferred Stock Valuation*) Pioneer's preferred stock is selling for $33 in the market and pays a $3.60 annual dividend.
   a. What is the expected rate of return on the stock?
   b. If an investor's required rate of return is 10 percent, what is the value of the stock for that investor?
   c. Should the investor acquire the stock?

8-14A. (*Common Stock Valuation*) The common stock of NCP paid $1.32 in dividends last year. Dividends are expected to grow at an 8 percent annual rate for an indefinite number of years.
   a. If NCP's current market price is $23.50, what is the stock's expected rate of return?
   b. If your required rate of return is 10.5 percent, what is the value of the stock for you?
   c. Should you make the investment?

8-15A. In October 1997, Briggs & Stratton, a small engine manufacturer, was expecting to pay an annual dividend of $1.12 in 1998. The firm's stock was selling for $49. The stock's beta is 1.10.

    a. What is Briggs & Stratton's dividend yield?

    b. Based on the Ibbotson Associates data presented in chapter 6 (Figure 6.8, p. 237), compute the expected rate of return for this stock. (Use the CAPM approach described in chapter 6.)

    c. What growth rate would you have to use in the multiple-period valuation model to get the same expected return as in part (b)?

8-16A. Access the Internet to gather the following information for Johnson & Johnson.

    a. The earnings per share and dividends per share for the past 5 years.

    b. The common stock price.

Assuming that the annual growth rate in earnings per share for the past 4 years is a reasonable estimate of the growth in share price for the indefinite future, which it may not be, estimate the expected rate of return for the stock.

You are considering three investments. The first is a bond that is selling in the market at $1,200. The bond has a $1,000 par value, pays interest at 14 percent, and is scheduled to mature in 12 years. For bonds of this risk class, you believe that a 12 percent rate of return should be required. The second investment that you are analyzing is a preferred stock ($100 par value) that sells for $90 and pays an annual dividend of $12. Your required rate of return for this stock is 14 percent. The last investment is a common stock ($25 par value) that recently paid a $3 dividend. The firm's earnings per share have increased from $4 to $8 in 10 years, which also reflects the expected growth in dividends per share for the indefinite future. The stock is selling for $25, and you think a reasonable required rate of return for the stock is 20 percent.

    1. Calculate the value of each security based on your required rate of return.

    2. Which investment(s) should you accept? Why?

    3. If your required rates of return changed to 14 percent for the bond, 16 percent for the preferred stock, and 18 percent for the common stock, how would your answers change to parts 1 and 2?

    4. Assuming again that your required rate of return for the common stock is 20 percent, but the anticipated constant growth rate changes to 12 percent, how would your answers to parts 1 and 2 change?

GO TO:
http://www.prenhall.com/bfm
For downloads and current events associated with this chapter

STUDY PROBLEMS (SET B)

8-1B. (*Preferred Stock Valuation*) Calculate the value of a preferred stock that pays a dividend of $7 per share when your required rate of return is 10 percent.

8-2B. (*Measuring Growth*) If the Stanford Corporation's return on equity is 24 percent and management plans to retain 70 percent of earnings for investment purposes, what will be the firm's growth rate?

8-3B. (*Preferred Stock Valuation*) What is the value of a preferred stock where the dividend rate is 16 percent on a $100 par value? The appropriate discount rate for a stock of this risk level is 12 percent.

8-4B. (*Preferred Stockholder Expected Return*) Shewmaker's preferred stock is selling for $55.16 and pays $2.35 in dividends. What is your expected rate of return if you purchase the security at the market price?

8-5B. (*Preferred Stockholder Expected Return*) You own 250 shares of McCormick Resources's preferred stock, which currently sells for $38.50 per share and pays annual dividends of $3.25 per share.

    a. What is your expected return?

    b. If you require an 8 percent return, given the current price, should you sell or buy more stock?

8-6B. (*Common Stock Valuation*) You intend to purchase Bama, Inc., common stock at $52.75 per share, hold it 1 year, and sell after a dividend of $6.50 is paid. How much will the stock price have to appreciate if your required rate of return is 16 percent?

8-7B. (*Common Stockholder Expected Return*) Blackburn & Smith's common stock currently sells for $23 per share. The company's executives anticipate a constant growth rate of 10.5 percent and an end-of-year dividend of $2.50.

    a. What is your expected rate of return?

    b. If you require a 17 percent return, should you purchase the stock?

8-8B. (*Common Stock Valuation*) Gilliland Motor, Inc., paid a $3.75 dividend last year. At a growth rate of 6 percent, what is the value of the common stock if the investors require a 20 percent rate of return?

8-9B. (*Measuring Growth*) Given that a firm's return on equity is 24 percent and management plans to retain 60 percent of earnings for investment purposes, what will be the firm's growth rate?

8-10B. (*Common Stockholder Expected Return*) The common stock of Bouncy-Bob Moore Co. is selling for $33.84. The stock recently paid dividends of $3 per share and has a projected growth rate of 8.5 percent. If you purchase the stock at the market price, what is your expected rate of return?

8-11B. (*Common Stock Valuation*) Honeybee common stock is expected to pay $1.85 in dividends next year, and the market price is projected to be $40 by year end. If the investors' required rate of return is 12 percent, what is the current value of the stock?

8-12B. (*Common Stock Valuation*) The market price for M. Simpson & Co.'s common stock is $44. The price at the end of 1 year is expected to be $47, and dividends for next year should be $2. What is the expected rate of return?

8-13B. (*Preferred Stock Valuation*) Green's preferred stock is selling for $35 in the market and pays a $4 annual dividend.

    a. What is the expected rate of return on the stock?

    b. If an investor's required rate of return is 10 percent, what is the value of the stock for that investor?

    c. Should the investor acquire the stock?

8-14B. (*Common Stock Valuation*) The common stock of KPD paid $1 in dividends last year. Dividends are expected to grow at an 8 percent annual rate for an indefinite number of years.

    a. If KPD's current market price is $25, what is the stock's expected rate of return?

    b. If your required rate of return is 11 percent, what is the value of the stock for you?

    c. Should you make the investment?

8-15B. In October 1997, CSX, a transportation firm (mostly railroads), was expecting to pay an annual dividend of $1.20 in 1998. The firm's stock was selling for $54. The stock's beta is 0.90.

    a. What is Briggs & Stratton's dividend yield?

    b. Based on the Ibbotson Associates data presented in chapter 6 (Figure 6.8, p. 237), compute the expected rate of return for this stock. (Use the CAPM approach described in chapter 6.)

    c. What growth rate would you have to use in the multiple-period valuation model to get the same expected return as in part (b)?

8-16B. Access the Internet to gather the following information for TCBY.

   a. The earnings per share and dividends per share for the past 5 years.

   b. The common stock price.

Assuming that the annual growth rate in earnings per share the past 4 years is a reasonable estimate of the growth in share price for the indefinite future, which it may not be, estimate the expected rate of return for the stock.

SELF-TEST SOLUTIONS

SS-1.

$$\text{Value } (V_{ps}) = \frac{.16 \times \$100}{.12}$$

$$= \frac{\$16}{.12}$$

$$= \$133.33$$

SS-2.

a. $\text{expected return} = \dfrac{\text{dividend}}{\text{market price}} = \dfrac{\$3.25}{\$38.50} = 0.0844 = 8.44\%$

b. Given your 8 percent required rate of return, the stock is worth $40.62 to you:

$$\text{value} = \frac{\text{dividend}}{\text{required rate of return}} = \frac{\$3.25}{0.08} = \$40.62$$

Because the expected rate of return (8.44%) is greater than your required rate of return (8%) or because the current market price ($38.50) is less than $40.62, the stock is undervalued and you should buy.

SS-3.

$$\text{Value } (V_{ps}) = \frac{\text{dividend}}{\text{required rate of return}} = \frac{\$2.75}{0.09} = \$30.56$$

SS-4.

$$\text{Value } (V_{cs}) = \left(\frac{\text{last year dividend } (1 + \text{growth rate})}{\text{required rate of return} - \text{growth rate}} \right)$$

$$= \frac{\$1.32(1.07)}{0.11 - 0.07}$$

$$= \$35.31$$

SS-5.

a. $\text{expected rate of return } (\bar{k}_{cs}) = \dfrac{\text{dividend in year 1}}{\text{market price}} + \text{growth rate}$

$$\bar{k}_{cs} = \frac{\$2.50}{\$23.00} + 0.105 = .2137$$

$$\bar{k}_{cs} = 21.37\%$$

b. The value of the stock for you would be $38.46. Thus the expected rate of return exceeds your required rate of return, which means that the value of the security to you is greater than the current market price. Thus you should buy the stock.

$$V_{cs} = \frac{\$2.50}{.17 - .105} = \$38.46$$

APPENDIX 8A

THE RELATIONSHIP BETWEEN VALUE AND EARNINGS

In understanding the relationship between a firm's earnings and the market price of its stock, it is helpful to look first at the relationship for a nongrowth firm and then expand our view to include the growth firm.

THE RELATIONSHIP BETWEEN EARNINGS AND VALUE FOR THE NONGROWTH COMPANY

When we speak of a nongrowth firm, we mean one that retains no profits for the purpose of reinvestment. The only investments made are for the purpose of maintaining status quo—that is, investing the amount of the depreciation taken on fixed assets so that the firm does not lose its current earnings capacity. The result is both constant earnings and a constant dividend stream to the common stockholder, because the firm is paying all earnings out in the form of dividends (dividend in year t equals earnings in year t). This type of common stock is essentially no different from a preferred stock. Recalling our earlier discussion about valuing a preferred stock, we may value the nongrowth common stock similarly, expressing our valuation in one of two ways:

$$\text{value of a nongrowth common stock } (V_{ng}) = \frac{\text{earnings per share}_1}{\text{required rate of return}} \tag{8A-1}$$

$$= \frac{\text{dividend per share}_1}{\text{required rate of return}} \tag{8A-2}$$

or

$$V_{ng} = \frac{EPS_1}{k_{cs}} = \frac{D_1}{k_{cs}}$$

EXAMPLE

The Reeves Corporation expects its earnings per share this year to be $12, which is to be paid out in total to the investors in the form of dividends. If the investors have a required rate of return of 14 percent, the value of the stock would be $85.71:

$$V_{ng} = \frac{\$12}{.14} = \$85.71$$

In this instance, the relationship between value and earnings per share is direct and unmistakable. If earnings per share increases (decreases) 10 percent, then the value of the share should increase (decrease) 10 percent; that is, the ratio of price to earnings will be a constant, as will the ratio of earnings to price. A departure from the constant relationship would occur only if the investors change their required rate of return, owing to a change in their perception about such things as risk or anticipated inflation. Thus there is good reason to perceive a relationship between next year's earnings and share price for the nongrowth company.

THE RELATIONSHIP BETWEEN EARNINGS AND VALUE FOR THE GROWTH FIRM

Turning our attention now to the growth firm, one that does reinvest its profits back into the business, we will recall that our valuation model depended on dividends and earnings increasing at a constant growth rate. Returning to equation (8-5), we valued a common stock where dividends were expected to increase at a constant growth rate as follows:

$$\text{value} = \frac{\text{dividend}_1}{\text{required rate of return} - \text{growth rate}}$$

or

$$V_{cs} = \frac{D_1}{k_{cs} - g}$$

Although equation (8-5) is certainly the conventional way of expressing value of the growth stock, it is not the only means. We could also describe the value of a stock as the present value of the dividend stream provided from the firm's existing assets plus the present value of any future growth resulting from the reinvestment of future earnings. We could represent this concept notationally as follows:

$$V_{cs} = \frac{EPS_1}{k_{cs}} + NVDG \qquad (8A\text{-}3)$$

where EPS_1/k_{cs} = the present value of the cash flow stream provided by the existing assets
$NVDG$ = the net value of any dividend growth resulting from the reinvestment of future earnings

The first term, EPS_1/k_{cs}, is immediately understandable given our earlier rationale about nongrowth stocks. The second term, the net value of future dividend growth ($NVDG$), needs some clarification.

To begin our explanation of $NVDG$, let r equal the fraction of a firm's earnings that are retained in the business, which implies that the dividend in year 1 (D_1) would equal $(1 - r) \times EPS_1$. Next assume that any earnings that are reinvested yield a rate of ROE (return on equity). Thus from the earnings generated in year 1, we would be investing the percentage of earnings retained, r, times the firm's earnings per share, EPS_1, or $r \times EPS_1$. In return, we should expect to receive a cash flow in all future years equal to the expected return on our investment, ROE, times the amount of our investment, or $r \times EPS_1 \times ROE$. Because cash inflows represent an annuity continuing in perpetuity, the present value from reinvesting a part of the firm's earnings in year 1 (PV_1) would be equal to the present value of the new cash flows less the cost of the investment:

$$PV_1 = \underbrace{\left(\frac{rEPS_1ROE}{k_{cs}} \right)}_{\substack{\text{present value} \\ \text{of increased} \\ \text{cash flows}}} - \underbrace{rEPS_1}_{\substack{\text{amount of cash} \\ \text{retained and} \\ \text{reinvested}}} \qquad (8A\text{-}4)$$

If we continued to reinvest a fixed percentage of earnings each year and earned ROE on these investments, there would also be a net present value in all the following years; that is, we would have a PV_2, PV_3, $PV_4 \ldots PV_\infty$. Also, because r and ROE are both constant, the series of PVs will increase at a constant growth rate of $r \times ROE$. We may therefore use the *constant-growth valuation model* to value $NVDG$ as follows:

$$NVDG = \frac{PV_1}{k_{cs} - g} \qquad (8A\text{-}5)$$

Thus we may now establish the value of a common stock as the sum of (1) a present value of a constant stream of earnings generated from the firm's assets already in place and (2) the present value of an increasing dividend stream coming from the retention of profits; that is,

$$V_{cs} = \frac{EPS_1}{k_{cs}} + \frac{PV_1}{k_{cs} - g}$$

(8A-6)

EXAMPLE

The Upp Corporation should earn $8 per share this year, of which 40 percent will be retained within the firm for reinvestment and 60 percent paid in the form of dividends to the stockholders. Management expects to earn an 18 percent return on any funds retained. Let us use both the constant-growth dividend model and the *NVDG* model to compute Upp's stock value, assuming the investors have a 12 percent required rate of return.

Constant-Growth Dividend Model

Because we are assuming that the Upp's *ROE* will be constant and that management faithfully intends to retain 40 percent of earnings each year to be used for new investments, the dividend stream flowing to the investor should increase by 7.2 percent each year, which we know by solving for $r \times ROE$, or $(.4)(18\%)$. The dividend for this year will be $4.80, which is the dividend-payout ratio of $(1 - r)$ times the expected earnings per share of $8 ($.60 \times \$8 = \$4.80$). Given a 12 percent required rate of return for the investors, the value of the security may be shown to be $100.

$$\begin{aligned} V_{cs} &= \frac{D_1}{k_{cs} - g} \\ &= \frac{\$4.80}{.12 - .072} \\ &= \$100 \end{aligned}$$

NVDG Model

Restructuring the problem to compute separately the present value of the no-growth stream and the present value of future growth opportunities, we may again determine the value of the stock to be $100. Solving first for value assuming a no-growth scenario,

$$\begin{aligned} V_{ng} &= \frac{EPS_1}{k_{cs}} \\ &= \frac{\$8}{.12} \\ &= \$66.67 \end{aligned}$$

(8A-7)

We next estimate the value of the future growth opportunities coming from reinvesting corporate profits each year, which is

$$NVDG = \frac{PV_1}{k_{cs} - g}$$

(8A-8)

Knowing k_c to be 12 percent and the growth rate to be 7.2 percent, we lack knowing only PV_1, which can easily be determined using equation (8A-4):

$$PV_1 = \left(\frac{rEPS_1 ROE}{k_{cs}}\right) - rEPS_1 \qquad\qquad (8A\text{-}4)$$

$$= \left(\frac{(.4)(\$8)(.18)}{.12}\right) - (.4)(\$8)$$

$$= \$4.80 - \$3.20$$

$$= \$1.60$$

The *NVDG* may now be computed:

$$NVDG = \frac{\$1.60}{.12 - .072}$$

$$= \$33.33$$

Thus the value of the combined streams is $100:

$$V_c = \$66.67 + \$33.33 = \$100$$

From the preceding example, we see that the value of the growth opportunities represents a significant portion of the total value, 33 percent to be exact. Furthermore, in looking at the *NVDG* model, we observe that value is influenced by the following: (1) the size of the firm's beginning earnings per share, (2) the percentage of profits retained, and (3) the spread between the return generated on new investments and the investor's required rate of return. The first factor relates to firm size; the second to management's decision about the firm's earnings retention rate. Although the first two factors are not unimportant, the last one is the key to wealth creation by management. *Simply, because management retains profits does not mean that wealth is created for the stockholders.* Wealth comes only if the return on equity from the investments, *ROE*, is greater than the investor's required rate of return, k_{cs}. Thus we should expect the market to assign value not only to the reported earnings per share for the current year but also to the anticipated growth opportunities that have a marginal rate of return that exceed the required rate of return of the firm's investors.

STUDY PROBLEMS

8A-1. (*Valuation of Common Stock—NVDG Model*) The Burgon Co. management expects the firm's earnings per share to be $5 this forthcoming year. The firm's policy is to pay out 35 percent of its earnings in the form of dividends. In looking at the investment opportunities available to the firm, the return on equity should be 20 percent for the foreseeable future. Use the *NVDG* model to find the value of the company's stock. The stockholders' required rate of return is 16 percent. Verify your results with the constant-growth dividend model.

8A-2. (*Valuation of Common Stock—NVDG Model*) You want to know the impact of retaining earnings on the value of your firm's stock. Given the information below, calculate the value of the stock under the different scenarios.

   a. Earnings per share on existing assets should be about $7 this forthcoming year.

   b. The stockholder's required rate of return is 18 percent.

   c. The expected return on equity may be as low as 16 percent or as high as 24 percent, with an expected return of 18 percent.

   d. You are considering three earnings-retention policies on a long-term basis: (1) retain no earnings, instead distributing all earnings to stockholders in the form of dividends; (2) retain 30 percent of earnings; or (3) retain 60 percent of earnings.

Learning Objectives

Active Applications

World Finance

Practice

CHAPTER 9

LEARNING OBJECTIVES

After reading this chapter, you should be able to

1. Discuss the difficulty of finding profitable projects in competitive markets.

2. Determine whether a new project should be accepted using the payback period.

3. Determine whether a new project should be accepted using the net present value.

4. Determine whether a new project should be accepted using the profitability index.

5. Determine whether a new project should be accepted using the internal rate of return.

6. Explain the importance of ethical considerations in capital-budgeting decisions.

7. Discuss the trends in the use of different capital-budgeting criteria.

CAPITAL-BUDGETING DECISION CRITERIA

INTRODUCTION

I n 1988, Ford Motor Company to made a decision to reenter the minivan market with a new challenger to Chrysler's Caravan and Voyager. Over the past decade, a number of challengers including the Ford Aerostar, GM's APV, and a number of Japanese models had entered the ring against the Chrysler minivan, all with the same result. The Chrysler minivan has scored a knockout against all comers and has continued to dominate the minivan market by a wide margin.

Given the history of challengers to Chrysler's minivan, it was not an easy decision to challenge the champ. Moreover, the stakes involved are so large that the outcome of this decision will have a major effect on Ford's future. To challenge Chrysler's dominance in this market, Ford committed $1.5 billion, with roughly $500 million going toward design, engineering, and testing. The end result of this is the Ford Windstar, which Ford unveiled in 1994. Whether this was a good decision or a bad decision, only time will tell, but early reports indicate that Ford has come up with a winner. General Motors, also looking for its share of the $28 billion minivan market, introduced the Chevy Venture in mid-1997, along with identical versions sold by Pontiac and Oldsmobile. Most early reports indicate that although these are good products, it's going to be tough to dethrone Chrysler as the minivan king. How did Ford and GM go about deciding to spend billions of dollars to introduce new minivans? They did it using the decision criteria we will examine in this chapter.

This chapter is actually the first of three chapters that deal with the process of decision making with respect to investment in fixed assets—that is, should a proposed project be accepted or should it be rejected? We will refer to this process as capital budgeting. In this chapter, we will look at evaluating a project. In deciding whether to accept a new project, we will focus on cash flows. Cash flows represent the benefits generated from accepting a capital-budgeting proposal. In this chapter, we will assume we know what level of cash flows are generated by a project and work on determining whether that project should be accepted. In the next chapter, we will examine what is a relevant cash flow and how we measure it. Then in chapter 11, we will look at how risk enters into this process.

Typically, these investments involve rather large cash outlays at the outset and commit the firm to a particular course of action over a relatively long period. Thus if a capital-budgeting decision is incorrect, reversing it tends to be costly. In evaluating capital investment proposals, we compare the costs and benefits of each in a number of ways. Some of these methods take into account the time value of money, one does not; however, each of these methods is used frequently in the real world. As you will see, our preferred method of analysis will be the net present value (NPV) method, which compares the present value of inflows and outflows.

CHAPTER PREVIEW

Capital budgeting is the process by which the firm renews and reinvents itself—adapting old projects to the times and finding new ones. It involves comparing cash inflows that may spread out over many years with cash outflows that generally occur close to the present. As a result, much of this chapter relies heavily on Axiom 2: The Time Value of Money—A Dollar Received Today Is Worth More Than a Dollar Received in the Future. We will begin this chapter with a look at finding profitable projects. As you will see, Axiom 5: The Curse of Competitive Markets—Why It's Hard to Find Exceptionally Profitable Projects helps explain this. Next we will look at the purpose and importance of capital budgeting. We will then consider four commonly used criteria for determining acceptability of investment proposals. Keep in mind during all this that what we are actually doing is developing a framework for decision making.

Capital budgeting

The decision-making process with respect to investment in fixed assets.

FINDING PROFITABLE PROJECTS

OBJECTIVE 1

Without question, it is easier to *evaluate* profitable projects than it is to *find* them. In competitive markets, generating ideas for profitable projects is extremely difficult. The competition is brisk for new profitable projects, and once they have been uncovered competitors generally rush in, pushing down prices and profits. For this reason, a firm must have a systematic strategy for generating capital-budgeting projects. Without this flow of new projects and ideas, the firm cannot grow or even survive for long, being forced to live off the profits from existing projects with limited lives. So where do these ideas come from for new products, for ways to improve existing products, or for ways to make existing products more profitable? The answer is from inside the firm—from everywhere inside the firm.

RELATE TO THE BIG PICTURE

The fact that profitable projects are difficult to find relates directly to Axiom 5: The Curse of Competitive Markets—Why It's Hard to Find Exceptionally Profitable Projects. When we introduced that axiom we stated that successful investments involve the reduction of competition by creating barriers to entry either through product differentiation or cost advantages. The key to locating profitable projects is to understand how and where they exist.

Typically, a firm has a research and development department that searches for ways to improve existing products or finding new products. These ideas may come from within the R&D department or be based on referral ideas from executives, sales personnel, anyone in the firm, or even from customers. For example, at Ford Motor Company prior to the 1980s, ideas for product improvement had typically been generated in Ford's research and development department. Unfortunately, this strategy was not enough to keep Ford from losing much of its market share to the Japanese. In an attempt to cut costs and improve product quality, Ford moved from strict reliance on an R&D department to seeking the input of employees at all levels for new ideas. Bonuses are now provided to workers for their cost-cutting suggestions, and assembly line personnel who can see the production process from a hands-on point of view are now brought into the hunt for new projects. The effect on Ford has been positive and significant. Although not all suggested projects prove to be profitable, many new ideas generated from within the firm turn out to be good ones.

Keep in mind that new capital-budgeting projects don't necessarily mean coming up with a new product, it may be taking an existing product and applying it to a new market. That's certainly been the direction that McDonald's has taken in recent years. Today, McDonald's operates in over 51 countries with more than 11,000 restaurants. One of the biggest is a 700-seat McDonald's in Moscow. Was this an expensive venture? It certainly was, in fact, the food plant that McDonald's built to supply burgers, buns, fries, and everything else sold there cost over $60 million. In addition to the costs, it differs from opening an outlet in the United States in a number of ways. First, in order to keep the quality of what McDonald's sells identical with what is served at any McDonald's anywhere in the world, McDonald's spent 6 years in putting together a supply chain that would provide the necessary raw materials at the quality level McDonald's demanded. On top of that, there are risks associated with the Russian economy and its currency that are well beyond the scope of what is experienced in the United States. However, since it opened, it has proven to be enormously successful. It all goes to show that not all capital budgeting projects have to be new products, they can also be existing products in new markets.

We will consider four commonly used criteria for determining acceptability of investment proposals. The first is the payback period and it is the least sophisticated, in that it does not incorporate the time value of money into its calculations; the remaining three do take it into account. For the time being, the problem of incorporating risk into the capital-budgeting decision is ignored. This issue will be examined in chapter 11. In addition, we will assume that the appropriate discount rate, required rate of return, or cost of capital is given. The determination of this rate is the topic of chapter 12.

OBJECTIVE 2

PAYBACK PERIOD

Payback period

A capital-budgeting criterion defined as the number of years required to recover the initial cash investment.

The **payback period** is the number of years needed to recover the initial cash outlay. As this criterion measures how quickly the project will return its original investment, it deals with cash flows, which measure the true timing of the benefits, rather than accounting profits. Unfortunately, it also ignores the time value of money and does not discount these cash flows back to the present. The accept-reject criterion centers on whether the project's payback period is less than or equal to the firm's maximum desired payback period. For example, if a firm's maximum desired payback period is 3 years and an investment proposal requires an initial cash outlay of $10,000 and yields the following set of annual cash flows, what is its payback period? Should the project be accepted?

WALL STREET JOURNAL, FEBRUARY 8, 1994

As Capital Spending Grows, Firms Take a Hard Look at Returns From the Effort

NEW YORK—As corporate America ratchets up its capital spending, it's doing so with a much keener eye to profiting from the effort.

"Chief executives are becoming much more disciplined about saying OK" to spending requests, says Ennius Bergsma of McKinsey & Co., the management consulting firm. "They want to know what will happen in year one, two and three, rather than plow money in and realize nothing materialized."

Notably, the sharper scrutiny isn't scaring spending projects away. Economists say that, for the second year in a row, companies this year are expected to boost spending on equipment by more than 12%.

DRI/McGraw Hill, which forecasts economic trends, sees capital spending on equipment in the U.S. reaching a record $457 billion this year. It expects capital spending in total, which includes the construction of new plants, to reach $610 billion, up 11% from 1993.

"We keep seeing new opportunities" for saving money through capital investments, says Reuben Mark, chief executive of Colgate-Palmolive Co., the big maker of household and personal-care products. One recent opportunity involved the company's Italian unit, where Colgate installed $1 million worth of new automated equipment for packaging the company's stand-up toothpaste tubes. The machines replaced some workers. Estimated savings to Colgate in the first year: $250,000.

The company is demanding more of this sort of cost-saving investment from its managers: In 1994, it wants total capital expenditures to equal 6% of sales, up from 5.2% of sales last year. When Mr. Mark became chief executive in 1984, roughly 13% of Colgate's total capital spending was going towards cost-saving ventures; the rest went into building new plants, among other things. Now the company is demanding that fully 60% of its capital spending be for cost-saving projects. Colgate even has assigned a force of spending police to track the rate of return on capital expenditures.

"This is not misty, Ingmar Bergman stuff," says Mr. Mark. In fact, part of a manager's compensation is determined by how well he or she meets the capital spending guidelines.

SOURCE: Fred R. Bleakley, "As Capital Spending Grows, Firms Take a Hard Look at Returns From the Effort," *The Wall Street Journal* (February 8, 1994): A2. Reprinted by permission of *The Wall Street Journal*, © 1994 Dow Jones & Co., Inc. All Rights Reserved Worldwide.

Analysis and Implications ...

A. Once a project is accepted, its progress is monitored throughout its life. The project's actual results are compared with the forecasted results. If there is a significant deviation between what was expected and what actually occurred, the forecasting process may be reexamined. Moreover, the project's cash flows will be reestimated, and the project may be reworked with cost cuts, modifications, and possibly early termination. The point here is that projects are always being reexamined and reevaluated, and the option to terminate them is always a possibility.

B. Much of the importance of capital-budgeting decisions comes from the amount of money spent on capital projects. The spending on equipment has been growing at an extremely rapid pace, from a level of just over $200 billion per year in 1980 to the expected level of $600 billion in 1998. Given the size of these investments and the difficulty in reversing them once they are made, capital-budgeting decisions take on even more importance.

C. In recent years, more and more capital expenditures have been directed at cost-saving and productivity-improving projects, rather than being aimed at introducing new products. For example, in 1994, RJR Nabisco issued a directive to its managers that new capital expenditures were to be made that would result in costs being cut by an amount equivalent of 20 percent of the dollar value of investment.

	After-Tax Cash Flow
Year 1	$ 2,000
Year 2	4,000
Year 3	3,000
Year 4	3,000
Year 5	10,000

In this case, after 3 years the firm will have recaptured $9,000 on an initial investment of $10,000, leaving $1,000 of the initial investment still to be recouped. During the fourth year, a total of $3,000 will be returned from this investment. Assuming cash will flow into the firm at a constant rate over the year, it will take one third of the year ($1,000/$3,000) to recapture the remaining $1,000. Thus the payback period on this project is 3⅓ years, which is more than the desired payback period. Using the payback period criterion, the firm would reject this project without even considering the $10,000 cash flow in year 5.

Although the payback period is used frequently, it does have some rather obvious drawbacks, which can best be demonstrated through the use of an example. Consider two investment projects, A and B, which involve an initial cash outlay of $10,000 each and produce the annual cash flows shown in Table 9.1. Both projects have a payback period of 2 years; therefore, in terms of the payback period criterion, both are equally acceptable. However, if we had our choice, it is clear we would select A over B, for at least two reasons. First, regardless of what happens after the payback period, project A returns our initial investment to us earlier within the payback period. Thus because there is a time value of money, the cash flows occurring within the payback period should not be weighted equally, as they are. In addition, all cash flows that occur after the payback period are ignored. This violates the principle that investors desire more in the way of benefits rather than less—a principle that is difficult to deny, especially when we are talking about money.

To deal with the criticism that the payback period ignores the time value of money, some firms use the **discounted payback period** approach. The discounted payback period method is similar to the traditional payback period except that it uses discounted net cash flows rather than actual undiscounted net cash flows in calculating the payback period. The discounted payback period is defined as the number of years needed to recover the initial cash outlay from the *discounted net cash flows*. The accept-reject criterion then becomes whether the project's discounted payback period is less than or equal to the firm's maximum desired discounted payback period. Using the assumption that the required rate of return on projects A and B illustrated in Table 9.1 is 17 percent, the discounted cash flows from these projects are given in Table 9.2. On project A, after 3 years, only $74 of the initial outlay remain to be recaptured, whereas year 4 brings in a

Discounted payback period

A variation of the payback period decision criterion defined as the number of years required to recover the initial cash outlay from the discounted net cash flows.

Table 9.1 Payback Period Example

Projects	A	B
Initial cash outlay	−$10,000	−$10,000
Annual net cash inflows:		
Year 1	$ 6,000	$ 5,000
2	4,000	5,000
3	3,000	0
4	2,000	0
5	1,000	0

Table 9.2 Discounted Payback Period Example Using a 17 Percent Required Rate of Return

Project A

Year	Undiscounted Cash Flows	$PVIF_{17\%,n}$	Discounted Cash Flows	Cumulative Discounted Cash Flows
0	−$10,000	1.0	−$10,000	−$10,000
1	6,000	.855	5,130	− 4,870
2	4,000	.731	2,924	− 1,946
3	3,000	.624	1,872	− 74
4	2,000	.534	1,068	994
5	1,000	.456	456	1,450

Project B

Year	Undiscounted Cash Flows	$PVIF_{17\%,n}$	Discounted Cash Flows	Cumulative Discounted Cash Flows
0	−$10,000	1.0	−$10,000	−$10,000
1	5,000	.855	4,275	− 5,725
2	5,000	.731	3,655	− 2,070
3	0	.624	0	− 2,070
4	0	.534	0	− 2,070
5	0	.456	0	− 2,070

discounted cash flow of $1,068. Thus if the $1,068 comes in a constant rate over the year, it will take 7/100s of the year ($74/$1,068) to recapture the remaining $74. The discounted payback period for Project A is 3.07 years, calculated as follows:

Discounted Payback Period$_A$ = 3.0 + $74/$1,068 = 3.07 years.

If Project A's discounted payback period was less than the firm's maximum desired discounted payback period, then Project A would be accepted. Project B, on the other hand, does not have a discounted payback period because it never fully recovers the project's initial cash outlay, and thus should be rejected. The major problem with the discounted payback period comes in setting the firm's maximum desired discounted payback period. This is an arbitrary decision that affects which projects are accepted and which ones are rejected. Thus although the discounted payback period is superior to the traditional payback period, in that it accounts for the time value of money in its calculations, its use is limited by the arbitrariness of the process used to select the maximum desired payback period. Moreover, as we will soon see, the net present value criterion is theoretically superior and no more difficult to calculate.

Although these deficiencies limit the value of the payback period and discounted payback period as tools for investment evaluation, these methods do have several positive features. First, they deal with cash flows, as opposed to accounting profits, and therefore focus on the true timing of the project's benefits and costs, even though the traditional payback period does not adjust the cash flows for the time value of money. Second, they are easy to visualize, quickly understood, and easy to calculate. Finally, although the payback period and discounted payback period methods have serious deficiencies, they are often used as rough screening devices to eliminate projects whose returns do not materialize until later years. These methods emphasize the earliest returns, which in all likelihood are less uncertain, and provide for the liquidity needs of the firm. Although their advantages are certainly significant, their disadvantages severely limit their value as discriminating capital-budgeting criteria.

OBJECTIVE 3

NET PRESENT VALUE

Net present value (NPV)

A capital-budgeting decision criterion defined as the present value of the future net cash flows after tax less the project's initial outlay.

The **net present value (NPV)** of an investment proposal is equal to the present value of its annual after tax net cash flows less the investment's initial outlay. The net present value can be expressed as follows:

$$NPV = \sum_{t=1}^{n} \frac{ACF_t}{(1+k)^t} - IO \tag{9-1}$$

where ACF_t = the annual after-tax cash flow in time period t
(this can take on either positive or negative values)
k = the appropriate discount rate; that is, the required rate of return or cost of capital[1]
IO = the initial cash outlay
n = the project's expected life

The project's net present value gives a measurement of the *net value* of an investment proposal in terms of today's dollars. Because all cash flows are discounted back to the present, comparing the difference between the present value of the annual cash flows and the investment outlay is appropriate. The difference between the present value of the annual cash flows and the initial outlay determines the net value of accepting the investment proposal in terms of today's dollars. Whenever the project's NPV is greater than or equal to zero, we will accept the project; and whenever the NPV is negative, we will reject the project. Note that if the project's net present value is zero, then it returns the required rate of return and should be accepted. This accept-reject criterion can be stated as:

NPV ≥ 0.0: Accept
NPV < 0.0: Reject

The following example illustrates the use of the net present value capital-budgeting criterion.

EXAMPLE

Ski-Doo is considering new machinery that would reduce manufacturing costs associated with its Mach Z snowmobile, for which the after-tax cash flows are shown in Table 9.3. If the firm has a 12 percent required rate of return, the present value of the after-tax cash flows is $47,678, as calculated in Table 9.4. Subtracting the $40,000 initial outlay leaves a net present value of $7,678. Because this value is greater than zero, the net present value criterion indicates that the project should be accepted.

---

[1]The required rate of return or cost of capital is the rate of return necessary to justify raising funds to finance the project or, alternatively, the rate of return necessary to maintain the firm's current market price per share. These terms will be defined in greater detail in chapter 12.

Table 9.3 NPV Illustration of Investment in New Machinery

	After-Tax Cash Flow		After-Tax Cash Flow
Initial outlay	−$40,000	Inflow year 3	13,000
Inflow year 1	15,000	Inflow year 4	12,000
Inflow year 2	14,000	Inflow year 5	11,000

Table 9.4 Calculation for NPV Illustration of Investment in New Machinery

	After-Tax Cash Flow	Present Value Factor at 12 Percent	Present Value
Inflow year 1	$15,000	.893	$13,395
Inflow year 2	14,000	.797	11,158
Inflow year 3	13,000	.712	9,256
Inflow year 4	12,000	.636	7,632
Inflow year 5	11,000	.567	6,237
Present value of cash flows			$47,678
Initial outlay			− 40,000
Net present value			$ 7,678

Note in the Ski-Doo example that the worth of the net present value calculation is a function of the accuracy of cash flow predictions.

The NPV criterion is the capital-budgeting decision tool we will find most favorable. First of all, it deals with cash flows rather than accounting profits. Also, it is sensitive to the true timing of the benefits resulting from the project. Moreover, recognizing that, the time value of money allows comparison of the benefits and costs in a logical manner. Finally, because projects are accepted only if a positive net present value is associated with them, the acceptance of a project using this criterion will increase the value of the firm, which is consistent with the goal of maximizing the shareholders' wealth.

The disadvantage of the NPV method stems from the need for detailed, long-term forecasts of cash flows accruing from the project's acceptance. Despite this drawback, the net present value is the theoretically correct criterion in that it measures the impact of a project's acceptance on the value of the firm's equity. The following example provides an additional illustration of its application.

EXAMPLE

A firm is considering the purchase of a new computer system, which will cost $30,000 initially, to aid in credit billing and inventory management. The after-tax cash flows resulting from this project are provided in Table 9.5. The required rate of return demanded by the firm is 10 percent. To determine the system's net present value, the 3-year $15,000 cash flow annuity is first discounted back to the present at 10 percent. From appendix E in the back of this book, we find that $PVIFA_{10\%,3yr}$ is 2.487. Thus the present value of this $15,000 annuity is $37,305 ($15,000 × 2.487).

Table 9.5 NPV Example Problem of Computer System

	After-Tax Cash Flow		After-Tax Cash Flow
Initial outlay	−$30,000	Inflow year 2	15,000
Inflow year 1	15,000	Inflow year 3	15,000

> Seeing that the cash inflows have been discounted back to the present, they can now be compared with the initial outlay, because both of the flows are now stated in terms of today's dollars. Subtracting the initial outlay ($30,000) from the present value of the cash inflows ($37,305) we find that the system's net present value is $7,305. Because the NPV on this project is positive, the project should be accepted.

OBJECTIVE 4

PROFITABILITY INDEX (BENEFIT/COST RATIO)

Profitability index (PI) (or Benefit/Cost Ratio)

A capital-budgeting decision criterion defined as the ratio of the present value of the future net cash flows to the initial outlay.

The **profitability index (PI)**, or **benefit/cost ratio**, is the ratio of the present value of the future net cash flows to the initial outlay. Although the net present value investment criterion gives a measure of the absolute dollar desirability of a project, the profitability index provides a relative measure of an investment proposal's desirability—that is, the ratio of the present value of its future net benefits to its initial cost. The profitability index can be expressed as follows:

$$PI = \frac{\sum_{t=1}^{n} \frac{ACF_t}{(1+k)^t}}{IO} \qquad (9\text{-}2)$$

where ACF_t = the annual after-tax cash flow in time period t
 (this can take on either positive or negative values)
  k = the appropriate discount rate; that is, the required rate of return or cost of capital
  IO = the initial cash outlay
  n = the project's expected life

The decision criterion is: Accept the project if the PI is greater than or equal to 1.00, and reject the project if the PI is less than 1.00.

PI ≥ 1.0: Accept
PI < 1.0: Reject

Looking closely at this criterion, we see that it yields the same accept-reject decision as the net present value criterion. Whenever the present value of the project's net cash flows is greater than its initial cash outlay, the project's net present value will be positive, signaling a decision to accept. When this is true, the project's profitability index will also be greater than 1, as the present value of the net cash flows (the PI's numerator) is greater than its initial outlay (the PI's denominator). Thus these two decision criteria will always yield the same accept/reject decision, although they will not necessarily rank acceptable projects in the same order. This problem of conflicting ranking will be dealt with at a later point.

Because the net present value and profitability index criteria are essentially the same, they have the same advantages over the other criteria examined. Both employ cash flows, recognize the timing of the cash flows, and are consistent with the goal of maximization of shareholders' wealth. The major disadvantage of this criterion, similar to the net present value criterion, is that it requires detailed cash flow forecasts over the entire life of the project.

EXAMPLE

A firm with a 10 percent required rate of return is considering investing in a new machine with an expected life of 6 years. The after-tax cash flows resulting from this investment are given in Table 9.6. Discounting the project's future net cash flows back to the present yields a present value of $53,667; dividing this value by the initial outlay of $50,000 gives a profitability index of 1.0733, as shown in Table 9.7. This tells us that the present value of the future benefits accruing from this project is 1.0733 times the level of the initial outlay. Because the profitability index is greater than 1.0, the project should be accepted.

Table 9.6 PI Illustration of Investment in New Machinery

	After-Tax Cash Flow		After-Tax Cash Flow
Initial outlay	−$50,000	Inflow year 4	12,000
Inflow year 1	15,000	Inflow year 5	14,000
Inflow year 2	8,000	Inflow year 6	16,000
Inflow year 3	10,000		

Table 9.7 Calculation for PI Illustration of Investment in New Machinery

	After-Tax Cash Flow	Present Value Factor at 10 Percent	Present Value
Initial outlay	−$50,000	1.000	−$50,000
Inflow year 1	15,000	0.909	13,635
Inflow year 2	8,000	0.826	6,608
Inflow year 3	10,000	0.751	7,510
Inflow year 4	12,000	0.683	8,196
Inflow year 5	14,000	0.621	8,694
Inflow year 6	16,000	0.564	9,024

$$PI = \frac{\sum_{t=1}^{n} \frac{ACF_t}{(1+k)^t}}{IO}$$

$$= \frac{\$13,635 + \$6,608 + \$7,510 + \$8,196 + \$8,694 + \$9,024}{\$50,000}$$

$$= \frac{\$53,667}{\$50,000}$$

$$= 1.0733$$

INTERNAL RATE OF RETURN

Internal rate of return (IRR)

A capital-budgeting decision criterion that reflects the rate of return a project earns. Mathematically, it is the discount rate that equates the present value of the inflows with the present value of the outflows.

The **internal rate of return (IRR)** attempts to answer this question: What rate of return does this project earn? For computational purposes, the internal rate of return is defined as the discount rate that equates the present value of the project's future net cash flows with the project's initial cash outlay. Mathematically, the internal rate of return is defined as the value of *IRR* in the following equation:

$$IO = \sum_{t=1}^{n} \frac{ACF_t}{(1 + IRR)^t} \tag{9-3}$$

where ACF_t = the annual after-tax cash flow in time period t
(this can take on either positive or negative values)
IO = the initial cash outlay
n = the project's expected life
IRR = the project's internal rate of return

In effect, the IRR is analogous to the concept of the yield to maturity for bonds, which was examined in chapter 7. In other words, a project's internal rate of return is simply the rate of return that the project earns.

The decision criterion is: Accept the project if the internal rate of return is greater than or equal to the required rate of return. We reject the project if its internal rate of return is less than this required rate of return. This accept-reject criterion can be stated as:

$IRR \geq$ required rate of return: Accept
$IRR <$ required rate of return: Reject

If the internal rate of return on a project is equal to the shareholders' required rate of return, then the project should be accepted, because the firm is earning the rate that its shareholders require. However, the acceptance of a project with an internal rate of return below the investors' required rate of return will decrease the firm's stock price.

If the NPV is positive, then the IRR must be greater than the required rate of return, k. Thus all the discounted cash flow criteria are consistent and will give similar accept-reject decisions. In addition, because the internal rate of return is another discounted cash flow criterion, it exhibits the same general advantages and disadvantages as both the net present value and profitability index, but has an additional disadvantage of being tedious to calculate if a financial calculator is not available.

An additional disadvantage of the IRR relative to the NPV deals with the implied reinvestment rate assumptions made by these two methods. The NPV method implicitly assumes that cash flows received over the life of the project are reinvested back in projects that earn the required rate of return. That is, if we have a mining project with a 10-year expected life that produces a $100,000 cash flow at the end of the second year, the NPV technique assumes that this $100,000 is reinvested over the period years 3 through 10 at the required rate of return. The use of the IRR, on the other hand, implies that cash flows over the life of the project can be reinvested at the IRR. Thus, if the mining project we just looked at has a 40 percent IRR, the use of the IRR implies that the $100,000 cash flow that is received at the end of year 2 could be reinvested at 40 percent over the remaining life of the project. In effect, *the NPV method implicitly assumes that cash flows over the life of the project can be reinvested at the firm's required rate of return, whereas the use of the IRR method implies that these cash flows could be reinvested at the IRR.* The better assumption is the one made by the NPV, that cash flows could be reinvested at the required rate of return, because these cash flows will either be (1) returned in the form of dividends to shareholders who demand the required rate of return on their investment, or (2) reinvested in a new investment project. If these cash flows are invested in a new project, then they are simply substituting for external funding on

AUGUST 1997

Inventing a Product: The Asia Car

Once a market is saturated, how do you go about expanding your sales? One answer is to go international and find new markets and new opportunities. It's consumers like Thaweesak Viravan, a shop owner who is a new member of Thailand's growing middle class, that are being targeted by Toyota and its "Asia car" which was unveiled in December 1996. How big are the opportunities for Toyota? In 1996 Southeast Asians bought 1.5 million cars and that figure is expected to grow by 50 percent in three years and double by early next century.

(A) In coming up with a new product, in this case a car, Toyota first went to the consumers to see what they wanted. They surveyed motorcyclists, students, shop keepers, and families that already owned cars. What they came up with was a car with an arctic strength air conditioner and built to withstand road conditions that terminate the typical American car. The "Asia car" was also built with higher ground clearance with the electronics placed high up in the car so that they wouldn't be damaged in the event of a flood. In addition, the "Asia car" comes without heaters (which simply aren't needed) or expensive anti-pollution equipment (which while probably needed, isn't required).

(B) Will this project be a gold mine for Toyota? Certainly it's a great opportunity, but as is the case with most golden opportunities in business this one has attracted competition—Honda. In April of 1996 Honda introduced "the City," which has already become the best selling passenger car in Thailand. In fact, some analysts are predicting a glut of new cars in this market as new entrants continue.

SOURCES: Based on Lisa Shuchman, "Shifting Gears: Japanese Auto Companies Map Out New Plans for Asia," *The Asian Wall Street Journal* (January 30, 1998): 1; Steven V. Brull, Robert Horn, and Bruce Einhorn, "No Heater, Great Suspension—It's The 'Asia Car'," *Business Week* (December 16, 1996): 31; Nopporn Wong-Anan, "Ford Aims for 'Utilitarian' Asia Vehicle," *The Asian Wall Street Journal* (November 25, 1996): 5; and "Japanese Automakers Seek to Keep Lead in Asian Market," *The Plain Dealer* (August 11, 1996): 4H.

Analysis and Implications ...

A. Capital budgeting involves not only evaluating new projects, but also finding them in the first place. Given the size of the emerging markets in Asia, it would be foolish not to look there for new business opportunities. However, products that work in the United States will likely have to be modified to fit those markets; in this case, that involved dropping the heater and putting in an industrial strength air conditioner.

B. Just as we learned in **Axiom 5: The Curse of Competitive Markets**, whenever there are lucrative opportunities, competition follows. As a result, it is important that the new product be developed and designed in such a way that it can't be easily one-upped by the competition. In effect, although our capital-budgeting techniques can do a good job of evaluating projects, a good product has its roots in good product development—knowing consumer wants and delivering it. From there, the sales forecasts have to be accurate—anticipating moves by competitors—because although our capital-budgeting criteria are good at evaluating proposals, the results are only as good as what is input into the models.

which the required rate of return is demanded. Thus the opportunity cost of these funds is the required rate of return. The bottom line to all this is that the NPV method makes the best reinvestment rate assumption and, as such, is superior to the IRR method. Why should we care which method is used if both methods give similar accept-reject decisions? The answer, as we will see in the next chapter, is that although they may give the same accept-reject decision, they may rank projects differently in terms of desirability.

Computing the IRR with a Financial Calculator

With today's calculators, the determination of an internal rate of return is merely a matter of a few keystrokes. In chapter 5, whenever we were solving time value of money problems for i, we were really solving for the internal rate of return. For instance, in chapter 5, when we solved for the rate that $100 must be compounded annually for it to grow to $179.10 in 10 years, we were actually solving for that problem's internal rate of return. Thus with financial calculators we need only input the initial outlay, the cash flows and their timing, and then press the function key **I/Y** or the **IRR** button to calculate the internal rate of return. On some calculators, it is necessary to press the compute key, **CPT**, before pressing the function key to be calculated.

Computing the IRR for Even Cash Flows

In this section, we are going to put our calculators aside and obtain a better understanding of the IRR by examining the mathematical process of calculating internal rates of return.

The calculation of a project's internal rate of return can either be very simple or relatively complicated. As an example of a straightforward solution, assume that a firm with a required rate of return of 10 percent is considering a project that involves an initial outlay of $45,555. If the investment is taken, the after-tax cash flows are expected to be $15,000 per annum over the project's 4-year life. In this case, the internal rate of return is equal to *IRR* in the following equation:

$$\$45,555 = \frac{\$15,000}{(1 + IRR)^1} + \frac{\$15,000}{(1 + IRR)^2} + \frac{\$15,000}{(1 + IRR)^3} + \frac{\$15,000}{(1 + IRR)^4}$$

From our discussion of the present value of an annuity in chapter 5, we know that this equation can be reduced to

$$\$45,555 = \$15,000 \left[\sum_{t=1}^{4} \frac{1}{(1 + IRR)^t} \right]$$

Appendix E gives values for the $PVIFA_{i,n}$ for various combinations of i and n, which further reduces this equation to

$$\$45,555 = \$15,000 \, (PVIFA_{i,4yr})$$

Dividing both sides by $15,000, this becomes

$$3.037 = PVIFA_{i,4yr}$$

Hence we are looking for a $PVIFA_{i,4yr}$ of 3.037 in the 4-year row of appendix E. This value occurs when i equals 12 percent, which means that 12 percent is the internal rate of return for the investment. Therefore, because 12 percent is greater than the 10 percent required return, the project should be accepted.

Computing the IRR for Uneven Cash Flows

Unfortunately, although solving for the IRR is quite easy when using a financial calculator or spreadsheet, it can be solved directly in the tables only when the future after-tax net cash flows are in the form of an annuity or a single payment. With a calculator, the process is simple: One need only key in the initial cash outlay, the cash flows, and their timing, and press the **IRR** button. When a financial calculator is not available and these flows are in the form of an uneven series of flows, a trial-and-error approach is necessary. To do this, we first determine the present value of the future after-tax net cash flows using an arbitrary discount rate. If the present value of the future cash flows at this discount rate is larger than the initial outlay, the rate is increased; if it is smaller than the initial outlay, the discount rate is lowered and the process begins again. This search routine is continued until the present value of the future after-tax cash flows is equal to the initial outlay. The interest rate that creates this situation is the internal rate of return. This is the same basic process that a financial calculator uses to calculate an IRR.

To illustrate the procedure, consider an investment proposal that requires an initial outlay of $3,817 and returns $1,000 at the end of year 1, $2,000 at the end of year 2, and $3,000 at the end of year 3. In this case, the internal rate of return must be determined using trial and error. This process is presented in Table 9.8, in which an arbitrarily selected discount rate of 15 percent was chosen to begin the process.

Table 9.8 Computing IRR for Uneven Cash Flows Without a Financial Calculator

Initial outlay	−$3,817	Inflow year 2	2,000
Inflow year 1	1,000	Inflow year 3	3,000

Solution:

Step 1: Pick an arbitrary discount rate and use it to determine the present value of the inflows.

Step 2: Compare the present value of the inflows with the initial outlay; if they are equal you have determined the IRR.

Step 3: If the present value of the inflows is larger (less than) than the initial outlay, raise (lower) the discount rate.

Step 4: Determine the present value of the inflows and repeat Step 2.

1. Try $i = 15$ percent:

	Net Cash Flows	Present Value Factor at 15 Percent	Present Value
Inflow year 1	$1,000	.870	$ 870
Inflow year 2	2,000	.756	1,512
Inflow year 3	3,000	.658	1,974
Present value of inflows			$4,356
Initial outlay			−$3,817

2. Try $i = 20$ percent:

	Net Cash Flows	Present Value Factor at 20 Percent	Present Value
Inflow year 1	$1,000	.833	$ 833
Inflow year 2	2,000	.694	1,388
Inflow year 3	3,000	.579	1,737
Present value of inflows			$3,958
Initial outlay			−$3,817

3. Try $i = 22$ percent:

	Net Cash Flows	Present Value Factor at 22 Percent	Present Value
Inflow year 1	$1,000	.820	$ 820
Inflow year 2	2,000	.672	1,344
Inflow year 3	3,000	.551	1,653
Present value of inflows			$3,817
Initial outlay			−$3,817

Obviously, 15 percent isn't the IRR for this project, because the present value of the inflows discounted back to present at 15 percent ($4,356) doesn't equal the initial outlay ($3,815). How do we make the present value of the future cash flows smaller? We raise the discount rate. Thus we tried 20 percent next. Again, 20 percent isn't the IRR for this project because the present value of the inflows discounted back to present at 20 percent ($3,958) doesn't equal the initial outlay ($3,815)—although it's closer than it was at 15 percent. Once more, we need to make the present value of the future cash flows smaller so we try a higher discount rate—22 percent. At 22 percent, we have found the project's internal rate of return, because the present value of the future cash flows equals the initial outlay. The project's internal rate of return is then compared with the firm's required rate of return, and if the IRR is the larger, the project is accepted.

EXAMPLE

A firm with a required rate of return of 10 percent is considering three investment proposals. Given the information in Table 9.9, management plans to calculate the internal rate of return for each project and determine which projects should be accepted.

Table 9.9 Three IRR Investment Proposal Examples

	A	B	C
Initial outlay	−$10,000	−$10,000	−$10,000
Inflow year 1	3,362	0	1,000
Inflow year 2	3,362	0	3,000
Inflow year 3	3,362	0	6,000
Inflow year 4	3,362	13,605	7,000

Because project A is an annuity, we can easily calculate its internal rate of return by determining the $PVIFA_{i,4yr}$ necessary to equate the present value of the future cash flows with the initial outlay. This computation is done as follows:

$$IO = \sum_{t=1}^{n} \frac{ACF_t}{(1 + IRR)^t}$$

$$\$10,000 = \sum_{t=1}^{4} \frac{\$3,362}{(1 + IRR)^t}$$

$$\$10,000 = \$3,362(PVIFA_{i,4yr})$$

$$2.974 = (PVIFA_{i,4yr})$$

We are looking for a $PVIFA_{i,4yr}$ of 2.974, in the 4-year row of appendix E, which occurs in the $i = 13$ percent column. Thus 13 percent is the internal rate of return. Because this rate is greater than the firm's required rate of return of 10 percent, the project should be accepted.

Project B involves a single future cash flow of $13,605, resulting from an initial outlay of $10,000; thus its internal rate of return can be determined directly from the present-value table in appendix C, as follows:

$$IO = \frac{ACF_t}{(1 + IRR)^t}$$

$$\$10,000 = \frac{\$13,605}{(1 + IRR)^4}$$

$$\$10,000 = \$13,605(PVIF_{i,4yr})$$

$$.735 = (PVIF_{i,4yr})$$

This tells us that we should look for a $PVIF_{i,4yr}$ of .735 in the 4-year row of appendix C, which occurs in the $i = 8$ percent column. We may therefore conclude that 8 percent is the internal rate of return. Because this rate is less than the firm's required rate of return of 10 percent, project B should be rejected.

The uneven nature of the future cash flows associated with project C necessitates the use of the trial-and-error method. The internal rate of return for project C is equal to the value of IRR in the following equation:

$$\$10,000 = \frac{\$1,000}{(1 + IRR)^1} + \frac{\$3,000}{(1 + IRR)^2} + \frac{\$6,000}{(1 + IRR)^3} + \frac{\$7,000}{(1 + IRR)^4}$$

Arbitrarily selecting a discount rate of 15 percent and substituting it for IRR reduces the right side of the equation to $11,090, as shown in Table 9.10 (page 338). Therefore, because the present value of the future cash flows is larger than the initial outlay, we must raise the discount rate to find the project's internal rate of return. Substituting 20 percent for the discount rate, the right side of the equation now becomes $9,763. As this is less than the initial outlay of $10,000, we must now decrease the discount rate. In other words, we know that the internal rate of return for this project is between 15 and 20 percent. Because the present value of the future flows discounted back to present at 20 percent was only $237 too low, a discount rate of 19 percent is selected. As shown in Table 9.10, a discount rate of 19 percent reduces the present value of the future inflows down to $10,009, which is approximately the same as the initial outlay. Consequently, project C's internal rate of return is approximately 19 percent.[2] Because the internal rate of return is greater than the firm's required rate of return of 10 percent, this investment should be accepted.

Viewing the NPV–IRR Relationship: The Net Present Value Profile

Perhaps the easiest way to understand the relationship between the internal rate of return the net present value is to view it graphically through the use of a **net present value profile**. A net present value profile is simply a graph showing how a project's net present value changes as the discount rate changes. To graph a project's net present value profile, you simply need to determine the project's net present value first using a zero percent discount rate, then slowly increase the discount rate until a representative curve has been plotted.

---

[2]If desired, the actual rate can be more precisely approximated through interpolation as follows:

Discount Rate	Present Value		
19%	$10,009	difference $9	difference $246
IRR	10,000		
20%	9,763		

Thus IRR = 19% + ($9/$246) · 1% = 19.04%

Table 9.10 Computing IRR for Project C

Try $i = 15$ percent:

	Net Cash Flows	Present Value Factor at 15 Percent	Present Value
Inflow year 1	$1,000	.870	$ 870
Inflow year 2	3,000	.756	2,268
Inflow year 3	6,000	.658	3,948
Inflow year 4	7,000	.572	4,004
Present value of inflows			$11,090
Initial outlay			−$10,000

Try $i = 20$ percent:

	Net Cash Flows	Present Value Factor at 20 Percent	Present Value
Inflow year 1	$1,000	.833	$ 833
Inflow year 2	3,000	.694	2,082
Inflow year 3	6,000	.579	3,474
Inflow year 4	7,000	.482	3,374
Present value of inflows			$ 9,763
Initial outlay			−$10,000

Try $i = 19$ percent:

	Net Cash Flows	Present Value Factor at 19 Percent	Present Value
Inflow year 1	$1,000	.840	$ 840
Inflow year 2	3,000	.706	2,118
Inflow year 3	6,000	.593	3,558
Inflow year 4	7,000	.499	3,493
Present value of inflows			$10,009
Initial outlay			−$10,000

How does the IRR enter into the net present value profile? The IRR is the discount rate at which the net present value is zero.

Let's look at an example of a project that involves an after-tax initial outlay of $105,517 with after-tax cash flows expected to be $30,000 per year over the project's 5-year life. Calculating the NPV of this project at several different discounts rates results in the following:

Discount Rate	Project's NPV
0%	$44,483
5%	$24,367
10%	$ 8,207
13%	$ 0
15%	−$ 4,952
20%	−$15,798
25%	−$24,839

Figure 9.1 Net Present Value Profile

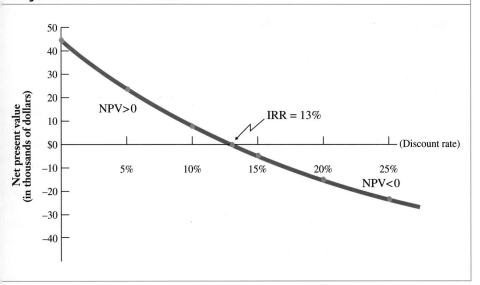

Plotting these values, we get the net present value profile in Figure 9.1.

Where is the IRR in this figure? Recall that the IRR is the discount rate that equates the present value of the inflows with the present value of the outflows, thus the IRR is the point where the NPV is equal to zero. In this case, 13 percent.

From the net present value profile, you can easily see how a project's net present value varies inversely with the discount rate—as the discount rate is raised, the net present value drops. From looking at a project's net present value profile, you can also see how sensitive the project is to your selection of the discount rate. The more sensitive the NPV is to the discount rate, the more important it is that you use the correct one in your calculations.

Complications with IRR: Multiple Rates of Return

Although any project can have only one NPV and one PI, a single project under certain circumstances can have more than one IRR. The reason for this can be traced to the calculations involved in determining the IRR. Equation (9-3) states that the IRR is the discount rate that equates the present value of the project's future net cash flows with the project's initial outlay:

$$IO = \sum_{t=1}^{n} \frac{ACF_t}{(1 + IRR)^t}$$

However, because equation (9-3) is a polynomial of a degree n, it has n solutions. Now if the initial outlay (IO) is the only negative cash flow and all the annual after-tax cash flows (ACF_t) are positive, then all but one of these n solutions is either a negative or imaginary number and there is no problem. But problems occur when there are sign reversals in the cash flow stream; in fact, there can be as many solutions as there are sign reversals. A normal pattern with a negative initial outlay and positive annual after-tax cash flows after that (−, +, +, …, +) has only one sign reversal, hence only one positive IRR. However, a pattern with more than one sign reversal can have more than one IRR.[3]

---

[3]This example is taken from James H. Lorie and Leonard J. Savage, "Three Problems in Rationing Capital," *Journal of Business* 28 (October 1955): 229–39.

	After-Tax Cash Flow
Initial outlay	–$ 1,600
Year 1	+$10,000
Year 2	–$10,000

In the preceding pattern of cash flows, there are two sign reversals, from –$1,600 to +$10,000 and then from +$10,000 to –$10,000, so there can be as many as two positive IRRs that will make the present value of the future cash flows equal to the initial outlay. In fact, two internal rates of return solve this problem, 25 and 400 percent. Graphically, what we are solving for is the discount rate that makes the project's NPV equal to zero; as Figure 9.2 illustrates, this occurs twice.

Which solution is correct? The answer is that neither solution is valid. Although each fits the definition of IRR, neither provides any insight into the true project returns. In summary, when there is more than one sign reversal in the cash flow stream, the possibility of multiple IRRs exists, and the normal interpretation of the IRR loses its meaning. In this case, try the NPV criterion instead.

Modified Internal Rate of Return

The primary drawback of the internal rate of return relative to the net present value method is the reinvestment rate assumption made by the internal rate of return. Recently, a new technique, the **modified internal rate of return (MIRR)**, has gained popularity as an alternative to the IRR method because it allows the decision-maker to directly specify the appropriate reinvestment rate. As a result, the MIRR provides the decision-maker with the intuitive appeal of the IRR coupled with an improved reinvestment rate assumption.

Modified internal rate of return (MIRR)

A variation of the IRR capital-budgeting decision criterion defined as the discount rate that equates the present value of the project's annual cash outlays with the present value of the project's terminal value, where the terminal value is defined as the sum of the future value of the project's cash inflows compounded to the project's termination at the project's required rate of return.

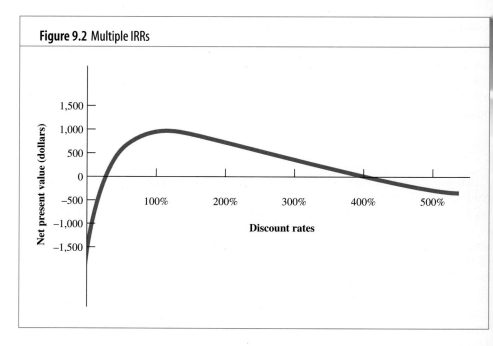

Figure 9.2 Multiple IRRs

The driving force behind the MIRR is the assumption that all cash inflows over the life of the project are reinvested at the required rate of return until the termination of the project. Thus to calculate the MIRR, we take all the annual after-tax cash *in*flows, $ACIF_t$s, and find their future value at the end of the project's life, compounded at the required rate of return. We will call this the project's *terminal value*, or *TV*. We then calculate the present value of the project's cash *out*flows. We do this by discounting all cash *out*flows, $ACOF_t$, back to present at the required rate of return. If the initial outlay is the only cash *out*flow, then the initial outlay is the present value of the cash *out*flows. The MIRR is the discount rate that equates the present value of the cash *out*flows with the present value of the project's *terminal value*.[4] Mathematically, the modified internal rate of return is defined as the value of MIRR in the following equation

$$PV_{outflows} = PV_{inflows}$$

$$\sum_{t=0}^{n} \frac{ACOF_t}{(1 + k)^t} = \frac{\displaystyle\sum_{t=0}^{n} ACIF_t(1 + k)^{n-t}}{(1 + MIRR)^n} \tag{9-4}$$

$$PV_{outflows} = \frac{TV}{(1 + MIRR)^n}$$

where $ACOF_t$ = the annual after-tax cash *out*flow in time period t
      $ACIF_t$ = the annual after-tax *in*flow in time period t
      TV = the terminal value of the $ACIF$s compounded at the required rate of return to the end of the project
      n = the project's expected life
      $MIRR$ = the project's modified internal rate of return
      k = the appropriate discount rate; that is, the required rate of return or cost of capital

EXAMPLE

Let's look at an example of a project with a 3-year life and a required rate of return of 10 percent assuming the following cash flows are associated with it:

	After-Tax Cash Flows		After-Tax Cash Flows
Initial outlay	–$6,000	Year 2	3,000
Year 1	2,000	Year 3	4,000

The calculation of the *MIRR* can be viewed as a three-step process, which is also shown graphically in Figure 9.3.

Step 1: Determine the present value of the project's cash *out*flows. In this case, the only *out*flow is the initial outlay of $6,000, which is already at the present, thus it becomes the present value of the cash *out*flows.

---

[4]You will notice that we differentiate between annual cash *in*flows and annual cash *out*flows, compounding all the *in*flows to the end of the project and bringing all the *out*flows back to present as part of the present value of the costs. Although there are alternative definitions of the MIRR, this is the most widely accepted definition. For an excellent discussion of the MIRR, see William R. McDaniel, Daniel E. McCarty, and Kenneth A. Jessell, "Discounted Cash Flow with Explicit Reinvestment Rates: Tutorial and Extension," *The Financial Review* (August 1988): 369–85.

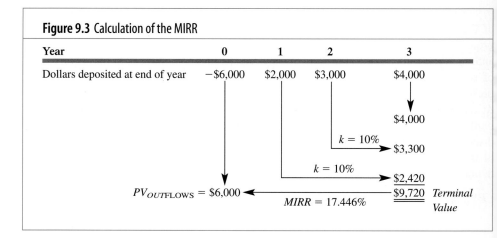

Figure 9.3 Calculation of the MIRR

Year	0	1	2	3
Dollars deposited at end of year	−$6,000	$2,000	$3,000	$4,000

$4,000

$k = 10\%$ → $3,300

$k = 10\%$ → $2,420

$PV_{OUTFLOWS} = \$6,000$ ← $MIRR = 17.446\%$ — $9,720 \underline{\underline{\quad}}$ *Terminal Value*

Step 2: Determine the terminal value of the project's cash *in*flows. To do this, we merely use the project's required rate of return to calculate the future value of the project's three cash *in*flows at the termination of the project. In this case, the *terminal value* becomes $9,720.

Step 3: Determine the discount rate that equates the present value of the *terminal value* and the present value of the project's cash *out*flows. Thus the *MIRR* is calculated to be 17.446 percent.

For our example, the calculations are as follows:

$$\$6,000 = \frac{\sum_{t=1}^{3} ACIF_t(1 + k)^{n-t}}{(1 + MIRR)^n}$$

$$\$6,000 = \frac{\$2,000(1 + .10)^2 + \$3,000(1 + .10)^1 + \$4,000(1 + .10)^0}{(1 + MIRR)^3}$$

$$\$6,000 = \frac{\$2,420 + \$3,300 + \$4,000}{(1 + MIRR)^3}$$

$$\$6,000 = \frac{\$9,720}{(1 + MIRR)^3}$$

$$MIRR = 17.446\%$$

Thus the MIRR for this project (17.446 percent) is less than its IRR which comes out to 20.614 percent. In this case, it only makes sense that the IRR should be greater than the MIRR, because the IRR allows intermediate cash *in*flows to grow at the IRR rather than the required rate of return.

In terms of decision rules, if the project's MIRR is greater than or equal to the project's required rate of return, then the project should be accepted; if not, it should be rejected:

MIRR ≥ required rate of return: Accept
MIRR < required rate of return: Reject

Because of the frequent use of the IRR in the real world as a decision-making tool and its limiting reinvestment rate assumption, the MIRR has become increasingly popular as an alternative decision-making tool.

ETHICS IN CAPITAL BUDGETING

OBJECTIVE 6

Although it may not seem obvious, ethics has a role in capital budgeting. Any actions that violate ethical standards can cause a loss of trust which can, in turn, have a negative and long-lasting effect on the firm. The "Bad Apple for Baby" story outlines one such violation. In this case, it deals with ethical lapses at Beech-Nut and demonstrates the consequences of those actions. No doubt the decisions of the Beech-Nut executives were meant to create wealth, but in fact, they cost Beech-Nut tremendously.

RELATE TO THE BIG PICTURE

*Ethics and ethical considerations continually crop up when capital-budgeting decisions are being made. This brings us back to the fundamental **Axiom 10: Ethical Behavior Is Doing the Right Thing, and Ethical Dilemmas Are Everywhere in Finance**. As "Bad Apple for Baby" points out, the most damaging event a business can experience is a loss of the public's confidence in its ethical standards. In making capital-budgeting decisions we must be aware of this, and that ethical behavior is doing the right thing and it is the right thing to do.*

A GLANCE AT ACTUAL CAPITAL-BUDGETING PRACTICES

OBJECTIVE 7

During the past 40 years, the popularity of each of the capital-budgeting methods has shifted rather dramatically. In the 1950s and 1960s, the payback period method dominated capital budgeting; but through the 1970s and 1980s, the internal rate of return and the net present value techniques slowly gained in popularity until they are today used by virtually all major corporations in decision making. Table 9.11 provides the results of a 1992 survey of the 100 largest Fortune 500 firms, showing the popularity of the internal rate of return and net present value methods.

Interestingly, although most firms use the NPV and IRR as their primary techniques, most firms also use the payback period as a secondary decision method for capital budgeting. In a sense, they are using the payback period to control for risk. The logic behind this is that because the payback period dramatically emphasizes early cash flows, which are presumably more certain—that is, have less risk—than cash flows occurring later in a project's life, managers believe its use will lead to projects with more certain cash flows.

Table 9.11 1992 Survey of Capital-Budgeting Practices of the 100 Largest Fortune 500 Industrial Firms

Investment Evaluation Methods Used:	Percent of Firms		
	A Primary Method	A Secondary Method	Total Using This Method
Internal rate of return	88%	11%	99%
Net present value	63%	22%	85%
Payback period	24%	59%	83%
Profitability index	15%	18%	33%

SOURCE: Harold Bierman, Jr., "Capital Budgeting in 1992: A Survey," *Financial Management* (Autumn 1993): 24.

FINANCIAL WORLD, JUNE 27, 1989

Bad Apple for Baby

(A) It's a widely held, but hard-to-prove belief that a company gains because it is perceived as more socially responsive than its competitors. Over the years, the three major manufacturers of baby food—Gerber Products, Beech-Nut Nutrition, and H. J. Heinz—had, with almost equal success, gone out of their way to build an image of respectability.

Theirs is an almost perfect zero-sum business. They know, at any given time, how many babies are being born. They all pay roughly the same price for their commodities, and their manufacturing and distribution costs are almost identical. So how does one company gain a market share edge over another, especially in a stagnant or declining market?

The answer for Beech-Nut was to sell a cheaper, adulterated product. Beginning in 1977, the company began buying a chemical concoction, made up mostly of sugar and water, and labeling it as apple juice. Sales of that product brought Beech-Nut an estimated $60 million between 1977 and 1982, while reducing material costs about $250,000 annually.

When various investigators tried to do something about it, the company stonewalled. Among other things, they shipped the bogus juice out of a plant in New York to Puerto Rico, to put it beyond the jurisdiction of federal investigators, and they even offered the juice as a give-away to reduce their stocks after they were finally forced to discontinue selling it.

(B) In the end, the company pleaded guilty to 215 counts of introducing adulterated food into commerce and violating the Federal Food Drug and Cosmetic Act. The FDA fined Beech-Nut $2 million.

In addition, Beech-Nut's president, Neils Hoyvald, and its vice president of operations, John Lavery, were found guilty of similar charges. Each faces a year and one day in jail and a $100,000 fine. Both are now out on appeal on a jurisdiction technicality.

Why did they do it? The Fort Washington, Pa.-based company will not comment. But perhaps some portion of motive can be inferred from a report Hoyvald wrote to Nestle, the company which had acquired Beech-Nut in the midst of his cover-up. "It is our feeling that we can report safely now that the apple juice recall has been completed. If the recall had been effectuated in early June [when the FDA had first ordered it], over 700,000 cases in inventory would have been affected; due to our many delays, we were only faced with having to destroy 20,000 cases."

One thing is clear: Two executives of a company with an excellent reputation breached a trust and did their company harm.

SOURCE: Stephen Kindel, "Bad Apple for Baby," *Financial World* (June 27, 1989): 48. Reprinted by permission. © 1989 *Financial World*.

Analysis and Implications . . .

A. When we introduced **Axiom 10: Ethical Behavior Is Doing the Right Thing, and Ethical Dilemmas Are Everywhere in Finance** in chapter 1, we noted that acting in an ethical manner is not only morally correct, but that it is congruent with our goal of maximization of shareholder wealth. In this case, we can directly relate unethical behavior to a loss of shareholder wealth.

B. The most damaging event a business can suffer is a loss of the public's confidence in its ethical standards. In the financial world, we have seen this happen with the insider trading scandal at Drexel Burnham Lambert that brought down the firm, and at Salomon Brothers with their attempt to corner the Treasury bill market. At Beech-Nut, the loss in consumer confidence that accompanied this scandal resulted in a drop of Beech-Nut's share of the overall baby food market from 19.1 percent to 15.8 percent. Thus although this violation of ethics resulted in a short-run gain for Beech-Nut, much more was lost in the long run for many years to come.

A reliance on the payback period came out even more dramatically in a study of the capital-budgeting practices of 12 large manufacturing firms.[5] This study also showed that, although the discounted cash flow methods are used at most firms, the simple payback criterion was the measure relied on primarily in one third of the firms examined. The use of the payback period seemed to be even more common for smaller projects, with firms severely simplifying the discounted cash flow analysis or relying primarily on the payback period. Thus, although discounted cash flow decision techniques have become more widely accepted, their use depends to an extent on the size of the project.

HOW FINANCIAL MANAGERS USE THIS MATERIAL

Without taking on new projects, a company simply wouldn't continue to exist. For example, Smith-Corona's inability to come up with a product to replace the typewriters that it produced resulted in that company going under in 1996. Finding new profitable projects and correctly evaluating them are central to the firms continued existence—and that's what capital budgeting is all about. It may be your decision to buy a Burger King franchise and open a Burger King restaurant. Or you may decide to help in Burger King's introduction of the Big King, a new burger that looks an awful lot like the Big Mac. Whatever your decision, when you're making an investment in fixed assets, it's a capital-budgeting decision. It may also involve taking a product that didn't work and trying to redesign it in such a way that it does. That's what 3Com Corporation did with the Palm Pilot electronic datebook and scheduler which succeeded with small size and simplicity where Apple's Newton and Motorola's Envoy failed.

Much of what is done within a business involves the capital-budgeting process. Many times it's referred to as strategic planning, but it generally involves capital-budgeting decisions. You may be involved in market research dealing with a proposed new product, on its marketing plan, or in analyzing its costs—these are all part of the capital-budgeting process. Once all this information has been gathered, it is analyzed using the techniques and tools that we have presented in this chapter. Actually, almost any decision can be analyzed using the framework we presented here. That's because the net present value method "values" the project under consideration. That is, it looks at the present value of its benefits relative to the present value of its costs and if the present value of the benefits outweigh the costs the project is accepted. That's a pretty good decision rule, and it can be applied to any decision a business faces.

SUMMARY

Before a profitable project can be adopted, it must be identified or found. Unfortunately, coming up with ideas for new products, for ways to improve existing products, or for ways to make existing products more profitable is extremely difficult. In general, the best source of ideas for these new, potentially profitable products is found within the firm.

The process of capital budgeting involves decision making with respect to investment in fixed assets. We examine four commonly used criteria for determining the acceptance or rejection of capital-budgeting proposals. The first method, the payback period, does not incorporate the time value of money into its calculations, although a variation of it, the discounted payback period, does. The discounted methods, net present value, profitability index, and internal rate of return, do account for the time value of money. These methods are summarized in Table 9.12.

OBJECTIVE 1

[5]Marc Ross, "Capital Budgeting Practices of Twelve Large Manufacturers," *Financial Management* 15 (Winter 1986): 15–22.

Table 9.12 Capital-Budgeting Criteria

1. A. Payback period = number of years required to recapture the initial investment

   Accept if payback ≤ maximum acceptable payback period
   Reject if payback > maximum acceptable payback period

   Advantages:
   - Uses cash flows.
   - Is easy to calculate and understand.
   - May be used as rough screening device.

   Disadvantages:
   - Ignores the time value of money.
   - Ignores cash flows occurring after the payback period.
   - Selection of the maximum acceptable payback period is arbitrary.

   B. Discounted payback period = the number of years needed to recover the initial cash outlay from the *discounted net cash flows*

   Accept if discounted payback ≤ maximum acceptable discounted payback period
   Reject if discounted payback > maximum acceptable discounted payback period

   Advantages:
   - Uses cash flows.
   - Is easy to calculate and understand.
   - Considers time value of money.

   Disadvantages:
   - Ignores cash flows occurring after the payback period.
   - Selection of the maximum acceptable discounted payback period is arbitrary.

2. Net present value = present value of the annual after-tax cash flows less the investment's initial outlay

$$NPV = \sum_{t=1}^{n} \frac{ACF_t}{(1 + k)^t} - IO$$

   where ACF_t = the annual after-tax cash flow in time period t (this can take on either positive or negative values)

   k = the appropriate discount rate; that is, the required rate of return or the cost of capital

   IO = the initial cash outlay

   n = the project's expected life

   Accept if $NPV \geq 0.0$
   Reject if $NPV < 0.0$

   Advantages:
   - Uses cash flows.
   - Recognizes the time value of money.
   - Is consistent with the firm's goal of shareholder wealth maximization.

   Disadvantages:
   - Requires detailed long-term forecasts of a project's cash flows.

3. Profitability index = the ratio of the present value of the future net cash flows to the initial outlay

$$PI = \frac{\sum_{t=1}^{n} \dfrac{ACF_t}{(1 + k)^t}}{IO}$$

Table 9.12 Capital-Budgeting Criteria (continued)

Accept if $PI \geq 1.0$
Reject if $PI < 1.0$

Advantages:
- Uses cash flows.
- Recognizes the time value of money.
- Is consistent with the firm's goal of shareholder wealth maximization.

Disadvantages:
- Requires detailed long-term forecasts of a project's cash flows.

4. A. Internal rate of return = the discount rate that equates the present value of the project's future net cash flows with the project's initial outlay

OBJECTIVE 5

$$IO = \sum_{t=1}^{n} \frac{ACF_t}{(1 + IRR)^t}$$

where IRR = the project's internal rate of return

Accept if $IRR \geq$ required rate of return
Reject if $IRR <$ required rate of return

Advantages:
- Uses cash flows.
- Recognizes the time value of money.
- Is in general consistent with the firm's goal of shareholder wealth maximization.

Disadvantages:
- Requires detailed long-term forecasts of a project's cash flows.
- Possibility of multiple IRRs.
- Assumes cash flows over the life of the project are reinvested at the IRR.

B. Modified internal rate of return = the discount rate that equates the present value of the project's cash *out*flows with the present value of the project's *terminal value*

$$\sum_{t=0}^{n} \frac{ACOF_t}{(1 + k)^t} = \frac{\sum_{t=0}^{n} ACIF_t (1 + k)^{n-t}}{(1 + MIRR)^n}$$

$$PV_{OUTFLOWS} = \frac{TV}{(1 + MIRR)^n}$$

where $ACOF_t$ = the annual after-tax cash *out*flow in time period t.
$ACIF_t$ = the annual after-tax cash *in*flow in time period t.
TV = the terminal value of $ACIF$s compounded at the required rate of return to the end of the project.

Accept if $MIRR \geq$ the required rate of return
Reject if $MIRR <$ required rate of return

Advantages:
- Uses cash flows.
- Recognizes the time value of money.
- In general, is consistent with the goal of maximization of shareholder wealth.

Disadvantages:
- Requires detailed long-term forecasts of a project's cash flows.

OBJECTIVE 6   Ethics and ethical decisions crop up in capital budgeting. Just as with all other areas of finance, violating ethical considerations results in a loss of public confidence which can have a significant negative effect on shareholder wealth.

OBJECTIVE 7   Over the past 40 years, the discounted capital-budgeting decision criteria have continued to gain in popularity and today dominate in the decision-making process.

KEY TERMS

Capital budgeting, 323

Discounted payback
period, 326

Internal rate of return
(IRR), 332

Modified internal rate of
return (MIRR), 340

Net present value (NPV), 328

Payback period, 324

Profitability index (PI)
(or benefit/cost ratio), 330

STUDY QUESTIONS

9-1. Why is the capital-budgeting decision so important? Why are capital-budgeting errors so costly?

9-2. What are the criticisms of the use of the payback period as a capital-budgeting technique? What are its advantages? Why is it so frequently used?

9-3. In some countries, expropriation of foreign investments is a common practice. If you were considering an investment in one of those countries, would the use of the payback period criterion seem more reasonable than it otherwise might? Why?

9-4. Briefly compare and contrast the NPV, PI, and IRR criteria. What are the advantages and disadvantages of using each of these methods?

9-5. What is the advantage of using the MIRR as opposed to the IRR decision criteria?

SELF-TEST PROBLEMS

ST-1. You are considering a project that will require an initial outlay of $54,200. This project has an expected life of 5 years and will generate after-tax cash flows to the company as a whole of $20,608 at the end of each year over its 5-year life. In addition to the $20,608 cash flow from operations during the fifth and final year, there will be an additional cash inflow of $13,200 at the end of the fifth year associated with the salvage value of a machine, making the cash flow in year 5 equal to $33,808. Thus the cash flows associated with this project look like this:

Year	Cash Flow	Year	Cash Flow
0	−$54,200	3	20,608
1	20,608	4	20,608
2	20,608	5	33,808

Given a required rate of return of 15 percent, calculate the following:

    a. Payback period

    b. Net present value

    c. Profitability index

    d. Internal rate of return

Should this project be accepted?

STUDY PROBLEMS (SET A)

9-1A. (*IRR Calculation*) Determine the internal rate of return on the following projects:

    a. An initial outlay of $10,000 resulting in a single cash flow of $17,182 after 8 years

    b. An initial outlay of $10,000 resulting in a single cash flow of $48,077 after 10 years

    c. An initial outlay of $10,000 resulting in a single cash flow of $114,943 after 20 years

    d. An initial outlay of $10,000 resulting in a single cash flow of $13,680 after 3 years

9-2A. (*IRR Calculation*) Determine the internal rate of return on the following projects:

    a. An initial outlay of $10,000 resulting in a cash flow of $1,993 at the end of each year for the next 10 years

    b. An initial outlay of $10,000 resulting in a cash flow of $2,054 at the end of each year for the next 20 years

    c. An initial outlay of $10,000 resulting in a cash flow of $1,193 at the end of each year for the next 12 years

    d. An initial outlay of $10,000 resulting in a cash flow of $2,843 at the end of each year for the next 5 years

9-3A. (*IRR Calculation*) Determine the internal rate of return to the nearest percent on the following projects:

    a. An initial outlay of $10,000 resulting in a cash flow of $2,000 at the end of year 1, $5,000 at the end of year 2, and $8,000 at the end of year 3

    b. An initial outlay of $10,000 resulting in a cash flow of $8,000 at the end of year 1, $5,000 at the end of year 2, and $2,000 at the end of year 3

    c. An initial outlay of $10,000 resulting in a cash flow of $2,000 at the end of years 1 through 5 and $5,000 at the end of year 6

9-4A. (*NPV, PI, and IRR Calculations*) Fijisawa, Inc., is considering a major expansion of its product line and has estimated the following cash flows associated with such an expansion. The initial outlay associated with the expansion would be $1,950,000 and the project would generate after-tax cash flows of $450,000 per year for 6 years. The appropriate required rate of return is 9 percent.

    a. Calculate the net present value.

    b. Calculate the profitability index.

    c. Calculate the internal rate of return.

    d. Should this project be accepted?

9-5A. (*Payback Period, Net Present Value, Profitability Index, and Internal Rate of Return Calculations*) You are considering a project with an initial cash outlay of $80,000 and expected after-tax cash flows of $20,000 at the end of each year for 6 years. The required rate of return for this project is 10 percent.

    a. What are the project's payback and discounted payback periods?

    b. What is the project's NPV?

    c. What is the project's PI?

    d. What is the project's IRR?

9-6A. (*Net Present Value, Profitability Index, and Internal Rate of Return Calculations*) You are considering two independent projects, Project A and Project B. The initial cash outlay associated with Project A is $50,000 and the initial cash outlay associated with Project B is $70,000. The required rate of return on both projects is 12 percent. The expected annual after-tax cash flows from each project are as follows:

Year	Project A	Project B
0	−$50,000	−$70,000
1	12,000	13,000
2	12,000	13,000
3	12,000	13,000
4	12,000	13,000
5	12,000	13,000
6	12,000	13,000

Calculate the NPV, PI, and IRR for each project and indicate if the project should be accepted.

9-7A. (*Payback Period Calculations*) You are considering three independent projects, Project A, Project B, and Project C. The required rate of return is 10 percent on each. Given the following cash flow information, calculate the payback period and discounted payback period for each.

Year	Project A	Project B	Project C
0	−$1,000	−$10,000	−$5,000
1	600	5,000	1,000
2	300	3,000	1,000
3	200	3,000	2,000
4	100	3,000	2,000
5	500	3,000	2,000

If you require a 3-year payback for both the traditional and discounted payback period methods before an investment can be accepted, which projects would be accepted under each criterion?

9-8A. (*NPV with Varying Rates of Return*) Dowling Sportswear is considering building a new factory to produce aluminum baseball bats. This project would require an initial cash outlay of $5,000,000 and will generate annual after-tax cash inflows of $1 million per year for 8 years. Calculate the project's NPV given:

    a. A required rate of return of 9 percent

    b. A required rate of return of 11 percent

    c. A required rate of return of 13 percent

    d. A required rate of return of 15 percent

9-9A. (*Internal Rate of Return Calculations*) Given the following cash flows, determine the internal rate of return for the three independent projects A, B, and C.

	Project A	Project B	Project C
Initial Investment:	−$50,000	−$100,000	−$450,000
Cash Inflows:			
Year 1	$10,000	$ 25,000	$200,000
Year 2	15,000	25,000	200,000
Year 3	20,000	25,000	200,000
Year 4	25,000	25,000	—
Year 5	30,000	25,000	—

9-10A. (*NPV with Varying Required Rates of Return*) Big Steve's, makers of swizzle sticks, is considering the purchase of a new plastic stamping machine. This investment requires an initial outlay of $100,000 and will generate after-tax cash inflows of $18,000 per year for 10 years. For each of the listed required rates of return, determine the project's net present value.

    a. The required rate of return is 10 percent.

    b. The required rate of return is 15 percent.

    c. Would the project be accepted under part (a) or (b)?

    d. What is this project's internal rate of return?

9-11A. (*MIRR Calculation*) Emily's Soccer Mania is considering building a new plant. This project would require an initial cash outlay of $10 million and will generate annual after-tax cash inflows of $3 million per year for 10 years.

Calculate the project's MIRR, given:

    a. A required rate of return of 10 percent

    b. A required rate of return of 12 percent

    c. A required rate of return of 14 percent

Your first assignment in your new position as assistant financial analyst at Caledonia Products is to evaluate two new capital-budgeting proposals. Because this is your first assignment, you have been asked not only to provide a recommendation, but also to respond to a number of questions aimed at judging your understanding of the capital-budgeting process. This is a standard procedure for all new financial analysts at Caledonia and will serve to determine whether you are moved directly into the capital-budgeting analysis department or are provided with remedial training. The memorandum you received outlining your assignment follows:

TO: The New Financial Analysts

FROM: Mr. V. Morrison, CEO, Caledonia Products

RE: Capital-Budgeting Analysis

    Provide an evaluation of two proposed projects, both with 5-year expected lives and identical initial outlays of $110,000. Both these projects involve additions to Caledonia's highly successful Avalon product line, and as a result, the required rate of return on both projects has been established at 12 percent. The expected after-tax cash flows from each project are as follows:

3	Project A	Project B
Initial Outlay	−$110,000	−$110,000
Year 1	20,000	40,000
Year 2	30,000	40,000
Year 3	40,000	40,000
Year 4	50,000	40,000
Year 5	70,000	40,000

In evaluating these projects, please respond to the following questions:

    1. Why is the capital-budgeting process so important?

    2. Why is it difficult to find exceptionally profitable projects?

    3. What is the payback period on each project? If Caledonia imposes a 3-year maximum acceptable payback period, which of these projects should be accepted?

    4. What are the criticisms of the payback period?

    5. What are the discounted payback periods for each of these projects? If Caledonia requires a 3-year maximum acceptable discounted payback period on new projects, which of these projects should be accepted?

6. What are the drawbacks or deficiencies of the discounted payback period? Do you feel either the payback or discounted payback period should be used to determine whether or not these projects should be accepted? Why or why not?

7. Determine the net present value for each of these projects. Should they be accepted?

8. Describe the logic behind the net present value.

9. Determine the profitability index for each of these projects. Should they be accepted?

10. Would you expect the net present value and profitability index methods to give consistent accept/reject decisions? Why or why not?

11. What would happen to the net present value and profitability index for each project if the required rate of return increased? If the required rate of return decreased?

12. Determine the internal rate of return for each project. Should they be accepted?

13. How does a change in the required rate of return affect the project's internal rate of return?

14. What reinvestment rate assumptions are implicitly made by the net present value and internal rate of return methods? Which one is better?

15. Determine the modified internal rate of return for each project. Should they be accepted? Do you feel it is a better evaluation technique than the internal rate of return? Why or why not?

STUDY PROBLEMS (SET B)

9-1B. (*IRR Calculation*) Determine the internal rate of return on the following projects:
  a. An initial outlay of $10,000 resulting in a single cash flow of $19,926 after 8 years
  b. An initial outlay of $10,000 resulting in a single cash flow of $20,122 after 12 years
  c. An initial outlay of $10,000 resulting in a single cash flow of $121,000 after 22 years
  d. An initial outlay of $10,000 resulting in a single cash flow of $19,254 after 5 years

9-2B. (*IRR Calculation*) Determine the internal rate of return on the following projects:
  a. An initial outlay of $10,000 resulting in a cash flow of $2,146 at the end of each year for the next 10 years
  b. An initial outlay of $10,000 resulting in a cash flow of $1,960 at the end of each year for the next 20 years
  c. An initial outlay of $10,000 resulting in a cash flow of $1,396 at the end of each year for the next 12 years
  d. An initial outlay of $10,000 resulting a cash flow of $3,197 at the end of each year for the next 5 years

9-3B. (*IRR Calculation*) Determine the internal rate of return to the nearest percent on the following projects:
  a. An initial outlay of $10,000 resulting in a cash flow of $3,000 at the end of year 1, $5,000 at the end of year 2, and $7,500 at the end of year 3
  b. An initial outlay of $12,000 resulting in a cash flow of $9,000 at the end of year 1, $6,000 at the end of year 2, and $2,000 at the end of year 3
  c. An initial outlay of $8,000 resulting in a cash flow of $2,000 at the end of years 1 through 5 and $5,000 at the end of year 6

9-4B. (*NPV, PI, and IRR Calculations*) Gecewich, Inc., is considering a major expansion of its product line and has estimated the following cash flows associated with such an expansion. The initial outlay associated with the expansion would be $2,500,000 and the project would generate incremental after-tax cash flows of $750,000 per year for 6 years. The appropriate required rate of return is 11 percent.
  a. Calculate the net present value.
  b. Calculate the profitability index.

c. Calculate the internal rate of return.

d. Should this project be accepted?

9-5B. (*Payback Period, Net Present Value, Profitability Index, and Internal Rate of Return Calculations*) You are considering a project with an initial cash outlay of $160,000 and expected after-tax cash flows of $40,000 at the end of each year for 6 years. The required rate of return for this project is 10 percent.

a. What is the project's payback period?

b. What is the project's NPV?

c. What is the project's PI?

d. What is the project's IRR?

9-6B. (*Net Present Value, Profitability Index, and Internal Rate of Return Calculations*) You are considering two independent projects, Project A and Project B. The initial cash outlay associated with Project A is $45,000, whereas the initial cash outlay associated with Project B is $70,000. The required rate of return on both projects is 12 percent. The expected annual after-tax cash inflows from each project are as follows:

Year	Project A	Project B	Year	Project A	Project B
0	−$45,000	−$70,000	4	$12,000	$14,000
1	12,000	14,000	5	12,000	14,000
2	12,000	14,000	6	12,000	14,000
3	12,000	14,000			

Calculate the NPV, PI, and IRR for each project and indicate if the project should be accepted.

9-7B. (*Payback Period Calculations*) You are considering three independent projects, Project A, Project B, and Project C. Given the following cash flow information calculate the payback period for each.

Year	Project A	Project B	Project C
0	−900	−$9,000	−$7,000
1	600	5,000	2,000
2	300	3,000	2,000
3	200	3,000	2,000
4	100	3,000	2,000
5	500	3,000	2,000

If you require a 3-year payback period before an investment can be accepted, which projects would be accepted?

9-8B. (*NPV with Varying Required Rates of Return*) Mo-Lee's Sportswear is considering building a new factory to produce soccer equipment. This project would require an initial cash outlay of $10,000,000 and will generate annual after-tax cash inflows of $2,500,000 per year for 8 years. Calculate the project's NPV given:

a. A required rate of return of 9 percent.

b. A required rate of return of 11 percent.

c. A required rate of return of 13 percent.

d. A required rate of return of 15 percent.

9-9B. (*Internal Rate of Return Calculations*) Given the following cash flows, determine the internal rate of return for Projects A, B, and C.

Year	Project A	Project B	Project C
Initial Investment:	−$75,000	−$95,000	−$395,000
Cash inflows:			
Year 1	$10,000	$25,000	$150,000
Year 2	10,000	25,000	150,000
Year 3	30,000	25,000	150,000
Year 4	25,000	25,000	—
Year 5	30,000	25,000	—

9-10B. (*NPV with Varying Required Rates of Return*) Bert's, makers of gourmet corn dogs, is considering the purchase of a new corn dog "molding" machine. This investment requires an initial outlay of $150,000 and will generate after-tax cash inflows of $25,000 per year for 10 years. For each of the listed required rates of return, determine the project's net present value.

    a. The required rate of return is 9 percent.

    b. The required rate of return is 15 percent.

    c. Would the project be accepted under part (a) or (b)?

    d. What is this project's internal rate of return?

9-11B. (*MIRR Calculation*) Artie's Soccer Stuff is considering building a new plant. This plant would require an initial cash outlay of $8 million and will generate annual after-tax cash inflows of $2 million per year for 8 years. Calculate the project's MIRR given:

    a. A required rate of return of 10 percent.

    b. A required rate of return of 12 percent.

    c. A required rate of return of 14 percent.

CASE PROBLEM

FORD'S PINTO

Ethics Case: The Value of Life

There was a time when the "made in Japan" label brought a predictable smirk of superiority to the face of most Americans. The quality of most Japanese products usually was as low as their price. In fact, few imports could match their domestic counterparts, the proud products of "Yankee know-how." But by the late 1960s, an invasion of foreign-made goods chiseled a few worry lines into the countenance of American industry. And in Detroit, worry was fast fading to panic as the Japanese, not to mention the Germans, began to gobble up more and more of the subcompact auto market.

Never one to take a back seat to the competition, Ford Motor Company decided to meet the threat from abroad head-on. In 1968, Ford executives decided to produce the Pinto. Known inside the company as "Lee's car," after Ford president Lee Iacocca, the Pinto was to weigh no more than 2,000 pounds and cost no more than $2,000.

Eager to have its subcompact ready for the 1971 model year, Ford decided to compress the normal drafting-board-to-showroom time of about three-and-a-half years into two. The compressed schedule meant that any design changes typically made before production-line tooling would have to be made during it.

Before producing the Pinto, Ford crash-tested eleven of them, in part to learn if they met the National Highway Traffic Safety Administration (NHTSA) proposed safety standard that all autos be able to withstand a fixed-barrier impact of 20 miles per hour without fuel loss. Eight standard-design Pintos failed the tests. The three cars that passed the test all had some kind of gas-tank modification. One had a plastic baffle between the front of the tank and the differential housing; the second had a piece of steel between the tank and the rear bumper; and the third had a rubber-lined gas tank.

Ford officials faced a tough decision. Should they go ahead with the standard design, thereby meeting the production time table but possibly jeopardizing consumer safety? Or should they delay production of the Pinto by redesigning the gas tank to make it safer and thus concede another year of subcompact dominance to foreign companies?

To determine whether to proceed with the original design of the Pinto fuel tank, Ford decided to use a capital-budgeting approach, examining the expected costs and the social benefits of making the change. Would the social benefits of a new tank design outweigh design costs, or would they not?

To find the answer, Ford had to assign specific values to the variables involved. For some factors in the equation, this posed no problem. The costs of design improvement, for example, could be estimated at eleven dollars per vehicle. But what about human life? Could a dollar-and-cents figure be assigned to a human being?

NHTSA thought it could. It had estimated that society loses $200,725 every time a person is killed in an auto accident. It broke down the costs as follows:

Future productivity losses	
Direct	$132,000
Indirect	41,300
Medical Costs	
Hospital	700
Other	425
Property damage	1,500
Insurance administration	4,700
Legal and court expenses	3,000
Employer losses	1,000
Victim's pain and suffering	10,000
Funeral	900
Assets (lost consumption)	5,000
Miscellaneous accident costs	200
Total per fatality	$200,725[a]

[a]Ralph Drayton, "One Manufacturer's Approach to Automobile Safety Standards," *CTLA News 8* (February 1968): 11.

Ford used NHTSA and other statistical studies in its cost-benefit analysis, which yielded the following estimates:

Benefits	
Savings:	180 burn deaths, 180 serious burn injuries, 2,100 burned vehicles
Unit cost:	$200,000 per death, $67,000 per injury, $700 per vehicle
Total benefit:	(180 × $200,000) + (180 × $67,000) + (2,100 × $700) = $49.5 million
Costs	
Sales:	11 million cars, 1.5 million light trucks
Unit cost:	$11 per car, $11 per truck
Total cost:	12.5 million × $11 = $137.5 million[a]

[a]Mark Dowie, "Pinto Madness," *Mother Jones* (September–October 1977): 20. See also Russell Mokhiber, *Corporate Crime and Violence* (San Francisco: Sierra Club Books, 1988): 373–82, and Francis T. Cullen, William J. Maakestad, and Gary Cavender, *Corporate Crime Under Attack: The Ford Pinto Case and Beyond* (Cincinnati: Anderson Publishing, 1987).

Because the costs of the safety improvement outweighed its benefits, Ford decided to push ahead with the original design. Here is what happened after Ford made this decision:

Between 700 and 2,500 persons died in accidents involving Pinto fires between 1971 and 1978. According to sworn testimony of Ford engineer Harley Copp, 95 percent of them would have survived if Ford had located the fuel tank over the axle (as it had done on its Capri automobiles).

NHTSA's standard was adopted in 1977. The Pinto then acquired a rupture-proof fuel tank. The following year Ford was obliged to recall all 1971–1976 Pintos for fuel-tank modifications.

Between 1971 and 1978, approximately fifty lawsuits were brought against Ford in connection with rear-end accidents in the Pinto. In the Richard Grimshaw case, in addition to awarding over $3 million in compensatory damages to the victims of a Pinto crash, the jury awarded a landmark $125 million in punitive damages against Ford. The judge reduced punitive damages to $3.5 million.

On August 10, 1978, eighteen-year-old Judy Ulrich, her sixteen-year-old sister Lynn, and their eighteen-year-old cousin Donna, in their 1973 Ford Pinto, were struck from the rear by a van near Elkhart, Indiana. The gas tank of the Pinto exploded on impact. In the fire that resulted, the three teenagers were burned to death. Ford was charged with criminal homicide. The judge presiding over the twenty-week trial advised jurors that Ford should be convicted if it had clearly disregarded the harm that might result from its actions and that disregard represented a substantial deviation from acceptable standards of conduct. On March 13, 1980, the jury found Ford not guilty of criminal homicide.

For its part, Ford has always denied that the Pinto is unsafe compared with other cars of its type and era. The company also points out that in every model year the Pinto met or surpassed the government's own standards. But what the company doesn't say is that successful lobbying by it and its industry associates was responsible for delaying for nine years the adoption of NHTSA's 20 miles-per-hour crash standard. And Ford critics claim that there were more than forty European and Japanese models in the Pinto price and weight range with a safer gas-tank position. "Ford made an extremely irresponsible decision," concludes auto safety expert Byron Bloch, "when they placed such a weak tank in such a ridiculous location in such a soft rear end."

Questions

1. Do you think Ford approached this question properly?
2. What responsibilities to its customers do you think Ford had? Were their actions ethically appropriate?
3. Would it have made a moral or ethical difference if the $11 savings had been passed on to Ford's customers? Could a rational customer have chosen to save $11 and risk the more dangerous gas tank? Would that have been similar to making air bags optional? What if Ford had told potential customers about its decision?
4. Should Ford have been found guilty of criminal homicide in the Ulrich case?
5. If you, as a financial manager at Ford, found out about what had been done, what would you do?

SOURCE: Reprinted by permission from William Shaw and Vincent Barry, "Ford's Pinto," *Moral Issues in Business*, 6th ed. (New York: Wadsworth, 1995), 84–86. © by Wadsworth, Inc.

SELF-TEST SOLUTIONS

SS-1.

a. Payback period $= \dfrac{\$54,200}{\$20,608} = 2.630$ years

b. $NPV = \sum\limits_{t=1}^{n} \dfrac{ACF_t}{(1+k)^t} - IO$

$\quad = \sum\limits_{t=1}^{4} \dfrac{\$20,608}{(1+.15)^t} + \dfrac{\$33,808}{(1+.15)^5} - \$54,200$

$\quad = \$20,608(2.855) + \$33,808\,(.497) - \$54,200$

$\quad = \$58,836 + \$16,803 - \$54,200$

$\quad = 21,439$

c. $PI = \dfrac{\sum\limits_{t=1}^{n} \dfrac{ACF_t}{(1+k)^t}}{IO}$

$\quad = \dfrac{\$75,639}{\$54,200}$

$\quad = 1.396$

d. $IO = \sum\limits_{t=1}^{n} \dfrac{ACF_t}{(1+IRR)^t}$

$\$54,200 = \$20,608\,(PVIFA_{IRR\%,\ 4yr}) + \$33,808\,(PVIF_{IRR\%,\ 5yr})$

Try 29 percent:

$\$54,200 = \$20,608\,(2.203) + \$33,808\,(.280)$

$\qquad = \$45,399 + 9,466$

$\qquad = \$54,865$

Try 30 percent:

$\$45,200 = \$20,608\,(2.166) + \$33,808\,(.269)$

$\qquad = \$44,637 + 9,094$

$\qquad = 53,731$

Thus the IRR is just below 30 percent. The project should be accepted because the NPV is positive, the PI is greater than 1.0, and the IRR is greater than the required rate of return of 15 percent.

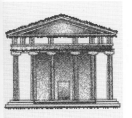

Learning Objectives

Active Applications

World Finance

Practice

CHAPTER 10

CASH FLOWS AND OTHER TOPICS IN CAPITAL BUDGETING

INTRODUCTION

I t was a major capital-budgeting decision that led the Ford Motor Company to introduce the Ford Windstar to its lineup of cars, trucks, and minivans. In the introduction to the previous chapter, we talked of the importance of this $1.5 billion investment by Ford that was targeted directly at Chrysler's Caravan/Voyager, which has been dominating the minivan market since its beginnings. Although this capital-budgeting decision may, on the surface, seem like a relatively simple decision, the forecasting of the expected cash flows associated with the Windstar were, in fact, quite complicated.

To begin with, Ford introduced a product that competed directly with some of its own products, the Ford Aerostar and the Mercury Villager. Thus some of the sales of the Windstar would cannibalize sales of other Ford products. In addition, Chrysler was in the process of a major redesign of their Caravan/Voyager product line—the first major redesign since its introduction. Given that fact, Ford may have its hands full trying to increase its market share in the minivan market above its current level.

From Ford's point of view, increasing the market share may not be the objective; simply preventing Ford from losing market share may be all that Ford is looking for from the Windstar. In fact, in many very competitive markets, the evolution and introduction of new products may serve more to preserve market share than to expand it. Certainly, that's the case in the computer market where Apple, Dell, Compaq, and IBM introduce upgraded models that continually render current models obsolete.

Does competing with yourself just to maintain market share make sense, or is it negative thinking that should be avoided? The answer to this deals with how we estimate a project's future cash flows. In the previous chapter, we looked at decision criterion, assuming the cash flows were known. In this chapter, we will see how difficult and complex it is estimating those cash flows. We will also gain an understanding of what a relevant cash flow is. We will evaluate projects relative to their base case—that is, what will happen if the project is not carried out. In the case of the Ford Windstar, we will ask what would happen to the Ford Aerostar and Mercury Villager sales that are expected to be captured by the Windstar if the Windstar was not introduced? Would they have been lost to a new generation of the Caravan/Voyager if the Windstar was not on the market? It is questions such as these, all leading us to an understanding of what are and are not relevant cash flows, that will be addressed in this chapter.

CHAPTER PREVIEW

This chapter continues our discussion of decision rules for deciding when to invest in new projects. First we will examine what is a relevant cash flow and how to calculate the relevant cash flow. This will be followed by a discussion of the problems created when the number of projects that can be accepted or the total budget is limited. This chapter will rely on **Axiom 3: Cash—Not Profits—Is King, Axiom 4: Incremental Cash Flows—It's Only What Changes That Counts**, and **Axiom 5: The Curse of Competitive Markets**. Be on the lookout for these important concepts.

OBJECTIVE 1   **GUIDELINES FOR CAPITAL BUDGETING**

To evaluate investment proposals, we must first set guidelines by which we measure the value of each proposal. In effect, we will be deciding what is and what isn't a relevant cash flow.

Use Cash Flows Rather than Accounting Profits

We will use cash flows, not accounting profits, as our measurement tool. The firm receives and is able to reinvest cash flows, whereas accounting profits are shown when they are earned rather than when the money is actually in hand. Unfortunately, a firm's accounting profits and cash flows may not be timed to occur together. For example, capital expenses, such as vehicles and plant and equipment, are depreciated over several years, with their annual depreciation subtracted from profit. Cash flows correctly reflect the timing of benefits and costs—that is, when the money is received, when it can be reinvested, and when it must be paid out.

RELATE TO THE BIG PICTURE

*If we are to make intelligent capital-budgeting decisions, we must accurately measure the timing of the benefits and costs, that is, when we receive money and when it leaves our hands. **Axiom 3: Cash—Not Profits—Is King** speaks directly to this. Remember, it is cash inflows that can be reinvested and cash outflows that involve paying out money.*

Think Incrementally

Unfortunately, calculating cash flows from a project may not be enough. Decision makers must ask: What new cash flows will the company as a whole receive if the company takes on a given project? What if the company does not take on the project? Interestingly, we may find that not all cash flows a firm expects from an investment proposal are incremental in nature. In measuring cash flows, however, the trick is to *think* incrementally. In doing so, we will see that only *incremental after-tax cash flows* matter. As such, our guiding rule in deciding if a cash flow is incremental will be to look at the company with, versus without, the new product. As you will see in the upcoming sections, this may be easier said than done.

> **RELATE TO THE BIG PICTURE**
>
> *In order to measure the true effects of our decisions, we will analyze the benefits and costs of projects on an incremental basis, which relates directly to **Axiom 4: Incremental Cash Flows—It's Only What Changes That Counts**. In effect, we will ask ourselves what the cash flows will be if the project is taken on versus what they will be if the project is not taken on.*

Beware of Cash Flows Diverted from Existing Products

Assume for a moment that we are managers of a firm considering a new product line that might compete with one of our existing products and possibly reduce its sales. In determining the cash flows associated with the proposed project, we should consider only the incremental sales brought to the company as a whole. New-product sales achieved at the cost of losing sales of other products in our line are not considered a benefit of adopting the new product. For example, when General Foods's Post Cereal Division introduced its Dino Pebbles in 1991, the product competed directly with the company's Fruity Pebbles. (In fact, the two were actually the same product, with an addition to the former of dinosaur-shaped marshmallows.) Post meant to target the market niche held by Kellogg's Marshmallow Krispies, but there was no question that sales recorded by Dino Pebbles bit into—literally cannibalized—Post's existing product line.

Remember that we are only interested in the sales dollars to the firm if this project is accepted, as opposed to what the sales dollars would be if the project is rejected. Just moving sales from one product line to a new product line does not bring anything new into the company, but if sales are captured from our competitors or if sales that would have been lost to new competing products are retained, then these are relevant incremental cash flows. In each case, these are the incremental cash flows to the firm—looking at the firm as a whole with the new product versus without the new product.

Look for Incidental or Synergistic Effects

Although in some cases, a new project may take sales away from a firm's current projects, in other cases, a new effort may actually bring new sales to the existing line. For example, in September 1991 USAir introduced service to Sioux City, Iowa. The new routes connecting this addition to the USAir system not only brought about new ticket sales on those routes, but also fed passengers to connecting routes. If managers were to look at only the revenue from ticket sales on the Sioux City routes, they would miss the incremental cash flow to USAir as a whole that results from taking on the new route. This is called a *synergistic* effect. The cash flow comes from *any* USAir flight that would not have occurred if service to Sioux City had not been available. The bottom line: Any cash flow to any part of the company that may result from the decision at hand must be considered when making that decision.

Bring in Working-Capital Requirements

Many times, a new project will involve additional investment in working capital. This may take the form of new inventory to stock a sales outlet, additional investment in accounts receivable resulting from additional credit sales, or increased investment in cash to operate additional cash registers, and more. Working-capital requirements are considered a cash flow even though they do not leave the company. How can investment in inventory be considered a cash outflow when the goods are still in the store? Because the firm does not have access to the inventory's cash value, the firm cannot use the money for other investments. Generally, working-capital requirements are tied up over the life of the project. When the project terminates, there is usually an offsetting cash inflow as the working capital is recovered. (Although this offset is not perfect because of the time value of money.)

Consider Incremental Expenses

Just as cash inflows from a new project are measured on an incremental basis, expenses should also be measured on an incremental basis. For example, if introducing a new product line necessitates training the sales staff, the after-tax cash flow associated with the training program must be considered a cash outflow and charged against the project. If accepting a new project dictates that a production facility be reengineered, the after-tax cash flows associated with that capital investment should be charged against the project. Again, any incremental after-tax cash flow affecting the company as a whole is a relevant cash flow whether it is flowing in or flowing out.

For example, shortly after Ford introduced the Windstar, Chrysler came out with redesigned versions of its Caravan and Voyager minivans with sliding doors on both sides, making it easy for passengers to enter and exit the rear seats. In response, Ford spent millions of dollars redesigning the Windstar and retooling its factories so that the driver's seat would fold up and make it easier for its rear passengers to get in and out. How did Ford make this capital-budgeting decision to redesign the Windstar and retool its factories? It looked at the incremental cash flows. That is, it looked at the cash flows to the company as a whole with this project versus the cash flows to the company as a whole without this project. It then based its decision on the difference in those cash flows, that is, on the incremental cash flows.

Remember That Sunk Costs Are Not Incremental Cash Flows

Only cash flows that are affected by the decision made at the moment are relevant in capital budgeting. The manager asks two questions: (1) Will this cash flow occur if the project is accepted? (2) Will this cash flow occur if the project is rejected? *Yes* to the first question and *no* to the second equals an incremental cash flow. For example, let's assume you are considering introducing a new taste treat called "Puddin' in a Shoe." You would like to do some test marketing before production. If you are considering the decision to test market and have not yet done so, the costs associated with the test marketing are relevant cash flows. Conversely, if you have already test marketed, the cash flows involved in test marketing are no longer relevant in project evaluation. It's a matter of timing. Regardless of what you might decide about future production, the cash flows allocated to marketing have already occurred. Cash flows that have already taken place are often referred to as "sunk costs" because they have been sunk into the project and cannot be undone. As a rule, any cash flows that are not affected by the accept-reject decision should not be included in capital-budgeting analysis.

Account for Opportunity Costs

Now we will focus on the cash flows that are lost because a given project consumes scarce resources that would have produced cash flows if that project had been rejected. This is the opportunity cost of doing business. For example, a product may use valuable floor space in a production facility. Although the cash flow is not obvious, the real question remains: What else could be done with this space? The space could have been rented out, or another product could have been stored there. The key point is that opportunity-cost cash flows should reflect net cash flows that would have been received if the project under consideration were rejected. Again, we are analyzing the cash flows to the company as a whole, with or without the project.

Decide If Overhead Costs Are Truly Incremental Cash Flows

Although we certainly want to include any incremental cash flows resulting in changes from overhead expenses such as utilities and salaries, we also want to make sure that these are truly incremental cash flows. Many times, overhead expenses—heat, light, rent—would occur whether a given project were accepted or rejected. There is often not a single specific project to which these expenses can be allocated. Thus the question is not whether the project benefits from overhead items, but whether the overhead costs are incremental cash flows associated with the project—and relevant to capital budgeting.

Ignore Interest Payments and Financing Flows

In evaluating new projects and determining cash flows, we must separate the investment decision from the financing decision. Interest payments and other financing cash flows that might result from raising funds to finance a project should not be considered incremental cash flows. If accepting a project means we have to raise new funds by issuing bonds, the interest charges associated with raising funds are not a relevant cash outflow. When we discount the incremental cash flows back to the present at the required rate of return, we are implicitly accounting for the cost of raising funds to finance the new project. In essence, the required rate of return reflects the cost of the funds needed to support the project. Managers first determine the desirability of the project and then determine how best to finance it.

MEASURING A PROJECT'S BENEFITS AND COSTS

OBJECTIVE 2

In measuring cash flows, we will be interested only in the *incremental,* or differential, *after-tax cash flows* that can be attributed to the proposal being evaluated. That is, we will focus our attention on the difference in the firm's after-tax cash flows *with* versus *without* the project. The worth of our decision depends on the accuracy of our cash flow estimates. For this reason, we first examined the question of what cash flows are relevant. Now we will see that, in general, a project's cash flows will fall into one of three categories: (1) the initial outlay, (2) the differential flows over the project's life, and (3) the terminal cash flow.

Initial Outlay

The **initial outlay** involves the immediate cash outflow necessary to purchase the asset and put it in operating order. This amount includes the cost of installing the asset (the asset's purchase price plus any expenses associated with shipping or installation) and any nonexpense cash outlays, such as increased working capital requirements. If we are considering a new sales outlet, there might be additional cash flows associated with investment in working capital in the form of increased inventory and cash necessary to operate the sales outlet. Although these cash flows are not included in the cost of the asset or even expensed on the books, they must be included in our analysis.

Initial outlay

The immediate cash outflow necessary to purchase the asset and put it in operating order.

> **Table 10.1** Summary of Calculation of Initial Outlay Incremental After-Tax Cash Flow
>
> 1. Installed cost of asset
> 2. Additional nonexpense outlays incurred (for example, working-capital investments)
> 3. Additional expenses on an after-tax basis (for example, training expenses)
> 4. In a replacement decision, the *after-tax* cash flow associated with the sale of the old machine

The after-tax cost of expense items incurred as a result of new investment must also be included as cash outflows—for example, any training expenses or special engineering expenses that would not have been incurred otherwise.

Finally, if the investment decision is a replacement decision, the cash inflow associated with the selling price of the old asset, in addition to any tax effects resulting from its sale, must be included.

Determining the initial outlay is a complex matter. Table 10.1 summarizes some of the more common calculations involved in determining the initial outlay. This list is by no means exhaustive, but it should give you a framework for thinking about the initial outlay and help simplify the calculations involved in the example that follows.

STOP AND THINK

At this point, we should realize that the incremental nature of the cash flow is of great importance. In many cases, if the project is not accepted, then status quo for the firm will simply not continue. In calculating incremental cash flows, we must be realistic in estimating what the cash flows to the company would be if the new project is not accepted.

Tax effects—sale of old machine. Potentially, one of the most confusing initial outlay calculations is for a replacement project involving the incremental tax payment associated with the sale of an old machine. There are three possible tax situations dealing with the sale of an old asset:

1. The old asset is sold for a price above the depreciated value. Here the difference between the old machine's selling price and its depreciated value is considered a taxable gain and taxed at the marginal corporate tax rate. If, for example, the old machine was originally purchased for $15,000, had a book value of $10,000, and was sold for $17,000, assuming the firm's marginal corporate tax rate is 34 percent, the taxes due from the gain would be ($17,000 − $10,000) × (.34), or $2,380.
2. The old asset is sold for its depreciated value. In this case, no taxes result, as there is neither a gain nor a loss in the asset's sale.
3. The old asset is sold for less than its depreciated value. In this case, the difference between the depreciated book value and the salvage value of the asset is a taxable loss and may be used to offset capital gains and thus results in tax savings. For example, if the depreciated book value of the asset is $10,000 and it is sold for $7,000 we have a $3,000 loss. Assuming the firm's marginal corporate tax rate is 34 percent, the cash inflow from tax savings is ($10,000 − $7,000) × (.34), or $1,020.

EXAMPLE

To clarify the calculation of the initial outlay, consider the example of Sibon Beverage, which is in the 34 percent marginal tax bracket. Sibon is considering the purchase of a new machine for $30,000 to be used in bottling. It has a 5-year life (according to IRS

Table 10.2 Calculation of Initial Outlay for Sibon Bottling

Outflows:		
Purchase price	$30,000	
Shipping fee	2,000	
Installation fee	3,000	
Installed cost of machine		$ 35,000
Increased taxes from sale of old machine		
($15,000 – $10,000)(.34)		1,700
Increased investment in inventory		5,000
Total outflows		$ 41,700
Inflows:		
Salvage value of old machine		–15,000
Net initial outlay		$ 26,700

guidelines) and will be depreciated using the *simplified straight-line method*, a method to be explained later. The useful life of this new machine is also 5 years. The new machine will replace an existing machine, originally purchased for $30,000 ten years ago, which currently has 5 more years of expected useful life. The existing machine will generate $2,000 of depreciation expenses for each of the next 5 years, at which time the book value will be equal to zero. To put the new machine in running order, it is necessary to pay after-tax shipping charges of $2,000 and installation charges of $3,000. Because the new machine will work faster than the old one, it will require an increase in goods-in-process inventory of $5,000. Finally, the old machine can be sold to a scrap dealer for $15,000.

As shown in Table 10.2, the installed cost of the new machine would be $30,000 plus $2,000 shipping and $3,000 installation fees, for a total of $35,000. Additional outflows are associated with taxes incurred on the sale of the old machine and with increased investment in inventory. Although the old machine has a book value of $10,000, it could be sold for $15,000. The increased taxes from the gain on the sale will be equal to the selling price of the old machine less its depreciated book value times the firm's marginal tax rate, or ($15,000 – $10,000) × (.34), or $1,700. The increase in goods-in-process inventory of $5,000 must also be considered part of the initial outlay, with an offsetting inflow of $5,000 corresponding to the recapture of this inventory occurring at the termination of the project. In effect, Sibon invests $5,000 in inventory now, resulting in an initial cash outlay, and liquidates this inventory in 5 years, resulting in a cash inflow at the end of the project. The total outlays associated with the new machine are $35,000 for its installed cost, $1,700 in increased taxes, and $5,000 in investment in inventory, for a total of $41,700. This is somewhat offset by the sale of the old machine for $15,000. Thus the net initial outlay associated with this project is $26,700. These calculations are summarized in Table 10.2.

Differential Flows over a Project's Life

The differential cash flows over the project's life involve the incremental after-tax cash flows resulting from increased revenues, plus savings in labor or material and reductions in selling expenses. Overhead items, such as utilities, heat, light, and executive salaries, are generally not affected. However, any resultant change in any of these categories must be included. Any increase in interest payments incurred as a result of issuing bonds to finance the project should *not* be included, as the costs of funds needed to support the project are implicitly accounted for by discounting the project back to the present using the required rate of return. Finally, an adjustment for the incremental change in taxes should be made, including any increase in taxes that might result from increased profits or any tax savings from an increase in depreciation expenses. Increased depreciation expenses affect tax-related cash flows by reducing taxable income and thus lowering taxes. Table 10.3 lists some of the factors that might be involved in determining a project's differential cash flows. However, before looking at an example, we will briefly examine the calculation of depreciation.

STOP AND THINK

Depreciation plays an important role in the calculation of cash flows. Although it is not a cash flow item, it lowers profits, which in turn lowers taxes. For students developing a foundation in corporate finance, it is the concept of depreciation, not the calculation of it, that is important. The reason the calculation of depreciation is deemphasized is that it is extremely complicated, and its calculation changes every few years as Congress enacts new tax laws. Through all this, bear in mind that although depreciation is not a cash flow item, it does affect cash flows by lowering the level of profits on which taxes are calculated.

The Revenue Reconciliation Act of 1993 largely left intact the modified version of the Accelerated Cost Recovery System introduced in the Tax Reform Act of 1986. Although this was examined in an appendix to chapter 1, a review is appropriate here. This modified version of the old accelerated cost recovery system (ACRS) is used for most tangible depreciable property placed in service beginning in 1987. Under this method, the life of the asset is determined according to the asset's class life, which is assigned by the IRS; for example, most computer equipment has a 5-year asset life. It also allows for only a half-year's deduction in the first year and a half-year's deduction in the year after the recovery period. The asset is then depreciated using the 200 percent declining balance method or an optional straight-line method.

Depreciation is calculated using a simplified straight-line method. This simplified process ignores the half-year convention that allows only a half-year's deduction in the year the project is placed in service and a half-year's deduction in the first year after the recovery period. By ignoring the half-year convention and assuming a zero salvage value, we are able to calculate annual depreciation by taking the project's initial depreciable value and dividing by its depreciable life as follows:

$$\text{annual depreciation using the simplified straight-line method} = \frac{\text{initial depreciable value}}{\text{depreciable life}}$$

The initial depreciable value is equal to the cost of the asset plus any expenses necessary to get the new asset into operating order.

THE WASHINGTON POST, APRIL 29, 1994

The Pentagon Bids to Pick a Winner

The Clinton administration ushered in a new era of government-business partnership yesterday as the Pentagon announced plans to spend $587 million over five years to try to create a new U.S. industry making flat-panel display screens for computers and televisions, a market now almost totally controlled by Japan.

It is perhaps the administration's most audacious stab at "industrial policy" in which government attempts to help distressed, strategically important industries compete in the marketplace.

(A) "We don't think our $587 million will buy the U.S. a display industry," says Kenneth S. Flamm, principal deputy assistant defense secretary, who is in charge of defense conversion. "But it will tip the balance for U.S. firms already considering entry."

"This is the form of industry-led government-industry partnership that we have been encouraging," said J. Richard Iverson, president of the American Electronics Association, which represents 3,000 computer companies.

The world's $4 billion market in flatpanel display screens—which are much thinner than the television picture tubes of yesteryear—is expecting to grow at $20 billion annually by the year 2010 as people communicate using personal computers and televisions.

Moreover, the screens will be a main component of the battlefield of the future, as more U.S. planes, tanks and individual soldiers receive data through ever-more sophisticated computers.

Japanese companies, led by Sharp Corp., control 95 percent of the flat-panel display screen market. U.S. military officials say Japanese companies do not inform the Pentagon about their technology plans—making it difficult for the military to plan its technology. Moreover, the U.S. government fears the Japanese may someday cut off supplies.

(B) "The demand for this technology is about to explode, but the structure of the global market is such that the U.S. could be left without any significant producers," said Flamm, adding that the administration's plan is "the only way we can guarantee the department has the access it needs to this critical technology."

SOURCE: Excerpted from John Mintz, "The Pentagon Bids to Pick a Winner," *The Washington Post* (April 29, 1994). © 1994 by *The Washington Post*. Reprinted with permission.

Analysis and Implications ...

A. Axiom 8 states that taxes bias business decisions. Just as tax breaks can tip the scales in favor of a project, government funding can do the same. In this case, government funding is creating investment that would not otherwise take place.

B. The decision to invest $587 million in the flat-panel display industry is, in effect, a capital-budgeting decision on the part of the government. In this case, the government's cash returns will be in the form of future taxes paid by firms in the display industry, taxes paid by individuals employed in that industry, and a reduction of welfare payments as a result of the increased employment.

This is not how depreciation would actually be calculated. The reason we have simplified the calculation is to allow you to focus directly on what should and should not be included in the cash flow calculations. Moreover, because the tax laws change rather frequently, we are more interested in recognizing the tax implications of depreciation than in understanding the specific depreciation provisions of the current tax laws.

Our concern with depreciation is to highlight its importance in generating cash flow estimates and to indicate that the financial manager must be aware of the current tax provisions when evaluating capital-budgeting proposals.

Extending the earlier example of Sibon Beverage, which illustrated the calculations of the initial outlay, suppose that purchasing the machine is expected to reduce salaries by $10,000 per year and fringe benefits by $1,000 annually, because it will take only one part-time person to operate, whereas the old machine requires two part-time operators. In addition, the cost of defects will fall from $8,000 per year to $3,000. However, maintenance expenses will increase by $4,000 annually. The annual depreciation on this new machine is $7,000 per year, whereas the depreciation expense lost with the sale of the old machine is $2,000 for each of the next 5 years. Annual depreciation on the new machine is calculated using the simplified straight-line method just described—that is, taking the cost of the new machine plus any expenses necessary to put it in operating order and dividing by its depreciable life. For the new bottling machine these calculations are reflected in Table 10.4.

Because the depreciation on the old machine is $2,000 per year, the increased depreciation will be from $2,000 per year to $7,000 per year, or an increase of $5,000 per year. Although this increase in depreciation expenses is not a cash flow item, it does affect cash flows by reducing book profits, which in turn reduces taxes.

To determine the annual net cash flows resulting from the acceptance of this project, the net savings *before* taxes using both book profit and cash flows must be found. The additional taxes are then calculated based on the before-tax book profit. For this example, Table 10.5 shows the determination of the differential cash flows on an after-tax basis. Thus the differential cash flows over the project's life are $9,620.

Terminal Cash Flow

The calculation of the terminal cash flow is in general quite a bit simpler than the preceding two calculations. Flows associated with the project's termination generally include the salvage value of the project plus or minus any taxable gains or losses associated with its sale.

Under the current tax laws, in most cases there will be tax payments associated with the salvage value at termination. This is because the current laws allow all projects to be depreciated to zero, and if a project has a book value of zero at termination and a positive salvage value, then that salvage value will be taxed. The tax effects associated

Table 10.4 Calculation of Depreciation for Sibon Using Simplified Straight-Line Method

New machine purchase price	$ 30,000
Shipping fee	2,000
Installation fee	3,000
Total depreciable value	$ 35,000
Divided by depreciable life	$35,000/5
Equals: Annual depreciation	$ 7,000

Table 10.5 Calculation of Differential Cash Flows for Sibon

		Book Profit	Cash Flow
Savings:	Reduced salary	$10,000	$10,000
	Reduced fringe benefits	1,000	1,000
	Reduced defects ($8,000 – $3,000)	5,000	5,000
Costs:	Increased maintenance expense	– 4,000	– 4,000
	Increased depreciation expense ($7,000 – $2,000)	– 5,000	
Net savings before taxes		$ 7,000	$12,000
Taxes (34%)		– 2,380 →	– 2,380
Net cash flow after taxes			$ 9,620

with the salvage value of the project at termination are determined exactly like the tax effects on the sale of the old machine associated with the initial outlay. The salvage value proceeds are compared with the depreciated value, in this case zero, to determine the tax.

In addition to the salvage value, there may be a cash outlay associated with the project termination. For example, at the close of a strip-mining operation, the mine must be refilled in an ecologically acceptable manner. Finally, any working capital outlay required at the initiation of the project—for example, increased inventory needed for the operation of a new plant—will be recaptured at the termination of the project. In effect, the increased inventory required by the project can be liquidated when the project expires. Table 10.6 provides a general list of some of the factors that might affect a project's terminal cash flow.

Continuing our example of Sibon Beverages to termination, the depreciated book value and salvage value of the machine at the termination date will be equal to zero. However, there will be a cash flow associated with the recapture of the initial outlay of work-in-process inventory of $5,000 as the inventory is liquidated. Therefore, the expected total terminal cash flow equals $5,000.

If we were to construct a cash flow diagram from this example (Figure 10.1), it would have an initial outlay of $26,700, differential cash flows during years 1 through 5 of $9,620, and an additional terminal cash flow at the end of year 5 of $5,000. The cash flow occurring in year 5 is $14,620, the sum of the differential cash flow in year 5 of $9,620, and the terminal cash flow of $5,000.

Cash flow diagrams similar to Figure 10.1 will be used through the remainder of this chapter with arrows above the time line indicating cash inflows and arrows below the time line denoting outflows.

Table 10.6 Summary of Calculation of Terminal Cash Flow on After-Tax Basis

1. The after-tax salvage value of the project
2. Cash outlays associated with the project's termination
3. Recapture of nonexpense outlays that occurred at the project's initiation (for example, working capital investments)

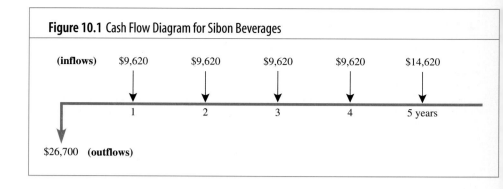

Figure 10.1 Cash Flow Diagram for Sibon Beverages

(inflows)	$9,620	$9,620	$9,620	$9,620	$14,620
	1	2	3	4	5 years

$26,700 **(outflows)**

Although the preceding calculations for determining the incremental, after-tax, net cash flows do not cover all possible cash flows, they do set up a framework in which almost any situation can be handled.

Capital Budgeting: A Comprehensive Example

Now let's put what we know about capital budgeting together and look at a manufacturing firm in the electronic components field that is in the 34 percent marginal tax bracket with a 15 percent required rate of return or cost of capital. Management is considering replacing a hand-operated assembly machine with a fully automated assembly operation. Given the information in Table 10.7, we want to determine the cash flows associated with this proposal, the project's net present value, profitability index, and internal rate of return, and then will apply the appropriate decision criteria.

Table 10.7 Comprehensive Capital-Budgeting Example

Existing situation:	One part-time operator—salary $12,000
	Variable overtime—$1,000 per year
	Fringe benefits—$1,000 per year
	Cost of defects—$6,000 per year
	Current book value—$10,000
	Expected life—15 years
	Expected salvage value—$0
	Age—10 years
	Annual depreciation—$2,000 per year
	Current salvage value of old machine—$12,000
	Annual maintenance—$0
	Marginal tax rate—34 percent
	Required rate of return—15 percent
Proposed situation:	Fully automated operation—no operator necessary
	Cost of machine—$50,000
	After-tax shipping fee—$1,000
	After-tax installation costs—$5,000
	Expected economic life—5 years
	Depreciation method—simplified straight-line over 5 years
	Salvage value after 5 years—$0
	Annual maintenance—$1,000 per year
	Cost of defects—$1,000 per year

The outflows associated with the initial outlay include the cost of the new machine plus the shipping and installation fee, in addition to any taxes on the sale of the old machine. Because the old machine is sold for more than its book value, that gain is taxed at the firm's marginal tax rate of 34 percent. The inflows associated with the initial outlay are then subtracted from the outflows to arrive at the net initial outlay of $44,680, as reflected in Table 10.8. Next the differential cash flows over the project's life are calculated as shown in Table 10.9, yielding an estimated $15,008 cash flow per annum. In making these computations, the incremental change in depreciation was determined by first calculating the original depreciable value, which is equal to the cost of the new machine ($50,000) plus any after-tax expense charges necessary to get the new machine in operating order (shipping fee of $1,000 plus the installation fee of $5,000). This depreciable amount was then divided by 5 years. The annual depreciation lost with the sale of the old machine was then subtracted out ($10,000/5 = $2,000 per year for the old machine's remaining 5 years of life). Once the

Table 10.8 Calculation of Initial Outlay for Comprehensive Example

Outflows:	Cost of new machine	$ 50,000
	Shipping fee	1,000
	Installation cost	5,000
	Increased taxes on sale of old machine	
	($12,000 – $10,000) (.34)	680
Inflows:	Salvage value—old machine	–12,000
	Net initial outlay	$ 44,680

Table 10.9 Calculation of Differential Cash Flows for Comprehensive Example

		Book Profit	Cash Flow
Savings:	Reduced salary	$12,000	$12,000
	Reduced variable overtime	1,000	1,000
	Reduced fringe benefits	1,000	1,000
	Reduced defects ($6,000 – $1,000)	5,000	5,000
Costs:	Increased maintenance expense	–1,000	–1,000
	Increased depreciation expense		
	($11,200 – $2,000)	–9,200	
Net savings before taxes		$ 8,800	$18,000
Taxes (34%)		–2,992 →	–2,992
Net cash flow after taxes			$15,008

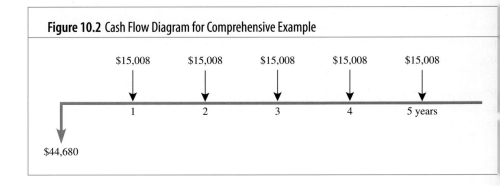

Figure 10.2 Cash Flow Diagram for Comprehensive Example

change in taxes is determined from the incremental change in book profit, it is subtracted from the net cash flow savings before taxes, yielding the $15,008 net cash flow after taxes.

Finally, the terminal cash flow associated with the project has to be determined. In this case, because the new machine is expected to have a zero salvage value, there will be no terminal cash flow. The cash flow diagram associated with this project is shown in Figure 10.2, with the inflows shown above the time line and the initial outlay below the line.

The net present value for this project is calculated as follows:

$$NPV = \sum_{t=1}^{n} \frac{ACF_t}{(1+k)^t} - IO$$

$$= \sum_{t=1}^{5} \frac{\$15,008}{(1+.15)^t} - \$44,680$$

$$= 15,008(PVIFA_{15\%,5yr}) - \$44,680$$

$$= \$15,008(3.352) - \$44,680$$

$$= \$50,307 - \$44,680$$

$$= \$5,627$$

Because its net present value is greater than zero, the project should be accepted. The profitability index, which gives a measure of relative desirability of a project, is calculated as follows:

$$PI = \frac{\sum_{t=1}^{n} \frac{ACF_t}{(1+k)^t}}{IO}$$

$$= \frac{\$50,307}{\$44,680}$$

$$= 1.13$$

Because the project's PI is greater than 1, the project should be accepted.

The internal rate of return can be determined directly from the *PVIFA* table, as follows:

$$IO = \sum_{t=1}^{n} \frac{ACF_t}{(1+IRR)^t}$$

$$\$44,680 = \$15,008(PVIFA_{i,5yr})$$

$$2.977 = PVIFA_{i,5yr}$$

Looking for the value of the $PVIFA_{i,5yr}$ in the 5-year row of the table in appendix E, we find that the value of 2.977 occurs between the 20 percent column (2.991) and the 21 percent column (2.926). As a result, the project's internal rate of return is between 20 percent and 21 percent, and the project should be accepted.

Applying the decision criteria to this example, we find that each of them indicates the project should be accepted, as the net present value is positive, the profitability index is greater than 1.0, and the internal rate of return is greater than the firm's required rate of return of 15 percent.

COMPLICATIONS IN CAPITAL BUDGETING: CAPITAL RATIONING AND MUTUALLY EXCLUSIVE PROJECTS

The use of our capital-budgeting decision rules implies that the size of the capital budget is determined by the availability of acceptable investment proposals. However, a firm may place a limit on the dollar size of the capital budget. This situation is called **capital rationing**. As we will see, an examination of capital rationing will not only enable us to deal with complexities of the real world but will serve to demonstrate the superiority of the NPV method over the IRR method for capital budgeting.

Using the internal rate of return as the firm's decision rule, a firm accepts all projects with an internal rate of return greater than the firm's required rate of return. This rule is illustrated in Figure 10.3, where projects A through E would be chosen. However, when capital rationing is imposed, the dollar size of the total investment is limited by the budget constraint. In Figure 10.3, the budget constraint of $X precludes the acceptance of an attractive investment, project E. This situation obviously contradicts prior decision rules. Moreover, the solution of choosing the projects with the highest internal rate of return is complicated by the fact that some projects may be indivisible; for example, it is meaningless to recommend that half of project D be acquired.

Capital rationing

The placing of a limit by the firm on the dollar size of the capital budget.

STOP AND THINK

It is somewhat uncomfortable to deal with problems associated with capital rationing because, under capital rationing, projects with positive net present values are rejected. This is a situation that violates the firm's goal of shareholder wealth maximization. However, in the real world, capital rationing does exist, and managers must deal with it. Often when firms impose capital constraints they are recognizing that they do not have the ability to handle more than a certain number (or certain number of large) new projects profitably.

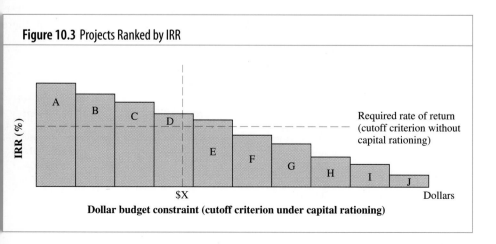

Figure 10.3 Projects Ranked by IRR

Rationale for Capital Rationing

We will first ask why capital rationing exists and whether or not it is rational. In general, three principal reasons are given for imposing a capital-rationing constraint. First, management may think market conditions are temporarily adverse. In the period surrounding the stock market crash of 1987, this reason was frequently given. At that time, interest rates were high, and stock prices were depressed, which made the cost of funding projects high. Second, there may be a shortage of qualified managers to direct new projects; this can happen when projects are of a highly technical nature. Third, there may be intangible considerations. For example, management may simply fear debt, wishing to avoid interest payments at any cost. Or perhaps issuance of common stock may be limited to maintain a stable dividend policy.

Despite strong evidence that capital rationing exists in practice, the question remains as to its effect on the firm. In brief, the effect is negative, and to what degree depends on the severity of the rationing. If the rationing is minor and short-lived, the firm's share price will not suffer to any great extent. In this case, capital rationing can probably be excused, although it should be noted that any capital rationing that rejects projects with positive net present values is contrary to the firm's goal of maximization of shareholders' wealth. If the capital rationing is a result of the firm's decision to limit dramatically the number of new projects or to limit total investment to internally generated funds, then this policy will eventually have a significantly negative effect on the firm's share price. For example, a lower share price will eventually result from lost competitive advantage if, owing to a decision to limit arbitrarily its capital budget, a firm fails to upgrade its products and manufacturing process.

Capital Rationing and Project Selection

If the firm decides to impose a capital constraint on investment projects, the appropriate decision criterion is to select the set of projects with the highest net present value subject to the capital constraint. In effect, you are selecting the projects that increase shareholder wealth the most, because the net present value is the amount of wealth that is created when a project is accepted. This guideline may preclude merely taking the highest-ranked projects in terms of the profitability index or the internal rate of return. If the projects shown in Figure 10.3 are divisible, the last project accepted may be only partially accepted. Although partial acceptances may be possible in some cases, the indivisibility of most capital investments prevents it. If a project is a sales outlet or a truck, it may be meaningless to purchase half a sales outlet or half a truck.

To illustrate this procedure, consider a firm with a budget constraint of $1 million and five indivisible projects available to it, as given in Table 10.10. If the highest-ranked projects were taken, projects A and B would be taken first. At that point, there

Table 10.10 Capital-Rationing Example of Five Indivisible Projects

Project	Initial Outlay	· Profitability Index	Net Present Value
A	$200,000	2.4	$280,000
B	200,000	2.3	260,000
C	800,000	1.7	560,000
D	300,000	1.3	90,000
E	300,000	1.2	60,000

would not be enough funds available to take project C; hence projects D and E would be taken. However, a higher total net present value is provided by the combination of projects A and C. Thus projects A and C should be selected from the set of projects available. This illustrates our guideline: to select the set of projects that maximizes the firm's net present value.

Project Ranking

In the past, we have proposed that all projects with a positive net present value, a profitability index greater than 1.0, or an internal rate of return greater than the required rate of return be accepted, assuming there is no capital rationing. However, this acceptance is not always possible. In some cases, when two projects are judged acceptable by the discounted cash flow criteria, it may be necessary to select only one of them, as they are mutually exclusive.

Mutually exclusive projects occur when a set of investment proposals perform essentially the same task; acceptance of one will necessarily mean rejection of the others. For example, a company considering the installation of a computer system may evaluate three or four systems, all of which may have positive net present values; however, the acceptance of one system will automatically mean rejection of the others. In general, to deal with mutually exclusive projects, we will simply rank them by means of the discounted cash flow criteria and select the project with the highest ranking. On occasion, however, problems of conflicting ranking may arise. As we will see, in general the net present value method is the preferred decision-making tool because it leads to the selection of the project that increases shareholder wealth the most.

Mutually exclusive projects

A set of projects that perform essentially the same task, so that acceptance of one will necessarily mean rejection of the others.

Problems in Project Ranking

There are three general types of ranking problems: the size disparity problem, the time disparity problem, and the unequal lives problem. Each involves the possibility of conflict in the ranks yielded by the various discounted cash flow capital-budgeting decision criteria. As noted previously, when one discounted cash flow criterion gives an accept signal, they will all give an accept signal, but they will not necessarily rank all projects in the same order. In most cases, this disparity is not critical; however, for mutually exclusive projects, the ranking order is important.

Size disparity. The *size disparity problem* occurs when mutually exclusive projects of unequal size are examined. This problem is most easily clarified with an example.

EXAMPLE

Suppose a firm is considering two mutually exclusive projects, A and B, both with required rates of return of 10 percent. Project A involves a $200 initial outlay and cash inflow of $300 at the end of 1 year, whereas project B involves an initial outlay of $1,500 and a cash inflow of $1,900 at the end of 1 year. The net present value, profitability index, and internal rate of return for these projects are given in Figure 10.4.

In this case, if the net present value criterion is used, project B should be accepted, whereas if the profitability index or the internal rate of return criterion is used, project A should be chosen. The question now becomes: Which project is better? The answer depends on whether capital rationing exists. Without capital rationing, project B is better because it provides the largest increase in shareholders' wealth; that is, it has a

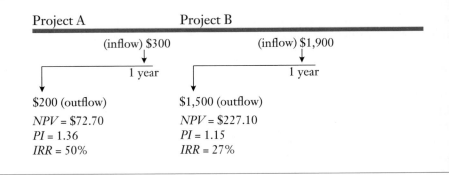

Figure 10.4 Size Disparity Ranking Problem

Project A	Project B
(inflow) $300	(inflow) $1,900
1 year	1 year
$200 (outflow)	$1,500 (outflow)
NPV = $72.70	*NPV* = $227.10
PI = 1.36	*PI* = 1.15
IRR = 50%	*IRR* = 27%

larger net present value. If there is a capital constraint, the problem then focuses on what can be done with the additional $1,300 that is freed if project A is chosen (costing $200, as opposed to $1,500). If the firm can earn more on project A plus the project financed with the additional $1,300 than it can on project B, then project A and the marginal project should be accepted. In effect, we are attempting to select the set of projects that maximize the firm's NPV. Thus if the marginal project has a net present value greater than $154.40 ($227.10 – $72.70), selecting it plus project A with a net present value of $72.70 will provide a net present value greater than $227.10, the net present value for project B.

In summary, whenever the size disparity problem results in conflicting rankings between mutually exclusive projects, the project with the largest net present value will be selected, provided there is no capital rationing. When capital rationing exists, the firm should select the set of projects with the largest net present value.

Time disparity. The *time disparity problem* and the conflicting rankings that accompany it result from the differing reinvestment assumptions made by the net present value and internal rate of return decision criteria. The NPV criterion assumes that cash flows over the life of the project can be reinvested at the required rate of return or cost of capital, whereas the IRR criterion implicitly assumes that the cash flows over the life of the project can be reinvested at the internal rate of return. Again, this problem may be illustrated through the use of an example.

Suppose a firm with a required rate of return or cost of capital of 10 percent and with no capital constraint is considering the two mutually exclusive projects illustrated in Figure 10.5. The net present value and profitability index indicate that project A is the better of the two, whereas the internal rate of return indicates that project B is the better. Project B receives its cash flows earlier than project A, and the different assumptions made as to how these flows can be reinvested result in the difference in rankings. Which criterion should be followed depends on which reinvestment assumption is used. The net present value criterion is preferred in this case because it makes the most acceptable assumption for the wealth-maximizing firm. It is certainly the most conservative assumption that can be made, because the required rate of return is the lowest possible reinvestment rate. Moreover, as we have already noted, the net present value method maximizes the value of the firm and the shareholders' wealth. An alternate solution, as discussed in chapter 9, is to use the MIRR method.

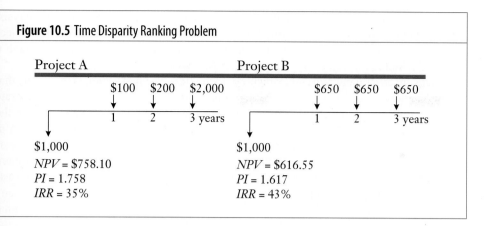

Figure 10.5 Time Disparity Ranking Problem

Project A

$100 $200 $2,000

1   2   3 years

$1,000
NPV = $758.10
PI = 1.758
IRR = 35%

Project B

$650 $650 $650

1   2   3 years

$1,000
NPV = $616.55
PI = 1.617
IRR = 43%

Unequal lives. The final ranking problem to be examined centers on the question of whether it is appropriate to compare mutually exclusive projects with different life spans.

Suppose a firm with a 10 percent required rate of return is faced with the problem of replacing an aging machine and is considering two replacement machines, one with a 3-year life and one with a 6-year life. The relevant cash flow information for these projects is given in Figure 10.6.

Examining the discounted cash flow criteria, we find that the net present value and profitability index criteria indicate that project B is the better project, whereas the internal rate of return favors project A. This ranking inconsistency is caused by the different life spans of the projects being compared. In this case, the decision is a difficult one because the projects are not comparable.

The problem of incomparability of projects with different lives arises because future profitable investment proposals may be rejected without being included in the analysis. This can easily be seen in a replacement problem such as the present example, in which two mutually exclusive machines with different lives are being considered. In this case, a comparison of the net present values alone on each of these projects would be misleading. If the project with the shorter life were taken, at its termination the firm could replace the machine and receive additional benefits, whereas acceptance of the project with the longer life would exclude this possibility, a possibility that is not included in the analysis. The key question thus becomes: Does today's investment decision include all future profitable investment proposals in its analysis? If not, the projects are not comparable. In this case, if project B is taken, then the project that could have been taken after 3 years when

Figure 10.6 Unequal Lives Ranking Problem

Project A

$500 $500 $500

1   2   3 years

$1,000
NPV = $243.50
PI = 1.2435
IRR = 23%

Project B

$300 $300 $300 $300 $300 $300

1   2   3   4   5   6 years

$1,000
NPV = $306.50
PI = 1.306
IRR = 20%

project A terminates is automatically rejected without being included in the analysis. Thus acceptance of project B not only forces rejection of project A, but also forces rejection of any replacement machine that might have been considered for years 4 through 6 without including this replacement machine in the analysis.

There are several methods to deal with this situation. The first option is to assume that the cash inflows from the shorter-lived investment will be reinvested at the required rate of return until the termination of the longer-lived asset. Although this approach is the simplest, merely calculating the net present value, it actually ignores the problem at hand—that of allowing for participation in another replacement opportunity with a positive net present value. The proper solution thus becomes the projection of reinvestment opportunities into the future—that is, making assumptions about possible future investment opportunities. Unfortunately, whereas the first method is too simplistic to be of any value, the second is extremely difficult, requiring extensive cash flow forecasts. The final technique for confronting the problem is to assume that reinvestment opportunities in the future will be similar to the current ones. The two most common ways of doing this are by creating a replacement chain to equalize life spans or calculating the project's equivalent annual annuity (EAA). Using a replacement chain, the present example would call for the creation of a two-chain cycle for project A; that is, we assume that project A can be replaced with a similar investment at the end of 3 years. Thus project A would be viewed as two A projects occurring back to back, as illustrated in Figure 10.7. The net present value on this replacement chain is $426.50, which can be compared with project B's net present value. Therefore, project A should be accepted because the net present value of its replacement chain is greater than the net present value of project B.

One problem with replacement chains is that, depending on the life of each project, it can be quite difficult to come up with equivalent lives. For example, if the two projects had 7- and 13-year lives, because the lowest common denominator is 7 × 13 = 91, a 91-year replacement chain would be needed to establish equivalent lives. In this case, it is easier to determine the project's **equivalent annual annuity (EAA)**. A project's EAA is simply an annuity cash flow that yields the same present value as the project's NPV. To calculate a project's EAA, we need only calculate a project's NPV and then divide that number by the $PVIFA_{i,n}$ to determine the dollar value of an n-year annuity that would produce the same NPV as the project. This can be done in two steps as follows:

Step 1: *Calculate the project's NPV.* In Table 10.14, we determined that project A had an NPV of $243.50, whereas project B had an NPV of $306.50.

Step 2: *Calculate the EAA.* The EAA is determined by dividing each project's NPV by the $PVIFA_{i,n}$ where i is the required rate of return and n is the project's life. This determines the level of an annuity cash flow that would produce the same

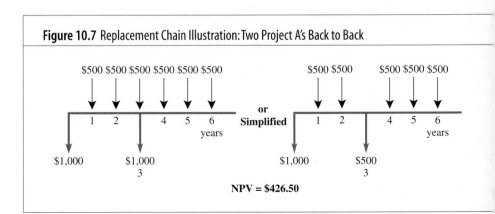

Figure 10.7 Replacement Chain Illustration: Two Project A's Back to Back

NPV = $426.50

NPV as the project. For project A the $PVIFA_{10\%,3yr}$ is equal to 2.487, whereas the $PVIFA_{10\%,6yr}$ for project B is equal to 4.355. Dividing each project's NPV by the appropriate $PVIFA_{i,n}$ we determine the EAA for each project:

$$EAA_A = NPV/PVIFA_{i,n}$$
$$= \$243.50/2.487$$
$$= \$97.91$$
$$EAA_B = \$306.50/4.355$$
$$= \$70.38$$

How do we interpret the EAA? For a project with an n-year life, it tells us what the dollar value is of an n-year annual annuity that would provide the same NPV as the project. Thus for project A, it means that a 3-year annuity of $97.91 given a discount rate of 10 percent would produce a net present value the same as project A's net present value, which is $243.50. We can now compare the equivalent annual annuities directly to determine which project is better. We can do this because we now have found the level of annual annuity that produces an NPV equivalent to the project's NPV. Thus because they are both annual annuities, they are comparable. An easy way to see this is to use the EAAs to create infinite-life replacement chains. To do this, we need only calculate the present value of an infinite stream or perpetuity of equivalent annual annuities. This is done by using the present value of an infinite annuity formula, that is, simply dividing the equivalent annual annuity by the appropriate discount rate. In this case we find:

$$NPV_{\infty,A} = \$97.91/.10$$
$$= \$979.10$$
$$NPV_{\infty,B} = \$70.38/.10$$
$$= \$703.80$$

Here we have calculated the present value of an infinite-life replacement chain. Because the EAA method provides the same results as the infinite-life replacement chain, it really doesn't matter which method you prefer to use.

HOW FINANCIAL MANAGERS USE THIS MATERIAL

Not only is the financial manager responsible for finding and then properly evaluating new projects, but the financial manager must be certain that the numbers going into the analysis are correct. Let's look at what the financial managers at Burger King faced when they decided to introduce the Big King, a new burger that looks an awful lot like the Big Mac. The first task they face is to estimate what the sales from this new product will be—a task that is easier said than done. Not only will sales be dependent upon how good the product is, or in this case, how good the product tastes, but they will also be dependent upon how good a job the marketing department does in selling the public on this new product. But just looking at sales is not enough. To properly perform the analysis on this product, Burger King needs to know what portion of sales will simply be sales diverted from Whoppers, and what portion of sales will be new to Burger King as a whole. In other words, when they introduce the Big King, how much of the sales are from new customers—those "Big Mac attack" eaters.

This is truly an area where finance and marketing meet. Much of the job of the financial manager is to make sure that the numbers are correct. That is, have the marketing people considered any synergistic effects? If new customers are drawn into Burger King, are they likely to buy a drink and some fries?—two very high markup sales. Will they bring in their families or friends when they make their Big King purchase? How about the increased inventory associated with carrying the Big King line? If it all sounds pretty complex, that's because it *is* complex. But more important, it is a decision that has a dramatic effect on the future direction of the firm, and it is an ongoing decision. That is, once the product is introduced and you see how the public reacts, you will continuously reevaluate the product to determine if it should be abandoned or expanded.

Look at the "New Coke." Cola-Cola spent an enormous amount of money test marketing and promoting that product, only to find the public didn't really like it after all. Once they realized that, the next capital-budgeting decision they made was, given the new sales estimates, to abandon the product. In effect, capital budgeting involves reinventing the company, and in order to make a good decision, you've got to have good information going into your capital-budgeting decision model. An awful lot of time and many jobs—maybe your job—revolve around making these decisions.

 OBJECTIVE 1

In this chapter, we examined the measurement of incremental cash flows associated with a firm's investment proposals which are used to evaluate those proposals. Relying on **Axiom 3: Cash—Not Profits—Is King**, and **Axiom 4: Incremental Cash Flows—It's Only What Changes That Counts**, we focused only on the incremental or different after-tax cash flows attributed to the investment proposal. Care was taken to be wary of cash flows diverted from existing products, look for incidental or synergistic effects, consider working capital requirements, consider incremental expenses, ignore sunk costs, account for opportunity costs, examine overhead costs carefully, and ignore interest payments and financing flows.

OBJECTIVE 2

In general, a project's cash flows fall into one of three categories: (1) the initial outlay, (2) the differential flows over the project's life, and (3) the terminal cash flow. A summary of the typical entries in each of these categories appears in Table l0.11.

Table 10.11 Summary of Calculation of Incremental After-Tax Cash Flows

A. Initial Outlay
1. Installed cost of asset
2. Additional nonexpense outlays incurred
   (for example, working-capital investments)
3. Additional expenses, on an after-tax basis (for example, training expenses)
4. In a replacement decision, the after-tax cash flow associated with the sale of the old machine

B. Differential Cash Flows over the Project's Life
1. Added revenue offset by increased expenses
2. Labor and material savings
3. Increases in overhead incurred
4. Tax savings from an increase in depreciation if the new project is accepted
5. Do not include interest expenses if the project is financed by issuing debt, as this is accounted for in the required rate of return

C. Terminal Cash Flow
1. The after-tax salvage value of the project
2. Cash outlays associated with the project's termination
3. Recapture of nonexpense outlays that occurred at the project's initiation
   (for example, working-capital investments)

We also examined capital rationing and the problems it can create by imposing a limit on the dollar size of the capital budget. Although capital rationing does not, in general, lead to the goal of maximization of shareholders' wealth, it does exist in practice. We discussed problems associated with the evaluation of mutually exclusive projects. Mutually exclusive projects occur when a set of investment proposals perform essentially the same task. In general, to deal with mutually exclusive projects, we rank them by means of the discounted cash flow criteria and select the project with the highest ranking. Conflicting rankings may arise because of the size disparity problem, the time disparity problem, and unequal lives. The problem of incomparability of projects with different lives is not simply a result of the different lives; rather, it arises because future profitable investment proposals may be rejected without being included in the analysis. Replacement chains and equivalent annual annuities are possible solutions to this problem.

OBJECTIVE 3

KEY TERMS

Capital rationing, 371

Equivalent annual annuity (EAA), 376

Initial outlay, 361

Mutually exclusive projects, 373

PHLIP

GO TO:
http://www.prenhall.com/bfm
For downloads and current events
associated with this chapter

STUDY QUESTIONS

10-1. Why do we focus on cash flows rather than accounting profits in making our capital-budgeting decisions? Why are we interested only in incremental cash flows rather than total cash flows?

10-2. If depreciation is not a cash flow item, does it affect the level of cash flows from a project in any way? Why?

10-3. If a project requires additional investment in working capital, how should this be treated in calculating cash flows?

10-4. How do sunk costs affect the determination of cash flows associated with an investment proposal?

10-5. What are mutually exclusive projects? Why might the existence of mutually exclusive projects cause problems in the implementation of the discounted cash flow capital-budgeting decision criteria?

10-6. What are common reasons for capital rationing? Is capital rationing rational?

10-7. How should managers compare two mutually exclusive projects of unequal size? Would your approach change if capital rationing existed?

10-8. What causes the time disparity ranking problem? What reinvestment rate assumptions are associated with the net present value and internal rate of return capital-budgeting criteria?

10-9. When might two mutually exclusive projects having unequal lives be incomparable? How should managers deal with this problem?

SELF-TEST PROBLEMS

ST-1. The Scotty Gator Corporation of Meadville, Pa., maker of Scotty's electronic components, is considering replacing one of its current hand-operated assembly machines with a new fully automated machine. This replacement would mean the elimination of one employee, generating salary and benefit savings. Given the following information, determine the cash flows associated with this replacement.

Existing situation:	One full-time machine operator—salary and benefits, $25,000 per year
	Cost of maintenance—$2,000 per year
	Cost of defects—$6,000 per year
	Original depreciable value of old machine—$50,000
	Annual depreciation—$5,000 per year
	Expected life—10 years
	Age—5 years old
	Expected salvage value in 5 years—$0
	Current salvage value—$5,000
	Marginal tax rate—34 percent
Proposed situation:	Fully automated machine—no operator required
	Cost of machine—$60,000
	After-tax installation fee—$3,000
	After-tax shipping fee—$3,000
	Cost of maintenance—$3,000 per year
	Cost of defects—$3,000 per year
	Expected life—5 years
	Salvage value—$20,000
	Depreciation method—simplified straight-line method over 5 years

ST-2. The J. Serrano Corporation is considering signing a 1-year contract with one of two computer-based marketing firms. Although one is more expensive, it offers a more extensive program and thus will provide higher after-tax net cash flows. Assume these two options are mutually exclusive and that the required rate of return is 12 percent. Given the following after-tax net cash flows:

Year	Option A	Option B
0	–$50,000	–$100,000
1	70,000	130,000

    a. Calculate the net present value.

    b. Calculate the profitability index.

    c. Calculate the internal rate of return.

    d. If there is no capital-rationing constraint, which project should be selected? If there is a capital-rationing constraint, how should the decision be made?

STUDY PROBLEMS (SET A)

10-1A. (*Capital Gains Tax*) The J. Harris Corporation is considering selling one of its old assembly machines. The machine, purchased for $30,000 five years ago, had an expected life of 10 years and an expected salvage value of zero. Assume Harris uses simplified straight-line depreciation, creating depreciation of $3,000 per year, and could sell this old machine for $35,000. Also assume a 34 percent marginal tax rate.

    a. What would be the taxes associated with this sale?

    b. If the old machine were sold for $25,000, what would be the taxes associated with this sale?

    c. If the old machine were sold for $15,000, what would be the taxes associated with this sale?

    d. If the old machine were sold for $12,000, what would be the taxes associated with this sale?

10-2A. (*Cash Flow Calculations*) The Winky Corporation, maker of electronic components, is considering replacing a hand-operated machine used in the manufacture of electronic components with a new fully automated machine. Given the following information, determine the cash flows associated with this replacement.

Existing situation:	One full-time machine operator—salary $20,000 per year
	Cost of maintenance—$5,000 per year
	Cost of defects—$5,000 per year
	Original cost of old machine—$30,000
	Expected life—10 years
	Age—5 years old
	Expected salvage value—$0
	Depreciation method—simplified straight-line over 10 years, $3,000 per year
	Current salvage value—$10,000
	Marginal tax rate—34 percent
Proposed situation:	Fully automated machine—no operator required
	Cost of machine—$55,000
	After-tax installation fee—$5,000
	Cost of maintenance—$6,000 per year
	Cost of defects—$2,000 per year
	Expected life—5 years
	Salvage value—$0
	Depreciation method—simplified straight-line method over 5 years

10-3A. (*Capital-Budgeting Calculation*) Given the cash flow information in problem 10-2A and a required rate of return of 15 percent, compute the following for the automated machine:

a. Payback period

b. Net present value

c. Profitability index

d. Internal rate of return

Should this project be accepted?

10-4A. (*New Project Analysis*) The Chung Chemical Corporation is considering the purchase of a chemical analysis machine. Although the machine being considered will not produce any increase in sales revenues, it will result in a before-tax reduction of labor costs by $35,000 per year. The machine has a purchase price of $100,000, and it would cost an additional $5,000 after tax to properly install this machine. In addition, to properly operate this machine, inventory must be increased by $5,000. This machine has an expected life of 10 years, after which it will have no salvage value. Also, assume simplified straight-line depreciation and that this machine is being depreciated down to zero, a 34 percent marginal tax rate, and a required rate of return of 15 percent.

a. What is the initial outlay associated with this project?

b. What are the annual after-tax cash flows associated with this project, for years 1 through 9?

c. What is the terminal cash flow in year 10 (what is the annual after-tax cash flow in year 10 plus any additional cash flows associated with termination of the project)?

d. Should this machine be purchased?

10-5A. (*New Project Analysis*) Raymobile Motors is considering the purchase of a new production machine for $500,000. Although the purchase of this machine will not produce any increase in sales revenues, it will result in a before-tax reduction of labor costs by $150,000 per year. To operate this machine properly, workers would have to go through a brief training session that would cost $25,000 after tax. In addition, it would cost $5,000 after tax to install this machine properly. Also, because this machine is extremely efficient, its purchase would necessitate an increase in inventory of $30,000. This machine has an expected life of 10 years, after which it will have no salvage value. Assume simplified straight-line depreciation and that this machine is being depreciated down to zero, a 34 percent marginal tax rate, and a required rate of return of 15 percent.

a. What is the initial outlay associated with this project?

b. What are the annual after-tax cash flows associated with this project, for years 1 through 9?

c. What is the terminal cash flow in year 10 (what is the annual after-tax cash flow in year 10 plus any additional cash flows associated with termination of the project)?

d. Should this machine be purchased?

10-6A. (*New Project Analysis*) Garcia's Truckin' Inc. is considering the purchase of a new production machine for $200,000. Although the purchase of this machine will not produce any increase in sales revenues, it will result in a before-tax reduction of labor costs by $50,000 per year. To operate this machine properly, workers would have to go through a brief training session that would cost $5,000 after tax. In addition, it would cost $5,000 after tax to install this machine properly. Also, because this machine is extremely efficient, its purchase would necessitate an increase in inventory of $20,000. This machine has an expected life of 10 years, after which it will have no salvage value. Finally, to purchase the new machine, it appears that the firm would have to borrow $100,000 at 8 percent interest from its local bank, resulting in additional interest payments of $8,000 per year. Assume simplified straight-line depreciation and that this machine is being depreciated down to zero, a 34 percent marginal tax rate, and a required rate of return of 10 percent.

a. What is the initial outlay associated with this project?

b. What are the annual after-tax cash flows associated with this project, for years 1 through 9?

c. What is the terminal cash flow in year 10 (what is the annual after-tax cash flow in year 10 plus any additional cash flows associated with termination of the project)?

d. Should this machine be purchased?

10-7A. (*Cash Flow—Capital-Budgeting Calculation*) The C. Duncan Chemical Corporation is considering replacing one of its machines with a new, more efficient machine. The old machine presently has a book value of $100,000 and could be sold for $60,000. The old machine is being depreciated on a simplified straight-line basis down to a salvage value of zero over the next 5 years, generating depreciation of $20,000 per year. The replacement machine would cost $300,000, and have an expected life of 5 years, after which it could be sold for $50,000. Because of reductions in defects and material savings, the new machine would produce cash benefits of $90,000 per year before depreciation and taxes. Assuming simplified straight-line depreciation, and that the replacement machine is being depreciated down to zero for tax purposes even though it can be sold at termination for $50,000, a 34 percent marginal tax rate, and a required rate of return of 15 percent, find:

a. The payback period

b. The net present value

c. The profitability index

d. The internal rate of return

10-8A. (*Cash Flow—Capital-Budgeting Calculation*) The Sumitomo Chemical Corporation is considering replacing a 5-year-old machine that originally cost $50,000, presently has a book value of $25,000, and could be sold for $60,000. This machine is currently being depreciated using the simplified straight-line method down to a terminal value of zero over the next 5 years, generating depreciation of $5,000 per year. The replacement machine would cost $125,000, and have a 5-year expected life over which it would be depreciated down using the simplified straight-line method and have no salvage value at the end of 5 years. The new machine would produce savings before depreciation and taxes of $45,000 per year. Assuming a 34 percent marginal tax rate and a required rate of return of 10 percent, calculate:

a. The payback period

b. The net present value

c. The profitability index

d. The internal rate of return

10-9A. (*Cash Flow—Capital-Budgeting Calculation*) Jabot Cosmetics Corporation is considering replacing a 10-year-old machine that originally cost $30,000, has a current book value of $10,000 with 5 years of expected life left, and is being depreciated using the simplified straight-line method over its 15-year expected life down to a terminal value of zero in 5 years, generating depreciation of $2,000 per year. The replacement machine being considered would cost $80,000 and have a 5-year expected life over which it would be depreciated using the simplified straight-line method down to zero. At termination in 5 years, the new machine would have a salvage value of $40,000. Material efficiencies resulting from the replacement would result in savings of $30,000 per year before depreciation and taxes. Currently, the old machine could be sold for $15,000. Assuming simplified straight-line depreciation, a 34 percent marginal tax rate, and a required rate of return of 20 percent, calculate:

a. The payback period

b. The net present value

c. The profitability index

d. The internal rate of return

10-10A. (*Size Disparity Ranking Problem*) The D. Dorner Farms Corporation is considering purchasing one of two fertilizer-herbicides for the upcoming year. The more expensive of the two is the better and will produce a higher yield. Assume these projects are mutually exclusive and that the required rate of return is 10 percent. Given the following after-tax net cash flows:

Year	Project A	Project B
0	−$500	−$5,000
1	700	6,000

a. Calculate the net present value.

b. Calculate the profitability index.

c. Calculate the internal rate of return.

d. If there is no capital-rationing constraint, which project should be selected? If there is a capital-rationing constraint, how should the decision be made?

10-11A. (*Time Disparity Ranking Problem*) The State Spartan Corporation is considering two mutually exclusive projects. The cash flows associated with those projects are as follows:

Year	Project A	Project B
0	−$50,000	−$50,000
1	15,625	0
2	15,625	0
3	15,625	0
4	15,625	0
5	15,625	$100,000

The required rate of return on these projects is 10 percent.

a. What is each project's payback period?

b. What is each project's net present value?

c. What is each project's internal rate of return?

d. What has caused the ranking conflict?

e. Which project should be accepted? Why?

10-12A. (*Unequal Lives Ranking Problem*) The B. T. Knight Corporation is considering two mutually exclusive pieces of machinery that perform the same task. The two alternatives available provide the following set of after-tax net cash flows:

Year	Equipment A	Equipment B
0	–$20,000	–$20,000
1	12,590	6,625
2	12,590	6,625
3	12,590	6,625
4		6,625
5		6,625
6		6,625
7		6,625
8		6,625
9		6,625

Equipment A has an expected life of 3 years, whereas equipment B has an expected life of 9 years. Assume a required rate of return of 15 percent.

a. Calculate each project's payback period.

b. Calculate each project's net present value.

c. Calculate each project's internal rate of return.

d. Are these projects comparable?

e. Compare these projects using replacement chains and EAA. Which project should be selected? Support your recommendation.

10-13A. (*EAAs*) The Andrzejewski Corporation is considering two mutually exclusive projects, one with a 3-year life and one with a 7-year life. The after-tax cash flows from the two projects are as follows:

Year	Project A	Project B
0	–$50,000	–$50,000
1	20,000	36,000
2	20,000	36,000
3	20,000	36,000
4	20,000	
5	20,000	
6	20,000	
7	20,000	

a. Assuming a 10 percent required rate of return on both projects, calculate each project's EAA. Which project should be selected?

b. Calculate the present value of an infinite-life replacement chain for each project.

10-14A. (*Capital Rationing*) Cowboy Hat Company of Stillwater, Oklahoma, is considering seven capital investment proposals, for which the funds available are limited to a maximum of $12 million. The projects are independent and have the following costs and profitability indexes associated with them:

Project	Cost	Profitability Index
A	$4,000,000	1.18
B	3,000,000	1.08
C	5,000,000	1.33
D	6,000,000	1.31
E	4,000,000	1.19
F	6,000,000	1.20
G	4,000,000	1.18

a. Under strict capital rationing, which projects should be selected?

b. What problems are there with capital rationing?

It's been 2 months since you took a position as an assistant financial analyst at Caledonia Products. Although your boss has been pleased with your work, he is still a bit hesitant about unleashing you without supervision. Your next assignment involves both the calculation of the cash flows associated with a new investment under consideration and the evaluation of several mutually exclusive projects. Given your lack of tenure at Caledonia, you have been asked not only to provide a recommendation, but also to respond to a number of questions aimed at judging your understanding of the capital budgeting process. The memorandum you received outlining your assignment follows:

TO: The Financial Analyst

FROM: Mr. V. Morrison, CEO, Caledonia Products

RE: Cash Flow Analysis and Capital Rationing

We are currently considering the purchase of a new fully automated machine to replace an older, manually operated one. The machine being replaced, now 5 years old, originally had an expected life of 10 years. It was being depreciated using the simplified straight-line method from $20,000 down to zero, thus generating $2,000 in depreciation per year, and could be sold for $25,000. The old machine took one operator, who earned $15,000 per year in salary and $2,000 per year in fringe benefits. Because the new machine is fully automated, this worker would no longer be needed. The annual costs of maintenance and defects associated with the old machine were $7,000 and $3,000, respectively. The replacement machine being considered has a purchase price of $50,000, a salvage value after 5 years of $10,000, and would be depreciated over 5 years using the simplified straight-line depreciation method down to zero. To get the automated machine in running order, there would be a $3,000 shipping fee and a $2,000 installation charge both on an after-tax basis. In addition, because the new machine would work faster than the old one, investment in raw materials and goods-in-process inventories would need to be increased by a total of $5,000. The annual costs of maintenance and defects on the new machine would be $2,000 and $4,000, respectively. The new machine also requires maintenance workers to be specially trained; fortunately, a similar machine was purchased 3 months ago, and at that time the maintenance workers went through the $5,000 training program needed to familiarize themselves with the new equipment. Caledonia's management is uncertain whether or not to charge half of this $5,000 after-tax training fee toward the new project. Finally, to purchase the new machine, it appears the firm would have to borrow an additional $20,000 at 10 percent interest from its local bank, resulting in additional interest payments of $2,000 per year. The required rate of return on projects of this kind is 20 percent and Caledonia is in the 34 percent marginal tax bracket.

1. Should Caledonia focus on cash flows or accounting profits in making our capital-budgeting decisions? Should we be interested in incremental cash flows, incremental profits, total cash flows, or total profits?

2. How does depreciation affect cash flows?

3. How do sunk costs affect the determination of cash flows?

4. What is the project's initial outlay?

5. What are the differential cash flows over the project's life?

6. What is the terminal cash flow?

7. Draw a cash flow diagram for this project.

8. What is its net present value?

9. What is its internal rate of return?

10. Should the project be accepted? Why or why not?

You have also been asked for your views on three unrelated sets of projects. Each set of projects involves two mutually exclusive projects. These projects follow:

11. Caledonia is considering two investments with 1-year lives. The more expensive of the two is the better and will produce more savings. Assume these projects are mutually exclusive and that the required rate of return is 10 percent. Given the following after-tax net cash flows:

Year	Project A	Project B
0	−$195,000	−$1,200,000
1	240,000	1,650,000

a. Calculate the net present value.

b. Calculate the profitability index.

c. Calculate the internal rate of return.

d. If there is no capital rationing constraint, which project should be selected? If there is a capital rationing constraint, how should the decision be made?

12. Caledonia is considering two additional mutually exclusive projects. The cash flows associated with these projects are as follows:

Year	Project A	Project B
0	−$100,000	−$100,000
1	32,000	0
2	32,000	0
3	32,000	0
4	32,000	0
5	32,000	$200,000

The required rate of return on these projects is 11 percent.

a. What is each project's payback period?

b. What is each project's net present value?

c. What is each project's internal rate of return?

d. What has caused the ranking conflict?

e. Which project should be accepted? Why?

13. The final two mutually exclusive projects that Caledonia is considering involve mutually exclusive pieces of machinery that perform the same task. The two alternatives available provide the following set of after-tax net cash flows:

Year	Equipment A	Equipment B
0	–$100,000	–$100,000
1	65,000	32,500
2	65,000	32,500
3	65,000	32,500
4		32,500
5		32,500
6		32,500
7		32,500
8		32,500
9		32,500

Equipment A has an expected life of 3 years, whereas equipment B has an expected life of 9 years. Assume a required rate of return of 14 percent.

a. Calculate each project's payback period.

b. Calculate each project's net present value.

c. Calculate each project's internal rate of return.

d. Are these projects comparable?

e. Compare these projects using replacement chains and EAAs. Which project should be selected? Support your recommendation.

STUDY PROBLEMS (SET B)

10-1B. (*Capital Gains Tax*) The R. T. Kleinman Corporation is considering selling one of its old assembly machines. The machine, purchased for $40,000 five years ago, had an expected life of 10 years and an expected salvage value of zero. Assume Kleinman uses simplified straight-line depreciation, creating depreciation of $4,000 per year, and could sell this old machine for $45,000. Also assume a 34 percent marginal tax rate.

a. What would be the taxes associated with this sale?

b. If the old machine were sold for $40,000, what would be the taxes associated with this sale?

c. If the old machine were sold for $20,000, what would be the taxes associated with this sale?

d. If the old machine were sold for $17,000, what would be the taxes associated with this sale?

10-2B. (*Cash Flow Calculations*) The Yonan Components Corporation, maker of electronic components, is considering replacing a hand-operated machine used in the manufacture of electronic components with a new fully automated machine. Given the following information, determine the cash flows associated with this replacement.

Existing situation:	Full-time machine operator—salary $24,000 per year
	Cost of maintenance—$6,000 per year
	Cost of defects—$5,000 per year
	Original cost of old machine—$40,000
	Expected life—10 years
	Age—5 years old
	Expected salvage value—$0
	Depreciation method—simplified straight-line over 10 years, $4,000 per year
	Current salvage value—$10,000
	Marginal tax rate—34 percent
	(continued)

10-3B. (*Capital-Budgeting Calculation*) Given the cash flow information in problem 10-2B and a required rate of return of 17 percent, compute the following for the automated machine:

a. Payback period

b. Net present value

c. Profitability index

d. Internal rate of return

Should this project be accepted?

10-4B. (*New Project Analysis*) The Guo Chemical Corporation is considering the purchase of a chemical analysis machine. Although the machine being considered will not produce any increase in sales revenues, it will result in a before-tax reduction of labor costs of $70,000 per year. The machine has a purchase price of $250,000, and it would cost an additional $10,000 after tax to install this machine properly. In addition, to operate this machine properly, inventory must be increased by $15,000. This machine has an expected life of 10 years, after which it will have no salvage value. Also, assume simplified straight-line depreciation and that this machine is being depreciated down to zero, a 34 percent marginal tax rate, and a required rate of return of 15 percent.

a. What is the initial outlay associated with this project?

b. What are the annual after-tax cash flows associated with this project, for years 1 through 9?

c. What is the terminal cash flow in year 10 (what is the annual after-tax cash flow in year 10 plus any additional cash flow associated with termination of the project)?

d. Should this machine be purchased?

10-5B. (*New Project Analysis*) El Gato's Motors is considering the purchase of a new production machine for $1 million. Although the purchase of this machine will not produce any increase in sales revenues, it will result in a before-tax reduction of labor costs by $400,000 per year. To operate this machine properly, workers would have to go through a brief training session that would cost $100,000 after tax. In addition, it would cost $50,000 after tax to install this machine properly. Also, because this machine is extremely efficient, its purchase would necessitate an increase in inventory of $150,000. This machine has an expected life of 10 years, after which it will have no salvage value. Assume simplified straight-line depreciation and that this machine is being depreciated down to zero, a 34 percent marginal tax rate, and a required rate of return of 12 percent.

a. What is the initial outlay associated with this project?

b. What are the annual after-tax cash flows associated with this project, for years 1 through 9?

c. What is the terminal cash flow in year 10 (what is the annual after-tax cash flow in year 10 plus any additional cash flows associated with termination of the project)?

d. Should this machine be purchased?

10-6B. (*New Project Analysis*) Weir's Truckin' Inc. is considering the purchase of a new production machine for $100,000. Although the purchase of this machine will not produce any increase in sales revenues, it will result in a before-tax reduction of labor costs by $25,000 per year. To operate this machine properly, workers would have to go through a brief training session that would cost $5,000 after tax. In addition, it would cost $5,000 after-tax to install this machine properly. Also, because this machine is extremely efficient, its purchase would necessitate an increase in inventory of $25,000. This machine has an expected life of 10 years, after which it will have no salvage value. Finally, to purchase the new machine, it appears that the firm would have to borrow $80,000 at 10 percent interest from its local bank, resulting in additional interest payments of $8,000 per year. Assume simplified straight-line depreciation and that this machine is being depreciated down to zero, a 34 percent marginal tax rate, and a required rate of return of 12 percent.

a. What is the initial outlay associated with this project?

b. What are the annual after-tax cash flows associated with this project, for years 1 through 9?

c. What is the terminal cash flow in year 10 (what is the annual after-tax cash flow in year 10 plus any additional cash flows associated with termination of the project)?

d. Should this machine be purchased?

10-7B. (*Cash Flow—Capital-Budgeting Calculations*) The Kensinger Corporation is considering replacing one of its machines with a new, more efficient machine. The old machine presently has a book value of $100,000 and could be sold for $60,000. The old machine is being depreciated on a simplified straight-line basis down to a salvage value of zero over the next 5 years, generating depreciation of $20,000 per year. The replacement machine would cost $350,000, and have an expected life of 5 years, after which it could be sold for $50,000. Because of reductions in defects and material savings, the new machine would produce cash benefits of $100,000 per year before depreciation and taxes. Assuming simplified straight-line depreciation, a 34 percent marginal tax rate, and a required rate of return of 15 percent, find

a. The payback period

b. The net present value

c. The profitability index

d. The internal rate of return

10-8B. (*Cash Flow—Capital-Budgeting Calculations*) The Taiheiyo Chemical Corporation is considering replacing a 5-year-old machine that originally cost $50,000, presently has a book value of $25,000, and could be sold for $60,000. This machine is currently being depreciated using the simplified straight-line method down to a terminal value of zero over the next 5 years, generating depreciation of $5,000 per year. The replacement machine would cost $100,000 and have a 5-year expected life over which it would be depreciated down using the simplified straight-line method and have no salvage value at the end of 5 years. The new machine would produce savings before depreciation and taxes of $35,000 per year. Assuming a 34 percent marginal tax rate and a required rate of return of 10 percent, calculate:

a. The payback period

b. The net present value

c. The profitability index

d. The internal rate of return

10-9B. (*Cash Flow—Capital-Budgeting Calculations*) The G. Rod Electronic Components Corporation is considering replacing a 10-year-old machine that originally cost $37,500, has a current book value of $12,500 with 5 years of expected life left, and is being depreciated using the simplified straight-line method over its 15-year expected life down to a terminal value of zero in 5 years, generating depreciation of $2,500 per year. The replacement machine being considered would cost $100,000 and have a 5-year expected life over which it would be depreciated using the simplified straight-line method down to zero. At termination in 5 years, the new machine would have a salvage value of $35,000. Material efficiencies resulting from the replacement would result in savings of $30,000 per year before depreciation and taxes. Currently, the old machine could be sold for $17,000. Assuming simplified straight-line depreciation, a 34 percent marginal tax rate, and a required rate of return of 20 percent, calculate:

a. The payback period

b. The net present value

c. The profitability index

d. The internal rate of return

10-10B. (*Size Disparity Ranking Problem*) The Unk's Farms Corporation is considering purchasing one of two fertilizer-herbicides for the upcoming year. The more expensive of the two is the better and will produce a higher yield. Assume these projects are mutually exclusive and that the required rate of return is 10 percent. Given the following after-tax net cash flows:

Year	Project A	Project B
0	−$650	−$4,000
1	800	5,500

a. Calculate the net present value.

b. Calculate the profitability index.

c. Calculate the internal rate of return.

d. If there is no capital-rationing constraint, which project should be selected? If there is a capital-rationing constraint, how should the decision be made?

10-11B. (*Time Disparity Ranking Problem*) The Z. Bello Corporation is considering two mutually exclusive projects. The cash flows associated with those projects are as follows:

Year	Project A	Project B
0	−$50,000	−$50,000
1	16,000	0
2	16,000	0
3	16,000	0
4	16,000	0
5	16,000	$100,000

The required rate of return on these projects is 11 percent.

a. What is each project's payback period?

b. What is each project's net present value?

c. What is each project's internal rate of return?

d. What has caused the ranking conflict?

e. Which project should be accepted? Why?

10-12B. (*Unequal Lives Ranking Problem*) The Battling Bishops Corporation is considering two mutually exclusive pieces of machinery that perform the same task. The two alternatives available provide the following set of after-tax net cash flows:

Year	Equipment A	Equipment B
0	−$20,000	−$20,000
1	13,000	6,500
2	13,000	6,500
3	13,000	6,500
4		6,500
5		6,500
6		6,500
7		6,500
8		6,500
9		6,500

Equipment A has an expected life of 3 years, whereas equipment B has an expected life of nine years. Assume a required rate of return of 14 percent.

    a. Calculate each project's payback period.

    b. Calculate each project's net present value.

    c. Calculate each project's internal rate of return.

    d. Are these projects comparable?

    e. Compare these projects using replacement chains and EAAs. Which project should be selected? Support your recommendation.

10-13B. (*EAAs*) The Anduski Corporation is considering two mutually exclusive projects, one with a 5-year life and one with a 7-year life. The after-tax cash flows from the two projects are as follows:

Year	Project A	Project B
0	–$40,000	–$40,000
1	20,000	25,000
2	20,000	25,000
3	20,000	25,000
4	20,000	25,000
5	20,000	25,000
6	20,000	
7	20,000	

    a. Assuming a 10 percent required rate of return on both projects, calculate each project's EAA. Which project should be selected?

    b. Calculate the present value of an infinite-life replacement chain for each project.

10-14B. (*Capital Rationing*) The Taco Toast Company is considering seven capital investment projects, for which the funds available are limited to a maximum of $12 million. The projects are independent and have the following costs and profitability indexes associated with them:

    a. Under strict capital rationing, which projects should be selected?

    b. What problems are associated with imposing capital rationing?

Project	Cost	Profitability Index
A	$4,000,000	1.18
B	3,000,000	1.08
C	5,000,000	1.33
D	6,000,000	1.31
E	4,000,000	1.19
F	6,000,000	1.20
G	4,000,000	1.18

DANFORTH & DONNALLEY LAUNDRY PRODUCTS COMPANY

Capital Budgeting: Relevant Cash Flows

O n April 14, 1998, at 3:00 P.M., James Danforth, president of Danforth & Donnalley (D&D) Laundry Products Company, called to order a meeting of the financial directors. The purpose of the meeting was to make a capital-budgeting decision with respect to the introduction and production of a new product, a liquid detergent called Blast.

D&D was formed in 1973 with the merger of Danforth Chemical Company, headquartered in Seattle, Washington, producers of Lift-Off detergent, the leading laundry detergent on the West Coast, and Donnalley Home Products Company, headquartered in Detroit, Michigan, makers of Wave detergent, a major Midwestern laundry product. As a result of the merger, D&D was producing and marketing two major product lines. Although these products were in direct competition, they were not without product differentiation: Lift-Off was a low-suds, concentrated powder, and Wave was a more traditional powder detergent. Each line brought with it considerable brand loyalty, and by 1998, sales from the two detergent lines had increased tenfold from 1973 levels, with both products now being sold nationally.

In the face of increased competition and technological innovation, D&D spent large amounts of time and money over the past 4 years researching and developing a new, highly concentrated liquid laundry detergent. D&D's new detergent, which they called Blast, had many obvious advantages over the conventional powdered products. It was felt that with Blast the consumer would benefit in three major areas. Blast was so highly concentrated that only 2 ounces was needed to do an average load of laundry as compared with 8 to 12 ounces of powdered detergent. Moreover, being a liquid, it was possible to pour Blast directly on stains and hard-to-wash spots, eliminating the need for a pre-soak and giving it cleaning abilities that powders could not possibly match. And, finally, it would be packaged in a lightweight, unbreakable plastic bottle with a sure-grip handle, making it much easier to use and more convenient to store than the bulky boxes of powdered detergents with which it would compete.

The meeting was attended by James Danforth, president of D&D; Jim Donnalley, director of the board; Guy Rainey, vice-president in charge of new products; Urban McDonald, controller; and Steve Gasper, a newcomer to D&D's financial staff, who was invited by McDonald to sit in on the meeting. Danforth called the meeting to order, gave a brief statement of its purpose, and immediately gave the floor to Guy Rainey.

Rainey opened with a presentation of the cost and cash flow analysis for the new product. To keep things clear, he passed out

Exhibit 1. D&D Laundry Products Company Annual Cash Flows from the Acceptance of Blast (Including flows resulting from sales diverted from the existing product lines)

Year	Cash Flows	Year	Cash Flows
1	$280,000	9	350,000
2	280,000	10	350,000
3	280,000	11	250,000
4	280,000	12	250,000
5	280,000	13	250,000
6	350,000	14	250,000
7	350,000	15	250,000
8	350,000		

Exhibit 2. D&D Laundry Products Company Annual Cash Flows from the Acceptance of Blast (Not including flows resulting from sales diverted from the existing product lines)

Year	Cash Flows	Year	Cash Flows
1	$250,000	9	315,000
2	250,000	10	315,000
3	250,000	11	225,000
4	250,000	12	225,000
5	250,000	13	225,000
6	315,000	14	225,000
7	315,000	15	225,000
8	315,000		

copies of the projected cash flows to those present (see Exhibits 1 and 2). In support of this information, he provided some insights as to how these calculations were determined. Rainey proposed that the initial cost for Blast include $500,000 for the test marketing, which was conducted in the Detroit area and completed in the previous June, and $2 million for new specialized equipment and packaging facilities. The estimated life for the facilities was 15 years, after which they would have no salvage value. This 15-year estimated life assumption coincides with company policy set by Donnalley not to consider cash flows occurring more than 15 years into the future, as estimates that far ahead "tend to become little more than blind guesses."

Rainey cautioned against taking the annual cash flows (as shown in Exhibit 1) at face value because portions of these cash flows actually are a result of sales that had been diverted from Lift-Off and Wave. For this reason, Rainey also produced the annual cash flows that had been adjusted to include only those cash flows incremental to the company as a whole (as shown in Exhibit 2).

At this point, discussion opened between Donnalley and McDonald, and it was concluded that the opportunity cost on funds is 10 percent. Gasper then questioned the fact that no costs were included in the proposed cash budget for plant facilities, which would be needed to produce the new product.

Rainey replied that, at the present time, Lift-Off's production facilities were being used at only 55 percent of capacity, and because these facilities were suitable for use in the production of Blast, no new plant facilities other than the specialized equipment and packaging facilities previously mentioned need be acquired for the production of the new product line. It was estimated that full production of Blast would only require 10 percent of the plant capacity.

McDonald then asked if there had been any consideration of increased working capital needs to operate the investment project. Rainey answered that there had and that this project would require $200,000 of additional working capital; however, as this money would never leave the firm and always would be in liquid form it was not considered an outflow and hence was not included in the calculations.

Donnalley argued that this project should be charged something for its use of the current excess plant facilities. His reasoning was that, if an outside firm tried to rent this space from D&D, it would be charged somewhere in the neighborhood of $2 million, and because this project would compete with the current projects, it should be treated as an outside project and charged as such. However, he went on to acknowledge that D&D has a strict policy that forbids the renting or leasing out of any of its production facilities. If they didn't charge for facilities, he concluded, the firm might end up accepting projects that under normal circumstances would be rejected.

From here, the discussion continued, centering on the questions of what to do about the "lost contribution from other projects," the test marketing costs, and the working capital.

Questions

1. If you were put in the place of Steve Gasper, would you argue for the cost from market testing to be included as a cash outflow?

2. What would your opinion be as to how to deal with the question of working capital?

3. Would you suggest that the product be charged for the use of excess production facilities and building?

4. Would you suggest that the cash flows resulting from erosion of sales from current laundry detergent products be included as a cash inflow? If there were a chance of competition introducing a similar product if you do not introduce Blast, would this affect your answer?

5. If debt is used to finance this project, should the interest payments associated with this new debt be considered cash flows?

6. What are the NPV, IRR, and PI of this project, including cash flows resulting from lost sales from existing product lines? What are the NPV, IRR, and PI of this project excluding these flows? Under the assumption that there is a good chance that competition will introduce a similar product if you don't, would you accept or reject this project?

HARDING PLASTIC MOLDING COMPANY

Capital Budgeting: Ranking Problems

On January 11, 1998, the finance committee of Harding Plastic Molding Company (HPMC) met to consider eight capital-budgeting projects. Present at the meeting were Robert L. Harding, president and founder, Susan Jorgensen, comptroller, and Chris Woelk, head of research and development. Over the past 5 years, this committee has met every month to consider and make final judgment on all proposed capital outlays brought up for review during the period.

Harding Plastic Molding Company was founded in 1970 by Robert L. Harding to produce plastic parts and molding for the Detroit automakers. For the first 10 years of operations, HPMC worked solely as a subcontractor for the automakers, but since then has made strong efforts to diversify in an attempt to avoid the cyclical problems faced by the auto industry. By 1998, this diversification attempt has led HPMC into the production of over 1,000 different items, including kitchen utensils, camera housings, and photographic equipment. It also led to an increase in sales of 800 percent during the 1980 to 1998 period. As this dramatic increase in sales was paralleled by a corresponding increase in production volume, in late 1996, HPMC was forced to expand production facilities. This plant and equipment expansion involved capital expenditures of approximately $10.5 million and resulted in an increase of production capacity of about 40 percent. Because of this increased production capacity, HPMC has made a concerted effort to attract new business and consequently has recently entered into contracts with a large toy firm and a major discount department store chain. Although non-auto-related business has grown significantly, it still only represents 32 percent of HPMC's overall business. Thus HPMC has continued to solicit nonautomotive business, and as a result of this effort and its internal research and development, the firm has four sets of mutually exclusive projects to consider at this month's finance committee meeting.

Over the past 10 years, HPMC's capital-budgeting approach has evolved into a somewhat elaborate procedure in which new proposals are categorized into three areas: profit, research and development, and safety. Projects falling into the profit or research and development areas are evaluated using present value techniques, assuming a 10 percent opportunity rate; those falling into the safety classification are evaluated in a more subjective framework. Although research and development projects have to receive favorable results from the present value criteria, there is also a total dollar limit assigned to projects of this category, typically running about $750,000 per year. This limitation was imposed by Harding primarily because of the limited availability of quality researchers in the plastics industry. Harding felt that if more funds than this were allocated, "we simply couldn't find the manpower to administer them properly." The benefits derived from safety projects, on the other hand, are not in terms of cash flows; hence present value methods are not used at all in their evaluation. The subjective approach used to evaluate safety projects is a result of the pragmatically difficult task of quantifying the benefits from these projects into dollar terms. Thus these projects are subjectively evaluated by a management-worker committee with a limited budget. All eight projects to be evaluated in January are classified as profit projects.

The first set of projects listed on the meeting's agenda for examination involve the utilization of HPMC's precision equipment. Project A calls for the production of vacuum containers for thermos bottles produced for a large discount hardware chain. The containers would be manufactured in five different size and color combinations. This project would be carried out over a 3-year period, for which HPMC would be guaranteed a minimum return plus a percentage of the sales. Project B involves the manufacture of inexpensive photographic equipment for a national photography outlet. Although HPMC currently has excess plant capacity, each of these projects would utilize precision equipment of which the excess capacity is limited. Thus adopting either project would tie up all precision facilities. In addition, the purchase of new equipment would be both prohibitively expensive and involve a time delay of approximately 2 years, thus making these projects mutually exclusive. (The cash flows associated with these two projects are given in Exhibit 1.)

The second set of projects involves the renting of computer facilities over a 1-year period to aid in customer billing and perhaps inventory control. Project C entails the evaluation of a customer billing system proposed by Advanced Computer Corporation. Under this system, all the bookkeeping and billing presently being done by HPMC's accounting department would be done by Advanced. In addition to saving costs involved in bookkeeping, Advanced would provide a more efficient billing system and do a credit analysis of delinquent customers, which could be used in the future for in-depth credit analysis. Project D is proposed by International Computer Corporation and includes a billing system similar to that offered by Advanced and, in addition, an inventory control system that will keep track of all raw materials and parts in stock and reorder when necessary, thereby reducing the likelihood of material stockouts, which has become more and more frequent over the past 3 years. (The cash flows for these projects are given in Exhibit 2.)

The third decision that faces the financial directors of HPMC involves a newly developed and patented process for molding hard plastics. HPMC can either manufacture and

market the equipment necessary to mold such plastics or it can sell the patent rights to Polyplastics Incorporated, the world's largest producer of plastics products. (The cash flows for projects E and F are shown in Exhibit 3.) At present, the process has not been fully tested, and if HPMC is going to market it itself, it will be necessary to complete this testing and begin production of plant facilities immediately. On the other hand, the selling of these patent rights to Polyplastics would involve only minor testing and refinements, which could be completed within the year. Thus a decision as to the proper course of action is necessary immediately.

The final set of projects up for consideration revolve around the replacement of some of the machinery. HPMC can go in one of two directions. Project G suggests the purchase and installation of moderately priced, extremely efficient equipment with an expected life of 5 years; project H advocates the purchase of a similarly priced, although less efficient, machine with life expectancy of 10 years. (The cash flows for these alternatives are shown in Exhibit 4.)

As the meeting opened, debate immediately centered on the most appropriate method for evaluating all the projects. Harding suggested that as the projects to be considered were mutually exclusive, perhaps their usual capital-budgeting criteria of net present value was inappropriate. He felt that, in examining these projects, perhaps they should be more concerned with relative

Exhibit 2. Harding Plastic Molding Company

| Year | Cash Flows | |
	Project C	Project D
0	$-8,000	$-20,000
1	11,000	25,000

Exhibit 3. Harding Plastic Molding Company

| Year | Cash Flows | |
	Project E	Project F
0	$-30,000	$-271,500
1	210,000	100,000
2		100,000
3		100,000
4		100,000
5		100,000
6		100,000
7		100,000
8		100,000
9		100,000
10		100,000

Exhibit 1. Harding Plastic Molding Company

| Year | Cash Flows | |
	Project A	Project B
0	$-75,000	$-75,000
1	10,000	43,000
2	30,000	43,000
3	100,000	43,000

Exhibit 4. Harding Plastic Molding Company

	Cash Flows	
Year	Project G	Project H
0	$–500,000	$–500,000
1	225,000	150,000
2	225,000	150,000
3	225,000	150,000
4	225,000	150,000
5	225,000	150,000
6		150,000
7		150,000
8		150,000
9		150,000
10		150,000

profitability or some measure of yield. Both Jorgensen and Woelk agreed with Harding's point of view, with Jorgensen advocating a profitability index approach and Woelk preferring the use of the internal rate of return. Jorgensen argued that the use of the profitability index would provide a benefit-cost ratio, directly implying relative profitability. Thus they merely need to rank these projects and select those with the highest profitability index. Woelk agreed with Jorgensen's point of view, but suggested that the calculation of an internal rate of return would also give a measure of profitability and perhaps be somewhat easier to interpret. To settle the issue, Harding suggested that they calculate all three measures, as they would undoubtedly yield the same ranking.

From here the discussion turned to an appropriate approach to the problem of differing lives among mutually exclusive projects

E and F, and G and H. Woelk argued that there really was not a problem here at all, that as all the cash flows from these projects can be determined, any of the discounted cash flow methods of capital budgeting will work well. Jorgensen argued that although this was true, some compensation should be made for the fact that the projects being considered did not have equal lives.

Questions

1. Was Harding correct in stating that the NPV, PI, and IRR necessarily will yield the same ranking order? Under what situations might the NPV, PI, and IRR methods provide different rankings? Why is it possible?
2. What are the NPV, PI, and IRR for projects A and B? What has caused the ranking conflicts? Should project A or B be chosen? Might your answer change if project B is a typical project in the plastic molding industry? For example, if projects for HPMC generally yield approximately 12 percent, is it logical to assume that the IRR for project B of approximately 33 percent is a correct calculation for ranking purposes? (*Hint:* Examine the implied reinvestment rate assumption.)
3. What are the NPV, PI, and IRR for projects C and D? Should project C or D be chosen? Does your answer change if these projects are considered under a capital constraint? What return on the marginal $12,000 not employed in project C is necessary to make one indifferent to choosing one project over the other under a capital-rationing situation?
4. What are the NPV, PI, and IRR for projects E and F? Are these projects comparable even though they have unequal lives? Why? Which project should be chosen? Assume that these projects are not considered under a capital constraint.
5. What are the NPV, PI, and IRR for projects G and H? Are these projects comparable even though they have unequal lives? Why? Which project should be chosen? Assume that these projects are not considered under a capital constraint.

SELF-TEST SOLUTIONS

SS-1: STEP 1: First calculate the initial outlay.

Initial outlay	
Outflows:	
Cost of machine	$60,000
Installation fee	3,000
Shipping fee	3,000
Inflows:	
Salvage value—old machine	–5,000
Tax savings on sale of old machine ($25,000 – $5,000) (.34)	–6,800
	$54,200

STEP 2: Calculate the differential cash flows over the project's life.

	Book Profit	Cash Flow
Savings:		
Reduced salary	$25,000	$25,000
Reduced defects	3,000	3,000
Costs:		
Increased maintenance	–1,000	–1,000
Increased depreciation		
($13,200 – $5000)[a]	–8,200	
Net savings before taxes	$18,800	$27,000
Taxes (.34)	–6,392 ⟶	–6,392
Annual net cash flow after taxes		$20,608

[a]Annual depreciation on the new machine is equal to the cost of the new machine ($60,000) plus any expenses necessary to get it in operating order (the shipping fee of $3,000 plus the installation fee of $3,000) divided by the depreciable life (5 years).

STEP 3: Calculate the terminal cash flow.

Salvage value—new machine	$20,000
Less: Taxes—recapture of depreciation ($20,000 × .34)	–6,800
	$13,200

Thus the cash flow in the final year will be equal to the annual net cash flow in that year of $20,608 plus the terminal cash flow of $13,200 for a total of $33,808.

SS-2. a. $NPV_A = \$70,000 \left[\dfrac{1}{(1+.12)^1}\right] - \$50,000$

$\qquad\qquad = \$70,000\,(.893) - \$50,000$

$\qquad\qquad = \$62,510 - \$50,000$

$\qquad\qquad = \$12,510$

$\qquad NPV_B = \$130,000 \left[\dfrac{1}{(1+.12)^1}\right] - \$100,000$

$\qquad\qquad = \$130,000\,(.893) - \$100,000$

$\qquad\qquad = \$116,090 - \$100,000$

$\qquad\qquad = \$16,090$

b. $PI_A = \dfrac{\$62,510}{\$50,000}$

$\qquad\quad = 1.2502$

$\qquad PI_B = \dfrac{\$116,090}{\$100,000}$

$\qquad\quad = 1.1609$

c. $\$50,000 = \$70,000\,(PVIF_{i,1\text{yr}})$

$\qquad .7143 = PVIF_{i,1\text{yr}}$

Looking for a value of $PVIF_{i,1yr}$ in appendix C, a value of .714 is found in the 40 percent column. Thus the IRR is 40 percent.

$100,000 = $130,000(PVIF_{i,1yr})$

$.7692 = PVIF_{i,1yr}$

Looking for a value of $PVIF_{i,1yr}$ in appendix C a value of .769 is found in the 30 percent column. Thus the IRR is 30 percent.

d. If there is no capital rationing, project B should be accepted because it has a larger net present value. If there is a capital constraint, the problem focuses on what can be done with the additional $50,000 (the additional money that could be invested if project A, with an initial outlay of $50,000, were selected over project B, with an initial outlay of $100,000). In the capital constraint case, if Serrano can earn more on project A plus the marginal project financed with the additional $50,000 than it can on project B, then project A and the marginal project should be accepted.

Learning Objectives

Active Applications

World Finance

Practice

CHAPTER 11

CAPITAL BUDGETING AND RISK ANALYSIS

INTRODUCTION

I
n the previous two chapters, we assumed that all projects had the same level of risk associated with them. In this chapter, we will discard that assumption and incorporate risk into the capital-budgeting decision. As international competition increases and technology changes at an ever quickening pace, risk and uncertainty play an increasingly important role in business decisions. In this chapter, we will examine problems in measuring risk and approaches for dealing with it as it affects business decisions.

We will look at the problems facing Judy Lewent, the chief financial officer at Merck & Co., the giant pharmaceutical firm. As we will see, it takes Merck an average of 10 years and an investment of $359 million to bring a new drug to market. Quite an investment, particularly when you consider the uncertainty involving what the competition will be like in 10 years and what constraints surrounding pricing might be in place as a result of possible health care reform. Moreover, not all new drugs introduced are profitable. In fact, only three out of ten new drugs that Merck introduces produce a positive net present value. How should Merck evaluate projects with uncertain returns that stretch out well into the future? Certainly, they shouldn't treat all projects in the same way, but how should they ensure that the decisions they make correctly reflect a project's uncertainty? Complicating Merck's task is the question of what is the appropriate measure of risk for a new project.

Axiom 1: The Risk-Return Trade-Off states that investors demand a higher return for taking on additional risk; in this chapter, we modify our capital-budgeting decision criterion to allow for different levels of risk for different projects. In fact, in so doing we will look directly at Judy Lewent at Merck and try to gain an understanding of how Merck deals with the risk and uncertainly that surrounds all its capital-budgeting decisions.

CHAPTER PREVIEW

This chapter completes our discussion of decision rules for when to invest in new projects. In chapter 9, we introduced the different capital-budgeting decision criteria, and in chapter 10, we looked at measuring a project's relevant cash flows. Through all of this discussion of capital-budgeting techniques, we implicitly assumed that the level of risk associated with each investment was the same. In this chapter, we lift that assumption. We begin with a discussion of what measure of risk is relevant in capital-budgeting decisions. We then look at various ways of incorporating risk into the capital-budgeting decision and how to measure that risk.

To do this, we will be relying heavily on **Axiom 1: The Risk Return Trade-Off—We Won't Take on Additional Risk Unless We Expect to Be Compensated with Additional Return and Axiom 9: All Risk Is Not Equal—Some Risk Can Be Diversified Away, and Some Cannot.**

RISK AND THE INVESTMENT DECISION

OBJECTIVE 1

Up to this point, we have ignored risk in capital budgeting; that is, we have discounted expected cash flows back to present and ignored any uncertainty that there might be surrounding that estimate. In reality, the future cash flows associated with the introduction of a new sales outlet or a new product are estimates of what is *expected* to happen in the future, not necessarily what *will* happen in the future. For example, when Coca-Cola decided to replace Classic Coke with its "New Coke," you can bet that the expected cash flows it based its decision on were nothing like the cash flows it realized. As a result, it didn't take Coca-Cola long to reintroduce Classic Coke. In effect, the cash flows we have discounted back to the present have been our best estimate of the expected future cash flows. A cash flow diagram based on the possible outcomes of an investment proposal rather than the expected values of these outcomes appears in Figure 11.1.

In this section, we will assume that under conditions of risk we do not know beforehand what cash flows will actually result from a new project. However, we do have expectations concerning the possible outcomes and are able to assign probabilities to these outcomes. Stated another way, although we do not know the cash flows resulting from the acceptance of a new project, we can formulate the probability distributions from which the flows will be drawn.

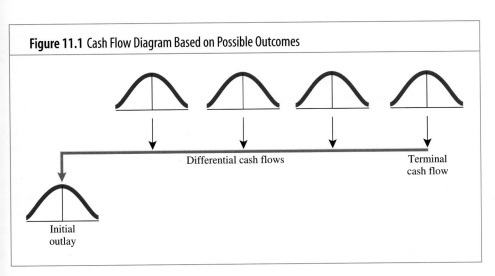

Figure 11.1 Cash Flow Diagram Based on Possible Outcomes

Differential cash flows

Terminal cash flow

Initial outlay

As we learned in chapter 6, risk occurs when there is some question as to the future outcome of an event. We will now proceed with an examination of the logic behind this definition. Again, risk is defined as the potential variability in future cash flows.

The fact that variability reflects risk can easily be shown with a coin toss. Consider the possibility of flipping a coin—heads you win, tails you lose—for 25 cents with your finance professor. Most likely, you would be willing to take on this game because the utility gained from winning 25 cents is about equal to the utility lost if you lose 25 cents. Conversely, if the flip is for $1,000, you may be willing to play only if you are offered more than $1,000 if you win—say, you win $1,500 if it turns out heads and lose $1,000 if it turns out tails. In each case, the probability of winning and losing is the same; that is, there is an equal chance that the coin will land heads or tails. In each case, however, the width of the dispersion changes, which is why the second coin toss is more risky and why you may not take the chance unless the payoffs are altered. The key here is the fact that only the dispersion changes; the probability of winning or losing is the same in each case. Thus the potential variability in future returns reflects the risk.

The final question to be addressed is whether or not individuals are in fact risk averse. Although we do see people gambling where the odds of winning are against them, it should be stressed that monetary return is not the only possible return they may receive. A nonmonetary, psychic reward accrues to some gamblers, allowing them to fantasize that they will break the bank, never have to work again, and retire to some island. Actually, the heart of the question is how wealth is measured. Although gamblers appear to be acting as risk seekers, they actually attach an additional nonmonetary return to gambling; the risk is in effect its own reward. When this is considered, their actions seem totally rational. It should also be noted that although gamblers appear to be pursuing risk on one hand, on the other hand in other endeavors they are also eliminating some risk by purchasing insurance and diversifying their investments.

In the remainder of this chapter, we assume that although future cash flows are not known with certainty, the probability distribution from which they come can be estimated. Also, as illustrated in chapter 6, because the dispersion of possible outcomes reflects risk, we are prepared to use a measure of dispersion or variability later in the chapter when we quantify risk.

In the pages that follow, there are only two basic issues that we address: (1) What is risk in terms of capital-budgeting decisions, and how should it be measured? (2) How should risk be incorporated into capital-budgeting analysis?

What Measure of Risk Is Relevant in Capital Budgeting?

Before we begin our discussion of how to adjust for risk, it is important to determine just what type of risk we are to adjust for. In capital budgeting, a project's risk can be looked at on three levels. First, there is the **project standing alone risk**, which is a project's risk ignoring the fact that much of this risk will be diversified away as the project is combined with the firm's other projects and assets.

Second, we have the project's **contribution-to-firm risk**, which is the amount of risk that the project contributes to the firm as a whole; this measure considers the fact that some of the project's risk will be diversified away as the project is combined with the firm's other projects and assets, but *ignores* the effects of diversification of the firm's shareholders. Finally, there is **systematic risk**, which is the risk of the project from the viewpoint of a well-diversified shareholder; this measure considers the fact that some of a project's risk will be diversified away as the project is combined with the firm's other projects, and, in addition, some of the remaining risk will be diversified away by shareholders as they combine this stock with other stocks in their portfolio. Graphically, this is shown in Figure 11.2.

Project standing alone risk

The risk of a project standing alone is measured by the variability of the asset's expected returns. That is, it is the risk of a project ignoring the fact that it is only one of many projects within the firm, and the firm's stock is but one of many stocks within a stockholder's portfolio.

Project's contribution-to-firm risk

The amount of risk that a project contributes to the firm as a whole. That is, it is a project's risk considering the effects of diversification among different projects within the firm, but ignoring the effects of shareholder diversification within the portfolio.

Systematic risk

The risk of a project measured from the point of view of a well-diversified shareholder. That is, it is a project's risk taking into account the fact that this project is only one of many projects within the firm, and the firm's stock is but one of many stocks within a stockholder's portfolio.

Figure 11.2 Looking at Three Measures of a Project's Risk

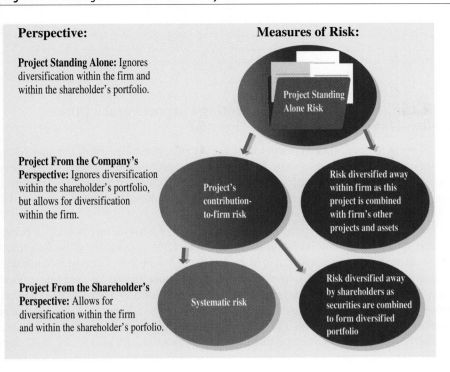

Perspective:

Project Standing Alone: Ignores diversification within the firm and within the shareholder's portfolio.

Project From the Company's Perspective: Ignores diversification within the shareholder's portfolio, but allows for diversification within the firm.

Project From the Shareholder's Perspective: Allows for diversification within the firm and within the shareholder's porfolio.

Measures of Risk:

Project Standing Alone Risk

Project's contribution-to-firm risk

Risk diversified away within firm as this project is combined with firm's other projects and assets

Systematic risk

Risk diversified away by shareholders as securities are combined to form diversified portfolio

Should we be interested in the project standing alone risk? The answer is *no*. Perhaps the easiest way to understand why not is to look at an example. Let's take the case of research and development projects at Johnson & Johnson. Each year, Johnson & Johnson takes on hundreds of new R&D projects, knowing that they only have about a 10 percent probability of being successful. If they are successful, the profits can be enormous; if they fail, the investment is lost. If the company has only one project, and it is an R&D project, the company would have a 90 percent chance of failure. Thus if we look at these R&D projects individually and measure their project standing alone risk, we would have to judge them to be enormously risky. However, if we consider the effect of the diversification that comes about from taking on several hundred independent R&D projects a year, all with a 10 percent chance of success, we can see that each R&D project does not add much in the way of risk to Johnson & Johnson. In short, because much of a project's risk is diversified away within the firm, project standing alone risk is an inappropriate measure of the level of risk of a capital-budgeting project.

Should we be interested in the project's contribution-to-firm risk? Once again, the answer is *no*, provided investors are well diversified, and there is no chance of bankruptcy. From our earlier discussion of risk in chapter 6, we saw that as shareholders, if we combined our stocks with other stocks to form a diversified portfolio, much of the risk of our security would be diversified away. Thus all that affects the shareholders is the systematic risk of the project and, as such, is all that is theoretically relevant for capital budgeting.

Measuring Risk for Capital-Budgeting Purposes and a Dose of Reality—Is Systematic Risk All There Is?

According to the capital asset pricing model (CAPM), systematic risk is the only relevant risk for capital-budgeting purposes; however, reality complicates this somewhat. In many instances, a firm will have undiversified shareholders, including owners of small corporations. Because they are not diversified, for those shareholders the relevant measure of risk is the project's contribution-to-firm risk.

The possibility of bankruptcy also affects our view of what measure of risk is relevant. Because the project's contribution-to-firm risk can affect the possibility of bankruptcy, this may be an appropriate measure of risk in the real world, where there is a cost associated with bankruptcy. First, if a firm fails, its assets, in general, cannot be sold for their true economic value. Moreover, the amount of money actually available for distribution to stockholders is further reduced by liquidation and legal fees that must be paid. Finally, the opportunity cost associated with the delays related to the legal process further reduces the funds available to the shareholder. Therefore, because there are costs associated with bankruptcy, reduction of the chance of bankruptcy has a very real value associated with it.

Indirect costs of bankruptcy also affect other areas of the firm, including production, sales, and the quality and efficiency of management. For example, firms with a higher probability of bankruptcy may have a more difficult time recruiting and retaining quality managers because jobs with that firm are viewed as being less secure. Suppliers also may be less willing to sell on credit. Finally, customers may lose confidence and fear that the firm may not be around to honor the warranty or to supply spare parts for the product in the future. As a result, as the probability of bankruptcy increases, the eventual bankruptcy may become self-fulfilling as potential customers and suppliers flee. The end result is that the project's contribution-to-firm risk is also a relevant risk measure for capital budgeting.

Finally, problems in measuring a project's systematic risk make its implementation extremely difficult. As we will see later on in this chapter, it is much easier talking about a project's systematic risk than it is measuring it.

Given all this, what do we use? The answer is that we will give consideration to both measures. We know in theory systematic risk is correct. We also know that bankruptcy costs and undiversified shareholders violate the assumptions of the theory, which brings us back to the concept of a project's contribution-to-firm risk. Still, the concept of systematic risk holds value for capital-budgeting decisions, because that is the risk for which shareholders are compensated. As such, we will concern ourselves with both the project's contribution-to-firm risk and the project's systematic risk, and not try to make any specific allocation of importance between the two for capital-budgeting purposes.

n the past two chapters, we ignored any risk differences between projects. This assumption is simple but not valid; different investment projects do in fact contain different levels of risk. We will now look at two methods for incorporating risk into the analysis. The first method, the *certainty equivalent approach*, attempts to incorporate the manager's utility function into the analysis. The second method, the *risk-adjusted discount rate*, is based on the notion that investors require higher rates of return on more risky projects.

Certainty Equivalent Approach

The **certainty equivalent approach** involves a direct attempt to allow the decision maker to incorporate his or her utility function into the analysis. The financial manager is allowed to substitute the certain dollar amount that he or she feels is equivalent to the expected but risky cash flow offered by the investment for that risky cash flow in the capital-budgeting analysis. In effect, a set of riskless cash flows is substituted for the original risky cash flows, between both of which the financial manager is indifferent. To a certain extent, this process is like the old television program "Let's Make a Deal." On that show, Monty Hall asked contestants to trade certain outcomes for uncertain outcomes. For example, he might give them the chance to trade a bedroom set worth $1,000 for what's behind the "door" of their choice. In some cases, contestants were willing to make a trade, and in some cases, they were not; it all depended upon how risk averse they were. The main difference between what we are doing and what was done on "Let's Make a Deal" is that on the TV show, contestants were in general not indifferent with respect to the certain outcome and the risky outcome, whereas in the certainty equivalent approach managers are indifferent.

To illustrate the concept of a **certainty equivalent**, let us look at a simple coin toss. Assume you can play the game only once and if it comes out heads, you win $10,000, and if it comes out tails, you win nothing. Obviously, you have a 50 percent chance of winning $10,000 and a 50 percent chance of winning nothing, with an expected value of $5,000. Thus $5,000 is your uncertain expected value outcome. The certainty equivalent then becomes the amount you would demand to make you indifferent with regard to playing and not playing the game. If you are indifferent with respect to receiving $3,000 for certain and not playing the game, then $3,000 is the certainty equivalent. However, someone else may not have as much fear of risk as you do and as a result, will have a different certainty equivalent.

To simplify future calculations and problems, let us define certainty equivalent coefficient (α_t) that represents the ratio of the certain outcome to the risky or expected outcome, between which the financial manager is indifferent. In equation form, α_t can be represented as follows:

$$\alpha_t = \frac{\text{certain cash flow}_t}{\text{risky or expected cash flow}_t} \tag{11-1}$$

Thus the alphas (α_t) can vary between 0, in the case of extreme risk, and 1, in the case of certainty. To obtain the value of the equivalent certain cash flow, we need only multiply the risky cash flow in years t times the α_t. When this is done, we are indifferent with respect to this certain cash flow and the risky cash flow. In the preceding example of the simple coin toss, the certain cash flow was $3,000, whereas the risky cash flow was $5,000, the expected value of the coin toss; thus the certainty equivalent coefficient is $3,000/$5,000 = 0.6. In summary, by multiplying the certainty equivalent coefficient (α_t) times the expected but risky cash flow, we can determine an equivalent certain cash flow.

Once this risk is taken out of the project's cash flows, those cash flows are discounted back to present at the risk-free rate of interest, and the project's net present value or

Certainty equivalent approach

A method for incorporating risk into the capital-budgeting decision in which the decision maker substitutes a set of equivalent riskless cash flows for the expected cash flows and then discounts these cash flows back to the present.

Certainty equivalents

The amount of cash a person would require with certainty to make him or her indifferent between this certain sum and a particular risky or uncertain sum.

profitability index is determined. If the internal rate of return is calculated, it is then compared with the risk-free rate of interest rather than the firm's required rate of return in determining whether or not it should be accepted or rejected. The certainty equivalent method can be summarized as follows:

$$NPV = \sum_{t=1}^{n} \frac{\alpha_t ACF_t}{(1 + k_{rf})^t} - IO \qquad (11\text{-}2)$$

where α_t = the certainty equivalent coefficient in period t
    ACF_t = the annual after-tax expected cash flow in period t
    IO = the initial cash outlay
    n = the project's expected life
    k_{rf} = the risk-free interest rate

The certainty equivalent approach can be summarized as follows:

Step 1: Risk is removed from the cash flows by substituting equivalent certain cash flows for the risky cash flows. If the certainty equivalent coefficient (α_t) is given, this is done by multiplying each risky cash flow by the appropriate α_t value.

Step 2: These riskless cash flows are then discounted back to the present at the riskless rate of interest.

Step 3: The normal capital-budgeting criteria are then applied, except in the case of the internal rate of return criterion, where the project's internal rate of return is compared with the risk-free rate of interest rather than the firm's required rate of return.

EXAMPLE

A firm with a 10 percent required rate of return is considering building new research facilities with an expected life of 5 years. The initial outlay associated with this project involves a certain cash outflow of $120,000. The expected cash inflows and certainty equivalent coefficients, α_t are as follows:

Year	Expected Cash Flow	Certainty Equivalent Coefficient, α_t
1	$10,000	0.95
2	20,000	0.90
3	40,000	0.85
4	80,000	0.75
5	80,000	0.65

The risk-free rate of interest is 6 percent. What is the project's net present value?

To determine the net present value of this project using the certainty equivalent approach, we must first remove the risk from the future cash flows. We do so by multiplying each expected cash flow by the corresponding certainty equivalent coefficient, α_t, as shown on the following page:

Expected Cash Flow	Certainty Equivalent Coefficient, α_t	α_t (Expected Cash Flow) = Equivalent Riskless Cash Flow
$10,000	0.95	$ 9,500
20,000	0.90	18,000
40,000	0.85	34,000
80,000	0.75	60,000
80,000	0.65	52,000

The equivalent riskless cash flows are then discounted back to the present at the risk-less interest rate, not the firm's required rate of return. The required rate of return would be used if this project had the same level of risk as a typical project for this firm. However, these equivalent cash flows have no risk at all; hence the appropriate discount rate is the riskless rate of interest. The equivalent riskless cash flows can be discounted back to present at the riskless rate of interest, 6 percent, as follows:

Year	Equivalent Riskless Cash Flow	Present Value Factor at 6 Percent	Present Value
1	$ 9,500	0.943	$ 8,958.50
2	18,000	0.890	16,020.00
3	34,000	0.840	28,560.00
4	60,000	0.792	47,520.00
5	52,000	0.747	38,844.00

NPV = –$120,000 + $8958.50 + $16,020 + $28,560 + $47,520 + $38,844 = $19,902.50

Applying the normal capital-budgeting decision criteria, we find that the project should be accepted, as its net present value is greater than zero.

The real problem with the certainty equivalent risk adjustment technique is that it is so arbitrary. That is, two excellent managers might look at the same project and come up with different certainty equivalent values. Which one is right? The answer is that they are both right, they just have different levels of risk aversion. Because it is so slippery, the certainty equivalent method is not used very often.

Risk-Adjusted Discount Rates

The use of risk-adjusted discount rates is based on the concept that investors demand higher returns for more risky projects. This is the basic principle behind **Axiom 1: The Risk Return Trade-Off** and the CAPM.

The required rate of return on any investment should include compensation for delay-ing consumption equal to the risk-free rate of return, plus compensation for any risk taken on. If the risk associated with the investment is greater than the risk involved in a typical endeavor, the discount rate is adjusted upward to compensate for this added risk. Once the firm determines the appropriate required rate of return for a project with a given level of risk, cash flows are discounted back to present at the **risk-adjusted discount rate**. Then the normal capital-budgeting criteria are applied, except in the case of the internal rate of return. For the IRR, the hurdle rate with which the project's internal rate of return is compared now becomes the risk-adjusted discount rate. Expressed mathemat-ically, the net present value using the risk-adjusted discount rate becomes

Risk-adjusted discount rate

A method for incorporating the project's level of risk into the capital-budgeting process, in which the discount rate is adjusted upward to compensate for higher than normal risk or downward to adjust for lower than normal risk.

$$NPV = \sum_{t=1}^{n} \frac{ACF_t}{(1 + k^*)^t} - IO \tag{11-3}$$

where ACF_t = the annual after-tax expected cash flow in time period t
IO = the initial cash outlay
k^* = the risk-adjusted discount rate
n = the project's expected life

The logic behind the risk-adjusted discount rate stems from the idea that if the level of risk in a project is different from that in the firm's typical project, then manage-ment must incorporate the shareholders' probable reaction to this new endeavor into the decision-making process. If the project has more risk than a typical project, then a higher required rate of return should apply. Otherwise, a project may appear to have a positive net present value, but if you had used the appropriate, higher required rate of return, the project may actually have a negative net present value. Thus marginal projects may lower the firm's share price—that is, reduce shareholders' wealth. This will occur as the market raises its required rate of return on the firm to reflect the addition of a more risky project, whereas the incremental cash flows resulting from the acceptance of the new project are not large enough to offset this change fully. By the same logic, if the project has less than normal risk, a reduction in the required rate of return is appropriate. Thus the risk-adjusted discount method attempts to apply more stringent standards—that is, require a higher rate of return—to projects that will increase the firm's risk level.

EXAMPLE

A toy manufacturer is considering the introduction of a line of fishing equipment with an expected life of 5 years. In the past, this firm has been quite conservative in its investment in new products, sticking primarily to standard toys. In this context, the introduction of a line of fishing equipment is considered an abnormally risky project. Management thinks that the normal required rate of return for the firm of 10 percent is not sufficient. Instead, the minimally acceptable rate of return on this project should be 15 percent. The initial outlay would be $110,000, and the expected cash flows from this project are as given below:

Year	Expected Cash Flow
1	$30,000
2	$30,000
3	$30,000
4	$30,000
5	$30,000

Discounting this annuity back to the present at 15 percent yields a present value of the future cash flows of $100,560. Because the initial outlay on this project is $110,000, the net present value becomes –$9,440, and the project should be rejected. If the normal required rate of return of 10 percent had been used as the discount rate, the project would have been accepted with a net present value of $3,730.

In practice, when the risk-adjusted discount rate is used, projects are generally grouped according to purpose, or risk class; then the discount rate preassigned to that purpose or risk class is used. For example, a firm with an overall required rate of return of 12 percent might use the following rate-of-return categorization:

Project	Required Rate of Return
Replacement decision	12%
Modification or expansion of existing product line	15
Project unrelated to current operations	18
Research and development operations	25

The purpose of this categorization of projects is to make their evaluation easier, but it also introduces a sense of the arbitrary into the calculations that makes the evaluation less meaningful. The trade-offs involved in the preceding classification are obvious; time and effort are minimized, but only at the cost of precision.

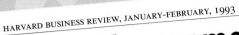

HARVARD BUSINESS REVIEW, JANUARY-FEBRUARY, 1993

Scientific Management at Merck: An Interview with CFO Judy Lewent

People who don't practice finance properly have done a great disservice to U.S. industry. Too often, when finance people are unleashed on operating people, an unhealthy tension develops between the need to invest in new projects and the need to have tight controls on spending. For that reason, finance people are often viewed as traffic cops: "You can't do this or go there." They keep the records straight, and that's that.

At Merck, we certainly work with a very sharp pencil. We are not lax. But instead of being an impediment to business, we attempt to work with the operating units and, in many cases, have been accepted as a partner in the business. I think that finance departments can take the nuances, the intuitive feelings that really fine businesspeople have and quantify them. In that way, they can capture both the hard financials of a project and the strategic intent.

For example, we had a development project for a nontraditional market segment, an antiparasitic agent called Avid that everyone was excited about. We collected the manufacturing and marketing elements and the research inputs, but the financial evaluation of the model showed a negative net present value for the project. If we had been traffic cops, we would have blown our whistle and gone home.

But instead, we started to take the project apart and talk more in-depth with marketing and with manufacturing. It turned out that the packaging costs were eating up the gross margins on the project. This was something that the original sponsors of the project had feared all along, but only on a conceptual level. We were able to give the project's sponsors, the marketing department, and manufacturing people a framework for talking about the product, and it suddenly became clear to all involved that the packaging size had to change. In this case, then, finance was a real resource in problem solving.

SOURCE: Nancy A. Nichols, "Scientific Management at the Merck: An Interview with CFO Judy Lewent," *Harvard Business Review* (January-February 1993). Reprinted by permission of *Harvard Business Review*. Copyright © 1993 by the President and Fellows of Harvard College, all rights reserved.

Analysis and Implications ...

A. For Merck and other pharmaceutical firms, taking on risk is simply part of the game. New products can only be generated through research and there is no guarantee that an R&D project will result in a profitable project. Complicating all this is the fact that, after a large investment in research, a good project may not generate profits for 10 to 15 years.

B. Since 1989, every significant research and development project at Merck has been analyzed over a 20-year time horizon.

C. Merck not only looks at the project's risk, but also tries to find what areas might be of financial concern to the project. This is done by changing one input while holding other inputs constant to determine what the effect is on the distribution of possible returns. In this case, Merck was able to spot an area in which the costs were so large as to turn a good project into a bad one. Once the problem area was spotted, it could be corrected. In this way, finance served not only as a method to evaluate and control the project, but also to refine it.

Table 11.1 Computational Steps in Certainty Equivalent and Risk-Adjusted Discount Rate Methods

Certainty Equivalent	Risk-Adjusted Discount Rate
STEP 1: Adjust the expected cash flows, ACF_t, downward for risk by multiplying them by the corresponding certainty equivalent coefficient, α_t.	STEP 1: Adjust the discount rate upward for risk, or down in the case of less than normal risk.
STEP 2: Discount the certainty equivalent riskless cash flows back to the present using the risk-free rate of interest.	STEP 2: Discount the expected cash flows back to present using the risk-adjusted discount rate.
STEP 3: Apply the normal decision criteria, except in the case of the internal rate of return, where the risk-free rate of interest replaces the required rate of return as the hurdle rate.	STEP 3: Apply the normal decision criteria except in the case of the internal rate of return, where the risk-adjusted discount rate replaces the required rate of return as the hurdle rate.

Certainty Equivalent versus Risk-Adjusted Discount Rate Methods

The primary difference between the certainty equivalent approach and the risk-adjusted discount rate approach involves the point at which the adjustment for risk is incorporated into the calculations. The certainty equivalent penalizes or adjusts downward the value of the expected annual after-tax cash flows, ACF_t which results in a lower net present value for a risky project. The risk-adjusted discount rate, conversely, leaves the cash flows at their expected value and adjusts the required rate of return, k, upward to compensate for added risk. In either case, the project's net present value is being adjusted downward to compensate for additional risk. The computational differences are illustrated in Table 11.1.

In addition to the difference in point of adjustment for risk, the risk-adjusted discount rate makes the implicit assumption that risk becomes greater as we move further out in time. Although this is not necessarily a good or bad assumption, we should be aware of it and understand it. Let's look at an example in which the risk-adjusted discount rate is used and then determine what certainty equivalent coefficients, α_t, would be necessary to arrive at the same solution.

EXAMPLE

Assume that a firm with a required rate of return of 10 percent is considering introducing a new product. This product has an initial outlay of $800,000, an expected life of 15 years, and after-tax cash flows of $100,000 each year during its life. Because of the increased risk associated with this project, management is requiring a 15 percent rate of return. Let us also assume that the risk-free rate of return is 6 percent.

If the firm chose to use the certainty equivalent method, the certainty equivalent cash flows would be discounted back to the present at 6 percent, the risk-free rate of interest. The present value of the $100,000 cash flow occurring at the end of the first year discounted back to present at 15 percent is $87,000. The present value of this $100,000 flow discounted back to present at the risk-free rate of 6 percent is $94,300.

Table 11.2 Certainty Equivalent Coefficients Yielding Same Results as Risk-Adjusted Discount Rate of 15 Percent in Illustrative Example

Year	1	2	3	4	5	6	7	8	9	10
α_t:	0.9226	0.8494	0.7833	0.7222	0.6653	0.6128	0.5654	0.5215	0.4797	0.4427

Thus, if the certainty equivalent approach were used, a certainty equivalent coefficient, α_1, of .9226 ($87,000 ÷ $94,300 = 0.9226) would be necessary to produce a present value of $87,000. In other words, the same results can be obtained in the first year by using the risk-adjusted discount rate and adjusting the discount rate up to 15 percent or by using the certainty equivalent approach and adjusting the expected cash flows by a certainty equivalent coefficient of 0.9226.

Under the risk-adjusted discount rate, the present value of the $100,000 cash flow occurring at the end of the second year becomes $75,600. To produce an identical present value under the certainty equivalent approach, a certainty equivalent coefficient of 0.8494 would be needed. Following this through for the life of the project yields the certainty equivalent coefficients given in Table 11.2.

What does this analysis suggest? It indicates that if the risk-adjusted discount rate method is used, we are adjusting downward the value of future cash flows that occur further in the future more severely than earlier cash flows.

In summary, the use of the risk-adjusted discount rate assumes that risk increases over time and that cash flows occurring further in the future should be more severely penalized.

STOP AND THINK

If performed properly, either of these methods can do a good job of adjusting for risk. However, by far the most popular method of risk adjustment is the risk-adjusted discount rate. The reason for the popularity of the risk-adjusted discount rate over the certainty equivalent approach is purely and simply its ease of implementation.

Risk-Adjusted Discount Rate and Measurement of a Project's Systematic Risk

When we initially talked about systematic risk or a beta, we were talking about measuring it for the entire firm. As you recall, although we could estimate a firm's beta using historical data, we did not have complete confidence in our results. As we will see, estimating the appropriate level of systematic risk for a single project is even more fraught with difficulties. To truly understand what it is that we are trying to do and the difficulties that we will encounter, let us step back a bit and examine systematic risk and the risk adjustment for a project.

What we are trying to do is to use the CAPM to determine the level of risk and the appropriate risk-return trade-offs for a particular project. We will then take the expected return on this project and compare it to the risk-return trade-offs suggested by the CAPM to determine whether or not the project should be accepted. If the project appears to be a typical one for the firm, using the CAPM to determine the appropriate risk-return trade-offs and then judging the project against them may be a warranted approach. But if the project is not a typical project, what do we do? Historical data generally do not exist for a new project. In fact, for some capital investments, for example, a truck or a new building, historical data would not have much meaning. What we need to do is make the best out of a bad situation. We either (1) fake it—that is, use historical accounting data, if available, to substitute for historical price data in estimating systematic risk; or (2) we attempt to find a substitute firm in the same industry as the capital budgeting project and use the substitute firm's estimated systematic risk as a proxy for the project's systematic risk.

Beta estimation using accounting data. When we are dealing with a project that is identical to the firm's other projects, we need only estimate the level of systematic risk for the firm and use that estimate as a proxy for the project's risk. Unfortunately, when projects are not typical of the firm, this approach does not work. For example, when R. J. Reynolds introduces a new food through one of its food products divisions, this new product most likely carries with it a different level of systematic risk than is typical for Reynolds as a whole.

To get a better approximation of the systematic risk level on this project, we could estimate the level of systematic risk for the food division and use that as a proxy for the project's systematic risk. Unfortunately, historical stock price data are available only for the company as a whole and, as you recall, historical stock return data are generally used to estimate a firm's beta. Thus we are forced to use *accounting return data* rather than historical stock return data for the division to estimate the division's systematic risk. To estimate a project's beta using accounting data we need only run a time series regression of the division's return on assets (net income/total assets) on the market index (the S&P 500). The regression coefficient from this equation would be the project's accounting beta and would serve as an approximation for the project's true beta or measure of systematic risk. Alternatively, a multiple regression model based on accounting data could be developed to explain betas. The results of this model could then be applied to firms which are not publicly traded to estimate their betas.

How good is the accounting beta technique? It certainly is not as good as a direct calculation of the beta. In fact, the correlation between the accounting beta and the beta calculated on historical stock return data is only about 0.6; however, better luck has been experienced with multiple regression models used to predict betas. Unfortunately, in many cases, there may not be any realistic alternative to the calculation of the accounting beta. Owing to the importance of adjusting for a project's risk, the accounting beta method is much preferred to doing nothing.

Pure play method

A method of estimating a project's beta that attempts to identify a publicly traded firm that is engaged solely in the same business as the project, and uses that beta as a proxy for the project's beta.

The pure play method for estimating a project's beta. Whereas the accounting beta method attempts to directly estimate a project or division's beta, the **pure play method** attempts to identify publicly traded firms that are engaged solely in the same business as the project or division. Once the proxy or pure play firm is identified, its systematic risk is determined and then used as a proxy for the project or division's level of systematic risk. What we are doing is looking for a publicly traded firm on the outside that looks like our project, and using that firm's required rate of return to judge our project. In doing so, we are presuming that the systematic risk of the proxy firm are identical to those of the project.

In using the pure play method, it should be noted that a firm's capital structure (that is, the way they raise money in the capital markets) is reflected in its beta. When the capital structure of the proxy firm is different from that of the project's firm, some adjustment must be made for this difference. Although not a perfect approach, it does provide some insights as to the level of systematic risk a project might have. In chapter 12, we will see how PepsiCo uses the pure play method to calculate a division's beta and required rate of return.

OTHER APPROACHES TO EVALUATING RISK IN CAPITAL BUDGETING

Simulation

Another method for evaluating risk in the investment decision is through the use of **simulation**. The certainty equivalent and risk-adjusted discount rate approaches provided us with a single value for the risk-adjusted net present value, whereas a simulation approach gives us a probability distribution for the investment's net present value or internal rate of return. Simulation imitates the performance of the project under evaluation. This is done by randomly selecting observations from each of the distributions that affect the outcome of the project, combining those observations to determine the final output of the project, and continuing with this process until a representative record of the project's probable outcome is assembled.

The easiest way to develop an understanding of the computer simulation process is to follow through an example simulation for an investment project evaluation. Suppose Merck is considering a new drug for the treatment of Alzheimer's disease. The simulation process is portrayed in Figure 11.3. First, the probability distributions are determined for all the factors that affect the project's returns; in this case, let us assume these include the market size, selling price, fixed costs, market growth rate, investment required, residual value of investment, share of market (which results in physical sales volume), operating costs, and useful life of facilities.

Then the computer randomly selects one observation from each of the probability distributions, according to its chance of actually occurring in the future. These nine observations are combined, and a net present value or internal rate of return figure is calculated. This process is repeated as many times as desired, until a representative distribution of possible future outcomes is assembled. Thus the inputs to a simulation include all the principal factors affecting the project's profitability, and the simulation output is a probability distribution of net present values or internal rates of return for the project. The decision maker bases the decision on the full range of possible outcomes. The project is accepted if the decision maker feels that enough of the distribution lies above the normal cutoff criteria ($NPV \geq 0$, $IRR \geq$ required rate of return).

Suppose that the output from the simulation of Merck's Alzheimer's disease drug project is as given in Figure 11.4. This output provides the decision maker with the probability of different outcomes occurring in addition to the range of possible outcomes. Sometimes called **scenario analysis**, this examination identifies the range of possible outcomes under the worst, best, and most likely case. Merck's management will examine the distribution to determine the project's level of risk and then make the appropriate adjustment.

You'll notice that although the simulation approach helps us to determine the amount of total risk that a project has, it does not differentiate between systematic and unsystematic risk. Because systematic risk cannot be diversified away for free, the simulation approach does not provide a complete method of risk assessment. However, it does provide important insights as to the total risk level of a given investment project. Now we will look briefly at how the simulation approach can be used to perform sensitivity analysis.

Sensitivity analysis through the simulation approach. **Sensitivity analysis** involves determining how the distribution of possible net present values or internal rates of returns for a particular project is affected by a change in one particular input variable. This is done by changing the value of one input variable while holding all other input variables constant. The distribution of possible net present values or internal rates of return that is

Simulation

The process of imitating the performance of an investment project under evaluation using a computer. This is done by randomly selecting observations from each of the distributions that affect the outcome of the project, combining those observations to determine the final output of the project, and continuing with this process until a representative record of the project's probable outcome is assembled.

Scenario analysis

Simulation analysis that focuses on an examination of the range of possible outcomes.

Sensitivity analysis

The process of determining how the distribution of possible returns for a particular project is affected by a change in one particular input variable.

Figure 11.3 Capital-Budgeting Simulation for Proposed New Alzheimers Drug

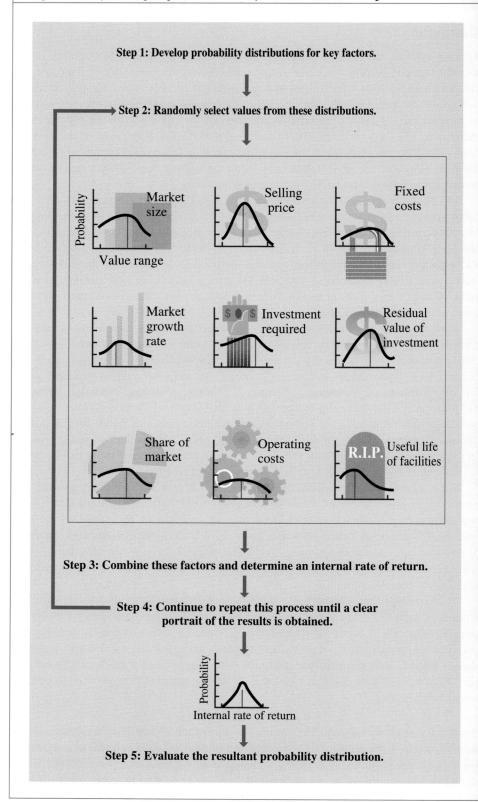

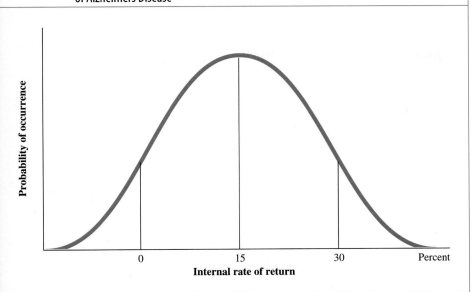

Figure 11.4 Output from Simulation of a Proposed New Drug for the Prevention of Alzheimers Disease

generated is then compared with the distribution of possible returns generated before the change was made to determine the effect of the change. For this reason, sensitivity analysis is commonly called "*What if?*" Analysis.

For example, in analyzing the proposal for a new drug for the prevention of Alzheimer's disease, Merck's management may wish to determine the effect of a more pessimistic forecast of the anticipated market growth rate. After the more pessimistic forecast replaces the original forecast in the model, the simulation is rerun. The two outputs are then compared to determine how sensitive the results are to the revised estimate of the market growth rate.

By modifying assumptions made about the values and ranges of the input factors and rerunning the simulation, management can determine how sensitive the outcome of the project is to these changes. If the output appears to be highly sensitive to one or two of the input factors, the financial managers may then wish to spend additional time refining those input estimates to make sure they are accurate.

Probability Trees

A **probability tree** is a graphic exposition of the sequence of possible outcomes; it presents the decision maker with a schematic representation of the problem in which all possible outcomes are pictured. Moreover, the computations and results of the computations are shown directly on the tree, so that the information can be easily understood.

To illustrate the use of a probability tree, suppose a firm is considering an investment proposal that requires an initial outlay of $1 million and will yield cash flows for the next 2 years. During the first year, let us assume there are three possible outcomes, as shown in Table 11.3. Graphically, each of these three possible alternatives is represented on the probability tree in Figure 11.5 as one of the three possible branches.

The second step in the probability tree is to continue drawing branches in a similar manner so that each of the possible outcomes during the second year is represented by a

Probability tree

A schematic representation of a problem in which all possible outcomes are graphically displayed.

Table 11.3 Possible Outcomes in Year 1

	Probability		
	.5	.3	.2
	Outcome 1	Outcome 2	Outcome 3
Cash flow	$600,000	$700,000	$800,000

Figure 11.5 First Stage of a Probability-Tree Diagram

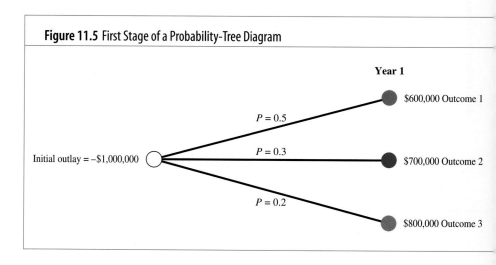

new branch. For example, if outcome 1 occurs in year 1, then there would be a 20 percent chance of a $300,000 cash flow and an 80 percent chance of a $600,000 cash flow in year 2 as shown in Table 11.4. Two branches would be sent out from the outcome 1 node, reflecting these two possible outcomes. The cash flows that occur if outcome 1 takes place and the probabilities associated with them are called *conditional outcomes* and *conditional probabilities* because they can occur only if outcome 1 occurs during the first year. Finally, to determine the probability of the sequence of a $600,000 flow in year 1 and a $300,000 outcome in year 2, the probability of the $600,000 flow (.5) is multiplied by the conditional probability of the second flow (.2), telling us that this sequence has a 10 percent chance of occurring; this is called its **joint probability**. Letting the values in Table 11.4 represent the conditional outcomes and their respective conditional probabilities, we can complete the probability tree, as shown in Figure 11.6.

The financial manager, by examining the probability tree, is provided with the expected internal rate of return for the investment, the range of possible outcomes, and a listing of each possible outcome with the probability associated with it. In this case, the

Joint probability

The probability of two different sequential outcomes occurring.

Table 11.4 Conditional Outcomes and Probabilities for Year 2

	If Outcome 1 $ACF_1 = \$600,000$		If Outcome 2 $ACF_1 = \$700,000$		If Outcome 3 $ACF_1 = \$800,000$	
Year 1	Then		Then		Then	
Year 2	ACF_2	Probability	ACF_2	Probability	ACF_2	Probability
	$300,000	.2	$300,000	.2	$400,000	.2
	600,000	.8	500,000	.3	600,000	.7
			700,000	.5	800,000	.1

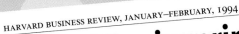

HARVARD BUSINESS REVIEW, JANUARY–FEBRUARY, 1994

Financial Engineering at Merck

(A) Last year Merck & Co., Inc., invested well over $2 billion in R&D and capital expenditures combined. The company spent much of the money on risky, long-term projects that are notoriously difficult to evaluate. Indeed, the critics of modern finance would argue that such projects should not be subjected to rigorous financial analysis, because such analysis fails to reflect the strategic value of long-term investments. Yet at Merck, it is those projects with the longest time horizon that receive the most intense and financially sophisticated analyses. In fact, Merck's financial function is active and influential with a highly quantitative, analytical orientation. The company is seldom, if ever, criticized for being shortsighted.

(B) Why doesn't all this analysis choke off long-term investing, as critics of modern finance theory say it should? In part because Merck is a leader in building financial models of scientific and commercial processes and in using those models to improve business decisions. Rather than relying on static, single-point forecasts, Merck's models use probability distributions for numerous variables and come up with a range of possible outcomes that both stimulate discussion and facilitate decision making.

For example, Merck's Research Planning Model, now ten years old, and its Revenue Hedging Model, now four years old, integrate economics, finance, statistics, and computer science to produce disciplined, quantitative analyses of specific elements of Merck's business. These models do not make decisions. Instead, **(C)** they provide Merck executives with cogent information both about risks and returns and about financial performance for specific projects and activities.

Analysis and Implications ...

A. The risks that pharmaceutical firms face in product development are great. It costs $359 million and takes 10 years to bring a new drug to market. Then once the drug has reached the market, 70 percent of the new drugs introduced do not cover their costs.

B. Rather than simply using an estimate of the project's expected net present value, Merck relies on a simulation approach. They examine the returns on proposed new drugs over a 20-year period, allowing for any and all complexities that they can foresee.

C. One of the key aspects of the simulation approach used by Merck is the ability to perform sensitivity analysis by changing the value of specific variables and seeing how the results are affected. In this way, Merck can determine where to spend more time in forecasting and where they should spend time and money trying to improve efficiency.

expected internal rate of return is 14.74 percent, and there is a 10 percent chance of incurring the worst possible outcome with an internal rate of return of −7.55 percent. There is a 2 percent probability of achieving the most favorable outcome, an internal rate of return of 37.98 percent.

Decision making with probability trees does not mean simply the acceptance of any project with an internal rate of return greater than the firm's required rate of return,

Figure 11.6 Probability Tree

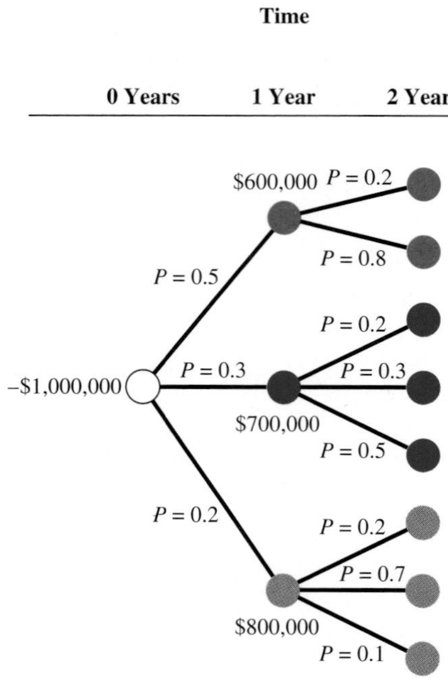

Time			(A) Internal rate of return for each branch	(B) Joint probability	(A) × (B)

	(A) Internal rate of return for each branch	(B) Joint probability	(A) × (B)
$300,000	−7.55	0.10	−0.7550
$600,000	13.07	0.40	5.2280
$300,000	0.00	0.06	0.0000
$500,000	13.90	0.09	1.2510
$700,000	25.69	0.15	3.8535
$400,000	14.83	0.04	0.5932
$600,000	27.18	0.14	3.8052
$800,000	37.98	0.02	0.7596
		1.00	

Expected internal rate of return = 14.7355%

because the project's required rate of return has not yet been adjusted for risk. As a result, the financial decision maker must examine the entire distribution of possible internal rates of return. Then based on that examination, he or she must decide, given her or his aversion to risk, if enough of this distribution is above the appropriate (risk-adjusted) required rate of return to warrant acceptance of the project. Thus the probability tree allows the manager to quickly visualize the possible future events, their probabilities, and their outcomes. In addition, the calculation of the expected internal rate of return and enumeration of the distribution should aid the financial manager in determining the risk level of the project. However, just as with the simulation approach, probability trees do not differentiate between systematic and unsystematic risk.

Other Sources of Risk: Time Dependence of Cash Flows

Up to this point, in all approaches other than the probability tree, we have assumed that the cash flow in one period is independent of the cash flow in the previous period. Although this assumption is appealing because it is simple, in many cases it is also invalid. For example, if a new product is introduced and the initial public reaction is poor, resulting in low initial cash flows, then cash flows in future periods are likely to be low. An extreme example of this is Coca-Cola's experience with the "New Coke." Poor consumer acceptance and sales in the first year were followed by even poorer results in the second year. If the New Coke had been received favorably during its first year, it quite likely would have done well in the second year. The end effect of time dependence of cash flows is to increase the risk of the project over time. That is, because large cash flows in the first period lead to large cash flows in the second period, and low cash flows in the first period lead to low cash flows in the second period, the probability distribution of possible net present values tends to be wider than if the cash flows were not dependent over time. The greater the degree of correlation between flows over time, the greater will be the dispersion of the probability distribution.

HOW FINANCIAL MANAGERS USE THIS MATERIAL

If financial managers could see into the future, the material in this chapter would be unnecessary. Unfortunately, they can't—in fact, no one can. What that means for capital-budgeting decision is that you're never really sure how the market will react to your new project. Moreover, not all projects have the same level of risk and, as a result, you have to look at each project individually and make some adjustment for risk. On top of all that, we have the problem of measuring risk.

What does all this mean for you as a financial manager? It means that you not only must understand how risk is measured and the fact that all risk is not the same (in effect, **Axiom 9**), but you must also make an adjustment for risk within the capital-budgeting process.

Looking back at Burger King and its introduction of the Big King burger aimed at competing with the McDonald's Big Mac, after all the test marketing, there is still a good deal of uncertainty as to how the public will react to this product. Remember, when McDonald's introduced the Arch Deluxe a couple years ago? That was McDonald's attempt to bring older customers back into McDonald's by providing a more sophisticated burger. They went through extensive test marketing and thought they had a winner, but it didn't sell that way. To determine how much risk and uncertainty there is with a new product, the financial manager much rely heavily on those making the sales forecast. Once they provide the estimate of risk, it is the financial manager's job to react to this and incorporate it into the capital-budgeting process, looking at the best and worst case scenarios and trying to determine just how risky the project is. That may be your job.

SUMMARY

In this chapter, we examine the problem of incorporating risk into the capital-budgeting decision. First we explore just what type of risk to adjust for: project standing alone risk, the project's contribution-to-firm risk, or the project's systematic risk. In theory, systematic risk is the appropriate risk measure, but bankruptcy costs and the issue of undiversified shareholders also give weight to considering a project's contribution-to-firm risk as the appropriate risk measure. Both measures of risk have merit, and we avoid making any specific allocation of importance between the two in capital budgeting.

OBJECTIVE 1

Two commonly used methods for incorporating risk into capital budgeting are (1) the certainty equivalent method and (2) risk-adjusted discount rates. The certainty equivalent approach involves a direct attempt to incorporate the decision maker's utility function into the analysis. Under this method, cash flows are adjusted downward by multiplying them by certainty equivalent coefficients, α_t's, which transform the risky cash flows into equivalent certain cash flows in terms of desirability. A project's net present value using the certainty equivalent method for adjusting for risk becomes

OBJECTIVE 2

$$NPV = \sum_{t=1}^{n} \frac{\alpha_t ACF_t}{(1 + k_{rf})^t} - IO \qquad (11\text{-}2)$$

The risk-adjusted discount rate involves an upward adjustment of the discount rate to compensate for risk. This method is based on the concept that investors demand higher returns for riskier projects.

 **OBJECTIVE 3**

The simulation and probability tree methods are used to provide information as to the location and shape of the distribution of possible outcomes. Decisions could be based directly on these methods, or they could be used to determine input into either certainty equivalent or risk-adjusted discount method approaches.

GO TO:
http://www.prenhall.com/bfm
For downloads and current events associated with this chapter

KEY TERMS

Certainty equivalent approach, 403

Certainty equivalents, 403

Joint probability, 414

Probability tree, 413

Project standing alone risk, 400

Project's contribution-to-firm risk, 400

Pure play method, 410

Risk-adjusted discount rate, 405

Scenario analysis, 411

Sensitivity analysis, 411

Simulation, 411

Systematic risk, 400

STUDY QUESTIONS

11-1. In chapter 9, we examined the payback period capital-budgeting decision criterion. Often this capital-budgeting criterion is used as a risk-screening device. Explain the rationale behind its use.

11-2. The use of the risk-adjusted discount rate assumes that risk increases over time. Justify this assumption.

11-3. What are the similarities and differences between the risk-adjusted discount rate and the certainty equivalent methods for incorporating risk into the capital-budgeting decision?

11-4. What is the value of using the probability tree method for evaluating capital-budgeting projects?

11-5. Explain how simulation works. What is the value in using a simulation approach?

11-6. What does time dependence of cash flows mean? Why might cash flows be time dependent? Give some examples.

SELF-TEST PROBLEMS

ST-1. G. Norohna and Co. is considering two mutually exclusive projects. The expected values for each project's cash flows are as follows:

Year	Project A	Project B
0	−$300,000	−$300,000
1	100,000	200,000
2	200,000	200,000
3	200,000	200,000
4	300,000	300,000
5	300,000	400,000

The company has decided to evaluate these projects using the certainty equivalent method. The certainty equivalent coefficients for each project's cash flows are as follows:

Year	Project A	Project B
0	1.00	1.00
1	.95	.90
2	.90	.80
3	.85	.70
4	.80	.60
5	.75	.50

Given that this company's normal required rate of return is 15 percent and the after-tax risk-free rate is 8 percent, which project should be selected?

STUDY PROBLEMS (SET A)

11-1A. (*Risk-Adjusted NPV*) The Hokie Corporation is considering two mutually exclusive projects. Both require an initial outlay of $10,000 and will operate for 5 years. The probability distributions associated with each project for years 1 through 5 are given as follows:

Probability Distribution for Cash Flow Years 1–5 (the same cash flow each year)			
Project A		**Project B**	
Probability	**Cash Flow**	**Probability**	**Cash Flow**
.15	$4,000	.15	$ 2,000
.70	5,000	.70	6,000
.15	6,000	.15	10,000

Because project B is the riskier of the two projects, the management of Hokie Corporation has decided to apply a required rate of return of 15 percent to its evaluation but only a 12 percent required rate of return to project A.

   a. Determine the expected value of each project's annual cash flows.

   b. Determine each project's risk-adjusted net present value.

   c. What other factors might be considered in deciding between these two projects?

11-2A. (*Risk-Adjusted NPV*) The Goblu Corporation is evaluating two mutually exclusive projects, both of which require an initial outlay of $100,000. Each project has an expected life of 5 years. The probability distributions associated with the annual cash flows from each project are as follows:

Probability Distribution for Cash Flow Years 1–5 (the same cash flow each year)			
Project A		**Project B**	
Probability	**Cash Flow**	**Probability**	**Cash Flow**
.10	$35,000	.10	$10,000
.40	40,000	.20	30,000
.40	45,000	.40	45,000
.10	50,000	.20	60,000
		.10	80,000

The normal required rate of return for Goblu is 10 percent, but because these projects are riskier than most, it is requiring a higher-than-normal rate of return on them. Project A requires a 12 percent and on project B a 13 percent rate of return.

a. Determine the expected value for each project's cash flows.

b. Determine each project's risk-adjusted net present value.

c. What other factors might be considered in deciding between these projects?

11-3A. (*Certainty Equivalents*) The V. Coles Corp. is considering two mutually exclusive projects. The expected values for each project's cash flows are as follows:

Year	Project A	Project B
0	–$1,000,000	–$1,000,000
1	500,000	500,000
2	700,000	600,000
3	600,000	700,000
4	500,000	800,000

Management has decided to evaluate these projects using the certainty equivalent method. The certainty equivalent coefficients for each project's cash flows are as follows:

Year	Project A	Project B
0	1.00	1.00
1	.95	.90
2	.90	.70
3	.80	.60
4	.70	.50

Given that this company's normal required rate of return is 15 percent and the after-tax risk-free rate is 5 percent, which project should be selected?

11-4A. (*Certainty Equivalents*) Neustal, Inc., has decided to use the certainty equivalent method in determining whether or not a new investment should be made. The expected cash flows associated with this investment and the estimated certainty equivalent coefficients are as follows:

Year	Expected Values for Cash Flows	Certainty Equivalent Coefficients
0	–$90,000	1.00
1	25,000	0.95
2	30,000	0.90
3	30,000	0.83
4	25,000	0.75
5	20,000	0.65

Given that Neustal's normal required rate of return is 18 percent and that the after-tax risk free rate is 7 percent, should this project be accepted?

11-5A. (*Risk-Adjusted Discount Rates and Risk Classes*) The G. Wolfe Corporation is examining two capital-budgeting projects with 5-year lives. The first, project A, is a replacement project; the second, project B, is a project unrelated to current operations. The G. Wolfe Corporation uses the risk-adjusted discount rate method and groups projects according to purpose and then uses a required rate of return or discount rate that has been preassigned to that purpose or risk class. The expected cash flows for these projects are as follows:

	Project A	Project B
Initial Investment:	$250,000	$400,000
Cash inflows:		
Year 1	$ 30,000	$135,000
Year 2	40,000	135,000
Year 3	50,000	135,000
Year 4	90,000	135,000
Year 5	130,000	135,000

The purpose/risk classes and preassigned required rates of return are as follows:

Purpose	Required Rate of Return
Replacement decision	12%
Modification or expansion of existing product line	15
Project unrelated to current operations	18
Research and development operations	20

Determine the project's risk-adjusted net present value.

11-6A. (*Certainty Equivalents*) Nacho Nachtmann Company uses the certainty equivalent approach when it evaluates risky investments. The company presently has two mutually exclusive investment proposals with an expected life of 4 years each to choose from with money it received from the sale of part of its toy division to another company. The expected net cash flows are as follows:

Year	Project A	Project B
0	-$50,000	-$50,000
1	15,000	20,000
2	15,000	25,000
3	15,000	25,000
4	45,000	30,000

The certainty equivalent coefficients for the net cash flows are as follows:

Year	Project A	Project B
0	1.00	1.00
1	.95	.90
2	.85	.85
3	.80	.80
4	.70	.75

Which of the two investment proposals should be chosen, given that the after-tax risk-free rate of return is 6 percent?

11-7A. (*Probability Trees*) The M. Solt Corporation is evaluating an investment proposal with an expected life of 2 years. This project will require an initial outlay of $1,200,000. The resultant possible cash flows are as follows:

Possible Outcomes in Year 1

	Probability		
	.6	.3	.1
	Outcome 1	Outcome 2	Outcome 3
Cash flow =	$700,000	$850,000	$1,000,000

Conditional Outcomes and Probabilities for Year 2

If $ACF_1 = \$700,000$		If $ACF_1 = \$850,000$		If $ACF_1 = \$1,000,000$	
ACF_2	Probability	ACF_2	Probability	ACF_2	Probability
$ 300,000	.3	$ 400,000	.2	$ 600,000	.1
700,000	.6	700,000	.5	900,000	.5
1,100,000	.1	1,000,000	.2	1,100,000	.4
		1,300,000	.1		

a. Construct a probability tree representing the possible outcomes.
b. Determine the joint probability of each possible sequence of events taking place.
c. What is the expected IRR of this project?
d. What is the range of possible IRRs for this project?

11-8A. (*Probability Trees*) Sega, Inc., is considering expanding its operations into computer-based lacrosse games. Sega feels that there is a 3-year life associated with this project, and it will initially involve an investment of $100,000. It also believes there is a 60 percent chance of success and a cash flow of $100,000 in year 1 and a 40 percent chance of failure and a $10,000 cash flow in year 1. If the project fails in year 1, there is a 60 percent chance that it will produce cash flows of only $10,000 in years 2 and 3. There is also a 40 percent chance that it will *really* fail and Sega will earn nothing in year 2 and get out of this line of business, with the project terminating and no cash flow occurring in year 3. If, conversely, this project succeeds in the first year, then cash flows in the second year are expected to be $200,000, $175,000, or $150,000 with probabilities of .30, .50, and .20, respectively. Finally, if the project succeeds in the third and final year of operation, the cash flows are expected to be either $30,000 more or $20,000 less than they were in year 2, with an equal chance of occurrence.

a. Construct a probability tree representing the possible outcomes.
b. Determine the joint probability of each possible sequence of events.
c. What is the expected IRR?
d. What is the range of possible IRRs for this project?

It's been 4 months since you took a position as an assistant financial analyst at Caledonia Products. During that time, you've had a promotion and now are working as a special assistant for capital budgeting to the CEO. Your latest assignment involves the analysis of several risky projects. Since this is your first assignment dealing with risk analysis, you have been asked not only to provide a recommendation on the projects in question, but also to respond to a number of questions aimed at judging your understanding of risk analysis and capital budgeting. The memorandum you received outlining your assignment follows:

GO TO:
http://www.prenhall.com/bfm
For downloads and current events associated with this chapter

TO: The Special Assistant for Capital Budgeting
FROM: Mr. V. Morrison, CEO, Caledonia Products
RE: Capital Budgeting and Risk Analysis

Provide a written response to the following questions:

1. In capital budgeting, risk can be measured from three perspectives. What are those three measures of a project's risk?

2. According to the CAPM, which measurement of a project's risk is relevant? What complications does reality introduce into the CAPM view of risk and what does that mean for our view of the relevant measure of a project's risk?

3. What are the similarities and differences between the risk-adjusted discount rate and certainty equivalent methods for incorporating risk into the capital-budgeting decision?

4. Why might we use the probability-tree technique for evaluating capital-budgeting projects?

5. Explain how simulation works. What is the value of using a simulation approach?

6. What is sensitivity analysis and what is its purpose?

7. What does time dependence of cash flows mean? Why might cash flows be time dependent? Give some examples.

8. Caledonia Products is using the certainty equivalent approach to evaluate two mutually exclusive investment proposals with an expected life of 4 years. The expected net cash flows are as follows:

Year	Project A	Project B
0	−$150,000	−$200,000
1	40,000	50,000
2	40,000	60,000
3	40,000	60,000
4	100,000	50,000

The certainty equivalent coefficients for the net cash flows are as follows:

Year	Project A	Project B
0	1.00	1.00
1	.90	.95
2	.85	.85
3	.80	.80
4	.70	.75

Which of the two investment proposals should be chosen, given that the after-tax risk-free rate of return is 7 percent?

9. Caledonia is considering an additional investment project with an expected life of 2 years and would like some insights on the level of risk this project has using the probability-tree method. The initial outlay on this project would be $600,000, and the resultant possible cash flows are as follows:

Possible Outcomes in Year 1

	Probability		
	.4	.4	.2
	Outcome 1	Outcome 2	Outcome 3
Cash flow =	$300,000	$350,000	$450,000

Conditional Outcomes and Probabilities for Year 2

If ACF$_1$ = $300,000		If ACF$_1$ = $350,000		If ACF$_1$ = $450,000	
ACF$_2$	Probability	ACF$_2$	Probability	ACF$_2$	Probability
$200,000	.3	$ 250,000	.2	$ 300,000	.2
300,000	.7	450,000	.5	500,000	.5
		650,000	.3	700,000	.2
				1,000,000	.1

a. Construct a probability tree representing the possible outcomes.

b. Determine the joint probability of each possible sequence of events taking place.

c. What is the expected IRR of this project?

d. What is the range of possible IRRs for this project?

STUDY PROBLEMS (SET B)

11-1B. (*Risk-Adjusted NPV*) The Cake-O-Las Corporation is considering two mutually exclusive projects. Each of these projects requires an initial outlay of $10,000 and will operate for 5 years. The probability distributions associated with each project for years 1 through 5 are given as follows:

Probability Distribution for Cash Flow Years 1–5 (the same cash flow each year)

Project A		Project B	
Probability	Cash Flow	Probability	Cash Flow
.20	$5,000	.20	$ 3,000
.60	6,000	.60	7,000
.20	7,000	.20	11,000

Because project B is the riskier of the two projects, the management of Cake-O-Las Corporation has decided to apply a required rate of return of 18 percent to its evaluation but only a 13 percent required rate of return to project A.

a. Determine the expected value of each project's annual cash flows.

b. Determine each project's risk-adjusted net present value.

c. What other factors might be considered in deciding between these two projects?

11-2B. (*Risk-Adjusted NPV*) The Dorf Corporation is evaluating two mutually exclusive projects, both of which require an initial outlay of $125,000. Each project has an expected life of

5 years. The probability distributions associated with the annual cash flows from each project are as follows:

Probability Distribution for Cash Flow Years 1–5 (the same cash flow each year)			
Project A		Project B	
Probability	Cash Flow	Probability	Cash Flow
.10	$40,000	.10	$20,000
.40	45,000	.20	40,000
.40	50,000	.40	55,000
.10	55,000	.20	70,000
		.10	90,000

The normal required rate of return for Dorf is 10 percent, but because these projects are riskier than most, Dorf is requiring a higher-than-normal rate of return on them. On project A, it is requiring an 11 percent; and on project B, a 13 percent rate of return.

a. Determine the expected value for each project's cash flows.

b. Determine each project's risk-adjusted net present value.

c. What other factors might be considered in deciding between these projects?

11-3B. (*Certainty Equivalents*) The Temco Corp. is considering two mutually exclusive projects. The expected values for each project's cash flows are as follows:

Year	Project A	Project B
0	−$1,000,000	−$1,000,000
1	600,000	600,000
2	750,000	650,000
3	600,000	700,000
4	550,000	750,000

Temco has decided to evaluate these projects using the certainty equivalent method. The certainty equivalent coefficients for each project's cash flows are as follows:

Year	Project A	Project B
0	1.00	1.00
1	.90	.95
2	.90	.75
3	.75	.60
4	.65	.60

Given that this company's normal required rate of return is 15 percent and the after-tax risk-free rate is 5 percent, which project should be selected?

11-4B. (*Certainty Equivalents*) Perumperal, Inc., has decided to use the certainty equivalent method in determining whether or not a new investment should be made. The expected cash flows associated with this investment and the estimated certainty equivalent coefficients are as follows:

Year	Expected Values for Cash Flows	Certainty Equivalent Coefficients
0	-$100,000	1.00
1	30,000	.95
2	25,000	.90
3	30,000	.83
4	20,000	.75
5	25,000	.65

Given that Perumperal's normal required rate of return is 18 percent and that the after-tax risk free rate is 8 percent, should this project be accepted?

11-5B. (*Risk-Adjusted Discount Rates and Risk Classes*) The Kick 'n' MacDonald Corporation is examining two capital-budgeting projects with 5-year lives. The first, project A, is a replacement project; the second, project B, is a project unrelated to current operations. The Kick 'n' MacDonald Corporation uses the risk-adjusted discount rate method and groups projects according to purpose and then uses a required rate of return or discount rate that has been preassigned to that purpose or risk class. The expected cash flows for these projects are as follows:

	Project A	Project B
Initial Investment:	$300,000	$450,000
Cash Inflows:		
Year 1	$ 30,000	$130,000
Year 2	40,000	130,000
Year 3	50,000	130,000
Year 4	80,000	130,000
Year 5	120,000	130,000

The purpose-risk classes and preassigned required rates of return are as follows:

Purpose	Required Rate of Return
Replacement decision	13%
Modification or expansion of existing product line	16
Project unrelated to current operations	18
Research and development operations	20

Determine the project's risk-adjusted net present value.

11-6B. (*Certainty Equivalents*) The M. Jose Company uses the certainty equivalent approach when it evaluates risky investments. The company presently has two mutually exclusive investment proposals, with an expected life of 4 years each, to choose from with money it received from the sale of part of its toy division to another company. The expected net cash flows are as follows:

Year	Project A	Project B
0	-$75,000	-$75,000
1	20,000	25,000
2	20,000	30,000
3	15,000	30,000
4	50,000	25,000

The certainty equivalent coefficients for the net cash flows are as follows:

Year	Project A	Project B
0	1.00	1.00
1	.95	.95
2	.85	.85
3	.80	.80
4	.70	.75

Which of the two investment proposals should be chosen, given that the after-tax risk-free rate of return is 7 percent?

11-7B. (*Probability Trees*) The Buckeye Corporation is evaluating an investment proposal with an expected life of 2 years. This project will require an initial outlay of $1,300,000. The resultant possible cash flows are as follows:

Possible Outcomes in Year 1

	Probability		
	.6	.3	.1
	Outcome 1	Outcome 2	Outcome 3
Cash flow =	$750,000	$900,000	$1,500,000

Conditional Outcomes and Probabilities for Year 2

If $ACF_1 = \$750,000$		If $ACF_1 = \$900,000$		If $ACF_1 = \$1,500,000$	
ACF_2	Probability	ACF_2	Probability	ACF_2	Probability
$ 300,000	.10	$ 400,000	.2	$ 600,000	.3
700,000	.50	700,000	.5	900,000	.6
1,100,000	.40	900,000	.2	1,100,000	.1
		1,300,000	.1		

a. Construct a probability tree representing the possible outcomes.

b. Determine the joint probability of each possible sequence of events taking place.

c. What is the expected IRR of this project?

d. What is the range of possible IRRs for this project?

11-8B. (*Probability Trees*) Mac's Buffaloes, Inc., is considering expanding its operations into computer-based basketball games. Mac's Buffaloes feels that there is a 3-year life associated with this project, and it will initially involve an investment of $120,000. It also feels there is a 70 percent chance of success and a cash flow of $100,000 in year 1 and a 30 percent chance of "failure" and a $10,000 cash flow in year 1. If the project "fails" in year 1, there is a 60 percent chance that it will produce cash flows of only $10,000 in years 2 and 3. There is also a 40 percent chance that it will really fail and Mac's Buffaloes will earn nothing in year 2 and get out of this line of business, with the project terminating and no cash flow occurring in year 3. If, on the other hand, this project succeeds in the first year, then cash flows in the second year are expected to be $225,000, $180,000, or $140,000 with probabilities of .30, .50, and .20, respectively. Finally, if the project succeeds in the third and final year of operation, the cash flows are expected to be either $30,000 more or $20,000 less than they were in year 2, with an equal chance of occurrence.

a. Construct a probability tree representing the possible outcomes.

b. Determine the joint probability of each possible sequence of events.

c. What is the expected IRR?

d. What is the range of possible IRRs for this project?

MADE IN THE U.S.A.: DUMPED IN BRAZIL, AFRICA . . .

Ethics in Dealing with Uncertainty in Capital Budgeting, or What Happens When a Project Is No Longer Sellable

In an uncertain world, capital budgeting attempts to determine what the future of a new product will bring and how then to act on that forecast. We never know for certain what the future will bring, but we do arrive at some idea of what the distribution of possible outcomes looks like. Unfortunately, when there is uncertainty, the outcome is not always a good one. For example, what happens if the government rules that our product is not safe? The answer is that we must abandon the product. The question then becomes what to do with the inventory we currently have on hand. We certainly want to deal with it in a way that is in the best interests of our shareholders. We also want to obey the law and act ethically. As with most ethical questions, there isn't necessarily a right or wrong answer.

When it comes to the safety of young children, fire is a parent's nightmare. Just the thought of their young ones trapped in their cribs and beds by a raging nocturnal blaze is enough to make most mothers and fathers take every precaution to ensure their children's safety. Little wonder that when fire-retardant children's pajamas hit the market in the mid-1970s, they proved an overnight success. Within a few short years, more than 200 million pairs were sold, and the sales of millions more were all but guaranteed. For their manufacturers, the future could not have been brighter. Then, like a bolt from the blue, came word that the pajamas were killers.

In June 1977, the U.S. Consumer Product Safety Commission (CPSC) banned the sale of these pajamas and ordered the recall of millions of pairs. Reason: The pajamas contained the flame-retardant chemical Tris (2,3-dibromoprophyl), which had been found to cause kidney cancer in children.

Whereas just months earlier the 100 medium- and small-garment manufacturers of the Tris-impregnated pajamas couldn't fill orders fast enough, suddenly they were worrying about how to get rid of the millions of pairs now sitting in warehouses. Because of its toxicity, the sleepwear couldn't even be thrown away, let alone be sold. Indeed, the CPSC left no doubt about how the pajamas were to be disposed of— buried or burned or used as industrial wiping cloths. All meant millions of dollars in losses for manufacturers.

The companies affected—mostly small, family-run operations employing fewer than 100 workers—immediately attempted to shift blame to the mills that made the cloth. When that attempt failed, they tried to get the big department stores that sold the pajamas and the chemical companies that produced Tris to share the financial losses. Again, no sale. Finally, in desperation, the companies lobbied in Washington for a bill making the federal government partially responsible for the losses. It was the government, they argued, that originally had required the companies to add Tris to pajamas and then had prohibited their sale. Congress was sympathetic; it passed a bill granting companies relief. But President Carter vetoed it.

While the small firms were waging their political battle in the halls of Congress, ads began appearing in the classified pages of *Women's Wear Daily*. "Tris-Tris-Tris . . . We will buy any fabric containing Tris," read one. Another said, "Tris—we will purchase any large quantities of garments containing Tris."[1] The ads had been placed by exporters, who began buying up the pajamas, usually at 10 to 30 percent of the normal wholesale price. Their intent was clear: to dump[2] the carcinogenic pajamas on overseas markets.[3]

Tris is not the only example of dumping. In 1972, 400 Iraqis died and 5,000 were hospitalized after eating wheat and barley treated with a U.S.-banned organic mercury fungicide. Winstrol, a synthetic male hormone that had been found to stunt the growth of American children, was made available in Brazil as an appetite stimulant for children. Depo-Provera, an injectable contraceptive known to cause malignant tumors in animals, was shipped overseas to 70 countries where it was used in U.S.-sponsored population control programs. And 450,000 baby pacifiers, of the type known to have caused choking deaths, were exported for sale overseas.

Manufacturers that dump products abroad clearly are motivated by profit or at least by the hope of avoiding financial losses resulting from having to withdraw a product from the market. For government and health agencies that cooperate in the exporting of dangerous products, the motives are more complex.

For example, as early as 1971, the dangers of the Dalkon Shield intrauterine device were well documented.[4] Among the adverse reactions were pelvic inflammation, blood poisoning, pregnancies resulting in spontaneous abortions, tubal pregnancies, and uterine perforations. A number of deaths were even attributed to the device. Faced with losing its domestic market, A. H. Robins Co., manufacturer of the Dalkon Shield, worked out a deal with the Office of Population within the U. S. Agency for International Development (AID), whereby AID bought thousands of the devices at a reduced price for use in population-control programs in 42 countries.

---

[1] Mark Hosenball, "Karl Marx and the Pajama Game," *Mother Jones* (November 1979): 47.

[2] "Dumping" is a term apparently coined by *Mother Jones* magazine to refer to the practice of exporting to overseas countries products that have been banned or declared hazardous in the United States.

[3] Unless otherwise noted, the facts and quotations reported in this case are based on Mark Dowie, "The Corporate Crime of the Century," *Mother Jones* (November 1971) and Russell Mokhiber, *Corporate Crime and Violence* (San Francisco: Sierra Club Books, 1988): 181–95. See also Jane Kay, "Global Dumping of U.S. Toxics Is Big Business," *San Francisco Examiner* (September 23, 1990): A2.

[4] See Mark Dowie and Tracy Johnston, "A Case of Corporate Malpractice," *Mother Jones* (November 1976).

Why do governmental and population-control agencies approve for sale and use overseas birth control devices proved dangerous in the United States? They say their motives are humanitarian. Because the rate of dying in childbirth is high in Third World countries, almost any birth control device is preferable to none. Third World scientists and government officials frequently support this argument. They insist that denying their countries access to the contraceptives of their choice is tantamount to violating their countries' national sovereignty.

Apparently this argument has found a sympathetic ear in Washington, for it turns up in the "notification" system that regulates the export of banned or dangerous products over-seas. Based on the principles of national sovereignty, self-determination, and free trade, the notification system requires that foreign governments be notified whenever a product is banned, deregulated, suspended, or canceled by an American regulatory agency. The State Department, which implements the system, has a policy statement on the subject that reads in part: "No country should establish itself as the arbiter of others' health and safety standards. Individual governments are generally in the best position to establish standards of public health and safety."

Critics of the system claim that notifying foreign health officials is virtually useless. For one thing, other governments rarely can establish health standards or even control imports into their countries. Indeed, most of the Third World countries where banned or dangerous products are dumped lack regulatory agencies, adequate testing facilities, and well-staffed customs departments.

Then there's the problem of getting the word out about hazardous products. In theory, when a government agency such as the Environmental Protection Agency or the Food and Drug Administration (FDA) finds a product hazardous, it is supposed to inform the State Department, which is to notify local health officials. But agencies often fail to inform the State Department of the product they have banned or found harmful. And when it is notified, its communiqués typically go no further than the U.S. embassies abroad. One embassy official even told the General Accounting Office that he "did not routinely forward notification of chemicals not registered in the host country because it may adversely affect U.S. exporting." When foreign officials are notified by U.S. embassies, they sometimes find the communiqués vague or ambiguous or too technical to understand.

In an effort to remedy these problems, at the end of his term in office, President Jimmy Carter issued an executive order that (1) improved export notice procedures; (2) called for publishing an annual summary of substances banned or severely restricted for domestic use in the United States; (3) directed the State Department and other federal agencies to participate in the development of international hazards alert systems; and (4) established procedures for placing formal export licensing controls on a limited number of extremely hazardous substances. In one of his first acts as president, however, Ronald Reagan rescinded the order. Later in his administration, the law that formerly prohibited U.S. pharmaceutical companies from exporting drugs that are banned or not registered in this country was weakened to allow the export to 21 countries of drugs not yet approved for use in the United States.

But even if communication procedures were improved or the export of dangerous products forbidden, there are ways that companies can circumvent these threats to their profits—for example, by simply changing the name of the product or by exporting the individual ingredients of a product to a plant in a foreign country. Once there, the ingredients can be reassembled and the product dumped.[5] Upjohn, for example, through its Belgian subsidiary, continues to produce Depo-Provera, which the FDA has consistently refused to approve for use in this country. And the prohibition on the export of dangerous drugs is not that hard to sidestep. "Unless the package bursts open on the dock," one drug company executive observes, "you have no chance of being caught."

Unfortunately for us, in the case of pesticides, the effects of overseas dumping are now coming home. The Environmental Protection Agency bans from the United States all crop uses of DDT and Dieldrin, which kill fish, cause tumors in animals, and build up in the fatty tissue of humans. It also bans heptachlor, chlordane, leptophos, endrin, and many other pesticides, including 2,4,5-T (which contains the deadly poison dioxin, the active ingredient in Agent Orange, the notorious defoliant used in Vietnam) because they are dangerous to human beings. No law, however, prohibits the sale of DDT and these other U.S.-banned pesticides overseas, where thanks to corporate dumping, they are routinely used in agriculture. The FDA now estimates, through spot checks, that 10 percent of our imported food is contaminated with illegal residues of banned pesticides. And the FDA's most commonly used testing procedure does not even check for 70 percent of the pesticides known to cause cancer.

SOURCE: Adapted by permission from William Shaw and Vincent Barry, "Made in the U.S.A.: Dumped in Brazil, Africa . . .", *Moral Issues in Business*, 6th ed. (New York: Wadsworth, 1995): 28–31. Copyright © 1995 by Wadsworth Inc.

Questions

1. Was the dumping in this case ethical? Those involved in the dumping might have argued that the people receiving the pajamas would not have otherwise had access to such clothing and were notified of the health and safety hazards. Does this affect your feelings about the case? What do you think about the exportation of the Dalkon Shield? Can it be justified because the rate of dying during childbirth in Third World countries is extremely high, and, as such, any effective birth control device is better than none?

2. What obligations did the financial managers have to their shareholders to do whatever is possible to avoid major financial losses associated with these products?

3. Is it still immoral or unethical to dump goods when doing so does not violate any U.S. laws? How about when those receiving the goods know the dangers? Why do you think dumpers dump? Do you think they believe what they are doing is ethically acceptable?

[5]Mark Dowie, "A Dumper's Guide to Tricks of the Trade," *Mother Jones* (November 1979): 25.

SELF-TEST SOLUTION

SS-1: Project A:

Year	(A) Expected Cash Flow	(B) α_t	(A · B) (Expected Cash Flow) × (α_t)	Present Value Factor at 8%	Present Value
0	−$300,000	1.00	−$300,000	1.000	−$300,000
1	100,000	.95	95,000	0.926	87,970
2	200,000	.90	180,000	0.857	154,260
3	200,000	.85	170,000	0.794	134,980
4	300,000	.80	240,000	0.735	176,400
5	300,000	.75	225,000	0.681	153,225
					$NPV_A = \$406,835$

Project B:

Year	(A) Expected Cash Flow	(B) α_t	(A · B) (Expected Cash Flow) × (α_t)	Present Value Factor at 8%	Present Value
0	−$300,000	1.00	−$300,000	1.000	−$300,000
1	200,000	.90	180,000	0.926	166,680
2	200,000	.80	160,000	0.857	137,120
3	200,000	.70	140,000	0.794	111,160
4	300,000	.60	180,000	0.735	132,300
5	400,000	.50	200,000	0.681	136,200
					$NPV_A = \$383,460$

Thus project A should be selected, because it has the higher NPV.

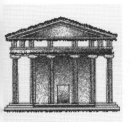
Learning Objectives

Active Applications

World Finance

Practice

CHAPTER 12

Cost of Capital

LEARNING OBJECTIVES

After reading this chapter, you should be able to

1. Describe the concepts underlying the firm's cost of capital (technically, its weighted average cost of capital) and the purpose for its calculation.

2. Calculate the after-tax cost of debt, preferred stock, and common equity.

3. Calculate a firm's weighted average cost of capital.

4. Describe the procedure used by PepsiCo to estimate the cost of capital for a multiple division firm.

5. Use the cost of capital to evaluate new investment opportunities.

6. Compute the economic profit earned by the firm and use quantity to calculate incentive-based compensation.

INTRODUCTION

Encore, Inc. and H&L Manufacturing are both faced with the need to assess financial performance. In one case, it is the anticipated performance of a new capital investment, and in the other, it is the performance of the firm as a whole. Consider the following scenarios:

- The Morristown division of Encore, Inc. is faced with an investment opportunity that requires the investment of $75 million to construct a new shipping and distribution facility. The new facility will free up existing factory space for additional productive capacity that the firm needs to meet growing demand.
- The management of H&L Manufacturing Company is trying to come to grips with the company's overall performance. Profits have grown by more than 20 percent per year over the past 5 years, but the firm's stock price has not kept pace with those of competitor firms.

Encore needs a benchmark return that can be used to evaluate whether the anticipated return from the new shipping and distribution investment is going to create or destroy shareholder wealth. H&L, on the other hand, needs a benchmark return to compare against the performance of the entire firm.

In this chapter, we will learn that the benchmark return that is appropriate in both instances is the firm's cost of capital. We recognize the first problem as the capital-budgeting problem introduced earlier in chapter 9. The second problem is the focal point of shareholder value based management (SVBM).

CHAPTER PREVIEW

Having studied the linkage between risk and rates of return for securities (chapter 6) and the valuation of bonds and stocks (chapters 7 and 8), we are prepared to consider the firm's cost of capital. A firm's cost of capital serves as the linkage between the firm's financing decisions and its investment decisions. The cost of capital becomes the hurdle rate that must be achieved by an investment before it will increase shareholder wealth. The term *cost of capital* is frequently used interchangeably with the firm's *required rate of return*, the *hurdle rate for new investments*, the *discount rate for evaluating a new investment,* and the firm's *opportunity cost of funds*. Regardless of the term used, the basic concept is the same. The cost of capital is that rate which must be earned on an investment project if the project is to increase the value of the common stockholder's investment in the project.

The cost of capital is also the appropriate basis for evaluating the performance of a division or even an entire firm. In this case, the cost of capital becomes the key determinant of the capital cost associated with a firm's investments. We will use economic profit to provide such a measure of performance.

In this chapter, we will discuss the fundamental determinants of a firm's cost of capital as well as the rationale for its calculation and use. This will entail developing the logic for estimating the cost of debt capital, preferred stock, and common stock. Chapter 14 takes up consideration of the impact of the firm's financing mix on the cost of capital.

This chapter emphasizes Axioms 1, 2, 3, 6, 8, and 9: Axiom 1: The Risk-Return Trade-Off—We Won't Take on Additional Risk Unless We Expect to Be Compensated with Additional Return; Axiom 2: The Time Value of Money—A Dollar Received Today Is Worth More Than a Dollar Received in the Future; Axiom 3: Cash—Not Profits—Is King; Axiom 6: Efficient Capital Markets—The Markets Are Quick and the Prices Are Right; Axiom 8: Taxes Bias Business Decisions; Axiom 9: All Risk Is Not Equal—Some Risk Can Be Diversified Away, and Some Cannot.

OBJECTIVE 1

THE COST OF CAPITAL: KEY DEFINITIONS AND CONCEPTS

Investor Opportunity Costs, Required Rates of Return, and the Cost of Capital

Investor's required rate of return

The minimum rate of return necessary to attract an investor to purchase or hold a security.

In chapter 9, we referred to the discount rate used in calculating NPV simply as the appropriate discount rate. In this chapter, we define what we mean by this term. Specifically, the appropriate discount rate primarily reflects the **investor's required rate of return**. In chapter 6, we defined the investor's required rate of return for a security as the *minimum rate of return necessary to attract an investor to purchase or hold a security.* This rate of return considers the investor's opportunity cost of making an investment; that is, if an investment is made, the investor must forgo the return available on the next-best investment. This forgone return is the opportunity cost of undertaking the investment and, consequently, is the investor's required rate of return.

Is the investor's required rate of return the same thing as the cost of capital? Not exactly. Two basic considerations drive a wedge between the investor's required rate of return and the cost of capital to the firm. First, there are taxes. When a firm borrows money to finance the purchase of an asset, the interest expense is deductible for federal income tax calculations. Consider a firm that borrows at 9 percent and then deducts its interest expense from its revenues before paying taxes at a rate of 34 percent. For each dollar of interest it pays, the firm reduces its taxes by $.34. Consequently, the actual cost of borrowing to the firm is only 5.94% [$.09 - (.34 \times .09) = .09(1 - .34) = 0.0594 = 5.94\%$]. The second thing that causes the firm's cost of capital to differ from the investor's required rate of return is any transaction costs incurred when a firm raises funds by issuing a particular type of security, sometimes called **flotation costs**. For example, if a firm sells new shares for $25 per share but incurs transaction costs of $5 per share, then the cost of capital for the new common equity is increased. Assume that the investor's required rate of return is 15 percent for each $25 share, then $.15 \times \$25 = \$3.75$ must be earned each year to satisfy the investor's required return. However, the firm has only $20 to invest, so the cost of capital (k) is calculated as the rate of return that must be earned on the $20 net proceeds, which will produce a dollar return of $3.75; that is,

$$\$20k = \$25 \times .15 = \$3.75$$

$$k = \frac{\$3.75}{\$20.00} = .1875 = 18.75\%$$

We will have more to say about both these considerations as we discuss the costs of the individual sources of capital to the firm.

Financial Policy and the Cost of Capital

A firm's **financial policy**—that is, the policies regarding the sources of finances it plans to use and the particular mix (proportions) in which they will be used, governs its use of debt and equity financing. The particular mixture of debt and equity that the firm utilizes can impact the firm's cost of capital. However, in this chapter, we will assume that the firm maintains a fixed financial policy that is reflected in a fixed debt-equity ratio. Determination of the target mix of debt and equity financing is the subject of chapter 14.

The firm's overall cost of capital will reflect the combined costs of all the sources of financing used by the firm. We will refer to this overall cost of capital as the firm's **weighted average cost of capital**. The weighted average cost of capital is the average of the after-tax costs of each of the sources of capital used by a firm to finance a project where the weights reflect the proportion of total financing raised from each source. Consequently, the weighted average cost of capital is the rate of return that the firm must earn on its investments so that it can compensate both its creditors and stockholders with their individual required rates of return. Let's now turn to a discussion of how the costs of debt and equity can be estimated.

Flotation costs

The underwriter's spread and issuing costs associated with the issuance and marketing of new securities.

Financial policy

The firm's policies regarding the sources financing and the particular mix in which they will be used.

Weighted average cost of capital

The average of the after-tax costs of each of the sources of capital used by a firm to finance a project. The weights reflect the proportion of the total financing raised from each source.

DETERMINING INDIVIDUAL COSTS OF CAPITAL

OBJECTIVE 2

In order to attract new investors, companies have created a wide variety of financing instruments or securities. In this chapter, we will stick to three basic types of financing instruments: debt, preferred stock, and common stock. In calculating the respective cost of financing from each of these types of financing instruments, we estimate the investor's required rate of return properly adjusted for any transaction or flotation costs associated with each funding source. In addition, because we will be discounting after-tax cash flows, we should adjust our cost of capital for any influence of corporate taxes. In summary, the cost of a particular source of capital is equal to the investor's required rate of return after adjusting for the effects of both flotation costs and corporate taxes.

The Cost of Debt

The investor's required rate of return on debt is simply the return that creditors demand on new borrowing. In chapter 7, we estimated this required rate of return by solving the following bond valuation equation:

$$P_d = \sum_{t=1}^{n} \frac{\text{interest paid in period } t(I_t)}{(1 + \text{bondholder's required rate of return } (k_d))^t} +$$
$$\frac{\text{maturity value of the debt } (\$M)}{(1 + \text{bondholder's required rate of return } (k_d))^n} \tag{12-1}$$

where P_d is the market price of the debt security and n is the number of periods to maturity. Should the firm incur flotation costs such as brokerage commissions and legal and accounting fees in issuing the debt, then the cost of debt capital, k_d, is found as follows:

$$\begin{array}{c}\text{net proceeds}\\\text{per bond } (NP_d)\end{array} = \sum_{t=1}^{n} \frac{\$I_t}{(1 + \$k_d)^t} + \frac{\$M}{(1 + k_d)^n} \tag{12-2}$$

The adjustment for flotation costs simply involves replacing the market price of the bond with the net proceeds per bond (NP_d) received by the firm after paying these costs. The result of this adjustment is that the discount rate that solves equation (12-2) is now the firm's cost of debt financing before adjusting for the effect of corporate taxes—that is, the before-tax cost of debt (k_d). The final adjustment we make is to account for the fact that interest is tax deductible. Thus the after-tax cost of debt capital is simply $k_d(1 - T_c)$, where T_c is the corporate tax rate.

As we learned in chapter 6, the interest payments on bonds are generally the same for each period. Under these conditions, equation (12-2) can be restated using the interest factors in the present value tables in appendices B and C as follows:

$$NP_d = \$I_t(PVIFAk_{d,n}) + \$M(PVIFk_{d,n}) \tag{12-2a}$$

RELATE TO THE BIG PICTURE

*When we calculate the bondholder's required rate of return, we are discounting the interest and principal payments to the bondholder back to the present using a discount rate that makes this present value equal the current price of the firm's bonds. In essence, we are valuing the bond, which relies on two basic axioms of finance: **Axiom 1: The Risk-Return Trade-Off—We Won't Take on Additional Risk Unless We Expect to Be Compensated with Additional Return**, and **Axiom 2: The Time Value of Money—A Dollar Received Today Is Worth More Than a Dollar Received in the Future.***

*In addition, the calculation of the bondholder's required rate of return relies on the observed market price of the firm's bonds to be an accurate reflection of their worth. Buyers and sellers only stop trading when they are convinced that the price properly reflects all available information. **Axiom 6: Efficient Capital Markets—The Markets Are Quick and the Prices Are Right**. What we mean here, very simply, is that investors are ever vigilant and quickly act on information that affects the riskiness and, consequently, the price of a firm's bonds and other securities.*

EXAMPLE: THE COST OF DEBT CAPITAL

Synopticom, Inc. plans a bond issue for the near future and wants to estimate its current cost of debt capital. After talking with the firm's investment banker, the firm's chief financial officer has determined that a 20-year maturity bond with a

$1,000 face value and 8 percent coupon (paying 8% × $1,000 = $80 per year in interest) can be sold to investors for $908.32. Equation (12–1) can be used to solve for the investor's required rate of return as we illustrated chapter 6. In this case, Synopticom's creditors require a 9 percent rate of return. The cost of capital to the firm is higher than 9 percent, however, because the firm will have to pay flotation costs of $58.32 per bond when it issues the securities. The flotation costs reduce the net proceeds to Synopticom to $850. Substituting into equation (12–2), we find that the before-tax cost of capital for the bond issue is 9.75 percent. Once again, we can solve equation (12–2) using a financial calculator as we illustrate in the margin.

One final adjustment is necessary to obtain the firm's after-tax cost of debt capital. Assuming that Synopticom is in the 34 percent corporate income tax bracket, we estimate the after-tax cost of debt capital as follows:

after-tax cost of debt = $k_d(1 - T_c)$

after-tax cost of debt = $9.75\%(1 - .34) = 6.435\%$

RELATE TO THE BIG PICTURE

*The tax deductibility of interest expense makes debt financing less costly to the firm. This is an example of **Axiom 8: Taxes Bias Business Decisions**. The tax deductibility of interest, other things remaining constant, serves to encourage firms to use more debt in their capital structure than they might otherwise use.*

The Cost of Preferred Stock

Determining the cost of preferred stock is very straightforward because of the simple nature of the cash flows paid to the holders of preferred shares. You will recall from chapter 7 that the value of a preferred stock is simply

$$\frac{\text{Price of}}{\text{preferred stock } (P_{ps})} = \frac{\text{preferred stock dividend}}{\text{required rate of return for preferred stockholder}} \quad (12\text{-}3)$$

where P_{ps} is the current market price of the preferred shares. Solving for the preferred stockholder's required rate of return, we get the following:

$$\frac{\text{Required rate of return}}{\text{for preferred stockholder}} = \frac{\text{preferred stock dividend}}{\text{price of preferred stock}} \quad (12\text{-}4)$$

Once again, where flotation costs are incurred when new preferred shares are sold, the investor's required rate of return is less than the cost of preferred capital to the firm. To calculate the cost of preferred stock, we must adjust the required rate of return to reflect these flotation costs. We replace the price of a preferred share in equation (12-4) with the net proceeds per share from the sale of new preferred shares (NP_{ps}). The resulting formula can be used to calculate the cost of preferred stock to the firm.

$$\text{cost of preferred stock } (k_{ps}) = \frac{\text{preferred stock dividend}}{\text{net proceeds per preferred share}} \quad (12\text{-}5)$$

What about corporate taxes? In the case of preferred stock, no tax adjustment must be made because preferred dividends are not tax deductible.

EXAMPLE: THE COST OF PREFERRED STOCK

On January 10, 1996, AmaxGold had an issue of preferred stock that traded on the NYSE. The issue paid an annual dividend of $3.75 per share and the preferred stock price closed at $60.375. Assume that if the firm were to sell an issue of preferred stock with the same characteristics as its outstanding issue, it would incur flotation costs of $2.375 per share and the shares would sell for their January 10, 1996, closing price. What is AmaxGold's cost of preferred stock?

Substituting into equation (12-5), we get the following cost of preferred stock for AmaxGold:

$$k_{ps} = \frac{\$3.75}{(\$60.375 - \$2.375)} = .06465 \text{ or } 6.465\%$$

Note that there is no adjustment for taxes, as preferred dividends are not tax deductible—that is, preferred dividends are paid after corporate taxes, unlike bond interest, which is paid with before-tax dollars.

The Cost of Common Equity

Common equity is unique in two respects. First, the cost of common equity is more difficult to estimate than the cost of debt or preferred stock because the common stockholder's required rate of return is not observable. This results from the fact that common stockholders are the residual owners of the firm, which means that their return is equal to what is left of the firm's earnings after paying the firm's bondholders their contractually set interest and principal payments and the preferred stockholders their promised dividends. Second, common equity can be obtained from either the retention of firm earnings or through the sale of new shares. The cost associated with each of these sources is different from one another because the firm does not incur any flotation costs when it retains earnings but does when it sells new common shares.

We discuss two methods for estimating the common stockholder's required rate of return, which is the foundation for our estimate of the firm's cost of equity capital. These methods are based on the dividend growth model and the capital asset pricing model, which were both discussed earlier in chapter 8 when we discussed stock valuation.

The Dividend Growth Model

Recall from chapter 8 that the value of a firm's common stock is equal to the present value of all future dividends. Where dividends are expected to grow at a rate g forever and this rate g is less than the investor's required rate of return, k_{cs}, then the value of a share of common stock, P_{cs}, can be written as:

$$P_{cs} = \frac{D_1}{k_{cs} - g} \tag{12-6}$$

where D_1 is the dividend expected to be received by the firm's common shareholders 1 year hence. The expected dividend is simply equal to the current dividend multiplied by 1 plus the annual rate of growth in dividends (i.e., $D_1 = D_0(1 + g)$). The investor's required rate of return then is found by solving equation (12-6) for k_{cs}.

$$k_{cs} = \frac{D_1}{P_{cs}} + g \tag{12-7}$$

Note that k_{cs} is the investor's required rate of return for investing in the firm's stock. It also serves as our estimate of the cost of equity capital, where new equity capital is obtained by retaining a part of the firm's current period earnings. Recall that common equity financing can come from one of two sources: the retention of earnings (i.e., earnings not paid out in dividends to the common stockholders) or from the sale of new common shares. When the firm retains earnings, it doesn't incur any flotation costs, thus the investor's required rate of return is the same as the firm's cost of new equity capital in this instance.

If the firm issues new shares to raise equity capital, then it incurs flotation costs. Once again we adjust the investor's required rate of return for flotation costs by substituting the net proceeds per share, NP_{cs}, for the stock price, P_{cs}, in equation (12-7) to estimate the cost of new common stock, k_{ncs}.

$$k_{ncs} = \frac{D_1}{NP_{cs}} + g \qquad (12\text{-}8)$$

EXAMPLE: ESTIMATING THE COST OF COMMON STOCK USING THE DIVIDEND GROWTH MODEL

The Talbot Corporation's common shareholders anticipate receiving a $2.20 per share dividend next year based on the fact that they received $2 last year and expect dividends to grow 10 percent next year. Furthermore, analysts predict that dividends will continue to grow at a rate of 10 percent into the foreseeable future. Given that the firm's stock is trading for $50 per share, we can calculate the investor's required rate of return (and the cost of retained earnings) as follows:

$$k_{cs} = \frac{D_1}{P_{cs}} + g = \frac{\$2.20}{\$50.00} + .10 = .144 \text{ or } 14.4\%$$

Should Talbot decide to issue new common stock, then it would incur a cost of $7.50 per share, or 15 percent of the current stock price. The resulting cost of new common equity capital would be:

$$k_{ncs} = \frac{D_1}{NP_{cs}} + g = \frac{\$2.20}{\$50 - 7.50} + .10 = .1518 \text{ or } 15.18\%$$

Thus Talbot faces two costs of capital with respect to common equity. If it retains earnings, then the cost of capital to the firm is 14.4 percent, and if it issues new common stock, the corresponding cost is 15.18 percent. This difference will prove to be important later when we calculate the overall or weighted average cost of capital for the firm.

RELATE TO THE BIG PICTURE

The dividend growth model for common stock valuation relies on three of the fundamental axioms of finance. First, stock value is equal to the present value of expected future dividends. This reflects **Axiom 2: The Time Value of Money—A Dollar Received Today Is Worth More Than a Dollar Received in the Future**. *Furthermore, dividends represent actual cash receipts to stockholders and are incorporated into the valuation model in a manner that reflects the timing of their receipt. This attribute of the dividend growth model reflects* **Axiom 3: Cash—Not Profits—Is King**. *Finally, the rate used to discount the expected future dividends back to the present reflects the riskiness of the dividends. The higher the riskiness of the dividend payments, the higher the investor's required rate of return. This reflects* **Axiom 1: The Risk-Return Trade-Off—We Won't Take on Additional Risk Unless We Expect to Be Compensated with Additional Return**.

Issues in Implementing the Dividend Growth Model

The principal advantage of the dividend growth model is its simplicity. To estimate an investor's required rate of return, the analyst needs only to observe the current dividend and stock price and to estimate the rate of growth in future dividends. The primary drawback relates to the applicability or appropriateness of the valuation model. That is, the dividend growth model is based on the fundamental assumption that dividends are expected to grow at a constant rate g forever. To avoid this assumption, analysts frequently utilize more complex valuation models in which dividends are expected to grow for, say, 5 years at one rate and then grow at a lower rate from year 6 forward. We will not consider these more complex models here.

Even if the constant growth rate assumption is acceptable, we must arrive at an estimate of that growth rate. We could estimate the rate of growth in historical dividends ourselves or go to published sources of growth rate expectations. Investment advisory services such as Value Line provide their own analysts' estimates of earnings growth rates (generally spanning up to 5 years), and the Institutional Brokers' Estimate System (I/B/E/S) collects and publishes earnings per share forecasts made by over 1,000 analysts for a broad list of stocks. These estimates are helpful but still require the careful judgment of the analyst in their use, because they relate to earnings (not dividends) and only extend 5 years into the future (not forever, as required by the dividend growth model). Nonetheless, these estimates provide a useful guide to making your initial dividend growth rate estimate.

We do have some scientific evidence regarding the usefulness of analysts' earnings growth rate estimates in the estimation of investors' required rates of return on common stocks. Although the period covered by the study is dated (1982 to 1984), it provides some interesting insights into investors' required rates of return for common stocks. Robert Harris studied the use of analysts' forecasts in conjunction with the dividend growth model to compute required rates of return for the stocks in the Standard and Poor's 500 Index.[1] In his study, Harris calculated an average of the analysts' forecasts of 5-year growth rates in earnings for all stocks in the S&P 500 Index for each quarter during 1982 to 1984. He then used these averages as proxies for the growth rates in dividends for each quarter. Second, using the dividend growth model, found in equation (12-7), he estimated an average cost of equity for all 500 stocks for each quarter in his study period. These costs of equity capital estimates were compared to the average yield on U.S. government bonds to calculate the implied risk premium for the average stock in the index. (Recall that a risk premium is simply the difference in the rate of return on a risky security such as a share of common stock and a less risky security such as a U.S. government bond.) The results, presented in Table 12.1, suggest that common stockholders had a required rate of return of 17.26 percent to 20.08 percent for the average stock in the S&P 500 Index throughout this time period. The average cost of equity capital over the entire period was 18.41 percent, and the average risk premium averaged 6.16 percent (ranging from 4.78 percent to 7.16 percent). These figures give us some insight into the basic magnitudes of the cost of equity capital for the very large and established companies that comprise the Standard and Poor's 500 Index and the corresponding risk premiums.

The Capital Asset Pricing Model

Capital asset pricing model

A statement of the relationship between expected returns and risk in which risk is captured by the systematic risk (beta) for the risky asset. The expected return is equal to the sum of the risk-free rate of interest and a risk premium equal to the product of beta and the market risk premium.

Recall from chapter 8 that the **capital asset pricing model (CAPM)** provides a basis for determining the investor's expected or required rate of return from investing in common stock. The model depends on three things:

1. the risk-free rate, k_{rf};
2. the systematic risk of the common stock's returns relative to the market as a whole or the stock's beta coefficient, β; and
3. the market risk premium, which is equal to the difference in the expected rate of return for the market as a whole; that is, the expected rate of return for the "average security" minus the risk-free rate, or in symbols, $k_m - k_{rf}$.

---

[1]Robert Harris, "Using Analysts' Forecasts to Estimate Shareholder Required Returns," *Financial Management* (Spring 1986): 510–67.

BASIC FINANCIAL MANAGEMENT IN PRACTICE

IPOs: Should a Firm Go Public?

(A) When a privately owned company decides to distribute its shares to the general public, it goes through a process known as initial public offering or IPO. There are a number of advantages to having a firm's shares traded in the public equity market. These include the following:

- **New capital is raised.** When the firm sells its shares to the public, it acquires new capital that can be invested in the firm.
- **The firm's owners gain liquidity of their share holdings.** Publicly traded shares are more easily bought and sold so that the owners can more easily liquidate all or a part of their interest in the firm.
- **The firm gains future access to the public capital market.** Once a firm has raised capital in the public markets, it is easier to go back a second and third time.
- **Being a publicly traded firm may benefit the firm's business.** Public firms tend to enjoy a higher profile than their privately held counterparts. This may make it easier to make sales and attract vendors to supply goods and services to the firm.

(B) However, all is not rosy as a publicly held firm. There are a number of potential disadvantages including the following:

- **Reporting requirements can be onerous.** Publicly held firms are required to file periodic reports with the Securities and Exchange Commission (SEC). This is not only onerous in terms of the time and effort required, but some business owners feel they must reveal information to their competitors that could be potentially damaging.

- Private equity investors now must share any new wealth with the new public investors. Now that the firm is a publicly held company, the new shareholders share on an equal footing with the company founders in the good (and bad) fortune of the firm.
- **The private investors lose a degree of control of the organization.** Outsiders gain voting control over the firm to the extent that they own its shares.
- **An IPO is expensive.** A typical firm may spend 15 to 25 percent of the money raised on expenses directly connected to the IPO. This cost is increased further if we consider the cost of lost management time and disruption of business associated with the IPO process.
- **Exit of company owners is usually limited.** The company founders may want to sell their shares through the IPO, but this is not allowed for an extended period of time. Therefore, the IPO is not usually a good mechanism for cashing out the company founders.
- **Everyone involved faces legal liability.** The IPO participants are jointly and severally liable for each others' actions. This means that they can be sued for any omissions from the IPO prospectus should the public market valuation fall below the IPO offering price.

A careful weighing of the financial consequences of each of these advantages and disadvantages can provide a company's owners (and management) with some basis for answering the question of whether they want to become a public corporation.

Other sources: Professor Ivo Welch's Web site at http://linux.agsm.ucla.edu/ipo/ provides a wealth of information concerning IPOs.

Analysis and Implications …

A. Many owners of small businesses believe than an IPO is the "Holy Grail" that marks the success of their businesses. This is a misleading view, however. In fact, not every firm should look toward the IPO as a desirable thing. To see if the IPO is right for your firm, you need to consider the importance of the advantages of public ownership. For example, does the firm need additional capital? Would public ownership benefit the firm's business? Is access to the public capital market necessary to provide capital in the amounts needed to meet the firm's future growth opportunities?

B. If none of the previous advantages of an IPO apply to your firm, then perhaps the IPO is not right for your firm. Furthermore, IPOs carry with them a number of costly disadvantages. Being a public firm requires that the firm file accounting information with the SEC. In addition, the new public market shareholders demand a "piece of the equity return pie" from the firm's current stockholders. They also gain a measure of control over the firm in proportion to the new shares issued. Finally, an IPO can be quite expensive.

Table 12.1 Required Rates of Return and Risk Premiums (%)

| | | S&P 500 | |
	Government Bond Yield	Required Return	Risk Premium
1982			
Quarter 1	14.27	20.81	6.54
Quarter 2	13.74	20.68	6.94
Quarter 3	12.94	20.23	7.29
Quarter 4	10.72	18.58	7.86
Average	12.92	20.08	7.16
1983			
Quarter 1	10.87	18.07	7.20
Quarter 2	10.80	17.76	6.96
Quarter 3	11.79	17.90	6.11
Quarter 4	11.90	17.81	5.91
Average	11.34	17.88	6.54
1984			
Quarter 1	12.09	17.22	5.13
Quarter 2	13.21	17.42	4.21
Quarter 3	12.83	17.34	4.51
Quarter 4	11.78	17.05	5.27
Average	12.48	17.26	4.78
Average 1982–1984	12.25	18.41	6.16

SOURCE: Robert Harris, "Using Analysts' Forecasts to Estimate Shareholder Required Returns," *Financial Management* (Spring 1986): 62. Used by permission of Financial Management Association International, College of Business Administration, University of South Florida, Tampa, FL 33620, (813) 974-2084.

Using the CAPM, the investor's required rate of return can be written as follows:

$$k_c = k_{rf} + \beta(k_m - k_{rf})$$

(12-9)

EXAMPLE: ESTIMATING THE COST OF COMMON STOCK USING THE CAPM

The Talbot Corporation's common stock has a beta coefficient of 0.82. Furthermore, the risk-free rate is currently 7 percent, and the expected rate of return on the market portfolio of all risky assets is 16 percent. Using the CAPM from equation (12-9), we can estimate Talbot's cost of capital as follows:

$$k_c = k_{rf} + \beta(k_m - k_{rf})$$
$$= 7\% + .82(16\% - 7\%) = .144 \text{ or } 14.4\%$$

Note that the required rate of return we have estimated is the cost of internal common equity, because no transaction costs are considered.

Issues in Implementing the CAPM

The CAPM approach has two primary advantages. First, the model is simple and easy to understand and implement. The model variables are readily available from public sources with the possible exception of beta coefficients for small and/or non–publicly traded firms. Second, because the model does not rely on dividends or any assumption about the growth rate in dividends, it can be applied to companies that do not currently pay dividends or are not expected to experience a constant rate of growth in dividends.

Using the CAPM requires that we obtain estimates of each of the three model variables—k_{rf}, β, and $(k_m - k_{rf})$. Let's consider each in turn. First, the analyst has a wide range of U.S. government securities upon which to base an estimate of the risk-free rate. Treasury securities with maturities from 30 days to 20 years are readily available, but the CAPM offers no guidance as to the appropriate choice. In fact, the model itself assumes that there is but one risk-free rate, and it corresponds to a one-period return (the length of the period is not specified, however). Consequently, we are left to our own judgment as to which maturity we should use to represent the risk-free rate. For applications of the cost of capital involving long-term capital expenditure decisions, it seems reasonable to select a risk-free rate of comparable maturity. So, if we are calculating the cost of capital to be used as the basis for evaluating investments that will provide returns over the next 20 years, it seems appropriate to use a risk-free rate corresponding to a U.S. Treasury bond of comparable maturity.

Second, estimates of security beta coefficients are available from a wide variety of investment advisory services, including Merrill Lynch and Value Line, among others. Alternatively, we could collect historical stock market returns for the company of interest as well as a general market index (such as the Standard and Poor's 500 Index) and estimate the stock's beta as the slope of the relationship between the two return series—as we did in chapter 6. However, because beta estimates are widely available for a large majority of publicly traded firms, analysts frequently rely on published sources for betas.

Finally, estimation of the market risk premium can be accomplished by looking at the history of stock returns and the premium earned over (under) the risk-free rate of interest. In chapter 6, we reported a summary of the historical returns earned on risk-free securities and common stocks in Figure 6.2. We saw that on average over the last 70 years, common stocks have earned a premium of roughly 7 percent over long-term government bonds. Thus, for our purposes, we will utilize this estimate of the market risk premium $(k_m - k_{rf})$ when estimating the investor's required rate of return on equity using the CAPM.

RELATE TO THE BIG PICTURE

*The capital asset pricing model, or CAPM, is a formal representation of **Axiom 1: The Risk-Return Trade-Off—We Won't Take on Additional Risk Unless We Expect to Be Compensated with Additional Return**. By "formal" we mean that the specific method of calculating the additional returns needed to compensate for additional risk is specified in the form of an equation—the CAPM. The CAPM's recognition of systematic or non-diversifiable risk as the source of risk that is rewarded in the capital market is a reflection of **Axiom 9: All Risk Is Not Equal—Some Risk Can Be Diversified Away, and Some Cannot**.*

THE WEIGHTED AVERAGE COST OF CAPITAL

OBJECTIVE 3

Now that we have calculated the individual costs of capital for each of the sources of financing the firm might use, we now turn to the combination of these capital costs into a single weighted average cost of capital. To estimate the weighted average cost of capital, we need to know the cost of each of the sources of capital used and the capital structure mix. We use the term **capital structure** to refer to the proportions of each source of financing used by the firm. Although a firm's capital structure can be quite complex, we will focus our examples on the three basic sources of capital: bonds, preferred stock, and common equity.

Capital structure

The mix of long-term sources of funds used by the firm.

In words, we calculate the weighted average cost of capital for a firm that uses only debt and common equity using the following equation:

$$\begin{matrix} \text{Weighted} \\ \text{Average Cost} \\ \text{of Capital} \end{matrix} = \begin{bmatrix} \text{After-Tax} & & \text{Proportion} \\ \text{Cost of} & \times & \text{of Debt} \\ \text{Debt} & & \text{Financing} \end{bmatrix} + \begin{bmatrix} \text{Cost of} & & \text{Proportion} \\ & \times & \text{of Equity} \\ \text{Equity} & & \text{Financing} \end{bmatrix}$$

For example, if a firm borrows money at 6 percent after taxes, pays 10 percent for equity, and raises its capital in equal proportions from debt and equity, its weighted average cost of capital is 8 percent, i.e.,

$$\begin{matrix} \text{Weighted} \\ \text{Average Cost} \\ \text{of Capital} \end{matrix} = [.06 \times .5] + [.10 \times .5] = .08 \ \text{ or } 8\%$$

In practice, the calculation of the cost of capital is generally more complex than this example. For one thing, firms often have multiple debt issues with different required rates of return, and they also use preferred equity as well as common equity financing. Furthermore, when new common equity capital is raised, it is sometimes the result of retaining and reinvesting the firm's current period earnings and, at other times, it involves a new stock offering. In the case of retained earnings, the firm does not incur the costs associated with selling new common stock. This means that equity from retained earnings is less costly than a new stock offering. In the examples that follow, we will address each of these complications.

Capital Structure Weights

We opened this chapter with a description of an investment opportunity faced by the Morristown division of Encore, Inc. A critical element in the analysis of that investment was an estimate of the cost of capital—the discount rate—to be used to calculate the NPV for the project. The reason we calculate a cost of capital is that it enables us to evaluate one or more of the firm's investment opportunities. Remember that the cost of capital should reflect the riskiness of the project being evaluated, so a firm may calculate multiple costs of capital where it makes investments in multiple divisions or business units having different risk characteristics. Thus for the calculated cost of capital to be meaningful, it must correspond directly to the riskiness of the particular project being analyzed. That is, in theory the cost of capital should reflect the particular way in which the funds are raised (the capital structure used) and the systematic risk characteristics of the project. Consequently, the correct way to calculate capital structure weights is to use the actual dollar amounts of the various sources of capital actually used by the firm.[2]

In practice, the mixture of financing sources used by a firm will vary from year to year. For this reason, many firms find it expedient to use **target capital structure proportions** in calculating the firm's weighted average cost of capital. For example, a firm might use its target mix of 40 percent debt and 60 percent equity to calculate its weighted average cost of capital even though, in that particular year, it raised the majority of its financing requirements by borrowing. Similarly, it would continue to use the target proportions in the subsequent year when it might raise the majority of its financing needs by reinvesting earnings or through a new stock offering.

Target capital structure proportions

The mix of financing sources that the firm plans to maintain through time.

---

[2]There are instances when we will want to calculate the cost of capital for the firm as a whole. In this case, the appropriate weights to use are based upon the market value of the various capital sources used by the firm. Market values rather than book values properly reflect the sources of financing used by a firm at any particular point in time. However, where a firm is privately owned, it is not possible to get market values of its securities, and book values are often used.

Table 12.2 Calculating the Weighted Average Cost of Capital

Panel A: Common equity raised by retaining earnings

Source of Capital	Capital Structure Weights	×	Cost of Capital	=	Product
Bonds	w_d		$k_d(1 - T_c)$		$w_d \cdot k_d(1 - T_c)$
Preferred stock	w_{ps}		k_{ps}		$w_{ps} \cdot k_{ps}$
Common equity					
Retained earnings	w_{cs}		k_{cs}		$w_{cs} \cdot k_{cs}$
Sum =	100%				k_{wacc}

Panel B: Common equity raised by selling new common stock

Source of Capital	Capital Structure Weights	×	Cost of Capital	=	Product
Bonds	w_d		$k_d(1 - T_c)$		$w_d \cdot k_d(1 - T_c)$
Preferred stock	w_{ps}		k_{ps}		$w_{ps} \cdot k_{ps}$
Common equity					
New stock offering	w_{ncs}		k_{ncs}		$w_{ncs} \cdot k_{ncs}$
Sum =	100%				k_{wacc}

Calculating the Weighted Average Cost of Capital

The weighted average cost of capital, k_{wacc}, is simply a weighted average of all the capital costs incurred by the firm. Table 12.2 illustrates the procedure used to esimate k_{wacc} for a firm that has debt, preferred stock, and common equity in its target capital structure mix. Note that in Panel A, the firm is able to finance all its target capital structure requirements for common equity through the retention of firm earnings, and in Panel B, it utilizes a new equity offering. For example, if the firm targets 75 percent equity financing and has current earnings of $750,000, then it can raise up to $750,000/.75 = $1,000,000 in new financing before it has to sell new equity. For $1,000,000 or less in capital spending, the firm's weighted average cost of capital would be calculated using the cost of equity from retained earnings (following Panel A of Table 12.2). For more than $1,000,000 in new capital, the cost of capital would rise to reflect the impact of the higher cost of using new common stock (following Panel B of Table 12.2).

EXAMPLE: ESTIMATING THE WEIGHTED AVERAGE COST OF CAPITAL

Ash, Inc.'s capital structure and estimated capital costs are found in Table 12.3. Note that sum of the capital structure weights must sum to 100 percent if we have properly accounted for all sources of financing and in the correct amounts. For example, Ash plans to invest a total of $3 million in common equity into the $5 million investment. Because Ash has earnings equal to the $3,000,000 it needs in new equity financing, the entire amount of new equity will be raised by retaining earnings.

We calculate the weighted average cost of capital following the procedure described in Panel A of Table 12.2 and using the information found in Table 12.3. The resulting calculations are found in Panel A of Table 12.4, in which Ash, Inc.'s weighted average cost of capital for up to $5,000,000 in new financing is found to be 12.7 percent.

If Ash needs more than $5,000,000, then it will not have any retained earnings to provide the additional equity capital. Thus, to maintain its desired 60 percent equity financing proportion, Ash will now have to issue new equity that costs 18 percent.

Table 12.3 Capital Structure and Capital Costs for Ash, Inc.

Source of Capital	Amount of Funds Raised ($)	Percentage of Total	Cost of Capital
Bonds	$1,750,000	35%	7%
Preferred stock	250,000	5%	13%
Common equity			
Retained earnings	3,000,000	60%	16%
	$5,000,000	100%	

Table 12.4 Weighted Average Cost of Capital for Ash, Inc.

Panel A: Cost of capital for $0 to $5,000,000 in new capital

Source of Capital	Capital Structure Weights	Cost of Capital	Product
Bonds	35%	7%	2.45%
Preferred stock	5%	13%	0.65%
Common equity			
Retained earnings	60%	16%	9.60%
	100%	k_{wacc} =	12.70%

Panel B: Cost of capital for more than $5,000,000

Source of Capital	Capital Structure Weights	Cost of Capital	Product
Bonds	35%	7%	2.45%
Preferred stock	5%	13%	0.65%
Common equity			
Common stock	60%	18%	10.80%
	100%		k_{wacc} = 13.90%

Panel B of Table 12.4 contains the calculation of Ash's weighted average cost of capital for more than $5,000,000. The resulting cost is 13.9 percent.

In practice, many firms calculate only one cost of capital using a cost of equity capital that ignores the transaction costs associated with raising new equity capital. In essence, they would use the capital cost calculated for Ash in Panel A Table 12.4 regardless of the level of new financing for the year. Although this is technically incorrect, it is understandable given the difficulties involved in estimating equity capital costs.[3]

COST OF CAPITAL IN PRACTICE: BRIGGS & STRATTON

Briggs & Stratton is the world's largest producer of air-cooled gasoline engines. For many years, the firm also was the world's largest producer of locks for automobiles and trucks. However, on February 27, 1995, the automobile lock business was spun off to the

---

[3]For a discussion of the imprecise nature of equity capital cost estimates, see Eugene F. Fama and Kenneth R. French, 1997 "Industry costs of equity," *Journal of Financial Economics* 43, 153–193.

stockholders, leaving Briggs & Stratton in a single business (producing air-cooled gasoline engines for outdoor power equipment).

Each year Briggs & Stratton engages in the exercise of estimating its cost of capital. The process entails a calculation very similar to that used by the hypothetical Ash, Inc. The differences, as we shall see, relate to simplifications, not additional complexities. The example calculations we present here are for 1995, but they reflect the procedure used by the firm today.

Cost of Equity

Briggs & Stratton uses the CAPM to estimate its cost of equity capital as follows:

$$k_c = k_{rf} + \beta(k_m - k_{rf}) \qquad (12\text{-}9)$$

$$k_c = .0727 + .95(.06) = .1297 \text{ or } 12.97\%$$

The risk-free rate (k_{rf}) is estimated as a weighted average of 30-year government bond interest rates from the April 1994 issues of *The Wall Street Journal*. The firm's beta coefficient (β) is taken from the February 1994 issue of *Value Line*. Finally, the market risk premium $(k_m - k_{rf})$ is estimated as the historical average difference in the return to equities and long-term government bonds.

Note that Briggs & Stratton does not make any adjustment for the influence of transaction costs nor does it bother with the nuance of estimating the fraction of its target equity component that could come from retained earnings.

Cost of Debt

At the close of 1994, Briggs & Stratton estimates the before-tax cost of debt financing to be 8.7 percent. The firm uses its statutory tax rate for fiscal 1994 of 39 percent to calculate the after-tax cost of debt financing as follows:

$$k_d (1 - \text{tax rate}) = .087 (1 - .39) = .0531 \text{ or } 5.31\%$$

Weighted Average Cost of Capital for 1995

The weighted average cost of capital is calculated using the formula very similar to the one laid out in equation (12-2). The only difference—as we see following—is the lumping of all equity financing into one component with no special consideration being given to the cost of retained earnings versus the sale of new equity, i.e.,

$$k_{wacc} = k_d (1 - T_c) w_d + k_c w_{cs} \qquad (12\text{-}10)$$

where k_d and k_c are the costs of debt and equity, T_c is the corporate tax rate, and w_d and w_{cs} are the weights attached to debt and equity, respectively.

Briggs & Stratton bases its capital structure weights upon its target capital structure. The weighted average cost of capital for 1995 is calculated in Table 12.5.

Table 12.5 Weighted Average Cost of Capital for Briggs & Stratton, 1995				
Source of Capital	1994 Capital Split	Percent of Capital	Cost of Capital	Weighted Cost of Capital
Debt	$93.9 million	16.4% ×	5.31% =	.87%
Equity	476.5 million	83.6% ×	12.97% =	10.84%
	$570.4 million	100.0%		11.71%

How Do Managers Resolve Ethical Decisions?

(A) What makes a managerial choice an ethical one? Brief et al.[a.] (1991) suggest that if the decision entails reflection on the moral significance of the choice, then the choice is an ethical one. How do managers resolve ethical dilemmas? There is some evidence suggesting that two factors come to bear on ethical choices: values and accountability.

We will consider two social value systems that are present in Western society, which are particularly relevant to the study of finance. These are the Smithian and Humanitarian value systems. The Smithian system is derived from the writings of the 19th-century moral philosopher and political economist Adam Smith. This value system is reflected in the current-day teachings of economists such as Milton Friedman[b] (1962). Briefly, this system holds that when individuals pursue their own self-interest in the marketplace, they contribute to the good of society. At the firm level, this system provides the basis for the market system and is used as the basis for corporate self-interest. In contrast, the Humanitarian system is based on the fundamental premise of the equality of individuals in society. This system seeks to protect individuals from the harshness of the market system and to promote equality of opportunity.

(B) Personal value systems are not the only influence on managerial decisions that have ethical implications. Managers are influenced by their perception of the value systems of the individuals to whom they are held accountable. That is, ethical choices made by managers are influenced by the values they believe are held by the person to whom they are accountable.[c] Arendt (1951, 1977) provides evidence that suggests that the effects of accountability may be more profound than those of the individual manager's values. Consequently, the potentially overpowering effects of hierarchical accountability may lead individual managers not to construe the moral significance attached to the choices they make. They may see no choice but to comply with the higher authority. Brief et al. (1991) provide empirical evidence bearing on the question of the relative importance of personal values versus accountability in the choices made by individuals. Using a set of experiments involving 135 M.B.A. students, they concluded that personal values may not be related to how an individual chooses to

---

OBJECTIVE 4

CALCULATING DIVISIONAL COSTS OF CAPITAL: PEPSICO, INC.

If a firm operates in multiple industries where each has its own particular risk characteristics, should it use different capital costs for each division? **Axiom 1** suggests that the financial manager should recognize these risk differences in estimating the cost of capital to use in each division. This is exactly what PepsiCo did prior to February 1997, when it operated in three basic industries.

PepsiCo goes to great lengths to estimate the cost of capital for each of its three major operating divisions (restaurants, snack foods, and beverages).[4] We will briefly summarize

---

[4]PepsiCo spun off its restaurants division in February 1997. However, the example used here was based on the pre-spinoff company.

resolve ethical dilemmas when the choices (values) of the higher authority are known explicitly.

© Note that we have not addressed the normative issue: How should ethical dilemmas be resolved? Instead, we have addressed the question, How do managers actually deal with ethical choices? The principal finding of the studies we have reviewed is that the *perceived values of one's superiors* have a profound impact on the way in which a subordinate resolves ethical dilemmas. So choose your superior carefully.

SOURCES: [a]A. Brief, J. M. Dukerich, and L. I. Doran, "Resolving Ethical Dilemmas in Management: Experimental Investigations of Values, Accountability and Choice," *Journal of Applied Social Psychology* 21 (1991): 380–96; [b]M. Friedman, *Capitalism and Freedom* (Chicago: University of Chicago Press, 1962); [c]H. Arendt, *The Origins of Totalitarianism* (New York: Harcourt Brace, 1951); H. Arendt, *Eichmann in Jerusalem* (New York: Penguin Books, 1977).

Analysis and Implications . . .

A. The notions of ethical decision making relies on one's sense of right and wrong which, in turn, influences how we each make judgements. There are two fundamental sources of value systems that have been considered in the analysis of ethical decisions. The first is the basic notion that by working hard to fulfill our own personal ambitions, we contribute not only to our own personal welfare but also to society as a whole. This is the idea of the "invisible hand" put forth by Adam Smith. The second fundamental value system that many of us have is based on our desire to be humane. Humanitarian values rest on the notion that we are all equal as human beings and should be protected from the harsh realities of a purely economic allocation system. This value system does not suggest that we should all be equally wealthy or that we should have equal earnings, but it does provide the basis for social welfare programs and other forms of economic safety nets for individuals in the society.

B. Our personal value system may be a combination of the Smithian and Humanitarian ideas, but these are not the only factors that influence our behavior. Specifically, research has found that individuals are influenced by the perceived values of the person to whom they are accountable. Very simply, subordinates often make choices that they feel are consistent with the values of their bosses rather than following their own values.

C. Positive refers to "what is" whereas normative is used here to refer to "what should be." It is much easier to talk about positive aspects of ethical issues than the normative side of things. The reason is that there is less room for disagreement about observations of actual decision-making practice than there is concerning how those decisions should have been made.

---

the basic elements of the calculations involved in these estimates, including the cost of debt financing, the cost of common equity, the target capital structure weights, and the weighted average cost of capital.

Table 12.6 contains the estimates of the after-tax cost of debt for each of PepsiCo's three divisions. Table 12.7 contains the estimates of the cost of equity capital for each of PepsiCo's three operating divisions using the CAPM. We will not explain the intricacies of their method for estimating divisional betas, except to say that they make use of beta estimates for a number of competitor firms from each of the operating divisions, which involves making appropriate adjustments for differences in the use of financial leverage across the competitor firms used in the analysis.[5]

---

[5]This method of using betas from comparable firms is sometimes referred to as the pure play method, because the analyst seeks independent beta estimates for firms engaged in only one business (i.e., restaurants or beverages). The betas for these pure play companies are then used to estimate the beta for a business or division.

Table 12.6 Estimating PepsiCo's Cost of Debt

	Pretax Cost of Debt	×	(1 − Tax Rate)	After-Tax Cost of Debt
Restaurants	8.93%	×	.62	5.54%
Snack foods	8.43%	×	.62	5.23%
Beverages	8.51%	×	.62	5.28%

Table 12.7 Cost of Equity Capital for PepsiCo's Operating Divisions

	Risk-Free Rate	+	Beta	Expected Market Return	−	Risk-Free Rate	=	Cost of Equity
Restaurants	7.28%	+	1.17	(11.48%	−	7.28%)	=	12.20%
Snack foods	7.28%	+	1.02	(11.48%	−	7.28%)	=	11.56%
Beverages	7.28%	+	1.07	(11.48%	−	7.28%)	=	11.77%

Table 12.8 PepsiCo's Weighted Average Cost of Capital for Each of Its Operating Divisions

	Cost of Equity Times the Target Equity Ratio	+	Cost of Debt Times the Target Debt Ratio	=	Weighted Average Cost of Capital
Restaurants	(12.20%)(0.70)	+	(5.54%)(0.30)	=	10.20%
Snack foods	(11.56%)(0.80)	+	(5.23%)(0.20)	=	10.29%
Beverages	(11.77%)(0.74)	+	(5.28%)(0.26)	=	10.08%

The weighted average cost of capital for each of the divisions is estimated in Table 12.8 using the capital costs estimated in Tables 12.6 and 12.7 and using PepsiCo's target capital structure weights for each operating division. Note that the weighted average costs of capital for all three divisions fall within a very narrow range, between 10.08 percent and 10.29 percent.

OBJECTIVE 5

USING A FIRM'S COST OF CAPITAL TO EVALUATE NEW CAPITAL INVESTMENTS

Now that we have learned the principles used to estimate a firm's cost of capital, it is tempting to use this capital cost to evaluate all the firm's investment opportunities. This can produce some very expensive mistakes. Recall that the cost of capital depends primarily on the use of the funds, not their source. Consequently, the appropriate cost of capital for individual investment opportunities should, in theory and practice, reflect the individual risk characteristics of the investment. With this principle in mind, we reason that the firm's weighted average cost of capital is the appropriate discount rate for estimating a project's NPV only when the project has similar risk characteristics to the firm. This would be true, for example, when the investment involves expanding an existing facility but would not be true when the investment involves entering into a completely new business with different risk characteristics.

What does it mean to say that a firm and an investment opportunity have similar risk characteristics? We can think of an investment's risk characteristics as coming from two sources: business risk and financial risk. By **business risk** we mean the potential variability in the firm's expected earnings before interest and taxes (EBIT). In chapter 6, we learned that investors should not be worried about total variability but should only be concerned about systematic variability. **Financial risk** refers to the added variability in earnings available to a firm's shareholders, and the added chance of insolvency caused by the use of securities bearing a limited rate of return in the firm's financial structure. For example, in chapter 3, we learned that firms that use higher levels of financial leverage also experience higher volatility in earnings available to the common stockholders. This higher volatility leads investors to require higher rates of return, which means a higher cost of capital for the project.

In summary, the firm's weighted average cost of capital is the appropriate discount rate for evaluating the NPV of investments whose business and financial risks are similar to those of the firm as a whole. See Table 12.9 on page 452 for a summary of the formulas involved in estimating the weighted average cost of capital. If either of these sources of project risk is different from the risks of the firm, then the analyst must alter the estimate of the cost of capital to reflect these differences. If financial risk is different, then this calls for the use of different financial mix ratios when calculating the weighted average cost of capital, as well as estimates of individual capital costs that properly reflect these financial risks. If operating-risk characteristics differ, then once again capital costs must be adjusted to reflect this difference. In our discussion of PepsiCo, we saw that it estimates three different weighted average costs of capital to reflect what it feels are meaningful differences in the operating and financial risk characteristics of its three operating divisions. This practice reflects PepsiCo's adherence to the principle that the cost of capital is primarily a function of the use of the capital (i.e., the riskiness of the different operating divisions).

Business risk

The potential variability in a firm's earnings before interest and taxes resulting from the nature of the firm's business endeavors.

Financial risk

The added variability in earnings available to a firm's shareholders and the additional risk of insolvency caused by the use of financing sources that require a fixed return.

RELATE TO THE BIG PICTURE

The firm's weighted average cost of capital provides the appropriate discount rate for evaluating new projects only where the projects offer the same riskiness as the firm as a whole. This limitation of the usefulness of the firm's weighted average cost of capital is a direct extension of **Axiom 1: The Risk-Return Trade-Off—We Won't Take on Additional Risk Unless We Expect to Be Compensated with Additional Return.** *If project risk differs from that of the firm, then the firm's cost of capital (which reflects the risk of the firm's investment portfolio) is no longer the appropriate cost of capital for the project. For this reason, firms that invest in multiple divisions or business units that have different risk characteristics should calculate a different cost of capital for each division. In theory, each individual investment opportunity has its own unique risk attributes and correspondingly should have a unique cost of capital. However, given the impreciseness with which we estimate the cost of capital, we generally calculate the cost of capital for each operating division of the firm, not each project.*

MARKET VALUE ADDED AND ECONOMIC PROFIT

OBJECTIVE 6

In the introduction, we described a firm, H&L Manufacturing, which was trying to come to grips with why its stock price was not growing as rapidly as its competitors. In essence, H&L needs to know whether it is creating or destroying shareholder wealth. How can we tell? The answer is **market value added**, or MVA. MVA is a very simple concept. It represents the difference in the current market value of the firm and the sum of all the funds that have been invested in the firm over its entire operating life. If the market

Market Value Added

Market value of a firm's assets minus the sum total of its invested capital.

Why Do Interest Rates Differ Between Countries?

If borrowers and lenders can freely obtain money in one country and invest it in another, why are interest rates not the same the world over? Stated somewhat differently, if capital markets are fully integrated and money flows to the highest rate of interest, it would seem that the forces of competition would make interest rates the same for a given risk borrower.

Let's consider a hypothetical example to see how this might work. Assume that a U.S. borrower can borrow 1,000 yen in Japan for a 5 percent interest paying back 1,050 yen in 1 year. Alternatively, the U.S. firm can borrow an equivalent amount in the United States and pay 15.5 percent interest. Why the big difference? Is capital 10.5 percent cheaper in Japan, and if so, why don't U.S. firms simply switch to the Japanese capital market for their funds? The answer, as we will now illustrate, lies in the differences in the anticipated rates of inflation for Japan versus the United States.

Although it was not obvious in the preceding example, we assumed a zero rate of inflation for the Japanese economy and a 10 percent rate of inflation for the U.S. economy. With a zero anticipated rate of inflation, the nominal rate of interest in Japan is equal to the real rate of 5 percent. Under these assumptions, the nominal rate in the United States can be calculated using the Fisher model as follows:[*]

$$\text{U.S. nominal rate of interest} = (1 + \text{real rate, U.S.})(1 + \text{inflation rate, U.S.}) - 1$$
$$= (1 + .05)(1.10) - 1 = .155 \text{ or } 15.5\%$$

_____

[*]The Fisher model or Fisher effect was introduced earlier in chapter 2.

To understand the reason for the different interest rates in Japan and the United States, we must extend the Fisher model to its international counterpart.

The International Fisher Effect

In an international context, we must recognize that there can be different rates of inflation among the different countries of the world. For example, the Fisher model for the nominal rate in the home or domestic country ($r_{n,h}$) is a function of the real interest rate in the home country ($r_{r,h}$) and the anticipated rate of inflation in the home country (i_h). For the rate of inflation in the home country, the Fisher relationship can be described as follows:

$$r_{n,h} = (1 + r_{r,h})(1 + i_h) - 1 = r_{r,h} + (i_h)(r_{r,h}) + i_h \quad (1a)$$

Using "f" as a subscript to denote a foreign country, we can define a similar relationship for any foreign country (Japan in our previous example):

$$r_{n,f} = (1 + r_{r,f})(1 + i_f) - 1 = r_{r,f} + (i_f)(r_{r,f}) + i_f \quad (1b)$$

The international version of the Fisher model prescribes that real returns will be equalized across countries through arbitrage, i.e.,

$$r_{r,h} = r_{r,f}$$

Solving for the real rates of interest in (1a) and (1b) and equating the results produces the international version of the Fisher model, i.e.,

$$r_{n,h} - (i_h)(r_{r,h}) - i_h = r_{n,f} - (i_f)(r_{r,f}) - i_f \quad (2)$$

value of the firm exceeds the investment made in the firm, then the firm has created shareholder wealth. MVA is calculated as follows:

$$\text{MVA} = \text{Total Market Value of the Firm} - \text{Invested Capital} \quad (12\text{-}10)$$

Total market value of the firm is simply the sum of the market value of the firm's outstanding shares of stock (current share price times the number of shares outstanding) plus the market value of the firm's debt (book value is frequently substituted). Invested capital is basically the sum total of the money invested in the firm to date. Invested capital is estimated

For simplicity analysts frequently ignore the intermediate product terms on both sides of equation (3) such that equation (2) reduces to the following:

$$r_{n,h} - i_h = r_{n,f} - i_f$$

Rearranging terms, we get the following relationship between nominal interest rates in the domestic and foreign country and the differences in anticipated inflation in the two countries:

$$r_{n,h} - r_{n,f} = i_h - i_f \qquad (3)$$

Thus differences in observed nominal rates of interest should equal differences in the expected rates of inflation between the two countries. This means that when we compare the interest rates for similar loans in two countries and they are not the same, we should immediately suspect that the expected rates of inflation for the two economies differs by an amount roughly equal to the interest rate differential!

Interest Rates and Currency Exchange Rates: Interest Rate Parity

Economists have formalized the relationship between interest rates of different countries in the interest rate parity theorem. This theorem is as follows:

$$\frac{(1 + r_{n,h})}{(1 + r_{n,f})} = \frac{E_1}{E_0} \qquad (4)$$

where $r_{n,h}$ is the domestic one-period rate of interest, $r_{n,f}$ is the corresponding rate of interest in a foreign

country and the E_j are exchange rates corresponding to the current period (i.e., the spot rate, E_0) and one-period hence (i.e., the one-period forward rate, E_1).

To illustrate, let's consider the previous example where the domestic one-period interest rate $(r_{n,h})$ is 15.5 percent, the Japanese rate of interest $(r_{n,f})$ is 5 percent, the spot exchange ratio (E_0) is \$1 to 1 yen and the forward exchange rate (E_1) is \$1.10 to 1 yen. Substituting into equation (1) produces the following result:

$$\frac{(1 + .155)}{(1 + .05)} = \frac{1.1}{1} = 1.10$$

The key thing to note here is that nominal interest rates are tied to exchange rates, and as we learned earlier, differences in nominal rates of interest are tied to expected rates of inflation.

Why would we expect the interest rate parity relationship to hold? The answer lies in the greed of investors who stand ready to engage in arbitrage (trading) to enforce this relationship (within the bounds of transaction costs). Formally, we rely on the fundamental dictum of an efficient market (the law of one price). Very simply, the exchange-adjusted prices of identical loand must be within transaction costs of equality or the opportunity exists for traders to buy the low cost loan and sell the higher priced loan for a profit.

SOURCE: W. Carl Kester and Timothy A. Luehrman, "What Makes You Think U.S. Capital Is So Expensive?" *Journal of Applied Corporate Finance* (Summer 1992): 29–41.

by adjusting the firm's book value of total assets for things such as R&D expense and allowances for doubtful accounts receivable, which are not included in the total assets of the firm but, nonetheless, represent dollars that have been invested in the firm.[6]

In essence, MVA is the net present value of all the firm's investments. A firm that is using its investments to produce what investors perceive to be positive net present values will have a positive MVA. Similarly, a firm that is using its invested capital in ways that investors feel destroys value will have a negative MVA. Note that because the market value of the firm's securities is based on expected future cash flows, MVA is a reflection of the

---

[6]We will not go into the adjustments that are made to a firm's book assets to measure invested capital. The adjustments add equity equivalent reserves to capital and periodic changes in those reserves to after-tax operating profits. For example, equivalent reserves include such items as the deferred income tax reserve, LIFO reserve, cumulative amortization of goodwill, capitalized intangibles (including R&D), allowance for doubtful accounts and warranty claim reserves.

Table 12.9 Summary of Cost of Capital Formulas

1. The After-Tax Cost of Debt, $k_d(1 - T_c)$
   a. Calculate the before-tax cost of debt, k_d, as follows:

   $$NP_d = \sum_{t=1}^{n} \frac{\$I_t}{(1 + k_d)^t} + \frac{\$M}{(1 + k_d)^n} \qquad (12\text{-}2)$$

   where NP_d is the net proceeds received by the firm from the sale of each bond; $\$I_t$ is the dollar amount of interest paid to the investor in period t for each bond; $\$M$ is the maturity value of each bond paid in period n; k_d is the before-tax cost of debt to the firm; and n is the number of periods to maturity.
   b. Calculate the after-tax cost of debt as follows:

   after-tax cost of debt $= k_d(1 - T_c)$
   where T_c is the corporate tax rate.

2. The Cost of Preferred Stock, k_p

   $$k_{ps} = \frac{\text{preferred stock dividend}}{NP_{ps}} \qquad (12\text{-}5)$$

   where NP_{ps} is the net proceeds per share of new preferred stock sold after flotation costs.

3. The Cost of Common Equity
   a. Method 1: dividend growth model
   Calculate the cost of internal common equity (retained earnings), k_c, as follows:

   $$k_{cs} = \frac{D_1}{P_{cs}} + g \qquad (12\text{-}7)$$

   where D_1 is the expected dividend for the next year, P_{cs} is the current price of the firm's common stock, and g is the rate of growth in dividends per year.
   Calculate the cost of external common equity (new stock offering), k_{ncs}, as follows:

   $$k_{ncs} = \frac{D_1}{NP_{cs}} + g \qquad (12\text{-}8)$$

   where NP_{cs} is the net proceeds to the firm after flotation costs per share of stock sold.
   b. Method 2: capital asset pricing model, k_c

   $$k_c = k_{rf} + \beta(k_m - k_{rf}) \qquad (12\text{-}9)$$

   where the risk-free rate is k_{rf}; the systematic risk of the common stock's returns relative to the market as a whole or the stock's beta coefficient is β; and the market risk premium, which is equal to the difference in the expected rate of return for the market as a whole (i.e., the expected rate of return for the "average security" minus the risk-free rate), is $k_m - k_{rf}$.

4. The Weighted Average Cost of Capital

   $$k_{wacc} = w_d \cdot k_d (1 - T_c) + w_{ps} \cdot k_{ps} + w_{cs}k_{cs} + w_{ncs}k_{ncs} \qquad (12\text{-}10)$$

   where the w_i terms represent the market value weights associated with the firm's use of each of its sources of financing. Note that we are simply calculating a weighted average of the costs of each of the firm's sources of capital where the weights reflect the firm's relative use of each source.

expected net present value. Because MVA is not a measure of historical performance but instead reflects anticipated future performance, it can change dramatically as a firm's fortunes change. For example, in 1988, IBM's MVA was the largest of any U.S. company. By 1990, the fortunes of IBM had changed dramatically as the personal computer became the computer of the future. In 1991, IBM ranked 31st and by 1996 its rank slipped to 997th.

Table 12.10 contains the top and bottom five firms in terms of their MVA for 1996. With the exception of super-performing Microsoft, all the top five wealth creators were ranked in the top 10 in 1991, which suggests that there is some stability among the top performers. However, only two of the bottom five performers were in the bottom five in 1991. The most dramatic change of fortune was IBM, which fell from 31st in 1991 to 997th in 1996.

MVA measures the wealth created by a firm at a particular point in time. However, the financial manager needs to evaluate the performance of the firm over a specific interval of time, say 1 year. For this purpose, we calculate the firm's **economic profit**. Economic profit is defined as follows:[7]

$$\text{Economic Profit} = \left(\begin{array}{c}\text{Net Operating}\\\text{Profit after-tax}\\\text{(NOPAT)}\end{array}\right) - \left(\begin{array}{c}\text{Invested}\\\text{Capital}\end{array} \times \begin{array}{c}\text{Cost of}\\\text{Capital}\end{array}\right) \qquad (12\text{-}11)$$

Economic profit

The difference in a firm's after-tax net operating income and an estimate of the cost of invested capital (invested capital times the firm's weighted average cost of capital).

Note that the distinction between economic and accounting profit (net operating profit) is the deduction of a return to the firm's invested capital. The product of the firm's invested capital (the total dollar investment made in the firm by its creditors and owners) and the cost of capital constitutes a capital charge. This capital charge is not a recognized accounting expense but it is a very real expense from the perspective of the firm's bondholders and stockholders. The firm's accounting profits must not only be positive but must cover the required rate of return on the firm's investment (the cost of capital) before shareholder value has been created. Thus economic profit is simply accounting profit (net operating profit or income) less a charge for the use of capital.

So what? How does the use of economic profit help the financial manager? The answer is surprisingly simple. Most firms manage to earn positive profits. However, earning positive profits is no assurance that the firm is creating shareholder wealth. Why? Because profits fail to incorporate any opportunity cost for the dollars that investors have tied up in the business. Economic profit, on the other hand, includes an explicit charge in the form of the capital charge, which recognizes the size of the investment made in the firm and the opportunity cost of that investment. Consider the case of Kmart (see Table 12.10). Using equation (12-11), we calculate Kmart's economic profit for 1996 as follows:

$$\text{Economic Profit} = \$188,840,000 - 16,476,000,000 \times .09 = (\$1,294,000,000)$$

How can this be? Kmart earned net operating profits after tax (NOPAT) of $188,840,000. The answer lies in the size of Kmart's NOPAT relative to its assets. In fact, from Table 12.10, we see that Kmart earned only 1.5 percent on its total asset investment, when its cost of capital was 9 percent. As long as a firm earns a return on its invested capital that is lower than its cost of capital it destroys shareholder wealth.

Economic profit has become an important tool for aligning shareholder and manager interests in the running of the company. This is accomplished by basing management's incentive compensation on economic profit. A very simple version of such a compensation scheme is illustrated in equation (12-12).

$$\begin{array}{c}\text{Incentive}\\\text{Compensation}\end{array} = \text{Base Pay} \times \begin{array}{c}\text{Percent}\\\text{Incentive}\\\text{Compensation}\end{array} \times \frac{\text{Actual Economic Profit}}{\text{Target Economic Profit}} \qquad (12\text{-}12)$$

---

[7]Stern Stewart & Co. have trademarked the term Economic Value Added or EVA™ to refer to their particular method for calculating a firm's economic profit using accounting statement results.

Table 12.10 Top and Bottom Wealth Creators for 1996			
1996 Rank	**1991 Rank**	**Company Name**	**MarketValue Added (MVA) $ Millions**
1	4	Coca-Cola	$87,820
2	6	General Electric	80,792
3	2	Merck	63,440
4	1	Philip Morris	51,628
5	20	Microsoft	44,850
996	978	Kmart	(4,190)
997	31	IBM	(5,878)
998	1,000	General Motors	(8,172)
999	-	RJR Nabisco Holdings	(11,882)
1,000	999	Ford Inc.	(12,915)

For example, consider the case of the assistant treasurer for NewCo Oil, Inc. The assistant treasurer's base pay is $80,000 a year and 20 percent of the total compensation for this position is designated by the company to be incentive based. If in a particular year, NewCo set a target economic profit of $1 million and earned $1.2 million, then the assistant treasurer's incentive compensation would be calculated as follows using equation (12-12):

$$\text{Incentive Compensation} = \text{Base Pay} \times \text{Percent Incentive Compensation} \times \frac{\text{Actual Economic Profit}}{\text{Target Economic Profit}}$$

$$= \$80,000 \times .20 \times (\$1.2 \text{ million}/\$1 \text{ million})$$

$$= \$19,200$$

In this case, the assistant treasurer's total annual compensation would be $99,200 = $80,000 + $19,200. If NewCo earned only $800,000 in economic profit, then the incentive compensation paid to the assistant treasurer would be $12,800 = $80,000 × .20 × ($800,000/$1,000,000).

Clearly, with this type of incentive compensation plan, the firm's managers will be very careful to manage for increased net operating profits while holding down the firm's invested capital and maintaining the lowest possible cost of capital. If they do this, then they will maximize the contribution to shareholder wealth and also maximize their own year-end bonuses.

HOW FINANCIAL MANAGERS USE THIS MATERIAL

The opportunity cost of capital is critically important for every firm, and most publicly traded firms estimate it at least annually and some revise their estimate quarterly. The cost of capital is not an abstract concept but a very important factor of corporate business decision making. Most firms rely on the weighted average cost of capital (calculated using current investor required rates of return and target financing proportions or weights).

Our discussion was kept purposely basic because this reflects the way in which the cost of capital is actually calculated. Specifically, firms that have two or more operating

Table 12.10 Top and Bottom Wealth Creators for 1996 (continued)

Economic Value Added (EVA) $ Millions	Invested Capital $ Millions	Return on Invested Capital	Cost of Capital
$2,140	$ 9,276	37.2%	12.0%
1,852	51,017	17.5%	13.5%
1,115	19,792	19.6%	13.5%
1,165	40,911	17.3%	14.4%
1,345	4,889	50.0%	13.1%
(1,294)	16,476	1.5%	9.0%
2,541	69,057	12.1%	8.9%
3,225	94,268	11.6%	8.1%
(1,390)	33,942	5.2%	9.3%
1,591	55,955	12.8%	9.8%

divisions will usually estimate a cost of capital for each division. However, when using the cost of capital for evaluating operating results and determining incentive compensation, even multi-division firms sometimes use a single weighted average cost of capital. This is sometimes done to simplify the basis for determining bonuses, and in other instances, it is done in an effort to remove the cost of capital as an element of discussion in determining compensation. The key fact here is that firms do calculate their cost of capital, they use it to make investment decisions and to determine incentive compensation, and they "try to keep it simple."

SUMMARY

OBJECTIVE 1

We opened our discussion of this chapter by discussing the investment opportunity facing Encore, Inc. The investment required that the firm invest $75 million to renovate a production facility that will provide after-tax savings to the firm of $25 million per year over the next 5 years. In chapter 9, we learned that the proper way to evaluate whether or not to undertake the investment involves calculating its net present value (NPV). To calculate NPV, we must estimate both project cash flows and an appropriate discount rate. In this chapter, we have learned that the proper discount rate is a weighted average of the after-tax costs of all the firm's sources of financing. In addition, we have learned that the cost of capital for any source of financing is estimated by first calculating the investor's required rate of return, then making appropriate adjustments for flotation costs and corporate taxes (where appropriate). If Encore's weighted average cost of capital is 10 percent, then the NPV of the plant renovation is $4,250 and the investment should be made. The reason is that the project is expected to increase the wealth of Encore's shareholders by $4,250. Very simply, the project is expected to return a present value amount of $4,250 more than Encore's sources of capital require, and since the common stockholders get any residual value left after returning the promised return to each of the other sources of capital, they receive the NPV.

To calculate the after-tax cost of debt capital, we must first calculate the before-tax cost of capital using the following formula:

$$NP_d = \sum_{t=1}^{n} \frac{\$I_t}{(1 + k_d)^t} + \frac{\$M}{(1 + k_d)^n} \tag{12-2}$$

where NP_d = the net proceeds received by the firm
from the sale of each bond

$\$I_t$ = the dollar amount of interest paid to the investor in period t for each bond

$\$M$ = the maturity value of each bond paid in period n

k_d = the before-tax cost of debt to the firm

n = the number of periods to maturity

Next, we adjust for the effects of corporate taxes because the bond interest is deducted from the firm's taxable income.

after-tax cost of debt = $k_d(1$ – corporate tax rate)

The cost of preferred stock is relatively easy to calculate. Below we calculate the dividend yield on the preferred issue using net proceeds from the sale of each new share as follows:

$$\text{cost of preferred stock} = \frac{\text{preferred stock dividend}}{\text{net proceeds per preferred share}} \tag{12-5}$$

Note that no adjustment is made for corporate taxes because preferred stock dividends, unlike bond interest, are paid with after-tax earnings.

Common equity can be obtained by the firm in one of two ways. First, the firm can retain a portion of its net income after paying common dividends. The retention of earnings constitutes a means of raising common-equity financing internally—that is, no capital market issuance of securities is involved. Second, the firm can also raise equity capital through the sale of a new issue of common stock.

We discussed two methods for estimating the cost of common equity. The first involved using the dividend growth model:

$$k_{cs} = \frac{D_1}{P_{cs}} + g \tag{12-7}$$

where g is the rate at which dividends are expected to grow forever, k_{cs} is the investor's required rate of return, and P_{cs} is the current price of a share of common stock. When a new issue of common shares is issued, the firm incurs flotation costs. These costs reduce the amount of funds the firm receives per share. Consequently, the cost of external common equity using the dividend growth model requires that we substitute the new proceeds per share, NP_{cs}, for share price:

$$k_{ncs} = \frac{D_1}{NP_{cs}} + g \tag{12-8}$$

The second method for estimating the cost of common equity involves the use of capital asset pricing model (CAPM), which we first discussed in chapter 8. There we learned that the CAPM provides a basis for evaluating investor's required rates of return on common equity, k_c, using three variables:

1. the risk-free rate, k_{rf};
2. the systematic risk of the common stock's returns relative to the market as a whole or the stock's beta coefficient, β; and

3. the market risk premium which is equal to the difference in the expected rate of return for the market as a whole—that is, the expected rate of return for the "average security" minus the risk-free rate, $k_m - k_{rf}$.

The CAPM is written as follows:

$$k_c = k_{rf} + \beta(k_m - k_{rf}) \tag{12-9}$$

We found that all of the variables on the right side of equation (12-9) could be obtained from public sources for larger, publicly traded firms. However, for non–publicly traded firms, the CAPM is more difficult to apply in the estimation of investor-required rates of return.

OBJECTIVE 3

The firm's weighted average cost of capital, k_{wacc}, can be defined as follows:

$$k_{wacc} = w_d \times k_d(1 - T_c) + w_{ps} \times k_{ps} + w_{cs}k_{cs} + w_{ncs}k_{ncs} \tag{12-10}$$

where the w terms represent the market value weights associated with the firm's use of each of its sources of financing. Note that we are simply calculating a weighted average of the costs of each of the firm's sources of capital where the weights reflect the firm's relative use of each source.

The weights used to calculate k_{wacc} should theoretically reflect the market values of each capital source as a fraction of the total market value of all capital sources (i.e., the market value of the firm). However, the analyst frequently finds the use of market value weights is impractical, either because the firm's securities are not publicly traded or because all capital sources are not used in proportion to their makeup of the firm's target capital structure in every financing episode. In these instances, we found that the weights should be the firm's long-term target financial mix.

OBJECTIVES 4, 5

The firm's weighted average cost of capital will reflect the operating or business risk of the firm's present set of investments and the financial risks attendant upon the way in which those assets are financed. Therefore, this cost of capital estimate is useful only for evaluating new investment opportunities that have similar business and financial risks. Remember that the primary determinant of the cost of capital for a particular investment is the risk of the investment itself, not the source of the capital. Multidivision firms such as PepsiCo resolve this problem by calculating a different cost of capital for each of their major operating divisions.

OBJECTIVE 6

How can we tell whether a firm's management is creating or destroying wealth? We found that a very common-sense measure known as market value added or MVA can be used for this purpose. MVA is simply the difference in the market value of the firm's securities (debt and equity) and the sum total of the funds that have been invested in the firm since its creation. If the market value of the firm's investments exceeds the total capital invested in the firm, then shareholder wealth has been created to the extent of this difference. Likewise, where the difference is negative, then shareholder wealth has been destroyed.

MVA measures the total shareholder wealth created by the firm at a particular point in time. How do we know whether shareholder wealth was created last year or last month? The answer is found in calculating the firm's economic profit, defined as follows:

$$\text{Economic Profit} = \begin{pmatrix} \text{Net Operating} \\ \text{Profit after-tax} \\ \text{(NOPAT)} \end{pmatrix} - \begin{pmatrix} \text{Invested} \\ \text{Capital} \times \frac{\text{Cost of}}{\text{Capital}} \end{pmatrix} \tag{12-11}$$

Thus a firm's management has successfully created shareholder wealth when its after-tax net operating profits are sufficient to cover the opportunity cost of its invested capital.

Firms are increasingly using the concept of economic profit to link employee compensation to shareholder interests. The following general model can be used for this purpose:

$$\frac{\text{Incentive}}{\text{Compensation}} = \text{Base Pay} \times \frac{\text{Percent}}{\text{Incentive}} \times \frac{\text{Actual Economic Profit}}{\text{Target Economic Profit}} \quad (12\text{-}12)$$

If the firm manages to earn higher economic profits than was targeted for the period, then employ incentive compensation rises. Similarly, higher economic profits lead to greater shareholder value being created.

GO TO:
http://www.prenhall.com/bfm
For downloads and current events
associated with this chapter

KEY TERMS

Business risk, 448

Capital asset pricing model, 438

Capital structure, 441

Economic profit, 452

Financial policy, 433

Financial risk, 448

Flotation costs, 433

Investor's required rate of return, 432

Market value added, 450

Target capital structure proportions, 442

Weighted average cost of capital, 433

FINCOACH PRACTICE EXERCISES FOR CHAPTER 12

To maximize your grades and master the mathematics discussed in this chapter, open *FINCOACH* on the *Finance Learning and Development Center* CD-ROM, and practice problems in the following categories: 1) CAPM 2) Bond Valuation 3) Stock Valuation 4) Cost of Capital I 5) Cost of Capital II

STUDY QUESTIONS

12-1. Define the term *cost of capital*.

12-2. Why do we calculate a firm's weighted average cost of capital?

12-3. In computing the cost of capital, which sources of capital do we consider?

12-4. How does a firm's tax rate affect its cost of capital? What is the effect of the flotation costs associated with a new security issue?

12-5. a. Distinguish between internal common equity and new common stock.

b. Why is a cost associated with internal common equity?

c. Describe the two approaches that could be used in computing the cost of common equity.

12-6. What might we expect to see in practice in the relative costs of different sources of capital?

SELF-TEST PROBLEMS

ST-1. (*Individual Costs of Capital*) Compute the cost for the following sources of financing:

a. A $1,000 par value bond with a market price of $970 and a coupon interest rate of 10 percent. Flotation costs for a new issue would be approximately 5 percent. The bonds mature in 10 years and the corporate tax rate is 34 percent.

b. A preferred stock selling for $100 with an annual dividend payment of $8. If the company sells a new issue, the flotation cost will be $9 per share. The company's marginal tax rate is 30 percent.

c. Internally generated common stock totaling $4.8 million. The price of the common stock is $75 per share, and the dividend per share was $9.80 last year. The dividend is not expected to change in the future.

d. New common stock where the most recent dividend was $2.80. The company's dividends per share should continue to increase at an 8 percent growth rate into the indefinite future. The market price of the stock is currently $53; however, flotation costs of $6 per share are expected if the new stock is issued.

ST-2. (*Weighted Average Cost of Capital*) The capital structure for the Carion Corporation is provided below. The company plans to maintain its debt structure in the future. If the firm has a 5.5 percent after-tax cost of debt, a 13.5 percent cost of preferred stock, and an 18 percent cost of common stock, what is the firm's weighted average cost of capital?

Capital Structure ($000)	
Bonds	$1,083
Preferred stock	268
Common stock	3,681
	$5,032

STUDY PROBLEMS

12-1A. (*Individual or Component Costs of Capital*) Compute the cost for the following:

a. A bond that has a $1,000 par value (face value) and a contract or coupon interest rate of 11 percent. A new issue would have a flotation cost of 5 percent of the $1,125 market value. The bonds mature in 10 years. The firm's average tax rate is 30 percent and its marginal tax rate is 34 percent.

b. A new common stock issue that paid a $1.80 dividend last year. The par value of the stock is $15, and earnings per share have grown at a rate of 7 percent per year. This growth rate is expected to continue into the foreseeable future. The company maintains a constant dividend-earnings ratio of 30 percent. The price of this stock is now $27.50, but 5 percent flotation costs are anticipated.

c. Internal common equity where the current market price of the common stock is $43. The expected dividend this coming year should be $3.50, increasing thereafter at a 7 percent annual growth rate. The corporation's tax rate is 34 percent.

d. A preferred stock paying a 9 percent dividend on a $150 par value. If a new issue is offered, flotation costs will be 12 percent of the current price of $175.

e. A bond selling to yield 12 percent after flotation costs, but prior to adjusting for the marginal corporate tax rate of 34 percent. In other words, 12 percent is the rate that equates the net proceeds from the bond with the present value of the future cash flows (principal and interest).

12-2A. (*Individual or Component Costs of Capital*) Compute the cost for the following:

a. A bond selling to yield 8 percent after flotation costs, but prior to adjusting for the marginal corporate tax rate of 34 percent. In other words, 8 percent is the rate that equates the net proceeds from the bond with the present value of the future cash flows (principal and interest).

b. A new common stock issue that paid a $1.05 dividend last year. The par value of the stock is $2, and the earnings per share have grown at a rate of 5 percent per year. This growth rate is expected to continue into the foreseeable future. The company maintains a constant dividend-earnings ratio of 40 percent. The price of this stock is now $25, but 9 percent flotation costs are anticipated.

c. A bond that has a $1,000 par value and a contract or coupon interest rate of 12 percent. A new issue would net the company 90 percent of the $1,150 market value. The bonds mature in 20 years, the firm's average tax rate is 30 percent, and its marginal tax rate is 34 percent.

d. A preferred stock paying a 7 percent dividend on a $100 par value. If a new issue is offered, the company can expect to net $85 per share.

e. Internal common equity where the current market price of the common stock is $38. The expected dividend this forthcoming year should be $3, increasing thereafter at a 4 percent annual growth rate. The corporation's tax rate is 34 percent.

12-3A. (*Cost of Equity*) Salte Corporation is issuing new common stock at a market price of $27. Dividends last year were $1.45 and are expected to grow at an annual rate of 6 percent forever. Flotation costs will be 6 percent of market price. What is Salte's cost of equity?

12-4A. (*Cost of Debt*) Belton is issuing a $1,000 par value bond that pays 7 percent annual interest and matures in 15 years. Investors are willing to pay $958 for the bond. Flotation costs will be 11 percent of market value. The company is in an 18 percent tax bracket. What will be the firm's after-tax cost of debt on the bond?

12-5A. (*Cost of Preferred Stock*) The preferred stock of Walter Industries sells for $36 and pays $2.50 in dividends. The net price of the security after issuance costs is $32.50. What is the cost of capital for the preferred stock?

12-6A. (*Cost of Debt*) The Zephyr Corporation is contemplating a new investment to be financed 33 percent from debt. The firm could sell new $1,000 par value bonds at a net price of $945. The coupon interest rate is 12 percent, and the bonds would mature in 15 years. If the company is in a 34 percent tax bracket, what is the after-tax cost of capital to Zephyr for bonds?

12-7A. (*Cost of Preferred Stock*) Your firm is planning to issue preferred stock. The stock sells for $115; however, if new stock is issued, the company would receive only $98. The par value of the stock is $100 and the dividend rate is 14 percent. What is the cost of capital for the stock to your firm?

12-8A. (*Cost of Internal Equity*) Pathos Co.'s common stock is currently selling for $21.50. Dividends paid last year were $.70. Flotation costs on issuing stock will be 10 percent of market price. The dividends and earnings per share are projected to have an annual growth rate of 15 percent. What is the cost of internal common equity for Pathos?

12-9A. (*Cost of Equity*) The common stock for the Bestsold Corporation sells for $58. If a new issue is sold, the flotation costs are estimated to be 8 percent. The company pays 50 percent of its earnings in dividends, and a $4 dividend was recently paid. Earnings per share 5 years ago were $5. Earnings are expected to continue to grow at the same annual rate in the future as during the past 5 years. The firm's marginal tax rate is 34 percent. Calculate the cost of (a) internal common and (b) external common.

12-10A. (*Cost of Debt*) Sincere Stationery Corporation needs to raise $500,000 to improve its manufacturing plant. It has decided to issue a $1,000 par value bond with a 14 percent annual coupon rate and a 10-year maturity. The investors require a 9 percent rate of return.

  a. Compute the market value of the bonds.

  b. What will the net price be if flotation costs are 10.5 percent of the market price?

  c. How many bonds will the firm have to issue to receive the needed funds?

  d. What is the firm's after-tax cost of debt if its average tax rate is 25 percent and its marginal tax rate is 34 percent?

12-11A. (*Cost of Debt*)

  a. Rework problem 12-10A assuming a 10 percent coupon rate. What effect does changing the coupon rate have on the firm's after-tax cost of capital?

  b. Why is there a change?

INTEGRATIVE PROBLEM

The capital structure for Nealon, Inc., follows. Flotation costs are (a) 15 percent of market value for a new bond issue, (b) $1.21 per share for common stock, and (c) $2.01 per share for preferred stock. The dividends for common stock were $2.50 last year and are projected to have an annual growth rate of 6 percent. The firm is in a 34 percent tax bracket. What is the weighted average cost of capital if the firm finances are in the following proportions?

Nealon, Inc., Balance Sheet		
Type of Financing		Percentage of Future Financing
Bonds (8%, $1,000 par, 16-year maturity)		38%
Preferred stock (5,000 shares outstanding,		
$50 par, $1.50 dividend)		15%
Common stock		47%
Total		100%

Market prices are $1,035 for bonds, $19 for preferred stock, and $35 for common stock. There will be sufficient internal common equity funding (i.e., retained earnings) available such that the firm does not plan to issue new common stocks.

STUDY PROBLEMS (SET B)

12-1B. (*Individual or Component Costs of Capital*) Compute the cost for the following:

a. A bond that has a $1,000 par value (face value) and a contract or coupon interior rate of 12 percent. A new issue would have a flotation cost of 6 percent of the $1,125 market value. The bonds mature in 10 years. The firm's average tax rate is 30 percent and its marginal tax rate is 34 percent.

b. A new common stock issue that paid a $1.75 dividend last year. The par value of the stock is $15, and earnings per share have grown at a rate of 8 percent per year. This growth rate is expected to continue into the foreseeable future. The company maintains a constant dividend/earnings ratio of 30 percent. The price of this stock is now $28, but 5 percent flotation costs are anticipated.

c. Internal common equity in which the current market price of the common stock is $43.50. The expected dividend this coming year should be $3.25, increasing thereafter at a 7 percent annual growth rate. The corporation's tax rate is 34 percent.

d. A preferred stock paying a 10 percent dividend on a $125 par value. If a new issue is offered, flotation costs will be 12 percent of the current price of $150.

e. A bond selling to yield 13 percent after flotation costs, but prior to adjusting for the marginal corporate tax rate of 34 percent. In other words, 13 percent is the rate that equates the net proceeds from the bond with the present value of the future cash flows (principal and interest).

12-2B. (*Individual or Component Costs of Capital*) Compute the cost of the following:

a. A bond selling to yield 9 percent after flotation costs, but prior to adjusting for the marginal corporate tax rate of 34 percent. In other words, 9 percent is the rate that equates the net proceeds from the bond with the present value of the future flows (principal and interest).

b. A new common stock issue that paid a $1.25 dividend last year. The par value of the stock is $2, and the earnings per share have grown at a rate of 6 percent per year. This growth rate is expected to continue into the foreseeable future. The company maintains a constant dividend/earnings ratio of 40 percent. The price of this stock is now $30, but 9 percent flotation costs are anticipated.

c. A bond that has a $1,000 par value (face value) and a contract or coupon interest rate of 13 percent. A new issue would net the company 90 percent of the $1,125 market value. The bonds mature in 20 years, and the firm's average tax rate is 30 percent and its marginal tax rate is 34 percent.

d. A preferred stock paying a 7 percent dividend on a $125 par value. If a new issue is offered, the company can expect to net $90 per share.

e. Internal common equity where the current market price of the common stock is $38. The expected dividend this coming year should be $4, increasing thereafter at 5 percent annual growth rate. This corporation's tax rate is 34 percent.

12-3B. (*Cost of Equity*) Falon Corporation is issuing new common stock at a market price of $28. Dividends last year were $1.30 and are expected to grow at an annual rate of 7 percent forever. Flotation costs will be 6 percent of market price. What is Falon's cost of equity?

12-4B. (*Cost of Debt*) Temple is issuing a $1,000 par value bond that pays 8 percent annual interest and matures in 15 years. Investors are willing to pay $950 for the bond. Flotation costs will be 11 percent of market value. The company is in a 19 percent tax bracket. What will be the firm's after-tax cost of debt on the bond?

12-5B. (*Cost of Preferred Stock*) The preferred stock of Gator Industries sells for $35 and pays $2.75 in dividends. The net price of the security after issuance costs is $32.50. What is the cost of capital for the preferred stock?

12-6B. (*Cost of Debt*) The Walgren Corporation is contemplating a new investment to be financed 33 percent from debt. The firm could sell new $1,000 par value bonds at a net price of $950. The coupon interest rate is 13 percent, and the bonds would mature in 15 years. If the company is in a 34 percent tax bracket, what is the after-tax cost of capital to Walgren for bonds?

12-7B. (*Cost of Preferred Stock*) Your firm is planning to issue preferred stock. The stock sells for $120; however, if new stock is issued, the company would receive only $97. The par value of the stock is $100, and the dividend rate is 13 percent. What is the cost of capital for the stock to your firm?

12-8B. (*Cost of Internal Equity*) The common stock for Oxford, Inc. is currently selling for $22.50. Dividends last year were $.80. Flotation costs on issuing stock will be 10 percent of market price. The dividends and earnings per share are projected to have an annual growth rate of 16 percent. What is the cost of internal common equity for Oxford?

12-9B. (*Cost of Equity*) The common stock for the Hetterbrand Corporation sells for $60. If a new issue is sold, the flotation cost is estimated to be 9 percent. The company pays 50 percent of its earnings in dividends, and a $4.50 dividend was recently paid. Earnings per share 5 years ago were $5. Earnings are expected to continue to grow at the same annual rate in the future as during the past 5 years. The firms' marginal tax rate is 35 percent. Calculate the cost of (a) internal common and (b) external common stock.

12-10B. (*Cost of Debt*) Gillian Stationery Corporation needs to raise $600,000 to improve its manufacturing plant. It has decided to issue a $1,000 par value bond with a 15 percent annual coupon rate and a 10-year maturity. If the investors require a 10 percent rate of return:

    a. Compute the market value of the bonds.

    b. What will the net price be if flotation costs are 11.5 percent of the market price?

    c. How many bonds will the firm have to issue to receive the needed funds?

    d. What is the firm's after-tax cost of debt if its average tax rate is 25 percent and its marginal tax rate is 34 percent?

12-11B. (*Cost of Debt*)

    a. Rework problem 12-10B assuming a 10 percent coupon rate. What effect does changing the coupon rate have on the firm's after-tax cost of capital?

    b. Why is there a change?

12-12B. (*Weighted Cost of Capital*) The capital structure for the Bias Corporation follows. The company plans to maintain its debt structure in the future. If the firm has a 6 percent after-tax cost of debt, a 13.5 percent cost of preferred stock, and a 19 percent cost of common stock, what is the firm's weighted cost of capital?

Capital Structure ($000)	
Bonds	$1,100
Preferred stock	250
Common stock	3,700
	$5,050

SELF–TEST SOLUTIONS

The following notations are used in this group of problems:

k_d = the before-tax cost of debt

k_{ps} = the cost of preferred stock

k_{cs} = the cost of internal common stock

k_{ncs} = the cost of new common stock

t = the marginal tax rate

D_t = the dollar dividend per share, where D_0 is the most recently paid dividend and D_1 is the forthcoming dividend

P_0 = the value (present value) of a security

NP_0 = the value of a security less any flotation costs incurred in issuing the security

SS–1.

a. $\$921.50 = \sum_{t=1}^{n} \dfrac{\$100}{(1 + k_d)^t} + \dfrac{\$1,000}{(1 + k_d)^{10}}$

	Rate	Value		
	11%	$940.90	} $19.40	
	k_d%	$921.50		} $53.90
	12%	$887.00		

$$k_d = 0.11 + \left(\dfrac{\$19.40}{\$53.90}\right)0.01 = .1136 = 11.36\%$$

$$k_{d(1-t)} = 11.36\% \ (1 - 0.34) = 7.50\%$$

b. $k_{ps} = \dfrac{D}{NP_0}$

$$k_{ps} = \dfrac{\$8}{\$100 - \$9} = .0879 = 8.79\%$$

c. $k_{cs} = \dfrac{D_1}{P_0} + g$

$$k_{cs} = \dfrac{\$9.80}{\$75} + 0\% = .1307 = 13.07\%$$

d. $k_{ncs} = \dfrac{D_1}{NP_0} + g$

$$k_{ncs} = \dfrac{\$2.80(1 + 0.08)}{\$53 - \$6} + 0.08 = .1443 = 14.43\%$$

SS–2.

Carion Corporation—Weighted Cost of Capital

	Capital Structure	Weights	Individual Costs	Weighted Costs
Bonds	$1,083	0.2152	5.5%	1.18%
Preferred stock	268	0.0533	13.5%	0.72%
Common stock	3,681	0.7315	18.0%	13.17%
	$5,032	1.0000		15.07%

Learning Objectives

Active Applications

World Finance

Practice

CHAPTER 13

LEARNING OBJECTIVES

After reading this chapter, you should be able to

1. Understand the difference between business risk and financial risk.

2. Use the technique of breakeven analysis in a variety of analytical settings.

3. Distinguish among the financial concepts of operating leverage, financial leverage, and combined leverage.

4. Calculate the firm's degree of operating leverage, financial leverage, and combined leverage.

5. Explain why a firm with a high business risk exposure might logically choose to employ a low degree of financial leverage in its financial structure.

ANALYSIS AND IMPACT OF LEVERAGE

INTRODUCTION

In 1996, the Coca-Cola Company posted only a moderate sales increase of 2.9 percent over the level of reported sales for 1995. This firm's change in net income, however, rose by a pleasant 16.9 percent over the same 1-year period. Thus the relative change in net income was 5.83 times the relative fluctuation in sales (i.e., 16.9 percent/2.9 percent). Such disparity in the relationship between sales fluctuations and net income fluctuations is not peculiar to Coca-Cola.

Consider that in 1993, Phillips Petroleum saw its sales rise by only 3.2 percent, yet its net income rose by a whopping 35 percent. Further, Archer Daniels Midland experienced a sales rise of 6.3 percent and a 12.7 percent increase in net income.

We know that sales fluctuations are not always in the positive direction. Over the 1992 to 1993 time frame, Chevron Corporation, the large integrated oil company, endured a 3.6 percent contraction in sales revenues; yet its net income contracted by a larger and more painful 19.4 percent.

What is it about the nature of businesses that causes changes in sales revenues to translate into larger variations in net income and finally the earnings available to the common shareholders? It would actually be a good planning tool for managers to be able to decompose such fluctuations into those policies that are associated with the operating side of the business, as distinct from those policies associated with the financing side of the business. Such knowledge could be put to effective use when the firm builds its strategic plan. This chapter will show you how to do just that.

CHAPTER PREVIEW

Our work in chapters 6, 7, and 12 allowed us to develop an understanding of how financial assets are valued in the marketplace. Drawing on the tenets of valuation theory, we presented various approaches to measuring the cost of funds to the business organization. This chapter presents concepts that relate to the valuation process and the cost of capital; it also discusses the crucial problem of planning the firm's financing mix.

The cost of capital provides a direct link between the formulation of the firm's asset structure and its financial structure. This is illustrated in Figure 13.1. Recall that the cost of capital is a basic input to the time-adjusted capital-budgeting models. It therefore affects the capital-budgeting, or asset-selection, process. The cost of capital is affected, in turn, by the composition of the right side of the firm's balance sheet—that is, its financial structure.

This chapter examines tools that can be useful aids to the financial manager in determining the firm's proper financial structure. First, we review the technique of breakeven analysis. This provides the foundation for the relationships to be highlighted in the remainder of the chapter. We then examine the concept of operating leverage, some consequences of the firm's use of financial leverage, and the impact on the firm's earnings stream when operating and financial leverage are combined in various patterns.

As you work through this chapter, you will be reminded of several of the axioms that form the basics of business financial management and decision-making. These will be emphasized: Axiom 1: The Risk-Return Trade-Off—We Won't Take on Additional Risk Unless We Expect to Be Compensated with Additional Return; Axiom 3: Cash—Not Profits—Is King; and Axiom 6: Efficient Capital Markets—The Markets Are Quick and the Prices Are Right. Our immediate tasks are to distinguish two types of risk that confront the firm and to clarify some key terminology that will be used throughout this and the subsequent chapter.

STOP AND THINK

In this chapter, we become more precise in assessing the causes of variability in the firm's expected revenue streams. It is useful to think of business risk as induced by the firm's investment decisions. That is, the composition of the firm's assets determines its exposure to business risk. In this way, business risk is a direct function of what appears on the left side of the company's balance sheet. Financial risk is properly attributed to the manner in which the firm's managers have decided to arrange the right side of the company's balance sheet. The choice to use more financial leverage means that the firm will experience greater exposure to financial risk. The tools developed here will help you quantify the firm's business and financial risk. A solid understanding of these tools will make you a better financial manager.

BUSINESS AND FINANCIAL RISK

OBJECTIVE 1

In studying capital-budgeting techniques, we referred to **risk** as the likely variability associated with expected revenue or income streams. As our attention is now focused on the firm's financing decision rather than its investment decision, it is useful to separate the income stream variations attributable to (1) the company's exposure to business risk, and (2) its decision to incur financial risk.

Business risk refers to the relative dispersion (variability) in the firm's expected earnings before interest and taxes (EBIT).[1] Figure 13.2 shows a subjectively estimated probability distribution of next year's EBIT for the Pierce Grain Company and the same

Risk

The likely variability associated with expected revenue or income streams.

Business risk

The relative dispersion in the firm's expected earnings before interest and taxes.

---

[1]If what the accountants call "other income" and "other expenses" are equal to zero, then EBIT is equal to net operating income. These terms will be used interchangeably.

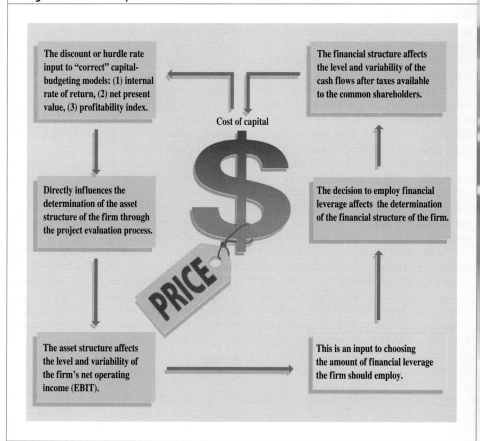

Figure 13.1 Cost of Capital as a Link between Firm's Asset Structure and Financial Structure

The discount or hurdle rate input to "correct" capital-budgeting models: (1) internal rate of return, (2) net present value, (3) profitability index.

Cost of capital

The financial structure affects the level and variability of the cash flows after taxes available to the common shareholders.

Directly influences the determination of the asset structure of the firm through the project evaluation process.

The decision to employ financial leverage affects the determination of the financial structure of the firm.

The asset structure affects the level and variability of the firm's net operating income (EBIT).

This is an input to choosing the amount of financial leverage the firm should employ.

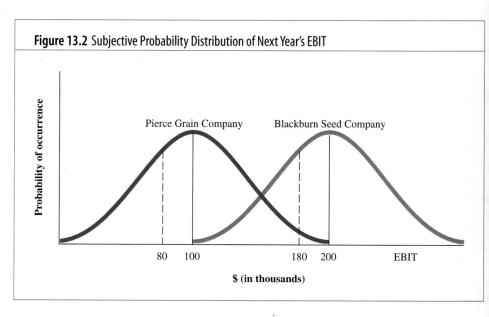

Figure 13.2 Subjective Probability Distribution of Next Year's EBIT

Probability of occurrence

Pierce Grain Company   Blackburn Seed Company

80   100   180   200   EBIT

$ (in thousands)

Table 13.1 Concept of Business Risk

Business Risk Attribute	Example[a]
1. Sensitivity of the firm's product demand to general economic conditions	If GNP declines, does the firm's sales level decline by a greater percentage?
2. Degree of competition	Is the firm's market share small in comparison with other firms that produce and distribute the same product(s)?
3. Product diversification	Is a large proportion of the firm's sales revenue derived from a single major product or product line?
4. Operating leverage	Does the firm utilize a high level of operating leverage resulting in a high level of fixed costs?
5. Growth prospects	Are the firm's product markets expanding and (or) changing, making income estimates and prospects highly volatile?
6. Size	Does the firm suffer a competitive disadvantage due to lack of size in assets, sales, or profits that translates into (among other things) difficulty in tapping the capital market for funds?

[a]Affirmative responses indicate greater business risk exposure.

type of projection for Pierce's larger competitor, the Blackburn Seed Company. The expected value of EBIT for Pierce is $100,000, with an associated standard deviation of $20,000. If next year's EBIT for Pierce fell one standard deviation short of the expected $100,000, the actual EBIT would equal $80,000. Blackburn's expected EBIT is $200,000, and the size of the associated standard deviation is $20,000. The standard deviation for the expected level of EBIT is the same for both firms. We would say that Pierce's degree of business risk exceeds Blackburn's because of its larger coefficient of variation of expected EBIT as follows:

$$\text{Pierce's coefficient of variation of expected EBIT} = \frac{\$20,000}{\$100,000} = .20$$

$$\text{Blackburn's coefficient of variation of expected EBIT} = \frac{\$20,000}{\$200,000} = .10$$

The relative dispersion in the firm's EBIT stream, measured here by its expected coefficient of variation, is the *residual* effect of several causal influences. Dispersion in operating income does not *cause* business risk; rather, this dispersion, which we call business risk, is the *result* of several influences. Some of these are listed in Table 13.1, along with an example of each particular attribute. Notice that the company's cost structure, product demand characteristics, and intra-industry competitive position all affect its business risk exposure. Such business risk is a direct result of the firm's investment decision. It is the firm's asset structure, after all, that gives rise to both the level and variability of its operating profits.

Financial risk, conversely, is a direct result of the firm's financing decision. In the context of selecting a proper financing mix, this risk applies to (1) the additional variability in earnings available to the firm's common shareholders; and (2) the additional

Financial risk

The additional variability in earnings available to the firm's common stockholder, and the additional chance of insolvency borne by the common stockholder caused by the use of financial leverage.

chance of insolvency borne by the common shareholder caused by the use of financial leverage.[2] **Financial leverage** means financing a portion of the firm's assets with securities bearing a fixed (limited) rate of return in hopes of increasing the ultimate return to the common stockholders. The decision to use debt or preferred stock in the financial structure of the corporation means that those who own the common shares of the firm are exposed to financial risk. Any given level of variability in EBIT will be *magnified* by the firm's use of financial leverage, and such additional variability will be embodied in the variability of earnings available to the common stockholder and earnings per share. If these magnifications are negative, the common stockholder has a higher chance of insolvency than would have existed had the use of fixed charge securities (debt and preferred stock) been avoided.

The closely related concepts of business and financial risk are crucial to the problem of financial structure design. This follows from the impact of these types of risk on the variability of the earnings stream flowing to the company's shareholders. In the rest of this chapter, we study techniques that permit a precise assessment of the earnings stream variability caused by (1) operating leverage and (2) financial leverage. We have already defined financial leverage. Table 13.1 shows that the business risk of the enterprise is influenced by the use of what is called operating leverage. **Operating leverage** refers to the incurrence of fixed operating costs in the firm's income stream. To understand the nature and importance of operating leverage, we need to draw upon the basics of cost-volume-profit analysis, or *breakeven analysis*.

> **STOP AND THINK**
>
> *The breakeven analysis concepts presented in the next section are often covered in many of your other classes, such as basic accounting principles and managerial economics. This just shows you how important and accepted this tool is within the realm of business decision making. The "Objective and Uses" section below identifies five typical uses of the breakeven model. You can probably add an application or two of your own. Hotels and motels, for instance, know exactly what their breakeven occupancy rate is. This breakeven occupancy rate gives them an operating target. This operating target, in turn, often becomes a crucial input to the hotel's advertising strategy. You may not want to become a financial manager—but you do want to understand how to compute breakeven points.*

OBJECTIVE 2

BREAKEVEN ANALYSIS

The technique of breakeven analysis is familiar to legions of businesspeople. It is usefully applied in a wide array of business settings, including both small and large organizations. This tool is widely accepted by the business community for two reasons: It is based on straightforward assumptions, and companies have found that the information gained from the breakeven model is beneficial in decision-making situations.

Objective and Uses

The objective of *breakeven analysis* is to determine the *breakeven quantity of output* by studying the relationships among the firm's cost structure, volume of output, and profit. Alternatively, the firm ascertains the breakeven level of sales dollars that corresponds to the breakeven quantity of output. We will develop the fundamental relationships by

---

[2]Note that the concept of financial risk used here differs from that used in our examination of cash and marketable securities management in chapter 17.

concentrating on units of output, and then extend the procedure to permit direct calcula-tion of the breakeven sales level.

What is meant by the breakeven quantity of output? It is that quantity of output, denominated in units, that results in an EBIT level equal to zero. Use of the break-even model, therefore, enables the financial officer (1) to determine the quantity of output that must be sold to cover all operating costs, as distinct from financial costs, and (2) to calcu-late the EBIT that will be achieved at various output levels.

The many actual and potential applications of the breakeven approach include the following:

1. **Capital expenditure analysis**. As a complementary technique to discounted cash flow evaluation models, the breakeven model locates in a rough way the sales volume needed to make a project economically beneficial to the firm. It should not be used to replace the time-adjusted evaluation techniques.
2. **Pricing policy**. The sales price of a new product can be set to achieve a target EBIT level. Furthermore, should market penetration be a prime objective, a price could be set that would cover slightly more than the variable costs of production and provide only a partial contribution to the recovery of fixed costs. The negative EBIT at several possible sales prices can then be studied.
3. **Labor contract negotiations**. The effect of increased variable costs resulting from higher wages on the breakeven quantity of output can be analyzed.
4. **Cost structure**. The choice of reducing variable costs at the expense of incurring higher fixed costs can be evaluated. Management might decide to become more capital-intensive by performing tasks in the production process through use of equipment rather than labor. Application of the breakeven model can indicate what the effects of this trade-off will be on the breakeven point for the given product.
5. **Financing decisions**. Analysis of the firm's cost structure will reveal the proportion that fixed operating costs bear to sales. If this proportion is high, the firm might reasonably decide not to add any fixed financing costs on top of the high fixed operating costs.

Essential Elements of the Breakeven Model

To implement the breakeven model, we must separate the production costs of the com-pany into two mutually exclusive categories: fixed costs and variable costs. You will recall from your study of basic economics that in the long run, all costs are variable. Breakeven analysis, therefore, is a short-run concept.

Assumed Behavior of Costs

Fixed costs. **Fixed costs**, also referred to as **indirect costs**, do not vary in total amount as sales volume or the quantity of output changes over some *relevant* range of output. Total fixed costs are independent of the quantity of product produced and equal some constant dollar amount. As production volume increases, fixed cost per unit of product falls, as fixed costs are spread over larger and larger quantities of output. Figure 13.3 graphs the behavior of total fixed costs with respect to the company's relevant range of output. This total is shown to be unaffected by the quantity of product that is manufac-tured and sold. Over some other relevant output range, the amount of total fixed costs might be higher or lower for the same company.

In a manufacturing setting, some specific examples of fixed costs are

1. Administrative salaries
2. Depreciation
3. Insurance
4. Lump sums spent on intermittent advertising programs
5. Property taxes
6. Rent

Fixed costs (indirect costs)

Costs that do not vary in total dollar amount as sales volume or quantity of output changes.

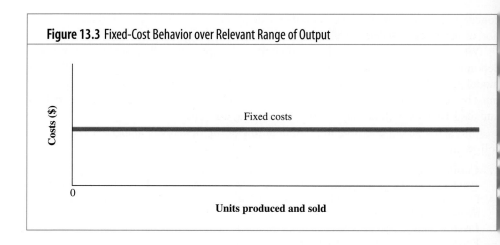

Figure 13.3 Fixed-Cost Behavior over Relevant Range of Output

Costs ($)

Fixed costs

0

Units produced and sold

Variable costs (direct costs)

Costs that are fixed per unit of output but vary in total as output changes.

Variable costs. **Variable costs** are sometimes referred to as **direct costs**. Variable costs are fixed per unit of output but vary in total as output changes. Total variable costs are computed by taking the variable cost per unit and multiplying it by the quantity produced and sold. The breakeven model assumes proportionality between total variable costs and sales. Thus, if sales rise by 10 percent, it is assumed that variable costs will rise by 10 percent. Figure 13.4 graphs the behavior of total variable costs with respect to the company's relevant range of output. Total variable costs are seen to depend on the quantity of product that is manufactured and sold. Notice that if zero units of the product are manufactured, then variable costs are zero, but fixed costs are greater than zero. This implies that some contribution to the coverage of fixed costs occurs as long as the selling price per unit exceeds the variable cost per unit. This helps explain why some firms will operate a plant even when sales are temporarily depressed—that is, to provide some increment of revenue toward the coverage of fixed costs.

For a manufacturing operation, some examples of variable costs include:

1. Direct labor
2. Direct materials
3. Energy costs (fuel, electricity, natural gas) associated with the production area
4. Freight costs for products leaving the plant
5. Packaging
6. Sales commissions

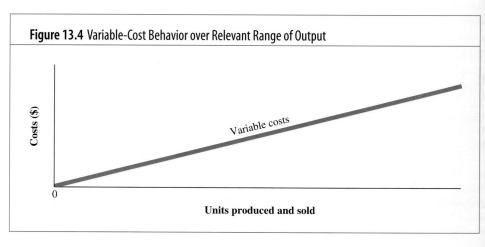

Figure 13.4 Variable-Cost Behavior over Relevant Range of Output

Costs ($)

Variable costs

0

Units produced and sold

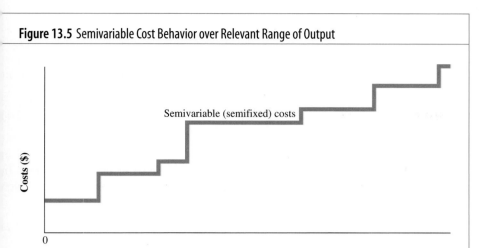

Figure 13.5 Semivariable Cost Behavior over Relevant Range of Output

Costs ($)

Semivariable (semifixed) costs

0

Units produced and sold

More on behavior of costs. No one believes that all costs behave as neatly as we have illustrated the fixed and variable costs in Figures 13.3 and 13.4. Nor does any law or accounting principle dictate that a certain element of the firm's total costs always be classified as fixed or variable. This will depend on each firm's specific circumstances. In one firm, energy costs may be predominantly fixed, whereas in another they may vary with output.[3]

Furthermore, some costs may be fixed for a while, then rise sharply to a higher level as a higher output is reached, remain fixed, and then rise again with further increases in production. Such costs may be termed either **semivariable** or **semifixed**.

The label is your choice, because both are used in industrial practice. An example might be the salaries paid production supervisors. Should output be cut back by 15 percent for a short period, the management of the organization is not likely to lay off 15 percent of the supervisors. Similarly, commissions paid to salespeople often follow a stepwise pattern over wide ranges of success. This sort of cost behavior is shown in Figure 13.5.

To implement the breakeven model and deal with such a complex cost structure, the financial manager must (1) identify the most relevant output range for planning purposes, and then (2) approximate the cost effect of semivariable items over this range by segregating a portion of them to fixed costs and a portion to variable costs. In the actual business setting this procedure is not fun. It is not unusual for the analyst who deals with the figures to spend considerably more time allocating costs to fixed and variable categories than in carrying out the actual breakeven calculations.

Semivariable costs (semifixed costs)

Costs that exhibit the joint characteristics of both fixed and variable costs over different ranges of output.

Total Revenue and Volume of Output

Besides fixed and variable costs, the essential elements of the breakeven model include total revenue from sales and volume of output. **Total revenue** means sales dollars and is equal to the selling price per unit multiplied by the quantity sold. The **volume of output** refers to the firm's level of operations and may be indicated either as a unit quantity or as sales dollars.

Total revenue

Total sales dollars.

Volume of output

The firm's level of operations expressed either in sales dollars or as units of output.

In a greenhouse operation, where plants are grown (manufactured) under strictly controlled temperatures, heat costs will tend to be fixed whether the building is full or only half full of seedlings. In a metal stamping operation, where levers are being produced, there is no need to heat the plant to as high a temperature when the machines are stopped and the workers are not there. In this latter case, the heat costs will tend to be variable.

Finding the Breakeven Point

Finding the breakeven point in terms of units of production can be accomplished in several ways. All approaches require the essential elements of the breakeven model just described. The breakeven model is a simple adaptation of the firm's income statement expressed in the following analytical format:

$$\text{sales} - (\text{total variable cost} + \text{total fixed cost}) = \text{profit} \qquad (13\text{-}1)$$

On a units of production basis, it is necessary to introduce (1) the price at which each unit is sold and (2) the variable cost per unit of output. Because the profit item studied in breakeven analysis is EBIT, we will use that acronym instead of the word "profit." In terms of units, the income statement shown in equation (13-1) becomes the breakeven model by setting EBIT equal to zero:

$$(\text{sales price per unit})\,(\text{units sold}) - [(\text{variable cost per unit})\,(\text{units sold}) \qquad (13\text{-}2)$$
$$+ (\text{total fixed cost})] = \text{EBIT} = \$0$$

Our task now becomes finding the number of units that must be produced and sold in order to satisfy equation (13-2)—that is, to arrive at an EBIT = $0. This can be done by (1) trial-and-error analysis, (2) contribution-margin analysis, or (3) algebraic analysis. Each approach will be illustrated using the same set of circumstances.

Problem Situation

Even though the Pierce Grain Company manufactures several different products, it has observed over a lengthy period that its product mix is rather constant. This allows management to conduct its financial planning by use of a "normal" sales price per unit and "normal" variable cost per unit. The "normal" sales price and variable cost per unit are calculated from the constant product mix. It is like assuming that the product mix is one big product. The selling price is $10 and the variable cost is $6. Total fixed costs for the firm are $100,000 per year. What is the breakeven point in units produced and sold for the company during the coming year?

Trial-and-error analysis. The most cumbersome approach to determining the firm's breakeven point is to employ the trial-and-error technique illustrated in Table 13.2.

Table 13.2 Pierce Grain Company Sales, Cost, and Profit Schedule

(1) Units Sold	(2) Unit Sales Price	(3) = (1) + (2) Sales	(4) Unit Variable Cost	(5) = (1) × (4) Total Variable Cost	(6) Total Fixed Cost	(7) = (5) + (6) Total Cost	(8) = (3) − (7) EBIT	
1. 10,000	$10	$100,000	$6	$ 60,000	$100,000	$160,000	$−60,000	1.
2. 15,000	10	150,000	6	90,000	100,000	190,000	−40,000	2.
3. 20,000	10	200,000	6	120,000	100,000	220,000	−20,000	3.
4. 25,000	10	250,000	6	150,000	100,000	250,000	0	4.
5. 30,000	10	300,000	6	180,000	100,000	280,000	20,000	5.
6. 35,000	10	350,000	6	210,000	100,000	310,000	40,000	6.

Input Data
Unit sales price   = $10
Unit variable cost = $6
Total fixed cost   = $100,000

Output Data
Breakeven point in units = 25,000 units produced and sold
Breakeven point in sales = $250,000

The process simply involves the arbitrary selection of an output level and the calculation of a corresponding EBIT amount. When the level of output is found that results in an EBIT = $0, the breakeven point has been located. Notice that Table 13.2 is just equation (13-2) in worksheet form. For the Pierce Grain Company, total operating costs will be covered when 25,000 units are manufactured and sold. This tells us that if sales equal $250,000, the firm's EBIT will equal $0.

Contribution-margin analysis. Unlike trial and error, use of the contribution-margin technique permits direct computation of the breakeven quantity of output. The **contribution margin** is the difference between the unit selling price and unit variable costs, as follows:

Contribution margin

Unit sales price minus unit variable cost.

Unit sales price
− Unit variable cost
= Unit contribution margin

The use of the word "contribution" in the present context means contribution to the coverage of fixed operating costs. For the Pierce Grain Company, the unit contribution margin is:

Unit sales price	$10
Unit variable cost	−6
Unit contribution margin	$ 4

If the annual fixed costs of $100,000 are divided by the unit contribution margin of $4, we find the breakeven quantity of output for Pierce Grain is 25,000 units. With much less effort, we have arrived at the identical result found by trial and error. Figure 13.6 portrays the contribution-margin technique for finding the breakeven point.

Algebraic analysis. To explain the algebraic method for finding the breakeven output level, we need to adopt some notation. Let

Q = the number of units sold
Q_B = the breakeven level of Q
P = the unit sales price
F = total fixed costs anticipated over the planning period
V = the unit variable cost

Equation (13-2), the breakeven model, is repeated below as equation (13-2a) with the model symbols used in place of words. The breakeven model is then solved for Q, the number of units that must be sold in order that EBIT will equal $0. We label the breakeven point quantity Q_B.

$$(P \cdot Q) - [(V \cdot Q) + (F)] = \text{EBIT} = \$0 \qquad \text{(13-2a)}$$

$$(P \cdot Q) - (V \cdot Q) - F = \$0$$

$$Q(P - V) = F$$

$$Q_B = \frac{F}{P - V} \qquad \text{(13-3)}$$

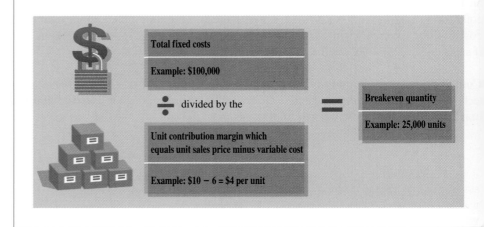

Figure 13.6 Contribution-Margin Approach to Breakeven Analysis

Total fixed costs

Example: $100,000

÷ divided by the

Unit contribution margin which
equals unit sales price minus variable cost

Example: $10 − 6 = $4 per unit

= Breakeven quantity

Example: 25,000 units

Observe that equation (13-3) says: divide total fixed operating costs, F, by the unit contribution margin, $P - V$, and the breakeven level of output, Q_B, will be obtained. The contribution-margin analysis is nothing more than equation (13-3) in different garb.

Application of equation (13-3) permits direct calculation of Pierce Grain's breakeven point, as follows:

$$Q_B = \frac{F}{P - V} = \frac{\$100,000}{\$10 - \$6} = 25,000 \text{ units}$$

Breakeven Point in Sales Dollars

In dealing with the multiproduct firm, it is convenient to compute the breakeven point in terms of sales dollars rather than units of output. Sales, in effect, become a common denominator associated with a particular product mix. Furthermore, an outside analyst may not have access to internal unit cost data. He or she may, however, be able to obtain annual reports for the firm. If the analyst can separate the firm's total costs as identified from its annual reports into their fixed and variable components, he or she can calculate a general breakeven point in sales dollars.

We will illustrate the procedure using the Pierce Grain Company's cost structure contained in Table 13.2. Suppose that the information on line 5 of Table 13.2 is arranged in the format shown in Table 13.3. We will refer to this type of financial statement as an **analytical income statement**. This distinguishes it from audited income statements published, for example, in the annual reports of public corporations. If we are aware of the simple mathematical relationships on which cost-volume-profit analysis is based, we can use Table 13.3 to find the breakeven point in sales dollars for the Pierce Grain Company.

First, let us explore the logic of the process. Recall from equation (13-1) that

sales − (total variable cost + total fixed cost) = EBIT

If we let total sales = S, total variable cost = VC, and total fixed cost = F, the preceding relationship becomes

$S - (VC + F) = \text{EBIT}$

Analytical income statement

A financial statement used by internal analysts that differs in composition from audited or published financial statements.

Table 13.3 Pierce Grain Company Analytical Income Statement

Sales	$300,000
Less: Total variable costs	180,000
Revenue before fixed costs	$120,000
Less: Total fixed costs	100,000
EBIT	$ 20,000

Because variable cost per unit of output and selling price per unit are *assumed* constant over the relevant output range in breakeven analysis, the ratio of total sales to total variable cost, VC/S, is a constant for any level of sales. This permits us to rewrite the previous expression as

$$S - \left[\left(\frac{VC}{S}\right)S\right] - F = \text{EBIT}$$

and

$$S - \left(1 - \frac{VC}{S}\right) - F = \text{EBIT}$$

At the breakeven point, however, EBIT = 0, and the corresponding breakeven level of sales can be represented as S^*. At the breakeven level of sales, we have

$$S^*\left(1 - \frac{VC}{S}\right) - F = 0$$

or

$$S^*\left(1 - \frac{VC}{S}\right) = F$$

Therefore,

$$S^* = \frac{F}{1 - \dfrac{VC}{S}} \tag{13-4}$$

The application of equation (13-4) to Pierce Grain's analytical income statement in Table 13.3 permits the breakeven sales level for the firm to be directly computed, as follows:

$$S^* = \frac{\$100,000}{1 - \dfrac{\$180,000}{\$300,000}}$$

$$= \frac{\$100,000}{1 - .60} = \$250,000$$

Notice that this is indeed the same breakeven sales level for Pierce Grain that is indicated on line 4 of Table 13.2.

Graphic Representation, Analysis of Input Changes, and Cash Breakeven Point

In making a presentation to management, it is often effective to display the firm's cost-volume-profit relationships in the form of a chart. Even those individuals who truly enjoy analyzing financial problems find figures and equations dry material at times. Furthermore, by quickly scanning the basic breakeven chart, the manager can approximate the EBIT amount that will prevail at different sales levels.

Such a chart has been prepared for the Pierce Grain Company. Figure 13.7 has been constructed for this firm using the input data contained in Table 13.2. Total fixed costs of $100,000 are added to the total variable costs associated with each production level to form the total costs line. When 25,000 units of product are manufactured and sold, the sales line and total costs line intersect. This means, of course, that the EBIT that would exist at that volume of output is zero. Beyond 25,000 units of output, notice that sales revenues exceed the total costs line. This causes a positive EBIT. This positive EBIT, or profits, is labeled "original EBIT" in Figure 13.7.

The unencumbered nature of the breakeven model makes it possible to quickly incorporate changes in the requisite input data and generate the revised output. Suppose a favorable combination of events causes Pierce Grain's fixed costs to decrease by $25,000. This would put total fixed costs for the planning period at a level of $75,000 rather than the $100,000 originally forecast. Total costs, being the sum of fixed and variable costs, would be lower by $25,000 at all output levels. The revised total costs line in

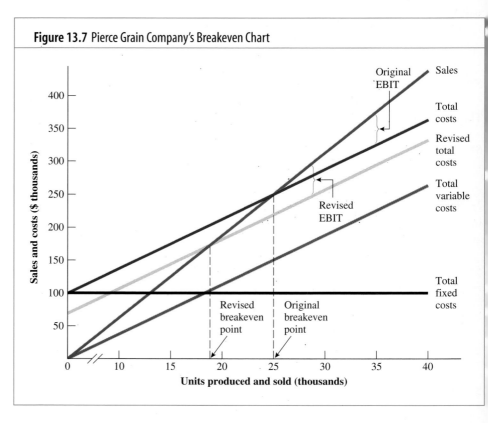

Figure 13.7 Pierce Grain Company's Breakeven Chart

Figure 13.7 reflects Pierce Grain's reduction in fixed costs. Under these revised conditions, the new breakeven point in units would be as follows:

$$Q_B = \frac{\$75,000}{\$10 - \$6} = 18,750 \text{ units}$$

The revised breakeven point of 18,750 units is identified in Figure 13.7, along with the revised EBIT amounts that would prevail at differing output and sales levels. The chart clearly indicates that at any specific production and sales level, the revised EBIT would exceed the original EBIT. This must be the case, as the revised total costs line lies below the original total costs line over the entire relevant output range. The effect on the breakeven point caused by other changes in (1) the cost structure or (2) the pricing policy can be analyzed in a similar fashion.

The data in Figure 13.7 can be used to demonstrate another version of basic cost-volume-profit analysis. This can be called **cash breakeven analysis**. If the company's fixed- or variable-cost estimates allow for any noncash expenses, then the resultant breakeven point is higher on an accounting profit basis than on a cash basis. This means the firm's production and sales levels do not have to be as great to cover the cash costs of manufacturing the product.

What are these noncash expenses? The largest and most significant is depreciation expense. Another category is prepaid expenses. Insurance policies are at times paid to cover a 3-year cycle. Thus the time period for which the breakeven analysis is being performed might *not* involve an actual cash outlay for insurance coverage.

For purposes of illustration, assume that noncash expenses for Pierce Grain amount to $25,000 over the planning period and that all these costs are fixed. We can compare the revised total costs line in Figure 13.7, which implicitly assumes a lower fixed *cash* cost line, with the sales revenue line to find the cash breakeven point. Provided Pierce Grain can produce and sell 18,750 units over the planning horizon, revenues from sales will be equal to cash operating costs.

Cash breakeven analysis

A variation from traditional breakeven analysis that removes (deducts) noncash expenses from the cost items.

RELATE TO THE BIG PICTURE

*The discussion above on cash breakeven analysis reinforces the importance of **Axiom 3: Cash—Not Profits—Is King**. By use of this modified version of regular breakeven analysis, we are reminded that only cash can be reinvested into the firm's operations, as distinct from retained earnings. Cash is used to pay operating expenses, acquire real capital, and distribute earnings in the form of cash dividends. Another way of understanding **Axiom 3** is as follows: Accounting profits are an opinion—cash is reality. Financial asset values are based on the firm's ability to generate cash flows. You cannot be misled over long time periods by cash flow generation. Note that this emphasis on reality also relates to our discussion of value-based management techniques (economic value added and market value added) in chapter 3.*

Limitations of Breakeven Analysis

Earlier we identified some of the applications of breakeven analysis. This technique is a useful tool in many settings. It must be emphasized, however, that breakeven analysis provides a *beneficial guide* to managerial action, not the final answer. The use of cost-volume-profit analysis has limitations, which should be kept in mind. These include the following:

1. The cost-volume-profit relationship is assumed to be linear. This is realistic only over narrow ranges of output.

2. The total revenue curve (sales curve) is presumed to increase linearly with the volume of output. This implies any quantity can be sold over the relevant output range at that *single* price. To be more realistic, it is necessary in many situations to compute *several* sales curves and corresponding breakeven points at differing prices.

3. A constant production and sales mix is assumed. Should the company decide to produce more of one product and less of another, a new breakeven point would have to be found. Only if the variable cost-to-sales ratios were identical for products involved would the new calculation be unnecessary.

4. The breakeven chart and the breakeven computation are static forms of analysis. Any alteration in the firm's cost or price structure dictates that a new breakeven point be calculated. Breakeven analysis is more helpful, therefore, in stable industries than in dynamic ones.

OBJECTIVE 3

OPERATING LEVERAGE

If *fixed* operating costs are present in the firm's cost structure, so is *operating leverage*. Fixed operating costs do not include interest charges incurred from the firm's use of debt financing. Those costs will be incorporated into the analysis when financial leverage is discussed.

So operating leverage arises from the firm's use of fixed operating costs. But what is operating leverage? **Operating leverage** is the responsiveness of the firm's EBIT to fluctuations in sales. By continuing to draw on our data for the Pierce Grain Company, we can illustrate the concept of operating leverage. Table 13.4 contains data for a study of a possible fluctuation in the firm's sales level. It is assumed that Pierce Grain is currently operating at an annual sales level of $300,000. This is referred to in the tabulation as the base sales level at t (time period zero). The question is: How will Pierce Grain's EBIT level respond to a positive 20 percent change in sales? A sales volume of $360,000, referred to as the forecast sales level at $t +1$, reflects the 20 percent sales rise anticipated over the planning period. Assume that the planning period is 1 year.

Operating leverage relationships are derived within the mathematical assumptions of cost-volume-profit analysis. In the present example, this means that Pierce Grain's variable cost-to-sales ratio of .6 will continue to hold during time period $t +1$, and the fixed costs will hold steady at $100,000.

Given the forecasted sales level for Pierce Grain and its cost structure, we can measure the responsiveness of EBIT to the upswing in volume. Notice in Table 13.4 that EBIT is expected to be $44,000 at the end of the planning period. The percentage change in EBIT from t to $t + 1$ can be measured as follows:

$$\text{percentage change in EBIT} = \frac{\$44,000_{t+1} - \$20,000_t}{\$20,000_t}$$

$$= \frac{\$24,000}{\$20,000}$$

$$= 120\%$$

We know that the projected fluctuation in sales amounts to 20 percent of the base period, $t,$ sales level. This is verified below:

$$\text{percentage change in sales} = \frac{\$360,000_{t+1} - \$300,000_t}{\$300,000_t}$$

$$= \frac{\$60,000}{\$300,000}$$

$$= 20\%$$

Table 13.4 Concept of Operating Leverage: Increase in Pierce Grain Company Sales

Item	Base Sales Level, t	Forecast Sales Level, $t + 1$
Sales	$300,000	$360,000
Less: Total variable costs	180,000	216,000
Revenue before fixed costs	$120,000	$144,000
Less: Total fixed costs	100,000	100,000
EBIT	$ 20,000	$ 44,000

By relating the percentage fluctuation in EBIT to the percentage fluctuation in sales, we can calculate a specific measure of operating leverage. Thus we have

OBJECTIVE 4

$$\text{degree of operating leverage from the base sales level}(s) = DOL_s = \frac{\text{percentage change in EBIT}}{\text{percentage change in sales}} \qquad (13\text{-}5)$$

Applying equation (13-5) to our Pierce Grain data gives

$$DOL_{\$300,000} = \frac{120\%}{20\%} = 6 \text{ times}$$

Unless we understand what the specific measure of operating leverage tells us, the fact that we may know it is equal to six times is nothing more than sterile information. For Pierce Grain, the inference is that for *any* percentage fluctuation in sales from the base level, the percentage fluctuation in EBIT will be six times as great. If Pierce Grain expected only a 5 percent rise in sales over the coming period, a 30 percent rise in EBIT would be anticipated as follows:

$$(\text{percentage change in sales}) \times (DOL_s) = \text{percentage change in EBIT}$$

$$(5\%) \times (6) = 30\%$$

We will now return to the postulated 20 percent change in sales. What if the direction of the fluctuation is expected to be negative rather than positive? What is in store for Pierce Grain? Unfortunately for Pierce Grain (but fortunately for the analytical process) we will see that the operating leverage measure holds in the negative direction as well. This situation is displayed in Table 13.5.

Table 13.5 Concept of Operating Leverage: Decrease in Pierce Grain Company Sales

Item	Base Sales Level, t	Forecast Sales Level, $t + 1$
Sales	$300,000	$240,000
Less: Total variable costs	180,000	144,000
Revenue before fixed costs	$120,000	$ 96,000
Less: Total fixed costs	100,000	100,000
EBIT	$ 20,000	$ −4,000

At the $240,000 sales level, which represents the 20 percent decrease from the base period, Pierce Grain's EBIT is expected to be –$4,000. How sensitive is EBIT to this sales change? The magnitude of the EBIT fluctuation is calculated as[4]

$$\text{percentage change in EBIT} = \frac{-\$4,000_{t+1} - \$20,000_t}{\$20,000_t}$$

$$= \frac{-\$24,000}{\$20,000}$$

$$= -120\%$$

Making use of our knowledge that the sales change was equal to –20 percent permits us to compute the specific measure of operating leverage as

$$DOL_{\$300,000} = \frac{-120\%}{-20\%} = 6 \text{ times}$$

What we have seen, then, is that the degree of operating leverage measure works in the positive or negative direction. A negative change in production volume and sales can be magnified severalfold when the effect on EBIT is calculated.

To this point, our calculations of the degree of operating leverage have required two analytical income statements: one for the base period and a second for the subsequent period that incorporates the possible sales alteration. This cumbersome process can be simplified. If unit cost data are available to the financial manager, the relationship can be expressed directly in the following manner:

$$DOL_s = \frac{Q(P - V)}{Q(P - V) - F} \tag{13-6}$$

Observe in equation (13-6) that the variables were all previously defined in our algebraic analysis of the breakeven model. Recall that Pierce sells its product at $10 per unit, the unit variable cost is $6, and total fixed costs over the planning horizon are $100,000. Still assuming that Pierce is operating at a $300,000 sales volume, which means output (Q) is 30,000 units, we can find the degree of operating leverage by application of equation (13-6):

$$DOL_{\$300,000} = \frac{30,000(\$10 - \$6)}{30,000(\$10 - \$6) - \$100,000} = \frac{\$120,000}{\$20,000} = 6 \text{ times}$$

Whereas equation (13-6) requires us to know unit cost data to carry out the computations, the next formulation we examine does not. If we have an analytical income statement for the base period, then equation (13-7) can be employed to find the firm's degree of operating leverage:

$$DOL_s = \frac{\text{revenue before fixed costs}}{\text{EBIT}} = \frac{S - VC}{S - VC - F} \tag{13-7}$$

Use of equation (13-7) in conjunction with the base period data for Pierce Grain shown in either Table 13.4 or 13.5 gives

$$DOL_{\$300,000} = \frac{\$120,000}{\$20,000} = 6 \text{ times}$$

---

[4]Some students have conceptual difficulty in computing these percentage changes when negative amounts are involved. Notice by inspection in Table 13.5 that the *difference* between an EBIT amount of +$20,000 at t and –$4,000 at $t+1$ is –$24,000.

The three versions of the operating leverage measure all produce the same result. Data availability will sometimes dictate which formulation can be applied. The crucial consideration, though, is that you grasp what the measurement tells you. For Pierce Grain, a 1 percent change in sales will produce a 6 percent change in EBIT.

STOP AND THINK

Before we complete our discussion of operating leverage and move on to the subject of financial leverage, ask yourself, "which type of leverage is more under the control of management?" You will probably (and correctly) come to the conclusion that the firm's managers have less control over its operating cost structure and almost complete control over its financial structure. What the firm actually produces, for example, will determine to a significant degree the division between fixed and variable costs. There is more room for substitution among the various sources of financial capital than there is among the labor and real capital inputs that enable the firm to meet its production requirements. Thus you can anticipate more arguments over the choice to use a given degree of financial leverage than the corresponding choice over operating leverage use.

Implications

As the firm's scale of operations moves in a favorable manner above the break-even point, the degree of operating leverage at each subsequent (higher) sales base will decline. In short, the greater the sales level, the lower the degree of operating leverage. This is demonstrated in Table 13.6 for the Pierce Grain Company. At the breakeven sales level for Pierce Grain, the degree of operating leverage is *undefined*, because the denominator in any of the computational formulas is zero. Notice that beyond the breakeven point of 25,000 units, the degree of operating leverage declines. It will decline at a decreasing rate and asymptotically approach a value of 1.00. As long as some fixed operating costs are present in the firm's cost structure, however, operating leverage exists, and the degree of operating leverage (DOL_s) will exceed 1.00. Operating leverage is present, then, whenever the firm faces the following situation:

$$\frac{\text{percentage change in EBIT}}{\text{percentage change in sales}} > 1.00$$

The data in Table 13.6 are presented in graphic form in Figure 13.8.

Table 13.6 Pierce Grain Company Degree of Operating Leverage Relative to Different Sales Bases

Units Produced and Sold	Sales Dollars	DOL_s
25,000	$ 250,000	Undefined
30,000	300,000	6.00
35,000	350,000	3.50
40,000	400,000	2.67
45,000	450,000	2.25
50,000	500,000	2.00
75,000	750,000	1.50
100,000	1,000,000	1.33

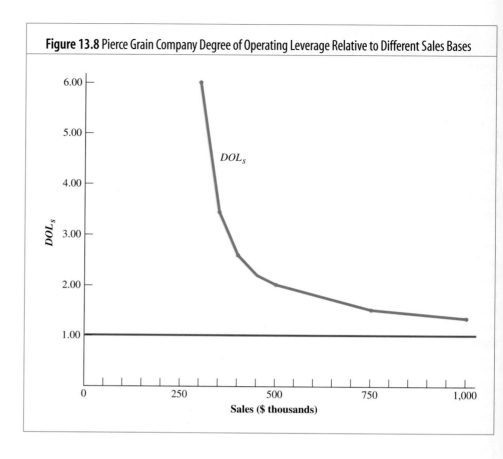

Figure 13.8 Pierce Grain Company Degree of Operating Leverage Relative to Different Sales Bases

The greater the firm's degree of operating leverage, the more its profits will vary with a given percentage change in sales. Thus operating leverage is definitely an attribute of the business risk that confronts the company. From Table 13.6 and Figure 13.8, we have seen that the degree of operating leverage falls as sales increase past the firm's breakeven point. The sheer size and operating profitability of the firm, therefore, affect and can lessen its business-risk exposure.

The manager considering an alteration in the firm's cost structure will benefit from an understanding of the operating leverage concept. It might be possible to replace part of the labor force with capital equipment (machinery). A possible result is an increase in fixed costs associated with the new machinery and a reduction in variable costs attributable to a lower labor bill. This conceivably could raise the firm's degree of operating leverage at a specific sales base. If the prospects for future sales increases are high, then increasing the degree of operating leverage might be a prudent decision. The opposite conclusion will be reached if sales prospects are unattractive.

STOP AND THINK

As you are introduced to the topic of financial leverage, remember that this is one of the most crucial policy areas on which a financial executive spends his or her time. We describe and measure here what happens to the firm's earnings per share when financial risk is assumed. Try to understand this effect. We demonstrate how actually to measure this effect in the next section. By now you should be realizing that variability of all types—be it in an earnings stream or in stock returns—is a central element of financial thought and the practice of financial management.

We have defined *financial leverage* as the practice of financing a portion of the firm's assets with securities bearing a fixed rate of return in hope of increasing the ultimate return to the common shareholders. In the present discussion, we focus on the responsiveness of the company's earnings per share to changes in its EBIT. For the time being, then, the return to the common stockholder being concentrated upon is earnings per share. We are *not* saying that earnings per share is the appropriate criterion for all financing decisions. In fact, the weakness of such a contention will be examined in the next chapter. Rather, the use of financial leverage produces a certain type of *effect*. This effect can be illustrated clearly by concentrating on an earnings-per-share criterion.

Let us assume that the Pierce Grain Company is in the process of getting started as a going concern. The firm's potential owners have calculated that $200,000 is needed to purchase the necessary assets to conduct the business. Three possible financing plans have been identified for raising the $200,000; they are presented in Table 13.7. In plan A, no financial risk is assumed: The entire $200,000 is raised by selling 2,000 common shares, each with a $100 par value. In plan B, a moderate amount of financial risk is assumed: 25 percent of the assets are financed with a debt issue that carries an 8 percent annual interest rate. Plan C would use the most financial leverage: 40 percent of the assets would be financed with a debt issue costing 8 percent.[5]

Table 13.8 presents the impact of financial leverage on earnings per share associated with each fund-raising alternative. If EBIT should increase from $20,000 to $40,000, then earnings per share would rise by 100 percent under plan A. The same positive fluctuation in EBIT would occasion an earnings per share rise of 125 percent under plan B, and 147 percent under plan C. In plans B and C, the 100 percent increase in EBIT (from $20,000 to $40,000) is magnified to a greater than 100 percent increase in earnings per

---

Table 13.7 Pierce Grain Company Possible Financial Structures

Plan A: 0% debt

		Total debt	$ 0
		Common equity	200,000[a]
Total assets	$200,000	Total liabilities and equity	$200,000

Plan B: 25% debt at 8% interest rate

		Total debt	$ 50,000
		Common equity	150,000[b]
Total assets	$200,000	Total liabilities and equity	$200,000

Plan C: 40% debt at 8% interest rate

		Total debt	$ 80,000
		Common equity	120,000[c]
Total assets	$200,000	Total liabilities and equity	$200,000

[a]2,000 common shares outstanding   [b]1,500 common shares outstanding   [c]1,200 common shares outstanding

---

[5]In actual practice, moving from a 25 to a 40 percent debt ratio would probably result in a higher interest rate on the additional bonds. That effect is ignored here to let us concentrate on the ramifications of using different proportions of debt in the financial structure.

Table 13.8 Pierce Grain Company Analysis of Financial Leverage at Different EBIT Levels

(1) EBIT	(2) Interest	(3) = (1) − (2) EBT	(4) = (3) × .5 Taxes	(5) = (3) − (4) Net Income to Common	(6) Earnings per Share
Plan A: 0% debt; $200,000 common equity; 2,000 shares					
$ 0	$ 0	$ 0	$ 0	$ 0	$ 0
20,000	0	20,000	10,000	10,000	5.00 ⎫
40,000	0	40,000	20,000	20,000	10.00 ⎬ 100%
60,000	0	60,000	30,000	30,000	15.00
80,000	0	80,000	40,000	40,000	20.00
Plan B: 25% debt; 8% interest rate; $150,000 common equity, 1,500 shares					
$ 0	$4,000	$ (4,000)	$ (2,000)ᵃ	$ (2,000)	$ (1.33)
20,000	4,000	16,000	8,000	8,000	5.33 ⎫
40,000	4,000	36,000	18,000	18,000	12.00 ⎬ 125%
60,000	4,000	56,000	28,000	28,000	18.67
80,000	4,000	76,000	38,000	38,000	25.33
Plan C: 40% debt; 8% interest rate; $120,000 common equity; 1,200 shares					
$ 0	$6,400	$ (6,400)	$ (3,200)ᵃ	$ (3,200)	$ (2.67)
20,000	6,400	13,600	6,800	6,800	5.67 ⎫
40,000	6,400	33,600	16,800	16,800	14.00 ⎬ 147%
60,000	6,400	53,600	26,800	26,800	22.33
80,000	6,400	73,600	36,800	36,800	30.67

ᵃThe negative tax bill recognizes the credit arising from the carryback and carryforward provision of the tax code. See chapter 1.

share. The firm is employing financial leverage, and exposing its owners to financial risk, when the following situation exists:

$$\frac{\text{percentage change in earnings per share}}{\text{percentage change in EBIT}} > 1.00$$

By following the same general procedures that allowed us to analyze the firm's use of operating leverage, we can lay out a precise measure of financial leverage. Such a measure deals with the sensitivity of earnings per share to EBIT fluctuations. The relationship can be expressed as

$$\text{degree of financial leverage (DFL) from base EBIT level} = DFL_{EBIT} = \frac{\text{percentage change in earnings per share}}{\text{percentage change in EBIT}} \quad (13\text{-}8)$$

Use of equation (13-8) with each of the financing choices outlined for Pierce Grain is shown subsequently. The base EBIT level is $20,000 in each case.

Plan A: $DFL_{\$20,000} = \dfrac{100\%}{100\%} = 1.00$ time

Plan B: $DFL_{\$20,000} = \dfrac{125\%}{100\%} = 1.25$ times

Plan C: $DFL_{\$20,000} = \dfrac{147\%}{100\%} = 1.47$ times

IBM: International Influences on Revenue Growth

(A) IBM's financial performance in 1996 reflects continued progress towards its strategic goals of revenue growth, an expanded portfolio of industry-specific customer solutions, (especially through network computing), and an increasingly competitive cost and expense structure.

(B) The company reported record revenue of nearly $76 billion, 30 percent net earnings growth over 1995, and ended the year with over $8 billion in cash. The company also continued to align itself for strategic growth by investing almost $20 billion in critical high-growth and advanced technology businesses, research and development, acquisitions, and repurchases of its common shares.

(C) The company's results were also affected adversely by the continued weakness of the European economy and the continued strengthening of the U.S. dollar. Without the currency effect, year-to-year revenue growth would have been 9 percent compared with the reported growth of 6 percent.

Although excellent progress was made in 1996, the company must continue to implement strategic actions to further improve its competitiveness. These actions include an ongoing focus on revenue growth and stable net income margins, while at the same time maintaining a strong balance sheet and cash flows for long-term growth. **(D)**

SOURCE: IBM *Annual Report* (1996): 44.

Analysis and Implications ...

In 1996, IBM posted an increase in sales of some 5.6 percent. But the company's change in net income was a much greater 30.0 percent. This is exactly the type of magnification effect that we are studying within this chapter. The management discussion from IBM's 1996 *Annual Report* highlights several concepts explored in this and other chapters of the text.

A. The emphasis here on "cost and expense structure" is directly related to our discussion of operating leverage and the precise measurement of it. Also notice how IBM management identifies revenue growth as one of its main corporate strategic goals. Successful sales growth, then, will generate larger fluctuations in earnings before interest and taxes and in net income.

B. Here the firm dwells on the increase in sales revenues and relates it to the aforementioned 30 percent increase in net earnings. A portion of this magnification effect is due to the firm's cost structure and resultant use of operating leverage—the material that we discussed in the previous section of chapter 13.

C. At this point, the management discussion dwells on international considerations. The firm asserts that sales growth would have been even better had the European economy been stronger. This means IBM feels the export of its products was dampened by the slow-growth status of several European countries. Further, IBM's management identifies the strong value of the dollar relative to European currencies as a factor that muted sales growth in 1996. The reason for this is, if the dollar is strong, the specific European currency is "weak." It takes more units of the foreign currency to buy 1 dollar. Thus it makes IBM's products more expensive; this tends to slow down sales growth.

D. Here IBM's management identifies the building blocks of its strategic plan. The emphasis on sales growth remains intact. Notice the closing reference to cash-flow generation—this should remind you of **Axiom 3: Cash— Not Profits—Is King**. Companies do, in fact, think about the important concepts that we discuss in this text.

Like operating leverage, the *degree of financial leverage* concept performs in the negative direction as well as the positive. Should EBIT fall by 10 percent, the Pierce Grain Company would suffer a 12.5 percent decline in earnings per share under plan B. If plan C were chosen to raise the necessary financial capital, the decline in earnings would be 14.7 percent. Observe that the greater the DFL, the greater the fluctuations (positive or negative) in earnings per share. The common stockholder is required to endure greater variations in returns when the firm's management chooses to use more financial leverage rather than less. The DFL measure allows the variation to be quantified.

OBJECTIVE 4

Rather than taking the time to compute percentage changes in EBIT and earnings per share, the DFL can be found directly, as follows:

$$DFL_{EBIT} = \frac{EBIT}{EBIT - I} \tag{13-9}$$

In equation (13-9) the variable, I, represents the total interest expense incurred on *all* the firm's contractual debt obligations. If six bonds are outstanding, I is the sum of the interest expense on all six bonds. If the firm has preferred stock in its financial structure, the dividend on such issues must be inflated to a before-tax basis and included in the computation of I.[6] In this latter instance, I is in reality the sum of all fixed financing costs.

Equation (13-9) has been applied to each of Pierce Grain's financing plans (Table 13.8) at a base EBIT level of $20,000. The results are as follows:

Plan A: $DFL_{\$20,000} = \dfrac{\$20,000}{\$20,000 - 0} = 1.00$ time

Plan B: $DFL_{\$20,000} = \dfrac{\$20,000}{\$20,000 - \$4,000} = 1.25$ times

Plan C: $DFL_{\$20,000} = \dfrac{\$20,000}{\$20,000 - \$6,400} = 1.47$ times

As you probably suspected, the measures of financial leverage shown previously are identical to those obtained by use of equation (13-8). This will always be the case.

RELATE TO THE BIG PICTURE

The effect on the earnings stream available to the firm's common stockholders from combining operating and financial leverage in large degrees is dramatic. When the use of both leverage types is indeed heavy, a large sales increase will result in a very large rise in earnings per share. Be aware, though, that the very same thing happens in the opposite direction should the sales change be negative! Piling heavy financial leverage use on a high degree of operating leverage, then, is a very risky way to do business.

---

[6]Suppose (1) preferred dividends of $4,000 are paid annually by the firm and (2) it faces a 40 percent marginal tax rate. How much must the firm earn *before* taxes to make the $4,000 payment out of after-tax earnings? Because preferred dividends are not tax deductible to the paying company, we have $4,000/(1 − .40) = $6,666.67. The Tax Reform Act of 1986 provided for the taxation of corporate incomes at a maximum rate of 34 percent for tax years beginning after June 30, 1987. This maximum rate applies to taxable incomes over $75,000. Under this new tax provision, the firm would need to earn only $6,060.61 before taxes to make the $4,000 preferred dividend payment. That is, $4,000/(1 − .34) = $6,060.61. Note that from a financial policy viewpoint, the 1986 tax act reduced *somewhat* the tax shield advantages of corporate debt financing and simultaneously reduced the tax bias against preferred stock and common stock financing.

*Thus the firm will not "fool the markets" by combining high degrees of operating and financial leverage. Recall **Axiom 6: Efficient Capital Markets—The Markets Are Quick and the Prices Are Right**. We stated in chapter 1 that efficient markets deal with the speed with which information is impounded into security prices. Should the firm become overlevered in the eyes of the markets, say, stemming from an overly large issue of new debt securities, then the company's stock price will quickly be adjusted downward. The capital markets fully understand the double-edged sword of leverage use. Things go well when revenues rise; things do not go well when revenues fall. And, leverage use, either operating or financial, magnifies the original fluctuations in the revenues. Be aware.*

COMBINATION OF OPERATING AND FINANCIAL LEVERAGE

OBJECTIVE 3

Changes in sales revenues cause greater changes in EBIT. Additionally, changes in EBIT translate into larger variations in both earnings per share (EPS) and total earnings available to the common shareholders (EAC), if the firm chooses to use financial leverage. It should be no surprise, then, to find out that combining operating and financial leverage causes further large variations in earnings per share. This entire process is visually displayed in Figure 13.9.

Because the risk associated with possible earnings per share is affected by the use of combined or total leverage, it is useful to quantify the effect. For an illustration, we refer once more to the Pierce Grain Company. The cost structure identified for Pierce Grain in our discussion of breakeven analysis still holds. Furthermore, assume that plan B, which carried a 25 percent debt ratio, was chosen to finance the company's assets. Turn your attention to Table 13.9.

In Table 13.9, an increase in output for Pierce Grain from 30,000 to 36,000 units is analyzed. This increase represents a 20 percent rise in sales revenues. From our earlier discussion of operating leverage and the data in Table 13.9, we can see that this 20 percent increase in sales is magnified into a 120 percent rise in EBIT. From this base sales level of $300,000 the degree of operating leverage is six times.

The 120 percent rise in EBIT induces a change in earnings per share and earnings available to the common shareholders of 150 percent. The degree of financial leverage is therefore 1.25 times.

Figure 13.9 Leverage and Earnings Fluctuations

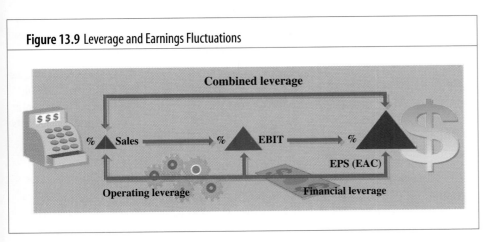

COCA-COLA COMPANY ANNUAL REPORT, 1993

The Coca-Cola Company Financial Policies

(A) Management's primary objective is to maximize shareowner value over time. To accomplish this objective, the Coca-Cola Company and subsidiaries (the Company) have developed a comprehensive business strategy that emphasizes maximizing long-term cash flows. This strategy focuses on continuing aggressive investment in the high-return soft drink business, increasing returns on existing investments and optimizing the cost of capital through appropriate financial policies. The success of this strategy is evidenced by the growth in the Company's cash flows and earnings, its increased returns on total capital and equity, and the total return to its share owners over time.

Management seeks investments that strategically enhance existing operations and offer cash returns that exceed the Company's long-term after-tax weighted average cost of capital, estimated by management to be approximately 11 percent as of January 1, 1994. The Company's soft drink business generates inherent high returns on capital, providing an attractive area for continued investment.

Maximizing share-owner value necessitates optimizing the Company's cost of capital through appropriate financial policies.

(B) The Company maintains debt levels considered prudent based on the Company's cash flows, interest coverage, and the percentage of debt to the Company's total capital. The Company's overall cost of capital is lowered by the use of debt financing, resulting in increased return to share owners.

The Company's capital structure and financial policies have resulted in long-term credit ratings of "AA" from Standard & Poor's and "Aa3" from Moody's, as well as the highest credit ratings available for its commercial paper programs. The Company's strong financial position and cash flows allow for opportunistic access to financing in financial markets around the world.

SOURCE: The Coca-Cola Company, *Annual Report* (1993): 44–46.

Analysis and Implications …

The fact that financial leverage effects can be measured provides management the opportunity to shape corporate policy formally around the decision to use or avoid the use of leverage-inducing financial instruments. The Coca-Cola Company has very specific policies on the use of financial leverage. The learning objectives of this chapter, then, comprise more than mere academic, intellectual exercises. The material is, in fact, the stuff of boardroom-level discussion.

A. We stated in chapter 1 that the goal of the firm is to maximize shareholder wealth, and this means maximizing the price of the firm's existing common stock. The Coca-Cola Company has accepted this approach to management as its "primary objective." To accomplish the objective, the Company has developed a strategy that centers on investment in its core business—the high-return soft drink business. Notice that Coca-Cola also speaks clearly about "optimizing" its cost of capital through properly designed financial policies. This is a good time to review the cost of capital linkage identified in Figure 13.1 and ponder its meaning.

B. Determining an appropriate (optimal) financing mix is a crucial activity of financial management. Companies use different approaches to seek an optimal range of financial leverage use. The Coca-Cola Company searches for a "prudent" level of debt use that is affected by (1) its projected cash flows, (2) interest coverage ratios, and (3) ratio of long-term debt to total capitalization. Further, the Company is highly concerned about the bond ratings that it receives from major rating agencies.

Table 13.9 Pierce Grain Company Combined Leverage Analysis

Item	Base Sales Level, t	Forecast Sales Level, $t + 1$	Selected Percentage Changes
Sales	$300,000	$360,000	+20
Less: Total variable costs	180,000	216,000	
Revenue before fixed costs	$120,000	$144,000	
Less: Total fixed costs	100,000	100,000	
EBIT	$ 20,000	$ 44,000	+120
Less: Interest expense	4,000	4,000	
Earnings before taxes (EBT)	$ 16,000	$ 40,000	
Less: Taxes at 50%	8,000	20,000	
Net income	$ 8,000	$ 20,000	+150
Less: Preferred dividends	0	0	
Earnings available to common (EAC)	$ 8,000	$ 20,000	+150
Number of common shares	1,500	1,500	
Earnings per share (EPS)	$ 5.33	$ 13.33	+150

$$\text{Degree of operating leverage} = \text{DOL}_{\$300,000} = \frac{120\%}{20\%} = 6 \text{ times}$$

$$\text{Degree of financial leverage} = \text{DFL}_{\$20,000} = \frac{150\%}{120\%} = 1.25 \text{ times}$$

$$\text{Degree of combined leverage} = \text{DCL}_{\$300,000} = \frac{150\%}{20\%} = 7.50 \text{ times}$$

The upshot of the analysis is that the 20 percent rise in sales has been magnified to 150 percent, as reflected by the percentage change in earnings per share. The formal measure of combined leverage can be expressed as follows:

$$\left(\begin{array}{c} \text{degree of combined} \\ \text{leverage from the} \\ \text{base sales level} \end{array} \right) = DCL_s = \left(\frac{\begin{array}{c}\text{percentage change in} \\ \text{earnings per share}\end{array}}{\text{percentage change in sales}} \right) \tag{13-10}$$

This equation was used in the bottom portion of Table 13.9 to determine that the degree of combined leverage from the base sales level of $300,000 is 7.50 times. Pierce Grain's use of both operating and financial leverage will cause any percentage change in sales (from the specific base level) to be magnified by a factor of 7.50 when the effect on earnings per share is computed. A 1 percent change in sales, for example, will result in a 7.50 percent change in earnings per share.

Notice that the degree of combined leverage is actually the *product* (not the simple sum) of the two independent leverage measures. Thus we have

$$(DOL_s) \times (DFL_{EBIT}) = DCL_s \tag{13-11}$$

or

$$(6) \times (1.25) = 7.50 \text{ times}$$

OBJECTIVE 4

It is possible to ascertain the degree of combined leverage in a direct fashion, without determining any percentage fluctuations or the separate leverage values. We need only substitute the appropriate values into equation (13-12):[7]

$$DCL_s = \frac{Q(P - V)}{Q(P - V) - F - I} \tag{13-12}$$

The variable definitions in equation (13-12) are the same ones that have been employed throughout this chapter. Use of equation (13-12) with the information in Table 13.9 gives

$$DCL_{\$300,000} = \frac{\$30,000(\$10 - \$6)}{\$30,000(\$10 - \$6) - \$100,000 - \$4,000}$$

$$= \frac{\$120,000}{\$16,000}$$

$$= 7.5 \text{ times}$$

OBJECTIVE 5

Implications

The total risk exposure the firm assumes can be managed by combining operating and financial leverage in different degrees. Knowledge of the various leverage measures aids the financial officer in determining the proper level of overall risk that should be accepted. If a high degree of business risk is inherent to the specific line of commercial activity, then a low posture regarding financial risk would minimize *additional* earnings fluctuations stemming from sales changes. Conversely, the firm that by its very nature incurs a low level of fixed operating costs might choose to use a high degree of financial leverage in the hope of increasing earnings per share and the rate of return on the common equity investment.

> **RELATE TO THE BIG PICTURE**
>
> *Our analysis of business risk, financial risk, and the three measurements of leverage use all relate directly to **Axiom 1: The Risk-Return Trade-Off—We Won't Take on Added Risk Unless We Expect to Be Compensated with Additional Return**. Should the firm decide to "pile on" heavy financial leverage use on top of a high degree of business risk exposure, then we would expect the firm's overall cost of capital to rise and its stock price to fall. This underscores the critical nature of designing the firm's financing mix to both the financial manager and the stockholders. This central area of financial decision making is explored further in the next chapter on "Planning the Firm's Financing Mix."*

HOW FINANCIAL MANAGERS USE THIS MATERIAL

The Introduction to this chapter pointed out how fluctuations of specific magnitudes in sales at Coca-Cola, Phillips Petroleum, Archer Daniels Midland, and Chevron actually became even *larger* relative changes in net income and earnings available to the respective firm's common stockholders. The material presented in the chapter allows financial managers to explain this phenomenon to various constituencies such as other managers, shareholders, and financial analysts who follow their firm's stock performance.

---

[7]As was the case with the degree of financial leverage metric, the variable, *I*, in the combined leverage measure, must include the before-tax equivalent of any preferred dividend payments when preferred stock is in the financial structure.

NEW ENGLAND ECONOMIC REVIEW, JANUARY/ FEBRUARY 1994

The Relationship Among Sales, Cash Flow, and Leverage

Perhaps it is not surprising that leverage, liquidity, and other variables should influence capital spending so little once the general business climate (represented by sales or cash flow) has been taken into account. The choice of leverage, like capital spending, depends on the prospect for profit. A good business climate can foster both investment and debt financing. In these cases, higher leverage does not deter investment; instead, it may appear to facilitate investment.

(A)

At other times, companies may increase their leverage while they reduce their capital spending, if the return on existing capital is great compared to that foreseen on new investments. In these cases, higher leverage may appear to deter investment. In any of these cases, appearances can be deceiving, because

(B)

investment and leverage jointly depend on business conditions, and this dependency entails no consistent relationship between indebtedness and investment.

For the making of economic policy, the evidence suggests that the familiar macroeconomic incentives for investment would be no less effective today than they have been in the past. In particular, the volume of investment spending would appear to respond to monetary and fiscal policies in the customary way. Profits and cash flow might increase as a result of either rising sales or a tax cut.

SOURCE: R. W. Kopcke with M. M. Howrey, "A Panel Study of Investment: Sales, Cash Flow, the Cost of Capital, and Leverage," *New England Economic Review* (January/February 1994): 23.

Analysis and Implications ...

We spent considerable time in earlier chapters studying capital-budgeting techniques and discussed the search by firms for projects with positive net present values. The spending by firms on real capital projects is an important topic not only for the specific firms involved, but also for the aggregate economy. This is because high levels of real capital spending over time are associated with high levels of societal wealth. Societies that do not invest tend to be poor. So, it follows that national economic policymaking is concerned with what variables do affect the spending by companies on projects.

Mr. Kopcke and Mr. Howrey of the Federal Reserve Bank of Boston studied the investment spending of 396 domestic manufacturing corporations and found some interesting relationships among the variables that seem to influence the size of firm's capital budgets.

A. The authors of this study have put forth a reasonable conclusion concerning the relationship between capital spending and the firm's choice to use or avoid financial leverage. They suggest that *both* capital budgets and financial leverage use depend on expected profits. This is close to asserting that the specific firm's capacity to generate future cash flows is a major determinant of its financing mix. This should remind you of **Axiom 3: Cash—Not Profits—Is King**. In the present context, the firm's ability to service its debt contracts depends on its ability to generate future cash flows.

B. Also, we see that these researchers suggest that general business conditions (that is, strong or weak) affect not only the size of the firm's capital budget, but also management's decision to use financial leverage in the financing of that capital budget. Such a logical combination of (1) the state of business conditions and (2) the expectation of future profits (cash flows) means that the underlying nature of the business in which the firm operates should be the most important factor affecting its ultimate financing mix. That is, *business risk* and commercial strategy directly affect the specific firm's decision to use financial leverage.

Based on the logic, models, and inherent assumptions within the models, managers can more precisely *estimate* the interaction that stems from combining operating leverage with financial leverage. The risks that shareholders are asked to assume because of management choices involving cost structure and financial structure are clarified.

Using some of the same theory and logic, managers develop a distinct linkage among the firm's forecasted sales revenues, cost structure, pricing decisions, and advertising programs. The breakeven model, although conceptually simple, is operationally powerful. Its understandability is its strength.

In the hotel industry, managers use the breakeven model to determine the property's breakeven occupancy rate. This becomes an input to the hotel's pricing policy. To achieve a desired total breakeven sales revenue might require a change in the rate charged per room night. In this instance, the hotel's competition has to be assessed and an advertising program put in place that on a forecast basis will permit the breakeven occupancy rate to be achieved.

Because firms are in business to generate a profit (and not just "breakeven"), the breakeven analysis will then extend into a format for achieving minimum target profit levels. So, the breakeven model is an essential part of the manager's strategy formulation toolkit.

SUMMARY

OBJECTIVE 1

In this chapter, we begin to study the process of arriving at an appropriate financial structure for the firm. We examine tools that can assist the financial manager in this task. We are mainly concerned with assessing the variability in the firm's residual earnings stream (either earnings per share or earnings available to the common shareholders) induced by the use of operating and financial leverage. This assessment builds on the tenets of breakeven analysis.

OBJECTIVE 2

Breakeven analysis permits the financial manager to determine the quantity of output or the level of sales that will result in an EBIT level of zero. This means the firm has neither a profit nor a loss before any tax considerations. The effect of price changes, cost structure changes, or volume changes on profits (EBIT) can be studied. To make the technique operational, it is necessary that the firm's costs be classified as fixed or variable. Not all costs fit neatly into one of these two categories. Over short planning horizons, though, the preponderance of costs can be assigned to either the fixed or variable classification. Once the cost structure has been identified, the breakeven point can be found by use of (1) trial-and-error analysis, (2) contribution-margin analysis, or (3) algebraic analysis.

OBJECTIVE 3

Operating leverage is the responsiveness of the firm's EBIT to changes in sales revenues. It arises from the firm's use of fixed operating costs. When fixed operating costs are present in the company's cost structure, changes in sales are magnified into even greater changes in EBIT. The firm's degree of operating leverage from a base sales level is the percentage change in EBIT divided by the percentage change in sales. All types of leverage are two-edged swords. When sales decrease by some percentage, the negative impact upon EBIT will be even larger.

OBJECTIVE 4

A firm employs financial leverage when it finances a portion of its assets with securities bearing a fixed rate of return. The presence of debt and/or preferred stock in the company's financial structure means that it is using financial leverage. When financial leverage is used, changes in EBIT translate into larger changes in earnings per share. The concept of the degree of financial leverage dwells on the sensitivity of earnings per share to changes in EBIT. The DFL from a base EBIT level is defined as the percentage change in earnings per share divided by the percentage change in EBIT. All other things equal, the more fixed-charge securities the firm employs in its financial structure, the greater its degree of financial leverage. Clearly, EBIT can rise or fall. If it falls, and financial leverage is used, the firm's shareholders endure negative changes in earnings per share that are larger than the relative decline in EBIT. Again, leverage is a two-edged sword.

Firms use operating and financial leverage in various degrees. The joint use of operating and financial leverage can be measured by computing the degree of combined leverage, defined as the percentage change in earnings per share divided by the percentage change in sales. This measure allows the financial manager to ascertain the effect on total leverage caused by adding financial leverage on top of operating leverage. Effects can be dramatic, because the degree of combined leverage is the product of the degrees of operating and financial leverage. Table 13.10 summarizes the salient concepts and calculation formats discussed in this chapter.

OBJECTIVE 5

Table 13.10 Summary of Leverage Concepts and Calculations

Technique	Description or Concept	Calculation	Text Reference
Breakeven Analysis			
1. Breakeven point quantity	Total fixed costs divided by the unit contribution margin	$Q_B = \dfrac{F}{P - V}$	(13-3)
2. Breakeven sales level	Total fixed costs divided by 1 minus the ratio of total variable costs to the associated level of sales	$S^* = \dfrac{F}{1 - \dfrac{VC}{S}}$	(13-4)
Operating Leverage			
3. Degree of operating leverage	Percentage change in EBIT divided by the percentage change in sales; or revenue before fixed costs divided by revenue after fixed costs	$DOL_s = \dfrac{Q(P - V)}{Q(P - V) - F}$	(13-6)
Financial Leverage			
4. Degree of financial leverage	Percentage change in earnings per share divided by the percentage change in EBIT; or EBIT divided by EBT.[a]	$DFL_{EBIT} = \dfrac{EBIT}{EBIT - I}$	(13-9)
Combined Leverage			
5. Degree of combined leverage	Percentage change in earnings per share divided by the percentage change in sales; or revenue before fixed costs divided by EBT.[a]	$DCL_s = \dfrac{Q(P - V)}{Q(P - V) - F - I}$	(13-12)

[a]The use of EBT here presumes no preferred dividend payments. In the presence of preferred dividend payments, replace EBT with earnings available to common stock (EAC).

GO TO:
http://www.prenhall.com/bfm
For downloads and current events
associated with this chapter

KEY TERMS

Analytical income
  statement, 474

Business risk, 465

Cash breakeven analysis, 477

Contribution margin, 473

Financial leverage, 468

Financial risk, 467

Fixed costs (indirect
  costs), 469

Operating leverage, 468

Risk, 465

Semivariable costs (semifixed
  costs), 471

Total revenue, 471

Variable costs (direct
  costs), 470

Volume of output, 471

STUDY QUESTIONS

13-1. Distinguish between business risk and financial risk. What gives rise to, or causes, each type of risk?

13-2. Define the term *financial leverage*. Does the firm use financial leverage if preferred stock is present in the capital structure?

13-3. Define the term *operating leverage*. What type of effect occurs when the firm uses operating leverage?

13-4. What is the difference between the (ordinary) breakeven point and the cash breakeven point? Which will be the greater?

13-5. A manager in your firm decides to employ breakeven analysis. Of what shortcomings should this manager be aware?

13-6. What is meant by total risk exposure? How may a firm move to reduce its total risk exposure?

13-7. If a firm has a degree of combined leverage of 3.0 times, what does a negative sales fluctuation of 15 percent portend for the earnings available to the firm's common stock investors?

13-8. Breakeven analysis assumes linear revenue and cost functions. In reality, these linear functions over large output and sales levels are highly improbable. Why?

SELF-TEST PROBLEMS

ST-1. (*Breakeven Point*) You are a hard-working analyst in the office of financial operations for a manufacturing firm that produces a single product. You have developed the following cost structure information for this company. All of it pertains to an output level of 10 million units. Using this information, find the breakeven point in units of output for the firm.

Return on operating assets	= 30%
Operating asset turnover	= 6 times
Operating assets	= $20 million
Degree of operating leverage	= 4.5 times

ST-2. (*Leverage Analysis*) You have developed the following analytical income statement for your corporation. It represents the most recent year's operations, which ended yesterday. Your supervisor in the financial studies office has just handed you a memorandum that asked for written responses to the following questions:

  a. At this level of output, what is the degree of operating leverage?

  b. What is the degree of financial leverage?

c. What is the degree of combined leverage?

d. What is the firm's breakeven point in sales dollars?

e. If sales should increase by 30 percent, by what percent would earnings before taxes (and net income) increase?

Sales	$20,000,000
Variable costs	12,000,000
Revenue before fixed costs	$ 8,000,000
Fixed costs	5,000,000
EBIT	3,000,000
Interest expense	1,000,000
Earnings before taxes	$ 2,000,000
Taxes (0.50)	1,000,000
Net income	$ 1,000,000

f. Prepare an analytical income statement that verifies the calculations from part (e) above.

ST-3. (*Fixed Costs and the Breakeven Point*) Bonaventure Manufacturing expects to earn $210,000 next year after taxes. Sales will be $4 million. The firm's single plant is located on the outskirts of Olean, New York. The firm manufactures a combined bookshelf and desk unit used extensively in college dormitories. These units sell for $200 each and have a variable cost per unit of $150. Bonaventure experiences a 30 percent tax rate.

a. What are the firm's fixed costs expected to be next year?

b. Calculate the firm's breakeven point in both units and dollars.

STUDY PROBLEMS (SET A)

13-1A. (*Sales Mix and Breakeven Point*) CheeMortal music store sells four kinds of musical instruments—pianos, violins, cellos, and flutes. The current sales mix for the store and the contribution margin ratio (unit contribution margin divided by unit sales price) for these product lines are as follows:

Product Line	Percent of Total Sales	Contribution Margin Ratio
Piano	24.5%	32%
Violin	15.0%	40%
Cello	39.5%	38%
Flute	21.0%	51%

Total sales for the next year are forecast to be $250,000. Total fixed costs will be $50,000.

a. Prepare a table showing (1) sales, (2) total variable costs, and (3) the total contribution margin associated with each product line.

b. What is the aggregate contribution margin ratio indicative of the sales mix? (Round off to two decimals.)

c. At this sales mix, what is the breakeven point in dollars?

13-2A. (*Breakeven Point*) Napa Valley Winery (NVW) is a boutique winery that produces a high-quality nonalcoholic red wine from organically grown cabernet sauvignon grapes. It sells each bottle for $30. NVW's chief financial officer, Jackie Cheng, has estimated variable costs to be 70 percent of sales. If NVW's fixed costs are $360,000, how many bottles of its wine must NVW sell to break even?

13-3A. (*Operating Leverage*) In light of a sales agreement that Napa Valley Winery (see description in Problem 13-2A) just signed with a national chain of health food restaurants, NVW's CFO Jackie Cheng is estimating that NVW's sales in the next year will be 50,000 bottles at $30 per bottle. If variable costs are expected to be 70 percent of sales, what is NVW's expected degree of operating leverage?

13-4A. (*Breakeven Point and Operating Leverage*) Some financial data for each of three firms are as follows:

	Jake's Lawn Chairs	Sarasota Sky Lights	Jefferson Wholesale
Average selling price per unit	$ 32.00	$ 875.00	$ 97.77
Average variable cost per unit	$ 17.38	$ 400.00	$ 87.00
Units sold	18,770	2,800	11,000
Fixed costs	$120,350	$850,000	$89,500

    a. What is the profit for each company at the indicated sales volume?
    b. What is the breakeven point in units for each company?
    c. What is the degree of operating leverage for each company at the indicated sales volume?
    d. If sales were to decline, which firm would suffer the largest relative decline in profitability?

13-5A. (*Leverage Analysis*) You have developed the following analytical income statement for your corporation. It represents the most recent year's operations, which ended yesterday.

Sales	$45,750,000
Variable costs	22,800,000
Revenue before fixed costs	$22,950,000
Fixed costs	9,200,000
EBIT	13,750,000
Interest expense	1,350,000
Earnings before taxes	$12,400,000
Taxes (.50)	6,200,000
Net income	$ 6,200,000

Your supervisor in the controller's office has just handed you a memorandum asking for written responses to the following questions:

    a. At this level of output, what is the degree of operating leverage?
    b. What is the degree of financial leverage?
    c. What is the degree of combined leverage?
    d. What is the firm's breakeven point in sales dollars?
    e. If sales should increase by 25 percent, by what percent would earnings before taxes (and net income) increase?

13-6A. (*Breakeven Point and Operating Leverage*) Footwear, Inc., manufactures a complete line of men's and women's dress shoes for independent merchants. The average selling price of its finished product is $85 per pair. The variable cost for this same pair of shoes is $58. Footwear, Inc., incurs fixed costs of $170,000 per year.

    a. What is the breakeven point in pairs of shoes for the company?

    b. What is the dollar sales volume the firm must achieve to reach the breakeven point?

    c. What would be the firm's profit or loss at the following units of production sold: 7,000 pairs of shoes? 9,000 pairs of shoes? 15,000 pairs of shoes?

    d. Find the degree of operating leverage for the production and sales levels given in part (c) above.

13-7A. (*Breakeven Point and Operating Leverage*) Zeylog Corporation manufactures a line of computer memory expansion boards used in microcomputers. The average selling price of its finished product is $180 per unit. The variable cost for these same units is $110. Zeylog incurs fixed costs of $630,000 per year.

    a. What is the breakeven point in units for the company?

    b. What is the dollar sales volume the firm must achieve to reach the breakeven point?

    c. What would be the firm's profit or loss at the following units of production sold: 12,000 units? 15,000 units? 20,000 units?

    d. Find the degree of operating leverage for the production and sales levels given in part (c) above.

13-8A. (*Breakeven Point and Operating Leverage*) Some financial data for each of three firms are as follows:

	Blacksburg Furniture	Lexington Cabinets	Williamsburg Colonials
Average selling price per unit	$ 15.00	$ 400.00	$ 40.00
Average variable cost per unit	$ 12.35	$ 220.00	$ 14.50
Units sold	75,000	4,000	13,000
Fixed costs	$35,000	$100,000	$70,000

    a. What is the profit for each company at the indicated sales volume?

    b. What is the breakeven point in units for each company?

    c. What is the degree of operating leverage for each company at the indicated sales volume?

    d. If sales were to decline, which firm would suffer the largest relative decline in profitability?

13-9. (*Fixed Costs and the Breakeven Point*) A & B Beverages expects to earn $50,000 next year after taxes. Sales will be $375,000. The store is located near the shopping district surrounding Blowing Rock University. Its average product sells for $27 a unit. The variable cost per unit is $14.85. The store experiences a 40 percent tax rate.

    a. What are the store's fixed costs expected to be next year?

    b. Calculate the store's breakeven point in both units and dollars.

13-10A. (*Breakeven Point and Profit Margin*) Mary Clark, a recent graduate of Clarion South University, is planning to open a new wholesaling operation. Her target operating profit margin is 26 percent. Her unit contribution margin will be 50 percent of sales. Average annual sales are forecast to be $3,250,000.

    a. How large can fixed costs be for the wholesaling operation and still allow the 26 percent operating profit margin to be achieved?

    b. What is the breakeven point in dollars for the firm?

13-11A. (*Leverage Analysis*) You have developed the following analytical income statement for your corporation. It represents the most recent year's operations, which ended yesterday. Your supervisor in the controller's office has just handed you a memorandum asking for written responses to the following questions:

a. At this level of output, what is the degree of operating leverage?

b. What is the degree of financial leverage?

Sales	$30,000,000
Variable costs	13,500,000
Revenue before fixed costs	$16,500,000
Fixed costs	8,000,000
EBIT	8,500,000
Interest expense	1,000,000
Earnings before taxes	7,500,000
Taxes (.50)	3,750,000
Net income	$ 3,750,000

c. What is the degree of combined leverage?

d. What is the firm's breakeven point in sales dollars?

e. If sales should increase by 25 percent, by what percent would earnings before taxes (and net income) increase?

13-12A. (*Breakeven Point*) You are a hard-working analyst in the office of financial operations for a manufacturing firm that produces a single product. You have developed the following cost struc-ture information for this company. All of it pertains to an output level of 10 million units. Using this information, find the breakeven point in units of output for the firm.

Return on operating assets	= 25%
Operating asset turnover	= 5 times
Operating assets	= $20 million
Degree of operating leverage	= 4 times

13-13A. (*Breakeven Point and Operating Leverage*) Allison Radios manufactures a complete line of radio and communication equipment for law enforcement agencies. The average selling price of its finished product is $180 per unit. The variable cost for these same units is $126. Allison Radios incurs fixed costs of $540,000 per year.

a. What is the breakeven point in units for the company?

b. What is the dollar sales volume the firm must achieve in order to reach the breakeven point?

c. What would be the firm's profit or loss at the following units of production sold: 12,000 units? 15,000 units? 20,000 units?

d. Find the degree of operating leverage for the production and sales levels given in par (c) above.

13-14A. (*Breakeven Point and Operating Leverage*) Some financial data for each of three firms are as follows:

	Oviedo Seeds	Gainesville Sod	Athens Peaches
Average selling price per unit	$ 14.00	$ 200.00	$ 25.00
Average variable cost per unit	$ 11.20	$ 130.00	$ 17.50
Units sold	100,000	10,000	48,000
Fixed costs	$25,000	$100,000	$35,000

a. What is the profit for each company at the indicated sales volume?

b. What is the breakeven point in units for each company?

c. What is the degree of operating leverage for each company at the indicated sales volume?

d. If sales were to *decline*, which firm would suffer the largest relative decline in profitability?

13-15A. (*Fixed Costs and the Breakeven Point*) Dot's Quik-Stop Party Store expects to earn $40,000 next year after taxes. Sales will be $400,000. The store is located near the fraternity-row district of Cambridge Springs State University and sells only kegs of beer for $20 a keg. The variable cost per keg is $8. The store experiences a 40 percent tax rate.

a. What are the Party Store's fixed costs expected to be next year?

b. Calculate the firm's breakeven point in both units and dollars.

13-16A. (*Fixed Costs and the Breakeven Point*) Albert's Cooling Equipment hopes to earn $80,000 next year after taxes. Sales will be $2 million. The firm's single plant is located on the edge of Slippery Rock, Pennsylvania, and manufactures only small refrigerators. These are used in many of the dormitories found on college campuses. Refrigerators sell for $80 per unit and have a variable cost of $56. Albert's experiences a 40 percent tax rate.

a. What are the firm's fixed costs expected to be next year?

b. Calculate the firm's breakeven point both in units and dollars.

13-17A. (*Breakeven Point and Selling Price*) Gerry's Tool and Die Company will produce 200,000 units next year. All of this production will be sold as finished goods. Fixed costs will total $300,000. Variable costs for this firm are relatively predictable at 75 percent of sales.

a. If Gerry's Tool and Die wants to achieve an earnings before interest and taxes level of $240,000 next year, at what price per unit must it sell its product?

b. Based on your answer to part (a), set up an analytical income statement that will verify your solution.

13-18A. (*Breakeven Point and Selling Price*) Parks Castings, Inc., will manufacture and sell 200,000 units next year. Fixed costs will total $300,000, and variable costs will be 60 percent of sales.

a. The firm wants to achieve an earnings before interest and taxes level of $250,000. What selling price per unit is necessary to achieve this result?

b. Set up an analytical income statement to verify your solution to part (a).

13-19A. (*Breakeven Point and Profit Margin*) A recent business graduate of Midwestern State University is planning to open a new wholesaling operation. His target operating profit margin is 28 percent. His unit contribution margin will be 50 percent of sales. Average annual sales are forecast to be $3,750,000.

a. How large can fixed costs be for the wholesaling operation and still allow the 28 percent operating profit margin to be achieved?

b. What is the breakeven point in dollars for the firm?

13-20A. (*Operating Leverage*) Rocky Mount Metals Company manufactures an assortment of woodburning stoves. The average selling price for the various units is $500. The associated variable cost is $350 per unit. Fixed costs for the firm average $180,000 annually.

a. What is the breakeven point in units for the company?

b. What is the dollar sales volume the firm must achieve to reach the breakeven point?

c. What is the degree of operating leverage for a production and sales level of 5,000 units for the firm? (Calculate to three decimal places.)

d. What will be the projected effect upon earnings before interest and taxes if the firm's sales level should increase by 20 percent from the volume noted in part (c) above?

13-21A. (*Breakeven Point and Operating Leverage*) The Portland Recreation Company manufactures a full line of lawn furniture. The average selling price of a finished unit is $25. The associated variable cost is $15 per unit. Fixed costs for Portland average $50,000 per year.

a. What is the breakeven point in units for the company?

b. What is the dollar sales volume the firm must achieve to reach the breakeven point?

c. What would be the company's profit or loss at the following units of production sold: 4,000 units? 6,000 units? 8,000 units?

d. Find the degree of operating leverage for the production and sales levels given in part (c) above.

e. What is the effect on the degree of operating leverage as sales rise above the breakeven point?

13-22A. (*Fixed Costs*) Detroit Heat Treating projects that next year its fixed costs will total $120,000. Its only product sells for $12 per unit, of which $7 is a variable cost. The management of Detroit is considering the purchase of a new machine that will lower the variable cost per unit to $5. The new machine, however, will add to fixed costs through an increase in depreciation expense. How large can the *addition to* fixed costs be to keep the firm's breakeven point in units produced and sold unchanged?

13-23A. (*Operating Leverage*) The management of Detroit Heat Treating did not purchase the new piece of equipment (see problem 13-22A). Using the existing cost structure, calculate the degree of operating leverage at 30,000 units of output. Comment on the meaning of your answer.

13-24A. (*Leverage Analysis*) An analytical income statement for Detroit Heat Treating is shown below. It is based on an output (sales) level of 40,000 units. You may refer to the original cost structure data in problem (13-22A).

Sales	$480,000
Variable costs	280,000
Revenue before fixed costs	$200,000
Fixed costs	120,000
EBIT	$ 80,000
Interest expense	30,000
Earnings before taxes	$ 50,000
Taxes	25,000
Net income	$ 25,000

a. Calculate the degree of operating leverage at this output level.

b. Calculate the degree of financial leverage at this level of EBIT.

c. Determine the combined leverage effect at this output level.

13-25A. (*Breakeven Point*) You are employed as a financial analyst for a single-product manufacturing firm. Your supervisor has made the following cost structure information available to you, all of which pertains to an output level of 1,600,000 units.

Return on operating assets	= 15%
Operating asset turnover	= 5 times
Operating assets	= $3 million
Degree of operating leverage	= 8 times

Your task is to find the breakeven point in units of output for the firm.

13-26A. (*Fixed Costs*) Des Moines Printing Services is forecasting fixed costs next year of $300,000. The firm's single product sells for $20 per unit and incurs a variable cost per unit of $14. The firm may acquire some new binding equipment that would lower variable cost per unit to $12. The new equipment, however, would add to fixed costs through the price of an annual maintenance agreement on the new equipment. How large can this increase in fixed costs be and still keep the firm's present breakeven point in units produced and sold unchanged?

13-27A. (*Leverage Analysis*) Your firm's cost analysis supervisor supplies you with the following analytical income statement and requests answers to the four questions listed below the statement.

Sales	$12,000,000
Variable costs	9,000,000
Revenue before fixed costs	$ 3,000,000
Fixed costs	2,000,000
EBIT	$ 1,000,000
Interest expense	200,000
Earnings before taxes	$ 800,000
Taxes	400,000
Net income	$ 400,000

a. At this level of output, what is the degree of operating leverage?

b. What is the degree of financial leverage?

c. What is the degree of combined leverage?

d. What is the firm's breakeven point in sales dollars?

13-28A. (*Leverage Analysis*) You are supplied with.the following analytical income statement for your firm. It reflects last year's operations.

Sales	$16,000,000
Variable costs	8,000,000
Revenue before fixed costs	$ 8,000,000
Fixed costs	4,000,000
EBIT	$ 4,000,000
Interest expense	1,500,000
Earnings before taxes	$ 2,500,000
Taxes	1,250,000
Net income	$ 1,250,000

a. At this level of output, what is the degree of operating leverage?

b. What is the degree of financial leverage?

c. What is the degree of combined leverage?

d. If sales should increase by 20 percent, by what percent would earnings before taxes (and net income) increase?

e. What is your firm's breakeven point in sales dollars?

13-29A. (*Sales Mix and Breakeven Point*) Toledo Components produces four lines of auto accessories for the major Detroit automobile manufacturers. The lines are known by the code letters A, B, C, and D. The current sales mix for Toledo and the contribution margin ratio (unit contribution margin divided by unit sales price) for these product lines are as follows:

Product Line	Percent of Total Sales	Contribution Margin Ratio
A	33⅓%	40%
B	41⅔	32
C	16⅔	20
D	8⅓	60

Total sales for next year are forecast to be $120,000. Total fixed costs will be $29,400.

a. Prepare a table showing (1) sales, (2) total variable costs, and (3) the total contribution margin associated with each product line.

b. What is the aggregate contribution margin ratio indicative of this sales mix?

c. At this sales mix, what is the breakeven point in dollars?

13-30A. (*Sales Mix and Breakeven Point*) Because of production constraints, Toledo Components (see problem 13-29A) may have to adhere to a different sales mix for next year. The alternative plan is outlined as follows:

Product Line	Percent of Total Sales
A	25%
B	36⅔
C	33⅓
D	5

a. Assuming all other facts in problem 13-29A remain the same, what effect will this different sales mix have on Toledo's breakeven point in dollars?

b. Which sales mix will Toledo's management prefer?

INTEGRATIVE PROBLEM

Imagine that you were hired recently as a financial analyst for a relatively new, highly leveraged ski manufacturer located in the foothills of Colorado's Rocky mountains. Your firm manufactures only one product, a state-of-the-art snow ski. The company has been operating up to this point without much quantitative knowledge of the business and financial risks it faces.

Ski season just ended, however, so the president of the company has started to focus more on the financial aspects of managing the business. He has set up a meeting for next week with the CFO, Maria Sanchez, to discuss matters such as the business and financial risks faced by the company. Accordingly, Maria has asked you to prepare an analysis to assist her in her discussions with the president.

As a first step in your work, you compiled the following information regarding the cost structure of the company.

Output level	50,000 units
Operating assets	$2,000,000
Operating asset turnover	7 times
Return on operating assets	35%
Degree of operating leverage	5 times
Interest expense	$ 400,000
Tax-rate	35%

As the next step, you need to *determine the breakeven point in units of output* for the company. One of your strong points has been that you always prepare supporting workpapers, which show how you arrive at your conclusions. You know Maria would like to see such workpapers for this analysis to facilitate her review of your work.

Thereafter you will have the information you require to *prepare an analytical income statement* for the company. You are sure that Maria would like to see this statement; in addition, you know that you need it to be able to answer the following questions. You also know Maria expects you to prepare, in a format that is presentable to the president, answers to the questions to serve as a basis for her discussions with the president.

1. What is the degree of financial leverage?
2. What is the degree of combined leverage?
3. What is the firm's breakeven point in sales dollars?
4. If sales should increase by 30 percent (as the president expects), by what percent would EBT (earnings before taxes) and net income increase?
5. Prepare another analytical income statement, this time to verify the calculations from part (4) above.

STUDY PROBLEMS (SET B)

13-1B. (*Breakeven Point*) Roberto Martinez is the chief financial analyst at New Wave Pharmaceuticals (NWP), a company that produces a vitamin claimed to prevent the common cold. Roberto has been asked to determine the company's breakeven point in units. He obtained the following information from the company's financial statements for the year just ended. In addition, he found out from NWP's production manager that the company produced 40 million units in that year. What will Roberto determine the breakeven point to be?

Sales	$20,000,000
Variable costs	16,000,000
Revenue before fixed costs	$ 4,000,000
Fixed costs	2,400,000
EBIT	$ 1,600,000

13-2B. (*Leverage Analysis*) New Wave Pharmaceuticals (see description and data in Problem 13-1B) is concerned that recent unfavorable publicity about the questionable medicinal benefits of other vitamins will temporarily hurt NWP's sales even though such assertions do not apply to NWP's vitamin. Accordingly, Roberto has been asked to determine the company's level of risk based on the financial information for the year just ended. In addition to the data described in Problem 13-1B, Roberto learned from the company's financial statements that the company incurred $800,000 of interest expense in the year just ended. What will Roberto determine the (a) degree of operating leverage, (b) degree of financial leverage, and (c) degree of combined leverage to be?

13-3B. (*Breakeven Point and Operating Leverage*) Avitar Corporation manufactures a line of computer memory expansion boards used in microcomputers. The average selling price of its finished product is $175 per unit. The variable cost for these same units is $115. Avitar incurs fixed costs of $650,000 per year.

a. What is the breakeven point in units for the company?
b. What is the dollar sales volume the firm must achieve to reach the breakeven point?
c. What would be the firm's profit or loss at the following units of production sold: 10,000 units? 16,000 units? 20,000 units?
d. Find the degree of operating leverage for the production and sales levels given in part (c) above.

13-4B. (*Breakeven Point and Operating Leverage*) Some financial data for each of three firms are as follows:

	Durham Furniture	Raleigh Cabinets	Charlotte Colonials
Average selling price per unit	$ 20.00	$ 435.00	$ 35.00
Average variable cost per unit	$ 13.75	$ 240.00	$ 15.75
Units sold	80,000	4,500	15,000
Fixed costs	$40,000	$150,000	$60,000

    a. What is the profit for each company at the indicated sales volume?

    b. What is the breakeven point in units for each company?

    c. What is the degree of operating leverage for each company at the indicated sales volume?

    d. If sales were to decline, which firm would suffer the largest relative decline in profitability?

13-5B. (*Fixed Costs and the Breakeven Point*) Cypress Books expects to earn $55,000 next year after taxes. Sales will be $400,008. The store is located near the shopping district surrounding Sheffield University. Its average product sells for $28 a unit. The variable cost per unit is $18. The store experiences a 45 percent tax rate.

    a. What are the store's fixed costs expected to be next year?

    b. Calculate the store's breakeven point in both units and dollars.

13-6B. (*Breakeven Point and Profit Margin*) A recent graduate of Neeley University is planning to open a new wholesaling operation. Her target operating profit margin is 28 percent. Her unit contribution margin will be 45 percent of sales. Average annual sales are forecast to be $3,750,000.

    a. How large can fixed costs be for the wholesaling operation and still allow the 28 percent operating profit margin to be achieved?

    b. What is the breakeven point in dollars for the firm?

13-7B. (*Leverage Analysis*) You have developed the following analytical income statement for your corporation. It represents the most recent year's operations which ended yesterday.

Sales	$40,000,000
Variable costs	16,000,000
Revenue before fixed costs	$24,000,000
Fixed costs	10,000,000
EBIT	$14,000,000
Interest expense	1,150,000
Earnings before taxes	$12,850,000
Taxes	3,750,000
Net income	$ 9,100,000

Your supervisor in the controller's office has just handed you a memorandum asking for written responses to the following questions:

    a. At this level of output, what is the degree of operating leverage?

    b. What is the degree of financial leverage?

    c. What is the degree of combined leverage?

    d. What is the firm's breakeven point in sales dollars?

    e. If sales should increase by 20 percent, by what percent would earnings before taxes (and net income) increase?

13-8B. (*Breakeven Point*) You are a hard-working analyst in the office of financial operations for a manufacturing firm that produces a single product. You have developed the following cost structure information for this company. All of it pertains to an output level of 7 million units. Using this information, find the breakeven point in units of output for the firm.

Return on operating assets	= 25%
Operating asset turnover	= 5 times
Operating assets	= $18 million
Degree of operating leverage	= 6 times

13-9B. (*Breakeven Point and Operating Leverage*) Matthew Electronics manufactures a complete line of radio and communication equipment for law enforcement agencies. The average selling price of its finished product is $175 per unit. The variable costs for these same units is $140. Matthew's incurs fixed costs of $550,000 per year.

  a. What is the breakeven point in units for the company?

  b. What is the dollar sales volume the firm must achieve to reach the breakeven point?

  c. What would be the firm's profit or loss at the following units of production sold: 12,000 units? 15,000 units? 20,000 units?

  d. Find the degree of operating leverage for the production and sales levels given in part (c) above.

13-10B. (*Breakeven Point and Operating Leverage*) Some financial data for each of three firms are as follows:

	Farm City Seeds	Empire Sod	Golden Peaches
Average selling price per unit	$ 15.00	$ 190.00	$ 28.00
Average variable cost per unit	$ 11.75	$ 145.00	$ 19.00
Units sold	120,000	9,000	50,000
Fixed costs	$30,000	$110,000	$33,000

  a. What is the profit for each company at the indicated sales volume?

  b. What is the breakeven point in units for each company?

  c. What is the degree of operating leverage for each company at the indicated sales volume?

  d. If sales were to *decline*, which firm would suffer the largest relative decline in profitability?

13-11B. (*Fixed Costs and the Breakeven Point*) Keller's Keg expects to earn $38,000 next year after taxes. Sales will be $420,002. The store is located near the fraternity-row district of Blue Springs State University and sells only kegs of beer for $17 a keg. The variable cost per keg is $9. The store experiences a 35 percent tax rate.

  a. What are Keller Keg's fixed costs expected to be next year?

  b. Calculate the firm's breakeven point both in units and in dollars.

13-12B. (*Fixed Costs and the Breakeven Point*) Mini-Kool hopes to earn $70,000 next year after taxes. Sales will be $2,500,050. The firm's single plant manufactures only small refrigerators. These are used in many recreational campers. The refrigerators sell for $75 per unit and have a variable cost of $58. Albert's experiences a 45 percent tax rate.

  a. What are the firm's fixed costs expected to be next year?

  b. Calculate the firm's breakeven point both in units and in dollars.

13-13B. (*Breakeven Point and Selling Price*) Heritage Chain Company will produce 175,000 units next year. All of this production will be sold as finished goods. Fixed costs will total $335,000. Variable costs for this firm are relatively predictable at 80 percent of sales.

a. If Heritage Chain wants to achieve an earnings before interest and taxes level of $270,000 next year, at what price per unit must it sell its product?

b. Based on your answer to part (a), set up an analytical income statement that will verify your solution.

13-14B. (*Breakeven Point and Selling Price*) Thomas Appliances will manufacture and sell 190,000 units next year. Fixed costs will total $300,000, and variable costs will be 75 percent of sales.

a. The firm wants to achieve an earnings before interest and taxes level of $250,000. What selling price per unit is necessary to achieve this result?

b. Set up an analytical income statement to verify your solution to part (a).

13-15B. (*Breakeven Point and Profit Margin*) A recent business graduate of Dewey University is planning to open a new wholesaling operation. His target operating profit margin is 25 percent. His unit contribution margin will be 60 percent of sales. Average annual sales are forecast to be $4,250,000.

a. How large can fixed costs be for the wholesaling operation and still allow the 25 percent operating profit margin to be achieved?

b. What is the breakeven point in dollars for the firm?

13-16B. (*Operating Leverage*) The B. H. Williams Company manufactures an assortment of woodburning stoves. The average selling price for the various units is $475. The associated variable cost is $350 per unit. Fixed costs for the firm average $200,000 annually.

a. What is the breakeven point in units for the company?

b. What is the dollar sales volume the firm must achieve to reach the breakeven point?

c. What is the degree of operating leverage for a production and sales level of 6,000 units for the firm? (Calculate to three decimal places.)

d. What will be the projected effect on earnings before interest and taxes if the firm's sales level should increase by 13 percent from the volume noted in part (c) above?

13-17B. (*Breakeven Point and Operating Leverage*) The Palm Patio Company manufactures a full line of lawn furniture. The average selling price of a finished unit is $28. The associated variable cost is $17 per unit. Fixed costs for Palm Patio average $55,000 per year.

a. What is the breakeven point in units for the company?

b. What is the dollar sales volume the firm must achieve to reach the breakeven point?

c. What would be the company's profit or loss at the following units of production sold: 4,000 units? 6,000 units? 8,000 units?

d. Find the degree of operating leverage for the production and sales levels given in part (c) above.

e. What is the effect on the degree of operating leverage as sales rise above the breakeven point?

13-18B. (*Fixed Costs*) Tropical Sun projects that next year its fixed costs will total $135,000. Its only product sells for $13 per unit, of which $6 is a variable cost. The management of Tropical is considering the purchase of a new machine that will lower the variable cost per unit to $5. The new machine however, will add to fixed costs through an increase in depreciation expense. How large can the *addition* to fixed costs be to keep the firm's breakeven point in units produced and sold unchanged?

13-19B. (*Operating Leverage*) The management of Tropical Sun did not purchase the new piece of equipment (see problem 13-18B). Using the existing cost structure, calculate the degree of operating leverage at 40,000 units of output. Comment on the meaning of your answer.

13-20B. (*Leverage Analysis*) An analytical income statement for Tropical Sun follows. It is based on an output (sales) level of 50,000 units. You may refer to the original cost structure data in problem (13-18B).

Sales	$650,000
Variable costs	300,000
Revenue before fixed costs	$350,000
Fixed costs	135,000
EBIT	$215,000
Interest expense	60,000
Earnings before taxes	$155,000
Taxes	70,000
Net income	$ 85,000

a. Calculate the degree of operating leverage at this output level.

b. Calculate the degree of financial leverage at this level of EBIT.

c. Determine the combined leverage effect at this output level.

13-21B. (*Breakeven Point*) You are employed as a financial analyst for a single-product manufacturing firm. Your supervisor has made the following cost structure information available to you, all of which pertains to an output level of 1,700,000 units.

Return on operating assets	= 16 percent
Operating asset turnover	= 6 times
Operating assets	= $3.25 million
Degree of operating leverage	= 9 times

Your task is to find the breakeven point in units of output for the firm.

13-22B. (*Fixed Costs*) Sausalito Silkscreen is forecasting fixed costs next year of $375,000. The firm's single product sells for $25 per unit and incurs a variable cost per unit of $13. The firm may acquire some new binding equipment that would lower variable cost per unit to $11. The new equipment, however, would add to fixed costs through the price of an annual maintenance agreement on the new equipment. How large can this increase in fixed costs be and still keep the firm's present breakeven point in units produced and sold unchanged?

13-23B. (*Leverage Analysis*) Your firm's cost analysis supervisor supplies you with the following analytical income statement and requests answers to the four questions listed below the statement.

Sales	$13,750,000
Variable costs	9,500,000
Revenue before fixed costs	$ 4,250,000
Fixed costs	3,000,000
EBIT	$ 1,250,000
Interest expense	250,000
Earnings before taxes	$ 1,000,000
Taxes	430,000
Net income	$ 570,000

a. At this level of output, what is the degree of operating leverage?

b. What is the degree of financial leverage?

c. What is the degree of combined leverage?

d. What is the firm's breakeven point in sales dollars?

13-24B. (*Leverage Analysis*) You are supplied with the following analytical income statement for your firm. It reflects last year's operations.

Sales	$18,000,000
Variable costs	7,000,000
Revenue before fixed costs	$11,000,000
Fixed costs	6,000,000
EBIT	$ 5,000,000
Interest expense	1,750,000
Earnings before taxes	$ 3,250,000
Taxes	1,250,000
Net income	$ 2,000,000

   a. At this level of output, what is the degree of operating leverage?

   b. What is the degree of financial leverage?

   c. What is the degree of combined leverage?

   d. If sales should increase by 15 percent, by what percent would earnings before taxes (and net income) increase?

   e. What is your firm's breakeven point in sales dollars?

13-25B. (*Sales Mix and the Breakeven Point*) Wayne Automotive produces four lines of auto accessories for the major Detroit automobile manufacturers. The lines are known by the code letters A, B, C, and D. The current sales mix for Wayne and the contribution margin ratio (unit contribution margin divided by unit sales price) for these product lines are as follows:

Product Line	Percent of Total Sales	Contribution Margin Ratio
A	25⅔%	40%
B	41⅓	32
C	19⅔	20
D	13⅓	60

Total sales for next year are forecast to be $150,000. Total fixed costs will be $35,000.

   a. Prepare a table showing (1) sales, (2) total variable costs, and (3) the total contribution margin associated with each product line.

   b. What is the aggregate contribution margin ratio indicative of this sales mix?

   c. At this sales mix, what is the breakeven point in dollars?

13-26B. (*Sales Mix and the Breakeven Point*) Because of production constraints, Wayne Automotive (see problem 13-25B) may have to adhere to a different sales mix for next year. The alternative plan is outlined as follows:

Product Line	Percent of Total Sales
A	33⅓%
B	41⅔
C	16⅔
D	8⅓

   a. Assuming all other facts in problem 13-25B remain the same, what effect will this different sales mix have on Wayne's breakeven point in dollars?

   b. Which sales mix will Wayne's management prefer?

ERIE GENERAL PRODUCERS

Breakeven Analysis, Operating Leverage,
Financial Leverage

Erie General Producers (EGP) is a medium-size public corporation that until recently consisted of two divisions. The Retail Furniture Group (RFG) has eight locations in the northeastern Ohio area, mostly concentrated around Cleveland. These retail outlets generate sales of contemporary, traditional, and early American furniture. In addition, casual and leisure furniture lines are carried by the stores. The other (old) division of EGP is its Concrete Group (CG). The CG operates three plants in the North Tonawanda area of western New York. These plants produce precast concrete wall panels and concrete stave farm silos. The company headquarters of EGP is located in Erie, Pennsylvania. This community touches Lake Erie in northwestern Pennsylvania and is about 140 miles north of Pittsburgh. Because Erie is almost equidistant from Cleveland and North Tonawanda and is a connecting hub for several interstate highways, it makes a sensible spot for the firm's home offices.

EGP was started 10 years ago as Erie Producers by its current president and board chairman, Anthony Toscano. During the firm's existence it has enjoyed periods of both moderate and strong growth in sales, assets, and earnings. Key managerial decisions have always been dominated by Toscano, who openly boasts of the fact that his company has never suffered through a year of negative earnings despite the often cyclical nature of both the retail furniture (RFG) and concrete (CG) divisions.

Recently, Mr. Toscano decided to acquire a third division for his firm. The division manufactures special machinery for the seafood processing industry and is appropriately called the Seafood Industry Group (SIG). The financial settlement for the acquisition took place yesterday. Currently, the SIG consists of one manufacturing plant in Erie. A single product is to be manufactured, assembled, and shipped from the facility. That product, however, represents a design breakthrough and carries with it a projected contribution margin ratio of .4000. This is greater than that enjoyed by either of EGP's other two divisions.

EGP's manufacturing operation in Erie will produce a new machine called "The Picker." The Picker was invented and successfully tested by Ben Pinkerton, the major stockholder and manager of a small seafood processing firm in Morattico, Virgina. Pinkerton plans and supervises all operations at Eastern Shore Processors. Eastern Shore specializes in freezing and pasteurizing crab meat. Freezing and pasteurizing procedures have been a boon to the seafood industry, for they permit the processor to retain a product without spoilage in hopes of higher prices at a later date. In comparing his industry to that of agriculture, Pinkerton aptly states: "The freezer is our grain elevator."

The seafood processing industry is characterized by a notable lack of capital equipment and a corresponding heavy use of human labor. Pinkerton will tell you that, at Eastern Shore Processors, a skilled crab meat picker will produce about 30 pounds of meat per day. No matter how skilled the human picker, however, he will leave about 10 pounds of meat per day in the top piece of the crab shell. This past year, after 5 years of trying, Pinkerton perfected a machine that would recover about 30 percent of this otherwise lost meat. In exchange for cash, Eastern Shore Processors sold all rights to The Picker to EGP. Thus Toscano established the SIG and immediately made plans to manufacture The Picker.

Recent income statements for the older divisions of EGP are contained in Exhibits 1 and 2. Toscano has now decided to assess more fully the probable impact of the decision to establish the SIG on the financial condition of EGP. Toscano knew that such figures should have been generated prior to the decision to enter this special field, but his seasoned judgment led him to a quick choice. He has requested several pieces of information, detailed as follows, from his chief financial officer.

Exhibit 1 Erie General Producers Retail Furniture Group Income Statement, December 31, Last Year

Sales	$12,000,000
Less: total variable costs	7,920,000
Revenue before fixed costs	$ 4,080,000
Less: total fixed costs	2,544,000
EBIT	$ 1,536,000
Less: interest expense	192,000
Earnings before taxes	$ 1,344,000
Less: taxes @ 50%	672,000
Net profit	$ 672,000

Exhibit 2 Erie General Producers Concrete Group Income Statement, December 31, Last Year

Sales	$8,000,000
Less: total variable costs	5,920,000
Revenue before fixed costs	$2,080,000
Less: total fixed costs	640,000
EBIT	$1,440,000
Less: interest expense	80,000
Earnings before taxes	$1,360,000
Less: taxes @ 50%	680,000
Net profit	$ 680,000

Questions and Problems

1. Using last year's results, determine the breakeven point in dollars for EGP (that is, before investing in the new SIG). The breakeven point is defined here in the traditional manner where EBIT = $0. (*Hint:* Use an aggregate contribution-margin ratio in your analysis.)

2. Using last year's results, determine what volume of sales must be reached to cover all before-tax costs.

3. Next year's sales for the SIG are projected to be $4,000,000. Total fixed costs will be $640,000. This division will have no outstanding debt on its balance sheet. EGP uses a 50 percent tax rate in all its financial projections. Using the format of Exhibits 1 and 2, construct a pro forma income statement for the SIG.

4. After the SIG begins operations, what will be EGP's breakeven point in dollars (a) as traditionally defined and (b) reflecting the coverage of *all* before-tax costs? Base the new sales mix on last year's sales performance for the older divisions plus that anticipated next year for the SIG. Using your answer to part (b) of this question, construct an analytical income statement demonstrating that earnings before taxes = $0.

5. Using next year's anticipated sales volume for EGP (including the SIG), compute (a) the degree of operating leverage, (b) the degree of financial leverage, and (c) the degree of combined leverage. Comment on the meaning of each of these statistics.

6. Using projected figures, determine whether acquisition of the SIG will increase or decrease the vulnerability of EGP's earnings before interest and taxes (EBIT) to cyclical swings in sales. Show your work.

7. Review the key assumptions of cost-volume-profit analysis.

SELF-TEST SOLUTIONS

SS-1. *Step 1: Compute the operating profit margin:*

$$(\text{margin}) \times (\text{turnover}) = \text{return on operating assets}$$

$$(M) \times (6) = 0.30$$

$$M = 0.30/6 = 0.05$$

Step 2: Compute the sales level associated with the given output level:

$$\frac{\text{sales}}{\$20,000,000} = 6$$

$$\text{sales} = \$120,000,000$$

Step 3: Compute EBIT:

$$(.05)\ (\$120,000,000) = \$6,000,000 = \text{EBIT}$$

Step 4: Compute revenue before fixed costs. Because the degree of operating leverage is 4.5 times, revenue before fixed costs (RBF) is 4.5 times EBIT, as follows:

$$\text{RBF} = (4.5)\ (\$6,000,000) = \$27,000,000$$

Step 5: Compute total variable costs:

$$(\text{sales}) - (\text{total variable costs}) = \$27,000,000$$

$$\$120,000,000 - (\text{total variable costs}) = \$27,000,000$$

$$\text{total variable costs} = \$93,000,000$$

Step 6: Compute total fixed costs:

$$\text{RBF} - \text{fixed costs} = \text{EBIT}$$

$$\$27,000,000 - \text{fixed costs} = \$6,000,000$$

$$\text{Fixed costs} = \$21,000,000$$

Step 7: Find the selling price per unit (P), and the variable cost per unit (V):

$$P = \frac{\text{sales}}{\text{output in units}} = \frac{\$120,000,000}{10,000,000} = \$12.00$$

$$V = \frac{\text{total variable costs}}{\text{output in units}} = \frac{\$93,000,000}{10,000,000} = \$9.30$$

Step 8: Compute the breakeven point:

$$Q_B = \frac{F}{P-V} = \frac{\$21,000,000}{\$12.00 - \$9.30}$$

$$= \frac{\$21,000,000}{\$2.70} = \$7,777,778 \text{ units}$$

The firm will break even when it produces and sells 7,777,778 units.

SS-2. a. $\dfrac{\text{Revenue before fixed costs}}{\text{EBIT}} = \dfrac{\$8,000,000}{\$3,000,000} = \underline{\underline{2.67 \text{ times}}}$

b. $\dfrac{\text{EBIT}}{\text{EBIT}-I} = \dfrac{\$3,000,000}{\$2,000,000} = \underline{\underline{1.50 \text{ times}}}$

c. $DCI_{\$20,000,000} = (2.67)(1.50) = \underline{4.00 \text{ times}}$

d. $S^* = \dfrac{F}{1 - \dfrac{VC}{S}} = \dfrac{\$5,000,000}{1 - \dfrac{\$12M}{\$20M}} = \dfrac{\$5,000,000}{1 - 0.60} = \dfrac{\$5,000,000}{0.40} = \underline{\underline{\$12,500,000}}$

e. $(30\%)(4.00) = 120\%$

f.

Sales	$26,000,000
Variable costs	15,600,000
Revenue before fixed costs	$10,400,000
Fixed costs	5,000,000
EBIT	$ 5,400,000
Interest expense	1,000,000
Earnings before taxes	$ 4,400,000
Taxes (0.50)	2,200,000
Net income	$ 2,200,000

We know that sales have increased by 30 percent to $26 million from the base sales level of $20 million.

Let us focus now on the change in earnings before taxes. We can compute that change as follows:

$$\frac{\$4,400,000 - \$2,000,000}{\$2,000,000} = \frac{\$2,400,000}{\$2,000,000} = 120\%$$

Because the tax rate was held constant, the percentage change in net income will also equal 120 percent. The fluctuations implied by the degree of combined leverage measure are therefore accurately reflected in this analytical income statement.

SS-3. a.
$$\{(P \cdot Q) - [V \cdot Q + (F)]\}(1 - T) = \$210,000$$
$$[(\$4,000,000) - (\$3,000,000) - F](.7) = \$210,000$$
$$(\$1,000,000 - F)(.7) = \$210,000$$
$$\$700,000 - .7F = \$210,000$$
$$.7F = \$490,000$$
$$F = \underline{\$700,000}$$

Fixed costs next year, then, are expected to be $700,000.

b.

$$Q_B = \frac{F}{P-V} = \frac{\$700,000}{\$50} = \underline{\underline{14,000 \text{ units}}}$$

$$S^* = \frac{F}{1 - \dfrac{VC}{S}} = \frac{\$700,000}{1 - .75} = \frac{\$700,000}{.25} = \underline{\underline{\$2,800,000}}$$

The firm will break even (EBIT = 0) when it sells 14,000 units. With a selling price of $200 per unit, the breakeven sales level is $2,800,000.

Learning Objectives

Active Applications

World Finance

Practice

CHAPTER 14

PLANNING THE FIRM'S FINANCING MIX

INTRODUCTION

The United States was recession-free from November 1982 until July 1990, when a general business contraction did occur. It officially lasted until the end of February 1991, and the nation's labor markets didn't regain full speed until the first half of 1994. Essentially, business enterprises were going through a once in a lifetime global realignment. This period was an essentially challenging one for many American business firms that had loaded their balance sheets with debt over the "good times."

Financial executives had to delicately manage cash flows to service existing debt contracts or face bankruptcy. These same executives had to give considerable thought as to how to finance the next (incremental) capital project.

Along these lines, one company that pays explicit attention to managing its financing mix is the Georgia-Pacific Corporation. This firm is one of the world's leaders in the manufacturing and distribution of building products, pulp, and paper. The firm employs about 47,500 individuals and ranked exactly 100 among the Fortune 500 largest domestic corporations at the end of 1996. Georgia-Pacific posted sales revenues of $13 billion for 1996 and possessed $12.8 billion in assets.

Georgia-Pacific's 1996 *Annual Report* contained a separate section on "Financial Strategy." On that subject, the management of the firm said: "Georgia-Pacific's objective is to provide superior returns to our shareholders. To achieve this goal, our financial strategy must complement our operating strategy. We must maintain a capital structure that minimizes our cost of capital while providing flexibility in financing our capital (expenditure) requirements."

LEARNING OBJECTIVES

After reading this chapter, you should be able to

1. Understand the concept of an optimal capital structure.

2. Explain the main underpinnings of capital structure theory.

3. Distinguish between the independence hypothesis and dependence hypothesis as these concepts relate to capital structure theory; and identify the Nobel Prize winners in economics who are the leading proponents of the independence hypothesis.

4. Understand and be able to graph the moderate position on capital structure importance.

5. Incorporate the concepts of agency costs and free cash flow into a discussion on capital structure management.

6. Use the basic tools of capital structure management.

7. Familiarize others with corporate financing policies in practice.

As you learn the material in this chapter, you will be able to make positive contributions to company financing strategies such as those put forth above by the Georgia-Pacific Corporation. In dealing with the firm's financing mix, you can help the firm avoid making serious financial errors, the consequences of which usually last for several years.

CHAPTER PREVIEW

In this chapter, we direct our attention to the determination of an appropriate financing mix for the firm. Think of the right side of the firm's balance sheet as a big pie. That pie can be sliced into different-sized pieces. One piece might be labeled *long-term debt*, another labeled *preferred equity*, and yet another, *common equity*. We want to mix the pieces together in an optimal fashion that will make the pie as large as possible.

That task is the focal point of this chapter, and it is one that all chief financial officers confront. In some instances, just changing the labels on the slices of the pie might not change its size—but in other cases, it might. That is the challenge of financial structure management. The total value of the firm is represented by the ultimate size of the pie. More value (pie) is better than less value (pie). Keep this in mind while you work through the chapter.

As you study this chapter on financial structure theory, decision making, and policy, you will be made aware of a full five of the ten axioms, first noted and explained in chapter 1, that underlie the basics of business financial management. Specifically, your attention will be directed to: Axiom 1: The Risk-Return Trade-Off—We Won't Take on Additional Risk Unless We Expect to Be Compensated with Additional Return; Axiom 3: Cash—Not Profits—Is King; Axiom 6: Efficient Capital Markets—The Markets Are Quick and Prices Are Right; Axiom 7: The Agency Problem—Managers Won't Work for the Owners Unless It's in Their Best Interest; and Axiom 8: Taxes Bias Business Decisions.

KEY TERMS AND GETTING STARTED

Financial structure

The mix of all funds sources that appear on the right side of the balance sheet.

Capital structure

The mix of long-term sources of funds used by the firm. Basically, this concept omits short-term liabilities.

Financial structure design

The management activity of seeking the proper mix of all financing components in order to minimize the cost of raising a given amount of funds.

We now direct our attention to the determination of an appropriate financing mix for the firm. First, we must distinguish between financial structure and capital structure. **Financial structure** is the mix of all items that appear on the right side of the company's balance sheet. **Capital structure** is the mix of the *long-term* sources of funds used by the firm. The relationship between financial and capital structure can be expressed in equation form:

(financial structure) − (current liabilities) = capital structure   (14-1)

Prudent **financial structure design** requires answers to the following two questions:

1. What should be the maturity composition of the firm's sources of funds; in other words, how should a firm best divide its total fund sources between short- and long-term components?
2. In what proportions relative to the total should the various forms of permanent financing be utilized?

The major influence on the maturity structure of the financing plan is the nature of the assets owned by the firm. A company heavily committed to real capital investment, represented primarily by fixed assets on its balance sheet, *should* finance those assets

Table 14.1 Balance Sheet

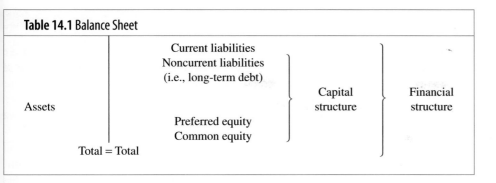

with permanent (long-term) types of financial capital. Furthermore, the permanent portion of the firm's investment in current assets should likewise be financed with permanent capital. Alternatively, assets held on a temporary basis are to be financed with temporary sources. The present discussion assumes that the bulk of the company's current liabilities are comprised of temporary capital.

This hedging concept is discussed in chapter 16. Accordingly, our focus in this chapter is an answer to the second of the two questions noted previously—this process is usually called *capital structure management*.

The *objective* of capital structure management is to mix the permanent sources of funds used by the firm in a manner that will maximize the company's common stock price. Alternatively, this objective may be viewed as a search for the funds mix that will minimize the firm's composite cost of capital. We can call this proper mix of funds sources the **optimal capital structure**.

Table 14.1 looks at equation (14-1) in terms of a simplified balance sheet format. It helps us visualize the overriding problem of capital structure management. The sources of funds that give rise to financing fixed costs (long-term debt and preferred equity) must be combined with common equity in the proportions most suitable to the investing marketplace. If that mix can be found, then, holding all other factors constant, the firm's common stock price will be maximized.

Whereas equation (14-1) quite accurately indicates that the corporate capital structure may be viewed as an absolute dollar *amount*, the *real* capital structure problem is one of balancing the array of funds sources in a proper manner. Our use of the term *capital structure* emphasizes this latter problem of relative magnitude, or proportions.

The rest of this chapter will cover three main areas. First, we discuss the theory of capital structure to provide a perspective. Second, we examine the basic tools of capital structure management. We conclude with a real-world look at actual capital structure management.

OBJECTIVE 1

Optimal capital structure

The unique capital structure that minimizes the firm's composite cost of long-term capital.

STOP AND THINK

It pays to understand the essential components of capital structure theory. The assumption of excessive financial risk can put the firm into bankruptcy proceedings. Some argue that the decision to use little financial leverage results in an undervaluation of the firm's shares in the marketplace. The effective financial manager must know how to find the area of optimum financial leverage use—this will enhance share value, all other considerations held constant. Thus grasping the theory will make you better able to formulate a sound financial structure policy.

An enduring controversy within financial theory concerns the effect of financial leverage on the overall cost of capital to the enterprise. The heart of the argument may be stated in the form of a question: Can the firm affect its overall cost of funds, either favorably or unfavorably, by varying the mixture of financing sources used?

This controversy has taken many elegant forms in the finance literature. Most of these presentations appeal more to academics than to financial management practitioners. To emphasize the ingredients of capital structure theory that have practical applications for business financial management, we will pursue an intuitive, or non-mathematical, approach to reach a better understanding of the underpinnings of this *cost of capital–capital structure argument*.

The Importance of Capital Structure

It makes economic sense for the firm to strive to minimize the cost of using financial capital. Both capital costs and other costs, such as manufacturing costs, share a common characteristic in that they potentially reduce the size of the cash dividend that could be paid to common stockholders.

We saw in chapter 8 that the ultimate value of a share of common stock depends in part on the returns investors expect to receive from holding the stock. Cash dividends comprise all (in the case of an infinite holding period) or part (in the case of a holding period less than infinity) of these expected returns. Now hold constant all factors that could affect share price except capital costs. If these capital costs could be kept at a minimum, the dividend stream flowing to the common stockholders would be maximized. This, in turn, would maximize the firm's common stock price.

If the firm's cost of capital can be affected by its capital structure, then capital structure management is clearly an important subset of business financial management.

Analytical Setting

The essentials of the capital structure controversy are best highlighted within a framework that economists would call a "partial equilibrium analysis." In a partial equilibrium analysis, changes that *do* occur in several factors and have an impact on a certain key item are ignored to study the effect of changes in a main factor on that same item of interest. Here, two items are simultaneously of interest: (1) K_0, the firm's composite cost of capital, and (2) P_0, the market price of the firm's common stock. The firm's use of financial leverage is the main factor that is allowed to vary in the analysis. This means that important financial decisions, such as investing policy and dividend policy, are held constant throughout the discussion. We are concerned with the effect of changes in the financing mix on share price and capital costs.

Our analysis will be facilitated if we adopt a *simplified* version of the basic dividend valuation model presented in chapter 8 in our study of valuation principles, and in chapter 12 in our assessment of the cost of capital. That model is shown below as equation (14-2):

$$P_0 = \sum_{t=1}^{\infty} \frac{D_t}{(1 + K_c)^t} \tag{14-2}$$

where P_0 = the current price of the firm's common stock

D_t = the cash dividend per share expected by investors during period t

K_c = the cost of common equity capital

We can strip away some complications by making the following assumptions concerning the valuation process implicit in equation (14-2):

1. Cash dividends paid will not change over the infinite holding period. Thus $D_1 = D_2 = D_3 = \ldots = D_\infty$. There is no expected growth by investors in the dividend stream.
2. The firm retains none of its current earnings. This means that *all* of each period's per-share earnings are paid to stockholders in the form of cash dividends. The firm's dividend payout ratio is 100 percent. Cash dividends per share in equation (14-2), then, also equal earnings per share for the same period.

Under these assumptions, the cash dividend flowing to investors can be viewed as a level payment over an infinite holding period. The payment stream is perpetual, and according to the mathematics of perpetuities, equation (14-2) reduces to equation (14-3), where E_t represents earnings per share during period t.

$$P_0 = \frac{D_t}{K_c} = \frac{E_t}{K_c} \qquad\qquad (14\text{-}3)$$

In addition to the suppositions noted above, the analytical setting for the discussion of capital structure theory includes the following assumptions:

1. Corporate income is not subject to any taxation. The major implication of removing this assumption is discussed later.
2. Capital structures consist of only stocks and bonds. Furthermore, the degree of financial leverage used by the firm is altered by the issuance of common stock with the proceeds used to retire existing debt, or the issuance of debt with the proceeds used to repurchase stock. This permits leverage use to vary but maintains constancy of the total book value of the firm's capital structure.
3. The expected values of all investors' forecasts of the future levels of net operating income (EBIT) for each firm are identical. Say that you forecast the average level of EBIT to be achieved by General Motors over a very long period ($n \to \infty$). Your forecast will be the same as our forecast, and both will be equal to the forecasts of all other investors interested in General Motors common stock. In addition, we do not expect General Motors's EBIT to grow over time. Each year's forecast is the same as any other year's. This is consistent with our assumption underlying equation (14-3), where the firm's dividend stream is not expected to grow.
4. Securities are traded in perfect or efficient financial markets. This means that transaction costs and legal restrictions do not impede any investors' incentives to execute portfolio changes that they expect will increase their wealth. Information is freely available. Moreover, corporations and individuals that are equal credit risks can borrow funds at the same rates of interest.

This completes our description of the analytical setting. We now discuss three differing views on the relationship between use of financial leverage and common stock value.

STOP AND THINK

The discussion and illustrations of the two extreme positions on the importance of capital structure that follow are meant to highlight the critical differences between differing viewpoints. This is not to say that the markets really behave in strict accordance with either position—they don't. The point is to identify polar positions on how things might work. Then by relaxing various restrictive assumptions, a more useful theory of how financing decisions are actually made becomes possible. That results in the third, or moderate, view.

Extreme Position 1: Independence Hypothesis (NOI Theory)[1]

The crux of this position is that the firm's composite cost of capital, K_0, and common stock price, P_0, are both *independent* of the degree to which the company chooses to use financial leverage. In other words, no matter how modest or excessive the firm's use of debt financing, its common stock price will not be affected. Let us illustrate the mechanics of this point of view.

Suppose that Rix Camper Manufacturing Company has the following financial characteristics:

Shares of common stock outstanding = 2,000,000 shares
Common stock price, P_0 = $ 10 per share
Expected level of net operating income (EBIT) = $2,000,000
Dividend payout ratio = 100 percent

Currently, the firm uses no financial leverage; its capital structure consists entirely of common equity. Earnings per share and dividends per share equal $1 each. When the capital structure is all common equity, the cost of common equity, K_c and the weighted cost of capital, K_0 are equal. If equation (14-3) is restated in terms of the cost of common equity, we have for Rix Camper

$$K_c = \frac{D_t}{P_0} = \frac{\$1}{\$10} = 10\%$$

Now, the management of Rix Camper decides to use some debt capital in its financing mix. The firm sells $8 million worth of long-term debt at an interest rate of 6 percent. With no taxation of corporate income, this 6 percent interest rate is the cost of debt capital, K_d. The firm uses the proceeds from the sale of the bonds to repurchase 40 percent of its outstanding common shares. After the capital-structure change has been accomplished, Rix Camper Manufacturing Company has the financial characteristics displayed in Table 14.2.

Based on the preceding data, we notice that the recapitalization (capital structure change) of Rix Camper will result in a dividend paid to owners that is 26.7 percent higher than it was when the firm used no debt in its capital structure. Will this higher dividend result in a lower composite cost of capital to Rix and a higher common stock price? According to the principles of the independence hypothesis, the answer is "No."

The independence hypothesis suggests that the total market value of the firm's outstanding securities is *unaffected* by the manner in which the right side of the balance sheet is arranged. That is, the sum of the market value of outstanding debt plus the sum of the market value of outstanding common equity will always be the *same* regardless of how much or little debt is actually used by the company. If capital structure has no impact on the total market value of the company, then that value is arrived at by the marketplace's capitalizing (discounting) the firm's expected net operating income stream. Therefore the independence hypothesis rests on what is called the **net operating income (NOI) approach to valuation**.

NOI approach to valuation

The concept from financial theory that suggests the firm's capital structure has no impact on its market valuation.

---

[1]The net operating income and net income capitalization methods, which are referred to here as "extreme positions 1 and 2," were first presented in comprehensible form by Durand. See David Durand, "Costs of Debt and Equity Funds for Business: Trends and Problems of Measurement," *Conference on Research in Business Finance* (New York: National Bureau of Economic Research, 1952), reprinted in Ezra Solomon, ed., *The Management of Corporate Capital* (New York: Free Press), 91–116. The leading proponents of the independence hypothesis in its various forms are Professors Modigliani and Miller. See Franco Modigliani and Merton H. Miller, "The Cost of Capital, Corporation Finance and Theory of Investment," *American Economic Review* 48 (June 1958): 261–97; Franco Modigliani and Merton H. Miller, "Corporate Income Taxes and the Cost of Capital: A Correction," *American Economic Review* 53 (June 1963): 433–43; and Merton H. Miller, "Debt and Taxes," *Journal of Finance* 32 (May 1977): 261–75.

The format is a very simple one, and the market value of the firm's common stock turns out to be a residual of the valuation process. Recall that before Rix Camper's recapitalization, the total market value of the firm was $20 million (2 million common shares times $10 per share). The firm's cost of common equity, K_c, and its weighted cost of capital, K_0, were each equal to 10 percent. The composite discount rate, K_0, is used to arrive at the market value of the firm's securities. After the recapitalization, we have for Rix Camper

Expected level of net operating income capitalized at $K_0 = 10$ percent	$ 2,000,000
= Market value of debt and equity	$20,000,000
− Market value of the new debt	8,000,000
= Market value of the common stock	$12,000,000

With this valuation format, what is the market price of each share of common stock? Because we know that 1.2 million shares of stock are outstanding after the capital-structure change, the market price per share is $10 ($12 million/1.2 million). This is exactly the market value per share, P_0, that existed *before* the change.

Now, if the firm is using some debt that has an *explicit cost* of 6 percent, K_d, and the weighted (composite) cost of capital, K_0, is 10 percent, it stands to reason that the cost of common equity, K_c, has risen above its previous level of 10 percent. What will the cost of common equity be in this situation? As we did previously, we can take equation (14-3) and restate it in terms of K_c, the cost of common equity. After the recapitalization, the cost of common equity for Rix Camper is shown to *rise* to 12.67 percent:

$$K_c = \frac{D_t}{P_0} = \frac{\$1.267}{\$10} = 12.67\%$$

The cost of common equity for Rix Camper is 26.7 percent higher than it was before the capital structure shift. Notice in Table 14.2 that this is *exactly* equal to the percentage increase in earnings and dividends per share that accompanies the same capital structure adjustment. This highlights a fundamental relationship that is an integral part of the independence hypothesis. It concerns the perceived behavior in the firm's cost of common equity as expected dividends (earnings) increase relative to a financing mix change:

percentage change in K_c = percentage change in D_t

Table 14.2 Rix Camper Company Financial Data Reflecting the Capital Structure Adjustment

Capital Structure Information	
Shares of common stock outstanding = 1,200,000	
Bonds at 6 percent = $8,000,000	
Earnings Information	
Expected level of net operating income (EBIT)	$ 2,000,000
Less: Interest expense	480,000
Earnings available to common stockholders	$ 1,520,000
Earnings per share (E_t)	$ 1.267
Dividends per share (D_t)	$ 1.267
Percentage change in both earnings per share and dividends per share relative to the unlevered capital structure	26.7 percent

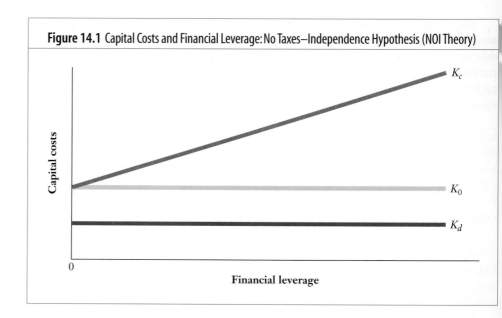

Figure 14.1 Capital Costs and Financial Leverage: No Taxes–Independence Hypothesis (NOI Theory)

K_c

K_0

K_d

Capital costs

0

Financial leverage

In this framework, the use of a greater degree of financial leverage may result in greater earnings and dividends, but the firm's cost of common equity will rise at precisely the same rate as the earnings and dividends do. Thus the inevitable trade-off between the higher expected return in dividends and earnings (D_t and E_t) and increased risk that accompanies the use of debt financing manifests itself in a linear relationship between the cost of common equity (K_c) and financial leverage use. This view of the relationship between the firm's cost of funds and its financing mix is shown graphically in Figure 14.1. Figure 14.2 relates the firm's stock price to its financing mix under the same set of assumptions.

In Figure 14.1, the firm's overall cost of capital, K_0, is shown to be unaffected by an increased use of financial leverage. If more debt is used in the capital structure, the cost of common equity will rise at the same rate additional earnings are generated. This will keep the composite cost of capital to the corporation unchanged. Figure 14.2 shows that because the cost of capital will not change with the leverage use, neither will the firm's stock price.

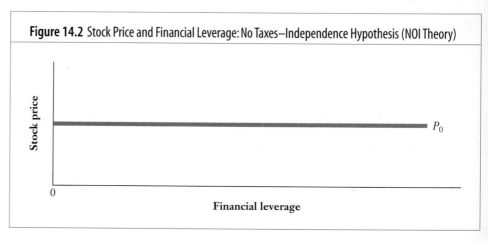

Figure 14.2 Stock Price and Financial Leverage: No Taxes–Independence Hypothesis (NOI Theory)

P_0

Stock price

0

Financial leverage

Debt financing, then, has two costs—its **explicit cost of capital**, K_d, calculated according to the formats outlined in chapter 12 and an implicit cost. The **implicit cost of debt** is the change in the cost of common equity brought on by using financial leverage (additional debt). The real cost of debt is the sum of these explicit and implicit costs. In general, the real cost of *any* source of capital is its explicit cost, plus the change that it induces in the cost of any other source of funds.

Followers of the independence hypothesis argue that the use of financial leverage brings a change in the cost of common equity large enough to offset the benefits of higher dividends to investors. Debt financing is not as cheap as it first appears to be. This will keep the composite cost of funds constant. The implication for management is that one capital structure is as good as any other; financial officers should not waste time searching for an optimal capital structure. One capital structure, after all, is as beneficial as any other, because all result in the same weighted cost of capital.

RELATE TO THE BIG PICTURE

*The suggestion from capital-structure theory that one capital structure is just as good as any other within a perfect ("pure") market framework relies directly on **Axiom 1: The Risk-Return Trade-Off—We Won't Take on Additional Risk Unless We Expect to Be Compensated with Additional Return**. This means that using more debt in the capital structure will not be ignored by investors in the financial markets. These rational investors will require a higher return on common stock investments in the firm that uses more leverage (rather than less), to compensate for the increased uncertainty stemming from the addition of the debt securities in the capital structure.*

Extreme Position 2: Dependence Hypothesis (NI Theory)

OBJECTIVE 3

The dependence hypothesis is at the opposite pole from the independence hypothesis. It suggests that both the weighted cost of capital, K_0, and common stock price, P_0, *are* affected by the firm's use of financial leverage. No matter how modest or excessive the firm's use of debt financing, both its cost of debt capital, K_d, and cost of equity capital, K_c, will not be affected by capital structure management. Because the cost of debt is less than the cost of equity, greater financial leverage will lower the firm's composite cost of capital indefinitely. Greater use of debt financing will thereby have a favorable effect on the company's common stock price. By returning to the Rix Camper situation, we can illustrate this point of view.

The same capital structure shift is being evaluated. That is, management will market $8 million of new debt at a 6 percent interest rate and use the proceeds to purchase its own common shares. Under this approach, the market is assumed to capitalize (discount) the expected earnings available to the common stockholders to arrive at the aggregate market value of the common stock. The market value of the firm's common equity is *not* a residual of the valuation process. After the recapitalization, the firm's cost of common equity, K_c, will still be equal to 10 percent. Thus a 10 percent cost of common equity is applied in the following format:

Expected level of net operating income	$ 2,000,000
− Interest expense	480,000
= Earnings available to common stockholders capitalized at	$ 1,520,000
$K_c = 10$ percent	
= Market value of the common stock	$15,200,000
+ Market value of the new debt	8,000,000
= Market value of debt and equity	$23,200,000

When we assume that the firm's capital structure consists only of debt and common equity, earnings available to the common stockholders is synonymous with net income. In the valuation process outlined above, it is net income that is actually capitalized to arrive at the market value of the common equity. Because of this, the dependence hypothesis is also called the **net income (NI) approach to valuation**.

Notice that the total market value of the firm's securities has risen to $23.2 million from the $20 million level that existed before the firm moved from the unlevered to the levered capital structure. The per-share value of the common stock is also shown to rise under this valuation format. With 1.2 million shares of stock outstanding, the market price per share is $12.67 ($15.2 million/1.2 million).

This increase in the stock price to $12.67 represents a 26.7 percent rise over the previous level of $10 per share. This is exactly equal to the percentage change in earnings per share and dividends per share calculated in Table 14.1. This permits us to characterize the dependence hypothesis in a very succinct fashion:

percentage change in K_c = 0 percent < percentage change in D_t
(over all degrees of leverage)

percentage change in P_0 = percentage change in D_t

The dependence hypothesis suggests that the *explicit and implicit* costs of debt are one and the same. The use of more debt does *not* change the firm's cost of common equity. Using more debt, which is explicitly cheaper than common equity, will lower the firm's composite cost of capital, K_0. If you take the market value of Rix Camper's common stock according to the net income theory of $15.2 million and express it as a percent of the total market value of the firm's securities, you get a market value weight of .655 ($15.2 million/$23.2 million). In a similar fashion, the market value weight of Rix Camper's debt is found to be .345 ($8 million/$23.2 million). After the capital structure adjustment, the firm's weighted cost of capital becomes

$$K_0 = (.345)(6.00\%) + (.655)(10.00\%) = 8.62\%$$

So, changing the financing mix from all equity to a structure including both debt and equity lowered the composite cost of capital from 10 percent to 8.62 percent. The ingredients of the dependence hypothesis are illustrated in Figures 14.3 and 14.4.

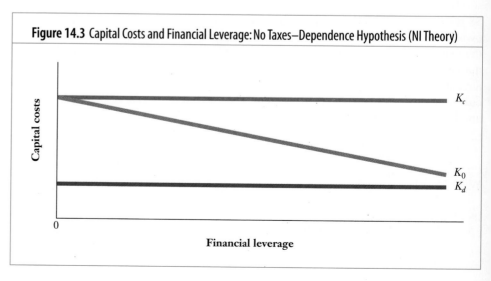

Figure 14.3 Capital Costs and Financial Leverage: No Taxes—Dependence Hypothesis (NI Theory)

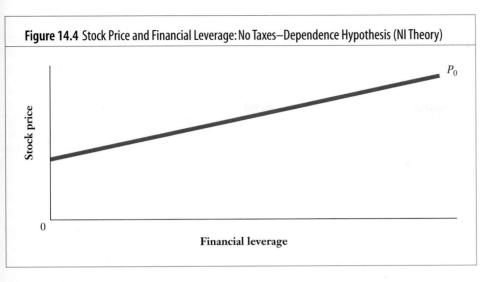

Figure 14.4 Stock Price and Financial Leverage: No Taxes–Dependence Hypothesis (NI Theory)

The implication for management from Figures 14.3 and 14.4 is that the firm's cost of capital, K_0, will decline as the debt-to-equity ratio increases. This also implies that the company's common stock price will rise with increased leverage use. Because the cost of capital decreases continuously with leverage, the firm should use as much leverage as is possible. Next we will move toward reality in the analytical setting of our capital structure discussion. This is accomplished by relaxing some of the major assumptions that surrounded the independence and dependence hypotheses.

Moderate Position: Corporate Income Is Taxed and Firms May Fail

In general, an analysis of extreme positions may be useful in that you are forced to sharpen your thinking not only about the poles, but also the situations that span the poles. In microeconomics, the study of perfect competition and monopoly provides a better understanding of the business activity that occurs in the wide area between these two model markets. In a similar fashion, the study of the independence and dependence hypotheses of the importance of capital structure helps us formulate a more informed view of the possible situations between those polar positions.

We turn now to a description of the cost of capital–capital structure relationship that has rather wide appeal to both business practitioners and academics. This moderate view (1) admits to the fact that interest expense is tax deductible, and (2) acknowledges that the probability of the firm's suffering bankruptcy costs is directly related to the company's use of financial leverage.

Tax deductibility of interest expense. This portion of the analysis recognizes that corporate income is subject to taxation. Furthermore, we assume that interest expense is tax deductible for purposes of computing the firm's tax bill. In this environment, the use of debt financing should result in a higher total market value for the firm's outstanding securities. We will see why subsequently.

We continue with our Rix Camper Manufacturing Company example. First, consider the total cash payments made to all security holders (holders of common stock plus holders of bonds). In the no-tax case, the sum of cash dividends paid to common shareholders plus interest expense amounted to $2 million both (1) when financing was all by common equity, and (2) after the proposed capital structure adjustment to a levered situation was

Table 14.3 Rix Camper Company Cash Flows to All Investors—The Case of Taxes		
	Unlevered Capital Structure	Levered Capital Structure
Expected level of net operating income	$2,000,000	$2,000,000
Less: Interest expense	0	480,000
Earnings before taxes	$2,000,000	$1,520,000
Less: Taxes at 50%	1,000,000	760,000
Earnings available to common stockholders	$1,000,000	$ 760,000
Expected payments to all security holders	$1,000,000	$1,240,000

accomplished. The *sum* of the cash flows that Rix Camper could pay to its contributors of debt and equity capital was not affected by its financing mix.

When corporate income is taxed by the government, however, the sum of the cash flows made to *all* contributors of financial capital *is* affected by the firm's financing mix. Table 14.3 illustrates this point.

If Rix Camper makes the capital structure adjustment identified in the preceding sections of this chapter, the total payments to equity and debtholders will be $240,000 *greater* than under the all-common-equity capitalization. Where does this $240,000 come from? The government's take, through taxes collected, is lower by that amount. This difference, which flows to the Rix Camper security holders, is called the **tax shield** on interest. In general, it may be calculated by equation (14-4), where r_d is the interest rate paid on the debt, M is the principal amount of the debt, and t is the firm's marginal tax rate:

Tax shield

The element from the federal tax code that permits interest costs to be deductible when computing the firm's tax bill. The dollar difference (the shield) flows to the firm's security holders.

$$\text{tax shield} = r_d(M)(t) \tag{14-4}$$

The moderate position on the importance of capital structure presumes that the tax shield must have value in the marketplace. Accordingly, this tax benefit will increase the total market value of the firm's outstanding securities relative to the all-equity capitalization. Financial leverage does affect firm value. Because the cost of capital is just the other side of the valuation coin, financial leverage also affects the firm's composite cost of capital. Can the firm increase firm value indefinitely and lower its cost of capital continuously by using more and more financial leverage? Common sense would tell us "No!" So would most financial managers and academicians. The acknowledgment of bankruptcy costs provides one possible rationale.

RELATE TO THE BIG PICTURE

*The section above on the "Tax Deductibility of Interest Expense" is a compelling example of **Axiom 8: Taxes Bias Business Decisions**. We have just seen that corporations have an important incentive provided by the tax code to finance projects with debt securities rather than new issues of common stock. The interest expense on the debt issue will be tax deductible. The common stock dividends will not be tax deductible. So firms can indeed increase their total after tax cash flows available to all investors in their securities by using financial leverage. This element of the U.S. tax code should also remind you of **Axiom 3: Cash—Not Profits—Is King**.*

The likelihood of firm failure. The probability that the firm will be unable to meet the financial obligations identified in its debt contracts increases as more debt is employed. The highest costs would be incurred if the firm actually went into bankruptcy proceedings. Here, assets would be liquidated. If we admit that these assets might sell for something

Figure 14.5 Capital Costs and Financial Leverage: The Moderate View, Considering Taxes and Financial Distress

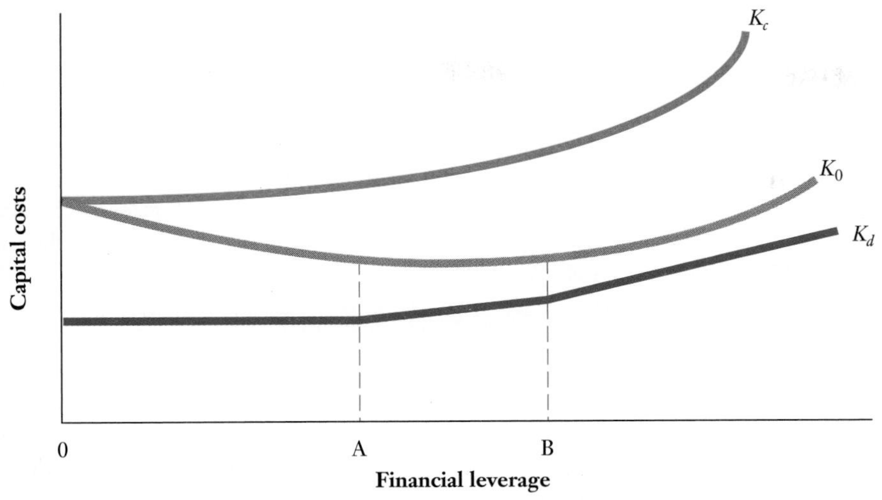

Graph showing Capital costs (vertical axis) versus Financial leverage (horizontal axis). Three curves are labeled: K_c (rising steeply), K_0 (saucer-shaped), and K_d (rising). Vertical dashed lines mark points A and B on the horizontal axis.

less than their perceived market values, equity investors and debtholders could both suffer losses. Other problems accompany bankruptcy proceedings. Lawyers and accountants have to be hired and paid. Managers must spend time preparing lengthy reports for those involved in the legal action.

Milder forms of financial distress also have their costs. As their firm's financial condition weakens, creditors may take action to restrict normal business activity. Suppliers may not deliver materials on credit. Profitable capital investments may have to be forgone, and dividend payments may even be interrupted. At some point, the expected cost of default will be large enough to outweigh the tax shield advantage of debt financing.[2] The firm will turn to other sources of financing, mainly common equity. At this point, the real cost of debt is thought to be higher than the real cost of common equity.

Moderate View: Saucer-Shaped Cost of Capital Curve

OBJECTIVE 4

This moderate view of the relationship between financing mix and the firm's cost of capital is depicted in Figure 14.5. The result is a saucer-shaped (or U-shaped) average cost of capital curve, K_0. The firm's average cost of equity, K_0, is seen to rise over all positive degrees of financial leverage use. For a while, the firm can borrow funds at a relatively low cost of debt, K_d. Even though the cost of equity is rising, it does not rise at a fast enough rate to offset the use of the less expensive debt financing. Thus, between points 0 and A on the financial-leverage axis, the average cost of capital declines and stock price rises.

Eventually, the threat of financial distress causes the cost of debt to rise. In Figure 14.5, this increase in the cost of debt shows up in the average cost of debt curve, K_d, at point A. Between points A and B, mixing debt and equity funds produces an average cost of capital

---

[2]Even this argument that the trade-off between bankruptcy costs and the tax shield benefit of debt financing can lead to an optimal structure has its detractors. See Robert A. Haugen and Lemma W. Senbet, "The Insignificance of Bankruptcy Costs to the Theory of Optimal Capital Structure," *Journal of Finance* 33 (May 1978): 383–93.

that is (relatively) flat. The firm's **optimal range of financial leverage** lies between points A and B. All capital structures between these two points are optimal because they produce the lowest composite cost of capital. As we said in the introduction to this chapter, finding this optimal range of financing mixes is the objective of capital structure management.

Point B signifies the firm's debt capacity. **Debt capacity** is the maximum proportion of debt the firm can include in its capital structure and still maintain its lowest composite cost of capital. Beyond point B, additional fixed-charge capital can be attracted only at very costly interest rates. At the same time, this excessive use of financial leverage would cause the firm's cost of equity to rise at a faster rate than previously. The composite cost of capital would then rise quite rapidly, and the firm's stock price would decline.

This version of the moderate view as it relates to the firm's stock price is characterized subsequently. The notation is the same as that found in our discussion of the independence and dependence hypotheses.

1. Between points 0 and A: $0 <$ percentage change in $P_0 <$ percentage change in D_t
2. Between points A and B: percentage change in $P_0 = 0$
3. Beyond point B: percentage change in $P_0 < 0$

STOP AND THINK

Given the same task or assignment, it is quite likely that you will do it better for yourself than for someone else. If you are paid well enough, you might do the job about as effectively for that other person. Once you receive compensation, your work will be evaluated by someone. This process of evaluation is called "monitoring" within most discussions on agency costs.

This describes the heart of what is called the "agency problem." As American businesses have grown in size, the owners and managers have become (for the most part) separate groups of individuals. An inherent conflict exists, therefore, between managers and shareholders for whom managers act as agents in carrying out their objectives (for example, corporate goals). The following discussion relates the agency problem to the financial decision-making process of the firm.

Firm Value, Agency Costs, Static Trade-Off Theory and the Pecking Order Theory

In chapter 1 of this text, we mentioned the *agency problem*. Recall that the agency problem gives rise to *agency costs*, which tend to occur in business organizations because ownership and management control are often separate. Thus the firm's managers can be properly thought of as agents for the firm's stockholders.[3] To ensure that agent-managers act in the stockholders' best interests requires that they have (1) proper incentives to do so and (2) that their decisions are monitored. The incentives usually take the form of executive compensation plans and perquisites. The perquisites might be a bloated support staff, country club memberships, luxurious corporate planes, or other amenities of a similar nature. Monitoring requires that certain costs be borne by the stockholders, such as (1) bonding the managers, (2) auditing financial statements, (3) structuring the organization in unique ways

---

[3]Economists have studied the problems associated with control of the corporation for decades. An early, classic work on this topic was A. A. Berle, Jr., and G. C. Means, *The Modern Corporation and Private Property* (New York: Macmillan, 1932). The recent emphasis in corporate finance and financial economics stems from the important contribution of Michael C. Jensen and William H. Meckling, "Theory of the Firm: Managerial Behavior, Agency Costs and Ownership Structure," *Journal of Financial Economics* 3 (October 1976): 306–60. Professors Jensen and Smith have analyzed the bondholder-stockholder conflict in a very clear style. See Michael C. Jensen and Clifford W. Smith, Jr., "Stockholder, Manager, and Creditor Interests: Applications of Agency Theory," in Edward I. Altman and Marti G. Subrahmanyam, eds., *Recent Advances in Corporate Finance* (Homewood, IL: Richard D. Irwin, 1985): 93–131.

Figure 14.6 Agency Costs of Debt: Trade-Offs

No Protective Bond Covenants	Many Protective Bonds Covenants
High interest rates	Low interest rates
Low monitoring costs	High monitoring costs
No lost operating efficiencies	Many lost operating efficiencies

that limit useful managerial decisions, and (4) reviewing the costs and benefits of management perquisites. This list is indicative, not exhaustive. The main point is that monitoring costs are ultimately covered by the owners of the company—its common stockholders.

Capital structure management also gives rise to agency costs. Agency problems stem from conflicts of interest, and capital-structure management encompasses a natural conflict between stockholders and bondholders. Acting in the stockholders' best interests might cause management to invest in extremely risky projects. Existing investors in the firm's bonds could logically take a dim view of such an investment policy. A change in the risk structure of the firm's assets would change the business risk exposure of the firm. This could lead to a downward revision of the bond rating the firm currently enjoys. A lowered bond rating in turn would lower the current market value of the firm's bonds. Clearly, bondholders would be unhappy with this result.

To reduce this conflict of interest, the creditors (bond investors) and stockholders may agree to include several protective covenants in the bond contract. These bond covenants were discussed in more detail in chapter 7, but essentially they may be thought of as restrictions on managerial decision making. Typical covenants restrict payment of cash dividends on common stock, limit the acquisition or sale of assets, or limit further debt financing. To make sure that the protective covenants are complied with by management means that monitoring costs are incurred. Like all monitoring costs, they are borne by common stockholders. Further, like many costs, they involve the analysis of an important trade-off.

Figure 14.6 displays some of the tradeoffs involved with the use of protective bond covenants. Note (in the left panel of Figure 14.6) that the firm might be able to sell bonds that carry no protective covenants only by incurring very high interest rates. With no protective covenants, there are no associated monitoring costs. Also, there are no lost operating efficiencies, such as being able to move quickly to acquire a particular company in the acquisitions market. Conversely, the willingness to submit to several covenants could reduce the explicit cost of the debt contract, but would involve incurring significant monitoring costs and losing some operating efficiencies (which also translates into higher costs). When the debt issue is first sold, then, a trade-off will be arrived at between incurring monitoring costs, losing operating efficiencies, and enjoying a lower explicit interest cost.

Next we have to consider the presence of monitoring costs at low levels of leverage and at higher levels of leverage. When the firm operates at a low debt-to-equity ratio, there is little need for creditors to insist on a long list of bond covenants. The financial risk is just not there to require that type of activity. The firm will likewise benefit from low explicit interest rates when leverage is low. When the debt-to-equity ratio is high, however, it is logical for creditors to demand a great deal of monitoring. This increase in agency costs will raise the implicit cost (the true total cost) of debt financing. It seems logical, then, to suggest that monitoring costs will rise as the firm's use of financial leverage increases. Just as the likelihood of firm failure (financial distress) raises a company's overall cost of capital (K_0), so do agency costs. On the other side of the coin, this means that total firm value (the total market value of the firm's securities) will be *lower* owing to the presence of agency costs of debt. Taken together, the presence of agency costs and the costs associated with financial distress argue in favor of the concept of an *optimal* capital structure for the individual firm.

This general approach to understanding or explaining capital-structure decision making has come to be known in the finance literature as the "static trade-off theory." The label follows the essential form of the implied model wherein the present value (benefits) of tax shields that stem from increased leverage use are "traded-off" against both the rising costs of the likelihood of financial distress and the rising agency costs associated with increased debt usage.[4]

This discussion can be summarized by introducing equation (14-5) for the value of the levered firm. It represents the static trade-off model.

$$\begin{array}{l}\begin{matrix}\text{market value} \\ \text{of levered firm}\end{matrix} = \begin{matrix}\text{market value of} \\ \text{unlevered firm}\end{matrix} + \begin{matrix}\text{present value} \\ \text{of tax shields}\end{matrix} \\ \\ \qquad\qquad -\left(\begin{matrix}\text{present value} \\ \text{of financial} \\ \text{distress costs}\end{matrix} + \begin{matrix}\text{present value} \\ \text{of agency} \\ \text{costs}\end{matrix}\right)\end{array} \qquad (14\text{-}5)$$

The relationship expressed in equation (14-5) is presented graphically in Figure 14.7. There we see that the tax shield effect is dominant until point *A* is reached. After point *A*, the rising costs of the likelihood of firm failure (financial distress) and agency costs cause the market value of the levered firm to decline. The objective for the financial manager here is to find point *B* by using all of his or her analytical skill; this must also include a good dose of seasoned judgment. At point *B*, the actual market value of the levered firm is maximized, and its composite cost of capital (K_0) is at a minimum. The implementation problem is that the precise costs of financial distress and monitoring can only be estimated by subjective means; a definite mathematical solution is not available. Thus planning the firm's financing mix always requires good decision making and management judgment.

An alternative view aimed at predicting how managers will finance their firm's capital budgets is now known in the financial-economics literature as the "pecking order theory." The germ of this approach is found in the works of Gordon Donaldson. Specifically, see his two volumes: *Corporate Debt Capacity* (Cambridge, MA: Division of Research, Harvard University, 1961), and *Strategy for Financial Mobility* (Cambridge, MA: Division of Research, Harvard University, 1969).

Myers then expanded on Donaldson's insights in the "Capital Structure Puzzle," noted below, and in several other places, including "Still Searching for Optimal Capital Structure," which appeared in R. W. Kopcke and E. S. Rosengren, eds., *Are the Distinctions between Debt and Equity Disappearing?* (Boston: Federal Reserve Bank of Boston, 1989): 80–95.

---

[4]Portions of the static trade-off model were contained in the original Modigliani and Miller 1958 article noted in footnote 1 in this chapter. It drew much increased attention, however, after the publication of Stewart C. Myers presidential address to the American Finance Association. See Stewart C. Myers's, "The Capital Structure Puzzle," *Journal of Finance* 39 (July 1984): 575–92. As might be expected, not all of the attention is complimentary concerning the usefulness of the static trade-off model.

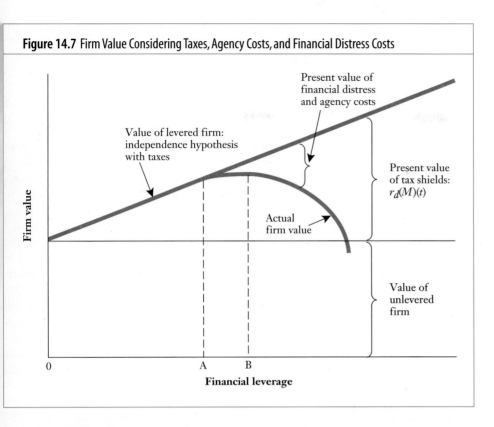

Figure 14.7 Firm Value Considering Taxes, Agency Costs, and Financial Distress Costs

Present value of
financial distress
and agency costs

Value of levered firm:
independence hypothesis
with taxes

Present value
of tax shields:
$r_d(M)(t)$

Actual
firm value

Value of
unlevered
firm

Firm value

0   A   B

Financial leverage

In this latter article, Myers succinctly summarized the pecking order theory of capital structure with these four points (see pages 84–85):

1. Firms adapt dividend policy to investment opportunities. Note that this assumption is close to the concept of the *residual dividend theory* discussed in chapter 15.
2. Firms prefer to finance investment opportunities with internally generated funds first; then external financial capital will be sought.
3. When external financing is needed, the firm will first choose to issue debt securtities; issuing equity-type securities will be done last.
4. As more external financing is required to fund projects with positive net present values, the financing pecking order will be followed. This means a preference toward more risky debt, then to convertibles, preferred equity, and common equity as the last preference.

The upshot of this pecking order theory is that *no* precisely defined target leverage ratio really exists. This is because observed leverage ratios (that is, total debt to total assets) merely reflect the cumulative external financing needs of the firm over time.

Agency Costs, Free Cash Flow, and Capital Structure

OBJECTIVE 5

In 1986, Professor Michael C. Jensen further extended the concept of agency costs into the area of capital structure management. The contribution revolves around a concept that Jensen labels "free cash flow." Professor Jensen defines free cash flow as follows:[5]

[5]Michael Jensen, "Agency Costs of Free Cash Flow, Corporate Finance, and Takeovers," *American Economic Review* 76 (May 1986): 323–29.

Free cash flow is cash flow in excess of that required to fund all projects that have positive net present values when discounted at the relevant cost of capital.

Jensen then puts forth that substantial free cash flow can lead to misbehavior by managers and poor decisions that are *not* in the best interests of the firm's common stockholders. In other words, managers have an incentive to hold on to the free cash flow and have "fun" with it, rather than "disgorging" it, say, in the form of higher cash dividend payments.

But all is not lost. This leads to what Jensen calls his "control hypothesis" for debt creation. By levering up, the firm's shareholders will enjoy increased control over their management team. For example, if the firm issues new debt and uses the proceeds to retire outstanding common stock, then management is obligated to pay out cash to service the debt—this simultaneously reduces the amount of free cash flow available to management with which to have fun.

We can also refer to this motive for financial leverage use as the "threat hypothesis." Management works under the threat of financial failure—therefore, according to the "free cash flow theory of capital structure," it works more efficiently. This is supposed to reduce the agency costs of free cash flow which will in turn be recognized by the marketplace in the form of greater returns on the common stock.

Note that the *free cash flow theory of capital structure* does not give a theoretical solution to the question of just how much financial leverage is enough. Nor does it suggest how much leverage is too much leverage. It is a way of thinking about why shareholders and their boards of directors might use more debt to control management behavior and decisions. The basic decision tools of capital structure management still have to be utilized. They will be presented later in this chapter.

Managerial Implications

Where does our examination of capital structure theory leave us? The upshot is that the determination of the firm's financing mix is centrally important to the financial manager. The firm's stockholders are affected by capital structure decisions.

At the very least, and before bankruptcy costs and agency costs become detrimental, the tax shield effect will cause the shares of a levered firm to sell at a higher price than they would if the company had avoided debt financing. Owing to both the risk of failure and agency costs that accompany the excessive use of leverage, the financial manager must exercise caution in the use of fixed-charge capital. This problem of searching for the optimal range of use of financial leverage is our next task.[6]

---

[6]The relationship between capital structure and enterprise valuation by the marketplace continues to stimulate considerable research output. The complexity of the topic is reviewed in Stewart C. Myers, "The Capital Structure Puzzle," *Journal of Finance* 39 (July 1984): 575–92. Ten useful papers are contained in Benjamin M. Friedman, ed., *Corporate Capital Structures in the United States* (Chicago: National Bureau of Economic Research and the University of Chicago Press, 1985).

BUSINESS REVIEW, FEDERAL RESERVE BANK OF PHILADELPHIA SEPTEMBER-OCTOBER 1989

Ben Bernanke on the Free Cash Theory of Capital Structure and the Buildup in Corporate Debt

The idea is that the financial structure of firms influences the incentives of "insiders" (managers, directors, and large shareholders with some operational interest in the business) and that, in particular, high levels of debt may increase the willingness of insiders to work hard and make profit-maximizing decisions. This incentive-based approach makes a valuable contribution to our understanding of a firm's capital structure. But while this theory might explain why firms like to use debt in general, does it explain why the use of debt has increased so much in recent years?

Michael Jensen, a founder and leading proponent of the incentive-based approach to capital structure, argues that it can. Jensen focuses on a recent worsening of what he calls the "free cash flow" problem. Free cash flow is defined as the portion of a corporation's cash flow that it is unable to invest profitably within the firm. Companies in industries that are profitable but no longer have much potential for expansion—the U.S. oil industry, for example—have a lot of free cash flow.

Why is free cash flow a problem? Jensen argues that managers are often tempted to use free cash flow to expand the size of the company, even if the expansion is not profitable. This is because managers feel that their power and job satisfaction are enhanced by a growing company; so given that most managers' compensation is at best weakly tied to the firm's profitability, Jensen argues that managers will find it personally worthwhile to expand even into money-losing operations. In principle, the board of directors and shareholders should be able to block these unprofitable investments; however, in practice, the fact that the management typically has far more information about potential investments than do outside directors and shareholders makes it difficult to second-guess the managers' recommendations.

How More Leverage Can Help

The company manager with lots of free cash flow may attempt to use that cash to increase his power and perquisites, at the expense of the shareholders. Jensen argues that the solution to the free cash-flow problem is more leverage. For example, suppose that management uses the free cash flow of the company, plus the proceeds of new debt issues, to repurchase stock from the outside shareholders—that is, to do a management buyout. This helps solve the free-cash-flow problem in several ways. The personal returns of the managers are now much more closely tied to the profits of the firm, which gives them incentives to be more efficient. Second, the releveraging process removes the existing free cash from the firm, so that any future investment projects will have to be financed externally; thus future projects will have to meet the market test of being acceptable to outside bankers or bond purchasers. Finally, the high interest payments implied by releveraging impose a permanent discipline on the managers; in order to meet these payments, they will have to ruthlessly cut money-losing operations, avoid questionable investments, and take other efficiency-promoting actions.

According to Jensen, a substantial increase in free-cash-flow problems—resulting from deregulation, the maturing of some large industries, and other factors—is a major source of the recent debt expansion. Jensen also points to a number of institutional factors that have promoted increased leverage. These include relaxed restrictions on mergers, which have lowered the barriers to corporate takeovers created by the antitrust laws and increased financial sophistication, such as the greatly expanded operations of takeover specialists like Drexel Burnham Lambert Inc. and the development of the market for "junk bonds."

Jensen's diagnosis is not controversial: it's quite plausible that these factors, plus changing norms about what constitutes an "acceptable" level of debt, explain at least part of the trend toward increased corporate debt. One important piece of evidence in favor of this explanation is that net equity issues have been substantially negative since 1983. This suggests that much of the proceeds of the new debt issues is being used to repurchase outstanding shares. This is what we would expect if corporations are attempting to re-leverage their existing assets, rather than using debt to expand their asset holdings. However, the implied conclusion—that the debt buildup is beneficial overall to the economy—is considerably more controversial.

Criticisms of the Incentive-Based Rationale for Increased Debt

Jensen and other advocates of the incentive-based approach to capital structure have made a cogent theoretical case for the beneficial effects of debt finance, and many architects of large-scale restructurings have given improved incentives and the promise of greater efficiency as a large part of the rationale for increased leverage. The idea that leverage is beneficial has certainly been embraced by the stock market: even unsubstantiated rumors of a potential leveraged buyout (LBO) have been sufficient to send the stock price of the targeted company soaring, often by 40 percent or more. At a minimum, this indicates that stock market participants *believe* that higher leverage increases profitability. Proponents of restructuring interpret this as evidence that debt is good for the economy.

There are, however, criticisms of this conclusion. First, the fact that the stock market's expectations of company profitability rise when there is a buyout is not proof that profits will rise in actuality. It is still too soon to judge whether the increased leverage of the 1980s will lead to a sustained increase in profitability. One might think of looking to historical data for an answer to this question. But buyouts in the 1960s and 1970s were somewhat different in character from more recent restructurings, and, in any case, the profitability evidence on the earlier episodes is mixed.

Even if the higher profits expected by the stock market do materialize, there is contention over where they are likely to come from. The incentive-based

theory of capital structure says they will come from improved efficiency. But some opponents have argued that the higher profits will primarily reflect transfers to the shareholders from other claimants on the corporation—its employees, customers, suppliers, bondholders, and the government. Customers may be hurt if takeovers are associated with increased monopolization of markets. Bondholders have been big losers in some buyouts, as higher leverage has increased bankruptcy risk and thus reduced the value of outstanding bonds. The government may have lost tax revenue, as companies, by increasing leverage, have increased their interest deductions (although there are offsetting effects here, such as the taxes paid by bought-out shareholders on their capital gains). The perception that much of the profits associated with releveraging and buyouts comes from "squeezing" existing beneficiaries of the corporation explains much of the recent political agitation to limit these activities.

The debt buildup can also be criticized from the perspective of incentive-based theories themselves. Two points are worth noting: first, the principal problem that higher leverage is supposed to address is the relatively weak connection between firms' profits and managers' personal returns, which reduces managers' incentives to take profit-maximizing actions. But if this is truly the problem, it could be addressed more directly—without subjecting the company to serious bankruptcy risk—simply by changing managerial compensation schemes to include more profit-based incentives.

The Downside of Debt Financing

Increased debt is not the optimal solution to all incentive problems. For example, it has been shown, as a theoretical proposition, that managers of debt-financed firms have an incentive to choose riskier projects over safe ones; this is because firms with fixed-debt obligations enjoy all of the upside potential of high-risk projects but share the downside losses with the debt holders, who are not fully repaid if bad investment outcomes cause the firm to fail.

That high leverage does not always promote efficiency can be seen when highly leveraged firms suffer losses and find themselves in financial distress. When financial problems hit, the need to meet interest payments may force management to take a very short-run perspective, leading them to cut back production and employment, cancel even potentially profitable expansion projects, and sell assets at fire-sale prices. Because the risk of bankruptcy is so great, firms in financial distress cannot make long-term agreements; they lose customers and suppliers who are afraid they cannot count on an ongoing relationship, and they must pay wage premiums to hire workers.

These efficiency losses, plus the direct costs of bankruptcy (such as legal fees), are the potential downside of high leverage.

SOURCE: Ben Bernanke, "Is There Too Much Corporate Debt?" *Business Review*, Federal Reserve Bank of Philadelphia (September–October 1989): 5–8.

Analysis and Implications . . .

A. Business journalists and academic researchers alike generated several explanations for the seemingly heavy use of debt financing by corporations that persisted over most of the 1980s. Not all analysts accepted Jensen's control hypothesis for debt creation. Professor Bernanke had his doubts. He reviews Jensen's free cash flow theory and comments on the 1980s buildup in corporate leverage. The "incentive-based approach" is Bernanke's term for the free cash flow theory of capital structure.

B. What is suggested here is that boards of directors and stockholders do *not* have equal access with management to the information that influences investment decisions. The outcome is that management may not actually make the best choices on behalf of its board or stockholders. When two groups (such as stockholders as opposed to managers) have unequal access to private information, it is referred to as *asymmetric information*. If both groups had access to the same information, it would be referred to as *symmetric information*. The presence of asymmetric information accentuates the agency problem that we have reviewed in this chapter. Because of it, some analysts refer to boards of directors as "boards of the directed." There is a difference.

C. It is being emphasized here that a host of explanations can be given for the 1980s debt buildup. All of these reasons in concert have caused the "free cash flow problem." Also observe the suggestion that leverage norms may have changed. This demonstrates the dynamic nature of capital structure management.

D. Recall that we showed in the previous chapter that using financial leverage is a two-edged sword; it magnifies profitability gains *and* losses to stockholders. The concept will be expanded on in the next section on the "Basic Tools of Capital Structure Management." We will see that using financial leverage can increase the firm's level of earnings per share provided that earnings before interest and taxes (EBIT) are above a critical level. Below a critical level, the opposite outcome occurs.

E. This discussion on where higher profits expected by the stock market will come from should remind you of **Axiom 5: The Curse of Competitive Markets—Why It's Hard to Find Exceptionally Profitable Projects.** The incentive-based theory that stresses improved profitability will follow improved efficiency may not happen unless competition in the product market is reduced by some barrier to entry. As we said in chapter 1, in competitive markets, extremely large profits cannot exist for very long. It follows from this line of thinking that the gains from employing the control hypothesis for debt creation may not last for very long.

F. The essential point here is that there may be more direct ways to motivate managers on the stockholders' behalf without exposing the entire firm to bankruptcy. The proposal is to alter management compensation packages so that managers act like owners. This is one approach to reducing agency costs.

Table 14.4 Pierce Grain Company Possible Capital Structures

Plan A: 0% debt

		Total debt	$ 0
		Common equity	200,000[a]
Total assets	$200,000	Total liabilities and equity	$200,000

Plan B: 25% debt at 8% interest rate

		Total debt	$ 50,000
		Common equity	150,000[b]
Total assets	$200,000	Total liabilities and equity	$200,000

Plan C: 40% debt at 8% interest rate

		Total debt	$ 80,000
		Common equity	120,000[c]
Total assets	$200,000	Total liabilities and equity	$200,000

[a]2,000 common shares outstanding
[b]1,500 common shares outstanding
[c]1,200 common shares outstanding

STOP AND THINK

You have now developed a workable knowledge of capital structure theory. This makes you better equipped to search for your firm's optimal capital structure. Several tools are available to help you in this search process and simultaneously help you make prudent financing choices. These tools are decision oriented. *They assist us in answering this question: "The next time we need $20 million, should we issue common stock or sell long-term bonds?"*

OBJECTIVE 6

BASIC TOOLS OF CAPITAL STRUCTURE MANAGEMENT

Recall from chapter 13 that the use of financial leverage has two effects on the earnings stream flowing to the firm's common stockholders. For clarity of exposition, Tables 13.7 and 13.8 are repeated here as Tables 14.4 and 14.5. Three possible financing mixes for the Pierce Grain Company are contained in Table 14.4, and an analysis of the corresponding financial leverage effects is displayed in Table 14.5.

The *first financial leverage effect* is the added variability in the earnings-per-share stream that accompanies the use of fixed-charge securities in the company's capital structure. By means of the degree-of-financial-leverage measure (DFL_{EBIT}) we explained how this variability can be quantified. The firm that uses more financial leverage (rather than less) will experience larger relative changes in its earnings per share (rather than smaller) following EBIT fluctuations. Assume that Pierce Grain elected financing plan C rather than plan A. Plan C is highly levered and plan A is unlevered. A 100 percent increase in EBIT from $20,000 to $40,000 would cause earnings per share to rise by 147 percent under plan C, but only 100 percent under plan A. Unfortunately, the effect would operate in the negative direction as well. A given change in EBIT is *magnified* by the use of financial leverage. This magnification is reflected in the variability of the firm's earnings per share.

The *second financial leverage effect* concerns the level of earnings per share at a given EBIT under a given capital structure. Refer to Table 14.5. At the EBIT level of $20,000, earnings per share would be $5, $5.33, and $5.67 under financing arrangements A, B, and C,

Table 14.5 Pierce Grain Company Analysis of Financial Leverage at Different EBIT Levels

(1)	(2)	(3) = (1) − (2)	(4) = (3) × .5	(5) = (3) − (4)	(6)
				Net Income	Earnings
EBIT	Interest	EBT	Taxes	to Common	per Share

Plan A: 0% debt; $200,000 common equity; 2,000 shares

EBIT	Interest	EBT	Taxes	Net Income to Common	EPS	
$ 0	$ 0	$ 0	$ 0	$ 0	$ 0	
20,000	0	20,000	10,000	10,000	5.00	
40,000	0	40,000	20,000	20,000	10.00	} 100%
60,000	0	60,000	30,000	30,000	15.00	
80,000	0	80,000	40,000	40,000	20.00	

Plan B: 25% debt; 8% interest rate; $150,000 common equity, 1,500 shares

EBIT	Interest	EBT	Taxes	Net Income to Common	EPS	
$ 0	$4,000	$ (4,000)	$ (2,000)[a]	$ (2,000)	$ (1.33)	
20,000	4,000	16,000	8,000	8,000	5.33	
40,000	4,000	36,000	18,000	18,000	12.00	} 125%
60,000	4,000	56,000	28,000	28,000	18.67	
80,000	4,000	76,000	38,000	38,000	25.33	

Plan C: 40% debt; 8% interest rate; $120,000 common equity; 1,200 shares

EBIT	Interest	EBT	Taxes	Net Income to Common	EPS	
$ 0	$6,400	$ (6,400)	$ (3,200)[a]	$ (3,200)	$ (2.67)	
20,000	6,400	13,600	6,800	6,800	5.67	
40,000	6,400	33,600	16,800	16,800	14.00	} 147%
60,000	6,400	53,600	26,800	26,800	22.33	
80,000	6,400	73,600	36,800	36,800	30.67	

[a]The negative tax bill recognizes the credit arising from the carryback and carryforward provision of the tax code. See chapter 1.

respectively. Above a critical level of EBIT, the firm's earnings per share will be higher if greater degrees of financial leverage are employed. Conversely, below some critical level of EBIT, earnings per share will suffer at greater degrees of financial leverage. Whereas the first financial-leverage effect is quantified by the degree-of-financial-leverage measure (DFL$_{EBIT}$), the second is quantified by what is generally referred to as EBIT–EPS analysis. EPS refers, of course, to earnings per share. The rationale underlying this sort of analysis is simple. Earnings is one of the key variables that influences the market value of the firm's common stock. The effect of a financing decision on EPS, then, should be understood because the decision will probably affect the value of the stockholders' investment.

EBIT–EPS Analysis

EXAMPLE

Assume that plan B in Table 14.5 is the existing capital structure for Pierce Grain Company. Furthermore, the asset structure of the firm is such that EBIT is expected to be $20,000 per year for a very long time. A capital investment is available to Pierce Grain that will cost $50,000. Acquisition of this asset is expected to raise the projected EBIT level to $30,000, permanently. The firm can raise the needed cash by (1) selling 500 shares of common stock at $100 each, or (2) selling new bonds that will net the firm $50,000 and carry an interest rate of 8.5 percent. These capital structures and corresponding EPS amounts are summarized in Table 14.6.

Table 14.6 Pierce Grain Company Analysis of Financing Choices

Part A: Capital Structures	Existing Capital Structure			With New Common Stock Financing			With New Debt Financing
Long-term debt at 8%	$ 50,000	Long-term debt at 8%	$ 50,000	Long-term debt at 8%	$ 50,000		
Common stock	150,000	Common stock	200,000	Long-term debt at 8.5%	50,000		
				Common stock	150,000		
Total liabilities and equity	$200,000	Total liabilities and equity	$250,000	Total liabilities and equity	$250,000		
Common shares outstanding	1,500	Common shares outstanding	2,000	Common shares outstanding	1,500		

Part B: Projected EPS Levels	Existing Capital Structure	With New Common Stock Financing	With New Debt Financing
EBIT	$ 20,000	$ 30,000	$ 30,000
Less: Interest expense	4,000	4,000	8,250
Earnings before taxes (EBT)	$ 16,000	$ 26,000	$ 21,750
Less: Taxes at 50%	8,000	13,000	10,875
Net Income	$ 8,000	$ 13,000	$ 10,875
Less: Preferred dividends	0	0	0
Earnings available to common	$ 8,000	$ 13,000	$ 10,875
EPS	$ 5.33	$ 6.50	$ 7.25

At the projected EBIT level of $30,000, the EPS for the common stock and debt alternatives are $6.50 and $7.25, respectively. Both are considerably above the $5.33 that would occur if the new project were rejected and the additional financial capital were not raised. Based on a criterion of selecting the financing plan that will provide the highest EPS, the bond alternative is favored. But what if the basic business risk to which the firm is exposed causes the EBIT level to vary over a considerable range? Can we be sure that the bond alternative will *always* have the higher EPS associated with it? The answer, of course, is "No." When the EBIT level is subject to uncertainty, a graphic analysis of the proposed financing plans can provide useful information to the financial manager.

Graphic analysis. The EBIT–EPS analysis chart allows the decision maker to visualize the impact of different financing plans on EPS over a range of EBIT levels. The relationship between EPS and EBIT is linear. Therefore, to construct the chart we only need two points for each alternative. Part B of Table 14.6 already provides us with one of these points. The answer to the following question for each choice gives us the second point: At what EBIT level will the EPS for the plan be exactly zero? If the EBIT level just covers the plan's financing costs (on a before-tax basis), then EPS will be zero. For the stock plan, an EPS of zero is associated with an EBIT of $4,000. The $4,000 is the interest expense incurred under the existing capital structure. If the bond plan is elected, the interest costs will be the present $4,000 plus $4,250 per year arising from the new debt issue. An EBIT of $8,250, then, is necessary to provide a zero EPS with the bond plan.

The EBIT–EPS analysis chart representing the financing choices available to the Pierce Grain Company is shown as Figure 14.8. EBIT is charted on the horizontal axis and EPS on the vertical axis. The intercepts on the horizontal axis represent the before-tax equivalent financing charges related to each plan. The straight lines for each plan tell us the EPS amounts that will occur at different EBIT amounts.

Notice that the bond-plan line has a *steeper slope* than the stock-plan line. This ensures that the lines for each financing choice will *intersect*. Above the intersection

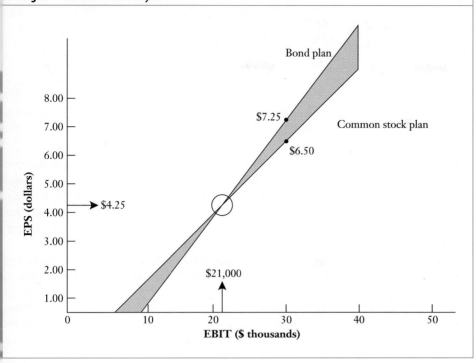

Figure 14.8 EBIT–EPS Analysis Chart

point, EPS for the plan with greater leverage will exceed that for the plan with lesser leverage. The intersection point, encircled in Figure 14.8, occurs at an EBIT level of $21,000 and produces EPS of $4.25 for each plan. When EBIT is $30,000, notice that the bond plan produces EPS of $7.25 and the stock plan, $6.50. Below the intersection point, EPS with the stock plan will *exceed* that with the more highly levered bond plan. The steeper slope of the bond-plan line indicates that with greater leverage, EPS is more sensitive to EBIT changes. This same concept was discussed in chapter 13 when we derived the degree of financial leverage measure.

Computing indifference points. The point of intersection in Figure 14.8 is called the **EBIT–EPS indifference point**. It identifies the EBIT level at which the EPS will be the same regardless of the financing plan chosen by the financial manager. This indifference point, sometimes called the breakeven point, has major implications for financial planning. At EBIT amounts in excess of the EBIT indifference level, the more heavily levered financing plan will generate a higher EPS. At EBIT amounts below the EBIT indifference level, the financing plan involving less leverage will generate a higher EPS. It is important, then, to know the EBIT indifference level.

We can find it graphically, as in Figure 14.8. At times it may be more efficient, though, to calculate the indifference point directly. This can be done by using the following equation:

EBIT–EPS indifference point

The level of earnings before interest and taxes (EBIT) that will equate earnings per share (EPS) between two different financing plans.

$$\overbrace{\frac{(EBIT - I)(1 - t) - P}{S_s}}^{\textit{EPS: Stock Plan}} = \overbrace{\frac{(EBIT - I)(1 - t) - P}{S_b}}^{\textit{EPS: Bond Plan}} \tag{14-6}$$

where S_s and S_b are the number of common shares outstanding under the stock and bond plans, respectively, I is interest expense, t is the firm's income tax rate, and P is preferred dividends paid. In the present case, P is zero because there is no preferred stock outstanding. If preferred stock is associated with one of the financing alternatives, keep in mind that the preferred dividends, P, are not tax deductible. Equation (14-6) *does* take this fact into consideration.

For the present example, we calculate the indifference level of EBIT as

$$\frac{(EBIT - \$4,000)(1 - 0.5) - 0}{2,000} = \frac{(EBIT - \$8,250)(1 - 0.5) - 0}{1,500}$$

When the expression above is solved for EBIT, we obtain $21,000. If EBIT turns out to be $21,000, then EPS will be $4.25 under both plans.

Uncommitted earnings per share and indifference points. The calculations that permitted us to solve for Pierce Grain's EBIT-EPS indifference point made no explicit allowance for the repayment of the bond principal. This procedure is not that unrealistic. It only presumes the debt will be perpetually outstanding. This means that when the current bond issue matures, a new bond issue will be floated. The proceeds from the newer issue would be used to pay off the maturity value of the older issue.

Many bond contracts, however, require that **sinking fund payments** be made to a bond trustee. A **sinking fund** is a real cash reserve that is used to provide for the orderly and early retirement of the principal amount of the bond issue. Most often the sinking fund payment is a mandatory fixed amount and is required by a clause in the bond indenture. Sinking fund payments can represent a sizable cash drain on the firm's liquid resources. Moreover, sinking fund payments are a return of borrowed principal, so they are *not* tax deductible to the firm.

Because of the potentially serious nature of the cash drain caused by sinking fund requirements, the financial manager might be concerned with the uncommitted earnings per share (UEPS) related to each financing plan. The calculation of UEPS recognizes that sinking fund commitments have been honored. UEPS can be used, then, for discretionary spending—such as the payment of cash dividends to common stockholders or investment in capital facilities.

If we let SF be the sinking fund payment required in a given year, the EBIT–UEPS indifference point can be calculated as

$$\underset{S_s}{\underbrace{\frac{(EBIT - I)(1 - t) - P - SF}{S_s}}_{\text{UEPS: Stock Plan}}} = \underset{S_b}{\underbrace{\frac{(EBIT - I)(1 - t) - P - SF}{S_b}}_{\text{UEPS: Bond Plan}}} \quad (14\text{-}7)$$

If several bond issues are already outstanding, then I in equations (14-6) and (14-7) for the stock plan consists of the sum of their related interest payments. For the bond plan, I would be the sum of existing plus new interest charges. In equation (14-7) the same logic applies to the sinking fund variable, SF. The indifference level of EBIT based on UEPS will always exceed that based on EPS.

A word of caution. Above the EBIT–EPS indifference point, a more heavily levered financial plan promises to deliver a larger EPS. Strict application of the criterion of selecting the financing plan that produces the highest EPS might have the firm issuing debt most of the time it raised external capital. Our discussion of capital structure theory taught us the dangers of that sort of action.

The primary weakness of EBIT–EPS analysis is that it disregards the implicit costs of debt financing. The effect of the specific financing decision on the firm's cost of common equity capital is totally ignored. Investors should be concerned with both the *level and variability* of the firm's expected earnings stream. EBIT–EPS analysis considers only the

Sinking fund

A cash reserve used for the orderly and early retirement of the principle amount of a bond issue. Payments into the fund are known as sinking fund payments.

level of the earnings stream and ignores the variability (riskiness) inherent in it. Thus this type of analysis must be used in conjunction with other basic tools in reaching the objective of capital-structure management.

RELATE TO THE BIG PICTURE

*The companion techniques of EBIT–EPS analysis and Uncommitted Earnings per Share analysis are well-known within the corporate financial planning groups of corporations. It is useful to emphasize that these tools of capital structure management are best utilized if we relate them to both **Axiom 3: Cash—Not Profits—Is King,** and **Axiom 6: Efficient Capital Markets—The Markets Are Quick and the Prices Are Right.***

Thus the cash flows, as opposed to accounting profits, that are available to the firm after a financing choice is made, will drive market prices. Recall from chapter 1 that we said efficient markets *will not be fooled by accounting changes that merely manipulate* reported earnings. *In the context of using these tools, then, the proper way to think of earnings per share and uncommitted earnings per share is on a cash basis rather than on an accounting accrual basis. The firm services its debt contracts not out of accounting earnings, but out of cash flows.*

Comparative Leverage Ratios

In chapter 3, we explored the overall usefulness of financial ratio analysis. Leverage ratios are one of the categories of financial ratios identified in that chapter. We emphasize here that the computation of leverage ratios is one of the basic tools of capital structure management.

Two types of leverage ratios must be computed when a financing decision faces the firm. We call these *balance sheet leverage ratios* and *coverage ratios*. The firm's balance sheet supplies inputs for computing the balance sheet leverage ratios. In various forms, these balance sheet metrics compare the firm's use of funds supplied by creditors with those supplied by owners.

Inputs to the coverage ratios *generally* come from the firm's income statement. At times, the external analyst may have to consult balance sheet information to construct some of these needed estimates. On a privately placed debt issue, for example, some fraction of the current portion of the firm's long-term debt might have to be used as an estimate of that issue's sinking fund. Coverage ratios provide estimates of the firm's ability to service its financing contracts. High coverage ratios, compared with a standard, imply unused debt capacity.

A worksheet. Table 14.7 is a sample worksheet used to analyze financing choices. The objective of the analysis is to determine the effect each financing plan will have on key financial ratios. The financial officer can compare the existing level of each ratio with its projected level, taking into consideration the contractual commitments of each alternative.

In reality, we know that EBIT might be expected to vary over a considerable range of outcomes. For this reason the coverage ratios should be calculated several times, each at a different level of EBIT. If this is accomplished over all possible values of EBIT, a probability distribution for each coverage ratio can be constructed. This provides the financial manager with much more information than simply calculating the coverage ratios based on the expected value of EBIT.

Industry norms. The comparative leverage ratios calculated according to the format laid out in Table 14.7, or in a similar format, have additional utility to the decision maker if they can be compared with some standard. Generally, corporate financial analysts, investment bankers, commercial bank loan officers, and bond-rating agencies rely on

Table 14.7 Comparative Leverage Ratios: Worksheet for Analyzing Financing Plans

Ratios	Computation Method	Existing Ratio	Ratio with New Common Stock Financing	Ratio with New Debt Financing
Balance sheet leverage ratios				
1. Debt ratio	$\dfrac{\text{total liabilities}}{\text{total assets}}$	___%	___%	___%
2. Long-term debt to total capitalization	$\dfrac{\text{long-term debt}}{\text{long-term debt + net worth}}$	___%	___%	___%
3. Total liabilities to net worth	$\dfrac{\text{total liabilities}}{\text{net worth}}$	___%	___%	___%
4. Common equity ratio	$\dfrac{\text{common equity}}{\text{total assets}}$	___%	___%	___%
Coverage ratios				
1. Times interest earned	$\dfrac{\text{EBIT}}{\text{annual interest expense}}$	___times	___times	___times
2. Times burden covered	$\dfrac{\text{EBIT}}{\text{interest} + \dfrac{\text{sinking fund}}{1-t}}$	___times	___times	___times
3. Cash flow overall coverage ratio	$\dfrac{\text{EBIT + lease expense + depreciation}}{\text{interest + lease expense} + \dfrac{\text{preferred dividends}}{1-t} + \dfrac{\text{principal payments}}{1-t}}$	___times	___times	___times

industry classes from which to compute "normal" ratios. Although industry groupings may actually contain firms whose basic business risk exposure differs widely, the practice is entrenched in American business behavior.[7] At the very least, then, the financial officer must be interested in *industry standards* because almost everybody else is.

Several published studies indicate that capital structure ratios vary in a significant manner among industry classes.[8] For example, random samplings of the common equity ratios of large retail firms seem to differ statistically from those of major steel producers. The major steel producers use financial leverage to a lesser degree than do the large retail organizations. On the whole, firms operating in the *same* industry tend to exhibit capital structure ratios that cluster around a central value, which we call a norm. Business risk

---

[7]An approach to grouping firms based on several component measures of business risk, as opposed to ordinary industry classes, is reported in John D. Martin, David F. Scott, Jr., and Robert F. Vandell, "Equivalent Risk Classes: A Multidimensional Examination," *Journal of Financial and Quantitative Analysis* 14 (March 1979): 101–18.

[8]See, for example, Eli Schwartz and J. Richard Aronson, "Some Surrogate Evidence in Support of the Concept of Optimal Financial Structure," *Journal of Finance* 22 (March 1967): 10–18; David F. Scott, Jr., "Evidence on the Importance of Financial Structure," *Financial Management* 1 (Summer 1972): 45–50; and David F. Scott, Jr., and John D. Martin, "Industry Influence on Financial Structure," *Financial Management* 4 (Spring 1975): 67–73.

Georgia-Pacific
on Capital Structure

The introduction to this chapter referred to the Georgia-Pacific Corporation's financial strategies and management of its capital structure. The following discussion further illustrates the care that this firm's key officers place on managing its financing mix and also alerts you to the subject of the next section.

Ⓐ Georgia-Pacific tries to balance the mix of debt and equity in a way that will benefit our shareholders, by keeping our weighted average cost of capital low, while retaining the flexibility needed to finance attractive internal projects or acquisitions. Risk factors that contribute to the volatility of our cash flows include economic cycles, changes in industry capacity, environmental regulations, and litigation.

On a market-value basis, our debt-to-capital ratio was 47 percent (year-end 1996). By employing this capital structure, we believe that our weighted average cost of capital is nearly optimized—at approximately 10 percent. Although reducing debt significantly would somewhat reduce the marginal cost of debt, significant debt reduction would likely increase our weighted average cost of capital by raising the proportion of higher-cost equity. Ⓑ

Considering Georgia-Pacific's ability to generate strong cash flow—even at the bottom of the cycle— we believe the current debt structure is quite manageable. In fact, combining the lowest full-year cash flows from building products and pulp and paper operations over recent business cycles would still provide enough cash to pay taxes, cover interest on $5.5 billion of debt, pay dividends and fund several hundred million dollars of reinvestment needed to maintain our facilities in competitive condition. Ⓒ

SOURCE: *Georgia-Pacific 1996 Annual Report*, 15.

Analysis and Implications ...

A. Notice how Georgia-Pacific actually uses the weighted average cost of concept that you learned how to estimate in chapter 12. Moreover, this company also focuses on the volatility (riskiness) of its cash flow stream as a key input to its capital structure planning. This volatility is directly related to the stage of the business (economic) cycle. We talked about the importance of the business cycle and economic contractions in the introduction to this chapter.

B. Georgia-Pacific subscribes to what we called the *moderate view* of the relationship between financing mix and the firm's average cost of capital. You might want to refer back to Figure 14.5 where this concept is graphed and the saucer-shaped cost of capital curve is depicted. The company measures its capital structure ratios at market value (as distinct from book value) and believes that it is operating near its optimal capital structure. In fact, Georgia-Pacific feels that reducing the proportion of debt in its capital structure would actually increase its average cost of capital.

C. Here the firm's management directly relates the stage of the aggregate business cycle to its capital structure planning process. Notice that by analyzing the "lowest full-year cash flows over recent business cycles" that Georgia-Pacific is employing a variation of the *Donaldson model* that is described and illustrated in the next section of this chapter. This model should remind you again of the importance of **Axiom 3: Cash—Not Profits—Is King**.

will vary from industry to industry. As a consequence, the capital structure norms will vary from industry to industry.

This is not to say that all companies in the industry will maintain leverage ratios "close" to the norm. For instance, firms that are very profitable may display *high* coverage ratios and *high* balance sheet leverage ratios. The moderately profitable firm, though, might find such a posture unduly risky. Here the usefulness of industry normal leverage ratios is clear. If the firm chooses to deviate in a material manner from the accepted values for the key ratios, it must have a sound reason.

Companywide Cash Flows: What Is the Worst that Could Happen?

In chapter 3, we noted that liquidity ratios are designed to measure the ability of the firm to pay its bills on time. Financing charges are just another type of bill that eventually comes due for payment. Interest charges, preferred dividends, lease charges, and principal payments all must be paid on time, or the company risks being caught in bankruptcy proceedings. To a lesser extent, dispensing with financing charges on an other than timely basis can result in severely restricted business operations. We have just seen that coverage ratios provide a measure of the safety of one general class of payment—financing charges. Coverage ratios, then, and liquidity ratios are very close in concept.

A more comprehensive method is available for studying the impact of capital structure decisions on corporate cash flows. The method is simple but nonetheless very valuable. It involves the preparation of a series of cash budgets under (1) different economic conditions and (2) different capital structures. The net cash flows under these different situations can be examined to determine if the financing requirements expose the firm to a degree of default risk too high to bear.

In work that has been highly acclaimed, Donaldson has suggested that the firm's debt-carrying capacity (defined in the broad sense here to include preferred dividend payments and lease payments) ought to depend on the net cash flows the firm could expect to receive during a recessionary period.[9] In other words, *target capital structure proportions* could be set by planning for the "worst that could happen." An example will be of help.

Suppose that a recession is expected to last for 1 year.[10] Moreover, the end of the year represents the bottoming-out, or worst portion of the recession. Equation (14-8) defines the cash balance, CB_r, the firm could expect to have at the end of the recession period.[11]

$$CB_r = C_0 + (C_s + OR) - (P_a + RM + \ldots + E_n) - FC \qquad (14\text{-}8)$$

where C_0 = the cash balance at the beginning of the recession
$\quad C_s$ = collection from sales
$\quad OR$ = other cash receipts
$\quad P_a$ = payroll expenditures
$\quad RM$ = raw material payments
$\quad E_n$ = the last of a long series of expenditures over which management has little control (nondiscretionary expenditures)
$\quad FC$ = fixed financial charges associated with a specific capital structure

---

[9] Refer to Gordon Donaldson, "New Framework for Corporate Debt Policy," *Harvard Business Review* 40 (March–April 1962): 117–31; Gordon Donaldson, *Corporate Debt Capacity* (Boston: Division of Research, Graduate School of Business Administration, Harvard University, 1961), chap. 7; and Gordon Donaldson, "Strategy for Financial Emergencies," *Harvard Business Review* 47 (November–December 1969): 67–79.

[10] The analysis can readily be extended to cover a recessionary period of several years. All that is necessary is to calculate the cash budgets over a similar period.

[11] For the most part, the present notation follows that of Donaldson.

If we let the net of total cash receipts and nondiscretionary expenditures be represented by NCF_r, then equation (14-8) can be simplified to

$$CB_r = C_0 + NCF_r - FC \qquad (14\text{-}9)$$

The inputs to equation (14-9) come from a detailed cash budget. The variable representing financing costs, FC, can be changed in accordance with several alternative financing plans to ascertain if the net cash balance during the recession, CB_r, might fall below zero.

Suppose that some firm typically maintains $500,000 in cash and marketable securities. This amount would be on hand at the start of the recession period. During the economic decline, the firm projects that its net cash flows from operations, NCF_r, will be $2 million. If the firm currently finances its assets with an unlevered capital structure, its cash balance at the worst point of the recession would be

$$CB_r = \$500,000 + \$2,000,000 - \$0 = \$2,500,000$$

This procedure allows us to study many different situations.[12] Assume that the same firm is considering a shift in its capitalization such that annual interest and sinking fund payments will be $2,300,000. If a recession occurred, the firm's cash balance at the end of the adverse economic period would be

$$CB_r = \$500,000 + \$2,000,000 - \$2,300,000 = \$200,000$$

The firm ordinarily maintains a liquid asset balance of $500,000. Thus the effect of the proposed capital structure on the firm's cash balance during adverse circumstances might seem too risky for management to accept. When the chance of being out of cash is too high for management to bear, the use of financial leverage has been pushed beyond a reasonable level. According to this tool, the appropriate level of financial leverage is reached when the chance of being out of cash is exactly equal to that which management will assume.

HOW FINANCIAL MANAGERS USE THIS MATERIAL

Our study of capital structure management has included examples of actual practice from several corporations including Georgia-Pacific, Texas Instruments, Medtronic, and General Mills. More emphasis and examples dealing with how financial managers use the main concepts from this chapter are presented in this section.

We have discussed (1) the concept of an optimal capital structure, (2) the search for an appropriate range of financial leverage, and (3) the fundamental tools of capital structure management. Now we will examine some opinions and practices of financial executives that support our emphasis on the importance of capital structure management.

OBJECTIVE 7

The Conference Board has surveyed 170 senior financial officers with respect to their capital structure practices.[13] Of these 170 executives, 102, or 60 percent, stated that they *do* believe there is an optimum capital structure for the corporation. Sixty-five percent of the responding practitioners worked for firms with annual sales in

---

[12]It is not difficult to improve the usefulness of this sort of analysis by applying the technique of simulation to the generation of the various cash budgets. This facilitates the construction of probability distributions of net cash flows under differing circumstances.

[13]Francis J. Walsh, Jr., *Planning Corporate Capital Structures* (New York: The Conference Board, 1972).

Corporate Policies on Using Financial Leverage

Managements continually face the challenge of determining how much financial leverage is enough. The statements that follow from Texas Instruments, General Mills, and Medtronic, Inc., deal with this difficult financial policy question.

Texas Instruments

TI's financial condition continued to strengthen in 1993. The company made further progress toward management's goal of reducing TI's debt-to-total capital ratio and generated positive cash flow net of additions to property, plant, and equipment.

Ⓐ TI's debt-to-total-capital ratio was .28 at the end of the year, down .01 from the third quarter and down .05 from year-end 1992. TI's goal is to reduce this ratio to about .25.

General Mills

Ⓑ Our major financial targets for top-decile performance include: Meeting or exceeding a 20 percent after-tax return on invested capital and 38 percent return on equity. Our ROC and ROE, before unusual items, have averaged 21 percent and 43 percent, respectively, during the past 3 years.

Maintaining a balance sheet with a strong A bond rating. Financial ratios, including a cash flow to debt ratio of 53 percent and a fixed charge coverage of 7.8 times, continued strong in 1993. The purchase of 6.3 million shares for our treasury, which both increased debt and reduced stockholders' equity, increased our debt-to-capital ratio to 63 percent.

Medtronic

Ⓒ The company's capital structure consists of equity and interest-bearing debt. The company utilizes long-term debt minimally. Interest-bearing debt as a percent of total capital was 10.9 percent at April 30, 1993, compared with 10.1 percent and 12.6 percent at April 30, 1992 and 1991, respectively. These ratios are well within the company's financial objective of maintaining a debt-to-total-capital ratio not exceeding 30 percent.

SOURCE: *Texas Instruments, 1993 Annual Report*, 36; *General Mills, 1993 Annual Report*, 19; and *Medtronic, 1993 Annual Report*, 36.

---

excess of $200 million. One executive who subscribed to the optimal capital structure concept stated:

> In my opinion, there is an optimum capital structure for companies. However, this optimum capital structure will vary by individual companies, industries, and then is subject to changing economies, by money markets, earnings trends, and prospects . . . the circumstances and the lenders will determine an optimum at different points in time.[14]

This survey and others consistently point out that (1) financial officers set target debt ratios for their companies, and (2) the values for those ratios are influenced by a conscious evaluation of the basic business risk to which the firm is exposed.

---

[14]Walsh, *Planning Corporate Capital Structures*, 14.

As you read the next section, "How Financial Managers Use This Material," it will be useful to reflect on the *breadth* of financial policy choices that are contained in these company statements. While we have studied several tools that assist the financial manager in planning the firm's financing mix, it is still a fact that no single tool or group of tools can with certainty locate the optimum capital structure. Most likely, the best that can be done is to get into the *optimum leverage range* by judiciously using several tools. Notice both the different metrics that are employed and the different policy stances that follow.

A. Texas Instruments has a clear-cut policy of trying to reduce its use of debt financing. This firm has reduced its debt-to-total-capital ratio to 28 percent at year-end 1993 from a much higher 33 percent at year-end 1992. Actually, over this 1-year period, Texas Instruments reduced its outstanding long-term debt from $909 million to $694 million.

The firm is precise about identifying its target long-term debt-to-total-capital-ratio. You will see in subsequent study of this chapter that a target long-term debt-to-total-capital-ratio is a favorite metric used by financial executives in assessing their firm's debt capacity.

B. General Mills is clear that it wants to be in the top 10 percent of major American companies when evaluated by its financial performance. The firm has five goals, of which two are present here; those two both relate to capital structure design. The firm's return on equity (ROE) can only exceed its return on invested capital (ROC) if it is favorably employing financial leverage. It is also seen that this firm makes the concept of debt capacity operational by being concerned about its bond rating (they seek a strong A rating). Further, note the concern over the times interest earned ratio (they call it fixed charge coverage). Both bond rating targets and coverage ratios are frequently used guides to financial managers in the present context.

C. Medtronic is much more conservative in its use of financial leverage than either Texas Instruments or General Mills. Observe that this firm specifically states that it uses long-term debt "minimally." This should tell you something about its concern (that is, lack of) for the *tax shield on interest* that we reviewed earlier. Similar to many other large firms, Medtronic also has a clearly stated debt-to-total-capital ratio.

Target Debt Ratios

Selected comments from financial executives point to the widespread use of target debt ratios. A vice-president and treasurer of the American Telephone and Telegraph Company (AT&T) described his firm's debt ratio policy in terms of a range:

> All of the foregoing considerations led us to conclude, and reaffirm for a period of many years, that the proper range of our debt was 30 percent to 40 percent of total capital. Reasonable success in meeting financial needs under the diverse market and economic conditions that we have faced attests to the appropriateness of this conclusion.[15]

---

[15]John J. Scanlon, "Bell System Financial Policies," *Financial Management* 1 (Summer 1972): 16–26.

Table 14.8 Setting Target Financial Structure Ratios

	Rank	
Type of Influence	1	2
Internal management and staff analysts	85%	7%
Investment bankers	3	39
Commercial bankers	0	9
Trade creditors	1	0
Security analysts	1	4
Comparative industry ratios	3	23
Other	7	18
Total	100%	100%

SOURCE: David F. Scott, Jr., and Dana J. Johnson, "Financing Policies and Practices in Large Corporations," *Financial Management* 11 (Summer 1982), p. 53.

In a similar fashion, the president of Fibreboard Corporation identified his firm's target debt ratio and noted how it is related to the uncertain nature of the company's business:

> Our objective is a 30 percent ratio of debt to capitalization. We need that kind of flexibility to operate in the cyclical business we are in.[16]

In the Conference Board survey mentioned earlier, 84 of the 102 financial officers who subscribed to the optimal capital structure concept stated that their firm *has* a target debt ratio.[17] The most frequently mentioned influence on the level of the target debt ratio was ability to meet financing charges. Other factors identified as affecting the target were (1) maintaining a desired bond rating, (2) providing an adequate borrowing reserve, and (3) exploiting the advantages of financial leverage.

Who Sets Target Debt Ratios?

From the preceding discussion, we know that firms *do* use target debt ratios in arriving at financing decisions. But who sets or influences these target ratios? This and other questions concerning corporate financing policy were investigated in one study published in 1982.[18] This survey of the 1,000 largest industrial firms in the United States (as ranked by total sales dollars) involved responses from 212 financial executives.

In one portion of this study, the participants were asked to rank several possible influences on their target leverage (debt) ratios. Table 14.8 displays the percentage of responses ranked either number one or number two in importance. Ranks past the second are omitted in that they were not very significant. Notice that the most important influence is the firm's own management group and staff of analysts. This item accounted for 85 percent of the responses ranked number one. Of the responses ranked number two in importance, investment bankers dominated the outcomes and accounted for 39 percent of such replies. The role of investment bankers in the country's capital market system is explored in some detail in chapter 2. Also notice that comparisons with ratios of industry competitors and commercial bankers have some impact on the determination of leverage targets.

---

[16]*Business Week* (December 6, 1976): 30.

[17]Walsh, *Planning Corporate Capital Structures,* 17.

[18]David F. Scott, Jr., and Dana J. Johnson, "Financing Policies and Practices in Large Corporations," *Financial Management* 11 (Summer 1982): 51–59.

Table 14.9 Definitions of Debt Capacity in Practice

Standard or Method	1,000 Largest Corporations (Percent Using)
Target percent of total capitalization (long-term debt to total capitalization)	27%
Long-term debt to net worth ratio (or its inverse)	14
Long-term debt to total assets	2
Interest (or fixed charge) coverage ratio	6
Maintain bond ratings	14
Restrictive debt covenants	4
Most adverse cash flow	4
Industry standard	3
Other	10
No response	16
Total	100%

SOURCE: Derived from David F. Scott, Jr., and Dana J. Johnson, "Financing Polices and Practices in Large Corporations," *Financial Management* 11 (Summer 1982), pp. 51–59.

Debt Capacity

Previously in this chapter, we noted that the firm's debt capacity is the maximum proportion of debt that it can include in its capital structure and still maintain its lowest composite cost of capital. But how do financial executives make the concept of debt capacity operational? Table 14.9 is derived from the same 1982 survey, involving 212 executives, mentioned previously. These executives defined debt capacity in a wide variety of ways. The most popular approach was as a target percentage of total capitalization. Twenty-seven percent of the respondents thought of debt capacity in this manner. Forty-three percent of the participating executives remarked that debt capacity is defined in terms of some balance-sheet-based financial ratio (see the first three items in Table 14.9). Maintaining a specific bond rating was also indicated to be a popular approach to implementing the debt capacity concept.

Business Cycles

Effective financial managers—those who assist in creating value for the firm's common shareholders—are perceptive about and in constant communication with the financial marketplace. When market conditions change abruptly, company financial policies and decisions must adapt to the new conditions. Some firms, however, do a better job of adjusting than others. Companies that are slow to adapt to changes in the aggregate, or overall, business environment face a lower level of cash flow generation and increased risk of financial distress.

Changes in the aggregate business environment are often referred to as *business cycles*. There are many useful definitions of such cycles. For example, Dr. Fischer Black, a former finance professor and later an executive with the well-known investment banking firm of Goldman, Sachs & Co., defined business cycles as follows:[19]

---

[19]Fischer Black, "The ABCs of Business Cycles," *Financial Analysts Journal* 37 (November–December 1981): 75–80. Dr. Black touched on similar points and other far-reaching points in his compelling presidential address to the American Finance Association; see Fischer Black, "Noise," *Journal of Finance* 41 (July 1986): 529–43.

Table 14.10 Post–World War II U.S Business Cycles

Start of Recession (Peaks)	End (Troughs)	Length (Months)
November 1948	October 1949	11
July 1953	May 1954	10
August 1957	April 1958	8
April 1960	February 1961	10
December 1969	November 1970	11
November 1973	March 1975	16
January 1980	July 1980	6
July 1981	November 1982	16
July 1990	March 1991	8

SOURCE: National Bureau of Economic Research (NBER).

Business cycles are fluctuations in economic activity. Business cycles show up in virtually all measures of economic activity—output, income, employment, unemployment, retail sales, new orders by manufacturers, even housing starts. When times are good, they tend to be good all over; and when times are bad, they tend to be bad all over.

A slightly different but compatible definition of business cycles that we will use is: **Business cycles** are a series of commercial adjustments to unanticipated, new information accentuated by *both* public policy decisions and private-sector decisions. When the decisions, on balance, are correct the economy expands. When the decisions, on balance, are incorrect, the economy contracts.

Since the end of World War II, the United States has endured nine recessions. Recessions are the contractionary or negative phase of the entire business cycle. Those nine recessions are documented in Table 14.10.

Typically, different stages of the business cycle induce a different set of relationships in the financial markets. These different relationships are reflected in the different capital structure decisions managers make. For example, relationships between interest rates and equity prices may differ sharply over different phases of the cycle. Some phases of the cycle favor the issuance of debt securities over equity instruments, and vice versa. Complicating the decision-making setting for the manager is the fact that financial relationships will be *dissimilar* over each cycle.[20]

The last "official" recession, which began in July 1990, produced its own set of unique financial characteristics. Accordingly, financial managers altered their firms' capital structures in response to new information that included capital cost relationships in the financial markets. Managers began to reverse some of the financial leverage buildup that occurred in the 1980s. Specifically, by early 1991, corporations began to take advantage of an improved market for common equities and brought to the marketplace substantial amounts of new common stock issues.

Business cycles

A series of commercial adjustments to unanticipated new information accentuated by both public policy decisions and private-sector decisions.

---

[20]Available discussions and studies on the relationship between business cycles and corporate financing patterns are not plentiful. One such study is Robert A. Taggart, Jr., "Corporate Financing: Too Much Debt?" *Financial Analysts Journal* 42 (May–June 1986): 35–42.

Business Risk

The single most important factor that should affect the firm's financing mix is the underlying nature of the business in which it operates. In chapter 13, we defined business risk as the relative dispersion in the firm's expected stream of EBIT. If the nature of the firm's business is such that the variability inherent in its EBIT stream is high, then it would be unwise to impose a high degree of financial risk on top of this already uncertain earnings stream.

Corporate executives are likely to point this out in discussions of capital structure management. A financial officer in a large steel firm related:

> The nature of the industry, the marketplace, and the firm tend to establish debt limits that any prudent management would prefer not to exceed. Our industry is capital intensive and our markets tend to be cyclical. . . . The capability to service debt while operating in the environment described dictates a conservative financial structure.[21]

Notice how that executive was concerned with both his firm's business risk exposure and its cash flow capability for meeting any financing costs. The AT&T financial officer referred to earlier also has commented on the relationship between business and financial risk:

> In determining how much debt a firm can safely carry, it is necessary to consider the basic risks inherent in that business. This varies considerably among industries and is related essentially to the nature and demand for an industry's product, the operating characteristics of the industry, and its ability to earn an adequate return in an unknown future.[22]

Also, refer back to the Introduction to this chapter. Recall that the management of Georgia-Pacific said:

> Georgia-Pacific's objective is to provide superior returns to our shareholders. To achieve this goal, our financial strategy must complement our operating strategy.[23]

It appears clear that the firm's capital structure cannot be properly designed without a thorough understanding of its commercial strategy.

Financial Managers and Theory

Earlier in this chapter, we discussed a moderate view of capital structure theory. The saucer-shaped cost of capital curve implied by this theory (Figure 14.9) predicts that managers will add debt to the firm's capital structure when current leverage use is *below* the firm's optimal range of leverage use at the base of the overall cost of capital curve. Conversely, managers will add equity when leverage use is above this optimal range. Under these conditions above *both* financing activities lower the cost of capital to the firm and increase shareholder wealth.

A 1991 survey of chief financial officers of the top (largest) nonfinancial, nonregulated U.S. firms addressed these predicted activities. Of the 800 firms surveyed, 117 responded, for a response rate of 14.6 percent. These decision makers were asked how their firms would respond if confronted with certain, specific financing situations.

It should be noted that the moderate view does not distinguish between internal equity (retained earnings and depreciation) and external equity (the sale of common stock). The questions posed to the financial managers, however, *do* make this distinction.

---

[21]Walsh, *Capital Structures*, 18.

[22]Scanlon, "Bell System Financial Policies," 19.

[23]*Georgia-Pacific 1996 Annual Report*, 15.

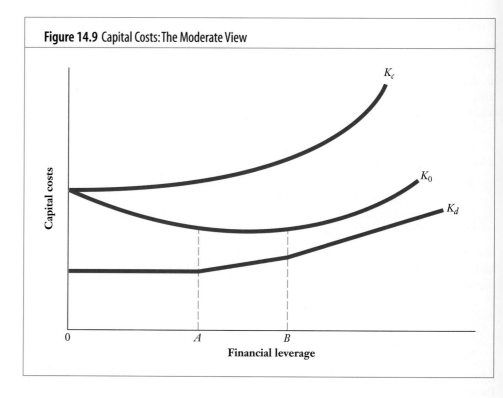

Figure 14.9 Capital Costs: The Moderate View

Based on our financial asset valuation models, common equity is generally considered the most *expensive* source of funds, exceeding the costs of both debt and preferred stock. The cost of external equity exceeds internal equity by the addition of flotation costs. (Recall our discussion in chapter 12 on these relationships.)

Addressing the downward-sloping portion of the cost of capital curve, managers were asked what their financing choice would be if (1) the firm has internal funds *sufficient* for investment requirements (capital budgeting needs), but (2) the debt ratio is *below* the level preferred by the firm. The moderate theory predicts that managers will add debt to the firm's capital structure in this situation. However, 81 percent of the respondents said they would use internal equity to finance their investments. Only 17 percent suggested they would use long-term debt, and 11 percent selected short-term debt. In this situation, most managers indicated they would choose to use the more expensive internal equity rather than the (seemingly) less expensive debt for investments.

Similarly, when internal funds are sufficient for new investment and the debt level *exceeds* the firm's optimum range of leverage use, managers again chose to use internal equity in 81 percent of the responses. Seventeen percent would issue new equity if market conditions were favorable. Because the debt level is currently excessive, the moderate theory would predict that external equity would be added to minimize the cost of capital. Instead, most firms preferred to fund investment with the internal funds. This is a prevalent tendency in American industry.

Responses to the preceding questions imply that, if managers follow the financing activity prescribed by the moderate view, it is *only* after internal funds have been exhausted. Because these internal funds are relatively expensive (compared with new debt), their use as the *initial* financing option indicates that either: (1) managers do not view their financing goal to be the minimization of the firm's cost of capital, or (2) the explicit and implicit costs of new security issues are understated. If this is actually the case, internal funds may be the *least* expensive source of funds from the perspective of

Table 14.11 Managers and Theory: Some Responses

Question

Your firm requires external funds to finance the next period's capital
   investments.
Financial leverage use exceeds that preferred by the firm.
Equity markets are underpricing your securities. Would your firm:

Choices	Responses
Reduce your investment plans?	68%
Obtain short-term debt?	28
Attempt to provide the market with adequate information to correctly price your securities before issuing equity?	13
Issue long-term debt?	13
Issue equity anyway?	4
Reduce your dividend payout?	4

SOURCE: Adapted from David F. Scott, Jr., and Nancy Jay, "Financial Managers and Capital Structure Theories,"
Working Paper 9203, Orlando, FL: Dr. Phillips Institute for the Study of American Business Activity, University of
Central Florida, March 1992.

financial managers. This may be a form of the agency problem that we previously discussed in this chapter.

The chief financial officers were also asked what their financing decision would be under these conditions: (1) the firm requires external funds, (2) financial leverage use *exceeds* the desired level, and (3) equity markets are underpricing the firm's stock. Table 14.11 contains the responses to this question.

In this difficult situation, 68 percent of the managers indicated that they would *reduce* their investment plans. That is, capital budgets would shrink. The primary explanations for such investment restriction were (1) that it was in the best interest of current shareholders, and (2) that it controlled risk.

The next-favored choice (28 percent) was the use of short-term debt, sometimes combined with investment reduction. This suggests that managers attempt to wait out difficult market conditions by adopting short-term solutions. The timing of security issues with favorable market conditions is a major objective of financial managers and entirely consistent with the optimal capital structure range defined under the moderate theory (Figure 14.9).

Some 4 percent of the respondents indicated that they would issue equity, despite the underpricing of the firm's stock. Thirteen percent of the firms indicated that they would attempt to correct the adverse pricing by providing the market with adequate information before attempting to issue equity.

Another 13 percent of the respondents indicated that they would add long-term debt, moving leverage use further beyond the optimal range.

Only 4 percent of the executives responding to this situation stated they would obtain needed funds by *reducing* the cash dividend payout. To managers, the shareholders' cash dividends are quite important. Firms prefer to forgo profitable projects rather than to reallocate the shareholders' expected cash dividends to investment. Dividend policies are discussed extensively in chapter 15.

You can see that our ability as analysts to *predict* financing choices, as opposed to *prescribing* them, is far from perfect. In many instances, managers appear to react as popular capital structure theories suggest. In other instances, though, managers either are rejecting some aspects of the theories, or the theories need more work. Understanding these aberrations is useful to the analyst.

A thorough grounding in both the theory of financing decisions and in the tools of capital structure management will assist you in making sound choices that maximize shareholder wealth. This combination of theory and practical tools also permits you to ask some very perceptive questions when faced with a decision-making situation.

SUMMARY

OBJECTIVE 1

This chapter deals with the design of the firm's financing mix, particularly emphasizing management of the firm's permanent sources of funds—that is, its capital structure. The objective of capital structure management is to arrange the company's sources of funds so that its common stock price will be maximized, all other factors held constant.

OBJECTIVES 2, 3, 4

Can the firm affect its composite cost of capital by altering its financing mix? Attempts to answer this question have comprised a significant portion of capital structure theory for over three decades. Extreme positions show that the firm's stock price is either unaffected or continually affected as the firm increases its reliance on leverage-inducing funds. In the real world, an operating environment where interest expense is tax deductible and market imperfections operate to restrict the amount of fixed-income obligations a firm can issue, most financial officers and financial academics subscribe to the concept of an optimal capital structure. The optimal capital structure minimizes the firm's composite cost of capital. Searching for a proper range of financial leverage, then, is an important financial management activity.

Complicating the manager's search for an optimal capital structure are conflicts that lead to agency costs. A natural conflict exists between stockholders and bondholders (the agency costs of debt). To reduce excessive risk taking by management on behalf of stockholders, it may be necessary to include several protective covenants in bond contracts that serve to restrict managerial decision making.

OBJECTIVE 5

Another type of agency cost is related to "free cash flow." Managers, for example, have an incentive to hold on to free cash flow and enjoy it, rather than paying it out in the form of higher cash-dividend payments. This conflict between managers and stockholders leads to the concept of the *free cash flow theory of capital structure*. This same theory is also known as the *control hypothesis* and the *threat hypothesis*. The ultimate resolution of these agency costs affects the specific form of the firm's capital structure.

OBJECTIVE 6

The decision to use senior securities in the firm's capitalization causes two types of financial leverage effects. The first is the added variability in the earnings-per-share stream that accompanies the use of fixed-charge securities. We explained in chapter 13 how this could be quantified by use of the degree of financial leverage metric. The second financial leverage effect relates to the level of earnings per share (EPS) at a given EBIT under a specific capital structure. We rely on EBIT–EPS analysis to measure this second effect. Through EBIT–EPS analysis the decision maker can inspect the impact of alternative financing plans on EPS over a full range of EBIT levels.

A second tool of capital structure management is the calculation of comparative leverage ratios. Balance sheet leverage ratios and coverage ratios can be computed according to the contractual stipulations of the proposed financing plans. Comparison of these ratios with industry standards enables the financial officer to determine if the firm's key ratios are materially out of line with accepted practice.

A third tool is the analysis of corporate cash flows. This process involves the preparation of a series of cash budgets that consider different economic conditions and different capital structures. Useful insight into the identification of proper target capital structure ratios can be obtained by analyzing projected cash flow statements that assume adverse operating circumstances.

OBJECTIVE 7

Surveys indicate that most financial officers in large firms believe in the concept of an optimal capital structure. The optimal capital structure is approximated by the identification of target debt ratios. The targets reflect the firm's ability to service fixed financing costs and also consider the business risk to which the firm is exposed.

Survey studies have provided information on who sets or influences the firm's target leverage ratios. The firm's own management group and staff of analysts are the major influence, followed in importance by investment bankers. Studies also show that executives operationalize the concept of debt capacity in many ways. The most popular approach is to define debt capacity in terms of a target long-term debt-to-total-capitalization ratio. Maintaining a specific bond rating (such as Aa or A) is also a popular approach to implementing the debt capacity concept.

Financing policies change in significant ways over time. During the 1980s, for example, most studies confirm that U.S. companies "levered up" when compared with past decades. Specifically, interest coverage ratios deteriorated during the 1980s when compared with the 1970s.

The early 1990s displayed a reversal of this trend. Effective financial managers have a sound understanding of business cycles. The recession that started in July 1990 produced a unique set of financial characteristics that led to relatively high common stock prices. Accordingly, financial managers reversed some of the leverage buildup incurred during the 1980s by bringing substantial amounts of new common stock to the marketplace.

Other studies of managers' financing tendencies suggest that (1) a tremendous preference for the use of internally generated equity to finance investments exists, (2) firms prefer to forgo seemingly profitable projects rather than reduce shareholders' expected cash dividends to finance a greater part of the capital budget, and (3) security issues are timed with favorable market conditions.

KEY TERMS

Business cycles, 548

Capital structure, 514

Debt capacity, 526

EBIT–EPS indifference point, 537

Explicit cost of capital, 521

Financial structure, 514

Financial structure design, 514

Implicit cost of debt, 521

Net income approach (NI), 522

Net operating income (NOI) approach, 519

Optimal capital structure, 515

Optimal range of financial leverage, 526

Sinking fund, 538

Tax shield, 524

GO TO:
http://www.prenhall.com/bfm
For downloads and current events associated with this chapter

STUDY QUESTIONS

14-1. Define the following terms:
   a. Financial structure
   b. Capital structure
   c. Optimal capital structure
   d. Debt capacity

14-2. What is the primary weakness of EBIT–EPS analysis as a financing decision tool?

14-3. What is the objective of capital structure management?

14-4. Distinguish between (a) balance sheet leverage ratios and (b) coverage ratios. Give two examples of each and indicate how they would be computed.

14-5. Why might firms whose sales levels change drastically over time choose to use debt only sparingly in their capital structures?

14-6. What condition would cause capital structure management to be a meaningless activity?

14-7. What does the term *independence hypothesis* mean as it applies to capital structure theory?

14-8. Who have been the foremost advocates of the independence hypothesis?

14-9. A financial manager might say that the firm's composite cost of capital is saucer-shaped or U-shaped. What does this mean?

14-10. Define the EBIT–EPS indifference point.

14-11. What is UEPS?

14-12. Explain how industry norms might be used by the financial manager in the design of the company's financing mix.

14-13. Define the term *free cash flow*.

14-14. What is meant by the *free cash flow theory of capital structure*?

14-15. Briefly describe the trend in corporate use of financial leverage during the 1980s.

14-16. Why should the financial manager be familiar with the business cycle?

14-17. In almost every instance, what funds source do managers use first in the financing of their capital budgets?

SELF-TEST PROBLEMS

ST-1. (*Analysis of Recessionary Cash Flows*) The management of Story Enterprises is considering an increase in its use of financial leverage. The proposal on the table is to sell $6 million of bonds that would mature in 20 years. The interest rate on these bonds would be 12 percent. The bond issue would have a sinking fund attached to it requiring that one-twentieth of the principal be retired each year. Most business economists are forecasting a recession that will affect the entire company in the coming year. Story's management has been saying, "If we can make it through this, we can make it through anything." The firm prefers to carry an operating cash balance of $750,000. Cash collections from sales next year will total $3 million. Miscellaneous cash receipts will be $400,000. Raw material payments will be $700,000. Wage and salary costs will be $1,200,000 on a cash basis. On top of this, Story will experience nondiscretionary cash outlays of $1.2 million, *including* all tax payments. The firm faces a 34 percent tax rate.

    a. At present, Story is unlevered. What will be the total fixed financial charges the firm must pay next year?

    b. If the bonds are issued, what is your forecast for the firm's expected cash balance at the end of the recessionary year (next year)?

    c. As Story's financial consultant, do you recommend that it issue the bonds?

ST-2. (*Assessing Leverage Use*) Some financial data and the appropriate industry norm for three companies are shown in the following table:

Measure	Firm X	Firm Y	Firm Z	Industry Norm
Total debt to total assets	20%	30%	10%	30%
Times interest and preferred dividend coverage	8 times	16 times	19 times	8 times
Price/earnings ratio	9 times	11 times	9 times	9 times

a. Which firm appears to be employing financial leverage to the most appropriate degree?

b. In this situation, which "financial leverage effect" appears to dominate the market valuation process?

ST-3. (*EBIT–EPS Analysis*) Four engineers from Martin-Bowing Company are leaving that firm in order to form their own corporation. The new firm will produce and distribute computer software on a national basis. The software will be aimed at scientific markets and at businesses desiring to install comprehensive information systems. Private investors have been lined up to finance the new company. Two financing proposals are being studied. Both of these plans involve the use of some financial leverage; however, one is much more highly levered than the other. Plan A requires the firm to sell bonds with an effective interest rate of 14 percent. One million dollars would be raised in this manner. In addition, under plan A, $5 million would be raised by selling stock at $50 per common share. Plan B also involves raising $6 million. This would be accomplished by selling $3 million of bonds at an interest rate of 16 percent. The other $3 million would come from selling common stock at $50 per share. In both cases, the use of financial leverage is considered to be a permanent part of the firm's capital structure, so no fixed maturity date is used in the analysis. The firm considers a 50 percent tax rate appropriate for planning purposes.

a. Find the EBIT indifference level associated with the two financing plans, and prepare an EBIT–EPS analysis chart.

b. Prepare an analytical income statement that demonstrates that EPS will be the same regardless of the plan selected. Use the EBIT level found in part (a) above.

c. A detailed financial analysis of the firm's prospects suggests that long-term EBIT will be above $1,188,000 annually. Taking this into consideration, which plan will generate the higher EPS?

d. Suppose that long-term EBIT is forecast to be $1,188,000 per year. Under plan A, a price/earnings ratio of 13 would apply. Under plan B, a price/earnings ratio of 11 would apply. If this set of financial relationships does hold, which financing plan would you recommend be implemented?

e. Again, assume an EBIT level of $1,188,000. What price/earnings ratio applied to the EPS of plan B would provide the same stock price as that projected for plan A? Refer to your data from part (d) above.

STUDY PROBLEMS (SET A)

14-1A. (*Analysis of Recessionary Cash Flows*) The management of Transpacific Inc. is considering an increase in its use of financial leverage to develop several investment projects. The proposal is to sell 15 million of bonds that would mature in 30 years. The interest rate on these bonds would be 18 percent. The bond issue would have a sinking fund attached to it requiring that one-thirtieth of the principal be retired each year. Most business economists are forecasting a recession that will affect the economy in the coming year. Transpacific's management has been maintaining an operating cash balance of $2 million. Cash collections from sales next year are estimated to be $4.5 million. Miscellaneous cash receipts will be $450,000. Raw material payments will be $900,000. Wage and salary cost will total $1.7 million on a cash basis. On top of this, Transpacific will experience nondiscretionary cash outflows of $1.4 million including all tax payments. The firm uses a 50 percent tax rate.

a. At present, Transpacific is unlevered. What will be the total fixed financial charges the firm must pay next year?

b. If the bonds are issued, what is your forecast for the firm's expected cash balance at the end of the recessionary year (next year)?

c. As Transpacific's financial consultant, do you recommend that it issue the bonds?

14-2A. (*Analysis of Recessionary Cash Flows*) Ontherise, Inc. is considering expanding its bagel bakery business with the acquisition of new equipment to be financed entirely with debt. The company does not have any other debt or preferred stock outstanding. The company currently has a cash balance of $200,000, which is the minimum Baruch Chavez, the CFO of Ontherise, believes to be desirable, Baruch has determined that the following relationships exist among the company's various items of cash flow (except as noted, all are expressed as a percentage of cash collections on sales):

Other cash receipts	5%
Cash Disbursements for:	
Payroll	30%
Raw Materials	25%
Nondiscretionary expenditures (essentially fixed, thus not percent of sales)	$500,000

The new debt would carry fixed financial charges of $140,000 the first year (interest, $90,000, plus principal—sinking fund, $50,000). To evaluate the sensitivity of the proposed debt plan to economic fluctuations, Baruch would like to determine how low cash collections from sales could be in the next year while ensuring that the cash balance at the end of the year is the minimum he considers necessary.

14-3A. (*EBIT–EPS Analysis with Sinking Fund*) Due to his concern over the effect of the "worst that could happen" if he finances the equipment acquisition only with debt (he believes cash collections on sales could be as low as $1,100,000 in the coming year), Baruch Chavez, the CFO of Ontherise, Inc., (see Problem 14-2A) also has decided to consider a part debt/part equity alternative to the proposed all-debt plan described above. The combination would include 60 percent equity and 40 percent debt. The equity part of the plan would provide $20 per share to the company for 30,000 new shares. The debt portion of this plan would include $400,000 of new debt with fixed financial charges of $52,000 for the first year (interest, $32,000, plus principal—sinking fund, $20,000). The company is in the 35 percent tax bracket. The company currently has 100,000 shares of stock outstanding. Baruch has asked you to determine the EBIT indifference level associated with the two financing alternatives.

14-4A. (*EBIT–EPS Analysis*) A group of retired college professors has decided to form a small manufacturing corporation. The company will produce a full line of traditional office furniture. Two financing plans have been proposed by the investors. Plan A is an all-common-equity alternative. Under this agreement, 1 million common shares will be sold to net the firm $20 per share. Plan B involves the use of financial leverage. A debt issue with a 20-year maturity period will be privately placed. The debt issue will carry an interest rate of 10 percent, and the principal borrowed will amount to $6 million. The corporate tax rate is 50 percent.

    a. Find the EBIT indifference level associated with the two financing proposals.

    b. Prepare an analytical income statement that proves EPS will be the same regardless of the plan chosen at the EBIT level found in part (a).

    c. Prepare an EBIT–EPS analysis chart for this situation.

    d. If a detailed financial analysis projects that long-term EBIT will always be close to $2.4 million annually, which plan will provide for the higher EPS?

14-5A. (*Capital Structure Theory*) Deep End Pools & Supplies has an all common equity capital structure. Some financial data for the company are as follows:

Shares of common stock outstanding = 900,000
Common stock price, $P_0 = \$30$ per share
Expected level of EBIT = $5,400,000
Dividend payout ratio = 100 percent

In answering the following questions, assume that corporate income is not taxed.

    a. Under the present capital structure, what is the total value of the firm?

    b. What is the cost of common equity capital, K_c? What is the composite cost of capital, K_0?

c. Now suppose Deep End sells $1.5 million of long-term debt with an interest rate of 8 percent. The proceeds are used to retire the outstanding common stock. According to the net operating income theory (the independence hypothesis), what will be the firm's cost of common equity after the capital structure change?

   1. What will be the dividend per share flowing to the firm's common shareholders?

   2. By what percentage has the dividend per share changed owing to the capital structure change?

   3. By what percentage has the cost of common equity changed owing to the capital structure change?

   4. What will be the composite cost of capital after the capital structure change?

14-6A. (*EBIT–EPS Analysis*) Four recent liberal arts graduates have interested a group of venture capitalists in backing a new business enterprise. The proposed operation would consist of a series of retail outlets to distribute and service a full line of vacuum cleaners and accessories. These stores would be located in Dallas, Houston, and San Antonio. Two financing plans have been proposed by the graduates. Plan A is an all-common-equity structure. Two million dollars would be raised by selling 80,000 shares of common stock. Plan B would involve the use of long-term debt financing. One million dollars would be raised by marketing bonds with an effective interest rate of 12 percent. Under this alternative, another million dollars would be raised by selling 40,000 shares of common stock. With both plans, then, $2 million is needed to launch the new firm's operations. The debt funds raised under Plan B are considered to have no fixed maturity date, in that this portion of financial leverage is thought to be a permanent part of the company's capital structure. The fledgling executives have decided to use a 40 percent tax rate in their analysis, and they have hired you on a consulting basis to do the following:

   a. Find the EBIT indifference level associated with the two financing proposals.

   b. Prepare an analytical income statement that proves EPS will be the same regardless of the plan chosen at the EBIT level found in part (a) above.

14-7A. (*EBIT–EPS Analysis*) Three recent graduates of the computer science program at Southern Tennessee Tech are forming a company to write and distribute software for various personal computers. Initially, the corporation will operate in the southern region of Tennessee, Georgia, North Carolina, and South Carolina. Twelve serious prospects for retail outlets have already been identified and committed to the firm. The firm's software products have been tested and displayed at several trade shows and computer fairs in the perceived operating region. All that is lacking is adequate financing to continue with the project. A small group of private investors in the Atlanta, Georgia, area is interested in financing the new company. Two financing proposals are being evaluated. The first (plan A) is an all common equity capital structure. Two million dollars would be raised by selling common stock at $20 per common share. Plan B would involve the use of financial leverage. One million dollars would be raised selling bonds with an effective interest rate of 11 percent (per annum). Under this second plan, the remaining $1 million would be raised by selling common stock at the $20 price per share. The use of financial leverage is considered to be a permanent part of the firm's capitalization, so no fixed maturity date is needed for the analysis. A 34 percent tax rate is appropriate for the analysis.

   a. Find the EBIT indifference level associated with the two financing plans.

   b. A detailed financial analysis of the firm's prospects suggests that the long-term EBIT will be above $300,000 annually. Taking this into consideration, which plan will generate the higher EPS?

   c. Suppose long-term EBIT is forecast to be $300,000 per year. Under plan A, a price/earnings ratio of 19 would apply. Under plan B, a price/earnings ratio of 15 would apply. If this set of financial relationships does hold, which financing plan would you recommend?

14-8A. (*EBIT–EPS Analysis*) Three recent liberal arts graduates have interested a group of venture capitalists in backing a new business enterprise. The proposed operation would consist of a series of retail outlets to distribute and service a full line of personal computer equipment. These stores would be located in southern New Jersey, New York, and Pennsylvania. Two financing plans have been proposed by the graduates. Plan A is an all common equity structure. Three million dollars would be raised by selling 75,000 shares of common stock. Plan B would involve the use of long-term debt financing. One million dollars would be raised by marketing bonds with an effective interest rate of 15 percent. Under this alternative, another $2 million would be raised by selling 50,000 shares of common stock. With both plans, then, $3 million is needed to launch the new firm's operations. The debt funds raised under plan B are considered to have no fixed maturity date, in that this proportion of financial leverage is thought to be a permanent part of the company's capital structure. The fledgling executives have decided to use a 34 percent tax rate in their analysis, and they have hired you on a consulting basis to do the following:

a. Find the EBIT indifference level associated with the two financing proposals.

b. Prepare an analytical income statement that proves EPS will be the same regardless of the plan chosen at the EBIT level found in part (a) above.

14-9A. (*EBIT–EPS Analysis*) Two recent graduates of the computer science program at Ohio Tech are forming a company to write, market, and distribute software for various personal computers. Initially, the corporation will operate in Illinois, Indiana, Michigan, and Ohio. Twelve serious prospects for retail outlets in these different states have already been identified and committed to the firm. The firm's software products have been tested and displayed at several trade shows and computer fairs in the perceived operating region. All that is lacking is adequate financing to continue the project. A small group of private investors in the Columbus, Ohio, area are interested in financing the new company. Two financing proposals are being evaluated. The first (plan A) is an all common equity capital structure. Four million dollars would be raised by selling stock at $40 per common share. Plan B would involve the use of financial leverage. Two million dollars would be raised by selling bonds with an effective interest rate of 16 percent (per annum). Under this second plan, the remaining $2 million would be raised by selling common stock at the $40 price per share. This use of financial leverage is considered to be a permanent part of the firm's capitalization, so no fixed maturity date is needed for the analysis. A 50 percent tax rate is appropriate for the analysis.

a. Find the EBIT indifference level associated with the two financing plans.

b. Prepare an analytical income statement that proves EPS will be the same regardless of the plan chosen at the EBIT level found in part (a) above.

c. A detailed financial analysis of the firm's prospects suggests that long-term EBIT will be above $800,000 annually. Taking this into consideration, which plan will generate the higher EPS?

d. Suppose that long-term EBIT is forecast to be $800,000 per year. Under plan A, a price/earnings ratio of 12 would apply. Under plan B, a price/earnings ratio of 10 would apply. If this set of financial relationships does hold, which financing plan would you recommend be implemented?

14-10A. (*Analysis of Recessionary Cash Flows*) The management of Idaho Produce is considering an increase in its use of financial leverage. The proposal on the table is to sell $10 million of bonds that would mature in 20 years. The interest rate on these bonds would be 15 percent. The bond issue would have a sinking fund attached to it requiring that one-twentieth of the principal be retired each year. Most business economists are forecasting a recession that will affect the entire economy in the coming year. Idaho's management has been saying, "If we can make it through this, we can make it through anything." The firm prefers to carry an operating cash balance of $1 million. Cash collections from sales next year will total $4 million. Miscellaneous cash receipts will be $300,000. Raw material payments will be $800,000. Wage and salary costs will total $1.4 million on a cash basis. On top of this, Idaho will experience nondiscretionary cash outflows of $1.2 million *including* all tax payments. The firm faces a 50 percent tax rate.

a. At present, Idaho is unlevered. What will be the total fixed financial charges the firm must pay next year?

b. If the bonds are issued, what is your forecast for the firm's expected cash balance at the end of the recessionary year (next year)?

c. As Idaho's financial consultant, do you recommend that it issue the bonds?

14-11A. (*EBIT–EPS Analysis*) Four recent business school graduates have interested a group of venture capitalists in backing a small business enterprise. The proposed operation would consist of a series of retail outlets that would distribute and service a full line of energy-conservation equipment.

These stores would be located in northern Virginia, western Pennsylvania, and throughout West Virginia. Two financing plans have been proposed by the graduates. Plan A is an all-common-equity capital structure. Three million dollars would be raised by selling 60,000 shares of common stock. Plan B would involve the use of long-term debt financing. One million dollars would be raised by marketing bonds with an interest rate of 10 percent. Under this alternative, another $2 million would be raised by selling 40,000 shares of common stock. With both plans, then, $3 million is needed to launch the new firm's operations. The debt funds raised under plan B are considered to have no fixed maturity date, in that this proportion of financial leverage is thought to be a permanent part of the company's capital structure. The fledgling executives have decided to use a 40 percent tax rate in their analysis.

a. Find the EBIT indifference level associated with the two financing proposals.

b. Prepare an analytical income statement that proves EPS will be the same regardless of the plan chosen at the EBIT level found in part (a).

14-12A. (*EBIT–EPS Analysis*) A group of college professors have decided to form a small manufacturing corporation. The company will produce a full line of contemporary furniture. Two financing plans have been proposed by the investors. Plan A is an all-common-equity alternative. Under this arrangement, 1,400,000 common shares will be sold to net the firm $10 per share. Plan B involves the use of financial leverage. A debt issue with a 20-year maturity period will be privately placed. The debt issue will carry an interest rate of 8 percent and the principal borrowed will amount to $4 million. The corporate tax rate is 50 percent.

a. Find the EBIT indifference level associated with the two financing proposals.

b. Prepare an analytical income statement that proves EPS will be the same regardless of the plan chosen at the EBIT level found in part (a).

c. Prepare an EBIT–EPS analysis chart for this situation.

d. If a detailed financial analysis projects that long-term EBIT will always be close to $1,800,000 annually, which plan will provide for the higher EPS?

14-13A. (*EBIT–EPS Analysis*) The professors in problem 14-12A contacted a financial consultant to provide them with some additional information. They felt that in a few years, the stock of the firm would be publicly traded over the counter, so they were interested in the consultant's opinion as to what the stock price would be under the financing plan outlined in problem 14-12A. The consultant agreed that the projected long-term EBIT level of $1,800,000 was reasonable. He also felt that if plan A were selected, the marketplace would apply a price/earnings ratio of 12 times to the company's stock; for plan B he estimated a price/earnings ratio of 10 times.

a. According to this information, which financing alternative would offer a higher stock price?

b. What price/earnings ratio applied to the EPS related to plan B would provide the same stock price as that projected for plan A?

c. Comment on the results of your analysis of problems 14-12A and 14-13A.

14-14A. (*Analysis of Recessionary Cash Flows*) Cavalier Agriculture Supplies is undertaking a thorough cash flow analysis. It has been proposed by management that the firm expand by raising $5 million in the long-term debt markets. All of this would be immediately invested in new fixed assets. The proposed bond issue would carry an 8 percent interest rate and have a maturity period of 20 years. The bond issue would have a sinking fund provision that one-twentieth of the principal would be retired annually. Next year is expected to be a poor one for Cavalier. The firm's management feels, therefore, that the upcoming year would serve well as a model for the worst possible operating conditions that the firm can be expected to encounter. Cavalier ordinarily carries a $500,000 cash balance. Next year sales collections are forecast to be $3 million. Miscellaneous cash receipts will total $200,000. Wages and salaries will amount to $1 million. Payments for raw materials used in the production process will be $1,400,000. In addition, the firm will pay $500,000 in nondiscretionary expenditures including taxes. The firm faces a 50 percent tax rate.

a. Cavalier currently has no debt or preferred stock outstanding. What will be the total fixed financial charges that the firm must meet next year?

b. What is the expected cash balance at the end of the recessionary period (next year), assuming the debt is issued?

c. Based on this information, should Cavalier issue the proposed bonds?

14-15A. (*Assessing Leverage Use*) Some financial data for three corporations are as follows:

Measure	Firm A	Firm B	Firm C	Industry Norm
Debt ratio	20%	25%	40%	20%
Times burden covered	8 times	10 times	7 times	9 times
Price/earnings ratio	9 times	11 times	6 times	10 times

    a. Which firm appears to be excessively levered?

    b. Which firm appears to be employing financial leverage to the most appropriate degree?

    c. What explanation can you provide for the higher price/earnings ratio enjoyed by firm B as compared with firm A?

14-16A. (*Assessing Leverage Use*) Some financial data and the appropriate industry norm are shown in the following table:

Measure	Firm X	Firm Y	Firm Z	Industry Norm
Total debt to total assets	35%	30%	10%	35%
Times interest and preferred dividend coverage	7 times	14 times	16 times	7 times
Price/earnings ratio	8 times	10 times	8 times	8 times

    a. Which firm appears to be using financial leverage to the most appropriate degree?

    b. In this situation which "financial leverage effect" appears to dominate the market's valuation process?

14-17A. (*Capital Structure Theory*) Boston Textiles has an all common equity capital structure. Pertinent financial characteristics for the company are shown below:

> Shares of common stock outstanding = 1,000,000
> Common stock price, P_0 = $20 per share
> Expected level of EBIT = $5,000,000
> Dividend payout ratio = 100 percent

In answering the following questions, assume that corporate income is not taxed.

    a. Under the present capital structure, what is the total value of the firm?

    b. What is the cost of common equity capital, K_c? What is the composite cost of capital, K_0?

    c. Now suppose that Boston Textiles sells $1 million of long-term debt with an interest rate of 8 percent. The proceeds are used to retire outstanding common stock. According to NOI theory (the independence hypothesis), what will be the firm's cost of common equity *after* the capital structure change?

       1. What will be the dividend per share flowing to the firm's common shareholders?

       2. By what percent has the dividend per share changed owing to the capital structure change?

       3. By what percent has the cost of common equity changed owing to the capital structure change?

       4. What will be the composite cost of capital after the capital structure change?

14-18A. (*Capital Structure Theory*) South Bend Auto Parts has an all common equity capital structure. Some financial data for the company are as follows:

> Shares of common stock outstanding = 600,000
> Common stock price, P_0 = \$40 per share
> Expected level of EBIT = \$4,200,000
> Dividend payout ratio = 100 percent

In answering the following questions, assume that corporate income is not taxed.

a. Under the present capital structure, what is the total value of the firm?

b. What is the cost of common equity capital, K_c? What is the composite cost of capital, K_0?

c. Now, suppose South Bend sells \$1 million of long-term debt with an interest rate of 10 percent. The proceeds are used to retire outstanding common stock. According to the net operating income theory (the independence hypothesis), what will be the firm's cost of common equity after the capital structure change?

1. What will be the dividend per share flowing to the firm's common shareholders?

2. By what percentage has the dividend per share changed owing to the capital structure change?

3. By what percentage has the cost of common equity changed owing to the capital structure change?

4. What will be the composite cost of capital after the capital structure change?

14-19A. (*EBIT–EPS Analysis*) Albany Golf Equipment is analyzing three different financing plans for a newly formed subsidiary. The plans are described as follows:

Plan A	Plan B	Plan C
Common stock:	Bonds at 9%: \$20,000	Preferred stock at 9%: \$20,000
\$100,000	Common stock: 80,000	Common stock: 80,000

In all cases, the common stock will be sold to net Albany \$10 per share. The subsidiary is expected to generate an average EBIT per year of \$22,000. The management of Albany places great emphasis on EPS performance. Income is taxed at a 50 percent rate.

a. Where feasible, find the EBIT indifference levels between the alternatives.

b. Which financing plan do you recommend that Albany pursue?

Several biking enthusiasts recently left their defense industry jobs and grouped together to form a corporation, Freedom Cycle, Inc. (FCI), which will produce a new type of bicycle. These new bicycles are to be constructed using space-age technologies and materials so they will never need repairs or maintenance. The FCI founders believe there is a need for such a bicycle due to their perception that many people today, especially middle-aged working couples such as themselves, really would like to ride bicycles for transportation as well as for pleasure, but are put off by the perceived high maintenance requirements of most bicycles today.

The founders believe such people would be quite willing to buy a maintenance-free bicycle for themselves as well as for their children, particularly after observing the repair and maintenance needs (for example, keeping spoked wheels trued and deraillers and brakes adjusted) of the bikes they already have purchased for their children. Accordingly, the FCI group feels certain that their new-age bicycles will meet the needs of this market and will be a tremendous hit.

To assist them with the financial management of the company, the FCI founders have hired Mabra Jordan to be CFO. Mabra has considerable experience with start-up companies such as FCI, and is well respected in the venture capital community. Indeed, based on the strength of her business plan, Mabra has convinced a local venture capital partnership to provide funding for FCI. Two alternatives have been proposed by the venture capitalists: a high leverage plan primarily using "junk" bonds (HLP), and a low leverage plan (LLP) primarily using equity.

HLP consists of $6 million of bonds carrying a 14 percent interest rate and $4 million of $20-per-share common stock. LLP, on the other hand, consists of $2 million of bonds with an interest rate of 11 percent and $8 million of common stock at $20 per share. Under either alternative, FCI is required to use a sinking fund to retire 10 percent of the bonds each year. FCI's tax rate is expected to be 35 percent.

1. Find the EBIT indifference level associated with the two financing alternatives, and prepare an EBIT–EPS analysis graph.

2. Prepare an analytical income statement that demonstrates that EPS will be the same regardless of the alternative selected. Use the EBIT level computed in part 1 above.

3. If an analysis of FCI's long-term prospects indicates that long-term EBIT will be $1,300,000 annually, which financing alternative will generate the higher EPS?

4. If the analysis of FCI's long-term prospects also shows that at a long-term EBIT of $1,300,000 a price/earnings ratio of 18 likely would apply under LLP, and a ratio of 14 would apply under HLP, which of the two financing plans would you recommend and why?

5. At an EBIT level of $1,300,000, what is the price/earnings ratio that would have to obtain under HLP for the EPS of HLP to provide the same stock price as that projected for LLP in part 4 above?

A concern of the venture capitalists, of course, is whether FCI would be able to survive its first year in business if for some reason—such as an economic recession or just an overly optimistic sales projection—the cash flow targets in FCI's business plan were not met. To allay such fears, Mabra included in the FCI business plan a worst-case scenario based on the following pessimistic projections.

Mabra believes FCI should maintain a $500,000 cash balance. Starting initially with zero cash, the company would obtain cash of $10,000,000 from either of the two financing alternatives described above. $9,500,000 of such financing would be used for capital acquisitions; the balance is intended to be available to provide initial working capital. The pessimistic sales forecast indicates cash receipts would be $4 million. Miscellaneous cash receipts (for example, from the sale of scrap titanium and other materials) would be $200,000. Cash payments on raw materials purchases would be $1 million; wage and salary cash outlays would be $1,500,000; nondiscretionary cash costs (not including tax payments) would be $700,000; and estimated tax payments would be $265,000 under LLP and $54,000 under HLP (note that the difference in estimated tax payments is attributable to the variation in taxable income, which reflects the difference in deductible interest expense).

6. What would be the total fixed financial charges under each of the two alternative financing plans being considered by FCI?

7. A significant issue is whether FCI will have a sufficient cash balance at the end of the possible recessionary year. What is your estimate of FCI's cash balance under each of the two financing plans at the end of such a year?

8. In light of the above and your knowledge of FCI's desired cash level, which financing plan, LLP or HLP, would you recommend?

STUDY PROBLEMS (SET B)

14-1B. (*Analysis of Recessionary Cash Flows*) Cappuccino Express, Inc., is considering expanding its cafe business by adding a number of new stores. Strong consideration is being given to financing the expansion entirely with debt. The company does not have any other debt or preferred stock outstanding. The company currently has a cash balance of $400,000, which is the minimum the CFO, Vanessa Jefferson, believes to be desirable. Vanessa has determined that the following relationships exist among the company's various items of cash flow (except as noted, all are expressed as a percentage of cash collections on sales):

Other cash receipts	5%
Cash Disbursements for:	
Payroll	40%
Coffee, pastries, and other costs of items sold	20%
Nondiscretionary expenditures (essentially fixed, thus not percent of sales)	$500,000

The new debt would carry fixed financial charges of $300,000 the first year (interest, $200,000, plus principal—sinking fund, $100,000). To evaluate the sensitivity of the proposed debt plan to economic fluctuations, Vanessa would like to determine how low cash collections from sales could be in the next year while ensuring that the cash balance at the end of the year is the minimum she considers necessary.

14-2B. (*EBIT–EPS Analysis with Sinking Fund*) Due to her concern over the effect of the "worst that could happen" if she finances the expansion only with debt (she believes cash collections on sales could be as low as $1,300,000 in the coming year), Vanessa Jefferson, the CFO of Cappuccino Express, Inc. (see Problem 14-1B) also has decided to consider a part debt/part equity alternative to the proposed all-debt plan described above. The combination would include 70 percent equity and 30 percent debt. The equity part of the plan would provide $20 per share to the company for 70,000 new shares. The debt portion of this plan would include $600,000 of new debt with fixed financial charges of $78,000 for the first year (interest, $48,000, plus principal—sinking fund, $30,000). The company is in the 35 percent tax bracket. The company currently has 100,000 shares of stock outstanding. Vanessa has asked you to determine the EBIT indifference level associated with the two financing alternatives.

14-3B. (*EBIT–EPS Analysis*) Three recent graduates of the computer science program at Midstate University are forming a company to write and distribute software for various personal computers. Initially, the corporation will operate in the region of Michigan, Illinois, Indiana, and Ohio. Twelve serious prospects for retail outlets have already been identified and committed to the firm. The firm's software products have been tested and displayed at several trade shows and computer fairs in the perceived operating region. All that is lacking is adequate financing to continue with the project. A small group of private investors in the Chicago, Illinois, area is interested in financing the new company. Two financing proposals are being evaluated. The first (plan A) is an all common equity capital structure. Three million dollars would be raised by selling common stock at $20 per common share. Plan B would involve the use of financial leverage. Two million dollars would be raised selling bonds with an effective interest rate of 11 percent (per annum). Under this second plan, the remaining $1 million would be raised by selling common stock at the $20 price per share. The use of financial leverage is considered to be a permanent part of the firm's capitalization, so no fixed maturity date is needed for the analysis. A 34 percent tax rate is appropriate for the analysis.

   a. Find the EBIT indifference level associated with the two financing plans.

   b. A detailed financial analysis of the firm's prospects suggests that the long-term EBIT will be above $450,000 annually. Taking this into consideration, which plan will generate the higher EPS?

   c. Suppose long-term EBIT is forecast to be $450,000 per year. Under plan A, a price/earnings ratio of 19 would apply. Under plan B, a price/earnings ratio of 12.39 would apply. If this set of financial relationships does hold, which financing plan would you recommend?

14-4B. (*EBIT–EPS Analysis*) Three recent liberal arts graduates have interested a group of venture capitalists in backing a new business enterprise. The proposed operation would consist of a series of retail outlets to distribute and service a full line of personal computer equipment. These stores would be located in Texas, Arizona, and New Mexico. Two financing plans have been proposed by the graduates. Plan A is an all-common-equity structure. Four million dollars would be raised by selling 80,000 shares of common stock. Plan B would involve the use of long-term debt financing. Two million dollars would be raised by marketing bonds with an effective interest rate of 16 percent. Under this alternative, another $2 million would be raised by selling 50,000 shares of common stock. With both plans, then, $4 million is needed to launch the new firm's operations.

The debt funds raised under plan B are considered to have no fixed maturity date, in that this proportion of financial leverage is thought to be a permanent part of the company's capital structure. The fledgling executives have decided to use a 34 percent tax rate in their analysis, and they have hired you on a consulting basis to do the following:

a. Find the EBIT indifference level associated with the two financing proposals.

b. Prepare an analytical income statement that proves EPS will be the same regardless of the plan chosen at the EBIT level found in part (a) above.

14-5B. (*EBIT–EPS Analysis*) Two recent graduates of the computer science program at Ohio Tech are forming a company to write, market, and distribute software for various personal computers. Initially, the corporation will operate in Missouri, Iowa, Nebraska, and Kansas. Eight prospects for retail outlets in these different states have already been identified and committed to the firm. The firm's software products have been tested. All that is lacking is adequate financing to continue the project. A small group of private investors are interested in financing the new company. Two financing proposals are being evaluated. The first (plan A) is an all common equity capital structure. Three million dollars would be raised by selling stock at $40 per common share. Plan B would involve the use of financial leverage. One million dollars would be raised by selling bonds with an effective interest rate of 14 percent (per annum). Under this second plan, the remaining $2 million would be raised by selling common stock at the $40 price per share. This use of financial leverage is considered to be a permanent part of the firm's capitalization, so no fixed maturity date is needed for the analysis. A 50 percent tax rate is appropriate for the analysis.

a. Find the EBIT indifference level associated with the two financing plans.

b. Prepare an analytical income statement that proves EPS will be the same regardless of the plan chosen at the EBIT level found in part (a) above.

c. A detailed financial analysis of the firm's prospects suggests that long-term EBIT will be above $750,000 annually. Taking this into consideration, which plan will generate the higher EPS?

d. Suppose that long-term EBIT is forecast to be $750,000 per year. Under plan A, a price/earnings ratio of 12 would apply. Under plan B, a price/earnings ratio of 9.836 would apply. If this set of financial relationships does hold, which financing plan would you recommend be implemented?

14-6B. (*Analysis of Recessionary Cash Flows*) The management of Cincinnati Collectibles (CC) is considering an increase in its use of financial leverage. The proposal on the table is to sell $11 million of bonds that would mature in 20 years. The interest rate on these bonds would be 16 percent. The bond issue would have a sinking fund attached to it requiring that one-twentieth of the principal be retired each year. Most business economists are forecasting a recession that will affect the entire economy in the coming year. CC's management has been saying, "If we can make it through this, we can make it through anything." The firm prefers to carry an operating cash balance of $500,000. Cash collections from sales next year will total $3.5 million. Miscellaneous cash receipts will be $300,000. Raw material payments will be $800,000. Wage and salary costs will total $1.5 million on a cash basis. On top of this, CC will experience nondiscretionary cash outflows of $1.3 million *including* all tax payments. The firm faces a 50 percent tax rate.

a. At present, CC is unlevered. What will be the total fixed financial charges the firm must pay next year?

b. If the bonds are issued, what is your forecast for the firm's expected cash balance at the end of the recessionary year (next year)?

c. As CC's financial consultant, do you recommend that it issue the bonds?

14-7B. (*EBIT–EPS Analysis*) Four recent business school graduates have interested a group of venture capitalists in backing a small business enterprise. The proposed operation would consist of a series of retail outlets that would distribute and service a full line of energy-conservation equipment. These stores would be located in northern California, western Nevada, and throughout Oregon. Two financing plans have been proposed by the graduates. Plan A is an all common equity capital structure. Five million dollars would be raised by selling 75,000 shares of common stock

Plan B would involve the use of long-term debt financing. Two million dollars would be raised by marketing bonds with an interest rate of 12 percent. Under this alternative, another $3 million would be raised by selling 55,000 shares of common stock. With both plans, then, $5 million is needed to launch the new firm's operations. The debt funds raised under plan B are considered to have no fixed maturity date, in that this proportion of financial leverage is thought to be a permanent part of the company's capital structure. The fledgling executives have decided to use a 40 percent tax rate in their analysis.

a. Find the EBIT indifference level associated with the two financing proposals.

b. Prepare an analytical income statement that proves EPS will be the same regardless of the plan chosen at the EBIT level found in part (a).

14-8B. (*EBIT–EPS Analysis*) A group of college professors have decided to form a small manufacturing corporation. The company will produce a full line of contemporary furniture. Two financing plans have been proposed by the investors. Plan A is an all-common-equity alternative. Under this arrangement 1,200,000 common shares will be sold to net the firm $10 per share. Plan B involves the use of financial leverage. A debt issue with 20-year maturity period will be privately placed. The debt issue will carry an interest rate of 9 percent and the principal borrowed will amount to $3.5 million. The corporate tax rate is 50 percent.

a. Find the EBIT indifference level associated with the two financing proposals.

b. Prepare an analytical income statement that proves EPS will be the same regardless of the plan chosen at the EBIT level found in part (a).

c. Prepare an EBIT–EPS analysis chart for this situation.

d. If a detailed financial analysis projects that long-term EBIT will always be close to $1,500,000 annually, which plan will provide for the higher EPS?

14-9B. (*EBIT–EPS Analysis*) The professors in problem 14-8B contacted a financial consultant to provide them with some additional information. They felt that in a few years, the stock of the firm would be publicly traded over the counter, so they were interested in the consultant's opinion as to what the stock price would be under the financing plan outlined in problem 14-8B. The consultant agreed that the projected long-term EBIT level of $1,500,000 was reasonable. He also felt that if plan A were selected, the marketplace would apply a price/earnings ratio of 13 times to the company's stock; for plan B he estimated a price/earnings ratio of 11 times.

a. According to this information, which financing alternative would offer a higher stock price?

b. What price/earnings ratio applied to the EPS related to plan B would provide the same stock price as that projected for plan A?

c. Comment upon the results of your analysis of problems 14-8B and 14-9B.

14-10B. (*Analysis of Recessionary Cash Flows*) Seville Cranes, Inc., is undertaking a thorough cash flow analysis. It has been proposed by management that the firm expand by raising $6 million in the long-term debt markets. All of this would be immediately invested in new fixed assets. The proposed bond issue would carry a 10 percent interest rate and have a maturity period of 20 years. The bond issue would have a sinking fund provision that one-twentieth of the principal would be retired annually. Next year is expected to be a poor one for Seville. The firm's management feels, therefore, that the upcoming year would serve well as a model for the worst possible operating conditions that the firm can be expected to encounter. Seville ordinarily carries a $750,000 cash balance. Next year sales collections are forecast to be $3.5 million. Miscellaneous cash receipts will total $200,000. Wages and salaries will amount to $1.2 million. Payments for raw materials used in the production process will be $1,500,000. In addition, the firm will pay $500,000 in nondiscretionary expenditures including taxes. The firm faces a 50 percent tax rate.

a. Seville currently has no debt or preferred stock outstanding. What will be the total fixed financial charges that the firm must meet next year?

b. What is the expected cash balance at the end of the recessionary period (next year), assuming the debt is issued?

c. Based on this information, should Seville issue the proposed bonds?

14-11B. (*Assessing Leverage Use*) Some financial data for three corporations are as follows:

Measure	Firm A	Firm B	Firm C	Industry Norm
Debt ratio	15%	20%	35%	25%
Times burden covered	9 times	11 times	6 times	9 times
Price/earnings ratio	10 times	12 times	5 times	10 times

a. Which firm appears to be excessively levered?

b. Which firm appears to be employing financial leverage to the most appropriate degree?

c. What explanation can you provide for the higher price/earnings ratio enjoyed by firm B as compared with firm A?

14-12B. (*Assessing Leverage Use*) Some financial data and the appropriate industry norm are shown in the following table:

Measure	Firm X	Firm Y	Firm Z	Industry Norm
Total debt to total assets	40%	35%	10%	35%
Times interest and preferred dividend coverage	8 times	13 times	16 times	7 times
Price/earnings ratio	8 times	11 times	8 times	8 times

a. Which firm appears to be using financial leverage to the most appropriate degree?

b. In this situation which "financial leverage effect" appears to dominate the market's valuation process?

14-13B. (*Capital Structure Theory*) Whittier Optical Labs has an all common equity capital structure. Pertinent financial characteristics for the company are as follows:

> Shares of common stock outstanding = 1,000,000
> Common stock price, P_0 = $22 per share
> Expected level of EBIT = $4,750,000
> Dividend payout ratio = 100 percent

In answering the following questions, assume that corporate income is not taxed.

a. Under the present capital structure, what is the total value of the firm?

b. What is the cost of common equity capital, K_c? What is the composite cost of capital, K_0?

c. Now suppose that Whittier sells $1 million of long-term debt with an interest rate of 9 percent. The proceeds are used to retire outstanding common stock. According to NOI theory (the independence hypothesis), what will be the firm's cost of common equity *after* the capital structure change?

1. What will be the dividend per share flowing to the firm's common shareholders?

2. By what percentage has the dividend per share changed owing to the capital structure change?

3. By what percentage has the cost of common equity changed owing to the capital structure change?

4. What will be the composite cost of capital after the capital structure change?

14-14B. (*Capital Structure Theory*) Fernando Hotels has an all common equity capital structure. Some financial data for the company are as follows:

> Shares of common stock outstanding = 575,000
> Common stock price, P_0 = $38 per share
> Expected level of EBIT = $4,500,000
> Dividend payout ratio = 100 percent

In answering the following questions, assume that corporate income is not taxed.

    a. Under the present capital structure, what is the total value of the firm?

    b. What is the cost of common equity capital, K_c? What is the composite cost of capital, K_0?

    c. Now suppose Fernando sells $1.5 million of long-term debt with an interest rate of 11 percent. The proceeds are used to retire outstanding common stock. According to the net operating income theory (the independence hypothesis), what will be the firm's cost of common equity after the capital structure change?

      1. What will be the dividend per share flowing to the firm's common shareholders?

      2. By what percent has the dividend per share changed owing to the capital structure change?

      3. By what percent has the cost of common equity changed owing to the capital structure change?

      4. What will be the composite cost of capital after the capital structure change?

14-15B. (*EBIT–EPS Analysis*) Mount Rosemead Health Services, Inc., is analyzing three different financing plans for a newly formed subsidiary. The plans are described as follows:

Plan A	Plan B	Plan C
Common stock:	Bonds at 10%: $ 50,000	Preferred stock at 10%: $ 50,000
$150,000	Common stock: $100,000	Common stock: $100,000

In all cases, the common stock will be sold to net Mount Rosemead $10 per share. The subsidiary is expected to generate an average EBIT per year of $36,000. The management of Mount Rosemead places great emphasis on EPS performance. Income is taxed at a 50 percent rate.

    a. Where feasible, find the EBIT indifference levels between the alternatives.

    b. Which financing plan do you recommend that Mount Rosemead pursue?

SPECIALTY AUTO PARTS:

Financial-Leverage Analysis

Specialty Auto Parts (SAP) is located in Toledo, Ohio. The firm was founded in 1919 by C. K. Blackburn, who served as president and chairman of the board until his death in early 1976. Both positions are now filled by Ken Blackburn, C. K.'s eldest son, who is carrying on his father's dogmatic tradition of "high quality products for a quality industry." Mark Dennis, vice-president of finance, often argued formally and informally against the total emphasis contained in the latter four words of that phrase, which trademarked all of SAP's advertisements. Dennis simply felt that by concentrating upon supplying component parts only to the auto industry, an undue exposure to basic business risk was assumed.

SAP manufactures a very wide range of component parts, subassemblies, and final assemblies for sale to the major automobile producers, who are largely concentrated 61 miles north, in Detroit. Standard items in the product line include hubs, rims, brakes, antiskid units, and mirrors. C. K. Blackburn had taken immense pride in all facets of SAP's activities, ranging from the early decision to locate in Toledo to the firm's solid reputation within key offices in Detroit's Fisher Building. In retrospect, the location decision was a fine one. An expressway connects Toledo with Detroit, making truck transportation extremely swift. Further, Toledo is located on the west end of Lake Erie, with a good port facility, enabling the firm to receive raw materials via marine transportation and to ship finished goods to other key automotive centers, such as Cleveland across the lake.

Blackburn family interests own 51 percent of the common stock of SAP. Over the years outside financing has been almost completely shunned by the organization. The SAP annual report of 4 years past contains this statement: "We will continue to finance corporate growth primarily through the internal generation of funds." Recent auto industry trends, however, have necessitated a shift by SAP management away from strict adherence to that policy. A national recession saw last year's motor vehicle factory sales of passenger cars drop 24 percent from the previous annual period. This, in turn, adversely affected the profitability and funds-generating capacity of SAP. On top of this, the officials of SAP have decided upon a major product mix shift. The firm underestimated the demand for disc brakes, which have been installed on about 84 to 86 percent of passenger cars in recent years (see Exhibit 1). SAP's capacity to produce in this area will be increased during the next year. The volume achieved on the sale of anti-skid units has proved to be a disappointment. Accordingly, some factory space and equipment devoted to this product line will be redeployed into other more profitable activities.

Noting the public's acceptance of rear window defoggers, the firm has developed the technology necessary to be competitive in this product. To effect this expertise, however, substantial equipment purchases will be required within the next 6 months. The end result is that SAP must raise $6 million in the capital markets through either the sale of new common stock or the issuance of bonds. The new common shares could be sold to net the firm $48 per share. The common stock price of SAP shares in the market place is now $54. Allen Winthrop, who is a partner in the investment banking house long used by SAP, has assured Mark Dennis that the new bond issue could be placed with an 8 percent interest rate. Winthrop's counsel always has been highly valued by Dennis and other members of the SAP top management team.

A preliminary meeting took place 1 week ago with Dennis, Winthrop and Ken Blackburn in attendance. The only topic

Exhibit 1 Specialty Auto Parts Factory Installations of Selected Equipment (Percent of Total Units Installed Upon)

Automobile equipment	Most recent year	One year earlier
Power brakes, 4-wheel drum	2.4	1.0
Power brakes, 2- or 4-wheel disc	64.8	74.5
Disc brakes manual	19.2	11.2
Skid control device	0.9	1.9
Rear window defogger	21.5	16.4

Exhibit 2 Specialty Auto Parts Abbreviated Balance Sheet, December 31, Last Year

Assets	
Current assets	$14,750,000
Net plant and equipment	19,000,000
Other	2,250,000
Total assets	$36,000,000
Liabilities and Equity	
Current liabilities	$ 4,920,000
Long-term debt	
First mortgage bonds, 20 years to maturity, at 7%	2,950,000
Common stock, $5 par	5,000,000
Capital surplus	10,000,000
Retained earnings	13,130,000
Total liabilities and equity	$36,000,000

Exhibit 3 Specialty Auto Parts Income Statement, December 31, Last Year

Sales	$112,000,000
Variable costs	88,476,520
Fixed costs (excluding interest)	12,064,980
Interest expense	206,500
Earnings before taxes	$ 11,252,000
Taxes (at 50%)	5,626,000
Net profit	$ 5,626,000

Exhibit 4 Main Competitors' Selected Financial Relationships

Firm	Debt ratio[a]	Tier[b]	P/E ratio[c]
Atlas Auto Components	32.7%	7	7.5
Autonite	20.1%	38	9.5
Kalsey-Ways, Ltd.	24.2%	14	9.0
L-G Parts	26.8%	14	9.0
Morgan-Wells, Inc.	19.0%	29	11.0
Simple average	24.6%	20.4	9.2

[a]Total debt divided by total assets.
[b]Times interest earned ratio.
[c]Price to earnings ratio.

discussed was the $6 million financing choice facing SAP. Exhibits 2, 3, and 4 were analyzed at length. Dennis felt that the firm's owners would benefit if the asset expansion were financed with debt capital. Also, Blackburn liked having total control over the firm's operations. With 51 percent of the common shares family owned, Blackburn knew that he could personally choose a course of action when a tough situation faced SAP. Incidentally, the corporate charter of SAP does not provide for the election of directors via a cumulative voting procedure.

Dennis pointed out to Blackburn that apart from the family, no "public" investor controlled as much as 5 percent of the outstanding common shares. Thus Dennis noted effective control

of the firm's operations would remain with the Blackburn family should the new common stock alternative be elected. Dennis did not think it would be prudent to elect the debt alternative *only* because it would ensure Blackburn family control over SAP in the strictest sense.

Both Dennis and Blackburn were concerned with the effect of additional financial leverage upon the firm's price/earnings ratio. To deal partially with this question, Winthrop's staff prepared Exhibit 4. Winthrop suggested to Blackburn that his firm prepare for the "worst that could happen." He stated that SAP's price/earnings ratio might remain unchanged from its present level of 9.59 times if the debt alternative were chosen. He did not, however, believe such an occurrence to be highly likely. Winthrop offered his best guess that SAP's price/earnings ratio will fall to 9.3 times if bonds are sold and will rise to 10 times if the common stock alternative is selected.

Before he took the question before the entire board, Ken Blackburn wanted to review a more substantial body of analysis with Dennis and Winthrop. He gave Dennis a week to prepare the information requested below.

Questions and Problems

1. Dennis has projected that the firm's variable cost to sales ratio will be .79 after the $6 million expansion is effected. In addition, fixed costs apart from interest will rise to an annual level of $13 million. Calculate the level of sales that will equate earnings per share regardless of whether the subject $6 million is financed with bonds or common stock.

2. Set up income statements for bond financing and common stock financing using the sales volume determined earlier, and demonstrate that earnings per share will indeed be the same under the assumed conditions.

3. Use last year's results as the base period. Compute earnings per share under each financing alternative for sales levels equal to (a) 70 percent, (b) 85 percent, (c) 100 percent, (d) 110 percent, and (e) 120 percent of the base period results.

4. Employing the price/earnings ratios suggested by Winthrop, project the common stock prices for each financing choice at the sales levels just analyzed.

5. Again taking Winthrop's "best guess" price/earnings ratios, determine the sales level that will equate market price per share regardless of the financing source chosen.

6. After reviewing recent marketing department forecasts of sales levels, Ken Blackburn concluded, "Rarely will SAP experience revenues below the $120 million mark." If Blackburn is correct, which financing alternative do you recommend?

SELF-TEST SOLUTIONS

SS-1. a. $FC = $ interest + sinking fund

$FC = (\$6,000,000)(.12) + (\$6,000,000/20)$

$FC = \$720,000 + \$300,000 = \underline{\underline{\$1,020,000}}$

b. $CB_r = C_0 + NCF_r - FC$

where $C_0 = \$750,000$

$FC = \$1,020,000$

and

$NCF_r = \$3,400,000 - \$3,100,000 = \$300,000$

so

$CB_r = \$750,000 + \$300,000 - \$1,020,000$

$CB_r = \underline{\underline{\$30,000}}$

c. We know that the firm has a preference for maintaining a cash balance of $750,000. The joint impact of the recessionary economic environment and the proposed issue of bonds would put the firm's recessionary cash balance (CB_r) at $30,000. Because the firm desires a minimum cash balance of $750,000 ($C_0$), the data suggest that the proposed bond issue should be postponed.

SS-2. a. Firm Y seems to be using financial leverage to the most appropriate degree. Notice that its price/earnings ratio of 16 times exceeds that of firm X (at 9 times) and firm Z (also at 9 times).

b. The first financial leverage effect refers to the added variability in the earnings per share stream caused by the use of leverage-inducing financial instruments. The second financial leverage effect concerns the level of earnings per share at a specific EBIT associated with a specific capital structure.

Beyond some critical EBIT level, earnings per share will be higher if more leverage is used. Based on the company data provided, the marketplace for financial instruments is weighing the second leverage effect more heavily. Firm Z, therefore, seems to be under-levered (is operating *below* its theoretical leverage capacity).

SS-3. a.

Plan A		Plan B
EPS: Less-Levered Plan		**EPS: More-Levered Plan**
$\dfrac{(EBIT - I)(1 - t) - P}{S_A}$	$=$	$\dfrac{(EBIT - I)(1 - t) - P}{S_B}$
$\dfrac{(EBIT - \$140,000)(1 - 0.5)}{100,000 \text{ (shares)}}$	$=$	$\dfrac{(EBIT - \$480,000)(1 - 0.5)}{60,000 \text{ (shares)}}$
$\dfrac{0.5\,EBIT - \$70,000}{10}$	$=$	$\dfrac{0.5\,EBIT - \$240,000}{6}$
$EBIT = \underline{\underline{\$990,000}}$		

b. The EBIT–EPS analysis chart for Martin-Bowing is presented in Figure 14.10.

	Plan A	Plan B
EBIT	$990,000	$990,000
I	140,000	480,000
EBT	$850,000	$510,000
T (.5)	425,000	255,000
NI	$425,000	$255,000
P	0	0
EAC	$425,000	$255,000
÷ No. of common shares	100,000	60,000
EPS	$ 4.25	$ 4.25

c. Because $1,188,000 exceeds the calculated indifference level of $990,000, the more highly levered plan (plan B) will produce the higher EPS.

d. At this stage of the problem, it is necessary to compute EPS under each financing alternative. Then the relevant price/earnings ratio for each plan can be applied to project the common stock price for the plan at a specific EBIT level.

Figure 14.10 EBIT–EPS Analysis Chart for Martin-Bowing Company

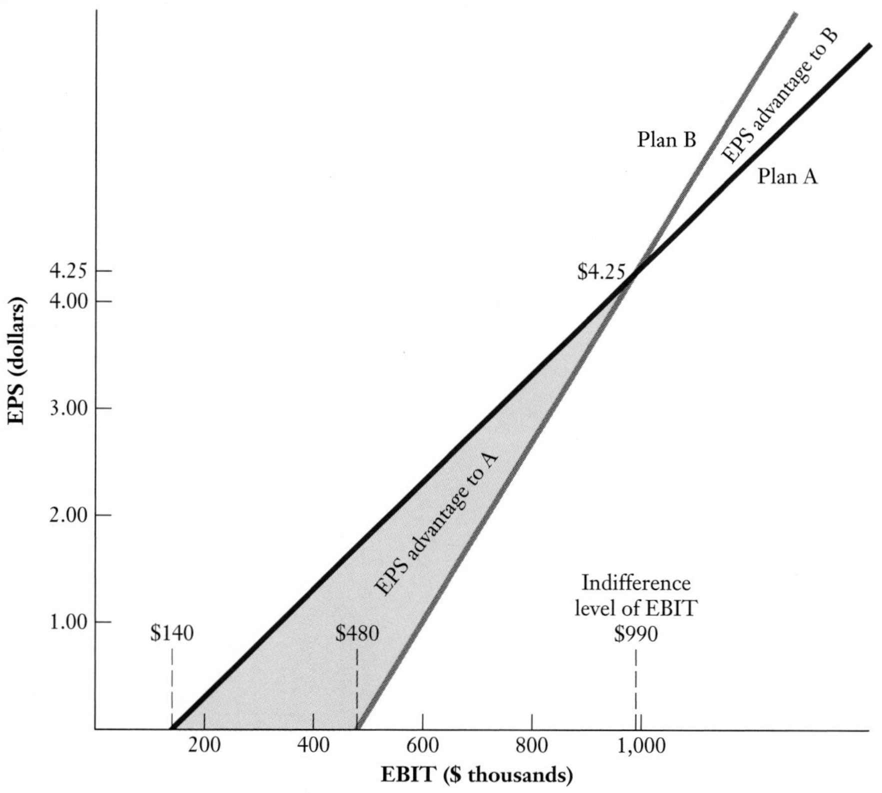

	Plan A	Plan B
EBIT	$1,188,000	$1,188,000
I	140,000	480,000
EBT	$1,048,000	$ 708,000
T (.5)	524,000	354,000
NI	$ 524,000	$ 354,000
P	0	0
EAC	$ 524,000	$ 354,000
÷ No. of common shares	100,000	60,000
EPS	$ 5.24	$ 5.90
× P/E ratio	13	11
= Projected stock price	$ 68.12	$ 64.90

Notice that the greater riskiness of plan B results in the market applying a lower price/earnings multiple to the expected EPS. Therefore, the investors would actually enjoy a higher stock price under plan A ($68.12) than they would under plan B ($64.90).

e. Here, we want to find the price/earnings ratio that would equate the common stock prices for both plans at an EBIT level of $1,188,000. All we have to do is take plan B's EPS and relate it to plan A's stock price. Thus:

$5.90 (P/E) = $68.12

(P/E) = $68.12/$5.90 = <u>11.546</u>.

A price/earnings ratio of 11.546 when applied to plan B's EPS would give the same stock price as that of plan A ($68.12).

Learning Objectives

Active Applications

World Finance

Practice

CHAPTER 15

DIVIDEND POLICY AND INTERNAL FINANCING

INTRODUCTION

T he corporate choice to pay or not to pay a cash dividend to stockholders and the further choice to increase the dividend, reduce the dividend, or keep it at the same dollar amount, represent one of the most challenging and perplexing areas of corporate financial policy. Because stockholder returns only come in two forms: stock price change and cash dividends received, it follows that the dividend decision directly impacts shareholder wealth.

We know that rational investors would rather be more wealthy rather than less wealthy. Accordingly, corporate boards of directors face a daunting decision every time the question of dividend policy and the possibility of changing the cash dividend is on the agenda.

In the simplest form, increasing the cash dividend simultaneously reduces the stock of internal financial capital (cash) available for capital expenditures. Thus the firm's stockholders find themselves smack in the middle of **Axiom 1: The Risk-Return Trade-Off—We Won't Take on Additional Risk Unless We Expect to Be Compensated with Additional Return**. The cash dividend, after all, is there in your hand to be spent today; the proposed capital expenditure is made based on the valuation of its expected incremental net cash flows. Recall **Axiom 4**.

The expected net present value of the proposed capital project will be impacted into the firm's stock price. But the arrival of new information over time about the success (or lack of success) of the capital project will be digested by the capital market

LEARNING OBJECTIVES

After reading this chapter, you should be able to

1. Describe the trade-off between paying dividends and retaining the profits within the company.

2. Explain the relationship between a corporation's dividend policy and the market price of its common stock.

3. Describe practical considerations that may be important to the firm's dividend policy.

4. Distinguish between the types of dividend policy corporations frequently use.

5. Specify the procedures a company follows in administering the dividend payment.

6. Describe why and how a firm might choose to pay non-cash dividends (stock dividends and stock splits) instead of cash dividends.

7. Explain the purpose and procedures related to stock repurchases.

and subsequently reflected in its stock price. So to be better off in a wealth context, the investor needs the firm to earn a higher rate of return on a dollar that is retained in the firm than that same investor could earn by investing that dollar elsewhere, given all economic considerations, such as having to pay a personal tax on the dollar of cash dividends received. It is indeed a perplexing corporate choice.

Over the years 1995 to 1997, the total return on the S&P 500 stock index equaled 37.4, 23.1, and 33.2 percent respectively.[1] These 3 years of abnormally high nominal returns followed 3 consecutive years, 1992 to 1994, where the total return on this same stock index never exceeded 10.0 percent. The recent history of lofty total returns on equity investments induced corporate executives and their boards of directors to rein in their dividend payout policies.

For example, in 1997, fewer firms increased their dividends from the previous year than had occurred since 1990. This tendency reflected widespread corporate sentiment that firms could increase shareholder wealth by retaining a larger proportion of earnings per share. Along these same lines, the management of the Coca-Cola Company said, "In 1996, our dividend payout ratio was approximately 36 percent of our net income. To free up additional cash for reinvestment in our high-return beverages business, our Board of Directors intends to gradually reduce our dividend payout ratio to 30 percent over time."[2] Here from Coca-Cola you have an explicit statement that describes the firm's dividend policy. Such is the focus of this chapter.

CHAPTER PREVIEW

The primary goal or objective of the firm should be to maximize the value, or price, of a firm's common stock. The success or failure of management's decisions can be evaluated only in light of their impact on the firm's common stock price. We observed that the company's investment (chapters 9, 10, and 11) and financing decisions (chapters 13 and 14) can increase the value of the firm. As we look at the firm's dividend and internal financing policies (*internal financing* means how much of the company's financing comes from cash flows generated internally), we return to the same basic question: "Can management influence the price of the firm's stock, in this case, through its dividend policies?" After addressing this important question, we then look at the practical side of the question, "What are the practices commonly followed by managers in making decisions about paying or not paying a dividend to the firm's stockholders?"

In the development of this chapter, you will be referred to several of the axioms that form the basics of business financial management and decision making. These are emphasized: **Axiom 1: The Risk-Return Trade-Off—We Won't Take on Additional Risk Unless We Expect to Be Compensated with Additional Return; Axiom 2: The Time Value of Money—A Dollar Received Today Is Worth More Than a Dollar Received in the Future; Axiom 4: Incremental Cash Flows—It's Only What Changes That Counts; Axiom 7: The Agency Problem—Managers Won't Work for Owners Unless It's in Their Best Interest; and Axiom 8: Taxes Bias Business Decisions.**

---

[1] *The Wall Street Journal* (January 2, 1998): R12.

[2] The Coca-Cola Company, *Annual Report* (1996), 42.

Before taking up the particular issues relating to dividend policy, we must understand several key terms and interrelationships.

A firm's dividend policy includes two basic components. First, the **dividend payout ratio** indicates the amount of dividends paid relative to the company's earnings. For instance, if the dividend per share is $2 and the earnings per share is $4, the payout ratio is 50 percent ($2 ÷ $4). The second component is the *stability* of the dividends over time. As will be observed later in the chapter, dividend stability may be almost as important to the investor as the amount of dividends received.

In formulating a dividend policy, the financial manager faces trade-offs. Assuming that management has already decided how much to invest and has chosen its debt-equity mix for financing these investments, the decision to pay a large dividend means simultaneously deciding to retain little, if any, profits; this in turn results in a greater reliance on external equity financing. Conversely, given the firm's investment and financing decisions, a small dividend payment corresponds to high profit retention with less need for externally generated equity funds. These trade-offs, which are fundamental to our discussion, are illustrated in Figure 15.1.

Dividend payout ratio

The amount of dividends relative to the company's net income or earnings per share.

Figure 15.1 Dividend-Retention-Financing Trade-Offs

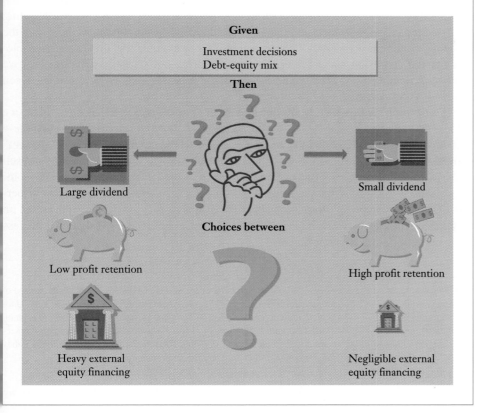

The fundamental question to be resolved in our study of the firm's dividend policy may be stated simply: What is a sound rationale or motivation for dividend payments? If we believe our objective should be to maximize the value of the common stock, we may restate the question as follows: Given the firm's capital-budgeting and borrowing decisions, what is the effect of the firm's dividend policies on the stock price? *Does a high dividend payment decrease stock value, increase it, or make no real difference?*

At first glance, we might reasonably conclude that a firm's dividend policy is important. We have already defined the value of a stock to be equal to the present value of future dividends (chapter 8). How can we now suggest that dividends are not important? Why do so many companies pay dividends, and why is a page in *The Wall Street Journal* devoted to dividend announcements? Based on intuition, we could quickly conclude that dividend policy is important. However, we might be surprised to learn that the dividend question has been a controversial issue for well over three decades. It has even been called the "dividend puzzle."[4]

Three Basic Views

Some would argue that the amount of the dividend is irrelevant, and any time spent on the decision is a waste of energy. Others contend that a high dividend will result in a high stock price. Still others take the view that dividends actually hurt the stock value. Let us look at these three views in turn.

View 1: Dividend policy is irrelevant. Much of the controversy about the dividend issue is based in the time-honored disagreements between the academic and professional communities. Some experienced practitioners perceive stock price changes resulting from dividend announcements and therefore see dividends as important. Many within the academic community—namely finance professors—who argue that dividends are irrelevant see the confusion about the matter resulting from not carefully defining what we mean by dividend policy. They would argue that the appearance of a relationship between dividends and stock price may be an illusion.[5]

The position that dividends are not important rests on two preconditions. First, we assume that investment and borrowing decisions have already been made, and that these decisions will not be altered by the amount of any dividend payments. Second, "**perfect**" **capital markets** are assumed to exist, which means that (1) investors can buy and sell stocks without incurring any transaction costs, such as brokerage commissions; (2) companies can issue stocks without any cost of doing so; (3) there are no corporate or personal taxes; (4) complete information about the firm is readily available; (5) there are no conflicts of interest between managements and stockholders; and (6) financial distress and bankruptcy costs are nonexistent.

Perfect capital markets

Capital markets where (1) investors can buy and sell stock without incurring any transaction costs, such as brokerage commissions; (2) companies can issue stocks without any cost of doing so; (3) there are no corporate or personal taxes; (4) complete information about the firm is readily available; (5) there are no conflicts of interest between management and stockholders; and (6) financial distress and bankruptcy costs are nonexistent.

---

[3]The concepts of this section draw heavily from Donald H. Chew, Jr., ed., "Do Dividends Matter? A Discussion of Corporate Dividend Policy," in *Six Roundtable Discussions of Corporate Finance with Joel Stern* (New York: Quorum Books, 1986): 67–101; and a book of readings edited by Joel M. Stern and Donald H. Chew, Jr., *The Revolution in Corporate Finance* (New York: Basil Blackwell, 1986). Specific readings included Merton Miller, "Can Management Use Dividends to Influence the Value of the Firm?" 299–303; Richard Brealey, "Does Dividend Policy Matter?" 304–9; and Michael Rozeff, "How Companies Set Their Dividend Payout Ratios," 320–26.

[4]See Fischer Black, "The Dividend Puzzle," *Journal of Portfolio Management* 2 (Winter 1976): 5–8.

[5]For an excellent presentation of this issue, see Merton Miller, "Can Management Use Dividends to Influence the Value of the Firm?" in Joel M. Stern and Donald H. Chew. Jr., eds., *The Revolution in Corporate Finance* (New York: Basil Blackwell, 1986): 299–305.

The first assumption—that we have already made the investment and financing decisions—simply keeps us from confusing the issues. We want to know the effect of dividend decisions on a stand-alone basis, without mixing in other decisions. The second assumption, that of perfect markets, also allows us to study the effect of dividend decisions in isolation, much like a physicist studies motion in a vacuum to avoid the influence of friction.

Given these assumptions, the effect of a dividend decision on share price may be stated unequivocally: *There is no relationship between dividend policy and stock value.* One dividend policy is as good as another one. In the aggregate, investors are concerned only with *total* returns from investment decisions; they are indifferent whether these returns come from capital gains or dividend income. They also recognize that the dividend decision, given the investment policy, is really a choice of financing strategy. Chapter 12 discussed the principles underlying growth. To finance growth, the firm (a) may choose to issue stock, allowing internally generated funds (profits) to be used to pay dividends; or (b) may use internally generated funds to finance its growth, while paying less in dividends, but not having to issue stock. In the first case, shareholders receive dividend income; in the second case, the value of their stock should increase, providing capital gains. The nature of the return is the only difference; total returns should be about the same. Thus to argue that paying dividends can make shareholders better off is to argue that paying out cash with one hand and taking it back with the other hand is a worthwhile activity for management.

The firm's dividend payout could affect stock price if the shareholder has no other way to receive income from the investment. However, assuming the capital markets are relatively efficient, a stockholder who needs current income could always sell shares. If the firm pays a dividend, the investor could eliminate any dividend received, in whole or in part, by using the dividend to purchase stock. The investor can thus personally create any desired dividend stream, no matter what dividend policy is in effect.

An example of dividend irrelevance. To demonstrate the argument that dividends may not matter, come to the Land of Ez (pronounced "ease"), where the environment is quite simple. First, the king, being a kind soul, has imposed no income taxes on his subjects. Second, investors can buy and sell securities without paying any sales commissions. In addition, when a company issues new securities (stocks or bonds), there are no flotation costs. Furthermore, the Land of Ez is completely computerized, so that all information about firms is instantaneously available to the public at no cost. Next, all investors realize that the value of a company is a function of its investment opportunities and its financing decisions. Therefore, the dividend policy offers no new information about either the firm's ability to generate earnings or the riskiness of its earnings. Finally, all firms are owned and managed by the same parties; thus we have no potential conflict between owners and managers.

Within this financial utopia, would a change in a corporation's dividend stream have any effect on the price of the firm's stock? The answer is no. To illustrate, consider Dowell Venture, Inc., a corporation that received a charter at the end of 1998 to conduct business in the Land of Ez. The firm is to be financed by common stock only. Its life is to extend for only 2 years (1999 and 2000) at which time it will be liquidated.

Table 15.1 presents Dowell Venture's balance sheet at the time of its formation, as well as the projected cash flows from the short-term venture. The anticipated cash flows are based on an expected return on investment of 20 percent, which is exactly what the common shareholders require as a rate of return on their investment in the firm's stock.

At the end of 1999, an additional investment of $300,000 will be required, which may be financed by (1) retaining $300,000 of the 1999 profits, or (2) issuing new common stock, or (3) some combination of both of these. In fact, two dividend plans for 1999 are under consideration. The investors would receive either $100,000 or $250,000 in dividends. If $250,000 is paid out of 1999's $400,000 in earnings, the company would be

Table 15.1 Dowell Venture, Inc., Financial Data

	December 31, 1998	
Total assets	$2,000,000	
Common stock (100,000 shares)	$2,000,000	
	1996	**1997**
Projected cash available from operations for paying dividends or for reinvesting	$400,000	$460,000

required to issue $150,000 in new stock to make up the difference in the total $300,000 needed for reinvestment versus the $150,000 that is retained. Table 15.2 depicts these two dividend plans and the corresponding new stock issue. Our objective in analyzing the data is to answer this question: Which dividend plan is preferable to the investors? In answering this question, we must take three steps: (1) Calculate the amount and timing of the dividend stream for the *original* investors. (2) Determine the present value of the dividend stream for each dividend plan. (3) Select the dividend alternative providing the higher value to the investors.

Step 1: *Computing the Dividend Streams*. The first step in this process is presented in Table 15.3. The dividends in 1999 (line 1, Table 15.3) are readily apparent from the data in Table 15.2. However, the amount of the dividend to be paid to the present shareholders in 2000 has to be calculated. To do so, we assume that investors receive (1) their original investments (line 2, Table 15.3), (2) any funds retained within the business in 1999 (line 3, Table 15.3), and (3) the profits for 2000 (line 4, Table 15.3). However, if additional stockholders invest in the company, as with plan 2, the dividends to be paid to these investors must be subtracted from the total available dividends (line 6, Table 15.3). The remaining dividends (line 7, Table 15.3) represent the amount current stockholders will receive in 1997. Therefore, the amounts of the dividend may be summarized as follows:

Dividend Plan	1999	2000
1	$1.00	$27.60
2	2.50	25.80

Table 15.2 Dowell Venture, Inc., 1999 Proposed Dividend Plans

	Plan 1	Plan 2
Internally generated cash flow	$400,000	$400,000
Dividend for 1999	100,000	250,000
Cash available for reinvestment	$300,000	$150,000
Amount of investment in 1999	300,000	300,000
Additional external financing required	$ 0	$150,000

Table 15.3 Dowell Venture, Inc., Step 1: Measurement of Proposed Dividend Streams

	Plan 1		Plan 2	
	Total Amount	Amount Per Share[a]	Total Amount	Amount Per Share[a]
Year 1 (1999)				
(1) Dividend	$ 100,000	$ 1.00	$ 250,000	$ 2.50
Year 2 (2000)				
Total dividend consisting of:				
(2) Original investment:				
(a) Old investors	$2,000,000		$2,000,000	
(b) New investors	0		150,000	
(3) Retained earnings from 1999	300,000		150,000	
(4) Profits for 2000	460,000		460,000	
(5) Total dividend to all investors in 2000	$2,760,000		$2,760,000	
(6) Less dividends to new investors:				
(a) Original investment	0		(150,000)	
(b) Profits for new investors				
(20% of $150,000 investment)	0		(30,000)	
(7) Liquidating dividends available to original investors in 2000	$2,760,000	$27.60	$2,580,000	$25.80

[a]Number of original shares outstanding equals 100,000.

Step 2: *Determining the Present Value of the Cash Flow Streams.* For each of the dividend payment streams, the resulting common stock value is

$$\text{stock price (plan 1)} = \frac{\$1.00}{(1+.20)^1} + \frac{\$27.60}{(1+.20)^2} = \$20$$

$$\text{stock price (plan 2)} = \frac{\$2.50}{(1+.20)^1} + \frac{\$25.80}{(1+.20)^2} = \$20$$

Therefore the two approaches provide the same end product; that is, the market price of Dowell Venture's common stock is $20 regardless of the dividend policy chosen.

Step 3: *Select the Best Dividend Plan.* If the objective is to maximize the shareholders' wealth, either plan is acceptable. Alternatively, shifting the dividend payments between years by changing the dividend policy does not affect the value of the security. Thus only if investments are made with expected returns exceeding 20 percent will the value of the stock increase. In other words, the only wealth-creating activity in the Land of Ez, where companies are financed entirely by equity, is management's investment decisions.

View 2: High dividends increase stock value. The belief that a firm's dividend policy is unimportant implicitly assumes that an investor should use the same required rate of return whether income comes through capital gains or through dividends. However, dividends are more predictable than capital gains; management can control dividends, but it cannot dictate the price of the stock. Investors are less certain of receiving income from capital gains than from dividends. The incremental risk associated with capital gains relative to dividend income implies a higher required rate for discounting a dollar of capital gains than for discounting a dollar of dividends. In other words, we would value a dollar of expected dividends more highly than a dollar of expected capital gains. We might, for example, require a 14 percent rate of return for a stock that pays its entire return from dividends, but a 20 percent return for a high-growth stock that pays no dividend. In so doing, we would give a higher value to the dividend income than we would to the capital gains. This view, which says dividends are more certain than capital gains, has been called the "**bird-in-the-hand**" **theory**.

The position that dividends are less risky than capital gains, and should therefore be valued differently, is not without its critics. If we hold to our basic decision not to let the firm's dividend policy influence its investment and capital-mix decisions, the company's operating cash flows, both in expected amount and variability, are unaffected by its dividend policy. Because the dividend policy has no impact on the volatility of the company's overall cash flows, it has no impact on the riskiness of the firm.

Increasing a firm's dividend does not reduce the basic riskiness of the stock; rather, if a dividend payment requires management to issue new stock, it only transfers risk *and* ownership from the current owners to new owners. We would have to acknowledge that the current investors who receive the dividend trade an uncertain capital gain for a "safe" asset (the cash dividend). However, if risk reduction is the only goal, the investor could have kept the money in the bank and not bought the stock in the first place.

We might find fault with this "bird-in-the-hand" theory, but there is still a strong perception among many investors and professional investment advisors that dividends are important. They frequently argue their case based on their own personal experience. As expressed by one investment advisor:

> In advising companies on dividend policy, we're absolutely sure on one side that the investors in companies like the utilities and the suburban banks want dividends. We're absolutely sure on the other side that . . . the high-technology companies should have no dividends. For the high earners—the ones that have a high rate of return like 20 percent, or more—we think they should have a low payout ratio. We think a typical industrial company which earns its cost of capital—just earns its cost of capital—probably should be in the average [dividend-payout] range of 40 to 50 percent.[6]

RELATE TO THE BIG PICTURE

The preceding discussion that specifies the "bird-in-the-hand" theory between the relationship of stock price and the firm's dividend policy relates directly to **Axiom 2: The Time Value of Money—A Dollar Received Today Is Worth More Than a Dollar Received in the Future.** *This theory suggests that because the dollar of dividends is received today it* should *be valued more highly than an uncertain capital gain that* might *be received in the future. The fundamental premise of this position is that the cash dividend in your hand (placed there today by the firm's payout policy) is more certain (less risky) than a possible capital gain. Many practitioners adhere to this theory; but many also adhere to the theory that is advanced in the next section. If nothing else, because it is controversial, dividend policy is important to the firm and its stockholders. And, in reality, many companies do pay cash dividends. Cash dividends are ubiquitous, so they are discussed in depth.*

View 3: Low dividends increase stock value. The third view of how dividends affect stock price proposes that dividends actually hurt the investor. This argument has largely been based on the difference in tax treatment for dividend income and capital gains. Unlike the investors in the great Land of Ez, most other investors do pay income taxes. For these taxpayers, the objective is to maximize the *after-tax* return on investment relative to the risk assumed. This objective is realized by *minimizing* the effective tax rate on the income and, whenever possible, by *deferring* the payment of taxes.

---

[6]From a discussion by John Childs, an investment adviser at Kidder Peabody, in Donald H. Chew, Jr., ed., "Do Dividends Matter? A Discussion of Corporate Dividend Policy," in *Six Roundtable Discussions of Corporate Finance with Joel Stern* (New York: Quorum Books, 1986): 83–84.

Like most tax code complexities, Congress over the years has altered the outcome of whether capital gains are taxed at either (1) a lower or (2) a similar rate as "earned income." Think of a water faucet being randomly turned on and then off. From 1987 through 1992, no federal tax advantage was provided for capital gains income relative to dividend income. A revision in the tax code that took effect beginning in 1993 did provide a preference for capital gains income. Then, the Taxpayer Relief Act of 1997 made the difference (preference) even more favorable for capital gains as opposed to cash dividend income. For some taxpayers, if a minimum holding period has been reached, the tax rate applied to capital gains was reduced to 20 percent from the previous level of 28 percent.

Further, another distinct benefit exists for capital gains vis-a-vis dividend income. Taxes on dividend income are paid when the dividend is received, while taxes on price appreciation (capital gains) are deferred until the stock is actually sold. Thus when it comes to tax considerations, most investors prefer the retention of a firm's earnings as opposed to the payment of cash dividends. If earnings are retained within the firm, the stock price increases, but the increase is not taxed until the stock is sold.

Although the majority of investors are subject to taxes, certain investment companies, trusts, and pension plans are exempt on their dividend income. Also, for tax purposes, a corporation may exclude 70 percent of the dividend income received from another corporation. In these cases, investors may prefer dividends over capital gains.

To summarize, when it comes to taxes, we want to maximize our *after-tax* return, as opposed to the *before-tax* return. Investors try to defer taxes whenever possible. Stocks that allow tax deferral (low dividends—high capital gains) will possibly sell at a premium relative to stocks that require current taxation (high dividends—low capital gains). In this way, the two stocks may provide comparable after-tax returns. This suggests that a policy of paying low dividends will result in a higher stock price. That is, high dividends hurt investors, whereas low dividends and high retention help investors. This is the logic of advocates of the low-dividend policy.

> **RELATE TO THE BIG PICTURE**
>
> *The presentation here of the argument that low cash dividends might increase common stock prices depends prominently on **Axiom 8: Taxes Bias Business Decisions.** For most individual economic units, income received in the form of cash dividends is subject to taxation at the relevant personal income tax rate. But the amount received from the sale of common stock that represents a "capital gain" is subject to a lower and, thus more favorable tax rate. So the argument suggests that taxpayers (investors) who find themselves in higher personal tax brackets will actually prefer to invest in companies that have dividend policies calling for low or no cash dividends being paid. Not only is the ultimate tax deferred until the gain is realized, but it enjoys a lower tax rate, leaving a larger residual gain for the investor who actually assumed the risk of the financial investment. **Axiom 8** is also an important underpinning of something called "the clientele effect" that will be discussed later in this chapter.*

Improving Our Thinking

We have now looked at three views on dividend policy. Which is right? The argument that dividends are irrelevant is difficult to refute, given the perfect market assumptions. However, in the real world, it is not always easy to feel comfortable with such an argument. Conversely, the high-dividend philosophy, which measures risk by how we split the firm's cash flows between dividends and retention, is not particularly appealing when studied carefully. The third view, which is essentially a tax argument against high dividends, is persuasive. However, if low dividends are so advantageous and generous dividends are so hurtful, why do companies continue to pay dividends? It is difficult to believe that managers would forgo such an easy opportunity to benefit their stockholders. What are we missing?

The need to find the missing elements in our "dividend puzzle" has not been ignored. When we need to understand better an issue or phenomenon, we have two options: improving our thinking or gathering more evidence about the topic. Scholars and practitioners have taken both approaches. Although no single definitive answer has yet been found that is acceptable to all, several plausible extensions have been developed. Some of the more popular additions include (1) the residual dividend theory, (2) the clientele effect, (3) information effects, (4) agency costs, and (5) expectations theory.

The residual dividend theory. Within the Land of Ez, companies were blessed with professional consultants who were essentially charitable in nature; they did not seek any compensation when they helped a firm through the process of issuing stock. (Even in the Land of Ez, managers needed help from investment bankers, accountants, and attorneys to sell a new issue.) However, in reality, the process is quite expensive and may cost as much as 20 percent of the dollar issue size.[7]

If a company incurs flotation costs, that may have a direct bearing on the dividend decision. Because of these costs, a firm must issue a larger amount of securities in order to receive the amount required for investment. For example, if $300,000 is needed to finance proposed investments, an amount exceeding the $300,000 will have to be issued to offset flotation costs incurred in the sale of the new stock issue. This means, very simply, that new equity capital raised through the sale of common stock will be more expensive than capital raised through the retention of earnings. (Remember what we learned in chapter 12?)

In effect, flotation costs eliminate our indifference between financing by internal capital and by new common stock. Earlier, the company could pay dividends and issue common stock or retain profits. However, when flotation costs exist, internal financing is preferred. Dividends are paid only if profits are not completely used for investment purposes; that is, only when there are "residual earnings" after the financing of new investments. This policy is called **residual dividend theory**.[8]

With the assumption of no flotation costs removed, the firm's dividend policy would be as follows:

1. Maintain the optimum debt ratio in financing future investments.
2. Accept an investment if the net present value is positive. That is, the expected rate of return exceeds the cost of capital.
3. Finance the equity portion of new investments first by internally generated funds. Only after this capital is fully utilized should the firm issue new common shares.
4. If any internally generated funds still remain after making all investments, pay dividends to the investors. However, if all internal capital is needed for financing the equity portion of proposed investments, pay no dividend.

In summary, dividend policy is influenced by (1) the company's investment opportunities, (2) the capital structure mix, and (3) the availability of internally generated capital. In the Krista Corporation example, dividends were paid *only* after all acceptable investments had been financed. This logic, called the residual dividend theory, implies that the dividends to be paid should equal the equity capital *remaining* after financing investments. According to this theory, dividend policy is a passive influence, having by itself no direct influence on the market price of the common stock.

Residual dividend theory

A theory asserting that the dividends to be paid should equal capital left over after the financing of profitable investments.

---

[7]We discussed the costs of issuing securities in chapter 12.

[8]The residual dividend theory is consistent with the "pecking order" theory of finance as described by Stewart Myers, "The Capital Structure Puzzle," *The Journal of Finance* (July 1984): 575–92.

Assume that the Krista Corporation finances 40 percent of its investments with debt and the remaining 60 percent with common equity. Two million dollars have been generated from operations and may be used to finance the common equity portion of new investments or to pay common dividends. The firm's management is considering five investment opportunities. Figure 15.2 graphs the expected rate of return for these investments, along with the firm's weighted marginal cost of capital curve. From the information contained in the figure, we would accept projects A, B, and C, requiring $2.5 million in total financing. Therefore, $1 million in new debt (40% × $2.5 million) would be needed, with common equity providing $1.5 million (60% × $2.5 million). In this instance, the dividend payment decision would be to pay $500,000 in dividends, which is the residual, or remainder, of the $2 million internally generated capital.

To illustrate further, consider the dividend decision if project D had also been acceptable. If this investment were added to the firm's portfolio of proposed capital expenditures, then $4 million in new financing would be needed. Debt financing would constitute $1.6 million (40% × $4 million) and common equity would provide the additional $2.4 million (60% × $4 million). Because only $2 million is available internally, $400,000 in new common stock would be issued. The residual available for dividends would be zero, and no dividend would be paid.

The clientele effect. What if the investors living in the Land of Ez did not like the dividend policy chosen by Dowell's management? No problem. They could simply satisfy their personal income preferences by purchasing or selling securities when the dividends received did not satisfy their current needs for income. If an investor did not view the dividends received in any given year to be sufficient, he or she could simply sell a portion of stock, thereby "creating a dividend." In addition, if the dividend were larger than the investor desired, he or she could purchase stock with the "excess cash" created by the dividend. However, once we leave the Land of Ez, we find that such adjustments in stock ownership

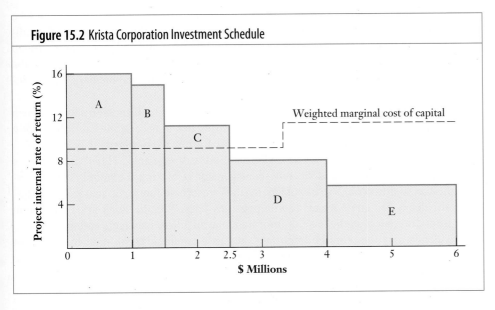

Figure 15.2 Krista Corporation Investment Schedule

are not cost-free. When an investor buys or sells stock, brokerage fees are incurred, ranging from approximately 1 to 10 percent. Even more costly, the investor who buys the stock with cash received from a dividend will have to pay taxes before reinvesting the cash. And when a stock is bought or sold, it must first be reevaluated. Acquisition of the information for decision making also may be time consuming and costly. Finally, aside from the cost of buying or selling part of the stock, some institutional investors, such as university endowment funds, are precluded from selling stock and "spending" the proceeds.

As a result of these considerations, investors may not be too inclined to buy stocks that require them to "create" a dividend stream more suitable to their purposes. Rather, if investors do in fact have a preference between dividends and capital gains, we could expect them to seek firms that have a dividend policy consistent with these preferences. They would, in essence, "sort themselves out" by buying stocks that satisfy their preferences for dividends and capital gains. Individuals and institutions that need current income would be drawn to companies that have high dividend payouts. Other investors, such as wealthy individuals, would much prefer to avoid taxes by holding securities that offer no or small dividend income but large capital gains. In other words, there would be a **clientele effect**: Firms draw a given clientele, given their stated dividend policy.

The possibility that clienteles of investors exist might lead us to believe that the firm's dividend policy matters. However, unless there is a greater aggregate demand for a particular policy than the market can satisfy, dividend policy is still unimportant; one policy is as good as the other. The clientele effect only warns firms to avoid making capricious changes in their dividend policy. Given that the firm's investment decisions are already made, the level of the dividend is still unimportant. The change in the policy matters only when it requires clientele to shift to another company.

The information effect. The investor in the Land of Ez would argue with considerable persuasion that a firm's value is determined strictly by its investment and financing decisions, and that the dividend policy has no impact on value. Yet we know from experience that a large, unexpected change in dividends can have a significant impact on the stock price. For instance, in August 1994, the Continental Corporation, a large insurance company, eliminated its annual dividend of $1. In response, the firm's stock price went from about $18 to $15. How can we suggest that dividend policy matters little, when we can cite numerous such examples of a change in dividend affecting the stock price, especially when the change is negative?

Despite such "evidence," we are not looking at the real cause and effect. It may be that investors use a change in dividend policy as a *signal* about the firm's financial condition, especially its earnings power. Thus a dividend increase that is larger than expected might signal to investors that management expects significantly higher earnings in the future. Conversely, a dividend decrease, or even a less than expected increase, might signal that management is forecasting less favorable future earnings.

Some would argue that management frequently has inside information about the firm that it cannot make available to investors. This difference in accessibility to information between management and investors, called **information asymmetry**, may result in a lower stock price than would occur under conditions of certainty. This reasoning says that, by regularly increasing dividends, management is making a commitment to continue these cash flows to the stockholders for the foreseeable future. So in a risky marketplace, dividends become a means to minimize any "drag" on the stock price that might come from differences in the level of information available to managers and investors.

Dividends may therefore be important only as a communication tool; management may have no other credible way to inform investors about future earnings, or at least no convincing way that is less costly.

Clientele effect

The belief that individuals and institutions that need current income will invest in companies that have high dividend payouts. Other investors prefer to avoid taxes by holding securities that offer only small dividend income, but large capital gains. Thus we have a "clientele" of investors.

Information asymmetry

The difference in accessibility to information between management and investors may result in a lower stock price than would occur under conditions of certainty.

Agency costs. Let us return again to the Land of Ez. We had avoided any potential conflict between the firm's investors and managers by assuming them to be one and the same. With only a cursory look at the real marketplace, we can see that managers and investors are typically not the same people, and as noted in the preceding section, these two groups do not have the same access to information about the firm. If the two groups are not the same, we must then assume that management is dedicated to maximizing shareholder wealth.[9] That is, we are making a presupposition that the market values of companies with separate owners and managers will not differ from those of owner-managed firms.

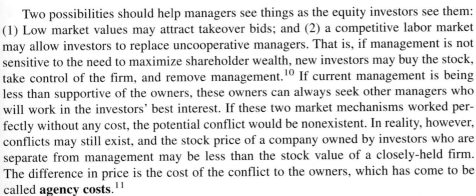

RELATE TO THE BIG PICTURE

Axiom 7 warned us there may be a conflict between management and owners, especially in large firms where managers and owners have different incentives. That is: **Managers Won't Work for Owners Unless It's in Their Best Interest.** *As we shall see in this section, the dividend policy may be one way to reduce this problem.*

Two possibilities should help managers see things as the equity investors see them: (1) Low market values may attract takeover bids; and (2) a competitive labor market may allow investors to replace uncooperative managers. That is, if management is not sensitive to the need to maximize shareholder wealth, new investors may buy the stock, take control of the firm, and remove management.[10] If current management is being less than supportive of the owners, these owners can always seek other managers who will work in the investors' best interest. If these two market mechanisms worked perfectly without any cost, the potential conflict would be nonexistent. In reality, however, conflicts may still exist, and the stock price of a company owned by investors who are separate from management may be less than the stock value of a closely-held firm. The difference in price is the cost of the conflict to the owners, which has come to be called **agency costs.**[11]

Recognizing the possible problem, management, acting independently or at the insistence of the board of directors, frequently takes action to minimize the cost associated with the separation of ownership and management control. Such action, which in itself is costly, includes auditing by independent accountants, assigning supervisory functions to the company's board of directors, creating covenants in lending agreements that restrict management's powers, and providing incentive compensation plans for management that help "bond" the management with the owners.

A firm's dividend policy may be perceived by owners as a tool to minimize agency costs. Assuming that the payment of a dividend requires management to issue stock to finance new investments, new investors may be attracted to the company only if management provides convincing information that the capital will be used profitably. Thus the payment of dividends indirectly results in a closer monitoring of management's investment activities. In this case, dividends may make a meaningful contribution to the value of the firm.

Agency costs

The costs, such as a reduced stock price, associated with potential conflict between managers and investors when these two groups are not the same.

---

[9]This issue was addressed briefly in chapter 1.

[10]The "corporate control hypothesis," especially as it relates to companies merging or being acquired, has generated a great amount of interest in recent years. For example, see the April 1983 issue of *Journal of Financial Economics.*

[11]See M. C. Jenson, and W. H. Meckling, "Theory of the Firm: Managerial Behavior, Agency Costs, and Ownership Structure," *Journal of Financial Economics* (October 1976): 305–60.

Expectations theory.[12] A common thread throughout much of our discussion of dividend policy, particularly as it relates to information effects, is the word *expected*. We should not overlook the significance of this word when we are making any financial decision within the firm. No matter what the decision area, how the market price responds to management's actions is not determined entirely by the action itself; it is also affected by investors' expectations about the ultimate decision to be made by management. This idea is called the **expectations theory**.

As the time approaches for management to announce the amount of the next dividend, investors form expectations as to how much that dividend will be. These expectations are based on several factors internal to the firm, such as past dividend decisions, current and expected earnings, investment strategies, and financing decisions. They also consider such things as the condition of the general economy, the strength or weakness of the industry at the time, and possible changes in government policies.

When the actual dividend decision is announced, the investor compares the actual decision with the expected decision. If the amount of the dividend is as expected, even if it represents an increase from prior years, the market price of the stock will remain unchanged. However, if the dividend is higher or lower than expected, investors will reassess their perceptions about the firm. They will question the meaning of the *unexpected* change in the dividend. They may use the unexpected dividend decision as a clue about unexpected changes in earnings; that is, the unexpected dividend change has information content about the firm's earnings and other important factors. In short, management's actual decision about the firm's dividend policy may not be terribly significant, unless it departs from investors' expectations. If there is a difference between actual and expected dividends, we will more than likely see a movement in the stock price.

The Empirical Evidence

Our search for an answer to the question of dividend relevance has been less than successful. We have given it our best thinking, but still no single definitive position has emerged. Maybe we could gather evidence to show the relationship between dividend practices and security prices. We might also inquire into the perceptions of financial managers who make decisions about dividend policies, with the idea that their beliefs affect their decision making. Then we could truly know that dividend policy is important or that it does not matter.

To test the relationship between dividend payments and security prices, we could compare a firm's dividend yield (dividend/stock price) and the stock's total return. The question is: Do stocks that pay high dividends provide higher or lower returns to investors? Such tests have been conducted with the use of highly sophisticated statistical techniques. Despite the use of these extremely powerful analytical tools, which involve intricate and complicated procedures, the results have been mixed.[13] However, over long periods, the results have given a slight advantage to the low-dividend stocks; that is, stocks that pay lower dividends appear to have higher prices. The findings are far from conclusive, however, owing to the relatively large standard errors of the estimates.

---

[12]Much of the thoughts in this section came from Merton Miller, "Can Management Use Dividends to Influence the Value of the Firm?" in *The Revolution in Corporate Finance*, Joel M. Stern, and Donald H. Chew, Jr., eds. (New York: Basil Blackwell, 1986): 299–303.

[13]See F. Black and M. Scholes, "The Effects of Dividend Yield and Dividend Policy on Common Stock Prices and Returns," *Journal of Financial Economics* 1 (May 1974), 1–22; P. Hess, "The Ex-Dividend Behavior of Stock Returns: Further Evidence on Tax Effects," *Journal of Finance* 37 (May 1982), 445–56; R. H. Litzenberger and K. Ramaswamy, "The Effect of Personal Taxes and Dividends on Capital Asset Prices: Theory and Empirical Evidence," *Journal of Financial Economics* 7 (June 1979), 163–95; and M. H. Miller and M. Scholes, "Dividends and Taxes: Some Empirical Evidence," *Journal of Political Economy* 90 (1982): 1118–41.

Table 15.4 Management Opinion Survey on Dividends

Statement of Managerial Beliefs	Level of Managers' Agreement		
	Agreement	No Opinion	Disagreement
1. A firm's dividend payout ratio affects the price of the common stock.	61%	33%	6%
2. Dividend payments provide a signaling device of future prospects.	52	41	7
3. The market uses dividend announcements as information for assessing security value.	43	51	6
4. Investors have different perceptions of the relative riskiness of dividends and retained earnings.	56	42	2
5. Investors are basically indifferent with regard to returns from dividends versus those from capital gains.	6	30	64
6. A stockholder is attracted to firms that have dividend policies appropriate to the stockholder's particular tax environment.	44	49	7
7. Management should be responsive to its shareholders' preferences regarding dividends.	41	49	10

SOURCE: Adapted from H. Kent Baker, Gail E. Farrelly, and Richard B. Edelman, "A Survey of Management Views on Dividend Policy," *Financial Management* (Autumn 1985): 81.

(The apparent differences may be the result of random sampling error and not real differences.) We simply have been unable to disentangle the effect of dividend policy from other influences.

Several reasons may be given for our inability to arrive at conclusive results. First, to be accurate, we would need to know the amount of dividends investors *expected* to receive. Because these expectations cannot be observed, we can only use historical data, which may or may not relate to current expectations. Second, most empirical studies have assumed a linear relationship between dividend payments and stock prices. The actual relationship may be nonlinear, possibly even discontinuous. Whatever the reasons, the evidence to date is inconclusive and the jury is still out.

Because our statistical prowess does not provide any conclusive evidence, let's turn to our last hope. What do the financial managers of the world believe about the relevance of dividend policy? Although we may not conclude that a manager's opinion is necessarily the "final word on the matter," having these insights is helpful. If financial managers believe that dividends matter and act consistently in accordance with that conviction, they could influence the relationship between stock value and dividend policy.

To help us gain some understanding of managements' perceptions, let's turn to a study by Baker, Farrelly, and Edelman, which surveyed financial executives at 318 firms listed on the New York Stock Exchange.[14] The study conducted in 1983 is summarized in Table 15.4. In looking at the Baker, Farrelly, and Edelman results, the evidence favors the relevance of dividend policy, but not overwhelmingly so. For the most part, managers are divided between believing that dividends are important and having no opinion in the matter.

---

[14]H. Kent Baker, Gail E. Farrelly, and Richard B. Edelman, "A Survey of Management Views on Dividend Policy," *Financial Management* (Autumn 1985): 78–84.

Do Dividends Matter? A Discussion of Corporate Dividend Policy

Joseph T. Willett, Moderator: I would like to welcome the participants and guests to this discussion, the subject of which is Corporate Dividend Policy. The general questions we want to address are these: Does dividend policy matter? And if so, why and how does it matter? Certain people argue that the theory of finance, combined with the treatment of dividends under U.S. tax law, would suggest that low dividends benefit investors. Others argue that because of the demand by some investors for current income, high dividends benefit investors. In the presence of these widely held views, I think it is fair to say that most carefully executed research has revealed no consistent relationship between dividends and share prices. From these studies, the market collectively appears to be "dividend neutral." That is, while individual investors may have preferences between dividends and capital gains, the results suggest neither a preference for nor an aversion to dividends. Which, of course, doesn't satisfy either the pro-dividend or anti-dividend group. Amid all this confusion, one observation stands out: nearly all successful firms pay dividends. And, furthermore, dividend policy is an important concern of most chief financial officers and financial managers generally. These facts of corporate practice, in light of all the evidence on the subject, present us with a puzzle—one which has continued to baffle the academic finance profession. In a paper written in 1976, entitled "The Dividend Puzzle," Fischer Black of MIT—one of the most widely respected researchers in the field, posed the question: "What should the individual investor do about dividends in his portfolio? What should the corporation do about dividend policy?

Joel Stern: I'd like to point out that the major reason why people like Fischer Black believe they don't know the answer to the question of the appropriate dividend policy is this: the evidence that has been accumulated in the academic community by serious researchers—by people that we have a lot of respect for, who are on the faculties of the premiere business schools—almost without exception, these academics find that there is no evidence to suggest that investors at the margin, where prices are set, have any preference for dividends over capital gains. This supports the point of view that the price-setting, marginal investor is "dividend-neutral," which means that a dollar of dividends gained is equal to a dollar of capital gains returned, while being indifferent how that return was divided between dividends and price appreciation. There is a second point of view, that has been expressed recently in research, which shows that investors who receive dividends cannot undo the harmful tax consequences of receiving that dividend. And, as a result, the market is actually "dividend averse," marking down prices of shares that pay cash dividends, so that the pretax returns that investors earn are high enough such that, post-tax, the returns are what they would have been had the company not paid cash dividends in the first place. But there is no creditable evidence that I am aware of—none that has been accepted by

---

Regarding the question about the price-dividend relationship, Baker et al. asked the financial managers straight up, "Does the firm's dividend policy affect the price of the common stock?" Slightly more than 60 percent of the responses were affirmative, which is significant, but there were still almost 40 percent who had no opinion or disagreed. Thus we could conclude that most managers think that dividends matter, but they have no mandate. Similarly, when asked if dividends provide informational content about the firm's future (Questions 2 and 3), the managers are basically split between "no opinion" and "agreement." When asked about the trade-off between dividends and capital gains (Questions 4 and 5),

the academic finance community—that shows that investors prefer dividends over capital gains.

If the evidence that has been published to date says that investors are dividend neutral or dividend averse, then how is it that somebody with the esteem of Fischer Black can come along and say: "We don't know what the right dividend policy is." The problem is that he is what we call a "positive economist." That doesn't mean that he is an economist who is positive about things. It means that he says the job of the economist is to account for what we see around us. He believes that markets behave in a sensible fashion at the margin; that under the guidance of the dominant price-setting investors, the market behaves in a rational manner, making the right choices for itself. Therefore, he is saying that there must be a reason why almost all companies for all time have been paying cash dividends. If a few companies paid dividends for all time, or almost all companies paid dividends only occasionally, then one could make the case that it is possible dividends are really not important. But, if we find that almost all companies pay dividends for almost all time, there must be a good reason why they are paying the dividends. Therefore, who are we, as financial advisors, to say to a company, "No, don't pay cash dividends. After all, it won't harm you very much despite the fact that almost all companies are paying dividends"? That wouldn't make very much sense.

(D)

SOURCE: *Six Roundtable Discussions of Corporate Finance with Joel Stern,* Donald H. Chew, Jr., ed., "Do Dividends Matter? A Discussion of Corporate Dividend Policy," 67–101. Copyright © 1986 by Quorum Books. Reproduced with permission of Greenwood Publishing Group, Inc., Westport, CT.

Analysis and Implications ...

A. This discussion on dividend policy involved a number of individuals, both from the academic community and from the business world. For our purposes, we have included only the moderator's introduction and the remarks of Joel Stern, one of the participants. These two individuals capture the essence of what is known or not known about the relationship between a firm's dividend policy and the preference of investors for dividend income.

B. Willett identifies the different views about dividend policy; that is, some believe that investor's desire current income (dividends)—View 2, as described in the chapter. Others, however, think that dividends are not preferred to capital gains, owing to their increasing the investor's tax liability—our View 3. Mostly, he concurs that dividends should not matter (View 1), but wonders why financial managers continue to act like they are important—a real puzzle, as they call it.

C. Stern leans toward View 3— do not pay dividends because they are taxable whereas capital gains are not taxed until the stock is sold. But he too cannot comfortably advise managers not to pay dividends, because almost all companies act as if dividends are important.

D. From these two discussions, we can see the confusion about whether dividends are preferred or capital gains are preferred. Our best logic says they are not important, but we see managers acting like they are important. Who is right?

almost two-thirds of the managers thought stockholders have a preference for dividend or capital gains, with a lesser number (56 percent) believing that investors perceive the relative riskiness of capital gains and dividends to be different. Interestingly enough, though, almost half of the managers felt no clear responsibility to be responsive to stockholders' preferences. Specifically, 56 percent of the financial executives either had no opinion or did not believe that stockholders are attracted to firms that have dividend policies appropriate to the stockholder's particular tax environment. Finally, Statement 7 suggests that the majority of managers are not true believers in the concept of a clientele effect.

What Are We to Conclude?

We have now looked carefully at the importance of a firm's dividend policy as management seeks to increase the shareholders' wealth. We have gone to great lengths to gain insight and understanding from our best thinking. We have even drawn from the empirical evidence on hand to see what the findings suggest.

A reasonable person cannot reach a definitive conclusion; nevertheless, management is left with no choice. A firm must develop a dividend policy, it is hoped, based on the best available knowledge. Although we can give advice only with some reservation, the following conclusions would appear reasonable:

1. As a firm's investment opportunities increase, the dividend payout ratio should decrease. In other words, an inverse relationship should exist between the amount of investments with an expected rate of return that exceeds the cost of capital and the dividends remitted to investors. Because of flotation costs associated with raising external capital, the retention of internally generated equity financing is preferable to selling stock (in terms of the wealth of the current common shareholders).
2. The firm's dividend policy appears to be important; however, appearances may be deceptive. The real issue may be the firm's *expected* earning power and the riskiness of these earnings. Investors may be using the dividend payment as a source of information about the company's *expected* earnings. Management's actions regarding dividends may carry greater weight than a statement by management that earnings will be increasing.
3. If dividends influence stock price, this is probably based on the investor's desire to minimize and defer taxes and from the role of dividends in minimizing agency costs.
4. If the expectations theory has merit, which we believe it does, management should avoid surprising investors when it comes to the firm's dividend decision. The firm's dividend policy might effectively be treated as a *long-term residual*. Rather than projecting investment requirements for a single year, management could anticipate financing needs for several years. Based upon the expected investment opportunities during the planning horizon, the firm's debt-equity mix, and the funds generated from operations, a *target* dividend payout ratio could be established. If internal funds remained after projection of the necessary equity financing, dividends would be paid. However, the planned dividend stream should distribute residual capital evenly to investors over the planning period. Conversely, if over the long term the entire amount of internally generated capital is needed for reinvestment in the company, then no dividend should be paid.

THE DIVIDEND DECISION IN PRACTICE

In setting a firm's dividend policy, financial managers must work in the world of reality with the concepts we have set forth so far in this chapter. Again, although these concepts do not provide an equation that explains the key relationships, they certainly give us a more complete view of the finance world, which can only help us make better decisions. Other considerations of a more practical nature also appear as part of the firm's decision making about its dividend policy.

OBJECTIVE 3

Other Practical Considerations

Many considerations may influence a firm's decision about its dividends, some of them unique to that company. Some of the more general considerations are given subsequently.

Legal restrictions. Certain legal restrictions may limit the amount of dividends a firm may pay. These legal constraints fall into two categories. First, *statutory restrictions* may prevent a company from paying dividends. Although specific limitations vary by state, generally a corporation may not pay a dividend (1) if the firm's liabilities exceed its assets, (2) if the amount of the dividend exceeds the accumulated profits (retained earnings), and (3) if the dividend is being paid from capital invested in the firm.

The second type of legal restriction is unique to each firm and results from restrictions in debt and preferred stock contracts. To minimize their risk, investors frequently impose restrictive provisions upon management as a condition to their investment in the company. These constraints may include the provision that dividends may not be declared prior to the debt being repaid. Also, the corporation may be required to maintain a given amount of working capital. Preferred stockholders may stipulate that common dividends may not be paid when any preferred dividends are delinquent.

Liquidity position. Contrary to common opinion, the mere fact that a company shows a large amount of retained earnings in the balance sheet does not indicate that cash is available for the payment of dividends. The firm's current position in liquid assets, including cash, is basically independent of the retained earnings account. Historically, a company with sizable retained earnings has been successful in generating cash from operations. Yet these funds are typically either reinvested in the company within a short period or used to pay maturing debt. Thus a firm may be extremely profitable and still be *cash poor*. Because dividends are paid with cash, and not with retained earnings, the firm must have cash available for dividends to be paid. Hence the firm's liquidity position has a direct bearing on its ability to pay dividends.

Absence or lack of other sources of financing. As already noted, a firm may (1) retain profits for investment purposes, or (2) pay dividends and issue new debt or equity securities to finance investments. For many small or new companies, this second option is not realistic. These firms do not have access to the capital markets, so they must rely more heavily upon internally generated funds. As a consequence, the dividend payout ratio is generally much lower for a small or newly established firm than for a large, publicly-owned corporation.

Earnings predictability. A company's dividend payout ratio depends to some extent on the predictability of a firm's profits over time. If earnings fluctuate significantly, management cannot rely on internally generated funds to meet future needs. When profits are realized, the firm may retain larger amounts to ensure that money is available when needed. Conversely, a firm with a stable earnings trend will typically pay a larger portion of its earnings out in dividends. This company has less concern about the availability of profits to meet future capital requirements.

Ownership control. For many large corporations, control through the ownership of common stock is not an issue. However, for many small and medium-sized companies, maintaining voting control takes a high priority. If the present common shareholders are unable to participate in a new offering, issuing new stock is unattractive, in that the control of the current stockholders is diluted. The owners might prefer that management finance new investments with debt and through profits rather than by issuing new common stock. This firm's growth is then constrained by the amount of debt capital available and by the company's ability to generate profits.

Inflation. Before the late 1970s, inflationary pressures had not been a significant problem for either consumers or businesses. However, during much of the 1980s, the deterioration of the dollar's purchasing power had a direct impact on the replacement of fixed assets. In a period of inflation, ideally, as fixed assets become worn and obsolete, the funds generated from depreciation are used to finance the replacements. As the cost of equivalent equipment continues to increase, the depreciation funds are insufficient. This requires a greater retention of profits, which implies that dividends have to be adversely affected. In the 1990s, inflation has not been a primary concern.

Alternative Dividend Policies

Regardless of a firm's long-term dividend policy, most firms choose one of several year-to-year dividend payment patterns:

Constant dividend payout ratio

A dividend payment policy in which the percentage of earnings paid out in dividends is held constant. The dollar amount fluctuates from year to year as profits vary.

Stable dollar dividend payout

A dividend policy that maintains a relatively stable dollar dividend per share over time.

Small regular plus year-end extra dividend payout

A dividend payment policy where the firm pays a small regular dividend plus an extra dividend only if the firm has experienced a good year.

1. **Constant dividend payout ratio**. In this policy, the percentage of earnings paid out in dividends is held constant. Although the dividend-to-earnings ratio is stable, the dollar amount of the dividend naturally fluctuates from year to year as profits vary.
2. **Stable dollar dividend per share**. This policy maintains a relatively stable dollar dividend over time. An increase in the dollar dividend usually does not occur until management is convinced that the higher dividend level can be maintained in the future. Management also will not reduce the dollar dividend until the evidence clearly indicates that a continuation of the present dividend cannot be supported.
3. **Small, regular dividend plus year-end extra**. A corporation following this policy pays a small regular dollar dividend plus a year-end *extra dividend* in prosperous years. The extra dividend is declared toward the end of the fiscal year, when the company's profits for the period can be estimated. Management's objective is to avoid the connotation of a permanent dividend. However, this purpose may be defeated if *recurring* extra dividends come to be expected by investors.

Of the three dividend policies, the stable dollar dividend is by far the most common. Figure 15.3 graphs the general tendency of companies to pay stable, but increasing, dividends, even though the profits fluctuate significantly. In a study by Lintner, corporate managers were found to be reluctant to change the dollar amount of the dividend in response to temporary fluctuations in earnings from year to year. This aversion was particularly evident when it came to decreasing the amount of the dividend from the previous level.[15] In a separate study, Smith explained the tendency for stable dividend in terms of his "**increasing-stream hypothesis of dividend policy**."[16] He proposed that dividend stability is essentially a smoothing of the dividend stream to minimize the effect of other types of company reversals. Thus corporate managers make every effort to avoid a dividend cut, attempting instead to develop a gradually increasing dividend series over the long-term future. However, if a dividend reduction is absolutely necessary, the cut should be large enough to reduce the probability of future cuts.

Increasing-stream hypothesis of dividend policy

A smoothing of the dividend stream in order to minimize the effect of company reversals. Corporate managers make every effort to avoid a dividend cut, attempting instead to develop a gradually increasing dividend series over the long-term future.

Dividend Policy and Corporate Strategy: Things Will Change—Even Dividend Policy

The recession of 1990 to 1991 induced a large number of American corporations to revisit their broadest corporate strategies that directly impact shareholder wealth. Today, the results of that "rethinking" are evident in many aspects of corporate behavior, including adjusted dividend policies.

One firm that altered its dividend policy in response to new strategies was W. R. Grace & Co., headquartered in Boca Raton, Florida. The firm's core businesses include packaging, catalysts and silica products, and construction products. Grace & Co. ranked number 271 within the 1997 *Fortune 500* list of the largest U.S. corporations, with sales of $5.26 billion.

The new corporate plans involved (1) divesting or discontinuing several product lines and (2) initiating a significant repurchase program of its own common stock. Stock repurchase programs are discussed in depth later in this chapter.

As a result, both the firm's payout ratio and actual cash dividend paid per share declined in significant fashion. The change in observed dividend policy is evident in Table 15.5. Notice that over the 1992 to 1994 period, Grace & Co. provided a good

---

[15]John Lintner, "Distribution of Income of Corporations Among Dividends, Retained Earnings, and Taxes," *American Economic Review* 46 (May 1956): 97–113.

[16]Keith V. Smith, "Increasing-Stream Hypothesis of Corporate Dividend Policy," *California Management Review* 15 (Fall 1971): 56–64.

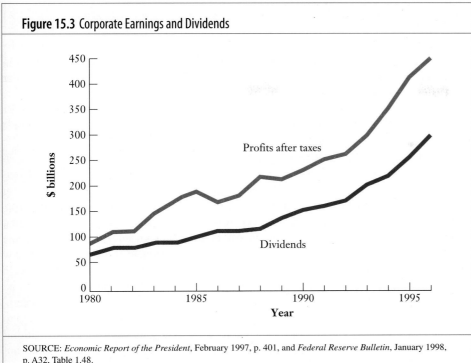

Figure 15.3 Corporate Earnings and Dividends

SOURCE: *Economic Report of the President*, February 1997, p. 401, and *Federal Reserve Bulletin*, January 1998, p. A32, Table 1.48.

example of what we have called a "stable dividend policy." During this period, the firm maintained a stable dollar dividend of $1.40 per share, whereas the payout ratio varied from 80.5 percent to 101.0 percent.

But when company policies changed dramatically, so did the associated dividend variables. The absolute dollar amount of the cash dividend per share was lowered to $0.50 in 1996 and the accompanying payout ratio fell to 20.7 percent. Importantly, the firm's total return to investors was a robust 30.9 percent during 1996, compared to its ten-year average of 16.4 percent. The market liked the change in dividend policy. So, although firms may be reluctant to change their dividend policies, with good planning and proper information dissemination it is possible to convince the financial markets that such a new direction might be good for investors.

Table 15.5 Earnings per Share, Dividends per Share and the Dividend Payout Ratio
W. R. Grace & Co., 1992–1996

Year	Earnings per share[a]	Dividends per Share	Payout Ratio
1992	$1.70	$1.40	82.3%
1993	1.39	1.40	101.0
1994	1.74	1.40	80.5
1995	2.14	1.175	54.9
1996	2.41	0.50	20.7

[a]This series represents earnings from continuing operations, but before special items.

SOURCE: Basic data from W. R. Grace & Co., *Annual Report* (1996), 55.

DIVIDEND PAYMENT PROCEDURES

After the firm's dividend policy has been structured, several procedural details must be arranged. For instance, how frequently are dividend payments to be made? If a stockholder sells the shares during the year, who is entitled to the dividend? To answer these questions, we need to understand dividend payment procedures.

Generally, companies pay dividends on a quarterly basis. To illustrate, IBM pays $1 per share in annual dividends. However, the firm actually issues a $.25 dividend for a total yearly dividend of $1 ($.25 × 4 quarters).

The final approval of a dividend payment comes from the board of directors. As an example, Abbot Labs, on December 12, 1994, announced that holders of record as of January 13, 1995 would receive a $.19 dividend. The dividend payment was to be made on February 15. December 12 is the **declaration date**—the date when the dividend is formally declared by the board of directors. The **date of record**, January 13, designates when the stock transfer books are to be closed. Investors shown to own stock on this date receive the dividend. If a notification of a transfer is recorded subsequent to January 13, the new owner is not entitled to the dividend. However, a problem could develop if the stock were sold on January 12, one day prior to the record date. Time would not permit the sale to be reflected on the stockholder list by the January 13 date of record. To avoid this problem, stock brokerage companies have uniformly decided to terminate the right of ownership to the dividend 2 working days prior to the record date. This prior date is the **ex-dividend date**. Therefore, any acquirer of Abbot Labs stock on January 11 or thereafter does not receive the dividend. Finally, the company mails the dividend check to each investor on February 15, the **payment date**. These events may be diagrammed as follows:

Declaration date

The date upon which a dividend is formally declared by the board of directors.

Date of record

Date at which the stock transfer books are to be closed for determining which investor is to receive the next dividend payment.

Ex-dividend date

The date upon which stock brokerage companies have uniformly decided to terminate the right of ownership to the dividend, which is 4 days prior to the record date.

Payment date

The date on which the company mails a dividend check to each investor.

Announcement Date	Ex-dividend Date	Record Date	Payment Date
December 12	January 11	January 13	February 15

STOCK DIVIDENDS AND STOCK SPLITS

An integral part of dividend policy is the use of **stock dividends** and **stock splits**. Both involve issuing new shares of stock on a pro rata basis to the current shareholders, while the firm's assets, its earnings, and the risk assumed and the investor's percentage of ownership in the company remain unchanged. The only *definite* result from either a stock dividend or stock split is the increase in the number of shares of stock outstanding.

To illustrate the effect of a stock dividend, assume that the Katie Corporation has 100,000 shares outstanding.[17] The firm's after-tax profits are $500,000, or $5 in earnings per share. At present, the company's stock is selling at a price/earnings multiple of 10, or $50 per share. Management is planning to issue a 20 percent stock dividend, so that a stockholder owning 10 shares would receive two additional shares. We might immediately conclude that this investor is being given an asset (two shares of stock) worth $100; consequently, his or her personal worth should increase by $100. This conclusion is erroneous. The firm will be issuing 20,000 new shares (100,000 shares × 20 percent). Because the $500,000 in after-tax profits does not change, the new earnings per share will be $4.167 ($500,000 ÷ 120,000 shares). If the price/earnings multiple remains at 10,

Stock dividend

A distribution of shares of up to 25 percent of the number of shares currently outstanding, issued on a pro rata basis to the current stockholders.

Stock split

A stock dividend exceeding 25 percent of the number of shares currently outstanding.

---

[17]The logic of this illustration is equally applicable to a *stock split*.

Table 15.6 L. Bernard Corporation Balance Sheet Before Stock Dividend	
Common stock	
Par value (1,000,000 shares outstanding; $2 par value)	$ 2,000,000
Paid-in capital	8,000,000
Retained earnings	15,000,000
Total equity	$25,000,000

the market price of the stock after the dividend should fall to $41.67 ($4.167 earnings per share × 10). The investor now owns 12 shares worth $41.67, which provides a $500 total value; thus he or she is neither better nor worse off than before the stock dividend.

This example may make us wonder why a corporation would even bother with a stock dividend or stock split if no one benefits. However, before we study the rationale for such distributions, we should understand the differences between a stock split and a stock dividend.

Stock Dividend versus Stock Split

The only difference between a stock dividend and a stock split relates to their respective accounting treatment. Stated differently, *there is absolutely no difference on an economic basis between a stock dividend and a stock split*. Both represent a proportionate distribution of additional shares to the present stockholders. However, *for accounting purposes*, the stock split has been defined as a stock dividend exceeding 25 percent.[18] Thus a stock dividend is arbitrarily defined as a distribution of shares up to 25 percent of the number of shares currently outstanding.

The accounting treatment for a stock dividend requires the issuing firm to capitalize the "market value" of the dividend. In other words, the dollar amount of the dividend is transferred from retained earnings to the capital accounts (par and paid-in capital). This procedure may best be explained by an example. Assume that the L. Bernard Corporation is preparing to issue a 15 percent stock dividend. Table 15.6 presents the equity portion of the firm's balance sheet prior to the distribution. The market price for the stock has been $14. Thus the 15 percent stock dividend increases the number of shares by 150,000 (1,000,000 shares × 15 percent). The "market value" of this increase is $2,100,000 (150,000 shares × $14 market price). To record this transaction, $2,100,000 would be transferred from retained earnings, resulting in a $300,000 increase in total par value (150,000 shares × $2 par value) and a $1,800,000 increment to paid-in capital. The $1,800,000 is the residual difference between $2,100,000 and $300,000. Table 15.7 shows the revised balance sheet.

What if the management of L. Bernard Corporation changed the plan and decided to split the stock two for one? In other words, a *100 percent increase* in the number of shares would result. In accounting for the split, the changes to be recorded are (1) the increase in the number of shares and (2) the decrease in the per-share par value from $2 to $1. The dollar amounts of each account do not change. Table 15.8 reveals the new balance sheet.

Thus for a stock dividend, an amount equal to the market value of the stock dividend is transferred from retained earnings to the capital stock accounts. When stock is split,

---

[18]The 25 percent standard applies only to corporations listed on the New York Stock Exchange. The American Institute of Certified Public Accountants states that a stock dividend greater than 20 or 25 percent is for all practical purposes a stock split.

Table 15.7 L. Bernard Corporation Balance Sheet After Stock Dividend

Common stock	
Par value (1,150,000 shares outstanding; $2 par value)	$ 2,300,000
Paid-in capital	9,800,000
Retained earnings	12,900,000
Total equity	$25,000,000

Table 15.8 L. Bernard Corporation Balance Sheet After Stock Split

Common stock	
Par value (2,000,000 shares outstanding; $1 par value)	$ 2,000,000
Paid-in capital	8,000,000
Retained earnings	15,000,000
Total equity	$25,000,000

only the number of shares changes, and the par value of each share is decreased proportionately. Despite this dissimilarity in accounting treatment, remember that no real economic difference exists between a split and a dividend.

Rationale for a Stock Dividend or Split

Although *stock* dividends and splits occur far less frequently than *cash* dividends, a significant number of companies choose to use these share distributions either with or in lieu of cash dividends. Because no economic benefit results, how do corporations justify these distributions?

Proponents of stock dividends and splits frequently maintain that stockholders receive a key benefit because the price of the stock will not fall precisely in proportion to the share increase. For a two-for-one split, the price of the stock might not decrease a full 50 percent, and the stockholder is left with a higher total value. There are two perceived reasons for this disequilibrium. First, many financial executives believe that an optimal price range exists. Within this range the total market value of the common stockholders is thought to be maximized. As the price exceeds this range, fewer investors can purchase the stock, thereby restraining the demand. Consequently, downward pressure is placed on its price. The second explanation relates to the *information content* of the dividend-split announcement. Stock dividends and splits have generally been associated with companies with growing earnings. The announcement of a stock dividend or split has therefore been perceived as favorable news. The empirical evidence, however, fails to verify these conclusions. Most studies indicate that investors are perceptive in identifying the true meaning of a share distribution. If the stock dividend or split is not accompanied by a positive trend in earnings and increases in cash dividends, price increases surrounding the stock dividend or split are insignificant.[19] Therefore, we should be suspicious of the assertion that a stock dividend or split can help increase the investors' worth.

A second reason for stock dividends or splits is the conservation of corporate cash. If a company is encountering cash problems, it may substitute a stock dividend for a cash

---

[19]See James A. Millar and Bruce D. Fielitz, "Stock Split and Stock-Dividend Decisions," *Financial Management* (Winter 1973): 35–45; and Eugene Fama, Lawrence Fisher, Michael Jensen, and Richard Roll, "The Adjustment of Stock Prices to New Information," *International Economic Review* (February 1969): 1–21.

dividend. However, as before, investors will probably look beyond the dividend to ascertain the underlying reason for conserving cash. If the stock dividend is an effort to conserve cash for attractive investment opportunities, the shareholder may bid up the stock price. If the move to conserve cash relates to financial difficulties within the firm, the market price will most likely react adversely.

STOCK REPURCHASES

OBJECTIVE 7

For well over three decades, corporate managements have been active in repurchasing their own equity securities. Several reasons have been given for a firm repurchasing its own stock. Examples of such benefits include:

1. Means for providing an internal investment opportunity
2. Approach for modifying the firm's capital structure
3. Favorable impact on earnings per share
4. Elimination of a minority ownership group of stockholders
5. Minimization of dilution in earnings per share associated with mergers and options
6. Reduction in the firm's costs associated with servicing small stockholders

Also, from the shareholders' perspective, a **stock repurchase**, as opposed to a cash dividend, has a potential tax advantage.

Stock repurchase (stock buyback)

The repurchase of common stock by the issuing firm for any of a variety of reasons resulting in a reduction of shares outstanding.

Share Repurchase as a Dividend Decision

Clearly, the payment of a common stock dividend is the conventional method for distributing a firm's profits to its owners. However, it need not be the only way. Another approach is to repurchase the firm's stock. The concept may best be explained by an example.

EXAMPLE

Telink, Inc., is planning to pay $4 million ($4 per share) in dividends to its common stockholders. The following earnings and market price information is provided for Telink:

Net income	$7,500,000
Number of shares	1,000,000
Earnings per share	$ 7.50
Price/earnings ratio	8
Expected market price per share after proposed dividend payment	$ 60

In a recent meeting, several board members, who are also major stockholders, questioned the need for a dividend payment. They maintain that they do not need the income, so why not allow the firm to retain the funds for future investments? In response, management contends that the available investments are not sufficiently profitable to justify retention of the income. That is, the investors' required rates of return exceed the expected rates of return that could be earned with the additional $4 million in investments.

Because management opposes the idea of retaining the profits for investment purposes, one of the firm's directors has suggested that the $4 million be used to repurchase the company's stock. In this way, the value of the stock should increase. This result may be demonstrated as follows:

1. Assume that shares are repurchased by the firm at the $60 market price (ex-dividend price) plus the contemplated $4 dividend per share, or for $64 per share.
2. Given a $64 price, 62,500 shares would be repurchased ($4 million ÷ $64 price).
3. If net income is not reduced, but the number of shares declines as a result of the share repurchase, earnings per share would increase from $7.50 to $8, computed as follows:

$$\text{earnings per share} = \text{net income/outstanding shares}$$
$$\text{(before repurchase)} = \$7,500,000/1,000,000$$
$$= \$7.50$$
$$\text{(after repurchase)} = \$7,500,000/(1,000,000 - 62,500)$$
$$= \$8$$

4. Assuming that the price/earnings ratio remains at 8, the new price after the repurchase would be $64, up from $60, where the increase exactly equals the amount of the dividend forgone.

In this example, Telink's stockholders are essentially provided the same value, whether a dividend is paid or stock is repurchased. If management pays a dividend, the investor will have a stock valued at $60 plus $4 received from the dividend. Conversely, if stock is repurchased in lieu of the dividend, the stock will be worth $64. These results were based upon assuming (1) the stock is being repurchased at the exact $64 price, (2) the $7,500,000 net income is unaffected by the repurchase, and (3) the price/earnings ratio of 8 does not change after the repurchase. Given these assumptions, however, the stock repurchase serves as a perfect substitute for the dividend payment to the stockholders.

The Investor's Choice

Given the choice between a stock repurchase and a dividend payment, which would an investor prefer? In perfect markets, where there are no taxes, no commissions when buying and selling stock, and no informational content assigned to a dividend, the investor would be indifferent with regard to the choices. The investor could create a dividend stream by selling stock when income is needed.

Because market imperfections do exist, the investor may have a preference for one of the two methods of distributing the corporate income. First, the firm may have to pay too high a price for the repurchased stock, which is to the detriment of the remaining stockholders. If a relatively large number of shares are being bought, the price may be bid up too high, only to fall after the repurchase operation. Second, as a result of the repurchase, the market may perceive the riskiness of the corporation as increasing, which would lower the price/earnings ratio and the value of the stock.

Financing or Investment Decision

Repurchasing stock when the firm has excess cash may be regarded as a dividend decision. However, a stock repurchase may also be viewed as a financing decision. By issuing debt and then repurchasing stock, a firm can immediately alter its debt-equity mix toward a higher proportion of debt. Rather than choosing how to distribute cash to the stockholders, management is using a stock repurchase as a means to change the corporation's capital structure.

In addition to dividend and financing decisions, many managers consider a stock repurchase an investment decision. When equity prices are depressed in the marketplace,

THE WALL STREET JOURNAL, SEPTEMBER 2, 1993

Many Concerns Use Excess Cash to Repurchase Their Shares

Stock buybacks are back. Faced with the prospect of only modest economic growth, many companies are using excess cash to buy their own shares rather than build new plants.

Consider the case of Mattel Inc., the El Segundo, Calif, toy maker. It just announced plans to buy 10 million shares during the next four years, even though its stock, 24 3/8, is selling at a healthy 16.6 times its past twelve month earnings. The reason: Plant capacity is sufficient to handle current sales growth of 10 percent to 12 percent yearly and excess cash is building up at the rate of $200 million a year.

(A) "We don't need the cash to grow so we've decided to give it back," says James Eskridge, Mattel's chief financial officer. Actually, Mattel plans to use about half of the $200 million each year for buybacks and dividends and the rest for growth.

The effect [of a stock repurchase] on individual stocks can be significant, says Robert Giordano, director of economic research at Goldman Sachs & Co.

(B) A case in point is General Dynamics Corp., which last summer began selling some divisions and using the proceeds to buy its stock when shares were trading at about $65 each. After nearly $1 billion in buybacks, the stock has gained about 37 percent, closing yesterday at 89 1/2.

"The market reacts positively to purchases, and it appreciates a firm that does not squander excess cash," says Columbia Business School professor Gailen Hite.

(C) Some of the buybacks have come from companies whose stock prices have been hurt. Drug makers, for example, have seen their stocks pummeled by fears that health-care reform will sap profits. As a result, pharmaceutical companies have been big players in the buyback game.

But economists and analysts are much more intrigued by companies that are awash in cash, thanks to improving sales and several years of cost cutting and debt reduction. At this stage of an economic recovery, many such companies would be investing heavily in plant and equipment. Not this time.

"Companies are throwing off more cash than they can ever hope to invest in plant, equipment, or inventories," says Charles Clough, chief investment strategist for Merrill Lynch Capital Markets. Companies already have pared down debt, and now they're turning to buy back their equity, he says. His prediction: "He who shrinks his balance sheet the fastest will win in the '90s."

SOURCE: Leslie Schism, "Many Concerns Use Excess Cash to Repurchase Their Shares," *The Wall Street Journal* (September 2, 1993): C1, C10. Reprinted by permission of *The Wall Street Journal*, © 1993 by Dow Jones & Co., Inc. All Rights Reserved Worldwide.

Analysis and Implications ...

A. Mattel is a good example of a firm that has used the technique of repurchasing its own shares as a way to give the shareholders a de facto dividend.

B. General Dynamics, a defense contractor, was in a declining industry where there were limited opportunities for reinvesting the firm's cash flows. GD's management could have continued to invest in missiles and other defense products, but to do so would have been disastrous given the surplus production in the industry at the time. Also, GD could have redeployed the money and invested in non-military business. Instead, management decided to give the money back to the shareholders and let them reinvest the money in other industries.

C. Here we see managers viewing the stock repurchase or buyback as in internal investment decision, which suggests that they believe the market has undervalued their shares. This logic for repurchasing shares does not have as sound a rationale as using the repurchase as a way to pay a dividend to shareholders.

management may view the firm's own stock as being materially undervalued and representing a good investment opportunity. While the firm's management may be wise to repurchase stock at unusually low prices, this decision cannot and should not be viewed in the context of an investment decision. Buying its own stock cannot provide expected returns as other investments do. No company can survive, much less prosper, by investing only in its own stock.

The Repurchase Procedure

If management intends to repurchase a block of the firm's outstanding shares, it should make this information public. All investors should be given the opportunity to work with complete information. They should be told the purpose of the repurchase, as well as the method to be used to acquire the stock.

Three methods for stock repurchase are available. First, the shares could be bought in the *market*. Here the firm acquires the stock through a stockbroker at the going market price. This approach may place an upward pressure on the stock price until the stock is acquired. Also, commissions must be paid to the stockbrokers as a fee for their services.

The second method is to make a tender offer to the firm's shareholders. A **tender offer** is a formal offer by the company to buy a specified number of shares at a predetermined and stated price. The tender price is set above the current market price in order to attract sellers. A tender offer is best when a relatively large number of shares are to be bought, because the company's intentions are clearly known and each shareholder has the opportunity to sell the stock at the tendered price.

The third and final method for repurchasing stock entails the purchase of the stock from one or more major stockholders. These purchases are made on a *negotiated basis*. Care should be taken to ensure a fair and equitable price. Otherwise, the remaining stockholders may be hurt as a result of the sale.

HOW FINANCIAL MANAGERS USE THIS MATERIAL

The Introduction to this chapter presented a definite statement from the management of Coca-Cola concerning its outlook for the firm's dividend policy that was framed within the concept of its dividend payout ratio. We learned that Coca-Cola plans to gradually reduce its payout ratio.

Coca-Cola management further has said: "We reinvest our operating cash flow principally in three ways: by pumping it back into our own business, by paying dividends, and by buying back our own stock."[20] Note that this latter use of the firm's cash flow relates to our discussion of "stock repurchases" (objective 7) towards the end of the chapter. Again, the differential tax treatment of cash dividends as opposed to capital gains can give investors a potential tax advantage when shares are repurchased. We are reminded once more of **Axiom 8: Taxes Bias Business Decisions**.

Another real example is provided by the Walt Disney Company. Recall our discussion of "Alternative Dividend Policies." Disney provides us with a concrete illustration of the stable dollar dividend per share approach in conjunction with an ongoing share repurchase program. Disney management said: "Disney paid out to its shareholders almost $1 billion through dividends and share repurchase in 1997. In January 1997, Disney's Board of Directors voted to increase the company *quarterly* dividend 20 percent from $0.11 to $0.1325 per share.[21]

---

[20]The Coca-Cola Company, *Annual Report* (1996), 27.

[21]The Walt Disney Company, *Annual Report* (1997), 18.

In February 1996, Disney common stock was trading at around $106 per share. This put the firm's annual dividend yield at a tiny 0.5 percent (i.e., $0.53/$106.0). By comparison, the dividend yield on the S&P 500 Index at that same point in time was 1.64 percent or 3.28 times that of Disney. Clearly, Disney management perceives that investors are more interested in expected capital gains than cash dividends, even if they did raise the absolute dollar value of the dividend payout.

SUMMARY

A company's dividend decision has an immediate impact upon the firm's financial mix. If the dividend payment is increased, less funds are available internally for financing investments. Consequently, if additional equity capital is needed, the company has to issue new common stock.

OBJECTIVE 1

In trying to understand the effect of the dividend policy on a firm's stock price, we must realize the following:

OBJECTIVE 2

- In perfect markets, the choice between paying or not paying a dividend does not matter. However, when we realize in the real world that there are costs of issuing stock, we have a preference to use internal equity to finance our investment opportunities. Here the dividend decision is simply a residual factor, where the dividend payment should equal the remaining internal capital after financing the equity portion of investments.
- Other market imperfections that may cause a company's dividend policy to affect the firm's stock price include: (1) the tax benefit of capital gains, (2) agency costs, (3) the clientele effect, and (4) the informational content of a given policy.

Other practical considerations that may affect a firm's dividend-payment decision include:

OBJECTIVE 3

- The firm's liquidity position
- The company's accessibility to capital markets
- Inflation rates
- Legal restrictions
- The stability of earnings
- The desire of investors to maintain control of the company

In practice, managers have generally followed one of three dividend policies:

OBJECTIVE 4

- Constant dividend payout ratio, where the percentage of dividends to earnings is held constant.
- Stable dollar dividend per share, where a relatively stable dollar dividend is maintained over time.
- Small, regular dividend plus a year-end extra, where the firm pays a small regular dollar dividend plus a year-end extra.

Of the three dividend policies, the stable dollar dividend is by far the most popular.

Generally, companies pay dividends on a quarterly basis. The final approval of a dividend payment comes from the board of directors. The critical dates in this process are as follows:

OBJECTIVE 5

- Declaration date—the date when the dividend is formally declared by the board of directors.
- Date of record—the date when the stock transfer books are to be closed to determine who owns the stock.
- Ex-dividend date—4 working days prior to the record date. After this date, the right to receive the dividend no longer goes with the stock.
- Payment date—the date the dividend check is mailed to the stockholders.

OBJECTIVE 6   Stock dividends and stock splits have been used by corporations either in lieu of or to supplement cash dividends. At the present, no empirical evidence identifies a relationship between stock dividends and splits and the market price of the stock. Yet a stock dividend or split could conceivably be used to keep the stock price within an optimal trading range. Also, if investors perceive that the stock dividend contained favorable information about the firm's operations, the price of the stock could increase.

OBJECTIVE 7   As an alternative to paying a dividend, management can repurchase stock. In perfect markets, an investor would be indifferent between receiving a dividend or a share repurchase. The investor could simply create a dividend stream by selling stock when income is needed. If, however, market imperfections exist, the investor may have a preference for one of the two methods of distributing the corporate income. A stock repurchase may also be viewed as a financing decision. By issuing debt and then repurchasing stock, a firm can immediately alter its debt-equity mix toward a higher proportion of debt. Also, many managers consider a stock repurchase an investment decision—buying the stock when they believe it to be undervalued.

GO TO:
http://www.prenhall.com/bfm
For downloads and current events
associated with this chapter

KEY TERMS

Agency costs, 585

Bird-in-the-hand dividend theory, 580

Clientele effect, 584

Constant dividend payout ratio, 592

Date of record, 594

Declaration date, 594

Dividend payout ratio, 575

Ex-dividend date, 594

Expectations theory, 586

Increasing-stream hypothesis of dividend policy, 592

Information asymmetry, 584

Payment date, 594

Perfect capital markets, 576

Residual dividend theory, 582

Small, regular dividend plus a year-end extra, 592

Stable dollar dividend per share, 592

Stock dividend, 594

Stock repurchase (stock buyback), 597

Stock split, 594

Tender offer, 600

STUDY QUESTIONS

15-1. What is meant by the term *dividend payout ratio*?

15-2. Explain the trade-off between retaining internally generated funds and paying cash dividends.

15-3. a. What are the assumptions of a perfect market?

   b. What effect does dividend policy have on the share price in a perfect market?

15-4. What is the impact of flotation costs on the financing decision?

15-5. a. What is the *residual dividend theory*?

   b. Why is this theory operational only in the long term?

15-6. Why might investors prefer capital gains to the same amount of dividend income?

15-7. What legal restrictions may limit the amount of dividends to be paid?

15-8. How does a firm's liquidity position affect the payment of dividends?

15-9. How can ownership control constrain the growth of a firm?

15-10. a. Why is a stable dollar dividend policy popular from the viewpoint of the corporation?

   b. Is it also popular with investors? Why?

15-11. Explain declaration date, date of record, and ex-dividend date.

15-12. What are the advantages of a stock split or dividend over a cash dividend?

15-13. Why would a firm repurchase its own stock?

SELF-TEST PROBLEMS

ST-1. (*Dividend Growth Rate*) Schutz, Inc., maintains a constant dividend payout ratio of 35 percent. Earnings per share last year were $8.20 and are expected to grow indefinitely at a rate of 12 percent. What will be the dividend per share this year? In 5 years?

ST-2. (*Residual Dividend Theory*) Britton Corporation is considering four investment opportunities. The required investment outlays and expected rates of return for these investments are shown on the next page. The firm's cost of capital is 14 percent. The investments are to be financed by 40 percent debt and 60 percent common equity. Internally generated funds totaling $750,000 are available for reinvestment.

    a. Which investments should be accepted? According to the residual dividend theory, what amount should be paid out in dividends?

    b. How would your answer change if the cost of capital were 10 percent?

Investment	Investment Cost	Internal Rates of Return
A	$275,000	17.50%
B	325,000	15.72
C	550,000	14.25
D	400,000	11.65

ST-3. (*Stock Split*) The debt and equity section of the Robson Corporation balance sheet follows. The current market price of the common shares is $20. Reconstruct the financial statement assuming that (a) a 15 percent stock dividend is issued, and (b) a two-for-one stock split is declared.

Robson Corporation	
Debt	$1,800,000
Common	
Par ($2 par; 100,000 shares)	200,000
Paid-in capital	400,000
Retained earnings	900,000
	$3,300,000

STUDY PROBLEMS (SET A)

15-1A. (*Dividend Policies*) The earnings for Harmony Pianos, Inc. have been predicted for the next 5 years and are listed below. There are 1 million shares outstanding. Determine the yearly dividend per share to be paid if the following policies are enacted:

    a. Constant dividend payout ratio of 40 percent.

    b. Stable dollar dividend targeted at 40 percent of the earnings over the 5-year period.

    c. Small, regular dividend of $.50 per share plus a year-end extra when the profits in any year exceed $1,500,000. The year-end extra dividend will equal 50 percent of profits exceeding $1,500,000.

Year	Profits after taxes
1	$1,000,000
2	2,000,000
3	1,600,000
4	900,000
5	3,000,000

15-2A. (*Flotation Costs and Issue Size*) Your firm needs to raise $10 million. Assuming that flotation costs are expected to be $15 per share and that the market price of the stock is $120, how many shares would have to be issued? What is the dollar size of the issue?

15-3A. (*Flotation Costs and Issue Size*) If flotation costs for a common stock issue are 18 percent, how large must the issue be so that the firm will net $5,800,000? If the stock sells for $85 per share, how many shares must be issued?

15-4A. (*Residual Dividend Theory*) Terra Cotta finances new investments by 40 percent debt and 60 percent equity. The firm needs $640,000 for financing new investments. If retained earnings available for reinvestment equal $400,000, how much money will be available for dividends in accordance with the residual dividend theory?

15-5A. (*Stock Dividend*) RCB has 2 million shares of common stock outstanding. Net income is $550,000, and the P/E ratio for the stock is 10. Management is planning a 20 percent stock dividend. What will be the price of the stock after the stock dividend? If an investor owns 100 shares prior to the stock dividend, does the total value of his or her shares change? Explain.

15-6A. (*Dividends in Perfect Markets*) The management of Harris, Inc., is considering two dividend policies for the years 1996 and 1997, 1 and 2 years away. In 1998, the management is planning to liquidate the firm. One plan would pay a dividend of $2.50 in 1996 and 1997 and a liquidating dividend of $45.75 in 1998. The alternative would be to pay out $4.25 in dividends in 1996, $4.75 in dividends in 1997, and a final dividend of $40.66 in 1998. The required rate of return for the common stockholders is 18 percent. Management is concerned about the effect of the two dividend streams on the value of the common stock.

    a. Assuming perfect markets, what would be the effect?

    b. What factors in the real world might change your conclusion reached in part (a)?

15-7A. (*Long-Term Residual Dividend Policy*) Stetson Manufacturing, Inc., has projected its investment opportunities over a 5-year planning horizon. The cost of each year's investment and the amount of internal funds available for reinvestment for that year as follows. The firm's debt-equity mix is 35 percent debt and 65 percent equity. There are currently 100,000 shares of common stock outstanding.

    a. What would be the dividend each year if the residual dividend theory were used on a year-to-year basis?

    b. What target stable dividend can Stetson establish by using the long-term residual dividend theory over the future planning horizon?

    c. Why might a residual dividend policy applied to the 5 years as opposed to individual years be preferable?

Year	Cost of Investments	Internal Funds Available for Reinvestment or for Dividends
1	$350,000	$250,000
2	475,000	450,000
3	200,000	600,000
4	980,000	650,000
5	600,000	390,000

15-8A. (*Stock Split*) You own 5 percent of the Trexco Corporation's common stock, which recently sold for $98 prior to a planned two-for-one stock split announcement. Before the split there are 25,000 shares of common stock outstanding.

    a. Relative to now, what will be your financial position after the stock split? (Assume the stock price falls proportionately.)

    b. The executive vice-president in charge of finance believes the price will only fall 40 percent after the split because she feels the price is above the optimal price range. If she is correct, what will be your net gain?

15-9A. (*Dividend Policies*) The earnings for Crystal Cargo, Inc., have been predicted for the next 5 years and follow. There are 1 million shares outstanding. Determine the yearly dividend per share to be paid if the following policies are enacted:

    a. Constant dividend payout ratio of 50 percent.

    b. Stable dollar dividend targeted at 50 percent of the earnings over the 5-year period.

    c. Small, regular dividend of $0.50 per share plus a year-end extra when the profits in any year exceed $1,500,000. The year-end extra dividend will equal 50 percent of profits exceeding $1,500,000.

Year	Profits After Taxes
1	$1,400,000
2	2,000,000
3	1,860,000
4	900,000
5	2,800,000

15-10A. (*Repurchase of Stock*) The Dunn Corporation is planning to pay dividends of $500,000. There are 250,000 shares outstanding, with an earnings per share of $5. The stock should sell for $50 after the ex-dividend date. If instead of paying a dividend, management decides to repurchase stock

    a. What should be the repurchase price?

    b. How many shares should be repurchased?

    c. What if the repurchase price is set below or above your suggested price in part (a)?

    d. If you own 100 shares, would you prefer that the company pay the dividend or repurchase stock?

15-11A. (*Flotation Costs and Issue Size*) D. Butler, Inc., needs to raise $14 million. Assuming that the market price of the firm's stock is $95 and flotation costs are 10 percent of the market price, how many shares would have to be issued? What is the dollar size of the issue?

15-12A. (*Residual Dividend Theory*) Martinez, Inc., finances new acquisitions with 70 percent debt and the rest in equity. The firm needs $1.2 million for a new acquisition. If retained earnings available for reinvestment are $450,000, how much money will be available for dividends according to the residual dividend theory?

15-13A. (*Stock Split*) You own 20 percent of Rainy Corp., which recently sold for $86 before a planned two-for-one stock split announcement. Before the split there are 80,000 shares of common stock outstanding.

    a. What is your financial position before the split, and what will it be after the stock split? (Assume the stock falls proportionately.)

    b. Your stockbroker believes the market will react positively to the split and that the price will fall only 45 percent after the split. If she is correct, what will be your net gain?

The following article appeared in the July 2, 1995, issue of the *Dallas Morning News*. Scott Burns, the author, argues the case for the importance of dividends.

Let us now praise the lowly dividend.

Insignificant to some. Small potatoes to others. An irksome sign of tax liability to many. However characterized, dividends are experiencing yet another round of defamation on Wall Street.

Why pay out dividends, the current argument goes, when a dollar of dividend can be retained as a dollar of book value that the market will value at two, three or four dollars? With the average stock now selling at more than three times book value, investors should prefer companies that retain earnings rather than pay them out, even if they do nothing more with the money than repurchase shares.

The New Wisdom

Instead, the New Wisdom says, the investor should go for companies that retain earnings, reinvest them and try to maximize shareholder value. Dividends should be avoided in the pursuit of long-term capital gains.

The only problem with this reasoning is that we've heard it before. And always at market tops.

- We heard it in the late 1960s as stock prices soared and dividend yields fell.
- We heard it again in the early '70s as investors fixated on the "Nifty Fifty" and analysts calmly projected that with growth companies yielding 1 percent or less, the most important part of the return was the certainty of 20 percent annual earnings growth.
- And we're hearing it now, with stock prices hitting new highs each day. The Standard & Poor's 500 Index, for instance, is up 19.7 percent since Dec. 31, the equivalent of more than seven years of dividends at the current yield of 2.6 percent.

Tilting the Yield

Significantly, we didn't hear that dividends were irrelevant in the late '70s, as stock valuations moved to new lows. At that time, portfolio managers talked about "yield tilt"—running a portfolio with a bias toward dividend return to offset some of the risk of continuing stock market decline. Indeed, many of the best performing funds in the late '70s were Equity-Income funds, the funds that seek above-average dividend income.

You can understand how much dividends contribute to long-term returns by taking a look at the performance of a major index, with and without dividend reinvestment. If you had invested $10,000 in the S&P's 500 Index in January 1982 and taken all dividends in cash, your original investment would have grown to $37,475 by the end of 1994.

It doesn't get much better than that.

The gain clocks a compound annual return of 10.7 percent, and total gain of $27,475. During the same period you would have collected an additional $14,244 in dividends.

Not a trivial sum, either.

In other words, during one of the biggest bull markets in history, unreinvested dividend income accounted for more than one-third of your total return.

If you had reinvested those dividends in additional stock, the final score would be even better: $60,303. The appreciation of your original investment would have been $27,475 while the growth from reinvested dividends would have been $22,828. Nearly half—45 percent—of your total return came from reinvested dividends. And this happened during a stellar period of rising stock prices.

Now consider the same investment during a period of misery. If you had invested $10,000 in the S&P's Index stocks in January 1968, your investment would have grown to only $14,073 over the next 13 years, a gain of only $4,073. During much of that time, the value of your original investment would have been less than $10,000. Dividends during the period would have totaled $7,088—substantially more than stock appreciation.

Reinvested, the same dividends would have grown to $9,705, helping your original investment grow to $23,778.

In a period of major ups and downs that many investors don't like to remember, dividends accounted for 70 percent of total return (see accompanying chart).

We could fiddle with these figures any number of ways. We could reduce the value of dividends by calculating income taxes. We could raise it by starting with the Dow Jones industrial average stocks, which tend to have higher dividends. But the point here is very simple: Whether you spend them or reinvest them, dividends are always an important part of the return on common stock.

A Close Look at Dividends in Two Markets

Anatomy of the bull market of 1982–1994

Original investment		$10,000
Gain on original investment		$27,475
Total dividends	$14,244	
Gain on reinvested dividends	$ 8,584	
Total gain from dividends		$22,828
Total		**$60,303**

Compound annualized return equals 14.8%; 45% from dividends

Anatomy of a bear market, 1968–1980

Original investment		$10,000
Gain on original investment		$ 4,073
Total dividends	$ 7,088	
Gain on reinvested dividends	$ 2,617	
Total gain from dividends		$ 9,705
Total		**$23,778**

Compound annualized return equals 6.9%; 70% from dividends.

SOURCE: Franklin/Templeton Group Hypothetical Illustration Program.

Based on your reading of this chapter, evaluate what Burns is saying. Do you agree or disagree with him? Why?

SOURCE: Scott Burns, "Those Lowly Dividends," *Dallas Morning News* (July 2, 1995): 1H. Web site www.scottburns.com.

STUDY PROBLEMS (SET B)

15-1B. (*Flotation Costs and Issue Size*) Your firm needs to raise $12 million. Assuming that flotation costs are expected to be $17 per share and that the market price of the stock is $115, how many shares would have to be issued? What is the dollar size of the issue?

15-2B. (*Flotation Costs and Issue Size*) If flotation costs for a common stock issue are 14 percent, how large must the issue be so that the firm will net $6,100,000? If the stock sells for $76 per share, how many shares must be issued?

15-3B. (*Residual Dividend Theory*) Steven Miller finances new investments by 35 percent debt and 65 percent equity. The firm needs $650,000 for financing new investments. If retained earnings available for reinvestment equal $375,000, how much money will be available for dividends in accordance with the residual dividend theory?

15-4B. (*Stock Dividend*) DCA has 2.5 million shares of common stock outstanding. Net income is $600,000, and the P/E ratio for the stock is 10. Management is planning an 18 percent stock dividend. What will be the price of the stock after the stock dividend? If an investor owns 120 shares before the stock dividend, does the total value of his or her shares change? Explain.

15-5B. (*Dividends in Perfect Markets*) The management of Montford, Inc., is considering two dividend policies for the years 1997 and 1998, 1 and 2 years away. In 1999, the management is planning to liquidate the firm. One plan would pay a dividend of $2.55 in 1997 and 1998 and a liquidating dividend of $45.60 in 1999. The alternative would be to pay out $4.35 in dividends in 1997, $4.70 in dividends in 1998, and a final dividend of $40.62 in 1999. The required rate of return for the common stockholders is 17 percent. Management is concerned about the effect of the two dividend streams on the value of the common stock.

    a. Assuming perfect markets, what would be the effect?

    b. What factors in the real world might change your conclusion reached in part (a)?

15-6B. (*Long-Term Residual Dividend Policy*) Wells Manufacturing, Inc., has projected its investment opportunities over a 5-year planning horizon. The cost of each year's investment and the amount of internal funds available for reinvestment for that year follow. The firm's debt-equity mix is 40 percent debt and 60 percent equity. There are currently 125,000 shares of common stock outstanding.

    a. What would be the dividend each year if the residual dividend theory were used on a year-to-year basis?

    b. What target stable dividend can Wells establish by using the long-term residual dividend theory over the future planning horizon?

    c. Why might a residual dividend policy applied to the 5 years as opposed to individual years be preferable?

Year	Cost of Investments	Internal Funds Available for Reinvestment or for Dividends
1	$360,000	$225,000
2	450,000	440,000
3	230,000	600,000
4	890,000	650,000
5	600,000	400,000

15-7B. (*Stock Split*) You own 8 percent of the Standlee Corporation's common stock, which most recently sold for $98 before a planned two-for-one stock split announcement. Before the split there are 30,000 shares of common stock outstanding.

    a. Relative to now, what will be your financial position after the stock split? (Assume the stock price falls proportionately.)

    b. The executive vice-president in charge of finance believes the price will only fall 45 percent after the split because she thinks the price is above the optimal price range. If she is correct, what will be your net gain?

15-8B. (*Dividend Policies*) The earnings for Carlson Cargo, Inc., have been predicted for the next 5 years and are listed below. There are 1 million shares outstanding. Determine the yearly dividend per share to be paid if the following policies are enacted:

    a. Constant dividend payout ratio of 40 percent.

    b. Stable dollar dividend targeted at 40 percent of the earnings over the 5-year period.

    c. Small, regular dividend of $0.50 per share plus a year-end extra when the profits in any year exceed $1,500,000. The year-end extra dividend will equal 50 percent of profits exceeding $1,500,000.

Year	Profits After Taxes
1	$1,500,000
2	2,000,000
3	1,750,000
4	950,000
5	2,500,000

15-9B. (*Repurchase of Stock*) The B. Phillips Corporation is planning to pay dividends of $550,000. There are 275,000 shares outstanding, with an earnings per share of $6. The stock should sell for $45 after the ex-dividend date. If instead of paying a dividend, management decides to repurchase stock

    a. What should be the repurchase price?

    b. How many shares should be repurchased?

    c. What if the repurchase price is set below or above your suggested price in part (a)?

    d. If you own 100 shares, would you prefer that the company pay the dividend or repurchase stock?

15-10B. (*Flotation Costs and Issue Size*) D. B. Fool, Inc., needs to raise $16 million. Assuming that the market price of the firm's stock is $100 and flotation costs are 12 percent of the market price, how many shares would have to be issued? What is the dollar size of the issue?

15-11B. (*Residual Dividend Theory*) Maness, Inc., finances new acquisitions with 35 percent in equity and the rest in debt. The firm needs $1.5 million for a new acquisition. If retained earnings available for reinvestment are $525,000, how much money will be available for dividends according to the residual dividend theory?

15-12B. (*Stock Split*) You own 25 percent of The Star Corporation, which recently sold for $90 before a planned two-for-one stock split announcement. Before the split there are 90,000 shares of common stock outstanding.

    a. What is your financial position before the split, and what will it be after the stock split? (Assume the stock falls proportionately.)

    b. Your stockbroker believes the market will react positively to the split and that the price will fall only 45 percent after the split. If she is correct, what will be your net gain?

SELF-TEST SOLUTIONS

SS-1. Dividend per share $= 35\% \times \$8.20$
$$= \$2.87$$

Dividends:

1 year $= \$2.87 \, (1 + 0.12)$
$$= \$3.21$$

5 years $= \$2.87 \, (1 + 0.12)^5$
$$= \$2.87 \, (1.762)$$
$$= \$5.06$$

SS-2. a. Investments A, B, and C will be accepted, requiring $1,150,000 in total financing. Therefore, 40 percent of $1,150,000 or $460,000 in new debt will be needed, and common equity will have to provide $690,000. The remainder of the $750,000 internal funds will be $60,000, which will be paid out in dividends.

b. Assuming a 10 percent cost of capital, all four investments would be accepted, requiring total financing of $1,550,000. Equity would provide 60 percent, or $930,000 of the total, which would not leave any funds to be paid out in dividends. New common would have to be issued.

SS-3. a. If a 15 percent stock dividend is issued, the financial statement would appear as follows:

Robson Corporation	
Debt	$1,800,000
Common	
Par ($2 par, 115,000 shares)	230,000
Paid-in capital	670,000
Retained earnings	600,000
	$3,300,000

b. A two-for-one split would result in a 100 percent increase in the number of shares. Because the total par value remains at $200,000, the new par value per share is $1 ($200,000 ÷ 200,000 shares). The new financial statement would be as follows:

Robson Corporation	
Debt	$1,800,000
Common	
Par ($1 par, 200,000 shares)	200,000
Paid-in capital	400,000
Retained earnings	900,000
	$3,300,000

Learning Objectives

Active Applications

World Finance

Practice

CHAPTER 16

WORKING-CAPITAL MANAGEMENT AND SHORT-TERM FINANCING

INTRODUCTION

A recent issue of Fortune *magazine noted that U. S. companies, on average, invest more than 15 cents in current assets from each $1 of sales. In 1990, American Standard fit into this mold very well with over $735 million invested in working capital. By 1993, American Standard had revenues totaling $4.2 billion but had reduced its net working capital (current assets–current liabilities) roughly in half.*

In 1990, American Standard had three primary product lines: plumbing supplies, air conditioners, and brakes for trucks and buses. The firm faced static sales and huge interest payments (the result of a $3.1 billion junk bond issue used to stave off a hostile takeover attempt by Black & Decker in 1989). To improve the firm's operating perfor-mance, its chairman, Emmanuel Kampouris, introduced a strategy aimed at reducing the firm's $735 million in net working capital to zero by 1996. This is feasible if the com-pany can reduce its inventories so low that they can be financed without borrowing. The idea is to deliver goods and bill customers more rapidly so that customer pay-ments are sufficient to pay for minimal stocks of inventories. Kampouris sought to accomplish this ambitious goal through implementation of a lean manufacturing system known as demand flow technology. Under this system, plants manufacture products as customers order them. Suppliers deliver straight to the assembly line, thus reducing stocks of parts, and plants ship the products as soon as they are completed. The system dramatically reduces inventories of both parts and finished goods. To date,

LEARNING OBJECTIVES

After reading this chapter, you should be able to

1. Define net working capital and explain its determinants.

2. Describe the risk-return trade-off involved in managing a firm's working capital.

3. List the advantages and disadvantages of using current liabilities to finance a firm's working-capital requirements.

4. Describe the hedging principle or principle of self-liquidating debt and the relevance of permanent and temporary sources of financing.

5. Calculate the effective cost of short-term credit.

6. List and describe the basic sources of short-term credit.

American Standard has reduced its inventories by more than one-half, down to $326 million since 1990. Thus American Standard invests only 5 cents out of each sales dollar in working capital compared to the norm of 15 cents. By saving interest payments on supplies, the company has increased its cash flow by $60 million a year.

CHAPTER PREVIEW

Chapter 16 is the first of three chapters that address short-term financing problems. Short-term financing decisions relate to the management of current assets which, by definition, are converted into cash within a period of 1 year or less and current liabilities, which must be repaid in 1 year or less. In contrast, capital budgeting is a long-term financing issue. We now want to look at short-term investing and financing issues. Short-term financing issues include such things as making sure that the firm has sufficient cash to pay its bills on time, managing the firm's collections of accounts receivable, extending credit to the firm's customers, and determining the proper amount and mix of short-term borrowing. Chapter 16 provides the framework for analyzing how much short-term financing the firm should use and what specific sources of short-term financing the firm should use. In chapter 17, we discuss the management of cash and marketable securities followed in chapter 18 by the discussion of managing the firm's investments in accounts receivable and inventories.

This chapter will emphasize these axioms: Axiom 1: The Risk-Return Trade-Off— We Won't Take on Additional Risk Unless We Expect to Be Compensated with Additional Return; Axiom 2: The Time Value of Money—A Dollar Received Today Is Worth More Than a Dollar Received in the Future; Axiom 3: Cash—Not Profits—Is King; and Axiom 4: Incremental Cash Flows—It's Only What Changes That Counts.

 OBJECTIVE 1

Working capital

The firm's total investment in current assets or assets which it expects to be converted into cash within a year or less.

Net working capital

The difference between the firm's current assets and its current liabilities. Frequently when the term working capital is used, it is actually intended to mean net working capital.

 OBJECTIVE 2

MANAGING CURRENT ASSETS AND LIABILITIES

Short-term financing problems arise in the management of a firm's investments in current assets (sometimes referred to as **working capital**) and its use of current liabilities. The firm's **net working capital** (which is the difference in a firm's current assets and its current liabilities) at any particular time provides a very useful summary measure of the firm's short-term financing decisions. As the firm's net working capital decreases, the firm's profitability tends to rise. However, this increase in profitability comes only at the expense of an increased risk of illiquidity. Consequently, short-term financing decisions impact a firm's net working capital and consequently entail a risk-return trade-off.

Working-Capital Management and the Risk-Return Trade-Off

Figure 16.1 illustrates the risk-return trade-off that arises in the management of a firm's net working capital. A firm can increase its net working capital by adding to its current assets relative to its current liabilities (for example, holding larger levels of inventories or marketable securities) or by decreasing its current liabilities relative to its current assets (for example, by using long-term sources of finance such as bonds rather than bank loans that must be repaid within the year).

Consider first the effects of increasing a firm's net working capital by holding larger investments in marketable securities and inventories without changing the firm's use of current liabilities. Other things remaining the same, this has the effect of increasing the firm's liquidity. That is, with the additional marketable securities, the firm has a ready source of funds should it experience an unexpected shortfall in its cash flow. In addition, the added inventories reduce the chance of production stoppages, the corresponding loss

Figure 16.1 The Risk-Return Trade-Off in Managing a Firm's Net Working Capital

	Firm Profitability	Firm Liquidity
Investing in additional marketable securities and inventories	Lower	Higher
Increasing the use of short- versus long-term sources of financing	Higher	Lower

of sales from inventory shortages. However, because these additional current asset investments earn very low returns, firm profitability is reduced.

Now consider the effects of reducing a firm's net working capital by substituting short-term financing such as notes payable that must be repaid in 1 year or less for long-term sources such as bonds. This has the net effects pointed out in Figure 16.1. The use of short-term sources such as bonds. This has the net effects pointed out in Figure 16.1. The use of short-term financing increases firm profitability for two reasons. First, short-term financing usually carries a lower rate of interest than long-term financing. In addition, when short-term sources of financing are used to finance a firm's seasonal needs for financing (such as the buildup of inventories for a retail firm prior to the Christmas season) the firm can repay the funds after the seasonal need has expired thus requiring the firm to pay interest only during the periods when the funds are needed. If long-term financing is used, the firm will end up holding excess cash during those times of the year when seasonal financing needs are zero thus incurring additional borrowing costs and reducing overall profitability.

Using short-term financing increases a firm's risk of not being able to pay its bills on time or the risk of illiquidity. This corresponds to the common sense notion that short-term financing must be repaid more frequently than long-term financing, thus exposing the firm to additional risk of having the financing come due at a time when its financial condition might make it difficult to repay the loan.

RELATE TO THE BIG PICTURE

*Working-capital decisions provide a classic example of the risk-return nature of financial decision making. Increasing the firm's net working capital (current assets less current liabilities) reduces the risk that the firm will not be able to pay its bills on time (i.e., the risk of illiquidity) but, at the same time, reduces the overall profitability of the firm. Thus working-capital decisions involve **Axiom 1: The Risk-Return Trade-Off—We Won't Take on Additional Risk Unless We Expect to Be Compensated with Additional Return**.*

Advantages of Current Liabilities: The Return

OBJECTIVE 3

Current liabilities offer the firm a more flexible source of financing than long-term liabilities or equity. They can be used to match the timing of a firm's needs for short-term financing. If, for example, a firm needs funds for a 3-month period during each year to finance a seasonal expansion in inventories, then a 3-month loan can provide substantial cost savings over a long-term loan (even if the interest rate on short-term financing should be higher). The use of long-term debt in this situation involves borrowing for the entire year rather than for the period when the funds are needed, which increases the amount of interest the firm must pay. This brings us to the second advantage generally associated with the use of short-term financing: interest cost.

In general, interest rates on short-term debt are lower than on long-term debt for a given borrower.

Disadvantages of Current Liabilities: The Risk

The use of current liabilities or short-term debt as opposed to long-term debt subjects the firm to a greater risk of illiquidity for two reasons. First, short-term debt, due to its very nature, must be repaid or rolled over more often, and so it increases the possibility that the firm's financial condition might deteriorate to a point where the needed funds might not be available.[1]

A second disadvantage of short-term debt is the uncertainty of interest costs from year to year. For example, a firm borrowing during a 6-month period each year to finance a seasonal expansion in current assets might incur a different rate of interest each year. This rate reflects the current rate of interest at the time of the loan, as well as the lender's perception of the firm's riskiness. If fixed rate long-term debt were used, the interest cost would be known for the entire period of the loan agreement.

OBJECTIVE 4

APPROPRIATE LEVEL OF WORKING CAPITAL

Managing the firm's net working capital (its liquidity) has been shown to involve simultaneous and interrelated decisions regarding investment in current assets and use of current liabilities. Fortunately, a guiding principle exists that can be used as a benchmark for the firm's working-capital policies: the **hedging principle**, or **principle of self-liquidating debt**. This principle provides a guide to the maintenance of a level of liquidity sufficient for the firm to meet its maturing obligations on time.[2]

Hedging principle or principle of self-liquidating debt

Financing maturity should follow the cash-flow-producing characteristics of the asset being financed.

> **STOP AND THINK**
>
> *In chapter 14, we discussed the firm's financing decision in terms of the choice between debt and equity sources of financing. There is, however, yet another critical dimension of the firm's financial policy. This relates to the maturity structure of the firm's debt. How should the decision be made as to whether to use short-term or current debt or longer-maturity debt? This is one of the fundamental questions addressed in this chapter and one that is critically important to the financial success of the firm. Basically, the hedging principle is one possible rule of thumb for guiding a firm's debt maturity financing decisions. This principle states that financing maturity*

---

[1]The dangers of such a policy are readily apparent in the experiences of firms that have been forced into bankruptcy. Penn Central, for example, had $80 million in short-term debt that it was unable to refinance (roll over) at the time of its bankruptcy.

[2]A value-maximizing approach to the management of the firm's liquidity involves assessing the value of the benefits derived from increasing the firm's investment in liquid assets and weighing them against the added costs to the firm's owners resulting from investing in low-yield current assets. Unfortunately, the benefits derived from increased liquidity relate to the expected costs of bankruptcy to the firm's owners, and these costs are "unmeasurable" by existing technology. Thus a "valuation" approach to liquidity management exists only in the theoretical realm.

should follow the cash-flow-producing characteristics of the asset being financed. For example, an asset that is expected to provide cash flows over an extended period such as 5 years should, in accordance with the hedging principle, be financed with debt with a pattern of similar cash flow requirements. Note that when the hedging principle is followed, the firm's debt will "self-liquidate" because the assets being financed will generate sufficient cash to retire the debt as it comes due.

HEDGING PRINCIPLE

Very simply, the hedging principle involves *matching* the cash-flow-generating characteristics of an asset with the maturity of the source of financing used to finance its acquisition. For example, a seasonal expansion in inventories, according to the hedging principle, should be financed with a short-term loan or current liability. The rationale underlying the rule is straightforward. Funds are needed for a limited period and when that time has passed, the cash needed to repay the loan will be generated by the sale of the extra inventory items. Obtaining the needed funds from a long-term source (longer than 1 year) would mean that the firm would still have the funds after the inventories they helped finance had been sold. In this case, the firm would have "excess" liquidity, which it either holds in cash or invests in low-yield marketable securities until the seasonal increase in inventories occurs again and the funds are needed. The result of all this would be an overall lowering of firm profits.

Consider an example in which a firm purchases a new conveyor belt system, which is expected to produce cash savings to the firm by eliminating the need for two laborers and, consequently, their salaries. This amounts to an annual savings of $14,000, whereas the conveyor belt costs $150,000 to install and will last 20 years. If the firm chooses to finance this asset with a 1-year note, then it will not be able to repay the loan from the $14,000 cash flow generated by the asset. In accordance with the hedging principle, the firm should finance the asset with a source of financing that more nearly matches the expected life and cash-flow-generating characteristics of the asset. In this case, a 15- to 20-year loan would be more appropriate.

Permanent and Temporary Assets

The notion of *maturity matching* in the hedging principle can be most easily understood when we think in terms of the distinction between **permanent** and **temporary asset investments** as opposed to the more traditional fixed and current asset categories. A permanent investment in an asset is an investment that the firm expects to hold for a period longer than 1 year. Note that we are referring to the period the firm plans to hold an investment, not the useful life of the asset. For example, permanent investments are made in the firm's minimum level of current assets, as well as in its fixed assets. Temporary asset investments, on the other hand, are composed of current assets that will be liquidated and not replaced within the current year. Thus some part of the firm's current assets is permanent and the remainder is temporary. For example, a seasonal increase in inventories is a temporary investment because the buildup in inventories will be eliminated when it is no longer needed.

Permanent asset investment

An investment in an asset that the firm expects to hold for the foreseeable future, whether fixed assets or current assets. For example, the minimum level of inventory the firm plans to hold for the foreseeable future is a permanent investment.

Temporary asset investment

Investments in assets that the firm plans to sell (liquidate) within a period no longer than 1 year. Although temporary investments can be made in fixed assets, this is not the usual case. Temporary investments generally are made in inventories and receivables.

Temporary, Permanent and Spontaneous Sources of Financing

Because total assets must always equal the sum of temporary, permanent, and spontaneous sources of financing, the hedging approach provides the financial manager with the basis for determining the sources of financing to use at any point.

FORTUNE AUGUST 22, 1994

Raiding a Company's Hidden Cash

Talk about stretch targets: Could any corporation operate without working capital? The answer may surprise you. A fast-growing number of companies are setting that audacious goal because pursuing it—even if they never attain it—unleashes efficiencies and savings that can dramatically improve corporate performance. In an era when global competition makes raising prices difficult and when companies need hefty cash flow to expand overseas, invest in new technologies, and pay down debt, this newly articulated discipline represents a managerial tool whose time has come.

(A) But c'mon—*zero* working capital? It isn't a fantasy. American Standard and Variety Corp., two diversified manufacturers, boast *negative* working capital in some of their businesses. At General Electric, CEO Jack Welch is making working-capital reduction a corporate crusade. Whirlpool, Quaker Oats, and Campbell Soup are driving in the same direction. Says Dennis Dammennan, GE's chief financial officer: "The concept not only generates cash, it also speeds up production, which helps you run your business far better."

Those who have been out of the game a while could perhaps use a definition about here. "Working capital is the grease that keeps the manufacturing motor running," says Harold Sirkin, a consultant with the Boston Consulting Group. It consists of inventories—raw materials, work-in process, and finished goods—as well as a company's receivables (what other companies owe it) minus its payables (what it owes other companies). On average, Fortune 500 companies use 20 cents of working capital for each dollar of sales—for all the companies on the list, a total of maybe $500 billion.

(B) Reducing working capital yields two powerful benefits. First, a dollar freed from inventories or receivables rings up a one-time $1 contribution to cash flow. Second, the quest for zero working capital permanently raises earnings. Like all capital, working capital costs money, so reducing it yields savings. In addition, cutting working capital forces companies to produce and deliver faster than the competition, enabling them to win new business and charge premium prices for filling rush orders. As inventories evaporate, warehouses disappear. Companies no longer need forklift drivers to shuttle supplies around the factory or schedulers to plan production months in advance.

Over the twelve months that ended last May, Campbell Soup pared working capital by $80 million. It used the cash to develop new products and buy companies in Britain, Australia, and other countries. But Campbell also expects to harvest an *extra* $50 million in profits over the next few years by lowering overtime, storage costs, and other expenses—savings that will persist year after year.

The most important discipline that zero working capital necessitates is speed. Many companies today produce elaborate long-term forecasts of orders. They then manufacture their product weeks or months in advance, creating big inventories; eventually they fill orders from the bulging stocks.

Where the Money Is		
	Working Capital	
Company	**In millions, as of 12/31/93**	**Per dollar of revenue**
Quaker	$ 399	$.07
Whirlpool	884	.12
Variety	361[a]	.13
American Standard	525	.14
Campbell	940	.14
Du Pont	6,222	.17
RJR Nabisco	3,041	.20[b]
GE	10,054	.27
Eastman Kodak	4,639	.28
McDonnell Douglas	4,139	.29

[a]As of 1/31/94 [b]Fortune 500 average

Minimizing working capital forces organizations to demolish that system. Scrapping forecasts, companies manufacture goods as they are ordered. The best companies start producing an auto braking system or cereal flavor after receiving an order and yet still manage to deliver just when the customer needs it.

The system, known as demand flow or demand-based management, builds on the familiar idea of just-in-time inventories but is far broader. Most companies achieve just-in-time in one or two areas. They demand daily shipments from suppliers, for example, or dispatch finished products the hour the customer wants them. But just-in-time deliveries don't guarantee efficiency. To meet the rapid schedule, many companies simply ship from huge inventories. They still manufacture weeks or months in advance.

Achieving zero working capital requires that every order and part move at maximum pace, never stopping. Orders streak from the processing department to the plant. Flexible factories manufacture each product every day. Finished goods flow from the assembly line onto waiting trucks. Manufacturers press suppliers to cut inventories as well, since minimal stocks translate into lower raw materials prices to the manufacturer. Instead of cluttering plants or warehouses, parts and products hurtle through the pipeline. As velocity rises, inventory—working capital—dwindles. That's why working capital levels are such a useful yardstick for efficiency and why, in the 1990s, manufacturers with the least working capital per dollar of sales will reign as the world's best-run companies.

SOURCE: Excerpted from Shawn Tully, "Raiding a Company's Hidden Cash," *Fortune* (August 22, 1994): 82–87. © 1994 Time Inc. All rights reserved.

Analysis and Implications . . .

A. How can a company actually have negative working capital? Simple: Current liabilities must be larger than current assets. Why do most firms have positive net working capital? The answer lies in inventories. Firms that smooth out their production in the face of seasonal or cyclical demand for their products will build up inventories when sales are down, and reduce those stocks of goods when sales expand. Thus inventories for manufacturing firms are related to production plans. What about retail firms, why do they have inventories? Part of the answer lies in the convenience of having items in stock for customers when they want it. However, manufacturers who want to maintain level production even during slack demand periods will either force or entice their retailers to purchase their product during these slack times. So, positive net working capital arises primarily out of the fact that production of goods is often times not synchronized with demand.

B. The two benefits that arise out of reducing working capital stem from the same source: the opportunity cost of money tied up in the business that is released when working capital is reduced. If a firm has net working capital of $100 million and interest rates are 10 percent, then the opportunity cost of this investment in the firm is $10 million per year.

C. How can a firm reduce its investment in working capital? If the source of inventories is a lack of synchronization between production and sales, synchronizing production and sales would reduce the need for inventories and consequently the firm's net investment in working capital. In the popular press, however, the term used to describe the synchronization process is an inventory system called "just-in-time" or "demand flow." Very simply, this means that products are produced when they are purchased and inputs are purchased only when they are needed to produce those products. Thus, instead of steady or level production throughout the ups and downs of the demand cycle, the firm engages in production only when orders are received. The result is a system of production that does not build up inventories of raw materials, work in process, or finished goods. You might ask why firms are now pursuing these dramatic reductions in working capital. The answer lies in two factors: First, the pressures of international competition has forced firms (particularly manufacturing firms) to seek out every operating efficiency. Second, the revolution in information technology now makes it possible to manage production processes much more efficiently.

Temporary sources of financing

Another term for current liabilities.

Permanent sources of financing

Sources of financing that do not mature or come due within the year, including intermediate term debt, long-term debt, preferred stock, and common stock.

Spontaneous sources of financing

Trade credit and other sources of accounts payable that arise in the firm's day-to-day operations.

Now, what constitutes a temporary, permanent, or spontaneous source of financing? **Temporary sources of financing** consist of current liabilities. Short-term notes payable constitute the most common example of a temporary source of financing. Notes payable include unsecured bank loans, commercial paper, and loans secured by accounts receivable and inventories. **Permanent sources of financing** include intermediate-term loans, long-term debt, preferred stock, and common equity.

Spontaneous sources of financing consist of trade credit and other accounts payable that arise in the firm's day-to-day operations. For example, as the firm acquires materials for its inventories, trade credit is often made available spontaneously or on demand from the firm's suppliers. Trade credit appears on the firm's balance sheet as accounts payable, and the size of the accounts payable balance varies directly with the firm's purchases of inventory items. In turn, inventory purchases are related to anticipated sales. Thus part of the financing needed by the firm is spontaneously provided in the form of trade credit.

In addition to trade credit, wages, and salaries payable, accrued interest and accrued taxes also provide valuable sources of spontaneous financing. These expenses accrue throughout the period until they are paid. For example, if a firm has a wage expense of $10,000 a week and pays its employees monthly, then its employees effectively provide financing equal to $10,000 by the end of the first week following a payday, $20,000 by the end of the second week, and so forth. Because these expenses generally arise in direct conjunction with the firm's ongoing operations, they too are referred to as *spontaneous*.

Hedging Principle: Graphic Illustration

The hedging principle can now be stated very succinctly: *Asset needs of the firm not financed by spontaneous sources should be financed in accordance with this rule: Permanent asset investments are financed with permanent sources, and temporary investments are financed with temporary sources.*

The hedging principle is depicted in Figure 16.2. Total assets are broken down into temporary and permanent asset investment categories. The firm's permanent investment in assets is financed by the use of permanent sources of financing (intermediate- and long-term debt, preferred stock, and common equity) or spontaneous sources (trade credit and other accounts payable). For illustration purposes, spontaneous sources of financing are treated as if their amount were fixed. In practice, of course, spontaneous sources of financing fluctuate with the firm's purchases and its expenditures for wages, salaries, taxes, and other items that are paid on a delayed basis. Its temporary investment in assets is financed with temporary (short-term) debt.

To summarize, note that the optimal financing mix involves the use of a combination of short- and long-term sources of financing. The particular mix according to the hedging principle relies on the nature of the firm's needs for financing. That is, the firm's assets needs.

RELATE TO THE BIG PICTURE

Although current liabilities provide financing for periods less than 1 year, the time value of money is still relevant and should be incorporated into our estimation of their cost. Thus estimating the cost of short-term credit provides yet another case where we rely on **Axiom 2: The Time Value of Money—A Dollar Received Today Is Worth More Than a Dollar Received in the Future.** *In addition, as we estimate the cost of credit, we will focus on cash received and paid. So we also rely on* **Axiom 3: Cash—Not Profits—Is King.** *Finally, we must be careful to consider all the cash flow consequences of the use of a particular source of short-term credit. In particular, we are interested in all the incremental cash inflows and outflows associated with the financing source. This reflects our use of* **Axiom 4: Incremental Cash Flows—It's Only What Changes That Counts.**

Figure 16.2 Hedging Principle: Financing Strategy

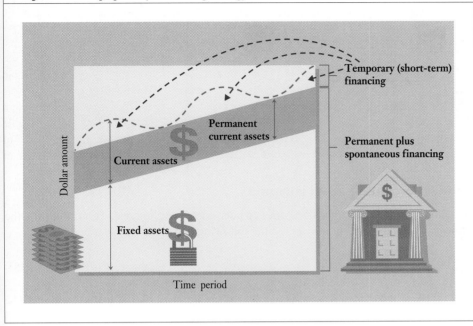

ESTIMATION OF THE COST OF SHORT-TERM CREDIT

There are a myriad of types of short-term financing sources. How is one to choose? A key factor is certainly the cost of credit.

Approximate Cost-of-Credit Formula

The procedure for estimating the cost of short-term credit is a very simple one and relies on the basic interest equation:

$$\text{interest} = \text{principal} \times \text{rate} \times \text{time} \tag{16-1}$$

where *interest* is the dollar amount of interest on a *principal* that is borrowed at some annual *rate* for a fraction of a year (represented by *time*). For example, a 6-month loan for $1,000 at 8 percent interest would require an interest payment of $40:

$$\text{interest} = \$1,000 \times .08 \times 1/2 = \$40$$

We use this basic relationship to solve for the cost of a source of short-term financing or the annual percentage rate (APR) where the interest amount, the principal sum, and the time period for financing are known. Thus solving the basic interest equation for APR produces[3]

$$\text{APR} = \frac{\text{interest}}{\text{principal} \times \text{time}} \tag{16-2}$$

or

$$\text{APR} = \frac{\text{interest}}{\text{principal}} \times \frac{1}{\text{time}}$$

---

[3]For ease of computation, we will assume a 30-day month and 360-day year in this chapter.

Annual Percentage Yield Formula

The simple APR calculation does not consider compound interest. To account for the influence of compounding, we can use the following equation:

$$\text{APY} = \left(1 + \frac{i}{m}\right)^m - 1 \tag{16-3}$$

where APY is the annual percentage yield, i is the nominal rate of interest per year (12 percent in the above example), and m is the number of compounding periods within a year [$m = 1/\text{TIME} = 1 \div (90/360) = 4$ in the preceding example]. Thus the effective rate of interest on the example problem, considering compounding, is

$$\text{APY} = \left(1 + \frac{.12}{4}\right)^4 - 1 = .126, \text{ or } 12.6\%$$

Compounding effectively raises the cost of short-term credit. Because the differences between APR and APY are usually small, we use the simple interest version of APR to compute the cost of short-term credit.

OBJECTIVE 6

SOURCES OF SHORT-TERM CREDIT

Secured and unsecured loans

Secured loans are backed by the pledge of specific assets as collateral whereas unsecured loans are only backed by the promise of the borrower to honor the loan commitment.

Short-term credit is offered by a wide variety of financial intermediaries in many different forms. For purposes of our review, we will find it useful to categorize them into two basic groups: unsecured and secured. **Unsecured loans** include all those sources that have as their security only the lender's faith in the ability of the borrower to repay the funds when due. Major sources of unsecured short-term credit include accrued wages and taxes, trade credit, unsecured bank loans, and commercial paper. **Secured loans** involve the pledge of specific assets as collateral in the event the borrower defaults in payment of principal or interest. Commercial banks, finance companies, and factors are the primary suppliers of secured credit. The principal sources of collateral are accounts receivable and inventories.

Unsecured Sources: Accrued Wages and Taxes

Because most businesses pay their employees only periodically (weekly, biweekly, or monthly), firms accrue a wages payable account that is, in essence, a loan from their employees. For example, if the wage expense for the Appleton Manufacturing Company is \$450,000 per week and it pays its employees monthly, then by the end of a 4-week month, the firm will owe its employees \$1.8 million in wages for services they have already performed during the month. Consequently, the employees finance their own efforts through waiting a full month for payment.

Similarly, firms generally make quarterly income tax payments for their estimated quarterly tax liability. This means that the firm has the use of the tax monies it owes based on quarterly profits up through the end of the quarter. In addition, the firm pays sales taxes and withholding (income) taxes for its employees on a deferred basis. The longer the period that the firm holds the tax payments, the greater the amount of financing they provide.

Note that these sources of financing *rise and fall spontaneously* with the level of firm sales. That is, as the firm's sales increase so do its labor expenses, sales taxes collected, and income taxes. Consequently, these accrued expense items provide the firm with automatic or spontaneous sources of financing.

Unsecured Sources: Trade Credit

Trade credit provides one of the most flexible sources of short-term financing available to the firm. We previously noted that trade credit is a primary source of spontaneous, or on-demand, financing. That is, trade credit arises spontaneously with the firm's purchases. To arrange for credit, the firm need only place an order with one of its suppliers. The supplier checks the firm's credit and, if it is good, sends the merchandise. The purchasing firm then pays for the goods in accordance with the supplier's credit terms.

Credit terms and cash discounts. Very often the credit terms offered with trade credit involve a cash discount for early payment. For example, a supplier might offer terms of 2/10, net 30, which means that a 2 percent discount is offered for payment within 10 days or the full amount is due in 30 days. Thus a 2 percent penalty is involved for not paying within 10 days or for delaying payment from the tenth to the thirtieth day (that is, for 20 days). The effective annual cost of not taking the cash discount can be quite severe. Using a $1 invoice amount, the effective cost of passing up the discount period using the preceding credit terms and our APR equation can be estimated:

$$\text{APR} = \frac{\$.02}{\$.98} \times \frac{1}{20/360} = .3673, \text{ or } 36.73\%$$

Note that the 2 percent cash discount is the *interest* cost of extending the payment period an *additional* 20 days. Note also that the principal amount of the credit is $.98. This amount constitutes the full principal amount as of the tenth day of the credit period, after which time the cash discount is lost. The effective cost of passing up the 2 percent discount for twenty days is quite expensive: 36.73 percent. Furthermore, once the discount period has passed, there is no reason to pay before the final due date (the thirtieth day). Table 16.1 lists the effective annual cost of alternative credit terms. Note that the cost of trade credit varies directly with the size of the cash discount and inversely with the length of time between the end of the discount period and the final due date.

Trade credit

Accounts payable that arise out of the normal course of business when the firm purchases from its suppliers who allow the firm to make payment after the delivery of the merchandise or services.

Table 16.1 Effective Rates of Interest on Selected Trade Credit Terms

Credit Terms	Effective Rate
2/10, net 60	14.69%
2/10, net 90	9.18
3/20, net 60	27.84
6/10, net 90	28.72

Stretching of trade credit. Some firms that use trade credit engage in a practice called *stretching* trade accounts. This practice involves delaying payments beyond the prescribed credit period. For example, a firm might purchase materials under credit terms of 3/10, net 60; however, when faced with a shortage of cash, the firm might extend payment to the eightieth day. Continued violation of trade terms can eventually lead to a loss of credit. However, for short periods, and at infrequent intervals, stretching may offer the firm an emergency source of short-term credit.

Advantages of trade credit. As a source of short-term financing, trade credit has a number of advantages. First, trade credit is conveniently obtained as a normal part of the firm's operations. Second, no formal agreements are generally involved in extending credit. Furthermore, the amount of credit extended expands and contracts with the needs of the firm; this is why it is classified as a spontaneous, or on-demand, source of financing.

Unsecured Sources: Bank Credit

Commercial banks provide unsecured short-term credit in two basic forms: lines of credit and transaction loans (notes payable). Maturities of both types of loans are usually 1 year or less, with rates of interest depending on the creditworthiness of the borrower and the level of interest rates in the economy as a whole.

Line of credit and revolving credit agreement

A line of credit agreement is an agreement between a firm and its banker to provide short-term financing to meet its temporary financing needs.

Revolving credit or revolver

A special type of line of credit agreement in which the line of credit is eventually converted into a term loan that requires periodic payments.

Line of credit. A **line of credit agreement** is a lending arrangement between a bank and a borrower in which the bank makes available a maximum amount of funds during a specified period of time. The actual borrowing is at the discretion of the borrowing firm and the bank usually requires that the line of credit have a zero balance for some specified period of time such as a month during each year. This requirement is designed to assure that the borrower is using the line of credit to finance working capital and not permanent asset acquisitions such as plant and equipment. **Revolving credit** or a **revolver** is a special type of line of credit agreement in which the line of agreements usually extend from 1 to 5 years in duration.

Credit terms. Lines of credit generally do not involve fixed rates of interest; instead they state that credit will be extended *at 1/2 percent over prime* or some other spread over the bank's prime rate.[4] Furthermore, the agreement usually does not spell out the specific use that will be made of the funds beyond a general statement, such as *for working-capital purposes.*

Lines of credit usually require that the borrower maintain a minimum balance in the bank throughout the loan period, called a compensating balance. This required balance (which can be stated as a percent of the line of credit or the loan amount) increases the effective cost of the loan to the borrower, unless a deposit balance equal to or greater than this balance requirement is ordinarily maintained in the bank.

EXAMPLE

M & M Beverage Company has a $300,000 line of credit that requires a compensating balance equal to 10 percent of the loan amount. The rate paid on the loan is 12 percent per annum, $200,000 is borrowed for a 6-month period, and

---

[4]The *prime rate of interest* is the rate that a bank charges its most creditworthy borrowers.

the firm does not currently have a deposit with the lending bank. The dollar cost of the loan includes the interest expense and, in addition, the opportunity cost of maintaining an idle cash balance equal to the 10 percent compensating balance. To accommodate the cost of the compensating balance requirement, assume that the added funds will have to be borrowed and simply left idle in the firm's checking account. Thus the amount actually borrowed (B) will be larger than the $200,000 needed. In fact, the needed $200,000 will constitute 90 percent of the total borrowed funds because of the 10 percent compensating balance requirement, hence $.90B = \$200,000$, such that $B = \$222,222$. Thus interest is paid on a $222,222 loan ($222,222 \times .12 \times 1/2 = \$13,333.32$) of which only $200,000 is available for use by the firm.[5] The effective annual cost of credit therefore is

$$APR = \frac{\$13,333.32}{\$200,000} \times \frac{1}{180/360} = 13.33\%$$

In the M & M Beverage Company example, the loan required the payment of principal ($222,222) plus interest ($13,333.32) at the end of the 6-month loan period. Frequently, bank loans will be made on a discount basis. That is, the loan interest will be deducted from the loan amount before the funds are transferred to the borrower. Extending the M & M Beverage Company example to consider discounted interest involves reducing the loan proceeds ($200,000) in the previous example by the amount of interest for the full 6 months ($13,333.32). The effective rate of interest on the loan is now:

$$APR = \frac{\$13,333.32}{\$200,000 - \$13,333.32} \times \frac{1}{180/360}$$

$$= .1429, \text{ or } 14.29\%$$

The effect of discounting interest raises the cost of the loan from 13.33 percent to 14.29 percent. This results from the fact that the firm pays interest on the same amount of funds as before ($222,222); however, this time it gets the use of $13,333.32 less, or $200,000 - \$13,333.32 = \$186,666.68$.

If M&M needs the use of a full $200,000, then it will have to borrow more than $222,222 to cover both the compensating balance requirement *and* the discounted interest. In fact, the firm will have to borrow some amount B such that

$$B - .10B - (.12 \times 1/2) B = \$200,000$$

$$.84B = \$200,000$$

$$B = \frac{\$200,000}{.84} = \$238,095$$

$$\text{and interest} = 0.06 \times \$238,095 = \$14,285.70$$

The cost of credit remains the same at 14.29 percent, as follows:

$$APR = \frac{\$14,285.70}{\$238,095 - \$23,810 - \$14,285.70} \times \frac{1}{180/360}$$

$$= .1429, \text{ or } 14.29\%$$

---

[5]The same answer would have been obtained by assuming a total loan of $200,000, of which only 90 percent or $180,000 was available for use by the firm; that is,

$$APR = \frac{\$12,000}{\$180,000} \times \frac{1}{180/360} = 13.33\%$$

Interest is now calculated on the $200,000 loan amount ($12,000 = \$200,000 \times 12 \times 1/2$).

Transaction Loans

Still another form of unsecured short-term bank credit can be obtained in the form of **transaction loans**. Here the loan is made for a specific purpose. This is the type of loan that most individuals associate with bank credit and is obtained by signing a promissory note.

Unsecured transaction loans are very similar to a line of credit regarding cost, term to maturity, and compensating balance requirements. In both instances, commercial banks often require that the borrower *clean up* its short-term loans for a 30- to 45-day period during the year. This means, very simply, that the borrower must be free of any bank debt for the stated period. The purpose of such a requirement is to ensure that the borrower is not using short-term bank credit to finance a part of its permanent needs for funds.

Unsecured Sources: Commercial Paper

Only the largest and most creditworthy companies are able to use **commercial paper**, which is simply a short-term *promise to pay* that is sold in the market for short-term debt securities.

The maturity of this credit source is generally 6 months or less, although some issues carry 270-day maturities. The interest rate on commercial paper is generally slightly lower (.5 percent to 1 percent) than the prime rate on commercial bank loans. Also, interest is usually discounted, although sometimes interest-bearing commercial paper is available.

New issues of commercial paper are either placed directly (sold by the issuing firm directly to the investing public) or dealer placed. Dealer placement involves the use of a commercial paper dealer, who sells the issue for the issuing firm. Many major finance companies, such as General Motors Acceptance Corporation, place their commercial paper directly. The volume of direct versus dealer placements is roughly 4 to 1 in favor of direct placements. Dealers are used primarily by industrial firms that either make infrequent use of the commercial paper market or, owing to their small size, would have difficulty placing the issue without the help of a dealer.

Several advantages accrue to the user of commercial paper:

1. **Interest rate**. Commercial paper rates are generally lower than rates on bank loans and comparable sources of short-term financing.
2. **Compensating balance requirements**. No minimum balance requirements are associated with commercial paper. However, issuing firms usually find it desirable to maintain lines of credit agreements sufficient to back up their short-term financing needs in the event that a new issue of commercial paper cannot be sold or an outstanding issue cannot be repaid when due.
3. **Amount of credit**. Commercial paper offers the firm with very large credit needs a single source for all its short-term financing. Because of loan restrictions placed on the banks by the regulatory authorities, obtaining the necessary funds from a commercial bank might require dealing with a number of institutions.[6]
4. **Prestige**. Because it is widely recognized that only the most creditworthy borrowers have access to the commercial paper market, its use signifies a firm's credit status.

Using commercial paper for short-term financing, however, involves a very important *risk*. That is, the commercial paper market is highly impersonal and denies even the most creditworthy borrower any flexibility in terms of repayment. When bank credit is used, the borrowing firm has someone with whom it can work out any temporary difficulties that might be encountered in meeting a loan deadline. This flexibility simply does not exist for the user of commercial paper.

---

[6]Member banks of the Federal Reserve System are limited to 10 percent of their total capital, surplus, and undivided profits when making loans to a single borrower. Thus when a corporate borrower's needs for financing are very large, it may have to deal with a group of participating banks to raise the needed funds.

The cost of commercial paper can be estimated using the simple effective cost-of-credit equation (APR). The key points to remember are that commercial paper interest is usually discounted and that a fee is charged if a dealer is used to place the issue. Even if a dealer is not used, the issuing firm will incur costs associated with preparing and placing the issue, and these costs must be included in estimating the cost of credit.

EXAMPLE

The EPG Mfg. Company uses commercial paper regularly to support its needs for short-term financing. The firm plans to sell $100 million in 270-day-maturity paper on which it expects to have to pay discounted interest at a rate of 12 percent per annum ($9,000,000). In addition, EPG expects to incur a cost of approximately $100,000 in dealer placement fees and other expenses of issuing the paper. The effective cost of credit to EPG can be calculated as follows:

$$\text{APR} = \frac{\$9,000,000 + \$100,000}{\$100,000,000 - \$100,000 - \$9,000,000} \times \frac{1}{270/360}$$

$$= .1335, \text{ or } 13.35\%$$

where the interest cost is calculated as $100,000,000 \times .12 \times [270/360]$ or $9,000,000 plus the $100,000 dealer placement fee. Thus the effective cost of credit to EPG is 13.35 percent.

Secured Sources: Accounts Receivable Loans

Secured sources of short-term credit have certain assets of the firm pledged as collateral to secure the loan. Upon default of the loan agreement, the lender has first claim to the pledged assets in addition to its claim as a general creditor of the firm. Hence the secured credit agreement offers an added margin of safety to the lender.

Generally, a firm's receivables are among its most liquid assets. For this reason, they are considered by many lenders to be prime collateral for a secured loan. Two basic procedures can be used in arranging for financing based on receivables: pledging and factoring.

Pledging accounts receivable. Under the pledging arrangement, the borrower simply pledges accounts receivable as collateral for a loan obtained from either a commercial bank or a finance company. The amount of the loan is stated as a percent of the face value of the receivables pledged. If the firm provides the lender with a *general line* on its receivables, then all of the borrower's accounts are pledged as security for the loan. This method of pledging is simple and inexpensive. However, because the lender has no control over the quality of the receivables being pledged, it will set the maximum loan at a relatively low percent of the total face value of the accounts, generally ranging downward from a maximum of around 75 percent.

Still another approach to pledging involves the borrower's presenting specific invoices to the lender as collateral for a loan. This method is somewhat more expensive in that the lender must assess the creditworthiness of each individual account pledged; however, given this added knowledge, the lender will be willing to increase the loan as a percent of the face value of the invoices. In this case, the loan might reach as high as 85 percent or 90 percent of the face value of the pledged receivables.

Accounts receivable loans generally carry an interest 2 percent to 5 percent higher than the bank's prime lending rate. Finance companies charge an even higher rate. In addition, the lender will usually charge a handling fee stated as a percent of the face value of the receivables processed, which may be as much as 1 percent to 2 percent of the face value.

The A. B. Good Company sells electrical supplies to building contractors on terms of net 60. The firm's average monthly sales are $100,000; thus given the firm's 2-month credit terms, its average receivables balance is $200,000. The firm pledges all its receivables to a local bank, which in turn advances up to 70 percent of the face value of the receivables at 3 percent over prime and with a 1 percent processing charge on all receivables pledged. A. B. Good follows a practice of borrowing the maximum amount possible, and the current prime rate is 10 percent.

The APR of using this source of financing for a full year is computed as follows:

$$\text{APR} = \frac{\$18,200 + \$12,000}{\$140,000} \times \frac{1}{360/360} = .2157, \text{ or } 21.57\%$$

where the total dollar cost of the loan consists of both the annual interest expense (.13 × .70 × $200,000 = $18,200) and the annual processing fee (.01 × $100,000 × 12 months = $12,000). The amount extended is .70 × $200,000 = $140,000. Note that the processing charge applies to all receivables pledged. Thus the A. B. Good Company pledges $100,000 each month, or $1,200,000 during the year, a 1 percent fee must be paid, for a total annual charge of $12,000.

One more point: The lender, in addition to making advances or loans, may be providing certain credit services to the borrower. For example, the lender may provide billing and collection services. The value of these services should be considered in computing the cost of credit. In the preceding example, A. B. Good Company may save credit department expenses of $10,000 per year by pledging all its accounts and letting the lender provide those services. In this case, the cost of short-term credit is only

$$\text{APR} = \frac{\$18,200 + \$12,000 - \$10,000}{\$140,000} \times \frac{1}{360/360} = .1443, \text{ or } 14.43\%$$

The primary advantage of pledging as a source of short-term credit is the flexibility it provides the borrower. Financing is available on a continuous basis. The new accounts created through credit sales provide the collateral for the financing of new production. Furthermore, the lender may provide credit services that eliminate or at least reduce the need for similar services within the firm. The primary disadvantage associated with this method of financing is its cost, which can be relatively high compared with other sources of short-term credit, owing to the level of the interest rate charged on loans and the processing fee on pledged accounts.

Factoring

The sale of a firm's accounts receivable to a financial intermediary known as a factor.

Factoring accounts receivable. Factoring accounts receivable involves the outright sale of a firm's accounts to a financial institution, called a *factor*. A factor is a firm that acquires the receivables of other firms. The factoring institution may be a commercial finance company that engages solely in factoring receivables (known as an *old-line factor*) or it may be a commercial bank. The factor, in turn, bears the risk of collection and services the accounts for a fee. The fee is stated as a percent of the face value of all receivables factored (usually from 1 percent to 3 percent).

The factor firm typically does not make payment for factored accounts until the accounts have been collected or the credit terms have been met. Should the firm wish to receive immediate payment for factored accounts, it can borrow from the factor, using the factored accounts as collateral. The maximum loan the firm can obtain is equal to the face value of its factored accounts less the factor's fee (1 percent to 3 percent), less a reserve (6 percent to 10 percent), less the interest on the loan. For example, if $100,000 in receivables is factored, carrying 60-day credit terms, a 2 percent factor's fee, a 6 percent reserve, and interest at 1 percent per month on advances, then the maximum loan or advance the firm can receive is computed as follows:

Face amount of receivables factored	$100,000
Less: Fee (.02 × $100,000)	(2,000)
Reserve (.06 × $100,000)	(6,000)
Interest (.01 × $92,000 × 2 months)	(1,840)
Maximum advance	$ 90,160

Note that interest is discounted and calculated based on a maximum amount of funds available for advance ($92,000 = $100,000 − $2,000 − $6,000). Thus the effective cost of credit can be calculated as follows:

$$\text{APR} = \frac{\$1,840 + \$2,000}{\$90,160} \times \frac{1}{60/360}$$

$$= .2555 \text{ or } 25.55\%$$

Secured Sources: Inventory Loans

Inventory loans provide a second source of security for short-term secured credit. The amount of the loan that can be obtained depends on both the marketability and perishability of the inventory. Some items, such as raw materials (grains, oil, lumber, and chemicals), are excellent sources of collateral, because they can easily be liquidated. Other items, such as work-in-process inventories, provide very poor collateral because of their lack of marketability.

There are several methods by which inventory can be used to secure short-term financing. These include a *floating or blanket lien, chattel mortgage, field warehouse receipt*, and *terminal warehouse receipt*.

Under a *floating lien* agreement, the borrower gives the lender a lien against all its inventories. This provides the simplest but least secure form of inventory collateral. The borrowing firm maintains full control of the inventories and continues to sell and replace them as it sees fit. Obviously, this lack of control over the collateral greatly dilutes the value of this type of security to the lender.

Under a *chattel mortgage agreement*, the inventory is identified (by serial number or otherwise) in the security agreement and the borrower retains title to the inventory but cannot sell the items without the lender's consent.

Under a *field warehouse financing agreement*, inventories used as collateral are separated from the firm's other inventories and placed under the control of a third-party field warehousing firm.

The *terminal warehouse agreement* differs from the field warehouse agreement in only one respect. Here the inventories pledged as collateral are transported to a public warehouse that is physically removed from the borrower's premises. The lender has an added degree of safety or security because the inventory is totally removed from the borrower's control. Once again, the cost of this type of arrangement is increased because the warehouse firm must be paid by the borrower; in addition, the inventory must be transported to and eventually from the public warehouse.

Inventory loans

Short-term loans that are secured by the pledge of inventories. The type of pledge or security agreement varies and can include floating liens, chattel mortgage agreements, field warehouse financing agreements, and terminal warehouse agreements.

The very existence of the firm depends upon the ability of its leadership to manage the firm's working capital. Working-capital management involves managing the process of converting investments in inventories and accounts receivable into cash, which the firm can use to pay its bills as investments mature. As such, working-capital management is at the very heart of the firm's day-to-day operating environment.

The firm's management is involved daily in making decisions that will impact this cash flow cycle. New items of inventory are acquired to replace ones that have been sold or to increase the firm's available stock. The inventory may be automatically financed through the creation of accounts payable or it may require that the firm seek out another source. As the firm sells its product or service, it frequently offers credit to its customers, which allows them to pay later. All these decisions impact the firm's financial obligations (debts) and its ability to meet those obligations when due (its liquidity).

The management of the firm's working capital is closely tied to the firm's financial planning process (chapter 4). Financial planning provides the firm with a means of foreseeing its future cash needs and sources of cash. Thus the financial planning process provides a tool for preparing for the future working-capital requirements of the firm.

SUMMARY

In this chapter, we studied the determinants of a firm's investment in working capital and the factors underlying the firm's choice among various sources of short-term financing. Working capital constitutes a significant determinant of most firms' total investment, and efforts to manage the level of the firm's investment can have a substantial impact on the firm's overall profitability.

OBJECTIVE 1

Traditionally, working capital is defined as the firm's total investment in current assets. Net working capital, on the other hand, is the difference between the firm's current assets and its current liabilities.

Net working capital arises out of a firm's investments in current assets and its decisions regarding the use of current liabilities. Investments in current assets are largely determined by the nature of the firm's business (that is, whether it is a manufacturing firm or a retail establishment) and how efficiently the firm is managed (see "Raiding a Company's Hidden Cash"). A firm's use of current liabilities is a function of the availability of short-term sources of financing to the firm and management's willingness to expose itself to the risks of insolvency posed by the use of short-term as opposed to longer-term or permanent sources of financing.

OBJECTIVE 2

Managing working capital can be thought of as managing the firm's liquidity which in turn entails managing the firm's investment in current assets, and its use of current liabilities. Each of these decisions involves risk-return trade-offs. Investing in current assets reduces the risk of illiquidity because current assets (generally) can be quickly turned into cash with little loss of value should the need arise. Using short-term sources of financing increases a firm's risk of illiquidity in that these sources of financing must be renegotiated or repaid more frequently than longer-term sources of financing such as bonds and equity.

OBJECTIVE 3

The principal advantage of using current liabilities for financing working capital is that their repayment term can be matched exactly to the period for which financing is needed. On the other hand, should the period for which funding is needed be uncertain, then the firm runs the risk of not having the necessary funds available to retire the short-term financing should it come due while the firm still needs the financing. A further disadvantage of using short-term financing arises when the need for funds extends beyond the term of the financing. This creates uncertainty with respect to the cost of financing. For example, should a firm borrow using a 6-month note and discover that it needs financing for a full year, then the firm not only must engage in the renegotiation of the terms of financing (or find a new source of financing), but it also faces the uncertainty as to the cost of credit 6 months hence. If the firm had borrowed with a 1-year maturity, it may have been able to lock in the rate of interest for the full year at the time the loan was taken out.

The hedging principle provides a benchmark for managing a firm's net working capital position. Very simply, the principle involves matching the cash-flow generating characteristics of an asset with the cash flow requirements of the financing source chosen.

OBJECTIVE 4

The effective cost of short-term credit can be calculated using the annual percentage rate (APR) formula:

OBJECTIVE 5

$$APR = \frac{interest}{principal} \times \frac{1}{time}$$

In this formulation, "interest" refers to the dollar amount of interest paid for the use of a sum equal to "principal" for the fraction of a year defined by "time." If interest is compounded, then the appropriate calculation involves computing the annual percentage yield (APY) using the following formula:

$$APY = \left(1 + \frac{i}{m}\right)^{m} - 1$$

where i is the rate of interest per year and m is the number of compounding periods within a year (that is, $m = 1 \div time$).

Short-term credit can be obtained from a variety of sources and in a wide array of forms. It is helpful to categorize these sources as either secured (repayment is assured by the pledge of specific assets) or unsecured (repayment is assured only by the pledge of the borrower to repay). Unsecured sources consist primarily of accrued expenses (such as wages and taxes) and accounts payable that arise in the normal course of business. Secured sources of short-term financing are generally secured by the pledge of a highly liquid asset. Frequently, the pledged asset is a current asset such as accounts receivable or inventories.

OBJECTIVE 6

KEY TERMS

Commercial paper, 624

Factoring, 626

Hedging principle, 614

Inventory loans, 627

Line of credit, 622

Net working capital, 612

Permanent asset investment, 615

Permanent sources of financing, 618

Revolving credit or revolver, 622

Secured and unsecured loans, 620

Spontaneous sources of financing, 618

Temporary asset investment, 615

Temporary sources of financing, 618

Trade credit, 621

Working capital, 612

GO TO:
http://www.prenhall.com/bfm
For downloads and current events associated with this chapter

STUDY QUESTIONS

16-1. Define and contrast the terms *working capital* and *net working capital.*

16-2. Discuss the risk-return relationship involved in managing the firm's working capital.

16-3. What is the primary advantage and disadvantage associated with the use of short-term debt? Discuss.

16-4. Explain what is meant by the statement, "The use of current liabilities as opposed to long-term debt subjects the firm to a greater risk of illiquidity."

16-5. Define the hedging principle. How can this principle be used in the management of working capital?

16-6. Define the following terms:
  a. Permanent asset investments
  b. Temporary asset investments
  c. Permanent sources of financing
  d. Temporary sources of financing
  e. Spontaneous sources of financing

16-7. What considerations should be used in selecting a source of short-term credit? Discuss each.

16-8. How can the formula "interest = principal × rate × time" be used to estimate the effective cost of short-term credit?

16-9. How can we accommodate the effects of compounding in our calculation of the effective cost of short-term credit?

16-10. What is meant by the following trade credit terms: 2/10, net 30? 4/20, net 60? 3/15, net 45?

16-11. Define the following:
  a. Line of credit
  b. Commercial paper
  c. Compensating balance
  d. Prime rate

16-12. List and discuss four advantages of the use of commercial paper.

16-13. What risk is involved in the firm's use of commercial paper as a source of short-term credit? Discuss.

16-14. List and discuss the distinguishing features of the principal sources of secured credit based on accounts receivable.

SELF-TEST PROBLEMS

ST-1. (*Analyzing the Cost of Commercial Paper*) The Marilyn Sales Company is a wholesale machine tool broker that has gone through a recent expansion of its activities resulting in a doubling of its sales. The company has determined that it needs an additional $200 million in short-term funds to finance peak season sales during roughly 6 months of the year. Marilyn's treasurer has recommended that the firm use a commercial paper offering to raise the needed funds. Specifically, he has determined that a $200 million offering would require 10 percent interest (paid in advance or discounted) plus a $125,000 placement fee. The paper would carry a 6-month (180-day) maturity. What is the effective cost of credit?

ST-2. (*Analyzing the Cost of Short-Term Credit*) The treasurer of the Lights-a-Lot Mfg. Company is faced with three alternative bank loans. The firm wishes to select the one that minimizes its cost of credit on a $200,000 note that it plans to issue in the next 10 days. Relevant information for the three loan configurations is as follows:

a. An 18 percent rate of interest with interest paid at the end of the loan period and no compensating balance requirement.

b. A 16 percent rate of interest and a 20 percent compensating balance requirement. This loan also calls for interest to be paid at the end of the loan period.

c. A 14 percent rate of interest that is discounted plus a 20 percent compensating balance requirement.

Analyze the cost of each of these alternatives. You may assume the firm would not normally maintain any bank balance that might be used to meet the 20 percent compensating balance requirements of alternatives (b) and (c).

STUDY PROBLEMS (SET A)

16-1A. (*Liquidity and Working-Capital Policy*) The balance sheets for two firms (A and B) are as follows:

Firm A			
Cash	$ 100,000	Accounts Payable	$ 200,000
Accounts Receivable	100,000	Notes Payable	200,000
Inventories	300,000	Bonds	600,000
Net Fixed Assets	1,500,000	Common Equity	1,000,000
Total	$2,000,000	Total	$2,000,000
Firm B			
Cash	$ 150,000	Accounts Payable	$ 400,000
Accounts Receivable	50,000	Notes Payable	200,000
Inventories	300,000	Bonds	400,000
Net Fixed Assets	1,500,000	Common Equity	1,000,000
Total	$2,000,000	Total	$2,000,000

Which of the two firms follows the most aggressive working-capital policy? Why?

16-2A. (*Cost of Trade Credit*) Sage Construction Company purchases $480,000 in doors and windows from Crenshaw Doors under credit terms of 1/15, net 45. Assuming that Sage takes advantage of the cash discount by paying on day 15, answer the following questions:

a. What is Sage's average monthly payables balance? You may assume a 360-day year and that the accounts payable balance includes the gross amount owed (that is, no discount has been taken).

b. If Sage were to decide to pass up the cash discount and extend payment until the end of the credit period, what would its payable balance become?

c. What is the opportunity cost of not taking the cash discount?

16-3A. (*Estimating the Cost of Bank Credit*) Paymaster Enterprises has arranged to finance its seasonal working-capital needs with a short-term bank loan. The loan will carry a rate of 12 percent per annum with interest paid in advance (discounted). In addition, Paymaster must maintain a minimum demand deposit with the bank of 10 percent of the loan balance throughout the term of the loan. If Paymaster plans to borrow $100,000 for a period of 3 months, what is the effective cost of the bank loan?

16-4A. (*Estimating the Cost of Commercial Paper*) On February 3, Burlington Western Company plans a commercial paper issue of $20 million. The firm has never used commercial paper before but has been assured by the firm placing the issue that it will have no difficulty raising the funds. The commercial paper will carry a 270-day maturity and will require interest based on a rate of 11 percent per annum. In addition, the firm will have to pay fees totaling $200,000 in order to bring the issue to market. What is the effective cost of the commercial paper issue to Burlington Western?

16-5A. (*Cost of Trade Credit*) Calculate the effective cost of the following trade credit terms where payment is made on the net due date, using the annual percentage rate (APR) formula.

    a. 2/10, net 30

    b. 3/15, net 30

    c. 3/15, net 45

    d. 2/15, net 60

16-6A. (*Annual Percentage Yield*) Compute the cost of the trade credit terms in problem 16-5A using the compounding formula, or annual percentage yield.

16-7A. (*Cost of Short-Term Financing*) The R. Morin Construction Company needs to borrow $100,000 to help finance a new $150,000 hydraulic crane used in the firm's commercial construction business. The crane will pay for itself in 1 year. The firm is considering the following alternatives for financing its purchase:

Alternative A—The firm's bank has agreed to lend the $100,000 at a rate of 14 percent. Interest would be discounted, and a 15 percent compensating balance would be required. However, the compensating balance requirement would not be binding on R. Morin because the firm normally maintains a minimum demand deposit (checking account) balance of $25,000 in the bank.

Alternative B—The equipment dealer has agreed to finance the equipment with a 1-year loan. The $100,000 loan would require payment of principal and interest totaling $116,300 at year end.

    a. Which alternative should R. Morin select?

    b. If the bank's compensating balance requirement were to necessitate idle demand deposits equal to 15 percent of the loan, what effect would this have on the cost of the bank loan alternative?

16-8A. (*Cost of Short-Term Bank Loan*) On July 1,1998, the Southwest Forging Corporation arranged for a line of credit with the First National Bank of Dallas. The terms of the agreement called for a $100,000 maximum loan with interest set at 1 percent over prime. In addition, the firm has to maintain a 20 percent compensating balance in its demand deposit account throughout the year. The prime rate is currently 12 percent.

    a. If Southwest normally maintains a $20,000 to $30,000 balance in its checking account with FNB of Dallas, what is the effective cost of credit through the line-of-credit agreement where the maximum loan amount is used for a full year?

    b. Re-compute the effective cost of credit to Southwest if the firm will have to borrow the compensating balance and it borrows the maximum possible under the loan agreement. Again, assume the full amount of the loan is outstanding for a whole year.

16-9A. (*Cost of Commercial Paper*) Tri-State Enterprises plans to issue commercial paper for the first time in the firm's 35-year history. The firm plans to issue $500,000 in 180-day maturity notes. The paper will carry a 10 1/4 percent rate with discounted interest and will cost Tri-State $12,000 (paid in advance) to issue

    a. What is the cost of credit to Tri-State?

    b. What other factors should the company consider in analyzing the use of commercial paper?

16-10A. (*Cost of Accounts Receivable*) Johnson Enterprises, Inc., is involved in the manufacture and sale of electronic components used in small AM-FM radios. The firm needs $300,000 to finance an anticipated expansion in receivables due to increased sales. Johnson's credit terms are net 60, and its average monthly credit sales are $200,000. In general, the firm's customers pay within the credit period; thus the firm's average accounts receivable balance is $400,000.

Chuck Idol, Johnson's comptroller, approached the firm's bank with a request for a loan for the $300,000 using the firm's accounts receivable as collateral. The bank offered to make the loan at rate of 2 percent over prime plus a 1 percent processing charge on all receivables pledged ($200,000 per month). Furthermore, the bank agreed to lend up to 75 percent of the face value of the receivables pledged.

   a. Estimate the cost of the receivables loan to Johnson where the firm borrows the $300,000. The prime rate is currently 11 percent.

   b. Idol also requested a line of credit for $300,000 from the bank. The bank agreed to grant the necessary line of credit at a rate of 3 percent over prime and required a 15 percent compensating balance. Johnson currently maintains an average demand deposit of $80,000. Estimate the cost of the line of credit to Johnson.

   c. Which source of credit should Johnson select? Why?

16-11A. (*Cost of Factoring*) MDM, Inc., is considering factoring its receivables. The firm has credit sales of $400,000 per month and has an average receivables balance of $800,000 with 60-day credit terms. The factor has offered to extend credit equal to 90 percent of the receivables factored less interest on the loan at a rate of 1-1/2 percent per month. The 10 percent difference in the advance and the face value of all receivables factored consists of a 1 percent factoring fee plus a 9 percent reserve, which the factor maintains. In addition, if MDM decides to factor its receivables, it will sell them all, so that it can reduce its credit department costs by $1,500 a month.

   a. What is the cost of borrowing the maximum amount of credit available to MDM, Inc., through the factoring agreement?

   b. What considerations other than cost should be accounted for by MDM, Inc., in determining whether to enter the factoring agreement?

16-12A. (*Cost of Secured Short-Term Credit*) The Sean-Janeow Import Co. needs $500,000 for the 3-month period ending September 30, 1998. The firm has explored two possible sources of credit:

   1. S-J has arranged with its bank for a $500,000 loan secured by accounts receivable. The bank has agreed to advance S-J 80 percent of the value of its pledged receivables at a rate of 11 percent plus a 1 percent fee based on all receivables pledged. S-J's receivables average a total of $1 million throughout the year.

   2. An insurance company has agreed to lend the $500,000 at a rate of 9 percent per annum, using a loan secured by S-J's inventory of salad oil. A field warehouse agreement would be used, which would cost S-J $2,000 a month.

Which source of credit should S-J select? Explain.

16-13A. (*Cost of Short-Term Financing*) You plan to borrow $20,000 from the bank to pay for a gift shop you have just opened. The bank offers to lend you the money at 10 percent annual interest for the 6 months the funds will be needed.

   a. Calculate the effective rate of interest on the loan.

   b. In addition, the bank requires you to maintain a 15 percent compensating balance in the bank. Because you are just opening your business, you do not have a demand deposit account at the bank that can be used to meet the compensating balance requirement. This means that you will have to put 15 percent of the loan amount from your own personal money (which you had planned to use to help finance the business) in a checking account. What is the cost of the loan now?

   c. In addition to the compensating balance requirement in (b), you are told that interest will be discounted. What is the effective rate of interest on the loan now?

16-14A. (*Cost of Factoring*) A factor has agreed to lend the JVC Corporation working capital by factoring $300,000 in receivables. JVC's receivables average $100,000 per month and have a ninety-day average collection period. (Note that JVC's credit terms call for payment in 90 days and accounts receivable average $300,000 because of the 90-day average collection period.) The factor will charge 12 percent interest on any advance (1 percent per month paid in advance), will charge a 2 percent factoring fee on all receivables factored, and will maintain a 20 percent reserve. If JVC undertakes the loan, it will reduce its own credit department expenses by $2,000 per month. What is the annual effective rate of interest to JVC on the factoring arrangement? Assume that the maximum advance is taken.

STUDY PROBLEMS (SET B)

16-1B. (*Liquidity and Working-Capital Policy*) The balance sheets for two firms (A and B) are as follows:

Firm A

Cash	$ 200,000	Accounts Payable	$ 400,000
Accounts Receivable	200,000	Notes Payable	400,000
Inventories	600,000	Bonds	1,200,000
Net Fixed Assets	3,000,000	Common Equity	2,000,000
Total	$4,000,000	Total	$4,000,000

Firm B

Cash	$ 200,000	Accounts Payable	$ 600,000
Accounts Receivable	400,000	Notes Payable	400,000
Inventories	400,000	Bonds	500,000
Net Fixed Assets	3,000,000	Common Equity	2,500,000
Total	$4,000,000	Total	$4,000,000

Which of the two firms follows the most aggressive working-capital policy? Why?

16-2B. (*Cost of Trade Credit*) Clearwater Construction Company purchases $600,000 in parts and supplies under credit terms of 2/30, net 60 every year. Assuming that Clearwater takes advantage of the cash discount by paying on day 30, answer the following questions:

a. What is Clearwater's average monthly payables balance? You may assume a 360-day year and that the accounts payable balance includes the gross amount owed (that is, no discount has been taken).

b. If Clearwater were to decide to pass up the cash discount and extend payment until the end of the credit period, what would its payable balance become?

c. What is the opportunity cost of not taking the cash discount?

16-3B. (*Estimating the Cost of Bank Credit*) Dee's Christmas Trees, Inc., is evaluating options for financing its seasonal working-capital needs. A short-term loan from Liberty Bank would carry a 14 percent annual interest rate, with interest paid in advance (discounted). If this option is chosen, Dee's would also have to maintain a minimum demand deposit equal to 10 percent of the loan balance, throughout the term of the loan. If Dee's needs to borrow $125,000 for the upcoming 3 months before Christmas, what is the effective cost of the loan?

16-4B. (*Estimating the Cost of Commercial Paper*) Duro Auto Parts would like to exploit a production opportunity overseas and is seeking additional capital to finance this expansion. The company plans a commercial paper issue of $15 million on February 3, 1998. The firm has never issued commercial paper before, but has been assured by the investment banker placing the issue that it will have no difficulty raising the funds, and that this method of financing is the least expensive option, even after the $150,000 placement fee. The issue will carry a 270-day maturity and will require interest based on an annual rate of 12 percent. What is the effective cost of the commercial paper issue to Duro?

16-5B. (*Cost of Trade Credit*) Calculate the effective cost of the following trade credit terms where payment is made on the net due date.

a. 1/10, net 30

b. 2/15, net 30

c. 2/15, net 45

d. 3/15, net 60

16-6B. (*Annual Percentage Yield*) Compute the cost of the trade credit terms in problem 16-5B using the compounding formula, or annual percentage yield.

16-7B. (*Cost of Short-Term Financing*) Vitra Glass Company needs to borrow $150,000 to help finance the cost of a new $225,000 kiln to be used in the production of glass bottles. The kiln will pay for itself in 1 year, and the firm is considering the following alternatives for financing its purchase:

Alternative A—The firm's bank has agreed to lend the $150,000 at a rate of 15 percent. Interest would be discounted, and a 16 percent compensating balance would be required. However, the compensating balance requirement would not be binding on Vitra, because the firm normally maintains a minimum demand deposit (checking account) balance of $25,000 in the bank.

Alternative B—The kiln dealer has agreed to finance the equipment with a 1-year loan. The $150,000 loan would require payment of principal and interest totaling $180,000.

    a. Which alternative should Vitra select?

    b. If the bank's compensating balance requirement were to necessitate idle demand deposits equal to 16 percent of the loan, what effect would this have on the cost of the bank loan alternative?

16-8B. (*Cost of Short-Term Bank Loan*) Lola's Ice Cream recently arranged for a line of credit with the Longhorn State Bank of Dallas. The terms of the agreement called for a $100,000 maximum loan with interest set at 2.0 percent over prime. In addition, Lola's must maintain a 15 percent compensating balance in its demand deposit throughout the year. The prime rate is currently 12 percent.

    a. If Lola's normally maintains a $15,000-to-$25,000 balance in its checking account with LSB of Dallas, what is the effective cost of credit through the line-of-credit agreement where the maximum loan amount is used for a full year?

    b. Recompute the effective cost of credit to Lola's Ice Cream if the firm has to borrow the compensating balance and it borrows the maximum possible under the loan agreement. Again, assume the full amount of the loan is outstanding for a whole year.

16-9B. (*Cost of Commercial Paper*) Luft, Inc., recently acquired production rights to an innovative sailboard design but needs funds to pay for the first production run, which is expected to sell briskly. The firm plans to issue $450,000 in 180-day maturity notes. The paper will carry an 11 percent rate with discounted interest and will cost Luft $13,000 (paid in advance) to issue.

    a. What is the effective cost of credit to Luft?

    b. What other factors should the company consider in analyzing whether to issue the commercial paper?

16-10B. (*Cost of Accounts Receivable*) TLC Enterprises, Inc., is a wholesaler of toys and curios. The firm needs $400,000 to finance an anticipated expansion in receivables. TLC's credit terms are net 60, and its average monthly credit sales are $250,000. In general, TLC's customers pay within the credit period; thus the firm's average accounts receivable balance is $500,000.

Kelly Leaky, TLC's comptroller, approached the firm's bank with a request for a loan for the $400,000, using the firm's accounts receivable as collateral. The bank offered to make the loan at a rate of 2 percent over prime plus a 1 percent processing charge on all receivables pledged ($250,000 per month). Furthermore, the bank agreed to lend up to 80 percent of the face value of the receivables pledged.

    a. Estimate the cost of the receivables loan to TLC where the firm borrows the $400,000. The prime rate is currently 11 percent.

    b. Leaky also requested a line of credit for $400,000 from the bank. The bank agreed to grant the necessary line of credit at a rate of 3 percent over prime and required a 15 percent compensating balance. TLC currently maintains an average demand deposit of $100,000. Estimate the cost of the line of credit.

    c. Which source of credit should TLC select? Why?

16-11B. (*Cost of Factoring*) To increase profitability, a management consultant has suggested to the Dal Molle Fruit Company that it consider factoring its receivables. The firm has credit sales of $300,000 per month and has an average receivables balance of $600,000 with 60-day credit terms. The factor has offered to extend credit equal to 90 percent of the receivables factored less interest on the loan at a rate of 1-1/2 percent per month. The 10 percent difference in the advance and the face value of all receivables factored consists of a 1 percent factoring fee plus a 9 percent reserve, which the factor maintains. In addition, if Dal Molle decides to factor its receivables, it will sell them all, so that it can reduce its credit department costs by $1,400 a month.

    a. What is the cost of borrowing the maximum amount of credit available to Dal Molle, through the factoring agreement?

    b. What considerations other than cost should be accounted for by Dal Molle, in determining whether or not to enter the factoring agreement?

16-12B. (*Cost of Secured Short-Term Credit*) DST, Inc., a producer of inflatable river rafts, needs $400,000 over the 3-month summer season, ending September 30, 1998. The firm has explored two possible sources of credit:

    1. DST has arranged with its bank for a $400,000 loan secured by accounts receivable. The bank has agreed to advance DST 80 percent of the value of its pledged receivables at a rate of 11 percent plus a 1 percent fee based on all receivables pledged. DST's receivables average a total of $1 million year-round.

    2. An insurance company has agreed to lend the $400,000 at a rate of 9 percent per annum, using a loan secured by DST's inventory. A field warehouse agreement would be used, which would cost DST $2,000 a month.

Which source of credit would DST select? Explain.

16-13B. (*Cost of Secured Short-Term Financing*) You are considering a loan of $25,000 to finance inventories for a janitorial supply store that you plan to open. The bank offers to lend you the money at 11 percent annual interest for the 6 months the funds will be needed.

    a. Calculate the effective rate of interest on the loan.

    b. In addition, the bank requires you to maintain a 15 percent compensating balance in the bank. Because you are just opening your business, you do not have a demand deposit at the bank that can be used to meet the compensating balance requirement. This means that you will have to put 15 percent of the loan amount from your own personal money (which you had planned to use to help finance the business) in a checking account. What is the cost of the loan now?

    c. In addition to the compensating balance requirement in (b), you are told that interest will be discounted. What is the effective rate of interest on the loan now?

16-14B. (*Cost of Financing*) Tanglewood Roofing Supply, Inc., has agreed to borrow working capital by factoring $450,000 in receivables on the following terms: Tanglewood's receivables average $150,000 per month and have a 90-day average collection period (note that the firm offers 90-day credit terms and its accounts receivable average $450,000 because of the 90-day collection period). The factor will charge 13 percent interest paid in advance, will charge a 2 percent factoring fee on all receivables factored, and will maintain a 15 percent reserve. If Tanglewood undertakes the loan, it will reduce its own credit department expenses by $2,000 per month. What is the annual effective rate of interest to Tanglewood on the factoring agreement? Assume that the maximum advance is taken.

SELF-TEST SOLUTIONS

SS-1. The discounted interest cost of the commercial paper issue is calculated as follows:

Interest expense $= .10 \times \$200,000,000 \times 180/360 = \$10,000,000$

The effective cost of credit can now be calculated as follows:

$$\text{APR} = \frac{\$10,000,000 + \$125,000}{\$200,000,000 - \$125,000 - \$10,000,000} \times \frac{1}{180/360}$$

$$= .1066, \text{ or } 10.66\%$$

SS-2.

a. $APR = \dfrac{.18 \times \$200,000}{\$200,000} \times \dfrac{1}{1}$

    $= .18$ or 18%

b. $APR = \dfrac{.16 \times \$200,000}{\$200,000 - (.20 \times \$200,000)} \times \dfrac{1}{1}$

    $= .20$ or 20%

c. $APR = \dfrac{.14 \times \$200,000}{\$200,000 - (.14 \times \$200,000) - (.2 \times \$200,000)} \times \dfrac{1}{1}$

    $= .2121$ or 21.21%

Alternative (a) offers the lower cost of financing, although it carries the highest stated rate of interest. The reason for this is that there is no compensating balance requirement, and interest is not discounted for this alternative.

Learning Objectives

Active Applications

World Finance

Practice

CHAPTER 17

LEARNING OBJECTIVES

After reading this chapter, you should be able to

1. Define liquid assets.

2. Understand why a firm holds cash.

3. Explain various cash-management objectives and decisions.

4. Describe and analyze the different mechanisms for managing the firm's cash collection and disbursement procedures.

5. Determine a prudent composition for the firm's marketable securities portfolio.

CASH AND MARKETABLE SECURITIES MANAGEMENT

INTRODUCTION

At the end of fiscal year 1997, the Walt Disney Company held 0.8 percent of its total assets in the form of cash and short-term marketable securities. During 1997, this same high-profile firm generated sales revenues of $22.5 billion. Based on a 365-day year, this means Disney "produced" $61,643,836 in sales revenues each day.

If Disney could have freed up only 1 day's worth of sales and invested it in 3-month U.S. Treasury bills in 1997 yielding 4.95 percent, the firm's before-tax profits would have jumped by $3,051,370. That is a tidy sum and demonstrates why firms like to have efficient treasury management departments in place. Shareholders enjoy the added profits.

Now, if Disney's management felt that its shareholders could stand the excitement and bear a little more risk, then the freed-up cash might be invested in bank certificates of deposit (CDs) of a similar 3-month maturity. At the same time in September 1997, the CDs of major money center banks were yielding 5.60 percent to investors.

That difference of 65 basis points (i.e., 5.60 − 4.95) may not seem like much, but when put to work on an investment of over $61 million, it produces a considerable income. In this case, the increased before-tax profits would total $3.45 million. So by investing the excess cash in CDs rather than in Treasury bills, Disney's before-tax profits would be $400,000 greater (i.e., $3.45 − $3.05).

Managing the cash and marketable securities portfolio are important tasks for the financial executive. This chapter will teach you about sophisticated cash management systems and about prudent places to "park" the firm's excess cash balances so they earn a positive rate of return and are also liquid at the same time. The firm's cash manager can make an important contribution to the organization's bottom line.

CHAPTER PREVIEW

Chapter 16 introduced the concept of working-capital management. Now we will consider the various elements of the firm's working capital in some depth. This chapter and its appendix center on the formulation of financial policies for management of cash and marketable securities. We explore three major areas: (1) techniques available to management for favorably influencing cash receipts and disbursements patterns, (2) sensible investment possibilities that enable the company to productively employ excess cash balances, and (3) some straightforward models that can assist financial officers in deciding on how much cash to hold. Appendix 17A presents these models.

In this chapter, three axioms will be relevant to our study: **Axiom 1: The Risk-Return Trade-Off—We Won't Take on Additional Risk Unless We Expect to Be Compensated with Additional Returns; Axiom 2: The Time Value of Money—A Dollar Received Today Is Worth More Than a Dollar Received in the Future; and Axiom 10: Ethical Behavior Is Doing the Right Thing, and Ethical Dilemmas Are Everywhere in Finance.**

You will see the importance of these axioms throughout this chapter.

WHAT ARE LIQUID ASSETS?

OBJECTIVE 1

To begin, it will be helpful to distinguish among some terms. **Cash** is the currency and coin the firm has on hand in petty cash drawers, in cash registers, or in checking accounts at the various commercial banks where its demand deposits are maintained. These cash balances earn no return, and are therefore the least desirable mechanism for holding excess cash. **Marketable securities** are those security investments the firm can quickly convert into cash balances. Most firms in the United States tend to hold marketable securities with very short maturity periods—less than 1 year. No law, of course, dictates that instruments with longer terms to maturity must be avoided. Rather, the decision to keep the average maturity quite short is based upon some sound business reasoning, which will be discussed later. Marketable securities are also referred to as **near cash** or **near-cash assets** because they can be turned into cash in a short period of time. Taken together, cash and near cash are known as **liquid assets**.

Our emphasis in this chapter is to learn how to effectively manage the firm's cash and marketable securities investments. We begin with a review of the basic cash flow process and the motives that economic units have for holding cash balances. In recent years, the financial function of cash management has grown in stature. Now trade associations and professional certifications exist just for this function, and cash management is usually part of treasury management within the company.

Cash

Currency and coin plus demand deposit accounts.

Marketable securities

Security investments (financial assets) the firm can quickly convert to cash balances. Also known as near cash or near-cash assets.

Liquid assets

The sum of cash and marketable securities.

STOP AND THINK

It is useful to think of the firm's cash balance as a reservoir that rises with cash inflows and falls with cash outflows. Any nonfinancial firm (in other words, any company that manufactures products, such as Ford Motor Company) desires to minimize its cash balances consistent with meeting its financial obligations in a timely manner.

Holding too much cash—what analysts tend to call "excess cash"—results in a loss of profitability to the firm. The auto manufacturer, for example, is not in business to build up its cash reservoir. Rather, it wants to manage its cash balance in order to maximize its financial returns—this will enhance shareholder wealth.

Figure 17.1 The Cash Generation and Disposition Process

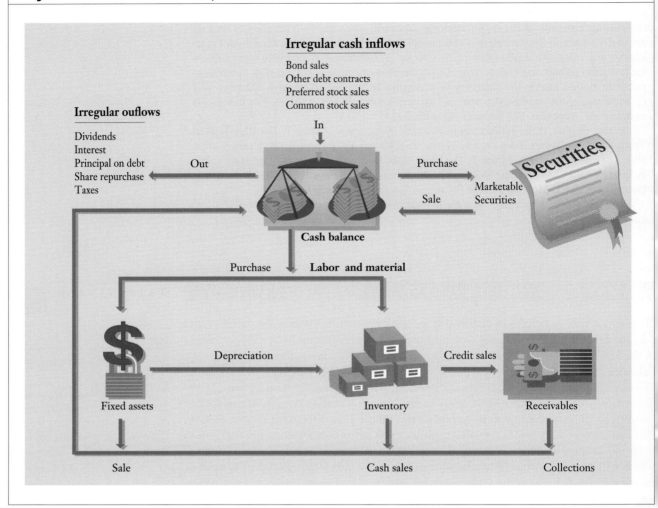

WHY A COMPANY HOLDS CASH

A thorough understanding of why and how a firm holds cash requires an accurate conception of how cash flows into and through the enterprise. Figure 17.1 depicts the process of cash generation and disposition in a typical manufacturing setting. The arrows designate the direction of the flow—that is, whether the cash balance increases or decreases.

Cash Flow Process

The firm experiences irregular increases in its cash holdings from several external sources. Funds can be obtained in the financial markets from the sale of securities, such as bonds, preferred stock, and common stock, or the firm can enter into nonmarketable debt contracts with lenders such as commercial banks. These irregular cash inflows do not occur on a daily basis. They tend to be episodic; the financing arrangements that give rise to them are effected at wide intervals. External financing contracts usually involve huge sums of money stemming from a major need identified by the company's management, and these needs do not occur every day. For example, a new product might have moved to the launching stage, or a plant expansion might be required to provide added productive capacity.

In most organizations, the financial officer responsible for cash management also controls the transactions that affect the firm's investment in marketable securities. As excess cash becomes temporarily available, marketable securities are purchased. When cash is in short supply, a portion of the marketable securities portfolio is liquidated.

Whereas the irregular cash inflows are from external sources, the other main sources of cash to the firm arise from internal operations and occur on a more regular basis. Over long periods, the largest receipts come from accounts receivable collections and, to a lesser extent, from direct cash sales of finished goods. Many manufacturing concerns also generate cash on a regular basis through the liquidation of scrap or obsolete inventory. At various times, fixed assets may also be sold, thereby generating some cash inflow. This is not a large source of funds except in unusual situations where, for instance, a complete plant renovation may be taking place.

Apart from the investment of excess cash in near-cash assets, the cash balance experiences reductions for three key reasons. First, on an irregular basis, withdrawals are made to (1) pay cash dividends on preferred and common stock shares; (2) meet interest requirements on debt contracts; (3) repay the principal borrowed from creditors; (4) buy the firm's own shares in the financial markets for use in executive compensation plans, or as an alternative to paying a cash dividend; and (5) pay tax bills. Again, by an *irregular basis*, we mean items *not* occurring on a daily or frequent schedule. Second, the company's capital expenditure program designates that fixed assets be acquired at various intervals. Third, inventories are purchased on a regular basis to ensure a steady flow of finished goods off the production line. Note that the arrow linking the investment in fixed assets with the inventory account is labeled *depreciation*. This indicates that a portion of the cost of fixed assets is charged against the products coming off the assembly line. This cost is subsequently recovered through the sale of the finished goods inventory, because the product selling price will be set by management to cover all the costs of production, including depreciation.

The variety of influences that constantly affect the cash balance held by the firm can be synthesized in terms of the classic motives for holding cash, as identified in the literature of economic theory.

Motives for Holding Cash

In a classic economic treatise, John Maynard Keynes segmented the firm's, or any economic unit's, demand for cash into three categories: (1) the transactions motive, (2) the precautionary motive, and (3) the speculative motive.[1]

Transactions motive. Balances held for transactions purposes allow the firm to meet cash needs that arise in the ordinary course of doing business. In Figure 17.1, transactions balances would be used to meet the irregular outflows as well as the planned acquisition of fixed assets and inventories.

The relative amount of cash needed to satisfy transactions requirements is affected by a number of factors, such as the industry in which the firm operates. It is well known that utilities can forecast cash receipts quite accurately, because of stable demand for their services. Computer software firms, however, have a more difficult time predicting their cash flows. New products are brought to market at a rapid pace, thereby making it difficult to project cash flows and balances very precisely.

---

[1]John Maynard Keynes, *The General Theory of Employment, Interest, and Money* (New York: Harcourt Brace Jovanovich, 1936).

The precautionary motive. Precautionary balances are a buffer stock of liquid assets. This motive for holding cash relates to the maintenance of balances to be used to satisfy possible, but as yet indefinite, needs.

In our discussion of transactions balances, we saw that cash flow predictability could affect a firm's cash holdings through synchronization of receipts and disbursements. Cash flow predictability also has a material influence on the firm's demand for cash through the precautionary motive. The airline industry provides a typical illustration. Air passenger carriers are plagued with a high degree of cash flow uncertainty. The weather, rising fuel costs, and continual strikes by operating personnel make cash forecasting difficult for any airline. The upshot of this problem is that because of all the things that *might* happen, the minimum cash balances desired by the management of the air carriers tend to be large.

In addition to cash flow predictability, the precautionary motive for holding cash is affected by access to external funds. Especially important are cash sources that can be tapped on short notice. Good banking relationships and established lines of credit can reduce the need to keep cash on hand. This unused borrowing power obviates somewhat the need to invest in precautionary balances.

In actual business practice, the precautionary motive is met to a large extent by the holding of a portfolio of *liquid assets*, not just cash. Notice in Figure 17.1 the two-way flow of funds between the company's holdings of cash and marketable securities. In large corporate organizations, funds may flow either into or out of the marketable securities portfolio on a daily basis. Because some actual rate of return can be earned on the near-cash assets, compared with a zero rate of return available on cash holdings, it is logical that investment in marketable securities will meet in part the firm's precautionary needs.

The speculative motive. Cash is held for speculative purposes in order to take advantage of potential profit-making situations. Construction firms that build private dwellings will at times accumulate cash in anticipation of a significant drop in lumber costs. If the price of building supplies does drop, the companies that built up their cash balances stand to profit by purchasing materials in large quantities. This will reduce their cost of goods sold and increase their net profit margin. Generally, the speculative motive is the least important component of a firm's preference for liquidity. The transactions and precautionary motives account for most of the reasons why a company holds cash balances.

STOP AND THINK

Any company can benefit from a properly designed cash-management system. If you identify what you believe to be a superbly run business organization, the odds are that firm has in place a sound cash-management system. Before we explore several cash-management techniques, it is necessary to introduce (1) the risk-return trade-off, (2) the objectives, and (3) the decisions that comprise the center of the cash-management process. Keep in mind that the billion-dollar company will save millions each year by grasping these concepts— whereas the small and midsized organization may actually enhance its overall chances of survival. The following section provides the rationale and structure for knowing about all of the techniques and financial instruments discussed in the remainder of the chapter.

OBJECTIVE 3 | **CASH-MANAGEMENT OBJECTIVES AND DECISIONS**

The degree to which a firm invests idle cash into marketable securities will be determined by the amount of insolvency risk the firm is willing to undergo in order to receive additional return on their cash balances. We will see that this trade-off is not easily balanced.

The Risk-Return Trade-Off

A company-wide cash management program must be concerned with minimizing the firm's risk of insolvency. In the context of cash management, the term **insolvency** describes the situation where the firm is unable to pay its bills on time. In such a case, the company is *technically insolvent* in that it lacks the necessary liquidity to make prompt payment on its current debt obligations. A firm could avoid this problem by carrying large cash balances to pay the bills that come due. Production, after all, would soon come to a halt should payments for raw material purchases be continually late or omitted entirely. The firm's suppliers would just cut off further shipments. In fact, fear of irritating a key supplier by being past due on the payment of a trade payable does cause some financial managers to invest in too much liquidity.

Insolvency

The firm is unable to pay its bills on time.

The management of the company's cash position, however, is one of those problem areas where you are criticized if you don't and criticized if you do. True, the production process will eventually be halted should too little cash be available to pay bills. But, if excessive cash balances are carried, the value of the enterprise in the financial marketplace will be suppressed because of the large cost of income forgone. The explicit return earned on idle cash balances is zero.

The financial manager must strike an acceptable balance between holding too much cash and too little cash. This is the focal point of the risk-return trade-off. A large cash investment minimizes the chances of insolvency, but penalizes company profitability. A small cash investment frees excess balances for investment in both marketable securities and longer-lived assets; this enhances company profitability and the value of the firm's common shares, but increases the chances of running out of cash.

RELATE TO THE BIG PICTURE

The dilemma faced by the financial manager is a clear example of the application of **Axiom 1: The Risk-Return Trade-Off—We Won't Take on Additional Risk Unless We Expect to Be Compensated with Additional Return.** *To accept the risk of not having sufficient cash on hand, the firm must be compensated with a return on the cash that is invested. Moreover, the greater the risk of the investment into which the cash is placed, the greater the return that the firm demands.*

The Objectives

The risk-return trade-off can be reduced to two prime objectives for the firm's cash-management system:

1. Enough cash must be on hand to meet the disbursal needs that arise in the course of doing business.
2. Investment in idle cash balances must be reduced to a minimum.

Evaluation of these operational objectives, and a conscious attempt on the part of management to meet them, gives rise to the need for some typical cash-management decisions.

The Decisions

Two conditions or ideals would allow the firm to operate for extended periods with cash balances near or at a level of zero: (1) a completely accurate forecast of net cash flows over the planning horizon and (2) perfect synchronization of cash receipts and disbursements. These ideals are *not* met in practice.

Cash flow forecasting is the initial step in any effective cash-management program. This is usually accomplished by the finance function's evaluation of data supplied by the marketing and production functions in the company. The *cash budget* is a device used to forecast the cash flows over the planning period. Here we must emphasize that the net cash flows pinpointed in the formal cash budget are only estimates, subject to considerable variation. A totally accurate cash flow projection is an ideal, not a reality.

Our discussion of the cash flow process depicted in Figure 17.1 showed that inflows and outflows are not synchronized. Some inflows and outflows are irregular; others are more continual. Some finished goods are sold directly for cash, but more likely the sales will be on account. The receivables, then, will have to be collected before a cash inflow is realized. Raw materials have to be purchased, but several suppliers are probably used, and each may have its own payment date. Further, no law of doing business fixes receivable collections to coincide with raw material payments dates. So the second criterion that would permit operation of the firm with extremely low cash balances is not met in actual practice either.

Given that the firm will, as a matter of necessity, invest in some cash balances, certain types of decisions related to the size of those balances dominate the cash-management process. These include decisions that answer the following questions:

1. What can be done to speed up cash collections and slow down or better control cash outflows?
2. What should be the composition of a marketable securities portfolio?
3. How should investment in liquid assets be split between actual cash holdings and marketable securities?

The remainder of this chapter dwells on the first two of these three questions. The third is explored in appendix 17A.

STOP AND THINK

Although the sheer number of cash collection and payment techniques is large, the concepts on which those techniques rest are quite simple. Controlling the cash inflow and outflow is a major theme of treasury management. But, within the confines of ethical management, the cash manager is always thinking (1) "How can I speed up the firm's cash receipts?" and (2) "How can I slow down the firm's cash payments and not irritate too many important constituencies—such as suppliers?"

The critical point is that cash saved becomes available for investment elsewhere in the company's operations, and at a positive rate of return this will increase total profitability. Grasping the elements of cash management requires that you understand the concept of cash "float," to which we now turn.

OBJECTIVE 4

COLLECTION AND DISBURSEMENT PROCEDURES

The efficiency of the firm's cash-management program can be enhanced by knowledge and use of various procedures aimed at (1) accelerating cash receipts and (2) improving the methods used to disburse cash. We will see that greater opportunity for corporate profit improvement lies with the cash receipts side of the funds flow process, although it would be unwise to ignore opportunities for favorably affecting cash-disbursement practices.

Managing the Cash Inflow[2]

In order to increase the speed in which we receive cash receipts, it is essential that we understand how to reduce float. **Float** is the length of time from when a check is written until the actual recipient can use the "good funds." Float (or total float) has four elements, as follows:

Float

The length of time from when a check is written until the actual recipient can draw upon or use the "good funds."

---

[2]The discussions on cash receipt and disbursement procedures draw heavily on materials that were provided by the managements of the Chase Manhattan Bank, Continental Bank, and First National Bank of Chicago.

1. **Mail float** is caused by the time lapse from the moment a customer mails a remittance check until the firm begins to process it.
2. **Processing float** is caused by the time required for the firm to process the customer's remittance checks before they can be deposited in the bank.
3. **Transit float** is caused by the time necessary for a deposited check from a customer to clear through the commercial banking system and become usable funds to the company. Credit is deferred for a maximum of two business days on checks that are cleared through the Federal Reserve System.
4. **Disbursing float** derives from the fact that the customer's funds are available in the company's bank account until the company's payment check has cleared through the banking system. Typically, funds available in the firm's banks *exceed* the balances indicated on its own books (ledgers).

We will use the term *float* to refer to the total of its four elements just described. Float reduction can yield considerable benefits in terms of usable funds that are released for company use and returns produced on such freed-up balances. As an example, for 1997, IBM reported total revenues of $79 billion. The amount of usable funds that would be released if IBM could achieve a 1-day reduction in float can be approximated by dividing annual revenues (sales) by the number of days in a year. In this case, 1 day's freed-up balances would be

$$\frac{\text{annual revenues}}{\text{days in year}} = \frac{\$79,000,000,000}{365} = \$216,438,356$$

If these released funds, which represent 1 day's sales, of approximately $216.4 million, could be invested to return 6 percent a year, then the annual value of the 1-day float reduction would almost be $13 million:

$$(\text{sales per day}) \times (\text{assumed yield}) = \$216,438,356 \times .06 = \$12,986,301$$

It is clear that effective cash management can yield impressive opportunities for profit improvement. Let us look now at specific techniques for reducing float.

The lock-box arrangement. The lock-box system is the most widely used commercial banking service for expediting cash gathering. Banks have offered this service since 1946. Such a system speeds up the conversion of receipts into usable funds by reducing both mail and processing float. Since the Federal Reserve System provides check-clearing facilities for depository institutions, it is possible to reduce transit float if lock boxes are located near Federal Reserve Banks and their branches. For large corporations that receive checks from all parts of the country, float reductions of 2 to 4 days are not unusual.

Figure 17.2 illustrates an elementary, but typical, cash collection system for a hypothetical firm. It also shows the origin of mail float, processing float, and transit float. In this system, the customer places his or her remittance check in the U.S. mail, which is then delivered to the firm's headquarters. This is mail float. On the check's arrival at the firm's headquarters (or local collection center), general accounting personnel must go through the bookkeeping procedures needed to prepare it for local deposit. The checks are then deposited. This is processing float. The checks are then forwarded for payment through the commercial bank clearing mechanism. The checks will be charged against the customer's own bank account. At this point, the checks are said to be "paid" and become "good" funds available for use by the company that received them. This bank clearing procedure represents transit float and, as we said earlier, can amount to a delay of up to two business days.

A lock-box arrangement is based on a simple procedure. The firm's customers are instructed to mail their remittance checks not to company headquarters or regional offices, but to a numbered Post Office box. This replaces step two in Figure 17.2, allowing mail to

Figure 17.2 Ordinary Cash-Gathering System

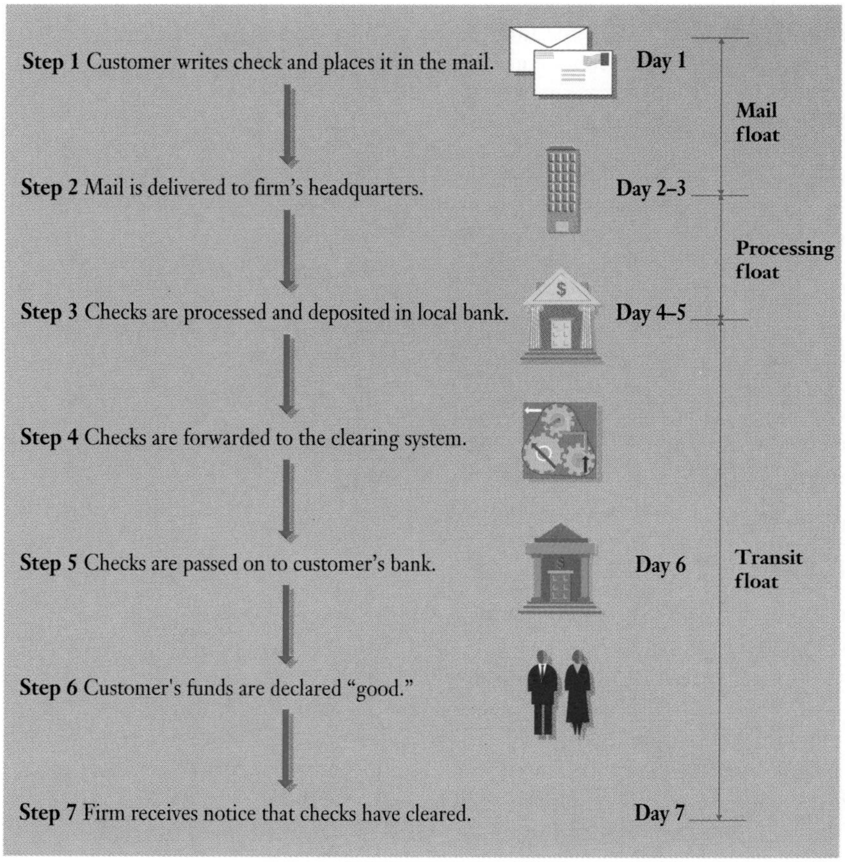

Step 1 Customer writes check and places it in the mail.	**Day 1**	**Mail float**
Step 2 Mail is delivered to firm's headquarters.	**Day 2–3**	
Step 3 Checks are processed and deposited in local bank.	**Day 4–5**	**Processing float**
Step 4 Checks are forwarded to the clearing system.		
Step 5 Checks are passed on to customer's bank.	**Day 6**	**Transit float**
Step 6 Customer's funds are declared "good."		
Step 7 Firm receives notice that checks have cleared.	**Day 7**	

travel a shorter distance and often cutting the mail float by 1 day. The bank that is providing the lock-box service is authorized to open the box, collect the mail, process the checks, and deposit the checks directly into the company's account. The bank, eliminating the processing float entirely, now performs step three functions and saves an additional 2 days. Furthermore, transit float (steps 4 to 7) can also be reduced by one day as a result of the lock-boxes being located near a Federal Reserve Bank or one of its branches.

Typically, a large bank will collect payments from the lock box at 1- to 2-hour intervals, 365 days of the year. During peak business hours, the bank may pick up mail every 30 minutes.

Once the mail is received at the bank, the checks will be examined, totaled, photocopied, and microfilmed. A deposit form is then prepared by the bank, and each batch of processed checks is forwarded to the collection department for clearance. Funds deposited in this manner are usually available for company use in one business day or less.

The same day deposits are made, the bank can notify the firm via some type of telecommunications system as to their amount. At the conclusion of each day, all check photocopies, invoices, deposit slips, and any other documents included with the remittances are mailed to the firm.

Note that the firm that receives checks from all over the country will have to use several lock boxes to take full advantage of a reduction in mail float. The firm's major bank should be able to offer as a service a detailed lock-box study, analyzing the company's receipt patterns to determine the proper number and location of lock-box receiving points.

The installation of the lock-box system can result in funds being credited to the firm's bank account a full 4 working days *faster* than is possible under the ordinary collection system.

When we first examined float, we calculated the 1997 sales per day for IBM to be $216.4 million and assumed that firm could invest its excess cash in marketable securities to yield 6 percent annually. If IBM could speed up its cash collections by 4 days the results would be startling. The gross annual savings to IBM (apart from operating the lock-box system) would amount to $49.97 million as follows:

(sales per day) × (days of float reduction) × (assumed yield)

$216,438,356 × (4) × .06 = $51,945,205

This is a large sum, which is noticed not only by the firms involved, but also by commercial banks that offer lock-box services.

In summary, the benefits of a lock-box arrangement are these:

1. **Increased working cash.** The time required for converting receivables into available funds is reduced. This frees up cash for use elsewhere in the enterprise.
2. **Elimination of clerical functions.** The bank takes over the tasks of receiving, endorsing, totaling, and depositing checks. With less handling of receipts by employees, better audit control is achieved and the chance of documents becoming lost is reduced.
3. **Early knowledge of dishonored checks.** Should a customer's check be uncollectible because of lack of funds, it is returned, usually by special handling, to the firm.

These benefits are not free. Usually, the bank levies a charge for each check processed through the system. The benefits derived from the acceleration of receipts must exceed the incremental costs of the lock-box system, or the firm would be better off without it. Companies that find the average size of their remittances to be quite small, for instance, might avoid a lock-box plan. Later in this chapter, we will illustrate how one calculates the costs and benefits of a specific cash-management service.

Preauthorized checks (PACs). Whereas the lock-box arrangement can often reduce total float by 2 to 4 days, for some firms the use of preauthorized checks (PACs) can be an even more effective way of converting receipts into working cash. A PAC resembles the ordinary check, but it does not contain nor require the signature of the person on whose account it is being drawn. A PAC is created only with the individual's legal authorization.

The PAC system is advantageous when the firm regularly receives a large volume of payments from the same customers. This type of cash-management service has proved useful to insurance companies, savings and loan associations, consumer credit firms, leasing enterprises, and charitable and religious organizations. The objective of this system is to reduce both mail and processing float. In relation to either the typical cash-gathering system or the lock-box system, the customer no longer (1) physically writes his or her own check or (2) deposits such a check in the mail. As a result, steps 1 to 3 (Figure 17.2) are reduced to less than 1 day.

The operation of a PAC system involves the following sequence of events:

1. The firm's customers authorize it to draw checks on their respective demand deposit accounts.
2. Indemnification agreements are signed by the customers and forwarded to the banks where they maintain their demand deposit accounts. These agreements authorize the banks to honor the PACs when they are presented for payment through the commercial bank clearing system.

3. The firm prepares a magnetic tape that contains all appropriate information about the regular payments.
4. At each processing cycle (monthly, weekly, semimonthly) the corporation retains a hard copy listing of all tape data for control purposes. Usually, the checks that are about to be printed will be deposited in the firm's demand deposit account, so a deposit ticket will also be forwarded to the bank.
5. Upon receipt of the tape, the bank will produce the PACs, deposit them to the firm's account, forward them for clearing through the commercial banking system, and return a control report to the firm.

For firms that can take advantage of a PAC system, the benefits include the following:

1. **Increased predictability of cash flows.** The collecting firm institutes the collection instead of the customer.
2. **Reduced expenses.** Billing and postage costs are eliminated, and the clerical processing of customer payments is significantly reduced.
3. **Customer preference.** Many customers prefer not to be bothered with a regular billing. With a PAC system, the check is actually written for the customer and the payment made even if he or she is on vacation or otherwise out of town.
4. **Increased working cash.** Mail float and processing float can be reduced in comparison with other payment processing systems.

Depository transfer checks. Both depository transfer checks and wire transfers are used in conjunction with what is known as **concentration banking**. A concentration bank is one where the firm maintains a major disbursing account.

In an effort to accelerate collections, many companies have established multiple collection centers. Regional lock-box networks are one type of approach to strategically located collection points. Even without lock boxes, firms may have numerous sales outlets throughout the country and collect cash over the counter. This requires many local bank accounts to handle daily deposits. Rather than have funds sitting in these multiple bank accounts in different geographic regions of the country, most firms will regularly transfer the surplus balances to one or more concentration banks. Centralizing the firm's pool of cash provides the following benefits:

1. **Lower levels of excess cash.** Desired cash balance target levels are set for each regional bank. These target levels consider both compensating balance requirements and necessary working levels of cash. Cash in excess of the target levels can be transferred regularly to concentration banks for deployment by the firm's top-level management.
2. **Better control.** With more cash held in fewer accounts, stricter control over available cash is achieved. Quite simply, there are fewer problems. The concentration banks can prepare sophisticated reports that detail corporate-wide movements of funds into and out of the central cash pool.
3. **More efficient investments in near-cash assets.** The coupling of information from the firm's cash forecast with data on available funds supplied by the concentration banks allows the firm quickly to transfer cash to the marketable securities portfolio.

Depository transfer checks provide a means for moving funds from local bank accounts to concentration accounts. The depository transfer check itself is an unsigned, non-negotiable instrument. It is payable only to the bank of deposit (the concentration bank) for credit to the firm's specific account. The firm files an authorization form with each bank from which it might withdraw funds. This form instructs the bank to pay the depository transfer checks without any signature.

Wire transfers. The fastest way to move cash between banks is by use of **wire transfers**, which eliminate transit float. Funds moved in this manner immediately become usable funds or "good funds" to the firm at the receiving bank. The following two major communication facilities are used to accommodate wire transfers:

Concentration banking

The selection of a few major banks where the firm maintains significant disbursing accounts.

Depository transfer checks

A non-negotiable instrument that provides the firm with a means to move funds from local bank accounts to concentration bank accounts.

Wire transfers

A method of moving funds electronically between bank accounts in order to eliminate transit float. The wired funds are immediately usable at the receiving bank.

1. **Bank Wire.** Bank Wire is a private wire service used and supported by approximately 250 banks in the United States for transferring funds, exchanging credit information, and effecting securities transactions.
2. **Federal Reserve Wire System.** The Fed Wire is directly accessible to commercial banks that are members of the Federal Reserve System. A commercial bank that is not on the Bank Wire or is not a member of the Federal Reserve System can use the wire transfer through its correspondent bank.

Managing the Cash Outflow

Significant techniques and systems for improving the firm's management of cash disbursements include (1) zero balance accounts, (2) payable-through drafts, and (3) remote disbursing. The first two offer markedly better control over companywide payments, and as a secondary benefit they *may* increase disbursement float. The last technique, remote disbursing, aims solely to increase disbursement float.

Zero balance accounts. Large corporations that operate multiple branches, divisions, or subsidiaries often maintain numerous bank accounts (in different banks) for the purpose of making timely operating disbursements. It does make good business sense for payments for purchased parts that go into, say, an automobile transmission to be made by the Transmission and Chassis Division of the auto manufacturer rather than its central office. The Transmission and Chassis Division originates such purchase orders, receives and inspects the shipment when it arrives at the plant, authorizes payment, and writes the appropriate check. To have the central office involved in these matters would be a waste of company time.

What tends to happen, however, is that with several divisions utilizing their own disbursal accounts, excess cash balances build up in outlying banks and rob the firm of earning assets. Zero balance accounts are used to alleviate this problem. The objectives of a zero balance account system are (1) for the firm to achieve better control over its cash payments, (2) to reduce excess cash balances held in regional banks for disbursing purposes, and (3) to increase disbursing float.

Zero balance accounts permit centralized control (at the headquarters level) over cash outflows while maintaining divisional disbursing authority. Under this system, the firm's authorized employees, representing their various divisions, continue to write checks on their individual accounts. Note that the numerous individual disbursing accounts are now *all* located in the same concentration bank. Actually, these separate accounts contain no funds at all, thus their appropriate label, "zero balance." These accounts have all of the other characteristics of regular demand deposit accounts including separate titles, numbers, and statements.

Zero balance accounts

A cash-management tool that permits centralized control over cash outflows but also maintains divisional disbursing authority.

Payable-through drafts. **Payable-through drafts** are legal instruments that have the physical appearance of ordinary checks but are *not* drawn on a bank. Instead, payable-through drafts are drawn on and payment is authorized by the issuing firm against its demand deposit account. Like checks, the drafts are cleared through the banking system and are presented to the issuing firm's bank. The bank serves as a collection point and passes the drafts on to the firm. The corporate issuer usually has to return all drafts it does not wish to cover (pay) by the following business day. Those documents not returned to the bank are automatically paid. The firm inspects the drafts for validity by checking signatures, amounts, and dates. Stop-payment orders can be initiated by the company on any drafts considered inappropriate.

The main purpose of using a payable-through draft system is *to provide for effective control over field payments.* Central office control over payments begun by regional units is provided as the drafts are reviewed in advance of final payment. Payable-through drafts, for example, are used extensively in the insurance industry. The claims agent does

Payable-through drafts

A payment mechanism that substitutes for regular checks in that drafts are not drawn on a bank, but instead are drawn on and authorized by the firm against its demand deposit account. The purpose is to maintain control over field-authorized payments.

not typically have check-signing authority against a corporate disbursement account. This agent can issue a draft, however, for quick settlement of a claim.

Remote disbursing. A few banks will provide the corporate customer with a cash-management service specifically designed to extend disbursing float. The firm's concentration bank may have a correspondent relationship with a smaller bank located in a distant city. In that remote city, the Federal Reserve System is unable to maintain frequent clearings of checks drawn on local banks. For example, a firm that is located in Dallas and maintains its master account there may open an account with a bank situated in, say, Amarillo, Texas. The firm will write the bulk of its payment checks against the account in the Amarillo bank. The checks will probably take at least 1 business day longer to clear, so the firm can "play the float" to its advantage.

A firm must use this technique of remote disbursing with extreme care. If a key supplier of raw materials located in Dallas has to wait the extra day for funds drawn on the Amarillo account, the possibility of incurring ill will might outweigh the apparent gain from an increase in the disbursing float. The impact on the firm's reputation of using remote disbursing should be explicitly evaluated.

> **RELATE TO THE BIG PICTURE**
>
> *The practice of remote disbursing has come under criticism by bank regulatory authorities. In early 1979, the Federal Reserve Bank of Dallas noted:*
>
> > *A policy discouraging remote disbursement—the use of remote banks by businesses, usually corporations, to delay payment of bills—has been adopted by the Board of Governors [of the Federal Reserve System]. The Board believes the banking industry has a public responsibility not to design, offer, promote or otherwise encourage the use of a service expressly intended to delay final settlement. The Board is calling on the nation's banks to join in the effort to eliminate remote disbursement practices.[3]*
>
> *The decision to use or not to use remote disbursing is a good example of **Axiom 9: Ethical Behavior Is Doing the Right Thing, and Ethical Dilemmas Are Everywhere in Finance**.*

Electronic Funds Transfer

In the purest economic sense, "total" float should equal zero days and therefore should be worth zero dollars to any business firm or other economic unit in the society. Float is really a measure of inefficiency of the financial system in an economy. It is a friction of the business environment that stems from the fact that all information arising from business transactions cannot be instantaneously transferred among the parties involved.

Today the extensive use of electronic communication equipment is serving to reduce float. The central concept of electronic funds transfer (EFT) is simple. If firm A owes money to firm B, this situation ought to be immediately reflected on both the books and the bank accounts of these two companies. Instantaneous transfer of funds would eliminate float. Of course, this ideal within the U.S. financial system has not been reached; the trend toward it, however, is readily observable.

Automated teller machines, like those imbedded in the wall of your supermarket or at the airline terminal, are familiar devices to most consumers. Businesses are now beginning to use even more advanced systems, such as terminal-based wire transfers, to move funds within their cash-management systems.

The heart of EFT is the elimination of the check as a method of transferring funds. The elimination of the check may never occur, but certainly a move toward a financial

---

[3]"Remote Disbursement Policy Adopted," *Voice of the Federal Reserve Bank of Dallas* (February 1979): 10.

system that uses fewer checks will. Transit, mail, and processing float become less important as EFT becomes more important. Simultaneously, this also implies that disbursing float becomes trivial.

STOP AND THINK

Our work in chapter 13 presented the popular breakeven model used by financial executives, accountants, and economists. The benefit to the firm of a given cash-management service can be assessed in a similar manner. Such a model follows. More complicated methods can be presented (some that involve use of an appropriate company discount rate), but the model below is used by managers and is easily explained to them. The important point is: Cash-management services are not free.

Evaluation of Costs of Cash-Management Services

A form of breakeven analysis can help the financial officer decide whether a particular collection or disbursement service will provide an economic benefit to the firm. The evaluation process involves a very basic relationship in microeconomics:

$$\text{added costs} = \text{added benefits} \tag{17-1}$$

If equation (17-1) holds exactly, then the firm is no better or worse off for having adopted the given service. We will illustrate this procedure in terms of the desirability of installing an additional lock box. Equation (17-1) can be restated on a per-unit basis as follows:

$$P = (D)(S)(i) \tag{17-2}$$

where P = increases in per-check processing cost if the new system is adopted
$\quad\quad D$ = days saved in the collection process (float reduction)
$\quad\quad S$ = average check size in dollars
$\quad\quad i$ = the daily, before-tax opportunity cost (rate of return) of carrying cash

Assume now that check processing cost, P, will rise by \$.18 a check if a lock box is used. The firm has determined that the average check size, S, that will be mailed to the lock-box location will be \$900. If funds are freed by use of the lock box, they will be invested in marketable securities to yield an *annual* before-tax return of 6 percent. With these data, it is possible to determine the reduction in check collection time, D, that is required to justify use of the lock box. That level of D is found to be

$$\$.18 = (D)(\$900)\left(\frac{.06}{365}\right)$$

$$1.217 \text{ days} = D$$

Thus the lock box is justified if the firm can speed up its collections by *more* than 1.217 days. This same style of analysis can be adapted to analyze the other methods of cash management.

Table 17.1 Features of Selected Cash-Collection and Disbursal Methods: A Summary

Method	Objective	How Accomplished
Cash-Collection Methods		
1. Lock-box system	Reduce (1) mail float, (2) processing float, and (3) transit float.	Strategic location of lock boxes to reduce mail float and transit float. Firm's commercial bank has access to lock box to reduce processing float.
2. Preauthorized checks	Reduce (1) mail float and (2) processing float.	The firm writes the checks (the PACs) for its customers to be charged against their demand deposit accounts.
3. (Ordinary) Depository transfer checks	Eliminate excess funds in regional banks.	Used in conjunction with concentration banking whereby the firm maintains several collection centers. The transfer check authorizes movement of funds from a local bank to the concentration bank.
4. Automated depository transfer check	Eliminate the mail float associated with the ordinary transfer check.	Telecommunications company transmits deposit data to the firm's concentration bank.
5. Wire transfers	Move funds immediately between banks. This eliminates transit float in that only "good funds" are transferred.	Use of Bank Wire or the Federal Reserve Wire System.
Cash-Disbursal Methods		
1. Zero balance accounts	(1) Achieve better control over cash payments, (2) reduce excess cash balances held in regional banks, and (3) possibly increase disbursing float.	Establish zero balance accounts for all of the firm's disbursing units, but in the same concentration bank. Checks are drawn against these accounts, with the balance in each account never exceeding $0. Divisional disbursing authority is thereby maintained at the local level of management.
2. Payable-through drafts	Achieve effective central office control over field-authorized payments.	Field office issues drafts rather than checks to settle payables.
3. Remote disbursing	Extend disbursing float.	Write checks against demand deposit accounts held in distant banks.

Before moving on to a discussion of the firm's marketable securities portfolio, it will be helpful to draw together the preceding material. Table 17.1 summarizes the key features of the cash-collection and disbursal techniques we have considered here.

> **STOP AND THINK**
>
> *Designing the marketable securities portfolio is one of the more pleasant tasks in financial management. This is because it is usually done with excess cash that is available for short periods of time. The firm typically has excess cash when operations are going well; some firms never get the opportunity to design such a near-cash portfolio or to spend much time even thinking about it.*
>
> *We will review the major securities that make up the portfolios designed by cash managers. Note that the firm's main line of business activity will have a key impact on how much risk is assumed in the portfolios.*
>
> *If the firm is in the business of manufacturing personal computers, it is likely management will feel that business itself is risky enough. Thus not much additional risk will be embedded in the marketable securities portfolio.*
>
> *In addition, observe how critical the concept of liquidity is to this aspect of cash management. Most large organizations will transfer funds into and out of the portfolio several times a day. Ready convertibility into cash, therefore, is a prime determinant of the final composition.*

Once the design of the firm's cash receipts and payments system has been determined, the financial manager faces the task of selecting appropriate financial assets for inclusion in the firm's marketable securities portfolio.

General Selection Criteria

Certain criteria can provide the financial manager with a useful framework for selecting a proper marketable securities mix. These considerations include evaluation of the (1) financial risk, (2) interest rate risk, (3) liquidity, (4) taxability, and (5) yields among different financial assets. We will briefly delineate these criteria from the investor's viewpoint.

Financial risk. *Financial risk*, as explained in chapter 6, refers to the uncertainty of expected returns from a security attributable to possible changes in the financial capacity of the security issuer to make future payments to the security owner. If the chance of default on the terms of the instrument is high (low), then the financial risk is said to be high (low). It is clear that the financial risk associated with holding commercial paper, which we will see shortly is nothing more than a corporate IOU, exceeds that of holding securities issued by the U.S. Treasury.

In both financial practice and research, when estimates of risk-free returns are desired, the yields available on Treasury securities are consulted and the safety of other financial instruments is weighed against them. Because the marketable securities portfolio is designed to provide a return on funds that would otherwise be tied up in idle cash held for transactions or precautionary purposes, the financial officer is not usually willing to assume much financial risk in the hope of greater return.

Interest rate risk. *Interest rate risk*, as defined in chapter 7, refers to the uncertainty of expected returns from a financial instrument attributable to changes in interest rates. Of particular concern to the corporate treasurer is the price volatility associated with instruments that have long, as opposed to short, terms to maturity. An illustration can help clarify this point.

Suppose the financial officer is weighing the merits of investing temporarily available corporate cash in a new offering of U.S. Treasury obligations that will mature in either (1) 90 days or (2) 1 year from the date of issue. Ninety-day and 1-year Treasury bills are issued at a discount from their maturity price of $1,000. The issue price of these bills is found by discounting at 7 percent, compounded annually.

If after 60 days from the date of purchase, prevailing interest rates rise to 9 percent, the market price of these currently outstanding Treasury securities will fall to bring the yields to maturity in line with what investors could obtain by buying a new issue of a given instrument. The market prices of *both* the 90-day and 1-year obligations will decline. The price of the 1-year instrument will decline by a greater dollar amount, however, than that of the 90-day instrument.

Sixty days from the date of issue, the price obtainable in the marketplace for the original 1-year instrument, which now has 305 days until maturity, can be found by computing P as follows:

$$P = \frac{\$1,000}{\left(1 + \frac{.09}{365}\right)^{305}} = \$926.59$$

If interest rates had remained at 7 percent:

$$P = \frac{\$1,000}{\left(1 + \frac{.07}{365}\right)^{305}} = \$943.19$$

Therefore, the rise in interest rates caused the price of the 1-year bill to fall by $16.60.

$943.19 − $926.59 = $16.60

Now, what will happen to the price of the bill that has 30 days remaining to maturity? In a similar manner, we can compute its price, P:

$$P = \frac{\$1,000}{\left(1 + \frac{.09}{365}\right)^{30}} = \$992.63$$

If interest rates had remained at 7 percent:

$$P = \frac{\$1,000}{\left(1 + \frac{.07}{365}\right)^{30}} = \$994.26$$

Therefore, the price of the Treasury bill falls $1.63:

$994.26 − $992.63 = $1.63

Thus the market value of the shorter-term security was penalized much less by the given rise in the general level of interest rates.

If we extended the illustration, we would see that, in terms of market price, a 1-year security would be affected less than a 2-year security, a 5-year security less than a 20-year security, and so on. Equity securities would exhibit the largest price changes because of their infinite maturity periods. To hedge against the price volatility caused by interest rate risk, the firm's marketable security portfolio will tend to be composed of instruments that mature over short periods.

Liquidity. In the present context of managing the marketable securities portfolio, *liquidity* refers to the ability to transform a security into cash. Should an unforeseen event require that a significant amount of cash be immediately available, then a sizable portion of the portfolio might have to be sold. The financial manager will want the cash *quickly* and will not want to accept a large *price concession* in order to convert the securities. Thus in the formulation of preferences for the inclusion of particular instruments in the portfolio, the manager must consider (1) the period needed to sell the security, and (2) the likelihood that the security can be sold at or near its prevailing market price. The latter element, here, means that "thin" markets, where relatively few transactions take place or where trades are accomplished only with large price changes between transactions, will be avoided.

Taxability. The tax treatment of the income a firm receives from its security investments does not affect the ultimate mix of the marketable securities portfolio as much as the criteria mentioned earlier. This is because the interest income from most instruments suitable for inclusion in the portfolio is taxable at the federal level. Still some corporate treasurers seriously evaluate the taxability of interest income and capital gains.

The interest income from only one class of securities escapes the federal income tax. That class of securities is generally referred to as *municipal obligations* or more simply as *municipals*. Because of the tax-exempt feature of interest income from state and local government securities, municipals sell at lower yields to maturity in the market than do securities that pay taxable interest. The after-tax yield on a municipal obligation, however, could be higher than the yield from a non-tax-exempt security. This would depend mainly on the purchasing firm's tax situation.

Consider Table 17.2. A firm is analyzing whether to invest in a 1-year tax-free debt issue yielding 6 percent on a $1,000 outlay or a 1-year taxable issue that yields 8 percent on a $1,000 outlay. The firm pays federal taxes at the rate of 34 percent. The yields quoted in the financial press and in the prospectuses that describe debt issues are *before-tax* returns.

Table 17.2 Comparison of After-Tax Yields

	Tax-exempt Debt Issue (6% Coupon)	Taxable Debt Issue (8% Coupon)
Interest income	$ 60.00	$ 80.00
Income tax (.34)	0.00	27.20
After-tax interest income	60.00	52.80
After-tax yield	$\dfrac{60.00}{\$1,000.00} = 6\%$	$\dfrac{52.80}{\$1,000.00} = 5.28\%$

Derivation of equivalent before-tax yield on a taxable debt issue:

$$r = \frac{r^*}{1-t} = \frac{.06}{1-.34} = 9.091\%$$

where

r = equivalent before-tax yield,
r^* = after-tax yield on tax-exempt security,
t = firm's marginal income tax rate.

Proof:

Interest income [$1,000 × .09091]	= $90.91
Income tax (.34)	30.91
After-tax interest income	$60.00

The actual *after-tax* return enjoyed by the firm depends on its tax bracket. Notice that the actual after-tax yield received by the firm is only 5.28 percent on the taxable issue versus 6 percent on the tax-exempt obligation. The lower portion of Table 17.2 shows that the fully taxed bond must yield 9.091 percent to make it comparable with the tax-exempt issue.

Another tax issue affecting our management of marketable securities is the distinction between capital gains and ordinary income. Capital gains are taxed at a lower rate than ordinary income (such as interest income). Under such circumstances, bonds selling at a discount from their face value may be attractive investments to tax-paying firms. Should a high level of interest rates currently exist, the market prices of debt issues that were issued in the past at low coupon rates will be depressed. This, as we said previously, brings their yield to maturity up to that obtainable on a new issue. Part of the yield to maturity on a bond selling at a discount is a *capital gain*, or the difference between the purchase price and the maturity value. Provided the firm held the fixed-income security for the requisite holding period, the return after tax could be higher than that derived from a comparable issue carrying a higher coupon but selling at par. We say *could* be higher, as the marketplace is rather efficient and recognizes this feature of taxability; consequently, discount bonds will sell at lower yields than issues that have similar risk characteristics but larger coupons. For short periods, however, a firm *might* find a favorable yield advantage by purchasing discount bonds.

Yields. The final selection criterion that we mention is a significant one—the yields that are available on the different financial assets suitable for inclusion in the near-cash portfolio. By now it is probably obvious that the factors of (1) financial risk, (2) interest rate risk, (3) liquidity, and (4) taxability all influence the available yields on financial instruments. The yield criterion involves an evaluation of the risks and benefits inherent in all of these factors. If a given risk is assumed, such as lack of liquidity, a higher yield may be expected on the nonliquid instrument.

Table 17.3 summarizes our framework for designing the firm's marketable securities portfolio. The four basic considerations are shown to influence the yields available on securities. The financial manager must focus on the risk-return trade-offs identified through

Table 17.3 Designing the Marketable Securities Portfolio

Considerations	→	Influence	→	Focus Upon	→	Determine
Financial risk Interest rate risk Liquidity Taxability		Yields		Risk vs. return preferences		Marketable securities mix

analysis. Coming to grips with these trade-offs will enable the financial manager to determine the proper marketable securities mix for the company. Let us look now at the marketable securities prominent in firms' near-cash portfolios.

Marketable Security Alternatives

Based on the foregoing discussion on the criteria to be used in selecting a security investment, let's now look at the investments that are commonly used.

U.S. Treasury bills. *U.S. Treasury bills* are the best-known and most popular short-term investment outlets among firms. A Treasury bill is a direct obligation of the U.S. government sold on a regular basis by the U.S. Treasury. New Treasury bills are issued in denominations of $10,000, $15,000, $50,000, $100,000, $500,000, and $1,000,000. In effect, therefore, one can buy bills in multiples of $5,000 above the smallest purchase price of $10,000 by combining $10,000 bills and $15,000 bills to reach the desired sum.

At present, bills are regularly offered with maturities of 91, 182, and 365 days. The 3-month and 6-month bills are auctioned weekly by the Treasury, and the 1-year bills are offered every 4 weeks. Bids (orders to purchase) are accepted by the various Federal Reserve Banks and their branches, which perform the role of agents for the Treasury. Each Monday, bids are received until 1:30 P.M. eastern time; after that time they are opened, tabulated, and forwarded to the Treasury for allocation (filling the purchase orders).

Treasury bills are sold on a discount basis; for that reason, the investor does not receive an actual interest payment. The return is the difference between the purchase price and the face (par) value of the bill.

Of prime importance to the corporate treasurer is the fact that a very active secondary market exists for bills. After a bill has been acquired by the firm, should the need arise to turn it into cash, a group of securities dealers stands ready to purchase it. This highly developed secondary market for bills not only makes them extremely liquid, but also allows the firm to buy bills with maturities of a week or even less.

As bills have the full financial backing of the U.S. government, they are, for all practical purposes, risk-free. This negligible financial risk and high degree of liquidity makes the yields lower than those obtainable on other marketable securities. The income from Treasury bills is subject to federal income taxes, but *not* to state and local government income taxes.

Federal agency securities. *Federal agency securities* are debt obligations of corporations and agencies that have been created to effect the various lending programs of the U.S. government. Five such government-sponsored corporations account for the majority of outstanding agency debt. The "big five" agencies are the Federal National Mortgage Association, the Federal Home Loan Banks, the Federal Land Banks, the Federal Intermediate Credit Banks, and the Banks for Cooperatives.

It is not true that the "big five" federally sponsored agencies are owned by the U.S. government and that the securities they issue are fully guaranteed by the government. The "big five" agencies are now entirely owned by their member associations or the general public. In addition, it is the issuing agency that stands behind its promises to pay, not the federal government.

These agencies sell their securities in a variety of denominations. The entry barrier caused by the absolute dollar size of the smallest available Treasury bill— $10,000— is not as severe in the market for agencies. A wide range of maturities is also available. Obligations can at times be purchased with maturities as short as 30 days or as long as 15 years.

Agency debt usually sells on a coupon basis and pays interest to the owner on a semiannual schedule, although there are exceptions. Some issues have been sold on a discount basis, and some have paid interest only once a year.

The income from agency debt that the investor receives is subject to taxation at the federal level. Of the "big five" agencies, only the income from FNMA issues is taxed at the state and local level.

The yields available on agency obligations will always exceed those of Treasury securities of similar maturity. This yield differential is attributable to lesser marketability and greater default risk. The financial officer might keep in mind, however, that none of these agency issues has ever gone into default.

Bankers' acceptances. *Bankers' acceptances* are one of the least understood instruments suitable for inclusion in the firm's marketable securities portfolio. Their part in U.S. commerce today is largely concentrated in the financing of foreign transactions. Generally, an acceptance is a draft (order to pay) drawn on a specific bank by an exporter in order to obtain payment for goods shipped to a customer, who maintains an account with that specific bank.

Because acceptances are used to finance the acquisition of goods by one party, the document is not "issued" in specialized denominations; its dollar size is determined by the cost of the goods being purchased. Usual sizes, however, range from $25,000 to $1 million. The maturities on acceptances run from 30 to 180 days, although longer periods are available from time to time. The most common period is 90 days.

Acceptances, like Treasury bills, are sold on a discount basis and are payable to the holder of the paper. A secondary market for the acceptances of large banks does exist.

The income generated from investing in acceptances is fully taxable at the federal, state, and local levels. Because of their greater financial risk and lesser liquidity, acceptances provide investors a yield advantage over Treasury bills and agency obligations. In fact, the acceptances of major banks are a very safe investment, making the yield advantage over Treasuries worth looking at from the firm's vantage point.

Negotiable certificates of deposit. A *negotiable certificate of deposit, CD*, is a marketable receipt for funds that have been deposited in a bank for a fixed time period. The deposited funds earn a fixed rate of interest. These are not to be confused with ordinary passbook savings accounts or nonmarketable time deposits offered by all commercial banks. CDs are offered by major money-center banks. We are talking here about "corporate" CDs—not those offered to individuals.

CDs are offered by key banks in a variety of denominations running from $25,000 to $10,000,000. The popular sizes are $100,000, $500,000, and $1,000,000. The original maturities on CDs can range from 1 to 18 months.

CDs are offered by banks on a basis differing from Treasury bills; that is, they are not sold at a discount. Rather, when the certificate matures, the owner receives the full amount deposited plus the earned interest.

A secondary market for CDs does exist, the heart of which is found in New York City. Even though the secondary market for CDs of large banks is well organized, it does not operate as smoothly as the aftermarket in Treasuries. CDs are more heterogeneous than Treasury bills. Treasury bills have similar rates, maturity periods, and denominations; more variety is found in CDs. This makes it harder to liquidate large blocks of CDs, because a more specialized investor must be found. The securities dealers who "make" the secondary market in CDs mainly trade in $1 million units. Smaller denominations can be traded but will bring a relatively lower price.

The income received from an investment in CDs is subject to taxation at all government levels. In recent years, CD yields have been above those available on bankers' acceptances.

Commercial paper. *Commercial paper* refers to short-term, unsecured promissory notes sold by large businesses to raise cash. These are sometimes described in the popular financial press as short-term corporate IOUs. Because they are unsecured, the issuing side of the market is dominated by large corporations, which typically maintain sound credit ratings. The issuing (borrowing) firm can sell the paper to a dealer who will in turn sell it to the investing public; if the firm's reputation is solid, the paper can be sold directly to the ultimate investor.

The denominations in which commercial paper can be bought vary over a wide range. At times, paper can be obtained in sizes from $5,000 to $5 million, or even more. Sometimes dealers will sell notes in multiples as small as $1,000 or $5,000 above the initial $5,000 denomination. This depends on the dealer. The usual denominations are $25,000, $50,000, $100,000, $250,000, $500,000, and $1 million. Major dealers in the dealer-placed market include the First Boston Corporation; Goldman, Sachs & Co.; Merrill Lynch, Pierce, Fenner & Smith, Inc.; and Salomon Brothers.

Commercial paper can be purchased with maturities that range from 3 to 270 days. Notes with maturities exceeding 270 days are very rare, because they would have to be registered with the Securities and Exchange Commission—a task firms avoid, when possible, because it is time consuming and costly.

These notes are *generally* sold on a discount basis, although sometimes paper that is interest bearing and can be made payable to the order of the investor is available.

The next point is of considerable interest to the financial officer responsible for management of the firm's near-cash portfolio. For practical purposes, there is *no* active trading in a secondary market for commercial paper. This distinguishes commercial paper from all the previously discussed short-term investment vehicles. On occasion, a dealer or finance company (the borrower) will redeem a note prior to its contract maturity date, but this is not a regular procedure. Thus when the corporation evaluates commercial paper for possible inclusion in its marketable securities portfolio, it should plan to hold it to maturity.

The return on commercial paper is fully taxable to the investor at all levels of government. Because of its lack of marketability, commercial paper in past years consistently provided a yield advantage over other near-cash assets of comparable maturity. The lifting of interest rate ceilings in 1973 by the Federal Reserve Board on certain large CDs, however, allowed commercial banks to make CD rates fully competitive in the attempt to attract funds. Over any time period, then, CD yields *may* be slightly above the rates available on commercial paper.

Repurchase agreements. *Repurchase agreements (repos)* are legal contracts that involve the actual sale of securities by a *borrower* to the *lender*, with a commitment on the part of the borrower to *repurchase* the securities at the contract price plus a stated interest charge. The securities sold to the lender are U.S. government issues or other instruments of the money market such as those described previously. The borrower is either a major financial institution—most often, a commercial bank—or a dealer in U.S. government securities.

Why might the corporation with excess cash prefer to buy repurchase agreements rather than a given marketable security? There are two major reasons. First, the original maturities of the instruments being sold can, in effect, be adjusted to suit the particular needs of the investing corporation. Funds available for very short time periods, such as 1 or 2 days, can be productively employed. The second reason is closely related to the first. The firm could, of course, buy a Treasury bill and then resell it in the market in a few days when cash was required. The drawback here would be the risk involved in liquidating the bill at a price equal to its earlier cost to the firm. The purchase of a repo removes this risk. The contract price of the securities that make up the arrangement is *fixed* for the duration of the transaction. The corporation that buys a repurchase agreement, then, is protected against market price fluctuations throughout the contract period. This makes it a sound alternative investment for funds that are freed up for only very short periods. For example mutual funds will buy repos as a way to "park" excess cash flows for a few days.

Money market mutual funds. Money market funds typically invest in a diversified portfolio of short-term, high-grade debt instruments such as those described previously. Some such funds, however, will accept more interest rate risk in their portfolios and acquire some corporate bonds and notes. The portfolio composition of 665 money market funds as of March 1997 is shown in Table 17.4. We see that commercial paper, repurchase agreements, plus all CDs (both domestic plus Eurodollar) represented 62.4 percent of money fund assets at this point in time. The average maturity period for these same 665 funds stood at 49 days at March 1997. The interest rate risk contained in this overall portfolio is, therefore, rather small.

The money market funds sell their shares to raise cash, and by pooling the funds of large numbers of small savers, they can build their liquid-asset portfolios. Many of these funds allow the investor to start an account with as little as $1,000. This small initial investment, coupled with the fact that some liquid-asset funds permit subsequent investments in amounts as small as $100, makes this type of outlet for excess cash well suited to the small firm and the individual. Furthermore, the management of a small enterprise may not be highly versed in the details of short-term investments. By purchasing shares in a liquid-asset fund, the investor is also buying managerial expertise.

Money market mutual funds offer the investing firm a high degree of liquidity. By redeeming (selling) shares, the investor can obtain cash quickly. Procedures for liquidation vary among the funds, but shares can usually be redeemed by means of (1) special redemption checks supplied by the fund, (2) telephone instructions, (3) wire instructions,

Table 17.4 Money Market Funds Asset Composition, Year-End 1996–1997

Type of Investment	Amount ($ billions)	Percent of Total
U.S. Treasury bills	41.96	5.5%
Other Treasury securities	49.64	6.5%
U.S. securities (agencies)	104.19	13.7%
Repurchase agreements	105.71	13.9%
Commercial bank CDs	16.54	2.2%
Other domestic CDs	52.78	6.9%
Eurodollar CDs	23.57	3.1%
Commercial paper	276.80	36.3%
Bankers' acceptances	2.62	0.3%
Cash reserves and other	87.94	11.5%
Total net assets	761.75	100.0%

SOURCE: Investment Company Institute, *1997 Mutual Fund Fact Book.*

or (4) a letter. When liquidation is ordered by telephone or wire, the mutual fund can remit to the investor by the next business day.

The returns earned from owning shares in a money market fund are taxable at all governmental levels. The yields follow the returns the investor could receive by purchasing the marketable securities directly.

HOW FINANCIAL MANAGERS USE THIS MATERIAL

Although a company's profitability is important, its ability to manage cash is vital. As a company becomes larger, cash management becomes more difficult and requires sophisticated systems to manage the firm's cash flows. Being effective in managing cash receipts and disbursements can mean thousands of dollars in savings to a larger company over a year's time.

The materials covered in this chapter have addressed many of the techniques used on a daily basis by almost all companies. These include:

- Check clearing mechanisms, electronic funds transfer systems, and float
- Collection (lock-box, preauthorized debits), concentration (branch banking, depository transfers), and disbursement (zero-balance accounts, remote and controlled disbursements)
- Use of excess funds through short-term investments, which requires written investment policies and guidelines and deciding where to invest excess cash, be it U.S. Treasury bills, CDs, commercial paper, repurchase agreements, banker's acceptances, money market funds, Munis, or other securities.
- Information management systems on deposit and balance reporting
- Selecting the right cash management bank

SUMMARY

 OBJECTIVE 1

Liquid assets are the summation of cash and marketable securities. Cash is the currency and coin the firm has on hand in cash drawers, cash registers, or checking accounts. Cash balances earn no return. Near-cash assets, also known as marketable securities, are security investments that earn a rate of return and that the firm can quickly convert into cash balances.

 OBJECTIVE 2

The firm experiences both regular and irregular cash flows. Once cash is obtained, the firm will have three motives for holding cash: to satisfy transactions, precautionary needs for liquidity, and speculative needs for liquidity. To a certain extent, such needs can be satisfied by holding readily marketable securities rather than cash.

 OBJECTIVE 3

The financial manager must (1) ensure that enough cash is on hand to meet the payment needs that arise in the course of doing business, and (2) attempt to maximize wealth by reducing the firm's idle cash balances to a minimum.

 OBJECTIVE 4

Float is the length of time from when a check is written until the actual recipient can use the "good funds." To reduce float, the firm can benefit considerably through the use of (1) lock-box arrangements, (2) preauthorized checks, (3) special forms of depository transfer checks, and (4) wire transfers. Lock-box systems and preauthorized checks serve to reduce mail and processing float. Depository transfer checks and wire transfers move funds between banks; they are often used in conjunction with concentration banking. Both the lock-box and preauthorized check systems can be employed as part of the firm's concentration banking setup to speed receipts to regional collection centers.

The firm can delay and favorably affect the control of its cash disbursements through the use of (1) zero balance accounts, (2) payable-through drafts, and (3) remote disbursing. Zero balance accounts allow the company to maintain central-office control over payments while permitting the firm's several divisions to maintain their own disbursing authority. Because key disbursing accounts are located in one major concentration bank, rather than in multiple banks across the country, excess cash balances that tend to build up in the outlying banks are avoided. Payable-through drafts are legal instruments that look like checks but are drawn on and paid by the issuing firm rather than its bank. The bank serves as a collection point for the drafts. Effective central-office control over field-authorized payments is the main reason such a system is used; it is not used as a major vehicle for extending disbursing float. Remote disbursing, however, is used to increase disbursing float. Remote disbursing refers to the process of writing payment checks on banks located in cities distant from the one where the check is originated.

Before any of these collection and disbursement procedures is initiated by the firm, a careful analysis should be undertaken to see if the expected benefits outweigh the expected costs.

The factors of (1) financial risk, (2) interest rate risk, (3) liquidity, and (4) taxability affect the yields available on marketable securities. By considering these four factors simultaneously with returns desired from the portfolio, the financial manager can design the mix of near-cash assets most suitable for a firm.

OBJECTIVE 5

We looked at several marketable securities. Treasury bills and federal agency securities are extremely safe investments. Bankers' acceptances, CDs, and commercial paper provide higher yields in exchange for greater risk assumption. Unlike the other instruments, commercial paper enjoys no *developed* secondary market. The firm can hedge against price fluctuations through the use of repurchase agreements. Money market mutual funds, a recent phenomenon of our financial market system, are particularly well suited for the short-term investing needs of small firms.

KEY TERMS

Cash, 639	**Float**, 644	**Payable-through drafts**, 649
Concentration banking, 648	**Insolvency**, 643	**Wire transfers**, 648
Depository transfer checks, 648	**Liquid assets**, 639	**Zero balance accounts**, 649
	Marketable securities, 639	

PHLIP

GO TO:
http://www.prenhall.com/bfm
For downloads and current events associated with this chapter

STUDY QUESTIONS

17-1. What is meant by the cash flow process?

17-2. Identify the principal motives for holding cash and near-cash assets. Explain the purpose of each motive.

17-3. What is concentration banking and how may it be of value to the firm?

17-4. Distinguish between depository transfer checks and automated depository transfer checks (ADTC).

17-5. In general, what type of firm would benefit from the use of a preauthorized check system? What specific types of companies have successfully used this device to accelerate cash receipts?

17-6. What are the two major objectives of the firm's cash-management system?

17-7. What three decisions dominate the cash-management process?

17-8. Within the context of cash management, what are the key elements of (total) float? Briefly define each element.

17-9. Distinguish between financial risk and interest rate risk as these terms are commonly used in discussions of cash management.

17-10. What is meant when we say, "A money market instrument is highly liquid"?

17-11. Which money market instrument is generally conceded to have no secondary market?

17-12. Your firm invests in only three different classes of marketable securities: commercial paper, Treasury bills, and federal agency securities. Recently, yields on these money market instruments of 3 months' maturity were quoted at 6.10, 6.25, and 5.90 percent. Match the available yields with the types of instruments your firm purchases.

17-13. What two key factors might induce a firm to invest in repurchase agreements rather than a specific security of the money market?

SELF-TEST PROBLEMS

ST-1. (*Costs of Services*) Creative Fashion Designs is evaluating a lock-box system as a cash receipts acceleration device. In a typical year, this firm receives remittances totaling $7 million by check. The firm will record and process 4,000 checks over the same time period. Ocala National Bank has informed the management of Creative Fashion Designs that it will process checks and associated documents through the lock-box system for a unit cost of $.25 per check. Creative Fashion Designs's financial manager has projected that cash freed by adoption of the system can be invested in a portfolio of near-cash assets that will yield an annual before-tax return of 8 percent. Creative Fashion Designs's financial analysts use a 365-day year in their procedures.

   a. What reduction in check collection time is necessary for Creative Fashion Designs to be neither better nor worse off for having adopted the proposed system?

   b. How would your solution to (a) be affected if Creative Fashion Designs could invest the freed balances only at an expected annual pre-tax return of 5.5 percent?

   c. What is the logical explanation for the differences in your answers to (a) and (b)?

ST-2. (*Cash Receipts Acceleration System*) Artie Kay's Komputer Shops is a large, national distributor and retailer of microcomputers, personal computers, and related software. The company has its central offices in Dearborn, Michigan, not far from the Ford Motor Company executive offices and headquarters. Only recently has Artie Kay's begun to pay serious attention to its cash-management procedures. Last week, the firm received a proposal from the Detroit National Bank. The objective of the proposal is to speed up the firm's cash collections.

Artie Kay's now uses a centralized billing procedure. All checks are mailed to the Dearborn headquarters office for processing and eventual deposit. Remittance checks now take an average of 5 business days to reach the Dearborn office. The in-house processing at Artie Kay's is quite slow. Once in Dearborn, another 3 days are needed to process the checks for deposit at Detroit National.

The daily cash remittances of Artie Kay's average $200,000. The average check size is $800. The firm currently earns 10.6 percent on its marketable securities portfolio and expects this rate to continue to be available.

The cash acceleration plan suggested by officers of Detroit National involves both a lock-box system and concentration banking. Detroit National would be the firm's only concentration bank. Lock boxes would be established in (1) Seattle, (2) San Antonio, (3) Chicago, and (4) Detroit. This would reduce mail float by 2.0 days. Processing float would be reduced to a level of 0.5 days. Funds would then be transferred twice each business day by means of automated depository transfer checks from local banks in Seattle, San Antonio, and Chicago to the Detroit National Bank. Each ADTC costs $20. These transfers will occur all 270 business days of the year. Each check processed through the lock-box system will cost Artie Kay's $.25.

a. What amount of cash balances will be freed if Artie Kay's adopts the system proposed by Detroit National?

b. What is the opportunity cost of maintaining the current banking arrangement?

c. What is the projected annual cost of operating the proposed system?

d. Should Artie Kay's adopt the new system? Compute the net annual gain or loss associated with adopting the system.

ST-3. (*Buying and Selling Marketable Securities*) Mountaineer Outfitters has $2 million in excess cash that it might invest in marketable securities. In order to buy and sell the securities, however, the firm must pay a transactions fee of $45,000.

a. Would you recommend purchasing the securities if they yield 12 percent annually and are held for

1. 1 month?
2. 2 months?
3. 3 months?
4. 6 months?
5. 1 year?

b. What minimum required yield would the securities have to return for the firm to hold them for 3 months (what is the breakeven yield for a 3-month holding period)?

STUDY PROBLEMS (SET A)

17-1A. (*Concentration Banking*) Healthy Herbal Beverage, Inc., produces a very healthy herbal beverage in Tupelo, Mississippi, that is distributed to health food stores primarily along the Gulf Coast, where many health-food aficionados seem to live. Until now, the company has received collections on its accounts receivable at its Tupelo headquarters. Such collections recently have been $40 million at an annual rate and are expected to remain at that level. The company's bank has suggested to Healthy Herbal's CFO, Wanda Jackson, that the bank could establish a concentration banking system for the company that would save the company 4 days in mail float, 3 days in processing float, and $35,000 in annual clerical costs. The bank would charge a flat fee per year of $40,000 to operate the system for Healthy Herbal. Wanda believes that the funds freed by such an arrangement could be invested at no transaction cost in the company's money market account and could earn an annual rate of return of 5 percent. Should Wanda accept the bank's proposal? Use a 365-day year in your analysis.

17-2A. (*Buying and Selling Marketable Securities*) An alternative to investing in a no-transaction-fee money market account under consideration by Wanda Jackson, the CFO at Healthy Herbal Beverage, Inc., (see Problem 17-1A) is direct investment in marketable securities. Assume for this problem that Wanda has determined that adoption of a concentration banking system could make $750,000 available for investment in marketable securities, but such direct investing would result in annual transaction fees of $15,000. Would you recommend that Wanda invest the funds in a money market account (at 5 percent per annum), or purchase the marketable securities directly if such securities yield 7.5 percent per annum and the expected holding period is for:

a. 1 month?

b. 2 months?

c. 6 months?

d. 1 year?

17-3A. (*Lock-Box System*) The Marino Rug Co. is located on the outskirts of Miramar, Florida. The firm specializes in the manufacture of a wide variety of carpet and tile. All of the firm's output is shipped to 12 warehouses, which are located in the largest metropolitan areas nationwide. National Bank of Miami is Marino Rug's lead bank. National Bank has just completed a study of Marino's cash collection system. Overall, National estimates that it can reduce Marino's total float by 3 days with the installation of a lock-box arrangement in each of the firm's 12 regions. The lock-box arrangement would cost each region $325 per month. Any funds freed up would be added to the firm's marketable securities portfolio and would yield 9.75 percent on an annual basis. Annual sales average $6,232,375 for each regional office. The firm and the bank use a 365-day year in their analyses. Should Marino's management approve the use of the proposed system?

17-4A. (*Marketable Securities Portfolio*) Mac's Tennis Racket Manufacturing Company currently pays its employees on a weekly basis. The weekly wage bill is $675,000. This means that on average, the firm has accrued wages payable of ($675,000 + $0)/2 = $337,500.

Jimmy McEnroe works as the firm's senior financial analyst and reports directly to his uncle, who owns all of the firm's common stock. Jimmy McEnroe wants to move to a monthly wage payment system. Employees would be paid at the end of every fourth week. Jimmy is aware that the labor union representing the company's workers will not permit the monthly payments system to take effect unless the workers are given some type of fringe-benefit compensation.

A plan has been worked out whereby the firm will make a contribution to the cost of life insurance coverage for each employee. This will cost the firm $50,775 annually. Jimmy McEnroe expects the firm to earn 8.5 percent annually on its marketable securities portfolio.

    a. Based on the projected information, should Mac's Tennis Racket Manufacturing Company move to the monthly wage payment system?

    b. What annual rate of return on the marketable securities portfolio would enable the firm just to breakeven on this proposal?

17-5A. (*Buying and Selling Marketable Securities*) Miami Dice & Card Company has generated $800,000 in excess cash that it could invest in marketable securities. In order to buy and sell the securities, the firm will pay total transactions fees of $20,000.

    a. Would you recommend purchasing the securities if they yield 10.5 percent annually and are held for

        1. 1 month?

        2. 2 months?

        3. 3 months?

        4. 6 months?

        5. 1 year?

    b. What minimum required yield would the securities have to return for the firm to hold them for 2 months (what is the breakeven yield for a 2-month holding period)?

17-6A. (*Cash Receipts Acceleration System*) James Waller Nail Corp. is a buyer and distributor of nails used in the home building industry. The firm has grown very quickly since it was established 8 years ago. Waller Nail has managed to increase sales and profits at a rate of about 18 percent annually, despite moderate economic growth at the national level. Until recently, the company paid little attention to cash-management procedures. James Waller, the firm's president, said: "With our growth—who cares?" Bending to the suggestions of several analysts in the firm's finance group, Waller did agree to have a proposal prepared by the Second National Bank in Tampa, Florida. The objective of the proposal is to accelerate the firm's cash collections.

At present, Waller Nail uses a centralized billing procedure. All checks are mailed to the Tampa office headquarters for processing and eventual deposit. Under this arrangement, all customers' remittance checks take an average of 5 business days to reach the Tampa office. Once in Tampa, another 2 days are needed to process the checks for deposit at the Second National Bank.

Daily cash remittances at Waller Nail average $750,000. The average check size is $3,750. The firm currently earns 9.2 percent annually on its marketable securities portfolio.

The cash-acceleration plan presented by the officers of Second National Bank involves both a lockbox system and concentration banking. Second National would be the firm's only concentration bank. Lock boxes would be established in (1) Los Angeles, (2) Dallas, (3) Chicago, and (4) Tampa. This would reduce funds tied up in mail float to 3.5 days. Processing float would be totally eliminated. Funds would then be transferred twice each business day by means of automated depository transfer checks from local banks in Los Angeles, Dallas, and Chicago to the Second National Bank.

Each ADTC costs $27. These transfers will occur all 270 business days of the year. Each check processed through the lock box will cost Waller Nail $.35.

  a. What amount of cash balances will be freed if Waller Nail adopts the system proposed by Second National Bank?

  b. What is the opportunity cost of maintaining the current banking arrangement?

  c. What is the projected annual cost of operating the proposed system?

  d. Should Waller Nail Corp. adopt the system? Compute the net annual gain or loss associated with adopting the system.

17-7A. (*Concentration Banking*) Walkin Chemicals operates in New Orleans. The firm produces and distributes industrial cleaning products on a nationwide basis. The firm presently uses a centralized billing system. Walkin Chemicals has annual credit sales of $438 million. Creole National Bank has presented an offer to operate a concentration banking system for the company. Walkin already has an established line of credit with Creole. Creole says it will operate the system on a flat fee basis of $250,000 per year. The analysis done by the bank's cash-management services division suggests that 2 days in mail float and 1 day in processing float can be eliminated.

Because Walkin borrows almost continuously from Creole National, the value of the float reduction would be applied against the line of credit. The borrowing rate on the line of credit is set at an annual rate of 11 percent. Further, because of a reduction in clerical help, the new system will save the firm $65,000 in processing costs. Walkin uses a 365-day year in analyses of this sort. Should Walkin accept the bank's offer to install the new system?

17-8A. (*Lock-Box System*) Advanced Electronics is located in Nashville, Tennessee. The firm manufactures components used in a variety of electrical devices. All the firm's finished goods are shipped to five regional warehouses across the United States.

First Volunteer Bank of Nashville is Advanced Electronics's lead bank. First Volunteer recently completed a study of Advanced Electronics's cash-collection system. First Volunteer estimates that it can reduce Advanced Electronics's total float by 2.5 days with the installation of a lock-box arrangement in each of the firm's five regions.

The lock-box arrangement would cost each region $500 per month. Any funds freed up would be added to the firm's marketable securities portfolio and would yield 11.75 percent on an annual basis. Annual sales average $10,950,000 for each regional office. The firm and the bank use a 365-day year in their analyses. Should Advance Electronics's management approve the use of the proposed system?

17-9A. (*Costs of Services*) The Mountain Furniture Company of Scranton, Pennsylvania, may install a lock-box system to speed up its cash receipts. On an annual basis, Mountain Furniture receives $40 million in remittances by check. The firm will record and process 15,000 checks over the year. The Third Bank of Scranton will administer the system at a cost of $.35 per check. Cash that is freed up by use of the system can be invested to yield 9 percent on an annual before-tax basis. A 365-day year is used for analysis purposes. What reduction in check collection time is necessary for Mountain Furniture to be neither better nor worse off for having adopted the proposed system?

17-10A. (*Buying and Selling Marketable Securities*) Saturday Knights Live Products, Inc., has $1 million in excess cash that it might invest in marketable securities. In order to buy and sell the securities, however, the firm must pay a transactions fee of $30,000.

  a. Would you recommend purchasing the securities if they yield 11 percent annually and are held for

  1. 1 month?

  2. 2 months?

  3. 3 months?

  4. 6 months?

  5. 1 year?

  b. What minimum required yield would the securities have to return for the firm to hold them for 3 months (what is the breakeven yield for a 3-month holding period?).

17-11A. (*Valuing Float Reduction*) Griffey Manufacturing Company is forecasting that next year's gross revenues from sales will be $890 million. The senior treasury analyst for the firm expects the marketable securities portfolio to earn 9.60 percent over this same time period. A 365-day year is used in all the firm's financial procedures. What is the value to the company of 1 day's float reduction?

17-12A. (*Costs of Services*) Mustang Ski-Wear, Inc., is investigating the possibility of adopting a lock-box system as a cash receipts acceleration device. In a typical year, this firm receives remittances totaling $12 million by check. The firm will record and process 6,000 checks over this same time period. The Colorado Springs Second National Bank has informed the management of Mustang that it will expedite checks and associated documents through the lock-box system for a unit cost of $.20 per check. Mustang's financial manager has projected that cash freed by adoption of the system can be invested in a portfolio of near-cash assets that will yield an annual before-tax return of 7 percent. Mustang financial analysts use a 365-day year in their procedures.

    a. What reduction in check collection time is necessary for Mustang to be neither better nor worse off for having adopted the proposed system?

    b. How would your solution to (a) be affected if Mustang could invest the freed balances only at an expected annual return of 4.5 percent?

    c. What is the logical explanation for the difference in your answers to (a) and (b)?

17-13A. (*Valuing Float Reduction*) The Columbus Tool and Die Works will generate $18 million in credit sales next year. Collections occur at an even rate, and employees work a 270-day year. At the moment, the firm's general accounting department ties up 5 days' worth of remittance checks. An analysis undertaken by the firm's treasurer indicates that new internal procedures can reduce processing float by 2 days. If Columbus Tool invests the released funds to earn 8 percent, what will be the annual savings?

17-14A. (*Valuing Float Reduction*) Montgomery Woodcraft is a large distributor of woodworking tools and accessories to hardware stores, lumber yards, and tradesmen. All its sales are on a credit basis, net 30 days. Sales are evenly distributed over its 12 sales regions throughout the United States. There is no problem with delinquent accounts. The firm is attempting to improve its cash-management procedures. Montgomery recently determined that it took an average of 3.0 days for customers' payments to reach their office from the time they were mailed and another day for processing before payments could be deposited. Annual sales average $5,200,000 for each region, and investment opportunities can be found to return 9 percent per year. What is the opportunity cost to the firm of the funds tied up in mailing and processing? In your calculations, use a 365-day year.

17-15A. (*Accounts Payable Policy and Cash Management*) Bradford Construction Supply Company is suffering from a prolonged decline in new construction in its sales area. In an attempt to improve its cash position, the firm is considering changes in its accounts payable policy. After careful study, it has been determined that the only alternative available is to slow disbursements. Purchases for the coming year are expected to be $37.5 million. Sales will be $65 million, which represents about a 20 percent drop from the current year. Currently, Bradford discounts approximately 25 percent of its payments at 3 percent 10 days, net 30, and the balance of accounts are paid in 30 days. If Bradford adopts a policy of payment in 45 days or 60 days, how much can the firm gain if the annual opportunity cost of investment is 12 percent? What will be the result if this action causes Bradford Construction suppliers to increase their prices to the company by 0.5 percent to compensate for the 60-day extended term of payment? In your calculations, use a 365-day year and ignore any compounding effects related to expected returns.

17-16A. (*Interest Rate Risk*) Two years ago, your corporate treasurer purchased for the firm a twenty-year bond at its par value of $1,000. The coupon rate on this security is 8 percent. Interest payments are made to bondholders once a year. Currently, bonds of this particular risk class are yielding investors 9 percent. A cash shortage has forced you to instruct your treasurer to liquidate his bond.

a. At what price will your bond be sold? Assume annual compounding.

b. What will be the amount of your gain or loss over the original purchase price?

c. What would be the amount of your gain or loss had the treasurer originally purchased a bond with a 4-year rather than a 20-year maturity? (Assume all characteristics of the bonds are identical except their maturity periods.)

d. What do we call this type of risk assumed by your corporate treasurer?

17-17A. (*Marketable Securities Portfolio*) Red Raider Feedlots has $4 million in excess cash to invest in a marketable securities portfolio. Its broker will charge $10,000 to invest the entire $4 million. The president of Red Raider wants at least half of the $4 million invested at a maturity period of 3 months or less; the remainder can be invested in securities with maturities not to exceed 6 months. The relevant term structure of short-term yields follows:

Maturity Period	Available Yield (Annual)
1 month	6.2%
2 months	6.4
3 months	6.5
4 months	6.7
5 months	6.9
6 months	7.0

a. What should be the maturity periods of the securities purchased with the excess $4 million to maximize the before-tax income from the added investment? What will be the amount of the income from such an investment?

b. Suppose that the president of Red Raider relaxes his constraint on the maturity structure of the added investment. What would be your profit-maximizing investment recommendation?

c. If one-sixth of the excess cash is invested in each of the preceding maturity categories, what would be the before-tax income generated from such an action?

17-18A. (*Comparison of After-Tax Yields*) The corporate treasurer of Aggieland Fireworks is considering the purchase of a BBB-rated bond that carries a 9 percent coupon. The BBB-rated security is taxable, and the firm is in the 46 percent marginal tax bracket. The face value of this bond is $1,000. A financial analyst who reports to the corporate treasurer has alerted him to the fact that a municipal obligation is coming to the market with a 5-1/2 percent coupon. The par value of this security is also $1,000.

a. Which one of the two securities do you recommend the firm purchase? Why?

b. What must the fully taxed bond yield before tax to make it comparable with the municipal offering?

17-19A. (*Comparison of Yields*) A large proportion of the marketable securities portfolio of Edwards Manufacturing is invested in Treasury bills yielding 6.52 percent before consideration of income taxes. Hoosierville Utilities is bringing a new issue of preferred stock to the marketplace. The new preferred issue will yield 9.30 percent before taxes. The corporate treasurer for Edwards wants to evaluate the possibility of shifting a portion of the funds tied up in Treasury bills to the preferred stock issue.

a. Calculate the ultimate yields available to Edwards from investing in each type of security. Edwards is in the 46 percent tax bracket.

b. What factors apart from the available yields should be analyzed in this situation?

17-20A. (*Forecasting Excess Cash*) The C. K. S. Stove Company manufactures wood-burning stoves in the Pacific Northwest. Despite the recent popularity of this product, the firm has experienced a very erratic sales pattern. Owing to volatile weather conditions and abrupt changes in new housing starts, it has been extremely difficult for the firm to forecast its cash balances. Still, the company president is disturbed by the fact that the firm has never invested in any marketable securities.

Instead, the liquid asset portfolio has consisted entirely of cash. As a start toward reducing the firm's investment in cash and releasing some of it to near-cash assets, a historical record and projection of corporate cash holdings is needed. Over the past 5 years, sales have been $10 million, $12 million, $11 million, $14 million, and $19 million, respectively. Sales forecasts for the next 2 years are $23 and $21 million. Total assets for the firm are 60 percent of sales. Fixed assets are the higher of 50 percent of total assets or $4 million. Inventory and receivables amount to 70 percent of current assets and are held in equal proportions.

a. Prepare a worksheet that details the firm's balance sheets for each of the past 5 years and for the forecast periods.

b. What amount of cash will the firm have on hand during each year for short-term investment purposes?

INTEGRATIVE PROBLEM

New Wave Surfing Stuff, Inc., is a manufacturer of surfboards and related gear that sells to exclusive surf shops located in several Atlantic and Pacific mainland coastal towns as well as several Hawaiian locations. The company's headquarters are located in Carlsbad, California, a small Southern California coastal town. True to form, the company's officers, all veteran surfers, have been somewhat laid back about various critical areas of financial management. With an economic downturn in California adversely affecting their business, however, the officers of the company have decided to focus intently on ways to improve New Wave's cash flows. The CFO, Willy Bonik, has been requested to forgo any more daytime surfing jaunts until he has wrapped up a plan to accelerate New Wave's cash flows.

In an effort to ensure his quick return to the surf, Willy has decided to focus on what he believes is one of the easiest methods of improving New Wave's cash collections, namely, adoption of a cash receipts acceleration system that includes a lock-box system and concentration banking. Willy is well aware that New Wave's current system leaves much room for improvement. The company's accounts receivable system currently requires that remittances from customers be mailed to the headquarters office for processing then for deposit in the local branch of the Bank of the U.S. Such an arrangement takes a considerable amount of time. The checks take an average of 6 days to reach the Carlsbad headquarters. Then, depending on the surf conditions, processing within the company takes anywhere from 3 to 5 days, with the average from the day of receipt by the company to the day of deposit at the bank being 4 days.

Willy feels fairly certain that such delays are costly. After all, New Wave's average daily collections are $100,000. The average remittance size is $1,000. If Willy could get these funds into his marketable securities account more quickly, he could earn 6 percent at an annual rate on such funds. In addition, if he could arrange for someone else to do the processing, Willy could save $50,000 per year in costs related to clerical staffing.

New Wave's banker was pleased to provide Willy with a proposal for a combination of a lock-box system and a concentration banking system. Bank of the U.S. would be New Wave's concentration bank. Lock boxes would be established in Honolulu, Newport Beach, and Daytona Beach. Each check processed through the lock-box system would cost New Wave $.25. This arrangement, however, would reduce mail float by an average 3.5 days. The funds so collected would be transferred twice each day, 270 days a year, using automated depository transfer checks from each of the local lock-box banks to Bank of the U.S. Each ADTC would cost $25. The combination of the lock-box system and concentration banking would eliminate the time it takes the company to process cash collections, thereby making the funds available for short-term investment.

1. What would be the average amount of cash made available if New Wave were to adopt the system proposed by Bank of the U.S.?

2. What is the annual opportunity cost of maintaining the current cash collection and deposit system?

3. What is the expected annual cost of the complete system proposed by Bank of the U.S.?

4. What is the net gain or loss that is expected to result from the proposed new system? Should New Wave adopt the new system?

STUDY PROBLEMS (SET B)

17-1B. (*Concentration Banking*) Sprightly Step, Inc, produces a line of walking shoes that has become extremely popular with aging baby boomers. The company's recent rapid growth to $80 million in annual credit sales to shoe stores around the country has made consideration of a more advanced billing and collection system worthwhile. Sprightly's bank has proposed a concentration banking system to Sprightly's CFO, Roberto Dylan, that would save the company 3 days in mail float, 2 days in processing float, and $50,000 in annual clerical costs. The bank would charge a flat fee per year of $80,000 to operate the system for Sprightly. Roberto believes that the funds freed by such an arrangement could be invested at no transaction cost in the company's money market account and could earn an annual rate of return of 5.5 percent. Should Roberto accept the bank's proposal? Use a 365-day year in your analysis.

17-2B. (*Buying and Selling Marketable Securities*) An alternative to investing in a no-transaction-fee money market account under consideration by Roberto Dylan, the CFO at Sprightly Step, Inc. (see Problem 17-1B, above), is direct investment in marketable securities. Assume for this problem that Roberto has determined that adoption of a concentration banking system could make $1,100,000 available for investment in marketable securities, but such direct investing would result in annual transaction fees of $15,000. Would you recommend that Roberto invest the funds in a money market account (at 5.5 percent per annum) or purchase the marketable securities directly if such securities yield 8 percent per annum and the expected holding period is for:

    a. 1 month?

    b. 2 months?

    c. 6 months?

    d. 1 year?

17-3B. (*Buying and Selling Marketable Securities*) Universal Concrete Company has generated $700,000 in excess cash that it could invest in marketable securities. In order to buy and sell the securities, the firm will pay total transaction fees of $25,000.

    a. Would you recommend purchasing the securities if they yield 11.5 percent annually and are held for

        1. 1 month?

        2. 2 months?

        3. 3 months?

        4. 6 months?

        5. 1 year?

    b. What minimum required yield would the securities have to return for the firm to hold them for 2 months (what is the breakeven yield for a 2-month holding period)?

17-4B. (*Cash Receipts Acceleration System*) Kobrin Door & Glass, Inc., is a buyer and distributor of doors used in the home building industry. The firm has grown very quickly since it was established 8 years ago. Kobrin Door has managed to increase sales and profits at a rate of about 18 percent annually, despite moderate economic growth at the national level. Until recently, the company paid little attention to cash-management procedures. Charles Kobrin, the firm's president, said: "With our growth—who cares?" Bending to the suggestions of several analysts in the firm's finance group, Kobrin did agree to have a proposal prepared by the First Citizens Bank in Tampa, Florida. The objective of the proposal is to accelerate the firm's cash collections.

At present, Kobrin Door uses a centralized billing procedure. All checks are mailed to the Tampa office headquarters for processing and eventual deposit. Under this arrangement, all customers' remittance checks take an average of 5 business days to reach the Tampa office. Once in Tampa, another 2 days are needed to process the checks for deposit at the First Citizens Bank.

Daily cash remittances at Kobrin Door average $800,000. The average check size is $4,000. The firm currently earns 9.5 percent annually on its marketable securities portfolio.

The cash-acceleration plan presented by the officers of First Citizens Bank involves both a lock-box system and concentration banking. First Citizens would be the firm's only concentration bank.

Lock boxes would be established in (1) Los Angeles, (2) Dallas, (3) Chicago, and (4) Tampa. This would reduce funds tied up in mail float to 3.5 days. Processing float would be totally eliminated. Funds would then be transferred twice each business day by means of automated depository transfer checks from local banks in Los Angeles, Dallas, and Chicago to the First Citizens Bank. Each depository transfer check (ADTC) costs $30. These transfers will occur all 270 business days of the year. Each check processed through the lock box will cost Kobrin Door $.40.

  a. What amount of cash balances will be freed if Kobrin Door adopts the system proposed by First Citizens Bank?

  b. What is the opportunity cost of maintaining the current banking arrangement?

  c. What is the projected annual cost of operating the proposed system?

  d. Should Kobrin Door & Glass adopt the system? Compute the net annual gain or loss associated with adopting the system.

17-5B. (*Concentration Banking*) Smith & Tucker (S&T) Enterprises operates in New Orleans. The firm manufactures and distributes quality furniture on a nationwide basis. The firm presently uses a centralized billing system. S&T has annual credit sales of $438 million. Bayou National Bank has presented an offer to operate a concentration banking system for the company. S&T already has an established line of credit with Bayou. Bayou says it will operate the system on a flat fee basis of $300,000 per year. The analysis done by the bank's cash-management services division suggests that 2 days in mail float and 1 day in processing float can be eliminated.

Because S&T borrows almost continuously from Bayou National, the value of the float reduction would be applied against the line of credit. The borrowing rate on the line of credit is set at an annual rate of 11 percent. Further, because of a reduction in clerical help, the new system will save the firm $68,000 in processing costs. S&T uses a 365-day year in analyses of this sort. Should S&T accept the bank's offer to install the new system?

17-6B. (*Lock-Box System*) Regency Components is located in Nashville, Tennessee. The firm manufactures components used in a variety of electrical devices. All the firm's finished goods are shipped to five regional warehouses across the United States.

Tennessee State Bank of Nashville is Regency Components's lead bank. Tennessee State recently completed a study of Regency's cash-collection system. Tennessee State estimates that it can reduce Regency's total float by 3.0 days with the installation of a lock-box arrangement in each of the firm's five regions.

The lock-box arrangement would cost each region $600 per month. Any funds freed up would be added to the firm's marketable securities portfolio and would yield 11.0 percent on an annual basis. Annual sales average $10,000,000 for each regional office. The firm and the bank use a 365-day year in their analyses. Should Regency Components's management approve the use of the proposed system?

17-7B. (*Costs of Services*) The Hallmark Technology Company of Scranton, Pennsylvania, may install a lock-box system in order to speed up its cash receipts. On an annual basis, Hallmark receives $50 million in remittances by check. The firm will record and process 20,000 checks over the year. The Third Bank of Scranton will administer the system at a cost of $.37 per check. Cash that is freed up by use of the system can be invested to yield 9 percent on an annual before-tax basis. A 365-day year is used for analysis purposes. What reduction in check collection time is necessary for Hallmark to be neither better nor worse off for having adopted the proposed system?

17-8B. (*Buying and Selling Marketable Securities*) Western Photo Corp. has $1 million in excess cash that it might invest in marketable securities. In order to buy and sell the securities, however, the firm must pay a transactions fee of $35,000.

  a. Would you recommend purchasing the securities if they yield 10 percent annually and are held for

  1. 1 month?

  2. 2 months?

  3. 3 months?

  4. 6 months?

  5. 1 year?

b. What minimum required yield would the securities have to return for the firm to hold them for 3 months (what is the breakeven yield for a 3-month holding period)?

17-9B. (*Valuing Float Reduction*) Brady Consulting Services is forecasting that next year's gross revenues from sales will be $900 million. The senior treasury analyst for the firm expects the marketable securities portfolio to earn 9.5 percent over this same time period. A 365-day year is used in all the firm's financial procedures. What is the value to the company of one day's float reduction?

17-10B. (*Costs of Services*) Colorado Communications is investigating the possibility of adopting a lock-box system as a cash receipts acceleration device. In a typical year, this firm receives remittances totaling $10 million by check. The firm will record and process 7,000 checks over this same time period. The Colorado Springs Second National Bank has informed the management of Colorado Comm that it will expedite checks and associated documents through the lock-box system for a unit cost of $.30 per check. Colorado Comm's financial manager has projected that cash freed by adoption of the system can be invested in a portfolio of near-cash assets that will yield an annual before-tax return of 7 percent. Colorado Comm's financial analysts use a 365-day year in their procedures.

a. What reduction in check collection time is necessary for Colorado Comm to be neither better nor worse off for having adopted the proposed system?

b. How would your solution to (a) be affected if Colorado Comm could invest the freed balances only at an expected annual return of 4.5 percent?

c. What is the logical explanation for the difference in your answers to (a) and (b)?

17-11B. (*Valuing Float Reduction*) Campus Restaurants, Inc., will generate $17 million in credit sales next year. Collections occur at an even rate, and employees work a 270-day year. At the moment, the firm's general accounting department ties up 4 days' worth of remittance checks. An analysis undertaken by the firm's treasurer indicates that new internal procedures can reduce processing float by 2 days. If Campus invests the released funds to earn 9 percent, what will be the annual savings?

17-12B. (*Lock-Box System*) Alpine Systems is a distributor of refrigerated storage units to the meat products industry. All its sales are on a credit basis, net 30 days. Sales are evenly distributed over its 10 sales regions throughout the United States. Delinquent accounts are no problem. The company has recently undertaken an analysis aimed at improving its cash-management procedures. Alpine determined that it takes an average of 3.2 days for customers' payments to reach the head office in Pittsburgh from the time they are mailed. It takes another full day in processing time prior to depositing the checks with a local bank. Annual sales average $5 million for each regional office. Reasonable investment opportunities can be found yielding 8 percent per year. To alleviate the float problem confronting the firm, the use of a lock-box system in each of the 10 regions is being considered. This would reduce mail float by 1.0 days. One day in processing float would also be eliminated, plus a full day in transit float. The lock-box arrangement would cost each region $225 per month.

a. What is the opportunity cost to Alpine Systems of the funds tied up in mailing and processing? Use a 365-day year.

b. What would the net cost or savings be from use of the proposed cash acceleration technique? Should Alpine adopt the system?

17-13B. (*Marketable Securities Portfolio*) Katz Jewelers currently pays its employees on a weekly basis. The weekly wage bill is $500,000. This means that on average the firm has accrued wages payable of $500,000 + $0)/2 = $250,000.

Harry Katz works as the firm's senior financial analyst and reports directly to his father, who owns all of the firm's common stock. Harry Katz wants to move to a monthly wage payment system. Employees would be paid at the end of every fourth week. The younger Katz is fully aware that the labor union representing the company's workers will not permit the monthly payments system to take effect unless the workers are given some type of fringe benefit compensation.

A plan has been worked out whereby the firm will make a contribution to the cost of life insurance coverage for each employee. This will cost the firm $40,000 annually. Harry Katz expects the firm to earn 8 percent annually on its marketable securities portfolio.

a. Based on the projected information, should Katz Jewelers move to the monthly wage payment system?

b. What annual rate of return on the marketable securities portfolio would enable the firm to just breakeven on this proposal?

17-14B. (*Valuing Float Reduction*) True Locksmith is a large distributor of residential locks to hardware stores, lumber yards, and tradesmen. All its sales are on a credit basis, net 30 days. Sales are distributed over its 10 sales regions throughout the United States. There is no problem with delinquent accounts. The firm is attempting to improve its cash-management procedures. True Locksmith recently determined that it took an average of 3.0 days for customers' payments to reach their office from the time they were mailed, and another day for processing before payments could be deposited. Annual sales average $5,000,000 for each region, and investment opportunities can be found to return 9 percent per year. What is the opportunity cost to the firm of the funds tied up in mailing and processing? In your calculations, use a 365-day year.

17-15B. (*Accounts Payable Policy and Cash Management*) Meadowbrook Paving Company is suffering from a prolonged decline in new development in its sales area. In an attempt to improve its cash position, the firm is considering changes in its accounts payable policy. After careful study, it has determined that the only alternative available is to slow disbursements. Purchases for the coming year are expected to be $40 million. Sales will be $65 million, which represents about a 15 percent drop from the current year. Currently, Meadowbrook discounts approximately 25 percent of its payments at 3 percent 10 days, net 30, and the balance of accounts are paid in 30 days. If Meadowbrook adopts a policy of payment in 45 days or 60 days, how much can the firm gain if the annual opportunity cost of investment is 11 percent? What will be the result if this action causes Meadowbrook Paving suppliers to increase their prices to the company by 0.5 percent to compensate for the 60-day extended term of payment? In your calculation, use a 365-day year and ignore any compounding effects related to expected returns.

17-16B. (*Interest Rate Risk*) Two years ago, your corporate treasurer purchased for the firm a twenty-year bond at its par value of $1,000. The coupon rate on this security is 8 percent. Interest payments are made to bondholders once a year. Currently, bonds of this particular risk class are yielding investors 9 percent. A cash shortage has forced you to instruct your treasurer to liquidate his bond.

    a. At what price will your bond be sold? Assume annual compounding.

    b. What will be the amount of your gain or loss over the original purchase price?

    c. What would be the amount of your gain or loss had the treasurer originally purchased a bond with a 4-year rather than a 20-year maturity? (Assume all characteristics of the bonds are identical except their maturity periods.)

    d. What do we call this type of risk assumed by your corporate treasurer?

17-17B. (*Marketable Securities Portfolio*) Spencer Pianos has $3.5 million in excess cash to invest in a marketable securities portfolio. Its broker will charge $15,000 to invest the entire $3.5 million. The president of Spencer wants at least half of the $3.5 million invested at a maturity period of 3 months or less; the remainder can be invested in securities with maturities not to exceed 6 months. The relevant term structure of short-term yields follows:

Maturity Period	Available Yield (Annual)
1 month	6.2%
2 months	6.4
3 months	6.5
4 months	6.7
5 months	6.9
6 months	7.0

    a. What should be the maturity periods of the securities purchased with the excess $3.5 million in order to maximize the before-tax income from the added investment? What will be the amount of the income from such an investment?

b. Suppose that the president of Spencer relaxes his constraint on the maturity structure of the added investment. What would be your profit-maximizing investment recommendation?

c. If one-sixth of the excess cash is invested in each of the preceding maturity categories, what would be the before-tax income generated from such an action?

17-18B. (*Comparison of After-Tax Yields*) The corporate treasurer of Ward Grocers is considering the purchase of a BBB-rated bond that carries an 8.0 percent coupon. The BBB-rated security is taxable, and the firm is in the 46 percent marginal tax bracket. The face value of this bond is $1,000. A financial analyst who reports to the corporate treasurer has alerted him to the fact that a municipal obligation is coming to the market with a 5-1/2 percent coupon. The par value of this security is also $1,000.

a. Which one of the two securities do you recommend the firm purchase? Why?

b. What must the fully taxed bond yield before tax to make it comparable with the municipal offering?

17-19B. (*Comparison of Yields*) A large proportion of the marketable securities portfolio of Bentley Boats is invested in Treasury bills yielding 7.0 percent before consideration of income taxes. Hoosierville Utilities is bringing a new issue of preferred stock to the marketplace. The new preferred issue will yield 9.30 percent before taxes. The corporate treasurer for Bentley wants to evaluate the possibility of shifting a portion of the funds tied up in Treasury bills to the preferred stock issue.

a. Calculate the ultimate yields available to Bentley from investing in each type of security. Bentley is in the 46 percent tax bracket.

b. What factors apart from the available yields should be analyzed in this situation?

17-20B. (*Forecasting Excess Cash*) Fashionable Floors, Inc., manufactures carpet in the Pacific Northwest. Despite the popularity of this product, the firm has experienced a very erratic sales pattern. Owing to volatile weather conditions and abrupt changes in new housing starts, it has been extremely difficult for the firm to forecast its cash balances. Still, the company president is disturbed by the fact that the firm has never invested in any marketable securities. Instead, the liquid asset portfolio has consisted entirely of cash. As a start toward reducing the firm's investment in cash and releasing some of it to near-cash assets, a historical record and projection of corporate cash holdings is needed. Over the past 5 years, sales have been $10 million, $12 million, $11 million, $14 million, and $19 million, respectively. Sales forecasts for the next 2 years are $24 and $20 million. Total assets for the firm are 65 percent of sales. Fixed assets are the higher of 50 percent of total assets or $4 million. Inventory and receivables amount to 70 percent of current assets and are held in equal proportions.

a. Prepare a worksheet that details the firm's balance sheets for each of the past 5 years and for the forecast periods.

b. What amount of cash will the firm have on hand during each year for short-term investment purposes?

SELF-TEST SOLUTIONS

SS-1. a. Initially, it is necessary to calculate Creative Fashions's average remittance check amount and the daily opportunity cost of carrying cash. The average check size is

$$\frac{\$7,000,000}{4,000} = \$1,750 \text{ per check}$$

The daily opportunity cost of carrying cash is

$$\frac{0.08}{365} = 0.0002192 \text{ per day}$$

Next, the days saved in the collection process can be evaluated according to the general format (see equation 17-1 in the text of this chapter) of

added costs = added benefits

or

$$P = (D)(S)(i) \quad \text{[see equation 17-2]}$$
$$\$0.25 = (D)(\$1{,}750)(.0002192)$$
$$0.6517 \text{ days} = D$$

Creative Fashion Designs therefore will experience a financial gain if it implements the lock-box system and by doing so will speed up its collections by more than 0.6517 days.

b. Here the daily opportunity cost of carrying cash is

$$\frac{0.055}{365} = 0.0001507 \text{ per day}$$

For Creative Fashion Designs to breakeven, should it choose to install the lock-box system, cash collections must be accelerated by 0.9480 days, as follows:

$$\$0.25 = (D)(\$1{,}750)(.0001507)$$
$$0.9480 \text{ days} = (D)$$

c. The breakeven cash-acceleration period of 0.9480 days is greater than the 0.6517 days found in (a). This is due to the lower yield available on near-cash assets of 5.5 percent annually, versus 8.0 percent. Because the alternative rate of return on the freed-up balances is lower in the second situation, more funds must be invested to cover the costs of operating the lock-box system. The greater cash-acceleration period generates this increased level of required funds.

SS-2. a. Reduction in mail float:

(2.0 days) ($200,000) = $400,000
+ reduction in processing float:
(2.5 days) ($200,000) = $500,000
total float reduction   = $900,000

b. The opportunity cost of maintaining the present banking arrangement is

$$\left(\begin{array}{c}\text{forecast yield on marketable}\\ \text{securities portfolio}\end{array}\right) \cdot \left(\begin{array}{c}\text{total float}\\ \text{reduction}\end{array}\right)$$
$$(.106)(\$900{,}000) = \underline{\$95{,}400}$$

c. The average number of checks to be processed each day through the lock-box arrangement is

$$\frac{\text{daily remittances}}{\text{average check size}} = \frac{\$200{,}000}{\$800} = 250 \text{ checks}$$

The resulting cost of the lock-box system on an annual basis is

(250 checks) ($0.25) (270 days) = $16,875

Next we must calculate the estimated cost of the ADTC system. Detroit National Bank will *not* contribute to the cost of the ADTC arrangement, because it is the lead concentration bank and thereby receives the transferred data. This means that Artie Kay's Komputer Shops will be charged for six ADTCs (three locations @ two checks each) each business day. Therefore, the ADTC system costs

(6 daily transfers) ($20 per transfer) (270 days) = $32,400

We now have the total cost of the proposed system:

Lock-box cost	$16,875
ADTC cost	32,400
Total cost	$49,275

d. Our analysis suggests that Artie Kay's Komputer Shops should adopt the proposed cash receipts acceleration system. The projected net annual gain is $46,125 as follows:

Projected return on freed balances	$95,400
Less: Total cost of new system	49,275
Net annual gain	$46,125

SS-3. a. Here we must calculate the dollar value of the estimated return for each holding period and compare it with the transactions fee to determine if a gain can be made by investing in the securities. Those calculations and the resultant recommendations follow:

					Recommendation
1. $2,000,000 (.12) (1/12)	=	$ 20,000	<	$45,000	No
2. $2,000,000 (.12) (2/12)	=	$ 40,000	<	$45,000	No
3. $2,000,000 (.12) (3/12)	=	$ 60,000	>	$45,000	Yes
4. $2,000,000 (.12) (6/12)	=	$120,000	>	$45,000	Yes
5. $2,000,000 (.12) (12/12)	=	$240,000	>	$45,000	Yes

b. Let (x) be the required yield. With $2 million to invest for 3 months we have

$200,000(x)(3/12) = $ 45,000
$200,000(x)   = $180,000
$200,000(x)   = $180,000/2,000,000 = 9%

The breakeven yield, therefore, is 9%.

APPENDIX 17A

CASH-MANAGEMENT MODELS: SPLIT BETWEEN CASH AND NEAR CASH

In this appendix, we continue our discussion of the management of the firm's cash position. We have dwelled on the overall objectives of company cash management, described some actual liquid asset holdings of selected industries and firms, and overviewed a wide array of cash-collection and disbursement procedures.

We now consider the problem of properly dividing the firm's liquid asset holdings between cash and near cash.

LIQUID ASSETS: CASH VERSUS MARKETABLE SECURITIES

Through use of the cash-budgeting procedures outlined in chapter 4, the financial manager can pinpoint time periods when funds will be in either short or excess supply. If a shortage of funds is expected, then alternative avenues of financing must be explored. Conversely, the cash-budget projections might indicate that large, positive net cash balances in excess of immediate transactions needs will be forthcoming. In this more pleasant situation, the financial manager ought to decide on the proper split of the expected cash balances between actual cash holdings and marketable securities. To hold all of the expected cash balances as actual balances would needlessly penalize the firm's profitability.

Let's look at various methods by which the financial manager can develop useful cash balance level benchmarks.

BENCHMARK 1: WHEN CASH NEED IS CERTAIN

A basic method for indicating the proper *average* amount of cash to have on hand involves use of the economic order quantity concept so familiar in discussions of inventory management as we will see in chapter 18.[4] The objective of this analysis is to balance the lost income that the firm suffers from holding cash rather than marketable securities against the transactions costs involved in converting securities into cash. The rudiments of this decision model can easily be introduced by the use of an illustration.

Suppose that the firm knows with certainty that it will need $250,000 in cash for transactions purposes over the next 2 months and that this much cash is currently available. This transactions demand for cash will be represented by the variable T. Let us assume, for purposes of this illustration, that when the firm requires cash for its transactions needs, it will sell marketable securities in any one of five lot sizes, ranging from $30,000 to $70,000. These cash conversion (order) sizes, C, are identified in line 1 of Table 17A.1.

Line 2 shows the number of times marketable securities will be turned into cash over the next 2 months for a particular order size. For example, should it be decided to liquidate securities in amounts of $40,000, then the number of cash conversions needed to meet transactions over the next 2 months is $250,000/$40,000 = 6.25. In general, the number of cash withdrawals from the near-cash portfolio can be represented as T/C.

---

[4]The roots of a quantitative treatment of the firm's cash balance as just another type of inventory are found in William J. Baumol, "The Transactions Demand for Cash: An Inventory Theoretic Approach," *Quarterly Journal of Economics* 66 (November 1952): 545–56.

Table 17A.1 Determination of Optimal Cash Order Size

1. Cash conversion size (the dollar amount of marketable securities that will be sold to replenish the cash balance)	$30,000	$40,000	$50,000	$60,000	$70,000
2. Number of cash orders per time period (the time period is two months in this example) ($250,000 ÷ line 1)	8.33	6.25	5.00	4.17	3.57
3. Average cash balance (line 1 ÷ 2)	$15,000	$20,000	$25,000	$30,000	$35,000
4. Interest income forgone (line 3 × .01)	$150.00	$200.00	$250.00	$300.00	$350.00
5. Cash conversion cost ($50 × line 2)	$416.50	$312.50	$250.00	$208.50	$178.50
6. Total cost of ordering and holding cash (line 4 + line 5)	$566.50	$512.50	$500.00	$508.50	$528.50

Next we assume that the firm's cash payments are of constant amounts and are made continually over the 2-month planning period. This implies that the firm's cash balance behaves in the sawtooth manner shown in Figure 17A.1. The assertion of regularity and constancy of payments allows the firm's average cash balance over the planning period to be measured as $C/2$ (see Figure 17A.1). When marketable securities are sold and cash flows into a demand deposit account, the cash balance is equal to C. As payments are made on a regular and constant basis, the cash balance is reduced to a level of zero. The average cash balance over the period is then

$$\frac{C+0}{2} = \frac{C}{2}$$

The average cash balances corresponding to the different cash conversion sizes in our example are noted in line 3 of Table 17A.1.

Line 4 measures the opportunity cost of earnings forgone based on holding the average cash balance recorded on line 3. If the *annual* yield available on marketable securities is

Figure 17A.1 Cash Balances According to Inventory Model

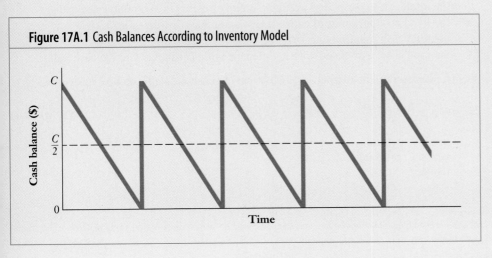

6 percent, then over the *two-month period* we are analyzing, the forfeited interest rate is .06/6 = .01.[5] Multiplying each average cash balance, C/2, by the .01 interest rate, *i*, available over the 2-month period produces the opportunity costs entered on line 4.

The very act of liquidating securities, unfortunately, is not without cost. Transacting conversions of marketable securities into cash can involve any of the following activities, each of which require the time of company employees as well as direct payment by the firm for various services:

1. Assistant treasurer's time to order the trade
2. Long-distance phone calls to effect the trade
3. Secretarial time to type authorization letters, make copies of the letters, and forward the letters to the company treasurer
4. Treasurer's time to read, approve, and sign the documents that authorize the trade
5. General accountant's time to record and audit the transaction
6. The value of fringe benefits incurred on the above times
7. The brokerage fee on each transaction

Suppose that the firm has properly studied the transaction costs, similar to those enumerated above, and finds they are of a fixed amount, *b*, per trade equal to $50. The transaction cost variable, *b*, is taken to be independent of the size of a particular securities order. Multiplying the transaction cost of $50 per trade by the number of cash orders that will take place during the planning period produces line 5. In general, the cash conversion cost (transaction cost) is equal to *b(T/C)*.

We are now down to the last line in Table 17A.1. This is the sum total of the income lost by holding cash rather than marketable securities and the cash-ordering costs. Line 6, then, is the total of lines 4 and 5. The inventory model seeks to *minimize* these *total costs* associated with holding cash balances. Table 17A.1 tells us, if cash is ordered on five occasions in $50,000 sizes over the 2-month period, the total costs of holding an average cash balance of $25,000 will be $500. This is less than the total costs associated with any other cash conversion size.

At the beginning of the 2-month planning horizon, all of the $250,000 available for transactions purposes need not be held in the firm's demand deposit account. To minimize the total costs of holding cash, only $50,000 should immediately be retained to transact business. The remaining $200,000 should be invested in income-yielding securities and then turned into cash as the firm's disbursal needs dictate.

It is useful to put our discussion of the inventory model for cash management into a more general form. Summarizing the definitions developed in the illustration, we have

C = the amount per order of marketable securities to be converted into cash
i = the interest rate per period available on investments in marketable securities
b = the fixed cost per order of converting marketable securities into cash
T = the total cash requirements over the planning period
TC = the total costs associated with maintenance of a particular average cash balance

As just pointed out, the total costs (TC) of having cash on hand can be expressed as

$$TC = i\left(\frac{C}{2}\right) \;+\; b\left(\frac{T}{C}\right) \tag{17A-1}$$

| total interest income forgone | total ordering costs |

---

[5]If we were studying a 1-month planning period, rather than the 2-month period being discussed, the annual yield would have to be stated on a monthly basis of .06/12 = .005.

If equation (17A-1) is applied to the $50,000 cash conversion size column in Table 17A.1, the total costs can be computed directly as follows:

$$TC = .01\left(\frac{\$50,000}{2}\right) + 50\left(\frac{\$250,000}{\$50,000}\right)$$

$$= \$250 + \$250 = \$500$$

You can see that the $500 total cost is the same as was found deductively in Table 17A.1. The optimal cash conversion size, C^*, can be found by use of equation (17A-2):

$$C^* = \sqrt{\frac{2bT}{i}} \qquad (17A-2)$$

When the data in our example are applied to equation (17A-2), the optimal cash order size is found to be

$$C^* = \sqrt{\frac{2(50)(250,000)}{.01}} = \$50,000$$

Figure 17A.2 displays this solution to our example problem graphically. Notice that the optimal cash order size of $50,000 occurs at the minimum point of the total cost curve associated with keeping cash on hand.

INVENTORY MODEL IMPLICATIONS

The solution to equation (17A-2) tells the financial manager that the optimal cash order size, C^*, varies directly with the square root of the order costs, bT, and inversely with the yield, i, available on marketable securities. Notice that as transactions requirements, T,

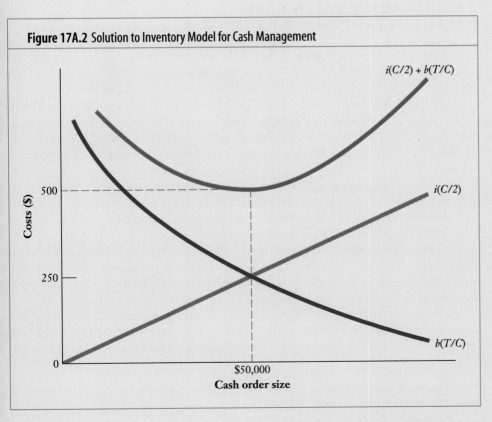

Figure 17A.2 Solution to Inventory Model for Cash Management

increase, owing perhaps to an augmented sales demand, the optimal cash order size does *not* rise proportionately.

The model also indicates that as interest rates rise on near-cash investments, the optimal cash order size decreases, with the effect dampened by the square-root sign as equation (17A-2) suggests. With higher yields to be earned on the marketable securities portfolio, the financial manager will be more reluctant to make large withdrawals because of the interest income that will be lost.

Some final perspectives on the use of the economic order quantity model in cash management can be obtained by reviewing the assumptions upon which it is derived. Among the more important of these assumptions are the following:

1. Cash payments over the planning period are (a) of a regular amount, (b) continuous, and (c) certain.
2. No unanticipated cash receipts will be received during the analysis period.
3. The interest rate to be earned on investments remains constant over the analysis period.
4. Transfers between cash and the securities portfolio may occur any time at a fixed cost, regardless of the amount transferred.

Clearly, the strict assumptions of the inventory model are not completely realized in actual business practice. For instance, the amount and timing of cash payments will not be known with certainty; nor are cash receipts likely to be as discontinuous or lumpy as is implied. If relaxation of the critical assumptions is not so prohibitive as to render the model useless, then the model can provide a benchmark for managerial decision making. The model's output is not intended to be a precise and inviolable rule. On the other hand, if the assumptions of the model cannot be reasonably approximated, the financial manager must look elsewhere for possible guides that indicate a proper split between cash and marketable securities.

BENCHMARK 2: WHEN CASH BALANCES FLUCTUATE RANDOMLY

It is entirely possible that the firm's cash balance pattern does *not at all* resemble that indicated in Figure 17A.1. The assumptions of certain regularity and constancy of cash payments may be unduly restrictive when applied to some organizations.[6]

Rather, the cash balance might behave more like the jagged line shown in Figure 17A.3. In this figure, it is assumed that the firm's cash balance changes in an irregular fashion from day to day. The changes are unpredictable; that is, they are random. Further, let us suppose the chances that a cash balance change will be either (1) positive or (2) negative are equal at .5 each.

As cash receipts exceed expenditures, the cash balance moves upward until it hits an upper control limit, *UL*, expressed in dollars. This occurs at point *A* in Figure 17A.3. At such time, the financial officer initiates an investment in marketable securities equal to *UL* − *RP* dollars, where *RP* is the cash return point.

If cash payments exceed receipts, the cash balance moves downward until it hits a lower control limit, *LL*. This situation is noted by point *B* in Figure 17A.3. When this occurs, the financial officer sells marketable securities equal to *RP* − *LL* dollars. This restores the cash balance to the return point, *RP*.

To make this application of control theory to cash management operational, we must determine the upper control limit, *UL*, the lower control limit, *LL*, and the cash return point, *RP*. For the present case, in which a net cash increase is as likely to occur

---

[6]This discussion is based upon Merton H. Miller and Daniel Orr, "A Model of the Demand for Money by Firms," *Quarterly Journal of Economics* 80 (August 1966): 413–35.

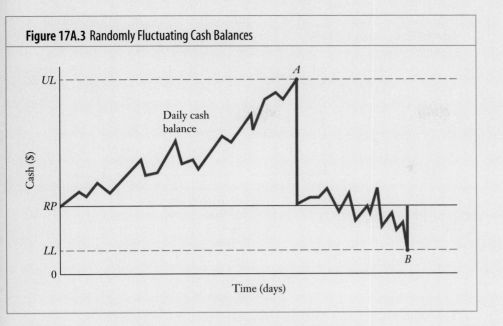

Figure 17A.3 Randomly Fluctuating Cash Balances

as a net cash decrease, use of the following variables will allow computation of the cash return point, RP.[7]

b = the fixed cost per order of converting marketable securities into cash

i = the daily interest rate available on investments in marketable securities

σ^2 = the variance of daily changes in the firm's expected cash balances (this is a measure of volatility of cash flow changes over time)

The optimal cash return point, RP, can be calculated as follows:

$$RP = \sqrt[3]{\frac{3b\sigma^2}{4i}} + 2LL \qquad (17A\text{-}3)$$

The upper control limit, UL, can be computed quite simply:

$$UL = 3RP - 2LL \qquad (17A\text{-}4)$$

The actual value for the lower limit, LL, is set by management. In business practice, a minimum is typically established below which the cash balance is not permitted to fall. Among other things, it will be affected by (1) the firm's banking arrangements, which may require compensating balances, and (2) management's risk-bearing tendencies.

To illustrate use of the model, suppose that the annual yield available on marketable securities is 9 percent. Over a 360-day year, i becomes .09/360 = .00025 per day. Assume that the fixed cost, b, of transacting a marketable securities trade is $50. Moreover, the firm has studied its past cash balance levels and has observed that the standard deviation, σ, in daily cash balance changes is equal to $800. The firm sees no reason why this variability should change in the future. It is the firm's policy to maintain $1,000 in its demand deposit account (LL) at all times. Finally, the firm has established that each day's actual cash balance is random. The equations that comprise this control limit system can be applied to provide guidelines for cash-management policy.

---

[7]Situations in which the probabilities of cash increases and decreases are not equal are extremely difficult to evaluate within the framework of the Miller-Orr decision model. See Miller and Orr, "A Model of the Demand for Money by Firms," *Quarterly Journal of Economics* 80 (August 1966): 427–29, 433–35.

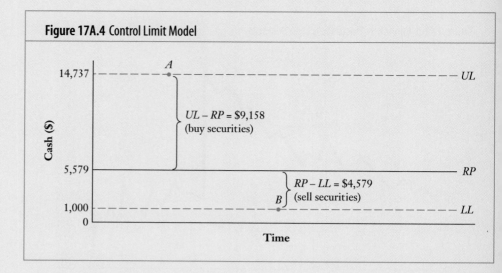

Figure 17A.4 Control Limit Model

The optimal cash return point for transactions purposes becomes

$$RP = \sqrt[3]{\frac{3(50)(800)^2}{4(.00025)}} + 1,000 = (4,579 + 1,000) = \$5,579$$

The upper cash balance limit that will trigger a transfer of cash to marketable securities is

$$UL = 3(5,579) - 2(1,000) = \$14,737$$

The cash balance control limits derived from this example are graphed in Figure 17A.4. Should the cash balance bump against the upper limit of $14,737 (point A), then the financial officer is instructed to buy $9,158 ($UL - RP$) of marketable securities. At the other extreme, if the cash balance should drop to the lower limit of $1,000 (point B), then the financial officer is instructed to sell $4,579 ($RP - LL$) of marketable securities to restore the cash balance level to $5,579. As long as the cash balance wanders *within* the UL to LL range, no securities transactions take place. By acting in this manner, the financial officer will *minimize* the sum of interest income forgone and the costs of purchasing and selling securities.[8]

CONTROL LIMIT MODEL IMPLICATIONS

Use of equation (17A-3) results in determination of the optimal cash return point within the framework of the control limit model. Inspection of this equation indicates to the financial officer that the optimal cash return level, RP, will vary directly with the cube root of both the transfer cost variable, b, and the volatility of daily cash balance changes, σ^2. Greater transfer costs or cash-balance volatility result in a greater *absolute dollar* spread between the upper control limit and the cash return point. This larger spread between UL and RP means that securities purchases are made in larger lot sizes. It is further evident that the optimal cash return point varies inversely with the cube root of the lost interest rate.

Similar to the basic inventory model reviewed in the preceding section, the control limit model implies that economies of scale are possible in cash management. In addition, the optimal cash return point always lies well below the midpoint of the range UL to LL, over which the cash balance is permitted to "walk." This means that the liquidation of

---

[8]As with the Baumol inventory model, the Miller-Orr control limit model seeks to minimize the total cost of managing the firm's cash balance over a finite planning horizon.

marketable securities occurs (1) more frequently and (2) in smaller lot sizes than purchases of securities. This suggests that firms with highly volatile cash balances must be acutely concerned with the liquidity of their marketable securities portfolio.

BENCHMARK 3: COMPENSATING BALANCES

An important element of the commercial banking environment that affects corporate cash management deserves special mention. This is the practice of the bank's requiring, either formally or informally, that the firm maintain deposits of a given amount in its demand deposit account. Such balances are referred to as *compensating balances*.

The compensating-balance requirement became typical banking practice after federal action forbade the payment of interest on demand deposits in the early 1930s.[9] In the face of prospective withdrawals the procedure allowed banks to maintain favorable levels of their basic raw material—deposits. Such balances are normally required of corporate customers in three situations: (1) where the firm has an established line of credit (loan commitment) at the bank but it is not entirely used, (2) where the firm has a loan outstanding at the bank, or (3) in exchange for various other services provided by the bank to its customer.

As you would expect, compensating-balance policies vary among commercial banks and, furthermore, are influenced by general conditions in the financial markets. Still, some tendencies can be identified. In the case of the unused portion of a loan commitment, the bank might require that the firm's demand deposits average anywhere from 5 to 10 percent of the commitment. If a loan is currently outstanding with the bank, the requirement will probably be 10 to 20 percent of the unpaid balance. During periods when monetary policy is restrictive, (so-called tight money periods) the ranges rise by about 5 percent across the board.

Instead of charging directly for certain banking services, the bank may ask the firm to "pay" for them by the compensating-balance approach. These services include check clearing, the availability of credit information, and any of the array of receipts-acceleration or payment-control techniques that we discussed in this chapter.

If the bank asks for compensation in the form of balances left on deposit rather than charging unit prices for services rendered, the requirement may be expressed as (1) an absolute amount or (2) an average amount. The latter is preferable to most firms, as it provides for some flexibility in use of the deposits. With the average balance requirement calculated over a month, and in some instances as long as a year, the balance can be low on occasion as long as it is offset with heavy balances in other time periods.

COMPENSATING-BALANCE REQUIREMENT IMPLICATIONS

In the analysis that the financial officer undertakes to determine the split between cash and near cash, explicit consideration must be given to compensating-balance requirements. This information can be used in conjunction with the basic inventory model (benchmark 1) or the control limit model (benchmark 2).

One approach is to use either of the models and in the calculations ignore the compensating-balance requirement. This is logical in many instances. Generally, the compensating balance required by the bank is beyond the firm's control.

In using the models, then, the focus is on the discretionary cash holdings above the required levels. Once the solution to the particular model is found, the firm's optimal

---

[9]Paul S. Nadler, "Compensating Balances and the Prime at Twilight," *Harvard Business Review* 50 (January–February 1972): 112.

average cash balance will be the *higher* of that suggested by the model or the balance requirement set by the bank.

A second approach is to introduce the size of the compensating balance into the format of the cash-management model and carry out the requisite calculations. We noted previously that in the control limit model, the lower control limit (LL) could be the compensating-balance requirement faced by the firm as opposed to a value of zero for LL. In the basic inventory-model the compensating balance can be treated as a safety stock. In Figure 17A.1, then, the cash balance would not touch the zero level and trigger a marketable securities purchase; rather, it would fall to the level of the compensating balance (some amount greater than zero) and initiate the securities purchase. Under ordinary circumstances, the calculated optimal order size of marketable securities is not altered by consideration of compensating balances in either model, so useful information on the proper split between near cash and discretionary cash (cash held in excess of compensating balances) is still provided by these two benchmarks.

Trends indicate that compensating balances are slowly giving way to unit pricing of bank services. Under unit pricing, the bank quotes a stated price for the service. The firm pays that rate only for the services actually used. Such a trend means that the importance of this third benchmark may diminish in the foreseeable future. At the same time, the policies suggested by application of cash-management models may well attract attention.

STUDY PROBLEMS

17A-1. (*Inventory Model*) The Richard Price Metal Working Company will experience $800,000 in cash payments next month. The annual yield available on marketable securities is 6.5 percent. The company has analyzed the cost of obtaining or investing cash and found it to be equal to $85 per transaction. Because cash outlays for Price Metal Working occur at a constant rate over any given month, the company has decided to apply the principles of the inventory model for cash management to provide answers to several questions.

    a. What is the optimal cash conversion size for the Price Metal Working Company?

    b. What is the total cost of having cash on hand during the coming month?

    c. How often (in days) will the firm have to make a cash conversion? Assume a 30-day month.

    d. What will be Price Metal Working's average cash balance?

17A-2. (*Control Limit Model*) The Edinboro Fabric Company manufactures 18 different final products, which are woven, cut, and dyed for use primarily in the clothing industry. Owing to the whimsical nature of the underlying demand for certain clothing styles, Edinboro Fabric has a most difficult time forecasting its cash balance levels. The company maintains $2,000 in its demand deposit account at all times. A detailed study of past cash balance levels has revealed that the standard deviation, σ, in daily cash balance changes has been equal to $600. The nature of the firm is not expected to undergo any structural changes in the foreseeable future, and for this reason the past volatility in cash balance levels is expected to continue in the future. Edinboro has determined that the cost of transacting a marketable securities trade is $85. Marketable securities are yielding 6 percent per annum. The firm always uses a 360-day year in its analysis procedures. Robert Cambridge, Edinboro's treasurer, has just returned from a 3-day cash management seminar in New York City. He has decided to apply the control limit model for cash management to his firm's situation.

    a. What is the optimal cash return point for Edinboro?

    b. What is the upper control limit?

    c. In what lot sizes will marketable securities be purchased? Sold?

    d. Graph your results.

Learning Objectives

Active Applications

World Finance

Practice

CHAPTER 18

ACCOUNTS RECEIVABLE, INVENTORY, AND TOTAL QUALITY MANAGEMENT

LEARNING OBJECTIVES

After reading this chapter, you should be able to

1. Discuss the determinants of the firm's investment in accounts receivable and how changes in credit policy are determined.

2. Discuss the reasons for carrying inventory and how inventory management decisions are made.

3. Discuss the changes that TQM and single-sourcing have had on inventory purchasing.

INTRODUCTION

In the fashion industry, it is not enough for a store to have inventory on hand; it also must have what is in style. As we all know, fashion trends can change overnight. This is particularly frustrating for fashion retailers, because traditionally, orders must be placed at least 6 months in advance. As a result, most fashion retailers have quite a challenge in reacting quickly to new trends and style changes.

The Limited, which has more than 3,000 retail outlets nationwide, including Express and Victoria's Secret, has set up an international inventory management system that allows the fashion cycle to be cut to 60 days. It does this by examining daily reports that are taken from point-of-sale computers, with information on items sold being fed back to company headquarters. Decisions are then made on what to produce, and those orders are sent by satellite to plants located in Hong Kong. The newly produced goods are then flown back to the United States on chartered flights that arrive four times a week. Once in the United States, the goods are sorted, priced, and shipped out to stores nationwide within 48 hours. As a result, the goods go on sale within 60 days of the order.

Although this is an expensive inventory system, the benefits from increased sales more than outweigh the costs of the chartered flights. In fact, it is this inventory stocking system that allows The Limited to be successful at keeping on top of trends. As we will see, inventory and also credit management play important roles in determining the success or failure of a company.

CHAPTER PREVIEW

In the two previous chapters, we developed a general overview of working-capital management and took an in-depth look at the management of cash and marketable securities. In this chapter, we will focus on the management of two more working-capital items: accounts receivable and inventory. Accounts receivable and inventory make up a large portion of the firm's assets; they actually compose on average 20.22 and 4.80 percent, respectively, of a typical firm's assets. Thus, because of their sheer magnitude, any changes in their levels will affect profitability.

In studying the management of these current assets, we first examine accounts receivable management, focusing on its importance, what determines investment in it, what the decision variables are, and how we determine them. Then we turn to inventory management, examine its importance, and discuss order quantity and order point problems, which in combination determine the level of investment in inventory. We also examine the relationship between inventory and total quality management.

As we will see, any changes in levels of accounts receivable and inventory will involve an application of Axiom 1: The Risk-Return Trade-Off—We Won't Take on Additional Risk Unless We Expect to Be Compensated with Additional Return. This chapter will also emphasize Axiom 4: Incremental Cash Flows—It's Only What Changes that Counts, and Axiom 5: The Curse of Competitive Markets—Why It's Hard to Find Exceptionally Profitable Projects.

OBJECTIVE 1 **ACCOUNTS RECEIVABLE MANAGEMENT**

All firms by their very nature are involved in selling either goods or services. Although some of these sales will be for cash, a large portion will involve credit. Whenever a sale is made on credit, it increases the firm's accounts receivable. Thus the importance of how a firm manages its accounts receivable depends on the degree to which the firm sells on credit. Table 18.1 lists, for selected industries, the percentage of total assets made up by accounts receivable. The more that is sold on credit, the higher the proportion of assets that are tied up in accounts receivable. Certainly for firms in the building construction business, managing accounts receivable is important because they make up almost 30 percent of a typical firm's assets.

From Table 18.1, we can see that accounts receivable typically comprise about 20 percent of a firm's assets. In effect, when we discuss management of accounts receivable, we are discussing the management of one-fifth of the firm's assets. Moreover, because cash flows from a sale cannot be invested until the account is collected, control of receivables takes on added importance; efficient collection determines both profitability and liquidity of the firm.

Size of Investment in Accounts Receivable

The size of the investment in accounts receivable is determined by several factors. First, the percentage of credit sales to total sales affects the level of accounts receivable held. Although this factor certainly plays a major role in determining a firm's investment in accounts receivable, it generally is not within the control of the financial manager. The nature of the business tends to determine the blend between credit sales and cash sales. A large grocery store tends to sell exclusively on a cash basis, whereas most construction-lumber supply firms make their sales primarily with credit. Actually, most large grocery stores allow you to use your credit card, but they receive immediate payment from the credit card company. Thus the nature of the business, and not the decisions of the financial manager, tends to determine the proportion of credit sales.

Table 18.1 Accounts Receivable as a Percentage of Total Assets for Major Industries

Industry	Accounts Receivable Relative to Total Assets
Total construction	29.30%
General merchandising stores—retail	18.80
Building materials, garden supplies, and mobile home dealers—retail	16.74
Automotive dealers and service stations—retail	13.54
Transportation	12.34
Apparel and accessory stores—retail	11.79
Agriculture, forestry, and fishing	9.84
Food stores	7.30
Hotels and other lodging places	5.64
All industries	20.33

SOURCE: Internal Revenue Service, U.S. Treasury Department, *Statistics of Income*, 1994, *Corporate Income Tax Returns* (Washington D.C.: Government Printing Office, 1997), 9–242.

The level of sales is also a factor in determining the size of the investment in accounts receivable. Very simply, the more sales, the greater accounts receivable. As the firm experiences seasonal and permanent growth in sales, the level of investment in accounts receivable will naturally increase. Thus, although the level of sales affects the size of the investment in accounts receivable, it is not a decision variable for the financial manager.

The final determinants of the level of investment in accounts receivable are the credit and collection policies—more specifically, the *terms of sale,* the *quality of customer,* and *collection efforts.* The terms of sale specify both the time period during which the customer must pay and the terms, such as penalties for late payments or discounts for early payments. The type of customer or credit policy also affects the level of investment in accounts receivable. For example, the acceptance of poorer credit risks and their subsequent delinquent payments may lead to an increase in accounts receivable. The strength and timing of the collection efforts can affect the period for which past-due accounts remain delinquent, which in turn affects the level of accounts receivable. Collection and credit policy decisions may further affect the level of investment in accounts receivable by causing changes in the sales level and the ratio of credit sales to total sales. However, the three credit and collection policy variables are the only true decision variables under the control of the financial manager. Figure 18.1 shows where the financial manager can—and cannot—make a difference.

STOP AND THINK

As we examine the credit decision, try to remember that our goal is not to minimize losses but to maximize profits. Although we will spend a good deal of time trying to sort out those customers with the highest probability of default, this analysis is only an input into a decision based on shareholder wealth maximization. Essentially, a firm with a high profit margin can tolerate a more liberal credit policy than a firm with a low profit margin.

Terms of sale—decision variable. The **terms of sale** identify the possible discount for early payment, the discount period, and the total credit period. They are generally stated in the form *a/b* net *c,* indicating that the customer can deduct *a* percent if the account is paid within *b* days; otherwise, the account must be paid within *c* days. Thus, for example,

Terms of sale
_____

The credit terms identifying the possible discount for early payment.

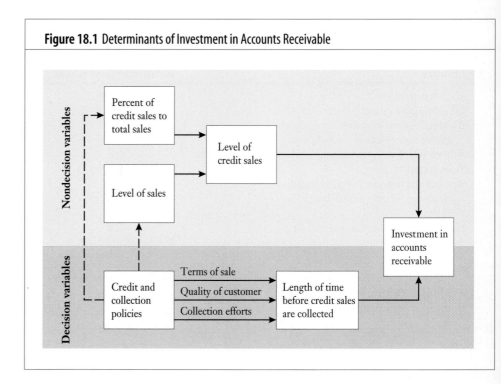

Figure 18.1 Determinants of Investment in Accounts Receivable

trade credit terms of 2/10, net 30 indicate that a 2 percent discount can be taken if the account is paid within 10 days; otherwise it must be paid within 30 days. What if the customer decides to forgo the discount and not pay until the final payment date? If such a decision is made, the customer has the use of the money for the time period between the discount date and the final payment date. However, failure to take the discount represents a cost to the customer. For instance, if the terms are 2/10, net 30, the annualized opportunity cost of passing up this 2 percent discount in order to withhold payment for an additional 20 days is 36.73 percent. This is determined as follows:

$$\begin{pmatrix} \text{annualized opportunity cost} \\ \text{of forgoing the discount} \end{pmatrix} = \frac{a}{1-a} \times \frac{360}{c-b} \tag{18-1}$$

Substituting the values from the example, we get

$$36.73\% = \frac{.02}{1 - .02} \times \frac{360}{30 - 10} \tag{18-2}$$

The typical discount ranges anywhere from one-half percent to 10 percent, whereas the discount period is generally 10 days and the total credit period varies from 30 to 90 days. Although the terms of credit vary radically from industry to industry, they tend to remain relatively uniform within any particular industry. Moreover, the terms tend to remain relatively constant over time, and they do not appear to be used frequently as a decision variable.

Type of customer—decision variable. A second decision variable involves determining the *type of customer* who is to qualify for trade credit. Several costs always are associated with extending credit to less credit-worthy customers (high-risk firms or individuals). First, as the probability of default increases, it becomes more important to identify which of the possible new customers would be a poor risk. When more time is spent investigating the less credit-worthy customer, the costs of credit investigation increase.

Default costs also vary directly with the quality of the customer. As the customer's credit rating declines, the chance that the account will not be paid on time increases. In the extreme case, payment never occurs. Thus taking on less credit-worthy customers results in increases in default costs.

Collection costs also increase as the quality of the customer declines. More delinquent accounts force the firm to spend more time and money collecting them. Overall, the decline in customer quality results in increased costs of credit investigation, collection, and default.

In determining whether or not to grant credit to an individual customer, we are primarily interested in the customer's short-run ability and inclination to pay. Thus liquidity ratios, other obligations, and the overall profitability of the firm become the focal point in this analysis. Credit-rating services, such as Dun & Bradstreet, provide information on the financial status, operations, and payment history for most firms. Other possible sources of information would include credit bureaus, trade associations, Chambers of Commerce, competitors, bank references, public financial statements, and, of course, the customer's past relationship with the firm.

One way in which both individuals and firms are often evaluated as credit risks is through the use of credit scoring. **Credit scoring** involves the numerical evaluation of each applicant. An applicant receives a score based on his or her answers to a simple set of questions. This score is then evaluated according to a predetermined standard, its level relative to the standard determining whether or not credit should be extended. The major advantage of credit scoring is that it is inexpensive and easy to perform. For example, once the standards are set, a computer or clerical worker without any specialized training could easily evaluate any applicant.

Credit scoring

The numerical credit evaluation of each candidate.

The techniques used for constructing credit-scoring indexes range from the simple approach of adding up default rates associated with the answers given to each question, to sophisticated evaluations using multiple discriminate analysis (MDA). MDA is a statistical technique for calculating the appropriate importance to be given to each question used in evaluating the applicant. Figure 18.2 shows a credit "scorecard" used by a large automobile dealer. The weights or scores attached to each answer are based on the auto dealer's past experience with credit sales. For example, the scorecard indicates that individuals with no telephone in their home have a much higher probability of default than those with a telephone. One caveat should be mentioned: Whenever this type of questionnaire is used to evaluate credit applicants, it should be examined carefully to be sure that it does not contain any illegal discriminatory questions.

Another model that could be used for credit scoring has been provided by Edward Altman, a Professor at New York University, who used multiple discriminant analysis to identify businesses that might go bankrupt. In his landmark study, Altman used financial ratios to predict which firms would go bankrupt over a 20-year period. Using multiple discriminant analysis, Altman came up with the following index:

$$Z = 3.3 \left(\frac{EBIT}{\text{total assets}} \right) + 1.0 \left(\frac{\text{sales}}{\text{total assets}} \right) + .06 \left(\frac{\text{market value of equity}}{\text{book value of debt}} \right)$$

$$+ 1.4 \left(\frac{\text{retained earnings}}{\text{total assets}} \right) + 1.2 \left(\frac{\text{working capital}}{\text{total assets}} \right) \qquad (18\text{-}3)$$

Altman found that of the firms that went bankrupt over this time period, 94 percent had Z scores of less than 2.7 one year prior to bankruptcy and only 6 percent had scores

Figure 18.2 Credit "Scorecard"

Telephone   Score

Home	Relative	None				
5	1	0				

Living quarters

Own home no mortgage	Own home mortgage	Rent a house	Live with someone	Rent an apartment	Rent a room	
6	3	2	1	0	0	

Bank accounts

None	1	More than 1				
0	4	6				

Years at present address

Under 1/2	1/2–2	3–7	8 or more			
0	1	3	4			

Size of family including customer

1	2	3–6	7 or more			
2	4	3	0			

Monthly income

Under $1,600	$1,601–$1,900	$1,901–$2,200	$2,201–$2,800	More than $2,800		
0	1	3	6	8		

Length of present employment

Under 1/2 year	1/2–2 years	3–7 years	8 years or more			
0	1	2	4			

Percent of selling price on credit

Under 50	50–69	70–84	85–99			
5	3	1	0			

Interview discretionary points (+5 to –5)

Total

Credit scorecard

_____
(Customer's name)

_____
(Street address)

_____
(City, State, Zip)

_____
(Home/Office telephone)

_____
(Credit scorer)

Credit scorecard evaluation

Dollar amount of loan: $0–$2,000

0–18	19–21	22 or more
Reject	Refer to main credit	Accept

Dollar amount of loan: $2,001–$5,000

0–21	22–24	25 or more
Reject	Refer to main credit	Accept

Dollar amount of loan: more than $5,000

0–23	24–27	27 or more
Reject	Refer to main credit	Accept

If a previous loan customer, were payments received promptly?   Yes ☐   No* ☐

Are you willing to take responsibility for authorizing this loan?   Yes ☐   No* ☐

*Refer to main credit if answer to either question is *No*.

above 2.7 percent. Conversely, of those firms that did not go bankrupt, only 3 percent had Z scores below 2.7 and 97 percent had scores above 2.7.

Again, the advantages of credit-scoring techniques are low cost and ease of implementation. Simple calculations can easily spot those credit risks that need more screening before credit should be extended to them.

Collection efforts—decision variable. The key to maintaining control over collection of accounts receivable is the fact that the probability of default increases with the age of the account. Thus control of accounts receivable focuses on the control and elimination of past-due receivables. One common way of evaluating the current situation is ratio analysis. The financial manager can determine whether or not accounts receivable are under control by examining the average collection period, the ratio of receivables to assets, the ratio of credit sales to receivables (called the accounts receivable turnover ratio), and the amount of bad debts relative to sales over time. In addition, the manager can perform what is called an aging of accounts receivable to provide a breakdown in both dollars and in percentages of the proportion of receivables that are past due. Comparing the current aging of receivables with past data offers even more control. An example of an *aging account* or *schedule* appears in Table 18.2.

The aging schedule provides you with a listing of how long your accounts receivable have been outstanding. Once the delinquent accounts have been identified, the firm's accounts receivable group makes an effort to collect them. For example, a past-due letter, called a *dunning letter*, is sent if payment is not received on time, followed by an additional dunning letter in a more serious tone if the account becomes 3 weeks past due, followed after 6 weeks by a telephone call. Finally, if the account becomes 12 weeks

Table 18.2 Aging Account

Age of Accounts Receivable (Days)		Dollar Value (00)	Percent of Total
0–30		$2,340	39%
31–60		1,500	25
61–90		1,020	17
91–120		720	12
Over 120		420	7
	Total	$6,000	100%

past due, it might be turned over to a collection agency. Again, a direct trade-off exists between collection expenses and lost goodwill on one hand and noncollection of accounts on the other, and this trade-off is always part of making the decision.

Thus far, we have discussed the importance and role of accounts receivable in the firm and then examined the determinants of the size of the investment in accounts receivable. We have focused on credit and collection policies, because these are the only discretionary variables for management. In examining these decision variables, we have simply described their traits. These variables are analyzed in a decision-making process called marginal or incremental analysis.

Credit Policy Changes: The Use of Marginal or Incremental Analysis

Changes in credit policy involve direct trade-offs between costs and benefits. When credit policies are eased, sales and profits from customers increase. Conversely, easing credit policies can also involve an increase in bad debts, additional funds tied up in accounts receivable and inventory, and additional costs from customers taking a cash discount. Given these costs, when is it appropriate for a firm to change its credit policy? The answer is when the increased sales generate enough in the way of new profit to more than offset the increased costs associated with the change. Determining whether this is so is the job of **marginal** or **incremental analysis**. In general, there are three categories of changes in credit policy that a firm can consider: a change in the risk class of the customer, a change in the collection process, or a change in the discount terms. To illustrate, let us follow through an example.

Marginal or incremental analysis

A method of analysis for credit policy changes in which the incremental benefits are compared to the added costs.

RELATE TO THE BIG PICTURE

*Marginal or incremental analysis is a direct application of **Axiom 4: Incremental Cash Flows—It's Only What Changes That Counts** into the credit analysis decision process. What we are really doing in marginal analysis is looking at all the cash flows to the company as a whole with the change in credit policy versus those cash flows without making the credit policy changes. Then, if the benefits resulting from the change outweigh the costs, the change should be made.*

EXAMPLE

Assume that Denis Electronics currently has annual sales, all credit, of $8 million and an average collection period of 30 days. The current level of bad debt is $240,000 and the firm's pre-tax opportunity cost or required rate of return is 15 percent. Further assume that the firm produces only one product, with variable costs equaling 75 percent of the selling price. The company is considering a change in the credit terms from the current terms of net 30 to 1/30 net 60. If this change is made, it is expected that half of the customers will take the discount and pay on the thirtieth day, whereas the other half will pass the discount and pay on the sixtieth day. This will increase the average collection period from 30 days to 45 days. The major reason Denis Electronics is considering this change is that it will generate additional sales of $1,000,000. Although the sales from these new customers will generate new profits, they will also generate more bad debts; however, it is assumed that the level of bad debts on the original sales will remain constant, and that the level of bad debts on the new sales will be 6 percent of those sales. In addition, to service the new sales, it will be necessary to increase the level of average inventory from $1,000,000 to $1,025,000.

Lets see how to evaluate this. Marginal or incremental analysis involves a comparison of the incremental profit contribution from new sales with the incremental costs resulting from the change in credit policy. If the benefits outweigh the costs, the change should be made. If not, the credit policy should remain as is. A four-step procedure for performing marginal or incremental analysis on a change in credit policy is:

Step 1: Estimate the change in profit.
Step 2: Estimate the cost of additional investment in accounts receivable and inventory.
Step 3: Estimate the cost of the discount (if a change in the cash discount is enacted).
Step 4: Compare the incremental revenues with the incremental costs.

Table 18.3 provides a summary of the relevant information concerning Denis's proposed credit change, whereas Table 18.4 provides the results of the incremental analysis.

In Step 1 of the analysis, the additional profits less bad debts from the new sales are calculated to be $190,000. In Step 2, the additional investment in accounts receivable and inventory is determined to be $458,340. Because the pre-tax required rate of return is 15 percent, the company's required return on this investment is $72,501. In Step 3, the cost of introducing a cash discount is determined to be $45,000. Finally, in Step 4, the benefits and costs are compared, and the net change in pre-tax profits are determined to be $72,499. Thus a change in the present credit policy is warranted.

In summary, the logic behind this approach to credit policy is to examine the incremental or marginal benefits from such a change and compare these with the incremental or marginal costs. If the change promises more benefits than costs, the change should be made. If, however, the incremental costs are greater than the benefits, the proposed change should not be made. Figure 18.3 graphs this process: The point where marginal costs equal marginal benefits occurs at credit policy A.

STOP AND THINK

The calculations associated with the incremental analysis of a change in credit policy illustrate the changes that occur when credit policy is adjusted. On the positive side, a loosening of credit policy should increase sales. On the negative side, bad debts, investment in accounts receivable and inventory, and costs associated with the cash discount all increase. The decision then boils down to whether the incremental benefits outweigh the incremental costs.

Table 18.3 Denis Electronics: Relevant Information for Incremental Analysis

New sales level (all credit):	$9,000,000
Original sales level (all credit):	$8,000,000
Contribution margin:	25%
Percent bad debt losses on new sales:	6%
New average collection period:	45 days
Original average collection period:	30 days
Additional investment in inventory:	$25,000
Pre-tax required rate of return:	15%
New percent cash discount:	1%
Percent of customers taking the cash discount:	50%

Table 18.4 Denis Electronics: Incremental Analysis of a Change in Credit Policy

Step 1: **Estimate the Change in Profit**. This is equal to the increased sales times the profit contribution on those sales less any additional bad debts incurred.

= (increased sales × contribution margin) − (increased sales × percent bad debt losses on new sales)

= ($1,000,000 × .25) − ($1,000,000 × .06)

= $190,000

Step 2: **Estimate the Cost of Additional Investment in Accounts Receivable and Inventory**. This involves first calculating the change in the investment in accounts receivable. The new and original levels of investment in accounts receivable are calculated by multiplying the daily sales level times the average collection period. The additional investment in inventory is added to this, and the sum is then multiplied by the pre-tax required rate of return.

$$= \begin{pmatrix} \text{additional} \\ \text{accounts} \\ \text{receivable} \end{pmatrix} + \begin{pmatrix} \text{additional} \\ \text{inventory} \end{pmatrix} \times \begin{pmatrix} \text{pre-tax required} \\ \text{rate of return} \end{pmatrix}$$

First, calculate the additional investment in accounts receivable.

$$\begin{pmatrix} \text{additional} \\ \text{accounts} \\ \text{receivable} \end{pmatrix} = \begin{pmatrix} \text{new level} \\ \text{of daily} \\ \text{sales} \end{pmatrix} \times \begin{pmatrix} \text{new average} \\ \text{collection} \\ \text{period} \end{pmatrix} - \begin{pmatrix} \text{original level} \\ \text{of daily} \\ \text{sales} \end{pmatrix} \times \begin{pmatrix} \text{original average} \\ \text{collection} \\ \text{period} \end{pmatrix}$$

$$= \left(\frac{\$9,000,000}{360} \times 45 \right) - \left(\frac{\$8,000,000}{360} \times 30 \right)$$

$$= \$458,340$$

Second, add additional investments in accounts receivable ($458,340) and inventory ($25,000) and multiply this total times the pre-tax required rate of return.

= ($458,340 + $25,000) × .15

= $72,501

Step 3: **Estimate the Change in the Cost of the Cash Discount (if a change in the cash discount is enacted)**. This is equal to the new level of sales times the new percent cash discount times the percent of customers taking the discount, less the original level of sales times the original percent cash discount times percent of customers taking the discount.

$$= \begin{pmatrix} \text{new} \\ \text{level} \\ \text{of} \\ \text{sales} \end{pmatrix} \times \begin{pmatrix} \text{new} \\ \text{percent} \\ \text{cash} \\ \text{discount} \end{pmatrix} \times \begin{pmatrix} \text{percent} \\ \text{customers} \\ \text{taking} \\ \text{discount} \end{pmatrix} - \begin{pmatrix} \text{original} \\ \text{level} \\ \text{of} \\ \text{sales} \end{pmatrix} \times \begin{pmatrix} \text{original} \\ \text{percent} \\ \text{cash} \\ \text{discount} \end{pmatrix} \times \begin{pmatrix} \text{original} \\ \text{percent} \\ \text{taking} \\ \text{discount} \end{pmatrix}$$

= ($9,000,000 × .01 × .50) − ($8,000 000 × .00 × .00)

= $45,000

Step 4: **Compare the Incremental Revenues with the Incremental Costs**.

$$\begin{matrix} \text{net change} \\ \text{in pre-tax} \\ \text{profits} \end{matrix} = \begin{matrix} \text{change} \\ \text{in} \\ \text{profits} \end{matrix} - \begin{pmatrix} \text{cost of new} \\ \text{investment in} \\ \text{accounts receivable} \\ \text{and inventory} \end{pmatrix} + \begin{matrix} \text{cost of} \\ \text{change in} \\ \text{cash} \\ \text{discount} \end{matrix}$$

= Step 1 − (Step 2 + Step 3)

= $190,000 − ($72,501 + $45,000)

= $72,499

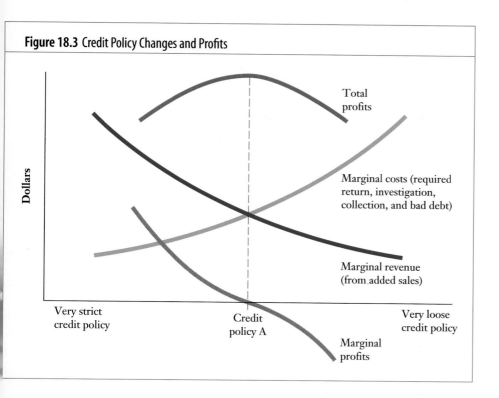

Figure 18.3 Credit Policy Changes and Profits

Total profits

Marginal costs (required return, investigation, collection, and bad debt)

Marginal revenue (from added sales)

Dollars

Very strict credit policy

Credit policy A

Very loose credit policy

Marginal profits

INVENTORY MANAGEMENT

Inventory management involves the control of the assets that are used in the production process or produced to be sold in the normal course of the firm's operations. The general categories of inventory include raw materials inventory, work-in-process inventory, and finished goods inventory. The importance of inventory management to the firm depends on the extent of the inventory investment. For an average firm, approximately 4.80 percent of all assets are in the form of inventory. However, the percentage varies widely from industry to industry, as Table 18.5 shows. Thus the importance of inventory management and control varies from industry to industry also. For example, it is much more important in the automotive dealer and service station trade, where inventories make up 54.21 percent of total assets, than in the hotel business, where the average investment in inventory is only 0.98 percent of total assets.

Purposes and Types of Inventory

The purpose of carrying inventories is to uncouple the operations of the firm—that is, to make each function of the business independent of each other function—so that delays or shutdowns in one area do not affect the production and sale of the final product. For example, in the auto industry, a strike or shutdown in a parts plant may shut down several assembly plants. Because production shutdowns result in increased costs, and because delays in delivery can lose customers, the management and control of inventory are important duties of the financial manager. To better illustrate the uncoupling function that inventories perform, we will look at several general types of inventories.

OBJECTIVE 2

Inventory management

The control of the assets used in the production process or produced to be sold in the normal course of the firm's operations.

Table 18.5 Inventory as a Percentage of Total Assets for Major Industries

Industry	Inventory Relative to Total Assets
Automotive dealers and service stations—retail	54.21%
Building materials, garden supplies, and mobile home dealers—retail	34.31
Apparel and accessory stores	32.07
Food stores	22.09
Total construction	13.54
Agriculture, forestry, and fishing	10.18
Electrical and electronic equipment	8.38
Petroleum and coal products	3.41
Eating and drinking places	3.25
Hotels and other lodging places	0.98
All industries	4.80

SOURCE: Internal Revenue Service, U.S. Treasury Department, *Statistics of Income*, 1994 *Corporate Income Tax Returns* (Washington D.C.: Government Printing Office, 1997), 9–242.

RELATE TO THE BIG PICTURE

The decision as to how much inventory to keep on hand is a direct application of **Axiom 1: The Risk-Return Trade-Off—We Won't Take on Additional Risk Unless We Expect to Be Compensated with Additional Return.** *The risk is that if the level of inventory is too low, the various functions of business do not operate independently and delays in production and customer delivery can result. The return results because reduced inventory investment saves money. As the size of inventory increases, storage and handling costs as well as the required return on capital invested in inventory rise. Therefore, as the inventory a firm holds is increased, the risk of running out of inventory is lessened, but inventory expenses rise.*

Raw materials inventory

This includes the basic materials purchased from other firms to be used in the firm's production operations.

Raw materials inventory. Raw materials inventory consists of basic materials purchased from other firms to be used in the firm's production operations. These goods may include steel, lumber, petroleum, or manufactured items such as wire, ball bearings, or tires that the firm does not produce itself. Regardless of the specific form of the raw materials inventory, all manufacturing firms by definition maintain a raw materials inventory. Its purpose is to uncouple the production function from the purchasing function—that is, to make these two functions independent of each other, so that delays in shipment of raw materials do not cause production delays. In the event of a delay in shipment, the firm can satisfy its need for raw materials by liquidating its inventory. During the 1991 war with Iraq, many firms that used petroleum as an input in production built up their petroleum inventories in anticipation of a slowdown or possibly a stoppage in the flow of oil from the Middle East. This buildup in raw material inventory would have allowed those firms with adequate inventories to continue production even if the war had severely cut the flow of oil.

Work-in-process inventory

Partially finished goods requiring additional work before they become finished goods.

Work-in-process inventory. Work-in-process inventory consists of partially finished goods requiring additional work before they become finished goods. The more complex and lengthy the production process, the larger the investment in work-in-process inventory. The purpose of work-in-process inventory is to uncouple the various operations in the production process so that machine failures and work stoppages in one operation will not affect the other operations. Assume, for example, there are 10 different production operations, each one involving the piece of work produced in the previous operation. If the machine performing the first production operation breaks down, a firm with no work-in-process inventory will have to shut down all 10 production operations. Yet if a firm has such inventory, the remaining nine operations can continue by drawing the input for the second operation from inventory rather than directly from the output of the first operation.

Finished-goods inventory. The **finished-goods inventory** consists of goods on which the production has been completed but that are not yet sold. The purpose of a finished-goods inventory is to uncouple the production and sales functions so that it is not necessary to produce the good before a sale can occur—sales can be made directly out of inventory. In the auto industry, for example, people would not buy from a dealer who made them wait weeks or months, when another dealer could fill the order immediately.

Finished-goods inventory

Goods on which the production has been completed but that are not yet sold.

Stock of cash. Although we discussed cash management at some length in chapter 17, it is worthwhile to mention cash again in the light of inventory management. This is because the *stock of cash* carried by a firm is simply a special type of inventory. In terms of uncoupling the various operations of the firm, the purpose of holding a stock of cash is to make the payment of bills independent of the collection of accounts due. When cash is kept on hand, bills can be paid without prior collection of accounts.

As we examine and develop inventory economic ordering quantity (EOQ) models, we will see a striking resemblance between the EOQ inventory and EOQ cash model; in fact, except for a minor redefinition of terms, they will be exactly the same.

Inventory-Management Techniques

The importance of effective inventory management is directly related to the size of the investment in inventory. Because, on average, approximately 4.80 percent of a firm's assets are tied up in inventory, effective management of these assets is essential to the goal of shareholder wealth maximization. To control the investment in inventory, management must solve two problems: the order quantity problem and the order point problem.

Order quantity problem. The **order quantity problem** involves determining the optimal order size for an inventory item given its expected usage, carrying costs, and ordering costs. Aside from a change in some of the variable names, it is exactly the same as the inventory model for cash management (EOQ model) presented in chapter 17.

The EOQ model attempts to determine the order size that will minimize total inventory costs. It assumes that

$$\text{total inventory costs} = \text{total carrying costs} + \text{total ordering costs} \tag{18-4}$$

Assuming that inventory is allowed to fall to zero and then is immediately replenished (this assumption will be lifted when we discuss the order point problem), the average inventory becomes $Q/2$, where Q is inventory order size in units. This can be seen graphically in Figure 18.4.

If the average inventory is $Q/2$ and the carrying cost per unit is C, then carrying costs become:

$$\begin{pmatrix}\text{total} \\ \text{carrying costs}\end{pmatrix} = \begin{pmatrix}\text{average} \\ \text{inventory}\end{pmatrix}\begin{pmatrix}\text{carrying cost} \\ \text{per unit}\end{pmatrix} \tag{18-5}$$

$$= \left(\frac{Q}{2}\right)C \tag{18-6}$$

Order quantity problem

Determining the optimal order size for an inventory item given its usage, carrying costs, and ordering costs.

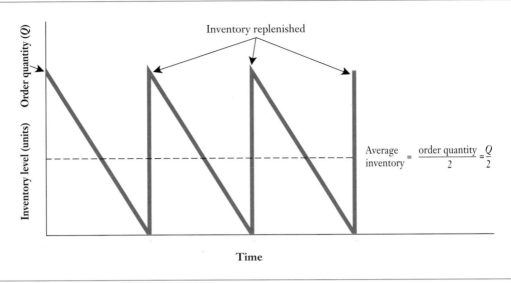

Figure 18.4 Inventory Level and the Replenishment Cycle

where Q = the inventory order size in units

C = carrying costs per unit

The carrying costs on inventory include the required rate of return on investment in inventory, in addition to warehouse or storage costs, wages for those who operate the warehouse, and costs associated with inventory shrinkage. Thus carrying costs include both real cash flows and opportunity costs associated with having funds tied up in inventory.

The ordering costs incurred are equal to the ordering costs per order times the number of orders. If we assume total demand over the planning period is S and we order in lot sizes of Q, then S/Q represents the number of orders over the planning period. If the ordering cost per order is O, then

$$\begin{matrix} \text{total} \\ \text{ordering costs} \end{matrix} = \left(\begin{matrix} \text{number} \\ \text{of orders} \end{matrix} \right) \left(\begin{matrix} \text{ordering cost} \\ \text{per order} \end{matrix} \right) \tag{18-7}$$

$$= \left(\frac{S}{Q} \right) O \tag{18-8}$$

where S = total demand in units over the planning period

O = ordering cost per order

Thus total costs in equation (18-4) become

$$\text{total costs} = \left(\frac{Q}{2} \right) C + \left(\frac{S}{Q} \right) O \tag{18-9}$$

Figure 18.5 illustrates this equation graphically. As you can see, as the order size increases, so does the carrying costs because you are holding more inventory. Eventually, the increased carrying costs outweigh the savings in ordering costs from not placing as many orders. At that point, total costs are minimized.

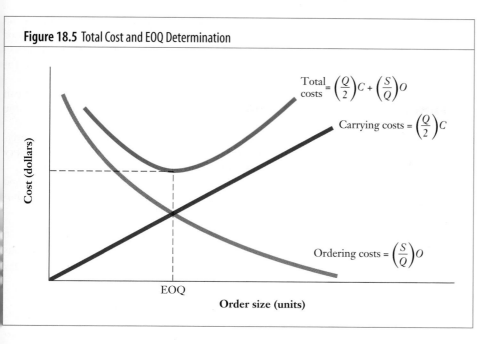

Figure 18.5 Total Cost and EOQ Determination

What we are looking for is the ordering size, Q^*, which provides the minimum total costs. By manipulating equation (18-9), we find that the optimal value of Q—that is, the economic ordering quantity (EOQ)— is

$$Q^* = \sqrt{\frac{2SO}{C}} \qquad \text{(18-10)}$$

The use of the EOQ model can best be illustrated through an example.

EXAMPLE

Suppose a firm expects total demand (S) for its product over the planning period to be 5,000 units, whereas the ordering cost per order (O) is $200, and the carrying cost per unit (C) is $2. Substituting these values into equation (18-10) yields

$$Q^* = \sqrt{\frac{2 \cdot 5,000 \cdot 200}{2}} = \sqrt{1,000,000} = 1,000 \text{ unit}$$

Thus, if this firm orders in 1,000-unit lot sizes, it will minimize its total inventory costs.

Despite the fact that the EOQ model tends to yield quite good results, there are weaknesses in the EOQ model associated with several of its assumptions. When its assumptions have been dramatically violated, the EOQ model can generally be modified to accommodate the situation. The model's assumptions are as follows:

1. **Constant or uniform demand**. Although the EOQ model assumes constant demand, demand may vary from day to day. If demand is stochastic—that is, not known in advance—the model must be modified through the inclusion of a **safety stock**.
2. **Constant unit price**. The inclusion of variable prices resulting from quantity discounts can be handled quite easily through a modification of the original EOQ model, redefining total costs and solving for the optimum order quantity.

Safety stock

Inventory held to accommodate any unusually large and unexpected usage during delivery time.

3. **Constant carrying costs.** Unit carrying costs may vary substantially as the size of the inventory rises, perhaps decreasing because of economies of scale or storage efficiency or increasing as storage space runs out and new warehouses have to be rented. This situation can be handled through a modification in the original model similar to the one used for variable unit price.
4. **Constant ordering costs.** Although this assumption is generally valid, its violation can be accommodated by modifying the original EOQ model in a manner similar to the one used for variable unit price.
5. **Instantaneous delivery.** If delivery is not instantaneous, which is generally the case, the original EOQ model must be modified through the inclusion of a safety stock, that is, the inventory held to accommodate any unusually large and unexpected usage during the delivery time.
6. **Independent orders.** If multiple orders result in cost savings by reducing paperwork and transportation cost, the original EOQ model must be further modified. Although this modification is somewhat complicated, special EOQ models have been developed to deal with it.

These assumptions illustrate the limitations of the basic EOQ model and the ways in which it can be modified to compensate for them. An understanding of the limitations and assumptions of the EOQ model provides the financial manager with more of a base for making inventory decisions.

Order Point Problem

The two most limiting assumptions—those of constant or uniform demand and instantaneous delivery—are dealt with through the inclusion of safety stock, which is the inventory held to accommodate any unusually large and unexpected usage during delivery time. The decision on how much safety stock to hold is generally referred to as the **order point problem**; that is, how low should inventory be depleted before it is reordered.

Two factors go into the determination of the appropriate order point: (1) the procurement or delivery-time stock and (2) the safety stock desired. Figure 18.6 graphs the process involved in order point determination. We observe that the order point problem can be decomposed into its two components, the **delivery-time stock**—that is, the inventory needed between the order date and receipt of the inventory ordered—and the safety stock. Thus the order point is reached when inventory falls to a level equal to the delivery-time stock plus the safety stock.

inventory order point:

$$\begin{bmatrix} \text{order new inventory} \\ \text{when the level of} \\ \text{inventory falls to} \\ \text{this level} \end{bmatrix} = \begin{pmatrix} \text{delivery-time} \\ \text{stock} \end{pmatrix} + \begin{pmatrix} \text{safety} \\ \text{stock} \end{pmatrix} \qquad (18\text{-}11)$$

As a result of constantly carrying safety stock, the average level of inventory increases. Whereas before the inclusion of safety stock the average level of inventory was equal to EOQ/2, now it will be

$$\text{average inventory} = \frac{EOQ}{2} + \text{safety stock} \qquad (18\text{-}12)$$

In general, several factors simultaneously determine how much delivery-time stock and safety stock should be held. First, the efficiency of the replenishment system affects how much delivery-time stock is needed. Because the delivery-time stock is the expected inventory usage between ordering and receiving inventory, efficient replenishment of inventory would reduce the need for delivery-time stock.

The uncertainty surrounding both the delivery time and the demand for the product affects the level of safety stock needed. The more certain the patterns of these inflows and

Order point problem

Determining how low inventory should be depleted before it is reordered.

Delivery-time stock

The inventory needed between the order date and the receipt of the inventory ordered.

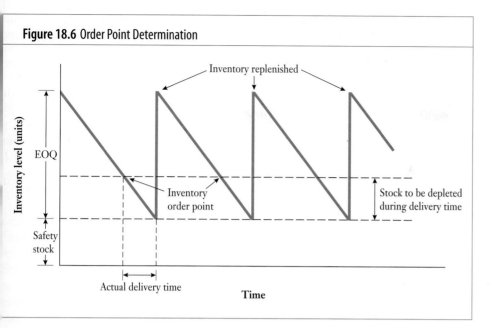

Figure 18.6 Order Point Determination

outflows from the inventory, the less safety stock required. In effect, if these inflows and outflows are highly predictable, then there is little chance of any stockout occurring. However, if they are unpredictable, it becomes necessary to carry additional safety stock to prevent unexpected stockouts.

The safety margin desired also affects the level of safety stock held. If it is a costly experience to run out of inventory, the safety stock held will be larger than it would be otherwise. If running out of inventory and the subsequent delay in supplying customers result in strong customer dissatisfaction and the possibility of lost future sales, then additional safety stock is necessary. A final determinant is the cost of carrying additional inventory, in terms of both the handling and storage costs and the opportunity cost associated with the investment in additional inventory. Very simply, the greater the costs, the smaller the safety stock.

The determination of the level of safety stock involves a basic trade-off between the risk of stock-out, resulting in possible customer dissatisfaction and lost sales, and the increased costs associated with carrying additional inventory.

Inflation and EOQ

Inflation affects the EOQ model in two major ways. First, although the EOQ model can be modified to assume constant price increases, often major price increases occur only once or twice a year and are announced ahead of time. If this is the case, the EOQ model may lose its applicability and may be replaced with **anticipatory buying**—that is, buying in anticipation of a price increase to secure the goods at a lower cost. Of course, as with most decisions, there are trade-offs. The costs are the added carrying costs associated with the inventory. The benefits, of course, come from buying at a lower price. The second way inflation affects the EOQ model is through increased carrying costs. As inflation pushes interest rates up, the cost of carrying inventory increases. In our EOQ model, this means that C increases, which results in a decline in Q^*, the optimal economic order quantity:

Anticipatory buying

Buying in anticipation of a price increase to secure goods at a lower cost.

$$\downarrow Q^* = \sqrt{\frac{2SO}{C\uparrow}}$$

(18-13)

Reluctance to stock large inventories because of high carrying costs became particularly prevalent during the late 1970s and early 1980s, when inflation and interest rates were at high levels.

Just-in-Time Inventory Control

The **just-in-time inventory control** is more than just an inventory control system, it is a production and management system. Not only is inventory cut down to a minimum, but the time and physical distance between the various production operations are also reduced. In addition, management is willing to trade off costs to develop close relationships with suppliers and promote speedy replenishment of inventory in return for the ability to hold less safety stock.

The just-in-time inventory control system was originally developed in Japan by Taiichi Okno, a vice-president of Toyota. Originally, the system was called the *kanban* system, named after the cards that were placed in the parts bins that were used to call for a new supply. The idea behind the system is that the firm should keep a minimum level of inventory on hand, relying on suppliers to furnish parts "just in time" for them to be assembled. This is in direct contrast to the traditional inventory philosophy of U.S. firms, which is sometimes referred to as a "just-in-case" system, which keeps healthy levels of safety stocks to ensure that production will not be interrupted. Although large inventories may not be a bad idea when interest rates are low, when interest rates are high they become very costly.

Although the just-in-time inventory system is intuitively appealing, it has not proved easy to implement. Long distances from suppliers and plants constructed with too much space for storage and not enough access (doors and loading docks) to receive inventory have limited successful implementation. But many firms have been forced to change their relationships with their suppliers. Because firms rely on suppliers to deliver high-quality parts and materials immediately, they must have a close, long-term relationship with them. Despite the difficulties of implementation, many U.S. firms have moved to cut inventory; in some cases, through the use of a just-in-time inventory system. General Motors and National Cash Register are just two of the many firms that have moved at least some of their operations to a just-in-time system. Dell Computer is a classic example of using a just-in-time inventory system for finished goods inventory. Dell doesn't carry any finished goods inventory, but instead won't assemble any computers until they are ordered. In fact, between 1982 and 1994, the average level of inventory relative to total assets for all American corporations fell by 34 percent, partly because of just-in-time systems.

Although the just-in-time system does not at first appear to bear much of a relationship to the EOQ model, it simply alters some of the assumptions of the model with respect to delivery time and ordering costs, and draws out the implications. Actually, it is just a new approach to the EOQ model that tries to produce the lowest average level of inventory possible. If we look at the average level of inventory as defined by the EOQ model, we find it to be

$$\text{average inventory} = \sqrt{\frac{2SO\downarrow}{C}} + \text{safety stock} \downarrow$$

The just-in-time system attacks this equation in two places. First, by locating inventory supplies in convenient locations, laying out plants in such a way that it is inexpensive and easy to unload new inventory shipments, and computerizing the inventory order system, the cost of ordering new inventory, O, is reduced. Second, by developing a strong relationship with suppliers located in the same geographical area and setting up restocking strategies that cut time, the safety stock is also reduced. The philosophy behind the just-in-time inventory system is that the benefits associated with reducing inventory and delivery time to a bare minimum through adjustment in the EOQ model will more than offset the costs associated with the increased possibility of stock-outs.

Although just-in-time inventory systems seem to do a great job of reducing inventory costs, if there is ever a breakdown in the supply of inventory to the system, the results can be catastrophic. Take, for example, General Motors, which has saved millions of dollars by going to a just-in-time system. In 1996, General Motors was hit by a strike that involved about 3,000 workers at two of its plants that produced brakes for the cars GM makes. As a result of not having brakes to put in cars, GM was forced to stop production and lay off over 177,000 workers. Moreover, because GM used a just-in-time inventory system, it didn't take long for the shutdown of the brake plant to affect all of GM's other operations.

Now let's take a look at exactly how a just-in-time inventory system works. Ford Motor Company's Avon Lake, Ohio plant, which produces the Mercury Villager and the Nissan Quest minivans, uses a just-in-time inventory system. In fact, some inventory is limited to a supply of only a few hours, whereas other inventory carries supplies up to several days. To allow for this constant resupply of inventory, Ford built the plant with 65 dock doors placed around the plant so that inventory would arrive as close as possible to the location where it was to be used.

In addition, Ford worked with suppliers so that much of the inventory would arrive partially assembled. For example, tires and wheels came pre-assembled by Bridgestone. These arrive several times a day delivered in the order in which they are to be used—with each fifth tire delivered being a spare. Seats also arrived hourly, already preassembled, from a supplier located just 25 miles away. In addition, the seats are arranged in the order they are to be used and arrive on the assembly line by conveyors directly from the delivery trucks ready to use. In effect, the only inventory time for tires and seats is when they are on the delivery truck waiting to be unloaded. Thus Ford's just-in-time inventory system allows for a dramatically reduced level of investment in inventory by allowing for a continuous flow and resupply of inventory. The end result of all this reduced investment is increased profits.

TQM AND INVENTORY-PURCHASING MANAGEMENT: THE NEW SUPPLIER RELATIONSHIPS

OBJECTIVE 3

Total quality management (TQM)

A company-wide systems approach to quality.

Out of the concept of **total quality management** (**TQM**), which is a company-wide systems approach to quality, has come a new philosophy in inventory management of "love thy supplier." Under this approach, the traditional antagonistic relationship between suppliers and customers, where suppliers are coldly dropped when a cheaper source can be found, is being replaced by a new order in customer–supplier relationships. In effect, what began as an effort to increase quality through closer supplier relations has turned out to have unexpected benefits. Close customer relationships have helped trim costs, in part, by allowing for the production of higher quality products. This close customer–supplier relationship has allowed the TQM philosophy to be passed across company boundaries to the supplier, enabling the firm to tap the supplier's expertise in designing higher-quality products. In addition, the interdependence between the supplier and customer has also allowed for the development and introduction of new products at a pace much faster than previously possible.

As we have seen, inventory can make up a rather large percentage of a firm's assets. That by itself lends importance to the role of inventory management and, more specifically, purchasing. In terms of manufacturing costs, purchased materials have historically accounted for 50 percent of U.S. and about 70 percent of Japanese manufacturing costs, and most manufacturers purchase more than 50 percent of their parts. Thus it is hard to overstate the importance of purchasing to the firm.

The traditional purchasing philosophy is to purchase a part or material from a variety of different suppliers, with the suppliers contracting out to a number of different firms. In fact, many companies put an upper limit of 10 or 20 percent on the purchases of any part from a single supplier. The reasoning behind this is that the company can diversify away the effects of poor quality by any one supplier. Thus, if one supplier was unable to meet delivery schedules, delivers a poor quality batch, or even goes out of business, this affects only a small percent of the total parts or material. However, efforts to raise quality have led to a new approach to the customer-supplier relationship called **single-sourcing**.

Under single-sourcing, a company uses very few suppliers or, in many cases, a single supplier, as a source for a particular part or material. In this way, the company has more direct influence and control over the quality performance of a supplier because the company accounts for a larger proportion of the supplier's volume. The company and supplier can then enter into a partnership, referred to as *partnering*, where the supplier agrees to meet the quality standards of the customer in terms of parts, material, service, and delivery. In this way, the supplier can be brought into the TQM program of the customer. In return, the company enters into a long-term purchasing agreement with the supplier that includes a stable order and delivery schedule. For example, on General Motor's Quad 4 engine (its first new engine in several decades), every part except the engine block is single-sourced, resulting in only 69 total suppliers—half the normal number for a production engine. In return for the suppliers' assurance of top quality and low cost, GM guaranteed the suppliers their jobs for the life of the engine. In the development of its new LH cars, the Chrysler Concorde, the Dodge Intrepid, and Eagle Vision, Chrysler trimmed its supplier base from 3,000 to less than 1,000 by the mid-1990s. Single-sourcing clearly creates an environment of cooperation between customers and suppliers where both share the common goal of quality.

Although the partnering relationship results in higher-quality parts, it can also improve the quality of the design process by allowing for the involvement of the supplier in production design. For example, the supplier may be given the responsibility of designing a new part or component to meet the quality standards and features outlined by the company. When Guardian Industries of Northville, Michigan, developed an oversized solar glass windshield for Chrysler's LH cars, their engineers met on almost a daily basis with the Chrysler design team to make sure the quality, features, and cost of the windshield met Chrysler standards. To produce the windshields, Guardian opened a new $35 million plant in Ligonier, Indiana. In a similar manner, Bailey Controls and Boise Cascade entered into a pact in which Bailey was the exclusive provider of control systems for eight of ten Boise plants. The two work together, reviewing and modifying the terms of the arrangement to ensure that they reflect the ever-changing business conditions and that the deal remains fair to both parties. In addition, recognizing the long-term nature of the relationship and that Boise's success would also benefit Bailey, Bailey worked with Boise—in fact, using a Boise plant on which to conduct experiments—to improve the software used to operate the Boise plants.

The concept of partnering has radically changed the way inventory is purchased. Moreover, it has turned the customer-supplier relationship from a formerly adversarial one into a cooperative one. The benefits in terms of increased quality of parts, materials, and design are so dramatic that partnering is not likely to fade away, but rather continue to evolve and take on even more importance in the future.

The Financial Consequences of Quality—The Traditional View

Traditionally, the cost of quality has been viewed as being made up of **preventive costs**, **appraisal costs**, and **failure costs**. The costs the firm incurs in running its quality management program include both preventive and appraisal costs. Preventive costs include

Single-sourcing

Using a single supplier as a source for a particular part or material.

Preventive costs

Costs resulting from design and production efforts on the part of the firm to reduce or eliminate defects.

Appraisal costs

Costs of testing, measuring, and analyzing to safeguard against possible defects going unnoticed.

those resulting from design and production efforts on the part of the firm to reduce or eliminate defects. Whereas preventive costs deal with the avoidance of defects the first time through, appraisal costs are associated with the detection of defects. Thus typical appraisal costs would include the costs of testing, measuring, and analyzing materials, parts, and products, as well as the production operations to safeguard against possible defective inventory going unnoticed. Together, preventive and appraisal costs make up much of what a typical total quality management program does.

Whereas preventive and appraisal costs deal with the costs associated with achieving good quality, failure costs refer to the costs resulting from producing poor-quality products. Failure costs can either occur within the firm, called **internal failure costs**, or once the product has left the firm, referred to as **external failure costs**. Internal failure costs are those costs associated with discovering the poor-quality product prior to delivery to the final customer. Internal failure costs include the costs of reworking the product, downtime costs, the costs of having to discount poorer quality products, and the costs of scrapping the product. External failure costs, on the other hand, come as a result of a poor-quality product reaching the customer's hands. Typical external failure costs would include product return costs, warranty costs, product liability costs, customer complaint costs, and lost sales costs.

> **Internal failure costs**
>
> Those costs associated with discovering poor quality products prior to delivery.
>
> **External failure costs**
>
> Costs resulting from a poor quality product reaching the customer's hands.

Traditionally, economists examined the trade-offs between quality and costs looking for the point where costs were minimized. The result of this is that some level of defects should be tolerated. That's because there comes a point when the costs associated with making the product right in the first place are more than the cost of poor quality—the failure costs.

RELATE TO THE BIG PICTURE

Axiom 5: The Curse of Competitive Markets—Why It's Hard to Find Exceptionally Profitable Projects examines how product differentiation can be used as a means of insulating a product from competition, thereby allowing prices to stay sufficiently high to support large profits. Producing a quality product is one of those ways to differentiate products. This strategy has been used effectively by Caterpillar Tractor, Toyota, and Honda Motors in recent years.

The Financial Consequences of Quality—The TQM View

In response to this traditional view, the TQM view argues that the traditional analysis is flawed in that it ignores the fact that increased sales and market share result from better-quality products, and that this increase in sales will more than offset the higher costs associated with increased quality. In effect, the TQM view argues that because lost sales resulting from a poor quality reputation and increased sales resulting from a reputation for quality are difficult to estimate, they tend to be underestimated or ignored in the traditional approach. In addition, the TQM view argues that the cost of achieving higher quality is less than economists have traditionally estimated. In fact, the benefits from quality improvement programs seem to have spillover effects resulting in increased worker motivation, higher productivity, and improved employee relations. Moreover, large increases in quality at minimum costs have been achieved with very low costs when companies focus on training and educating the production workers.

Thus the TQM view concludes that traditional analysis underestimates the cost of producing a poor-quality product, while it overestimates the cost of producing a high-quality product. As a result, under this new TQM view of the quality-costs trade-offs, the optimal quality level moves much closer to 100 percent quality.

The adoption of total quality management programs by many firms has borne out this TQM view of the quality-cost relationship. For example, after Xerox Corporation introduced TQM it experienced a decline of 90 percent in defective items. For Xerox, the end result of this was a 20 percent drop in manufacturing costs over that same period.

HOW FINANCIAL MANAGERS USE THIS MATERIAL

Given the fact that the total investment in both accounts receivable and inventory represents approximately one-quarter of a typical firm's assets, it's no surprise that a good deal of time goes into managing them. This includes deciding who should be able to buy on credit, trying to collect on overdue accounts, managing inventory to make sure you don't run out of any products, and overseeing quality control. But more than just managing these accounts and items, inventory and accounts receivable policies are increasingly used as sales tools. In effect, you sell your product, but you make that sale based upon your accounts receivable policy, your inventory policy, or the quality of your goods.

For example, Mitsubishi has an annual sale on its large screen projection televisions where prices aren't cut. Instead, the projection televisions are offered at zero percent interest with the first payments not due until the following year. In effect, Mitsubishi uses its accounts receivable policy as a marketing tool. If you're working for Mitsubishi, your job may be to set standards as to who qualifies for this deal, or to oversee the collection of those accounts.

Inventory policy is also used as a marketing tool. Having the product available for immediate delivery may be your sales gimmick. Other companies don't keep any inventory on hand and pass the savings that are produced on to the customers. For example, Dell computer doesn't produce any computers until they are sold, which allows it to keep costs down to a minimum and pass those cost savings on to the customers. In fact, this stratetgy has proved so profitable that in late 1997, Apple announced it was also going to start selling over the Internet using the same "build-when-ordered" approach. If you took a job for another firm that sells directly out of inventory, your job might be managing that inventory—making sure you don't run out of anything while keeping your investment in inventory down to a minimum. Is inventory management complicated? The answer is yes. Just look at IBM, which has about 1,000 products currently in service with over 200,000 different inventoried parts supporting those products. To provide customers with prompt service, IBM has developed an inventory system that includes 2 central warehouses, 21 field distribution centers, 64 parts stations, and 15,000 outside locations with over 15,000 customer engineers, not to mention all those involved in managing the inventory.

As for quality control, again, for many firms it is a marketing strategy—"Quality is Job 1" touts Ford Motor Company. ITT Electro-Optical Products Division, which manufacturers night vision products including pilots goggles, aviator's night vision imaging systems, and night goggles, is another company to benefit from a TQM approach to business. Complicating ITT's task is the fact that manufacturing these systems is extremely complex, involving over 200 different chemicals and 400 different processes. This production complexity has led to an industry average production level of good units of only 10 to 40 percent. Prior to implementing a TQM program, which involved continuous process involvement, statistical process control, and employee involvement, only 35 percent of the units ITT produced were good. Implementing the TQM approach raised the percent of good units produced to 75 percent. The savings from reducing the proportion of bad units produced were passed on in lower prices, resulting in a 60-fold increase of the number of units sold over 5 years. To say the least, there are an awful lot of people inspecting products and working on ways to improve their quality—and that may be your job.

FORTUNE, FEBRUARY 21, 1994

The New Golden Rule of Business

(A) In that battle-scarred landscape where suppliers and their corporate customers meet and deal, lions are lying down with lambs, and swords are being beaten into plowshares. Hard-nosed businessmen use embarrassingly romantic terms to describe the new order in supplier–customer relationships. "It's like a marriage," croons a big-league purchasing executive. Companies that succeed at partnerships like this usually set them up routinely, not as exceptions, and with customers and suppliers alike. Sitting in the middle of a web of such relationships is Bailey Controls, an Ohio-headquartered, $300-million-a-year manufacturer of control systems for big factories, from steel and paper mills to chemical and pharmaceutical plants.

(B) To spin its web, Bailey, a unit of Elsag Bailey Process Automation, treats some suppliers almost like departments of its own company.

Bailey has physically plugged two of its main electronics distributors into itself. Montreal-based Future Electronics is hooked on with an electronic data interchange system. Every week, Bailey electronically sends Future its latest forecasts of what material it will need for the next six months, so that Future can stock up in time. (C) Bailey itself stocks only enough inventory for a few days of operation, as opposed to the two to three months' worth it used to carry. Whenever a bin of parts falls below a designated level, a Bailey employee passes a laser scanner over the bin's bar code, instantly alerting Future to send the parts at once.

Arrow Electronics, headquartered on Long Island, is plugged in even more closely: It has a warehouse in Bailey's factory, stocked according to Bailey's twice monthly forecasts. Bailey provides the space, Arrow the warehouseman and the $500,000 inventory.

SOURCE: Excerpted from Myron Magnet, "The New Golden Rule of Business," *Fortune* (February 21, 1994): 60–64. © 1994 Time Inc. All rights reserved.

Analysis and Implications …

A. Why are suppliers willing to provide this service to customers? First, while it may be more expensive, it also results in higher volume, with customers relying on fewer suppliers and establishing stronger ties with them. In addition, the need for a large sales staff to service customers is also eliminated. More important, suppliers can take comfort in reduced variability of demand and less reliance on competitive bids for sales and the variability in sales that accompanies winning and losing bids.

B. The close relationships spawned in this new customer–supplier inventory relationship not only results in increased speed of replenishment of inventory and reduced costs, but also in increased quality. By wedding suppliers and customers, the firms are able to tap into the suppliers' technological expertise in designing and making parts. Moreover, these close relationships allow for the dissemination of quality management techniques across company lines and into the supplier's domain.

C. Not only does Bailey save money by passing on the costs of carrying its large inventory to its suppliers, but it also saves money by reductions in the workforce needed to run the purchasing department.

OBJECTIVE 1

The size of the investment in accounts receivable depends on three factors: the percentage of credit sales to total sales, the level of sales, and the credit and collection policies. However, only the credit and collection policies are decision variables open to the financial manager. The policies that the financial manager has control over include the terms of sale, the quality of customer, and the collection efforts.

OBJECTIVE 2

Although the typical firm has fewer assets tied up in inventory (4.80%) than it does in accounts receivable (20.22%), inventory management and control is still an important function of the financial manager. The purpose of holding inventory is to make each function of the business independent of the other functions—that is, to uncouple the firm's operations. Inventory-management techniques primarily involve questions of how much inventory should be ordered and when the order should be placed. The answers directly determine the average level of investment in inventory. The EOQ model is employed in answering the first of these questions. This model attempts to calculate the order size that minimizes the sum of the inventory carrying and ordering costs. The order point problem attempts to determine how low inventory can drop before it is reordered. The order point is reached when the inventory falls to a level equal to the delivery-time stock plus the safety stock. Determining the level of safety stock involves a direct trade-off between the risk of running out of inventory and the increased costs associated with carrying additional inventory.

The just-in-time inventory control system lowers inventory by reducing the time and distance between the various production functions. The idea behind the system is that the firm should keep a minimum level of inventory on hand and rely on suppliers to furnish parts "just in time" for them to be assembled.

OBJECTIVE 3

The TQM philosophy affects the way the purchasing portion of inventory management is handled. The traditional adversarial purchaser/supplier relationship has given way to close customer relationships, which have in turn helped trim costs by allowing for the production of higher-quality products. This close customer–supplier relationship has allowed the TQM philosophy to be passed across company boundaries to the supplier, and has also allowed the firm to tap the supplier's expertise in designing higher-quality products. In addition, this interdependence between the supplier and customer has allowed for the development and introduction of new products much quicker than previously possible. The use of single-sourcing (where a company uses a very few suppliers or, in many cases, a single supplier, as a source for a particular part or material) has helped align the interests of the supplier and customer.

The movement toward a policy of 100 percent quality has been fueled by the realization that quality can be used as a means of differentiating products. The TQM view concludes that traditional quality-cost analysis underestimates the cost of producing a poor-quality product, while it overestimates the cost of producing a high-quality product. As a result, under this new TQM view of the quality-costs trade-offs, the low point in the total cost curve moves to an optimal quality level of 100 percent quality.

KEY TERMS

Anticipatory buying, 701

Appraisal costs, 704

Credit scoring, 689

Delivery-time stock, 700

External failure costs, 705

Finished-goods inventory, 697

Internal failure costs, 705

Inventory management, 695

Just-in-time inventory control problem, 702

Marginal or incremental analysis, 692

Order point problem, 700

Order quantity problem, 697

Preventive costs, 704

Raw materials inventory, 696

Safety stock, 699

Single-sourcing, 704

Terms of sale, 687

Total quality management
(TQM), 703

Work-in-process
inventory, 696

STUDY QUESTIONS

18-1. What factors determine the size of the investment a firm makes in accounts receivable? Which of these factors are under the control of the financial manager?

18-2. What do the following trade credit terms mean?

a. 1/20, net 50

b. 2/30, net 60

c. net 30

d. 2/10, 1/30, net 60

18-3. What is the purpose of an aging account in the control of accounts receivable? Can this same function be performed through ratio analysis? Why or why not?

18-4. If a credit manager experienced no bad debt losses over the past year, would this be an indication of proper credit management? Why or why not?

18-5. What is the purpose of credit scoring?

18-6. What are the risk-return trade-offs associated with adopting a more liberal trade credit policy?

18-7. Explain the purpose of marginal analysis.

18-8. What is the purpose of holding inventory? Name several types of inventory and describe their purpose.

18-9. Can cash be considered a special type of inventory? If so, what functions does it attempt to uncouple?

18-10. To control investment in inventory effectively, what two questions must be answered?

18-11. What are the major assumptions made by the EOQ model?

18-12. What are the risk-return trade-offs associated with inventory management?

18-13. How might inflation affect the EOQ model?

18-14. How does single-sourcing and closer customer–supplier relationships contribute to the firm?

18-15. What does the TQM view of the quality-cost relationship say is mistated by the traditional economic view of trade-offs between quality and cost?

SELF-TEST PROBLEMS

ST-1. (*EOQ Calculations*) A local gift shop is attempting to determine how many sets of wine glasses to order. The store feels it will sell approximately 800 sets in the next year at a price of $18 per set. The wholesale price that the store pays per set is $12. Costs for carrying one set of wine glasses are estimated at $1.50 per year whereas ordering costs are estimated at $25.

a. What is the economic order quantity for the sets of wine glasses?

b. What are the annual inventory costs for the firm if it orders in this quantity? (Assume constant demand and instantaneous delivery and thus no safety stock is carried.)

ST-2. (*EOQ Calculations*) Given the following inventory information and relationships for the F. Beamer Corporation:

1. Orders can be placed only in multiples of 100 units.
2. Annual unit usage is 300,000. (Assume a 50-week year in your calculations.)
3. The carrying cost is 30 percent of the purchase price of the goods.
4. The purchase price is $10 per unit.
5. The ordering cost is $50 per order.
6. The desired safety stock is 1,000 units. (This does not include delivery-time stock.)
7. Delivery time is 2 weeks.

Given this information

      a. What is the optimal EOQ level?

      b. How many orders will be placed annually?

      c. At what inventory level should a reorder be made?

STUDY PROBLEMS (SET A)

18-1A. (*Trade Credit Discounts*) If a firm buys on trade credit terms of 2/10 net 50 and decides to forgo the trade credit discount and pay on the net day, what is the effective annualized cost of forgoing the discount?

18-2A. (*Trade Credit Discounts*) If a firm buys on trade credit terms of 2/20 net 30 and decides to forgo the trade credit discount and pay on the net day, what is the effective annualized cost of forgoing the discount?

18-3A. (*Trade Credit Discounts*) Determine the effective annualized cost of forgoing the trade credit discount on the following terms:

      a. 1/10, net 20

      b. 2/10, net 30

      c. 3/10, net 30

      d. 3/10, net 60

      e. 3/10, net 90

      f. 5/10, net 60

18-4A. (*Altman Model*) The following ratios were supplied by six loan applicants. Given this information and the credit-scoring model developed by Altman (equation 18-3), which loans have a high probability of defaulting next year?

	$\dfrac{\text{EBIT}}{\text{Total Assets}}$	$\dfrac{\text{Sales}}{\text{Total Assets}}$	$\dfrac{\text{Market Value of Equity}}{\text{Book Value of Debt}}$	$\dfrac{\text{Retained Earnings}}{\text{Total Assets}}$	$\dfrac{\text{Working Capital}}{\text{Total Assets}}$
Applicant 1	.2	.2	1.2	.3	.5
Applicant 2	.2	.8	1.0	.3	.8
Applicant 3	.2	.7	.6	.3	.4
Applicant 4	.1	.4	1.2	.4	.4
Applicant 5	.3	.7	.5	.4	.7
Applicant 6	.2	.5	.5	.4	.4

18-5A. (*Ratio Analysis*) Assuming a 360-day year, calculate what the average investment in inventory would be for a firm, given the following information in each case:

a. The firm has sales of $600,000, a gross profit margin of 10 percent, and an inventory turnover ratio of 6.

b. The firm has a cost of goods sold figure of $480,000 and an average age of inventory of 40 days.

c. The firm has a cost of goods sold figure of $1,150,000 and an inventory turnover ratio of 5.

d. The firm has a sales figure of $25 million, a gross profit margin of 14 percent, and an average age of inventory of 45 days.

18-6A. (*Marginal Analysis*) The Bandwagonesque Corporation is considering relaxing its current credit policy. Currently, the firm has annual sales (all credit) of $5 million and an average collection period of 60 days (assume a 360-day year). Under the proposed change, the trade credit terms would be changed from net 60 to net 90 days and credit would be extended to a riskier class of customer. It is assumed that bad debt losses on current customers will remain at their current level. Under this change, it is expected that sales will increase to $6 million. Given the following information, should the firm adopt the new policy?

New sales level (all credit):	$6,000,000
Original sales level (all credit):	$5,000,000
Contribution margin:	20%
Percent bad debt losses on new sales:	8%
New average collection period:	90 days
Original average collection period:	60 days
Additional investment in inventory:	$50,000
Pre-tax required rate of return:	15%

18-7A. (*Marginal Analysis*) The Foxbase Alpha Corporation is considering a major change in credit policy. Managers are considering extending credit to a riskier class of customer and extending their credit period from net 30 days to net 45 days. They do not expect bad debt losses on their current customers to change. Given the following information, should they go ahead with the change in credit policy?

New sales level (all credit):	$12,500,000
Original sales level (all credit):	$11,000,000
Contribution margin:	20%
Percent bad debt losses on new sales:	9%
New average collection period:	45 days
Original average collection period:	30 days
Additional investment in inventory:	$75,000
Pre-tax required rate of return:	15%

18-8A. (*EOQ Calculations*) A downtown comic shop is trying to determine the optimal order quantity for the reprint of a first issue of a popular comic book. It is expected to sell approximately 3,000 copies in the next year at a price of $1.50. The store buys the comic at a wholesale figure of $1. Costs for carrying the comic are estimated at $.10 a copy per year, and it costs $10 to order more comics.

a. Determine the EOQ.

b. What would be the total costs for ordering the comics one, four, five, ten, and fifteen times a year?

c. What questionable assumptions are being made by the EOQ model?

18-9A. (*EOQ Calculations*) The local hamburger fast-food restaurant purchases 20,000 boxes of hamburger rolls every month. Order costs are $50 an order, and it costs $.25 a box for storage.

   a. What is the optimal order quantity of hamburger rolls for this restaurant?

   b. What questionable assumptions are being made by the EOQ model?

18-10A. (*EOQ Calculations*) A local car manufacturing plant has a $75 per-unit per-year carrying cost on a certain item in inventory. This item is used at a rate of 50,000 per year. Ordering costs are $500 per order.

   a. What is the EOQ for this item?

   b. What are the annual inventory costs for this firm if it orders in this quantity? (Assume constant demand and instantaneous delivery.)

18-11A. (*EOQ Calculations*) Swank Products is involved in the production of camera parts and has the following inventory, carrying, and storage costs:

1. Orders must be placed in round lots of 200 units.
2. Annual unit usage is 500,000. (Assume a 50-week year in your calculations.)
3. The carrying cost is 20 percent of the purchase price.
4. The purchase price is $2 per unit.
5. The ordering cost is $90 per order.
6. The desired safety stock is 15,000 units. (This does not include delivery time stock.)
7. The delivery time is 1 week.

Given the preceding information:

   a. Determine the optimal EOQ level.

   b. How many orders will be placed annually?

   c. What is the inventory order point? (That is, at what level of inventory should a new order be placed?)

   d. What is the average inventory level?

18-12A. (*EOQ Calculations*) Toledo Distributors has determined the following inventory information and relationships:

1. Orders can be placed only in multiples of 200 units.
2. Annual unit usage is 500,000 units. (Assume a 50-week year in your calculations.)
3. The carrying cost is 10 percent of the purchase price of the goods.
4. The purchase price is $5 per unit.
5. The ordering cost is $100 per order.
6. The desired safety stock is 5,000 units. (This does not include delivery-time stock.)
7. Delivery time is 4 weeks.

Given this information:

   a. What is the EOQ level?

   b. How many orders will be placed annually?

   c. At what inventory level should a reorder be made?

   d. Now assume the carrying costs are 50 percent of the purchase price of the goods and recalculate (a), (b), and (c). Are these the results you anticipated?

INTEGRATIVE PROBLEM

Your first major assignment after your recent promotion at Ice Nine involves overseeing the management of accounts receivable and inventory. The first item that you must attend to involves a proposed change in credit policy that would involve relaxing credit terms from the existing terms of 1/50 net 70 to 2/60 net 90 in hopes of securing new sales. The management at Ice Nine does not expect bad debt losses on their current customers to change under the new credit policy. The following information should aid you in the analysis of this problem.

New sales level (all credit):	$8,000,000
Original sales level (all credit):	$7,000,000
Contribution margin:	25%
Percent bad debt losses on new sales:	8%
New average collection period:	75 days
Original average collection period:	60 days
Additional investment in inventory:	$50,000
Pre-tax required rate of return:	15%
New percent cash discount:	2%
Percent of customers taking the new cash discount:	50%
Original percent cash discount:	1%
Percent of customers taking the old cash discount:	50%

To help in your decision on relaxing credit terms, you have been asked to respond to the following questions:

1. What factors determine the size of investment Ice Nine makes in accounts receivable?

2. If a firm currently buys from Ice Nine on trade credit with the present terms of 1/50 net 70 and decides to forgo the trade credit discount and pay on the net day, what is the effective annualized cost to that firm of forgoing the discount?

3. If Ice Nine changes its trade credit terms to 2/60 net 90, what is the effective annualized cost to a firm that buys on credit from Ice Nine and decides to forgo the trade credit discount and pay on the net day?

4. What is the estimated change in profits resulting from the increased sales less any additional bad debts associated with the proposed change in credit policy?

5. Estimate the cost of additional investment in accounts receivable and inventory associated with this change in credit policy.

6. Estimate the change in the cost of the cash discount if the proposed change in credit policy is enacted.

7. Compare the incremental revenues with the incremental costs. Should the proposed change be enacted?

You have also been asked to deal with some questions dealing with inventory management at Ice Nine. Presently, Ice Nine is involved in the production of musical products with its German engineered Daedlufetarg music line. Production of this product involves the following inventory, carrying, and storage costs:

a. Orders must be placed in round lots of 100 units.

b. Annual unit usage is 250,000. (Assume a 50-week year in your calculations.)

c. The carrying cost is 10 percent of the purchase price.

d. The purchase price is $10 per unit.

e. The ordering cost is $100 per order.

f. The desired safety stock is 5,000 units. (This does not include delivery time stock.)

g. The delivery time is 1 week.

Given the preceding information:

1. Determine the optimal EOQ level.

2. How many orders will be placed annually?

3. What is the inventory order point? (That is, at what level of inventory should a new order be placed?)

4. What is the average inventory level?

5. What would happen to the EOQ if annual unit sales doubled (all other unit costs and safety stocks remaining constant)? What is the elasticity of EOQ with respect to sales? (That is, what is the percent change in EOQ divided by the percent change in sales?)

6. If carrying costs double, what would happen to the EOQ level? (Assume the original sales level of 250,000 units.) What is the elasticity of EOQ with respect to carrying costs?

7. If the ordering costs double, what would happen to the level of EOQ? (Again assume original levels of sales and carrying costs.) What is the elasticity of EOQ with respect to ordering costs?

8. If the selling price doubles, what would happen to EOQ? What is the elasticity of EOQ with respect to selling price?

9. What assumptions are being made by the EOQ model that has been used here?

10. How would the results of this model change if carrying cost were to increase, perhaps because of increased inflation?

11. How would an improvement in the relationship that Ice Nine has with its suppliers resulting in a decrease in the average delivery time for replenishment of inventory affect your answer?

12. If Ice Nine could decrease its ordering costs, perhaps by improving its relationship with suppliers, how would this affect your answer?

STUDY PROBLEMS (SET B)

18-1B. (*Trade Credit Discounts*) If a firm buys on trade credit terms of 2/10 net 60 and decides to forgo the trade credit discount and pay on the net day, what is the effective annualized cost of forgoing the discount?

18-2B. (*Trade Credit Discounts*) If a firm buys on trade credit terms of 2/20 net 40 and decides to forgo the trade credit discount and pay on the net day, what is the effective annualized cost of forgoing the discount?

18-3B. (*Trade Credit Discounts*) Determine the effective annualized cost of forgoing the trade credit discount on the following terms:

    a. 1/5, net 20

    b. 2/20, net 90

    c. 1/20, net 100

    d. 4/10, net 50

    e. 5/20, net 100

    f. 5/30, net 50

18-4B. (*Altman Model*) The following ratios were supplied by six loan applicants. Given this information and the credit-scoring model developed by Altman [equation (18-3)], which loans have a high probability of defaulting next year and thus should be avoided?

	$\dfrac{\text{EBIT}}{\text{Total Assets}}$	$\dfrac{\text{Sales}}{\text{Total Assets}}$	$\dfrac{\text{Market Value of Equity}}{\text{Book Value of Debt}}$	$\dfrac{\text{Retained Earnings}}{\text{Total Assets}}$	$\dfrac{\text{Working Capital}}{\text{Total Assets}}$
Applicant 1	.3	.4	1.2	.3	.5
Applicant 2	.2	.6	1.3	.4	.3
Applicant 3	.2	.7	.6	.3	.2
Applicant 4	.1	.5	1.8	.5	.4
Applicant 5	.5	.7	.5	.4	.6
Applicant 6	.2	.4	.2	.4	.4

18-5B. (*Ratio Analysis*) Assuming a 360-day year, calculate what the average investment in inventory would be for a firm, given the following information in each case.

    a. The firm has sales of $550,000, a gross profit margin of 10 percent, and an inventory turnover ratio of 5.

    b. The firm has a cost of goods sold figure of $480,000 and an average age of inventory of 35 days.

    c. The firm has a cost of goods sold figure of $1,250,000 and an inventory turnover ratio of 6.

    d. The firm has a sales figure of $25 million, a gross profit margin of 15 percent, and an average age of inventory of 50 days.

18-6B. (*Marginal Analysis*) The Hyndford Street Corporation is considering relaxing its current credit policy. Currently the firm has annual sales (all credit) of $6 million and an average collection period of 40 days (assume a 360-day year). Under the proposed change the trade credit terms would be changed from net 40 days to net 90 days and credit would be extended to a riskier class of customer. It is assumed that bad debt losses on current customers will remain at their current level. Under this change, it is expected that sales will increase to $7 million. Given the following information, should the firm adopt the new policy?

New sales level (all credit):	$7,000,000
Original sales level (all credit):	$6,000,000
Contribution margin:	20%
Percent bad debt losses on new sales:	8%
New average collection period:	90 days
Original average collection period:	40 days
Additional investment in inventory:	$40,000
Pre-tax required rate of return:	15%

18-7B. (*Marginal Analysis*) The Northern Muse Corporation is considering a major change in credit policy. Managers are considering extending credit to a riskier class of customer and extending their credit period from net 30 days to net 50 days. They do not expect bad debt losses on their current customers to change. Given the following information, should they go ahead with the change in credit policy?

New sales level (all credit):	$18,000,000
Original sales level (all credit):	$17,000,000
Contribution margin:	20%
Percent bad debt losses on new sales:	8%
New average collection period:	50 days
Original average collection period:	30 days
Additional investment in inventory:	$60,000
Pre-tax required rate of return:	15%

18-8B. (*EOQ Calculations*) A downtown bookstore is trying to determine the optimal order quantity for a reprint of a first issue of a popular comic book. It is expected to sell approximately 3,500 copies in the next year at a price of $1.50. The store buys the comic at a wholesale figure of $1. Costs for carrying the comic are estimated at $.20 a copy per year, and it costs $9 to order more comics.

    a. Determine the EOQ.

    b. What would be the total costs for ordering the comics one, four, five, ten, and fifteen times a year?

    c. What questionable assumptions are being made by the EOQ model?

18-9B. (*EOQ Calculations*) The local hamburger fast-food restaurant purchases 21,000 boxes of hamburger rolls every month. Order costs are $55 an order, and it costs $.20 a box for storage.

    a. What is the optimal order quantity of hamburger rolls for this restaurant?

    b. What questionable assumptions are being made by the EOQ model?

18-10B. (*EOQ Calculations*) A local car manufacturing plant has a $70 per-unit per-year carrying cost on a certain item in inventory. This item is used at a rate of 55,000 per year. Ordering costs are $500 per order.

    a. What is the economic order quantity for this item?

    b. What are the annual inventory costs for this firm if it orders in this quantity? (Assume constant demand and instantaneous delivery.)

18-11B. (*EOQ Calculations*) Swank Products is involved in the production of camera parts and has the following inventory, carrying, and storage costs:

1. Orders must be placed in round lots of 200 units.
2. Annual unit usage is 600,000. (Assume a 50-week year in your calculations.)
3. The carrying cost is 15 percent of the purchase price.
4. The purchase price is $3 per unit.
5. The ordering cost is $90 per order.
6. The desired safety stock is 15,000 units. (This does not include delivery-time stock.)
7. The delivery time is 1 week.

Given the preceding information:

    a. Determine the optimal EOQ level.

    b. How many orders will be placed annually?

    c. What is the inventory order point? (That is, at what level of inventory should a new order be placed?)

    d. What is the average inventory level?

18-12B. (*EOQ Calculations*) Toledo Distributors has determined the following inventory information and relationships:

1. Orders can be placed only in multiples of 200 units.
2. Annual unit usage is 500,000 units. (Assume a 50-week year in your calculations.)
3. The carrying cost is 9 percent of the purchase price of the goods.
4. The purchase price is $5 per unit.
5. The ordering cost is $75 per order.
6. The desired safety stock is 5,000 units. (This does not include delivery-time stock.)
7. Delivery time is 4 weeks.

Given this information:

    a. What is the EOQ level?

    b. How many orders will be placed annually?

    c. At what inventory level should a reorder be made?

    d. Now assume the carrying costs are 50 percent of the purchase price of the goods and recalculate (a), (b), and (c). Are these the results you anticipated?

SELF-TEST SOLUTIONS

SS-1. a. The economic order quantity is

$$Q^* = \sqrt{\frac{2SO}{C}}$$

    where S = total demand in units over the planning period
                O = ordering cost per order
                C = carrying costs per unit

Substituting the values given in the self-test problem into the EOQ equation we get

$$Q^* = \sqrt{\frac{2 \cdot 800 \cdot 25}{1.50}}$$

$$= \sqrt{26{,}667}$$

$$= 163 \text{ units per order}$$

Thus 163 units should be ordered each time an order is placed. Note that the EOQ calculations occur based on several limiting assumptions such as constant demand, constant unit price, and constant carrying costs, which may influence the final decision.

b. Total costs = carrying costs + ordering costs

$$= \left(\frac{Q}{2}\right)C + \left(\frac{S}{Q}\right)O$$

$$= \left(\frac{163}{2}\right)\$1.50 + \left(\frac{800}{163}\right)\$25$$

$$= \$122.25 + \$122.70$$

$$= \$244.95$$

Note that carrying costs and ordering costs are the same (other than a slight difference caused by having to order in whole rather than fractional units). This is because the total costs curve is at its minimum when ordering costs equal carrying costs.

SS-2. a.

$$EOQ = \sqrt{\frac{2SO}{C}}$$

$$= \sqrt{\frac{2(300{,}000)(50)}{3}}$$

$$= 3{,}162 \text{ units, but because orders must be placed in 100 unit lots, the effective EOQ}$$
becomes 3,200 units

b. $\dfrac{\text{Total usage}}{\text{EOQ}} = \dfrac{300{,}000}{3{,}200} = 93.75$ orders per year

c. Inventory order point = delivery time + safety stock

$$= \frac{2}{50} \times 300{,}000 + 1{,}000$$

$$= 12{,}000 + 1{,}000$$

$$= 13{,}000 \text{ units}$$

Learning Objectives

Active Applications

World Finance

Practice

LEARNING OBJECTIVES

After reading this chapter, you should be able to

1. Describe the basic characteristics of a term loan.

2. Calculate the principal and interest components of an installment loan.

3. List and define the basic types of lease arrangements.

4. Calculate the net advantage of leasing versus purchasing an asset.

5. Describe the potential sources of economic benefit derived from leasing versus purchasing.

TERM LOANS AND LEASES

INTRODUCTION

Virtually everyone has rented something at one time or another. With renting, just like owning, you get to use the asset. What distinguishes renting or leasing from owning is that when you rent, you don't actually obtain ownership of the thing being rented and must return it to the owner at the end of the agreement.

Firms lease all types of capital equipment as an alternative to purchasing it. For example, they lease computers, trucks, and railroad cars. The U.S. Navy has even leased minesweepers. The total amount spent on leasing by U.S. companies now exceeds $400 billion annually.

Why lease—why not purchase? Some companies lease because they think they can avoid investing in equipment that faces the risk of rapid obsolescence, whereas others think that they are conserving their cash. As we learn in this chapter, these and many other reasons for leasing are subject to quantitative analysis, which reduces the decision down to an analysis of the net present value of leasing versus owning.

CHAPTER PREVIEW

Chapter 19 contains a discussion of two sources of *intermediate term financing*: *term loans* and *leases*. Intermediate term financing consists of all those sources of financing with maturities longer than 1 year and shorter than 10 years. This maturity range is bracketed by short-term sources of financing such as bank notes, trade credit, and commercial paper (discussed in chapters 16, 17, and 18) and long-term sources of financing such as bonds and stock (discussed in chapters 7 and 8).

Our discussion of term loans, an important source of financing for machinery and equipment, will focus on the various *sources of term financing* and their basic characteristics as well as the *calculation of installment payments* (including the decomposition of those payments into their principal and interest components). We then categorize leases as *operating* or *financial leases* and focus on the latter, because operating leases are short-term in nature. We evaluate the merits of *leasing versus purchasing* by first evaluating the viability of purchasing via the project's net present value and then analyzing the incremental benefits of leasing by calculating the *net advantage of leasing*.

This chapter will emphasize these axioms: **Axiom 1: The Risk-Return Trade-Off—We Won't Take on Additional Risk Unless We Expect to Be Compensated with Additional Return; Axiom 2: The Time Value of Money—A Dollar Received Today Is Worth More Than a Dollar Received in the Future; Axiom 3: Cash—Not Profits—Is King; Axiom 4: Incremental Cash Flows—It's Only What Changes That Counts; and Axiom 8: Taxes Bias Business Decisions.**

TERM LOANS

OBJECTIVE 1

Term loans generally share three common characteristics: They (1) have maturities of 1 to 10 years; (2) are repaid in periodic installments (such as quarterly, semiannual, or annual payments) over the life of the loan; and (3) are usually secured by a chattel mortgage on equipment or a mortgage on real property. The principal suppliers of term credit are commercial banks, insurance companies, and (to a lesser extent) pension funds.

We will consider briefly some of the more common characteristics of term loan agreements.

Term loans

Loans that have maturities of 1 to 10 years and are repaid in periodic installments over the life of the loan; usually secured by a chattel mortgage on equipment or a mortgage on real property.

Maturities

Commercial banks generally restrict their term lending to 1- to 5-year maturities. Insurance companies and pension funds with their longer-term liabilities generally make loans with 5- to 15-year maturities. Thus the term lending activities of commercial banks actually complement rather than compete with those of insurance companies and pension funds. In fact, commercial banks very often cooperate with both insurance companies and pension funds in providing term financing for very large loans.

Collateral

Term loans are generally backed by some form of collateral. Shorter-maturity loans are frequently secured with a *chattel mortgage* (a mortgage on machinery and equipment) or with securities such as stocks and bonds. Longer-maturity loans are frequently secured by mortgages on real estate.

There is also a form of term credit that requires no collateral that can be used by only the largest blue-chip companies. These unsecured **medium-term notes (MTNs)** were created as a result of the introduction of shelf-registration by the Securities and Exchange Commission in 1982. Shelf registration permits companies to file a single registration statement for a series of similar issues. Once registered, the MTNs can be sold as funds are required, giving the issuer a ready source of term financing. The key thing to recognize here is that unsecured term financing, like similar forms of unsecured short-term financing (e.g., commercial paper) is available to only the most creditworthy borrowers.

Restrictive Covenants

In addition to requiring collateral, the lender in a term loan agreement often places restrictions on the borrower that, when violated, make the loan immediately due and payable. These restrictive covenants are designed to prohibit the borrower from engaging in any activities that would increase the likelihood of loss on the loan. There are some common restrictions:

1. **Working-capital requirement.** This restriction takes the form of a minimum current ratio, such as 2 to 1 or $3\frac{1}{2}$ to 1, or a minimum dollar amount of net working capital. The actual requirement would reflect the norm for the borrower's industry, as well as the lender's desires.
2. **Additional borrowing.** This type of restriction requires the lender's approval before any additional debt can be issued. Furthermore, a restriction on additional borrowing is often extended to long-term lease agreements, which are discussed later in this chapter.
3. **Periodic financial statements.** A standard covenant in most term loan agreements includes a requirement that the borrower supply the lender with financial statements on a regular basis. These generally include annual or quarterly income statements and balance sheets.
4. **Management.** Term loan agreements sometimes include a provision that requires prior approval by the lender of major personnel changes. In addition, the borrower may be required to insure the lives of certain key personnel, naming the lender as beneficiary.

We have presented only a partial listing of restrictions commonly found in term loan agreements. The number and form of such provisions are limited only by the scope of the law and the imagination of the parties involved. It should be noted, however, that restrictive covenants are subject to negotiation. The specific agreement that results reflects the relative bargaining strengths of the borrower and lender. Marginal borrowers are more likely to find their loan agreements burdened with restrictive covenants than more creditworthy borrowers.

Term loan agreements can be very technical and are generally tailored to the situation. Therefore, it is difficult to generalize about their content. However, many banks rely on standardized *worksheets* or *checksheets* to aid in the preparation of the document.

RELATE TO THE BIG PICTURE

*When we determine the loan payments for an installment loan, we are solving for a series of annuity payments (installment or loan payments) whose present value equals the face value of the loan when discounted using the borrowing rate on the loan. Thus we are valuing a series of future cash flows. The valuation process utilizes a number of our axioms: **Axiom 1: The Risk-Return Trade-Off—We Won't Take on Additional Risk Unless We Expect to Be Compensated with Additional Return** comes into play in determining the rate of interest for the loan. **Axiom 2: The Time Value of Money—A Dollar Received Today Is Worth More Than a Dollar Received in the Future** provides the basis for finding the present value of future payments. Finally, **Axiom 3: Cash—Not Profits—Is King** tells us that what matters to both the lender and borrower is the cash received and cash paid.*

Repayment Schedules

Term loans are generally repaid with periodic installments, which include both an interest and a principal component. Thus the loan is repaid over its life with equal annual, semiannual, or quarterly payments.

To illustrate how the repayment procedure works, let us assume that a firm borrows $15,000, which is to be repaid in five annual installments. The loan will carry an 8 percent rate of interest, and payments will be made at the end of each of the next 5 years. The following diagram shows the cash flows to the lender:

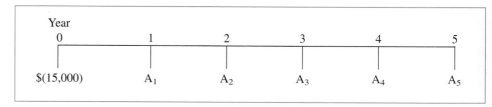

The $15,000 cash flow at period zero is placed in parentheses to indicate an outflow of cash by the lender, whereas the annual installments, A_1 through A_5, represent cash inflows (of course, the opposite is true for the borrower). The lender must determine the annual installments that will give an 8 percent return on the outstanding balance over the life of the loan. This problem is very similar to the internal rate of return problem encountered in chapter 9, where we discussed capital-budgeting decisions and had to determine the rate of interest that would make the present value of a stream of future cash flows equal to some present sum. Here we want to determine the future cash flows whose present value, when discounted at 8 percent, is equal to the $15,000 loan amount. Thus we must solve for those values of A_1 through A_5 whose present value when discounted at 8 percent is $15,000. In equation form,

$$\$15,000 = \sum_{t=1}^{5} \frac{A_t}{(1+.08)^t} \tag{19-1}$$

Where we assume equal annual installments, A, for all 5 years, we can solve for A as follows:

$$\$15,000 = A \sum_{t=1}^{5} \frac{1}{(1+.08)^t}$$

or

$$A = \frac{\$15,000}{\displaystyle\sum_{t=1}^{5} \frac{1}{(1+.08)^t}} = \frac{\$15,000}{\text{PVIF}_{8\%,\ 5\ \text{yrs}}} \tag{19-2}$$

The term that is divided into that $15,000 loan amount is the present value factor for a 5-year annuity carrying an 8 percent rate of interest. Thus,

$$A = \frac{\$15,000}{3.993} = \$3,756.57$$

Therefore, if the borrower makes payments of $3,756.57 each year, then the lender will receive an 8 percent return on the outstanding loan balance. To verify this assertion, check Table 19.1, which contains the principal and interest components of the annual loan payments. We see that the $3,756.57 installments truly provide the lender with an 8 percent return on the outstanding balance of a $15,000 loan.

Loan Participations among Banks

The demand for loans is not evenly dispersed across banks; heavier demand is placed on large money center banks and banks in regions of the country that are experiencing strong economic growth. This frequently means that these banks cannot provide all the necessary funds, so they share the loan demand with one or more participating banks. This shared lending has grown rapidly in recent years and has served to promote the flow of funds from banks with excess lending capacity to those with excess loan demand. The participating banks work out an agreement and receive a certificate of participation, which states that the lead bank will pay a portion of the loan cash flows as they are received.

Eurodollar Loans

Eurodollar loans are intermediate term loans made by major international banks to businesses based on foreign deposits that are denominated in dollars. These loans are generally made in amounts ranging from $1 million to $1.5 billion with the rate based on a certain amount above the London Interbank Offered Rate (LIBOR). The rate on these loans is adjusted periodically (generally every 6 months), and there is a wide range of

Eurodollar loans

Intermediate term loans made by major international banks to businesses based on foreign deposits that are denominated in dollars.

Table 19.1 Term Loan Amortization Schedule				
End of Year t	Installment Payment[a] A	Interest[b] I_t	Principal Repayment[c] P_t	Remaining Balance[d] RB_t
0	—	—	—	$15,000.00
1	$3,756.57	$1,200.00	$2,556.57	12,443.43
2	3,756.57	995.47	2,761.10	9,682.33
3	3,756.57	774.59	2,981.98	6,700.35
4	3,756.57	536.03	3,220.54	3,479.81
5	3,756.57	278.38	3,478.19	1.62[e]

[a]The annual installment payment, A, is found as follows:

$$A = \frac{\$15,000}{\sum_{t=1}^{5} \frac{1}{(1+.08)^t}} = \$3,756.57$$

[b]Annual interest expense is equal to 8 percent of the outstanding loan balance. Thus for year 1, the interest expense, I_1, is found as follows:

$I_1 = .08(\$15,000) = \$1,200$

[c]Principal repayment for year t, P_t is the difference in the loan payment, A, and interest for the year. Thus for year 1, we compute

$P_1 = A - I_1, = \$3,756.57 - \$1,200 = \$2,556.57$

[d]The remaining balance of the end of year 1, RB_t, is the difference in the remaining balance for the previous year, RB_t, and the principal payment in year 1, P_1. Thus at the end of year 1,

$RB_1 = RB_0 - P_1 = \$15,000 - \$2,556.57 = \$12,443.43$

[e]The $1.62 difference in RB_4 and P_5 is due to rounding error.

maturities. Eurodollar lending has become a major source of commercial lending with the total volume of lending being measured in trillions of dollars.

The attraction of the Eurodollar market relates to the fact that this market is subject to very limited official regulation. It has been suggested, in fact, that some investors use the market to avoid home country taxes. For example, Eurobonds (which are long-term bonds sold outside the country in whose currency the bond is denominated) are sold in bearer rather than registered form. This means that there is no record of who owns the bonds and receives the interest payments.

STOP AND THINK

Term loans provide the firm with an important source of financing for machinery and equipment whose useful lives extend beyond 1 year but are less than 10 years. Term loans with their annual installments offer the firm a financing alternative that closely matches the cash flow generating characteristics of the machinery and equipment. Thus term loan financing can be a useful financing instrument in trying to implement the hedging financing principle discussed in chapter 16.

OBJECTIVE 3   **LEASES**

Leasing provides an alternative to buying an asset to acquire its services. Although some leases involve maturities of more than ten years, most do not. Thus lease financing is classified as a source of intermediate term credit. Today, virtually any type of asset can be acquired through a lease agreement. The recent growth in lease financing has been phenomenal, with more than $200 billion in assets (based on original cost) now under lease in the United States.

A **lease** is simply a contract between a **lessee**, who acquires the services of a leased asset by making a series of payments to the **lessor**, who is the owner of the asset. The contract provides the lessee with the right to use the asset for the term of the lease agreement, at the end of the term of the lease, the lessee must return the asset to the lessor. However, leases frequently contain an option for the lessee to purchase the asset at the termination of the lease agreement. Lessees can be just about anyone (an individual, a business, or a government agency). Lessors are generally the manufacturer of the leased asset or an independent leasing company.

The primary difference between leasing and buying an asset relates to the rights that transfer to the lessee versus the owner. The lessee obtains the right to use the asset up until the term of the agreement. The owner, on the other hand, receives both the right to use the asset and the title to the asset so that, when he or she decides to sell, the owner can dispose of the asset and realize the proceeds from its sale.

Types of Lease Arrangements

There are three major types of lease agreements: direct leasing, sale and leaseback, and leveraged leasing. Most lease agreements fall into one of these categories. However, the particular lease agreement can take one of two forms. (1) The **financial lease** constitutes a noncancelable contractual commitment on the part of the firm leasing the asset (the lessee) to make a series of payments to the firm that actually owns the asset (the lessor) for use of the asset. (2) The **operating lease** differs from the financial lease only with respect to its cancelability. An operating lease can be canceled after proper notice to the lessor any time during its term. Thus operating leases are by their very nature sources of short-term financing. The balance of this chapter is concerned with the financial lease, which provides the firm with a form of intermediate-term financing most comparable with debt financing.

In the jargon of the leasing industry, a financial lease can take one of two basic forms: a **net lease** or a **net-net lease**. In a net lease agreement, the lessee firm assumes the risk and burden of ownership over the term of the lease. That is, the lessee must maintain the asset, as well as pay insurance and taxes on the asset. A net-net lease requires that the lessee meet all the requirements of the net lease as well as return the asset, still worth a *preestablished value*, to the lessor at the end of the lease term.

Direct Leasing

In a *direct lease*, the firm acquires the services of an asset it did not previously own. Direct leasing is available through several financial institutions, including manufacturers, banks, finance companies, independent leasing companies, and special-purpose leasing companies.[1] In the lease arrangement, the lessor purchases the asset and leases it to the lessee. In the case of a manufacturer lessor, however, the lessor has already produced the asset.

Sale and Leaseback

A **sale and leaseback arrangement** arises when a firm sells land, buildings, or equipment that it already owns to a lessor and simultaneously enters into an agreement to lease the property back for a specified period under specific terms. The lessor involved in the sale and leaseback varies with the nature of the property involved and the lease period. When land is involved and the corresponding lease is long term, the lessor is generally a

---

[1]Many leasing companies specialize in the leasing of a single type of asset. For example, several firms lease computers exclusively, and others lease only automobiles.

Lease

A contract between a lessee, who acquires the services of a leased asset by making a series of rental payments and the lessor, who is the owner of the asset.

Lessee and lessor

The user of the leased asset, who agrees to make periodic lease or rental payments to the lessor, who owns the asset.

Financial lease

A noncancelable contractual commitment on the part of the firm leasing the asset (the lessee) to make a series of payments to the firm that actually owns the asset (the lessor) for the use of the asset over the period of the agreement.

Operating lease

A lease agreement (see financial lease) in which the lessee can cancel the agreement at any time after giving proper notice to the lessor.

Net and net-net leases

In a net lease agreement, the lessee assumes the risk and burden of ownership over the term of the lease. This means that the lessee must pay insurance and taxes on the asset as well as maintain the operating condition of the asset. In a net-net lease, the lessee must, in addition to the requirements of a net lease, return the asset to the lessor at the end of the lease still worth a preestablished value.

Sale and leaseback arrangement

An arrangement arising when a firm sells land, buildings, or equipment that it already owns and simultaneously enters into an agreement to lease the property back for a specified period, under specific terms.

life insurance company. If the property consists of machinery and equipment, then the maturity of the lease will probably be intermediate term, and the lessor could be an insurance company, commercial bank, or leasing company.

The lessee firm receives cash in the amount of the sales price of the assets sold and the use of the asset over the term of the lease. In return, the lessee must make periodic rental payments through the term of the lease and give up any salvage or residual value to the lessor.

Leveraged Leasing

In the leasing arrangements discussed thus far, only two participants have been identified: the lessor and lessee. In leveraged leasing, a third participant is added: the lender, who helps finance the acquisition of the asset to be leased. From the viewpoint of the lessee, there is no difference in a leveraged lease, direct lease, or sale and leaseback arrangement. However, with a leveraged lease, the method of financing used by the lessor in acquiring the asset receives specific consideration. The lessor generally supplies equity funds up to 20 to 30 percent of the purchase price and borrows the remainder from a third-party lender, which may be a commercial bank or insurance company. In some arrangements, the lessor firm sells bonds, which are guaranteed by the lessee. This guarantee serves to reduce the risk and thus the cost of the debt. The majority of financial leases are leveraged leases.

Leases and Financial Reporting

Any lease that meets one or more of the following criteria is a *capital lease* and must be included in the body of the balance sheet of the lessee according to the Financial Accounting Standards Board (FASB). All other lease agreements are classified as *operating leases* for accounting purposes. In a capital lease:

1. The lease transfers ownership of the property to the lessee by the end of the lease term.
2. The lease contains a bargain repurchase option.
3. The lease term is equal to 75 percent or more of the estimated economic life of the leased property.
4. The present value of the minimum lease payments equals or exceeds 90 percent of the excess of the fair value of the property over any related investment tax credit retained by the lessor.

The last two requirements are the most stringent elements in the board's statement. The first two have been applicable to most leases for many years because of the Internal Revenue Service's "true" lease requirements. However, the last two apply to most financial leases written in the United States. As a result, the board now requires capitalization of all leases meeting one or more of these criteria.

Table 19.2 is a sample balance sheet for the Alpha Mfg. Company. Alpha has entered into capital leases whose payments have a present value of $4 million.

Note that the asset "leased property" is matched by a liability, "capital lease obligations." The specific entries recorded for the lease obligation equal the present value of minimum lease payments the firm must pay over the term of the lease. The discount rate used is the lower of either the lessee's incremental borrowing rate or the lessor's implicit interest rate (where that rate can be determined).

Operating leases are not disclosed in the body of the balance sheet. Instead, these lease obligations must be reported in a footnote to the balance sheet.

The Lease-versus-Purchase Decision

The lease-versus-purchase decision is a hybrid capital-budgeting problem that forces the analyst to consider the consequences of alternative forms of financing on the investment decision. When we discussed capital budgeting in chapter 9 and the cost of capital in chapter 12,

Table 19.2 Alpha Manufacturing Company Balance Sheet December 31, 1995 (Millions of Dollars)

Assets

Current assets	$14
Plant and equipment	20
Leased property (capital leases)	4
Total	$38

Liabilities and stockholders' equity

Current liabilities	$ 8
Long-term debt	9
Capital lease obligations	4
Stockholders' equity	17
Total	$38

we assumed that all new financing would be undertaken in accordance with the firm's optimal capital structure. When analyzing an asset that is to be leased, the analysis must be altered to consider financing through leasing as opposed to the use of the more traditional debt and equity sources of funds. Thus the lease-versus-purchase decision requires a standard capital-budgeting type of analysis, as well as an analysis of two alternative financing *packages*. The lease-purchase decision involves the analysis of two basic issues:

1. Should the asset be purchased using the firm's optimal financing mix?
2. Should the asset be financed using a financial lease?

The answer to the first question can be obtained through an analysis of the project's NPV, following the method laid out in chapter 9. There are times when it might be advantageous to lease an asset, even when the NPV for its purchase is negative. The cost savings of a lease more than offsets the negative NPV of purchase. For example, the Alpha Mfg. Co. is considering the acquisition of a new computer-based inventory and payroll system. The computed net present value of the new system based on normal purchase financing is –$40, indicating that acquisition of the system through purchasing or ownership is not warranted. However, an analysis of the cost savings resulting from leasing the system (referred to here as the *net advantage of leasing* or *NAL*) indicates that the lease alternative will produce a present value cost saving of $60 over normal purchase financing. Therefore, the net present value of the system if leased is $20 (the net present value if leased equals the NPV of a purchase *plus* the net advantage of leasing, or – $40 + $60). Thus the system's services should be acquired via the lease agreement.

RELATE TO THE BIG PICTURE

A primary motivating factor behind leasing is the opportunity to transfer the tax consequences of ownership (i.e., interest and depreciation expenses) from a firm that is either not currently paying taxes because of prior year losses or is paying them at a very low rate to another firm (the lessor), who is paying taxes at a much higher rate. This is a direct application of **Axiom 8: Taxes Bias Business Decisions***.*

The Lease-Purchase Algorithm

OBJECTIVE 4

Figure 19.1 contains a flow chart that can be used in performing lease-purchase analyses. The analyst first calculates *NPV(P)*. If the project's net present value is positive, then the left branch of Figure 19.1 should be followed. Tracing through the left branch, we now compute *NAL*. If *NAL* is positive, the lease alternative offers a positive present-

Figure 19.1 Lease-Purchase Analysis

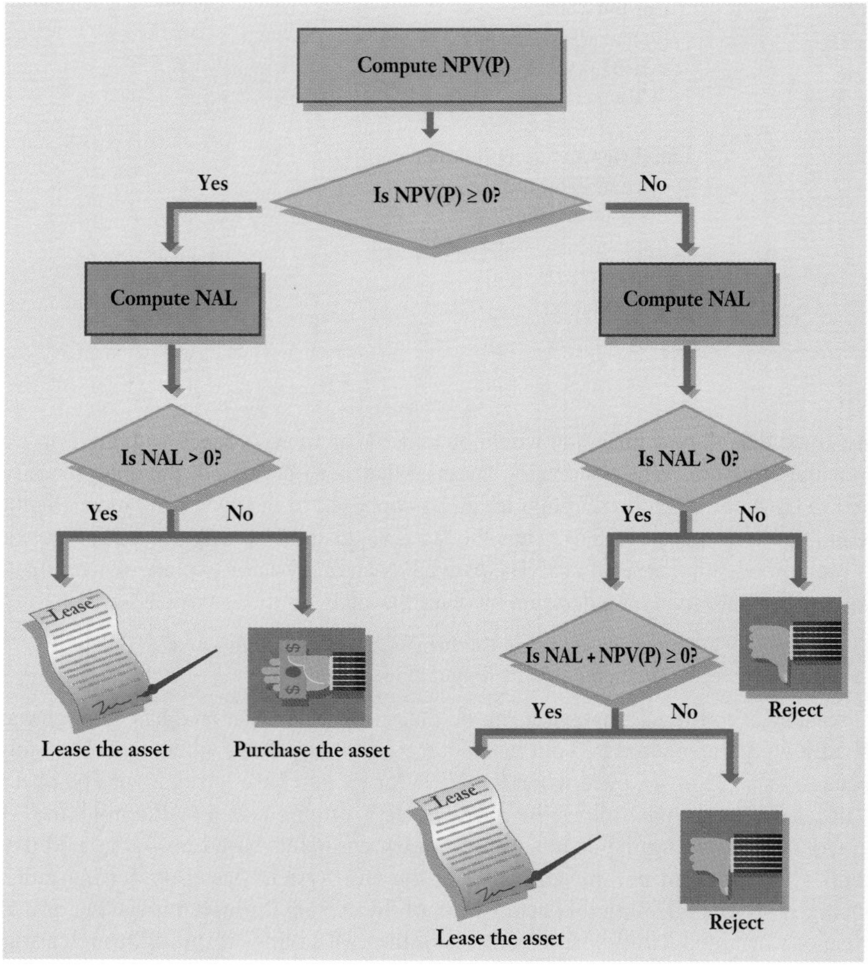

value cost advantage over normal purchase financing, and the asset should be leased. Should *NAL* be negative, then the purchase alternative should be selected. If *NPV(P)* is negative, then return to the top of Figure 19.1 and go to the right side of the flow chart. The only hope for the project's acceptance at this point is a favorable set of lease terms. In this circumstance, the project would be acceptable and thus leased *only* if *NAL* were large enough to offset the negative *NPV(P)* [that is, where *NAL* was greater than the absolute value of *NPV(P)* or, equivalently, where *NAL* + *NPV(P)* ≥ 0].[2]

The lease-versus-purchase problem is analyzed using the equations (19-3) and (19-4) found in Table 19.3. The first equation is simply the net present value of purchasing the

---

[2]That is, *NAL* = *NPV(L)* − *NPV(P)*, where *NPV(L)* is the net present value of the asset if leased. Thus the sum of *NPV(P)* and *NAL* is the net present value of the asset if leased. See Lawrence D. Schall, "The Lease-or-Buy and Asset Acquisition Decisions," *Journal of Finance* 29 (September 1974): 1203–14, for a development of net present value of leasing and purchasing equations.

Table 19.3 Lease-Purchase Model

Equation One—Net present value of purchase [NPV(P)]:

$$NPV(P) = \sum_{t=1}^{n} \frac{ACF_t}{(1 + K)^t} - IO \qquad (19\text{-}3)$$

where ACF_t = the annual after-tax cash flow in period t resulting from the asset's purchase (note that ACF_n also includes any after-tax salvage value expected from the project).

K = the firm's cost of capital applicable to the project being analyzed and the particular mix of financing used to acquire the project.

IO = the initial cash outlay required to purchase the asset in period zero (now).

n = the productive life of the project.

Equation Two—Net Advantage of Leasing (NAL):

$$NAL = \sum_{t=1}^{n} \frac{O_t(1 - T) - R_t(1 - T) - T \cdot I_t - I \cdot D_t}{(1 + r_b)^t} - \frac{V_n}{(1 + K_s)^n} + IO \qquad (19\text{-}4)$$

where O_t = any operating cash flows incurred in period t that are incurred only when the asset is purchased. Most often this consists of maintenance expenses and insurance that would be paid by the lessor.

R_t = the annual rental for period t.

T = the marginal tax rate on corporate income.

I_t = the tax-deductible interest expense forfeited in period t if the lease option is adopted. This represents the interest expense on a loan equal to the full purchase price of the asset being acquired.[a]

D_t = depreciation expense in period t for the asset.

V_n = the after-tax salvage value of the asset expected in year n.

K_s = the discount rate used to find the present value of V_n. This rate should reflect the risk inherent in the estimated V_n. For simplicity the after-tax cost of capital (K) is often used as a proxy for this rate. Also, note that this rate is the same one used to discount the salvage value in $NPV(P)$.

IO = the purchase price of the asset, which is not paid by the firm in the event the asset is leased.

r_b = the after-tax rate of interest on borrowed funds (i.e., $r_b = r(1 - T)$ where r is the before-tax borrowing rate for the firm). This rate is used to discount the relatively certain after-tax cash flow savings that accrue through the leasing of the asset.

[a]This analysis makes the implicit assumption that a dollar of lease financing is equivalent to a dollar of loan. This form of equivalence is only one of several that might be used.

proposed project, discussed in chapter 9. The second equation calculates the net present value advantage of leasing or NAL. NAL represents an accumulation of the cash flows (both inflows and outflows) associated with leasing *as opposed* to purchasing the asset. Specifically, through leasing, the firm avoids certain operating expenses, O_t, but incurs the after-tax rental expense, $R_t(1 - T)$. By leasing, furthermore, the firm loses the tax-deductible expense associated with interest, $T \cdot I_t$, and depreciation, $T \cdot D_t$. Finally, the firm does not receive the salvage value from the asset, V_n, if it is leased, but it does not have to make the initial cash outlay to purchase the asset, IO. Thus NAL reflects the cost savings associated with leasing, net of the opportunity costs of not purchasing.

Table 19.4 Computing Project Annual After-Tax Cash Flows (ACF_t) Associated with Asset Purchase

	Year			
	1		**2**	
	Book Profits	**Cash Flow**	**Book Profits**	**Cash Flow**
Annual cash revenues	$ 5,000	$ 5,000	$ 5,000	$ 5,000
Less: depreciation	(3,000)	—	(3,000)	—
Net revenues before taxes	$ 2,000	$ 5,000	$ 2,000	$ 5,000
Less: taxes (50%)	(1,000) →	(1,000)	(1,000) →	(1,000)
Annual after-tax cash flow		$ 4,000		$ 4,000

Note that the before-tax cost of new debt is used to discount the *NAL* cash flows other than the salvage value, V_n. This is justified because the affected cash flows are very nearly riskless and certainly no more risky than the interest and principal accruing to the firm's creditors (which underlie the rate of interest charged to the firm for its debt).[3] Because V_n is not a risk-free cash flow but depends on the market price for the leased asset in year n, a rate higher than r is appropriate. Because the salvage value of the leased asset was discounted using the cost of capital when determining $NPV(P)$, we use this rate here when calculating *NAL*.

Case Problem in Lease-Purchase Analysis

The Waynesboro Plastic Molding Company (WPM) is now deciding whether to purchase an automatic casting machine. The machine will cost $15,000 and for tax purposes will be depreciated toward a zero salvage value over a 5-year period. However, at the end of 5 years, the machine actually has an expected salvage value of $2,100. Because the machine is depreciated toward a zero book value at the end of 5 years, the salvage value is fully taxable at the firm's marginal tax rate of 50 percent. Hence the after-tax salvage value of the machine is only $1,050.[4] The firm uses the simple straight-line depreciation method to depreciate the $15,000 asset toward a zero salvage value. Furthermore, the project is expected to generate annual cash revenues of $5,000 per year over the next 5 years (net of cash operating expenses but before depreciation and taxes). For projects of this type, WPM has a target debt ratio of 40 percent that is impounded in its after-tax cost-of-capital estimate of 12 percent. Finally, WPM can borrow funds at a before-tax rate of 8 percent.

---

[3]The argument for using the firm's borrowing rate to discount these tax shelters goes as follows: The tax shields are relatively free of risk in that their source (depreciation, interest, rental payments) can be estimated with a high degree of certainty. There are, however, two sources of uncertainty regarding these tax shelters: (1) the possibility of a change in the firm's tax rate or the tax benefits of leasing, and (2) the possibility that the firm might become bankrupt at some future date. If we attach a very low probability to the likelihood of a reduction in the tax rate, then the prime risk associated with these tax shelters is the possibility of bankruptcy wherein they would be lost forever (certainly, all tax shelters after the date of bankruptcy would be lost). We now note that the firm's creditors also faced the risk of the firm's bankruptcy when they lent the firm funds at the rate r. If this rate, r, reflects the market's assessment of the firm's bankruptcy potential as well as the time-value of money, then it offers an appropriate rate for discounting the interest shelters generated by the firm. Note also that the O_t cash flows are generally estimated with a high degree of certainty (in the case in which they represent insurance premiums they may be contractually set) such that r is appropriate as a discount rate here also. Of course, r is adjusted for taxes to discount the after-tax cash flows.

[4]The problem example is a modification of the well-known example from R. W. Johnson and W. G. Lewellen, "Analysis of the Lease-or-Buy Decision," *Journal of Finance* 27 (September 1972): 815–23.

Year					
3		4		5	
Book Profits	Cash Flow	Book Profits	Cash Flow	Book Profits	Cash Flow
$ 5,000	$ 5,000	$ 5,000	$ 5,000	$ 5,000	$ 5,000
(3,000)	—	(3,000)	—	(3,000)	—
$ 2,000	$ 5,000	$ 2,000	$ 5,000	$ 2,000	$ 5,000
(1,000) →	(1,000)	(1,000) →	(1,000)	(1,000) →	(1,000)
	$ 4,000		$ 4,000		$ 4,000

Step 1: Computing NPV(P)—should the asset be purchased? The first step in analyzing the lease-purchase problem involves computing the net present value under the purchase alternative. The relevant cash flow computations are presented in Table 19.4.

The $NPV(P)$ is found by discounting the annual cash flows (ACF_t) in Table 19.3 back to the present at the firm's after-tax cost of capital of 12 percent, adding this sum to the present value of the salvage value, and subtracting the initial cash outlay. These calculations are shown in Table 19.5. The project's $NPV(P)$ is a positive $15.35, indicating that the asset should be acquired.

The second question concerns whether the asset should be leased. This can be answered by considering the net advantage to leasing (NAL).

Step 2: Computing NAL—should the asset be leased? The computation of NAL is shown in Table 19.6. The resulting NAL is a negative $(1,121), which indicates that leasing is not preferred to the normal debt-equity method of financing. In fact, WPM will be $(1,121) worse off, in present value terms, if it chooses to lease rather than purchase the asset.

Calculating NAL involves solving equation (19-4) presented earlier in Table 19.2. To do this, we first estimate all those cash flows that are to be discounted at the firm's after-tax cost of debt, r_b. These include $O_t(1 - T)$, $R_t(1 - T)$, $I_t \cdot T$, and $T \cdot D_t$.

The operating expenses associated with the asset that will be paid by the lessor if we lease—that is, the O_t—generally consist of certain maintenance expenses and insurance. WPM estimates them to be $1,000 per year over the life of the project. The annual rental or lease payments, R_t, are given and equal $4,200.

Table 19.5 Calculating $NPV(P)$

Year t	Annual CashFlow ACF_t	Discount Factor for 12 Percent	Present Value
1	$4,000	.893	$ 3,572
2	4,000	.797	3,188
3	4,000	.712	2,848
4	4,000	.636	2,544
5	4,000	.567	2,268
5 (Salvage – V_n)	1,050	.567	595.35
		Present value of $ACFs$ and V_n	= $15,015.35
		$NPV(P) = \$15,015.35 - \$15,000 = \$$	15.35

Table 19.6 Computing *NAL*

Overview: To solve for *NAL*, we use equation (19-4), which was discussed in Table 19.2. This equation contains three terms and is repeated below for convenience.

$$NAL = \underbrace{\sum_{t=1}^{n} \frac{O_t(1-T) - R_t(1-T) - I_t \cdot T - D_t \cdot T}{(1+r_b)^t}}_{\text{Term 1}} - \underbrace{\frac{V_n}{(1+K_s)^n}}_{\text{Term 2}} + \underbrace{IO}_{\text{Term 3}}$$

Step 1: Solving for Term 1 $= \sum_{t=1}^{n} \dfrac{O_t(1-T) - R_t(1-T) - I_t - T - D_t \cdot T}{(1+r_b)^t}$

Year t	After-Tax Operating Expenses Paid by Lessor[a] $O_t(1-T)$	−	After-Tax Rental Expense[b] $R_t(1-T)$	−	Tax Shelter on Loan Interest[c] I_tT	=	Tax Shelter on Depreciation[d] D_tT	−	Sum	×	Discount Factor[e] DF	=	Present Value PV
1	$500		$2,100		$600		$1,500		−$3,700		.962		−$ 3,558
2	500		2,100		498		1,500		− 3,598		.925		− 3,326
3	500		2,100		387		1,500		− 3,487		.889		− 3,100
4	500		2,100		268		1,500		− 3,368		.855		− 2,879
5	500		2,100		140		1,500		− 3,240		.822		− 2,662
													− 15,525

Step 2: Solving for term 2 $= - \left[\dfrac{V_n}{(1+K_s)^n} \right] = \dfrac{\$1,050}{(1+.12)^5} = \$1,050 \times .567^f =$ $ 596

Step 3: Term 3 = *IO* $15,000

Step 4: Calculate *NAL* = $15,525 − $596 + $15,000 = −$ 1,121

[a]After-tax lessor-paid operating expenses are found by $O_t(1-T) = \$1,000(1-.5) = \$500$.
[b]After-tax rent expense for year 1 is computed as follows: $R_t(1-T) = \$4,200(1-.5) = \$2,100$.
[c]Interest expense figures were calculated in Table 19.1 for a $15,000 loan. For year 1 the interest tax shelter is $0.5 \times \$1,200 = \$600$.
[d]The tax shelter from depreciation is found as follows: $D_1T = \$3,000 \times 0.5 = \$1,500$.
[e]Based on the after-tax borrowing rate, i.e., .08 (1 − .5) = .04.
[f]K_s was estimated to be the same as the firm's after-tax cost of capital, 12 percent.

The interest tax shelter lost because the asset is leased and not purchased must now be estimated. This tax shelter is lost because the firm does not borrow any money if it enters into the lease agreement. Table 19.1 contains the principal and interest components for a 5-year $15,000 loan. Note that the interest column supplies the needed information for the interest tax shelter that is lost if the asset is leased, I_t.[5]

---

[5]Technically, the firm does not lose the interest tax shelter on a $15,000 loan if it leases. In fact, the firm would lose the tax shelter on only that portion of the $15,000 purchase price that it would have financed by borrowing, for example, 40 percent of the $15,000 investment, or $6,000. However, if the firm leases the $15,000 asset, it has effectively used 100 percent levered (nonowner) financing. This means that the leasing of this project uses not only its 40 percent allotment of levered (debt) financing, but an additional 60 percent as well. Thus by leasing the $15,000 asset the lessee forfeits the interest tax shelter on a 40 percent or $6,000 loan plus an additional 60 percent of the $15,000 purchase price, or an additional $9,000 loan. In total, leasing has caused the firm to forgo the interest tax savings on a loan equal to 100 percent of the leased asset's purchase price. Once again, we note that this analysis presumes $1 of lease financing is equivalent to $1 of loan financing.

The next step in calculating *NAL* involves finding the present value of the after-tax salvage value. Earlier when we computed *NPV(P)*, we found this to equal $15.35. Because *NPV(P)* is positive, the purchase would increase shareholder wealth. Now, substituting the results of our calculations into equation (19-4) produces the *NAL* of $(1,121). Because *NAL* is negative, the asset should not be leased.

Note that the lease payments used in this example were made at the end of each year. In practice, lease payments are generally made at the beginning of each year (that is, they constitute an *annuity due* rather than an ordinary annuity, as used here). The *NAL* for the example used here is even more negative if we assume beginning of year lease payments. That is, with beginning of year payments *NAL* = − $1,495. You can easily verify this result as follows: Note first that changing from a regular annuity to an annuity due affects only the first and last annuity payments. In this example, this means that the first lease payment of $2,100 (after tax) is paid immediately such that its present value is $2,100. However, the final lease payment is now made at the beginning of year 5 (or at the end of year 4). The present value of the fifth-year after-tax lease payment is therefore $2,100 × .822 = $1,726. To summarize, by changing from a regular annuity set of lease payments to an annuity due, we must include a −$2,100 immediate cash flow at time $t = 0$, and we exchange this for the fifth-year present-value after-tax lease payment of $1,726. Therefore, the *NAL* with annuity due lease payments is *NAL* (annuity due) = (1,121) + 1,726 − 2,100 = (1,495). Hence, if the lease payments are an annuity due, the asset should be purchased [because *NPV(P)* = $15.35] and not leased (because *NAL* = −$1,495).

Let's recap the lease-purchase analysis: First the project's net present value was computed. This analysis produced a positive *NPV(P)* equal to $15.35, which indicated that the asset should be acquired. On computing the net advantage to leasing, we found that the financial lease was not the preferred method of financing the acquisition of the asset's services. Thus the asset's services should be purchased using the firm's normal financing mix.

Our analysis of the lease-purchase choice found in Tables 19.3, 19.4, and 19.5 illustrates the application of the following axioms: Note that in Table 19.3, we are careful to identify the cash flow consequences of asset ownership even though this requires that we evaluate profits for purposes of determining tax liabilities. This illustrates the use of **Axiom 3: Cash—Not Profits—Is King**. We then discount the cash flows associated with both purchasing and leasing which reflects **Axiom 2: The Time Value of Money—A Dollar Received Today Is Worth More Than a Dollar Received in the Future**. In Table 19.5, we see two axioms at work. First, we are careful to properly adjust all expenses for their tax consequences, which reflects **Axiom 8: Taxes Bias Business Decisions**. Finally, we discount the after-tax expenses associated with leasing versus purchasing, using the firm's borrowing rate, and discount the salvage value using the firm's weighted average cost of capital. Using a higher rate to discount the riskier salvage value reflects **Axiom 1: The Risk-Return Trade-Off—We Won't Take on Additional Risk Unless We Expect to Be Compensated with Additional Return**.

The Economics of Leasing versus Purchasing

OBJECTIVE 5

Let's now review briefly the economic attributes of leasing and purchasing. Figure 19.2 summarizes the participants and transactions involved in leasing (the right side of the figure) and purchasing (the left side). In purchasing, the asset is financed via the sale of securities and the purchaser acquires title to the asset (including both the use and salvage value of the asset). In leasing, the lessee acquires the use value of the asset but uses the lessor as an *intermediary* to finance and purchase the asset. The key feature of leasing as opposed to purchasing is the interjection of a financial intermediary (the lessor) into the scheme used to acquire the asset's services. Thus the basic question that arises in

Figure 19.2 Comparison of Purchasing with Simple Financial Lease Agreement

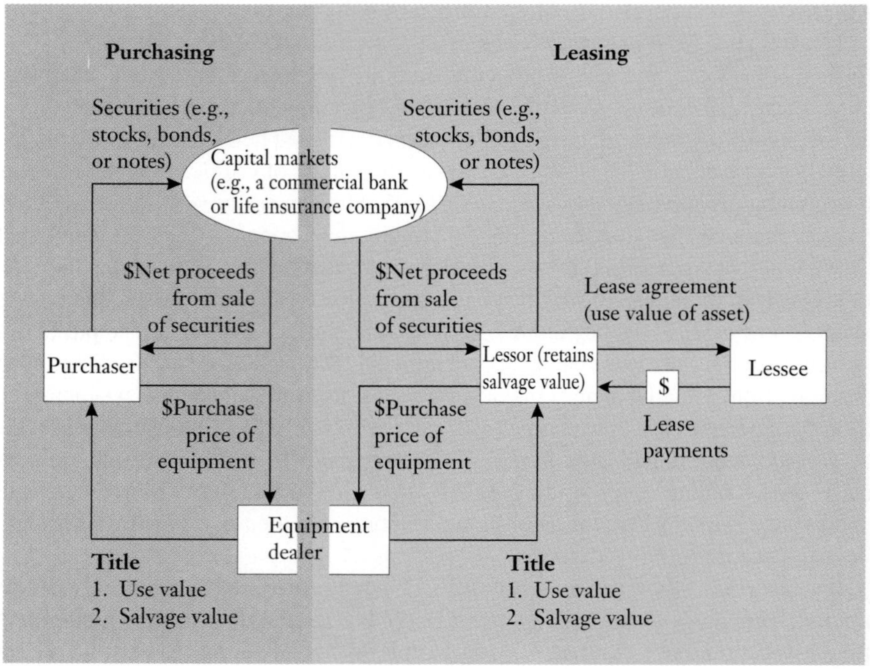

lease-purchase analysis is one of "Why does adding another financial intermediary (the lessor) save the lessee money?" Some of the traditional answers to this question are discussed subsequently. As you read through each, simply remember that the lessee is hiring the lessor to perform the functions associated with ownership that he or she would perform if the asset were purchased. Thus for the lease to be "cheaper" than owning, the lessor must be able to perform these functions of ownership at a lower cost than the lessee could perform them and be willing to pass a portion of these savings along to the lessee in the form of lower rental rates.

Potential Benefits from Leasing[6]

Several purported advantages have been associated with leasing as opposed to debt financing. These benefits include flexibility and convenience, lack of restrictions, avoiding the risk of obsolescence, conservation of working capital, 100 percent financing, tax savings, and availability of credit.

Flexibility and Convenience

A variety of potential benefits are often included under the rubric of flexibility and convenience. It is argued, for example, that leasing provides the firm with flexibility because it allows for piecemeal financing of relatively small asset acquisitions. Debt financing of such acquisitions can be costly and difficult to arrange. Leases, conversely, may be arranged more quickly and with less documentation.

---

[6]The contributions of Paul F. Anderson in the preparation of this discussion are gratefully acknowledged.

Another flexibility argument notes that leasing may allow a division or subsidiary manager to acquire equipment without the approval of the corporate capital-budgeting committee. Depending on the firm, the manager may be able to avoid the time-consuming process of preparing and presenting a formal acquisition proposal.

A third flexibility advantage relates to the fact that some lease payment schedules may be structured to coincide with the revenues generated by the asset, or they may be timed to match seasonal fluctuations in a given industry. Thus the firm is able to synchronize its lease payments with its cash cycle—an option rarely available with debt financing.

Arguments for the greater convenience of leasing take many forms. It is sometimes stated that leasing simplifies bookkeeping for tax purposes because it eliminates the need to prepare time-consuming depreciation tables and subsidiary fixed asset schedules. Finally, leasing allows the firm to avoid the "problems" and "headaches" associated with ownership. Executives often note that leasing "keeps the company out of the real estate business." Implicit in this argument is the assumption that the firm's human and material resources may be more profitably allocated to its primary line of business and that it is better to allow the lessor to deal with the obligations associated with ownership.

It is difficult to generalize about the validity of the various arguments for greater flexibility and convenience in leasing. Some companies, under specific conditions, may find leasing advantageous for some of the reasons listed earlier. In practice, the trade-offs are likely to be different for every firm. The relevant issue is often that of shifting functions. By leasing a piece of capital equipment, the firm may effectively shift bookkeeping, disposal of used equipment, and other functions to the lessor. The lessee will benefit in these situations if the lessor is able to perform the functions at a lower cost than the lessee and is willing to pass on a portion of the savings in lower lease rate.

The arguments that follow should be viewed in a similar vein. In many cases, the benefits the firm is able to attain are not worth the cost. Compounding the problem is the fact that it is often difficult for a lessee firm to quantify such cost-benefit trade-offs.

Lack of Restrictions

Another suggested advantage of leasing relates to the lack of restrictions associated with a lease. Unlike term loan agreements or bond indentures, lease contracts generally do not contain protective covenant restrictions. Furthermore, in calculating financial ratios under existing covenants, it is sometimes possible to exclude lease payments from the firm's debt commitments. Once again, the extent to which lack of restrictions benefits a lessee will depend on the price it must pay. If a lessor views its security position to be superior to that of a lender, it may not require a higher return on the lease to compensate for the lack of restrictions on the lessee. Conversely, if the prospective lessee is viewed as a marginal credit risk, a higher rate may be charged.

Avoidance of Risk of Obsolescence

Similar reasoning applies to another popular argument for leasing. This argument states that a lease is advantageous because it allows the firm to avoid the risk that the equipment will become obsolete. In actuality, the risk of obsolescence is passed on to the lessee in any financial lease. Because the original cost of the asset is fully amortized over the basic lease term, all of the risk is borne by the lessee. Only in a cancelable operating lease is it sometimes possible to avoid the risk of obsolescence.

A related argument in favor of leasing states that a lessor will generally provide the firm with better and more reliable service to maintain the resale value of the asset. The extent to which this is true depends on the lessor's own cost-benefit trade-off. If the lessor is a manufacturing or a leasing company that specializes in a particular type of equipment, it may be profitable to maintain the equipment's resale value by ensuring that it is properly repaired and maintained. Because of their technical and marketing expertise, these types of lessors may be able to operate successfully in the secondary market for the equipment. Conversely, bank lessors or independent financial leasing companies would probably find it too expensive to follow this approach.

Conservation of Working Capital

One of the oldest and most widely used arguments in favor of leasing is the assertion that a lease conserves the firm's working capital. The conservation argument runs as follows: Because a lease does not require an immediate outflow of cash to cover the full purchase price of the asset, funds are retained in the business.

It is clear that a lease does require a lower initial outlay than a cash purchase. However, the cash outlay associated with the purchase option can be reduced or eliminated by borrowing the down payment from another source. This argument leads us directly into the next purported advantage of lease financing.

One Hundred Percent Financing

Another alleged benefit of leasing is embodied in the argument that a lease provides the firm with 100 percent financing. It is pointed out that the borrow-and-buy alternative generally involves a down payment, whereas leasing does not. Given that investors and creditors are reasonably intelligent, however, it is sensible to conclude that they consider similar amounts of lease and debt financing to add equivalent amounts of risk to the firm. Thus a firm uses up less of its capacity to raise nonequity funds with debt than with leasing. In theory, it could issue a second debt instrument to make up the difference—that is, the down payment.

Tax Savings

It is also argued that leasing offers an economic advantage in that the tax shield generated by the lease payments usually exceeds the tax shield from depreciation that would be available if the asset were purchased. The extent to which leasing provides a tax-shield benefit is a function of many factors. The *NAL* equation (19-4), discussed earlier, is the basis for weighing these differences in tax shields.

Ease of Obtaining Credit

Another purported advantage of leasing is that firms with poor credit ratings are able to obtain assets through leases when they are unable to finance the acquisitions with debt capital. The counter argument is that the firm will certainly face a high lease interest rate to compensate the lessor for bearing this higher risk of default.

Why Do Firms Lease?

Several researchers have asked firms why they use financial leases as opposed to purchasing. For example, in a study by Ferrara, Thies, and Dirsmith[7] the following factors were found to affect the leasing decision:

---

[7]W. L. Ferrara, J. B. Thies, and M. W. Dersmith, "The Lease-Purchase Decision," National Association of Accountants, 1980. Cited in "Leasing—A Review of the Empirical Studies," *Managerial Finance* 15, 1 and 2 (1989): 13–20.

Factor	Rank	Percent of Respondents
Implied interest rate	1	52
Threat of obsolescence	2	37
Income taxes	3	33
Maintain flexibility	4	12
Conserve working capital	5	12
Less restrictive financing	6	6
Off balance sheet finance	7	7

Interestingly, the factor most often mentioned was the implied cost of financing. That is, 52 percent of the lessees considered the cost of lease financing to be an important factor in determining their decision to use lease financing. This factor was followed by concern over the risk of obsolescence followed by tax considerations. In light of the theoretical significance given to tax considerations in the theoretical literature on lease financing, it is interesting to note that only 33 percent of the respondents felt that tax considerations were a factor in their decision to lease.

Ferrara, Thies, and Dersmith also provide evidence concerning the motives underlying a firm's decision to use lease financing and its financial characteristics.[8] Specifically, they observed that smaller and financially weaker firms tended to justify the use of lease financing based on qualitative benefits. These included flexibility, the conservation of working capital, financing restrictions, off balance sheet financing, and transference of the risk of obsolescence. Conversely, larger and financially stronger firms tended to base their leasing decisions on more quantitative considerations. That is, this latter group tended to use more formal comparisons of the cost of leasing versus other forms of intermediate-term financing.

HOW FINANCIAL MANAGERS USE THIS MATERIAL

Firms can and do lease just about everything. So, how do they decide when to lease? The answer is that for big-ticket items, a formal analysis is used, along the lines of the net advantage of leasing model discussed in this chapter. However, for smaller expenditures, often no formal model is used.

When you discuss the decision to lease with a financial analyst, he or she will often cite the types of points we made in our discussion of the potential benefits from leasing. That is, leasing is simply easier than purchasing because of internal controls within the firm regarding asset purchases. In addition, it is commonplace to hear analysts suggesting that by leasing, the firm can avoid the risk of obsolescence. As we learned earlier, however, the firm simply transfers the risk of obsolescence to the lessor (presumably for a fee). Analysts also point out that by leasing, the firm

---

[8]Anderson and Bird also investigated the reasons why lessees lease. They used a survey in which the respondents were asked to indicate both the extent to which they agreed or disagreed with the advantages attributed to leasing and the extent to which a particular advantage was important to their lease decisions. One of the purported advantages to leasing was the following: "All things considered, leasing is less expensive than debt as a means of acquiring equipment." The respondents accorded the lowest agreement rating to this statement (that is they disagreed that this was true), yet they ranked this same statement third in overall importance in terms of their decision to lease. The authors interpret this finding as evidence that lessees believe that it is important that the cost of leasing be less than the cost of debt financing, but they do not expect to find this to be so in practice.

has to invest less of its own money as there is no associated down payment (or at least a minimal one). Once again, we know that this ignores the fact that the firm receives only the use value and not the salvage value of the asset through the lease and often uses more financial leverage (non-owner financing) than it would if it purchased the asset. The point is that many of the potential advantages of leasing fail to make the leasing alternative truly comparable to purchasing the asset. So, when analyzing a lease financing alternative, be careful to compare "apples to apples" and not be fooled by the claims of an overly zealous lessor.

SUMMARY

OBJECTIVE 1

Intermediate financing is any source of financing with a final maturity greater than 1 year but less than 10. The two major sources of intermediate financing are term loans and financial leases.

Term loans are available from commercial banks, life insurance companies, and pension funds. Although the specifics of each agreement vary, they share a common set of general characteristics. These include:

1. A final maturity of 1 to 10 years
2. A requirement of some form of collateral
3. A body of restrictive covenants designed to protect the security interests of the lender
4. A loan amortization schedule whereby periodic loan payments, comprised of both principal and interest components, are made over the life of the loan.

OBJECTIVE 2

Term loans generally require the borrower to repay them by making level monthly (quarterly or annual) payments or installments. These payments include two components: (1) the interest owed on the loan balance outstanding at the time of the last loan payment, and (2) the difference in the installment payment and the interest component. This difference goes toward reducing the principal amount of the loan.

Installment payments are calculated using present value analysis. They constitute the periodic (monthly, quarterly, annual, and so on) payment whose present value, when discounted back to the present using the loan rate of interest, equals the face amount of the loan.

OBJECTIVE 3

There are three basic types of lease arrangements:

1. Direct lease
2. Sale and leaseback
3. Leveraged lease

The lease agreement can further be classified as a financial or operating lease; we focused on the financial lease. Current reporting requirements of the FASB virtually ensure the inclusion of all financial leases in the body of the lessee firm's balance sheet.

OBJECTIVE 4

The lease-versus-purchase decision is a hybrid capital-budgeting problem wherein the analyst must consider both the investment and financing aspects of the decision. The method we recommend for analyzing the lease-versus-purchase choice involves first calculating the net present value of the asset if it were purchased. Next we calculate the net advantage of leasing over purchasing.

OBJECTIVE 5

Many and varied factors are often claimed as advantages of leasing the firm's usual debt-equity financing mix. However, a complete lease-purchase analysis using a model similar to the one discussed here is needed to provide a rational basis for uncovering the true advantages of lease financing.

KEY TERMS

Capital lease, 724

Eurodollar loans, 721

Financial lease, 723

Lease, 723

Lessee, 723

Lessor, 723

Leveraged lease, 724

Net leases, 723

Net-net leases, 723

Operating lease, 723

Sale and leaseback
arrangement, 723

Term loans, 719

GO TO:
http://www.prenhall.com/bfm
For downloads and current events
associated with this chapter

FINCOACH PRACTICE EXERCISES FOR CHAPTER 19:

To maximize your grades and master the mathematics discussed in this chapter, open *FINCOACH* on the **Finance Learning and Development Center** CD and practice problems in the following categories: 1)*Present Value Basics I* 2) *Present Value Basics II* 3) *Project and Firm Valuation I* 4) *Project and Firm Valuation II*

STUDY QUESTIONS

19-1. What characteristics distinguish intermediate-term debt from other forms of debt instruments?

19-2. List and discuss the major types of restrictions generally found in the covenants of term loan agreements.

19-3. Define each of the following:

    a. Direct lease

    b. Sale and leaseback arrangement

    c. Net-net lease

    d. Operating lease

19-4. How are financial leases handled in the financial statements of the lessee firm?

19-5. List and discuss each of the potential benefits from lease financing.

SELF-TEST PROBLEMS

ST-1. (*Analyzing a Term Loan*) Calculate the annual installment payment and the principal and interest components of a 5-year loan carrying a 10 percent rate of interest. The loan amount is $50,000.

ST-2. (*Analyzing an Installment Loan*) The S. P. Sargent Sales Company is contemplating the purchase of a new machine. The total cost of the machine is $120,000 and the firm plans to make a $20,000 cash downpayment. The firm's bank has offered to finance the remaining $100,000 at a rate of 14 percent. The bank has offered two possible loan repayment plans. Plan A involves equal annual installments payable at the end of each of the next 5 years. Plan B requires five equal annual payments plus a balloon payment of $20,000 at the end of year 5.

    a. Calculate the annual payment on the loan in plan A.

    b. Calculate the principal and interest components of the plan A installment loan.

    c. Calculate the annual installments for plan B where the loan carries a 14 percent rate.

ST-3. (*Lease versus Purchase Analysis*) Jensen Trucking, Inc., is considering the possibility of leasing a $100,000 truck-servicing facility. This newly developed piece of equipment facilitates the cleaning and servicing of diesel tractors used on long-haul runs. The firm has evaluated the possible purchase of the equipment and found it to have an $8,000 net present value. However, an equipment leasing company has approached Jensen with an offer to lease the equipment for an annual rental charge of $24,000 payable at the beginning of each of the next 5 years. In addition, should Jensen lease the equipment, it would receive insurance and maintenance valued at $4,000 per year (assume that this amount would be payable at the beginning of each year if purchased separately from the lease agreement). Also, for simplicity you may assume that tax savings are realized immediately. Additional information pertaining to the lease and purchase alternatives is found in the following table:

Acquisition price	$100,000
Useful life (used in analysis)	5 years
Salvage value (estimated)	$0
Depreciation method	Straight-line
Borrowing rate	12%
Marginal tax rate	40%
Cost of capital (based on a target debt/total asset ratio of 30%)	16%

a. Calculate the net advantage of leasing (*NAL*) the equipment.

b. Should Jensen lease the equipment?

STUDY PROBLEMS (SET A)

19-1A. (*Calculation of Balloon Payment for a Term Loan*) The First State Bank has offered to lend $325,000 to Jamie Tulia to help him purchase a group home for handicapped persons. The bank loan officer (Chris Turner) has structured the loan to include four installments of $50,000 each followed in year 5 by a balloon payment. The loan is to carry a 10 percent rate of interest with annual compounding. What is the fifth year balloon payment?

19-2A. (*Calculating Lease Payments*) Apple Leasing, Inc. calculates its lease payments such that they provide the firm with a 12 percent pre-tax return. The firm has been asked to quote rental payments on a $100,000 piece of equipment which is to include ten payments spread over the next 9 years (the first payment is made immediately upon signing of the agreement with the remaining payments coming at the end of each of the next 9 years). What amount should Apple quote on the lease?

19-3A. (*Installment Payments*) Compute the annual payments for an installment loan carrying an 18 percent rate of interest, a 5-year maturity, and a face amount of $100,000.

19-4A. (*Principal and Interest Components of an Installment Loan*) Compute the annual principal and interest components of the loan in problem 19-3A.

19-5A. (*Cost of an Intermediate-Term Loan*) The J. B. Marcum Company needs $250,000 to finance a new minicomputer. The computer sales firm has offered to finance the purchase with a $50,000 down payment followed by five annual installments of $59,663.11 each. Alternatively, the firm's bank has offered to lend the firm $250,000 to be repaid in five annual installments based on an annual rate of interest of 16 percent. Finally, the firm has arranged to finance the needed $250,000 through a loan from an insurance company requiring a lump-sum payment of $385,080 in 5 years.

a. What is the effective annual rate of interest on the loan from the computer sales firm?

b. What will the annual payments on the bank loan be?

c. What is the annual rate of interest for the insurance company term loan?

d. Based on cost considerations only, which source of financing should Marcum select?

19-6A. (*Cost of Intermediate-Term Credit*) Charter Electronics is planning to purchase a $400,000 burglar alarm system for its southwestern Illinois plant. Charter's bank has offered to lend the firm the full $400,000. The note would be paid in one payment at the end of 4 years and would require payment of interest at a rate of 14 percent compounded annually. The manufacturer of the alarm system has offered to finance the $400,000 purchase with an installment loan. The loan would require four annual installments of $140,106 each. Which method of financing should Charter select?

19-7A. (*Lease-versus-Purchase Analysis*) S. S. Johnson Enterprises (SSJE) is evaluating the acquisition of a heavy-duty forklift with 20,000- to 24,000-pound lift capacity. SSJE can purchase the forklift through the use of its normal financing mix (30 percent debt and 70 percent common equity) or lease it. Pertinent details follow:

Acquisition price of the forklift	$20,000
Useful life	4 years
Salvage value (estimated)	$ 4,000
Depreciation method	Straight-line
Annual cash savings before-tax and depreciation from the forklift	$ 6,000
Rate of interest on a 4-year installment loan	10 percent
Marginal tax rate	50 percent
Annual rentals (4-year lease)	$ 6,000
Annual operating expenses included in the lease	$ 1,000
Cost of capital	12 percent

a. Evaluate whether the forklift acquisition is justified through normal purchase financing.

b. Should SSJE lease the asset?

19-8A. (*Installment Loan Payment*) Calculate the annual installment payments for the following loans:

a. A $100,000 loan carrying a 15 percent annual rate of interest and requiring 10 annual payments.

b. A $100,000 loan carrying a 15 percent annual rate of interest with quarterly payments over the next 5 years. (*Hint:* Refer to chapter 5 for discussion of semiannual compounding and discounting.)

c. A $100,000 loan requiring annual installments for each of the next 5 years at a 15 percent rate of interest. However, the annual installments are based on a 30-year loan period. In year 5, the balance of the loan is due in a single (balloon) payment. (*Hint:* Calculate the installment payments using $n = 30$ years. Next use the procedure given in Table 19.1 to determine the remaining balance of the loan at the end of the fifth year.)

Early in the spring of 1998, the Jonesboro Steel Corporation (JSC) decided to purchase a small computer. The computer is designed to handle the inventory, payroll, shipping, and general clerical functions for small manufacturers like JSC. The firm estimates that the computer will cost $60,000 to purchase and will last 4 years, at which time it can be salvaged for $10,000. The firm's marginal tax rate is 50 percent, and its cost of capital for projects of this type is estimated to be 12 percent. Over the next 4 years, the management of JSC thinks the computer will reduce operating expenses by $27,000 a year before depreciation and taxes. JSC uses straight-line depreciation.

JSC is also considering the possibility of leasing the computer. The computer sales firm has offered JSC a 4-year lease contract with annual payments of $18,000. In addition, if JSC leases the computer, the lessor will absorb insurance and maintenance expenses valued at $2,000 per year. Thus JSC will save $2,000 per year if it leases the asset (on a before-tax basis).

1. Evaluate the net present value of the computer purchase. Should the computer be acquired via purchase? (*Hint:* Refer to Tables 19.3 and 19.4.)

2. If JSC uses a 40 percent target debt to total assets ratio, evaluate the net present value advantage of leasing. JSC can borrow at a rate of 8 percent with annual installments paid over the next 4 years. (*Hint:* Recall that the interest tax shelter lost through leasing is based on a loan equal to the full purchase price of the asset or $60,000.)

3. Should JSC lease the asset?

STUDY PROBLEMS (SET B)

19-1B. (*Calculation of Balloon Payment for a Term Loan*) In March, the Cross National Bank agreed to finance the purchase of a new building for Harris Tweed's men's wear shop. The loan is for $300,000 and will carry a 12 percent annual rate of interest with annual compounding. The loan will require that Harris make four annual installments of $60,000 at the end of years 1 through 4. In year 5, Harris must make a large balloon payment which will fully retire the outstanding loan balance. What is the fifth-year balloon payment?

19-2B. (*Calculating Lease Payments*) Raucher Leasing, Inc. calculates its lease payments with a 15 percent pre-tax return. The firm has been asked to quote rental payments on a $250,000 piece of equipment which is to include ten payments spread over 9 years (the first payment is made immediately upon signing of the agreement with the remaining payments coming at the end of each of the next 9 years). What amount should Raucher quote on the lease?

19-3B. (*Installment Payments*) Compute the annual payments for an installment loan carrying a 16 percent rate of interest, a 7-year maturity, and a face amount of $100,000.

19-4B. (*Principal and Interest Components of an Installment Loan*) Compute the annual principal and interest components of the loan in problem 19-3B.

19-5B. (*Cost of an Intermediate Loan*) Azteca Freight Forwarding Company of Laredo, Texas needs $300,000 to complete the construction of several prefabricated metal warehouses. The firm that produces the warehouses has offered to finance the purchase with a $50,000 downpayment followed by 5 annual installments of $69,000 each. Alternatively, Azteca's bank has offered to lend the firm $300,000 to be repaid in 5 annual installments based on an annual rate of interest of 16 percent. Finally, the firm could finance the needed $300,000 through a loan from an insurance company requiring a lump-sum payment of $425,000 in 5 years.

a. What is the effective annual rate of interest on the loan from the warehouse producer?

b. What will the annual payments on the bank loan be?

c. What is the annual rate of interest for the insurance company term loan?

d. Based on cost considerations only, which source of financing should Azteca select?

19-6B. (*Intermediate-Term Credit*) Powder Meadows, a western ski resort, is planning to purchase a $500,000 ski lift. Powder Meadows' bank has offered to lend it the full $500,000. The note would be paid in one payment at the end of 4 years and would require payment of interest at a rate of 14 percent compounded annually. The manufacturer of the ski lift has offered to finance the $500,000 purchase with an installment loan. The loan would require 4 annual installments of $175,000 each. Which method of financing should Powder Meadows select?

19-7B. (*Lease-versus-Purchase Analysis*) KKR Live, Inc., a carnival operating firm based in Laramie, Wyoming, is considering the acquisition of a new German-made carousel, with a passenger capacity of 30. KKR can purchase the carousel through the use of its normal financing mix (30 percent debt and 70 percent common equity) or lease it. Pertinent details follow:

Acquisition price of the carousel	$25,000
Useful life	4 years
Salvage value	$5,000
Depreciation method	Straight-line
Annual cash savings before-tax and depreciation from the carousel	$7,000
Rate of interest on a 4-year installment loan	11 percent
Marginal tax rate	50 percent
Annual rentals (4-year lease)	$7,000
Annual operating expenses included in the lease	$1,250
Cost of capital	13 percent

    a. Evaluate whether the carousel acquisition is justified through normal purchase financing.

    b. Should KKR lease the asset?

19-8B. (*Installment Loan Payment*) Calculate the annual installment payments for the following loans:

    a. A $125,000 loan carrying a 13 percent annual rate of interest and requiring 12 annual payments.

    b. A $125,000 loan carrying a 13 percent annual rate of interest with quarterly payments over the next 6 years. (*Hint*: Refer to chapter 5 for a discussion of semiannual compounding and discounting.)

    c. A $125,000 loan requiring annual installments for each of the next 5 years at a 13 percent rate of interest. However, the annual installments are based on a 30-year loan period. In year 5, the balance of the loan is due in a single (balloon) payment. (*Hint:* Calculate the installment payments using $n = 30$ years. Next use the procedure given in Table 19.1 to determine the remaining balance of the loan at the end of the fifth year.)

19-9B. (*Lease-versus-Purchase Analysis*) Lubin Landscaping, Inc. has decided to purchase a truck-mounted lawn fertilizer tank and spray unit. The truck would replace its hand-held fertilizer tanks, providing substantial reductions in labor expense. The firm estimates that the truck will cost $65,000 to purchase and will last 4 years, at which time it can be salvaged for $8,000. The firm's tax rate is 50 percent, and its cost of capital for projects of this type is estimated to be 14 percent. Over the next 4 years, the management of Lubin estimates that the truck will reduce operating expenses by $29,000 a year before depreciation and taxes. Lubin uses straight-line depreciation.

Lubin is also considering the possibility of leasing the truck. The truck sales firm has offered Lubin a 4-year lease contract with annual payments of $20,000. In addition, if Lubin leases the truck, the lessor will absorb insurance and maintenance expenses valued at $2,250 per year. Thus Lubin will save $2,250 per year if it leases the asset (on a before-tax basis).

    a. Evaluate the net present value of the truck purchase. Should the truck be acquired via purchase? (*Hint*: Refer to Tables 19.3 and 19.4.)

    b. If Lubin uses a 40 percent target debt to total assets ratio, evaluate the net present value advantage of leasing. Lubin can borrow at a rate of 8 percent with annual installments paid over the next 4 years. (*Hint:* Recall that the interest tax shelter lost through leasing is based on a loan equal to the full purchase price of the asset or $65,000.)

    c. Should Lubin lease the asset?

SELF-TEST SOLUTIONS

SS-1.

Time	Payment	Principal	Interest	Remaining Balance
0				$50,000.00
1	$13,189.83	$ 8,189.83	$5,000.00	41,810.17
2	13,189.83	9,008.81	4,181.02	32,801.36
3	13,189.83	9,909.69	3,280.14	22,891.67
4	13,189.83	10,900.66	2,289.17	11,991.01
5	13,189.83	11,990.73	1,199.10	0.28[a]

[a]Rounding error.

SS-2. a. $\text{Payment} = \$100,000 \div \sum_{t=1}^{5} \frac{1}{(1.14)^t}$

$= \$29,128.35$

b.

Time	Payment	Principal	Interest	Remaining Balance
0	—	—	—	$100,000
1	$29,128.35	$15,128.35	$14,000.00	84,871
2	29,128.35	17,246.32	11,882.03	67,625
3	29,128.35	19,660.80	9,467.55	47,964
4	29,128.35	22,413.32	6,715.03	25,551
5	29,128.35	25,551.18	3,577.17	.03[a]

[a]Rounding error.

c. Because the plan B loan includes a $20,000 balloon payment, the 5 annual installments have a present value of only

$\$89,613 = \$100,000 - \$20,000/(1.14)^5$

Therefore, the annual installments can be calculated as follows:

$\text{Payment} = \$89,613 \div \sum_{t=1}^{5} \frac{1}{(1.14)^t}$

$= \$26,102.79$

SS-3. a. *NAL* = $1,772.69. (Calculations are found in the following table.)

b. The *NAL* is positive, indicating that the lease would offer cost savings over a purchase and therefore should be used.

Year	After-Tax Operating Expenses Paid by Lessor[a]		After-Tax Rental Expense[b]		Tax Shelter on Depreciation[c]		Tax Shelter on Loan Interest[d]		Sum		Discount Factor at Borrowing Rate (12%)		Present Value
t	$O_t(1-T)$	$-$	$R_t(1-T)$	$-$	D_tT	$-$	I_tT	$=$	Sum	$\times$	DF	$=$	PV
0	$2,400		-$14,400.000						-$12,000.000		1.000		-$ 12,000.00
1	2,400		- 14,400.000		-$8,000.000		-4,800.00		- 24,800.000		0.933		-$ 23,134.33
2	2,400		- 14,400.000		- 8,000.000		-4,044.43		- 24,044.433		0.870		-$ 20,923.05
3	2,400		- 14,400.000		- 8,000.000		-3,198.20		- 23,198.199		0.812		-$ 18,830.85
4	2,400		- 14,400.000		- 8,000.000		-2,250.42		- 22,250.416		0.757		-$ 16,848.41
5					- 8,000.000		-1,188.90		- 9,188.899		0.706		-$ 6,490.67
											Total		-$ 98,227.31
											Plus: initial outlay		100,000.00
											NAL		=$ 1,772.69

[a]$4,000 (1 − .4) = $2,400. For simplicity we assume that the tax shields on expenses paid at the beginning of the year are realized immediately.
[b]$14,400 = $24,000 (1 − .4).
[c]The machine has a zero salvage value. Thus its annual depreciation expense is $100,000/5 = $20,000.
[d]Based on a $100,000 loan with four end-of-year installments and a 12 percent rate of interest. The loan payments equal $27,740.97.

Learning Objectives

Active Applications

World Finance

Practice

CHAPTER 20

LEARNING OBJECTIVES

After reading this chapter, you should be able to

1. Explain the difference between a commodity future and a financial future and how they might be used by a financial manager to control risk.

2. Explain what put and call options are and how they might be used by a financial manager to control risk.

3. Explain what a currency swap is and how it might be used to eliminate exchange rate risk.

THE USE OF FUTURES, OPTIONS, AND CURRENCY SWAPS TO REDUCE RISK

INTRODUCTION

This chapter will focus on how financial managers use futures, options, and currency swaps to eliminate risk. Although it looks easy, as many a firm has seen, it's a dangerous undertaking if done incorrectly. It's also an area that needs a good deal of supervision. While hedging can reduce risk, speculating, which involves investing in futures simply because you think the price will go up or down, can open a firm up to tremendous risks. For example, with futures contracts, you only put down a small amount and later—regardless of what happens to the price of the underlying asset—have to buy or sell that asset.

What do we mean by tremendous risks? Let's look at the example of Nick Leeson, a 27-year-old futures trader stationed in Singapore for Barings Bank. Nick began his career with Barings Bank in 1989 as a clerk, settling transactions. After a few years as a clerk, he had gained the reputation as a hard worker and an exceptional organizer. At his request, Leeson was transferred to Singapore, where he got the chance to trade futures contracts in Tokyo and Osaka, Japan. Leeson's job was to buy and sell Japanese stock index futures in a relatively safe arbitrage strategy—simultaneously buying and selling the same contract in Tokyo and Osaka whenever the prices were out of line with each other. In January 1995, however, Leeson had a hunch that Japanese stocks were going to climb and, without the knowledge of Barings Bank, started the wholesale buying of Japanese stock index futures. To say the least, his timing was poor—on January 17 an earthquake struck the city of Kobe, Japan and the Japanese stock *market fell by about 13 percent. To cover this loss, he doubled his bets and in just over a month, by the time he fled to Germany, he had lost about $1.2 billion dollars and caused the collapse of Barings Bank. It was quite a month's work for a 27-year-old trader. In 1995, Leeson was returned to Singapore where he plea bargained his sentence down to 6-1/2 years for fraud.*

The point is that, if used improperly, these tools for reducing risk may do just the opposite. That means that you as a financial manager must have an understanding not only of the proper use of these tools, but of their risk potential and limitations.

CHAPTER PREVIEW

In this chapter, we examine two financial instruments that are not created by the firm: futures and options. These financial instruments are commonly referred to as "derivative securities" in that their value or price is determined by, or "derived" from, the price of another asset, exchange rate, commodity price, or interest rate. It is important for us to be familiar with them for two reasons. First, these instruments can be used to reduce the risks associated with interest and exchange rate and commodity price fluctuations. Second, as you will see in future finance courses, an understanding of the pricing of options is extremely valuable because many different financial assets can be viewed as options. In fact, risky bonds, common stock, and the abandonment decision can all be thought of as types of options. We also examine currency swaps which are used to hedge exchange rate risk over longer periods of time.

This chapter will emphasize **Axiom 1: The Risk-Return Trade-Off—We Won't Take on Additional Risk Unless We Expect to Be Compensated with Additional Return.** Be on the lookout for this concept.

FUTURES

OBJECTIVE 1

Commodity and financial futures are perhaps the fastest-growing and most exciting new financial instrument today. Financial managers who only a few years ago would not have considered venturing into the futures market are now actively using this market to eliminate risk. As the number of participants in this market has grown, so has the number of items on which future contracts are offered, the old standbys such as coffee and soybeans to newer ones such as U.S. Treasury bonds, sorghum, municipal bonds, and diammonium phosphate.

A **future**, or **futures contract**, is a contract to buy or sell a stated commodity (such as soybeans or corn) or financial claim (such as U.S. Treasury bonds) at a specified price at some future specified time. They are used by the financial manager to lock in future prices of raw materials, interest rates, or exchange rates. As you saw in the introduction to this chapter, if not controlled or understood, there are also dangers associated with their use. It is important to note here that this is a contract that *requires* its holder to buy or sell the asset, regardless of what happens to its value during the interim. The importance of a futures contract is that it can be used by financial managers to lock in the price of a commodity or an interest rate and thereby eliminate one source of risk. For example, if a corporation is planning on issuing debt in the near future and is concerned about a possible rise in interest rates between now and when the debt will be issued, it might sell a U.S. Treasury bond futures contract with the same face value as the proposed debt offering and a delivery date the same as when the debt offering is to occur. Alternatively, with the use of a futures contract, Ralston-Purina or Quaker Oats can lock in the future

Futures contract

A contract to buy or sell a stated commodity or financial claim at a specified price at some future, specified time.

price of corn or oats whenever they wish. Because a futures contract locks in interest rates or commodity prices, the costs associated with any possible rise in interest rates or commodity prices are completely offset by the profits made by writing the futures contract. In effect, futures contracts allow the financial manager to lock in future interest and exchange rates or prices for a number of agricultural commodities such as corn and oats.

As the use of futures contracts becomes more common in the financial management of the firm, it is important for the financial manager to be familiar with the operation and terminology associated with these financial instruments.

STOP AND THINK

Although there are many uses for futures, options, and currency swaps, our interest focuses on how financial managers use them to reduce risk. Keep in mind that the financial manager can use them to effectively offset future movements in the price of commodities or interest rates and thereby eliminate risk.

An Introduction to Futures Markets

The futures markets originated in medieval times. In fact, England, France, and Japan all developed futures markets of their own. Here in the United States, several futures markets sprang up in the early years, but it was not until the establishment of the Chicago Board of Trade (CBT) in 1848 that the futures markets were provided with their true roots. As we will see, although this market has been in operation for 150 years, it was not until the early 1970s—when the futures markets expanded from agricultural commodities to financial futures—that financial managers began to regularly venture into this market.

To develop an understanding of futures markets, let us examine several distinguishing features of futures contracts. A *futures contract* is distinguished by (1) an organized exchange, (2) a standardized contract with limited price changes and margin requirements, (3) a clearinghouse in each futures market, and (4) daily resettlement of contracts. Remember, a futures contract is legally binding. That means you must buy or sell a commodity some time in the future.

The organized exchange. Although the Chicago Board of Trade is the oldest and largest of the futures exchanges, it is certainly not the only exchange. In fact, there are more than 10 different futures exchanges in operation in the United States today. The importance of having organized exchanges associated with the futures market is that they provide a central trading place. If there were no central trading place, then there would be no potential to generate the depth of trading necessary to support a secondary market; and in a very circular way, the existence of a secondary market encourages more traders to enter the market and in turn provides additional liquidity.

An organized exchange also encourages confidence in the futures market by allowing for the effective regulation of trading. The various exchanges set and enforce rules and collect and disseminate information on trading activity and the commodities being traded. Together, the liquidity generated by having a central trading place, effective regulation, and the flow of information through the organized exchanges, has effectively fostered their development.

Standardized contracts. To develop a strong secondary market in any security, there must be many identical securities—or in this case, futures contracts—outstanding. In effect, standardization of contracts leads to more frequent trades on that contract, leading to greater liquidity in the secondary market for that contract, which in turn draws more traders into the market. This is why futures contracts are highly standardized and very specific with respect to the description of the goods to be delivered and the time and place of delivery. Let's look at a Chicago Board of Trade oats contract, for example. This contract calls for the delivery of 5,000 bushels of No. 2 heavy or No. 1 grade oats to Chicago or to Minneapolis–St. Paul at a 7.5 cents per bushel discount. In addition, these contracts are written to come due in March, May, July, September, and December. Through this standardization of contracts, trading has built up in enough identical contracts to allow for the development of a strong and highly liquid secondary market.

To encourage investors to participate in the futures market, daily price limits are set on most futures contracts (for some contracts coming due in the next two months, limits are not imposed). Without these limits, it is thought that there would be more price volatility on most futures contracts than many investors would be willing to accept. These daily price limits are set to protect investors, maintain order on the futures exchanges, and encourage the level of trading volume necessary to develop a strong secondary market. For example, the Chicago Board of Trade imposes a 10 cents per bushel ($500 per contract) price movement limit above and below the previous day's settlement price of oats contracts. This limit protects against runaway price movements. These daily price limits do not halt trading once the limit has been reached, but they do provide a boundary within which trading must occur. The price of an oats contract may rise 10 cents very early in the trading day—"up the limit," in futures jargon. This will not stop trading; it only means that no trade can take place above that level. As a result, any dramatic shifts in the market price of a futures contract must take place over a number of days, with the price of the contract going "up the limit" each day.

Futures clearinghouse. The main purpose of the futures clearinghouse is to guarantee that all trades will be honored. This is done by having the clearinghouse interpose itself as the buyer to every seller and the seller to every buyer. Because of this substitution of parties, it is not necessary for the original seller (or buyer) to find the original buyer (or seller) when he or she decides to clear his or her position. As a result, all an individual has to do is make an equal and opposite transaction that will provide a net zero position with the clearinghouse and cancel out that individual's obligation.

Because no trades occur directly between individuals, but between individuals and the clearinghouse, buyers and sellers realizing gains in the market are assured that they will be paid. Because futures contracts are traded with minimal "good faith" money, as we will see in the next section, it is necessary to provide some security to traders so that when money is made, it will be paid. There are other important benefits of a clearinghouse, including providing a mechanism for the delivery of commodities and the settlement of disputed trades, but these benefits also serve to encourage trading in the futures markets and thereby create a highly liquid secondary market.

Daily resettlement of contracts. Another safeguard of the futures market is a margin requirement. Although margin requirements on futures resemble stock margin requirements in that there is an initial margin and a maintenance margin that comes into play when the value of the contract declines, similarities between futures and stock margins end there.

Before we explore margin requirements on futures, it would be helpful to develop an understanding of the meaning of a margin on futures. The concept of a margin on futures contracts has a meaning that is totally different from its usage in reference to common stocks. The margin on common stocks refers to the amount of equity the investor has invested in the stocks. With a futures contract, no equity has been invested, because nothing has been bought. All that has happened is that a contract has been signed obligating the two parties to a future transaction and defining the terms of that transaction. This is an important thought: There is no actual buying or selling occurring with a futures contract; it is merely an agreement to buy or sell some commodity in the future. As a result, the term **futures margin** refers to "good faith" money the purchaser puts down to ensure that the contract will be carried out.

The initial margin required for commodities (deposited by both buyer and seller) is much lower than the margin required for common stock, generally amounting to only 3 to 10 percent of the value of the contract. For example, if September oats contracts on the CBT were selling at $1.65 per bushel, then one contract for 5,000 bushels would be selling for $1.65 × 5,000 = $8,250. The initial margin on oats is $400 per contract, which represents only about 4.85 percent of the contract price. Needless to say, the leverage associated with futures trading is tremendous—both on the up and down sides. Small changes in the price of the underlying commodity result in very large changes in the value of the futures contract, because very little has to be put down to "own" a contract. Moreover, for many futures contracts, if the financial manager can satisfy the broker that he or she is not engaged in trading as a speculator, but as a hedger, the manager can qualify for reduced initial margins. Because of the low level of the initial margin, there is also a *maintenance* or *variation margin* requirement that forces the investor or financial manager to replenish the margin account to a level specified by the exchange after any market loss.

One additional point related to margins deserves mention. The initial margin requirement can be fulfilled by supplying Treasury bills instead of cash. These Treasury bills are valued at 90 percent of their value for margin purposes, so it takes $100,000 worth of Treasury bills to provide a $90,000 margin. The advantage of using Treasury bills as margin is that the investor earns money on them, whereas brokerage firms do not pay interest on funds in commodity cash accounts. Moreover, if the financial manager is going to carry Treasury bills anyway, he or she can just deposit the Treasury bills with the broker and purchase the futures contracts with no additional cash outlay.

Suppose you are a financial manager for Ralston-Purina. You are in charge of purchasing raw materials—in particular, oats. Currently, a September futures contract for the delivery of oats has a price of $1.65 per bushel. You need oats in September, and feel that this is an exceptional price—oats will probably be selling for more than that per bushel in September. Thus you want to lock in this price, and to do this you purchase one contract for 5,000 bushels at 165 cents or $1.65 per bushel. On purchasing the September oats contract, the only cash you would have to put up would be the initial margin of $400. Let's further assume that the price of oats futures then falls to a level of 161 cents per bushel the day after you make your purchase. In effect, you have incurred a loss of 4 cents per bushel on 5,000 bushels, for a total loss on your investment of $200.

At this point, the concept of daily resettlement comes into play. What this means is that all futures positions are brought to the market at the end of each trading day and all gains and losses, in this case a loss, are then settled. You have lost $200, which is then subtracted from your margin account, lowering it to $200 ($400 initially, less the $200 loss). Because the margin account has fallen below the maintenance margin on oats, which is $250, you would have to replenish the account back to its initial level of $400. If on the following day the price of September oats contracts fell another cent to 160 cents per bushel, you would have lost another 1 cent on 5,000 bushels for a loss of $50. This would then be subtracted from your margin account during the daily resettlement at the end of the trading day, leaving $350 in the account. Because your margin account would not be below the maintenance margin requirement of $250, you would not have to add any additional funds to the account. Let's carry our example one day further, this time to the upbeat side, and put some profits in. Let's assume that on the third day, the price of September oats contract is up 5 cents per bushel. This means that you have made 5 cents on 5,000 bushels, for a total profit of $250. This brings your margin account up from

$350 to $600, which is $200 above the initial margin of $400. You can withdraw this $200 from your margin account.

Obviously, the purpose of margin requirements is to provide some measure of safety for futures traders; and despite the very small level of margin requirements imposed, they do a reasonable job. They are set in accordance with the historical price volatility of the underlying commodity in such a way that it is extremely unlikely that a trader will ever lose more than is in his or her margin account in any one day.

Commodity Futures

In general, when people talk about commodities, they are referring to nonfinancial futures. This includes agricultural commodities as well as metals, wood products, and fibers. Although there are several new commodity futures contracts now being traded, such as lumber and orange juice, much of the trading in the commodities futures markets involves such traditional favorites as corn and wheat. For the financial manager, these markets provide a means of offsetting the risks associated with future price changes. Here the financial manager is securing a future price for a good that is currently in production, or securing a future price for some commodity that must be purchased in the future. In either case, the manager is using the futures market to eliminate the effects of future price changes on the future purchase or sale of some commodity.

Hedging with Futures

Although there are many different futures contracts available, it's not always possible to find what you're looking for. For example, you may have a manufacturing plant that uses petroleum as its primary raw material. However, there may not be futures contracts available on the specific grade of petroleum that you use. If you want to reduce risk by using the futures market to lock in a future price for petroleum, are you out of luck? Not really. Because all petroleum prices tend to move together, you could hedge away the risk of petroleum price rises using futures contracts on other grades of petroleum.

This use of futures contracts on similar but not identical commodities is referred to as cross hedging. With cross hedging, you don't actually want the commodity for which you've entered into a futures contract. What you're trying to do is lock in a price on a commodity whose price moves as close to identically as possible with the commodity you're interested in. As a result, you don't want to hold the futures contract to maturity and actually receive delivery of the commodity. The way you reverse your futures position is by taking an opposite and canceling position. That is, if you had earlier bought a futures contract, you would now sell the same contract and allow the two contracts to cancel each other out.

Is there danger in this? Not if it's done correctly. But that doesn't mean that companies haven't been burned when they thought they were using the futures market to hedge away risks. An example of a billion-dollar mistake is Metallgesellschaft AG, a German firm, that lost over $1 billion in 1993. One of its U.S. subsidiaries had entered into 10-year contracts to supply oil and gasoline at fixed prices. That meant that as long as petroleum prices didn't rise, they would make money, but if petroleum prices rose, they'd be in trouble. To eliminate the risk from price rises, they turned to the futures market, buying short-term futures contracts. As it turned out, petroleum prices dropped and the subsidiary suffered enormous losses on these futures contracts. Unfortunately, because Metallgesellschaft AG's petroleum contracts were over 10 years, there weren't offsetting gains on them. The result was a billion-dollar loss. They hedged the right product, but they didn't hedge for the right maturity. The bottom line here is that, although futures contracts can reduce risk, you've got to make sure you know what you're doing with them.

Financial Futures

Financial futures come in a number of different forms, including futures on Treasury bills, notes and bonds, GMNAs, certificates of deposit, Eurodollars, foreign currencies, and stock indices. These financial newcomers first appeared in 1972, when foreign currencies were introduced; interest rate futures did not appear until 1975. The growth in financial futures has been phenomenal, and today they dominate the futures markets. Our discussion of financial futures will be divided into three sections: (1) interest rate futures, (2) foreign exchange futures, and (3) stock index futures.

Interest rate futures. Currently, Treasury bond futures are the most popular of all futures contracts in terms of contracts issued. In fact on October 15, 1987, 659,487 contracts were traded with a face value of $65.94 billion! Although Treasury (or T-bond) futures are just one of several interest rate futures contracts, the fact that they are risk-free, long-term bonds with a maturity of at least 15 years has been the deciding factor in making them the most popular of the interest rate futures.

For the financial manager, interest rate futures provide an excellent means for eliminating the risks associated with interest rate fluctuations. As we learned earlier, there is an inverse relationship between bond prices in the secondary market and yields—that is, when interest rates fall bond prices rise, and when interest rates rise bond prices fall. If you think back to the chapter on valuation, you will recall that this inverse relationship between bond prices and yield is a result of the fact that when bonds are issued, their coupon rate is fixed. However, once the bond is issued, it must compete in the market with other financial instruments. Because new bonds are issued to yield the current interest rate, yields on old bonds must adjust to remain competitive with the newer issues. Thus when interest rates rise, the price of an older bond with a lower coupon interest rate must decline to increase the yield on the old bond, making it competitive with the return on newly issued bonds.

Interest rate futures offer investors a very inexpensive way of eliminating the risks associated with interest rate fluctuations. For example, banks, pension funds, and insurance companies all make considerable use of the interest rate futures market to avoid paper losses that might otherwise occur when interest rates unexpectedly increase. Corporations also use interest rate futures to lock in interest rates when they are planning to issue debt. If interest rates rise before the corporation has the opportunity to issue the new debt, the profits on the interest rate futures contracts they have sold will offset the increased costs associated with the proposed debt offering.

Foreign exchange futures. Of all the financial futures, foreign exchange futures have been around the longest, first appearing in 1972. Foreign exchange futures work in the same way as other futures, but in this case the commodity is German marks, British pounds, or some other foreign currency. As we will see, the similarities between these futures and the others we have examined are great. Not only do foreign exchange futures work in the same way as other futures, but they also are used by financial managers for the same basic reasons—to hedge away risks, in this case, exchange rate risks. One of the major participants in the foreign exchange futures market is the exporter who will receive foreign currency when its exported goods are finally received and who uses this market to lock in a certain exchange rate. As a result, the exporter is unaffected by any exchange rate fluctuations that might occur before it receives payment. Foreign exchange futures are also used to hedge away possible fluctuations in the value of earnings of foreign subsidiaries.

In the 1980s and 90s, fluctuations in exchange rates became common. With exchange rate futures, a financial manager could eliminate the effects—good or bad—of exchange rate fluctuation with a relatively small investment. The extremely high degree of leverage that was available coupled with the dramatic fluctuations in foreign exchange rates encouraged many financial managers to consider entering the exchange rate futures market. One example of a dramatic price movement came as the British pound dropped to a value of just over $1.07 in early 1985. To get a feel for the degree of leverage experienced in the foreign exchange futures market and the large profits and losses that can occur in this market, let's look at Figure 20.1, which examines profits and losses resulting from buying and selling British pound futures.

As Figure 20.1 shows, fortunes could have been lost and made by those investing in British pound futures. Some firms no doubt saved themselves enormous losses by hedging away exchange rate risk, whereas others would have benefited by the dramatic swing in the exchange rate. Over just 5 trading days, the value of an investment in British pound futures went down almost threefold. A more recent example of the dramatic fluctuations that can occur in exchange rates is the dramatic drop in Asian currencies in 1998. Needless to say, the foreign exchange futures market is a very risky market, characterized by extreme leverage both on the up and down side and periodic major movements in the underlying values of the foreign exchange currencies. To the financial manager, this market provides a perfect mechanism for eliminating the effect of exchange rate fluctuations.

Stock index futures. Stock indexes have been around for many years, but it has only been recently that financial managers and investors have had the opportunity to trade them directly. In fact, despite only first appearing in February 1982, by 1984 they became the second most widely traded futures contract of all, exceeded in trading volume only by T-bond futures contracts.

At this point, after looking at other futures contracts, the workings of stock index futures should be clear. They work basically the same way, with one major exception: Stock index

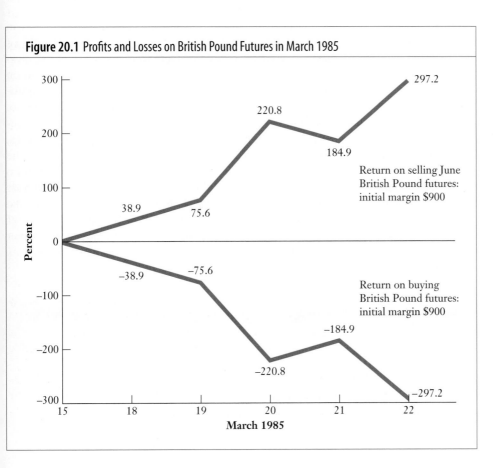

Figure 20.1 Profits and Losses on British Pound Futures in March 1985

futures contracts allow only for cash settlement. There is no delivery, because what is being traded is the *future price* of the index, not the underlying stocks in the index. Currently there are several stock index futures available, with futures on the S&P 500 index clearly dominating in terms of volume. However, in mid-1997, futures trading on the Dow Jones Industrial Average (DJIA) was initiated. Given that the DJIA is perhaps the most recognized stock market index, this is almost certain to be a popular stock index future.

Let's examine exactly what an S&P 500 index futures contract involves. The S&P 500 index is a broad-based index made up of 400 industrials, 40 utilities, 20 transportations, and 40 financial companies. These companies represent about 80 percent of the value of all issues traded on the NYSE. This is a value-weighted index; the weight each stock takes on in the index is determined by the market value of that stock. The contract size or value of each contract is 500 times the S&P 500 index, which puts it at about $577,500 in mid-1998.

Just as with currency futures, when there is a major fluctuation in the stock market, entire fortunes can be made or lost in the stock index futures market. Take, for example, trading on October 22, 1987, during the week of the great crash. That day one trader, Albert "Bud" Furman III, made $900,000 in 90 seconds by buying 303 S&P 500 futures contracts at $196.00 a contract and selling 300 futures contracts 90 seconds later at $202.00 per contract (500 × $6/contract × 300 contracts = $900,000).

After the 1987 crash, a system of shock absorber limits and circuit breakers were introduced to most index futures markets. These serve the same purpose as do daily price limits, but they are not as strict. For example, the New York Futures Exchange has 10-minute, 30-minute, 1-hour, and 2-hour trading halts that result from wide swings in the stock market. The purpose of these programmed trading halts is to allow investors to rationally appraise the market during periods of large price swings.

To the financial manager, the great popularity of these financial newcomers lies in their ability to reduce or eliminate systematic risk. When we talked about the variability or risk associated with common stock returns, we said that there were two types of risk: systematic and unsystematic risk. Unsystematic risk, although accounting for a large portion of the variability of an individual security's returns, is largely eliminated in large portfolios through random diversification, leaving only systematic or market risk in a portfolio. As a result, we said that a portfolio's returns are basically determined by market movements, as modified by the portfolio's beta. Before the introduction of stock index futures, a portfolio or pension fund manager was forced to adjust the portfolio's beta if he or she anticipated a change in the direction of the market. Stock index futures allow the portfolio or pension fund manager to eliminate or mute the effects of swings in the market without the large transactions costs that would be associated with the trading needed to modify the portfolio's beta. Unfortunately, although stock index futures allow for the elimination of the unwanted effects of market downswings, they also eliminate the effects of market upswings. In other words, they allow the portfolio or pension fund manager to eliminate as much of the effect of the market as he or she wishes from his or her portfolio.

RELATE TO THE BIG PICTURE

*The area of risk management has grown rapidly over the last decade. In response to volatile interest rates, commodity prices, and exchange rates of the late 1970s through the 1990s, financial managers turned to the futures, options, and swap markets for relief. Once again, the financial markets demonstrated their dynamic and adaptive nature in finding new ways of reducing risk without affecting return. The inspiration for such behavior, of course, finds its roots in **Axiom 1: The Risk-Return Trade-Off—We Won't Take on Additional Risk Unless We Expect to Be Compensated with Additional Return.***

An **option**, or **option contract**, gives its owner the right to buy or sell a fixed number of shares of stock at a specified price over a limited time period. Although trading in option contracts has existed for many years, it was not until the Chicago Board Options Exchange (CBOE) began trading in listed options in 1973 that the volume of trading reached any meaningful level. During the years since the CBOE first listed options on 16 stocks, volume has grown at a phenomenal rate, with over 10,000 different active option contracts on over 800 stocks listed today. Trading volume has also grown to such an extent that, on a typical day, trading in options involves numbers equal to half the volume of trading on the NYSE. Still, to many financial managers, options remain a mystery, viewed as closer to something one would find in Las Vegas than on Wall Street.

> **Option contract**
>
> An option contract gives its owner the right to buy or sell a fixed number of shares of stock at a specified price over a limited time period.

Clearly, there is too much going on in the options markets not to pay attention to them. Financial managers are just beginning to turn to them as an effective way of eliminating risk for a small price. As we will see, they are fascinating, but they are also confusing—with countless variations and a language of their own. Moreover, their use is not limited to speculators; options are also used by the most conservative financial managers to eliminate unwanted risk. In this section, we will discuss the fundamentals of options, their terminology, and how they are used by financial managers.

The Fundamentals of Options

Although the market for options seems to have a language of its own, there are only two basic types of options: puts and calls. Everything else involves some variation. A **call option** gives its owner the right to purchase a given number of shares of stock or some other asset at a specified price over a given period. Thus if the price of the underlying common stock or asset goes up, a call purchaser makes money. This is essentially the same as a "rain check" or guaranteed price. You have the option to buy something, in this case common stock, at a set price.

> **Call option**
>
> A call option gives its owner the right to purchase a given number of shares of stock or some other asset at a specified price over a given time period.

In effect, a call option gives you the right to buy, but it is not a promise to buy. A **put**, on the other hand, gives its owner the right to sell a given number of shares of common stock or some other asset at a specified price over a given period. A put purchaser is betting that the price of the underlying common stock or asset will drop. Just as with the call, a put option gives its holder the right to sell the common stock at a set price, but it is not a promise to sell. Because these are just options to buy or sell stock or some other asset, they do not represent an ownership position in the underlying corporation, as does common stock. In fact, there is no direct relationship between the underlying corporation and the option. An option is merely a contract between two investors.

> **Put option**
>
> A put option gives its owner the right to sell a given number of shares of common stock or some other asset at a specified price over a given time period.

Because there is no underlying security, a purchaser of an option can be viewed as betting against the seller or *writer* of the option. For this reason, the options markets are often referred to as a zero sum game. If someone makes money, then someone must lose money; if profits and losses were added up, the total for all options would equal zero. If commissions are considered, the total becomes negative, and we have a "negative sum" game. As we will see, the options markets are quite complicated and risky. Some experts refer to them as legalized institutions for transferring wealth from the unsophisticated to the sophisticated. However, for the financial manager, they can be tools for eliminating risk.

THE NEW YORK TIMES, JUNE 28, 1994

Coffee Futures Soar 25%
Biggest Daily Rise in Seven Years

Coffee prices surged more than 25 percent yesterday, the largest one-day rise in more than seven years, as a damaging frost struck much of the coffee-growing areas of Brazil.

(A) "We are going to see this market skyrocket," said Judith Ganes, coffee analyst for Merrill Lynch. "Consumers are likely to feel it at the retail level." Coffee for July delivery jumped 33.8 cents to $1.5975 a **(B)** pound—after peaking earlier at $1.80—its highest price since November 1986.

(C) Coffee futures prices have risen 73 percent since May amid declining supplies, increased consumption and smaller than expected harvests in Brazil and Colombia. The gains have brought the prices of coffee beans back to their level before the International Coffee Agreement collapsed in 1989,

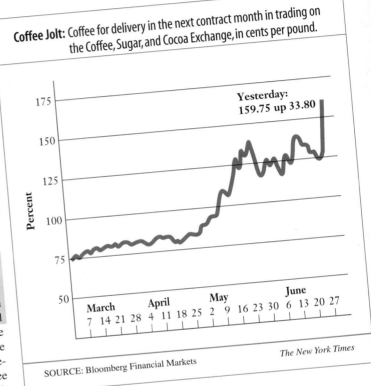

Coffee Jolt: Coffee for delivery in the next contract month in trading on the Coffee, Sugar, and Cocoa Exchange, in cents per pound.

Yesterday: 159.75 up 33.80

SOURCE: Bloomberg Financial Markets

The New York Times

The contract. When an option is purchased, it is nothing more than a contract that allows the purchaser to either buy in the case of a call, or sell in the case of a put, the underlying stock or asset at a predetermined price. That is, no asset has changed hands, but the price has been set for a future transaction that will occur *only if and when* the option purchaser wants it to. In this section, we will refer to the process of selling puts and calls as *writing*. Often, selling options is referred to as *shorting* or *taking a short position* in those options, whereas buying an option is referred to as *taking a long position*.

sending prices plunging below 50 cents a pound in August 1992.

Brazil is the world's biggest coffee producer, accounting for about 25 percent of the world harvest. Crop losses there from frost, now estimated at 15 percent, are expected to tighten global output—already relatively scarce because of bad weather elsewhere—and reduce worldwide supplies by about 4 percent.

Ⓓ

Coffee beans take years to mature, so next year's Brazilian crop will be most affected by the frost. AccuWeather said the temperature was as low as 29 degrees on Saturday night, when a mass of cold air moved north from Antarctica. It was the worst frost in more than a decade.

SOURCE: Leonard Sloane, "Coffee Futures Soar 25%, Biggest Daily Rise in 7 Years," *The New York Times* (June 28,1994): D1. Copyright © 1994 by The New York Times Co. Reprinted by permission.

Analysis and Implications . . .

A. The futures markets provide the financial manager the opportunity to lock in the price of a commodity, thereby eliminating exposure to price fluctuations both up and down. By purchasing futures contracts on coffee, a financial manager at Maxwell House could hedge away the risk associated with price fluctuations on its primary raw material.

B. Coffee, like most other futures contracts, has a daily limit, but with coffee the daily price limit of 6 cents per contract does not apply to contracts on the 2 nearby months. For this reason, coffee futures contracts were free to jump by 25 percent. Interestingly, because of the limits, no trading occurred on any contracts maturing in three months or longer. They merely went "up the limit" without any trading occurring.

C. We should keep in mind that the futures market is a zero sum game. When someone does well, there is also someone on the other end doing poorly. Who sold these futures contracts in the first place? Some were sold by coffee growers trying to lock in a price for their crops, others were sold by speculators betting that coffee prices would go down.

D. This wasn't the last freeze to hit Brazil in 1994. In July another mass of cold air caused more damage to the coffee crop, driving prices even higher—up to $2.74 per pound. Within 2 weeks of peaking out, coffee future prices dropped to just over $2 per pound. Needless to say, a lot of money changed hands in the coffee futures market during this time period.

The exercise or striking price. The **option striking price** is the price at which the stock or asset may be purchased from the writer in the case of a call or sold to the writer in the case of a put.

Option premium. The **option premium** is merely the price of the option. It is generally stated in terms of dollars per share rather than per option contract which covers 100 shares. Thus if a call option premium is $2, then an option contract would cost $200 and allow the purchase of 100 shares of stock at the exercise price.

Option striking price

The price at which the stock or asset may be purchased from the writer in the case of a call, or sold to the writer in the case of a put.

Option premium

The price of the option.

Option expiration date

The date on which the option expires.

Expiration date. The **option expiration date** is the date on which the option contract expires. An American option is one that can be exercised any time up to the expiration date. A European option can be exercised only on the expiration date.

Covered and naked options. If a call writer owns the underlying stock or asset on which he or she writes a call, the writer is said to have written a *covered call*. Conversely, if the writer writes a call on a stock or asset that he or she does not own, he or she is said to have written a *naked call*. The difference is that if a naked call is exercised, the call writer must deliver stock or assets that he or she does not own.

Open interest. The term *open interest* refers to the number of option contracts in existence at one point in time. The importance of this concept comes from the fact that open interest provides the investor with some indication of the amount of liquidity associated with that particular option.

In-, out-of, and at-the-money. A call (put) is said to be out-of-the-money if the underlying stock is selling below (above) the exercise price of the option. Alternatively, a call (put) is said to be in-the-money if the underlying stock is selling above (below) the exercise price of the option. If the option is selling at the exercise price, it is said to be selling at-the-money. For example, if Ford Motor's common stock was selling for $22 per share, a call on Ford with an exercise price of $20 would be in-the-money, whereas a call on Ford with an exercise price of $30 would be out-of-the-money.

Option's intrinsic value

The minimum value of the option.

Intrinsic and time (or speculative) value. The term **intrinsic value** refers to the minimum value of the option—that is, the amount by which the stock is in-the-money. Thus for a call, the intrinsic value is the amount by which the stock price exceeds the exercise price. If the call is out-of-the-money—that is, the exercise price is above the stock price—then its intrinsic value is zero. Intrinsic values can never be negative. For a put, the intrinsic value is again the minimum value the put can sell for, which is the exercise price less the stock price. For example, a Ford April 20 put, that is, a put on Ford stock with an exercise price of $20 that expires in April, when Ford's common stock was selling for $12 per share would have an intrinsic value of $8. If the put was selling for anything less than $8, investors would buy puts and sell the stock until all profits from this strategy were exhausted. Arbitrage, this process of buying and selling like assets for different prices, keeps the price of options at or above their intrinsic value. If an option is selling for its intrinsic value, it is said to be selling at *parity*.

Option's time (or speculative) value

The amount by which the option premium exceeds the intrinsic value of the option.

The **time value**, or **speculative value**, of an option is the amount by which the option premium exceeds the intrinsic value of the option. The time value represents the amount above the intrinsic value of an option that an investor is willing to pay to participate in capital gains from investing in the option. At expiration, the time value of the option falls to zero and the option sells for its intrinsic value, because the chance for future capital gains has been exhausted. These relationships are as follows:

call intrinsic value = stock price − exercise price
put intrinsic value = exercise price − stock price
call time value = call premium − (stock price − exercise price)
put time value = put premium − (exercise price − stock price)

Perhaps the easiest way to gain an understanding of the pricing of options is to look at them graphically. Figure 20.2 presents a profit and loss graph for the purchase of a call on Ford stock with an exercise price of $20 that is bought for $4. This is termed a Ford 20 call. In Figure 20.2 and all other profit and loss graphs, the vertical axis represents the profits or losses realized on the option's expiration date, and the horizontal axis represents the stock price on the expiration date. Remember that because we are viewing the value of the option at expiration, the option has no time value and therefore it sells for exactly its intrinsic value. To keep things simple, we will also ignore any transaction costs.

For the Ford 20 call shown in Figure 20.2, the call will be worthless at expiration if the value of the stock is less than the exercise or striking price. This is because it would make no sense for an individual to exercise the call option to purchase Ford stock for $20 per share if he or she could buy the same Ford stock from a broker at a price less than $20. Although the option will be worthless at expiration, if the stock price is below the exercise price, the most that an investor can lose is the option premium—that is, how much he or she paid for the option, which in this case was $4. Although this may be the entire investment in the option, it is also generally only a fraction of the stock's price. Once the stock price climbs above the exercise price, the call option takes on a positive value and increases in a linear one-to-one basis as the stock price increases. Moreover, there is no limit on how high the profits can climb. In the case of the Ford 20 call, once the price of Ford stock rises above $20, the call begins taking on value, and once it hits $24, the investor breaks even. The investor has earned enough in the way of profits to cover the $4 premium she paid for the option in the first place.

To the call writer, the profit and loss graph is the mirror image of the call purchaser's graph. As we noted earlier, the options market is a zero sum game in which

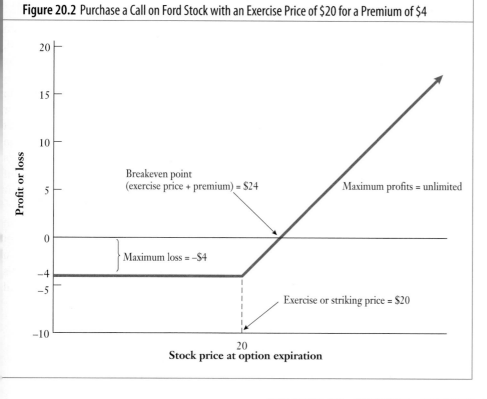

Figure 20.2 Purchase a Call on Ford Stock with an Exercise Price of $20 for a Premium of $4

one individual gains at the expense of another. Figure 20.3 shows the profits and losses at expiration associated with writing a call option. Once again, we will look at the profits and losses at expiration, because at that point in time options have no time value. The maximum profit to the call writer is the premium, or how much the writer received when the option was sold, whereas the maximum loss is unlimited.

Looking at the profit and loss graph presented in Figure 20.4 for the purchase of a Ford 20 put that is bought for $3, we see that the lower the price of the Ford stock, the more the put is worth. Here the put only begins to take on value once the price of the Ford stock drops below the exercise price, which in this case is $20. Then for every dollar that the price of the Ford stock drops, the put increases in value by one dollar. Once the Ford stock drops to $17 per share, the put purchaser breaks even by making $3 on the put, which exactly offsets what was initially paid for the put. Here, as with the purchase of a call option, the most an investor can lose is the premium, which although small in dollar value relative to the potential gains, still represents 100 percent of the investment. The maximum gain associated with the purchase of a put is limited only by the fact that the lowest a stock's price can fall to is zero.

To a put writer, the profit and loss graph is the mirror image of the put purchaser's graph. This is shown in Figure 20.5. Here the most a put writer can earn is the premium or amount for which the put was sold. The potential losses for the put writer are limited only by the fact that the stock price cannot fall below zero.

All of our graphs have shown the price of the option at expiration. When we reexamine these relationships at a time before expiration, we find that the options now take on some time value. In other words, investors are willing to pay more than the intrinsic value for an option because of the uncertainty of the future stock price. That is, although the stock price may fluctuate, the possible losses on the option are limited, whereas the possible gains are almost unlimited.

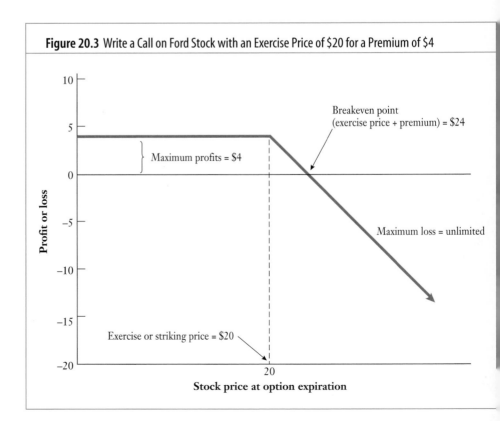

Figure 20.3 Write a Call on Ford Stock with an Exercise Price of $20 for a Premium of $4

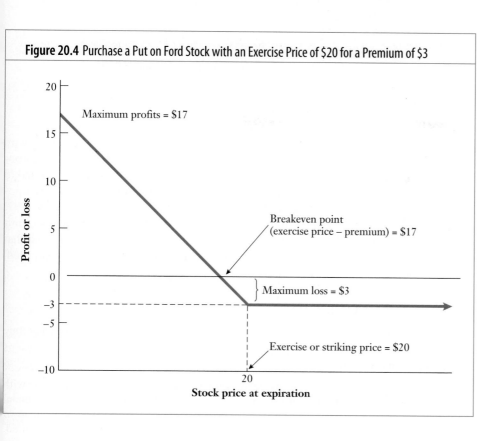

Figure 20.4 Purchase a Put on Ford Stock with an Exercise Price of $20 for a Premium of $3

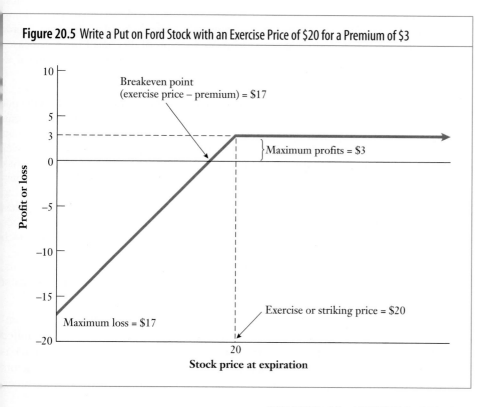

Figure 20.5 Write a Put on Ford Stock with an Exercise Price of $20 for a Premium of $3

This feature in which the potential loss is limited to the amount invested along with unlimited returns is what draws many speculators to options. Although the biggest corporate losses have been associated with futures contracts, in which losses are not limited to the amount invested, options speculation has produced its share of huge losses for corporations. Look at NatWest which lost £90 million in interest rate options in February 1997, or Dell Computer which lost $8 million in 1992. No doubt, these companies didn't understand the degree of risk that they had exposed themselves to. Keep in mind that options should be used to reduce risk, but if they aren't fully understood or controlled, they can produce results opposite from those intended.

Characteristics of Options

As we examine options from the viewpoint of the financial manager, we will see that they have some attractive features that help explain their popularity. There are three reasons for the popularity of options:

1. **Leverage.** Calls allow the financial manager the chance for unlimited capital gains with a very small investment. Because a call is only an option to buy, the most a financial manager can lose is what was invested, which is usually a very small percentage of what it would cost to buy the stock itself, whereas the potential for gain is unlimited. As we will see, when a financial manager owns a call, he or she controls or benefits directly from any price increases in the stock. The idea of magnifying the potential return is an example of leverage. It is similar to the concept of leverage in physics, where a small amount of force can lift a heavy load. Here a small investment is doing the work of a much larger investment. Unfortunately, leverage is a double-edged sword: Small price increases can produce a large percentage profit, but small price decreases can produce large percentage losses. With an option, the maximum loss is limited to the amount invested.

2. **Financial insurance.** For the financial manager, this is the most attractive feature of options. A put can be looked on as an insurance policy, with the premium paid for the put being the cost of the policy. The transactions costs associated with exercising the put can then be looked on as the deductible. When a put with an exercise price equal to the current stock price is purchased, it insures the holder against any declines in the stock price over the life of the put. Through the use of a put, a pension fund manager can reduce the risk exposure in a portfolio with little in cost and little change to the portfolio. One dissimilarity between a put and an insurance policy is that with a put an investor does not need to own the asset, in this case the stock, before buying the insurance. A call, because it has limited potential losses associated with it, can also be viewed as an investment insurance policy. With a call, the investor's potential losses are limited to the price of the call, which is quite a bit below the price of the stock itself.

3. **Investment alternative expansion.** From the viewpoint of the investor, the use of puts, calls, and combinations of them can materially increase the set of possible investment alternatives available.

Again, an understanding of the popularity of both puts and calls to the financial manager involves understanding (1) the concept of leverage—in the case of calls unlimited and in the case of puts very large potential gains with limited and relatively small maximum potential losses—and (2) the concept of financial insurance. These two factors combined allow for an expansion of the available investment alternatives. Remember, both puts and calls are merely options to buy or sell the stock at a specified price. The worst that can happen is that the options become worthless and the financial manager loses the investment.

The Chicago Board Options Exchange

Prior to 1973, when the CBOE opened, there was no central marketplace for put and call options. At that time, put and call options transactions took place on the over-the-counter market through what was called the Put and Call Dealers Association, with only about 20 active brokers and dealers in the market. Through a telephone hookup, these dealers acted as middlemen, matching up potential writers and purchasers of options.

Because the specifics of each option were negotiated directly between the writer and the purchaser of the option, very seldom were any two options alike. Generally, every option written had a different expiration date and a different exercise price. As a result, there was little in the way of a secondary market for these individualized options, and the writers and purchasers generally had to hold their position until expiration or until the options were exercised.

With the creation of the CBOE, all this began to change. In 1973, the CBOE began trading listed options on 16 different stocks. Today there are four different exchanges that list and trade options—the CBOE, the AMEX, the Philadelphia, and the Pacific—with over 800 different stocks having listed options. Although the over-the-counter market run by the Put and Call Association is still in operation for stocks that are not listed on the CBOE or any other exchange, it now handles less than 10 percent of all traded options.

This dramatic growth in the trading of options is almost entirely due to the several developments brought on by exchange-listed trading that the CBOE initiated, including the following:

1. **Standardization of the option contracts.** Today, the expiration dates for all options are standardized. As a result, there is only 1 day per month on which a listed option on any stock can expire. The number of shares that a call allows its owner to purchase, and a put allows its owner to sell, has also been standardized to 100 shares per option contract. In addition, the striking prices have been standardized, generally at five-point intervals, so that there are more identical options. Through this standardization, the number of different option contracts on each stock is severely limited. The result is that more options are identical and the secondary market is made more liquid.
2. **Creation of a regulated central marketplace.** The exchange listing of options provides a central location for continuous trading in options, both newly issued and in the secondary market. The CBOE and the exchanges that followed in listing options also imposed strong surveillance and disclosure requirements.
3. **Creation of the options clearinghouse corporation (OCC).** The OCC bears full responsibility for honoring all options issued on the CBOE. In effect, all options held by individuals have been written by the OCC, and alternatively all options written by individuals are held by the OCC. The purpose of creating a buffer between individual buyers and sellers of options is to provide investors with confidence in the market, in addition to facilitating the clearing and settlement of options. Because of the importance of the OCC, let us look for a moment at its operation.

   When an options transaction is agreed upon, the seller writes an option contract to the OCC, which in turn writes an identical option contract to the buyer. If the buyer later wants to exercise the option, he or she gives the OCC the exercise price associated with the option, which in turn provides the buyer with stock. To get the stock to cover the option, the OCC simultaneously exercises a call option it has on this stock. Because of the operation of the OCC and the strong secondary market created by the CBOE, options are not exercised very frequently but are generally sold. Rather than exercise an option, an investor or financial manager usually just sells the option to another investor and realizes the profits in that manner. Writers of options clear their position by buying an option identical to the one they wrote. As a result, the writer has two identical contracts on both sides of the market with the OCC. These positions then cancel each other out.

4. **Trading was made certificateless.** Instead of issuing certificates, the OCC maintains a continuous record of trader's positions. In addition to making the clearing of positions (the canceling out of an option writer's obligation when an identical option is purchased) easier, it has also allowed for an up-to-date record of existing options to be maintained.

5. **Creation of a liquid secondary market with dramatically decreased transactions costs.** There also has been a self-fulfilling generation of volume adding to the liquidity of the secondary market. That is, the innovations created a liquid secondary market for options, and this liquid secondary market attracted more investors into the options market, which in turn created even more liquidity in the secondary market.

Innovations in the Options Market

Recently, five additional variations of the traditional option have appeared: the stock index option, the interest rate option, the foreign currency option, the Treasury bond futures option, and Leaps.

Stock index options. The options on stock indexes were first introduced on the CBOE in 1983 and have since proved extremely popular. Although there are a variety of different index options, based on several different broad stock market indexes and also industry indexes such as a computer industry index, it has been the broader stock market indexes that have carried the bulk of the popularity of index options. Although the industry-based index options have received a somewhat mixed reception, stock index options, in particular the S&P 100 index on the CBOE, have proved to be extremely popular. In fact, more than 80 percent of all stock index options trading involves the S&P 100 index. Currently it accounts for over half of the volume of all option trading, and has made the CBOE the second largest U.S. securities market, with daily trading occasionally reaching nearly 700,000 contracts (remember each contract involves an option on 100 "shares" of the index).

The reason for this popularity is quite simple. These options allow portfolio managers and other investors holding broad portfolios cheaply and effectively to eliminate or adjust the market risk of their portfolios. When we talked about systematic and unsystematic risk, we noted that in a large and well-diversified portfolio, unsystematic risk was effectively diversified away, leaving only systematic risk. Thus the return on a large and well-diversified portfolio was a result of the portfolio's beta and the movement of the market. As a result, because the movements of the market cannot be controlled, portfolio managers periodically attempt to adjust the beta of the portfolio when they think a change in the market's direction is at hand. Index options allow them to make this change without the massive transaction costs that would otherwise be incurred.

In general, stock index options are used in exactly the same way traditional options are used: for leverage and for investment insurance. However, because of the unusual nature of the "underlying stock," these concepts take on a different meaning. In the case of leverage, the portfolio manager is speculating that the market will head either up or down and is able to cash in on any market volatility with a relatively small investment. In fact, the ability to enjoy the leverage of an option while being concerned with broad market movements has resulted in much of the popularity of stock index options, as small changes in the market can result in very large changes in the price of these options. To get an idea of exactly what we mean, let us look at what happened in early 1985, when the stock market moved ahead.

On January 21, 1985, when the S&P 100 was at 169.27, an investor could have bought a February call with an exercise price of 170 and paid 2 3/4, or $275.00, as shown

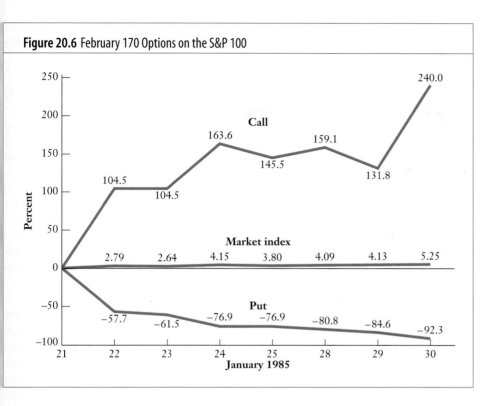

Figure 20.6 February 170 Options on the S&P 100

in Figure 20.6. Ten days later, it was worth 9 3/8, or $937.50, when the index closed at 178.14. Conversely, an investor who purchased a put for 3 1/4, or $325, would have had the value of the investment drop to $25. All this dramatic price movement was the result of only a 5.24 percent change in the underlying index.

In the case of the investment insurance motive for holding index options, the financial manager is really using them to eliminate the effects of a possible downward movement in the market. For example, a portfolio manager who wants to insure the portfolio against a downturn in the market might purchase a put on the S&P 100 or S&P 500 index. Thus, if the market declines, the put will appreciate in value, offsetting the loss in the investor's portfolio.

In effect, index options can be used in the same way as the more traditional options. The only difference is that here the profits or losses depend on what happens to the value of the index rather than to one stock.

Interest rate options. Options on 30-year Treasury bonds are also traded on the CBOE. Although the trading appeal of interest rate options is somewhat limited, they do open some very interesting doors to the financial manager. In terms of the insurance and leverage traits, they allow the financial manager to insure against the effects of future changes in interest rates. We know that as interest rates rise, the market value of outstanding bonds falls; thus through the purchase of an interest rate put, the market value of a portfolio manager's bonds can be protected. Alternatively, a financial manager who is about to raise new capital through a debt offering and who is worried about a possible rise in interest rates before the offering occurs may purchase an interest rate put. This would have the effect of locking in current interest rates at the maximum level that the firm would have to pay.

Foreign currency options. Foreign currency options are the same as the other options we have examined, except the underlying asset is the British pound, the Japanese yen, or some other foreign currency. Although foreign currency options are limited to the Philadelphia Exchange, there is a considerable amount of interest in them largely because of the wide fluctuations foreign currency has had in recent years relative to the dollar. In terms of the insurance and leverage traits, these options allow multinational firms to guard against fluctuations in foreign currencies that might adversely affect their operations. The leverage trait allows investors to speculate in possible future foreign currency fluctuations with a minimum amount of exposure to possible losses.

Let's look at an example of how foreign currency options might be used. As firms trade more and more internationally, the need to protect sales against undesirable currency fluctuations becomes increasingly important. For example, Cessna might use currency options to protect sales on its Citation V aircraft, which are sold in Europe to Swiss customers. Because the Citation V is built in the United States and sold abroad, its costs in labor and materials are based on the dollar. However, as the dollar fluctuates relative to the Swiss franc, so must the sales price in Swiss francs for Cessna to receive the same amount of dollars on each sale in Switzerland.

Problems surface when the value of the Swiss franc falls relative to that of the dollar. For each sale to bring the same amount of dollars back to Cessna, the selling price in Swiss francs would have to be *increased*. Unfortunately, increasing prices may lead to lost sales. To guard against this situation, Cessna may purchase *put options* on the Swiss franc to cover the anticipated Swiss sales. These puts give Cessna the option to sell or convert Swiss francs into dollars at a preset price. If after the put options are purchased, the Swiss franc falls, Cessna could keep its selling prices constant in terms of the Swiss franc and make up for the loss in the currency exchange with the profits on the puts. Conversely, if the value of the Swiss franc rises relative to the value of the dollar, Cessna could lower its Swiss price, sell more aircraft, and still bring home the same dollars per sale—all that would be lost is the price paid for the put options.

> **STOP AND THINK**
>
> *An option on a Treasury bond future really holds little advantage over an option on a Treasury bond in terms of ability to reduce interest rate risk. Its advantages stem mainly from the great depth of the Treasury bond futures market.*

Options on treasury bond futures. Options on Treasury bond futures work the same way as any other option. The only difference between them and other bond options is that they involve the acquisition of a futures position rather than the delivery of actual bonds. To the creative financial manager, they provide a flexible tool to insure against adverse changes in interest rates while retaining the opportunity to benefit from any favorable interest rate movement that might occur. Although a futures contract establishes an obligation for both parties to buy and sell at a specified price, an option only establishes a right. It is therefore exercised only when it is to the option holder's advantage to do so. In effect, a call option on a futures contract does not establish a price obligation, but rather a maximum purchase price. Conversely, a put option on a futures contract is used to establish a minimum selling price. Thus the buyer of an option on a futures contract can achieve immunization against any unfavorable price movements, whereas the buyer of the futures contract can achieve immunization against any price movements, regardless of whether they are favorable or unfavorable.

In their short history, options on U.S. Treasury bond futures have proved to be extremely popular, with the majority of institutions choosing to trade options on bond futures rather than options on actual bonds. Their extreme popularity can be traced to several important advantages they possess:

1. **Efficient price determination of the underlying instrument.** The U.S. Treasury bond futures contract on the Chicago Board of Trade is the most widely traded futures contract of all. As a result, there is a continuous stream of market-determined price information concerning these contracts. Conversely, price information on most other bonds is generally somewhat sketchy at best, with substantial time between trades and generally a wide gap between existing bid and ask prices.
2. **Unlimited deliverable supply.** Because the Clearing Corporation can create as many futures contracts as are needed, the process of exercising an option is made extremely simple. When an option on a futures contract is exercised, the buyer simply assumes a futures position at the exercise price of the option. Because the Clearing Corporation can create as many futures contracts as are needed, the market price of these contracts is not affected by the exercise of the options on them. Conversely, if an option holder on an actual bond were to exercise his or her option, he or she would have to take delivery of the underlying bond. Because the supply of any particular bond is limited, a serious price pressure might be placed on that bond, provided the bond does not enjoy sufficient liquidity. Thus, because of the unlimited deliverable supply of futures contracts, the exercise of options on futures does not affect the price of those futures.
3. **Greater flexibility in the event of exercise.** If the option proves to be profitable, the purchaser or writer can settle the transaction in cash by offsetting the futures position acquired by exercise, or do nothing temporarily and assume the futures position and make or take delivery of the actual bonds when the futures contract comes due.
4. **Extremely liquid market.** Because of the other advantages of options on Treasury bond futures, a great number of these options have been created and are traded daily. As a result of the large volume, options on Treasury bond futures have developed a very liquid and active secondary market, which has encouraged other traders to enter this market.

Financial institutions seem to be major participants in the options on Treasury bond futures market, although there are many potential users of financial futures. They use futures options to alter the risk-return structure of their investment portfolios and actually reduce their exposure to downside risk. A common strategy is to purchase put options and thereby eliminate the possibility of large losses while retaining the possibility of large gains. There is a cost associated with this strategy, because the option premium must be paid regardless of whether or not the option is exercised. An additional return is also generated by those who write call options against a bond portfolio. With this strategy, the premium increases the overall return if bond yields remain stable or rise; however, a maximum return is also established for the portfolio, because it is this tail of the distribution that is sold with the option.

Leaps—long-term options. Long-term Equity Anticipation Securities or "Leaps" are long-term options—both puts and calls—with expiration dates that go out as far as 3 years in the future. Because they are longer term than traditional options, they can be used to hedge against longer term movements in stocks. Leaps calls allow the investor to benefit from a stock price increase without purchasing the stock, whereas Leaps puts provide a hedge against stock price declines over the long run. As with other options, they expire on the Saturday following the third Friday of the expiration month, with all Leaps expiring in January.

Currency swap

An exchange of debt obligations in different currencies.

The currency swap is another technique for controlling exchange rate risk. Whereas options and futures contracts generally have a fairly short duration, a currency swap provides the financial manager with the ability to hedge away exchange rate risk over longer periods. It is for that reason that currency swaps have gained in popularity. A **currency swap** is simply an exchange of debt obligations in different currencies. Interest rate swaps are used to provide long-term exchange rate risk hedging. Actually, a currency swap can be quite simple, with two firms agreeing to pay each other's debt obligation.

How does this serve to eliminate exchange rate risk? If I am an American firm with much of my income coming from sales in England, I might enter in a currency swap with an English firm. If the value of the British pound depreciates from 1.90 dollars to the pound to 1.70 dollars to the pound, then each dollar of sales in England will bring fewer dollars back to the parent company in the United States. This would be offset by the effects of the currency swap because it costs the U.S. firm less dollars to fulfill the English firm's interest obligations. That is, pounds cost less to purchase, and the interest payments owed are in pounds. The nice thing about a currency swap is that it allows the firm to engage in long-term exchange rate risk hedging, because the debt obligation covers a relatively long time period.

Needless to say, there are many variations of the currency swap. One of the more popular is the interest rate currency swap, where the principal is not included in the swap. That is, only interest payment obligations in different currencies are swapped. The key to controlling risk is to get an accurate estimate on the net exposure level to which the firm is subjected. Then the firm must decide whether it feels it is prudent to subject itself to the risk associated with possible exchange rate fluctuations.

These look like great ideas—enter into a contract that reduces risk—but just as with the other derivative securities, they are dangerous if used by those who don't understand their risks. For example, in 1994 Procter & Gamble Corporation lost $157 million on swaps that involved interest rate payments made in German marks and U.S. dollars. How did this happen? Exchange rates and interest rates didn't go the way Procter & Gamble had anticipated and the costs were a lot more than they thought they might ever be. In effect, Procter & Gamble simply got talked into something they didn't understand.

HOW FINANCIAL MANAGERS USE THIS MATERIAL

Over the past 10 years, the use of futures and options by corporations has exploded. The primary way they are used is to hedge away risk in commodity markets, foreign exchange rates, and interest rates. How might you become involved in them? Maybe your first job will be working for McDonald's. To say the least, McDonald's, with operations in 91 countries, gets much of its income from its overseas operations. As a result, currency fluctuations can have a dramatic effect on their profits. With profits from abroad coming in currencies such as the baht (Thailand), the won (Korea), and the ringgit (Malaysia), things got pretty scary in late 1997, when all of these currencies collapsed. How does a company such as McDonald's protect itself and take some of the risk out of its international operations? The answer is, by using futures and options to hedge away the interest rate risk.

Similarly, manufacturing firms use futures to hedge away price fluctuations in their raw materials. Kellogg's may buy futures in rice for Rice Krispies if they feel

FORTUNE MARCH 7, 1994

The Risk That Won't Go Away

To all generally well-informed business people, a few words of semicomfort about financial derivatives: First, if you don't really understand what these are, don't fret. Most of your colleagues, top brass included, are equally baffled. Second, if ten years from now—despite periodic booster shots from articles like this one—you still can't keep these things in focus, then cheer! That will mean derivatives have not been forcibly brought to your attention by bad, bad news, in which they make headlines as a villain, or even *the* villain, in some financial crisis that sweeps the world.

(A) That possibility must be entertained because derivatives have grown with stunning speed into an enormous, pervasive, and controversial financial force.

Derivatives are contracts whose value is derived—the key word—from the value of some underlying asset, such as currencies, equities, or commodities; from an indicator like interest rates; or from a stock market or other index. The derivative instruments that result—variously called swaps, forwards, futures, puts, calls, swaptions, caps, floors, collars, captions, *(B)* floortions, spreadtions, lookbacks, and other neverland names—keep bursting into the news as they did recently when the Federal Reserve raised interest rates and share prices sank, costing some traders of derivatives huge amounts that in some cases surely ran into many millions. The "counter-parties" to these contracts customarily use them to hedge some business risk they don't want to bear, such as a jump in interest rates or a fall in the value of a currency.

(C) But transferring such a risk doesn't wipe it away. The risk simply gets passed by the initial contract to a dealer, who in turn may hedge it by a separate contract with still another dealer, who for his part may haul in yet another dealer or maybe a speculator who *wants* the risk. In the words of Roger & Hammerstein's King of Siam: "et cetera, et cetera, et cetera." What results is a tightly wound market of many, many, interconnections—*global* interconnections—that is altogether quite different from anything that has ever existed before.

Most chilling, derivatives hold the possibility of systematic risk—the danger that these contracts might directly or indirectly cause some localized or particularized trouble in the financial markets to spread uncontrollably. An imaginable scenario is some deep crisis at a major dealer that would cause it to default on its contracts and be the instigator of a chain reaction bringing down other institutions and sending paroxysms of fear through a financial market that lives on the expectation of prompt payments. Inevitably, that would put deposit-insurance funds, and the taxpayers behind them, at risk.

SOURCE: Carol J. Loomis, "The Risk That Won't Go Away," *Fortune* (March 7, 1994): 40–57. © 1994 Time Inc. All rights reserved.

Analysis and Implications ...

A. It has been estimated that the derivatives market has been growing at a rate of about 40 percent per year. Examples of losses in this market abound, with Metallgesellschaft (AG), Germany's 14th largest industrial corporation, which we discussed earlier, leading the way with losses. One of MG's subsidiaries, a U.S. marketing organization and part owner of an oil refinery, reported losses approaching $1.3 billion.

B. It is hard to fully understand the scope of this market with the worldwide total of derivatives estimated to be about $16 trillion.

C. The worry is that although regulators can control problems of banks and other financial institutions by walling off the troubled institutions from the rest of the market, the problems of derivatives may carry over these walls. In short, derivatives, because of their interconnections leading to securities firms and other non-banks, make the process of "walling off" almost impossible. It is the interlockings of businesses and the ripple effect from a major failure that regulators worry about.

rice prices are low, and they want to lock in those prices. Delta may buy futures on oil to lock in the price of its fuel. Your job may involve making those purchases, analyzing prices to determine if your company should lock in the prices of its raw materials, or it may involve determining how many futures and options you should buy. Unfortunately, some firms use futures and options for speculative purposes rather than to hedge away risk. For example, Sumitomo Bank lost $1.8 billion in June 1996 in copper futures.

Still, given the risks that globalization brings, futures and options are a great tool to use in reducing those risks. It's important to keep in mind that they can also be used by smaller firms. For example, if you have a small specialty bakery with customers in England, France, and Germany, you could easily eliminate your exchange rate risk with currency options. In addition, you could lock in the future price of your raw materials in the futures markets.

SUMMARY

OBJECTIVE 1

Futures, options, and currency swaps are important for the financial manager due to their ability to reduce risks associated with interest and exchange rate and commodity price fluctuations.

A futures contract is a contract to buy or sell a stated commodity (such as soybeans or corn) or financial claim (such as U.S. Treasury bonds) at a specified price at some future specified time. This contract requires its holder to buy or sell the asset regardless of what happens to its value during the interim. The importance of a futures contract is that it can be used by financial managers to lock in the price of a commodity or an interest rate and thereby eliminate one source of risk. A futures contract is a specialized form of a forward contract distinguished by (1) an organized exchange, (2) a standardized contract with limited price changes and margin requirements, (3) a clearinghouse in each futures market, and (4) daily resettlement of contracts.

OBJECTIVE 2

A call option gives its owner the right to purchase a given number of shares of stock at a specified price over a given period. Thus, if the price of the underlying common stock goes up, a call purchaser makes money. A put, conversely, gives its owner the right to sell a given number of shares of common stock at a specified price over a given period. Thus a put purchaser is betting that the price of the underlying common stock will drop. Because these are just options to buy or sell stock, they do not represent an ownership position in the underlying corporation, as does common stock.

OBJECTIVE 3

A currency swap is an exchange of debt obligations in different currencies. Exchange rate variations are offset by the effects of the swap. One major advantage of a currency swap is that it allows for the hedging of exchange rate risk over a long period of time.

GO TO:
http://www.prenhall.com/bfm
For downloads and current events associated with this chapter

KEY TERMS

call option, 753

currency swap, 766

futures contract, 745

futures margin, 748

option contract, 753

option expiration date, 756

option premium, 755

option striking price, 755

option's intrinsic value, 756

option's time (or speculative) value, 756

put option, 753

STUDY QUESTIONS

20-1. What is the difference between a commodity future and financial future? Give an example of each.

20-2. Describe a situation in which a financial manager might use a commodity future. Assume that during the period following the transaction the price of that commodity went up. Describe what happened. Now assume that the price of that commodity went down. Now what happened?

20-3. Describe a situation in which a financial manager might use an interest rate future. Assume that during the period following the transaction the interest rates went up. Describe what happened. Now assume that interest rates went down following the transaction. Now what happened?

20-4. Define a call option.

20-5. Define a put option.

20-6. What innovative developments were brought on by exchange-listed trading that the CBOE initiated that led to the dramatic growth in the trading of options?

20-7. What is an option on a futures contract? Give an example of one.

20-8. Compare the two strategies of buying a call and writing a put. What are the differences between the two?

20-9. What is a currency swap and why has it gained so in popularity?

STUDY PROBLEMS (SET A)

20-1A. Draw a profit or loss graph (similar to Figure 20.2) for the purchase of a call contract with an exercise price of $65 for which a $9 premium is paid. Identify the breakeven point, maximum profits, and maximum losses. Now draw the profit or loss graph assuming an exercise price of $70 and a $6 premium.

20-2A. Repeat problem 20-1A, but this time draw the profit or loss graph (similar to Figure 20.3) for the call writer.

20-3A. Draw a profit or loss graph (similar to Figure 20.4) for the purchase of a put contract with an exercise price of $45 for which a $5 premium is paid. Identify the breakeven point, maximum profits, and maximum losses.

20-4A. Repeat problem 20-3A, but this time draw the profit or loss graph (similar to Figure 20.5) for the put writer.

INTEGRATIVE PROBLEM

For your job as the business reporter for a local newspaper, you are given the task of putting together a series of articles on the derivatives markets. Much recent local press coverage has been given to the dangers and the losses that some firms have experienced in those markets. Your editor would like you to address several specific questions in addition to demonstrating the use of futures contracts and options and applying them to several problems.

Please prepare your response to the following memorandum from your editor:

TO: Business Reporter

FROM: Perry White, Editor, Daily Planet

RE: Upcoming Series on the Derivative Securities Market

In your upcoming series on the derivative markets, I would like to make sure you cover several specific points. In addition, before you begin this assignment, I want to make sure we are all reading from the same script, as accuracy has always been the cornerstone of the Daily Planet. As such I'd like a response to the following questions before we proceed:

1. What opportunities do the derivative securities markets (i.e., the futures and options markets) provide to the financial manager?

2. When might a firm become interested in purchasing interest rate futures? Foreign exchange futures? Stock index futures?

3. What can a *firm* do to reduce exchange risk?

4. How would Treasury bond futures and options on Treasury bond futures differ?

5. What is an option on a futures contract? Give an example of one and explain why it exists.

6. Draw a profit or loss graph (similar to Figure 20.2) for the purchase of a call contract with an exercise price of $25 for which a $6 premium is paid. Identify the breakeven point, maximum profits, and maximum losses.

7. Repeat question 6, but this time draw the profit or loss graph (similar to Figure 20.3) for the call writer.

8. Draw a profit or loss graph (similar to Figure 20.4) for the purchase of a put contract with an exercise price of $30 for which a $5 premium is paid. Identify the breakeven point, maximum profits, and maximum losses.

9. Repeat question 8, but this time draw the profit or loss graph (similar to Figure 20.5) for the put writer.

10. What is a currency swap and who might use one?

STUDY PROBLEMS (SET B)

20-1B. Draw a profit or loss graph (similar to Figure 20.2) for the purchase of a call contract with an exercise price of $50 for which a $5 premium is paid. Identify the breakeven point, maximum profits, and maximum losses. Now draw the profit or loss graph assuming an exercise price of $55 and a $6 premium.

20-2B. Repeat problem 20-1B, but this time draw the profit or loss graph (similar to Figure 20.3) for the call writer.

20-3B. Draw a profit or loss graph (similar to Figure 20.4) for the purchase of a put contract with an exercise price of $60 for which a $4 premium is paid. Identify the breakeven point, maximum profits, and maximum losses.

20-4B. Repeat problem 20-3B, but this time draw the profit or loss graph (similar to Figure 20.5) for the put writer.

CONVERTIBLE SECURITIES AND WARRANTS

In September of 1997, Costco Companies, Incorporated issued $900 million of zero coupon bonds that mature in 2017. What made these bonds interesting is that they were zero coupon convertible bonds, that is, each bond could be traded in for 11.3545 shares of Costco's common stock any time on or prior to maturity. In effect, this financing package put together by Costco looked more like options than normal bonds.

In this appendix, we will examine how convertibles and warrants can be used to raise money. Both of these financing methods contain elements of an option in that they can be exchanged at the owner's discretion for a specified number of shares of common stock. In investigating each financing alternative, we look first at its specific characteristics and purpose; then we focus on any special considerations that should be examined before the convertible security or the warrant is issued.

CONVERTIBLE SECURITIES

A **convertible security** is a preferred stock or a debt issue that can be exchanged for a specified number of shares of common stock at the will of the owner. In effect, it contains elements of an option. It provides the stable income associated with preferred stock and bonds in addition to the possibility of capital gains associated with common stock. This combination of features has led convertibles to be called *hybrid* securities.

When the convertible is initially issued, the firm receives the proceeds from the sale, less flotation costs. This is the only time the firm receives any proceeds from issuing convertibles. The firm then treats this convertible as if it were normal preferred stock or debentures, paying dividends or interest regularly. If the security owner wishes to exercise an option to exchange the convertible for common stock, he or she may do so at any time according to the terms specified at the time of issue. The desire to convert generally follows a rise in the price of the common stock. Once the convertible owner trades the convertibles in for common stock, the owner can never trade the stock back for convertibles. From then on, the owner is treated as any other common stockholder and receives only common stock dividends.

Convertible security

Preferred stock or debentures that can be exchanged for a specified number of shares of common stock at the will of the owner.

CHARACTERISTICS AND FEATURES OF CONVERTIBLES

Conversion ratio. The number of shares of common stock for which the convertible security can be exchanged is set out when the convertible is initially issued. On some convertible issues, this **conversion ratio** is stated directly. For example, the convertible may state that it is exchangeable for 15 shares of common stock. Some convertibles give only a **conversion price**, stating, for example, that the security is convertible at $39 per share. This tells us that for every $39 of par value of the convertible security, one share of common stock will be received.

Conversion ratio

The number of shares of common stock for which a convertible security can be exchanged.

$$\text{conversion ratio} = \frac{\text{par value of convertible security}}{\text{conversion price}} \qquad (20A\text{-}1)$$

For example, in 1987, Union Carbide issued $350 million of convertible debentures that mature in 2012. These convertibles have a $1,000 par value, a 7-1/2 percent coupon interest rate, and a conversion price of $35.50. Thus the conversion ratio—the number of shares to be received upon conversion—is $1,000/$35.50 = 28.169 shares. The security owner has the option of holding the 7-1/2 percent convertible debenture or trading it in for 28.169 shares of Union Carbide common stock.

Conversion value. The **conversion value** of a convertible security is the total market value of the common stock for which it can be exchanged. This can be calculated as follows:

$$\begin{matrix} \text{conversion} \\ \text{value} \end{matrix} = \begin{pmatrix} \text{conversion} \\ \text{ratio} \end{pmatrix} \times \begin{pmatrix} \text{market value per share} \\ \text{of the common stock} \end{pmatrix} \quad (20A\text{-}2)$$

If the Union Carbide common stock were selling for, say, $24 per share, then the conversion value for the Union Carbide convertible would be (28.169)($24.00) = $676.06, that is, the market value of the common stock for which the convertible could be exchanged would be $676.06. Thus, regardless of what this convertible debenture was selling for, it could be converted into $676.06 worth of common stock.

Security value. The **security value** (or bond value, as it is sometimes called) of a convertible security is the price the convertible security would sell for in the absence of its conversion feature. This is calculated by determining the required rate of return on a straight (nonconvertible) issue of the same quality and then determining the present value of the interest and principal payments at this rate of return. Thus, regardless of what happens to the value of the firm's common stock, the lowest value to which the convertible can drop should be its value as a straight bond or preferred stock.

Conversion period. On some issues, the time period during which the convertible can be exchanged for common stock is limited. Many times conversion is not allowed until a specified number of years have passed, or is limited by a terminal conversion date. Still other convertibles may be exchanged at any time during their life. In either case, the **conversion period** is specified when the convertible is originally issued.

Conversion premium. The **conversion premium** is the difference between the convertible's market price and the higher of its security value and its conversion value. It can be expressed as an absolute dollar value, in which case it is defined as

$$\begin{matrix} \text{conversion} \\ \text{premium} \end{matrix} = \begin{pmatrix} \text{market price of} \\ \text{the convertible} \end{pmatrix} - \begin{pmatrix} \text{higher of the security value} \\ \text{and conversion value} \end{pmatrix} \quad (20A\text{-}3)$$

In describing convertibles, we have introduced a number of terms. To eliminate confusion, Table 20A.1 summarizes them.

STOP AND THINK

As you recall, the agency problem deals with conflicts of interest between stockholders, bondholders, and managers. Convertible bonds, which allow bondholders to benefit from the price appreciation of equity, help align the interests of stockholders and bondholders and reduce the agency problem.

WHY ISSUE CONVERTIBLES?

The major reason for choosing to issue convertibles rather than straight debt, preferred stock, or common stock is the fact that interest rates on convertibles are indifferent to the issuing firm's risk level.

While higher risk and uncertainty bring on higher interest costs in straight debt, this is not necessarily the case with convertibles. If we think about a convertible as a package of straight debt and a convertible feature allowing the holder to purchase common stock at a set price, an

Conversion value

The total market value of the common stock for which it can be exchanged.

Security value

The price the convertible security would sell for in the absence of its conversion feature.

Conversion period

The time period during which the convertible can be exchanged for common stock.

Conversion premium

The difference between the convertible's market price and the higher of its security value and its conversion value.

increase in risk and uncertainty certainly raises the cost of the straight-debt portion of the convertible. However, the convertibility feature benefits from this increase in risk and uncertainty and the increase in stock price volatility that follows. In effect, the conversion feature only has value if the stock price rises; otherwise it has zero value. The more risk and stock price volatility, the greater the likelihood that the conversion feature will be of value at some point before the expiration date. As a result, more risk and uncertainty increase the value of the conversion feature of the convertible. Thus the negative effect of an increase in risk and uncertainty on the straight-debt portion of a convertible is partially offset by the positive effect on the conversion feature. The result of all this is that the interest rate associated with convertible debt is, to an extent, indifferent to the risk level of the issuing firm. The coupon rates for medium- and high-risk companies issuing convertibles and straight debt might be as follows:

	Company Risk	
	Medium	**High**
Convertible debt	8%	8.25%
Straight debt	11	13

Thus convertible debt may allow companies with a high level of risk to raise funds at a relatively favorable rate.

STOP AND THINK

Given what you have learned so far about convertibles, it makes sense that convertibles tend to be issued most frequently by smaller firms with lower bond ratings, high growth rates, and more than average leverage. In addition, convertibles tend to be subordinated and unsecured.

VALUATION OF A CONVERTIBLE

The valuation of a convertible depends primarily upon two factors: the value of the straight debenture or preferred stock and the value of the security if it were converted into common stock. Complicating the valuation is the fact that investors are in general willing to pay a premium for the conversion privilege, which allows them to hedge against the future. If the price of the common stock should rise, the investor would participate in capital gains; if it should decline, the convertible security will fall only to its value as a straight debenture or preferred stock.

In examining the Union Carbide convertible debenture, let us assume that if it were selling as a straight debenture, its price would be $785.46. Thus, regardless of what happens to its common stock, the lowest value the convertible can drop to is $785.46. The conversion value, on the other hand, is $676.06, so this convertible is worth more as straight debt than if it were common stock. However, the real question is: Why are investors willing to pay a conversion premium of 16.1 percent over its security or conversion value for this Union Carbide debenture? Quite simply—because investors are willing to pay for the chance for capital gains without the large risk of loss.

Figure 20A.1 graphically depicts the relationship between the value of the convertible and the price of its common stock. The bond value of the convertible serves as a floor for the value of the investment: When the conversion value reaches the convertible's security value (point *A*), the value of the convertible becomes dependent upon its conversion value. In effect, the convertible security is valued as a bond when the price of the common stock

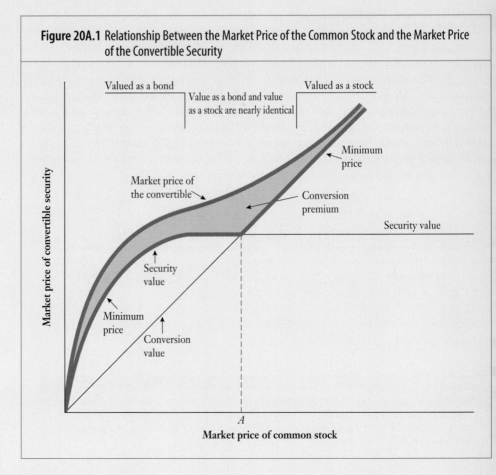

Figure 20A.1 Relationship Between the Market Price of the Common Stock and the Market Price of the Convertible Security

is low and as common stock when the price of the common stock rises. Of course, if the firm is doing poorly and in financial distress, both the common stock price and the security value will suffer. In the extreme, when the firm's total value falls to zero both the common stock and any debt that the firm had issued would have no value. Although the minimum price of the convertible is determined by the higher of either the straight bond or preferred stock price or the conversion value, investors also pay a premium for the conversion option. Again, this premium results because convertible securities offer investors stable income from debenture or preferreds—and thus less risk of price decline due to adverse stock conditions—while retaining capital gains prospects from stock price gains. In effect, downside stock price variability is hedged away, whereas upside variability is not.

STOP AND THINK

As you look at the convertible and warrant markets, as well as the options and futures markets covered earlier in this chapter, keep in mind the fact that these markets are continuously evolving. For example, recently a variation of the convertible debenture called an exchangeable debenture has gained popularity. An exchangeable debenture is similar to a convertible debenture except that it can be exchanged at the option of the holder for the common stock of another company. For example, in late 1989, Millicom, Inc., issued $60 million of subordinated exchangeable debentures due in 2014. These debentures are identical to convertibles except that they can be exchanged for stock in Racal Electronics, of which Millicom owns 30 million shares. Here, then, we are only describing several basic securities of which there are unlimited variations in the financial markets.

WARRANTS

A **warrant** provides the investor with an option to purchase a fixed number of shares of common stock at a predetermined price during a specified time period. Warrants have been used in the past primarily by weaker firms as sweetener attachments to bonds or preferred stock to improve their marketability. However, in April 1970, when AT&T included them as a part of a major financing package, warrants achieved a new level of respectability.

Warrant

An option to purchase a fixed number of shares of common stock at a predetermined price during a specified time period.

Only recently have warrants been issued in conjunction with common stock. Their purpose is essentially the same as when they are issued in conjunction with debt or preferred stock; that is, to improve the reception in the market of the new offering or make a tender offer too attractive to turn down.

Although warrants are similar to convertibles in that both provide investors with a chance to participate in capital gains, the mechanics of the two instruments differ greatly. From the standpoint of the issuing firm, there are two major differences. First, when convertibles are exchanged for common stock, debt is eliminated and fixed finance charges are reduced; whereas when warrants are exchanged, fixed charges are not reduced. Second, when convertibles are exchanged, there is no cash inflow into the firm—the exchange is merely one type of security for another. But with warrants, because they are merely an option to buy the stock at a set price, a cash flow accompanies the exchange.

CHARACTERISTICS AND FEATURES OF WARRANTS

Exercise price. The **exercise price** is that at which the warrant allows its holder to purchase the firm's common stock. The investor trades a warrant plus the exercise price for common stock. Typically, when warrants are issued, the exercise price is set above the current market price of the stock. Thus, if the stock price does not rise above the exercise price, the warrant will never be converted. In addition, there can also be a step-up exercise price, where the warrant's exercise price changes over time.

Warrant exercise price

The price at which a warrant allows its holder to purchase the firm's common stock.

Warrant expiration date. Although some warrants are issued with no warrant expiration date, most warrants are set to expire after a number of years. In issuing warrants as opposed to convertibles, the firm gives up some control over when the warrants will be exercised. With convertibles, the issuing company can force conversion by calling the issue or using step-up conversion prices, whereas with warrants only the approach of the expiration date or the use of step-up exercise prices can encourage conversion.

Detachability. Most warrants are said to be detachable in that they can be sold separately from the security to which they were originally attached. Thus, if an investor purchases a primary issuance of a corporate bond with a warrant attached, he or she has the option of selling the bond alone, selling the warrant alone, or selling the combination intact. *Nondetachable* warrants cannot be sold separately from the security to which they were originally attached. Such a warrant can be separated from the senior security only by being exercised.

Exercise ratio. The **exercise ratio** states the number of shares that can be obtained at the exercise price with one warrant. If the exercise ratio on a warrant were 1.5, one warrant would entitle its owner to purchase 1.5 shares of common stock at its exercise price.

REASONS FOR ISSUING WARRANTS

Sweetening debt. Warrants attached to debt offerings provide a feature whereby investors can participate in capital gains while holding debt. The firm can thereby increase the demand for the issue, increase the proceeds, and lower the interest costs. Attaching warrants to long-term debt is a sweetener, performing essentially the same function that the convertibility feature on debt performs; that is, giving investors something they want and thereby increasing the marketability and demand for the bonds.

Additional cash inflow. If warrants are added to sweeten a debt offering, the firm will receive an eventual cash inflow when and if the warrants are exercised; a convertibility feature would not provide this additional inflow.

Valuation of a warrant. Because the warrant is an option to purchase a specified number of shares of stock at a specified price for a given length of time, the market value of the warrant will be primarily a function of the common stock price. To understand the valuation of warrants, we must define two additional terms, the minimum price and the premium. Let us look at the Photon Pharmaceutical warrants with an expiration date of December 31, 2001, an exercise ratio of 1.00, and let's assume an exercise price of $80 through the expiration date. This means that any time until expiration on December 31, 2001, an investor with one warrant can purchase one share of Photon Pharmaceutical stock at $80 regardless of the market price of that stock. Let's assume these Photon Pharmaceutical warrants were selling at $5.50, and the Photon Pharmaceutical stock was selling for $56.75 per share.

Minimum price. The *minimum price* of a warrant is determined as follows:

$$\text{minimum price} = \left(\begin{array}{c}\text{market price of}\\\text{common stock}\end{array}\right) - \left(\begin{array}{c}\text{exercise}\\\text{price}\end{array}\right) \times \text{exercise ratio} \qquad (20A\text{-}4)$$

In the Photon Pharmaceutical example, the exercise price is greater than the price of the common stock ($80 as opposed to $56.75). In this case, the minimum price of the warrant is considered to be zero, because things simply do not sell for negative prices [($56.75 − $80) × 1.00 = −$23.25]. If, for example, the price of the Photon

Pharmaceutical common stock rose to $86 per share, the minimum price on the warrant would become ($86 − $80) × 1.00 = $6. This would tell us that this warrant could not fall below a price of $6.00, because if it did, investors could realize immediate trading profits by purchasing the warrants and converting them along with the $80 exercise price into common stock until the price of the warrant was pushed up to the minimum price. This process of simultaneously buying and selling equivalent assets for different prices is called *arbitrage*.

Premium. The premium is the amount above the minimum price for which the warrant sells:

$$\text{premium} = \left(\begin{array}{c}\text{market price}\\ \text{of warrant}\end{array}\right) - \left(\begin{array}{c}\text{minimum price}\\ \text{of warrant}\end{array}\right)$$

In the case of the Photon Pharmaceutical warrant, the premium is $5.50 − $0 = $5.50. Investors are paying a premium of $5.50 above the minimum price for the warrant. They are willing to do so because the possible loss is small although the warrant price is only about 9.69 percent of the common stock; in turn, the possible return is large because, if the price of the common stock climbs, the value of the warrant also will climb.

Figure 20A.2 graphs the relationships among the warrant price, the minimum price, and the premium. Point *A* represents the exercise price on the warrant. Once the price of the stock is above the exercise price, the warrant's minimum price takes on positive or nonzero values.

Although the stock price/exercise price ratio is one of the most important factors in determining the size of the premium, several other factors also affect it. One such factor is the time left to the warrant expiration date. As the warrant's expiration date approaches, the size of the premium begins to shrink, approaching zero. A second factor is investors' expectations concerning the capital gains potential of the stock. If they feel favorably about the prospects for price increases in the common stock, a large warrant premium will result, because a stock price increase will effect a warrant price increase. Finally, the degree of price volatility on the underlying common stock affects the size of the warrant premium. The more volatile the common stock price, the higher the warrant premium. As price volatility increases, so does the probability of and potential size of profits.

Figure 20A.2 Valuation of Warrants

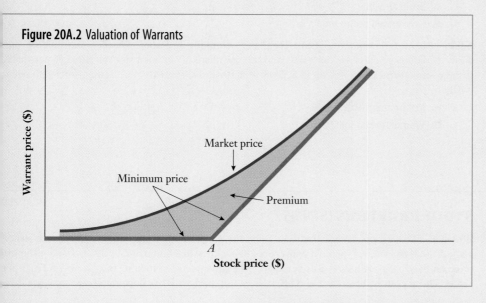

STUDY QUESTIONS

20A-1. Define the following terms:

    a. Conversion ratio

    b. Conversion value

    c. Conversion premium

20A-2. What is a reason for issuing convertible securities?

20A-3. Why does a convertible bond sell at a premium above its value as a bond or common stock?

20A-4. Convertible bonds are said to provide the capital gains potential of common stock and the security of bonds. Explain this statement both verbally and graphically. What happens to the graph when interest rates rise? When they fall?

20A-5. Convertible bonds generally carry lower coupon interest rates than do nonconvertible bonds. If this is so, does it mean that the cost of capital on convertible bonds is lower than on nonconvertible? Why or why not?

20A-6. Explain the difference between a convertible security and a warrant.

20A-7. Explain the valuation of warrants both verbally and graphically.

20A-8. What factors affect the size of the warrant premium? How?

SELF-TEST PROBLEMS

ST-1. (*Convertible Terminology*) In 1999, Winky's Cow Paste, Inc., issued $10 million of $1,000 par value, 10 percent semiannual convertible debentures that come due in 2019. The conversion price on these convertibles is $16.75 per share. The common stock was selling for $14-3/4 per share on a given date shortly after these convertibles were issued. These convertibles have a B– rating, and straight B– debentures were yielding 14 percent on that date. The market price of the convertible was $970 on that date. Determine the following:

    a. Conversion ratio

    b. Conversion value

    c. Security value

    d. Conversion premium

ST-2. (*Warrant Terminology*) Petro-Tech, Inc., currently has some warrants outstanding that allow the holder to purchase, with one warrant, one share of common stock at $18.275 per share. If the common stock was selling at $25 per share and the warrants were selling for $9.50, what would be the

    a. Minimum price?

    b. Warrant premium?

STUDY PROBLEMS (SET A)

20A-1A. (*Convertible Terminology*) In 1999, the Andy Fields Corporation of Delaware issued some $1,000 par value, 6 percent convertible debentures that come due in 2019. The conversion price on these convertibles is $40 per share. The price of the common stock is now $27.25 per share. These convertibles have a BBB rating, and straight BBB debentures are now yielding

9 percent. The market price of the convertible is now $840.25. Determine the following (assume bond interest payments are made annually):

a. Conversion ratio

b. Conversion value

c. Security value

d. Conversion premium

20A-2A. (*Convertible Terminology*) The L. Padis, Jr., Corporation has an issue of 5 percent convertible preferred stock outstanding. The conversion price on these securities is $27 per share to 9/30/03. The price of the common stock is now $13.25 per share. The preferred stock is selling for $17.75. The par value of the preferred stock is $25 per share. Similar quality preferred stock without the conversion feature is currently yielding 8 percent. Determine the following:

a. Conversion ratio

b. Conversion value

c. Conversion premium

20A-3A. (*Warrant Terminology*) The T. Kitchel Corporation has a warrant that allows the purchase of one share of common stock at $30 per share. The warrant is currently selling at $4 and the common stock is priced at $25 per share. Determine the minimum price and the premium of the warrant.

20A-4A. (*Warrant Terminology*) Cobra Airlines has some warrants outstanding that allow the purchase of common stock at the rate of one warrant for each share of common stock at $11.71 per share.

a. Given that the warrants were selling for $3 each and the common stock was selling for $10 per share, determine the minimum price and warrant premium as of that date.

b. Given that the warrants were selling for $9.75 each, and the common stock was selling for $16.375 per share, determine the minimum price and warrant premium as of that date.

20A-5A. (*Warrant Terminology*) International Corporation has some warrants outstanding that allow the purchase of common stock at the price of $22.94 per share. These warrants are somewhat unusual in that one warrant allows for the purchase of 3.1827 shares of common stock at the exercise price of $22.94 per share. Given that the warrants were selling for $6.25 each, and the common stock was selling for $7.25 per share, determine the minimum price and the warrant premium as of that date.

20A-6A. (*Warrants and Their Leverage Effect*) A month ago, you purchased 100 Bolster Corporation warrants at $3 each. When you made your purchase, the market price of Bolster's common stock was $40 per share. The exercise price on the warrants is $40 per share whereas the exercise ratio is 1.0. Today, the market price of Bolster's common stock has jumped up to $45 per share, whereas the market price of Bolster's warrants has climbed to $7.50 each. Calculate the total dollar gain that you would have received if you had invested the same dollar amount in common stock versus warrants. What is this in terms of return on investment?

STUDY PROBLEMS (SET B)

20A-1B. (*Convertible Terminology*) In 1999, the P. Mauney Corporation of Virginia issued some $1,000 par value, 7 percent convertible debentures that come due in 2019. The conversion price on these convertibles is $45 per share. The price of the common stock is now $26 per share. These convertibles have a BBB rating, and straight BBB debentures are now yielding 9 percent. The market price of the convertible is now $840.25. Determine the following (assume bond interest payments are made annually):

a. Conversion ratio

b. Conversion value

c. Security value

d. Conversion premium

20A-2B. (*Convertible Terminology*) The Ecotosleptics Corporation has an issue of 6 percent convertible preferred stock outstanding. The conversion price on these securities is $28 per share to 9/30/03. The price of the common stock is now $14 per share. The preferred stock is selling for $20. The par value of the preferred stock is $25 per share. Similar quality preferred stock without the conversion feature is currently yielding 8 percent. Determine the following:

    a. Conversion ratio

    b. Conversion value

    c. Conversion premium

20A-3B. (*Warrant Terminology*) The Megacorndoodles Corporation has a warrant that allows the purchase of one share of common stock at $32 per share. The warrant is currently selling at $5 and the common stock is priced at $24 per share. Determine the minimum price and the premium of the warrant.

20A-4B. (*Warrant Terminology*) Taco Fever has some warrants outstanding that allow the purchase of common stock at the rate of one warrant for each share of common stock at $11.75 per share.

    a. Given that the warrants were selling for $4 each, and the common stock was selling for $9 per share, determine the minimum price and warrant premium as of that date.

    b. Given that the warrants were selling for $7 each, and the common stock was selling for $15.375 per share, determine the minimum price and warrant premium as of that date.

20A-5B. (*Warrant Terminology*) Fla'vo'phone Corporation has some warrants outstanding that allow the purchase of common stock at the price of $22.94 per share. These warrants are somewhat unusual in that one warrant allows for the purchase of 4.257 shares of common stock at the exercise price of $22.94 per share.

    a. Given that the warrants were selling for $6.75 each, and the common stock was selling for $8 per share, determine the minimum price and the warrant premium as of that date.

20A-6B. (*Warrants and Their Leverage Effect*) A month ago, you purchased 100 Annie Kay's Corporation warrants at $2.75 each. When you made your purchase, the market price of Annie Kay's common stock was $35 per share. The exercise price on the warrants is $35 per share whereas the exercise ratio is 1.0. Today, the market price of Annie Kay's common stock has jumped up to $40 per share, whereas the market price of Annie Kay's warrants has climbed to $6.75 each. Calculate the total dollar gain that you would have received if you had invested the same dollar amount in common stock versus warrants. What is this in terms of return on investment?

SELF-TEST SOLUTIONS

SS-1. a. conversion ratio = par value of convertible security/conversion price

$$= \frac{\$1,000}{\$16.75}$$

$$= 59.70 \text{ shares}$$

b. conversion value $= \left(\begin{array}{c}\text{conversion} \\ \text{ratio}\end{array}\right) \times \left(\begin{array}{c}\text{market value per share} \\ \text{of common stock}\end{array}\right)$

$$= 59.70 \text{ shares} \times \$14.75/\text{share}$$

$$= \$880.58$$

c. security value $= \displaystyle\sum_{t=1}^{40} \dfrac{\$50}{(1+.07)^t} + \dfrac{\$1,000}{(1+.07)^{40}}$

$\qquad\qquad\qquad = \$50(13.332) + \$1,000(.067)$

$\qquad\qquad\qquad = \$666.60 + \$67$

$\qquad\qquad\qquad = \$733.60$

(*Note:* Because this debenture pays interest semiannually, $t = 20$ years $\times 2 = 40$ and $i = 14\%/2 = 7\%$ in the calculations.)

d. conversion premium $= \left(\begin{array}{c}\text{market price of}\\ \text{the convertible}\end{array}\right) - \left(\begin{array}{c}\text{higher of the security value}\\ \text{and conversion value}\end{array}\right)$

$\qquad\qquad\qquad\qquad = \$970.00 - \$880.58$

$\qquad\qquad\qquad\qquad = \$89.42$

SS-2. a. minimum price $= \left(\begin{array}{c}\text{market price of}\\ \text{common stock}\end{array} - \begin{array}{c}\text{exercise}\\ \text{price}\end{array}\right) \times \left(\begin{array}{c}\text{exercise}\\ \text{ratio}\end{array}\right)$

$\qquad\qquad\qquad = (\$25.00 - \$18.275) \times (1.0)$

$\qquad\qquad\qquad = \$6.725$

b. warrant premium $= \left(\begin{array}{c}\text{market price}\\ \text{of warrant}\end{array}\right) - \left(\begin{array}{c}\text{minimum price}\\ \text{of warrant}\end{array}\right)$

$\qquad\qquad\qquad = (\$9.50 - \$6.725)$

$\qquad\qquad\qquad = \$2.775$

Learning Objectives

Active Applications

World Finance

Practice

CHAPTER 21

CORPORATE RESTRUCTURING: COMBINATIONS AND DIVESTITURES

INTRODUCTION

History shows us that mergers and acquisitions come in waves. During the 1960s and early 1970s, there was the diversification wave during which firms acquired very divergent businesses and combined them into huge conglomerates. This period saw the building of corporate giants that later became the target for bust-up mergers of the 1980s. During this period, corporate raiders such as Carl Icahn and Sir James Goldsmith acquired many of the corporate behemoths formed during the earlier merger wave and busted them up, selling off the pieces as independent companies in the belief that the corporate giants were worth more dead than alive. The 1990s have given rise to the largest merger wave of all. This merger wave has been characterized as one driven by strategic acquisitions whereby the buyer hopes that, by merging with the seller, the value of the whole (merged firm) will be greater than the sum of the values of the parts (the buyer and seller firms).

If we gauge mergers in terms of their impact on the stock prices of the merging firms at the time of the merger announcement, many of the mergers of the 1990s have destroyed rather than created value. The following mergers provide interesting cases in point:

Acquiring Company	Target Company	Acquisition Price	Year Completed	CAGR*
Quaker Oats	Snapple Beverage	$ 1.70 billion	1994	.726
Novell	Wordperfect	1.42 billion	1994	.773
Time Inc.	Warner Communications	12.84 billion	1990	.790
Eli Lilly	PCS Health	4.10 billion	1994	.971
AT&T	NCR	7.53 billion	1991	1.02

*CAGR is the compound annual growth rate in market value divided by industry index, based on acquirer total return 3 months before announcement and 36 months thereafter, or longest time period available.

SOURCE: Phillip L. Zweig, Judy Perlman Kline, Stephanie Anderson Forest, and Kevin Gudridge, "Special Report: The Case Against Mergers," *Business Week* (October 30, 1995): 123–130. Reprinted from the October 30 issue of Business Week by special permission. © 1995 by McGraw-Hill Companies.

In the last column of the preceding exhibit, we see the ratio of the compound annual rate of growth in market value divided by that of the firm's industry growth rate for the period beginning 3 months before the announced merger and ending 36 months afterwards. Note that in only one case is the ratio greater than 1, thus indicating that the merged firm outperformed its industry counterparts. This is a limited sample of transactions but it does raise the important question: Do mergers destroy shareholder wealth? The answer is a simple one: only when you pay too much. Thus in this chapter, we will address two fundamental questions: "What are good (shareholder wealth enhancing) reasons for mergers?" and "How much is a potential acquisition worth?"

CHAPTER PREVIEW

Chapter 21 presents an overview of corporate restructuring. Corporate restructuring can be thought of in terms of two broad categories of activities: combining or merging independent firms into a single entity and breaking up or de-merging firms into multiple independent components. The restructuring of the nineties provides an example of the former whereas the restructuring of the eighties was all about the latter.

Our discussion of corporate restructuring begins with a discussion of why mergers might create value. As the term "might" suggests, not all mergers do create value. Next we discuss alternative methods for valuing an entire business enterprise. This chapter will emphasize these axioms: Axiom 1: The Risk-Return Trade-Off—We Won't Take on Additional Risk Unless We Expect to Be Compensated with Additional Return; Axiom 2: The Time Value of Money—A Dollar Received Today Is Worth More Than a Dollar Received in the Future; Axiom 3: Cash—Not Profits—Is King; Axiom 4: Incremental Cash Flows—It's Only What Changes That Counts; Axiom 7: The Agency Problem—Managers Won't Work for the Owners Unless It's in Their Best Interest; and Axiom 8: Taxes Bias Business Decisions.

> **STOP AND THINK**
>
> *Mergers and acquisitions are frequently justified by management on the grounds that merging diversifies the firm, thus reducing risk. However, because the stockholder can diversify personally with more ease and less expense by buying stock in the two companies, there must be other reasons for the merger if it is to add value.*

WHY MERGERS MIGHT CREATE WEALTH

Clearly, for a merger to create wealth, it would have to provide shareholders with something they could not get by merely holding the individual shares of the merging firms. The anticipated benefits from merging are referred to as synergies. There are many potential sources of synergy as we will now discuss.

Economies of Scale

Wealth can be created in a merger through economies of scale. For example, administrative expenses including accounting, data processing, or simply top-management costs, may fall as a percentage of total sales as a result of sharing these resources following a merger.

The sharing of resources can also lead to an increase in the firm's productivity. For example, if two firms sharing the same distribution channels merge, distributors carrying one product may now be willing to carry the other, thereby increasing the sales outlets for the products.

Tax Benefits

If a merger were to result in a reduction of taxes that is not otherwise possible, then wealth is created by the merger. This can be the case with a firm that has lost money and thus generated tax credits but does not currently have a level of earnings sufficient to use those tax credits. Operating losses can be carried back 3 years and forward a total of 15 years. As a result, tax credits that cannot be used and have no value to one firm can take on value when that firm is acquired by another firm that has earnings sufficient to employ the tax credits. In addition, a merger allows for previously depreciated assets to be revalued; wealth is created from the tax benefits arising from the increased depreciation associated with this revaluation of assets.

RELATE TO THE BIG PICTURE

*Once again, we see that tax policy influences business decisions. Sometimes this is the intended consequence of fiscal policies of the federal government, and at others, it is an unanticipated reaction. We find that **Axiom 8: Taxes Bias Business Decisions** provides at least some partial explanation for corporate restructuring activities.*

Unused Debt Potential

Some firms simply do not exhaust their debt capacity. If a firm with unused debt capacity is acquired, the new management can then increase debt financing, and reap the tax benefits associated with the increased leverage.

Complementarity in Financial Slack

When cash-rich bidders and cash-poor targets are combined, wealth may be created. This is particularly true where the cash-poor firm is a small business with limited access to capital markets. In effect, the merger allows positive NPV projects to be accepted that would have been rejected if the merger had not occurred.

ANNUAL REPORT OF BERKSHIRE HATHAWAY, 1981

Of Toads and Princes

Ⓐ Many managements apparently were overexposed in impressionable childhood years to the story in which the imprisoned handsome prince is released from a toad's body by a kiss from a beautiful princess. Consequently, they are certain their managerial kiss will do wonders for the profitability of Company T(arget) . . . investors can always buy toads at the going price for toads. If investors instead bankroll princesses who wish to pay double for the right to kiss the toad, those kisses had better pack some real dynamite. We've observed many kisses but very few miracles. Nevertheless, many managerial princesses remain serenely confident about the future potency of their kisses—even after their corporate backyards are knee-deep in unresponsive toads . . .

We have tried occasionally to buy toads at bargain Ⓑ prices with results that have been chronicled in past reports. Clearly, our kisses fell flat. We have done well with a couple of princes—but they were princes when purchased. At least our kisses didn't turn them into toads. And, finally, we have occasionally been quite successful in purchasing fractional interests in easily identifiable princes at toad-like prices.

SOURCE: Warren Buffett, *1981 Annual Report of Berkshire Hathaway*, 4–5. Copyrighted material. Reprinted with permission of author.

Analysis and Implications . . .

A. A wide variety of "strategies" have been tried to acquire companies that add value. On average, the stockholders of acquiring firms merely break even, and the acquired firm's stockholders realize an average return of 30 percent. So where is the logic to making corporate acquisitions of other corporations? For Berkshire Hathaway and Warren Buffett, the preferred strategy has been to acquire good companies, not "fixer uppers."

B. The key to success in corporate acquisitions is acquiring a business for the right price. The simple truth is that if the acquisition does not offer a positive net present value to the acquiring firm's stockholders, it should not be made.

RELATE TO THE BIG PICTURE

*Sometimes the only hope for returning a firm to strong financial performance involves changing the firm's management. To assure that the new management will act in the best interests of the firm's owners, these changes in management are frequently accompanied by changes in the means by which management is compensated. These changes are aimed at aligning managerial and stockholder interests such that the managers will find it in their best interest to make managerial choices that lead to a maximization of share value. Thus changes in a firm's management and the method of managerial compensation is frequently a reflection of an agency problem which forms the basis for **Axiom 7: The Agency Problem—Managers Won't Work for Owners Unless It's in Their Best Interest**.*

Removal of Ineffective Management

A merger can result in the replacement of inefficient operations, whether in production or management. If a firm with ineffective management can be acquired, it may be possible to replace the current management with a more efficient management team, and thereby create wealth. This may be the case with firms that have grown from solely production into production and distribution companies, or R & D firms that have expanded into production and distribution; the managers simply may not know enough about the new aspects of the firm to manage it effectively.

Increased Market Power

The merger of two firms can result in an increase in market or monopoly power. Although this can result in increased wealth, it may also be illegal. The Clayton Act, as amended by the Celler-Kefauver Amendment of 1950, makes any merger illegal that results in a monopoly or substantially reduces competition. The Justice Department and the Federal Trade Commission monitor all mergers to ensure that they do not result in a reduction of competition.

Reduction in Bankruptcy Costs

There is no question that diversification can reduce the chance of financial failure and bankruptcy. Furthermore, there is a cost associated with bankruptcy. First, if a firm fails and the firm's assets are liquidated, the forced sale frequently results in depressed prices. Moreover, the amount of money actually available for distribution to stockholders is further reduced by selling costs and legal fees that must be paid. Finally, the opportunity cost associated with the delays related to the legal process further reduces the funds available to the shareholder. Therefore, because costs are associated with bankruptcy, reduction of the chance of bankruptcy adds value.

The risk of bankruptcy also entails indirect costs associated with changes in the firm's debt capacity and the cost of debt. As the firm's cash flow patterns stabilize, the risk of default will decline, giving the firm an increased debt capacity and possibly reducing the cost of its debt. Because interest payments are tax deductible, they provide valuable tax savings. Thus monetary benefits are associated with an increased debt capacity. These indirect costs of bankruptcy also spread out into other areas of the firm, affecting things like production and the quality and efficiency of management. Firms with higher probabilities of bankruptcy may have a more difficult time recruiting and retaining quality managers and employees because jobs with that firm are viewed as less secure. This in turn may result in less productivity for these firms. In addition, firms with higher probabilities of bankruptcy may have a more difficult time marketing their product because of customer concern over future availability of the product. In short, there are real costs to bankruptcy. If a merger reduces this possibility of bankruptcy, it creates wealth.

"Chop-Shop" Approach—Buying Below Replacement Cost

The "chop-shop" approach suggests that the sum of the individual parts of a firm may be worth more than the current value of the whole. In the 1980s, many corporate raiders were driven by the fact that it was less expensive to purchase assets through an acquisition than it was to obtain those assets in any other way. This was particularly true of both conglomerates and oil companies. For conglomerates, corporate raiders found that they often sold for less than the sum of the market value of their parts. Much of the merger and acquisition activity associated with oil companies was driven by the fact that it was cheaper to acquire new oil reserves by purchasing a rival oil company than it was through exploration. If assets are mispriced, as this approach seems to suggest, then identifying those assets and revealing this information about the undervalued assets to an investor may result in the creation of wealth.

It should be noted that the free cash flow theory could explain this creation of wealth as easily as a mispricing theory. In particular, the oil industry was characterized in the late 1970s and early 1980s by high prices that provided high levels of cash flow.

These resources were used to finance overexploration and drilling activity in the face of falling oil consumption. In addition, many oil firms engaged in diversification programs in which they acquired retail, computer software, and other very diverse firms. Thus as mergers and restructuring raged through the oil industry, wealth was created through the elimination of wasteful exploration expenditures and the divesture of unrelated businesses.

DETERMINATION OF A FIRM'S VALUE

One of the first problems in analyzing a potential merger involves placing a value on the acquired firm. This task is not easy. The value of a firm depends not only on its cash flow generation capabilities, but also upon the operating and financial characteristics of the acquiring firm. As a result, no single dollar value exists for a company. Instead, a range of values is determined that would be economically justifiable to the prospective acquirer. The final price is then negotiated by the two managements.

To determine a reasonable price for a corporation, several factors are carefully evaluated. We know that the objective of the acquiring firm should be maximization of its stockholders' wealth (stock price). However, quantifying the relevant variables for this purpose is difficult at best. For instance, the primary reason for a merger might be to acquire managerial talent or to complement a strong sales staff with an excellent production department. These *synergistic effects* are difficult to measure using the historical data of the companies involved. We consider four approaches to valuing an acquisition candidate. These include (1) book value, (2) appraisal value, (3) "chop-shop" or "break-up" value and (4) "cash flow" or "going concern" value.

Book Value

The **book value** of a firm's net worth is simply the owner's equity account on the balance sheet. That is, the balance sheet amount of the assets less its outstanding liabilities. For example, if a firm's assets measured at their historical cost less accumulated depreciation is $10 million and the firm's debt totals $4 million, the aggregate book value of the firm's equity is $6 million. Furthermore, if 100,000 shares of common stock are outstanding, the book value per share is $60 ($6 million ÷ 100,000 shares).

Book value does not measure the market value of a company's net worth because it is based on the historical cost of the firm's assets. Seldom do such costs bear a relationship to the value of the organization or its ability to produce earnings.

Although the book value of an enterprise is clearly not the most important factor, it should not be overlooked. It can be used as a starting point to be compared with other analyses. Also, a study of the firm's working capital is particularly important to acquisitions involving a business consisting primarily of liquid assets like financial institutions. Furthermore, in industries where the ability to generate earnings requires large investments in such items as steel, cement, and petroleum, the book value could be a critical factor, especially where plant and equipment are relatively new.

> **Book value**
>
> Generally used in this context to refer to the book or historical cost value of the firm's net worth.

Appraisal Value

An *appraisal value* of a company may be acquired from an independent appraisal firm. The techniques used by appraisers vary widely; however, this value is often closely tied to the replacement cost of the firm's assets. This method of analysis is not adequate by itself, because the value of individual assets may have little relation to the firm's overall ability to generate cash flow, and thus the going-concern value of the firm. However, the appraised value of an enterprise may be beneficial when used in conjunction with other valuation methods. Also, the appraised value may be an important factor in special situations, such as in financial companies, natural resource enterprises, or organizations that have been operating at a loss.[1]

The use of appraisal values does yield several additional advantages. The value according to independent appraisers may permit the reduction of accounting goodwill by increasing the recognized worth of specific assets. *Goodwill* results when the purchase price of a firm exceeds the book value of the assets. Consider a company having a book value of $60,000 that is purchased for $100,000 (the $40,000 difference is goodwill). The $60,000 book value consists of $20,000 in working capital and $40,000 in fixed assets. However, an appraisal might suggest that the current values of these assets are $25,000 and $55,000, respectively. The $15,000 increase ($55,000 − $40,000) in fixed assets permits the acquiring firm to record a larger depreciation expense than would otherwise be possible, thereby reducing taxes. A second reason for an appraisal is to provide a test of the reasonableness of results obtained through methods based upon the going-concern concept. Third, the appraiser may uncover strengths and weaknesses that otherwise might not be recognized, such as in the valuation of patents, secret processes, and partially completed R & D expenditures.

"Chop-Shop" or Break-up Value

The "chop-shop" approach to valuation was first proposed by Dean Lebaron and Lawrence Speidell of Batterymarch Financial Management. Specifically, it attempts to identify multi-industry companies that are undervalued and would be worth more if separated into parts. Very simply, this approach entails attempting to buy assets below their replacement cost.

Any time we confront a technique that suggests that stocks may be inefficiently priced, we should be skeptical. In the case of a multi-industry firm, inefficiency in pricing may be brought on by the high cost of obtaining information. Alternatively, these firms may be worth more if split up because of agency problems. Shareholders of multi-industry companies may feel they have less control of the firm's managers, because additional layers of management may have developed with multi-industry firms. These agency costs may take the form of increased expenditures necessary to monitor the managers, costs associated with organizational change, and opportunity costs associated with poor decisions made as a result of the manager acting in his or her own best interests rather than the best interest of the shareholders.

The "chop-shop" approach attempts to value companies by their various business segments. As it is implemented by Batterymarch, it first attempts to find "pure-play" companies—that is, companies in a single industry from which it computes average "valuation ratios." The ratios frequently used compare total capitalization (debt plus equity) to total sales, to assets, and to income. In effect, these ratios represent the average value of a dollar of sales, a dollar of assets, and a dollar of income for a particular industry based on the average of all pure play companies in that industry. Assuming that these ratios apply to the various business segments of a multi-industry firm, the firm can then be valued by its parts.

For the chop-shop valuation technique to be feasible, we must naturally have information about the various business segments within the firm. This requirement is fulfilled, at least in part, by the reporting rules set forth in *Statement 14* of the Financial Accounting Standards Board (the public accountants governing group). This standard requires that firms provide detailed accounting statements along the various lines of

---

[1] The assets of a financial company and a natural resources firm largely consist of securities and natural reserves, respectively. The value of these individual assets has a direct bearing on the firm's earning capacity. Also, a company operating at a loss may only be worth its liquidation value, which would approximate the appraisal value.

business or what is called Standard Industrial Codes (SIC). Of course, we know that not all firms in the same industry are in fact the same—some have more growth potential or earning ability than others. As such, this methodology should be used cautiously.

The "chop-shop" approach involves three steps.

Step 1: Identify the firm's various business segments and calculate the average capitalization ratios for firms in those industries.

Step 2: Calculate a "theoretical" market value based upon each of the average capitalization ratios.

Step 3: Average the "theoretical" market values to determine the "chop-shop" value of the firm.

EXAMPLE

To illustrate the chop-shop approach, consider Cavos, Inc., with common stock currently trading at a total market price of $13 million. For Cavos, the accounting data set forth four business segments: industrial specialties, basic chemicals, consumer specialties, and basic plastics. Data for these four segments are as follows:

Business Segment	Sales ($000)	Assets ($000)	Income ($000)
Industrial specialties	$ 2,765	$2,206	$186
Basic chemicals	5,237	4,762	165
Consumer specialties	2,029	1,645	226
Basic plastics	1,506	1,079	60
Total	$11,537	$9,692	$637

The three steps for valuing Cavos would be

Step 1: We first identify "pure" companies, that being firms that operate solely in one of the above industries; we then calculate the average capitalization ratios for those firms. This could easily be done using a computer database, such as the Computstat tapes, which provide detailed financial information on most publicly traded firms. The average capitalization ratios for Cavos's four business segments have been determined and are as shown in Table 21.1.

Step 2: Once we have calculated the average market capitalization ratios for the various market segments, we need only multiply Cavos's segment values (that is, segment sales, segment assets, and segment income) times the corresponding capitalization ratios to determine the theoretical market values. This is done in Table 21.2.

Step 3: Finally, the theoretical values must be averaged to calculate the "chop-shop" value of the firm. The average of the three theoretical values in Table 21.2 is $18,923,000, computed as follows:

$$\frac{\text{value based on sales} + \text{value based on assets} + \text{value based on income}}{3}$$

or

$$\frac{(\$23,518,500 + \$21,087,700 + \$12,132,800)}{3}$$

$$= \$18,913,000$$

Hence Cavos, Inc. is selling for significantly less than its chop-shop value—$13 million compared with $18.9 million.

Table 21.1 Average Capitalization Ratios for Industries in Which Cavos, Inc., Is Active

Business Segment	Capitalization Sales	Capitalization Assets	Capitalization Operating Income
Industrial specialties	0.61	1.07	21.49
Basic chemicals	2.29	2.43	17.45
Consumer specialties	3.58	2.92	19.26
Basic plastics	1.71	2.18	15.06

The major limitation of a valuation model such as the chop-shop approach is that it is not derived from any theoretical basis. What it does is assume that average industry capitalization relationships—in this case, ratios of capitalization to sales, assets, and operating income—hold for all firms in a particular industry. Of course, this is frequently not the case. It is easy to identify specific companies that simply produce superior products and whose future earnings growth is, as a result, higher. These companies, because of their expected future growth, should have their sales, assets, and operating income valued higher.

Table 21.2 Calculation of the "Theoretical Values" for Cavos, Inc., Using Market Capitalization Ratios

	Value Based on Market Capitalization/Sales		
Business Segment	(A) Market Capitalization/Sales	(B) Segment Sales	(A) × (B) Theoretical Market Value
Industrial specialties	0.61	$2,765	$ 1,686.7
Basic chemicals	2.29	5,237	11,992.7
Consumer specialties	3.58	2,029	7,263.8
Basic plastics	1.71	1,506	2,575.3
Total			$23,518.5

	Value Based on Market Capitalization/Assets		
Business Segment	(A) Market Capitalization/Assets	(B) Segment Assets	(A) × (B) Theoretical Market Value
Industrial specialties	1.07	$2,206	$ 2,360.4
Basic chemicals	2.43	4,762	11,571.7
Consumer specialties	2.92	1,645	4,803.4
Basic plastics	2.18	1,079	2,352.2
Total			$21,087.7

	Value Based on Market Capitalization/Income		
Business Segment	(A) Market Capitalization/Income	(B) Segment Income	(A) × (B) Theoretical Market Value
Industrial specialties	21.49	$186	$ 3,997.1
Basic chemicals	17.45	165	2,879.3
Consumer specialties	19.26	226	4,352.8
Basic plastics	15.06	60	903.6
Total			$12,132.8

Given this limitation of the chop-shop valuation approach, why have we dealt with it in such detail? The reason is that it reflects a view among some investors and corporate raiders that the replacement value of a firm's assets may exceed the value placed on the firm as a whole in the market. The chop-shop method attempts to value the multi-industry firm by its parts. Moreover, as we will see when we explore the cash flow approach to valuation, there simply is no way to estimate the value of a takeover candidate with complete confidence. Thus this method provides the decision maker with additional information.

RELATE TO THE BIG PICTURE

*Estimation of the value of a firm entails use of four of the fundamental axioms of finance. Specifically, **Axiom 1: The Risk-Return Trade-Off—We Won't Take on Additional Risk Unless We Expect to Be Compensated with Additional Return**, when assessing the proper opportunity cost for the investment. **Axiom 2: The Time Value of Money**, along with **Axiom 4: Incremental Cash Flows** and **Axiom 3: Cash—Not Profits—Is King**, provide guidance in determining that it is cash flows adjusted to reflect their present value that determine firm value.*

The Cash Flow or "Going Concern" Value

This final valuation approach is familiar to us from our study of capital budgeting. Using the cash flow approach to merger valuation requires that we estimate the incremental net cash flows available to the bidding firm as a result of the merger or acquisition. The present value of these cash flows then will be determined, and this will be the maximum amount that should be paid for the target firm. The initial outlay then can be subtracted out to calculate the net present value from the merger. Although this is very similar to a capital-budgeting problem, there are differences, particularly in estimating the initial outlay.

Finding the present value of the cash flows for a merger involves a five-step process:

Step 1: Estimate the incremental after-tax cash flows available from the target firm. This includes all synergistic cash flows (including those to both the bidding and target firms) created as a result of the acquisition. It should also be noted that interest expenses are not included in these cash flows, as they are accounted for in the required rate of return.

Step 2: Estimate the after-tax risk-adjusted discount rate associated with cash flows from the target firm. The target firm's, not the bidding firm's, required rate of return is appropriate here. The reason is that we are acquiring the target firm thus its financial and operating risk characteristics are relevant to its valuation. If there is any anticipated change in financing policy associated with the target firm as a result of the acquisition, this change should also be considered.

Step 3: Calculate the present value of the incremental cash flows from the target firm.

Step 4: Estimate the initial outlay associated with the acquisition. The initial outlay is defined here as the market value of all securities and cash paid out plus the market value of all liabilities assumed.

Step 5: Calculate the net present value of the acquisition by subtracting the initial outlay from the present value of the incremental cash flows from the target firm.

Estimation of the incremental after-tax cash flows resulting from an acquisition is often difficult. Thus a certain lack of precision is inherent in these calculations because of the problem of estimating the synergistic gains from combining the two firms. For example, it is very difficult to estimate the gains that might be expected from any reduction in bankruptcy costs, increased market power, or reduction in agency costs that might occur. Still, it is imperative that we attempt to estimate these gains if we are to place a proper value on the target firm. Once the required rate of return is determined, the present value of the incremental cash flows from acquiring the target firm can then be calculated. The final step then becomes the calculation of the initial outlay associated with the acquisition.

EXAMPLE

Let's look at the valuation of Tabbypaw Pie, Inc., which is being considered as a possible takeover target by ALF, Inc. as an illustration of cash flow or going concern valuation. Currently, Tabbypaw Pie uses 30 percent debt in its capital structure, but ALF plans on increasing the debt ratio to 40 percent (we will assume that only debt and equity are used) once the acquisition is completed. The after-tax cost of debt capital for Tabbypaw Pie is estimated to be 7 percent, and we will assume that this rate does not change as Tabbypaw's capital structure changes. The cost of equity after the acquisition is expected to be 20.8 percent. The current market value of Tabbypaw's debt outstanding is $110 million, all of which will be assumed by ALF. Also, let's assume that ALF intends to pay $260 million in cash and common stock for all of Tabbypaw Pie's stock in addition to assuming all of Tabbypaw's debt. Currently, the market price of Tabbypaw Pie's common stock is $210 million.

Step 1: Estimate the incremental cash flows from the target firm, including the synergistic flows, such as any possible flows from tax credits. This estimation for Tabbypaw is provided in Table 21.3. Here we are assuming that any cash flows after 2002 will be constant at $75 million. Also, we subtract any funds that must be reinvested in the firm in the form of capital expenditures that are required to support the firm's increasing profits.

Step 2: Determine an appropriate risk-adjusted discount rate for evaluating Tabbypaw. Here we will use the weighted cost of capital (k_0) for Tabbypaw as our discount rate, where the weighted cost of capital is calculated as

$$k_0 = W_d K_d (1 - T) + W_c K_c$$

Table 21.3 Estimated Incremental Cash Flows from Tabbypaw Pie, Inc. ($ millions)

	1998	1999	2000	2001	2002 and Thereafter
Net sales	$496	$536	$606	$670	$731
Cost of goods sold	354	385	444	500	551
Administrative and selling expenses	28	30	32	35	38
Earnings before depreciation and interest	114	121	130	135	142
Depreciation	39	40	41	42	43
Earnings before interest and taxes	75	81	89	93	99
Taxes (incremental)	27	30	34	36	39
Net income	48	51	55	57	60
+ Depreciation	39	40	41	42	43
− Capital expenditures	24	25	26	27	28
Net after-tax cash flow (before interest)	$ 63	$ 66	$ 70	$ 72	$ 75

where W_d, W_c = the percentage of funds provided by debt and common, respectively, and K_d, K_c = the cost of debt and common, respectively, and $T =$ the corporate tax rate.

For Tabbypaw,

$$k_0 = (.40)(.07) + (.60)(.208) = .1528, \text{ or } 15.28\%$$

Step 3: Next we must calculate the present value of the incremental cash flows expected from the target firm, as given in Table 21.3. Assuming that cash flows do not change after 2002, but continue at the 2002 level in perpetuity, and discounting these cash flows at the 15.28 percent weighted average cost of capital, we get

$$\begin{pmatrix} \text{present value} \\ \text{of all cash flows} \end{pmatrix} = \begin{pmatrix} \text{present value} \\ \text{of 1995–1998} \\ \text{cash flows} \end{pmatrix} + \begin{pmatrix} \text{present value} \\ \text{of cash flows} \\ \text{after 1998} \end{pmatrix}$$

where the present value of cash flows for 1998 through 2001 would be $190.772 million, determined as follows:

$$\frac{\$63}{(1+.1528)} + \frac{\$66}{(1+.1528)^2} + \frac{\$70}{(1+.1528)^3} + \frac{\$72}{(1+.1528)^4} = \$190.772 \text{ million}$$

and the present value of the $75 million cash flow stream, beginning in 2002, is computed to be $277.921 million.[2]

$$\frac{\dfrac{\$75}{.1528}}{(1+.1528)^4} = \$277.921$$

Thus the present value of the cash inflows associated with the acquisition of Tabbypaw Pie by ALF is $468.693 million, or $468,693,000; that is, the sum of $190.772 million and $277.921 million.

Step 4: Next we estimate the initial outlay associated with the acquisition. As already noted, the initial outlay is defined as the market value of all securities and cash paid out plus the market value of all debt liabilities assumed. In this case, the market value of the assumed debt obligations is $110 million. This amount, along with the acquisition price of $260 million, comprise the initial outlay of $370 million.

Step 5: Finally, the net present value of the acquisition is calculated by subtracting the initial outlay (calculated in step 4) from the present value of the incremental cash flows from the target firm (calculated in step 3):

$$\text{NPV acquisition} = \text{PV inflows} - \text{initial outlay}$$

$$= \$468,693,000 - \$370,000,000$$

$$= \$98,693,000$$

Thus the acquisition should be undertaken because it has a positive net present value. In fact, ALF could pay up to $468.693 million for Tabbypaw Pie.

---

[2]Remember that we find the present value of an infinite stream of cash flows, where the amount is constant in each year, as follows:

$$\text{value} = \frac{\text{annual cash flow}}{\text{required rate of return}}$$

Because the cash flows do not begin until the fifth year, our equation is finding the value at the end of the fourth year; thus, we must discount the value back for 4 years.

THE NEW YORK TIMES, AUGUST 15, 1994

Tough Leader Wields the Ax at Scott

The two brass ornaments that decorate the desk of Albert J. Dunlap are circling sharks. A pouncing brass lion rules his conference table. And a brass eagle stoops to its prey in his reception room. "I like predators," said Mr. Dunlap, the chief executive of the Scott Paper Company, fixing an office visitor with steely blue eyes. "I like them because they live by their wits."

To be sure, the 57-year-old turn-around specialist, who announced the biggest corporate revamping in Scott's history, has acquired a few predatory nicknames himself. When asked about them, he smiled, paused, and said: "On the whole, I prefer to be called Rambo in Pinstripes rather than Chainsaw. That makes me sound like a serial killer, don't you think?"

Ⓐ Mr. Dunlap said both sobriquets were quite popular in England, where he lived for eight years while turning around Crown Zellerbach and Diamond International for Sir James Goldsmith, the British-French financier. Then Mr. Dunlap restructured units of Consolidated Press Holdings, the Australian media company led by Kerry Packer.

Cutting 10,500 Jobs

Now Mr. Dunlap, a perpetual-motion machine with a bulldozer voice and a caustic wit, is applying his intensity to the world's largest producer of tissue products. In early August, Mr. Dunlap announced that 10,500 jobs—nearly a third of the company's work force—would be eliminated by the end of year. The cutback superseded the more gradual three-year reduction of 8,300 jobs announced last November. In scope and in number of jobs, Mr. Dunlap said, this is the largest revamping he has ever tried.

Mr. Dunlap, who came out of retirement to join Scott in April, trained as a paratrooper before he graduated from West Point in 1960. (He continues to wear his class ring.) And though he no longer jumps out of airplanes, he is still "taking frightening jumps out of the sky into strange corporations," he said.

Ⓑ After touchdown, instead of sinking in the quicksands of corporate culture, Mr. Dunlap has sought to transform the companies he heads. "You must get rid of the people who represent the old culture, or they will fight you," he said. "And you have to get rid of all the old symbols."

Many Scott employees are in a state of shock, dread, and anger as they wait for their managers to decide who will go and who will stay. "Hundreds of people are already cleaning out their offices, and most people are assuming they're not staying," said Susan Kent, a 10-year employee on the corporate human relations staff. Ms. Kent has already learned her fate: she was let go last week.

Dottie Carrigan, a purchasing specialist who has worked for Scott for 19 years, did not know if she would be dismissed but found the courage to say that Mr. Dunlap "has no idea of the quality or the spirit or the integrity of the people he's letting go." "It's a very painful thing," she said.

But Mr. Dunlap says he sympathizes with the pain of his workers. "I come from a working-class family, and lots of times my father was out of work due to no fault of his own," referring to Albert Sr., a shop steward at Todd Shipyards in Hoboken, N.J. where Mr. Dunlap survived what he called an inner-city childhood.

"They call me abrasive, but I'm really just a catalyst," Mr. Dunlap added. "It doesn't make any sense to sacrifice 100 percent of the people at this company to save 30 percent of the people we have to let go."

When he came aboard at Scott, Mr.Dunlap bought $2 million worth of stock at $38 a share. When the stock price rose above $50 in June, he bought another $2 million, because he believed in the company.

Praise from Wall Street

The stock is now trading for more than $69, not only because Wall Street loves blood, but because Mr. Dunlap "has been extremely successful in restructuring and is very conservative about the balance sheet," said Kathryn McAuley, an analyst who follows Scott for Brown Brothers Harriman & Company.

Mr. Dunlap said earlier this month that his shrinking of Scott would save $420 million in operating costs next year before taxes. Scott's second-quarter earnings rose 71 percent, to $40.2 million, or 54 cents a share, from $23.5 million, or 32 cents per share, in the quarter a year earlier. Sales, however, declined 2 percent, to $1.18 billion in the quarter.

Scott "was a stodgy old company, and they decided to go outside to someone from a totally different management culture," Mr. Dunlap said. The tough, brash raider described his arrival in the comfortable, patrician offices of Scott as "a strange marriage, born out of desperation."

"It was call me, or call Dr. Kevorkian," he added.

Scott was "in jeopardy of losing our investment-grade rating on our bonds," he asserted. Annual shareholder returns were down 1.9 percent, in comparison with returns in the rest of the paper and forest-products industry, which were up 9.6 percent. "Debt had ballooned, there was a high cost structure, there was no vision and no leadership," he said. "If you ask me about the shareholders, they would have been abused less if they had been captured by terrorists."

A Hands-On Manager

Since his arrival, Mr. Dunlap has been a ubiquitous presence in Scott's corporate suites as he charges down corridors for face-to-face meetings with his managers. "I walked into my office today, and Al was there, sitting in my chair," said Basil L. Anderson, Scott's chief financial officer, one of the few former senior Scott executives to make the new team. (Seven other senior executives were not so lucky.) Mr. Dunlap sat to scribble out a memo.

Internationally, Scott is the market leader in sales of toilet paper, facial tissues, paper towels, napkins, and wet wipes. But domestically, it has been vying for second place with James River, the maker of Northern brand products, while Procter & Gamble is No. 1.

(D) Mr. Dunlap has already put up for sale Scott's S. D. Warren subsidiary, which produces coated printing papers, and other paper-industry businesses, because, he said, "our emphasis will no longer be as a forest-products company."

"We are no longer solely in the business of pumping out tons of paper," he said.

Also on the block is the 55-acre Scott World Headquarters, a symbol of the order he is changing. "It has lovely walking paths, fountains, a pond and geese, too," Mr. Dunlap said of the corporate park with its three squat, modernistic buildings that sit like three boxes of Scott tissues adjacent to the Philadelphia airport. Everything must go: "The pond, the flags, and we'll throw in the geese."

The corporate headquarters staff will be reduced to 200 from 1,600 initially, employees will be consolidated in a building in Philadelphia. Mr. Dunlap would not say how long the company would honor its marriage vows to Philadelphia.

Focus on Signature Brands

Beyond cost-cutting, Mr. Dunlap's vision is to focus on Scott signature brands, he said, reorienting the corporation as a global consumer-product company selling not only to individuals but also to offices, factories, institutions and hotels, a market that accounts for 40 percent of domestic sales.

Emphasizing this core business will enable Scott "to work out our debt reduction and future possible stock buybacks," he said, adding that he intends to create a new corporate culture from the ground up, "building on the adversity that the new team has shared."

(E) There is a belief among workers at Scott that Mr. Dunlap is a short-time hit man who will not fulfill his five-year contract and who took the job to make a lot of money. Their view is that Salomon Brothers and Coopers & Lybrand, the reorganization consultants, are calling the tune.

"Al is hardly a puppet dancing to our tune—boy, let me tell you, with Al, it's just the opposite," said C. Don Burnett, a senior partner at Coopers & Lybrand. "There's no question that Al is in charge."

By the accounts of executives who have worked for him, Mr. Dunlap is an exacting leader whose dressing-down of a manager can be as surgical as his rejuggling of a balance sheet.

Mr. Dunlap "Is No Diplomat"

Mr. Dunlap "is no diplomat," Sir James Goldsmith said in a telephone interview from Spain.

Sir James also has high praise for Mr. Dunlap's skills. "At the particular task of repositioning a company, and taking the hard decisions to get it right, I've never met anyone better," Sir James said. "He is a surgeon in the sense that he has to cause bleeding to get the patient right."

To Mr. Dunlap, the huge work-force reduction is not uninhibited bloodletting, but carefully targeted laser surgery. Those who survive it can reap great rewards. More than a decade ago, when Mr. Dunlap brought the near-moribund Lily-Tulip Inc., the paper cup maker, back from the living dead, "everyone was shaking in their boots," said John P. Murtagh, whom Mr. Dunlap brought in as Scott's general counsel in June. "I thought my number was up. But he took me from a low-level lawyer and elevated me above my boss."

"It's a Sin to Lose Money"

As for charges that he is making money off the painful restructuring Mr. Dunlap said: "Scott should be making money for its shareholders. It's a sin to lose money, a mortal sin."

Mr. Dunlap is not among the sinners but the saved. He denied published reports that his net worth is $50 million; he put it at twice that, and several executives he has worked with confirmed that figure.

His wealth gave him a lavish retirement. But by all accounts, Mr. Dunlap did not flourish in it for long. "Al gets bored when all he has to do is go to the golf course or play tennis," Judy, his wife of 26 years, said.

Why, then, did he come out of retirement to head Scott? "He wants to show people, this time, that he is more than Rambo in Pinstripes," said Mr. Burnett of Coopers & Lybrand. "He wants to show the world that he knows how to build a company."

Standing at parade rest behind his desk with the circling sharks, Mr. Dunlap supplied his own answer. "Jimmy said to me once, 'You have a fire in the belly,'" he said, referring to Sir James. "I feel that he was absolutely right."

SOURCE: Glen Collins, "Tough Leader Wields the Ax at Scott," *The New York Times* (August 15, 1994): C1, C6. Copyright © 1994 by The New York Times Co. Reprinted by permission.

Analysis and Implications...

A. Corporate restructuring is simply another term for major change to the business. In this instance, Scott Paper Company is downsizing its workforce dramatically to improve its profitability.

B. The human side of restructuring can be devastating. When a firm finds itself no longer able to compete effectively with its industry peers, drastic measures are frequently required to make the firm competitive again. In this instance, one third of the firm's workforce will be eliminated.

C. When drastic cost cutting is undertaken, the result is improved earnings and improved prospects of future cash flow. Wall Street discounts these additional expected cash flows back to the present, and the resulting present value becomes the basis for an increase in the firm's stock price. In this instance, the source of the increase in share price can be traced directly to the firm's cost cutting efforts which focus primarily on reducing the firm's workforce.

D. In addition to reductions in workforce, other tools of restructuring typically include refocusing on the firm's core business by selling off subsidiaries and divisions that are not tied directly on the core business. In addition, lavish corporate assets such as corporate jets, apartment complexes in resort areas, and plush corporate headquarters, are frequently sold.

E. In 1998, Sunbeam's board of directors fired Mr. Dunlap.

DIVESTITURES

Although the merger-and-acquisition phenomenon has been a major influence in restructuring the corporate sector, divestitures, or what we might call "reverse mergers," may have become an equally important factor. In fact, preliminary research to date would suggest that we may be witnessing a new era in the making—one where the public corporation has become a more efficient vehicle for increasing and maintaining stockholder wealth.[3] Whereas corporate management once seemed to behave as if 2 + 2 were equal to 5, especially during the conglomerate heyday of the 1960s, the wave of reverse mergers seems based on the counter proposition that 5 − 1 is 5. And the market's consistently positive response to such deals seems to be providing broad confirmation of the "new math."[4]

A successful divestiture allows the firm's assets to be used more efficiently and therefore to be assigned a higher value by the market forces. It essentially eliminates a division or subsidiary that does not fit strategically with the rest of the company; that is, it removes an operation that does not contribute to the company's basic purposes.

The different types of divestitures may be summarized as follows:

1. **Selloff.** A selloff is the sale of a subsidiary, division, or product line by one company to another. For example, Radio Corporation of America (RCA) sold its finance company and General Electric sold its metallurgical coal business.

2. **Spinoff.** A spinoff involves the separation of a subsidiary from its parent, with no change in the equity ownership. The management of the parent company gives up operating control of the subsidiary, but the shareholders retain the same percentage ownership in both firms. New shares representing ownership in the diverted assets are issued to the original shareholders on a pro-rata basis.

3. **Liquidation.** A liquidation in this context is not a decision to shut down or abandon an asset. Rather, the assets are sold to another company, and the proceeds are distributed to the stockholders.

4. **Going private.** A company goes private when its stock that has traded publicly is purchased by a small group of investors, and the stock is no longer bought and sold on a public exchange. The ownership of the company is transferred from a diverse group of outside stockholders to a small group of private investors, usually including the firm's management. The leveraged buyout is a special case of going private. As noted earlier in the chapter, the existing shareholders sell their shares to a small group of investors. The purchasers of the stock use the firm's unused debt capacity to borrow the funds to pay for the stock. Thus the new investors acquire the firm with little, if any, personal investment. However, the firm's debt ratio may increase by as much as tenfold. Often the objective is to reorganize the company (sometimes selling of unrelated businesses) and bringing the company back public in a few years.

Selloff

The sale of a subsidiary, division, or product line by one firm to another.

Spinoff

The separation of a subsidiary from its parent, with no change in the equity ownership. The management of the parent company gives up operating control over the assets involved in the spinoff but the stockholders retain ownership, albeit through shares of the newly created spinoff company.

HOW FINANCIAL MANAGERS USE THIS MATERIAL

Businesses grow in one of two ways. They acquire assets, or they acquire operating firms. This chapter is about the latter method and focuses on the financial consequences of acquiring and selling whole firms. The 1990s have seen the largest wave of mergers and acquisitions ever in recorded economic history. In every transaction, there is a buyer and a seller who must come to agreement on the price at which the transaction will take place.

---

[3]See Robert Comment and Gregg A. Jarrell, 1995, "Corporate Focus and Stock Returns," *Journal of Financial Economics* 37: 67–87; and Kose John and Eli Ofek, 1995, "Asset Sales and Increase in Focus," *Journal of Financial Economics* 37: 105–126.

[4]Joel M. Stern, and Donald H. Chew, Jr. (eds.), *The Revolution in Corporate Finance* (New York: Basis Blackwell, 1986): 416.

The Growing Importance of Multinational Corporations in the World Economy

Multinational corporations are an important force behind the integration of world markets, and they are growing rapidly. In 1996, the most recent year for which the United Nations has figures, the rate of growth in investment by these firms was roughly three times as fast as total investment.

Approximately half of all foreign direct investment involves mergers and acquisitions. This activity allows the multinational firms to quickly achieve a presence in another market and acquire economies of scale in marketing and distribution. However, a disproportionate portion of all international mergers-and-acquisitions activity takes place among developed as opposed to undeveloped countries. As a consequence, the United States is frequently a leading recipient of foreign direct investment as foreign enterprises acquire U.S.-based companies.

Even multinational firms tend to do most of their business within their home market. The typical multinational firm produces more than two-thirds of its output and has two-thirds of its employees in its home country. The five largest multinational corporations are described as follows:

Company	Industry	Foreign assets as % of total	Foreign sales as % of total	Foreign employment as % of total
Royal Dutch/Shell	Energy	67.8	73.3	77.9
Ford	Automotive	29.0	30.6	29.8
General Electric	Electronics	30.4	24.4	32.4
Exxon	Energy	73.1	79.6	53.7
General Motors	Automotive	24.9	29.2	33.9
Averages		45.0	47.4	45.5

SOURCE: UNCTAD.

These firms on average invest 45 percent of their assets out-of-country, receive 47.4 percent of their sales revenues from abroad, and have 45.5 percent of their total workforce employed in a foreign country.

Investment bankers as well as internal company analysts spend countless hours trying to arrive at what they think is the economic value of the target firm. We discussed four basic approaches to valuing a business, and each is widely used in financial practice. In fact, because business valuation is very difficult, the analyst will frequently use multiple methods in an effort to learn more about the economic worth of the enterprise. Frequently, the final valution will be compared with market values of similar firms of similar transactions relative to earnings or cash flow. These market value multiples in conjunction with discounted cash flow estimates provide the backbone of the valuation process.

SUMMARY

Corporate restructuring involves the combination of two or more businesses to form a new firm (merging) and the separation of a single firm into multiple new firms. The process of corporate restructuring has been a critically important facet of the U.S. corporate system. It provides a means for incorporating change into the economic system in ways that facilitate the reallocation of resources toward more productive uses.

Corporate restructuring activities tend to come in waves. During the 1960s, restructuring led to the formation of some of the largest conglomerate firms in U.S. financial history. In the 1980s, behemoth corporate enterprises were bought (frequently in hostile takeovers) and then broken up as a part of what has come to be known as the bust-up takeover wave. In the nineties, we find ourselves in the midst of what has already proven to be the largest restructuring wave in U.S. history. This wave is marked by mergers resulting from consolidations of certain key industries such as banking and financial services, telecommunications, and defense contracting. Throughout all of these periods, the basic question is the same: Does the restructuring create shareholder wealth? So in this chapter, we have focused on two basic issues: "When does it make sense to engage in a merger (or its reverse)?" and "How much should the firm pay for an acquisition or demand for a divestiture?"

The assertion that merger activity creates wealth for the shareholder cannot be maintained with certainty. Only if the merger provides something that the investor cannot do on his or her own can a merger or acquisition be of financial benefit.

OBJECTIVE 1

Determining the value of a firm is a difficult task. In addition to projecting the firm's future profitability, which is a cornerstone in valuation, the acquirer must consider the effects of joining two businesses into a single operation. What may represent a good investment may not be a good merger.

OBJECTIVE 2

Valuing a potential acquisition, like valuing a proposed capital-budgeting expenditure, is both an art and a science. We are essentially trying to forecast the future consequences of ownership, which can never be known with precision. Consequently, we discussed four approaches to determining the value of a company: (1) book value, (2) appraisal value, (3) "chop-shop" or break-up value, and (4) cash flow or "going concern" value. Because there is always a margin of error in the application of any valuation method, we suggested that the methods be used in conjunction with one another in an effort to learn more about the possible range of values for the firm being valued.

KEY TERMS

Appraisal value, 787
Book value, 787

Cash flow or going concern value, 791
Chop-shop or break-up value, 788

Selloff, 798
Spinoff, 798

GO TO:
http://www.prenhall.com/bfm
For downloads and current events associated with this chapter

FINCOACH PRACTICE EXERCISES FOR CHAPTER 21

To maximize your grades and master the mathematics discussed in this chapter, open *FINCOACH* on the **Finance Learning and Development Center** CD and practice problems in the following categories: 1) *Portfolio Diversification* 2) *CAPM* 3) *Project and Firm Valuation II*

STUDY QUESTIONS

21-1. Why might merger activities create wealth?

21-2. Why is book value alone an imperfect measure of the worth of a company?

21-3. What advantages are provided by the use of an appraisal value in valuing a firm?

21-4. What is the concept of the chop-shop valuation procedure?

21-5. Compare the NPV approach used in valuing a merger with the same approach in capital budgeting.

21-6. Explain the different types of divestitures.

SELF-TEST PROBLEMS

ST-1. Using the chop-shop approach, assign a value for the Calvert Corporation, where its common stock is currently trading at a total market price of $5 million. For Calvert, the accounting data set forth two business segments: auto sales and auto specialties. Data for the firm's two segments are as follows:

Business Segment	Segment Sales ($000)	Segment Assets ($000)	Segment Income ($000)
Auto sales	$3,000	$1,000	$150
Auto specialties	2,500	3,000	500
Total	$5,500	$4,000	$650

Industry data for "pure-play" firms have been compiled and are summarized as follows:

Business Segment	Capitalization/ Sales	Capitalization/ Assets	Capitalization/ Operating Income
Auto sales	1.40	3.20	18.00
Auto specialties	.80	.90	8.00

STUDY PROBLEMS (SET A)

21-1A. (*Chop-Shop Valuation*) Using the chop-shop method, determine a value for Aramus, Inc., whose common stock is trading at a total market price of $15 million. For Aramus, the accounting data are divided into three business segments: sunglasses distribution, reading glasses distribution, and technical products. Data for the firm's three segments are as follows:

Business Segment	Segment Sales ($000)	Segment Assets ($000)	Segment Income ($000)
Sunglasses distribution	$ 3,500	$ 1,000	$ 350
Reading glasses distribution	2,000	1,500	250
Technical products	6,500	8,500	1,200
Total	$12,000	$11,000	$1,800

Industry data for "pure-play" firms have been computed and are summarized as follows:

Business Segment	Capitalization/ Sales	Capitalization/ Assets	Capitalization/ Operating Income
Sunglasses distribution	1.0	.8	8.0
Reading glasses distribution	.9	.8	10.0
Technical products	1.2	1.0	7.0

21-2A. (*Free Cash Flow Valuation*) The Argo Corporation is viewed as a possible takeover target by Hilary, Inc. Currently, Argo uses 20 percent debt in its capital structure, but Hilary plans to increase the debt ratio to 30 percent if the acquisition is consummated. The after-tax cost of debt capital for Argo is estimated to be 8 percent, with either 20 or 30 percent debt financing. The cost of equity after the acquisition is expected to be 18 percent. The current market value of Argo's outstanding debt is $40 million, all of which will be assumed by Hilary. Hilary intends to pay $250 million in cash and common stock for all of Argo's stock in addition to assuming all of Argo's debt. Currently, the market price of Argo's common stock is $200 million. Selected items from Argo's financial data are as follows:

	1995	1996	1997	1998	Thereafter
			(Millions)		
Net sales	$200	$225	$240	$250	$275
Administrative and selling expenses	15	20	27	28	30
Depreciation	10	15	17	20	24
Capital expenditures	12	13	15	17	20

In addition, the cost of goods sold runs 60 percent of sales and the marginal tax rate is 34 percent. Compute the net present value of the acquisition.

21-3A. (*Free Cash Flow Valuation*) The Prime Corporation is viewed as a possible takeover target by TVC Enterprises, Inc. Currently, Prime uses 25 percent debt in its capital structure, but TVC plans to increase the debt ratio to 40 percent if the acquisition is consummated. Prime's after-tax cost of debt is 10 percent, which should hold constant. The cost of equity after the acquisition is expected to be 20 percent. The current market value of Prime's debt outstanding is $30 million, all of which will be assumed by TVC. TVC intends to pay $150 million in cash and common stock for all of Prime's stock in addition to assuming all of its debt. Currently, the market price of Prime's common stock is $125 million. Selected items from Prime's financial data are as follows:

	1998	1999	2000	2001	Thereafter
			(Millions)		
Net sales	$300	$330	$375	$400	$425
Administrative and selling expenses	40	50	58	62	65
Depreciation	25	30	35	38	40
Capital expenditures	30	37	45	48	50

In addition, the cost of goods sold runs 60 percent of sales, and the marginal tax rate is 34 percent. Compute the NPV of the acquisition.

STUDY PROBLEMS (SET B)

21-1B. (*Chop-Shop Valuation*) Using the chop-shop approach, assign a value for Cornutt, Inc., whose stock is currently trading at a total market price of $4 million. For Cornutt, the accounting data set forth three business segments: consumer wholesaling, specialty services, and retirement centers. Data for the firm's three segments are as follows:

Business Segment	Segment Sales ($000)	Segment Assets ($000)	Segment Income ($000)
Consumer wholesaling	$1,500	$ 750	$100
Specialty services	800	700	150
Retirement centers	2,000	3,000	600
Total	$4,300	$4,450	$850

Industry data for "pure-play" firms have been compiled and are summarized as follows:

Business Segment	Capitalization/ Sales	Capitalization/ Assets	Capitalization/ Operating Income
Consumer wholesaling	.75	.60	10.00
Specialty services	1.10	.90	7.00
Retirement centers	1.00	.60	6.00

21-2B. (*Chop-Shop Valuation*) Using the chop-shop method, determine a value for Wrongway, Inc., whose common stock is trading at a total market price of $10 million. For Wrongway, the accounting data are divided into three business segments: sunglasses distribution, reading glasses distribution, and technical products. Data for the firm's three segments are as follows:

Business Segment	Segment Sales ($000)	Segment Assets ($000)	Segment Income ($000)
Sunglasses distribution	$2,200	$ 600	$200
Reading glasses distribution	1,000	700	150
Technical products	3,500	5,000	500
Total	$6,700	$6,300	$850

Industry data for "pure-play" firms have been computed and are summarized as follows:

Business Segment	Capitalization/ Sales	Capitalization/ Assets	Capitalization/ Operating Income
Sunglasses distribution	.8	1.0	8.0
Reading glasses distribution	1.2	.9	10.0
Technical products	1.2	1.1	12.0

21-3B. (*Free Cash Flow Valuation*) The Brown Corporation is viewed as a possible takeover target by Cicron, Inc. Currently, Brown uses 20 percent debt in its capital structure, but Cicron plans to increase the debt ratio to 25 percent if the acquisition is consummated. The after-tax cost of debt capital for Brown is estimated to be 8 percent, which holds constant under either capital structure. The cost of equity after the acquisition is expected to be 22 percent. The current market value of Brown's outstanding debt is $75 million, all of which will be assumed by Cicron. Cicron intends to pay $225 million in cash and common stock for all of Brown's stock in addition to assuming all of Brown's debt. Currently, the market price of Brown's common stock is $200 million. Selected items from Brown's financial data are as follows:

	1995	1996	1997	1998	Thereafter
			(Millions)		
Net sales	$260	$265	$280	$290	$300
Administrative and					
selling expenses	25	25	25	30	30
Depreciation	15	17	18	23	30
Capital expenditures	22	18	18	20	22

In addition, the cost of goods sold runs 50 percent of sales and the marginal tax rate is 34 percent. Compute the net present value of the acquisition.

21-4B. (*Free Cash Flow Valuation*) Little Corp. is viewed as a possible takeover target by Big, Inc. Currently, Little uses 20 percent debt in its capital structure, but Big plans to increase the debt ratio to 50 percent if the acquisition goes through. The after-tax cost of debt is 15 percent, which should hold constant. The cost of equity after the acquisition is expected to be 25 percent. The current market value of Little's debt outstanding is $12 million, all of which will be assumed by Big. Big intends to pay $25 million in cash and common stock for all of Little's stock in addition to assuming all of Little's debt. Currently, the market price of Little's common stock is $20 million. Selected items from Little's financial data are as follows:

	1995	1996	1997	1998	Thereafter
			(Millions)		
Net sales	$200	$220	$245	$275	$300
Administrative and					
selling expenses	30	35	38	40	45
Depreciation	18	20	22	25	30
Capital expenditures	20	22	25	28	30

In addition, the cost of goods sold is 70 percent of sales, and the marginal tax rate is 34 percent. Compute the NPV of the acquisition.

SELF-TEST SOLUTION

SS-1.

	Capital-to- Sales	Segment Sales	Theoretical Values
Auto sales	1.40	$3,000	$4,200
Auto specialties	0.80	2,500	2,000
			$6,200

	Capital-to- Assets	Segment Assets	Theoretical Values
Auto sales	3.20	$1,000	$3,200
Auto specialties	0.90	3,000	2,700
			$5,900

	Capital-to- Income	Segment Income	Theoretical Values
Auto sales	18.00	$ 150	$2,700
Auto specialties	8.00	500	4,000
			$6,700

Theoretical Value based on	
Sales	$6,200
Assets	5,900
Income	6,700
Average value	$6,267

Learning Objectives

Active Applications

World Finance

Practice

CHAPTER 22

INTERNATIONAL BUSINESS FINANCE

INTRODUCTION

Over the years 1994 to 1997, a group of Asian countries known as the "Asian tigers" enjoyed aggregate economic growth rates that were eye-popping to the rest of the world and to global investors. For example, over this 4-year period ended in 1997, the real (i.e., inflation-adjusted) gross domestic product (GDP) of Malaysia expanded by an average of 8.6 percent per year, whereas that of Thailand grew by 6.6 percent per year. Now, you have the right to say: "So what?" Well, by comparison, the GDP of the United States, which was enjoying a fine aggregate economic expansion, grew by an average of 3.03 percent over the same 4 years.

Due primarily to numerous internal challenges, both political and economic, to these Asian countries, foreign investors lost faith in the ability of these economies to continue to perform at such lofty levels over the short term. Some of the triggers for concern on the part of global investors included (1) uncomfortably high rates of inflation at the consumer level, (2) a rapid expansion of domestic credit coupled with loose borrowing standards, (3) soft banking supervision, and (4) especially unwise real estate investments and excess investment in industries already dealing with excess production capacity.[1]

Now remember our **Axiom 6: Efficient Capital Markets—The Markets Are Quick and the Prices Are Right**. Global investors quickly ceased to invest so

---

[1] A useful summary of the 1997 to 1998 Asian economic challenge is provided in Jane Little, "Anatomy of a Currency Crisis," *Regional Review*, Federal Reserve Bank of Boston (Fall 1997): 10–13.

LEARNING OBJECTIVES

After reading this chapter, you should be able to

1. Discuss the internationalization of business.

2. Explain why foreign exchange rates in two different countries must be in line with each other.

3. Discuss the concept of interest rate parity.

4. Explain the purchasing-power parity theory and the law of one price.

5. Explain what exchange rate risk is and how it can be controlled.

6. Identify working-capital management techniques that are useful for international businesses to reduce exchange rate risk and potentially increase profits.

7. Explain how the financing sources available to multinational corporations differ from those available to domestic firms.

8. Discuss the risks involved in direct foreign investment.

ebulliently in the economies of the Asian tigers. This change in confidence resulted in a slack in demand for their specific foreign currencies, which devalued that currency relative to the U.S. dollar. The changes were dramatic. The currencies of Malaysia and Thailand are tracked in the following table.

Southeast Asia Currency Crisis				
Country	Currency	06-27-97 Units to Buy 1 Dollar	02-06-98 Units to Buy 1 Dollar	Percentage Change (%)
Malaysia	Ringgit	2.5230	3.8200	51.4
Thailand	Baht	24.300	48.100	97.9

SOURCE: Federal Reserve Statistical Release H.10 (512), respective dates.

In the table, note that it took 51.4 percent more units of the Malaysian ringgit and 97.9 percent more units of the Thai baht to acquire 1 dollar over the short time span from June 27, 1997 to February 6, 1998. In the context of international business, foreign trade, and global investing, currency gyrations of this magnitude are considered massive and induce significant economic dislocations.

The short-term effect was that U.S. goods became significantly more expensive to the Asian countries, and goods produced in the Asian countries became cheaper to U.S. buyers. The internal adjustments required by the affected Asian countries, however, were massive. It was sadly reminiscent of the petroleum shortages endured by the United States during the middle 1970s. As a point of comparison, even household supplies of a staple such as cooking oil became the cause of small riots in Indonesia during early 1998.

As we have just illustrated, American business activity is not constrained by mere geographic boundaries. Merchandise trade and financial asset investing are now continuous global activities. Adjustments occur instantly and can be quite painful, but can also be quite profitable, depending on precisely where you sit. You want to be "sitting pretty." Such is the focus of this chapter on international business finance.

CHAPTER PREVIEW

This chapter highlights the complications that an international business faces when it deals in multiple currencies. Effective strategies for the reduction of foreign exchange risk are discussed. Working-capital management and capital structure decisions in the international context are also covered. For the international firm, direct foreign investment is a capital-budgeting decision—with some additional complexities.

As you study this chapter on international business finance, you will be reminded of two of the axioms that tie this entire text together. These are highlighted: Axiom 1: The Risk-Return Trade-Off—We Won't Take on Additional Risk Unless We Expect to Be Compensated with Additional Return; and Axiom 3: Cash—Not Profits—Is King. Look for them as you work through the several discussions.

THE GLOBALIZATION OF PRODUCT AND FINANCIAL MARKETS

World trade has grown much faster over the last few decades than world aggregate output (global gross domestic product or *GDP*). The dollar value of world exports has grown from $129.5 billion in 1962 to an estimated $5.5 *trillion* in 1998. This remarkable increase in international trade is reflected in the increased openness of almost all national economies to international influences. For example, the proportion of U.S. GDP accounted for by exports and imports (about one-fifth) is now double what it was two decades ago, and is even higher for manufactured goods (see Figure 22.1). The U.S. Department of Commerce estimates that the United States exports about one-fifth of its industrial production and that about 70 percent of all U.S. goods compete directly with foreign goods.

There has also been a rise in the global level of international portfolio and direct investment. Both direct and portfolio investment in the United States have been increasing faster than U.S. investment overseas. Direct investment occurs when the **multinational corporation (MNC)**, a corporation with holdings and/or operations in more than one country, has control over the investment, such as when it builds an offshore manufacturing facility. Portfolio investment involves financial assets with maturities greater than 1 year, such as the purchase of foreign stocks and bonds. Total foreign investment in the United States now exceeds such U.S. investment overseas.

A major reason for long-run overseas investments of U.S. companies is the high rates of return obtainable from these investments. The amount of U.S. *direct foreign investment (DFI)* abroad is large and growing. Significant amounts of the total assets, sales, and profits of American MNCs are attributable to foreign investments and foreign operations. Direct foreign investment is not limited to American firms. Many European and Japanese firms have operations abroad, too. During the last decade, these firms have been increasing their sales and setting up production facilities abroad, especially in the United States.

Capital flows between countries for international financial investment purposes have also been increasing. Many firms, investment companies, and individuals invest in the

Multinational corporation (MNC)

A corporation with holdings and/or operations in one or more countries.

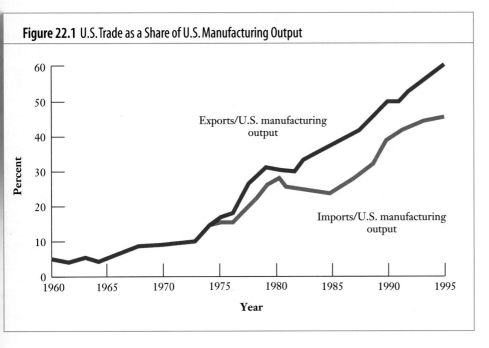

Figure 22.1 U.S. Trade as a Share of U.S. Manufacturing Output

capital markets in foreign countries. The motivation is twofold: to obtain returns higher than those obtainable in the domestic capital markets and to reduce portfolio risk through international diversification. The increase in world trade and investment activity is reflected in the recent globalization of financial markets. The Eurodollar market is larger than any domestic financial market. U.S. companies are increasingly turning to this market for funds. Even companies and public entities that have no overseas presence are beginning to rely on this market for financing.

In addition, most national financial markets are becoming more integrated with global markets because of the rapid increase in the volume of interest rate and currency swaps. Because of the widespread availability of these swaps, the currency denomination and the source country of financing for many globally integrated companies are dictated by accessibility and relative cost considerations regardless of the currency ultimately needed by the firm.

The foreign exchange markets have also grown rapidly, and the weekly trading volume in these globally integrated markets (between $3 and $5 trillion) exceeds the annual trading volume on the world's securities markets. Even a purely domestic firm that buys all its inputs and sells all its output in its home country is not immune to foreign competition, nor can it totally ignore the workings of the international financial markets.

OBJECTIVE 2

EXCHANGE RATES

Recent History of Exchange Rates

Between 1949 and 1970, the exchange rates between the major currencies were fixed. All countries were required to set a specific *parity rate* for their currency vis-à-vis the U.S. dollar. For example, consider the German currency, the deutsche mark (DM). In 1949, the parity rate was set at DM4.0 per dollar (DM4.0/$). The actual exchange rate prevailing on any day was allowed to lie within a narrow band around the parity rate. The DM was allowed to fluctuate between DM4.04 and DM3.96/$. A country could effect a major adjustment in the exchange rate by changing its parity rate with respect to the dollar. When the currency was made cheaper with respect to the dollar, this adjustment was called a *devaluation*. A *revaluation* resulted when a currency became more expensive with respect to the dollar. In 1969, the DM parity rate was adjusted to DM3.66/$. This adjustment was a revaluation of the DM parity by 9.3 percent. The new bands around the parity were DM3.7010 and DM3.6188/$. The DM strengthened against the dollar because fewer DM were needed to buy a dollar.

Floating rate international currency system

An international currency system in which exchange rates between different national currencies are allowed to fluctuate with supply and demand conditions. This contrasts with a fixed rate system in which exchange rates are pegged for extended periods of time and adjusted infrequently.

Since 1973, a **floating-rate international currency system**, a system in which exchange rates between different national currencies are allowed to fluctuate with supply and demand conditions, has been operating. For most currencies, there are no parity rates and no bands within which the currencies fluctuate.[2] Most major currencies, including the U.S. dollar, fluctuate freely, depending upon their values as perceived by the traders in foreign exchange markets. The country's relative economic strengths, its level of exports and imports, the level of monetary activity, and the deficits or surpluses in its balance of payments (BOP) are all important factors in the determination of exchange rates.[3] Short-term, day-to-day fluctuations in exchange rates are caused by changing supply and demand conditions in the foreign exchange market.

---

[2]The system of floating rates is referred to as the "floating-rate regime."

[3]The balance of payments for the United States reflects the difference between the import and export of goods (the trade balance) and services. Capital inflows and outflows are tabulated in the capital account.

The Foreign Exchange Market

The foreign exchange market provides a mechanism for the transfer of purchasing power from one currency to another. This market is not a physical entity such as the New York Stock Exchange; it is a network of telephone and computer connections among banks, foreign exchange dealers, and brokers. The market operates simultaneously at three levels. At the first level, customers buy and sell foreign exchange (that is, foreign currency) through their banks. At the second level, banks buy and sell foreign exchange from other banks in the same commercial center. At the last level, banks buy and sell foreign exchange from banks in commercial centers in other countries. Some important commercial centers for foreign exchange trading are New York, London, Zurich, Frankfurt, Hong Kong, Singapore, and Tokyo.

An example will illustrate this multilevel trading. A trader in Texas may buy foreign exchange (pounds) from a bank in Houston for payment to a British supplier against some purchase made. The Houston bank, in turn, may purchase the foreign currency (pounds) from a New York bank. The New York bank may buy the pounds from another bank in New York or from a bank in London.

Because this market provides transactions in a continuous manner for a very large volume of sales and purchases, the currency markets are efficient: In other words, it is difficult to make a profit by shopping around from one bank to another. Minute differences in the quotes from different banks are quickly eliminated. Because of the arbitrage mechanism, simultaneous quotes to different buyers in London and New York are likely to be the same.

Two major types of transactions are carried out in the foreign exchange markets: spot and forward transactions.

Spot Exchange Rates

A typical spot transaction involves an American firm buying foreign currency from its bank and paying for it in dollars. The price of foreign currency in terms of the domestic currency is the **exchange rate**. Another type of spot transaction is when an American firm receives foreign currency from abroad. The firm typically would sell the foreign currency to its bank for dollars. These are both **spot transactions** because one currency is traded for another currency today. The actual exchange rate quotes are expressed in several different ways, as discussed later. To allow time for the transfer of funds, the *value date* when the currencies are actually exchanged is 2 days after the spot transaction occurs. Four banks could easily be involved in the transactions: the local banks of the buyer and seller of the foreign exchange, and the money-center banks that handle the purchase and sale in the interbank market. Perhaps the buyer or seller will have to move the funds from one of its local banks to another, bringing even more banks into the transaction. A forward transaction entails an agreement today to deliver a specified number of units of a currency on a future date in return for a specified number of units of another currency.

On the spot exchange market, contrasted with the over-the-counter market, the quoted exchange rate is typically called a direct quote. A **direct quote** indicates the number of units of the home currency required to buy one unit of the foreign currency. That is, in New York the typical exchange-rate quote indicates the number of dollars needed to buy one unit of a foreign currency: dollars per pound, dollars per mark, and so on. The spot rates in columns 2 and 3 of Table 22.1 are the direct exchange quotes taken from *The Wall Street Journal* on January 24, 1996. To buy £1 on January 23, 1996, $1.5145 was needed. To buy FFI and DMI, $.1975 and $.6761 were needed, respectively. The quotes in the spot market in Paris are given in terms of francs and those in Frankfurt in terms of deutsche marks.

Exchange rate

The price of a foreign currency stated in terms of the domestic or home currency.

Spot transaction

A transaction made immediately in the market place at the market price.

Direct quote

The exchange rate that indicates the number of units of the home currency required to buy one unit of foreign currency.

An **indirect quote** indicates the number of units of foreign currency that can be bought for one unit of the home currency. This reads as francs per dollar, marks per dollar, and so forth. An indirect quote is the general method used in the over-the-counter market. Exceptions to this rule include British pounds, Irish punts, Australian dollars, and New Zealand dollars, which are quoted via direct quote for historical reasons. Indirect quotes are given in the last two columns of Table 22.1.

Table 22.1 Foreign Exchange Rates Reported on January 24, 1996

Country	U.S. $ Equiv.		Currency per U.S. $	
	Tue	Mon	Tue	Mon
Argentina (Peso)	1.0007	1.0007	.9992	.9993
Australia (Dollar)	.7334	.7323	1.3635	1.3656
Austria (Schilling)	.09654	.09613	10.358	10.403
Bahrain (Dinar)	2.6532	2.6532	.3769	.3769
Belgium (Franc)	.03305	.03289	30.260	30.400
Brazil (Real)	1.0288	1.0288	.9720	.9720
Britain (Pound)	1.5145	1.5117	.6603	.6615
30-Day Forward	1.5134	1.5106	.6608	.6620
90-Day Forward	1.5116	1.5088	.6616	.6628
180-Day Forward	1.5088	1.5061	.6628	.6640
Canada (Dollar)	.7309	.7298	1.3681	1.3701
30-Day Forward	.7309	.7298	1.3682	1.3702
90-Day Forward	.7308	.7297	1.3684	1.3705
180-Day Forward	.7302	.7291	1.3696	1.3715
Chile (Peso)	.002439	.002429	409.95	411.65
China (Renminbl)	.1202	.1206	8.3170	8.2928
Colombia (Peso)	.0009820	.0009818	1018.33	1018.50
Czech. Rep. (Koruna)	...	...	...	...
Commercial rate	.03683	.03666	27.154	27.276
Denmark (Krone)	.1756	.1749	5.6948	5.7187
Ecuador (Sucre)	...	...	...	...
Floating Rate	.0003455	.0003455	2894.50	2894.50
Finland (Markka)	.2214	.2208	4.5167	4.5285
France (Franc)	.1975	.1980	5.0630	5.0512
30-Day Forward	.1977	.1980	5.0589	5.0510
90-Day Forward	.1979	.1984	5.0528	5.0395
180-Day Forward	.1982	.1988	5.0465	5.0313
Germany (Mark)	.6761	.6768	1.4790	1.4775
30-Day Forward	.6773	.6779	1.4765	1.4751
90-Day Forward	.6794	.6801	1.4718	1.4703
180-Day Forward	.6827	.6834	1.4649	1.4634
Greece (Drachma)	.004117	.004104	242.90	243.67
Hong Kong (Dollar)	.1294	.1293	7.7280	7.7331
Hungary (Forint)	.006974	.006965	143.39	143.57
India (Rupee)	.02790	.02792	35.842	35.820
Indonesia (Ruplah)	.0004359	.0004369	2294.00	2289.00
Ireland (Punt)	1.5735	1.5691	.6355	.6373
Israel (Shekel)	.3199	.3199	3.1260	3.1257

Table 22.1 Foreign Exchange Rates Reported on January 24, 1996 (*continued*)

Country	U.S. $ Equiv.		Currency per U.S. $	
	Tue	Mon	Tue	Mon
Italy (Lira)	.0006270	.0006285	1595.00	1591.00
Japan (Yen)	.009465	.009454	105.65	105.78
30-Day Forward	.009508	.009497	105.18	105.30
90-Day Forward	.009585	.009574	104.33	104.45
180-Day Forward	.009698	.009686	103.12	103.25
Jordan (Dinar)	1.4104	1.4104	.7090	.7090
Kuwait (Dinar)	3.3322	3.3325	.3001	.3001
Lebanon (Pound)	.0006279	.0006279	1592.50	1592.50
Malaysia (Ringgit)	.3917	.3916	2.5530	2.5534
Malta (Lira)	2.7809	2.7682	.3596	.3612
Mexico (Peso)	…	…	…	…
Floating rate	.1347	.1365	7.4250	7.3250
Netherlands (Guilder)	.6038	.6045	1.6561	1.6543
New Zealand (Dollar)	.6614	.6647	1.5119	1.5044
Norway (Krone)	.1548	.1544	6.4599	6.4774
Pakistan (Rupee)	.02920	.02920	34.247	34.250
Peru (new Sol)	.4292	.4292	2.3299	2.3300
Philippines (Peso)	.03820	.03821	26.178	26.170
Poland (Zloty)	.3948	.3948	2.5330	2.5330
Portugal (Escudo)	.006553	.006533	152.60	153.07
Russia (Ruble) (a)	.0002128	.0002132	4700.00	4691.00
Saudi Arabia (Riyal)	.2666	.2666	3.7509	3.7503
Singapore (Dollar)	.7052	.7027	1.4180	1.4230
Slovak Rep. (Koruna)	.03322	.03321	30.098	30.108
South Africa (Rand)	.2742	.2741	3.6467	3.6480
South Korea (Won)	.001270	.001267	787.40	789.20
Spain (Peseta)	.008055	.008020	124.15	124.69
Sweden (Krona)	.1460	.1467	6.8493	6.8168
Switzerland (Franc)	.8413	.8414	1.1886	1.1885
30-Day Forward	.8441	.8442	1.1847	1.1846
90-Day Forward	.8491	.8491	1.1777	1.1777
180-Day Forward	.8565	.8564	1.1675	1.1677
Taiwan (Dollar)	.03646	.03646	27.430	27.430
Thailand (Baht)	.03959	.03959	25.259	25.260
Turkey (Lira)	.00001632	.00001636	61279.50	61113.00
United Arab (Dirham)	.2724	.2724	3.6711	3.6710
Uruguay (New Peso)	…	…	…	…
Financial	.1387	.1393	7.2100	7.1788
Venezuela (Bolivar)	.003448	.003448	290.00	290.00
Brady Rate	.002740	.002740	365.00	365.00
SDR	1.4626	1.4588	.6837	.6855
ECU	1.2428	1.2458		

[a]Exchange rates: Tuesday, January 23, 1996. Federal Reserve Statistical Release H.10 (512), January 1996.

[b]Special Drawing Rights (SDR) are based on exchange rates for the U.S., German, British, French, and Japanese currencies. Source: International Monetary Fund.

[c]European Currency Unit (ECU) is based on a basket of community currencies.
a-fixing, Moscow Interbank Currency Exchange

In summary, a direct quote is the dollar/foreign currency rate ($/FC), and an indirect quote is the foreign currency/dollar (FC/$). Therefore, an indirect quote is the reciprocal of a direct quote and vice versa. The following example illustrates the computation of an indirect quote from a given direct quote.

EXAMPLE

Suppose you want to compute the indirect quotes from the direct quotes of spot rates for pounds, francs, and marks given in column 2 of Table 22.1. The direct quotes are pound, 1.5145; French franc, .1975; and deutsche mark, .6761. The related indirect quotes are calculated as the *reciprocal* of the direct quote as follows:

$$\text{indirect quote} = \frac{1}{\text{direct quote}}$$

Thus,

pounds $\qquad \dfrac{1}{\$1.5145/\pounds} = \pounds.6603/\$$

francs $\qquad \dfrac{1}{\$.1975/FF} = FF5.0630/\$$

deutsche marks $\dfrac{1}{\$.6761/DM} = DM1.4790/\$$

Notice that the above direct quotes and indirect quotes are identical to those shown in columns 2 and 4 of Table 22.1.

Direct and indirect quotes are useful in conducting international transactions, as the following examples show.

EXAMPLE

An American business must pay DM1,000 to a German firm on January 23, 1996. How many dollars will be required for this transaction?

$\$.6761/DM \times DM1,000 = \$676.10$

EXAMPLE

An American business must pay $2,000 to a British resident on January 23, 1996. How many pounds will the British resident receive?

$\pounds.6603/\$ \times \$2,000 = \pounds1,520.60$

Exchange Rates and Arbitrage

The foreign exchange quotes in two different countries must be in line with each other. The direct quote for U.S. dollars in London is given in pounds per dollar. Because the foreign exchange markets are efficient, the direct quotes for the per U.S. dollar in London, on January 23, 1996, must be very close to the indirect rate of £.6603/$ prevailing in New York on that date.

If the exchange-rate quotations between the London and New York spot exchange markets were out of line, then an enterprising trader could make a profit by buying in the market where the currency was cheaper and selling it in the other. Such a buy-and-sell strategy would involve a zero net investment of funds and no risk bearing yet would provide a sure profit. Such a person is called an **arbitrageur**, and the process of buying and selling in more than one market to make a riskless profit is called arbitrage. Spot exchange markets are efficient in the sense that arbitrage opportunities do not persist for any length of time. That is, the exchange rates between two different markets are quickly brought in line, aided by the arbitrage process. **Simple arbitrage** eliminates exchange rate differentials across the markets for a single currency, as in the preceding example for the New York and London quotes. **Triangular arbitrage** does the same across the markets for all currencies. **Covered-interest arbitrage** eliminates differentials across currency and interest rate markets.

Suppose that London quotes £.6700/$ instead of £.6603/$. If you simultaneously bought a pound in New York for £.6603/$ and sold a pound in London for £.6700/$, you would have (1) taken a zero net investment position since you bought £1 and sold £1, (2) locked in a sure profit of £.0097/$ no matter which way the pound subsequently moves, and (3) set in motion the forces that will eliminate the different quotes in New York and London. As others in the marketplace learn of your transaction, they will attempt to make the same transaction. The increased demand to buy pounds in New York will lead to a higher quote there and the increased supply of pounds will lead to a lower quote in London. The workings of the market will produce a new spot rate that lies between £.6603/$ and £.6700/$ and is the same in New York and in London.

Asked and Bid Rates

Two types of rates are quoted in the spot exchange market: the asked and the bid rates. The **asked rate** is the rate the bank or the foreign exchange trader "asks" the customer to pay in home currency for foreign currency when the bank is selling and the customer is buying. The asked rate is also known as the **selling rate** or the *offer rate*. The **bid rate** is the rate at which the bank buys the foreign currency from the customer by paying in home currency. The bid rate is also known as the **buying rate**. Note that Table 22.1 contains only the selling, offer, or asked rates, and not the buying rate.

The bank sells a unit of foreign currency for more than it pays for it. Therefore, the direct asked quote ($/FC) is greater than the direct bid quote. The difference between the asked quote and the bid quote is known as the **bid-asked spread**. When there is a large volume of transactions and the trading is continuous, the spread is small and can be less than −1 percent (.001) for the major currencies. The spread is much higher for infrequently traded currencies. The spread exists to compensate the banks for holding the risky foreign currency and for providing the service of converting currencies.

Cross Rates

A **cross rate** is the computation of an exchange rate for a currency from the exchange rates of two other currencies. The following example illustrates how this works.

> ### EXAMPLE
>
> **Taking the dollar/pound and the mark/dollar rates from columns 2 and 4 of Table 22.1, determine the mark/pound and pound/mark exchange rates. We see that**
>
> $$(\$/£) \times (DM/\$) = (DM/£)$$
>
> **or**
>
> $$1.5145 \times 1.4790 = DM2.2399$$
>
> **Thus the pound/mark exchange rate is**
>
> $$1/2.2399 = £.4464/DM$$

Sidebar definitions

Arbitrageur

A person involved in the process of buying and selling in more than one market to make riskless profits.

Simple arbitrage

Trading to eliminate exchange rate differentials across the markets for a single currency, e.g., for the New York and London markets.

Triangular arbitrage

Arbitrage across the markets for all currencies.

Covered-interest arbitrage

Arbitrage designed to eliminate differentials across currency and interest rate markets.

Asked rate

The rate a bank or foreign exchange trader "asks" the customer to pay in home currency for foreign currency when the bank is selling and the customer is buying.

Selling rate

Same as the asked rate.

Bid rate

The rate at which the bank buys the foreign currency from the customer by paying in home currency.

Buying rate

The bid rate in a currency transaction.

Bid-asked spread

The difference between the asked quote and the bid quote.

Cross rate

The computation of an exchange rate for a currency from the exchange rates of two other currencies.

Cross-rate computations make it possible to use quotations in New York to compute the exchange rate between pounds, marks, and francs. Arbitrage conditions hold in cross rates, too. For example, the pound exchange rate in Frankfurt (the direct quote marks/pound) must be 2.2399. The mark exchange rate in London must be .4464 pounds/mark. If the rates prevailing in Frankfurt and London were different from the computed cross rates, using quotes from New York, a trader could use three different currencies to lock in arbitrage profits through a process called triangular arbitrage.

Forward Exchange Rates

A **forward exchange contract** requires delivery, at a specified future date, of one currency for a specified amount of another currency. The exchange rate for the forward transaction is agreed on today; the actual payment of one currency and the receipt of another currency take place at the future date. For example, a 30-day contract on March 1 is for delivery on March 31. Note that the forward rate is not the same as the spot rate that will prevail in the future. The actual spot rate that will prevail is not known today; only the forward rate is known. The actual spot rate will depend on the market conditions at that time; it may be more or less than today's forward rate. **Exchange rate risk** is the risk that tomorrow's exchange rate will differ from today's rate.

As indicated earlier, it is extremely unlikely that the future spot rate will be exactly the same as the forward rate quoted today. Assume that you are going to receive a payment denominated in pounds from a British customer in 30 days. If you wait for 30 days and exchange the pounds at the spot rate, you will receive a dollar amount reflecting the exchange rate 30 days hence (that is, the future spot rate). As of today, you have no way of knowing the exact dollar value of your future pound receipts. Consequently, you cannot make precise plans about the use of these dollars. If, conversely, you buy a future contract, then you know the exact dollar value of your future receipts, and you can make precise plans concerning their use. The forward contract, therefore, can reduce your uncertainty about the future, and the major advantage of the forward market is that of risk reduction.

Forward contracts are usually quoted for periods of 30, 90, and 180 days. A contract for any intermediate date can be obtained, usually with the payment of a small premium. Forward contracts for periods longer than 180 days can be obtained by special negotiations with banks. Contracts for periods greater than 1 year can be costly.

Forward rates, like spot rates, are quoted in both direct and indirect form. The direct quotes for the 30-day and 90-day forward contracts on pounds, francs, and marks are given in column 2 of Table 22.1. The indirect quotes for forward contracts, like spot rates, are reciprocals of the direct quotes. The indirect quotes are indicated in column 4 of Table 22.1. The direct quotes are the dollar/foreign currency rate, and the indirect quotes are the foreign currency/dollar rate similar to the spot exchange quotes.

The 30-day forward quote for pounds is $1.5134 per pound. This means that if one purchases the contract for forward pounds on January 23, 1996, the bank will deliver £1 against the payment of $1.5134 on January 22, 1996. The bank is contractually bound to deliver £1 at this price, and the buyer of the contract is legally obligated to buy it at this price on February 22, 1996. Therefore, this is the price the customer must pay regardless of the actual spot rate prevailing on February 22, 1996. If the spot price of the pound is less than $1.5134, then the customer pays *more* than the spot price. If the spot price is greater than $1.5234, then the customer pays *less* than the spot price.

The forward rate is often quoted at a premium to or discount from the existing spot rate. For example, the 30-day forward rate for the pound may be quoted as

.0011 premium (1.5134 forward rate − 1.5145 spot rate). If the forward contract is selling for more dollars than the spot—that is, a larger direct quote—the pound is said to be selling at a discount, which means the dollar is selling at a premium to the pound. Consider another example: If the indirect spot and forward quotes for the mark are 1.4790 and 1.4800, respectively, the mark is selling at a premium to the dollar and the dollar at a discount to the mark. When the forward contract sells for fewer dollars than the spot—a smaller direct quote—the pound is said to be at a discount from the dollar. Notice in column 2 of Table 22.1 that the forward contracts are selling at a discount for pounds and French francs. This premium or discount is also called the **forward-spot differential**.

Forward-spot differential

The premium or discount between forward and spot currency exchange rates.

Notationally, the relationship may be written

$$F - S = \text{premium } (F > S) \text{ or discount } (S > F) \tag{22-1}$$

where F = the forward rate, direct quote
S = the spot rate, direct quote

The premium or discount can also be expressed as an annual percentage rate, computed as follows:

$$\frac{F - S}{S} \times \frac{12}{n} \times 100 = \text{annualized percentage} \tag{22-2}$$

premium $(F > S)$ or discount $(S > F)$

where n = the number of months of the forward contract

EXAMPLE

Compute the percent-per-annum premium on the 30-day pound.

Step 1: Identify F, S, and n.

   $F = 1.5134$, $S = 1.5145$, $n = 1$ month

Step 2: Because S is greater than F, we compute the annualized percentage discount:

$$D = \frac{1.5134 - 1.5145}{1.5145} \times \frac{12 \text{ months}}{1 \text{ month}} \times 100$$

$$= -0.87\%$$

The percent-per-annum discount on the 30-day pound is −0.87 percent. The percent-per-annum discount on the 30-day and 90-day pound and franc contracts are computed similarly. The results are given in Table 22.2.

Table 22.2 Percent-per-Annum (Discount)

	30-Day	90-Day
British pound	−0.87%	−0.77%
French franc	−1.22%	−0.81%

Examples of Exchange Rate Risk

The concept of exchange rate risk applies to all types of international businesses. The measurement of these risks, and the type of risk, may differ among businesses. Let us see how exchange risk affects international trade contracts, international portfolio investments, and direct foreign investments.

Exchange rate risk in international trade contracts. The idea of exchange rate risk in trade contracts is illustrated in the following situations.

Case I. An American automobile distributor agrees to buy a car from the manufacturer in Detroit. The distributor agrees to pay $6,500 on delivery of the car, which is expected to be 30 days from today. The car is delivered on the thirtieth day and the distributor pays $6,500. Notice that from the day this contract was written until the day the car was delivered, the buyer knew the exact dollar amount of the liability. There was, in other words, no uncertainty about the value of the contract.

Case II. An American automobile distributor enters into a contract with a British supplier to buy a car from Britain for £3,500. The amount is payable on the delivery of the car, 30 days from today. From Figure 22.2, we see the range of spot rates that we believe can occur on the date the contract is consummated. On the thirtieth day, the American importer will pay some amount in the range of $4,600.75 (3,500 × 1.3145) to $6,000.75 (3,500 × 7.7145) for the car. Today, the American firm is not certain what its future dollar outflow will be 30 days hence. That is, the dollar value of the contract is uncertain.

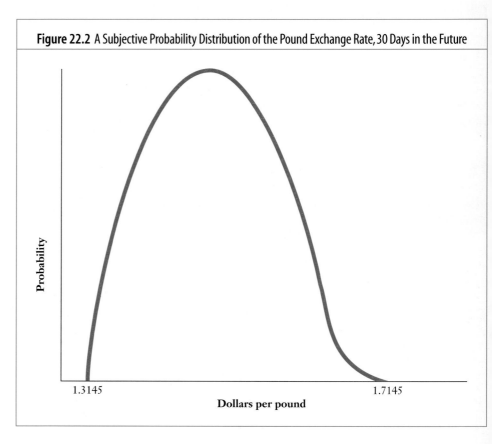

Figure 22.2 A Subjective Probability Distribution of the Pound Exchange Rate, 30 Days in the Future

These two examples help illustrate the idea of foreign exchange risk in international trade contracts. In the domestic trade contract (Case I), the exact dollar amount of the future dollar payment is known today with certainty. In the case of the international trade contract (Case II), where the contract is written in the foreign currency, the exact dollar amount of the contract is not known. The variability of the exchange rate induces variability in the future cash flow.

Exchange rate risk exists when the contract is written in terms of the foreign currency or *denominated* in foreign currency. There is no direct exchange risk if the international trade contract is written in terms of the domestic currency. That is, in Case II, if the contract were written in dollars, the American importer would face no direct exchange risk. With the contract written in dollars, the British exporter would bear all the exchange rate risk because the British exporter's future pound receipts would be uncertain. That is, the British exporter would receive payment in dollars, which would have to be converted into pounds at an unknown (as of today) pound/dollar exchange rate. In international trade contracts of the type discussed here, at least one of the two parties to the contract always bears the exchange rate risk.

Certain types of international trade contracts are denominated in a third currency, different from either the importer's or the exporter's domestic currency. In Case II, the contract might have been denominated in, say, the deutsche mark. With a mark contract, both importer and exporter would be subject to exchange rate risk.

Exchange rate risk is not limited to the two-party trade contracts; it exists also in foreign portfolio investments and direct foreign investments.

Exchange rate risk in foreign portfolio investments. Let us look at an example of exchange rate risk in the context of portfolio investments. An American investor buys a German security. The exact return on the investment in the security is unknown. Thus the security is a risky investment. The investment return in the holding period of, say, 3 months stated in marks could be anything from −2 to +8 percent. In addition, the mark/dollar exchange rate may depreciate by 4 percent or appreciate by 6 percent in the 3-month period during which the investment is held. The return to the American investor, in dollars, will therefore be in the range of −6 to +14 percent.[4] Notice that the return to a German investor, in marks, is in the range of −2 to +8 percent. Clearly, for the American investor, the exchange factor induces a greater variability in the dollar rate of return. Hence the exchange rate fluctuations may increase the riskiness of the investments.

Exchange rate risk in direct foreign investment. The exchange rate risk of a direct foreign investment (DFI) is more complicated. In a DFI, the parent company invests in assets denominated in a foreign currency. That is, the balance sheet and the income statement of the subsidiary are written in terms of the foreign currency. The parent company receives the repatriated profit stream in dollars. Thus the exchange rate risk concept applies to fluctuations in the dollar value of the assets located abroad as well as to the fluctuations in the home currency-denominated profit stream. Exchange risk not only affects immediate profits, it may affect the future profit stream as well.

Although exchange rate risk can be a serious complication in international business activity, remember the principle of the risk-return trade-off: Traders and corporations find numerous reasons that the returns from international transactions outweigh the risks.

---

[4]Example: Assume the spot exchange rate is $.50/DM. In 3 months, the exchange rate would be $.50 \times (1 - .04) = .48$ to $.50 \times (1 + .06) = .53$. A $50 investment today is equivalent to a DM100 investment. The DM100 investment would return DM98 to DM108 in 3 months. The return, in the worst case is DM98 × .48 = $47.04. The return, in the best case, is DM108 × .53 = $57.24. The holding-period return, on the $50 investment, will be between −6 percent ($47.04 − $50)/$50) and +14 percent ($57.24 − $50)/$50).

OBJECTIVE 3

INTEREST-RATE PARITY THEORY

Interest-rate parity (IRP)

States that (except for the effect of small transaction costs) the forward premium or discount should be equal and opposite in size to the differences in the national interest rates for securities of the same maturity.

Forward rates generally entail a premium or a discount relative to current spot rates. However, these forward premiums and discounts differ between currencies and maturities (see Table 22.2). These differences depend solely on the difference in the level of interest rates between the two countries, called the *interest rate differential*. The value of the premium or discount can be theoretically computed from the **interest-rate parity (IRP) theory**. This theory states that (except for the effects of small transaction costs) the forward premium or discount should be equal and opposite in size to the difference in the national interest rates for securities of the same maturity.

Stated very simply, what does all this mean? It means that because of arbitrage, the interest rate differential between two countries must be equal to the difference between the forward and spot exchange rates. If this were not true, arbitrageurs would buy in the forward market and sell in the spot market (or vice versa) until prices were back in line and there were no profits left to be made. For example, if prices in the forward market were too low, arbitrageurs would enter the market, increase the demand for the forward foreign currency, and drive up the prices in the forward market until those prices obeyed the interest-rate parity theory.

OBJECTIVE 4

PURCHASING POWER PARITY

Purchasing-power parity (PPP) theory

In the long run, exchange rates adjust so that the purchasing power of each currency tends to remain the same. Thus exchange rate changes tend to reflect international differences in inflation rates. Countries with high rates of inflation tend to experience declines in the value of their currency.

Long-run changes in exchange rates are influenced by international differences in inflation rates and the purchasing power of each nation's currency. Exchange rates of countries with high rates of inflation will tend to decline. According to the **purchasing-power parity (PPP) theory**, in the long run, exchange rates adjust so that the purchasing power of each currency tends to be the same. Thus, exchange rate changes tend to reflect international differences in inflation rates. Countries with high rates of inflation tend to experience declines in the value of their currency. Thus, if Britain experiences a 10 percent rate of inflation in a year that Germany experiences only a 6 percent rate, the UK currency (the pound) will be expected to decline in value approximately by 3.77 percent (1.10/1.06) against the German currency (the deutsche mark). More accurately, according to the PPP

$$\text{expected spot rate} = \text{current spot rate} \times \text{expected difference in inflation rate}$$

$$\begin{array}{l}\text{expected spot rate} \\ \text{(domestic currency} \\ \text{per unit of foreign} \\ \text{currency)}\end{array} = \begin{array}{l}\text{current spot rate} \\ \text{(domestic currency} \\ \text{per unit of foreign} \\ \text{currency)}\end{array} \times \frac{(1 + \text{expected domestic inflation rate})}{(1 + \text{expected foreign inflation rate})}$$

Thus, if the beginning value of the mark were £.40, with a 6 percent inflation rate in Germany and a 10 percent inflation rate in Britain, according to the PPP, the expected value of the deutsche mark at the end of that year will be £.40 × [1.10/1.06], or £.4151.

THE WALL STREET JOURNAL, JULY 25, 1994

Traders Say Dollar May Have Hit Bottom

LONDON—The dollar's latest ten-day rally, following its stunning declines earlier this year, has foreign-exchange experts struggling to determine whether the U.S. currency has finally hit bottom.

A sustained dollar recovery isn't considered likely until other ingredients are present. Besides investor confidence that the Clinton administration wants a stable dollar, a broad rally would require higher U.S. interest rates, lower German rates, and settlement of the U.S. trade dispute with Japan, analysts say.

The interest rate outlook, at least, does seem to promise some relief for the dollar. Short-term German rates are currently higher than their U.S. equivalents, a difference that contributes to the mark's strength. But Hermann Remsperger, chief economist at Berliner Handles & Frankfurter Bank in Frankfurt, expects that to be reversed by year end as the Fed raises rates to damp U.S. inflation and lower German inflation possibly allows the Bundesbank to cut rates.

Economists add that further Fed tightening could stabilize the U.S. bond market, which would further draw back investors, lending further support to the dollar. "For the dollar to strengthen in the long run, there must be the expectation that capital gains in the U.S. are in the offing—especially for foreign investors" says Remsperger.

The U.S.-Japan trade front is more problematic. While many economists and traders are skeptical that U.S.-Japanese tensions will ease sufficiently enough to allow a resolution soon, "Sentiment can't turn fully positive for the dollar until the Clinton administration achieves satisfaction from the Japanese government on measures to stimulate domestic demand in Japan and to afford greater access to U.S. exports."

Meanwhile, a strong yen is hurting the competitiveness of Japan's exports, and weighing down the country's already weak economy. "The very strong yen is a burden for the Japanese economy," says Mr. Remsperger. "If you look at the trade account in yen terms, you see that this burden has ready been shown in the figures—in other words they are exporting less." But the weak Japanese economy is also cutting Japanese demand for U.S. imports.

SOURCE: Excerpted from Michael R. Sesit, "Traders Say Dollar May Have Hit Bottom," *The Wall Street Journal* (July 25, 1994): C1, 15. Reprinted by permission of *The Wall Street Journal*, © 1994 by Dow Jones & Co., Inc. All Rights Reserved Worldwide.

Analysis and Implications ...

A. As you recall, the interest rate parity theory states that the forward premium or discount should be equal to the difference in national interest rates for securities of the same maturity. As a result, if U.S. interest rates increase while German interest rates fall, the dollar should increase in value relative to the German mark.

B. In order for the dollar to strengthen, there must be increased demand for dollars. Perhaps the largest draw of money into any economy deals with investors' expectations regarding possible capital gains. As investors' expectations increase regarding capital gains in the U.S., more dollars will be purchased, thus strengthening the dollar.

C. Over the past 4 years, the dollar has dropped 35 percent versus the Japanese yen. The key here is the persistent and massive trade deficit with Japan, now at around $60 billion per year, which has pushed the dollar down versus the yen. Before the dollar can strengthen against the yen, the trade gap must be controlled. For this to happen, U.S. firms must gain access to Japanese markets.

D. As the dollar drops in value against the yen, Japanese goods become more expensive and less attractive to Americans. Likewise, U.S. goods sold in Japan become less expensive, increasing their desirability—although this is somewhat tempered by the weakness in the Japanese economy.

Stated very simply, what does this mean? It means that a dollar should have the same purchasing power anywhere in the world—well, at least on average. Obviously, this is not quite true. However, what the purchasing-power parity theory tells us is that we should expect, on average, that differences in inflation rates between two countries should be reflected in changes in the exchange rates. In effect, the best forecast of the difference in inflation rates between two countries should also be the best forecast of the change in the spot rate of exchange.

The Law of One Price

Law of one price

The proposition that in competitive markets the same goods should sell for the same price where prices are stated in terms of a single currency.

Underlying the PPP relationship is the **law of one price**. This law is actually a proposition that in competitive markets where there are no transportation costs or barriers to trade, the same goods sold in different countries sells for the same price if all the different prices are expressed in terms of the same currency. The idea is that the worth, in terms of marginal utility, of a good does not depend on where it is bought or sold. Because inflation will erode the purchasing power of any currency, its exchange rate must adhere to the PPP relationship if the law of one price is to hold over time.

There are enough obvious exceptions to the concept of purchasing-power parity that it may, at first glance, seem difficult to accept. For example, in the spring of 1996, a Big Mac cost $2.36 in the United States, and given the then existing exchange rates, it cost an equivalent of $2.02 in Mexico, $2.70 in Japan, and $3.22 in Germany. On the surface this might appear to violate the purchasing-power parity theory and the law of one price; however, we must remember that this theory is based upon the concept of arbitrage. In the case of a Big Mac, it's pretty hard to imagine buying Big Macs in Mexico for $2.02, shipping them to Germany, and reselling them for $3.22. But for commodities such as gold and other items that are relatively inexpensive to ship and do not have to be consumed immediately, the law of one price holds much better.

International Fisher Effect

According to the domestic Fisher effect (FE) (remember our discussion in chapter 2), nominal interest rates reflect the expected inflation rate and a real rate of return. In other words,

$$\frac{\text{nominal}}{\text{interest rate}} = \frac{\text{expected}}{\text{inflation rate}} + \frac{\text{real rate}}{\text{of interest}}$$

Although there is mixed empirical support for the international Fisher effect (IFE), it is widely thought that, for the major industrial countries, the real rate of interest is about 3 percent when a long-term period is considered. In such a case, with the previous assumption regarding inflation rates, interest rates in Britain and Germany would be (.10 + .03 + .003) or 13.3 percent and (.06 + .03 + .0018) or 9.18 percent, respectively.

In effect, the IFE states that the real interest rate should be the same all over the world, with the difference in nominal or stated interest rates simply resulting from the difference in expected inflation rates. As we look at interest rates around the world, this tells us that we should not necessarily send our money to a bank account in the country with the highest interest rates. That course of action might only result in sending our money to a bank in the country with the highest expected level of inflation.

OBJECTIVE 5 **EXPOSURE TO EXCHANGE RATE RISK**

An asset denominated or valued in terms of foreign-currency cash flows will lose value if that foreign currency declines in value. It can be said that such an asset is exposed to exchange rate risk. However, this possible decline in asset value may be offset by the decline in value of any liability that is also denominated or valued in terms of that foreign currency. Thus a firm would normally be interested in its net exposed position (exposed assets − exposed liabilities) for each period in each currency.

Although expected changes in exchange rates can often be included in the cost-benefit analysis relating to such transactions, in most cases, there is an unexpected component in exchange rate changes and often the cost-benefit analysis for such transactions does not fully capture even the expected change in the exchange rate. For example, price increases for the foreign operations of many MNCs often have to be less than those necessary to fully offset exchange rate changes, owing to the competitive pressures generated by local businesses, as the Japanese car makers found in 1988 for their U.S. sales.

Three measures of foreign exchange exposure are translation exposure, transactions exposure, and economic exposure. Translation exposure arises because the foreign operations of MNCs have accounting statements denominated in the local currency of the country in which the operation is located. For U.S. MNCs, the *reporting currency* for its consolidated financial statements is the dollar, so the assets, liabilities, revenues, and expenses of the foreign operations must be translated into dollars. International transactions often require a payment to be made or received in a foreign currency in the future, so these transactions are exposed to exchange rate risk. Economic exposure exists over the long term because the value of future cash flows in the reporting currency (that is, the dollar) from foreign operations are exposed to exchange rate risk. Indeed, the whole stream of future cash flows is exposed. The Japanese automaker situation highlights the effect of economic exposure on an MNC's revenue stream. The three measures of exposure now are examined more closely.

Translation Exposure

Foreign currency assets and liabilities are considered exposed if their foreign currency value for accounting purposes is to be translated into the domestic currency using the currency exchange rate—the exchange rate in effect on the balance sheet date. Other assets and liabilities and equity amounts that are translated at the historic exchange rate—the rate in effect when these items were first recognized in the company's accounts—are not considered to be exposed. The rate (current or historic) used to translate various accounts depends on the translation procedure used.

Although transaction exposure can result in exchange rate change-related losses and gains that are realized and have an impact on both reported and taxable income, translation exposure results in exchange rate losses and gains that are reflected in the company's accounting books, but are unrealized and have little or no impact on taxable income. Thus, if financial markets are efficient and managerial goals are consistent with owner wealth maximization, a firm should not have to waste real resources hedging against possible paper losses caused by translation exposure. However, if there are significant agency or information costs or if markets are not efficient, a firm may indeed find it economical to hedge against translation losses or gains.

Transaction Exposure

Receivables, payables, and fixed-price sales or purchase contracts are examples of foreign currency transactions whose monetary value was fixed at a time different from the time when these transactions are actually completed. **Transaction exposure** is a term that describes the net contracted foreign currency transactions for which the settlement amounts are subject to changing exchange rates. A company normally must set up an additional reporting system to track transaction exposure, because several of these amounts are not recognized in the accounting books of the firm.

Exchange rate risk may be neutralized or hedged by a change in the asset and liability position in the foreign currency. An exposed asset position (such as an account receivable)

Transaction exposure

The net contracted foreign currency transactions for which the settlement amounts are subject to changing exchange rates.

can be hedged or covered by creating a liability of the same amount and maturity denominated in the foreign currency (such as a forward contract to sell the foreign currency). An exposed liability position (such as an account payable) can be covered by acquiring assets of the same amount and maturity in the foreign currency (such as a forward contract to buy the foreign currency). The objective is to have a zero net asset position in the foreign currency. This eliminates exchange rate risk, because the loss (gain) in the liability (asset) is exactly offset by the gain (loss) in the value of the asset (liability) when the foreign currency appreciates (depreciates). Two popular forms of hedge are the money-market hedge and the exchange-market or forward-market hedge. In both types of hedge, the amount and the duration of the asset (liability) positions are matched. Note as you read the next two subsections how IRP theory assures that each hedge provides the same cover.

Money-market hedge. In a money-market hedge, the exposed position in a foreign currency is offset by borrowing or lending in the money market. Consider the case of the American firm with a net liability position (that is, the amount it owes) of £3,000. The firm knows the exact amount of its pound liability in 30 days, but it does not know the liability in dollars. Assume that the 30-day money-market rates in both the United States and Britain are, respectively, 1 percent for lending and 1.5 percent for borrowing. The American business can take the following steps:

Step 1: Calculate the present value of the foreign currency liability (£3,000) that is due in 30 days. Use the money-market rate applicable for the foreign country (1 percent in the United Kingdom). The present value of £3,000 is £2,970.30, computed as follows: 3,000/(1 + .01).

Step 2: Exchange dollars on today's spot market to obtain the £2,970.30. The dollar amount needed today is $4,498.52 (2,970.30 × 1.5145).

Step 3: Invest £2,970.30 in a United Kingdom 1-month money-market instrument. This investment will compound to exactly £3,000 in 1 month. The future liability of £3,000 is covered by the £2,970.30 investment.[5]

Note: If the American business does not own this amount today, it can borrow $4,498.52 from the U.S. money market at the going rate of 1.5 percent. In 30 days, the American business will need to repay $4,566.00 [$4,498.52 × (1 + .015)].

Assuming that the American business borrows the money, its management may base its calculations on the knowledge that the British goods, on delivery in 30 days, will cost it $4,566.00. The British business will receive £3,000. The American business need not wait for the future spot exchange rate to be revealed. On today's date, the future dollar payment of the contract is known with certainty. This certainty helps the American business in making its pricing and financing decisions.

Many businesses hedge in the money market. The firm needs to borrow (creating a liability) in one market, lend or invest in the other money market, and use the spot exchange market on today's date. The mechanics of covering a net asset position in the foreign currency are the exact reverse of the mechanics of covering the liability position. With a net asset position in pounds: Borrow in the United Kingdom money market in pounds, convert to dollars on the spot exchange market, invest in the U.S. money market. When the net assets are converted into pounds (i.e., when the firm receives what it is owed), pay off the loan and the interest. The cost of hedging in the money market is the cost of doing business in three different markets. Information about the three markets is needed, and analytical calculations of the type indicated here must be made.

---

[5]Observe that £2,970.30 × (1 + .01) = £3,000.

Many small and infrequent traders find the cost of the money-market hedge prohibitive, owing especially to the need for information about the market. These traders use the exchange-market or the forward-market hedge, which has very similar hedging benefits.

The forward-market hedge. The forward market provides a second possible hedging mechanism. It works as follows: A net asset (liability) position is covered by a liability (asset) in the forward market. Consider again the case of the American firm with a liability of £3,000 that must be paid in 30 days. The firm may take the following steps to cover its liability position:

Step 1: Buy a forward contract today to purchase £3,000 in 30 days. The 30-day forward rate is $1.5134/£.

Step 2: On the thirtieth day pay the banker $4,540.20 (3,000 × $1.5134) and collect £3,000. Pay these pounds to the British supplier.

By the use of the forward contract the American business knows the exact worth of the future payment in dollars ($4,540.20). The exchange rate risk in pounds is totally eliminated by the net asset position in the forward pounds. In the case of a net asset exposure, the steps open to the American firm are the exact opposite: Sell the pounds forward, and on the future day receive and deliver the pounds to collect the agreed-on dollar amount.

The use of the forward market as a hedge against exchange rate risk is simple and direct. That is, match the liability or asset position against an offsetting position in the forward market. The forward-market hedge is relatively easy to implement. The firm directs its banker that it needs to buy or sell a foreign currency on a future date, and the banker gives a forward quote.

The forward-market hedge and the money-market hedge give an identical future dollar payment (or receipt) if the forward contracts are priced according to the interest-rate parity theory. The alert student may have noticed that the dollar payments in the money-market hedge and the forward-market hedge examples were, respectively, $4,566.00 and $4,540.20. Recall from our previous discussions that in efficient markets, the forward contracts do indeed conform to IRP theory. However, the numbers in our example are not identical because the forward rate used in the forward-market hedge is not exactly equal to the interest rates in the money-market hedge.

Currency-futures contracts and options. The forward-market hedge is not adequate for some types of exposure. If the foreign currency asset or liability position occurs on a date for which forward quotes are not available, the forward-market hedge cannot be accomplished. In certain cases, the forward-market hedge may cost more than the money-market hedge. In these cases, a corporation with a large amount of exposure may prefer the money-market hedge. In addition to forward-market and money-market hedges, a company can also hedge its exposure by buying (or selling) some relatively new instruments—foreign currency futures contracts and foreign currency options. Although futures contracts are similar to forward contracts in that they provide fixed prices for the required delivery of foreign currency at maturity, exchange traded options permit fixed (strike) price foreign currency transactions anytime before maturity. Futures contracts and options differ from forward contracts in that, unlike forward contracts, which are customized regarding amount and maturity date, futures and options are traded in standard amounts with standard maturity dates. In addition, although forward contracts are written by banks, futures and options are traded on organized exchanges, and individual traders deal with the exchange-based clearing organization rather than with each other. The purchase of futures requires the fulfillment of margin requirements (about 5 to 10 percent of the face amount), whereas the purchase of forward contracts requires only good credit standing with a bank. The purchase of options requires an immediate outlay that reflects a premium above the strike price and an outlay equal to the strike price when and if the option is executed.

Economic Exposure

The economic value of a company can vary in response to exchange rate changes. This change in value may be caused by a rate change-induced decline in the level of expected cash flows and/or by an increase in the riskiness of these cash flows. *Economic exposure* refers to the overall impact of exchange rate changes on the value of the firm and includes not only the strategic impact of changes in competitive relationships that arise from exchange rate changes, but also the economic impact of transactions exposure, and if any, translation exposure.

Economic exposure to exchange rate changes depends on the competitive structure of the markets for a firm's inputs and outputs and how these markets are influenced by changes in exchange rates. This influence, in turn, depends on several economic factors, including price elasticities of the products, the degree of competition from foreign markets and direct (through prices) and indirect (through incomes) impact of exchange rate changes on these markets. Assessing, the economic exposure faced by a particular firm thus depends on the ability to understand and model the structure of the markets for its major inputs (purchases) and outputs (sales).

A company need not engage in any cross-border business activity to be exposed to exchange rate changes, because product and financial markets in most countries are related and influenced to a large extent by the same global forces. The output of a company engaged in business activity only within one country may be competing with imported products, or it may be competing for its inputs with other domestic and foreign purchasers. For example, a Canadian chemical company that did no cross-border business nevertheless found that its profit margins depended directly on the U.S. dollar/Japanese yen exchange rate. The company used coal as an input in its production process, and the Canadian price of coal was heavily influenced by the extent to which the Japanese bought U.S. coal, which in turn depended on the dollar/yen exchange rate.

Although translation exposure need not be managed, it might be useful for a firm to manage its transaction and economic exposures because they affect firm value directly. In most companies, transaction exposure is generally tracked and managed by the office of the corporate treasurer. Economic exposure is difficult to define in operating terms, and very few companies manage it actively. In most companies, economic exposure is generally considered part of the strategic planning process, rather than a treasurer's or finance function.

OBJECTIVE 6 MULTINATIONAL WORKING-CAPITAL MANAGEMENT

The basic principles of working-capital management for a multinational corporation are similar to those for a domestic firm. However, tax and exchange rate factors are additional considerations for the MNC. For an MNC with subsidiaries in many countries, the optimal decisions in the management of working capital are made by considering the market as a whole. The global or centralized financial decisions for an MNC is superior to the set of independent optimal decisions for the subsidiaries. This is the control problem of the MNC. If the individual subsidiaries make decisions that are best for them individually, the consolidation of such decisions may not be best for the MNC as a whole. To effect global management, sophisticated computerized models—incorporating many variables for each subsidiary—are solved to provide the best overall decision for the MNC.

Before considering the components of working-capital management, we examine two techniques that are useful in the management of a wide variety of working-capital components.

Leading and Lagging

Two important risk-reduction techniques for many working-capital problems are called leading and lagging. Often forward-market and money-market hedges are not available to eliminate exchange risk. Under such circumstances, leading and lagging may be used to reduce exchange risk.

Recall that a net asset (long) position is not desirable in a weak or potentially depreciating currency. If a firm has a net asset position in such a currency, it should expedite the disposal of the asset. The firm should get rid of the asset earlier than it otherwise would have, or *lead*, and convert the funds into assets in a relatively stronger currency. By the same reasoning, the firm should *lag*, or delay the collection against a net asset position in a strong currency. If the firm has a net liability (short) position in the weak currency, then it should delay the payment against the liability, or lag, until the currency depreciates. In the case of an appreciating or strong foreign currency and a net liability position, the firm should lead the payments—that is, reduce the liabilities earlier than it would otherwise have.

These principles are useful in the management of working capital of an MNC. They cannot, however, eliminate the foreign exchange risk. When exchange rates change continuously, it is almost impossible to guess whether or when the currency will depreciate or appreciate. This is why the risk of exchange rate changes cannot be eliminated. Nevertheless, the reduction of risk, or the increased gain from exchange rate changes, via the lead and lag is useful for cash management, accounts-receivable management, and short-term liability management.

Cash Management and Positioning of Funds

Positioning of funds takes on an added importance in the international context. Funds may be transferred from a subsidiary of the MNC in country A to another subsidiary in country B such that the foreign exchange exposure and the tax liability of the MNC as a whole are minimized. It bears repeating that, owing to the global strategy of the MNC, the tax liability of the subsidiary in country A may be greater than it would otherwise have been, but the overall tax payment for all units of the MNC is minimized.

The transfer of funds among subsidiaries and the parent company is done by royalties, fees, and transfer pricing. A **transfer price** is the price a subsidiary or a parent company charges other companies that are part of the MNC for its goods or services. A parent that wishes to transfer funds from a subsidiary in a depreciating-currency country may charge a higher price on the goods and services sold to this subsidiary by the parent or by subsidiaries from strong-currency countries.

Transfer price

The price a subsidiary or a parent company charges other companies that are part of the same MNC for its goods or services.

INTERNATIONAL FINANCING AND CAPITAL STRUCTURE DECISIONS

OBJECTIVE 7

An MNC has access to many more financing sources than a domestic firm. It can tap not only the financing sources in its home country that are available to its domestic counterparts, but also sources in the foreign countries in which it operates. Host countries often provide access to low-cost subsidized financing to attract foreign investment.

In addition, the MNC may enjoy preferential credit standards because of its size and investor preference for its home currency. An MNC may be able to access third-country capital markets—countries in which it does not operate but which may have large, well-functioning capital markets. Finally, an MNC can also access external currency markets: Eurodollar, Eurocurrency, or Asian dollar markets. These external markets are unregulated, and because of their lower spread, can offer very attractive rates for financing *and* for investments. With the increasing availability of interest rate and currency swaps, a firm can raise funds in the lowest-cost maturities and currencies and swap them into funds with the maturity and currency denomination it requires. Because of its ability to tap a larger number of financial markets, the MNC may have a lower cost of capital; and because it may be better able to avoid the problems or limitations of any one financial market, it may have a more continuous access to external finance compared to a domestic company.

Access to national financial markets is regulated by governments. For example, in the United States, access to capital markets is governed by SEC regulations. Access to Japanese capital markets is governed by regulations issued by the Ministry of Finance. Some countries have extensive regulations; other countries have relatively open markets. These regulations may differ depending on the legal residency terms of the company raising funds. A company that cannot use its local subsidiary to raise funds in a given market will be treated as foreign. In order to increase their visibility in a foreign capital market, a number of MNCs are now listing their equities on the stock exchanges of many of these countries.

The external currency markets are predominantly centered in Europe, and about 80 percent of their value is denominated in terms of the U.S. dollar. Thus most external currency markets can be characterized as Eurodollar markets. Such markets consist of an active short-term money market and an intermediate-term capital market with maturities ranging up to 15 years and averaging about 7 to 9 years. The intermediate-term market consists of the Eurobond and the Syndicated Eurocredit markets. Eurobonds are usually issued as unregistered bearer bonds and generally tend to have higher flotation costs but lower coupon rates compared to similar bonds issued in the United States. A Syndicated Eurocredit loan is simply a large-term loan that involves contributions by a number of lending banks.

In arriving at its capital-structure decisions, an MNC has to consider a number of factors. First, the capital structure of its local affiliates is influenced by local norms regarding capital structure in that industry and in that country. Local norms for companies in the same industry can differ considerably from country to country. Second, the local affiliate capital structure must also reflect corporate attitudes toward exchange rate and political risk in that country, which would normally lead to higher levels of local debt and other local capital. Third, local affiliate capital structure must reflect home country requirements with regard to the company's consolidated capital structure. Finally, the optimal MNC capital structure should reflect its wider access to financial markets, its ability to diversify economic and political risks, and its other advantages over domestic companies.

RELATE TO THE BIG PICTURE

Investment across international boundaries gives rise to special risks not encountered when investing domestically. Specifically, political risks and exchange rate risk are unique to international investing. Once again, **Axiom 1: The Risk-Return Trade-Off—We Won't Take on Additional Risk Unless We Expect to Be Compensated with Additional Return** *provides a rationale for evaluating these considerations. Where added risks are present, added rewards are necessary to induce investment.*

THE NEW YORK TIMES, JUNE 1, 1994

Ukraine: Not for the Fainthearted

KIEV, UKRAINE—S. C. Johnson & Son Inc., the $3 billion family-owned company that makes clothes, floor wax, furniture cleaners, bug killers, and air fresheners, has traditionally been challenged by new frontiers.

When the company opened a plant in Britain 80 years ago, it was one of the first American corporations to go abroad. At the end of the cold war, it trailblazed again this time into the uncertain precincts of the Ukraine.

Johnson Wax's experience since 1990—when the company started to make and bottle detergents and furniture polish in a renovated corner of a ramshackle factory on the outskirts of Kiev—helps explain the reluctance of other consumer-products companies to jump in.

(A) A few months after Ukraine joined Russia and Belarus in leaving the crumbling Soviet Union, it introduced a coupon currency to replace the ruble. In relatively short order, the coupons became all but worthless. By late last year, inflation had reached about 100 percent a month, from almost zero two years before. A fierce credit squeeze by the government left wholesalers little money to buy Johnson's products. And a government that had initially promised to create a friendly environment for Western investors became encrusted with old style—many say corrupt—former Communists.

Last year, Johnson Wax halved its production from that of 1992. And almost half of 1993's 10 million bottles that came off the assembly line had to be sold in Russia, where the economy, however turbulent, is far stronger than Ukraine's.

(B) A major attraction for Western manufacturers here is low wages. Johnson would like to raise the pay of some workers above the monthly $150 that the best get, but a 92 percent tax rate on earned income above $150 makes it impossible to do so.

Some improvements in everyday life make the difficulty of doing business here a little easier. To make an overseas telephone call took two days several years ago. Now they can be made on the spot. And there are more flights in and out of the country.

(C) But unpredictability prevails. In the last six months, the Ukrainian government has raised or lowered the value-added tax rate three times. Now there are worries that the government might impose an excise tax on supplies coming across the border from Russia. And still another currency is expected, prompting further headaches.

Analysis and Implications ...

A. Pricing, along with almost every other aspect of business, becomes increasingly complicated when inflation rates become both unpredictable and high. In the year ending in June 1993, inflation in Russia was running at 839 percent per year.

B. Unforeseen dilemmas seem to pop up with some regularity when dealing in the international arena. For example, the notion of a government-dictated upper end on wages, in this case imposed by a 92 percent tax rate, is hard to imagine beforehand.

C. From **Axiom 1: The Risk-Return Trade-Off** we learned that investors demand a return for delaying consumption as well as an additional return for taking on added risk. The discount rate that we use to move money through time should reflect anticipated inflation along with the level of risk. In Russia, the difficulty of determining the appropriate discount rate is compounded by the fact that risk abounds, taking the form of instability in terms of taxes, unchecked corruption, and difficulties in obtaining raw materials.

An MNC often makes direct foreign investments abroad in the form of plants and equipment. The decision process for this type of investment is very similar to the capital-budgeting decision in the domestic context—with some additional twists. Most real-world capital-budgeting decisions are made with uncertain future outcomes. Recall that a capital-budgeting decision has three major components: the estimation of the future cash flows (including the initial cost of the proposed investment), the estimation of the risk in these cash flows, and the choice of the proper discount rate. We will assume that the NPV criterion is appropriate as we examine (1) the risks associated with direct foreign investment, and (2) factors to be considered in making the investment decision that may be unique to the international scene.

Risks in Direct Foreign Investments

Risks in domestic capital budgeting arise from two sources: business risk and financial risk. The international capital-budgeting problem incorporates these risks as well as political risk and exchange risk.

Business risk and financial risk. International business risk is due to the response of business to economic conditions in the foreign country. Thus the U.S. MNC needs to be aware of the business climate in both the United States and the foreign country. Additional business risk is due to competition from other MNCs, local businesses, and imported goods. Financial risk refers to the risks introduced in the profit stream by the firm's financial structure. The financial risks of foreign operations are not very different from those of domestic operations.

Political risk. Political risk arises because the foreign subsidiary conducts its business in a political system different from that of the home country. Many foreign governments, especially those in the Third World, are less stable than the U.S. government. A change in a country's political setup frequently brings a change in policies with respect to businesses—and especially with respect to foreign businesses. An extreme change in policy might involve nationalization or even outright expropriation of certain businesses. These are the political risks of conducting business abroad. A business with no investment in plant and equipment is less susceptible to these risks. Some examples of political risk are as follows:

1. Expropriation of plants and equipment without compensation.
2. Expropriation with minimal compensation that is below actual market value.
3. Nonconvertibility of the subsidiary's foreign earnings into the parent's currency—the problem of *blocked funds*.
4. Substantial changes in the laws governing taxation.
5. Governmental controls in the foreign country regarding the sale price of the products, wages, and compensation to personnel, hiring of personnel, making of transfer payments to the parent, and local borrowing.
6. Some governments require certain amounts of local equity participation in the business. Some require that the majority of the equity participation belong to their country.

All these controls and governmental actions introduce risks in the cash flows of the investment to the parent company. These risks must be considered before making the foreign investment decision. The MNC may decide against investing in countries with risks of types 1 and 2. Other risks can be borne—provided that the returns from the foreign investments are high enough to compensate for them. Insurance against some types of political risks may be purchased from private insurance companies or from the U.S. government Overseas Private Investment Corporation. It should be noted that although an MNC cannot protect itself against all foreign political risks, political risks are also present in domestic business.

Exchange rate risk. The exposure of the fixed assets is best measured by the effects of the exchange rate changes on the firm's future earnings stream: that being economic exposure rather than translation exposure. For instance, changes in the exchange rate may adversely affect sales by making competing imported goods cheaper. Changes in the cost of goods sold may result if some components are imported and their price in the foreign currency changes because of exchange rate fluctuations. The thrust of these examples is that the effect of exchange rate changes on income statement items should be properly measured to evaluate exchange risk. Finally, exchange rate risk affects the dollar-denominated profit stream of the parent company, whether or not it affects the foreign-currency profits.

HOW FINANCIAL MANAGERS USE THIS MATERIAL

As the magnitude of international trade has expanded over the past two decades, so has the role of the multinational corporation. Firms routinely report their operating results by breaking-out revenues *both* from major product lines *and* country-of-origin where direct foreign investment has taken place.

U.S. companies have diversified by competing directly in overseas markets. In 1995, for example, the direct foreign investment of U.S. firms generated an impressive $1.8 trillion in overseas (in-country) sales. By comparison, the exports of U.S. goods from American trade ports totaled $575.9 billion for this same 1995 year—or, about one-third of the amount of in-country sales.[6] U.S. firms realize full well the importance of a global presence.

The expanded U.S. multinational presence has made financial executives acutely aware of the problems associated with foreign exchange rate risk. Management of the Walt Disney Company has said: "The Company's objective in managing the exposure to foreign currency fluctuations is to reduce earnings and cash flow volatility associated with foreign exchange rate changes to allow management to focus its attention on its core business issues and challenges."[7]

The preponderance of multinational corporations do indeed focus on their main lines of business and do not, therefore, voluntarily enter into either foreign currency transactions or interest rate transactions for purposes of speculation on possible profit-making opportunities.

SUMMARY

The growth of our global economy, the increasing number of multinational corporations, and the increase in foreign trade itself underscore the importance of the study of international finance.

OBJECTIVE 1

Exchange rate mechanics are discussed in the context of the prevailing floating rates. Under this system, exchange rates between currencies vary in an apparently random fashion in accordance with the supply and demand conditions in the exchange market. Important economic factors affecting the level of exchange rates include the relative economic strengths of the countries involved, the balance-of-payments mechanism, and the countries' monetary policies. Several important exchange rate terms are introduced. These include the asked and the bid rates, which represent the selling and buying rates of

OBJECTIVE 2

[6]*Economic Report of the President* (February 1997): Table B-101, 414. Also see J. P. Quinlan, "Europe, Not Asia, Is Corporate America's Key Market," *The Wall Street Journal* (January 12, 1998): A 20.

[7]The Walt Disney Company, *Annual Report*, 1997, 58–59.

currencies. The direct quote is the units of home currency per unit of foreign currency, and the indirect quote is the reciprocal of the direct quote. Cross-rate computations reflect the exchange rate between two foreign currencies.

The forward exchange market provides a valuable service by quoting rates for the delivery of foreign currencies in the future. The foreign currency is said to sell at a discount (premium) forward from the spot rate when the forward rate is greater (less) than the spot rate, in direct quotation. In addition, the influences of purchasing-power parity (PPP) and the international Fisher effect (IFE) in determining the exchange rate are discussed. In rational and efficient markets, forward rates are unbiased forecasts of future spot rates that are consistent with the PPP.

Exchange rate risk exists because the exact spot rate that prevails on a future date is not known with certainty today. The concept of exchange rate risk is applicable to a wide variety of businesses, including export-import firms and firms involved in making direct foreign investments or international investments in securities. Exchange exposure is a measure of exchange rate risk. There are different ways of measuring the foreign exposure, including the net asset (net liability) measurement. Different strategies are open to businesses to counter the exposure to this risk, including the money-market hedge, the forward-market hedge, futures contracts, and options. Each involves different costs.

In discussing working-capital management in an international environment, we find leading and lagging techniques useful in minimizing exchange rate risks and increasing profitability. In addition, funds positioning is a useful tool for reducing exchange rate risk exposure. The MNC may have a lower cost of capital because it has access to a larger set of financial markets than a domestic company. In addition to the home, host, and third-country financial markets, the MNC can tap the rapidly growing external currency markets. In making capital structure decisions, the MNC must consider political and exchange rate risks and host and home country capital structure norms.

The complexities encountered in the direct foreign investment decision include the usual sources of risk—business and financial—and additional risks associated with fluctuating exchange rates and political factors. Political risk is due to differences in political climates, institutions, and processes between the home country and abroad. Under these conditions, the estimation of future cash flows and the choice of the proper discount rates are more complicated than for the domestic investment situation.

GO TO:
http://www.prenhall.com/bfm
For downloads and current events associated with this chapter

KEY TERMS

Arbitrageur, 814

Asked rate, 814

Bid-rate, 815

Bid-asked spread, 815

Buying rate, 815

Covered-interest arbitrage, 814

Cross rate, 815

Direct quote, 811

Exchange rate, 811

Exchange rate risk, 815

Floating-rate international currency system, 810

Forward exchange contract, 815

Forward-spot differential, 816

Indirect quote, 811

Interest rate parity (IRP) theory, 819

Law of one price, 820

Multinational corporation (MNC), 807

Purchasing power parity (PPP) theory, 820

Selling rate, 815

Simple arbitrage, 814

Spot transactions, 811

Transaction exposure, 823

Transfer price, 827

Triangular arbitrage, 814

STUDY QUESTIONS

22-1. What additional factors are encountered in international as compared with domestic financial management? Discuss each briefly.

22-2. What different types of businesses operate in the international environment? Why are the techniques and strategies available to these firms different?

22-3. What is meant by *arbitrage profits*?

22-4. What are the markets and mechanics involved in generating (a) simple arbitrage profits, (b) triangular arbitrage profits?

22-5. How do the purchasing power parity, interest rate parity, and the Fisher effect explain the relationships between the current spot rate, the future spot rate, and the forward rate?

22-6. What is meant by (a) exchange risk, (b) political risk?

22-7. How can exchange risk be measured?

22-8. What are the differences between transaction, translation, and economic exposures? Should all of them be ideally reduced to zero?

22-9. What steps can a firm take to reduce exchange risk? Indicate at least two different techniques.

22-10. How are the forward market and the money market hedges affected? What are the major differences between these two types of hedges?

22-11. In the New York exchange market, the forward rate for the Indian currency, the rupee, is not quoted. If you were exposed to exchange risk in rupees, how could you cover your position?

22-12. Compare and contrast the use of forward contracts, futures contracts, and options to reduce foreign exchange exposure. When is each instrument most appropriate?

22-13. Indicate two working-capital management techniques that are useful for international businesses to reduce exchange risk and potentially increase profits.

22-14. How do the financing sources available to an MNC differ from those available to a domestic firm? What do these differences mean for the company's cost of capital?

22-15. What risks are associated with direct foreign investment? How do these risks differ from those encountered in domestic investment?

22-16. How is the direct foreign investment decision made? What are the inputs to this decision process? Are the inputs more complicated than those to the domestic investment problem? If so, why?

22-17. A corporation desires to enter a particular foreign market. The DFI analysis indicates that a direct investment in the plant in the foreign country is not profitable. What other course of action can the company take to enter the foreign market? What are the important considerations?

22-18. What are the reasons for the acceptance of a sales office or licensing arrangement when the DFI itself is not profitable?

SELF-TEST PROBLEM

The data for Self-Test Problem ST-1 are given in the following table:

Selling Quotes for the German Mark in New York		
Country	**Contract**	**$/Foreign Currency**
Germany—mark	Spot	.3893
	30-day	.3910
	90-day	.3958

ST-1. You own $10,000. The dollar rate on the German mark is $2.5823/DM. The German mark rate is given in the preceding table. Are arbitrage profits possible? Set up an arbitrage scheme with your capital. What is the gain (loss) in dollars?

STUDY PROBLEMS (SET A)

The data for Study Problems 22-1 through 22-6 are given in the following table:

Selling Quotes for Foreign Currencies in New York		
Country	**Contract**	**$/Foreign Currency**
Canada—dollar	Spot	.8437
	30-day	.8417
	90-day	.8395
Japan—yen	Spot	.004684
	30-day	.004717
	90-day	.004781
Switzerland—franc	Spot	.5139
	30-day	.5169
	90-day	.5315

22-1. An American business needs to pay (a) 10,000 Canadian dollars, (b) 2 million yen, and (c) 50,000 Swiss francs to businesses abroad. What are the dollar payments to the respective countries?

22-2. An American business pays $10,000, $15,000, and $20,000 to suppliers, in, respectively, Japan, Switzerland, and Canada. How much, in local currencies, do the suppliers receive?

22-3. Compute the indirect quote for the spot and forward Canadian dollar, yen, and Swiss franc contracts.

22-4. The spreads on the contracts as a percent of the asked rates are 2 percent for yen, 3 percent for Canadian dollars, and 5 percent for Swiss francs. Show, in a table similar to the preceding one, the bid rates for the different spot and forward rates.

22-5. You own $10,000. The dollar rate in Tokyo is 216.6743. The yen rate in New York is given in the previous table. Are arbitrage profits possible? Set up an arbitrage scheme with your capital. What is the gain (loss) in dollars?

22-6. Compute the Canadian dollar/yen and the yen/Swiss franc spot rate from the data in the preceding table.

INTEGRATIVE PROBLEM

For your job as the business reporter for a local newspaper, you are given the assignment of putting together a series of articles on the multinational finance and the international currency markets for your readers. Much recent local press coverage has been given to losses in the foreign exchange markets by JGAR, a local firm that is the subsidiary of Daedlufetarg, a large German manufacturing firm. Your editor would like you to address several specific questions dealing with multinational finance. Prepare a response to the following memorandum from your editor:

TO: Business Reporter

FROM: Perry White, Editor, *Daily Planet*

RE: Upcoming Series on Multinational Finance

In your upcoming series on multinational finance, I would like to make sure you cover several specific points. In addition, before you begin this assignment, I want to make sure we are all reading from the same script, as accuracy has always been the cornerstone of the *Daily Planet*. I'd like a response to the following questions before we proceed:

1. What new problems and factors are encountered in international as opposed to domestic financial management?
2. What does the term *arbitrage profits* mean?
3. What can a firm do to reduce exchange risk?
4. What are the differences between a forward contract, a futures contract, and options?

Use the following data in your response to the remaining questions:

Selling Quotes for Foreign Currencies in New York

Country–Currency	Contract	$/Foreign
Canada—dollar	Spot	.8450
	30-day	.8415
	90-day	.8390
Japan—yen	Spot	.004700
	30-day	.004750
	90-day	.004820
Switzerland—franc	Spot	.5150
	30-day	.5182
	90-day	.5328

5. An American business needs to pay (a) 15,000 Canadian dollars, (b) 1.5 million yen, and (c) 55,000 Swiss francs to businesses abroad. What are the dollar payments to the respective countries?
6. An American business pays $20,000, $5,000, and $15,000 to suppliers in, respectively, Japan, Switzerland, and Canada. How much, in local currencies, do the suppliers receive?
7. Compute the indirect quote for the spot and forward Canadian dollar contract.
8. You own $10,000. The dollar rate in Tokyo is 216.6752. The yen rate in New York is given in the preceding table. Are arbitrage profits possible? Set up an arbitrage scheme with your capital. What is the gain (loss) in dollars?
9. Compute the Canadian dollar/yen spot rate from the data in the preceding table.

STUDY PROBLEMS (SET B)

The data for Study Problems 22-1B through 22-6B are given in the following table:

Selling Quotes for Foreign Currencies in New York

Country	Contract	$/Foreign Currency
Canada—dollar	Spot	.8439
	30-day	.8410
	90-day	.8390
Japan—yen	Spot	.004680
	30-day	.004720
	90-day	.004787
Switzerland—franc	Spot	.5140
	30-day	.5179
	90-day	.5335

22-1B. An American business needs to pay (a) 15,000 Canadian dollars, (b) 1.5 million yen, and (c) 55,000 Swiss francs to businesses abroad. What are the dollar payments to the respective countries?

22-2B. An American business pays $20,000, $5,000, and $15,000 to suppliers in, respectively, Japan, Switzerland, and Canada. How much, in local currencies, do the suppliers receive?

22-3B. Compute the indirect quote for the spot and forward Canadian dollar, yen, and Swiss franc contracts.

22-4B. The spreads on the contracts as a percent of the asked rates are 4 percent for yen, 3 percent for Canadian dollars, and 6 percent for Swiss francs. Show, in a table similar to the previous one, the bid rates for the different spot and forward rates.

22-5B. You own $10,000. The dollar rate in Tokyo is 216.6752. The yen rate in New York is given in the previous table. Are arbitrage profits possible? Set up an arbitrage scheme with your capital. What is the gain (loss) in dollars?

22-6B. Compute the Canadian dollar/yen and the yen/Swiss franc spot rate from the data in the preceding table.

SELF-TEST SOLUTION

SS-1. The German rate is 2.5823 marks/$1, while the (indirect) New York rate is 1/.3893 = 2.5687 marks/$.

Assuming no transaction costs, the rates between German and New York are out of line. Thus arbitrage profits are possible.

Step 1: Because the mark is cheaper in Germany, buy $10,000 worth of marks in Germany.
The number of marks purchased would be $10,000 × 2.5823 = 25,823 marks

Step 2: Simultaneously sell the marks in New York at the prevailing rate. The amount received upon the sale of the marks would be:

25,823 marks × $.3893/mark = $10,052.89
net gain is $10,052.89 − $10,000 = $52.89

USING A CALCULATOR

As you prepare for a career in business, the ability to use a financial calculator is essential, whether you are in the finance division or the marketing department. For most positions, it will be assumed that you can use a calculator in making computations that at one time were simply not possible without extensive time and effort. The following examples let us see what is possible, but they represent only the beginning of using the calculator in finance.

With just a little time and effort, you will be surprised at how much you can do with the calculator, such as calculating a stock's beta, or determining the value of a bond on a specific day given the exact date of maturity, or finding net present values and internal rates of return, or calculating the standard deviation. The list is almost endless.

In demonstrating how calculators may make our work easier, we must first decide which calculator to use. The options are numerous and largely depend on personal preference. We have chosen the Texas Instruments BAII Plus.

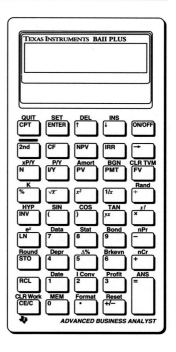

We will limit our discussion to the following issues:

  I. Introductory Comments
  II. An Important Starting Point
  III. Calculating Table Values for:
    A. Appendix B (Compound sum of $1)
    B. Appendix C (Present value of $1)
    C. Appendix D (Sum on an annuity of $1 for *n* periods)
    D. Appendix E (Present value of an annuity for $1 for *n* periods)
  IV. Calculating Present Values
  V. Calculating Future Values (Compound sum)
  VI. Calculating the Number of Payments or Receipts
  VII. Calculating the Payment Amount
  VIII. Calculating the Interest Rate
  IX. Bond Value
    A. Computing the value of a bond
    B. Calculating the yield to maturity on a bond
  X. Computing the Net Present Value and Internal Rate of Return
    A. Where future cash flows are equal amounts in each period (annuity)
    B. Where future cash flows are unequal amounts in each period.

I. INTRODUCTORY COMMENTS

In the examples that follow, you are told (1) which keystrokes to use, (2) the resulting appearance of the calculator display, and (3) a supporting explanation.

The keystrokes column tells you which keys to press. The keystrokes shown in an unshaded box tell you to use one of the calculator's dedicated or "hard" keys. For example, if +/− is shown in the keystrokes instruction column, press that key on the keyboard of the calculator. To use a function printed in gray lettering above a dedicated key, always press the gray key 2nd first, then the function key.

II. An Important Starting Point

Example: You want to display four numbers to the right of the decimal.

Keystrokes	Display	Explanation
2nd		
FORMAT	DEC =	
4 ENTER	DEC = 4.0000	Sets display to show four numbers to the right of the decimal
CE/C CE/C	0.0000	Clears display

Example: You want to display two payments per year to be paid at the end of each period.

Keystrokes	Display	Explanation
2nd		
P/Y	P/Y =	
2 ENTER	P/Y = 2.0000	Sets number of payments per year at 2
2nd		
BGN	END	Sets timing of payment at the end of each period
CE/C CE/C	0.0000	Clears display

III. Calculating Table Values

A. The compound sum of $1 (Appendix B)

Example: What is the table value for the compound sum of $1 for 5 years at a 12 percent annual interest rate?

Keystrokes	Display	Explanation
2nd		
P/Y	P/Y =	
1 ENTER	P/Y = 1.0000	Sets number of payments per year at 1
2nd		
BGN	END	Sets timing of payment at the end of each period
CE/C CE/C	0.0000	Clears display
2nd		
CLR TVM	0.0000	Clears TVM variables
1 +/−	PV = −1.0000	Stores initial $1 as a negative present value
PV		Otherwise, the answer will appear as a negative
5 N	N = 5.0000	Stores number of periods
12 I/Y	I/Y = 12.0000	Stores interest rate
CPT FV	FV = 1.7623	Table value

III. Calculating Table Values (continued)

B. The present value of $1 (Appendix C)

Example: What is the table value for the present value of $1 for 8 years at a 10 percent annual interest rate?

Keystrokes	Display	Explanation
2nd		
P/Y	P/Y =	
1 ENTER	P/Y = 1.0000	Sets number of payments per year at 1
2nd		
BGN	END	Sets timing of payment at the end of each period
CE/C CE/C	0.0000	Clears display
2nd		
CLR TVM	0.0000	Clears TVM variables
1 +/− FV	FV = −1.0000	Stores future amount as negative value
8 N	N = 8.0000	Stores number of periods
10 I/Y	I/Y = 10.0000	Stores interest rate
CPT PV	PV = 0.4665	Table value

C. The sum of an annuity of $1 for *n* periods (Appendix D)

Example: What is the table value for the compound sum of an annuity of $1 for 6 years at a 14 percent annual interest rate?

Keystrokes	Display	Explanation
2nd		
P/Y	P/Y =	
1 ENTER	P/Y = 1.0000	Sets number of payments per year at 1
2nd		
BGN	END	Sets timing of payment at the end of each period
CE/C CE/C	0.0000	Clears display
2nd		
CLR TVM	0.0000	Clears TVM variables
1 +/− PMT	PMT = −1.0000	Stores annual payment (annuity) as a negative number. Otherwise, the answer will appear as a negative.
6 N	N = 6.0000	Stores number of periods
14 I/Y	I/Y = 14.0000	Stores interest rate
CPT FV	FV = 8.5355	Table value

III. Calculating Table Values (continued)

D. The present value of an annuity of $1 for *n* periods (Appendix E)

Example: What is the table value for the present value of an annuity of $1 for 12 years at 9 percent annual interest rate?

Keystrokes	Display	Explanation
2nd		
P/Y	P/Y =	
1 ENTER	P/Y = 1.0000	Sets number of payments per year at 1
2nd		
BGN	END	Sets timing of payment at the end of each period
CE/C CE/C	0.0000	Clears display
2nd		
CLR TVM	0.0000	Clears TVM variables
1 +/− PMT	PMT = −1.0000	Stores annual payment (annuity) as a negative number. Otherwise, the answer will appear as a negative.
12 N	N = 12.0000	Stores number of periods
9 I/Y	I/Y = 9.0000	Stores interest rate
CPT PV	PV = 7.1607	Table value

IV. Calculating Present Values

Example: You are considering the purchase of a franchise of quick oil-change locations, which you believe will provide an annual cash flow of $50,000. At the end of 10 years, you believe that you will be able to sell the franchise for an estimated $900,000. Calculate the maximum amount you should pay for the franchise (present value) in order to realize at least an 18 percent annual yield.

Keystrokes	Display	Explanation
2nd		
BGN	END	Sets timing of payment at the end of each period
CE/C CE/C	0.0000	Clears display
2nd		
CLR TVM	0.0000	Clears TVM variables
10 N	N = 10.0000	Stores *n*, the holding period
18 I/Y	I/Y = 18.0000	Stores *i*, the required rate of return

IV. Calculating Present Values (continued)

50,000 [PMT]	PMT = 50,000.0000	Stores PMT, the annual cash flow to be received
900,000 [FV]	FV = 900,000.0000	Stores FV, the cash flow to be received at the end of the project
[CPT] [PV]	PV = −396,662.3350	The present value, given a required rate of return of 18 percent. (Note: The present value is displayed with a minus sign because it represents cash paid out.)

V. Calculating Future Values (Compound Sum)

Example: If you deposit $300 a month (at the beginning of each month) into a new account that pays 6.25% annual interested compounded monthly, how much will you have in the account after 5 years?

Keystrokes	Display	Explanation
[2nd] [BGN]	END	Sets timing of payment at the end of each period
[2nd] [SET]	BGN	Sets timing of payments to beginning of each period
[2nd] [P/Y]	P/Y =	
12 [ENTER]	P/Y = 12.0000	Sets 12 payments per year
[CE/C] [CE/C]	0.0000	Clears display
[2nd] [CLR TVM]	0.0000	Clears TVM variables
60 [N]	N = 60.0000	Stores n, the number of months for the investment
6.25 [I/Y]	I/Y = 6.2500	Stores i, the annual rate
300 [+/−] [PMT]	PMT = −300.0000	Stores PMT, the monthly amount invested (with a minus sign for cash paid out)
[CPT] [FV]	FV = 21,175.7613	The future value after 5 years

VI. Calculating the Number of Payments or Receipts

Example: If you wish to retire with $500,000 saved, and can only afford payments of $500 each month, how long will you have to contribute toward your retirement if you can earn a 10 percent return on your contributions?

Keystrokes	Display	Explanation
2nd BGN	BGN	Verifies timing of payment at the beginning of each period
2nd P/Y	P/Y = 12.0000	
12 ENTER	P/Y = 12.0000	Sets 12 payments per year
CE/C CE/C	0.0000	Clears display
2nd CLR TVM	0.0000	Clears TVM variables
10 I/Y	I/Y = 10.0000	Stores i, the interest rate
500 +/− PMT	PMT = −500.0000	Stores PMT, the monthly amount invested (with a minus sign for cash paid out)
500,000 FV	FV = 500,000.0000	The value we want to achieve
CPT N	N = 268.2539	Number of months (because we considered monthly payments) required to achieve our goal

VII. Calculating the Payment Amount

Example: Suppose your retirement needs were $750,000. If you are currently 25 years old and plan to retire at age 65, how much will you have to contribute each month for retirement if you can earn 12.5% on your savings?

Keystrokes	Display	Explanation
2nd BGN	BGN	Verifies timing of payment at the beginning of each period
2nd P/Y	P/Y = 12.0000	
12 ENTER	P/Y = 12.0000	Sets 12 payments per year
CE/C CE/C	0.0000	Clears display

VII. Calculating the Payment Amount (continued)

Keystrokes	Display	Explanation
2nd CLR TVM	0.0000	Clears TVM variables
12.5 I/Y	I/Y = 12.5000	Stores *i*, the interest rate
480 N	N = 480.0000	Stores *n*, the number of periods until we stop contributing (40 years × 12 months/years = 480 months)
750,000 FV	FV = 750,000.0000	The value we want to achieve
CPT PMT	PMT = −53.8347	Monthly contribution required to achieve our ultimate goal (shown as negative because it represents cash paid out)

VIII. Calculating the Interest Rate

Example: If you invest $300 at the end of each month for 6 years (72 months) for a promised $30,000 return at the end, what interest rate are you earning on your investment?

Keystrokes	Display	Explanation
2nd BGN	BGN	Sets timing of payments to beginning of each period
2nd SET	END	Sets timing of payments to end of each period
2nd P/Y	P/Y = 12.0000	
12 ENTER	P/Y = 12.0000	Sets 12 payments per year
CE/C CE/C	0.0000	Clears display
2nd CLR TVM	0.0000	Clears TVM variables
72 N	N = 72.0000	Stores N, the number of deposits (investments)
300 +/− PMT	PMT = −300.0000	Stores PMT, the monthly amount invested (with a minus sign for cash paid out)
30,000 FV	FV = 30,000.0000	Stores the future value to be received in 6 years
CPT I/Y	I/Y = 10.5892	The annual interest rate earned on the investment

IX. Bond Valuation

A. Computing the value of a bond

Example: Assume the current date is January 1, 1993, and that you want to know the value of a bond that matures in 10 years and has a coupon rate of 9 percent (4.5% semi-annually). Your required rate of return is 12 percent.

Keystrokes	Display	Explanation
2nd BGN	END	Verifies timing of payments to end of each period
2nd P/Y	P/Y = 12.0000	
2 ENTER	P/Y = 2.0000	Sets 2 payments per year; end mode (END) assumes cash flows are at the end of each 6-month period
CE/C CE/C	0.0000	Clears display
2nd CLR TVM	0.0000	Clears TVM variables
20 N	N = 20.0000	Stores the number of semiannual periods (10 years × 2)
12 I/Y	I/Y = 12.0000	Stores annual rate of return
45 PMT	PMT = 45.0000	Stores the semiannual interest payment
1,000 FV	FV = 1,000.0000	Stores the bond's maturity or par value
CPT PV	PV = −827.9512	Value of the bond, expressed as a negative number

---

Solution using the bond feature:

CE/C CE/C	0.0000	Clears display
2nd BOND	STD = 1-01-1970	(This will be the last date entered)
2nd CLR WORK	STD = 1-01-1970	Clears BOND variables
1.01.93 ENTER	STD = 1-01-1993	Stores the current date (month, day, year)
↓	CPN = 0.0000	
9 ENTER	CPN = 9.0000	Stores the coupon interest rate
↓	RDT = 12-31-1990	(This will be the last date entered)
1.01.03 ENTER	RDT = 1-01-2003	Stores the maturity date in 10 years

Solution using the bond feature: (continued)

Keystrokes	Display	Explanation
↓	RV = 100.0000	Verifies bonds maturity or par value
↓	ACT	
2nd		
SET	360	Sets calculations to be based on 360-day year
↓	2/Y	Verifies semiannual compounding rate
↓	YLD = 0.0000	
12 ENTER	YLD = 12.0000	Stores the investor's required rate of return
↓	PRI = 0.0000	
CPT	PRI = 82.7951	Value of bond as a % of par value; i.e., value of bond is $827.95

IX. Bond Valuation

B. Computing the yield to maturity on a bond

Example: Assume the current date is January 1, 1994, and that you want to know your yield to maturity on a bond that matures in 8 years and has a coupon rate of 12% (6% semiannually). The bond is selling for $1,100.

Keystrokes	Display	Explanation
2nd BGN	END	Verifies timing of payments to end of each period
2nd P/Y	P/Y = 12.0000	
2 ENTER	P/Y = 2.0000	Sets 2 payments per year; end mode (END) assumes cash flows are at the end of each 6-month period
CE/C CE/C	0.0000	Clears display
2nd CLR TVM	0.0000	Clears TVM variables
16 N	N = 16.0000	Stores the number of semiannual periods (8 years × 2)
1100 +/− PV	PV = −1,100.0000	Value of the bond, expressed as a negative number
60 PMT	PMT = 60.0000	Stores the semiannual interest payments
1,000 FV	FV = 1,000.0000	Stores the bond's maturity or par value
CPT I/Y	I/Y = 10.1451	The yield to maturity, expressed on an annual basis

Solution using the bond feature:

Keystrokes	Display	Explanation
CE/C CE/C	0.0000	Clears display
2nd		
BOND	SDT = 1-01-1993	(This will be the last date entered)
2nd		
CLR WORK	SDT = 1-01-1993	Clears BOND variables
1.03.94 ENTER	SDT = 1-03-1994	Stores the current date (month, day, year)
↓	CPN = 0.0000	
12 ENTER	CPN = 12.0000	Stores the coupon interest rate
↓	RDT = 1-01-2003	(This will be the last date entered)
1.03.02 ENTER	RDT = 1-03-2002	Stores the maturity date in 8 years
↓	RV = 100.0000	Verifies bonds maturity or par value
↓	360	
2nd		
SET	ACT	Sets calculations to be based on 360-day year
↓	2/Y	Verifies semiannual compounding rate
↓	YLD = 0.0000	
↓	PRI = 0.0000	
110 ENTER	PRI = 110.0000	Stores the bond value as a percentage of par value
↑	YLD = 0.0000	
CPT	YLD = 10.1451	Bond's yield to maturity

X. Computing the Net Present Value and Internal Rate of Return

A. Where future cash flows are equal amounts in each period (annuity)

Example: The firm is considering a capital project that would cost $80,000. The firm's cost of capital is 12 percent. The project life is 10 years, during which time the firm expects to receive $15,000 per year. Calculate the NPV and the IRR.

Keystrokes	Display	Explanation
2nd		
BGN	END	Verifies timing of payments to end of each period
2nd		
P/Y		
1 ENTER	P/Y = 1.0000	Sets 1 payment per year; end mode (END) assumes cash flows are at the end of each year

X. Computing the Net Present Value and Internal Rate of Return (continued)

Keystrokes	Display	Explanation
CE/C CE/C	0.0000	Clears display
2nd		
CLR TVM	0.0000	Clears TVM variables
15,000 PMT	PMT = 15.0000	Stores the annual cash flows of $15,000
10 N	N = 10.0000	Stores the life of the project
12 I/Y	I/Y = 12.0000	Stores the cost of capital
CPT PV	PV = −84,753.3454	Calculates present value
+/−	PV = 84,753.3454	Changes PV to positive
− 80,000 =	4,753.3454	Calculates net present value by subtracting the cost of the project
80,000 +/−	−80,000.0000	
PV	PV = −80,000.0000	
CPT I/Y	I/Y = 13.4344	Calculates the IRR

B. Where future cash flows are unequal amounts in each period

Example: The firm is considering a capital project that would cost $110,000. The firm's cost of capital is 15 percent. The project life is 5 years, with the following expected cash flows: $ − 25,000, $50,000, $60,000, $60,000, and $70,000. In addition, you expect to receive $30,000 in the last year from the salvage value of the equipment. Calculate the NPV and IRR.

Keystrokes	Display	Explanation
CE/C CE/C	0.0000	Clears display
CF	CF$_0$ = 0.0000	
2nd		
CLR WORK	CF$_0$ = 0.0000	Clears cash flow variables
110,000 +/− ENTER	CF$_0$ = −110,000.0000	Stores CF$_0$, the initial investment (with a minus sign for a negative cash flow)
↓	C01 = 0.0000	Stores CF$_1$, the first year's cash flow (with a minus sign for a negative cash flow)
25,000 +/− ENTER	C01 = −25,000.0000	
↓ ENTER	F01 = 1.0000	Stores the number of years CF$_1$ is repeated (in this case, 1 year only)
↓	C02 = 0.0000	
50,000 ENTER	C02 = 50,000.0000	Stores CF$_2$
↓	F0$_2$ = 1.0000	

X. Computing the Net Present Value and Internal Rate of Return (continued)

ENTER	F02 = 1.0000	Stores the number of years CF_2 is repeated
↓	C03 = 0.0000	
60,000	C03 = 60,000.0000	Stores CF_3
ENTER		
↓	F03 = 2.0000	Stores the number of years CF_3 is repeated (here, 2 years, so our response is 2 to the $F0_3$ prompt)
2 ENTER		
↓	C04 = 0.0000	
100,000	C04 = 100,000.0000	Stores CF_4, $70,000 plus expected $30,000
ENTER		
↓	F04 = 1.0000	Stores the number CF_4 is repeated
ENTER		
2nd		
QUIT	0.0000	Ends storage of individual cash flows
NPV	I = 0.0000	
15 ENTER	I = 15.0000	Stores interest rate
↓	NPV = 0.0000	
CPT	NPV = 29,541.8951	Calculates the project's NPV at the stated interest rate
IRR	IRR = 0.0000	
CPT	IRR = 22.0633	Calculates the project's IRR

COMPOUND SUM OF $1

n	1%	2%	3%	4%	5%	6%	7%	8%	9%	10%
1	1.010	1.020	1.030	1.040	1.050	1.060	1.070	1.080	1.090	1.100
2	1.020	1.040	1.061	1.082	1.102	1.124	1.145	1.166	1.188	1.210
3	1.030	1.061	1.093	1.125	1.158	1.191	1.225	1.260	1.295	1.331
4	1.041	1.082	1.126	1.170	1.216	1.262	1.311	1.360	1.412	1.464
5	1.051	1.104	1.159	1.217	1.276	1.338	1.403	1.469	1.539	1.611
6	1.062	1.126	1.194	1.265	1.340	1.419	1.501	1.587	1.677	1.772
7	1.072	1.149	1.230	1.316	1.407	1.504	1.606	1.714	1.828	1.949
8	1.083	1.172	1.267	1.369	1.477	1.594	1.718	1.851	1.993	2.144
9	1.094	1.195	1.305	1.423	1.551	1.689	1.838	1.999	2.172	2.358
10	1.105	1.219	1.344	1.480	1.629	1.791	1.967	2.159	2.367	2.594
11	1.116	1.243	1.384	1.539	1.710	1.898	2.105	2.332	2.580	2.853
12	1.127	1.268	1.426	1.601	1.796	2.012	2.252	2.518	2.813	3.138
13	1.138	1.294	1.469	1.665	1.886	2.133	2.410	2.720	3.066	3.452
14	1.149	1.319	1.513	1.732	1.980	2.261	2.579	2.937	3.342	3.797
15	1.161	1.346	1.558	1.801	2.079	2.397	2.759	3.172	3.642	4.177
16	1.173	1.373	1.605	1.873	2.183	2.540	2.952	3.426	3.970	4.595
17	1.184	1.400	1.653	1.948	2.292	2.693	3.159	3.700	4.328	5.054
18	1.196	1.428	1.702	2.026	2.407	2.854	3.380	3.996	4.717	5.560
19	1.208	1.457	1.753	2.107	2.527	3.026	3.616	4.316	5.142	6.116
20	1.220	1.486	1.806	2.191	2.653	3.207	3.870	4.661	5.604	6.727
21	1.232	1.516	1.860	2.279	2.786	3.399	4.140	5.034	6.109	7.400
22	1.245	1.546	1.916	2.370	2.925	3.603	4.430	5.436	6.658	8.140
23	1.257	1.577	1.974	2.465	3.071	3.820	4.740	5.871	7.258	8.954
24	1.270	1.608	2.033	2.563	3.225	4.049	5.072	6.341	7.911	9.850
25	1.282	1.641	2.094	2.666	3.386	4.292	5.427	6.848	8.623	10.834
30	1.348	1.811	2.427	3.243	4.322	5.743	7.612	10.062	13.267	17.449
40	1.489	2.208	3.262	4.801	7.040	10.285	14.974	21.724	31.408	45.258
50	1.645	2.691	4.384	7.106	11.467	18.419	29.456	46.900	74.354	117.386

n	11%	12%	13%	14%	15%	16%	17%	18%	19%	20%
1	1.110	1.120	1.130	1.140	1.150	1.160	1.170	1.180	1.190	1.200
2	1.232	1.254	1.277	1.300	1.322	1.346	1.369	1.392	1.416	1.440
3	1.368	1.405	1.443	1.482	1.521	1.561	1.602	1.643	1.685	1.728
4	1.518	1.574	1.630	1.689	1.749	1.811	1.874	1.939	2.005	2.074
5	1.685	1.762	1.842	1.925	2.011	2.100	2.192	2.288	2.386	2.488
6	1.870	1.974	2.082	2.195	2.313	2.436	2.565	2.700	2.840	2.986
7	2.076	2.211	2.353	2.502	2.660	2.826	3.001	3.185	3.379	3.583
8	2.305	2.476	2.658	2.853	3.059	3.278	3.511	3.759	4.021	4.300
9	2.558	2.773	3.004	3.252	3.518	3.803	4.108	4.435	4.785	5.160
10	2.839	3.106	3.395	3.707	4.046	4.411	4.807	5.234	5.695	6.192
11	3.152	3.479	3.836	4.226	4.652	5.117	5.624	6.176	6.777	7.430
12	3.498	3.896	4.334	4.818	5.350	5.936	6.580	7.288	8.064	8.916
13	3.883	4.363	4.898	5.492	6.153	6.886	7.699	8.599	9.596	10.699
14	4.310	4.887	5.535	6.261	7.076	7.987	9.007	10.147	11.420	12.839
15	4.785	5.474	6.254	7.138	8.137	9.265	10.539	11.974	13.589	15.407
16	5.311	6.130	7.067	8.137	9.358	10.748	12.330	14.129	16.171	18.488
17	5.895	6.866	7.986	9.276	10.761	12.468	14.426	16.672	19.244	22.186
18	6.543	7.690	9.024	10.575	12.375	14.462	16.879	19.673	22.900	26.623
19	7.263	8.613	10.197	12.055	14.232	16.776	19.748	23.214	27.251	31.948
20	8.062	9.646	11.523	13.743	16.366	19.461	23.105	27.393	32.429	38.337
21	8.949	10.804	13.021	15.667	18.821	22.574	27.033	32.323	38.591	46.005
22	9.933	12.100	14.713	17.861	21.644	26.186	31.629	38.141	45.923	55.205
23	11.026	13.552	16.626	20.361	24.891	30.376	37.005	45.007	54.648	66.247
24	12.239	15.178	18.788	23.212	28.625	35.236	43.296	53.108	65.031	79.496
25	13.585	17.000	21.230	26.461	32.918	40.874	50.656	62.667	77.387	95.395
30	22.892	29.960	39.115	50.949	66.210	85.849	111.061	143.367	184.672	237.373
40	64.999	93.049	132.776	188.876	267.856	378.715	533.846	750.353	1051.642	1469.740
50	184.559	288.996	450.711	700.197	1083.619	1670.669	2566.080	3927.189	5988.730	9100.191

COMPOUND SUM OF $1 (continued)

n	21%	22%	23%	24%	25%	26%	27%	28%	29%	30%
1	1.210	1.220	1.230	1.240	1.250	1.260	1.270	1.280	1.290	1.300
2	1.464	1.488	1.513	1.538	1.562	1.588	1.613	1.638	1.664	1.690
3	1.772	1.816	1.861	1.907	1.953	2.000	2.048	2.097	2.147	2.197
4	2.144	2.215	2.289	2.364	2.441	2.520	2.601	2.684	2.769	2.856
5	2.594	2.703	2.815	2.932	3.052	3.176	3.304	3.436	3.572	3.713
6	3.138	3.297	3.463	3.635	3.815	4.001	4.196	4.398	4.608	4.827
7	3.797	4.023	4.259	4.508	4.768	5.042	5.329	5.629	5.945	6.275
8	4.595	4.908	5.239	5.589	5.960	6.353	6.767	7.206	7.669	8.157
9	5.560	5.987	6.444	6.931	7.451	8.004	8.595	9.223	9.893	10.604
10	6.727	7.305	7.926	8.594	9.313	10.086	10.915	11.806	12.761	13.786
11	8.140	8.912	9.749	10.657	11.642	12.708	13.862	15.112	16.462	17.921
12	9.850	10.872	11.991	13.215	14.552	16.012	17.605	19.343	21.236	23.298
13	11.918	13.264	14.749	16.386	18.190	20.175	22.359	24.759	27.395	30.287
14	14.421	16.182	18.141	20.319	22.737	25.420	28.395	31.691	35.339	39.373
15	17.449	19.742	22.314	25.195	28.422	32.030	36.062	40.565	45.587	51.185
16	21.113	24.085	27.446	31.242	35.527	40.357	45.799	51.923	58.808	66.541
17	25.547	29.384	33.758	38.740	44.409	50.850	58.165	66.461	75.862	86.503
18	30.912	35.848	41.523	48.038	55.511	64.071	73.869	85.070	97.862	112.454
19	37.404	43.735	51.073	59.567	69.389	80.730	93.813	108.890	126.242	146.190
20	45.258	53.357	62.820	73.863	86.736	101.720	119.143	139.379	162.852	190.047
21	54.762	65.095	77.268	91.591	108.420	128.167	151.312	178.405	210.079	247.061
22	66.262	79.416	95.040	113.572	135.525	161.490	192.165	228.358	271.002	321.178
23	80.178	96.887	116.899	140.829	169.407	203.477	244.050	292.298	349.592	417.531
24	97.015	118.203	143.786	174.628	211.758	256.381	309.943	374.141	450.974	542.791
25	117.388	144.207	176.857	216.539	264.698	323.040	393.628	478.901	581.756	705.627
30	304.471	389.748	497.904	634.810	807.793	1025.904	1300.477	1645.488	2078.208	2619.936
40	2048.309	2846.941	3946.340	5455.797	7523.156	10346.879	14195.051	19426.418	26520.723	36117.754
50	13779.844	20795.680	31278.301	46889.207	70064.812	104354.562	154942.687	229345.875	338440.000	497910.125

n	31%	32%	33%	34%	35%	36%	37%	38%	39%	40%
1	1.310	1.320	1.330	1.340	1.350	1.360	1.370	1.380	1.390	1.400
2	1.716	1.742	1.769	1.796	1.822	1.850	1.877	1.904	1.932	1.960
3	2.248	2.300	2.353	2.406	2.460	2.515	2.571	2.628	2.686	2.744
4	2.945	3.036	3.129	3.224	3.321	3.421	3.523	3.627	3.733	3.842
5	3.858	4.007	4.162	4.320	4.484	4.653	4.826	5.005	5.189	5.378
6	5.054	5.290	5.535	5.789	6.053	6.328	6.612	6.907	7.213	7.530
7	6.621	6.983	7.361	7.758	8.172	8.605	9.058	9.531	10.025	10.541
8	8.673	9.217	9.791	10.395	11.032	11.703	12.410	13.153	13.935	14.758
9	11.362	12.166	13.022	13.930	14.894	15.917	17.001	18.151	19.370	20.661
10	14.884	16.060	17.319	18.666	20.106	21.646	23.292	25.049	26.924	28.925
11	19.498	21.199	23.034	25.012	27.144	29.439	31.910	34.567	37.425	40.495
12	25.542	27.982	30.635	33.516	36.644	40.037	43.716	47.703	52.020	56.694
13	33.460	36.937	40.745	44.912	49.469	54.451	59.892	65.830	72.308	79.371
14	43.832	49.756	54.190	60.181	66.784	74.053	82.051	90.845	100.509	111.120
15	57.420	64.358	72.073	80.643	90.158	100.712	112.410	125.366	139.707	155.567
16	75.220	84.953	95.857	108.061	121.713	136.968	154.002	173.005	194.192	217.793
17	98.539	112.138	127.490	144.802	164.312	186.277	210.983	238.747	269.927	304.911
18	129.086	148.022	169.561	194.035	221.822	253.337	289.046	329.471	375.198	426.875
19	169.102	195.389	225.517	260.006	299.459	344.537	395.993	454.669	521.525	597.625
20	221.523	257.913	299.937	348.408	404.270	468.571	542.511	627.443	724.919	836.674
21	290.196	340.446	398.916	466.867	545.764	637.256	743.240	865.871	1007.637	1171.343
22	380.156	449.388	530.558	625.601	736.781	865.668	1018.238	1194.900	1400.615	1639.878
23	498.004	593.192	705.642	838.305	994.653	1178.668	1394.986	1648.961	1946.854	2295.829
24	652.385	783.013	938.504	1123.328	1342.781	1602.988	1911.129	2275.564	2706.125	3214.158
25	854.623	1033.577	1248.210	1505.258	1812.754	2180.063	2618.245	3140.275	3761.511	4499.816
30	3297.081	4142.008	5194.516	6503.285	8128.426	10142.914	12636.086	15716.703	19517.969	24201.043
40	49072.621	66519.313	89962.188	121388.437	163433.875	219558.625	294317.937	393684.687	525508.312	700022.688

APPENDIX C

PRESENT VALUE OF $1

n	1%	2%	3%	4%	5%	6%	7%	8%	9%	10%
1	.990	.980	.971	.962	.952	.943	.935	.926	.917	.909
2	.980	.961	.943	.925	.907	.890	.873	.857	.842	.826
3	.971	.942	.915	.889	.864	.840	.816	.794	.772	.751
4	.961	.924	.888	.855	.823	.792	.763	.735	.708	.683
5	.951	.906	.863	.822	.784	.747	.713	.681	.650	.621
6	.942	.888	.837	.790	.746	.705	.666	.630	.596	.564
7	.933	.871	.813	.760	.711	.665	.623	.583	.547	.513
8	.923	.853	.789	.731	.677	.627	.582	.540	.502	.467
9	.914	.837	.766	.703	.645	.592	.544	.500	.460	.424
10	.905	.820	.744	.676	.614	.558	.508	.463	.422	.386
11	.896	.804	.722	.650	.585	.527	.475	.429	.388	.350
12	.887	.789	.701	.625	.557	.497	.444	.397	.356	.319
13	.879	.773	.681	.601	.530	.469	.415	.368	.326	.290
14	.870	.758	.661	.577	.505	.442	.388	.340	.299	.263
15	.861	.743	.642	.555	.481	.417	.362	.315	.275	.239
16	.853	.728	.623	.534	.458	.394	.339	.292	.252	.218
17	.844	.714	.605	.513	.436	.371	.317	.270	.231	.198
18	.836	.700	.587	.494	.416	.350	.296	.250	.212	.180
19	.828	.686	.570	.475	.396	.331	.277	.232	.194	.164
20	.820	.673	.554	.456	.377	.312	.258	.215	.178	.149
21	.811	.660	.538	.439	.359	.294	.242	.199	.164	.135
22	.803	.647	.522	.422	.342	.278	.226	.184	.150	.123
23	.795	.634	.507	.406	.326	.262	.211	.170	.138	.112
24	.788	.622	.492	.390	.310	.247	.197	.158	.126	.102
25	.780	.610	.478	.375	.295	.233	.184	.146	.116	.092
30	.742	.552	.412	.308	.231	.174	.131	.099	.075	.057
40	.672	.453	.307	.208	.142	.097	.067	.046	.032	.022
50	.608	.372	.228	.141	.087	.054	.034	.021	.013	.009

n	11%	12%	13%	14%	15%	16%	17%	18%	19%	20%
1	.901	.893	.885	.877	.870	.862	.855	.847	.840	.833
2	.812	.797	.783	.769	.756	.743	.731	.718	.706	.694
3	.731	.712	.693	.675	.658	.641	.624	.609	.593	.579
4	.659	.636	.613	.592	.572	.552	.534	.516	.499	.482
5	.593	.567	.543	.519	.497	.476	.456	.437	.419	.402
6	.535	.507	.480	.456	.432	.410	.390	.370	.352	.335
7	.482	.452	.425	.400	.376	.354	.333	.314	.296	.279
8	.434	.404	.376	.351	.327	.305	.285	.266	.249	.233
9	.391	.361	.333	.308	.284	.263	.243	.225	.209	.194
10	.352	.322	.295	.270	.247	.227	.208	.191	.176	.162
11	.317	.287	.261	.237	.215	.195	.178	.162	.148	.135
12	.286	.257	.231	.208	.187	.168	.152	.137	.124	.112
13	.258	.229	.204	.182	.163	.145	.130	.116	.104	.093
14	.232	.205	.181	.160	.141	.125	.111	.099	.088	.078
15	.209	.183	.160	.140	.123	.108	.095	.084	.074	.065
16	.188	.163	.141	.123	.107	.093	.081	.071	.062	.054
17	.170	.146	.125	.108	.093	.080	.069	.060	.052	.045
18	.153	.130	.111	.095	.081	.069	.059	.051	.044	.038
19	.138	.116	.098	.083	.070	.060	.051	.043	.037	.031
20	.124	.104	.087	.073	.061	.051	.043	.037	.031	.026
21	.112	.093	.077	.064	.053	.044	.037	.031	.026	.022
22	.101	.083	.068	.056	.046	.038	.032	.026	.022	.018
23	.091	.074	.060	.049	.040	.033	.027	.022	.018	.015
24	.082	.066	.053	.043	.035	.028	.023	.019	.015	.013
25	.074	.059	.047	.038	.030	.024	.020	.016	.013	.010
30	.044	.033	.026	.020	.015	.012	.009	.007	.005	.004
40	.015	.011	.008	.005	.004	.003	.002	.001	.001	.001
50	.005	.003	.002	.001	.001	.001	.000	.000	.000	.000

PRESENT VALUE OF $1 (continued)

n	21%	22%	23%	24%	25%	26%	27%	28%	29%	30%
1	.826	.820	.813	.806	.800	.794	.787	.781	.775	.769
2	.683	.672	.661	.650	.640	.630	.620	.610	.601	.592
3	.564	.551	.537	.524	.512	.500	.488	.477	.466	.455
4	.467	.451	.437	.423	.410	.397	.384	.373	.361	.350
5	.386	.370	.355	.341	.328	.315	.303	.291	.280	.269
6	.319	.303	.289	.275	.262	.250	.238	.227	.217	.207
7	.263	.249	.235	.222	.210	.198	.188	.178	.168	.159
8	.218	.204	.191	.179	.168	.157	.148	.139	.130	.123
9	.180	.167	.155	.144	.134	.125	.116	.108	.101	.094
10	.149	.137	.126	.116	.107	.099	.092	.085	.078	.073
11	.123	.112	.103	.094	.086	.079	.072	.066	.061	.056
12	.102	.092	.083	.076	.069	.062	.057	.052	.047	.043
13	.084	.075	.068	.061	.055	.050	.045	.040	.037	.033
14	.069	.062	.055	.049	.044	.039	.035	.032	.028	.025
15	.057	.051	.045	.040	.035	.031	.028	.025	.022	.020
16	.047	.042	.036	.032	.028	.025	.022	.019	.017	.015
17	.039	.034	.030	.026	.023	.020	.017	.015	.013	.012
18	.032	.028	.024	.021	.018	.016	.014	.012	.010	.009
19	.027	.023	.020	.017	.014	.012	.011	.009	.008	.007
20	.022	.019	.016	.014	.012	.010	.008	.007	.006	.005
21	.018	.015	.013	.011	.009	.008	.007	.006	.005	.004
22	.015	.013	.011	.009	.007	.006	.005	.004	.004	.003
23	.012	.010	.009	.007	.006	.005	.004	.003	.003	.002
24	.010	.008	.007	.006	.005	.004	.003	.003	.002	.002
25	.009	.007	.006	.005	.004	.003	.003	.002	.002	.001
30	.003	.003	.002	.002	.001	.001	.001	.001	.000	.000
40	.000	.000	.000	.000	.000	.000	.000	.000	.000	.000
50	.000	.000	.000	.000	.000	.000	.000	.000	.000	.000

n	31%	32%	33%	34%	35%	36%	37%	38%	39%	40%
1	.763	.758	.752	.746	.741	.735	.730	.725	.719	.714
2	.583	.574	.565	.557	.549	.541	.533	.525	.518	.510
3	.445	.435	.425	.416	.406	.398	.389	.381	.372	.364
4	.340	.329	.320	.310	.301	.292	.284	.276	.268	.260
5	.259	.250	.240	.231	.223	.215	.207	.200	.193	.186
6	.198	.189	.181	.173	.165	.158	.151	.145	.139	.133
7	.151	.143	.136	.129	.122	.116	.110	.105	.100	.095
8	.115	.108	.102	.096	.091	.085	.081	.076	.072	.068
9	.088	.082	.077	.072	.067	.063	.059	.055	.052	.048
10	.067	.062	.058	.054	.050	.046	.043	.040	.037	.035
11	.051	.047	.043	.040	.037	.034	.031	.029	.027	.025
12	.039	.036	.033	.030	.027	.025	.023	.021	.019	.018
13	.030	.027	.025	.022	.020	.018	.017	.015	.014	.013
14	.023	.021	.018	.017	.015	.014	.012	.011	.010	.009
15	.017	.016	.014	.012	.011	.010	.009	.008	.007	.006
16	.013	.012	.010	.009	.008	.007	.006	.006	.005	.005
17	.010	.009	.008	.007	.006	.005	.005	.004	.004	.003
18	.008	.007	.006	.005	.005	.004	.003	.003	.003	.002
19	.006	.005	.004	.004	.003	.003	.003	.002	.002	.002
20	.005	.004	.003	.003	.002	.002	.002	.002	.001	.001
21	.003	.003	.003	.002	.002	.002	.001	.001	.001	.001
22	.003	.002	.002	.002	.001	.001	.001	.001	.001	.001
23	.002	.002	.001	.001	.001	.001	.001	.001	.001	.000
24	.002	.001	.001	.001	.001	.001	.001	.001	.000	.000
25	.001	.001	.001	.001	.001	.000	.000	.000	.000	.000
30	.000	.000	.000	.000	.000	.000	.000	.000	.000	.000
40	.000	.000	.000	.000	.000	.000	.000	.000	.000	.000

SUM OF AN ANNUITY OF $1 FOR *n* PERIODS

n	1%	2%	3%	4%	5%	6%	7%	8%	9%	10%
1	1.000	1.000	1.000	1.000	1.000	1.000	1.000	1.000	1.000	1.000
2	2.010	2.020	2.030	2.040	2.050	2.060	2.070	2.080	2.090	2.100
3	3.030	3.060	3.091	3.122	3.152	3.184	3.215	3.246	3.278	3.310
4	4.060	4.122	4.184	4.246	4.310	4.375	4.440	4.506	4.573	4.641
5	5.101	5.204	5.309	5.416	5.526	5.637	5.751	5.867	5.985	6.105
6	6.152	6.308	6.468	6.633	6.802	6.975	7.153	7.336	7.523	7.716
7	7.214	7.434	7.662	7.898	8.142	8.394	8.654	8.923	9.200	9.487
8	8.286	8.583	8.892	9.214	9.549	9.897	10.260	10.637	11.028	11.436
9	9.368	9.755	10.159	10.583	11.027	11.491	11.978	12.488	13.021	13.579
10	10.462	10.950	11.464	12.006	12.578	13.181	13.816	14.487	15.193	15.937
11	11.567	12.169	12.808	13.486	14.207	14.972	15.784	16.645	17.560	18.531
12	12.682	13.412	14.192	15.026	15.917	16.870	17.888	18.977	20.141	21.384
13	13.809	14.680	15.618	16.627	17.713	18.882	20.141	21.495	22.953	24.523
14	14.947	15.974	17.086	18.292	19.598	21.015	22.550	24.215	26.019	27.975
15	16.097	17.293	18.599	20.023	21.578	23.276	25.129	27.152	29.361	31.772
16	17.258	18.639	20.157	21.824	23.657	25.672	27.888	30.324	33.003	35.949
17	18.430	20.012	21.761	23.697	25.840	28.213	30.840	33.750	36.973	40.544
18	19.614	21.412	23.414	25.645	28.132	30.905	33.999	37.450	41.301	45.599
19	20.811	22.840	25.117	27.671	30.539	33.760	37.379	41.446	46.018	51.158
20	22.019	24.297	26.870	29.778	33.066	36.785	40.995	45.762	51.159	57.274
21	23.239	25.783	28.676	31.969	35.719	39.992	44.865	50.422	56.764	64.002
22	24.471	27.299	30.536	34.248	38.505	43.392	49.005	55.456	62.872	71.402
23	25.716	28.845	32.452	36.618	41.430	46.995	53.435	60.893	69.531	79.542
24	26.973	30.421	34.426	39.082	44.501	50.815	58.176	66.764	76.789	88.496
25	28.243	32.030	36.459	41.645	47.726	54.864	63.248	73.105	84.699	98.346
30	34.784	40.567	47.575	56.084	66.438	79.057	94.459	113.282	136.305	164.491
40	48.885	60.401	75.400	95.024	120.797	154.758	199.630	295.052	337.872	442.580
50	64.461	84.577	112.794	152.664	209.341	290.325	406.516	573.756	815.051	1163.865

n	11%	12%	13%	14%	15%	16%	17%	18%	19%	20%
1	1.000	1.000	1.000	1.000	1.000	1.000	1.000	1.000	1.000	1.000
2	2.110	2.120	2.130	2.140	2.150	2.160	2.170	2.180	2.190	2.200
3	3.342	3.374	3.407	3.440	3.472	3.506	3.539	3.572	3.606	3.640
4	4.710	4.779	4.850	4.921	4.993	5.066	5.141	5.215	5.291	5.368
5	6.228	6.353	6.480	6.610	6.742	6.877	7.014	7.154	7.297	7.442
6	7.913	8.115	8.323	8.535	8.754	8.977	9.207	9.442	9.683	9.930
7	9.783	10.089	10.405	10.730	11.067	11.414	11.772	12.141	12.523	12.916
8	11.859	12.300	12.757	13.233	13.727	14.240	14.773	15.327	15.902	16.499
9	14.164	14.776	15.416	16.085	16.786	17.518	18.285	19.086	19.923	20.799
10	16.722	17.549	18.420	19.337	20.304	21.321	22.393	23.521	24.709	25.959
11	19.561	20.655	21.814	23.044	24.349	25.733	27.200	28.755	30.403	32.150
12	22.713	24.133	25.650	27.271	29.001	30.850	32.824	34.931	37.180	39.580
13	26.211	28.029	29.984	32.088	34.352	36.786	39.404	42.218	45.244	48.496
14	30.095	32.392	34.882	37.581	40.504	43.672	47.102	50.818	54.841	59.196
15	34.405	37.280	40.417	43.842	47.580	51.659	56.109	60.965	66.260	72.035
16	39.190	42.753	46.671	50.980	55.717	60.925	66.648	72.938	79.850	87.442
17	44.500	48.883	53.738	59.117	65.075	71.673	78.978	87.067	96.021	105.930
18	50.396	55.749	61.724	68.393	75.836	84.140	93.404	103.739	115.265	128.116
19	56.939	63.439	70.748	78.968	88.211	98.603	110.283	123.412	138.165	154.739
20	64.202	72.052	80.946	91.024	102.443	115.379	130.031	146.626	165.417	186.687
21	72.264	81.698	92.468	104.767	118.809	134.840	153.136	174.019	197.846	225.024
22	81.213	92.502	105.489	120.434	137.630	157.414	180.169	206.342	236.436	271.028
23	91.147	104.602	120.203	138.295	159.274	183.600	211.798	244.483	282.359	326.234
24	102.173	118.154	136.829	158.656	184.166	213.976	248.803	289.490	337.007	392.480
25	114.412	133.333	155.616	181.867	212.790	249.212	292.099	342.598	402.038	471.976
30	199.018	241.330	293.192	356.778	434.738	530.306	647.423	790.932	966.698	1181.865
40	581.812	767.080	1013.667	1341.979	1779.048	2360.724	3134.412	4163.094	5529.711	7343.715
50	1668.723	2399.975	3459.344	4994.301	7217.488	10435.449	15088.805	21812.273	31514.492	45496.094

SUM OF AN ANNUITY OF $1 FOR *n* PERIODS (continued)

n	21%	22%	23%	24%	25%	26%	27%	28%	29%	30%
1	1.000	1.000	1.000	1.000	1.000	1.000	1.000	1.000	1.000	1.000
2	2.210	2.220	2.230	2.240	2.250	2.260	2.270	2.280	2.290	2.300
3	3.674	3.708	3.743	3.778	3.813	3.848	3.883	3.918	3.954	3.990
4	5.446	5.524	5.604	5.684	5.766	5.848	5.931	6.016	6.101	6.187
5	7.589	7.740	7.893	8.048	8.207	8.368	8.533	8.700	8.870	9.043
6	10.183	10.442	10.708	10.980	11.259	11.544	11.837	12.136	12.442	12.756
7	13.321	13.740	14.171	14.615	15.073	15.546	16.032	16.534	17.051	17.583
8	17.119	17.762	18.430	19.123	19.842	20.588	21.361	22.163	22.995	23.858
9	21.714	22.670	23.669	24.712	25.802	26.940	28.129	29.369	30.664	32.015
10	27.274	28.657	20.113	31.643	33.253	34.945	36.723	38.592	40.556	42.619
11	34.001	35.962	38.039	40.238	42.566	45.030	47.639	50.398	53.318	56.405
12	42.141	44.873	47.787	50.895	54.208	57.738	61.501	65.510	69.780	74.326
13	51.991	55.745	59.778	64.109	68.760	73.750	79.106	84.853	91.016	97.624
14	63.909	69.009	74.528	80.496	86.949	93.925	101.465	109.611	118.411	127.912
15	78.330	85.191	92.669	100.815	109.687	119.346	129.860	141.302	153.750	167.285
16	95.779	104.933	114.983	126.010	138.109	151.375	165.922	181.867	199.337	218.470
17	116.892	129.019	142.428	157.252	173.636	191.733	211.721	233.790	258.145	285.011
18	142.439	158.403	176.187	195.993	218.045	242.583	269.885	300.250	334.006	371.514
19	173.351	194.251	217.710	244.031	273.556	306.654	343.754	385.321	431.868	483.968
20	210.755	237.986	268.783	303.598	342.945	387.384	437.568	494.210	558.110	630.157
21	256.013	291.343	331.603	377.461	429.681	489.104	556.710	633.589	720.962	820.204
22	310.775	356.438	408.871	469.052	538.101	617.270	708.022	811.993	931.040	1067.265
23	377.038	435.854	503.911	582.624	673.626	778.760	900.187	1040.351	1202.042	1388.443
24	457.215	532.741	620.810	723.453	843.032	982.237	1144.237	1332.649	1551.634	1805.975
25	554.230	650.944	764.596	898.082	1054.791	1238.617	1454.180	1706.790	2002.608	2348.765
30	1445.111	1767.044	2160.459	2640.881	3227.172	3941.953	4812.891	5873.172	7162.785	8729.805
40	9749.141	12936.141	17153.691	22728.367	30088.621	39791.957	52570.707	69376.562	91447.375	120389.375

n	31%	32%	33%	34%	35%	36%	37%	38%	39%	40%
1	1.000	1.000	1.000	1.000	1.000	1.000	1.000	1.000	1.000	1.000
2	2.310	2.320	2.330	2.340	2.350	2.360	2.370	2.380	2.390	2.400
3	4.026	4.062	4.099	4.136	4.172	4.210	4.247	4.284	4.322	4.360
4	6.274	6.362	6.452	6.542	6.633	6.725	6.818	6.912	7.008	7.104
5	9.219	9.398	9.581	9.766	9.954	10.146	10.341	10.539	10.741	10.946
6	13.077	13.406	13.742	14.086	14.438	14.799	15.167	15.544	15.930	16.324
7	18.131	18.696	19.277	19.876	20.492	21.126	21.779	22.451	23.142	23.853
8	24.752	25.678	26.638	27.633	28.664	29.732	30.837	31.982	33.167	34.395
9	33.425	34.895	36.429	38.028	39.696	41.435	43.247	45.135	47.103	49.152
10	44.786	47.062	49.451	51.958	54.590	57.351	60.248	63.287	66.473	69.813
11	59.670	63.121	66.769	70.624	74.696	78.998	83.540	88.335	93.397	98.739
12	79.167	84.320	89.803	95.636	101.840	108.437	115.450	122.903	130.822	139.234
13	104.709	112.302	120.438	129.152	138.484	148.474	159.166	170.606	182.842	195.928
14	138.169	149.239	161.183	174.063	187.953	202.925	219.058	236.435	255.151	275.299
15	182.001	197.996	215.373	234.245	254.737	276.978	301.109	327.281	355.659	386.418
16	239.421	262.354	287.446	314.888	344.895	377.690	413.520	452.647	495.366	541.985
17	314.642	347.307	383.303	422.949	466.608	514.658	567.521	625.652	689.558	759.778
18	413.180	459.445	510.792	567.751	630.920	700.935	778.504	864.399	959.485	1064.689
19	542.266	607.467	680.354	761.786	852.741	954.271	1067.551	1193.870	1334.683	1491.563
20	711.368	802.856	905.870	1021.792	1152.200	1298.809	1463.544	1648.539	1856.208	2089.188
21	932.891	1060.769	1205.807	1370.201	1556.470	1767.380	2006.055	2275-982	2581.128	2925.862
22	1223.087	1401.215	1604.724	1837.068	2102.234	2404.636	2749.294	3141.852	3588.765	4097.203
23	1603.243	1850.603	2135.282	2462.669	2839.014	3271.304	3767.532	4336.750	4989.379	5737.078
24	2101.247	2443.795	2840.924	3300.974	3833.667	4449.969	5162.516	5985.711	6936.230	8032.906
25	2753.631	3226.808	3779.428	4424.301	5176.445	6052.957	7073.645	8261.273	9642.352	11247.062
30	10632.543	12940.672	15737.945	19124.434	23221.258	28172.016	34148.906	41357.227	50043.625	60500.207

PRESENT VALUE OF AN ANNUITY OF $1 FOR *n* PERIODS

n	1%	2%	3%	4%	5%	6%	7%	8%	9%	10%
1	.990	.980	.971	.962	.952	.943	.935	.926	.917	.909
2	1.970	1.942	1.913	1.886	1.859	1.833	1.808	1.783	1.759	1.736
3	2.941	2.884	2.829	2.775	2.723	2.673	2.624	2.577	2.531	2.487
4	3.902	3.808	3.717	3.630	3.546	3.465	3.387	3.312	3.240	3.170
5	4.853	4.713	4.580	4.452	4.329	4.212	4.100	3.993	3.890	3.791
6	5.795	5.601	5.417	5.242	5.076	4.917	4.767	4.623	4.486	4.355
7	6.728	6.472	6.230	6.002	5.786	5.582	5.389	5.206	5.033	4.868
8	7.652	7.326	7.020	6.733	6.463	6.210	5.971	5.747	5.535	5.335
9	8.566	8.162	7.786	7.435	7.108	6.802	6.515	6.247	5.995	5.759
10	9.471	8.983	8.530	8.111	7.722	7.360	7.024	6.710	6.418	6.145
11	10.368	9.787	9.253	8.760	8.306	7.887	7.499	7.139	6.805	6.495
12	11.255	10.575	9.954	9.385	8.863	8.384	7.943	7.536	7.161	6.814
13	12.134	11.348	10.635	9.986	9.394	8.853	8.358	7.904	7.487	7.103
14	13.004	12.106	11.296	10.563	9.899	9.295	8.746	8.244	7.786	7.367
15	13.865	12.849	11.938	11.118	10.380	9.712	9.108	8.560	8.061	7.606
16	14.718	13.578	12.561	11.652	10.838	10.106	9.447	8.851	8.313	7.824
17	15.562	14.292	13.166	12.166	11.274	10.477	9.763	9.122	8.544	8.022
18	16.398	14.992	13.754	12.659	11.690	10.828	10.059	9.372	8.756	8.201
19	17.226	15.679	14.324	13.134	12.085	11.158	10.336	9.604	8.950	8.365
20	18.046	16.352	14.878	13.590	12.462	11.470	10.594	9.818	9.129	8.514
21	18.857	17.011	15.415	14.029	12.821	11.764	10.836	10.017	9.292	8.649
22	19.661	17.658	15.937	14.451	13.163	12.042	11.061	10.201	9.442	8.772
23	20.456	18.292	16.444	14.857	13.489	12.303	11.272	10.371	9.580	8.883
24	21.244	18.914	16.936	15.247	13.799	12.550	11.469	10.529	9.707	8.985
25	22.023	19.524	17.413	15.622	14.094	12.783	11.654	10.675	9.823	9.077
30	25.808	22.397	19.601	17.292	15.373	13.765	12.409	11.258	10.274	9.427
40	32.835	27.356	23.115	19.793	17.159	15.046	13.332	11.925	10.757	9.779
50	39.197	31.424	25.730	21.482	18.256	15.762	13.801	12.234	10.962	9.915

n	11%	12%	13%	14%	15%	16%	17%	18%	19%	20%
1	.901	.893	.885	.877	.870	.862	.855	.847	.840	.833
2	1.713	1.690	1.668	1.647	1.626	1.605	1.585	1.566	1.547	1.528
3	2.444	2.402	2.361	2.322	2.283	2.246	2.210	2.174	2.140	2.106
4	3.102	3.037	2.974	2.914	2.855	2.798	2.743	2.690	2.639	2.589
5	3.696	3.605	3.517	3.433	3.352	3.274	3.199	3.127	3.058	2.991
6	4.231	4.111	3.998	3.889	3.784	3.685	3.589	3.498	3.410	3.326
7	4.712	4.564	4.423	4.288	4.160	4.039	3.922	3.812	3.706	3.605
8	5.146	4.968	4.799	4.639	4.487	4.344	4.207	4.078	3.954	3.837
9	5.537	5.328	5.132	4.946	4.772	4.607	4.451	4.303	4.163	4.031
10	5.889	5.650	5.426	5.216	5.019	4.833	4.659	4.494	4.339	4.192
11	6.207	5.938	5.687	5.453	5.234	5.029	4.836	4.656	4.487	4.327
12	6.492	6.194	5.918	5.660	5.421	5.197	4.988	4.793	4.611	4.439
13	6.750	6.424	6.122	5.842	5.583	5.342	5.118	4.910	4.715	4.533
14	6.982	6.628	6.303	6.002	5.724	5.468	5.229	5.008	4.802	4.611
15	7.191	6.811	6.462	6.142	5.847	5.575	5.324	5.092	4.876	4.675
16	7.379	6.974	6.604	6.265	5.954	5.669	5.405	5.162	4.938	4.730
17	7.549	7.120	6.729	6.373	6.047	5.749	5.475	5.222	4.990	4.775
18	7.702	7.250	6.840	6.467	6.128	5.818	5.534	5.273	5.033	4.812
19	7.839	7.366	6.938	6.550	6.198	5.877	5.585	5.316	5.070	4.843
20	7.963	7.469	7.025	6.623	6.259	5.929	5.628	5.353	5.101	4.870
21	8.075	7.562	7.102	6.687	6.312	5.973	5.665	5.384	5.127	4.891
22	8.176	7.645	7.170	6.743	6.359	6.011	5.696	5.410	5.149	4.909
23	8.266	7.718	7.230	6.792	6.399	6.044	5.723	5.432	5.167	4.925
24	8.348	7.784	7.283	6.835	6.434	6.073	5.747	5.451	5.182	4.937
25	8.442	7.843	7.330	6.873	6.464	6.097	5.766	5.467	5.195	4.948
30	8.694	8.055	7.496	7.003	6.566	6.177	5.829	5.517	5.235	4.979
40	8.951	8.244	7.634	7.105	6.642	6.233	5.871	5.548	5.258	4.997
50	9.042	8.305	7.675	7.133	6.661	6.246	5.880	5.554	5.262	4.999

PRESENT VALUE OF AN ANNUITY OF $1 FOR *n* PERIODS (continued)

n	21%	22%	23%	24%	25%	26%	27%	28%	29%	30%
1	.826	.820	.813	.806	.800	.794	.787	.781	.775	.769
2	1.509	1.492	1.474	1.457	1.440	1.424	1.407	1.392	1.376	1.361
3	2.074	2.042	2.011	1.981	1.952	1.923	1.896	1.868	1.842	1.816
4	2.540	2.494	2.448	2.404	2.362	2.320	2.280	2.241	2.203	2.166
5	2.926	2.864	2.803	2.745	2.689	2.635	2.583	2.532	2.483	2.436
6	3.245	3.167	3.092	3.020	2.951	2.885	2.821	2.759	2.700	2.643
7	3.508	3.416	3.327	3.242	3.161	3.083	3.009	2.937	2.868	2.802
8	3.726	3.619	3.518	3.421	3.329	3.241	3.156	3.076	2.999	2.925
9	3.905	3.786	3.673	3.566	3.463	3.366	3.273	3.184	3.100	3.019
10	4.054	3.923	3.799	3.682	3.570	3.465	3.364	3.269	3.178	3.092
11	4.177	4.035	3.902	3.776	3.656	3.544	3.437	3.335	3.239	3.147
12	4.278	4.127	3.985	3.851	3.725	3.606	3.493	3.387	3.286	3.190
13	4.362	4.203	4.053	3.912	3.780	3.656	3.538	3.427	3.322	3.223
14	4.432	4.265	4.108	3.962	3.824	3.695	3.573	3.459	3.351	3.249
15	4.489	4.315	4.153	4.001	3.859	3.726	3.601	3.483	3.373	3.268
16	4.536	4.357	4.189	4.033	3.887	3.751	3.623	3.503	3.390	3.283
17	4.576	4.391	4.219	4.059	3.910	3.771	3.640	3.518	3.403	3.295
18	4.608	4.419	4.243	4.080	3.928	3.786	3.654	3.529	3.413	3.304
19	4.635	4.442	4.263	4.097	3.942	3.799	3.664	3.539	3.421	3.311
20	4.657	4.460	4.279	4.110	3.954	3.808	3.673	3.546	3.427	3.316
21	4.675	4.476	4.292	4.121	3.963	3.816	3.679	3.551	3.432	3.320
22	4.690	4.488	4.302	4.130	3.970	3.822	3.684	3.556	3.436	3.323
23	4.703	4.499	4.311	4.137	3.976	3.827	3.689	3.559	3.438	3.325
24	4.713	4.507	4.318	4.143	3.981	3.831	3.692	3.562	3.441	3.327
25	4.721	4.514	4.323	4.147	3.985	3.834	3.694	3.564	3.442	3.329
30	4.746	4.534	4.339	4.160	3.995	3.842	3.701	3.569	3.447	3.332
40	4.760	4.544	4.347	4.166	3.999	3.846	3.703	3.571	3.448	3.333
50	4.762	4.545	4.348	4.167	4.000	3.846	3.704	3.571	3.448	3.333

n	31%	32%	33%	34%	35%	36%	37%	38%	39%	40%
1	.763	.758	.752	.746	.741	.735	.730	.725	.719	.714
2	1.346	1.331	1.317	1.303	1.289	1.276	1.263	1.250	1.237	1.224
3	1.791	1.766	1.742	1.719	1.696	1.673	1.652	1.630	1.609	1.589
4	2.130	2.096	2.062	2.029	1.997	1.966	1.935	1.906	1.877	1.849
5	2.390	2.345	2.302	2.260	2.220	2.181	2.143	2.106	2.070	2.035
6	2.588	2.534	2.483	2.433	2.385	2.339	2.294	2.251	2.209	2.168
7	2.739	2.677	2.619	2.562	2.508	2.455	2.404	2.355	2.308	2.263
8	2.854	2.786	2.721	2.658	2.598	2.540	2.485	2.432	2.380	2.331
9	2.942	2.868	2.798	2.730	2.665	2.603	2.544	2.487	2.432	2.379
10	3.009	2.930	2.855	2.784	2.715	2.649	2.587	2.527	2.469	2.414
11	3.060	2.978	2.899	2.824	2.752	2.683	2.618	2.555	2.496	2.438
12	3.100	3.013	2.931	2.853	2.779	2.708	2.641	2.576	2.515	2.456
13	3.129	3.040	2.956	2.876	2.799	2.727	2.658	2.592	2.529	2.469
14	3.152	3.061	2.974	2.892	2.814	2.740	2.670	2.603	2.539	2.477
15	3.170	3.076	2.988	2.905	2.825	2.750	2.679	2.611	2.546	2.484
16	3.183	3.088	2.999	2.914	2.834	2.757	2.685	2.616	2.551	2.489
17	3.193	3.097	3.007	2.921	2.840	2.763	2.690	2.621	2.555	2.492
18	3.201	3.104	3.012	2.926	2.844	2.767	2.693	2.624	2.557	2.494
19	3.207	3.109	3.017	2.930	2.848	2.770	2.696	2.626	2.559	2.496
20	3.211	3.113	3.020	2.933	2.850	2.772	2.698	2.627	2.561	2.497
21	3.215	3.116	3.023	2.935	2.852	2.773	2.699	2.629	2.562	2.498
22	3.217	3.118	3.025	2.936	2.853	2.775	2.700	2.629	2.562	2.498
23	3.219	3.120	3.026	2.938	2.854	2.775	2.701	2.630	2.563	2.499
24	3.221	3.121	3.027	2.939	2.855	2.776	2.701	2.630	2.563	2.499
25	3.222	3.122	3.028	2.939	2.856	2.776	2.702	2.631	2.563	2.499
30	3.225	2.124	3.030	2.941	2.857	2.777	2.702	2.631	2.564	2.500
40	3.226	3.125	3.030	2.941	2.857	2.778	2.703	2.632	2.564	2.500
50	3.226	3.125	3.030	2.941	2.857	2.778	2.703	2.632	2.564	2.500

Solutions for Selected End-of-Chapter Problems

CHAPTER 1

1-1A. Taxable income = $526,800
Tax liability = $179,112
1-3A. Taxable income = $365,000
Tax liability = $124,100
1-5A. Taxable income = ($38,000)
Tax liability = $0
1-7A. Taxable income = $153,600
Tax liability = $43,154
1-9A. Taxable income = $370,000
Tax liability = $125,800
1-11A. Taxable income = $1,813,000
Tax liability = $616,420

CHAPTER 2

2-2A. Nominal rate = 12.13%.
2-4A. Nominal rate = 11.28%.
2-6A. Nominal rate = 12.35%.

CHAPTER 3

3-1A. Net Profit Margin = 8.0%
3-5A. **a.** Total Asset Turnover = 2X
c. Operating Return on Investment = 35%
3-7A.

	1997	1998
Current Ratio	6x	4x
ACP	137 days	107 days
Fixed Asset T/O	1x	1.04x
Operating Profit Margin	20.8%	24.8%

3-9A. Cash flow from:

Operations	$87,000
Investing	(142,500)
Financing	63,000

3-11A. **a.** 2.25x; 11.11%; 25%

CHAPTER 4

4-1A. Discretionary Financing Needed = ($0.5 million)
4-3A. Total Assets = $1.8 million
4-5A. Total Assets = $2 million
4-9A. **a.** Notes Payable = $1.11 million
b. Current Ratio = 2x and 1.12x
4-11A.

	January	February	March
Net Monthly Change	$65,500	(1,000)	(127,500)
Cumulative Borrowing	$-0-	-0-	61,000

4-13A. **a.** Debt to Assets = 61.1%, 61.9%, 59.4%, 50.4%, 44.4%

CHAPTER 5

5-1A. **a.** $12,970
c. $3,019.40
5-2A. **a.** $n = 15$ years

5-3A. **b.** 5%
c. 9%
5-4A. **b.** $PV = $235.20
5-5A **a.** $6,289
c. $302.89
5-6A. **c.** $1,562.96
5-7A. **a.** $FV_1 = $10,600
$FV_5 = $13,380
$FV_{15} = $23,970
5-9A. **a.** $6,690
b. Semiannual: $6,720
Bimonthly: $6,740
5-11A. Year 1: 18,000 books
Year 2: 21,600 books
Year 3: 25,920 books
5-13A. $6,108.11
5-15A. 8%
5-17A. $658,197.85
5-21A. **b.** $8,333.33
5-26A. $6,509
5-28A. 22%
5-29A. $6,934.81
5-32A. **a.** $1,989.73
5-35A. $15,912

CHAPTER 6

6-1A. $\bar{k} = 9.1\%$; $\sigma = 3.06\%$
6-3A. Security A: $\bar{k} = 16.7\%$; $\sigma = 10.12\%$
Security B: $\bar{k} = 9.2\%$: $\sigma = 3.57\%$
6-5A. About 0.5.
6-7A. 10.56%
6-9A.

	Asman
Time	Return
2	20.0%

6-11A **a.** 15.8%
b. 0.95
6-12A. S&P 500: $\bar{k} = 1.40\%$;
$\sigma = 3.80\%$
Deere: $\bar{k} = 0.59\%$
$\sigma = 7.0\%$

CHAPTER 7

7-1A. $752.52
7-3A. 4.8%
7.8%
7-7A. **a.** $ 863.78
b. Market Value $707.63 when required rate of return is 15%; Market Value $1,171.19 when required rate of return is 8%
7-9A. **a.** $1,182.57
b. (i) $925.31; (ii) $1,573.50

CHAPTER 8

8-1A.	$50
8-3A.	$116.67
8-5A.	**a.** 8.5%
	b. $42.50
8-7A.	**a.** 18.9%
	b. $28.57
8-9A.	7.2%
8-11A.	$39.96
8-13A.	**a.** 10.91%
	b. $36

CHAPTER 9

9-1A.	**a.** IRR = 7%
	b. IRR = 17%
9-3A.	**a.** IRR = approximately 19%
9-5A.	**a.** Payback Period = $80,000/$20,000 = 4 years
	Discounted Payback Period = 5.0 + 4,200/11,280 = 5.37 years.
	c. PI = 1.0888
9-7A.	Project C:
	Payback Period = 3.5 years
	Discounted Payback Period = 4.0 + 397/1,242 = 4.32 years.
9-9A.	Project C: IRR = 16%

CHAPTER 10

10-1A.	**a.** $6,800
	b. $3,400
	c. No taxes.
	d. $1,020 refund
10-3A.	**a.** 2.75 years
	b. $10,628.16
10-5A.	**a.** $560,000
	b. Annual net cash flow after taxes = $116,170
10-7A.	**a.** Payback Period = 3.10 years
10-9A	**b.** NPV = $17,371.76
10-11A.	**b.** NPV_B = $12,100
10-13A.	**a.** EAA_A = $9,729

CHAPTER 11

11-1A.	**b.** NPV_A = $8,025
	NPV_B = $10,112
11-3A.	NPV_A = $726,380
11-5A.	NPV_A = – $24,780

CHAPTER 12

12-1A.	**a.** After-tax cost of debt = 6.53%
	b. k_{nc} = 14.37%
	c. k_c = 15.14%
	d. k_{ps} = 8.77%
12-3A.	k_{nc} = 12.06%
12-5A.	k_{ps} = 7.69%
12-7A.	k_{ps} = 14.29%

12-9A.	**a.** k_{cs} = 17.59%
	b. k_{nc} = 18.25%
12-11A.	**a.** V_b = $1,063.80
	b. NP_o = $952.10
	c. 525 bonds

CHAPTER 13

13-2A.	Breakeven point = 40,000 bottles.
13-4A.	**a.** Jake's EBIT = $154,067.40
	Sarasota = 480,000
	Jefferson = 28,970
	b. Jake's = 8,232
	Sarasota = 1,789
	Jefferson = 8,310
	c. Jake's = 1.78 times
	Sarasota = 2.77 times
	Jefferson = 4.09 times
	d. Jefferson Wholesale would suffer the largest decline in profitability.
13-6A.	**a.** 6,296 pairs of shoes
	b. $534,591.19
	c. At 7,000, EBIT = $19,000
	At 9,000, EBIT = $73,000
	At 15,000, EBIT = $235,000
	d. 9.95 times; 3.33 times; 1.72 times
13-7A.	**a.** 9,000 units
	b. $1,620,000
13-9A.	**a.** $85,416.67
	b. 7,030 units; $189,815
13-11A.	**a.** 1.94 times
13-13A.	**a.** 10,000 units
	b. $1,800,000
13-15A.	**a.** F = $173,333.33
	b. 14,444 units; S* = $288,888.88
13-21A.	**a.** 5,000 units
	b. $125,000
	c. –$10,000; $10,000; $30,000
13-23A.	5 times
13-25A.	1,400,000 units
13-27A.	**a.** 3 times
	b. 1.25 times
	c. 3.75 times
	d. $8 million

CHAPTER 14

14-2A.	Cash collection from sales = $1,280,000
14-4A.	**a.** EBIT = $2,000,000
	b. EPS will be $1.00 for each plan.
	d. Plan B
14-6A.	**a.** EBIT = $240,000
	b. EPS will be $1.80 for each plan.
14-7A.	**a.** EBIT = $220,000
	b. Plan B.
14-9A.	**a.** $640,000
	b. EPS = $3.20
14-11A.	**a.** $300,000
	b. EPS = $3.00

14-13A. **a.** Plan A = $7.68
       b. 10.378
14-17A. **a.** $20,000,000
       b. $k_c = 25\%$; $k_o = 25\%$
14-19A. **a.** Plan A vs. Plan B = $9,000
          Plan A vs. Plan C = $18,000

CHAPTER 15

15-2A. 95,238 shares
15-4A. Dividend = $16,000
15-6A. Value of stock both plans = $31.76
15-8A. **b.** Net gain = $24,500
15-10A. **b.** 9,615 shares
15-12A. Dividend = $90,000

CHAPTER 16

16-1A.

	Firm A	Firm B
Working Capital	$500,000	550,000
Current Ratio	1.25x	.917x

16-3A. APR = 13.79%
16-5A. **a.** 36.73%
      b. 74.23%
      c. 37.11%
      d. 16.33%
16-7A. **a.** APR = 16.3%
      b. APR = 19.7%
16-9A. **a.** APR = 16.27%
16-11A. **a.** APR = 22.85%
16-13A. **a.** APR = 10%
      b. APR = 11.76%
      c. APR = 12.5%

CHAPTER 17

17-1A. Yes, the projected net annual gain from using the new system is $33,356.
17-4A. **a.** Yes, the firm will generate $35,288 in net annual savings.
      b. 5.01%
17-6A. **a.** $2,625,000
      b. $241,500
17-7A. Yes; annual savings = $211,000
17-9A. .5322 days
17-13A. $10,667

17-16A. **a.** $912.44
      b. $87.56
      c. $17.59

CHAPTER 18

18-3A. **a.** 36.36%
      b. 36.73%
18-5A. **a.** $90,000
      b. $53,333
18-7A. $56,875
18-8A. **a.** 775 units
18-10A. **a.** 816 units
      b. $61,237
18-12A. **b.** 35.2 orders per year

CHAPTER 19

19-1A. Balloon = $268,160.75
19-3A. Payment = $31,977.78
19-5A. **a.** 15%
      b. Payment = $76,359.19
      c. 9%
19-7A. **a.** NPV (P) = – $2,271
      b. NAL = – $874

CHAPTER 20

no solutions provided

CHAPTER 21

21-1A. Average theoretical value = $12,433
21-3A. Net present value = – $14.87

CHAPTER 22

22-1A. **a.** $8,437
      b. $9,368
      c. $25,695
22-3A. Canada: 1.1853; 1.1881; 1.1912
      Japan: 213.4927: 211.9992; 209.1613
      Switzerland: 1.9459, 1.9346: 1.8815
22-5A. Net gain = $149.02

GLOSSARY

Accounts receivable turnover ratio Accounts receivable turnover ratio indicates how rapidly the firm is collecting its credit, as measured by the number of times its accounts receivable are collected or "rolled over" during the year.

Acid-test ratio Acid-test ratio indicates a firm's liquidity, as measured by its liquid assets, excluding inventories, relative to its current liabilities.

Adjustable rate preferred stock Preferred stock intended to provide investors with some protection against wide swings in the stock value that occur when interest rates move up and down. The dividend rate changes along with prevailing interest rates.

Agency costs The costs, such as a reduced stock price, associated with potential conflict between managers and investors when these two groups are not the same.

Agency problem Problem resulting from conflicts of interest between the manager (the stockholder's agent) and the stockholders.

Amortized loan A loan paid off in equal installments.

Analytical income statement A financial statement used by internal analysts that differs in composition from audited or published financial statements.

Annual percentage yield (APY) or effective annual rate The annual compound rate that produces the same return as the nominal or quoted rate.

Annuity A series of equal dollar payments for a specified number of years.

Annuity due An annuity in which the payments occur at the beginning of each period.

Anticipatory buying Buying in anticipation of a price increase to secure goods at a lower cost.

Appraisal costs Costs of testing, measuring, and analyzing to safeguard against possible defects going unnoticed.

Arbitrage-pricing model (APM) An alternative theory to the capital asset pricing model for relating stock returns and risk. The theory maintains that security returns vary from their expected amounts when there are unanticipated changes in basic economic forces.

Arbitrageur A person involved in the process of buying and selling in more than one market to make riskless profits.

Asked rate The rate a bank or foreign exchange trader "asks" the customer to pay in home currency for foreign currency when the bank is selling and the customer is buying.

Asset allocation Identifying and selecting the asset classes appropriate for a specific investment portfolio and determining the proportions of these assets within the given portfolio.

Auction rate preferred stock Variable rate preferred stock in which the dividend rate is set by an auction process.

Average collection period Average collection period indicates how rapidly a firm is collecting its credit, as measured by the average number of days it takes to collect its accounts receivable.

Balance sheet A statement of financial position at a particular date. The form of the statement follows the balance sheet equation: total assets = total liabilities + owner's equity.

Beta A measure of the relationship between an investment's returns and the market returns. This is a measure of the investment's nondiversifiable risk.

Bid-asked spread The difference between the asked quote and the bid quote.

Bid rate The rate at which the bank buys the foreign currency from the customer by paying in home currency.

Bird-in-the-hand dividend theory The belief that dividend income has a higher value to the investor than does capital gains income, because dividends are more certain than capital gains.

Bond A type of debt or a long-term promissory note, issued by the borrower, promising to pay its holder a predetermined and fixed amount of interest each year.

Bondholder's expected rate of return The discount rate that equates the present value of the future cash flows (interest and maturity value) with the current market price of the bond. It is the rate of return an investor will earn if a bond is held to maturity.

Book value The value of an asset as shown on a firm's balance sheet. It represents the historical cost of the asset rather than its current market value or replacement cost.

Business cycles A series of commercial adjustments to unanticipated new information accentuated by both public policy decisions and private-sector decisions.

Business risk The potential variability in a firm's earnings before interest and taxes resulting from the nature of the firm's business endeavors.

Buying rate The bid rate in a currency transaction.

Call option A call option gives its owner the right to purchase a given number of shares of stock or some other asset at a specified price over a given time period.

Call provision Lets the company buy its preferred stock back from the investor, usually at a premium price above the stock's par value.

Capital asset pricing model (CAPM) An equation stating that the expected rate of return on a project is a function of (1) the risk-free rate, (2) the investment's systematic risk, and (3) the expected risk premium for the market portfolio of all risky securities.

Capital budgeting The decision-making process with respect to investment in fixed assets.

Capital gain or loss As defined by the revenue code, a gain or loss resulting from the sale or exchange of a capital asset.

Capital market All institutions and procedures that facilitate transactions in long-term financial instruments.

Capital rationing The placing of a limit by the firm on the dollar size of the capital budget.

Capital structure The mix of long-term sources of funds used by the firm. Basically, this concept omits short-term liabilities.

Cash Currency and coin plus demand deposit accounts.

Cash breakeven analysis A variation from traditional breakeven analysis that removes (deducts) noncash expenses from the cost items.

Cash budget A detailed plan of future cash receipts and disbursements.

Cash flows from financing activities Cash flow that includes proceeds from long-term debt or issuing common stock, and payments made for stock dividends.

Cash flows from investment activities Cash flows that include the purchase of fixed assets and other assets.

Cash flows from operations Cash flow that consists of (1) collections from customers; (2) payments to suppliers for the purchase of materials; (3) other operating cash flows such as marketing and administrative expenses and interest payments; and (4) cash tax payments.

Certainty equivalent approach A method for incorporating risk into the capital-budgeting decision in which the decision maker substitutes a set of equivalent riskless cash flows for the expected cash flows and then discounts these cash flows back to the present.

Certainty equivalents The amount of cash a person would require with certainty to make him or her indifferent between this certain sum and a particular risky or uncertain sum.

Characteristic line The line of "best fit" through a series of returns for a firm's stock relative to the market returns. The slope of the line, frequently called beta, represents the average movement of the firm's stock returns in response to a movement in the market's returns.

Clientele effect The belief that individuals and institutions that need current income will invest in companies that have high dividend payouts. Other investors prefer to avoid taxes by holding securities that offer only small dividend income, but large capital gains. Thus we have a "clientele" of investors.

Commercial paper Short-term loans by the most creditworthy borrowers that are bought and sold in the market for short-term debt securities.

Common stock Common stock shares represent the ownership in a corporation.

Compound annuity Depositing an equal sum of money at the end of each year for a certain number of years and allowing it to grow.

Compound interest Interest that occurs when interest paid on the investment during the first period is added to the principal; then, during the second period, interest is earned on this new sum.

Concentration banking The selection of a few major banks where the firm maintains significant disbursing accounts.

Constant dividend payout ratio A dividend payment policy in which the percentage of earnings paid out in dividends is held constant. The dollar amount fluctuates from year to year as profits vary.

Contribution margin Unit sales price minus unit variable cost.

Conversion period The time period during which the convertible can be exchanged for common stock.

Conversion premium The difference between the convertible's market price and the higher of its security value and its conversion value.

Conversion ratio The number of shares of common stock for which a convertible security can be exchanged.

Conversion value The total market value of the common stock for which it can be exchanged.

Convertible preferred stock Convertible preferred stock allows the preferred stockholder to convert the preferred stock into a predetermined number of shares of common stock, if he or she so chooses.

Convertible security Preferred stock or debentures that can be exchanged for a specified number of shares of common stock at the will of the owner.

Corporation An entity that *legally* functions separate and apart from its owners.

Coupon interest rate A bond's coupon interest rate indicates what percentage of the par value of the bond will be paid out annually in the form of interest.

Covered-interest arbitrage Arbitrage designed to eliminate differentials across currency and interest rate markets.

Credit scoring The numerical credit evaluation of each candidate.

Cross rate The computation of an exchange rate for a currency from the exchange rates of two other currencies.

Cumulative preferred stock Requires all past unpaid preferred stock dividends be paid before any common stock dividends are declared.

Cumulative voting Each share of stock allows the shareholder a number of votes equal to the number of directors being elected. The shareholder can then cast all of his or her votes for a single candidate or split them among the various candidates.

Currency swap An exchange of debt obligations in different currencies.

Current assets Current assets consist primarily of cash, marketable securities, accounts receivable, inventories, and prepaid expenses.

Current ratio Current ratio indicates a firm's liquidity, as measured by its liquid assets (current assets) relative to its liquid debt (short-term or current liabilities).

Current yield The ratio of the annual interest payment to the bond's market price.

Date of record Date at which the stock transfer books are to be closed for determining which investor is to receive the next dividend payment.

Debenture Any unsecured long-term debt.

Debt Consists of such sources as credit extended by suppliers or a loan from a bank.

Debt capacity The maximum proportion of debt that the firm can include in its capital structure and still maintain its lowest composite cost of capital.

Debt ratio Debt ratio indicates how much debt is used to finance a firm's assets.

Declaration date The date upon which a dividend is formally declared by the board of directors.

Delivery-time stock The inventory needed between the order date and the receipt of the inventory ordered.

Depository transfer checks A non-negotiable instrument that provides the firm with a means to move funds from local bank accounts to concentration bank accounts.

Depreciation The means by which an asset's value is expensed over its useful life for federal income tax purposes.

Direct method A statement of cash flow that begins with sales and converts the income statement from an accrual basis to a cash basis.

Direct quote The exchange rate that indicates the number of units of the home currency required to buy one unit of foreign currency.

Direct sale The sale of securities by the corporation to the investing public without the services of an investment banking firm.

Direct securities The pure financial claims issued by economic units to savers. These can later be transformed into indirect securities.

Discount bond A bond that is selling below its par value.

Discounted payback period A variation of the payback period decision criterion defined as the number of years required to recover the initial cash outlay from the discounted net cash flows.

Discretionary financing Sources of financing that require an explicit decision on the part of the firm's management every time funds are raised.

Dividend payout ratio The amount of dividends relative to the company's net income or earnings per share.

duPont analysis The duPont analysis is an approach to evaluate a firm's profitability and return on equity.

Duration A measure of how responsive a bond's price is to changing interest rates. Also, it is a weighted average time to maturity in which the weight attached to each year is the present value of the cash flow for that year.

Earnings before taxes Operating income minus interest expense.

EBIT–EPS indifference point The level of earnings before interest and taxes (EBIT) that will equate earnings per share (EPS) between two different financing plans.

Economic profit The difference in a firm's after-tax net operating income and an estimate of the cost of invested capital (invested capital times the firm's weighted average cost of capital).

Efficient market A market in which the values of securities at any instant in time fully reflect all available information, which results in the market value and the intrinsic value being the same.

Equity Stockholder's investment in the firm and the cumulative profits retained in the business up to the date of the balance sheet.

Equivalent annual annuity (EAA) An annual cash flow that yields the same present value as the project's NPV. It is calculated by dividing the project's NPV by the appropriate $PVIFA_{i,n}$.

Eurobonds Bonds issued in a country different from the one in whose currency the bond is denominated—for instance, a bond issued in Europe or in Asia by an American company that pays interest and principal to the lender in U.S. dollars.

Eurodollar loans Intermediate term loans made by major international banks to businesses based on foreign deposits that are denominated in dollars.

Exchange rate The price of a foreign currency stated in terms of the domestic or home currency.

Exchange rate risk The risk that tomorrow's exchange rate will differ from today's.

Ex-dividend date The date upon which stock brokerage companies have uniformly decided to terminate the right of ownership to the dividend, which is 4 days prior to the record date.

Exercise ratio The number of shares of common stock that can be obtained at the exercise price with one warrant.

Expectations theory The effect of new information about a company on the firm's stock price depends more on how the new information compares to expectations than on the actual announcement itself.

Expected rate of return The weighted average of all possible returns where the returns are weighted by the probability that each will occur.

Explicit cost of capital The cost of capital for any funds source considered in isolation from other funds sources.

External failure costs Costs resulting from a poor quality product reaching the customer's hands.

Factoring The sale of a firm's accounts receivable to a financial intermediary known as a factor.

Financial assets Claims for future payment by one economic unit on another.

Financial lease A noncancelable contractual commitment on the part of the firm leasing the asset (the lessee) to make a series of payments to the firm that actually owns the asset (the lessor) for the use of the asset over the period of the agreement.

Financial leverage Financing a portion of the firm's assets with securities bearing a fixed or limited rate of return.

Financial markets Those institutions and procedures that facilitate transactions in all types of financial claims (securities).

Financial policy The firm's policies regarding the sources financing and the particular mix in which they will be used.

Financial ratios Restating the accounting data in relative terms to identify some of the financial strengths and weaknesses of a company.

Financial risk The additional variability in earnings available to the firm's common stockholder, and the additional chance of insolvency borne by the common stockholder caused by the use of financial leverage.

Financial structure The mix of all funds sources that appear on the right side of the balance sheet.

Financial structure design The management activity of seeking the proper mix of all financing components in order to minimize the cost of raising a given amount of funds.

Financing costs Costs incurred by a company that often include interest expenses and preferred dividends.

Finished-goods inventory Goods on which the production has been completed but that are not yet sold.

Firm-specific risk or company-unique risk (diversifiable risk or unsystematic risk) The portion of the variation in investment returns that can be eliminated through investor diversification. This diversifiable risk is the result of factors that are unique to the particular firm.

Fixed costs (indirect costs) Costs that do not vary in total dollar amount as sales volume or quantity of output changes.

Fixed or long-term assets Assets comprising equipment, buildings, and land.

Float The length of time from when a check is written until the actual recipient can draw upon or use the "good funds."

Floating rate international currency system An international currency system in which exchange rates between different national currencies are allowed to fluctuate with supply and demand conditions. This contrasts with a fixed rate system in which exchange rates are pegged for extended periods of time and adjusted infrequently.

Flotation costs The underwriter's spread and issuing costs associated with the issuance and marketing of new securities.

Forward exchange contract A contract that requires delivery on a specified future date of one currency in return for a specified amount of another currency.

Forward-spot differential The premium or discount between forward and spot currency exchange rates.

Future-value interest factor ($FVIF_{i,n}$) The value $(1 + i)^n$ used as a multiplier to calculate an amount's future value.

Future-value interest factor of an annuity ($FVIFA_{i,n}$) The value $\left[\sum_{t=0}^{n-1}(1 + i)^t\right]$ used as a multiplier to calculate the future value of an annuity.

Futures contract A contract to buy or sell a stated commodity or financial claim at a specified price at some future, specified time.

Futures margin Good faith money the purchaser puts down to ensure that the contract will be carried out.

Hedging principle or principle of self-liquidating debt Financing maturity should follow the cash-flow-producing characteristics of the asset being financed.

Holding-period return The return an investor would receive from holding a security for a designated period of time. For example, a monthly holding-period return would be the return for holding a security for a month.

Implicit cost of debt The change in the cost of common equity caused by the choice to use additional debt.

Income statement The statement of profit or loss for the period is comprised of net revenues less expenses for the period.

Increasing-stream hypothesis of dividend policy A smoothing of the dividend stream in order to minimize the effect of company reversals. Corporate managers make every effort to avoid a dividend cut, attempting instead to develop a gradually increasing dividend series over the long-term future.

Indenture The legal agreement or contract between the firm issuing the bonds and the bond trustee who represents the bondholders.

Indirect method A statement of cash flow that beings with net income and then adds back the non-cash expenses, and other items that affect a company's cash flows.

Indirect quote The exchange rate that expresses the required number of units of foreign currency to buy one unit of home currency.

Indirect securities The unique financial claims issued by financial intermediaries. Mutual fund shares are an example.

Information asymmetry The difference in accessibility to information between management and investors may result in a lower stock price than would occur under conditions of certainty.

Initial outlay The immediate cash outflow necessary to purchase the asset and put it in operating order.

Insolvency The firm is unable to pay its bills on time.

Interest-rate parity (IRP) States that (except for the effect of small transaction costs) the forward premium or discount should be equal and opposite in size to the differences in the national interest rates for securities of the same maturity.

Interest-rate risk The variability in a bond's value (risk) caused by changing interest rates.

Interest tax shield The savings in taxes resulting from the tax deductibility of the interest expense.

Internal failure costs Those costs associated with discovering poor quality products prior to delivery.

Internal rate of return (IRR) A capital-budgeting decision criterion that reflects the rate of return a project earns. Mathematically, it is the discount rate that equates the present value of the inflows with the present value of the outflows.

Intrinsic or economic value The present value of the asset's expected future cash flows. This value is the amount the investor considers to be a fair value, given the amount, timing, and riskiness of future cash flows.

Inventory loans Short-term loans that are secured by the pledge of inventories. The type of pledge or security agreement varies and can include floating liens, chattel mortgage agreements, field warehouse financing agreements, and terminal warehouse agreements.

Inventory management The control of the assets used in the production process or produced to be sold in the normal course of the firm's operations.

Inventory turnover ratio Inventory turnover indicates the relative liquidity of inventories, as measured by the number of times a firm's inventories are replaced during the year.

Investment banker A financial specialist who underwrites and distributes new securities and advises corporate clients about raising external financial capital.

Investor's required rate of return The minimum rate of return necessary to attract an investor to purchase or hold a security. It is also the discount rate that equates the present value of the cash flows with the value of the security.

Joint probability The probability of two different sequential outcomes occurring.

Junk or high-yield bonds Bonds rated BB or below.

Just-in-time inventory control system Keeping inventory to a minimum and relying on suppliers to furnish parts "just in time."

Law of one price The proposition that in competitive markets the same goods should sell for the same price where prices are stated in terms of a single currency.

Lease A contract between a lessee, who acquires the services of a leased asset by making a series of rental payments and the lessor, who is the owner of the asset.

Lessee and lessor The user of the leased asset, who agrees to make periodic lease or rental payments to the lessor, who owns the asset.

Line of credit and revolving credit agreement A line of credit agreement is an agreement between a firm and its banker to provide short-term financing to meet its temporary financing needs.

Liquid assets The sum of cash and marketable securities.

Liquidation value The amount that could be realized if an asset were sold individually and not as a part of a going concern.

Liquidity The ability of a firm to pay its bills on time, and how quickly a firm converts its liquid assets (accounts receivables and inventories) into cash.

Majority voting Each share of stock allows the shareholder one vote, and each position on the board of directors is voted on separately. As a result, a majority of shares has the power to elect the entire board of directors.

Marginal or incremental analysis A method of analysis for credit policy changes in which the incremental benefits are compared to the added costs.

Marginal tax rate The tax rate that would be applied to the next dollar of income.

Marketable securities Security investments (financial assets) the firm can quickly convert to cash balances. Also known as near cash or near-cash assets.

Market-related risk (nondiversifiable risk or systematic risk) The portion of variations in investment returns that cannot be eliminated through investor diversification. This variation results from factors that affect all stocks.

Market value The observed value for the asset in the marketplace.

Market Value Added Market value of a firm's assets minus the sum total of its invested capital.

Maturity The length of time until the bond issuer returns the par value to the bondholder and terminates the bond.

Modified internal rate of return (MIRR) A variation of the IRR capital-budgeting decision criterion defined as the discount rate that equates the present value of the project's annual cash outlays with the present value of the project's terminal value, where the terminal value is defined as the sum of the future value of the project's cash inflows compounded to the project's termination at the project's required rate of return.

Money market All institutions and procedures that facilitate transactions in short-term credit instruments.

Mortgage bond A bond secured by a lien on real property.

Multinational corporation (MNC) A corporation with holdings and/or operations in one or more countries.

Mutually exclusive projects A set of projects that perform essentially the same task, so that acceptance of one will necessarily mean rejection of the others.

Net and net-net leases In a net lease agreement, the lessee assumes the risk and burden of ownership over the term of the lease. This means that the lessee must pay insurance and taxes on the asset as well as maintain the operating condition of the asset. In a net-net lease, the lessee must, in addition to the requirements of a net lease, return the asset to the lessor at the end of the lease still worth a preestablished value.

Net income available to common stockholders (net income) A figure representing the firm's profit or loss for the period. It also represents the earnings available to the firm's common and preferred stockholders.

Net operating loss carryback and carryforward A tax provision that permits the taxpayer first to apply a loss against the profits in the 2 prior years (carryback). If the loss has not been completely absorbed by the profits in these 2 years, it may be applied to taxable profits in each of the 20 following years (carryforward).

Net present value (NPV) A capital-budgeting decision criterion defined as the present value of the future net cash flows after tax less the project's initial outlay.

Net profit margin Net profit margin measures the net income of a firm as a percent of sales.

Net working capital The difference between the firm's current assets and its current liabilities. Frequently when the term working capital is used, it is actually intended to mean net working capital.

NI approach to valuation The concept from financial theory that suggests the firm's capital structure has a direct impact upon and can increase its market valuation.

NOI approach to valuation The concept from financial theory that suggests the firm's capital structure has no impact on its market valuation.

Nominal or quoted interest rate The stated rate of interest on the contract.

Nominal rate of interest The observed rate of interest on a specific fixed-income security; no adjustment is made for expected inflation.

Operating income (earnings before interest and taxes) Profit from sales minus total operating expenses.

Operating income return of investment Operating income return on investment indicates the effectiveness of management at generating operating profits on the firm's assets, as measured by operating profits relative to the total assets.

Operating lease A lease agreement (see financial lease) in which the lessee can cancel the agreement at any time after giving proper notice to the lessor.

Operating leverage The incurrence of fixed operating costs in the firm's income stream.

Operating profit margin Operating profit margin indicates management's effectiveness in managing the firm's income statement, as measured by operating profits relative to sales.

Opportunity cost of funds The next best rate of return available to the investor for a given level of risk.

Optimal capital structure The unique capital structure that minimizes the firm's composite cost of long-term capital.

Optimal range of financial leverage The range of various financial structure combinations that generate the lowest composite cost of capital for the firm.

Option contract An option contract gives its owner the right to buy or sell a fixed number of shares of stock at a specified price over a limited time period.

Option expiration date The date on which the option expires.

Option premium The price of the option.

Option's intrinsic value The minimum value of the option.

Option's time (or speculative) value The amount by which the option premium exceeds the intrinsic value of the option.

Option striking price The price at which the stock or asset may be purchased from the writer in the case of a call, or sold to the writer in the case of a put.

Order point problem Determining how low inventory should be depleted before it is reordered.

Order quantity problem Determining the optimal order size for an inventory item given its usage, carrying costs, and ordering costs.

Ordinary annuity An annuity in which the payments occur at the end of each period.

Organized security exchanges Formal organizations involved in the trading of securities. They are tangible entities that conduct auction markets in listing securities.

Other assets Assets not included in current assets or fixed assets.

Over-the-counter markets All security markets except the organized exchanges.

Participating preferred stock Allows the preferred stockholder to participate in earnings beyond the payment of the stated dividend.

Partnership An association of two or more individuals joining together as co-owners to operate a business for profit.

Par value of a bond The bond's face value that is returned to the bondholder at maturity, usually $1,000.

Payable-through drafts A payment mechanism that substitutes for regular checks in that drafts are not drawn on a bank, but instead are drawn on and authorized by the firm against its demand deposit account. The purpose is to maintain control over field-authorized payments.

Payback period A capital-budgeting criterion defined as the number of years required to recover the initial cash investment.

Payment date The date on which the company mails a dividend check to each investor.

Percent of sales method Estimating the level of an expense, asset, or liability for a future period as a percent of the sales forecast.

Perfect capital markets Capital markets where (1) investors can buy and sell stock without incurring any transaction costs, such as brokerage commissions; (2) companies can issue stocks without any cost of doing so; (3) there are no corporate or personal taxes; (4) complete information about the firm is readily available; (5) there are no conflicts of interest between management and stockholders; and (6) financial distress and bankruptcy costs are nonexistent.

Permanent asset investment An investment in an asset that the firm expects to hold for the foreseeable future, whether fixed assets or current assets. For example, the minimum level of inventory the firm plans to hold for the foreseeable future is a permanent investment.

Permanent sources of financing Sources of financing that do not mature or come due within the year, including intermediate term debt, long-term debt, preferred stock, and common stock.

PIK preferred stock Investors receive no dividends initially; they merely get more preferred stock, which in turn pays dividends in even more preferred stock.

Plowback ratio The percent of a firm's earnings that are reinvested in the firm.

Portfolio beta The relationship between a portfolio's returns and the market returns. It is a measure of the portfolio's nondiversifiable risk.

Preemptive rights The right of a common shareholder to maintain a proportionate share of ownership in the firm. When new shares are issued, common shareholders have the first right of refusal.

Preferred stock A hybrid security with characteristics of both common stock and bonds. It is similar to common stock because it has

no fixed maturity date, the nonpayment of dividends does not bring on bankruptcy, and dividends are not deductible for tax purposes. Preferred stock is similar to bonds in that dividends are limited in amount.

Premium bond A bond that is selling above its par value.

Present value The current value of a future sum.

Present-value interest factor ($PVIF_{i,n}$) The value $[1/(1 + i)^n]$ used as a multiplier to calculate an amount's present value.

Present-value interest factor for an annuity ($PVIFA_{i,n}$) The value $\left[\sum_{t=1}^{n} \dfrac{1}{(1+i)^t}\right]$ used as a multiplier to calculate the present value of an annuity.

Preventive costs Costs resulting from design and production efforts on the part of the firm to reduce or eliminate defects.

Primary market Transactions in securities offered for the first time to potential investors.

Private placement A security offering limited to a small number of potential investors.

Priviliged subscription The process of marketing a new security issue to a select group of investors.

Probability tree A schematic representation of a problem in which all possible outcomes are graphically displayed.

Profitability index (PI) (or Benefit/Cost Ratio) A capital-budgeting decision criterion defined as the ratio of the present value of the future net cash flows to the initial outlay.

Project's contribution-to-firm risk The amount of risk that a project contributes to the firm as a whole. That is, it is a project's risk considering the effects of diversification among different projects within the firm, but ignoring the effects of shareholder diversification within the portfolio.

Project standing alone risk The risk of a project standing alone is measured by the variability of the asset's expected returns. That is, it is the risk of a project ignoring the fact that it is only one of many projects within the firm, and the firm's stock is but one of many stocks within a stockholder's portfolio.

Protective provisions Provisions for preferred stock that are included in the terms of the issue to protect the investor's interest.

Proxy A proxy gives a designated party the temporary power of attorney to vote for the signee at the corporation's annual meeting.

Proxy fight When rival groups compete for proxy votes in order to control the decisions made in a stockholder meeting.

Public offering A security offering where all investors have the opportunity to acquire a portion of the financial claims being sold.

Purchasing-power parity (PPP) theory
In the long run, exchange rates adjust so that the purchasing power of each currency tends to remain the same. Thus exchange rate changes tend to reflect international differences in inflation rates. Countries with high rates of inflation tend to experience declines in the value of their currency.

Pure play method   A method of estimating a project's beta that attempts to identify a publicly traded firm that is engaged solely in the same business as the project, and uses that beta as a proxy for the project's beta.

Put option   A put option gives its owner the right to sell a given number of shares of common stock or some other asset at a specified price over a given time period.

Raw materials inventory   This includes the basic materials purchased from other firms to be used in the firm's production operations.

Real assets   Tangible assets such as houses, equipment, and inventories.

Real rate of interest   The nominal rate of interest less the expected rate of inflation over the maturity of the fixed-income security. This represents the expected increase in actual purchasing power to the investor.

Residual dividend theory   A theory asserting that the dividends to be paid should equal capital left over after the financing of profitable investments.

Retained earnings   The cumulative earnings that have been retained and reinvested in the firm over its life.

Return on assets   Return on assets determines the amount of net income produced on a firm's assets by relating net income to total assets.

Return on common equity   Return on common equity indicates the accounting rate of return on the stockholders' investment, as measured by net income relative to common equity.

Revolving credit or revolver   A special type of line of credit agreement in which the line of credit is eventually converted into a term loan that requires periodic payments.

Rights   Certificates issued to shareholders giving them an option to purchase a stated number of new shares of stock at a specified price during a 2- to 10-week period.

Risk   The prospect of an unfavorable outcome. This concept has been measured operationally as the standard deviation or beta, which will be explained later.

Risk-adjusted discount rate   A method for incorporating the project's level of risk into the capital-budgeting process, in which the discount rate is adjusted upward to compensate for higher than normal risk or downward to adjust for lower than normal risk.

Risk-free or riskless rate of return   The rate of return on risk-free investments. The interest rate on short-term U.S. government securities are commonly used to measure this rate.

Risk premium   The additional rate of return we expect to earn above the risk-free rate for assuming risk.

Safety stock   Inventory held to accommodate any unusually large and unexpected usage during delivery time.

Sale and leaseback arrangement   An arrangement arising when a firm sells land, buildings, or equipment that it already owns and simultaneously enters into an agreement to lease the property back for a specified period, under specific terms.

Scenario analysis   Simulation analysis that focuses on an examination of the range of possible outcomes.

Secondary market   Transactions in currently outstanding securities.

Secured and unsecured loans   Secured loans are backed by the pledge of specific assets as collateral whereas unsecured loans are only backed by the promise of the borrower to honor the loan commitment.

Security market line   The return line that reflects the attitudes of investors regarding the minimal acceptable return for a given level of systematic risk.

Security value   The price the convertible security would sell for in the absence of its conversion feature.

Selling rate   Same as the asked rate.

Selloff   The sale of a subsidiary, division, or product line by one firm to another.

Semivariable costs (semifixed costs)   Costs that exhibit the joint characteristics of both fixed and variable costs over different ranges of output.

Sensitivity analysis   The process of determining how the distribution of possible returns for a particular project is affected by a change in one particular input variable.

Shelf registration   A procedure for issuing new securities where the firm obtains a master registration statement approved by the SEC.

Simple arbitrage   Trading to eliminate exchange rate differentials across the markets for a single currency, e.g., for the New York and London markets.

Simulation   The process of imitating the performance of an investment project under evaluation using a computer. This is done by randomly selecting observations from each of the distributions that affect the outcome of the project, combining those observations to determine the final output of the project, and continuing with this process until a representative record of the project's probable outcome is assembled.

Single-sourcing   Using a single supplier as a source for a particular part or material.

Sinking fund   A fund that requires the firm periodically to set aside an amount of money for the retirement of its preferred stock. This money is then used to purchase the preferred stock in the open market or through the use of the call provision, whichever method is cheaper.

Small regular plus year-end extra dividend payout   A dividend payment policy where the firm pays a small regular dividend plus an extra dividend only if the firm has experienced a good year.

Sole proprietorship   A business owned by a single individual.

Spinoff   The separation of a subsidiary from its parent, with no change in the equity ownership. The management of the parent company gives up operating control over the assets involved in the spinoff but the stockholders retain ownership, albeit through shares of the newly created spinoff company.

Spontaneous financing   Sources of financing that arise naturally during the course of business. Accounts payable is a primary example.

Spot transaction   A transaction made immediately in the market place at the market price.

Stable dollar dividend payout   A dividend policy that maintains a relatively stable dollar dividend per share over time.

Standard deviation   A measure of the spread or dispersion about the mean of a probability distribution. We calculate it by squaring the difference between each outcome and its expected value, weighting each squared difference by its associated probability, summing over all possible outcomes, and taking the square root of this sum.

Statement of cash flows   The statement of cash flow enumerates the cash receipts and cash disbursements for a specified interval of time (usually 1 year).

Stock dividend   A distribution of shares of up to 25 percent of the number of shares currently outstanding, issued on a pro rata basis to the current stockholders.

Stock repurchase (stock buyback)   The repurchase of common stock by the issuing firm for any of a variety of reasons resulting in a reduction of shares outstanding.

Stock split   A stock dividend exceeding 25 percent of the number of shares currently outstanding.

Subchapter S Corporation   A corporation that, because of specific qualifications, is taxed as though it were a partnership.

Subordinated debenture   A debenture that is subordinated to other debentures in being paid in the case of insolvency.

Sustainable rate of growth   The maximum rate of growth in sales that the firm can sustain while maintaining its present capital structure (debt and equity mix) and without having to sell new common stock.

Syndicate   A group of investment bankers who contractually assist in the buying of a new security issue.

Systematic risk   The risk of a project measured from the point of view of a well-diversified shareholder. That is, it is a project's risk taking into account the fact that this project is only one of many projects within the firm, and the firm's stock is but one of many stocks within a stockholder's portfolio.

Target capital structure proportions   The mix of financing sources that the firm plans to maintain through time.

Tax expenses   Tax liability determined by earnings before taxes.

Tax shield   The element from the federal tax code that permits interest costs to be deductible when computing the firm's tax bill. The dollar difference (the shield) flows to the firm's security holders.

Temporary asset investment   Investments in assets that the firm plans to sell (liquidate) within a period no longer than 1 year. Although temporary investments can be made in fixed assets, this is not the usual case. Temporary investments generally are made in inventories and receivables.

Temporary sources of financing   Another term for current liabilities.

Tender offer   The formal offer by the company to buy a specified number of shares at a predetermined and stated price.

Term loans   Loans that have maturities of 1 to 10 years and are repaid in periodic installments over the life of the loan; usually secured by a chattel mortgage on equipment or a mortgage on real property.

Terms of sale   The credit terms identifying the possible discount for early payment.

Times interest earned   Times interest earned indicates a firm's ability to cover its interest expense, as measured by its earnings before interest and taxes relative to the interest expense.

Total asset turnover   Total asset turnover indicates management's effectiveness at managing a firm balance sheet—its assets—as indicated by the amount of sales generated per 1 dollar of assets.

Total quality management (TQM)   A company-wide systems approach to quality.

Total revenue   Total sales dollars.

Trade credit   Accounts payable that arise out of the normal course of business when the firm purchases from its suppliers who allow the firm to make payment after the delivery of the merchandise or services.

Transaction exposure   The net contracted foreign currency transactions for which the settlement amounts are subject to changing exchange rates.

Transfer price   The price a subsidiary or a parent company charges other companies that are part of the same MNC for its goods or services.

Triangular arbitrage   Arbitrage across the markets for all currencies.

Underwriting   The purchase and subsequent resale of a new security issue. The risk of selling the new issue at a profitable price is assumed (underwritten) by an investment banker.

Variable costs (direct costs)   Costs that are fixed per unit of output but vary in total as output changes.

Volume of output   The firm's level of operations expressed either in sales dollars or as units of output.

Warrant   An option to purchase a fixed number of shares of common stock at a predetermined price during a specified time period.

Warrant exercise price   The price at which a warrant allows its holder to purchase the firm's common stock.

Weighted average cost of capital   The average of the after-tax costs of each of the sources of capital used by a firm to finance a project. The weights reflect the proportion of the total financing raised from each source.

Wire transfers   A method of moving funds electronically between bank accounts in order to eliminate transit float. The wired funds are immediately usable at the receiving bank.

Working capital   The firm's total investment in current assets or assets which it expects to be converted into cash within a year or less.

Work-in-process inventory   Partially finished goods requiring additional work before they become finished goods.

Yield to maturity   The same as the expected rate of return (see above).

Zero and very low coupon bonds   Bonds issued at a substantial discount from their $1,000 face value that pay no or little interest.

Zero balance accounts   A cash-management tool that permits centralized control over cash outflows but also maintains divisional disbursing authority.

ORGANIZATION INDEX

A

Abbot Labs, 594
Alaska Airlines, 272–274
Alpha Manufacturing Company, 724, 725
Alphatec Electronics PCL, 103
AmaxGold, 436
Amazon.com, 290
American Airlines, 240
American Electronics Association, 365
American Standard, 611–612, 616
American Stock Exchange (AMEX), 49, 761
American Telephone and Telegraph Company (AT&T), 48, 295, 296, 545, 549, 775, 783
Anderson Publishing, 355n
Apple Computers, 24, 345, 357, 706
Appleton Manufacturing Company, 620
Archer-Daniels-Midland, 300, 464, 490
Arrow Electronics, 707
Ash, Inc., 442–443

B

Bailey Controls, 704, 707
Baker, Farrelly, and Edelman, 587
BankAmerica, 293
Banks for Cooperatives, 656
Barings Bank, 744–745
Batterymarch Financial Management, 788
Beech-Nut Nutrition, 343, 344
Berkshire Hathaway, Inc., 79, 215, 298
Berliner Handles & Frankfurter Bank, 819
Bernard, L., Corporation, 595, 596
Blackburn Seed Company, 467
Black & Decker, 611
Boise Cascade, 704
Boston Consulting Group, 616
Boston Stock Exchange, 49
Briggs & Stratton, 444–446
Brister Corporation, 274, 276
Bristol-Myers, 227

Bristol-Myers Squibb Co., 21–22
Burger King, 345, 377–378, 417
Burlington Northern, 3

C

Campbell Soup, 18, 616
Caterpillar, Inc., 269
Cavos, Inc., 789, 790
Central Florida, University of, 551n
Cessna, 764
Chase Manhattan Bank, 644n
Chevron Corporation, 464, 490
Chicago Board of Trade (CBT), 49n, 746–748
Chicago Board Options Exchange (CBOE), 49n
Chrysler Corporation, 177, 211, 259, 322, 357–358, 360, 704
Cincinnati Stock Exchange, 49
Citibank, 219
Citizens National Bank of Leesburg, 63
Clearing Corporation, 765
Coca-Cola Company, 93, 213, 219, 378, 399, 416, 464, 488, 490, 576, 600
Colgate-Palmolive Co., 325
College Bound, 309
CommNet, 271
Compaq, 357
Consolidated Press Holdings, 794
Continental Bank, 644n
Continental Corporation, 584
Coopers & Lybrand, 93, 795
Corporate Citizen, 5
Costco Companies, Incorporated, 771
Crown Zellerbach, 794

D

Daimler-Benz, 87
Danforth Chemical Company, 392
Danforth & Donnalley Laundry Products Company, 392–393
D&B Benchmark Data, 111n
Debartolo Realty, 93
Dell Computers, 219, 357, 702, 760

Delta, 768
Denis Electronics, 692–694
Diamond International, 794
Donnalley Home Products Company, 392
Dowell Venture, Inc., 577, 578, 579
Dow Jones Industrial Average, 41
Drexel Burnham Lambert, Inc., 21, 58, 269–270, 344, 531
DRI/McGraw Hill, 325
Dun and Bradstreet, 95, 96, 111n
Du Pont, 616

E

Eastman Kodak, 616
Eli Lilly, 783
Encore, Inc., 431, 442, 454
Equitable, 93
Erie General Producers (EGP), 509–510
Exxon, 219, 226

F

Federal Home Loan banks, 656
Federal Intermediate Credit Banks, 656
Federal Land Banks, 656
Federal National Mortgage Association, 656
Federal Power Commission, 57
Federal Reserve Bank of Atlanta, 71n
Federal Reserve Bank of Boston, 491, 528, 805n
Federal Reserve Bank of Dallas, 650
Federal Reserve Bank of Philadelphia, 533n
Federal Reserve Bank of Richmond, 71n
Fibreboard Corporation, 546
Fidelity, 223
First Boston Corporation, 658
First National Bank of Chicago, 644n
Fitch Investor Services, 266
Florida Marlins, 24

Ford Motor Company, 226, 260, 322, 324, 354–355, 357–358, 360, 639, 703, 706, 757–759
FPA Medical Management, 290
Franklin Union, 172
Friendly Ice Cream, 24, 197
Future Electronics, 707

G

General Dynamics Corp., 599
General Electric, 6, 213, 299, 616, 797
General Foods, 359
General Mills, 15–16, 543, 544–545
General Motors, 14, 44, 233, 322, 517, 702, 703, 704
General Motors Acceptance Corporation, 624
Georgia-Pacific Corporation, 513–514, 541, 543, 549
Gerber Products, 344
Giant Eagle, 93
Gillette Company, 108
Goldman Sachs & Co., 47, 599, 658
Good, A. B., Company, 626
Gottschalks, 309
Grace, W. R., & Co., 592–593
Granger, C. W. J., 144n
Great Atlantic and Pacific Tea Co. (A&P), 298
Griggs Corporation, 12, 13
GTE, 233
Guardian Industries, 704
Gucci, 87

H

Hanover Direct, 211
Harding Plastic Molding Company, 393–397
Heinz, H. J., 344
Hershey Foods, 226
H&L Manufacturing, 431, 450
Hoffman-La Roche, 17
Honda, 17, 333
Honolulu Stock Exchange, 49n
Humbrecht & Quist, 303

I

Ibbotson Associates, 59n, 236, 237n, 239, 242
IBM, 2, 226, 259, 357, 452, 485, 645, 647, 706
Intel, 101
IntelComm, 268
International Accounting Standards Committee (IASC), 87
International Harvester, 53
Interstate Commerce Commission, 57
Iomega Corporation, 303

J

Johnson, S. C. & Son Inc., 827
Johnson & Johnson, 401
Johnson Wax, 827

K

Katie Corporation, 594
Kellogg's, 359, 766, 768
Kmart, 93, 453
Kohlberg Kravis Roberts (KKR), 261, 269
Krista Corporation, 582, 583

L

Land of Ez, 577, 582–585
Lehman Brothers, 103
Levi, 17
Lily-Tulip Inc., 796
The Limited, 685
Lipper Analytical Services, 239
Louisiana Gas, 20
Lowe's Cos., 146

M

Marriott, 197
Marshall, Thurgood, Scholarship Fund, 5
Massachusetts Institute of Technology (MIT), 588
Mattel Inc., 599
McDonald's Corporation, 17, 83, 83n, 85–86, 87–89, 90–91, 92, 94–95, 96, 98, 99, 100, 101–102, 104–108, 109–112, 114, 225, 226, 324, 417, 766
McDonnell Douglas, 616

MCI, 24
McKinsey & Co., 325
Meade Johnson, 227
Medtronic, 543, 544–545
Merck & Co., Inc., 2, 398, 407, 411–413, 415
Mercury, 358
Merrill Lynch, 212, 438, 441, 754
Merrill Lynch, Pierce, Fenner & Smith, 658
Merrill Lynch Capital Markets, 47, 599
Metallgesellschaft (AG), 749, 767
Microsoft, 219
Midwest Stock Exchange, 49
Miller Brewing, 5
Millicom, Inc., 775
Mitsubishi, 706
Mobil Oil, 53
Moody's, 266, 268
Morgan Stanley & Company, 223
Motorola, 218–219, 345

N

National Cash Register, 702
National Highway Traffic Safety Administration (NHTSA), 354, 355
National Quotation Bureau, 51
NatWest, 760
Navistar, 53
NCR, 783
Netscape Communications Corporation, 290, 305
Nevada Power, 226
NewCo Oil, Inc., 453
New York Stock Exchange (NYSE), 49n, 50, 63, 219, 220, 234, 236, 269, 436, 587, 752, 809
New York University, 689
Nike, 218–219
Novell, 783

O

Overseas Private Investment Corporation, 828

P

Pacific Bell, 259
Pacific Stock Exchange, 49
Parker Pen Co., 298
PCS Health, 783

Penn Central, 614n
Penney, J. C., 260
PepsiCo., Inc., 220–227, 223–226, 240, 302, 446–447
Pfizer, 212
Phar-Mor, Inc., 93, 309
Philadelphia Electric, 292
Philadelphia Stock Exchange, 49
Philip Morris, 5
Phillips Petroleum, 464, 490
Photon Pharmaceutical, 776–777
Pierce Grain Company, 465, 472–484, 474–475, 486–490, 534–538
Prentice Hall, 95
Price Waterhouse, 103
Procter & Gamble Corporation, 766

Q

Quaker Oats, 294, 616, 745–746, 783

R

Radio Corporation of America, 797
Ralston-Purina, 745–746, 748
Reynolds Metals, 292
Rix Camper Manufacturing Company, 518–519, 521–524
RJR Nabisco, 261, 269, 325, 616
Robins, A. H., Company, 428
Rosewood Corporation, 260

S

Salco Furniture Company, Inc., 153–155
Salomon Brothers, Inc., 21, 58, 298, 344, 658, 795
Schering-Plough, 16
Scott Paper Company, 113, 794–796
Sears, Roebuck & Company, 93
Securities and Exchange Commission (SEC), 49, 54, 57, 270, 294, 309, 439
Securities Class Action Alert, 309
Securities Data Company, 54n
Sharp Corporation, 365
Sibon Beverage, 362–363, 366–368
Sierra Club Books, 355n
SKC Corporation, 620
Ski-Doo, 328, 329
Smith-Corona, 345

Smith Kline, 212
Snapple Beverage, 783
Specialty Auto Parts (SAP), 568–569
Starbucks coffee, 16
Stern Stewart & Co., 112, 452n
Stock Exchange of Thailand, 103
Sumitomo Bank, 768
SunTrust Bank, 63
Synopticom, Inc., 434–435

T

Tabbypaw Pie, Inc., 792–793
Talbot Corporation, 437, 440
Telink, Inc, 597–598
Tenneco Corporation, 292
Texaco, 53, 261
Texas Instruments, 543, 544–545
Texas Power and Light, 291
3Com Corporation, 345
Toledo Edison, 291
Touche Ross & Co., 301n
Toyota, 17, 333, 702

U

Union Carbide, 771–772, 774
United Negro College Fund (UNCF), 5
USAir, 359

V

Value Line, 438, 441
Variety Corp., 616
Virginia State Lottery, 192

W

Wall Street Journal, reading stock quote in, 299
Wal-Mart, 17, 93, 229n
Walt Disney Company, 1, 73, 113, 600–601, 638, 829
Warner Communications, 783
Waynesboro Plastic Molding Company (WPM), 728
Westinghouse Electric, 93
Whirlpool, 616
Wordperfect, 783
WorldCom, 24

X

Xerox Corporation, 233, 706

SUBJECT INDEX

A

Accelerated cost recovery system (ACRS), 364
Accounting data, beta estimation using, 410
Accounting profits, 3, 15
  cash flows versus, 358
Accounts receivable
  factoring, 626–627
  loans on, 625
  management of, 686–695
  pledging, 625–626
  size of investment in, 686–687
Accrued wages and taxes, 620–621
Accumulated earnings tax, 11–12
Acid-test ratio, 96
Adjustable rate preferred stock, 293
Advising, 52
After-tax cost of debt, 449
Agency costs, 526–528, 585
  and capital structure management, 529–530
Agency problem, 18–19, 526
Algebraic method for finding breakeven output, 473–474
Amortized loans, 192–193
Analytical income statement, 474
Analytical setting, 516–517
Andreessen, Marc L., 305
Annual percentage yield (APY), 196
  formula for, 620
Annuities
  compound, 184–186
  definition of, 184
  infinite, 195
  ordinary, 184, 191
  present value of an, 188–191
Annuities due, 184, 191, 731
Anticipatory buying, 701
Appraisal costs, 704
Appraisal value, 787–788
Approximate cost-of-credit formula, 619
Arbitrage
  covered-interest, 813
  and exchange rates, 812–813
  simple, 813
  triangular, 813
Arbitrage pricing model (APM), 235
Arbitrageur, 813
Asked rate, 813

Asset allocation, 240
Asset depreciation range (ADR) system, 34
Assets
  financial, 43
  financing, 102–104
  real, 43
Asymmetric information, 533
At-the-money option, 756
Auction rate preferred stock, 293
Automated teller machines, 650
Averaging conventions, 34

B

Balance of payments (BOP), 808
Balance sheet, 84–87
Balance sheet leverage ratios, 539
Bank credit, 622–623
Bankers' acceptances, 657
Banking Act (1933), 51
Bankruptcy
  indirect costs of, 402
  possibility of, 402
  reduction in costs, 786
Bank wire, 649
Behavior, ethical, 21–22
Benefit/cost ratio, 330–331
Bergsma, Ennius, 325
Bernanke, Ben, 531–534
Best-efforts basis, 53
Beta, 225
  measuring portfolio's, 226–227
Beta estimation
  accounting data in, 410
  pure play method for, 410
Bid-asked spread, 813
Bird-in-the-hand dividend theory, 580
Blocked funds, 828
Blumkin, Rose, 215
Boesky, Ivan F., 21, 56, 57n
Bond covenants, 527
Bondholder's expected rate of return, 274
Bond ratings, 261, 266
Bonds
  characteristics of, 264–266
  definition of, 266
  discount, 279
  mortgage, 267
  premium, 279
  zero and very low coupon, 268

Bond valuation, 259–283, 271–274
  important relationships in, 277–282
Book value, 260, 787
Breakeven analysis
  assumed behavior of costs, 468–470
  essential elements of, 468
  limitations of, 477–478
  objective and uses, 468
Breakeven point
  finding, 472
  in sales dollars, 474–475
Break-up value, 788–791
Breeden, Richard C., 309
Bressler, Richard C., 3
Broker-dealers, 50
Brokers, 50
Budget period, 155
Budgets
  cash, 153
  definition of, 153
  fixed versus flexible, 155
  functions of, 153
Buffett, Warren, 80, 215, 298
Business, legal forms of
  comparison of, 6
  corporation, 6
  partnership, 4, 6
  sole proprietorship, 4
Business cycles, 547–548
  definition of, 548
Business risk, 448, 465–467, 549, 828
Buying rate, 813

C

Calculator. See Financial calculator
Call
  covered, 756
  naked, 756
Call option, 753
Call provision, 294
Capital
  calculating divisional costs of, 446–447
  cost of, 431–454
  determining individual costs of, 433–434
  explicit cost of, 521
  net working, 612

  weighted average cost of, 449
  working, 612
Capital asset pricing model (CAPM), 231–232, 402, 438, 440
  defense of, 234
  Fama and French attack on, 232–235
  issues in implementing, 440–441
Capital budgeting
  comprehensive example, 368–371
  decision criteria, 322–345
    benefit/cost ratio, 330–331
    finding profitable projects, 323–324
    internal rate of return, 332, 334–341
    net present value, 328–330
    payback period, 324–327
    profitability index, 330–331
  definition of, 323
  ethics in, 343
    dealing with uncertainty in, 428–429
  glance at actual practices, 343, 345
  guidelines for, 358–361
  measuring project's benefits and costs, 361–371
  measuring risk for purposes, 402
  methods for incorporating risk into, 403–410
  rationing and mutually exclusive projects, 371–377
  relevance of risk in, 400–401
Capital expenditure analysis, 469
Capital flows between countries, 807–808
Capital gains, 11
  distinction between ordinary income and, 655
Capital investment, using firm's cost of capital to evaluate new, 448–449
Capital lease, 724
Capital losses, 11
Capital markets, 48–49
  investor's experience in, 235–240
  mix of corporate securities sold in, 41–42
  perfect, 576

Capital rationing
 definition of, 371
 and mutually exclusive projects,
  371–377
 and project selection, 372–373
 rationale for, 372
Capital structure, 441, 514
 decisions and international
  financing, 825–826
 importance of, 516
Capital structure management,
  515, 527
 and agency costs, 529–530
 basic tools of, 534–543
Capital structure theory, 516–530
Capital structure weights, 442
Carty, Lea, 271
Cash, 639
 motives for holding, 641–642
 random fluctuation of balances,
  680–682
 reasons for holding, 640–642
Cash breakeven analysis, 477
Cash budget, 153
Cash discounts, 621
Cash flows, 15, 213–214
 companywide, 542–543
 computing internal rate of return
  for even, 334
  for uneven, 334–337
 diversion of, from existing
  products, 359
 from financing activities, 91
 forecasting, 643–644
 incremental, 15–16, 361
 interpreting statement, 94–95
 from investment activities, 91
 measuring, from operations,
  91–92
 from operations, 89–91
 or "going concern" value,
  791–793
 process of, 640–641
 terminal, 366–368
 time dependence of, 416–417
 use of, versus accounting
  profits, 358
Cash inflow, managing, 644–649
Cash management, 825
 evaluation of costs of, 651–652
 models for, 676
 objectives and decisions,
  642–644
Cash need, certainty of, 676–679
Cash outflow, managing, 649–650
Celler-Kefauver Amendment
  (1950), 786
Certainty equivalent approach,
  403–405
 versus risk-adjusted discount
  rate methods, 408–409
Certificates of deposit (CDs), 658

Chattel mortgage, 719
 agreement for, 627
Chicago Board Options Exchange
  (CBOE), 761–762
Chop-shop approach, 786–787
Chop-shop value, 788–791
Clark, James H., 305
Clayton Act, 786
Clientele effect, 583–584
Collateral, 719
Collection procedures, 644–652
Commercial paper, 624–625,
  658, 719
Commission basis, 53
Commodity futures, 749
Common stock
 characteristics of, 296–300
 cost of, 436, 449
 estimating cost of, using divi-
  dend growth model, 437
 expected rate of return, 308–310
 promoting, on Internet, 303
 rationale for dividend or split,
  596–597
 valuing, 301–307
  growth factor in, 302
  multiple holding periods,
   304, 306–307
  single holding period, 304
Company-unique risk, 219–220
Companywide cash flows, 542–543
Comparative leverage ratios,
  539–540, 542
Compensating balances, 683–684
Competitive bid purchase, 53
Competitive markets, 16–17
Complementarity in financial, 784
Complex stream, present value of,
  193–195
Compound annuities, 184–186
Compound interest, 173–181
 with nonannual periods, 179–181
Concentration banking, 648
Conditional outcomes, 414
Conditional probabilities, 414
Constant carrying costs, 700
Constant demand, 699
Constant dividend payout ratio, 592
Constant-growth dividend
  model, 320
Constant ordering costs, 700
Constant unit price, 699
Contracts
 daily resettlement of, 747–749
 option, 753
Contribution-margin analysis, 473
Contribution-to-firm risk, 400
Control limit model, 682–683
Conversion period, 772
Conversion premium, 772
Conversion price, 771
Conversion ratio, 771

Conversion value, 772
Convertible preferred stock, 293
Convertible securities, 771
 characteristics and features of,
  771–773
 reasons for issuing, 772–773
 valuation of, 774–775
Corporate bonds, 41–42
Corporate dividend policy, 588–589
Corporate profitability, 40
Corporate strategy and dividend
  policy, 592–593
Corporations, 6
 Subchapter S, 12
 taxation of, 7
Costs
 of capital, 431–454, 525–526
 of common equity, 449
 of debt, 446
 of equity, 445–446
 external failure, 705
 internal failure, 705
 overhead, 361
 of preferred stock, 449
 sunk, 360
Cost structure, 469
Counter-parties, 767
Coupon interest rate, 265
Coverage ratios, 539
Covered call, 756
Covered-interest arbitrage, 813
Credit, ease of obtaining, 734
Credit policy changes, 692–695
Credit scoring, 689
Credit terms, 621, 622
Cross rates, 813–814
Cumulative preferred stock, 292
Cumulative voting, 300
Currency exchange rates and
  interest rates, 451
Currency-futures contracts and
  options, 823–824
Currency swaps, 766
Current assets, 84
 managing, 612–614
Current liabilities
 advantages, 613–614
 disadvantages of, 614
 managing, 612–614
Current ratio, 96
Current yield, 265

D

Daily resettlement of contracts,
  747–749
Dartmouth College, Trustees of,
 v. *Woodard, 6n*
Date of record, 594
Dealer placement, 624
Debentures, 267
 subordinated, 268

Debt, 84
 after-tax cost of, 449
 cost of, 434
 criticisms of incentive-based
  rationale for increased, 532
 implicit cost of, 521
Debt capacity, 547
Debt capital, cost of, 434–435
Debt financing, downside of,
  532–533
Debt ratio, 103–104
Debt-to-equity ratio, 527–528
Declaration date, 594
Default-risk premium, 62
Degree-of-financial-leverage mea-
  sure (DFL-$_{EBIT}$), 534, 535
Delivery-time stock, 700
Demand-based management, 617
Demand flow management, 617
Dependence hypothesis, 521–523
Depository transfer checks, 648
Depreciation, 10–11, 641
 methods of, 33–34
Derivatives, 767
Devaluation, 808
Differential cash flows over pro-
  ject's life, 363–364, 366
Direct costs, 470
Direct foreign investment, 828–829
 exchange rate risk in, 817
Direct leasing, 723
Direct method, 91
Direct placement, 48
Direct quote, 809
Direct sale, 53
Direct securities, 45
Disbursement procedures, 644–652
Disbursing float, 645
Discount bond, 279
Discounted net cash flows, 326
Discounted payback period,
  326–327
Discount rate, 68
 changes in, 69
Discretionary financing, 145–147
Discretionary financing needed
  (DFN) model, 148
 analyzing effects of profitability
  and dividend policy on,
  148–149
Distributing, 52
Diversifiable risk, 219–220
Diversification and risk, 218–219,
  237–240
Divestitures, 797
Dividend decision
 in practice, 590–593
 share repurchase as, 597–598
Dividend exclusion, 10
Dividend growth model, 436–437
 estimating cost of common
  stock using, 437

issue in implementing, 437–438
issues in implementing, 437–438
Dividend payment
    procedures, 594
    versus profit retention, 575
Dividend payout ratio, 575
Dividend policies
    alternative, 592
    and corporate strategy, 592–593
    effects of, on discretionary
        financing needed (DFN)
        model, 148–149
    impact of, on stock price,
        576–590
Dividend rate band, 293
Divisional costs of capital, calcu-
    lating, 446–447
Dollar, value of, 819
Dorrance, John, Jr., 18
Double-declining balance (DDB)
    depreciation, 33–34
Dunlap, Al, 113
DuPont analysis, 108–111
Duration, 282
Dwyer, Dan, 271

E

Earnings before interest and tax
    (EBIT), 81, 82
    earnings per share (EPS) analy-
        sis, 535–539
    earnings per share (EPS) indif-
        ference point, 537–538
Earnings predictability, 591
Economic exposure, 824
Economic ordering quantity (EOQ)
    model, 697–700, 702
    and inflation, 701–702
Economic profit, 452
Economic value, 260
Economies of scale, 784
Economy, movement of funds
    through, 45–47
Effective annual rate, 196
Efficient markets, 17–18, 260–262
Eisner, Michael, 1, 113
Electronic funds transfer, 650–651
Equity, 84
Equivalent annual annuity (EAA),
    375–377
Ethical behavior, 21–22, 103
Ethical decisions, resolving,
    444–445
Ethical dilemmas, 30–32
Ethics, 301
    in capital budgeting, 343
Eurobonds, 270
Eurodollar loans, 721–722
Exchange rate risk, 814, 829
    examples of, 816–818
    exposure to, 820–824

Exchange rates, 808, 809
    and arbitrage, 812–813
    forward, 814–815
    recent history of, 808
    spot, 809–812
Ex-dividend date, 594
Exercise ratio, 776
Expectations theory, 586
Expected rate of return, 214
    stockholder's, 307–310
Expenses
    incremental, 360
    interest, 8
Expiration date, 756
Explicit cost of capital, 521
External failure costs, 705
Externally generated funds, 39n

F

Factoring, accounts receivable,
    626–627
Failure costs, 704
Fair value, 260
Federal agency securities, 656–657
Federal funds rate, 68
Federal Reserve System, 650
    and federal funds rate, 37–38
    and interest rates, 68–71
Federal Reserve Wire System, 649
Federal Trade Commission (FTC),
    57, 786
Fiduciaries, taxation of, 7
Field warehouse financing
    agreement, 627
Financial assets, 43
Financial calculator
    computing internal rate of return
        on, 334
    moving money through time
        with aid of, 178–179
Financial decisions, influence of
    taxes on, 19
Financial forecasting, 142, 143–151
Financial futures, 750–752
Financial insurance, 760
Financial intermediary, indirect
    transfer using, 47
Financial lease, 723
Financial leverage, 468, 483–484,
    486
    analysis of, 568–572
    corporate policies on using,
        544–545
Financial management
    basics of, 12–22
    definition of, 2
    information in, 73
    theory in, 549–552
Financial markets, 40
    components of United States,
        48–51

definition of, 42
globalization of, 807–808
rates of return in, 59–63
reasons for existence of, 42–45
Financial planning and budgeting,
    152–154
Financial policy, 433
Financial ratio analysis, 95–108
Financial risk, 448, 467–468, 653,
    828
Financial statements
    balance sheet, 84–87
    of cash flows, 87–88
    cash flows from operations,
        89–91
    income, 81–83
Financial structure, 514
    design of, 514–515
Financial variables, forecasting, 144
Financing
    cash flows from activities, 91
    permanent sources of, 618
    planning firm's mix, 513–552
    spontaneous sources of, 618
    temporary sources of, 618
Financing costs, 81–82
Financing decisions, 469
Financing process, 45–46
Finished-goods inventory, 697
Firms
    goal of, 2–4
    measuring performance,
        112–113
    planning financial mix for,
        513–552
    reasons for holding cash,
        640–642
Firm-specific risk, 219–220
Firm value, 526–527
    determination of, 787–793
Fisher effect, 67
    international, 450–451, 820
Fixed assets, 84
Fixed costs, 469
Float, 644–645
Floating lien agreement, 627
Floating-rate international cur-
    rency system, 808
Flotation costs, 56, 433
Foreign currency options, 764
Foreign exchange futures,
    750–751
Foreign exchange market, 809
Foreign portfolio investments,
    exchange rate risk in, 817
Forward exchange contract, 814
Forward exchange rates, 814–815
Forward-market hedge, 823
Forward-spot differential, 815
Franklin, Benjamin, 172
Free cash flow as problem, 531–534
Friedman, Milton, 444

Funds
    direct transfer of, 47
    effect of changes in rate on
        short-term rates, 69
Futures, 745–752
    foreign exchange, 750–751
    hedging with, 749
    interest rate, 750
    stock index, 751–752
Futures clearinghouse, 747
Futures margin, 748
Futures markets, 746–749
Future value, 173–181
Future-value interest factor, 176

G

Generally accepted accounting
    principles (GAAP), 80
General partnership, 4
Glass-Steagall Act (1933), 51
Globalization of product and
    financial markets, 807–808
Going private, 797
Graphic analysis, 536–537
Gross domestic product (GDP), 805
Gross income, 8
Growth factor in valuing common
    stock, 302
Growth firm, relationship between
    earnings and value for,
    319–321

H

Half-year convention, 34
Harper, Charles, 309
Hedge
    forward-market, 823
    money-market, 822
Hedging principle, 615, 617
Hidden cash, 616–617
High-yield bonds, 268–270,
    271, 531
Holding-period returns, 220
Hoyvald, Neils, 344

I

Implicit cost of debt, 521
Income
    gross, 8
    objectives of taxation, 7
Income statement, 81–83
Increasing-stream hypothesis of
    dividend policy, 592
Incremental after-tax cash flows,
    359
Incremental analysis, 692–695
Incremental cash flows, 15–16, 361
Incremental expenses, 360
Indenture, 265

Independence hypothesis, 518–521
Independent orders, 700
Indirect costs, 469
Indirect method, 91–92
Indirect quote, 810
Indirect securities, 44–45
Industry leaders, 54
Industry norms, 539–541
Industry standards, 540
Infinite annuities, 195
Inflation, 61, 591
  and economic ordering quantity,
      701–702
  effects of, on rates of return and
      Fisher-effect, 67
  and real rates of return, 72–73
Information asymmetry, 584
Information effect, 584
Initial outlay, 361–363
Initial public offering (IPO), 439
In-money option, 756
Insider trading, 57n
Insolvency, 643
Instantaneous delivery, 700
Institutional Brokers' Estimate
      System (I/B/E/S), 438
Interest expense, 8
  tax deductibility of, 523–524
Interest rate determinants, 63–64,
      66–67
Interest rate futures, 750
Interest rate options, 763
Interest rate parity, 451, 818
Interest-rate risk, 278, 653–654
Interest rates
  compound, 173–181
  and currency exchange rates, 451
  and Federal Reserve System,
      68–71
  making comparable, 196
  and monetary policy, 68
  nominal, 61
  reasons for differences in
      between countries, 450–451
  risk premiums in estimating, 64
Interest tax shield, 266
Internal failure costs, 705
Internally generated funds, 39n
Internal rate of return (IRR), 332,
      334–341
  modified, 340–342
International financing and capital
      structure decisions, 825–826
International Fisher effect,
      450–451, 820
International trade contracts,
      exchange rate risk in,
      816–817
Internet, promoting stock on, 303
Intrinsic value, 260, 262
Inventory
  finished-goods, 697

just-in-time, 702–703
purpose and types of, 695
raw materials, 696
work-in-process, 696–697
Inventory loans, 627
Inventory management, 695–703
  techniques in, 697–700
Inventory model for cash manage-
      ment, 679–680
Inventory policy, 706
Inventory turnover ratio, 98
Investment
  cash flows from activities, 91
  direct foreign, 828–829
Investment alternative expansion,
      760
Investment banker
  definition of, 51
  distribution methods, 52–54
  functions of, 52
  indirect transfer using, 47
Investment banking firm, 51
Investment banking house, 51
Investors
  experience in capital markets,
      235–240
  required rate of return, 432
Iverson, J. Richard, 365

J

Jensen, Michael, 275, 531
Joint probability, 414
Junk bonds, 268–270, 271, 531
Just-in-time inventory control,
      702–703

K

Kanban system, 702
Keynes, John Maynard, 641

L

Labor contract negotiations, 469
Lagging, 825
La Rouchefoucauld, 259
Lavery, John, 344
Law of one price, 820
Leading, 825
Lease arrangements, types of, 723
Lease-purchase algorithm,
      725–728
Lease-purchase analysis, case
      problem in, 728–731
Leases, 722–723
  capital, 724
  direct, 723
  financial, 723
  net, 723
  net-net, 723
  operating, 723, 724

purchase algorithm, 725–728
  versus purchase decision,
      724–725
  sale and leaseback, 723–724
Lease-versus-purchase decision,
      724–725
Leasing
  direct, 723
  economics of, versus purchasing,
      731–732
  leveraged, 724
  potential benefits from, 732
  reasons for, 734
Lessee, 723
Lessor, 723
Leverage, 760
  financial, 468
  impact of, 531–532
  operating, 468
Leveraged leasing, 724
Limited partnership, 6
Line of credit, 622
Liquid assets, 676–684
  definition of, 639
Liquidation, 797
Liquidation value, 260
Liquidity, 95–98, 654
  measuring, 96–97
Liquidity position, 591
Liquidity premium, 63
Lizerbram, Sol, 290
Loan amortization, 192–193
  schedule for, 193
Lock-box arrangement, 645–648
London Interbank Offered Rate
      (LIBOR), 721
Long-term assets, 84
Long-term Equity Anticipation
      Securities (Leaps), 765

M

Mail float, 645
Maintenance margin, 748
Malkiel, Burton G., 227
Management, removal of ineffec-
      tive, 785–786
Marginal analysis, 692–695
Marginal tax rates, 9–10
Mark, Reuben, 325
Marketable securities, 639
  alternatives to, 656
  composition of portfolio, 653–660
Market portfolio, 220
Market power, increased, 786
Market-related risk, 219
Market risk, measuring, 220–226
Markets
  competitive, 16–17
  efficient, 17–18
Market value, 260
Market value added, 450–452

Marshall, John, 6
Maturities, 265, 719
Maturity premium, 63
Maximization of shareholder
      wealth, 3–4
Medium-term notes (MTNs), 719
Mergers in creating wealth,
      784–787
Microeconomics, 523
  profit maximization in, 2–3
Mid-month convention, 34
Milken, Michael, 269, 270
Modified accelerated cost recovery
      system, 34–36
Modified internal rate of return,
      340–342
Monetary policy and interest
      rates, 68
Money market, 48
Money-market hedge, 822
Mortgage bonds, 267
Multinational corporations
      (MNC), 807, 825–826
  growing importance, in world
      economy, 798
Multinational working-capital
      management, 824–825
Multiple discriminate analysis
      (MDA), 689
Multiple holding periods, 304,
      306–307
Multiple rates of return, 339–340
Municipal obligations, 654
Municipals, 654
Mutually exclusive projects, 373

N

Nakagama, Mary Frances, 212
Naked call, 756
National Association of Security
      Dealers Automated
      Quotation System
      (NASDAQ), 51
National market system, 58
Negotiable certificates of deposit,
      657–658
Negotiated purchase, 52–53
Net advantage of leasing (NAL),
      725
Net cash flows, discounted, 326
Net income, 82
Net income approach to valuation,
      522–523
Net lease, 723
Net-net lease, 723
Net operating income (NOI)
      approach to valuation,
      518–521
Net operating loss
  carryback and carryforward, 11
  deduction, 11

Net present value (NPV),
    328–330, 725
Net present value profile, 337–339
Net profit margin, 100*n*
Net working capital, 612
NI theory, 521–523
Nominal interest rates, 61, 63–64,
    196
Nondetachable warrants, 776
Nondiversifiable risk, 219–220
Nongrowth company, relationship
    between earnings and value
    for, 318–321
NVDG model, 320–321

O

Obsolescence, avoidance of risk
    of, 733–734
One hundred percent financing, 734
Open interest, 756
Operating and financial leverage,
    combination of, 487–490
Operating income, 81
Operating income return on invest-
    ment (OIROI), 99–102
Operating leases, 723, 724
Operating leverage, 468, 478–482
Operating profit margin, 99
Operating profits, 98–102
Operations, cash flows from, 91–92
Opportunity costs
    accounting for, 360–361
    of funds, 59, 230
Optimal capital structure, 515
Option contracts, 753
    standardization of, 761
Option premium, 755
Options, 753–765
    at-the-money, 756
    call, 753
    characteristics of, 760–761
    contract, 754
    foreign currency, 764
    fundamentals of, 753–760
    innovations in market, 762–765
    interest rate, 763
    in-the-money, 756
    out-of-money, 756
    put, 753
    stock index, 762–763
    striking price, 755
    on treasury bond futures,
        764–765
Options clearinghouse corporation
    (OCC), creation of, 761
Order point problem, 700–701
Order quantity problem, 697–700
Ordinary annuities, 184, 191
Ordinary income, distinction
    between capital gains
    and, 655

Organized security exchanges,
    49–50
Out-of-money option, 756
Overhead costs, 361
Over-the-counter markets, 49, 50–51
Ownership control, 591

P

Parity rate, 808
Partial equilibrium analysis, 516
Participating preferred stock, 293
Partnering, 704
Partnership, 4, 6
    taxation of, 7
Par value of bond, 265
Payable-through drafts, 649–650
Payback period, 324–327
Payment date, 594
Payment-in-kind (PIK) preferred
    stock, 294
Pecking order theory, 528–529
Peer group, 96
Percent of sales forecast method,
    144–148
    limitations of, 149–151
Perfect capital markets, 576
Periodic financial statements, 720
Permanent asset investment, 615
Permanent sources of financing, 618
Perpetuity, 195
Perritt, Gerald, 229
Pledging, accounts receivable,
    625–626
Plowback ratio, 151
Political risk, 828
Portfolio beta, measuring, 226–227
Positioning of funds, 825
Preauthorized checks (PACs),
    647–648
Precautionary motive for holding
    cash, 642
Preemptive rights, 300
Preferred stock
    adjustable rate, 293
    auction rate, 293
    convertible, 293
    cost of, 435–436, 449
    definition of, 291
    expected rate of return, 308
    features and types of, 291–294
    participating, 293
    payment-in-kind (PIK), 294
    valuing, 294–296
Preliminary prospectus, 57
Premium, option, 755
Premium bond, 279
Present value, 181–184
    of annuity, 188–191
    of complex stream, 193–195
Present-value interest factor
    (PVIF), 182

Preventive costs, 704
Price quotes, 51
Pricing policy, 469
Primary markets, 48
    regulations for, 56–57
Private placements, 48, 54–55
Privileged subscription, 53
Probability trees, 413–416
Processing float, 645
Product differentiation, 16–17
Product markets, globalization of,
    807–808
Profitability, effects of, on
    discretionary financing
    needed (DFN) model,
    148–149
Profitability index, 330–331
Profit maximization, 2–3
Profit retention, dividend payment
    versus, 575
Profits
    accounting, 3, 15
    operating, 98–102
Project ranking, 373
    problems in, 373–377
Projects
    finding profitable, 323–324
    measuring benefits and costs of,
        361–371
    selection and capital rationing,
        372–373
    standing alone risk, 400
    systematic risk, measurement
        of, and risk-adjusted
        discount rate, 409–410
Protective provisions, 292–293
Proxy, 300
Proxy fights, 300
Public offering, 48
Public Utility Holding Company
    Act (1935), 298
Purchasing, economics of leasing
    versus, 731–732
Purchasing power parity, 818, 820
Pure play method for estimating
    project's beta, 410
Put option, 753

Q

Quality, financial consequences of,
    704–706
Quoted interest rate, 196

R

Rates of return
    effects of inflation on, 67
    in financial markets, 59–63
    investor's required, 228, 230–232
    relationship between risk and,
        236–237

Ratio analysis
    integrative approach to, 108–111
    limitations of, 111
Raw materials inventory, 696
Real assets, 43
Real rates
    of interest, 67
    of return and inflation, 72–73
Real return, 59
Recessions, 548
Red herring, 57
Regulations
    primary market, 56–57
    secondary market, 57
Rekenthaler, John, 229
Remote disbursing, 650
Repayment schedules, 720–721
Replacement cost, buying below,
    786–787
Repurchase, procedure, 600
Repurchase agreements, 658–660
Required rate of return, 230
    measuring, 230–231
Residual dividend theory, 582
Restrictive covenants, 719–720
Retained earnings, 84–85
Return on assets, 99*n*
Return on common equity, 104–106
Revaluation, 808
Revenue Reconciliation Act
    (1993), 8, 11, 364
Rights, 300
Rights offerings, 53
Risk, 214–228, 465
    and being patient, 240
    business, 465–467, 828
    definition of, 216
    diversifiable, 219–220
    and diversification, 218–219,
        237–240
    exchange rate, 829
    financial, 467–468, 828
    and investment decision,
        399–402
    measuring, for capital-budgeting
        purposes, 402
    methods for incorporating, into
        capital budgeting, 403–410
    nondiversifiable, 219–220
    political, 828
    relationship between rates of
        return and, 236–237
    and single investment, 216–218
Risk-adjusted discount rates,
    405–407
    versus certainty equivalent,
        408–409
    and measurement of project's
        systematic risk, 409–410
Risk premiums, 230
    estimating specific interest rates
        using, 64

Risk return trade-off, 13–14, 19–20, 399, 405, 612–613, 643–644

S

Safety margin, 700–701
Safety stock, 699
Sale and leaseback, 723–724
Sales forecast, 144
Savings, movement of, 46–47
Scenario analysis, 411
Secondary markets, 44, 48
  regulations of, 57
Securities
  direct, 45
  indirect, 44–45
Securities Act (1933), 56
Securities Acts Amendments (1975), 58
Securities Exchange Act (1934), 57
Security market line, 232
Security value, 772
Self-liquidating debt, principle of, 614
Selling rate, 813
Selloff, 797
Semiannual interest payments, 274
Semifixed costs, 471
Semivariable costs, 471
Sensitivity analysis through simulation approach, 411–413
Shareholder value based management (SVBM), 431
Shareholder wealth, maximization of, 3–4
Share repurchase as dividend decision, 597–598
Shelf offering, 58
Shelf registration, 58, 719
Short-term credit
  estimation of cost of, 619–620
  sources of, 620–627
Simple arbitrage, 813
Simplified straight-line method, 364
Simulation, 411
  sensitivity analysis through, 411–413
Single holding period, 304
Single-sourcing, 704
Sinking fund, 294, 538
Sinking fund payments, 538
Siracusano, Luciano, 211–212
Size disparity problem, 373–374
Small regular plus year-end extra dividend payout, 592
Smith, Adam, 444

Sole proprietorship, 4
Solon, 214
Speculative motive for holding cash, 642
Speculative value, 756
Spinoff, 797
Spontaneous sources of financing, 144–145, 618
Spot exchange rates, 809–812
Spot transaction, 809
Stable dollar dividend payout, 592
Standard deviation, 216–218
Standard Industrial Codes (SIC), 789
Standardized contracts, 746–747
Standby agreement, 53
Statement of cash flows, 87–88
Static trade-off theory, 528
Statutory restrictions, 590–591
Stock dividend
  definition of, 594
  versus stock split, 595–596
Stockholder, expected rate of return, 307–310
Stock index futures, 751–752
Stock index options, 762–763
Stock of cash, 697
Stock prices, impact of dividend policy on, 576–590
Stock repurchases, 597
Stock split
  definition of, 594
  versus stock dividend, 595–596
Stock valuation, 290–310
Straight-line depreciation, 33–34
Striking price, option, 755
Subchapter S Corporation, 12
Subordinated debentures, 268
Sunk costs, 360
Sustainable rate of growth, 151–152
Swaps, 767
  currency, 766
Syndicate, 52
Synergistic effects, 359, 787
Systematic risk, 400

T

Target capital structure mix, 442
Target capital structure proportions, 542
Target debt ratios, 545, 546
Taxability, 654
Taxable income, computing, 8
Taxes
  accumulated earnings, 11–12
  deductibility of interest expense, 523–524

environment of, 7
  influence of, on financial decisions, 19
Tax expenses, 82
Taxpayer Relief Act (1997), 11n, 581
Taxpayers, types of, 7–8
Tax rates, marginal, 9–10
Tax Reform Act (1986), 11, 364
Tax shield, 524
Temporary asset investment, 615
Temporary sources of financing, 618
Tender offer, 600
Terminal cash flow, 366–368
Terminal warehouse agreement, 627
Term loans, 719
  collateral, 719
  maturities, 719
  participations among banks, 721
  repayment schedules, 720–721
  restrictive covenants, 719–720
Terms of sale, 686–688
Threat hypothesis, 530
Time dependence of cash flows, 416–417
Time disparity problem, 374–375
Times interest earned, 104
Time value of money, 14–15, 172–197, 756
Tobias, Andrew, 172–173
Total asset turnover, 100
Total quality management (TQM), 703–706
Total revenue, 471
Trade credit, 621–622
  advantages of, 622
  stretching of, 622
Transaction exposure, 821–824
Transaction loans, 624
Transaction motive for holding cash, 641
Transfer price, 825
Transit float, 645
Translation exposure, 821
Treasury bills, United States, 656
Treasury bond futures, options on, 764–765
Trial-and-error analysis, 472–473
Triangular arbitrage, 813

U

Uncertainty, ethics in dealing with, in capital budgeting, 428–429
Underwriting, 44, 52
Uniform demand, 699
Unsecured loans, 620

V

Valuation, process of, 262–264
Value
  appraisal, 787–788
  book, 260, 787
  cash flow or "going concern," 791–793
  chop-shop or break-up, 788–791
  conversion, 772
  economic, 260
  fair, 260
  intrinsic, 260, 262, 756
  liquidation, 260
  market, 260
  security, 772
  time, 756
Value at risk (VAR), 233
Variable costs, 470
Variation margin, 748
Volume of output, 471
Voting rights, 298–300

W

Warrants, 775
  characteristics and features of, 775–776
  expiration date, 776
  nondetachable, 776
  reasons for issuing, 776–777
Weight average cost of capital, 433, 441–442, 446, 449
  calculating, 442–443
"What if?" analysis, 413
Wire transfers, 648
Working capital, 612
  appropriate level of, 614–615
  conservation, 734
  zero, 617
Working-capital management, 612–613
  multinational, 824–825
Working-capital requirements, 360, 720
Work-in-process inventory, 696–697

Y

Yields, 655–656
  to maturity, 274, 276–277

Z

Zero balance accounts, 649
Zero coupon bonds, 268
Zero working capital, 617

THE PRENTICE HALL FINANCE CENTER CD-ROM
Prentice Hall, Inc.

LICENSE AGREEMENT AND LIMITED WARRANTY
READ THE FOLLOWING TERMS AND CONDITIONS CAREFULLY BEFORE OPENING THIS DISK PACKAGE. THIS LEGAL DOCUMENT IS AN AGREEMENT BETWEEN YOU AND PRENTICE-HALL, INC. (THE COMPANY). BY OPENING THIS SEALED DISK PACKAGE, YOU ARE AGREEING TO THE TERMS AND CONDITIONS OF THIS AGREEMENT . IF YOU DO NOT AGREE WITH THESE TERMS AND CONDITIONS, DO NOT OPEN THE DISK PACKAGE. PROMPTLY RETURN THE UNOPENED DISK PACKAGE AND ALL ACCOMPANYING ITEMS TO THE PLACE YOU OBTAINED THEM. [[FOR A FULL REFUND OF ANY SUMS YOU HAVE PAID FOR THE SOFTWARE.]] THESE TERMS APPLY TO ALL LICENSED SOFTWARE ON THE DISK EXCEPT THAT THE TERMS FOR USE OF ANY SHAREWARE OR FREEWARE ON THE DISKETTES ARE AS SET FORTH IN THE ELECTRONIC LICENSE LOCATED ON THE DISK:

GRANT OF LICENSE:
In consideration of your adoption of textbooks and/or other materials published by the Company, and your agreement to abide by the terms and conditions of this Agreement, the Company grants to you the Company grants to you a nonexclusive, nontransferable, permanent license to use and display the copy of the enclosed software program (hereinafter the SOFTWARE) on a single computer (i.e., with a single CPU) at a single location so long as you comply with the terms of this Agreement. The Company reserves all rights not expressly granted to you under this Agreement.

OWNERSHIP OF SOFTWARE:
You own only the magnetic or physical media (the enclosed disks) on which the SOFTWARE is recorded or fixed, but the Company retains all the rights, title, and ownership to the SOFTWARE recorded on the original disk copy(ies) and all subsequent copies of the SOFTWARE, regardless of the form or media on which the original or other copies may exist. This license is not a sale of the original SOFTWARE or any copy to you.

RESTRICTIONS ON COPYING, USE AND TRANSFER:
This SOFTWARE and the accompanying printed materials and user manual (the Documentation) are the subject of copyright and is licensed to you only. You may not copy the documentation or the Software except that you may make a single copy of the SOFTWARE for backup or archival purposes only. You may not network the SOFTWARE or otherwise use it on more than one computer or computer terminal at the same time. You may physically transfer the SOFTWARE from one computer to another provided that the SOFTWARE is used on only one computer at a time. You may not distribute copies of the SOFTWARE or Documentation to others. You may not reverse engineer, disassemble, decompile, modify, adapt, translate, or create derivative works based on the SOFTWARE or the Documentation without the prior written consent of the Company. The enclosed SOFTWARE may not be transferred to any one else without the prior written consent of the Company. Any unauthorized transfer of the SOFTWARE shall result in the immediate termination of this Agreement. You may be held legally responsible for any copying or copyright infringement which is caused or encouraged by your failure to abide by the terms of these restrictions.

TERMINATION:
This license is effective until terminated. This license will terminate automatically without notice from the Company and become null and void if you fail to comply with any provisions or limitations of this license. Upon termination, you shall destroy the Documentation and all copies of the SOFTWARE. All provisions of this Agreement as to warranties, limitation of liability, remedies or damages, and our ownership rights shall survive termination.

MISCELLANEOUS:
THIS AGREEMENT SHALL BE CONSTRUED IN ACCORDANCE WITH THE LAWS OF THE UNITED STATES OF AMERICA AND THE STATE OF NEW YORK, APPLICABLE TO CONTRACTS MADE IN NEW YORK, AND SHALL BENEFIT THE COMPANY, ITS AFFILIATES AND ASSIGNEES.

LIMITED WARRANTY AND DISCLAIMER OF WARRANTY:
The Company warrants that the SOFTWARE, when properly used in accordance with the Documentation, will operate in substantial conformity with the description of the SOFTWARE set forth in the Documentation. The Company does not warrant that the SOFTWARE will meet your requirements or that the operation of the SOFTWARE will be uninterrupted or error-free. The Company warrants that the media on which the SOFTWARE is delivered shall be free from defects in materials and workmanship under normal use for a period of thirty (30) days from the date of your purchase. Your only remedy and the Company's only obligation under these limited warranties is [[, at the Company's option,]] return of the warranted item [[for a refund of any amounts paid by you or]] replacement of the item. Any replacement of SOFTWARE or media under the warranties shall not extend the original warranty period. The limited warranty set forth above shall not apply to any SOFTWARE which the Company determines in good faith has been subject to misuse, neglect, improper installation, repair, alteration, or damage by you. EXCEPT FOR THE EXPRESSED WARRANTIES SET FORTH ABOVE, THE COMPANY DISCLAIMS ALL WARRANTIES, EXPRESS OR IMPLIED, INCLUDING WITHOUT LIMITATION, THE IMPLIED WARRANTIES OF MERCHANTABILITY AND FITNESS FOR A PARTICULAR PURPOSE. EXCEPT FOR THE EXPRESS WARRANTY SET FORTH ABOVE, THE COMPANY DOES NOT WARRANT, GUARANTEE, OR MAKE ANY REPRESENTATION REGARDING THE USE OR THE RESULTS OF THE USE OF THE SOFTWARE IN TERMS OF ITS CORRECTNESS, ACCURACY, RELIABILITY, CURRENTNESS, OR OTHERWISE. IN NO EVENT, SHALL THE COMPANY OR ITS EMPLOYEES, AGENTS, SUPPLIERS, OR CONTRACTORS BE LIABLE FOR ANY INCIDENTAL, INDIRECT, SPECIAL, OR CONSEQUENTIAL DAMAGES ARISING OUT OF OR IN CONNECTION WITH THE LICENSE GRANTED UNDER THIS AGREEMENT, OR FOR LOSS OF USE, LOSS OF DATA, LOSS OF INCOME OR PROFIT, OR OTHER LOSSES, SUSTAINED AS A RESULT OF INJURY TO ANY PERSON, OR LOSS OF OR DAMAGE TO PROPERTY, OR CLAIMS OF THIRD PARTIES, EVEN IF THE COMPANY OR AN AUTHORIZED REPRESENTATIVE OF THE COMPANY HAS BEEN ADVISED OF THE POSSIBILITY OF SUCH DAMAGES. [[IN NO EVENT SHALL LIABILITY OF THE COMPANY FOR DAMAGES WITH RESPECT TO THE SOFTWARE EXCEED THE AMOUNTS ACTUALLY PAID BY YOU, IF ANY, FOR THE SOFTWARE.]]

SOME JURISDICTIONS DO NOT ALLOW THE LIMITATION OF IMPLIED WARRANTIES OR LIABILITY FOR INCIDENTAL, INDIRECT, SPECIAL, OR CONSEQUENTIAL DAMAGES, SO THE ABOVE LIMITATIONS MAY NOT ALWAYS APPLY. THE WARRANTIES IN THIS AGREEMENT GIVE YOU SPECIFIC LEGAL RIGHTS AND YOU MAY ALSO HAVE OTHER RIGHTS WHICH VARY IN ACCORDANCE WITH LOCAL LAW.

ACKNOWLEDGMENT
YOU ACKNOWLEDGE THAT YOU HAVE READ THIS AGREEMENT, UNDERSTAND IT, AND AGREE TO BE BOUND BY ITS TERMS AND CONDITIONS. YOU ALSO AGREE THAT THIS AGREEMENT IS THE COMPLETE AND EXCLUSIVE STATEMENT OF THE AGREEMENT BETWEEN YOU AND THE COMPANY AND SUPERSEDES ALL PROPOSALS OR PRIOR AGREEMENTS, ORAL, OR WRITTEN, AND ANY OTHER COMMUNICATIONS BETWEEN YOU AND THE COMPANY OR ANY REPRESENTATIVE OF THE COMPANY RELATING TO THE SUBJECT MATTER OF THIS AGREEMENT. Should you have any questions concerning this agreement or if you wish to contact the Company for any reason, please contact in writing: [Name of Company Representative, address]